EUROPEAN WRITERS

The Twentieth Century

EUROPEAN WRITERS
The Twentieth Century

GEORGE STADE

EDITOR IN CHIEF

Volume 8

SIGMUND FREUD

TO

PAUL VALÉRY

CHARLES SCRIBNER'S SONS / NEW YORK

Copyright © 1989 Charles Scribner's Sons

Library of Congress Cataloging-in-Publication Data
(Revised for volumes 8–9)

European writers.

    Vols. 5– . Jacques Barzun, editor, George Stade, editor in chief.
    Vols. 8– . George Stade, editor in chief.
    Includes bibliographies.
    Contents: v. 1–2. The Middle Ages and the Renaissance:
Prudentius to Medieval Drama. Petrarch to Renaissance
Short Fiction—v. 3–4. The Age of Reason and the
Enlightenment: René Descartes to Montesquieu.
Voltaire to André Chénier.—v. 5–7. The Romantic
Century: Goethe to Pushkin. Hugo to Fontane.
Baudelaire to the Well-Made Play—v. 8–9. The
Twentieth Century: Sigmund Freud to Paul Valéry.
Pío Baroja to Franz Kafka.
    1. European literature—History and criticism—
Addresses, essays, lectures. I. Jackson, W. T. H.
(William Thomas Hobdell), 1915– . II. Stade,
George. III. Barzun, Jacques, 1907– .
PN501.E9 1983   809'.894   83–16333
ISBN 0–684–16594–5 (v. 1–2)
ISBN 0–684–17914–8 (v. 3–4)
ISBN 0–684–17915–6 (v. 5–7)
ISBN 0–684–18923–2 (v. 8)
ISBN 0–684–18924–0 (v. 9)

Published simultaneously in Canada
by Collier Macmillan Canada Inc.
Copyright under the Berne Convention.

3 5 7 9 11 13 15 17 19   B/C   20 18 16 14 12 10 8 6 4

PRINTED IN THE UNITED STATES OF AMERICA

The following pamphlets in the Columbia University Press Series "Columbia
Essays on Modern Writers" have been reprinted in this volume by special
arrangement with Columbia University Press, the publisher:

Bien, Peter: *Constantine Cavafy.* Copyright © 1964 Columbia University Press.
Lima, Robert: *Ramón del Valle-Inclán.* Copyright © 1972 Columbia University Press.
Ragusa, Olga: *Luigi Pirandello.* Copyright © 1968 Columbia University Press.
Goldsmith, Ulrich K.: *Stefan George.* Copyright © 1970 Columbia University Press.
Rossi, Vinio: *André Gide.* Copyright © 1968 Columbia University Press.

EDITORIAL STAFF

DANIEL J. CALTO, *MANAGING EDITOR*

JONATHAN ARETAKIS, *Associate Editor*

JOHN F. FITZPATRICK, *Associate Editor*

BRIGITTE M. GOLDSTEIN, *Editorial Assistant*

BETH ANN MCCABE, *Associate Editor*

JOAN ZSELECZKY, *Associate Editor*

EMILY GARLIN, *Proofreader*

GRETCHEN GORDON, *Proofreader*

ERIC HARALSON, *Copyeditor*

CAROL HOLMES, *Proofreader*

TATIANA HOLWAY, *Copyeditor*

W. KIRK REYNOLDS, *Proofreader*

LUCY RINEHART, *Copyeditor*

EMILY WRIGHT, *Copyeditor*

MATTHEW M. KARDOVICH, *Director of Production*

CHARLES E. SMITH, *PUBLISHER*

LIST OF SUBJECTS

Volume 8

LIST OF SUBJECTS

INTRODUCTION

FROM ITS INCEPTION, *European Writers* was designed as a companion to the eight-volume *American Writers* (1974–1981) and to the nine-volume *British Writers* (1979–1987), as well as a continuation of the two-volume *Ancient Writers: Greece and Rome* (1982). Another companion reference set, *Latin-American Writers,* is in progress. These five reference sets constitute, so far, the Scribners World Literature series.

Seven volumes of *European Writers* have already been published: the two-volume *The Middle Ages and the Renaissance* (1983), the two-volume *The Age of Reason and the Enlightenment* (1984), and the three-volume *The Romantic Century* (1985). With the publication of the six volumes that make up *The Twentieth Century* plus the planned series index, the set will be complete, although supplementary volumes may be added at some time in the future.

Each of the six volumes contains approximately twenty articles. Each article is roughly 15,000 words long. Each is devoted to a single writer; articles on writers such as Hans Arp, André Breton, and Filippo Marinetti, however, are also devoted to the literary movements these writers helped found. In style and scope, the articles are expressly written for that mythical but inspiring figure, the general reader, rather than for the specialist. But the article that can at once inform the beginner and stimulate the specialist will have achieved its goal. In pursuit of this goal, the articles each present an account of a writer's works, his life, his relations to his time, his place, his literary surroundings. But from article to article the emphasis varies, as from writer to writer the relative interest or importance of his life, works, and situation varies. Whatever the relative emphasis, the works come first; other matters are discussed to the extent that they form or inform the works. All translations of quoted passages are by the authors of the articles, unless otherwise stated.

Of the figures to whom articles in *The Twentieth Century* are devoted, Sigmund Freud (1856–1939) is the oldest and Milan Kundera (b. 1929) is the youngest. For the most part, then, the articles in these volumes are devoted to writers whose major works were published toward the end of the last century and during the first three-quarters of this century, eras of transition, of modernism, and of what has increasingly come to be called post-modernism. (Freud's *The Interpretation of Dreams* was first published at the end of 1899, but the title page was dated 1900, as though the publisher had intuited that the book would inaugurate a new era.) The articles are arranged chronologically, according to the dates of birth of the writers discussed.

Any project of this sort is likely to provoke questions as to why so-and-so was included when so-and-so was not. To the inquiring reader the editor can only answer that he has often questioned his own decisions, that he has often revised them and then revised his revisions, that he has consulted widely, that he has applied a number of overlapping criteria in an attempt to offset his ignorance or prejudice. The criteria included whether the writer under consideration was someone that American readers were likely to look up, and whether American readers were likely to look the writer up in twenty years, whether, that is, the writer's work was of enduring interest. The editor informed himself about the status of any writer under consideration within world literature and within his nation's literature. Above all, the works of the writers finally selected are in the editor's opinion either very important or very good—for not everything that is important is good, and vice versa.

Some writers, such as Thomas Mann and Marcel Proust, satisfied all of the criteria. Some did not. American readers are not at the moment very likely to look up the Greek writer Yannos Ritsos, but there is good reason for believing that in the near future his international reputation will be more in accord with his great accomplishments. As much can be said about Gunnar Ekelöf, Miroslav Krleža, and Dezső Kostalányi, for example. On the other hand, if the reputations of Vicente Blasco Ibáñez and Sigrid Undset are not what they once were, readers are still likely to look up these authors of international best-sellers that were turned into popular movies. In any case, the articles are all designed both to provide a frame for works the reader may well already know, say, the tales of Franz Kafka, and to provide an introduction to works the reader may well want to know firsthand, once he has read about them—the varied and equally strange productions of Ramón del Valle-Inclán, say.

There is not yet any generally recognized canon of European modernists. There is no common denominator by virtue of which the modernist writers and their immediate predecessors and successors group themselves in the mind. Attempts to isolate the modern element in modern literature are at all angles to each other. In their methods and matter, the modernists are even more diverse than the romantics. For all that, there are family resemblances, enough of them so that from our perspective there seems to have been something like a community among writers of the modernist era, even among those who were not aware of each other. The community was one not so much of interests or goals or even of lines of descent as of features shaped by common environmental pressures, political and intellectual.

The world wars and their tremendous aftermaths, the Russian Revolution and the spread of Communism, the rise and fall of Fascism, the gradual dissolution of overseas empires and the ideologies that supported them—stages in one (so far) endless crisis—dislocated more Europeans, intellectually and materially, than did the Protestant Reformation or the French

Revolution. There were other dislocations. The conclusions of mathematicians and physicists, of philosophers and historiographers, of psychologists and anthropologists, whose alarming news spread quickly, cast new doubt on the ability of the human mind to understand the world around it, to define its past, to examine its own activity. The notion of an unconscious internalized the Uncertainty Principle. The demonstration by anthropologists of primitive rites behind civilized institutions, their demonstration of the merely relative value of any nation's institutions, led some writers to question not only their own forms of civilization, but the thing itself. Some championed primitivism as more authentic. Others reasserted civilized values according to *Die Philosophie des Als Ob,* as if, that is, the values were not suspended over the void. The effect was that no institution or value, whether religious or political or ethical, whether regulating the relations between the classes, the sexes, parents and children, the individual and his society, or writers and readers, could be taken for granted.

All ages, in Europe at least, have been ages of dislocation to those who lived in them, of artists who saw what a dubious figure the emperor cut without his clothes. But the exemplary modern writers thought of their own blindness and insight, their own estrangement from institutional authority, as differing from that of their predecessors not just in degree, but in kind. The modernists for the most part did not see themselves as standing within the most recent phase of an evolving literary tradition that may or may not have gone awry, but that would continue beyond them. The modernists more often saw themselves as standing on this side of an unbreachable chasm, one that cut them off from the traditions that led to them. Tradition was to the modernists not a ladder one climbed as onto the shoulders of giants, from where one could see a little farther, but a museum, a chest of souvenirs. Or if it was a ladder, it had fallen away. Anyone who has understood his propositions, said Ludwig Wittgenstein, must see them "as steps to climb up beyond them." He must, so to speak, throw away the ladder after he has climbed up. "Do not come down the ladder," says a character in Samuel Beckett's *Watt,* "I haf taken it away." Thus the learned quality of much modernist writing: you have to study the past if you want to make sure you don't repeat it; you have to know past literature if you want to cite telling fragments ripped from their original contexts, so as to "strip them of their aura," in Walter Benjamin's phrase, so as to destroy their authority. That writer, as Hannah Arendt neatly phrased it, "discovered that the transmissibility of the past has been replaced by its citability."

The modernists, then, did not see themselves as reformers, as renovators whose task was to add new rungs to the ladder or to shore up the old ones; they saw their task as to dramatize the breach, to "make it new," to start from scratch, to engage in a permanent revolution of the self, the world, and, above all, the word. For it is words that express, represent, and even constitute the world—so many modern writers felt. Past uses of words, conventional styles, traditional literary forms, so the argument goes, retain obsolete values, maintain discredited institutions, sustain ossified relations of power. These were at best merely appropriate to some other time or place; at worst, they have become odious, life-denying. Thus the many movements and manifestos of modern literature. Different personalities and circumstances might generate naturalism here and symbolism there, here formalism and there Dada, or futurism or surrealism or Acmeism, all with different programs. But the participants in these movements and the others agreed that whatever *was,* when they began writing, was wrong.

One does not have to endorse these presumptions to feel the specific power of modern European literature. Reading the writers discussed in these articles can be as disorienting, as wrenching and exhilarating, as falling in love. An immersion in modern literature can leave you no longer quite sure where or what you are, but freer, more energized, to go where you want, to become what you choose to be. The articles in *The Twentieth Century* try to explain how and why the proto-modernists and modernists, anti-modernists and post-modernists, tried in various ways to free us from the stock response, from the taskmasters outside us and the censors within. The editor of these volumes and the staff at Scribners also hope that these articles will lead readers back to the original writers, whose words may not reconstitute a world, but whose works take us out of this world or take the old world out of us.

GEORGE STADE

CHRONOLOGY OF
THE TWENTIETH CENTURY

1848	Karl Marx and Friedrich Engels publish the *Communist Manifesto.*
	Liberal democratic and socialist revolutions break out on the Continent. The "spring of the people" turns in many areas into national revolts.
1849	In France, Louis Bonaparte is elected president of the Second Republic by universal manhood suffrage.
	In Germany, the Frankfurt Parliament seeks a formula for the unification of all German-speaking lands.
	After initial success, liberal and national aspirations are defeated—the conservative reaction triumphs everywhere.
1852	Louis Bonaparte proclaims the Second Empire and takes the name Napoleon III.
1854	The Crimean War pits France and England against Russia and involves the European powers in the affairs of the Ottoman Empire.
1856–1939	Sigmund Freud
1859	Charles Darwin publishes his work *The Origin of Species.*
1859–1861	Camillo Benso di Cavour unifies most of Italy under King Victor Emmanuel.
1859–1952	Knut Hamsun
1861	Serfdom is abolished in the Russian Empire by imperial decree.
1861–1865	Civil War divides the United States; slavery is abolished in 1863, and President Abraham Lincoln is assassinated in the war's aftermath (1865).
1862–1931	Arthur Schnitzler
1862–1946	Gerhart Hauptmann
1862–1949	Maurice Maeterlinck
1866	Austria is defeated in war with Prussia and excluded from German affairs, increasing Prussian power in Central Europe.
1867	The dual monarchy of Austria-Hungary is created.
1866–1936	Ramón del Valle-Inclán
1866–1952	Benedetto Croce
1867–1928	Vicente Blasco Ibáñez
1867–1936	Luigi Pirandello
1868–1933	Stefan George
1868–1936	Maxim Gorky
1868–1955	Paul Claudel
1869–1951	André Gide

1870–1871	Napoleon III's Second Empire is defeated in the Franco-Prussian War. The Third Republic of France is founded. Germany is unified by Otto von Bismarck, and the king of Prussia becomes German emperor.
1871–1922	Marcel Proust
1871–1945	Paul Valéry
1871–1950	Heinrich Mann
1872–1956	Pío Baroja
1873–1907	Alfred Jarry
1873–1954	Colette
1873–1967	Azorín
1874	The first exhibition of impressionist art opens in Paris.
	Henry Stanley's expedition opens the interior of Africa.
1874–1929	Hugo von Hofmannsthal
1875–1926	Rainer Maria Rilke
1875–1939	Antonio Machado
1875–1955	Thomas Mann
1876	Alexander Graham Bell invents the telephone.
1876–1944	Filippo Marinetti
1877–1919	Endre Ady
1877–1962	Hermann Hesse
1878–1900	Germany becomes the dominant political and economic power on the Continent, making it a close rival of Great Britain.
	The major European Powers embark on a new phase of imperialist expansionism and vie intensely for spheres of influence and overseas possessions, particularly in Africa.
1880–1918	Guillaume Apollinaire
1880–1921	Alexander Blok
1880–1934	Andrey Bely
1880–1942	Robert Musil
1881–1958	Juan Ramón Jiménez
1882	The new nation of Italy joins Germany and Austria-Hungary in the Triple Alliance.
1882–1944	Jean Giraudoux
1882–1949	Sigrid Undset
1883–1923	Jaroslav Hašek
1883–1924	Franz Kafka
1883–1955	José Ortega y Gasset
1883–1957	Nikos Kazantzakis
1884–1885	The Berlin Conference abolishes the slave trade in Africa, but seals European domination over the entire continent.
1884–1937	Yevgeny Zamyatin
1885–1922	Velemir Khlebnikov
1885–1939	Dezső Kosztolányi
1885–1939	Stanislaw Witkiewicz
1885–1962	Isak Dinesen
1885–1970	François Mauriac
1885–1971	Gyorgy Lukács
1886	The Second International strengthens the bonds among socialists of varying outlook and national origin.
	Gottlieb Daimler constructs the first gasoline-powered motor.
1886–1951	Hermann Broch
1886–1966	Hans Arp
1887–1914	Georg Trakl

1887–1975	Saint-John Perse
1888	George Eastman's box camera makes photography widely available to the public.
1888–1935	Fernando Pessoa
1888–1970	Giuseppe Ungaretti
1889–1964	Jean Cocteau
1889–1966	Anna Akhmatova
1889–1975	Gunnar Gunnarsson
1890–1938	Karel Čapek
1890–1960	Boris Pasternak
1891–1938	Osip Mandelshtam
1891–1967	Pavlo Tychnya
1891–1974	Pär Lagerkvist
1892–1923	Edith Södergran
1892–1940	Walter Benjamin
1892–1941	Marina Tsvetayeva
1892–1975	Ivo Andrič
1893	Karl Benz constructs a four-wheel, gasoline-driven motor car.
1893–1894	France and Russia form a military alliance after a similar agreement between Russia and Germany lapses.
1893–1930	Vladimir Mayakovsky
1893–1981	Miroslav Krleza
1894–1906	The Dreyfus Affair reveals deep divisions within French politics and society; anti-Semitic and anti-republican sentiments are vented in often violent confrontations.
1894–1941	Isaac Babel
1894–1961	Louis-Ferdinand Céline
1895	Auguste and Louis Lumière invent the cinématographe and give a public motion picture demonstration in Paris.
1895–1896	Knowledge of radioactivity is advanced with Wilhelm Röntgen's discovery of X rays and Marie and Pierre Curie's success in isolating the radioactive element in uranium.
1896–1948	Antonin Artaud
1896–1957	Giuseppe Tomasi di Lampedusa
1896–1966	André Breton
1896–1972	Henry de Montherlant
1896–1981	Eugenio Montale
1896–1970	Tarjei Vesaas
1897–1936	Federico García Lorca
1898	Max Planck formulates his quantum theory in physics.
1898–1956	Bertolt Brecht
1898–1962	Michel de Ghelderode
1898–1973	Wilhelm Moberg
1898–1974	José María Ferreira de Castro
1899–1944	Antoine de Saint-Exupéry
1900–1960	Yury Olesha
1900–1971	George Seferis
1900–1976	Eyvind Johnson
1900–1978	Ignazio Silone
1900–1968	Salvatore Quasimodo
1901–1976	André Malraux
1901–1967	Marcel Aymé
1902–1976	Raymond Queneau

1902–	Halldór Laxness
1902–	Nathalie Sarraute
1903–1987	Marguerite Yourcenar
1903–	Georges Simenon
1904	Great Britain and France resolve their differences over colonial interests and conclude the Entente Cordiale.
1904–1969	Witold Gombrowicz
1905	The Russian Empire is defeated in war with Japan.
	Revolution breaks out in Russia, and Tsar Nicholas II concedes to the creation of a legislative body, the Duma.
	Great Britain, France, and Russia form the Triple Entente.
1905–1980	Jean-Paul Sartre
1905–	Elias Canetti
1907	Pablo Picasso's painting *Les demoiselles d'Avignon* creates a sensation at the first cubist exhibition, held in Paris.
1907–1968	Gunnar Ekelöf
1907–	Alberto Moravia
1908–1950	Cesare Pavese
1908–1966	Elio Vittorini
1908–1986	Simone de Beauvoir
1909–1943	Simone Weil
1909–	Yannis Ritsos
1910–1911	Italy defeats Turkey in war and annexes Tripoli.
1910–1986	Jean Genet
1910–1987	Jean Anouilh
1911	Arnold Schoenberg expounds the twelve-tone scale in music.
1911–	Odysseus Elytis
1911–	Max Frisch
1911–	Czesław Miłosz
1912–	Eugène Ionesco
1913–1960	Albert Camus
1913–	Claude Simon
1914	World War I breaks out in August; the Central Powers, Germany and Austria-Hungary, face the Entente of France, Russia, and Great Britain.
1915	Turkey carries out mass killings of the Armenian people. Carl Jung's *The Unconscious* is published.
1915–1916	Italy declares war against her former allies Germany and Austria.
1915–1980	Roland Barthes
1916	Chemical weapons are introduced on the battlefield at Ypres.
1916–	Camilo José Cela
1916–	Natalia Ginzburg
1917	The tsarist regime in Russia is overthrown in February; the provisional social democratic government continues the war. In October, the Bolsheviks, under Vladimir Ilyich Lenin, seize power and negotiate peace with Germany at Brest-Litovsk.
	The United States enters the war on the side of the Entente.
1917–1985	Heinrich Böll
1918	President Woodrow Wilson presents his Fourteen Points, calling for the creation of a League of Nations and the reorganization of Eastern Europe based on national self-determination.
	The imperial government of Germany sues for peace.
	The German and Austro-Hungarian Empires crumble under pressure of revolution and are replaced by republics.

1918–	Alexander Solzhenitsyn
1919	The Treaty of Versailles imposes punitive peace terms on Germany.
	The National Socialist Party is organized in Munich; Mussolini organizes the Italian Fascist movement.
	The Third International is founded in Moscow.
1919–1922	Women are granted the right to vote in most European countries and in the United States.
	Walter Gropius establishes the Bauhaus school of design.
1921–	Friedrich Dürrenmatt
1922	The four-year civil war between Bolshevik and White Russian forces ends with the creation of the Union of Soviet Socialist Republics.
1922–	Alain Robbe-Grillet
1923	Hyperinflation in Germany causes severe economic hardship.
1923–1985	Italo Calvino
1924	A republic is declared in Greece.
1926	John L. Baird invents television.
1926–1984	Michel Foucault
1926–	Michel Butor
1927	Werner Karl Heisenberg elaborates the uncertainty principle in physics.
	The film industry is revolutionized by the introduction of sound.
1927–	Günter Grass
1928	Agricultural collectivization begins in the Soviet Union; peasant resistance is brutally suppressed.
1929	The stock market crash in the United States acts as a catalyst for worldwide economic depression.
1929–	Milan Kundera
1933	The National Socialists, led by Adolf Hitler, come to power in Germany. They suppress all rival political parties and gain dictatorial powers.
1934	Joseph Stalin initiates the Great Purge of the Communist Party in Russia; thousands of people are tried for treason and executed.
1935	The Nuremberg Laws deprive German Jews of their citizenship; Jews and other "undesirables" are subjected to widening persecution.
	Mussolini's army invades Abyssinia.
	The monarchy is restored in Greece.
1936	The Spanish army, under Francisco Franco, revolts against the elected Republican government, setting off the Spanish Civil War. The conflict attracts international political and military support from the right and the left.
	Hitler's troops occupy the Rhineland, violating the Treaty of Versailles.
	In France, Léon Blum forms a Popular Front government, uniting moderate socialists and Communists.
1938	The Anschluss incorporates Austria into the German Reich.
	Britain's attempts to mediate the Sudenten Crisis through negotiations with Hitler fail, and Germany proceeds to invade and divide Czechoslovakia.
1939	Hitler and Stalin conclude a non-aggression pact between Germany and the Soviet Union.
	On September 1, German troops invade Poland; Britain and France declare war in protest. World War II begins.
	Germany and Russia partition Poland.
1940	The Blitzkrieg extends German control over most of Western Europe.
1941	The war continues to expand: Germany invades Russia in June, and Japan bombs Pearl Harbor in December, bringing the United States into the war.
1942	Germany puts in operation the "Final Solution," the systematic deportation and annihilation of the Jewish population in the areas under its control.

1942	A team of scientists in the United States succeeds in splitting the atom.
	ENIAC, the first electronic computer, is developed.
1943	Germany suffers severe setbacks on the Eastern Front. The Allies land in Sicily and Mussolini is removed from power in Italy.
1944	In June, a massive Allied army lands at Normandy and moves to liberate Nazi-held Europe.
1945	Germany surrenders to the Allies in May and is divided into four occupation zones controlled by the United States, England, France, and the Soviet Union.
	Japan surrenders in August, after the United States drops atom bombs on Hiroshima and Nagasaki.
1947	India gains independence from British rule; a thirty-year period begins in which many European colonies throughout the world become independent.
	President Harry Truman pronounces a doctrine promising military and economic aid to any country under threat from Communism.
1948	The Berlin Blockade by the Soviet Union and East Germany cuts off access to the city from the West and escalates the Cold War.
1949	In April and May, Chinese Communists win decisive victories over the Nationalists; the four-year Chinese Civil War ends in October with the establishment of the People's Republic of China.
	The Korean War breaks out between Communists in the north and non-Communists in the south, eventually involving the United States and China in the conflict.
	Mahatma Gandhi is assassinated in India.
	The United Nations votes to partition Palestine, creating the state of Israel.
	South Africa institutes the policy of apartheid.
1953	Soviet dictator Joseph Stalin dies.
1954	France ends colonial control over Indochina after the fall of Dien Bien Phu to Communist forces.
1956	Revolts break out in Poland and Hungary against the Communist regimes in these countries. After initial success, the uprisings are suppressed by the Soviet military.
	French and British troops land at Port Said to prevent Egypt from taking control of the Suez Canal.
1957	The Soviet Union launches the first space satellite.
1958	Charles de Gaulle establishes the Fifth Republic of France.
1961	East Germany erects a wall across Berlin.
1962	The French possessions in West Africa gain independence. France withdraws from Algeria after losing a colonial war there, thus bringing to a close an internally divisive sixteen-year period of colonial warfare
1963	Martin Luther King, Jr., leads the massive March on Washington for Jobs and Freedom.
	President John F. Kennedy is assassinated.
1964	China denounces the Soviet Union and challenges its dominant position in the Communist world.
	United States involvement in the Vietnam War escalates.
1965–1968	In China, supporters of Mao Tse-tung wage the Cultural Revolution against foreign influences on Chinese life, precipitating violent internal power struggles.
1967	Army generals stage a coup in Greece and set up a military dictatorship.
1968	Opposition to the war in Vietnam grows in the United States and abroad. Student revolts spread in the United States and Europe, particularly in France and West Germany.
	Martin Luther King, Jr., and Robert F. Kennedy are assassinated.
	The "Prague Spring," a popular movement for greater liberties in Czechoslovakia, is suppressed by Warsaw Pact forces.
1969	U.S. astronaut Neil Armstrong becomes the first man to walk on the moon.
1974	President Richard Nixon resigns from office under threat of impeachment for collusion in the Watergate scandal.

1975	The Vietnam War ends when the South Vietnamese city of Saigon falls to Communist forces.
	Spanish dictator Francisco Franco dies.
	The military dictatorship in Greece is overthrown.
1976	The first International Women's Year Conference convenes in Mexico City.
1978	Spain holds free parliamentary elections for the first time since the Civil War in the 1930's.
1979	Soviet troops invade Afghanistan.
1980	The United States and China establish full diplomatic relations.
	Religious fundamentalism and terrorism become increasingly potent political forces in many parts of the world.
1981	In Poland, the Solidarity movement demands governmental and economic reforms.
1984	The European peace movement protests deployment of nuclear weapons on the Continent.
1986	Radioactive contamination across Europe results from an accident at the Chernobyl nuclear power plant in the Soviet Union.

CONTRIBUTORS TO VOLUMES 8 AND 9

ALBERT BADES FERNANDEZ
Cornell University
JOSÉ ORTEGA Y GASSET

JARED M. BECKER
Columbia University
ITALO SVEVO

ALBERT BERMEL
*The Graduate School and
University Center of the
City University of New York*
JEAN GIRAUDOUX

PETER BIEN
Dartmouth College
CONSTANTINE CAVAFY
NIKOS KAZANTZAKIS

MARIANNA D. BIRNBAUM
*University of California,
Los Angeles*
ENDRE ADY

LeROY C. BREUNIG
Barnard College
GUILLAUME APOLLINAIRE

MARLENE CIKLAMINI
Rutgers University
SIGRID UNDSET

PELLEGRINO D'ACIERNO
Hofstra University
FILIPPO TOMMASO MARINETTI

HERMAN K. DOSWALD
*Virginia Polytechnic
Institute and
State University*
HUGO VON HOFMANNSTHAL

ULRICH K. GOLDSMITH
University of Colorado
STEFAN GEORGE

ANTHONY HEILBUT
New York City
HEINRICH MANN

F. W. J. HEMMINGS
University of Leicester
MARCEL PROUST

ROBERTA JOHNSON
Scripps College
PÍO BAROJA

CHARLES KLOPP
Ohio State University
GABRIELE D'ANNUNZIO

ROBERT LIMA
*Pennsylvania State
University*
RAMÓN DEL VALLE-INCLÁN

ROBERT E. LOTT
University of Illinois
AZORÍN

PATRICK J. MAHONY
Université de Montréal
SIGMUND FREUD

JAMES R. McWILLIAMS
University of Oregon
ARTHUR SCHNITZLER

JEREMY T. MEDINA
Hamilton College
VICENTE BLASCO IBÁÑEZ

PHILIP MELLEN
*Virginia Polytechnic
Institute and
State University*
GERHART HAUPTMANN

CIRIACO MORÓN ARROYO
Cornell University
ANTONIO MACHADO

HELEN MUCHNIC
Smith College
ANDREY BELY

HARALD S. NÆSS
*University of Wisconsin,
Madison*
KNUT HAMSUN

MANFREDI PICCOLOMINI
*City University of
New York, Herbert
H. Lehman College*
BENEDETTO CROCE

GERALD PIROG
Rutgers University
ALEXANDER BLOK

ROBERT PYNSENT
University of London
JAROSLAV HAŠEK

OLGA RAGUSA
Columbia University
LUIGI PIRANDELLO

PETER S. ROGERS
Texas A & M University
PAUL CLAUDEL

JAMES ROLLESTON
Duke University
RAINER MARIA RILKE

VINIO ROSSI
Oberlin College
ANDRÉ GIDE

SANFORD R. SCHWARTZ
*Pennsylvania State
University*
HENRI BERGSON

HAROLD B. SEGEL
Columbia University
MAXIM GORKY

MICHAEL SEIDEL
Columbia University
ALFRED JARRY

LEROY R. SHAW
*University of Illinois
at Chicago*
FRANK WEDEKIND

WALTER H. SOKEL
University of Virginia
FRANZ KAFKA

J. P. STERN
*University College
of London*
THOMAS MANN

JOAN HINDE STEWART
*North Carolina
State University*
COLETTE

RICHARD S. STOWE
Lawrence University
MAURICE MAETERLINCK

STEVEN WINSPUR
Columbia University
PAUL VALÉRY

VICTORIA YABLONSKY
Los Angeles, California
ROBERT MUSIL

HOWARD T. YOUNG
Pomona College
JUAN RAMÓN JIMÉNEZ
MIGUEL DE UNAMUNO

THEODORE ZIOLKOWSKI
Princeton University
HERMANN HESSE

SIGMUND FREUD

(1856–1939)

IT HAS BEEN rightly said that we know more about Freud than about any other person in the history of mankind, and yet an extraordinary amount of primary material about him has not yet been brought to light. Freud's contemporaries had the advantage of listening to him, but it always remains for a succeeding age to be able to read more of his writings. Relative to Freud's contemporaries, we are privileged, even though a great part of Freud's works have still not been published. We may safely estimate that most of the unpublished writing consists of correspondence; indeed, Freud stands as one of the most prolific letter-writers in all of world literature.

No one else discovered so much about the workings of the human mind as did Freud. He gave us an unmatched method for studying the mind at its deepest levels; he explored and formulated the sexual complexity of individual and family life as no one else had previously done, and in so doing he revolutionized the entire field of psychopathology. It is one thing when a scientist invents a new instrument; it is quite another to proceed from that to make discoveries and construct a body of theory. Freud did both and more; with a knowledge that can be described as encyclopedic, he extended his findings in all kinds of directions in a profound way. He not only added considerably to the accumulated store of human knowledge but also radically altered the manner in which we look at our lives. Of all people

living in our century, Freud was the one who most influenced it in various cultural ways. Such influence had both inspiring and unsettling aspects. Although Freud elaborated a dream theory that was a veritable rhetoric of the unconscious and that discovered poetry in each one of us, he also troubled the sleep of the world, ranking among the three men who have dealt severe blows to its narcissism. The first blow was a cosmological one administered by the sixteenth-century astronomer Nicholas Copernicus; he refuted geocentric theory and showed instead that we live on a relatively small fragment of matter revolving around the sun. Man's importance was next belittled by the biological findings of Charles Darwin, whose demonstration of evolution undercut our detachment from the animal world. Finally, Freud convincingly proved that man is not the master that he thinks he is over his own consciousness, rationality, and will.

Because of the particular nature of Freud's writings, they are still read as pertinent and timely classics in the field of psychoanalysis, which is thus singular among the sciences, whose founders are usually studied today merely for their historical interest. This fact, along with Freud's gigantic stature and the capital importance he ascribed to early development, helps to explain the surprising kinship between psychoanalysis and theology: they are both fields whose practitioners constantly have their originator in mind. It is certainly revelatory that a Jew, and not a Christian, discovered psychoanalysis; as Freud said in "Die Widerstände gegen die Psychoanalyse" ("Resistances to Psychoanalysis," 1925), it was his experience of social ostracism as a Jew and his consequent situation of solitary opposition that contributed to his founding a new science. Freud's discovery was facilitated because the prejudice of European Christians against the Jews placed the latter at a vantage point from which it was easier to examine the vicious irrationality of oppressors' self-justifying invocation of morality and supreme reason. The latter point may help to correct an all too common belief that the psychoanalyst's novel instruments are introspection and empathy—an injustice to mystical traditions that predate psychoanalysis by many centuries and that have formulated delicately honed procedures to refine one's introspection and empathy. Freud's contribution, in relation to these traditions, is to turn self-examination toward the unconscious traces of drive and defense. Freud's great historical innovation is to enhance introspection and empathy by self-analysis in its technical sense, that is, by the analysis of one's constellations of drive and defense.

In spite of his epochal brilliance as a scientist, the only prize Freud received while living was the Goethe Prize for literature. Albert Einstein's praise is confirmatory: "I do not know any contemporary who has presented his subject in the German language in such a masterly fashion." Other writers, such as Thomas Mann and Stefan Zweig, joined in the consensus that Freud was one of the exemplary masters of German prose. His writing shows a superb artistry in an astonishing number of different genres, from history, biography, autobiography, and letters to lectures, dialogues, case histories, and scientific treatises.

An account of Freud's life begins appropriately with his father. Jakob Freud (1815–1896) married his first wife, Sally Kramer, in 1831; they had two sons, Emmanuel (1833–1914) and Philipp (1836–1911). In 1852 Jakob's first

wife died and it seems that he remarried, only to become a widower again not long afterward; then in 1855 he entered into marriage with Amalie Nathansohn (1835–1930). On 6 May of the next year Jakob and Amalie had their first child, Sigmund, who was born in Freiberg, a small Moravian village of less than five thousand people. (Today it is called Přibor and is located in Czechoslovakia.) In the next ten years Sigmund's mother had seven other children, five of whom were girls; one of her two sons, Julius, died at the age of eight months, when Sigmund himself was slightly less than two years old. Much has been said about the fact that Sigmund's uncles and half brothers, Emmanuel and Philipp, were approximately the age of his mother and that Sigmund was just a little older than his nephew John. This unusual familial entanglement undoubtedly influenced Freud's later explanation of the family romance, which is a child's fantasy that he is of noble lineage and that those claiming to be his parents are imposters. Before we follow Jakob Freud as he left with his family for Leipzig in 1859, we should mention another significant detail in the life of young Sigmund in Freiberg: he had an unforgettable Roman Catholic nanny who took him to mass and who talked to him of hell and heaven.

In 1860, after a short stay in Leipzig, Jakob took his family to Vienna, where he continued with his struggling merchant business. Not surprisingly, young Sigmund proved to be a brilliant student, usually coming out at the top of his class. In 1873 he enrolled for a medical doctor's degree at the University of Vienna, but because of his passion for research and for further study both inside and outside of medicine, he completed his medical training in eight years instead of the usual five. From 1876 to 1882 he worked in the physiological laboratory of the famous Ernst Brücke, who, along with Hermann Helmholtz, had propounded a biophysics and a mechanistic determinism of the human organism. Then Freud studied for a while under Theodor Meynert, the most famous specialist in brain anatomy of the day; thanks to Meynert's influence, Freud went on to become a neurologist (he was never a psychiatrist), eventually establishing himself as an authority on children's cerebral palsy. A third influential figure was Jean-Martin Charcot, at whose Parisian clinic Freud trained for several months during 1885 and 1886; there he became more alert to the psychological aspect of hysterical manifestations. When Freud returned from Paris, he married Martha Bernays, ending a four-year engagement.

A special place must be reserved for another of Freud's teachers, Josef Breuer. From 1880 to 1882 Breuer treated a woman now known by her pseudonym, Anna O. Breuer confided to Freud that he had hypnotized her, that she then recalled the original situations in which her several hysterical symptoms arose, and that her symptoms putatively disappeared when she expressed the suppressed emotion attached to the original causes. (Thus the term "cathartic therapy" was derived.) Gradually Freud became convinced of the far-reaching implications of this case. It was partly due to his own growing clinical convictions and partly due to Breuer's diminished objection to publicity that the case only appeared in print over ten years later (along with explanatory essays and other cases) in a collaborative work called *Studien über Hysterie* (*Studies in Hysteria,* 1893–1895). Despite their differences, Freud and the older Breuer agreed on two important notions that informed their co-authored venture: rather than being nonsensical, hysterical symptoms are fully meaningful and stand as substitutes for other mental acts, and as the patient discovers their meaning, the relevant symptoms disappear.

A key area of disagreement between Breuer and Freud concerned the importance of sexuality in the origin of neuroses. When the two went their separate professional ways, Freud felt more able to pursue his intuitions and observations about sexuality's decisive role. He became convinced that hysteria was traceable to a real sexual trauma experienced in one's life. (This theory is known as the seduc-

tion hypothesis.) But within a short time, Freud came to doubt this hypothesis and, after a period of self-doubt, proclaimed that fantasy might serve just as well as a trigger to neurotic formation.

As Freud's association with Breuer foundered, his friendship with Wilhelm Fliess intensified, so much so that Freud's semi-official biographer Ernest Jones called it the only truly unusual experience in Freud's life. Freud found Fliess much more ready than Breuer to accord sexuality a central position, even though Fliess's approach to the subject was predominantly physiological rather than psychological. For a number of years Freud devalued himself in comparison with Fliess, whom he elevated unrealistically. Fliess acted not only as Freud's personal physician but also as a sort of personal savior. It was as though, in order to sustain the audacity of his originality and to alleviate his attendant guilt and shame, Freud had to cast Fliess in the role of supreme authority. By 1900 the intense friendship between Freud and Fliess was essentially over, after thirteen years. The split came as a result of Freud's growing independence and his skepticism about Fliess's powerful physiological theories.

During that friendship Freud started his self-analysis, which, from 1897 on, evolved into a systematic one. It was a heroic, painful experience, an unrepeatable one, for no one after Freud can be so innocent again; it was excruciating for a man of Freud's conservative background to acknowledge his murderous wishes against his deceased, beloved father and to confront in such solitude the longstanding variety and extent of his sexual longings. Besides improving his personal life in certain respects, the self-analysis facilitated his discovery of the importance of infantile sexuality, the functioning of bisexuality in neurosis, and some of the psychic significance of dreams.

From 1900 to 1905 Freud published a series of five distinguished works, which were influenced in various ways by his self-analysis: *Die Traumdeutung* (*The Interpretation of Dreams,*

1900), *Zur Psychopathologie des Alltagsle- bens* (*The Psychopathology of Everyday Life*, 1901), a case history of a female hysteric entitled "Bruchstück einer Hysterie-Analyse" ("Fragment of an Analysis of a Case of Hyste- ria," 1905), *Drei Abhandlungen zur Sexual- theorie* (*Three Essays on the Theory of Sexu- ality*, 1905), and *Der Witz und seine Beziehung zum Unbewussten* (*Jokes and Their Relation to the Unconscious*, 1905). Except for the case history, a common concern runs through the above texts. In the book on dreams Freud showed that although the technique of free association was first enlisted in relation to symptoms, it was potentially more revelatory when he applied it to dreams. Dreams were not pathological processes in themselves, and it was in interpreting those phenomena that Freud discovered the most about unconscious processes in normal as well as pathological psychic life. In *The Psychopathology of Every- day Life*, Freud investigated the unconscious processes underlying verbal slips, slips of the pen, and the like, committed by healthy people, thereby demonstrating again the continuity between normal and pathological mental events. In the *Three Essays*, Freud propounded a larger view of sexuality, one that established a continuity between infantile, normal adult, and perverse sexual life. Likewise, in the book on jokes, Freud demonstrated that the same processes that formed dreams went into the making of jokes.

In the opening years of the twentieth cen- tury, Freud was ending the period of his self- described "splendid isolation." The small group gathered around him slowly increased to include Alfred Adler, Karl Abraham, Sándor Ferenczi, Otto Rank, Carl Jung, and Jones. In 1909 Freud and Jung went to the United Sates, where they lectured and received honorary doctorates at Clark University. In 1910 the International Psychoanalytic Association was founded, and organizational splits soon fol- lowed—first Adler in 1911, then Jung in 1914, and Rank years afterward. Predictably, when World War I broke out, organized psychoanal- ysis suffered; yet it was precisely during that time that Freud wrote up his papers on meta- psychology, which framed psychoanalytic the- ory in a highly abstract language dealing with conflict and psychic energy. Slightly later he delivered at the University of Vienna the *Vor- lesungen zur Einführung in die Psychoanalyse* (*Introductory Lectures on Psycho-Analysis*, 1916–1917), a brilliant general presentation that still retains its usefulness.

When the war ended, Freud was over sixty years old, but that did not prevent him from entering into one of his most prolific periods. In 1920 he promulgated a new theory of the drives in *Jenseits des Lustprinzips* (*Beyond the Pleasure Principle*, 1920). In 1923 his *Das Ich und das Es* (*The Ego and the Id*) offered a novel picture of the mind according to which there are three agencies, the ego, the id, and the superego, the latter two threatening to overpower the ego. In 1926 Freud published his last major theoretical work, which he titled *Hemmung, Symptom und Angst* (*Inhibitions, Symptoms and Anxiety*). In it Freud revised his theory of anxiety, now seeing it as a signal by which the ego indicates some imminent danger; he also disputed Rank's idea that the trauma of human birth was the source of all subsequent anxiety. Then, in 1933, Freud pub- lished the *Neue Folge der Vorlesungen zur Einführung in die Psychoanalyse* (*New Intro- ductory Lectures on Psycho-Analysis*), a sup- plementary series profitable to both the begin- ning and more advanced student and a locus of some controversial Freudian remarks on female psychology.

Starting in 1923, Freud was also preoccu- pied in another way—he had cancerous tu- mors in the palatal region, which necessitated over thirty operations before his death in 1939. Throughout this period, he tolerated the pain with an astounding courage, which even grew when he confronted the dispossessing Ge- stapo in 1938. Thanks to international cooper- ation, Freud was able to leave Vienna and settle down in England for his last days. It is entirely in keeping with Freud's strong moral personality that the last item he published in his lifetime—a letter that appeared in the review *Time and Tide* in 1938—dealt with anti-Semitism in England.

A further word might be said about Freud's character. Perhaps his most outstanding personal trait was his courage. It was that quality, along with his enormous intellectual powers of observation, analysis, imagination, and memory (photographic and phonographic), that enabled him to create the discipline of psychoanalysis. Overall, he was a rather stoic man of exceptional industry and determination; he also combined a revolutionary spirit with a firm belief in the triumph of reason and experiment. To family, friends, and needy visitors Freud repeatedly evinced extraordinary financial generosity, accompanied by his typical self-effacement, which partially explains why that quality of his has all too often gone unappreciated by commentators. On the other hand, if he was considerate, he could often be stern and harsh to a degree that intensified his problematic relationships with many of his male friends. Apparently Freud's relationships with women were not so affected by the deep-seated ambivalence revealed in his self-confessed need to always have both an intimate friend and a detested enemy.

Although Freud enjoys classic stature as a world writer, he is primarily important for having founded the psychoanalytic movement. Without understanding that, we hardly render appreciative justice to Freud, not only as the pioneer in a new science but also as a peerless expounder of that science.

The science Freud founded embodies more than a theory of the mind; psychoanalysis is a theory of repression and resistance as well as an explanation of the crucial role of sexuality and of the Oedipus complex. First, in conformity with its character as a depth psychology, traditional psychoanalysis considered the processes of the mind from three points of view: the dynamic, the economic, and the topographical (this triad constitutes Freud's so-called metapsychology). According to the dynamic stand-

point, all mental processes—apart from the reception of external stimuli—interplay and form compromises with each other. The contents of these mental processes are governed by the compulsion to repeat and are represented as persistent images or ideas that are emotionally charged (e.g., the image of a hostile parent). In terms of Freud's final theoretical formulations, these investments derive from two possible drives: Thanatos, or the drive toward destruction and the dissolution of life, and Eros, the striving of all living things for closer union. (The manifestation of Eros as mental energy is called the libido.) In sum, the dynamic standpoint refers to psychic conflict that is based on the interaction of the two drives and their mental and affective derivatives.

From the economic point of view, the mental representatives of the drives are invested by the mind's instinctive tendency to reduce unpleasure and increase pleasure. The purpose of the mind or psychic apparatus is to keep the amount of excitation as low as possible in accordance with the pleasure principle, unpleasure being related to an increase of excitation and pleasure to a decrease. In the regular course of development, the pleasure principle is modified by its encounters with the external world and yields its place to the reality principle; according to the latter, the mind tolerates transient feelings of unpleasure in order to achieve the even greater, if delayed, pleasure of satisfaction.

We now come to the third or topographical point of view from which Freud theoretically considered the mental processes. Topographically, the mind is divisible into the conscious, preconscious, and unconscious. The great division here exists between the conscious and the unconscious, the latter consisting of repressed material and therefore incapable of being brought to consciousness by an act of volitional attention. On the other hand, the preconscious relates to those mental contents of which we are not aware at any particular moment but that are capable of achieving consciousness by an act of volitional attention.

Later, without abandoning the duality of the topographical theory of the mind, Freud proposed a tripartite categorization, generally known as the structural theory. In the structural sense, the mind is comprised of: the id, the repository of the drives, whose processes are fully unconscious; the ego, the site of reason, common sense, and perception of the external world, whose processes and contents nevertheless are mostly unconscious; and the superego, the site of self-observation and self-criticism, whose processes and contents are partly conscious but mostly unconscious.

There is finally the psychoanalytic theory of neuroses, which is founded on three cornerstones: the importance of repression, of the sexual drives, and of transference. Any attempt on the part of the psychoanalyst to dislodge the repressed from the patient's unconscious encounters resistance. At the same time, those unconscious impulses undergo what Freud described as "the return of the repressed" ("Weitere Bemerkungen über die Abwehrneuropsychosen" ["Further Remarks on the Neuropsychoses of Defence," 1896]). In such instances, the repressed material makes a compromise that alone allows it to enter consciousness. Neurotic symptoms, then, are compromise formations that stand as moderated satisfactions substituting for the full satisfactions that would result from an unconditional lifting of repression.

It is the sexual drive that is subject to the most repression throughout the various stages of life. Developmentally, psychosexual life is divisible into three stages: (1) the oral stage, extending into the second year of life and centering on the mouth and lips as erogenous zones; (2) the anal phase, lasting until the age of four, focusing on the anal erogenous zone, first in terms of pleasurable retention and later in terms of pleasurable elimination, and involving significant sadistic strivings and the voluntary control of the sphincter; and (3) the genital phase, beginning around the age of three and lasting approximately until the end of the fifth year, during which time there is a chiefly genital focus of sexual stimulation. Proper to this latter phase is the child's nuclear neurosis and most important conflict, the Oedipus complex, which consists of mainly unconscious ideas and feelings attending the wish to possess the parent of the opposite sex and to eliminate that of the same sex. (The term "Oedipus complex" applies to both sexes; the more accurate term for females, the Electra complex, has not gained wide currency.) In this Oedipal period the superego begins to assume its final form as the internalization of parental prohibition. Through internalization the superego becomes heir to the Oedipus complex; it forces the child to forsake certain gratifications and, in the case of violations of the internalized prohibitions, to be subject to self-guilt.

The so-called pregenital organizations, the oral and anal phases, are points at which the libido may become fixated and to which, if triggered by repression, it may regress; the form of any subsequent neurosis is determined by these infantile libidinal fixations. On the other hand, resolving the Oedipus complex involves the successful passage from autoerotic love to one capable of mature, true intimacy with another.

A further remark: transference is not restricted to the analytic setting; rather, being a universal phenomenon, it bears traces and patterns of the affectionate and hostile relationship that the child had with his parental figures and that he repeats variously with others in his later life.

Under the definition of psychoanalysis as a method of treating psychological disorders, it is appropriate to consider the evolution of psychoanalytic technique from its crude beginnings to its later refinements. Only toward the very end of 1887 did Freud try to treat patients with hypnosis; before that he used the standard techniques of massage, hydrotherapy, and electric stimulation. Although spurred on by Breuer, Freud gradually realized that using hypnosis to achieve catharsis did not produce the long-lasting desired results; that is, the catharsis or discharge of emotion attached to a previously repressed experience did not necessarily make symptoms disappear. Other factors involved in Freud's disillusionment with hypnosis were that not all patients could be hypnotized and that he himself was not a good hypnotist.

At this point Freud recalled that during his second stay in France, Hippolyte Bernheim had demonstrated that patients could be made to remember merely by the therapist's suggestion. Convinced, then, that patients really retained everything that was pathologically important and that it was merely a matter of obliging them to express it verbally, Freud commanded his patients to lie down, to shut their eyes, and, aided by the pressure of his hand on their foreheads, to communicate their emerging memories.

The next great technical step was the discovery of free association, which, according to many, ranks as the greatest of all Freud's discoveries. The endorsement of free association and the patient's attendant free choice to cooperate or not shows how far Freud moved away from the authoritarianism of hypnotic technique, which also had the disadvantages of concealing the patient's resistances and psychic processes from the therapist. With Freud's technique of free association, on the other hand, the patient was invited to put himself in a self-observing state and to say whatever came to him, even though he felt it to be disagreeable, reprehensible, nonsensical, trivial, or irrelevant. Freud called the reliance on free association the fundamental technical rule of analysis. He was not, however, oblivious to the paradoxical link between free association and determinism in that the ideas dredged up by the patient are really not free but are interconnected and linked in a determined way back to basic starting points. Such determinism permitted Freud to detect fundamental laws governing psychological life.

In this therapeutic venture, Freud proposed that the analyst be seated out of sight behind the reclining patient, maintaining himself in an evenly suspended attention in order to capture the drift of the patient's unconscious with his own unconscious. Aided by an *Einfühlung* (empathy) by which he would "feel" his way into the patient's psychic life, the analyst would present his interpretations; by means of them, he would explain the unconscious meanings found in the patient's symptoms, dreams, associations, and most important of all, the transference. It was in treating Dora that Freud learned that transference—the process by which a patient displaces onto his analyst his reactions to significant figures from his past life—is not only the greatest obstacle to obtaining a cure but also the analyst's most powerful therapeutic instrument. Transference functions ambiguously in the clinical working-through of the patient's resistances to the emergence of unconscious content into the conscious sphere. Looking back on Freud's technical evolution up to this point, we can see that he shifted his analytic focus from interpreting drive derivatives to interpreting resistances; concurrently, removing symptoms was no longer his primary aim per se, for overcoming a patient's resistances was thought to bring about the disappearance of symptoms as a secondary result.

Between 1910 and 1915 Freud introduced the notion of countertransference, i.e., the analyst's transference onto the patient ("Die zukünftigen Chancen der psychoanalytischen Therapie" ["The Future Prospects of Psycho-Analytic Therapy," 1910]), and also wrote six papers on technique. Though far from being a systematic elaboration of psychoanalytic technique, these papers give valuable guidelines about conducting a psychoanalytic treatment and understanding its phenomena. With notable emphasis, he pointed out that "every single association, every act of the person under treatment must reckon with the resistance," that transference emerges "as the most powerful resistance" ("Zur Dynamik der Übertragung" ["The Dynamics of Transference," 1912]) and is a piece of repetition, that a patient begins treatment by repeating instead of remembering, and that his ordinary illness acquires new meaning and is recapitulated as a "transference neurosis" whereby the analyst becomes the focal figure at whom the patient's conflicts are directed. By way of essential clarification, I should add that the foregoing remarks represent Freud's textual exposition but not necessarily his practice—how one theorizes and how one applies one's theories may be two different matters. In actual fact, despite his growing awareness of the transference, Freud continued to ascribe importance to memory retrieval and reconstruction of past events to a far greater degree than would many contemporary analysts, who ascribe greater importance to the transference and interaction in the current analytic setting.

We should not leave the consideration of psychoanalytic technique without trying to capture afresh some of its novelty. Due to many causes, including a benumbing popularization arising from the mass media, the originality of the psychoanalytic setting has been, in Erik Erikson's words, undercut and made subject to the "metabolism of the generations." But to realize the true meaning of that setting, we must appreciate the Renaissance openness of Freud—nothing alien was alien to him. Accordingly, he constructed a situation in which one was invited to complete freedom of expression without the constraints of criticism and condemnation; those who had previously risked being social outcasts for their bizarre, irrational, asocial behavior could now find out, in a context of cooperation and respect, that such behavior was indeed full of human meanings.

The undeniable value of psychoanalysis as a therapy, though, should not tempt us to neglect its pertinence to other fields. Indeed, a number of scholars specialize in what they call Freud's works of applied psychoanalysis, in which Freud applied psychoanalytic techniques to other disciplines. This descriptive epithet, however, is quite misleading. On the one hand, applied psychoanalysis is to be found in various remarks strewn throughout Freud's entire opus and hence is erroneously restricted to selected works. On the other hand and more significantly, the term "applied psychoanalysis" has a unidirectional, imperialistic note to it; more accurately and democratically, we ought to speak of psychoanalysis being variously co-involved or, better yet, co-applicable with a number of other disciplines.

This said, because of limited space, only the briefest mention can be made of some of Freud's writings in the fields of aesthetics, the social sciences, and religion. In *Der Wahn und die Träume in W. Jensens "Gradiva"* (*Delusions and Dreams in Jensen's "Gradiva,"* 1907), Freud showed how the structures of the dreams and delusions of the novel's protagonist correspond to those encountered in psychoanalytic practice. Turning to sculpture, Freud offered a fascinating, detailed study of the artist's conception in "Der Moses des Michelangelo" ("The Moses of Michelangelo," 1914). Freud's personal favorite among his works was his first elaborate psychoanalytic biography, *Eine Kindheitserinnerung des Leonardo da Vinci* (*Leonardo da Vinci and a Memory of His Childhood,* 1910). Freud examined the unconscious erotic ties that bind a group to its leader in *Massenpsychologie und Ich-Analyse* (*Group Psychology and the Analysis of the Ego,* 1921), his most outstanding contribution to social psychology. Two texts on religion may also be mentioned here. In *Die Zukunft einer Illusion* (*The Future of an Illusion,* 1927), Freud asserted that religion was an illusion arising from an infantile belief in the omnipotence of thought; and one of the highly contested claims Freud made in his *Der Mann Moses und die Monotheistische Religion* (*Moses and Monotheism,* 1939) was that Moses was really an Egyptian. In comparing the two latter works, Freud described himself as progressing from a conception of religion as sheer illusion to a conception of religion as embodying historical truth.

After the foregoing bird's-eye view of Freud's writing, we can move on to a more detailed study of five of his central works for the different blending of content and form in each. (One preliminary word of caution about the possibility of drawing inaccurate conclusions: the indication of multiple instinctual traces in Freud's writings does not necessarily disprove their propositions.) A masterpiece in psychoanalytic theory is *The Interpretation of Dreams,* by far the greatest of Freud's works, and a classic of world literature. The work is sui generis, blending autobiography, biography, literary analysis, history, and science, and brilliantly combining introspection, analysis, synthesis, imagination, and speculation. Starting from the tranquil assurance of the definite article in its title, *The Interpretation of Dreams* relentlessly overpowers the reader with insights and startling conclusions.

During the composition of his masterpiece, Freud was reportedly in a kind of waking dream state. To his friend Fliess, Freud confessed that when he sat down to write a paragraph he did not know where it would end. As a further illustration of his compositional freedom, he cited the joke about the horseman Itzig: "Itzig, where are you going?" "I don't know, but ask the horse." And yet, because of Freud's awesome intelligence, memory, and powers of concentration, there was an overriding expository control that counterpointed the oneiric, or dreamlike, drift of his work. Indeed, Freud's comment on *Oedipus Rex* in chapter 5 of *The Interpretation of Dreams* reflects also on his own writing:

> The action of the play consists in nothing other than a disclosure that is gradually increased and artistically delayed (a procedure comparable to psychoanalysis) telling us that Oedipus himself is the murderer of Laius and also that he is the son of the murdered man and Jocasta.
>
> (*Gesammelte Werke,* vols. 2–3, p. 268)

Parallel to the measured revelations of Sophocles is the incremental orchestration of Freud's theses. Thus his second chapter ends: "When the work of interpretation has been completed, we perceive that a dream is the fulfillment of a wish." The fourth chapter adds: "A dream is a (disguised) fulfillment of a (suppressed or repressed) wish." In the fifth chapter we read: "A succession of meanings or wish-fulfillments may be superimposed on one another, the bottom one being the fulfillment of a wish dating from earliest childhood." Then, in the final chapter, the simple formula is firmly fleshed out: "A wish that is represented in a dream must be an infantile one."

There is even a more striking organization to be found in the seven chapters of *The Interpretation of Dreams* when we realize that Freud associates the dream with a maternal identification. In chapters 2 and 7 Freud refers to the unfathomable core of the dream as its *Nabel* ("navel") and in the second instance it is further described as an inextricable point in a "tangle of dream-thoughts." Not only did Freud make an imaginative return to the womb in some particular dream or in his attempts to fathom it down to the navel, but he also arranged the book on dreams so that chapter by chapter he gets closer to understanding the navel. In the light of this maternal return, the book's whole is thus more than the sum of its parts.

Moreover, the nature imagery, which ranges from references to woods to references to high ground and which unifies *The Interpretation of Dreams,* symbolizes the body of a woman, precisely that of Freud's mother. Twice in his work Freud explicitly states that wood symbolizes the female, and in the *Introductory Lectures* he makes these pertinent statements about universal symbolism:

> The complicated topography of the female genital parts makes it understandable that they are very often represented as landscapes, with rocks, woods, and water. . . . *"Materia"* is derived from *"mater,"* "mother," and the material out of which anything originates is, so to speak, a mother to it. This ancient conception survives, therefore, in the symbolic use of wood for "woman" or "mother."
>
> (*Gesammelte Werke,* vol. 11, pp. 158–162)

Let us turn now to a well-known passage in Freud's letter to Fliess that imagistically describes the organization of the book on dreams:

> The whole thing is planned on the model of an imaginary walk. First comes the dark forest of authors (who do not see the trees), hopeless in a place where it is very easy to go astray. Then there is a ravine through which I lead the reader—my dream specimen with its peculiarities, its details, its indiscretions, and its bad jokes—and then suddenly the high ground and the view, and the question: "Which way do you want to go?"
>
> (*Briefe an Wilhelm Fliess,* p. 400)

Part of this passage is repeated verbatim in the initial lines of chapter 3 of *The Interpretation of Dreams,* where Freud and the reader suddenly emerge on high ground, and he proposes following one path among many. With chapter 5, he opens a new trail: "Now that we have reached our goal on this one path, we may return and choose a new starting-point for our rambles through the problems of the dream." At the opening of chapter 7, Freud looks back on the arduous journey: each path he has taken hitherto has led to light, but from now on every path will lead him back into darkness. It is highly meaningful that the dream's navel is mentioned in the seventh and last chapter for the second time. The previous chapters have prepared for an unprecedented theoretical examination of dream life in its depths.

Thus the journeying back and forth in the book on dreams involves Freud symbolically journeying inside and outside himself and his fantasized mother. In the specimen dream analysis in chapter 2, Freud associates his pregnant wife with the dream's heroine Irma and looks into her mouth-vagina. In an act of self-delivery, Freud emerges from this uterine chapter to the outer world, where he eventually encounters Oedipus in chapter 5. In terms of fantasy, then, *The Interpretation of Dreams* depicts a growing mastery over dreams and maternal figures and a development from the uterine to the pre-Oedipal and Oedipal stages of human maturation. All three stages figure imagistically in the final exploration of the mother's body in chapter 7, which, in the investigation of dream processes, reverts to their moment of inauguration, to the first memory trace and wish of the newborn child, and magnificently concludes that dreams of the future are molded by indestructible wishes into "a perfect likeness of the past."

To state it differently: dream processes are at once the book's subject and object, container and contained, form and matter. In composing this book, Freud confided to Fliess that he could make himself dream appropriate dreams—as if they were self-commanded performances. By the same token, he later recognized (as he wrote to Jung in 1911) a self-reflexiveness in what he himself censored and was defensive about: "The book proves the principles of dream interpretation by its own nature, so to speak, through its own deficiencies." The book on dreams not only describes but enacts what it describes. And it is this characteristic of enactive discourse that further ensures the unique position of *The Interpretation of Dreams* in the history of autobiography, and indeed in the whole of world literature, whether imaginative or scientific.

The foregoing examination prepares us to consider Freud's more strictly scientific analysis of dream formation. Within his enterprise of showing that dreams were anything but trivial and that they had profound meaning, Freud divides the dream into two basic parts, the manifest dream and the latent dream. The manifest dream is the dream dreamt, which the dreamer may be able to recall to various degrees in his waking state. The latent dream may draw upon nocturnal sensory stimuli, and more importantly, day residues, and most importantly, repressed infantile drives. The nocturnal sensory stimuli include such impressions as thirst and pain. For example, the dreamer may dream that he is slaking his thirst; in this sense, dreams may truly function as the guardians of sleep. Day residues are memory traces of experiences lived during the day or days prior to the dream; remaining active in the unconscious, they may, like the nocturnal sensory stimuli, appear in varying disguises in the manifest dream.

The core of the latent dream, however, is a wish or several wishes arising from the repressed infantile drives in the unconscious. The two qualifiers of the word "drives" must be seen in all their significance: the drives are repressed because the drive-related wishes were forbidden and therefore had to be driven away from consciousness; and they are infantile because the dream has a sedimented age, extending from the most recent to the most remote past. We might note that Freud insists that the repressed infantile wishes are not necessarily always of a sexual nature.

The manifest dream is the hallucinated expression of an unconscious wish or fantasy that is kept away from conscious waking life. The construction of the dream takes an appreciably longer period of time than the period of its actual staging—Freud makes the apt analogy of the relatively long preparation of fireworks and their short-lived explosion. Two other remarks are appropriate here: first, the "normal" hallucinatory nature of dreams in some ways is similar to the pathological thoughts of psychotic individuals in their waking state; and second, given the much lesser structuring in the child's mind in its process of development, the division of the dream into its manifest and latent parts is less pertinent for children's dreams than for adults'.

The passage from the latent to the manifest dream is effected by dreamwork, which Freud considered the quintessence of the dream. Even though sleep brings about a relaxation of repression so that unconscious wishes and fantasies may press forward for gratification, there is an alert censorship that ordinarily prevents their undisguised expression. It is here that the four principles of dreamwork come into play: displacement, condensation, symbolization, and representability. By virtue of the mechanism of displacement, affective energy formerly invested in a forbidden person is transferred onto a more neutral individual. Condensation, on the other hand, is the process whereby two or more images can be combined into a single image. (Conversely, a single latent wish may be distributed through several representations in the manifest content.) In symbolization, a fairly neutral object is substituted for one that is conflictingly charged and bears forbidden meanings. (For example, a tree stands for a penis.) Representability pertains ordinarily to the translatability of the latent content into the visual image of the manifest dream. (For example, the notion of understanding may be translated in the manifest dream as a person literally standing under something.)

To explain the effect of dreamwork, Freud invoked the military analogy of soldiers trying to pass beyond the enemy lines. Given the resistance at the line, the soldiers might well disguise themselves, preferably with the clothes of their enemy. Likewise, because of censorship, material cannot ordinarily pass into the manifest dream without undergoing various degrees of distortion. Thus the warded-off impulses may have recourse to the use of relatively neutral day residues and in that way pass into the manifest dream as compromise formations. Hence dream images are overdetermined in that they bear multiple meanings derived from multiple unconscious sources. A further difficulty in retrieving the original manifest dream is that sometime after it is dreamt, it is subject to what is called secondary elaboration, which imposes a logical coherence over the absurd and bizarre oneiric material. In the final analysis, then, the dream emerges as an extraordinarily complex phenomenon in mental life and testifies to the marvelous ways in which prohibited wishes may be fulfilled. In this regard, dreams of punishment do not really form an exception, for they may satisfy feelings of guilt and the attendant desire for reparative punishment.

Invaluable as what Freud called the royal road to the unconscious, the dream simultaneously manifests itself in three regressive ways: as a temporal regression from adulthood to childhood, as a topical regression from the conscious to the unconscious, and as a formal regression from the level of verbal language to the pictorial and symbolic representations proper to early life. In conclusion, we find it easy to agree with Freud's own estimate of *The Interpretation of Dreams:* "It contains, even according to my present-day judgment, the most valuable of all the discoveries it has been my good fortune to make. Insight such as this falls to one's lot but once in a lifetime."

Totem und Tabu (*Totem and Taboo,* 1913) comprises Freud's chief contribution to social anthropology, and it also constitutes a diptych with *The Interpretation of Dreams.* As Jones reports, Freud himself said that in the book on dreams he described the wish to kill the father, whereas in *Totem and Taboo* he portrayed the actual deed. It might additionally be noted that Thomas Mann admired the aesthetic quality of the prose of *Totem and Taboo,* and Freud held its fourth and last book to be the stylistic high point of his career.

Concentrating on the Australian aborigines, Freud makes conclusions about totemistic religion in general. For the aborigines, a totem, usually an animal, is venerated as the primeval ancestor of each entire clan. Where there are totems, there are usually interdictions against sexual or marital union among members of the same clan—thus the stricture to marry outside the totem (totemic exogamy) and thereby avoid group incest.

In its original sense, a taboo was an object or person who supposedly possessed mysterious powers and who was not to be touched—a situation provoking an ambivalent reaction of veneration and horror from tribal members. The principal prohibition regarding the taboo—that of touching—reminds us also of similar restraints in phobias and obsessional neuroses. By extension, taboos applied to actions, and even hostile thoughts about certain enemies, were gravely forbidden. If that hostility were carried to the point of killing an enemy, then the taboo broadened to include not only everything that came from the dead body but also its vindictive ghost. In the fear of that vindictiveness Freud sees the origin of conscience, for the death of the awesome other was both wanted and yet feared and not wanted. Sometimes, too, living rulers were the objects of the same ambivalence: if they were hated, they were also given mysterious powers; and if they were exalted above the lot of common mortals, they were also made to live a tormented, restricted existence tantamount to bondage.

But Freud's most daring hypothesis concerns the existence of the primal horde, and it is in the story of that horde that Freud first attempts to analyze the whole of man's social history. He sees totemism, therefore, as a decisive step in a hypothetical reconstruction linking the individual Oedipus complex and the prehistory of man. Indeed, Freud concludes that the origins not only of neurosis but also of religion, morals, society, and art converged in the Oedipus complex. Much of this is spelled out in Freud's famous and oft-cited passage about the primal horde:

> [In the primal horde] there was a violent, jealous father who kept all the females for himself and drove away his sons as they grew up. . . . One day the brothers who had been driven out came together, killed and devoured their father, and so made an end of the patriarchal horde. . . . The violent primal father had surely been the envied and feared model of each one of the company of brothers; and in the act of devouring him they accomplished their identification with him, and each one of them acquired a part of his strength. The totem meal, which is perhaps mankind's earliest festival, would be a repetition and a commemoration of this memorable and criminal deed, which was the beginning of so many things—social organization, moral restrictions and religion. . . . [Hence, according to what is now named deferred obedience, the sons] revoked their deeds in that they forbade the killing of the totem, the substitute for their father; and they renounced its fruits in that they resigned their claim to the women who were set free. They

thus created out of their filial sense of guilt the two fundamental taboos of totemism, which on that very account had to correspond to the two repressed wishes of the Oedipus complex.

(*Gesammelte Werke*, vol. 9, pp. 171–173)

My major concern is to show how the very writing of *Totem and Taboo* not only was retrospective but also acquired the value of a symbol of castration among the members of the growing psychoanalytic movement at the time. Awareness of the relevance of the treatise to Freud as father in relation to the surrounding analysts as sons is indispensable for any well-rounded appreciation of the treatise and accurately reveals it to be a current as well as retrospective reflection.

First of all, some dates are important. From 1910 to 1913 Freud wrote and completed *Totem and Taboo*. In the first of those years, 1910, Freud organized and chaired the international psychoanalytic congress at which the International Psychoanalytic Association was founded. In the last of those years, the rebellious Jung (whose name means "young" in German) resigned from the editorship of the main psychoanalytic journal and in 1914 resigned from the International Psychoanalytic Association. Those are the main temporal coordinates of the story Freud obliquely told about himself as the primal father of the psychoanalytic horde.

From early on, Freud's patriarchal role was explicitly acknowledged by his close followers, who proclaimed themselves to be his sons. By 1911 there was overt rebellion among the flock of Freud's disciples that he called "the wild hunt": Alfred Adler, Wilhelm Stekel, and Victor Tausk displayed their scientific and personal hostility. Meanwhile it was Jung whom Freud privately named as his successor. However, age, succession, and father-son rivalry were subjects that had haunted the relationship of Freud and Jung from its very beginning and that tolled like a ceaseless bell throughout their correspondence. Although Freud in fact nominated Jung in 1910 as the first president of the International Psychoanalytic Association, Freud—as his biographer Jones says—remained the real power behind the throne. Besides that, there is the little-known fact (radically distorted by Jones, a "faithful" son) that Freud had proposed that the president retain his title for life and be empowered to name or depose any analyst in the world; also, any speech to be given by an analyst or any article to be published by him would first have to be approved by the president. Fortunately, the Viennese analysts, mostly Jews, successfully rebelled against the transfer of presidential power, however token a power it was, to the Christian bastion of Jung's Zurich. Freud's outlook was broader than the sectarianism of his Viennese colleagues because he feared that his science would be labeled a Jewish discipline; yet, as history has shown, Vienna proved a better home for psychoanalysis.

Meanwhile, another story was emerging. Jung was contesting Freud's theory of the Oedipus complex and was writing *Wandlungen und Symbole des Libido* (*Psychology of the Unconscious*, 1912), a work that investigates the background of the mythological hero. Jung avowed that writing the last chapter, entitled "The Sacrifice," would involve the "sacrifice" of his friendship with Freud. Freud for his part was writing *Totem and Taboo*, thereby stepping into the field of anthropology and mythology, which he had formerly left to Jung.

Freud had unambiguously identified psychoanalytic doctrine as female ("Lady Psychoanalysis") and described his writing of *Totem and Taboo* as a casual liaison that turned into marriage; and he even dubbed the fourth book of his treatise a veritable "princess." Freud had also indicated that his working on the last part of *Totem and Taboo* was evidence that his death, impatiently awaited by his Viennese foes, was not yet realized. When Freud's opus was finally finished and published, some interpreted it also as a gesture of vengeance whereby Freud followed Jung into the domain of folk psychology and there annihilated him, symbolically castrated him, on his own ground. Thus the father killed the venturous son and kept Lady Psychoanalysis all to himself. Others among Freud's faithful followers—the self-styled "happy brothers"—formally celebrated the publication of *Totem and Taboo* by inviting Freud to a dinner, which they overtly called a totemic festival.

Thus *Totem and Taboo* is not merely a work of exposition or of self-reflection. Its very writing was a symbolic act in itself, castrating the "young" son who was not submissive; hence the work goes beyond description and stands forth as a piece of enactive discourse, performing the decisive role of restoring paternal authority in the psychoanalytic community of its time.

One of the most intriguing and fascinating texts in the whole of Freud's work is *Beyond the Pleasure Principle;* it is also Freud's most controversial text, repudiated by many of his faithful followers. Changing his former theory of drives, Freud made a new basic division between Thanatos and Eros. The latter is much more than the sexual drive Freud had identified earlier, for it exists in each cell and drives living substances to unite into larger entities, and in that way constitutes a flight forward. Ultimately, however, victory goes to Thanatos, which is the drive in all life to return to a previous inanimate state. Like Arthur Schopenhauer, Freud believed that the aim of life is death; this was a pessimistic view, to be sure, and one that undercut the romantic notion of the basic innocence of man and life.

Among the evidence for his theory of Eros, Freud cites the Upanishads and Plato's *Symposium.* Among the stronger evidence for the death drive is a phenomenon inferred from various clinical material: the compulsion to repeat (more ancient than the pleasure principle), as manifested in recurrent dreams proper to traumatic neuroses and in patients' tendency to repeat painful experiences in their lives.

We may now ask ourselves why it took Freud so many years to see aggression as a drive, especially since in the early 1890's Breuer had twice posited the aggressive drive in one of the sections he individually wrote for *Studies in Hysteria.* Searching for an answer to our question will also reveal that the delayed postulation of the death drive was a return to Freud's own repressed drives and that he wrote a text that proceeded as its own metaphor. The text not only described its subject but also enacted it.

To illustrate this, let us begin with the opening word of the text's title, "beyond," which means "farther on" or "on the other side" as opposed to "on this side." By the middle of chapter 1, Freud declares that the pleasure principle does not dominate the mental processes. Aided by various examples of repetition, the text gathers its own momentum, so that by the end of chapter 2 we read that there is something, yet nameless, that is "more primitive" than the pleasure principle. After naming the compulsion to repeat, Freud ends in chapter 3 by saying that we must further study the repetitive force, "which is more primitive, more elementary, more instinctual than the pleasure principle . . . to which . . . we have hitherto attributed dominance." By now, the "beyond" has clearly become "before" or "prior to" the pleasure principle. Freud's text is, like Eros itself, a series of progressive detours that eventually yield to a retrogressive direction. Freud's final arrival at a concept that is by definition retrogressive stands as a moment of irony as it refers us back to a radically progressive beginning. Such an expository gesture is paralleled by Freud's explanations of the origin of consciousness and of the compulsion to repeat, explanations that themselves are resumed and reexplained.

Consider Freud's *repeated* observation of his one-and-a-half-year-old grandson Ernst, who *repeatedly* played with a wooden reel and string when his mother was absent. Ernst would throw the reel away and cry "o-o-o-o," his way of saying the German word *fort* (gone); he then would retrieve the stringed reel and joyfully cry "da" (there), thus playing out his mother's absence and joyful return. Another game little Ernst played was to crouch below a full-length mirror that did not quite reach to the floor and periodically pop up to see his image in the mirror. Thus he was able to make his own image disappear from the mirror and return to it. We might remark that in writing this account, Freud (whose name means "joy" in German) twice inscribes his name in his grandson's game: Ernst's *freudig* (joyful) "da" was a substitute for his mother's *erfreulich* (joyful) return. Our reflection on the writing of this episode leads us to wonder about the autobiographical traces compulsively embedded in Freud's biographical account.

Another insightful example of Freud's multiple repetitions concerns the fact that *Beyond the Pleasure Principle* has seven chapters. Freud's preoccupation with numbers had the makings of a compulsive symptom: he had seven brothers and sisters; he thought that his life was characterized by seven-year cycles; and he associated the number seven with the prediction of death and the struggle of his seven internal organs to direct his life to an end. Freud's regular correspondence with his great friend Fliess lasted nearly fourteen years, and the correspondence with Jung nearly seven. There were exactly seven members of the Secret Committee (a committee ruling the International Psychoanalytic Association and unknown to its rank-and-file members until 1944). For years Freud felt strongly inhibited from visiting the forbidden city of Rome with its seven hills, and once he did, he returned for a sum of seven visits in all. Finally, there are other works in the Freudian canon that have seven chapters: *The Interpretation of Dreams, Jokes and Their Relation to the Unconscious,* the pivotal essay "Das Unbewusste" ("The Unconscious," 1915), *Die Frage der Laienanalyse* (*The Question of Lay Analysis,* 1926), and *New Introductory Lectures.* Moreover, the first two of the *Three Essays on the Theory of Sexuality* have seven parts each, as does Freud's own favorite among his writings, part 4 of *Totem and Taboo.*

I have left for the end one of the most significant details about *Beyond the Pleasure Principle:* although Freud repeatedly mentions Eros in it, he does not once use the term "Thanatos" to name the death drive, a significant omission in that the term had been used years before at the Vienna Psychoanalytic Society. A possible reason for Freud's omission is that he did not, consciously or unconsciously, want to have the name of his preferred child, Anna, formally inscribed in Th*anat*os. For an explanation, we must return to Freud's unforgettable essay "Das Motiv der Kästchenwahl" ("The Theme of Three Caskets," 1913), which deals with the themes of love and death. Analyzing Shakespeare's *King Lear,* Freud asserts on the concluding page:

> Lear carries Cordelia's corpse on to the stage. Cordelia is Death. If one reverses the situation, it becomes understandable and familiar. She is the Goddess of Death, who takes away the dead hero from the battlefield, much as the Valkyrie do in German mythology. Eternal wisdom in the dress of primeval myth advises the old man to renounce love, to elect death and to make friends with the necessity of dying.
>
> (*Gesammelte Werke,* vol. 10, p. 36)

In a private letter to Ferenczi written around the time of "The Three Caskets," Freud acknowledged that its subject concerned his daughter Anna and death. These interconnections make it all the more significant that when Freud was composing *Beyond the Pleasure Principle,* he was at the same time attempting the impossible—he was trying to analyse his own daughter Anna. In that impossible adventure between father and daughter, the very oedipal drama of Eros and Thanatos could only be bizarrely repeated. Both Sigmund and Anna were caught in the progressive and retrogressive movements of striving for union and mortal dissolution, both of which were encapsulated orthographically by the palindrome "Anna," which reads the same backward and forward. As a self-defeating venture in which present and past were inevitably so fundamentally dislocated and distorted, this intrafamilial therapy was an anachronism and a pseudo-*analysis*, yet it constituted the compulsive backdrop to *Beyond the Pleasure Principle*, which, in chapter 2, united grandfather Freud with one of his specifically mentioned daughters and grandchildren. The treatise is a repetitive exposition and enactment of an eternal return in autobiography and familial biography authored ultimately, according to the implications of the text, by an eternal ghostwriter in whom generations meet.

Freud wrote five great case histories, each of them unparalleled in psychiatric or psychoanalytic literature for analytic and literary power. Each of them also presents a rich mixture of clinical and theoretical material that never fails to offer a profound experience to the reader. The Schreber case is unique among these five cases in that Freud never saw its protagonist. Fascinated by the *Memoirs* of Daniel Schreber, a distinguished German judge whose serious illness had led to hospitalizations, Freud decided to write "Psychoanalytische Bemerkungen über einen autobiographisch beschriebenen Fall von Paranoia" ("Psychoanalytic Notes upon an Autobiographical Account of a Paranoid Case," 1911); Freud's account still remains a classic commentary on the psychodynamics of paranoia. Another case, "Analyse der Phobie eines fünfjährigen Knaben" ("Analysis of a Phobia of a Five-Year-Old Boy," 1909), deals with little Hans, whom Freud saw only once and otherwise treated through the reporting father. Thanks to the treatment of this little boy who so feared that a horse would bite him that he would not go outdoors, Freud for the first time directly demonstrated the existence of infantile sexuality and the Oedipus complex in a child. In "Fragment of an Analysis of a Case of Hysteria," Freud described his treatment of Dora, who suddenly and without explanation left him after the eleventh week of sessions. Although Freud admitted having realized the treatment's transferential implications too late, especially the negative paternal transference, he managed to use the case to write a remarkable, condensed synthesis of *Studies on Hysteria* and *The Interpretation of Dreams* that at the same time is a transitional piece anticipating some of the findings in *Three Essays on the Theory of Sexuality.*

The Rat Man figures as the subject of "Bemerkungen über einen Fall von Zwangsneurose" ("Notes upon a Case of Obsessional Neurosis," 1909). The case is singular in that it is generally alleged to be Freud's only complete one; it stands also as a matchless description of the phenomenology of obsessional neurosis and contains some theoretical statements on the neurosis that are still authoritative. Just before consulting Freud, the patient was on maneuvers, during one moment of which a "cruel captain" had told with relish the story of an oriental torture in which a pot of rats was affixed to the anus of the victim. Immediately the Rat Man (whence his name) fantasized that the torture was applied both to his beloved lady friend and to his long-deceased father. It was not long before rats began to symbolize many things for the Rat Man, including money, feces, gambling, penis, baby, and marriage.

At the center of the patient's pathology was a considerable unconscious hostility toward his father, whom he consciously loved. For some time after his father's demise, he refused to accept the death as fact; when he finally did, he manifested an intense ambivalence and pathological mourning in constantly visiting bereaved relatives to express his sympathy, for which he was nicknamed "carrion crow" in his family. Also, he habitually imagined people as dying so he could share heartfelt sympathy with the affected relatives. One classic obsessional gesture he directed to his lady friend was the following: after a serious disagreement with her, he happened to walk on a road over which the carriage of his departing lady was to pass, and he removed a stone that he felt to be lying dangerously in the middle of the road; next, overcome by hostility and thinking his action to be absurd, he went back and placed the stone in its original position.

Freud found that for the Rat Man, "looking took the place of touching" and carnal contiguity; his case involved an overdetermined use of the eye, for, as Freud stresses elsewhere, the optical zone is "perhaps the zone most remote from the sexual object." Also part and parcel of the Rat Man's obsessiveness was his reliance on defensive isolation. According to one of the meanings of this isolation, the Rat Man experienced ideas without the appropriate accompanying feeling, resulting in a severance of causal connections (contiguity) between ideas. According to another meaning of isolation, this time dealing with the articulation of ideas, the Rat Man inserted an interval of time between his utterances in order to lead astray any conscious investigation of their causal connections.

When we turn from the Rat Man as patient to Freud's exposition of the case as such, we come upon a surprise: the case is characterized by disconnectedness to such an extent that we must suspect some interference from Freud's unconscious and that we must finally identify the case not only as one of exposition but also as one of enactment. In this case, the gaps and disjunctions in Freud's text enact the discontinuities involved in the Rat Man's defensive isolation. Both in his correspondence with Jung and in the introduction to the case, Freud writes of its disconnected and aphoristic nature (aphorisms being broad statements that exist independently and have no ligatures or connections with other statements). And indeed, in the Rat Man case, instead of encountering the familiar Freud with his superb articulateness, we come upon a writer who, amid his many moments of brilliance, confuses the precipitating causes of his patient's illnesses, elaborates little on the links between the Rat Man's early and later loved objects, does not firmly correlate the clinical and theoretical considerations as he does in his other cases, and does not succeed in neatly tying together child and adult symptomatology. In sum, the isolation of causal connections, along with a theoretical doing and undoing (the alternating affirmation and withdrawal of propositions), punctuates Freud's text and exhibits its dual

nature as subject and object, as exposition and enactment.

By general agreement, Freud's greatest case history is about the Wolf Man, the hero of "Aus der Geschichte einer infantilen Neurose" ("From the History of an Infantile Neurosis," 1918). The Wolf Man was a Russian patient whom Freud followed in treatment for four-and-a-half years; the Russian returned to Freud a second time, and then was treated afterward by others at irregular intervals for over fifty years. He literally became a ward of psychoanalysis.

The Wolf Man was twenty-three when he first consulted Freud for a psychoanalysis that in great part turned on a dream that the patient had had at the age of four:

> I dreamt that it is night and I lie in my bed. (My bed stood with its foot towards the window, and in front of the window was a row of old walnut trees. I know that it was winter and nighttime when I dreamt.) Suddenly the window opens by itself, and I see with great fright that on the big walnut tree before the window some white wolves are sitting. There were six or seven of them. The wolves were entirely white and looked like foxes rather than sheep-dogs, for they had large tails like foxes and their ears were pointed up like dogs when they pay attention to something. With great terror, obviously about being eaten up by the wolves, I scream and wake up.
>
> (*Gesammelte Werke,* vol. 12, p. 54)

Using other data arising from the analysis, Freud tries to trace the dream to a time two-and-a-half years earlier when the eighteen-month-old boy had witnessed his parents engaged in intercourse (the so-called primal scene). In the most audacious gesture to be found in his writings, Freud attempts to reconstruct a host of details attending that event: his patient's infantile age, his physical sickness at the time, the season of the year, the time of day, its general temperature, the place of the action, the state and color of his parents' clothes, the color of the bedclothes, the quality of the child's attention, his detection of his father's sounds and of the emotional expression on his mother's face, his observation of their genitals, their coital position, the number of occurrences of intercourse, the general nature of the witness's reaction, the specific manner in which the child interrupted his parents' lovemaking, and the tonal quality of his ensuing reaction. More specifically, Freud imagines the previous postulates to form the following scenario: one hot summer day, the eighteen-month-old boy, afflicted with malaria, was sleeping in a cot in his parents' bedroom, where the parents retired, half dressed, for a siesta; possibly at the height of a fever, at five in the afternoon the young child woke up and with strained attention watched his parents, half-dressed in white underclothes and kneeling on white bedclothes, engage in tergal coitus three times; while noticing his parents' genitalia, his father's heavy breathing, and his mother's facial expression of enjoyment, the generally passive baby suddenly had a bowel movement and screamed, thereby interrupting the young couple.

There are many reasons for distrusting the plausibility of Freud's reconstruction: to name but two, a young baby sorely afflicted with malaria and its distortion of the sensorium is incapable of prolonged, strained attention, and intercourse from the rear as a position precludes a child from seeing at any angle the genitalia of his parents. But what is so fascinating is that again and again Freud tries to "persuade" us of his interpretation. As a matter of fact, the word "persuade" occurs more frequently in the Wolf Man case than in Freud's other writings, and when one remembers what the term means in German, Freud's peculiar lexical insistence becomes clear. In German, the word is *überzeugen,* whose root, *zeugen,* means either to witness or to procreate. Those two actions, witnessing and procreating, constitute the two events of the primal scene—the witnessing of the child and the copulating of the parents. This, then, is but one indication—and there are others—that the subject of Freud's claims is intermingled with his strategy of rhetoric or persuasion. Once

more, the division between subject and means, exposition and enactment, dwindles away. To put it another way, Freud's discourse is both a narrative of the past and a staging in the present, both a dramatic representation and a re-presentation.

A mention of the apocalyptic relevance of Freud will serve as a timely though uncomfortable conclusion. While creating a science that constantly distinguishes fantasy from reality in a variety of spheres, Freud enjoyed the painful distinction of living through a series of historical terrors: racial and religious persecution, the unscrupulousness of organized capitalism and Marxism, world war, the rise of Nazism, and so forth. One may wonder how Freud would have reflected on our nuclear era, which has its own ultimate distinction: namely, the psychotic-like fantasies of man's annihilating the universe might equally be sober considerations grounded in reality—for yesterday's nightmare is potentially today's reality. It was precisely within the legacy of the Freudian tradition that the British psychoanalyst Edward Glover wrote in 1946: "The capacity so painfully acquired by normal man to distinguish between sleep, hallucination, delusion and the objective reality has for the first time in history been seriously weakened."

Selected Bibliography

EDITIONS

INDIVIDUAL WORKS
Studien über Hysterie. Vienna, 1893–1895.
Die Traumdeutung. Vienna, 1900.
Zur Psychopathologie des Alltagslebens. Vienna, 1901.
Drei Abhandlungen zur Sexualtheorie. Vienna, 1905.
Der Witz und seine Beziehung zum Unbewussten. Vienna, 1905.
Der Wahn und die Träume in W. Jensen's "Gradiva." Vienna, 1907.
Eine Kindheitserinnerung des Leonardo da Vinci. Vienna, 1910.
Totem und Tabu. Vienna, 1913.

SIGMUND FREUD

Vorlesungen zur Einführung in die Psychoanalyse. Vienna, 1916–1917.

Jenseits des Lustprinzips. Vienna, 1920.

Massenpsychologie und Ich-Analyse. Vienna, 1921.

Das Ich und das Es. Vienna, 1923.

Die Frage der Laienanalyse. Vienna, 1926.

Hemmung, Symptom, und Angst. Vienna, 1926.

Die Zukunft einer Illusion. Vienna, 1927.

Neue Folge der Vorlesungen zur Einführung in die Psychoanalyse. Vienna, 1933.

"Ein Wort zum Antisemitismus." In *Die Zukunft,* November 1938.

Der Mann Moses und die Monotheistische Religion. Amsterdam, 1939.

COLLECTED WORKS

Sigmund Freud: Gesammelte Werke. 18 vols. Frankfurt am Main, 1940–1968.

Sigmund Freud: Studienausgabe. 10 vols. Frankfurt am Main, 1969–1975.

CORRESPONDENCE

The Freud–Jung Letters. Edited by William McGuire and translated by Ralph Manheim and R. C. Hull. Princeton, N.J., 1974.

Sigmund Freud: Briefe an Wilhelm Fliess (1887–1904). Edited by J. Masson, M. Schröter, and G. Fichtner. Frankfurt am Main, 1986.

TRANSLATIONS

The Freud–Jung Letters. Edited by William McGuire and translated by Ralph Manheim and R. C. Hull. Princeton, N.J., 1974.

A General Introduction to Psychoanalysis. Translated by Joan Riviere. New York, 1952. Freud's *Introductory Lectures* also appear under this title.

The Pelican Freud Library. 14 vols. Translated by Angela Richards, James Strachey, et al. London, 1962–1985.

Sigmund Freud: Three Case Histories. Edited by Philip Rieff. New York, 1963. Contains case histories of Dora, the Rat Man, and the Wolf Man.

The Standard Edition of the Complete Psychological Works of Sigmund Freud. 24 vols. Translated by James Strachey, et al. London, 1953–1974.

BIOGRAPHICAL AND CRITICAL STUDIES

Andersson, Ola. *Studies in the Prehistory of Psychoanalysis.* Stockholm, 1962.

Anzieu, Didier. *Freud's Self-Analysis and the Discovery of Psychoanalysis.* Translated by Peter Graham. New York, 1986.

Bernheimer, Charles, and Clare Kahane, eds. *In Dora's Case: Freud—Hysteria—Feminism.* New York, 1985.

Blanton, Smiley. *Diary of My Analysis with Sigmund Freud.* New York, 1971.

Brenner, Charles. *An Elementary Textbook of Psychoanalysis.* New York, 1955.

Clark, Ronald W. *Freud: The Man and the Cause.* New York, 1980.

Eagle, Morris N. *Recent Developments in Psychoanalysis.* New York, 1984.

Eissler, Kurt R. *Medical Orthodoxy and the Future of Psychoanalysis.* New York, 1965.

————. *Talent and Genius.* New York, 1971.

————. *Victor Tausk's Suicide.* New York, 1983.

Ellenberger, Henri F. *The Discovery of the Unconscious: The History and Evolution of Dynamic Psychiatry.* New York, 1970.

Gardiner, Muriel, ed. *The Wolf-Man and Sigmund Freud.* New York, 1971.

Gay, Peter. *Freud, Jews and Other Germans: Masters and Victims in Modernist Culture.* New York, 1978.

Gilman, Sandra L., ed. *Introducing Psychoanalytic Theory.* New York, 1982.

Glover, Edward. *Freud or Jung?* London, 1950.

Hyman, Stanley Edgar. *The Tangled Bank: Darwin, Marx, Frazer and Freud as Imaginative Writers.* New York, 1962.

Janik, Allan, and Stephen Toulmin. *Wittgenstein's Vienna.* London, 1973.

Johnston, William M. *The Austrian Mind: An Intellectual and Social History, 1848–1938.* Berkeley, Calif., 1972.

Jones, Ernest. *Sigmund Freud: Life and Work.* 3 vols. New York, 1953–1957.

Kanzer, Mark, and Jules Glenn, eds. *Freud and His Self-Analysis.* New York, 1979.

————, eds. *Freud and His Patients.* New York, 1980.

Kardiner, Abram. *My Analysis with Freud: Reminiscences.* New York, 1977.

Kaufmann, Walter Arnold. *Discovering the Mind, Vol. 3: Freud Versus Adler and Jung.* New York, 1980.

Klein, Dennis B. *Jewish Origins of the Psychoanalytic Movement.* New York, 1981.

Kris, Ernst. *Psychoanalytic Explorations in Art.* New York, 1952.

Laplanche, Jean, and J. B. Pontalis. *The Language of Psychoanalysis.* Translated by Donald Nicholson-Smith. New York, 1973.

McGrath, William J. *Freud's Discovery of Psychoanalysis: The Politics of Hysteria.* Ithaca, N.Y., 1986.

Mahony, Patrick J. *Freud as a Writer.* New York, 1982.

————. *The Cries of the Wolf Man.* New York, 1984.

————. *Freud and the Rat Man.* New Haven, Conn., 1986.

Marcus, Steven. *Freud and the Culture of Psychoanalysis.* Boston, Mass., 1984.

Mehlman, J., ed. *French Freud: Structural Studies in Psychoanalysis.* Yale French Studies, no. 48. New Haven, Conn., 1972.

Meissner, W. W. *Psychoanalysis and Religious Experience.* New Haven, Conn., 1984.

Reik, Theodor. *From Thirty Years with Freud.* London, 1942.

Ricoeur, Paul. *Freud and Philosophy.* Translated by D. Savage. New Haven, Conn., 1970.

Rieff, Philip. *Freud: The Mind of the Moralist.* London, 1960.

Roazen, Paul. *Freud and His Followers.* New York, 1971.

Ruitenbeek, Hendrik Marinus., ed. *Freud as We Knew Him.* Detroit, 1973.

Schur, Max. *Freud: Living and Dying.* London, 1972.

Skura, Meridith Anne. *The Literary Use of the Psychoanalytic Process.* New Haven, Conn., 1981.

Spector, Jack J. *The Aesthetics of Freud: A Study in Psychoanalysis and Art.* London, 1972.

Stepansky, Paul E., ed. *Freud: Appraisals and Reappraisals.* Hillsdale, N.J., 1986.

Sterba, Richard F. *Reminiscences of a Viennese Psychoanalyst.* Detroit, 1982.

Sulloway, Frank J. *Freud, Biologist of the Mind: Beyond the Psychoanalytic Legend.* New York, 1979.

Wallace, Edwin R. *Freud and Anthropology: A History and Reappraisal.* New York, 1983.

Weber, Samuel. *The Legend of Freud.* Minneapolis, 1982.

Wollheim, Richard. *Freud.* London, 1971.

Wright, Elizabeth. *Psychoanalytic Criticism: Theory in Practice.* London, 1984.

PATRICK J. MAHONY

KNUT HAMSUN
(1859–1952)

THE AUTHOR of *Sult* (*Hunger*, 1890) and *Pan* (1894), Knut Hamsun is Norway's best-known novelist and one of the major writers of modern times. He is commonly ranked immediately below the four great names of Scandinavian literature, Hans Christian Andersen, Søren Kierkegaard, Henrik Ibsen, and August Strindberg; his works are available in more than thirty languages and he has won many admirers among European and American men of letters. Germany's Thomas Mann saw in Hamsun a direct descendant of Feodor Dostoevsky and Friedrich Nietzsche; the Russians celebrated him for his drama; Arthur Koestler praised his tender love stories and H. G. Wells his powerful prose epic, *Markens grøde* (*Growth of the Soil,* 1917), for which he won the Nobel Prize. Isaac Bashevis Singer has spoken with admiration of Hamsun's modern subjectiveness, his fragmentariness, his use of flashbacks, and his lyricism, and it has recently been recognized that Hamsun was indeed a precursor of European modernism, with a literary technique anticipating Marcel Proust, James Joyce, and Virginia Woolf.

Even to those of his countrymen who do not read literature, Hamsun's name means something: after World War II, at the age of eighty-nine, he was accused of collaboration with the German occupation forces in Norway and sentenced to pay the Norwegian government practically everything he owned. Norwegians have since begun to doubt whether their treatment of the old novelist was appropriate, but in the bitterness and disappointment of the postwar years it is understandable: this was the betrayal of a man who had been his country's most beloved writer. It is not difficult to see why: despite its often sordid details and tragic tone, the typical Hamsun novel has humor, charm, love of life, and, above all, a joy in nature that can be appreciated by readers everywhere.

Knut Pedersen—as Hamsun was known before he changed his name—was born on 4 August 1859 in Lom, Gudbrandsdal. This is the heart of Norway, known both for its scenic beauty and for its acclaimed artists and cultural achievements—two of Norway's best twentieth-century poets (Olav Aukrust and Tor Jonsson) came from the same little parish. On his mother's side Hamsun belonged to an old and respected farming family, although his immediate relatives had recently come down in the world. Hamsun's father was an itinerant tailor from a neighboring community. When Hamsun was four years old the family moved six hundred miles north to the island of Hamarøy in Nordland, where Hamsun's uncle, Hans Olsen, worked as a shopkeeper and postmaster and had acquired a farm called Hamsund, from which Hamsun later took his name. Northern Norway, with its midnight sun and its snow-clad peaks rising out of the ocean, is even more of a fairy-tale land than Gudbrandsdal. In Hamsun's day the people living there were mostly poor fishermen and small-holders, while in a few large estates along the coast wealthy merchants plied their trade, imitating the life-style of the Oslo bourgeoisie and enjoying the same privileges as nobility elsewhere. Although Hamsun never became a genuine Nordlander, he studied the mannerisms and language of his northern neighbors and used this material in his later work.

As payment for what they owed Hans Olsen, Hamsun's parents had little Knut work for this uncle, who was crippled with arthritis but still a hard taskmaster with no understanding of children. In his service Knut learned to grit his teeth, a sign of determination that later stood him in good stead. These years with Uncle Hans have since been explored by psychoanalysts and by critics trying to explain Hamsun's curious hatred of "old imperialist" England. Hamsun received no education beyond grade school, and after confirmation spent five years working as a peddler, a shoemaker's apprentice, a bailiff's assistant, and a schoolteacher. The experience from these and other professions served him well in his writing career, which began when at eighteen he published a short novel called *Den Gaadefulde* (The Enigmatic Man, 1877). Hamsun's next novel, *Bjørger* (1878), is more ambitious in that it consciously imitates the prose of Bjørnstjerne Bjørnson (1832–1910), who in his so-called rustic novels had tried to revive the old Icelandic saga narrative. Despite Hamsun's attempt to create a new style here, his melodramatic story of love between a young poet and his admired Laura is interesting mainly as a study for Hamsun's most famous love story, *Victoria,* written ten years later.

Hamsun then realized he wanted to become a professional writer and, with a loan from the Nordland merchant E. B. K. Zahl, spent the summer of 1879 in southern Norway, where he completed a novel, "Frida," for which he was unable to find a publisher and which has since been lost. After a brief attempt to become an actor, in 1880–1881 Hamsun worked on road construction north of Oslo, where he met friends who were willing to pay for his ticket to America. There he hoped to find a future as a poet among the Norwegian immigrants. Before leaving for the United States, Hamsun sought the advice of Norway's best-known writer, Bjørnstjerne Bjørnson.

Bjørnson had visited America in 1880–1881 and, unlike many Scandinavian visitors to the New World, was enthusiastic about its democratic experiment. At the invitation of Professor Rasmus B. Anderson of Madison, Wisconsin, he had undertaken a lecture tour of the Midwest and suggested to Hamsun that he also turn to Professor Anderson. When he called in Madison in February of 1882, Hamsun did not receive the help he had hoped for, and in the following months he worked on farms around Elroy, Wisconsin, and later at a store in the town. He also lectured on literary topics and nurtured plans to become a writer. In December of 1882, in the autograph album of a young friend, he penned his so-called Elroy Manifesto: "My life is a peaceless flight through all the land, my religion is the moral of the wildest naturalism but my world is the aesthetical literatur [*sic*]."

Early in 1884, after he had moved to the little town of Madelia, Minnesota, Hamsun met the Norwegian poet and Unitarian minister Kristofer Janson, whose secretary he became. In Janson's home in Minneapolis he found a good library and a stimulating literary milieu, and Janson's wife, Drude, herself a frustrated artist, fell in love with the young writer. In the late spring of 1884, Hamsun became ill and was told by his doctor that he suffered from terminal tuberculosis. Since he wished to return to Norway to die, friends offered to pay for his ticket, and in August Hamsun arrived in Oslo, where his disease was diagnosed as nothing more than a case of bronchitis. He was advised to move inland, where the mountain air would be beneficial.

Hamsun spent the next year and a half in Valdres, where he worked as a postal clerk, made good friends, and acquired the final version of his name when, in an article on

Mark Twain, a printer accidentally left out the "d" in Hamsund. A lecture tour to the small towns of eastern Norway ended in disappointment when he realized that more profitable work would be needed to keep him alive. He was often without food and sometimes had to spend his nights in a shack or even at the police station, experiences that he later used in his first great novel, *Hunger.* In July 1886 he fled from his creditors and returned to America. This time he was determined not to be waylaid by literary ambitions: he would make money, return to Norway, pay his debts, and then live as a writer.

Hamsun's second stay in America began quite auspiciously. He worked on the construction of a new cable car line in Chicago; it was very hard work but paid well, and later that same fall he was employed as a conductor on the Halsted Line. However, he was still unable to put any money aside, and in the end he appealed to no less a person than Philip Armour of the Chicago stockyards. Apparently touched by the helpless tone of Hamsun's letter, Armour paid his ticket so that he could join his old friends in Minneapolis. During the summer of 1887 Hamsun worked on one of the bonanza farms in North Dakota, but in the fall he was back in Minneapolis.

With the help of friends he organized a series of literary lectures to be held at Dania Hall during the winter of 1887–1888. His subjects were the great French writers, Honoré de Balzac, Gustave Flaubert, Émile Zola, and later the new realist writers of Scandinavia—Bjørnson, Ibsen, Jonas Lie, Janson, Alexander M. Kielland, and Strindberg. His last lecture in March, "Aesthetic Reflections—Life in Minneapolis," was an amusing assessment of America's cultural life.

He left the U.S. in the summer of 1888 and on his way to New York was able to place an article on Strindberg—the first ever published in English on the Swedish writer—in a Chicago journal. When his ship docked in Oslo, Hamsun did not go ashore; the memory of the rough days he had spent in that city two years earlier was too painful, and he continued to Copenhagen. Here once more he lived in poverty, yet he wrote to a friend in America: "How I find this country agreeable! I assure you, the whole existence—way of life—here is in deep harmony with my temperament, my nature. Here is Europe, and I am a European, thank God!"

During the fall of 1888 Hamsun managed to turn out an article on Janson and a chapter of what later became the novel *Hunger*, which made him famous almost overnight. He was invited to the homes of well-known literati, to lecture at the Student Union on his experiences in America, and to have these lectures published as a book—*Fra det moderne Amerikas Aandsliv* (*The Cultural Life of Modern America*), which appeared in April of 1889. Of Hamsun's formative years as a writer, the four-and-a-half he spent in America were of major importance, although he at first denied this was so. His attitude toward America changed over the years from positive to negative to somewhat positive, but as the symbol of a materialist view of life the country remained problematic to him throughout his writing career.

In 1889, when Hamsun wrote his amusing book about America's cultural life, he aimed to devastate, not only because he hoped to entertain the Copenhagen students with humorous accounts of an outlandish place, but also because he was himself disillusioned. He had gone to America as a man of no distinguished family background or education and with some of Bjørnson's belief in democracy, and he returned to Europe as an elitist who was soon to embrace Nietzsche's ideas on the *Übermensch*. In his book he attacks America's obsession with profit, growth, and speed, and on this point he never changed his critical stance. Democracy he attacked because it led to isolationism and provincialism and so did not further the arts, which more and more became Hamsun's major concern: "I have never met anyone who has had as morbid a passion for aesthetic beauty as he and whose whole way of thinking has been to such an extent dominated by that passion," Janson wrote in his memoirs.

In his chapters on American literature Hamsun left out Twain, whom he admired, and spoke of Walt Whitman as a barbarian and Ralph Waldo Emerson as a poor philosopher. He singled out Whitman's rhetorical repetitions for ridicule, although he gradually adopted this stylistic feature in his own prose. On the other hand, he praised Emerson for being a fine orator whose sentences sometimes "whip like a silken banner in the wind." Otherwise he associated American literature first and foremost with Henry Wadsworth Longfellow's poetry, which to him seemed overly romantic and old-fashioned. He praised American newspapers, however, not for their editorials, but for their daily reporting: "American journalism is still the most distinctive and vigorous intellectual manifestation of the American people. In its boldness, its realistic intensity, it is also from a literary standpoint the most modern."

Hamsun's statements may seem arrogant coming from a representative of a small, backward country, but it should be remembered that during these years the Scandinavian countries were leaders in Western literature, with names such as Jens Peter Jacobsen, Ibsen, and Strindberg to their credit. The realism of the major European literatures had been channeled into the Nordic countries through the efforts of the great Danish critic Georg Brandes. He asked that Scandinavian writers leave their old romanticism behind and use their gifts in the service of society by attacking old prejudices and questioning existing institutions. In Norway Lie wrote about marriage; Kielland attacked the school system, Bjørnson the state church; and Ibsen, in his shocking play *Ghosts* (1881) about marriage and hereditary venereal disease, showed how far the new iconoclasts were willing to go. This is the "wildest naturalism" Hamsun speaks about in his "Elroy Manifesto," and which he had found in America's newspapers but not in its literature.

Nevertheless, Hamsun learned from American literature. It is true that after his return from the United States he used every opportunity to ridicule the Yankees, but it is equally true that his colleagues in Scandinavia looked upon him as an "American." His need to be in the news and to attack the old and clear ground for the young, for instance, was seen as an American characteristic. Indeed, a word often applied to him during the early 1890's was "Yankee." Brandes, in his review of *The Cultural Life of Modern America,* found that Hamsun's consistent hunting for effect was an American feature in his style. More particularly he may have meant the rhetorical use of repetition, questions and answers, and antithetical constructions, which Hamsun had heard American orators use and practiced himself as a lecturer on many occasions. These features are especially pronounced in *The Cultural Life of Modern America,* although they color his prose style from beginning to end. The following two quotations—written more than fifty years apart—show Hamsun's lifelong ambition to write sentences that "whip like a silken banner in the wind":

> The other loved him as a slave, as a mad man and as a beggar. Why? Ask the dust of the road and the leaves that fall, ask the mysterious God of Life; for none other knows these things. She gave him nothing; no, nothing did she give him and yet he thanked her. She said: "Give me your peace and your reason." And he grieved only that she did not ask his life.
>
> (*Pan,* translated by James McFarlane; p. 147)

> Even now I have reminders of what my stay there at Psychiatric Clinic in Oslo destroyed for me. It cannot be measured, it has nothing to do with weight and measure. It was a slow, slow pulling up by the roots. Where does the blame lie? No one person, no one thing: a system. Domination over a living being, regulations lacking mercy and tact, a psychology of blank spaces and labels, a whole science bristling defiance.
>
> (*On Overgrown Paths,* translated by Carl L. Anderson; p. 91)

In his attack on American literature, Hamsun is not unlike Ibsen's Peer Gynt, who denounced the trolls but actually wrote their motto behind his ear and lived accordingly.

The 1890's is the most important decade in Hamsun's literary career. He published six novels, three plays, and a collection of short stories, and he lectured widely on the new trends in European literature. His tone in these lectures was much more aggressive than in his Minneapolis talks of three years earlier. Thus in September 1891 he attacked Ibsen and other great writers of his generation and stated that he wanted to clear the ground for fresh ideas. Ibsen, who was in the audience, later used the incident in his famous play *The Master Builder* (1892), in a scene where the aging architect expresses his fear of young competitors. But Hamsun definitely did bring in something new during those years. Indeed, when his name is associated with European literary modernism, one thinks first and foremost of his works from the 1890's, in particular of his novels *Hunger, Mysterier* (*Mysteries,* 1892), and *Pan.*

Toward the end of Hamsun's American stay, Brandes, who had brought naturalism and problem literature to Scandinavia, altered his signals. Gradually tiring of his utilitarian past and turning his attention to the great men who fought alone in the vanguard of progress, he had taken up contact with Nietzsche and in the spring of 1888 gave a series of lectures on the German genius, which were followed by a protracted newspaper discussion of his work. Unknown elsewhere, Nietzsche received his first public attention in Copenhagen. Hamsun arrived on the scene when the discussion was still going on, but the new ideas were not new to him—what Nietzsche had done to make Brandes an elitist, America had already done to Hamsun. To him the aim of literature was not to reform society but to create a new kind of nobility.

Already in 1885 Hamsun had praised Twain for his ability "to strike"; two years later he praised Strindberg for "his rude force" and elaborated Strindberg's notions of a different hero. The new hero was not to be a man with dominant personality traits—what the French literary critic Hippolyte Taine had called the "faculté maîtresse"; rather he was to be without character in the traditional sense, split and complex, not good, not bad, but both, subtly differentiated in his nature, changing in his actions. Finally, in his important article "Fra det ubevidste sjæleliv" (From the Unconscious Life of the Mind), published in the journal *Samtiden* in 1890, Hamsun launched his idea of a new literature:

> Now what if literature on the whole began to deal a little more with mental states than with engagements and balls and hikes and accidents as such? Then one would, to be sure, have to relinquish creating types, as all have been created before, "characters" whom one meets every day in the fishmarket. . . . But in return . . . we would experience a little more of the secret movements which are unnoticed in the remote places of the soul, the capricious disorder of perception, the wandering of these thoughts and feelings out of the blue; motionless, trackless journeys with the brain and the heart, strange activities of the nerves, the whispering of the blood, the pleading of the bone, the entire unconscious life.
>
> (p. 325–326)

For those who wondered what he might have meant by "the whispering of the blood," Hamsun provided an explanation six months later when *Hunger* appeared—beside *Growth of the Soil,* Hamsun's most widely known novel and, some would argue, his best. Like many first novels it contains all the central elements of its author's later fiction—a tragic love story, poetic rendering of natural scenery, shockingly realistic detail—and is related in a manner that reveals the special fluctuations of a youthful temperament: the book has humor, exuberance, hope, and despair in a combination never fully repeated by the more mature Hamsun. It is also special in being more directly autobiographical than anything Hamsun wrote before his autobiography, *På gjenrodde stier* (*On Overgrown Paths*). The novel is set in Christiania (Oslo), where the royal palace, Saint Olaf Square, and the East Station are well-known places. The hero's address, Tomtegaten no. 11, was also Hamsun's during his stay in Christiania in 1880. Like the hero of his novel, he lived in a shack in Møllergaten and spent a night at the police station, as we know from letters. The hero's final escape on board a ship bound for Leith resembles Hamsun's own flight to America in 1886. Also different from the practice in novels of the naturalistic period is the use of a first-person narrator—as in Whitman's poetry or Strindberg's *The Son of a Servant* (1886–1887), which Hamsun had studied in Minneapolis. However, unlike Strindberg, Hamsun is concerned not with an individual's growth or development, but rather with a soul's dialogue with its alter ego.

A first reading of *Hunger* confirms Hamsun's own claim that with regard to plot he was playing on one string. The four parts that make up the novel seem much alike both in mood and content. They tell of the young man Andreas Tangen's search for food, lodging, and part-time work in a big, unfriendly city where he wishes to try his luck as a writer, but where gradually he finds himself with no place to stay and nothing to eat. His attempts to get a job are all unsuccessful, but in each of the four parts, when catastrophe is close, he is saved by a newspaper editor who buys an article, or by an old friend who has a dollar to spare, or, at the end, by taking a job on a ship and sailing away from the city. The novel, like others by Hamsun, describes an "experiment in living," here on the most elemental level: how to support the body—with food, rest, sex— in order that it can support an exceptional mind. As in most of Hamsun's early work, the experiment is unsuccessful for the protagonist, whose body and soul are finally at the point of breaking down. The reader, however, follows his course with undivided attention, fascinated alternately by the interplay of crass realism in the description of his physical decline and the astounding turns of his sparkling imagination.

Even in this continuous flow of scenes it is possible to discern a certain structuring of events. The first expository part offers the general pattern: the search for food, money, and work. Part 2, describing a night spent in a cell at the city jail, marks the first low point in the protagonist's misery and shows how easily his hunger pains are overshadowed by his fear of death. Part 3 contains the climax, with the expectation and excitement of the two meetings with a woman whom he calls, fantastically, Ylajali, and part 4 the catastrophe in which, after losing Ylajali and tearing up his drama, the protagonist gives up the whole experiment.

Such a horizontal development, despite Hamsun's wish to obtain the synchronic effect of an orchestral score, is also evident in other ways. The change of time from fall to winter; the change of the protagonist's residence from Oslo's west to its east end; the drop in social status from having belonged in the company of the city's intellectual elite (when Ylajali first sees him in the theater) to a position where even servants laugh at him; and finally, his own moral fall when he accepts unearned money—all this reinforces the impression of a planned steady decline. It is true that in part 4 the protagonist does not suffer from lack of food the way he does in the earlier sections, but we have already learned that there are worse pains than hunger. The ugliness of his surroundings and particularly his own inability to produce beauty in any form finally leave this hero completely without hope.

He is an artist-hero of the kind psychiatrists might label schizoid, manic-depressive, or sado-masochistic. Ibsen's statement that "to be a poet is to see" applies to this hero to an extraordinary degree, for under the influence of hunger, in mental states that today might be called "psychedelic," he registers objects and events with the fidelity of the most sensitive camera: "Nothing escaped my eyes. I was sharp and my brain was very much alive, everything poured in toward me with a staggering distinctness as if a strong light had fallen on everything around me." Despite the many illustrations of states of mind where the hero is described as being in the power of forces beyond his control, he is not always a mere medium. He can analyze the workings of the camera he is, so that by creating special conditions, he can make it yield extraordinary impressions, sometimes dreamlike, sometimes grotesque.

He is definitely an aesthete: the sight of an invalid, a toothless woman, or an old man strikes him with a revulsion that he tries unsuccessfully to counteract with his daydreams of beauty—of Ylajali, elevated in his dreams to a "princess," reclining on a bed of yellow roses. In his desperate fight to preserve his life he cannot avoid the constant reminders of death: fearful in the prison scene, grotesque in the newspaper advertisement for shrouds, peaceful in the book's many graveyard scenes. He sees life as irony—on the first page we find him reading advertisements for newly baked bread and for shrouds—and he practices such irony in his endless play acting. He simulates in order to confuse his enemy, who are the various representatives of Christiania's bourgeoisie. But at the same time his is a compulsive make-believe: the hero pretends to be experiencing life, whereas he is in fact a voyeur, deriving vicarious pleasures and pains (except for his hunger pains) from observing others.

His real antagonist is still Christiania, "the city no one leaves until it has left a mark on him," and in *Hunger* it assumes personality as in few other Norwegian novels. Actually, there is little description of the city, only glimpses from endless walks in the streets: one or two drab interiors, an occasional view from a window, or else a lyric snapshot from the harbor quarter, where the sea shines like mother of pearl. This highly accomplished impressionism gives way, when hunger affects the protagonist, to expressionism: inanimate objects assume personality; people become animals and incidents symbols. He experiences his shoes as old friends, as a soft, whispering sound coming toward him; the fall roses seem to take on a fever, their leaves a strange and unnatural flush; silent couples and noisy groups on Karl Johan Street remind him of mating times, of a warm swamp, of cats making love with high-pitched shrieks; and he sees his own predicament in the following scene:

> A small boy had been sitting, playing by himself on the far sidewalk; he was playing peacefully, expecting no harm—fastening together some long strips of paper. Suddenly he jumped up swearing; he walked backwards out on the street, keeping his eyes on a grown man with a red beard who was leaning out of a second-story window, spitting down on his head; the child sobbed with anger, and, unable to move, swore up at the window, while the man laughed in his face—five minutes perhaps went by this way. I turned so as not to see the boy sobbing.
>
> (Bly trans., pp. 217–218)

As the plot progresses, it becomes increasingly difficult to decide whether God or the city is bringing about the protagonist's final defeat. The play he is writing about a prostitute sinning at the high altar of a church looks like an attempt to get even with God, but the incident with the red-bearded man and the little boy also seems to be an allegory of how the unfriendly city of Christiania treats its well-meaning visitors. Typically—and all Hamsun heroes have this touch—the protagonist's final act before his departure is to "set his house in order": he leaves his last cake, even though he is still hungry, for the unknown little boy.

Hunger can be read as an example of Scandinavian naturalism from the 1880's. Hamsun wanted to be direct in his new novel, and for stark realism some of its scenes are still unsurpassed in Norwegian literature. But the book also marks the end of the naturalistic period in the north. The hero is finally felled by inner and outer circumstances, but in his attempt to overcome the weakness of his body, there is a victory for the free human spirit. Even more than its hero, however, the style of Hamsun's *Hunger* brought something new. The message is transmitted in a medium in which the old romantic rhetoric, with its emphasis on color and rhythm, comes to life in a new way: the sentence "I tried to liven up the dead points with a colorful word" applies not only to the artist-hero of *Hunger,* but also to Hamsun's writing of the novel, as do the kind words of the newspaper editor: "There is too much fever in all you write."

However, what makes *Hunger* different from other "rhetorical" books by Hamsun, such as *Pan,* is its humor, which gives a special irony to scenes that would otherwise be merely pathetic or theatrical. The "Russian" quality of *Hunger* has often been pointed out—the gray, ultimately resigned despair that appears in Dostoevsky's work (and in Edvard Munch's painting "The Sick Child" [1885])—but equally important is a sense of absurdity in the style of Twain. This above all singles out *Hunger* as a classical Hamsun novel, not only in its being his first great novel or indeed a novel of some historical significance, but also in its having a wonderful balance of naturalism and romanticism, of humor and despair, which Hamsun never quite achieved again.

In the summer of 1890, after completing *Hunger,* Hamsun left Copenhagen to look for a small, quiet place where he could work on his next book, originally intended to be a selection of "strange," or weird, stories. He settled in the tiny town of Lillesand on the south coast of Norway until money problems once more sent him out on the lecture tour. He ridiculed Lillesand in the article "Smaabyliv" (Small-Town Life), although he was attracted by its young ladies and intrigued by a housemate called Grøgaard, a destitute creature of good family background. After a few weeks in Lillesand, Hamsun abandoned his plans for a volume of stories and instead began writing his novel *Mysteries,* in which Nagel, a disillusioned young man traveling along the south coast of Norway on a steamer, is struck by the idyllic appearance of a small town and persuades himself to try life one final time there. He has already sized up the place and its inhabitants, who are confused by his curious dress and odd behavior, when he falls in love with Dagny Kielland, a young woman of ex-

traordinary charm and beauty. She finds him interesting, but since she is already engaged to a naval officer now on cruise and decides to remain faithful to him, Nagel's wooing is unsuccessful; from despair or spite he proposes to an older woman, the spinster Martha, with whom he hopes to live a simple cotter's life. However, because Dagny prevents this union, he is cut off on all sides and ends his life by drowning himself. In the denouement the two survivors, Dagny and Martha, walk arm in arm and comment on the unusual qualities of the departed protagonist.

Nagel is indeed an enigmatic man, and *Mysteries* a novel in which Hamsun's ambition to become a myth, a subject for storytellers, is particularly well exemplified. In a letter to Bollette Pavels Larsen, Hamsun described his "ambition to arrive in a small town completely unannounced, live there incognito for some time, and then disappear as mysteriously as I came" (10 October 1890). The theme is central in Hamsun's first novel, *The Enigmatic Man,* as it is also in *Mysteries.* It is a much larger book than *Hunger,* and although the point of view is consistently that of the protagonist, it has the greater distance of a third-person narrative. It is also more of a social novel in that Nagel, unlike Tangen of *Hunger,* acquires a number of friends and acquaintances with whom he discusses politics and poetry—somewhat along the lines of Hamsun's own argumentation in his lectures. Finally, *Mysteries* differs from *Hunger* in its many tales (told by Nagel), which are fully incorporated into the text, although originally they may have been some of the "strange" stories Hamsun had hoped to publish after *Hunger.*

In *Hunger* the hero is plagued by a crippled man who walks in front of him, stops when he stops, walks when he walks, as if he were his double. This technique is employed as a motif and it is developed into a central theme in *Mysteries,* setting it apart from Hamsun's other major novels. In Ibsen's *Rosmersholm* (1886), which was a target in one of his lectures, Hamsun had rediscovered some of the novelist Janson's Christian socialism. Rosmer, a minister of aristocratic background and independent means, wishes to be active in his community. His goal is to create "happy noblemen" around him, but unfortunately he is a decadent dreamer who is swindled by his fellow idealists. Hamsun, whose notion of nobility was "rude force" and "the ability to strike," resented Ibsen's rather sympathetic picture of a weak aristocrat and may have wanted to set the record straight in *Mysteries* by showing the Rosmers of this world to be moral swindlers. Strindberg, too, was intrigued by *Rosmersholm,* particularly by the way in which Rebecca gradually drives Beate to her suicide in the millrace: he speaks of Rebecca's "psychic murder" and, in the Nietzschean spirit of the times, later developed it into a "battle of the brains" theme in some of his works. A similar intellectual hide-and-seek lies behind the action in *Mysteries,* which is on one level a detective story.

In *Mysteries* the former aristocrat Grøgaard becomes the Midget, a clown or village idiot, who seems willing to dance in the market square for whoever pays him a penny. Nagel befriends the Midget and pays him to keep him from debasing himself by his ridiculous performance, but at the same time he watches him carefully as if he were a criminal. He suspects him because the Midget has the reputation for being "good" and "humble," and as a Nietzsche disciple, Nagel takes this to mean he is covering up some secret crime. *Mysteries* is not successful as a detective story, and Nagel the investigator never catches the Midget redhanded. However, in the end he is proven right: the Midget, we are told, is guilty of some secret crime against Martha. More interesting, though, is the way in which the Midget represents another side of the hero—not the proud elitist who is Nagel/Hamsun, but the provocative humbug who is also Nagel/Hamsun, and who will do anything to be in the news. Nagel speaks about his "mission," which may have been to create a new nobility or, on a lower level, to instill pride in people like the Midget.

Hence his final defeat is marked not only by losing Dagny and Martha, but by seeing toward the end of the novel the Midget once more playing the buffoon in the market square.

Although at the time of its writing *Mysteries* was Hamsun's most ambitious novel, he later criticized it for its excessive "talk," meaning presumably its long discussions of politics and poetry and the importance of great men. It has not been one of Hamsun's popular novels, but it has always been a favorite among discriminating readers, probably because it contains so much of what they admire: the love story, the beautifully wrought language, and particularly the quintessential Hamsun hero, Johan Nilsen Nagel.

Knut Hamsun spent the years from 1893 to 1896 in Paris, associating with Strindberg and other writers, and working on two plays; but he did not learn French as he had hoped, and the stay apparently did not influence his literary production. He had chosen the city as the stronghold of culture and intellectuality, but like Jean-Jacques Rousseau, he realized that men are not meant to be crowded together in anthills. "I belong to the forests and the solitude," he wrote in *Pan,* his most beautiful book, which he began in Paris and completed in Norway's southernmost town, although it is a novel about northern Norway, the world of his childhood.

For Hamsun to write a novel about a hunter was indeed unusual. He always claimed that he belonged to the woods rather than to the city, but even though he spent long periods of his life as a tramp in Norway and America and in later years led the life of a country gentleman, he was never a sportsman; he had no practical knowledge of traps, guns, fishing flies, or hunting dogs, and one might well ask where he got both his information and his inspiration. One likely source could be the *Jagtbreve* (Hunting Letters, 1889–1892) of Vilhelm Dinesen (Isak Dinesen's father), which we know Hamsun read. There were also the hunting memoirs from the *Blomstermålningar* (Flower Paintings, 1888) of Strindberg, whom Hamsun later described as "an animal longing for the woods." Strindberg wrote: "Nature can be very charming, but when it behaves threateningly, dangerously, unfeelingly, then it is frightening. And at such times I felt the terror, which from the nature god Pan received its name of panic."

Pan is the diary of Thomas Glahn, a retired lieutenant who has received a letter containing two green feathers once presented by him to a young woman in northern Norway. To while away his time, he now (1857) sits down to write about his summer there two years ago, playing with memories that seemingly left little impression, but in fact marked him for life. A city dweller of good family background and education, Glahn in 1855 had rented a forest hut from a rich merchant, Ferdinand Mack of Sirilund, and was busy with his spiritual return to nature when he fell in love with Mack's twenty-year-old daughter, Edvarda. The two experienced a period of intense happiness that was soon interrupted by misunderstanding and acrimony. Glahn comforted himself with another woman, Eva—"a young girl with a white woolen scarf, she had very dark hair." Later he learned that she was the wife of the local blacksmith and Herr Mack's mistress. Edvarda, on the other hand, was seen more and more in the company of a Finnish baron to whom she was later married. When the baron prepared for his return to Finland, Glahn gave him a good-riddance salute by blasting a cliff and sending boulders crashing into the sea as his ship was passing by. Herr Mack, however, knowing of the plan, had set Eva to work tarring a boat on the beach right beneath that part of the mountain, and she was killed by the rockfall. In the autumn when Glahn was about to leave, Edvarda asked to keep his dog, Aesop, in memory of him, but fearing that she would mistreat the dog, he shot it and sent her the dead body.

Pan is an unusual novel, since it is supplied with an epilogue in the short story "Glahns Død" (Glahn's Death), which Hamsun published in a periodical one year before the novel. In the epilogue, Glahn, now (1859) in India,

again receives a letter from Edvarda, this time saying she is a widow and free to marry him. Glahn dresses up as if for a wedding, then provokes his estranged hunting companion to shoot him.

Northern Norway's magnificent scenery and provincial social life provide the background and framework of the novel. The plot is organized around two island picnics and two Sirilund parties—social occasions on which either Glahn or Edvarda or both fail to maintain community standards. During the first outing Edvarda exclaims quite unabashedly, "I love only Glahn." During the second an annoyed Glahn throws Edvarda's shoe overboard. After the first Sirilund gathering, frustrated by Edvarda's cold and erratic behavior and jealous of a little lame doctor whom Edvarda seems to admire, Glahn forces the doctor to jump like a dog over the barrel of his outstretched gun; and at the last ball Glahn, pretending to whisper something to the baron, spits into his ear.

As so often in Hamsun's novels, the climax of the romance is reached fairly soon—one-third of the way through the plot—and is followed by painful and prolonged scenes of love-hate. As in *Hunger,* the development of the love story is accompanied by a seasonal movement—the transformation of the natural landscape from spring to winter—but it is more pronounced in this hunting diary. Here the progression of the seasons, and in particular the arrival of the fall with its first killing frost (the "Iron Nights"), pushes the pitch of Hamsun's prose to heights it never reached before or after. Finally winter arrives, with its first northern lights.

The ruler of the district is Ferdinand Mack, a powerful merchant somewhat in the style of Zahl from Hamsun's own youth. Age (he is forty-six) has not reduced his sexual prowess, nor his inclination to jealousy and hatred. When Mack's mistress Eva (the smith's wife) gives him up for Glahn, he arranges to have her killed and burns down Glahn's hut in the woods. Mack's style, including his poise and sharp intelligence, is reminiscent of an Eastern potentate's, and Glahn seems to respect him as a worthy antagonist. Mack's daughter, Edvarda, feels differently about him. No love is lost between them, although she is willing to consider the eligible suitors he brings to the place: a lame doctor and a pedantic natural scientist, the baron whom she finally marries.

But as Glahn loves Edvarda, so she loves him; since their love does not succeed, the book sets out to show what is wrong with one or both of them. Edvarda is a woman afraid to break away from the norms of society, although she is much more a true daughter of nature than her literary predecessors, Dagny and Ylajali. As an only child brought up by her father to be the local princess, she is pert, proud, generous, and impulsive, but lacking in education and social graces, weaknesses that cause her much humiliation and that she sets out to remedy. Edvarda, who looks and acts like a teenager and who begins by publicly confessing her love for Glahn and ends by marrying the Finnish baron, seems to be the usual Hamsun heroine who is spoiled by social ambition. She waits for her hero, but finds that Glahn does not measure up to her dream picture.

Glahn is handsome and likable and, if not learned, able to read the minds of people around him. Socially he is the opposite of Edvarda. Formerly a gallant Christiania lieutenant, he is driven by a melancholy weariness of the world to the forests of northern Norway, where he seeks an unspoiled nature and tries unsuccessfully to unlearn his city manners. He manages to upset glasses and feel awkward in the company of young society women, but he is not free from the traces of social polish. Whenever he hates Edvarda, he thinks of her as an uneducated fisherlass, and in the end he is not above sending for his uniform to impress the stubborn "princess" with his military splendor. More particularly he is unable to shed his social training in treating women. It costs him nothing to seduce the shepherd girl Henriette or to become Eva's lover, but he is deeply embarrassed by Edvarda's uninhibited declaration of love; and although they later meet every night for a week, there is no direct indication of a sexual relationship. Glahn's reluctance with the "princess" may be the reason for Edvarda's erratic behavior, which finally changes their friendship into mutual hatred. When Edvarda hears of Glahn's meetings with Eva, her love is reawakened by jealousy, and she comes back wearing a white scarf like her rival (in *Mysteries,* the frustrated Dagny had suddenly appeared in a white hat, simulating Martha's white hair). But it is too late. Glahn's cruel treatment by the fickle Edvarda now makes him deaf to her moving confession of love.

Glahn, like Nagel, has been "half in love with easeful death," and his comparison of its beauty with the joy of continued living is rendered more poetically in *Pan* than anywhere else in Hamsun's prose. Death is viewed as an island existence and the image, probably inspired by Arnold Böcklin's 1880 painting "Island of the Dead," is later repeated in Hamsun's poem "Skjærgaardsø" ("Island Off the Coast"). Glahn is the Pan-Narkissos, referred to in the text as "crouching so that he seemed to sit and drink out of his own belly." But in the novel the general temper is rather that of Nietzsche's Dionysian spirit, the goat-god Pan, from which the word "panic" is derived. Glahn's development describes a gradual unbalancing of the mind. He knows that Mack has spied on his blasting project, and he has seen Eva tarring the boat at the foot of the mountain; yet, although he used to be particularly astute in reading all manner of signs, Glahn takes no heed, and the catastrophe resulting in Eva's death cannot be prevented.

Actually, it has been in preparation for a long time. When Glahn, for no apparent reason, throws Edvarda's shoe into the sea, shoots himself in the foot, spits in the baron's ear, and sends Edvarda a dead dog, these acts are only stations on a well-mapped way to defeat. He tells Eva:

> There are times when it is a bliss to be dragged along by the hair. So distorted can the mind

become. One can be dragged by the hair up hill and down dale, and if anybody asks what is happening, then one answers in ecstasy: "I am being dragged along by the hair!"

(McFarlane trans., p. 125)

On his last day Glahn dresses up like a bridegroom, knowing that only death can be his true bride.

In the midst of all this melodrama, with the faithful maiden brutally killed, the proud heroine married off to a wizened scientist, and the hero slowly losing his mind, Hamsun's joy of life is still present. *Pan* owes its Norwegian popularity less to its tale of passion than to Glahn's eloquent declaration of his love of nature, in a manner closer to Nietzsche's Zarathustra than to Rousseau: "A toast to the merciful stillness over the earth, to the stars and the crescent moon, yes to it and to them!" Hamsun's fascination with autumn, already indicated in *Hunger*, is especially evident in *Pan*. But even if autumn hits Glahn harder—like an alcoholic bout—during the so-called Iron Nights, he is always roused by nature, and his language assumes its rhythms. Instead of the long, involved periods of a discursive style with its many subordinate clauses (hypotaxis), coordinated sentences are favored (parataxis). Short sentences, often completely without conjunctions (asyndeton) or else studded with conjunctions (polysyndeton), characterize this kind of prose, which is reminiscent of the Bible's, particularly in such poetic books as the Song of Solomon:

> I give thanks for the lovely night, for the hills, for the whispering of the darkness and the sea. . . . It whispers within my heart. I give thanks for my life, for my breathing, for the grace of being alive tonight, for these things I give thanks from my heart. Listen in the east and listen in the west, but listen! That is the everlasting God! This stillness murmuring in my ear is the blood of all nature seething, is God weaving through the world and through me. I see a gossamer thread glistening in the fire's light, I hear the rowing of a boat in the harbor, the Northern lights arise against the northern sky. Oh, I give thanks by my immortal soul that it is I who am sitting here!

(p. 125)

Arthur Koestler called Hamsun's next novel, *Victoria*, "one of the great love stories of world literature." The sweetest of Hamsun's books, it used to be considered a suitable confirmation present in Norway. Its lovers torment each other, but not unendingly and not unnaturally. The atmosphere is relatively harmonious, reflecting Hamsun's own happiness and peace of mind after he married (May 1898) and spent his honeymoon with old friends in Valdres. Unlike Nagel and Glahn, the novel's hero, Johannes, is a real writer, and the young woman he loves is as close to a real princess as possible in a country without nobility. Victoria is the daughter of an estate owner whose home is referred to as "The Castle," while Johannes is only the son of a neighboring tenant farmer and miller. Their childhood love is like a charming rose garden, but for Johannes one not without thorns. As they grow up it becomes increasingly clear there can be no marriage: Victoria's father needs a rich son-in-law to save his estate. Hence, like a true princess, Victoria is made to sacrifice her happiness to her family and becomes engaged to the wealthy but unattractive Otto. When Otto dies unexpectedly and she is free to marry Johannes, he in the meantime has found another woman—just as Nagel finds Martha, and Glahn, Eva. Johannes' new friend, Camilla, although she is very patient with her writing fiancé, is no slave of love: when he seems to have less time for her than for his books, she finds another friend, which gives Hamsun the opportunity to bring in the melodrama of cheating women and jealous husbands.

But there is more melodrama to come. Without Johannes knowing it, Victoria has contracted tuberculosis, and he never sees her again; so that what we have here is Hamsun's early story of Bjørger and Laura in new dress. An interesting innovation occurs at the end of the book, however, when Johannes reads a long letter from Victoria, now dead, that explains everything: how she had always loved only Johannes but had to give him up when her father had implored her to help save the family honor. As in *Pan,* in which the epilogue is told by Glahn's hunting companion, the point of view changes, an additional unusual feature because Hamsun, the male chauvinist, lets a woman have the last word. As in *Mysteries, Victoria* has a number of stories or allegories woven into the text. Furthermore, it offers insights into the creative process, describing Johannes' way of writing and, presumably, Hamsun's own.

In contemporary Norwegian painting, a comparison of Edvard Munch's "The Sick Child" with his "Dance of Life" (1899–1900) shows the development of a simplified iconography. After the scrupulous realism of *Hunger,* a similar reduction of detail has clearly taken place in *Victoria:* we do not know the second name of either Johannes or Victoria; their parents are referred to as the miller and the castle master, respectively; there are a tutor, the mother in blue, the mother in black, the lord and the lady, and other allegorical designations. The subtle psychology Hamsun calls for in his article on the unconscious life of the mind had finally given way to tale, allegory, mood, color, ornament—a lighter and more sentimental kind of literature that Hamsun himself called "just a little poetry." And he described poetry at the time (1898) as "the only form of writing that is not both pretentious and inconsequential, but merely inconsequential." *Victoria* lacks the power of Hamsun's other great novels from the 1890's, but it is still the quintessential Hamsun love story: with nothing really new to say, the author has stated his case more simply, clearly, economically, and as beautifully. In the words of Johannes, the miller's son who becomes a writer: "Love is creation's source, creation's ruler; but all of love's ways are strewn with blossoms and blood, blossoms and blood."

Knut Hamsun's literary landscape has three major series of peaks—the great novels of the 1890's, the social novels written during World War I, and the Vagabond trilogy dating from around 1930. In between are two valleys with foothills: his production from the years 1900 to 1912 and two novels from the early 1920's. These two lower ranges are associated with crises in Hamsun's life—the end of his youth at around forty and the beginning of old age at around seventy—and are characterized by depressions and, in the case of the first crisis, by extreme restlessness, which did not bode well for his family life. Since his stay in America he had longed to travel in the East, and in 1899 took off for Finland, Russia, and the Near East. After his return he spent most of his wife's fortune at a casino in Ostende and was later known for his wild parties at Bernina, a restaurant in Copenhagen. He tried to salvage his marriage by designing and building a home on the Oslo fjord, but it was too late, and in 1906 he was divorced. In honor of the poet, dramatist, and novelist Bjørnson on his seventieth birthday in 1902, Hamsun had written a magnificent poem, and he slowly came to realize how Bjørnson, a fighter and traveler like himself, had drawn his strength from family life and his country home. In 1909, when he was fifty, Hamsun married a young actress with a farming background, Marie Andersen. Two years later they bought and moved to a farm in northern Norway, where the first of their four children was born.

During these years Hamsun continued to produce work. He published two collections of short stories (1903, 1905), three plays (1902, 1903, 1910), a travelog (1903), a book of verse (1904), and six novels. Although Hamsun's plays—six in all—were well received in Russia and for years supplied him with a steady income, they have never had any lasting life on stages elsewhere. His book of verse, taken as a whole, is also unremarkable, although in its day it did bring something new, both unusual rhythms and a pleasing singability. All in all Hamsun's fame rests on his novels, of which during these years he wrote two kinds, both different from anything he had done earlier.

One type—*Sværmere* (*Dreamers,* 1903), *Benoni* (1908), *Rosa* (1908)—has the same setting as *Pan,* northern Norway and the house of Mack (but now the hero is an upstart businessman or inventor who even manages to win the "princess"). Tragedy in these novels has given way to humor, and psychology to the simple typology and plot development of the fairy tale. With their emphasis on local color, including dialect, these novels mark a new departure in Hamsun's work.

Very different is the Wanderer trilogy—*Under høststjernen* (*Under the Autumn Star,* 1906), *En vandrer spiller med sordin* (*With Muted Strings,* 1909), and *Den siste glede* (*Look Back on Happiness,* 1912), in which the enigmatic main theme of *Mysteries* is repeated in a new manner. This time the hero is not like Nagel, an agronomist in a striking yellow suit, but a middle-aged writer dressed as a tramp who pretends to be looking for work as a woodsman, but who is really a refugee from the wasting café life of big cities hoping to find new inspiration in the country. Furthermore, his name is not aristocratic like Nagel or Glahn, but is the very prosaic Pedersen, Hamsun's own original name. A humorous low style has replaced the high melodrama of *Mysteries* and *Pan.* Pedersen digs ditches, cuts cordwood, and makes love to the minister's wife—in the barn.

However, these books differ from the folksy Benoni novels in being sentimental. During a church service Pedersen is overcome with emotion, and he loves the wife of his employer, Captain Falkenberg, with a hopeless never-ending passion. Finally he acts as a god in disguise, helping the farmers with good advice and serving as a matchmaker for a neurotic city girl, whom he manages to marry off to a healthy farm boy.

Of these books, the first two (translated into English as *The Wanderer*) are minor masterworks, mixing realism and romanticism in their prose, which sometimes breaks into poetry. The last novel of the trilogy is more didactic and, instead of poetry, has an epilogue in which Hamsun addresses gainfully employed women with his typically sexist attitudes. It reads like a reprimanding letter to his wife, Marie, a former actress with a B.A., who, Hamsun thought, missed her city days and deplored that, as a farmer's wife, her liberal arts education was being wasted. Actually she was the farmer of the two, he the footloose, neurotic artist, who more and more took on the guise of Rousseau, seeing man's only salvation in a return to nature and the soil.

Hamsun first heard about Rousseau and his back-to-nature call when he read Strindberg's autobiography in Minneapolis. Although he understood Rousseau's and Strindberg's longing for rural simplicity, he did not then share their cultural pessimism. Thus, in *Mysteries,* he writes that farmers are "nothing but lice, peasant cheese, and Luther's catechism."After visiting America around the turn of the century, Hamsun's Danish colleague Johannes V. Jensen had written a book praising what he called "the farmer spirit," which he found in President Theodore Roosevelt and Bjørnson, as well as in Hamsun, whom he referred to as the essential farmer (although admittedly Hamsun had been caught by the enticements of the city). Hamsun did not then agree with Jensen's characterization and claimed that whatever culture he possessed he had acquired in the city, and indeed by eliminating the farmer in him. But in 1919 he told a Danish woman writer: "You and I should not live on poetry and emptiness, we should play our part as human beings, marry and have children, build homes and till the soil."

Hamsun's journey into middle age, then, was accompanied not only by a love of wild nature, but also by a condemnation of the city and an idealization of life in the country. Despite his years in cities—New York, Copenhagen, Paris, Moscow—Hamsun's urban experience was superficial. Cities, whether large or small, were inimical to him; he was drawn reluctantly by their cultural attractions, but he had no understanding of their social importance as places for emigrants from the countryside to find work and security. Rather they were like anthills, as he writes in *Konerne ved vandposten* (*The Women at the Pump,* 1920), with "everyone busy with his own affairs, crossing each other's path, elbowing each other aside, sometimes even trampling on each other. That's the way it is, sometimes they even trample on each other."

In two novels, *Børn av tiden* (*Children of the Age,* 1913) and *Segelfoss by* (*Segelfoss Town,* 1915), Hamsun set out to chronicle the industrialization of the Segelfoss estate, formerly a northern Norwegian feudal community ruled by Lieutenant Willatz Holmsen III, a generous but extremely arrogant gentleman. To this area comes an enterprising man—formerly of the district—who has worked himself up from nothing. Little by little he buys most of Holmsen's land, harnesses the waterfall, and builds his mill. Lieutenant Holmsen, after he has sold or mortgaged most of his property, finds the old family treasure, pays all his debts, and dies a proud and honest man, the closest to a conventional hero in all of Hamsun's work. In the second volume the urban development is completed. A lawyer arrives as well as a doctor, a local newspaper is established, and traveling salesmen begin to visit the town, in the end even a traveling theater group.

Both books have dozens of characters, several plotlines, local color, and humorous dialogue. Hamsun seems to have accepted the general structure of the social novel from the 1880's (which he earlier criticized), so that these books show an inverted form of *Mysteries,* with the love story distanced and the small-town background made central. Hamsun has little sympathy for his city dwellers, particularly the university trained immigrants from the south, but the satire is good-humored rather than bitter. Hamsun continued his jeremiad against the urban experience in several other books. First, however, he wrote his novel in praise of a simple country life, *Growth of the Soil,* for which he received the Nobel Prize in 1920.

Growth of the Soil has been called Hamsun's greatest novel, which it is not; it has also

been seen as atypical, which in many ways it is, although the idea that he wrote the book simply to win over the Nobel committee is not tenable. The novel probably arose out of a newspaper discussion of unwed mothers who secretly killed and buried their newborn children in order to hide their shame. Writing during World War I, Hamsun used the occasion to provide an effective peace message to his readers; hence the simple psychology and the low-keyed rhetoric. The book has a style very different from that of *Pan,* and yet the two novels are related, as if Hamsun had rewritten the earlier romantic work in a classical mode.

The story is about Isak, "a lumbering barge of a man" who looks for homesteading land in northern Norway. He needs a woman to help him at his new settlement and mentions it to the Lapps who walk past his place; soon Inger arrives from the nearest parish. With her harelip she is not much to look at (neither is he, for that matter), but she is a good worker and, what is more, she owns a cow. Isak eventually gets himself a horse, and Inger has her first children, Eleseus and Sivert. When her third child is born—a girl with a harelip—Inger, thinking of what she has suffered because of her blemish, kills the baby. The little grave is discovered, and Inger goes to prison for six years, to come back a different person: she has learned reading, writing, and dressmaking; she likes to have people around her; she even dances with the newly arrived telegraph workers; and she wants Eleseus to accept the engineer's offer of an office job in town. This turns out to be a very costly decision for the parents. Eleseus not only spends his time and their money on useless things, he grows restless at home, emigrates to America, and is never heard from again.

Geissler, the bailiff, is a curious character. To Isak he acts as a providential benefactor, helping him in his homesteading and discovering and later buying the copper mountain on Isak's estate. But, by bringing miners and industry to the place, he also acts as a scourge to the settlers, and finally, he is responsible for

Eleseus' fate. But to Sivert he says: "You be content! You've everything to live on, everything to believe in, being born and bringing forth, you are the needful on earth. . . . Generation to generation, breeding ever anew; and when you die, the new stock goes on. That's the meaning of eternal life."

In the newspaper discussion of unwed mothers who kill their babies, Hamsun the journalist takes a very harsh stand: "Hang the mother, hang the father too!" On the other hand, as an artist, in *Growth of the Soil* his sympathy with the unfortunate woman is striking. He arranges his novel in two parts. In book 2, the account of Axel and Barbro is a darker and more realistic variation of Isak and Inger's story. As a farmer, Axel is less generous and good-humored than Isak, and as a child murderer, Barbro is ruthless compared to Inger. Yet even for Barbro there is hope once she settles for good in the countryside. "Nature alone can heal all wounds" seems to be Hamsun's message.

Most of the characters in this book are psychologically uninteresting. Isak is curiously uncomplicated, and Eleseus' tragic fate is treated without sympathy by the narrator, which makes a reader wonder whether indeed this narrator should be taken seriously, and whether his and Geissler's praise of simple farming life really represents Hamsun's own view. After all, agriculture is culture, the beginning of a development that ends with the creation of cities and their emptiness and corruption; so Isak can be seen as the first link in a chain that ends with Geissler, who speaks of farming as the meaning of eternal life, while at the same time bringing industry and destruction to the area.

But this view, however attractively modern, is not borne out by Hamsun's other writings. He never had any understanding of primitive peoples, of such true children of nature as the Lapps, but in the years before World War I he came to look on farming as the only viable compromise between the ills of wild nature and the city, and he wanted to make his new message simple, beautiful, and free from doubt. Hence, despite its many dark scenes and seemingly worthless characters, *Growth of the Soil* has the outline structure and the optimism of myth and fairy tale rather than the close-up perspective and resignation of true realism. The author tells the sad tale of Eleseus with considerable detail, yet he seems lacking in understanding of the young man and makes his story merely incidental in the unfolding of the book's tremendous life force. Other writers, themselves in need of optimism, may have sensed Hamsun's intentions. H. G. Wells wrote about *Growth of the Soil:* "I am not usually lavish with my praise, but indeed the book impresses me as among the very greatest novels I have ever read. It is wholly beautiful; it is saturated with wisdom and humor and tenderness."

Readers who had expected a permanent change in Hamsun's writing after *Growth of the Soil* were surprised by the pessimism of his next novel, *The Women at the Pump.* But there was a personal reason for this: *Growth of the Soil* was written while the outcome of World War I was still undecided. *The Women at the Pump,* with its openly anti-English sentiment, came after Hamsun's favorite foreign country, Germany, had been completely defeated. The bitterness of this small-town satire (*Mysteries* once more, without Nagel and the Midget as its central characters) is further increased in Hamsun's next book, *Siste kapitel* (*Chapter the Last,* 1923), about life in a sanatorium. The prospect of advancing old age apparently added to Hamsun's depression over the European situation. Although the book can hardly have influenced Thomas Mann's somewhat similar *Magic Mountain* of only one year later, Hamsun had used the sanatorium as a symbol of modern times in other books known to the German novelist. *The Women at the Pump* has humor, and *Chapter the Last* has a growth-of-the-soil theme as part of its plot; nevertheless the two novels were commonly regarded as Hamsun's darkest, and in his next work few of his readers expected to find a revival of the

36

exuberance and poetry of his Benoni and Wanderer books.

In 1926 Knut Hamsun received psychoanalytic treatment (one of the first in Norway to do so), and toward the end of the following year he completed his longest novel, the inspiration for which he felt he owed his analyst. The trilogy about August and his friends consists of the novels *Landstrykere* (*Wayfarers*, 1927), *August* (1930), and *Men livet lever* (*The Road Leads On*, 1933). *Wayfarers* is the story of Edevart Andersen (born in the 1850's), a big, strong farmboy from Polden in northern Norway. He is slow at school and a little naive, but as he watches two mountebanks who are on a visit north with their barrel organ, he begins discovering that out in the world most things are not what they seem. Edevart befriends the sailor August, two years older than himself, who has already seen most parts of the world. The two begin a vagabond existence, involving anything from modest peddling in the countryside to business projects full of daring and imagination and, sometimes, handsome rewards—a lifelong companionship providing the narrator with many opportunities to offer scenes of colorful, quixotic humor. But Edevart, the disillusioned idealist, is marked for tragedy from the beginning. He falls in love with a married woman, Lovise Magrete—the description of their first meeting at Lovise Magrete's little farm is one of the finest and most touching in all of Hamsun's works. However, like Hamsun's other women, Lovise Magrete wants something in return for her love, this time money so that she can leave for America with her family; and although she later returns to Edevart without her husband, the once innocent, happy, and industrious Lovise Magrete has acquired the restlessness of the New World.

Edevart marries her and they spend years on small farms in America. In volume 2 of the trilogy—the novel *August*—they return to settle, as Edevart hopes, permanently, in Polden; but Lovise Magrete wants to be with her children in America, and when Edevart, restless as always, finally decides to follow her once more

to the West, he perishes in a storm at sea trying to sail out to meet the ocean liner. August in the meantime has carried on with his endless enterprise, everything from a tobacco plantation to a herring-meal factory. In volume 3, *The Road Leads On,* he begins sheep farming in the grand style known from his days on the pampas of Argentina. However, one day in a tight spot on August's newly constructed mountain road, his thousand sheep are scared by an automobile and jump off the road over a 900-foot precipice—with the old salt August borne along in their midst. The novel ends with a quote from the (fictional) "Ballad of August": "An ocean of sheep was the sailor's death."

Some of the optimism of *Growth of the Soil* is present in the August trilogy, but there is a much wider range of characters and ideas. Hamsun had left behind him the mythlike structure of his back-to-nature novel and written a much more realistic book about the spirit of rootlessness. The novel does have farmers who represent a wholesome return to nature, and some of them, like Ezra, are very much like Isak Sellanraa, but these characters are not central to the plot as the vagabonds Edevart and August are. Edevart is destroyed by his disillusionment and apathy, but he is made into a much more finely nuanced character than Eleseus of *Growth of the Soil*. Furthermore, August, although embodying the very spirit of industry that the narrator condemns, is not written off like Eleseus. Indeed, Hamsun's dialectical method, in which the protagonist is accused and excused like the defendant in a court case, is nowhere more evident than in the trilogy, and it is not easy to sort out the author's opinions among the many voices that speak from the text.

Hamsun wrote to his wife, Marie, about *August:* "It is an attack upon industry. Now, that is all right, but whether I have managed it from a literary point of view is another matter." He probably did not manage it quite the way he wished. The coming and going of industry has since become a commonplace phenomenon, and few readers will heed the author's warning in this regard. In 1930 August was a man of the future; half a century later, despite the "green wave" movements and the attempt to make Hamsun a modern ecologist, August, as a representative of industry and enterprise, is not a man of the past. People in northern Norway, like twentieth-century people generally, cannot enjoy a high standard of living without some form of industry, and even if August's herring-meal factory does not succeed, many other factories have.

Much more convincingly argued is the book's major theme of emigration. Hamsun's book appeared immediately after Norwegian immigration to America had received its finest treatment in the work of O. E. Rölvaag. Hamsun may not have had Rölvaag's knowledge of nineteenth-century Norwegian homesteaders in the American Midwest, but he knew from personal experience what it means to be uprooted. He used this knowledge and his superior art to transcend the scope of conventional immigration novels by giving his readers not only the specific truth about the rootlessness of many nineteenth-century Norwegian immigrants in the American Midwest, but the much more general truth about a sense of displacement that characterizes all human life in the twentieth century. This is why Lovise Magrete's case, unlike Barbro's, is irremediable and tragic; also why the trilogy—much more than *Growth of the Soil*—expresses our present reality; and why August, despite the danger he is said to represent, is closer to us than the farmer Ezra.

The optimism that followed Hamsun's successful treatment by a psychoanalyst did not last; during the 1930's he became increasingly isolated both from his country, with its young social democratic government, and from his family. At the end of World War I, Hamsun's only hope for a better Europe, a youthful Germany, had been defeated by what he called "old imperialist England," and his bitterness is noticeable in his books from the early 1920's. His attitude to Hitler's Germany became known during the so-called Ossietzky affair. In 1934 Carl von Ossietzky, a German pacifist whom the Nazis had placed in a concentration camp, was proposed by some Norwegians for the Nobel Prize for Peace. Hamsun attacked the proposal as an insult to a young European nation and was in turn attacked publicly by all his colleagues in the Norwegian Authors Union. At home his relationship to his wife and children was less than ideal. He was more than fifty years older than his children and found them to be excessively spoiled, with their young mother to blame. They tried to emulate their famous father— as artists, actresses, writers—but when they did not succeed and became depressed, they seemed to find no sympathy. How well Hamsun nevertheless understood young people's problems can be seen from his last novel, *Ringen sluttet* (*The Ring Is Closed*, 1936). Hamsun was a famous and wealthy man, he had achieved his goal, yet he felt barren and bitter, realizing that the want and misery of the hungry years of his youth had been more productive for him as an artist. For Hamsun it was a question of age: he wanted to stay modern, to be a fighter for youth and youthful ideas, but he was very old and did not like what he saw around him. He became more and more reactionary and authoritarian, while as an artist, incredibly, he was still able to side with the young in their struggle against the repressive older generation.

The Ring Is Closed is set in a small southern Norwegian coastal town. Abel Brodersen, because he lives out at the lighthouse and is the son of an old and niggardly sea captain and his alcoholic wife, is not accepted as an equal by the pharmacist's daughter, Olga, whom he loves. He goes to sea and after his parents are dead returns to his hometown, where he shows little enterprise and lives off his inheritance until it is all spent. Once a rich man's son, he must live in a shack with nothing to eat, like the hero of Hamsun's early novel *Hunger*. It gradually transpires that he had previously lived quite happily at Green

Ridge, Kentucky, married to an American woman, Angèle, until she was killed in an unspecified accident. Later we are told the truth, that Abel himself had shot her after finding her with his best friend, Lawrence, and that Lawrence had been accused of the crime and later sentenced to death in the electric chair. At the end of the first part of the novel—Hamsun never completed the second part—Abel leaves one final time for America. Hamsun's son Tore has said that his father had intended to let Abel confess his crime and accept his sentence in America, then return home for good.

Abel's curious defeatism was not accepted by Norwegians in the optimistic and enterprising 1930's. They regarded him as something close to an animal, and the book as nothing but an ugly picture of the future—this despite the narrator's praise of Abel: "But in the depths of his obscurity, he was not lacking in character. . . . He possessed a sublime indifference toward all conditions he encountered. . . . It rendered him independent—a sovereign in his own way." What Hamsun describes in his last novel is something remarkably modern—a hippie from Green Ridge, Kentucky, a person who might not be understood even in the oil-rich Norway of the 1980's. Henry Miller, praising Hamsun on the occasion of his centennial in 1959, compared the typical Hamsun protagonist to some of his own countrymen:

> In present-day America these rebellious exceptional people are becoming more common probably because of the intolerable, senseless way of life we have created for ourselves. To act as if the world had already gone to pot, that is their attitude. To create their own life in the midst of death and destruction, that is their wish.
>
> (*Dagens nyheter,* 3 August 1959)

The Ring Is Closed is Hamsun's last novel. For the historian and biographer it offers a remarkably close picture of old Hamsun's times and his family situation, particularly the parent-child relationship. It is modern in the sense of being based on contemporary life and also in the sense that it belongs to literary modernism, showing a reaction against conventional society and a concern about art for its own sake, much as in the great works of Hamsun's youth. Indeed, the title *The Ring Is Closed* shows that Hamsun, after more than thirty books, returned to the sentiments of his first masterpiece, *Hunger.* The central love story is the same as in most of his works, but there are important differences in social philosophy. Consider, for instance, Hamsun's ambivalent attitude toward art: the basic idea of the artist as restless and inauthentic, an idea that is normally worked out as a vacillation within the protagonist between city and nature. For one period in Hamsun's production—the years between 1911 and 1933 and most emphatically in the novel *Growth of the Soil* from 1917—there is a temporary compromise in that the family farm is accepted as a solution to the dilemma: agriculture is seen as the only acceptable form of culture; farming is, as it were, poetry made respectable. But this view is abandoned in *The Ring Is Closed.* Here Hamsun returns to the antisocial attitudes of *Hunger;* farming no longer holds a promise for the future, and for the first time in his work, truly primitive people, who live from hand to mouth on almost nothing except sunshine, are praised: "With them the thought of coming up is meaningless. . . . Their lives are simple, they wear flowers for their adornment. . . . They were so beautiful to look at."

However, while the city and wild nature are no longer happily united in the utopian family farm, *The Ring Is Closed* contains a compromise between polarities in Hamsun's universe—the opposition between West and East, between restless activity and passive contemplation. We have learned that the two shall never meet, but in Hamsun's last novel these opposites—August and Edevart, enterprise and defeatism—are united within the character of Abel.

If Knut Hamsun had not survived his eightieth birthday in 1939, he would have died the most popular of Norway's great writers. This was not to be. From 1940 until 1945 Hitler's soldiers occupied Norway, and while the king and Norway's exiled government in London encouraged Norwegians to continue their resistance to the enemy forces, Hamsun let himself be used by the Germans to produce propaganda for the Nazi regime. But he also worked for Norwegians who had been imprisoned by the occupation forces, and his efforts in this respect have not received the attention they deserve. In January 1941 Hamsun met with Joseph Terboven, the Reichskommissar for Norway, to discuss the release of one of his colleagues, the Norwegian writer Ronald Fangen. Two years later in an article entitled "Nu igjen—!" (Now once more—!), dealing with letters he had received from parents whose sons had been sentenced to death for collaboration with the enemy, Hamsun deplored not only that these men had sided with England, but that they were young and had to die. The article seems inspired by genuine pity, and it is reasonable to think that Hamsun now saw Terboven as a man Norway did not need, a person who should be removed.

In June 1943 Hamsun met Hitler in Germany. After polite introductory remarks, the conversation turned to politics, in particular to Terboven, whose actions Hamsun criticized: "The methods of the Reichskommissar are not appropriate in our country. His Prussian manner is not acceptable to us, and then all these executions—it's enough!" Hamsun wept; Hitler asked the interpreter to calm down the old novelist and left the meeting. Although Hamsun is known not to have been impressed by Hitler, in May 1945, when Germany had lost the war, he composed an incredible obituary, describing the German dictator as "a warrior for mankind and a preacher of the gospel of right for all nations."

Three weeks after Hamsun had published his eulogy of Hitler (and explained it to his son Tore as an example of his wish to be consistent to the end), he and his wife, Marie, were interned at their estate, Nørholm, near Grimstad.

After three weeks Hamsun was transferred to the Grimstad hospital and three months later to the Landvik old-age home, a short distance from the town. On two occasions he was interrogated by the magistrate at Grimstad. Hamsun did not deny his sympathy for Germany, but he did not consider himself guilty of treason, because his conscience told him he had worked for his country. The result of the hearing, however, was that Hamsun was indicted in accordance with a new law concerning treason whereby membership in the Nasjonal Samling (Norwegian Nazi party) was punishable with prison or fines up to one million Norwegian crowns. Nørholm was confiscated and Hamsun placed under arrest.

However, in October 1945, before the charges were brought against him by the magistrate, Hamsun was moved to the psychiatric clinic in Oslo, where he was examined by Professor Gabriel Langfeldt and Dr. Ørnulv Ødegård. Whether the attorney general actually had doubts about Hamsun's ability to stand trial, or whether he just wanted to see the case shelved, is not known, but in February 1946, after what Hamsun later described as four terrible months at the psychiatric clinic, he was returned to the old-age home at Landvik. Doctors Langfeldt and Ødegård had then signed a report declaring that they did not consider Hamsun to be insane or to have been insane at the time of his offensive actions, but that they considered him to be—and the phrase has since become famous in Norway—"a person with permanently impaired mental faculties." Two weeks later the attorney general announced that although Hamsun must be considered to be responsible for his actions since he was not insane, the government did not wish to bring a criminal case against him because of his permanent impairment and because the old man was practically deaf. However, the directorate for reparations would be responsible for the reparations question; Hamsun would not be sent to prison, but might lose his money.

Hamsun had to wait for two years—until December 1947—before his case came up. In a moving speech to the court he explained why he had written his wartime articles: it had been to save Norwegian lives. He had also sent innumerable telegrams to Terboven and to Hitler asking for clemency. The jury, however, found that although Hamsun had not technically been a member of the Nasjonal Samling, he had supported the enemy throughout the war, a transgression all the more serious since the novelist had a high social position in Norway. He was sentenced to pay a fine of 425,000 Norwegian crowns, or eighty-five percent of what the court considered him to be worth. Two years later Hamsun published a brilliant and moving account of his trial, *On Overgrown Paths,* which was well received by critics and made readers wonder what Dr. Langfeldt had meant by "permanently impaired mental faculties."

A 175-page chronicle of contemporary events and impressions without chapter divisions, *On Overgrown Paths* lacks the intensity and artistic form of Hamsun's earlier work. However, *Hunger's* chief compositional device—the protagonist's gradual displacement from the pleasures of the Palace Gardens to the slums behind the East Station—is similarly felt in the changing places and fortunes of the old author Hamsun, who is endlessly moved around as a political prisoner. Also, what seems at first nothing but a day-to-day account of trivial events suddenly reveals the art of the great novelist, his sense of scene and dialogue, of humor and pathos, and beneath it all a disturbing question to the reader: "Did I, Knut Hamsun, deserve this?"

In a play (and film) called *Eiszeit* (Ice Age, 1973), about the old Knut Hamsun, Germany's Tankred Dorst emphasizes above all the author's intense stubbornness; indeed, his deafness is seen as symbolic. Dorst's Hamsun does not *want* to hear, and he includes scenes showing the old novelist's pedantic preoccupation with meaningless detail. A one-sided reading of Hamsun's biography could present the old artist as a cold and isolated man, but many people who were Hamsun's friends knew him as a warm person, and no one who reads his books can avoid hearing the message of joy that strangely accompanies his lifelong theme of alienation.

On Overgrown Paths also shows Hamsun's Renaissance mind at work in a positive manner. He inspects new and old buildings, criticizes people's carpentry as well as their vocabulary, and deplores the new spelling as well as the lack of old-fashioned respect in modern forms of greeting. There are also cases of direct involvement, as when he takes great pains to guard a young pine tree against an old poplar; and there are scenes showing some of Hamsun's former ecstasy over the mysteries of nature, as when he watches the first open water on the Nørholm inlet with the moon "climbing up from the sea like a jellyfish dripping with gold." Finally, although it deals with a very old man in icy isolation, *On Overgrown Paths* exudes a warmth that served to remind Norwegian readers of what they owed this once so beloved writer and to ask them whether the old sinner could not have been treated more generously.

"I can wait, I have time on my side" were Hamsun's proud words to the Grimstad court in 1947. But in 1950, at the news that the Gyldendal publishing house would begin printing his books again, the ninety-year-old novelist broke down and cried: his worst torture had been his total neglect by readers and scholars in the postwar years. After all, Hamsun had had a name and lost it. His novels had been discovered by the Germans in the 1890's, and from Germany their fame spread to the Mediterranean countries and to the Middle and Far East. After receiving the Nobel Prize in 1920 he also won a name for himself in the English-speaking world. By 1939 his works had appeared in more than thirty languages. Of Scandinavian writers who have won the Nobel Prize, some are already totally forgotten. Hamsun, on the other hand, seems to have profited from the enforced neglect after World War II: since his death at 92 on 19 January 1952, an increasing number of books and articles on his life and works have appeared every year in many countries. Today he is the only Norwegian writer besides Ibsen and Sigrid Undset who belongs to world literature.

Hamsun's new position receives its strength from two sources. One is his position in literary modernism. His manic-depressive heroes, his elitism, his emphasis on the unconscious life of the mind, his stream-of-consciousness techniques—these make him a pioneer in the development of twentieth-century European writing. Very different is his popular appeal, resulting from the melodrama of his love stories and, above all and particularly for Norwegian readers, from the central place of nature in all his work. Furthermore, to Norwegians it is not only Hamsun's "I belong to the woods" that speaks to their hearts. Equally important is his idealization of a simple life-style, his emphasis on *trivsel*—a pan-Scandinavian word denoting well-being and peace of mind—and his insistence that in the last resort industry and materialism do not hold a promise for the future.

Hamsun's appeal, however, is universal. The American novelist Henry Miller once wrote to a Norwegian friend:

> It was from Knut Hamsun that I derived much of my love of life, love of nature, love of men. All I have done, or hope I have, in relating the distressing story of my life, is to increase that love of life, nature and all of God's creatures in those who read me.
>
> (*Henry Miller on Writing,* [New York, 1964]; p. 209)

Selected Bibliography

EDITIONS

COLLECTED WORKS
Artikler. Oslo, 1939.
Samlede verker. 15 vols. Oslo, 1954–1956.
Paa Turné. Tre foredrag om litteratur. Oslo, 1960. Includes lectures from 1891.

CORRESPONDENCE
Brev til Marie. Oslo, 1970.
Knut Hamsum som han var. Oslo, 1956.

TRANSLATIONS

August. Translated by Eugene Gay-Tifft. New York, 1931.
Benoni. Translated by Arthur G. Chater. New York, 1925.
Chapter the Last. Translated by Arthur G. Chater. New York, 1929.
Children of the Age. Translated by J. S. Scott. New York, 1924.
The Cultural Life of Modern America. Translated by Barbara Gordon Morgridge. Cambridge, Mass., 1969.
Dreamers. Translated by W. W. Worster. New York, 1921.
Growth of the Soil. Translated by W. W. Worster. New York, 1925.
Hunger. Translated by Robert Bly. New York, 1967.
Look Back on Happiness. Translated by Paula Wiking. New York, 1940.
Mysteries. Translated by Gerry Bothmer. New York, 1971.
On Overgrown Paths. Translated by Carl L. Anderson. New York, 1967.
Pan. Translated by James McFarlane. New York, 1956.
The Ring Is Closed. Translated by Eugene Gay-Tifft. New York, 1937.
The Road Leads On. Translated by Eugene Gay-Tifft. New York, 1934.
Rosa. Translated by Arthur G. Chater. New York, 1926.
Segelfoss Town. Translated by Oliver Stallybrass. New York, 1969.
Victoria. Translated by J. S. Scott. New York, 1925.
The Wanderer. Translated by Oliver and Gunnvor Stallybrass. New York, 1975.
Wayfarers. Translated by James McFarlane. New York, 1980.
The Woman at the Pump. Translated by Oliver and Gunnvor Stallybrass. New York, 1978.

BIOGRAPHICAL AND CRITICAL STUDIES

Berendsohn, Walter. *Knut Hamsun.* Munich, 1929.
Braatøy, Trygve. *Livets cirkel.* Oslo, 1929.
Brynildsen, Aasmund. *Svermeren og hans demon.* Oslo, 1973.
Ferguson, Robert. *Enigma: The Life of Knut Hamsun.* New York, 1987.
Gustafson, Alrik. *Six Scandinavian Novelists.* New York, 1940.

Hamsun, Marie. *Regnbuen.* Oslo, 1953.
——————. *Under gullregnen.* Oslo, 1959.
Hamsun, Tore. *Knut Hamsun.* Oslo, 1959.
Hansen, Thorkild. *Prosessen mot Hamsun.* Oslo, 1959.
Ingwersen, Faith. "The Truthful Liars." Ph.D. dissertation, University of Chicago, 1974.
Kierkegaard, Peter. *Knut Hamsun som modernist.* Copenhagen, 1976.
Kittang, Atle. *Luft, vind, ingenting.* Oslo, 1984.
Landquist, John. *Knut Hamsun.* Tübingen, 1927.
Larsen, Hanna Astrup. *Knut Hamsun.* New York, 1922.
Lowenthal, Leo. *Literature and the Image of Man.* Boston, 1957.
McFarlane, James. "The Whisper of the Blood." *PMLA* 71:563–594 (1956).
Marstrander, Jan. *Det ensomme menneske i Knut Hamsuns diktning.* Oslo, 1959.
Næss, Harald S. *Knut Hamsun.* Boston, 1984.
Nettum, Rolf Nyboe. *Konflikt og visjon.* Oslo, 1970.
Nilson, Sten Sparre. *En ørn i uvær.* Oslo, 1960.
Nybø, Gregory. *Knut Hamsuns "Mysterier."* Oslo, 1969.

Øyslebø, Olaf. *Knut Hamsun gjennom stilen.* Oslo, 1964.
Popperwell, Ronald. "Critical Attitudes to Knut Hamsun." *Scandinavica* 9:1–23 (1970).
Rottem, Øystein. *Knut Hamsuns "Landstrykere."* Oslo, 1978.
Sehmsdorf, Henning. "Knut Hamsun's *Pan."* *Edda,* 345–393 (1974).
Simpson, Allen. *Knut Hamsuns "Landstrykere."* Oslo, 1973.
Skavlan, Einar. *Knut Hamsun.* Oslo, 1929.
Stray, Sigrid. *Min klient Knut Hamsun.* Oslo, 1979.
Tiemroth, Jørgen. *Illusionens vej.* Copenhagen, 1974.
Vige, Rolf. *Knut Hamsuns "Pan."* Oslo, 1963.
Wiehr, Joseph. "Knut Hamsun: His Personality and His Outlook Upon Life." *Smith College Studies in Modern Languages* 3:1–129 (1921–1922).

BIBLIOGRAPHIES

Østby, Arvid. *Knut Hamsun—En bibliografi.* Oslo, 1972.

HARALD S. NÆSS

HENRI BERGSON

(1859–1941)

HENRI BERGSON WAS one of the most influential philosophers of the early twentieth century. He rose to preeminence in the first decade of the century, enjoying an extraordinary vogue in the years just prior to World War I, and remained a significant presence throughout the 1920's and 1930's. He was a gifted writer who was admired for his clear and graceful prose; and his influence extended far beyond philosophical circles to artists, scientists, theologians, and at the peak of his fame to educated society in general. To younger intellectuals such as the philosopher Jacques Maritain and the poet and essayist Charles Péguy, Bergson was known as the "liberator"—the man who had redeemed Western thought from the nineteenth-century "religion of science." Many believed that Bergson's efforts to mark the limits of scientific explanation had conclusively dispelled the specter of mechanistic determinism. This immense prestige did not last, however. Bergson's reputation began to wane slowly after World War I and has declined precipitously since World War II. Although he prepared the way for subsequent developments in continental thought, his name has virtually disappeared from current philosophical discussion. Today it requires an exercise in historical imagination to appreciate the extraordinary role he once played in the intellectual life of our century.

LIFE

Bergson was born in Paris on 18 October 1859, the son of Jewish parents. His mother was English, while his father, a talented musician and once the director of the Geneva Conservatory, was descended from a wealthy Polish family—the sons of Berek, or Bereksons, from which the name Bergson is derived. The young Bergson attended the Lycée Condorcet, where he excelled equally in science and the humanities. In 1878 the family moved to England, while he remained in France and went on to the École Normale Supérieure, a classmate of the sociologist Émile Durkheim, the Socialist leader Jean Jaurès, and other future luminaries of the Third Republic. Here he displayed exceptional promise in mathematics but eventually decided to pursue a career in philosophy.

After leaving the École Normale in 1881, Bergson spent the next sixteen years teaching at various lycées in Angers, Clermont-Ferrand, and finally Paris. In 1891 he married a cousin of Marcel Proust, Louise Neuburger, who bore a single child, a daughter deaf from birth who later became a painter. It was during his years at the lycée that Bergson wrote his first two books, *Essai sur les données immédiates de la conscience* (*Time and Free Will: An Essay on the Immediate Data of Conciousness*, 1889) and *Matière et mémoire* (*Matter and Memory*,

1896), which contributed to his growing esteem in the academy. In 1897 he returned to the École Normale as professor of philosophy, and three years later was called to the prestigious Collège de France, where he retained a chair until his retirement in 1921.

At the beginning of the new century Bergson's reputation began its remarkable ascent. The appeal of his lectures extended far beyond the university: a course by Bergson was a Parisian social event, and the auditorium was often so crowded that special arrangements were required to seat his own students. His popularity grew even more dramatically with the appearance of *L'Évolution créatrice* (*Creative Evolution,* 1907), which made him the most celebrated philosopher in Europe and extended his reputation across the seas. The years just before the outbreak of World War I mark the high tide of Bergsonism, as his books were rapidly translated into other languages and discussions of his work began to abound.

In 1914 Bergson retired from active duty at the Collège de France, and for the duration of the war he devoted himself to the French cause, first in patriotic essays and then in official diplomatic missions to Spain and the United States. After the war he played an active role in the new League of Nations, serving as the first president of the League's Commission for Intellectual Cooperation. At the same time, he continued his philosophical pursuits and produced an extended critique of Einstein's theory of relativity, *Durée et Simultanéité* (*Duration and Simultaneity,* 1922). In 1924, however, Bergson was suddenly stricken with crippling arthritis that forced his retirement from public life. He was awarded the Nobel Prize for Literature in 1927, and despite the difficulties of declining health devoted himself to his last major project, *Les deux sources de la morale et de la religion* (*The Two Sources of Morality and Religion*), which appeared in 1932. This book attests to his personal allegiance to Catholicism, though in his final years he refrained from formal conversion because he foresaw the imminent tribula-tion of the Jews. He declared in his will, dated 8 February 1937: "I would have been converted had I not seen being prepared for many years the terrible wave of anti-Semitism about to break upon the world. I have preferred to remain with those who tomorrow will be the persecuted." He remained true to his word. After the fall of France he refused to accept an exemption from the new authorities, and in December 1940, at the age of eighty-one, he lined up outdoors to register as a Jew. A few weeks later he was dead of pneumonia.

INTELLECTUAL HERITAGE

To appreciate Bergson's impact on modern thought we must consider the situation of French intellectual life around the turn of the century. Throughout the nineteenth century the French intelligentsia had been divided into two opposing camps. On one side were those committed to the scientific humanism that perpetuated the rationalist ideals of the Enlightenment. Proponents of this tradition, which was associated with the prestigious names of Auguste Comte, Hippolyte Taine, and Ernest Renan, advanced a thoroughly naturalistic understanding of the universe. They anticipated the day when the methods of modern science, which had proven so successful in physics and chemistry, would provide a definitive explanation not only of the physical world but also of human thought and action. On the other side were religious humanists who sought to preserve or reconstitute the spiritual heritage of the church. French spiritualism or voluntarism, as it is alternatively called, is largely forgotten today, but it was a major and at times the prevailing philosophical current in nineteenth-century France. This tradition originated with the works of Maine de Biran, and then was developed further by Felix Ravaisson, and eventually by several late-nineteenth-century philosophers, including two of Bergson's teachers at the École Normale, Jules Lachelier and Émile Boutroux.

These philosophers distinguished sharply between mental and physical processes, arguing that the activities of the mind are irreducible to physical explanation. They emphasized the spontaneity of the human will—the free act of spirit that cannot be predicted by the knowledge of antecedent conditions—and claimed that natural scientific method ignores the element of spontaneity in nature itself. All of these points were incorporated and further developed in Bergson's philosophy.

Of the two main currents in French intellectual life, it was scientific humanism that dominated the third quarter of the century. Charles Darwin's *The Origin of Species* was published in 1859—the year of Bergson's birth—and the ethos of scientific naturalism continued to reign supreme for the next few decades. In France Taine and Renan were the guiding lights of the age, and positivism—the use of scientific method to investigate every facet of existence—the preeminent intellectual tendency. For a time Bergson himself was attracted to Herbert Spencer's mechanistic view of evolution, and according to his own account, it was his disenchantment with Spencer that led to his radical revaluation of the concept of time.

Bergson's reaction to Spencer was one expression of a major revolt against positivism near the end of the nineteenth century. Philosophers and students of the human sciences began to question the use of natural scientific method to explain human thought and action. Psychologists, for example, attempted to rid their discipline of the mechanistic notions employed by their predecessors. They were urged on by philosophers such as Wilhelm Dilthey, who declared that we must replace "explanatory" psychology, which is modeled on the natural sciences, with a "descriptive" psychology that captures the actual *Erlebnis* (lived experience) of human beings. Historians made a similar effort to free their enterprise from the constraints of positivism. Taine, Henry Buckle, and other historians were accused of distorting historical reality in the process of adapting it to natural scientific method. The anti-positivist turn among historians was endorsed by the philosopher Wilhem Windelband, who asserted that history is not, like physics or chemistry, a "nomothetic" discipline that searches for general laws but rather an "ideographic" discipline that deals with unique experiences and events. In history as in psychology and other fields it became increasingly common to assert that the methods appropriate to the study of physical processes cannot be extended to the investigation of human processes. Manifestations of "life" are not reducible to mechanical explanation.

Late-nineteenth-century intellectuals challenged not only the encroachments of natural science into other domains but also its pretensions to certainty within its own domain—the physical universe. Philosophers as well as scientists began to doubt whether scientific formulations truly reflect the reality of the physical world. In Austria the physicist Ernst Mach, in the process of questioning the conceptual foundations of Newtonian mechanics, disputed the widespread belief that scientific knowledge can reveal the actual forms of nature itself. In France the mathematician Henri Poincaré argued that Euclidean geometry, which for two millennia had been considered a literal transcipt of external space, was merely one "convention" for organizing spatial relations. The Euclidean system, which we use at the scale of ordinary experience, is no more true than a non-Euclidean system; it is simply more convenient. Mach and Poincaré were certainly minority voices in the scientific community, but they were joined by a growing number of philosophers, including Bergson, Friedrich Nietzsche, William James, and many others. By the turn of the century philosophers and scientists from different and often competing traditions were converging on the same instrumental theory of knowledge—the view that scientific systems are not so much faithful representations of external reality as human inventions or instruments that help order experience in a convenient and efficacious manner.

Bergson played a major role in all these intellectual developments. In his first book, *Time and Free Will,* he demonstrates that the mechanistic notions employed by psychologists distort the nature of human experience, while in later works he shows that scientific reasoning misrepresents even the activities of the natural universe. Throughout his career, however, Bergson held that his aim was not to reject scientific inquiry but rather to free it from certain philosophical prejudices that distort its results. Like Nietzsche he saw that these prejudices are older than science itself and were woven into the fabric of Western philosophy from the very beginning. Hence his philosophical project extends beyond the critique of nineteenth-century positivism to a critical analysis of some enduring and unexamined assumptions of Western thought.

Bergson once remarked that most major philosophers have only one essential insight and spend their entire career attempting to work out its implications. This statement applies to no one more than Bergson himself. He began in the 1880's with the problem of time, and the germ of his entire oeuvre lies in his initial encounter with this one fundamental concept. Although each of his books addresses a different issue, taken together in their order of appearance his works display the progressive unfolding of a single inspiration. In this respect, the course of his career seems to exemplify the principal and seemingly paradoxical insight of his first book—that the growth of the mind is a process of continuous organic development whereby our ability to preserve the past enables us to develop freely into the future.

TIME AND FREE WILL

Time and Free Will is the translator's title of Bergson's doctoral thesis, *Essai sur les données immédiates de la conscience,* which was presented and published in 1889. In this book and its sequel, *Matter and Memory,* Bergson posits a sharp distinction between physical and psychological processes, demonstrating that procedures designed to explore the physical world are inappropriate to the study of mental life. He attacks various schools of psychology that depend upon the methods of natural science and for that reason obsure the distinctive qualities of consciousness: the psycho-physical school, which establishes quantitative laws correlating changes in external stimuli with variations in sensory response; the associationist doctrine, which employs a model derived from the laws of mechanics to describe the operations of the psyche; and less directly in his thesis than in *Matter and Memory,* the materialist position, which treats the mind as an epiphenomenon of the brain's activity and maintains, in the words of one proselyte, that the brain secretes thought just as the liver secretes bile. Bergson shows that each of these approaches leads to a distorted view of consciousness and in their place he proposes a radically different alternative.

In the first part of his thesis Bergson considers the issues raised by the psycho-physical school, which attempts to quantify changes in psychic intensity by correlating them with measurable changes in external stimuli. He argues that psycho-physics relies upon an erroneous assumption embedded in everyday speech—the habit of treating differences in psychic intensity as if they were differences in magnitude. We speak, for instance, of greater or lesser feelings of love, assuming that as our feelings vary we experience merely changes of degree in the same emotion. But for Bergson differences in psychic intensity are changes not in degree but in kind. What we refer to as an increase in joy or sorrow is really a qualitative change that we "interpret as a change in magnitude." Misled by our tendency to use the same word to cover a wide range of psychic states, we mistake one type of difference for another and thereby misconceive the nature of our mental life. The psycho-physical method also depends on another common error—the habit of confusing psychological changes with the physical changes that cause them. Consider our perception of a colored surface under the influence of a brighter or dimmer light. Most of us would say that the color remains the same—only our sensation of luminous intensity increases or diminishes. But, if we pay close attention to the surface, we can see that the variation is not quantitative but qualitative:

> As the luminous source is brought nearer, violet takes a bluish tinge, green tends to become a whitish yellow, and red a brilliant yellow. Inversely, when the light is moved away, ultramarine passes into violet and yellow into green; finally, red, green and violet tend to become a whitish yellow.
>
> (Pogson trans., p. 51)

Under ordinary circumstances we fail to perceive these differences because we habitually equate psychological effects with their physical causes. Knowing that the change has been produced by the increase or diminution of light, we assert that we perceive a difference in luminous intensity rather than a difference in color. We replace "the qualitative impression received by our consciousness" with "the quantitative interpretation given by our understanding." Psycho-physics merely systematizes this common confusion, assuming that it can measure psychological changes by correlating them with quantifiable changes in physical stimuli. Bergson, for his part, emphasizes the distinction between qualitative and quantitative differences, psychological effects and their physical causes. He grants that we can for certain purposes interpret one in terms of the other, but "sooner or later . . . we shall have to recognize the conventional character of this assimilation."

In the next section of his thesis, Bergson examines a related confusion between psychological and physical processes—the tendency to consider our psychic experience in terms that are borrowed from the perception of physical objects. He starts with the seemingly innocent concept of number, which presupposes a capacity to conceive a collection of separate

but identical units. In order to count a flock of sheep, for example, we must be able to reduce heterogeneity to homogeneity—that is, to ignore qualitative differences among the sheep and regard all of them as quantitatively identical. In addition, we must be able to imagine successive units juxtaposed side by side in space:

> If we picture to ourselves each of the sheep in the flock in succession and separately, we shall never have to do with more than a single sheep. In order that the number should go on increasing in proportion as we advance, we must retain the successive images and set them alongside each of the new units which we picture to ourselves: now, it is in space that such a juxtaposition takes place and not in pure duration.
>
> (Pogson trans., p. 77)

Bergson is arguing that human beings possess a unique capacity to project a principle of purely quantitative differentiation—an empty, homogeneous space composed of individual units that are at once identical and distinct. In his view, the significance of this point cannot be overestimated: the faculty for comprehending a "space without quality" is not only the basis of the ability to count but also the foundation of many of our most valued cognitive functions. The capacity to project a homogeneous medium, "clearly conceived by the human intellect, enables us to use clean-cut distinctions, to count, to abstract, and perhaps also to speak." Conceptual abstraction, for instance, "already implies the intuition of a homogeneous medium," since it "assumes clean-cut distinctions and a kind of externality of the concepts or their symbols with regard to one another." The same statement would also apply to the terms of ordinary language.

"Space without quality," however, is far better suited to the perception of the external world, where we attend to discrete and stable objects, than to the internal life of the psyche. This becomes apparent when we examine our own immediate experience as it progresses over time. Consider our consciousness of a chiming bell. I may decide explicitly to count the individual sounds, in which case "I shall have to separate them, and this separation must take place within some homogeneous medium in which the sounds, stripped of their qualities, and in a manner emptied, leave traces of their presence which are absolutely alike." Or alternatively, I may retain each successive sensation "in order to combine it with the others and form a group which reminds me of an air or rhythm which I know: in that case I do not *count* the sounds, I limit myself to gathering, so to speak, the qualitative impression produced by the whole series." In the latter instance we do not attend to each sound as a discrete individual unit external to all the others. Instead, we hear a melody or rhythm in which the individual notes seem to melt or flow into one another to form an organic whole. Even though the sounds appear individually in succession, "we perceive them in one another, and . . . their totality may be compared to a living being whose parts, although distinct, permeate one another just because they are so closely connected." Thus, in addition to our capacity to project a homogeneous medium that creates a succession of distinct and identical units, we can also imagine a "succession without distinction, and think of it as a mutual penetration, an interconnexion and organization of elements, each one of which represents the whole, and cannot be distinguished or isolated from it except by abstract thought."

According to Bergson, this "succession without distinction" is the fundamental feature of consciousness as it exists in *durée réelle* (real duration). At the deepest level our mental life is a qualitative rather than a quantitative progression. Since we are endowed with memory, which preserves the past into the present and makes possible their mutual interpenetration, consciousness is not a series of separate individual states but a seamless whole in which each state flows into all of the others. Instead of a mere accumulation of distinct bits of experience, consciousness is a process of continuous, organic development in which each new moment is permeated by all that has come before it.

In everyday life, however, we remain largely unaware of this deeper current of psychic life. For the most part we are directed not to heterogeneous duration but to homogeneous space. We apprehend permanent external objects rather than our changing impressions of them, since we are usually more concerned with finding points of stability in the outer environment than with following the ceaseless flux of our own psychic life. Moreover, our practical orientation toward the external world exerts a significant influence on consciousness itself. As in the example of the colored surface, where our knowledge of the physical cause overwhelms our immediate experience, the homogeneous medium through which we perceive external reality slowly replaces the awareness of real duration. Bergson argues in *Matter and Memory* that

> our ego comes in contact with the external world at its surface; our successive sensations, although dissolving into one another, retain something of the mutual externality which belongs to their objective causes; and thus our superficial psychic life comes to be pictured without any great effort as set out in a homogeneous medium.
> (Paul and Palmer trans., p. 125)

As a result of this conditioning, we lose contact with real duration and the mind begins to look at itself "not directly, but by a kind of refraction through the forms which it has lent to external perception." Reversing Immanuel Kant's emphasis on the forms through which we apprehend external reality, Bergson maintains that we end up grasping our own psychic life "through the medium of certain forms borrowed from the external world, which thus gives us back what we have lent it."

At this point the distinction between external and internal perception, homogeneous space and heterogeneous duration, has developed into a distinction within consciousness itself. We possess, so to speak, two different selves, or rather two different levels of self: a superficial level that is assimilated to external space and a more profound level that exists in real duration. We are generally quite content with the superficial self, which is well adapted to the demands of everyday life, and rarely attend to our deeper mental life. And yet the consequences of ignoring real duration are momentous. To the degree that consciousness adapts itself to homogeneous space, our behavior becomes as mechanical and predictable as that of material objects. It is only in real duration that we act as free agents and become our authentic selves.

The common practice of identifying the psyche entirely with its more superficial stratum is the error made by association psychology, to which Bergson turns in the last part of his thesis. Associationism first flourished in the eighteenth century but, despite the efforts of Samuel Taylor Coleridge and others, remained very much alive in the nineteenth. In Bergson's view, the associationists reduce the mind to a collection of discrete, impersonal elements, the stronger of which prevail over the weaker: " 'I could have abstained from murder,' says Stuart Mill, 'if my aversion to the crime and my dread of its consequences had been weaker than the temptation which impelled me to commit it.' " Associationists like Mill conceive the mind in terms of a homogeneous space in which distinguishable feelings or ideas are juxtaposed side by side. Aversion and temptation, fear and desire, are presented as though they were separable units mutually external to one another. Bergson grants that this picture may apply to our superficial psychic states but contends that it misrepresents our deeper mental activities. As we delve beneath the surface of the mind, individual elements of consciousness "cease to stand in juxtaposition and begin to permeate and melt into one another, and each [is] tinged with the colouring of all the others." It is an inaccurate psychology that shows us the soul "determined by sympathy, aversion, or hate as though by so many forces pressing upon it. These feelings, provided that they go deep enough, each make up the whole soul, since the whole content of the soul is reflected in each of them." Associationist psychology resolves this unified personal whole into a series of discrete, impersonal elements, thereby replacing the concrete reality of psychic life with a symbolic translation that is used to dissect it.

This distorted image of psychic life leads ultimately to the denial of moral freedom. Once he reduces the mind to a series of impersonal elements, the associationist proceeds to approach consciousness in the same way that the physicist approaches matter. Adopting the scientist's assumption that the same causes always produce the same effects, the associationist believes that if he identifies the existing system of psychic elements, he can then calculate the course of future action. His ultimate aim is the reduction of moral life to a system of laws as determinate as the laws of mechanics.

Bergson insists that this sort of reasoning is fatally flawed. His main objection is that the principal assumption of mechanics—that identical causes will always produce identical effects—cannot be translated to the psychological realm, since identical conditions never reappear on the stage of consciousness, except at the superficial level. Our deeper mental life is "in a constant state of becoming, and the same feeling, by the mere fact of being repeated, is a new feeling." The mind that develops in real duration is therefore irreducible to a determinate calculus, which means that our moral decisions are free to the extent that they issue from a unique personality that develops and changes over time. From this point of view, free will is nothing other than "the relation of the concrete self to that act which it performs." This relation is indefinable, and any attempt to define it requires that we ignore the uniqueness of each individual and, like the associationists, adopt an impersonal terminology that misrepresents the very process wherein our freedom lies.

Bergson acknowledges that our moments of freedom are rare, since we are ordinarily detached from our own immediate experience. Most of the time we dwell at the superficial level of the mind, projecting ourselves into the homogeneous space through which we deal with the external world. Instead of attending to our deeper psychic states, which are perpetually changing in time, we apprehend a world of discrete and stable objects laid out before us in space. As a result of this adaptation to external conditions, our thoughts come to operate according to laws as determinate as those that govern material objects. But beneath this level of awareness, there is still the deeper life of the mind, which we, like the associationists, generally overlook. And it is here, in the dynamic temporality of real duration, that we are restored to our authentic selves. "To act freely," Bergson concludes, is simply "to recover possession of oneself, and to get back into pure duration."

Bergson went on to develop the distinction between homogeneous space and heterogeneous duration over the course of his entire career. As he turned to other problems, he continued to show how the mind's spatial orientation conditions our everyday experiences and consequently the assumptions of scientists and philosophers, leading the scientist to mechanism and determinism and the philosopher to misconceived and insoluble problems. But the idea of real duration has implications that go beyond its significance for Bergson's own career. Seen in retrospect, Bergson's thesis represents a major shift in nineteenth-century intellectual life. A few years earlier James had published a similar critique of associationism, "On Some Omissions of Introspective Psychology" (1884), and presented his now-famous image of psychic life as an unbroken "stream of consciousness." James and Bergson, together with Dilthey and several others, were inciting a revolt against positivism by liberating the study of consciousness from methods derived from physical science. They were also opening up a new frontier—the exploration of "lived experience"—that has played a major role in twentieth-century philosophy, expecially in existentialism and phenomenology. In their attempt to delineate the distinctive features of consciousness, these late-nineteenth-century philosophers anticipate the efforts of Edmund Husserl and later of Martin Heidegger, Jean-Paul Sartre, Maurice Merleau-Ponty, and others to describe the modalities through which human beings apprehend and participate in the world around them.

MATTER AND MEMORY

Bergson's second book, *Matter and Memory,* develops the line of inquiry begun in the first. Real duration presupposes a capacity to retain past experiences, and once *Time and Free Will* was completed Bergson devoted himself to a full-length study of memory. In the late nineteenth century the study of memory was dominated by psychologists and physiologists who believed that memory-images were a mere epiphenomenon of brain states or else corresponded to them exactly. This belief was reinforced by developments in neurophysiology, which had demonstrated precise correlations between particular kinds of brain damage and specific disorders of recollection. Bergson does not question the validity of neurophysiological research but challenges the assumption that the faculty of recollection is merely a function of the cerebral apparatus. In contrast to the prevailing view he argues that memory is irreducible to the physiology of the brain, which is not so much the repository of memory as a bodily mechanism for limiting and directing it to practical ends. In the same way that *Time and Free Will* distinguishes between superficial and deeper consciousness, *Matter and Memory* distinguishes between brain and memory, or more generally between bodily and spiritual processes. While the brain governs our practical dealings with the external environment, memory is a spiritual phenomenon that transcends the instrumental functions of the body.

Bergson first considers the role of the brain in the process of perception. He questions the widespread belief that the cerebral apparatus records impressions from the external world and then stores them in the form of memory-images. This view, he maintains, depends upon the assumption that the brain is a neutral register of sensory impressions and perception a purely contemplative process. He proposes instead that the role of the cerebral apparatus is not to record images but to coordinate the body's response to sensory stimuli. The brain has an instrumental rather than a speculative function; it is directed not toward knowledge but toward action. The same is true of perception, which is an instrumental process that is designed not to store internal images but to prepare us for external movement. We misconceive perception because in actual experience it is always interlaced with memory, which informs present action by providing images from the past, and it is the presence of these images that "lends to perception its subjective character." If "pure perception" were possible, however, it would be "a part of things" rather than ourselves, since in its essence perception is nothing other than "a system of nascent acts which plunges roots deep into the real."

Although perception and memory are intermingled in practice, Bergson holds that they are fundamentally different in principle. Perception is a bodily mechanism that expedites transactions with the environment, whereas memory is a spiritual phenomenon that influences the body but is irreducible to its functions. Because scientists and philosophers begin with the mixed state of actual experience, they blur the distinction between perception and memory, assuming that perception involves the registration of images in the mind and memory the subsequent retrieval of these same images. They see in perception and memory a difference only in degree rather than in kind. This mistake leads them, in Bergson's view, to a distorted explanation of mental life.

Bergson then turns to memory itself. The past, he maintains, survives in two forms: in movements that have become bodily habits and in recollected images that arise in the mind. Here the initial distinction between perception

and memory reappears as a division between two kinds of memory: habit memory, which is bodily function, and pure memory, which is the repository of our entire past. Suppose I memorize a poem and then recite it on several occasions. Bergson notes that there is a crucial difference between my ability to recite the poem and my ability to recollect each occasion on which I recited it. To recite the poem is to perform a habitual action that is learned through constant repetition. But the act of recalling a particular recitation has none of the marks of habit: it involves the representation of a unique and unrepeatable event in my life. This representation arises from pure memory, which preserves the events of our life history as we have lived them in time.

If our past survives in pure memory, why at any given moment are we unaware of all but a mere fraction of it? Here Bergson emphasizes the role of the brain, which he regards as a bodily mechanism that limits memory to what is useful in the present. As a result of the selective action of the brain, pure memory does not manifest itself directly but rather in the form of images that have bearing on the current situation. Actual remembrance arises from the tension between pure memory and the requirements of present action:

> On the one hand, the memory of the past offers to the sensory-motor mechanisms, all the recollections capable of guiding them in their task and of giving to the motor reaction the direction suggested by the lessons of experience. . . . On the other hand, the sensory-motor apparatus furnishes to ineffective, that is unconscious, memories, the means of taking on a body, of materializing themselves, in short of becoming present. For, that a recollection should reappear in consciousness, it is necessary that it should descend from the heights of pure memory down to the precise point where the *action* is taking place.
> (Paul and Palmer trans., p. 197)

This process may be visualized by imagining an inverted cone, the top of which represents the totality of my experiences, and the bottom

53

the point at which my body interacts with the external environment. My actual recollections appear in the form of images somewhere between the two extremes. The closer the mind moves toward the circle at the top, the more it is detached from the current situation and the nearer it approximates the random life of dreams. Likewise, the closer it comes to the point at the bottom, the more it is focused on the immediate problem at hand. Bergson complicates the picture by asserting that in any one situation the mind may pass through an indefinite number of positions between the two ends of the cone. It may also approach the bottom point from a variety of different angles depending on the character of the tension between pure memory and the requirements of action. This means that in response to a given set of circumstances, the mind may traverse many levels of recollection, calling up numerous images that shed light on different aspects of the current problem and influence the action we perform.

Seen from this perspective, memory is not a mere function of the brain, which only selects the memories most appropriate to our momentary concerns, but an independent reality that is limited by the brain. Although neurophysiologists have identified certain types of memory loss with specific lesions of the cerebral apparatus, brain damage does not impair pure memory. Injury to the brain may affect habit memory, or it may upset the mechanisms through which memories are selected, but in neither case is pure memory destroyed. Properly interpreted, the evidence of neurophysiology supports the hypothesis that the source of memory lies outside the brain. Although its activation depends upon a bodily mechanism, pure memory points to a spiritual reality that transcends the body itself.

Matter and Memory focuses on scientific studies of memory, but it goes beyond psychology and neurophysiology to consider some perennial problems of philosophy. Throughout the book Bergson criticizes philosophers who rely on the traditional division between mind and matter, paying special attention to the classical antinomy between idealism and realism. Both idealists and realists, he claims, are misled by the assumption that perception is an internal rather than an external process, a speculative faculty for acquiring knowledge rather than an instrumental function that prepares us for action. The result of this error is that both groups must struggle to account for the way in which mind and matter are related, and each concludes by translating one into the terms of the other: idealists grant priority to internal perceptions and then try to account for external reality by reducing it to the ideas we have of it; realists begin with external reality and then account for internal perceptions by reducing them to impressions we receive from without. Bergson opts for neither alternative and argues instead that the insoluble antinomy between idealism and realism is based on a faulty view of perception common to both positions, which in the end are merely two sides of the same coin. Here as elsewhere Bergson attempts to demonstrate that the traditional impasses of philosophy, like the one that sets idealism and realism in irreconcilable opposition, derive not from the intrinsic limitations of philosophy itself, but from assumptions that have led to the erroneous formulation of some basic philosophical distinctions.

At first glance, *Matter and Memory* seems to perpetuate the dualism that marks *Time and Free Will.* As he does in his first book, Bergson initially distinguishes between physical and psychological realms and then elaborates this distinction into a division between two processes within the psyche itself: instrumental functions that coordinate our responses to the physical world and a deeper stratum of mental life associated with real duration and memory. In *Time and Free Will* he makes some effort to mitigate this dualism, since his ultimate concern is the relationship between real duration and the moral choices that determine our impact on the world around us. But this effort hardly offsets the impression created by the project of establishing a sharp distinction between physical and psychological domains, a distinction expressed in the opposition between homogeneous space and heterogeneous duration. In *Matter and Memory* Bergson takes additional measures to overcome the dualistic character of his work. Although he continues to distinguish between physical and mental processes, he begins to focus more on the points at which they intersect. Whereas *Time and Free Will* emphasizes the recovery of pure duration, *Matter and Memory* is concerned less with pure memory in itself than with the means by which it informs our dealings with external reality. Our actions, he claims, transcend predictable mechanical response to the extent that we bring our accumulated experiences to bear on a given situation. In this respect, memory is synonymous with free will: it is by means of the faculty of recollection that human beings introduce an element of indeterminacy to their actions and therefore to the external world. Memory is the "inner energy" that frees us "from the rhythm of the flow of things" and allows us "to retain in an ever higher degree the past in order to influence ever more deeply the future." To state it in somewhat different terms, "Spirit borrows from matter the perceptions on which it feeds, and restores them to matter in the form of movements which it has stamped with its own freedom." This image of spirit infusing matter proceeds from, but eventually replaces, the initial duality between perception and memory. It is an image that plays an important role in Bergson's later works.

LAUGHTER *AND THE THEORY OF ART*

In the decade between *Matter and Memory* and *Creative Evolution* Bergson wrote numerous essays, many of which were later collected under the title *L'Énergie spirituelle* (*Mind-Energy*, 1919). One of the most notable pieces of this period, however, was his treatise on laughter, *Le rire* (*Laughter*), published in 1900. Here Bergson exhibits the formidable range of his thought by turning to a pervasive but unexamined phenomenon of social life. His thesis is that laughter is produced by seeing human beings display the mechanical behavior we ordinarily associate with machines and other inanimate objects. A man running along the street suddenly trips and falls, and bystanders begin to laugh as they see his body momentarily continue the running motion before it adjusts to the situation. According to Bergson, the laughter is aroused by the perception of absentmindedness or inelasticity—the fact that the muscles continue to perform the same movements when the circumstances require their flexible adjustment. Consider also a comic scene in which an officious character, who conducts his daily affairs with mathematical precision, becomes the victim of a prankster who has tampered with the objects on the stage. The character's actions have become so habitual that when he dips his pen into the inkstand and draws out only mud, he fails to notice any peculiarity and so continues to perform his automatic routines. Later, as he goes to sit down on his customary chair, he overlooks the fact that the furniture has been moved and ends up sprawled across the floor. In both street and stage scenes the laughable element consists in a "mechanical inelasticity, just where one would expect to find the wide-awake adaptability and the living pliableness of a human being." We laugh when we see the human form acting in a fashion that suggests the rigidity and automatism of a machine.

Bergson's theory of laughter rests on the distinction between the psychical and the physical, mind and matter, that appears in his earlier works. In *Time and Free Will* he shows that in our more superficial states we are less like "vital" beings who are free and constantly developing and more like "mechanical" entities that are determined and predictable. In *Matter and Memory* he claims that freedom is dependent on memory, and to the extent that memory withdraws from the plane of action, our responses become as predictable as those of inanimate objects. This reduction of the vital to the mechanical also accounts for the phenomenon of laughter. We expect other persons to display the flexibility appropriate to human beings and laugh when they exhibit the behavior we associate with lifeless things.

The behavior that provokes laughter comes from an "inattention to life," a withdrawal of spirit from the plane of action. When the mind is not infusing existence with its vitality, our actions become increasingly mechanical. They lose their supple quality and begin to assume mechanical characteristics. In this view laughter is a biosocial device for restoring and preserving attention to the world around us. As innocent as it may seem, laughter is first and foremost a corrective for those who ignore the social demand for responsive behavior and a warning to the rest of us who are tempted to do the same.

Laughter is filled with fine observations on comic drama, especially the plays of Molière. It is a mistake, however, to assume that Bergson's approach to comedy is representative of his approach to art in general. From his own remarks it is clear that he regarded comedy as an impure form of art. Pure art detaches us from the instrumental mechanisms that condition everyday life; it frees us from our social selves by awakening our deepest emotions or by refining our external perceptions beyond the requirements of practical existence. Comedy, by this definition, stands midway between art and life. Unlike those forms that detach us from the social world, comedy is a social function designed to preserve our ties to the community.

Bergson wrote no sustained treatise on aesthetics, but reflections on art are scattered throughout his work. They appear quite prominently in *Time and Free Will*, where art is defined with the recovery of real duration:

> Now, if some bold novelist, tearing aside the cleverly woven curtain of our conventional ego, shows us under this appearance of logic a fundamental absurdity, under this juxtaposition of simple states an infinite permeation of a thousand different impressions which have already ceased to exist the instant they are named, we commend him for having known us better than we know ourselves.
>
> (Brereton and Rothwell trans., p. 133)

Anticipating the stream-of-consciousness novel, Bergson envisions a mode of writing that reveals the flow of experience beneath the surface of ordinary awareness. As we encounter this artistic rendering of real duration, we in turn become more aware of our deeper selves: "Encouraged by him [the novelist], we have put aside for an instant the veil which we interposed between our consciousness and ourselves. He has brought us back into our own presence."

Bergson acknowledges that the novelist cannot present real duration directly. Language by its very nature detaches us from immediate experience; it is designed not to express the deeper life of the mind but to simplify it for practical purposes. In *Time and Free Will* language is closely identified with homogeneous space, since it requires that we "establish between our ideas the same sharp and precise distinctions, the same discontinuity, as between material objects." Here language is conceived as a homogeneous medium that we project upon the heterogeneous flux of experience, a system of discrete individual tokens that organizes the otherwise continuous stream of sensations. These tokens allow us to communicate efficiently, but they ignore the subtle shades of personal experience:

> Each of us has his own way of loving and hating; and this love or this hatred reflects his whole personality. Language, however, denotes these states by the same words in every case: so that it has been able to fix only the objective and impersonal aspect of love, hate, and the thousand emotions which stir the soul.
>
> (Brereton and Rothwell trans., p. 164)

Although we esteem the writer who strives to present the flow of immediate experience, it is impossible "to translate completely what our soul experiences: there is no common measure between mind and language." Hence the artist is engaged in a constant struggle to make language convey the very thing it is designed to distort. In slightly different terms, art involves an inescapable compromise between spirit and matter: just as memory-images arise from the tension between pure memory and the demands of external action, so the work of art emerges from the interaction between personal insight and the impersonal medium of language.

The problem of language raises the issue of literary technique, but Bergson usually refrains from prescriptive statement, confining himself to some reflections on image and rhythm. He is well aware of the power of images and often uses them to illustrate the process of real duration. But he warns us that images must be used with caution, since they can easily insert themselves between the reader and the intuition to which the writer is directing him. No image, he maintains, can "reproduce exactly the original feeling I have of the flow of my own conscious life." His discussions of literary language, however, are less likely to emphasize precise visual images, which depend upon spatial perception, than the rhythmic movement of verbal sequences as we experience them in time:

> The words may then have been well chosen, [but] they will not convey the whole of what we wish to make them say if we do not succeed by the rhythm, by the punctuation, by the relative lengths of the sentence and parts of the sentences, by a particular dancing of the sentences, in making the reader's mind, continually guided by a series of nascent movements, describe a curve of thought and feeling analogous to that we ourselves describe. . . . The words, taken individually, no longer count: there is nothing left but the flow of meaning which runs through the words, nothing but two minds which, without intermediary, seem to vibrate directly in unison with one another.
>
> (Carr trans., pp. 56–57)

Artists cannot entirely overcome the externality of language, but they can to a degree overcome its intrinsic limitations. Just as memory attempts to infuse matter with spirit, the artist struggles to make the impersonal medium of language the outward expression of a unique personal insight.

In Bergson's view, the function of art is to release us from the instrumental mechanisms—psychic, linguistic, and social—that condition everyday existence. These mechanisms simplify our experience by isolating those elements from the psychic flux that serve our practical needs and then screening us from the rest. The artist, who is free from the constraints of ordinary life and attends more closely to immediate experience, enables us "to brush aside the utilitarian symbols, the conventional and socially accepted generalities, in short, everything that veils reality from us, in order to bring us face to face with reality itself." The words "face to face with reality itself" may be somewhat misleading, however, especially when we consider the visual arts. A superior landscapist does not try to duplicate external reality as it ordinarily appears; instead, he infuses the landscape with a unique emotion that transforms the way we apprehend the world around us. Art may bring us "face to face with reality," but it is a reality infused with personal feelings and revealed only through the work of art itself.

INTELLECT AND INTUITION

In 1903 Bergson published a long essay, "Introduction à la métaphysique" (*An Introduction to Metaphysics*), which lays out his theory of knowledge. This essay has been reprinted many times and is often used, somewhat misleadingly, as a general introduction to his work (the introduction to *La pensée et le mouvant* [*The Creative Mind*, 1934] serves this purpose much better). *An Introduction to Metaphysics* is not so much an overview of Bergson's thought as a new development that prepares the way for *Creative Evolution*. The significance of the essay is twofold. First, it posits his now well-known distinction between intellect, which provides relative knowledge, and intuition, which leads to absolute knowledge. Second, *An Introduction to Metaphysics* shows Bergson extending the idea of real duration from the human psyche to the natural world itself. In this work intuition becomes the means through which we grasp durations other than our own; it is the faculty that enables us to pass from our own psychic stream to the mobile reality of the external universe.

The intellect offers us only relative knowledge of objects. It is an instrumental rather than a speculative faculty, and its purpose is to replace the stream of immediate experience with a network of stable and useful concepts:

> We do not aim generally at knowledge for the sake of knowledge, but in order to take sides, to draw profit—in short, to satisfy an interest. We inquire up to what point the object we seek to know is *this* or *that*, to what known class it belongs, and what kind of action, bearing or attitude it should suggest to us. . . . All knowledge, properly so called, is then oriented in a certain direction, or taken from a certain point of view.
>
> (Hulme trans., pp. 38–39)

The intellect is not a dispassionate register of sensory impressions, but a practical mechanism for selectively arranging them. Contrary to traditional belief, it is designed not to reflect reality itself but to project a useful grid upon it.

Intuition, by contrast, leads us directly to the real. Whereas the intellect places the object within one or another system that isolates a feature it shares with other objects, intuition aims at the object in itself. Bergson defines intuition as a kind of "intellectual sympathy by which one places oneself within an object in order to coincide with what is unique in it and consequently inexpressible." Intuition reverses the habitual tendency of the mind

to simplify and, in a sense, distort reality and enables us to apprehend the object as it really is.

Once his principal distinction is established, Bergson considers the process of real duration and claims that the intellect, which reduces the unique and novel to the repeatable and recognizable, is incapable of grasping the psychic flux as it develops in time. He then suggests that the intellect is similarly limited in its apprehension of the external world. The reality given to us in immediate experience is dynamic rather than static—a shifting, mobile flux rather than a system of unchanging forms. Ordinarily we rely on the intellect to immobilize this dynamic flux, and as a result we come to believe that reality itself is essentially unchanging. Intuition reverses this process and restores us to the fluid reality that is evident in immediate experience. This faculty makes it possible for us to overcome the limitations of the intellect and to develop "fluid concepts, capable of following reality in all its sinuosities and of adopting the very movement of the inward life of things."

The distinction between intellect and intuition has given rise to certain misconceptions, some of which derive from apparent inconsistencies in Bergson himself. In *An Introduction to Metaphysics* Bergson clearly subordinates intellect to intuition, arguing that conceptual knowledge is merely relative and only intuition can penetrate to reality itself. But at other times he seems to regard intellect and intuition as complementary functions: the intellect provides knowledge of external matter, whereas intuition reveals the internal movement of real duration. Such is the view implied in *Time and Free Will,* which distinguishes sharply between physical and psychological processes, homogeneous space and heterogeneous duration. The same idea appears in some later works, especially in passages where Bergson is defending himself against the charge of irrationalism and must acknowledge the adequacy of scientific knowledge to the physical world. It seems, then, as if Bergson holds two incompatible views of external reality, one of which sees it as a dynamic flux that we grasp through intuition, the other conceiving it as a collection of material objects that we comprehend through the intellect. *An Introduction to Metaphysics* clearly espouses the former view: it shows Bergson extending the idea of real duration from the internal to the external world. The apparent contradiction between this position and the other is resolved in *Creative Evolution,* where Bergson shows how his vision of a dynamic natural flux grasped solely by the intuition may be reconciled with the presence of stable material objects that are the province of the intellect.

CREATIVE EVOLUTION

In his first two books Bergson is concerned principally with the sciences of the mind: *Time and Free Will* is devoted to contemporary psychology, *Matter and Memory* to neurophysiology. In his third and most popular book, *Creative Evolution,* he turns from the psyche to the natural world and takes on the theory of biological evolution. Here he openly embraces the idea of evolutionary development but maintains that it has been distorted by the mechanistic assumptions of natural science. Such assumptions are the inevitable product of the intellect, a faculty that must project a mechanistic form upon reality in order to comprehend it. *Creative Evolution* is therefore as much an inquiry into the nature of intellect as it is a study of evolution, since the theory of biological development cannot be dissociated from the mental apparatus we have used to create it.

As in *An Introduction to Metaphysics,* Bergson starts with the idea of real duration and then proposes that we consider the natural world *sub specie durationis.* If we put aside our habitual ways of thinking, we can observe in the development of organic life a process of continuous creation like that of consciousness itself, a process "in which the past presses against the present and causes the upspring-

ing of a new form of consciousness, incommensurable with its antecedent." Real duration thus provides us with a model through which to envision the development of life itself.

The rational intellect, in Bergson's view, has no better grasp of evolutionary development than it does of real duration. It is a practical instrument more suited for classifying forms that already exist than for comprehending the process through which genuinely new forms emerge. By its very nature the intellect reduces time to a function of space, treating the past and future as calculable functions of the present. The intellect is compelled to regard novelty as a mere rearrangement of existing elements, and cannot imagine continuous and unforeseeable change. This failure to comprehend true novelty characterizes the prevailing views of evolution, mechanistic and teleological alike. Mechanistic theories by definition seek to explain future states on the basis of antecedent conditions in the present. Teleological theories appear to be different, but are only mechanistic theories in reverse. Since they assume that evolution involves the realization of "a programme previously arranged," they too fail to grasp the continual emergence of that which is radically new.

In response to both mechanistic and teleological views Bergson postulates the existence of a spontaneous creative impetus—the *élan vital*—that produces ever new forms of life and raises creation to progressively higher levels of development. The *élan vital* is a speculative notion, but Bergson repeatedly demonstrates that it accounts for biological facts that other theories fail to explain. He also marshals evidence to show that evolution progresses not in a linear development from one stage to the next, but through the divergence of the original impetus into distinct and specialized tendencies. In the animal kingdom, for example, the vital impetus has advanced through the division into two especially successful lines of development: the arthropods, best represented by social insects such as bees and ants, and the vertebrates, which achieve their highest form in the human species. *Hymenoptera* and *homo sapiens* each exhibit the fullest development of a fundamental organ of life: bees and ants manifest the triumph of instinct, whereas humanity displays the highest realization of the intellect.

Instinct, according to Bergson, is a faculty for using the organic instruments of the body. It is perfectly suited to its function—"molded on the very form of life"—and seizes its object spontaneously without the intervention of consciousness. Intellect, on the other hand, is a faculty for manufacturing artificial instruments out of inanimate matter. It presupposes consciousness, and the instruments it produces are ingenious but imperfect. Each faculty has virtues that the other lacks. Instinct is one with life itself, but lacks any impulsion to go beyond its existing functions. Intellect is marvelously innovative but is marked by "a natural inability to comprehend life"; that is to say, the intellect is designed not to comprehend the creative impetus itself but to organize the material objects this impetus has produced.

The intellect, Bergson contends, evolves simultaneously with the genesis of matter, and the two have "progressively adapted themselves one to the other in order to attain at last a common form." The intellectuality of mind is closely tied to the materiality of things:

> Our intellect, in the narrow sense of the word, is intended to secure the perfect fitting of our body to its environment, to represent the relations of external things among themselves—in short, to think matter. . . . We shall see that the human intellect feels at home among inanimate objects, more especially among solids, where our action finds its fulcrum and our industry its tools; that our concepts have been formed on the model of solids; that our logic is, pre-eminently, the logic of solids; that, consequently, our intellect triumphs in geometry, wherein is revealed the kinship of logical thought with unorganized matter.
> (Mitchell trans., p. ix)

This "logic of solids" has shaped the entire course of Western philosophy, which has traditionally favored space over time and granted ontological priority to things over actions, to static essences over dynamic flux. The intellect, which is adapted to the organization of material things, cannot reveal the mobile nature of reality itself. It is a product of evolutionary development, but is incapable of grasping the dynamic process which produced it.

The human mind is not purely intellect, however. Although the *élan vital* has diverged into highly specialized tendencies, traces of the whole may be found in each of its parts. As Bergson puts it, there is surrounding our intellect "an indistinct fringe which recalls its origins." This "vague nebulosity" contains elements of instinct, which in the human species has evolved into the faculty of intuition. The latter is akin to instinct, but it is "instinct that has become disinterested, self-conscious, capable of reflecting upon its object and of enlarging it indefinitely." Intuition surpasses instinct in its capacity to interact with intelligence and produce new and unforeseeable developments in the human mind. Bergson suggests that the future of the human species, and perhaps the evolutionary process itself, lies in the further development of intuition, which will not only reveal the true character of the natural order but also advance it to a higher though as yet indefinable level of development.

Creative Evolution was a huge popular success, and its widespread appeal tells us something about the cultural conditions of the age. Despite the reaction against positivism, the triumphs of natural science still weighed heavily on the minds of many people. To those for whom science and spirituality seemed irreconcilably opposed, Bergson appeared as a mediating agent who dispelled the threatening implications of Darwinism. He did this by simultaneously spiritualizing biology and naturalizing the spiritual. After reading Bergson's book one could believe that Darwinian evolution is essentially a consequence of the mechanistic nature of intellect and that the *élan vital* makes far more sense of the entire evolutionary process. One could also view the traditional conception of God as a product of intellect and reconceive the divine as a creative spirit that realizes itself progressively in the natural order. The previously unbridgeable gap between science and spirituality, naturalistic and religious points of view, seemed to dissolve into mere illusion.

The response to *Creative Evolution* was not uniformly favorable, however. By intimating that the vital impetus may be equated with God, Bergson offended many Catholics and entered into a collision course with church doctrine just at the moment when it was enjoying a major revival in France. Catholics inspired by Bergson's earlier studies of the psyche were less receptive to his speculative cosmology. They included some of his most significant disciples, such as Péguy in France and T. E. Hulme in England, who strongly preferred the Bergson of *Time and Free Will* and *Matter and Memory*. Péguy and Hulme praised Bergson for restoring the distinction between the mechanistic realm of matter and the vital realm of human existence but accused him of collapsing the equally important distinction between the human and the divine. From their perspective *Creative Evolution* denied the transcendence of the spiritual realm by reducing God to an immanent life force realizing itself through the course of evolutionary development. Bergson was also criticized by other influential Catholics such as Maritain, and by 1914 his works were placed on the church's Index of Prohibited Books. The same year also dealt a more powerful and perhaps fatal blow to the success of *Creative Evolution*. With the outbreak of World War I the cultural climate of Europe began to change dramatically, and by the time it was over the ethos that could support a vision of progressive cosmic development had been entirely eliminated. From then on the vogue of Bergsonism began its steady descent.

THE TWO SOURCES OF MORALITY AND RELIGION

After ill health forced his retirement in 1924, Bergson turned his attention to his last major work, *The Two Sources of Morality and Religion*. In his previous books he addresses the problems of psychology, neurophysiology, and evolutionary biology, exposing the assumptions that led them to erroneous conclusions about human nature and the physical universe. In his final book he considers in a similar manner the science of ethnology, in particular the naturalistic approach to religion advanced by Durkheim and Lucien Lévy-Bruhl, who reduce religious beliefs and rituals to a social function. Bergson grants the partial validity of this view of religion but claims that it overlooks a crucial dimension of spiritual life. As in *Time and Free Will* and *Matter and Memory,* he distinguishes between superficial and deeper levels of the psyche, the first associated with mechanisms through which we adapt to the external world, the other bearing witness to spiritual reality. The science of ethnology, he claims, observes only the more superficial aspect of the human mind and therefore fails to comprehend the more profound significance of religious inspiration.

Bergson begins by distinguishing between two types of morality, the closed and the open. Closed morality is designed to preserve the solidarity of the social group, and its function is akin to that of other instrumental mechanisms that facilitate adaptation to the surrounding environment. The sense of moral obligation, Bergson claims, is not merely the product of social pressure, but a habit that approximates an instinctive tendency. We are by nature gregarious beings: our feelings of obligation proceed as much from internal as from external compulsion, and we usually bind ourselves with little effort or awareness to the norms of society. Closed morality may be described as the process through which this binding takes place. It is a quasi-instinctual function that maintains the cohesion of a community and protects it against the threat of others.

Thus far Bergson's views correspond closely to those of Durkheim and Lévy-Bruhl. But Bergson goes on to argue that morality is not fully reducible to a social function. Open morality, as he calls it, proceeds from a source entirely different from that of its counterpart. It arises only in exceptional individuals—the great prophets, saints, and mystics—who have occasionally inspired humanity to pursue a higher spiritual calling. Whereas closed morality is "a system of *orders* dictated by *impersonal* social requirements," open morality is "a series of *appeals* made to the conscience of each of us by *persons* who represent the best there is in humanity." This type of morality is not a means of consolidating a particular clan but a spiritual emotion that awakens us to the brotherhood of all mankind. In Bergson's view there is no direct passage from love of one's own family, town, or nation to love of all humanity: the spirit that gives rise to universal love differs not in degree but in kind from the others. The first type of love solidifies a group against its potential adversaries, whereas the other type requires a leap of creative sympathy that reaches across the gulf that separates one group from another. Bergson identifies universal love with the development of the *élan vital:* our spiritual leaders bear the progressive current of the vital impetus by calling us to a higher realization of our humanity. As in *Creative Evolution,* where future cosmic development seems to depend on the ability of our species to infuse matter with spirit, Bergson envisions the bearer of open morality infusing a resistant society with the spirit of universal brotherhood.

Corresponding to the two kinds of morality are two kinds of religion—the static and the dynamic. Static religion, like closed morality, performs an important social function: it generates images and myths that counteract the propensity of the intellect to destabilize the social order. For all its benefits, the intellect produces effects that are potentially detrimental to life. First, it encourages the growth of individuality, which poses a serious threat to communal solidarity. Secondly, the intellect has debilitating psychological consequences: intelligent beings are conscious of the gap be-

tween their goals and their capabilities and in addition are uniquely burdened by the knowledge of their inevitable deaths. As a result of this awareness, they are prone to discouragement and inaction. In order to counteract these tendencies, nature has provided us with *la fonction fabulatrice* (the myth-making faculty) through which to overcome the temptation to solitude and despair. This faculty offsets excessive individuality by producing images that help consolidate social identity. It also neutralizes the fear of ultimate annihilation by creating images of life after death and wards off the awareness of frailty through images of beneficent deities that sustain our efforts. The production of these images is similar to the production of laughter in that both are quasi-instinctive functions: laughter is designed to overcome inattention to social norms, religious images to counteract that which is "depressing for the individual, and dissolvent for society, in the exercise of intelligence." From this point of view, religion may be defined as "a defensive reaction of nature" against the damaging consequences of the intellect. By creating the myth-making faculty, the *élan vital* has removed an obstacle to its advance by providing us with a means of using the intellect without suffering the harmful effects of its activity.

Our myth-making faculty, however, is only one source of religious experience. If closed morality finds its counterpart in the bio-social functions of static religion, open morality has its counterpart in the purely spiritual principle of dynamic religion. Static religion is associated with the operations of intellect, dynamic religion with intuition and the *élan vital.* This second source of religion is manifest in the religious mystic, who brings us closer to "the creative effort," which is "of God, if it is not God himself." The task of the mystic is to advance the progress of creation through the spiritual transformation of humanity. Bergson is thinking primarily of Christ, the model of those who are consumed by "the love of God for all men," a love that seeks "to complete the creation of the human species and make of humanity what it would have straightaway become, had it been able to assume its final shape without the assistance of man himself." Dynamic religion thus strives to overcome the limitations of our present stage of development by infusing human nature with the abiding love of God.

At the end of *The Two Sources of Morality and Religion* Bergson contemplates the prospects of a world transformed by love. He looks foward to a time when the perennial hostility between nations will have yielded to the reign of universal peace. The obstacles to the realization of this dream are admittedly great. The effect of closed morality is to set one group against another, and efforts to achieve universal harmony must struggle against this "deep-rooted war-instinct underlying civilization." And yet, he hopes, the same progressive spirit that founded the League of Nations may ultimately prevail over the intransigence of human nature. The extraordinary development of technology in recent centuries has been a mixed blessing, but it has given us the potential to eliminate some of the material conditions that give rise to war. And if the material side of our nature has witnessed such a dramatic transformation, it is at least conceivable that our spiritual nature may undergo a transformation of similar proportions. Moreover, with the material forces now at our disposal, the cost of spiritual failure could be immense. In his final appeal Bergson reminds us that the very survival of humanity depends upon the course we decide to take:

> Mankind lies groaning, half crushed beneath the weight of its own progress. Men do not sufficiently realize that their future is in their own hands. Theirs is the task of determining first of all whether they want to go on living or not. Theirs the responsibility, then, for deciding if they want merely to live, or intend to make just the extra effort required for fulfilling, even on their refractory planet, the essential function of the universe, which is a machine for the making of gods.
>
> (Audra and Brereton trans., p. 306)

The book concludes with this image of cosmic progression toward the divine, though the utopian vision is heavily qualified by the sense of impending crisis.

The Two Sources of Morality and Religion was published long after the cult of Bergsonism had disappeared and therefore the book had none of the cultural impact of the earlier works. Moreover, in the wake of continuing economic depression and the rise of Fascism there was little receptivity to the optimistic spirit of Bergson's cosmology. By the later 1930's Bergson himself recognized that the clouds were darkening over Europe, and he lived to see the outbreak of a second great war in many ways more savage than the first. In terms of its popular reception, then, Bergson's last book was virtually stillborn, certainly by comparison to *Creative Evolution*. Yet some readers have found *The Two Sources of Morality and Religion* the most moving of all his works. Here the pervasive dichotomy between spirit and matter is expressed in the collision between our progressive aspiration for universal peace and the terrible reality of our warlike instincts. None of Bergson's other books touches so directly on our ultimate concerns as human beings, and none evokes so deeply the spiritual crisis of the twentieth century.

LEGACY

Bergson was one of the most celebrated intellectuals of the early twentieth century. His writings seemed to illuminate virtually every sphere of knowledge and to resolve the most pressing intellectual issues of the day. To a culture still laboring under the burden of positivism, he offered a means of reconciling the substantial achievements of modern science with the spiritual heritage of the church. Some admirers saw an even greater significance in his work, regarding him not merely as a major critic of positivism but as the herald of a decisive transformation of Western thought. It appeared as if Bergson had uncovered the crucial and long-hidden assumptions of the Western philosophical tradition and had begun to steer it in a fundamentally new direction. Such extraordinary acclaim is all the more remarkable when we realize that Bergson's reputation declined almost as quickly as it had risen and that his writings play little if any role in contemporary intellectual life. To the degree that his books are still read today, they are treated more as documents of turn-of-the-century cultural history than as enduring works of philosophy.

Despite this loss of esteem, Bergson's works have had a significant impact on modern thought, though his influence has varied from country to country. In France he is the unacknowledged forerunner of existential philosophy: his critique of scientific rationalism, as well as his emphasis on immediate experience and personal authenticity, clearly anticipates the works of Sartre, Gabriel Marcel, and Merleau-Ponty. His ideas have also resurfaced in post-structuralist thought, especially in the writings of Gilles Deleuze. In the English-speaking world, however, the situation is quite different. Berson was at first greeted enthusiastically by philosophers such as James, but his reputation was soon eclipsed by the rise of the analytic tradition. He maintained a small following outside the philosophical mainstream, and influenced the later works of Alfred North Whitehead, but his role in recent Anglo-American philosophy has otherwise been minimal.

Although his book on religion did not appear until the 1930's, Bergson influenced the course of French religious thought from the outset of the century. Maritain was one of many young intellectuals who found spiritual inspiration in Bergson's lectures. Although Maritain eventually rejected Bergsonism, he acknowledged that Bergson's works had rescued him from scientific naturalism and prepared the way for his conversion to Catholicism. Bergson was also a major influence on Catholic modernism, the significant if short-lived attempt by Alfred Loisy, Édouard Le Roy, and others to bring church doctrine into line with modern thought. In 1907 this movement was condemned by Rome, which placed Bergson's own books on the Index seven years later. Yet Bergsonian ideas continued to inspire Catholic writers who believed that the church must eventually come to terms with the intellectual currents of modernity. His presence is especially evident in the works of Teilhard de Chardin, whose cosmological speculations are heavily indebted to *Creative Evolution*.

Bergson has often been called the artist's philosopher, and to trace his impact on modern authors would require nothing less than an extensive survey of early-twentieth-century literature. The question is not whether Bergson was known to a particular writer, but how well he was known and where to draw the line between influence and affinity. In the case of acknowledged disciples, such as Péguy, there is very little ambiguity. But when it comes to writers like Proust, whose concerns are closely related to Bergson's but not clearly derived from them, the question of indebtedness remains a matter of perpetual debate. The same is true of Bergson's relationship to stream-of-consciousness fiction, where it is difficult to determine the significance of his influence even when a definite link can be established. Nevertheless, it is fair to say that Bergson's account of real duration anticipates the attempts of James Joyce, Virginia Woolf, and William Faulkner to render artistically the flux of psychic life, and that his works, which were widely discussed in the early twentieth century, helped to create the cultural environment in which stream-of-consciousness narration arose.

The precipitous decline of Bergson's reputation leaves us with a peculiar problem of assessment. Does the value of his works transcend his own times, or was he, somewhat like Spencer, merely the intellectual spokesman of a particular generation? Does current disfavor attest to his inadequacies as a philosopher, or does it tell us something about the limitations of our own cultural environment? There are no simple answers to these questions, though the shifting fortunes of Bergsonism are clearly symptomatic of changes that have occurred since the beginning of the century. One approach to these questions might be to distinguish between the critical and speculative sides of Bergson's thought. It is one of the misfortunes of Bergson's career that he came to be associated almost exclusively with cosmological speculations for which he is now summarily dismissed. Speculative philosophy is an especially risky business in periods of rapid intellectual change, and Bergson has become increasingly vulnerable to the charge that his views are fatally dependent on outdated scientific research. The disrepute of Bergsonian speculation is compounded by the fact that most modern philosophers have simply grown weary of this kind of enterprise and have all but abandoned it. What seems to have been forgotten, however, is the critical dimension of Bergson's thought, which helped to establish the ethos of contemporary philosophy. Throughout his career Bergson exposed the assumptions that are built into the way we talk about ourselves and the world around us. He recognized that these assumptions regulate our theoretical as well as our practical discourses, and his principal aim was to reveal how the world would look once we stripped away the obfuscations of our linguistic and conceptual apparatus. In this respect his work is closely allied with the critical projects of philosophers such as Heidegger and the Ludwig Wittgenstein of *Philosophical Investigations* (1953). What Bergson eventually claimed to discover about the world has gained little assent from contemporary philosophers and scientists, but his analysis of the snares of ordinary language, and the effects of these snares on theoretical inquiry, place him firmly in the mainstream of modern philosophy.

Selected Bibliography

EDITIONS

INDIVIDUAL WORKS

Essai sur les données immédiates de la conscience. Paris, 1889.

Matière et mémoire. Paris, 1896.

Le rire: Essai sur la signification du comique. Paris, 1900.

"Introduction à la métaphysique." *Revue de metaphysique et de morale* 29:1–36 (1903).

L'Évolution créatrice. Paris, 1907.

L'Énergie spirituelle: Essais et conférences. Paris, 1919.

Durée et simultanéité: A propos de la théorie d'Einstein. Paris, 1922; 2d ed., 1924.

Les deux sources de la morale et de la religion. Paris, 1932.

La pensée et le mouvant: Essais et conférences. Paris, 1934.

COLLECTED WORKS

Écrits et paroles. Edited by R.-M. Mossé-Bastide. 3 vols. Paris, 1957–1959.

Oeuvres. Édition du centenaire. Edited by André Robinet and Henri Gouhier. Paris, 1959.

Mélanges. Edited by André Robinet. Paris, 1972.

TRANSLATIONS

"Aristotle's Concept of Place." Translated by John K. Ryan. In *Ancients and Moderns,* edited by John K. Ryan. Washington, D.C., 1970.

Creative Evolution. Translated by Arthur Mitchell. New York, 1911.

The Creative Mind. Translated by Mabelle L. Andison. New York, 1946.

Duration and Simultaneity with Reference to Einstein's Theory. 2d ed. Translated by Leon Jacobson. Indianapolis, 1965.

An Introduction to Metaphysics. Translated by T. E. Hulme. New York, 1912.

Laughter: An Essay on the Meaning of the Comic. Translated by Cloudesley Brereton and Fred Rothwell. New York, 1911. Reprinted in *Comedy,* edited by Wylie Sypher. Garden City, N.Y., 1956.

Matter and Memory. Translated by Nancy Margaret Paul and W. Scott Palmer. New York, 1911.

Mind-Energy: Lectures and Essays. Translated by H. Wildon Carr. New York, 1920.

Time and Free Will: An Essay on the Immediate Data of Consciousness. Translated by F. L. Pogson. New York, 1910.

The Two Sources of Morality and Religion. Translated by R. Ashley Audra and Cloudesley Brereton. London, 1935.

BIOGRAPHICAL AND CRITICAL STUDIES

Alexander, Ian W. *Bergson: Philosopher of Reflection.* New York, 1957.

Arbour, Romeo. *Henri Bergson et les lettres françaises.* Paris, 1955.

Bachelard, Gaston. *La dialectique de la durée.* Paris, 1936.

Béguin, Albert, and Pierre Thévenaz, eds. *Henri Bergson: Essais et témoignages.* Neuchâtel, 1943.

Benda, Julien. *Le Bergsonisme, ou une philosophie de la mobilité.* Paris, 1912.

Capek, Milič. *Bergson and Modern Physics: A Reinterpretation and Re-evaluation.* New York, 1971.

Carr, H. Wildon. *Henri Bergson: The Philosophy of Change.* London, 1912.

Chevalier, Jacques. *Henri Bergson.* Translated by Lilian A. Clare. New York, 1928.

Copleston, Frederick. *From Maine de Biran to Sartre.* In *A History of Philosophy,* vol. 9. New York, 1975.

Deleuze, Gilès. *Le Bergsonisme.* Paris, 1966.

Douglass, Paul. *Bergson, Eliot, and American Literature.* Lexington, Ky., 1986.

Les études Bergsoniennes. Paris, 1948–.

Gunter, P. A. Y., ed. *Bergson and the Evolution of Physics.* Knoxville, Tenn., 1969.

Hanna, Thomas, ed. *The Bergsonian Heritage.* New York, 1962.

Jankélévitch, Vladimir. *Henri Bergson.* Paris, 1959.

Kolakowski, Leszek. *Bergson.* Oxford, 1985.

Kumar, Shiv K. *Bergson and the Stream of Consciousness Novel.* London, 1962.

Le Roy, Édouard. *Une philosophie nouvelle: Henri Bergson.* Paris, 1914. Translated by Vincent Benson as *The New Philosophy of Henri Bergson.* New York, 1913.

Lindsay, A. D. *The Philosophy of Bergson.* London, 1911.

Maritain, Jacques. *La philosophie Bergsonienne: Études critiques:* Paris, 1914. 2d ed. Translated by Mabelle L. Andison as *Bergsonian Philosophy and Thomism.* New York, 1955.

Pilkington, A. E. *Bergson and His Influence: A Reassessment.* Cambridge, Eng., 1976.

Russell, Bertrand. *The Philosophy of Bergson, with a Reply by Mr. H. Wildon Carr and a Rejoinder by Mr. Russell.* Cambridge, Eng., 1914.

Santayana, George. "The Philosophy of M. Henri Bergson." In *Winds of Doctrine: Studies in Contemporary Opinion.* New York, 1912.

Scharfstein, Ben-Ami. *Roots of Bergson's Philosophy.* New York, 1943.

BIBLIOGRAPHIES

Gunter, P. A. Y. *Henri Bergson: A Bibliography.* 2d ed. Bowling Green, Ohio, 1986.

SANFORD R. SCHWARTZ

ITALO SVEVO
(1861–1928)

I N ANY CULTURAL atlas Trieste would figure as a speck rather than as a capital. No match for the enchanting decadence of Venice, certainly not an artistic or intellectual metropolis like Paris or Vienna, it was, at the end of the nineteenth century, a small, bustling commercial center, the Austro-Hungarian Empire's chief port on the Adriatic. Yet the confluence of languages and cultures in the little city did make it a promising vantage point from which to regard the upheavals of modern European art and science. Books and magazines issued in Paris were on sale in Trieste literally within hours of their publication, while Middle Europe's Friedrich Nietzsche, Sigmund Freud, and Franz Kafka could be absorbed by the Triestine intelligentsia virtually as local influences, before they were known across the world. Perhaps it was serendipity that brought James Joyce there for several years just after the turn of the century, but it might also be something more than accident that the quintessential modernist should have come to rest at an important stage of his development in a province crisscrossed by so many significant lines of European innovation. At any rate the Irishman's arrival in Trieste became a happy chance for the local writer Italo Svevo, whose novels, thanks to generous Joycean promotion in Paris, emerged after twenty-five years of neglect to be recognized as indispensable works of Italian modernism.

Svevo's real name was Ettore Schmitz, his father being of German-Italian Jewish stock. The pen name he adopted was a bow to his hybrid national background, for "Italo" is a way of saying "the Italian," while "Svevo" refers to the Swabians, a South German ethnic group. The large Italian population of Trieste fervently aspired to be joined to Italy from the mid-nineteenth century until World War I, in the wake of which war the union was finally effected. Although nationalistic rhetoric and bravado were not congenial to him, Svevo did gravitate toward the Mediterranean side of his heritage, as even the choice of Italian for his writing testifies. At the same time, however, he appeared for a long while out of phase with the literary culture of Italy, partly because he came from a Middle European background permeated by ideas and sensibilities that reached the peninsula only later.

Svevo's childhood and youth acquainted him with diverse experiences of social class as well, since his family's fortunes fluctuated considerably. While still a teenager, his father had been obliged to earn a living as a peddler, and only in mid-life did the elder Schmitz arrive at a comfortable situation; but then in his declining years he suffered business reverses. Thus Svevo and his brothers passed from being privileged children who could be sent at their father's whim to an expensive boarding school in Germany to being pinched young men compelled to take dreary jobs as clerks in order to survive. Svevo's own position rose again when, in his mid-thirties, he married a distant cousin, Livia Veneziani, whose family had become extremely successful at marketing all across Europe a marine paint that provided superior protection for the hulls of ships. (The British Admiralty was one of their most enthusiastic customers.) But, at least through his twenties and early thirties, Svevo lived on the boundary between middle-class respectability and bohemianism. He wrote assiduously and eventually published a first novel, *Una vita* (*A Life*) in 1892. During this period his closest friend and confidant— aside from his brother Elio, who had always encouraged him to write—was Umberto Veruda, a painter who believed fanatically in his art and who both professed and practiced an irregular life. Svevo was a fellow traveler in this bohemianism for some years, frequenting the cafés hospitable to Trieste's artists and conducting a madcap love affair with a temperamental woman named Giuseppina Zergol, who later ran off to join the circus—an experience that was evidently transposed into his second novel, *Senilità* (*As a Man Grows Older*), which appeared in 1898.

Like Thomas Mann, Svevo felt the call of the anti-bourgeois artistic existence without ever going so far as to choose, say, Arthur Rimbaud's completely unconventional *poète maudit* as his model, either in life or in art. Both Svevo and Mann favored an irony toward middle-class rituals and expectations, but they were definitely not members of any violent avant-garde that promised to demolish the old and invent a radically new vision of the world. Their biographies may perhaps run parallel in this respect, for on the threshhold of maturity both abandoned an unsettled life to marry into a well-off family.

Unluckily for Svevo his two novels of the 1890's did not find favorable or even understanding reviewers. Partly it was a question of a language that lacked finesse; indeed, as critics complained, his prose seemed to have been translated from a foreign idiom. In his youth Svevo had studied for years in Germany, and at home he generally spoke the Triestine dialect; Italian consequently was not really a native language to him, and a certain clumsiness of expression, even downright grammatical errors, blots his prose. At a later point in the development of Italy's literary tastes, these defects came to be considered as less momentous. But Svevo's awkward composition had the bad fortune to run counter to prevailing expectations, imposed almost singlehandedly by the virtuoso poet, novelist, and dramatist Gabriele D'Annunzio, whose polished, elegant style had been defined in his phrase "beauty is all." Only subsequent generations less enamored of D'Annunzian splendor could value Svevo's plain language and cease to regard it as a monstrosity.

Furthermore, as the sparse critical reaction to *A Life* and *As a Man Grows Older* suggests, a related problem existed for Svevo's plots and characters: his heroes were unprepossessing, inept—quite out of step with a very significant cultural mood of Italy in the 1890's, D'Annunzio's vision of the artist-as-Superman. To an Italian reading public surfeited with naturalism's stories of the lower classes and of the cruel destiny that oppressed them, D'Annunzio offered an alternative, beginning with his 1889 novel *Il piacere* (Pleasure; translated into English as *A Child of Pleasure*). Here was a refined, upper-class hero haughty enough to model himself without embarrassment on the geniuses and universal men of the Renaissance. After a brief excursion into Dostoevsky worship, from which he took away an admiration for Raskolnikov's justification of murder, D'Annunzio arrived at an explicit homage to Nietzsche's Superman in the preface to his novel of 1894, *Il trionfo della morte* (*The Triumph of Death*). A dash of social Darwinism completed D'Annunzio's cultural potpourri and made him the leading representative of an anti-populist, narcissistic egomania that, as off-putting as it may sound, became a chief inspiration for a large segment of the Italian middle class between the end of the nineteenth century and the beginning of the twentieth. Svevo swam in these same intellectual currents (Nietzscheanism and social Darwinism especially) but reacted quite differently to them than did his more famous contemporary.

It is easy to guess why, later in life, Svevo lost no opportunity to puncture the D'Annunzian myth. The young Joyce's passionate admiration for D'Annunzio's style nettled Svevo until one day he challenged his friend to scrutinize a random sample of that magniloquent prose. Upon opening *Il fuoco* (The Fire, or *The Flame of Life* [1900], as it was called in a contemporary British translation: this was D'Annunzio's portrait of the artist as an extraordinarily vain young man, which for a while exercised influence over the creator of Stephen Dedalus), they found, to Svevo's satisfaction, that the first phrase to meet their eyes was a vacuous paean to a woman's smile. Presumably the apostle of "beauty" shrank somewhat in Joyce's eyes after this test. A second episode reveals the other aspect of Svevo's intolerance for the D'Annunzian vogue. Corresponding with a young Italian writer named Valerio Jahier, the Triestine novelist, by this time finally in possession of a reputation of his own, confessed that he had always found the figure of D'Annunzio's Superman pretentious and absurd. Svevo's disposition never allowed him to esteem the aristocratic pose that had so infected Italian letters and even the popular mind in the preceding decades.

For twenty-five years after the failure of *As a Man Grows Older,* Svevo did not write another novel; instead, he dedicated himself to the manufacture of marine paints and the pleasures of a relatively serene family life. His career with the firm owned by his wife's parents often took him abroad, usually to Great Britain, where a new factory was established to meet the booming demand. So it was that in 1907, to improve his business English, Svevo began lessons with Joyce, a twenty-five-year-old footloose artist who had chanced to arrive in Trieste. The young teacher believed in cre-

ative pedagogy, and thus the pupil was asked to produce such exercises as a critique in English of the first three chapters of *A Portrait of the Artist as a Young Man* (1916), Joyce's current work in progress. Probably it was significant that Svevo objected to the first chapter of the novel as too rigorously descriptive in its approach and not sufficiently informed by moral perspective. That, at bottom, was the same kind of reservation Svevo felt regarding D'Annunzio: a fantastic beauty of language rang hollow without a complete moral life behind it.

Joyce also read his student's novels, which by then had long been forgotten. He admired and remembered them, and when Svevo published his third work of fiction, *La coscienza di Zeno* (*The Confessions of Zeno*), in 1923, Joyce, by now lionized in Paris, steered French critics to the neglected Triestine. That marked the beginning of Svevo's fame. As he himself put it in a preface to the reissued *As a Man Grows Older* (1927), Joyce had made him feel like a Lazarus resurrected from the dead. Not only was he fully appreciated for the first time, but his reputation had miraculously sprung up in the very center of the cultural world, in fabled Paris.

Joyce's role in creating Svevo's renown is well known. More shadowy is another outcome of the two novelists' meeting. Stanislaus, James's brother, suggested that Leopold Bloom in *Ulysses* (1922) was a figure who owed much to the real-life Svevo. And Stanislaus was no distant observer. Having followed his brother to Trieste, he took a teaching job intended for James and passed his adult life in Svevo's city. Certainly Leopold Bloom and Svevo are both Jews who married Gentiles (we know that Joyce questioned Svevo on Jewish customs, most likely in preparation for his novel), and perhaps they share a wry humor exercised through wordplay and irony. But the most intriguing connection between life and the art of *Ulysses* is the contrast between the reckless and ebullient young Stephen and the phlegmatic, world-weary, but no less intelligent "parent," Leopold Bloom. Svevo had a somewhat similar relationship with Veruda—pieces of it had filtered into his second novel—and a similar counterpoint existed between Joyce and Svevo. The Irishman certainly had his penchant for the bohemian life. He was not married to his companion Nora Barnacle, and he was a blithe spirit when it came to borrowing money and drowning himself in liquor. Svevo, by the time Joyce got to know him, was ensconced in a well-appointed villa, bemused perhaps by his material good fortune, but with no real will to resist it. The contrast extends even to the artistic temperaments of the two. Svevo did not match the radical inventiveness in language and in narrative technique that Joyce displayed; nor did he want to. He stood back from the most daring forms of experimentation in the moderns, not because he was a classicist but because, cognizant of his world's disorder, he still fretted over whether that chaos might not be due to some incompetence in man and made himself anxious wondering whether things could still be somehow rectified. Thus the disintegration of traditional syntax found in Joyce's *Ulysses* and especially in his *Finnegan's Wake* (1939) has no equivalent in Svevo's prose, and even if the Triestine novelist shares some of the Joycean fascination for dreams and the unconscious, he does not abandon conventionally chronological narrative to imitate the "stream of consciousness" that Joyce uses to shape his storytelling. Leopold/Svevo, in short, seems a good deal less daring than the bold young Stephen/Joyce.

The "resurrection" of Svevo in 1925 is a curious episode, the significance of which has often been debated. For Antonio Gramsci, a leader of the Italian Communist Party in the 1920's and 1930's as well as an influential cultural critic, the fact that Joyce and Parisian literary circles seemed to have introduced Svevo to Italy attested to a woefully abstracted Italian intelligentsia, incapable of recognizing native talents, reliant for every insight and advance on the more vigorous foreign com-

mentators. There may be some justice in the complaint that Svevo's long obscurity was one of many proofs of the Italian intellectuals' blindness to their own nation. But Svevo's "discovery" in Italy in 1925 contained more than had met Gramsci's eye. Eugenio Montale, who was chiefly responsible for promoting interest in Svevo in Italy during the late 1920's, had come to read the Triestine novelist not through slavish imitation of Parisian fashions but because he had learned of the unknown from Roberto Bazlen, a critic sensitive to modernism and one who, significantly enough, was a Triestine himself—heir, that is, to the same mix of Middle European interests and Italian identity as Svevo. More importantly, as Montale implied in the pieces he published in 1925 and later, the recognition accorded Svevo really signaled the belated reunion of two fraternal movements in Italian literature. Like the "Twilight" poets of the century's first decade or like Montale himself, Svevo represented the antithesis of the powerful D'Annunzian aura. After D'Annunzio's personae with their grandiose projects for reviving classical tragedy and restoring Italy to a preeminent position in European culture, it was a relief to see Svevo, in a maneuver similar to that of the "Twilight" writers, raise the weak and contradictory man to the status of worthy protagonist and representative figure. D'Annunzio's overwhelming influence on Italian letters may have helped to deprive Svevo of an earlier fame, but in retrospect it was clear that the Triestine author had not been alone in resisting the example of the Superman. Likewise, it obviously pleased Montale to discover a writer so deliberately inelegant as Svevo. D'Annunzio had vaunted his ability to summon from the Italian language a music to rival the Wagnerian orchestra; but the "Twilight" poets, and then Montale after them, had turned away from this ambition to sublimity, seeking more prosaic tones. (Guido Gozzano, in Montale's judgment the most interesting of the "Twilight" generation, had referred to his language as that of a schoolboy who has been corrected by the family maid: hardly exalted speech.) For the leading Italian promoter of Svevo, the Triestine novelist served as encouraging confirmation that the nation's literature was taking a salutary turn toward modesty in the wake of D'Annunzio.

As if to compensate for all the years his writing had been ignored, destiny made Svevo the cynosure of the literary world in his last few years. Feted in Paris, he was the subject of numerous essays in France as well as in Italy. The writers who collaborated on the Florentine review *Solaria* played a special role in spreading his reputation. (An homage to Svevo appeared in its pages shortly after his death following an automobile accident in 1928.) *Solaria* attracted contributors who were not in line with the ideology of the young Fascist regime. Its ideals comprised a cosmopolitan, Europeanized point of view and an art that centered on psychological analysis and self-exploration. Given Fascism's designs for a celebratory, nationalistic, and ultimately an imperial culture, it is easy to see why *Solaria* was regarded as a nonconformist publication. Svevo's writings jibed well with the spirit of the review. At odds with the self-glorification of D'Annunzio, he was equally out of step with Fascist cultural trends, which had borrowed much from the magniloquent poet who had contended with Benito Mussolini after World War I for the privilege of interpreting the state of mind of the Italian nation. Svevo's anti-heroes did not belong in these lofty circles; instead they found their warmest welcome at the margins of Italian culture during the regime.

It is typical of the sense of alienation attaching to *Solaria* that in the late 1920's Montale discussed in its pages Charlie Chaplin's film *The Gold Rush* (1926), stressing what he saw as the Jewish roots of the sad clown's art and asserting that the deepest levels of Chaplin's humor were bound to remain impenetrable to a mass audience. A decade later the Fascist regime followed Nazi Germany in adopting anti-Semitic legislation, and Chaplin's films,

as works of a supposedly Jewish artist (Chaplin in fact was not Jewish), were banned in Italy, even before his scathing film of 1940, *The Great Dictator,* in which Mussolini figures as Benzini Napaloni from the land of Bacteria and his partner, the autocrat Adenoid Hynkel, makes the microphones droop with his withering orations against a certain ethnic group. Montale consistently gravitated toward the anti-heroic character in art, whether it was Svevo's bumbler, Chaplin's self-deprecatory, anti-authoritarian persona, or the timid and withdrawn alter ego appearing in Gozzano's verse. He himself had invented a variant on this type with his character Arsenio, who, in a poem of 1928 ("Arsenio"), shows himself to be the epitome of indecisiveness and dashed hopes. The world views incarnated in all of these personages were antithetical to Fascism, so it is no surprise that so much of their spirit tended to congregate in a few places, such as *Solaria.* Theirs was a minority view hanging on persistently in an unfriendly environment, and the mere fact that the magazine's circulation never exceeded seven or eight hundred copies gives an idea of their isolation.

After Svevo's death in 1928, his widow, whose long hair and first name Joyce used for his creature Anna Livia Plurabelle in *Finnegan's Wake,* devoted her energies to proselytizing on behalf of her husband's work. Leonard Woolf, for instance, recalls her dressed in widow's weeds when she came to England about the time that the Hogarth Press issued a translation of a Svevo short story in 1929. (Svevo's short fiction, like his plays, was collected only after death and remains far overshadowed by his three novels.) Perhaps Veneziani's most important effort at preserving and magnifying her husband's reputation occurred during World War II, when she was obliged to go into hiding to escape Fascist racial persecution. During the two difficult years in concealment she never parted with a precious trunkful of Svevo's letters and papers. In the postwar years these became the basis for her biography of her husband and eventually were included in his collected works. This trove of documents is indispensable in assessing the novelist's relationship with friends such as Veruda, Joyce, and Montale as well as fathoming Svevo's reactions, favorable and not, to influences such as Arthur Schopenhauer, Nietzsche, Freud, and D'Annunzio. Moreover, the numerous letters to his wife give an absorbing picture of Ettore Schmitz as the neurotic husband—a portrait that often mirrors in an appealingly odd way the adventures of the writer's confused protagonists. Svevo thus leaves us not just his works but a life and works that complement one another and engage us equally.

THE THREE NOVELS

A Life, published when Svevo was just past thirty, has been criticized as being an awkwardly stitched together first novel, a collection of diverse inspirations that range from the naturalistic, almost clinical account of a woman dying to a psychological portrait that traces in intricate detail the comically mistaken assumptions of a shy young clerk striving to find his way in the world and always taking a wrong turn. Tragedy and comedy, impersonal naturalism and psychological analysis do come together in unusual ways in Svevo's novel, and perhaps it is best to see this first major work as both a farewell to the popular naturalistic vein of the second half of the nineteenth century and a foray into a new kind of writing concerned with exploring the psyche of a character. Late-nineteenth-century naturalism in Italy is almost inevitably associated with a tragic outlook: disease, animal instincts in man, and the struggle for material survival are its typical situations. On the other hand, Svevo generally employs his psychological penetration to create a comedy of errors, to show a fantastic card house of delusions and how it topples on contact with reality. It is the blend of these two modes of writing and thinking that makes up Svevo's unique world, and if

the mixture is somewhat awkward in *A Life,* that is not the case in his later works.

In *A Life* Alfonso Nitti is a country boy who has come to make a career in a city bank. He might be the paradigm of a humble rural family's intelligent son, on whom high hopes are pinned, but his is not a story of the naif's education and rise in the great metropolis, because the protagonist only dreams his conquests. While he sits at his desk imagining himself rich and noble, treating his employer Maller with the condescension only a superior can be permitted, his correspondence piles up and he cannot complete it; the disorganization on his desk multiplies, and he never manages to sort it out. In his daydreams Alfonso makes brilliant conversation, but when he is invited to a tea for employees at Maller's home he is monosyllabic in company and makes a painful impression on the banker's daughter Annetta. During his free evening hours he plans a vast work of moral philosophy, fancying that both its conception and style will dazzle the world. But as the months wear on, he barely gets beyond a few pages of rough outline. Even intermittent impulses to help the foundering family with whom he boards are whims, and in the cold light of day his imaginary noble sacrifices for a dowerless daughter are never translated into a marriage proposal—which, after all, would put a gloomy end to a career he sees as potentially brilliant.

In all these dreams—the word "dream" is a leitmotif in the novel—Svevo has us read not only ingenuousness but also at least a dim aspiration to do good. If we are to find coherence in the diverse sections of *A Life,* we must note from the outset that Alfonso aims at being not merely a success in the world but also a moral hero, a Robin Hood who will succor the defenseless and give a comeuppance to the powerful. Unfortunately, he never quite screws up enough resolve for these acts of courage. He often dreams of forging ahead through his beneficence, but in reality he steadily gives ground to those who exploit.

Alfonso's ineptitude finds a contrast in Macario, a cousin of Annetta, who becomes the clerk's friend and mentor. Macario is a dandy, cutting an elegant figure in Annetta's salon and demonstrating himself to be an intrepid boatsman on marine expeditions that leave Alfonso only queasy. Macario affects the Superman's philosophy, admiring eagles and scorning as nature's rubbish those who were not born with the wings to soar. Alfonso, half eager to learn, half dubious at his friend's argonaut ethos, trots beside him, wondering whether he himself could ever be capable of such bravado.

A chance to test himself comes when the capricious Annetta decides to convert her weekly tea into a literary salon. Suddenly Alfonso finds himself flattered by the banker's daughter for his literary efforts (Macario has spread word of his philosophical treatise), and he is enlisted to help her write a novel. Not only does Annetta defer to him but his stature at the bank rises as well, and his fellow employees begin to regard him as the favorite of Maller. But even though others resent his social ascent, Alfonso's real condition is hardly changed. Very soon Annetta grows impatient with the snail's pace of his composition and his hapless wandering from the main theme of the novel. Rather than revising them, she practically discards all the pieces he writes, replacing them with her own. With her plots as well she dominates the feckless Alfonso. He wishes to write the story of a clerk whose business acumen wins him a fortune and the right to marry the boss's daughter. But he is too timid to show this story to Annetta, fearing that she will find it presumptuous. In the meantime she insists that they compose a tale obviously dear to her: a noble woman charms and manipulates a wealthy industrialist who is caught helplessly in her web.

Here Svevo plays with the conventional plots of nineteenth-century fiction, especially those with typically middle-class concerns such as the social climb of the son and the proper marriage of the daughter. Indeed, his entire work is studded with parodies of these standard models of the bourgeois epic. As Zeno says in Svevo's later novel *The Confessions of Zeno,* the career of a young man from a good family is normally conceived as a parallel to Napoleon's: a meteoric rise, years of splendor, and perhaps, if he is unlucky, a catastrophic fall. Not so in his own case, Zeno continues, for his life, much to his chagrin, knew no rise and no fall, but simply settled at a single intermediate pitch and never modulated. It is a commonplace to say that the novel as a genre is a debased epic, a bourgeois version of the hero's quest enacted in the parlor and at the stock exchange rather than on the battlefield. But Svevo takes this insight further and has his heroes incompetent to enact even the lowly middle-class conquest of prosperity and domestic tranquillity. So it is that Alfonso can only dream of writing about the great exploits of the hungry young man from the provinces come to make his fortune in the city. In fact he is too shy to play that role, and what is more, he cannot even propose it in fiction, so cowed is he by Annetta.

Novel-writing eventually becomes only a pretext for the encounters between Annetta and Alfonso, for the latter, encouraged by Macario, has decided that he is in love with his collaborator. Furtive touches and kisses follow, then uncertainty about Annetta's sentiments, and finally, just as abruptly as she had embarked on the novel, Annetta admits Alfonso to her bedroom for a night of love. The problem is that Alfonso cannot explain to himself this sudden development. Half tied to moral considerations but also half cynical, thanks to Macario's instruction, he torments himself first with guilt at having led the girl into temptation and then also with doubts about whether she is really his, and if not, then how to exploit her passion further. In the long run, however, it is the moral Alfonso who prevails. Whereas he might have happily lived out part of his plot, winning the banker's daughter and assuring himself a comfortable existence, he is now assaulted by scruples and draws back.

At this juncture the story grows more complicated, for Alfonso finally discovers (the obvious in social situations always eludes him till the last minute, no doubt because he is so engrossed in idealized conceptions of how humans behave) why it is that Francesca, Annetta's governess, has been following the course of the affair with such intensity. Hers is not disinterested observation. She is the mistress of the widower Maller and has calculated that if Annetta and Alfonso's irregular affair can be translated into legitimate matrimony, she too may have a chance at gaining more than her present backstairs position in the household. So when she sees Alfonso unaccountably hesitate on the brink of triumph, she urges him with all her might not to be a fool but to seize the prey before it can flutter away. Francesca, unlike Alfonso, is too down-to-earth to entertain illusions about why Annetta fell into bed with such a clumsy suitor: she attributes it to sheer caprice, a powerful enough force, but likely to change direction on another day.

The clearer Francesca's calculations become to him, the more Alfonso recoils. He cannot be an enterprising character like Macario, who delivers lectures on how to manipulate others. Guilt for his success at seduction overcomes him, and he runs away, vowing to return only if Annetta commands him. He had dreamed of boldly ascending the social ladder, but now that he has stepped on the first rung, he freezes, unable to move himself higher. He takes a leave of absence from the bank and removes himself to his country town, where, moreover, his mother is dying.

The weeks he spends at his mother's bedside and the fever he undergoes after her death have the effect of burning away any residual worldly desires in Alfonso. The tiny town in the hinterland, the stark house, and the agonizing wait for his mother's end do not make the city glitter in his eyes, but only inspire repugnance in him. He is actually satisifed to receive word that Annetta has abandoned her interest in him; this proof of her frivolity renders his devotion to his mother in her last days more virtuous. He has discovered his vocation in life, and it is a self-sacrificing one.

The first part of *A Life* gives us an Alfonso who is so comically bumbling in his attempts to get ahead in the world that we are not prepared for the high moral seriousness to which Svevo's protagonist converts at the time of his mother's death. We are accustomed to the idea that a great sinner may become, through the miracle of repentance, a very holy man. But that a rather flimsy clown may turn into a virtuous sage does not strike us as being so likely. A disjointedness thus hangs over the middle of *A Life,* and only in Svevo's next novel, *As a Man Grows Older,* does a really convincing fusion of the comic and tragic occur.

In the first half of the book Alfonso toys with the ethos of the Superman; at times he thinks he would like to practice Macario's confident philosophy. But there is something in him that prevents him—and we are always left wondering whether at the deepest level this something is not simply congenital ineptitude rather than ethical principle. His long vigil by his mother's bedside further solidifies the sense of resignation in him. Upon his return to the city he no longer seeks conquest but dedicates himself to quietude. Annetta, having dropped him, is now engaged to none other than Macario, yet instead of being rankled at her fickleness and his former comrade's cynical usurpation, he resolves to make a virtue of his humiliation; his character will be all the more sterling if, having known the allure of sexual conquest and ambitions fulfilled, he now renounces every desire. Looking around, he observes his fellow workers in the bank ceaselessly struggling for advancement, sometimes using cut-throat methods. Alfonso, however, strives to remain indifferent to both defeats and triumphs. He aims at a Buddhistic peace through the annihilation of his will, and as several commentators, such as P. N. Furbank, have noted, Svevo draws on Schopenhauer at this point to describe his protagonist's stance.

Disciplining himself to self-abnegation, he submits almost without a whimper when Maller, evidently aware of what has transpired between his employee and his daughter, consigns him to the most cramped office and the most menial clerk's duties in the bank. When disaster strikes the family he boards with, he prepares to sacrifice himself again. The daughter that he had once vaguely intended to rescue from her dowerless straits has now been gotten pregnant by an unscrupulous suitor who will marry her only for a price, and it is Alfonso who pulls from his own pocket the money from his small inheritance to save what is left of the girl's honor.

Like a monk, Alfonso mortifies his desires and worldly goals. To all the exploiters, all the calculating schemers he has known—Macario, Francesca, the seducer of the dowerless daughter—he offers the other cheek. Yet this humility remains flawed. Alfonso's will is never pure in whatever direction it drives him. When he thought he wanted to soar to success and fortune, he faltered and changed course at the last moment. Now, when he desires to foreswear all his former passions, he cannot quite manage; he must have a final interview with Annetta. Not even the purpose of the encounter is clear to him: should he respectfully assure her of his eternal silence about her moment of weakness, or should he sound out her feelings for him again? Annetta does not appear at the appointment, but her outraged brother arrives to insult him and challenge him to a duel. Alfonso's fluctuating will has led him once more to Annetta, but this time his endless changeability is not permissible. Fleeing back to self-abnegation, he returns to his room and kills himself. The story concludes with a chilly letter from Maller to Alfonso's guardian in his native village. The banker expresses regret at his employee's death and advises that he has no information to suggest why Alfonso committed suicide. Even at his end, Alfonso cannot assert his will, and the shrewder characters around him easily suppress the last traces of his desires.

In sharp contrast to the Schopenhauerian quietude that Alfonso attempts to make his credo in the last part of *A Life* are the novel's abundant Darwinian- or Nietzschean-inspired celebrations of the strongest, the Superman. Indeed, the Darwinian and Nietzschean world views surround and for a while entice Alfonso. At first in Annetta's salon he finds himself the least fit, for he is not a brilliant talker, and others easily outclass him in the struggle to win attention. But when Annetta's whimsy elevates him to chief literary adviser to the house, Alfonso quickly modifies his ethical system to fit his changed circumstances— even though he plainly has had no hand in producing his abrupt rise in status. The original plan for his work of moral philosophy was simply to demonstrate that the collectivity's interests must always come first; but, no doubt excited by his success with the banker's daughter, he now represents his ethics to her as a hymn to the exceptional man who scorns the many and places himself above their laws. (This system, of course, is the equivalent of the bold plot that he does not have the courage to present for inclusion in their jointly written novel: his plot of the entrepreneur triumphant.) Svevo uses a fine irony at this point, for Alfonso's change of heart provides the least convincing endorsement of the Superman imaginable. Nothing could be more pathetic than the naive clerk's momentary willingness to believe that his good fortune in salon society proves the extraordinary man's right to trample on others. Svevo has simultaneously reinforced his portrait of Alfonso as deluded and weak and offered a deflating gibe at those who are anxious to set themselves at the crown of the pyramid and deride the lower orders.

At any rate, it is not long before doubts overtake our hero, for he soon sees himself more the toy of Annetta, Macario, and Francesca than the manipulator, and anyway the notion of exploiting his employer's daughter to get ahead has come to seem reprehensible to him. In the second half of *A Life* Alfonso thus views the Darwinian-Nietzschean contests with no admiration for the strong. In his native village the spectacle of his mother's decline, as well as the memory of a savage outbreak of typhus years before, inspires in him a sad meditation on all those healthy organisms, created, it would seem, for no purpose and destroyed without mercy. On the train returning to the city he witnesses a painful scene as the conductor roughly ejects a beggar from the car, leaving the vagabond to face a cold welcome in a town of the hinterland. Meanwhile, at Maller's bank, even as Alfonso steels himself to accept his own demotion with humility, he sees enacted a brutal struggle for position: an energetic youth pitilessly shoulders aside the ancient factotum of the establishment, who no longer has the strength or concentration to do his chores efficiently.

Alfonso's ultimate flaw, as we have seen, is to believe that he can abstain from these combats and can set himself apart from all the other players. At least for a time he is allowed to think that he "could judge the others from above, serenely, because he himself had once taken part in that battle, and knew what it was like. For both the vanquished and the victors he felt a fervent compassion." These lines recall Giovanni Verga's famous preface to his novel *I Malavoglia* (*The House by the Medlar Tree,* 1882), in which the author enunciates as a poetics his will to stand outside the struggles of his poor, ruined Sicilian fishermen, simply registering, camera-like, the defeated as well as their antagonists, the conquerors. But while it is Verga the artist who aspires to a dispassionate recording of his characters' battle for survival, Svevo only attributes this aspiration to his weak and wavering protagonist Alfonso, who, moreover, is drawn back into the fray from his neutral pose and then destroyed. Thus it seems that with his first novel Svevo intends to bid farewell to the canons of naturalism, for the objective reading of life's Darwinian struggle is demonstrated, through Alfonso's cautionary tale, to be impossible. The echoes of an impersonal viewpoint in *A Life*'s picture of the dying mother are only a last

homage to the age of Émile Zola and Verga. Svevo the narrator infiltrates himself into the vicissitudes of his personages' lives; his writing increasingly relies on the introspective and confessional modes of the psychological novel. In the early and mid-1890's, with characteristically portentous tones, D'Annunzio also had proclaimed the demise of naturalistic fiction and the birth of psychological narrative. In his quiet provincial corner Svevo, almost unnoticed, makes the same transition, the difference being that while he chooses to penetrate the psychology of the weak, his better-known contemporary assays a portrayal of the conquerors.

Like *A Life,* Svevo's second novel, *As a Man Grows Older* (the English translation of the title was suggested by Joyce), is the story of a love affair in which the female outmaneuvers and devastates the male. Emilio Stefani bears some kinship to Alfonso Nitti, for he too is a sensitive soul, a literary man full of vague dreams and intentions but possessing precious little ability to convert his resolves into real accomplishments. This time Svevo's protagonist falls in love with a lower-class woman, not the banker's daughter, but there is in both female figures an elusiveness that never allows the baffled male any peace of mind.

The first page of the novel depicts an Emilio confident of his ability to exploit his relationship with the beautiful blond Angiolina. Emilio wants no entangling involvement, only sweet pleasures absorbed without guilt or commitments. He assumes the posture of the playboy who asks favors of the lower-class girl without accepting any responsibilities toward her. But his capacity for self-delusion is immense. Very soon Emilio's jealous temperament and lack of self-control emerge, while the apparently modest, naive Angiolina turns out to be inscrutable, strong-willed, and perhaps the most artfully deceptive female in all the city. We realize how fatally Emilio has fallen under her spell when we see him anguishing over her collection of photographs, which includes several portraits of other men-about-town. It is not that these souvenirs of past relationships shock Emilio, for he knows that Angiolina has passed through two or three other affairs. But he makes himself vulnerable by supposing that he can react rationally to Angiolina's free and easy ways. She insouciantly dismisses the photographs as trifling mementos, while he has the obsessive's capacity for storing up such little pricks as these and tormenting himself endlessly with them. The lecture to Angiolina about avoiding serious obligations and emotional entanglements now sounds absurd because it was not she who needed to guard against making too much of their affair.

Svevo and his fellow anti-D'Annunzian, the "Twilight" poet Gozzano, share an interesting predilection in their writing for the woman who has more strength than the man. Gozzano's poem "Invernale" (Winter Scene, 1911), for instance, contrasts the intrepid female ice-skater with the timorous male standing on the shore. The situation has paradigmatic value because here, as elsewhere in his poetry, Gozzano's male is troubled by an excess of consciousness, an inhibiting self-awareness. He cannot be the lively, untrammeled spirit that the woman is; rather he envies her and longs for her as a way of embracing the liberty of an unexamined life. Svevo's Emilio also meets his antithesis in Angiolina in that whereas he is besieged by qualms and contradictory resolutions, she proceeds without any apparent burden of conscience at all. Caught in an obvious lie by her jealous lover, she shows no embarrassment about replacing it with another falsehood, hoping that the second will absolve her. However Emilio tries to imitate this unconcern—as when he asks for a relationship without dependency—he cannot muster the nonchalance of Angiolina. This, then, is the great invention of the generation that follows D'Annunzio: an anti-hero plagued by doubts and weakness, regarding with a mixture of awe and revulsion the feats of the uninhibited. D'An-

nunzio had pumped up his Superman with so much self-assurance that confidence had been given a bad name; his successors could only look upon it with a jaundiced eye.

A temporary rupture between the lovers occurs when one evening a friend of Emilio's spots Angiolina being escorted through town by another man. Even in breaking off with her, however, Emilio seems a pathetic and ridiculous figure. He strains for a high moral tone in reproaching her for this infidelity, only to discover Angiolina is not conscious of having done anything offensive. Moreover, Emilio's dignified withdrawal covers over but hardly disposes of his frantic passion for her. After a short while he inevitably returns to her, and she, lighthearted as ever, briefly excusing herself for not having repented and sought him out earlier, agrees to pick up the relationship once more. But by now Emilio's destiny is certain: he has put more into this love than it can bear, and in fact his futile hopes for halcyon days of pleasure grow in perverse reaction to each new sign of Angiolina's mutability.

The too obvious variance between Emilio's conception of his love and its reality makes for a comical spectacle. Don Quixote was never more persistent in idealizing his passions, nor was Miguel de Cervantes' knight more unceremoniously abused by the objects of his desire. Inspired by the account of a German astronomer who takes a country girl as his bride and lives with her in an ethereal Alpine observatory, Emilio one day elaborately fantasizes a similar aerie in which to dwell with his beloved Angiolina. But this magical vision of a mountaintop love nest bores her, and her polite attention instantly dissolves a moment later when she hears that Emilo's friend, the sculptor Stefano Balli, would like to meet her and perhaps have her pose for him. Another social opening excites Angiolina far more than her lover's most inventive romance.

But the core of the novel is tragic, and the tragedy is worked out in the classic manner: the protagonist wantonly persists in his belief that he can control events, venting first his arrogance and then his frustration on others until he finds, only too late, that he has destroyed both them and himself. Emilio's cruelest act of destruction involves his sister Amalia, a sad figure, very plain, devoted to her brother because she has no one else in the world. When Emilio embarks on his adventure with Angiolina, Amalia suffers to see her brother neglect her. Just as this gloom settles over her life, however, an unexpected reprieve arrives in the person of Balli who, drawn into the role of advising Emilio about his escapade, finds himself also regaling the sister with his worldliness and flamboyance.

Balli has a more casual approach to life than Emilio. Instead of wrestling to influence the course of events and being upset when they escape his command, he opens himself to all possibilities and ends up getting at least as much if not more of what he wants than his friend. When as a young man he was on the verge of abandoning sculpture, he chanced to meet a benefactor who made it possible for him to continue his art for many years. He has never known great triumphs with the public but proceeds anyway, fairly indifferent to success, sufficiently exalted by his work alone. In social relations he shows an equal expansiveness and independence, for which Emilio envies him. Balli can pursue a woman without being obsessed by her, whereas Emilio, against his will, is immediately ensnared by Angiolina. Showing great good nature toward the plain Amalia, Balli plays the raconteur and lightens her dismal existence. Emilio, the brother supposedly dedicated to his sister's well-being, grows irritated by even this harmless diversion from her gray routine. Having broken with Angiolina because of her evening with another, his jealousy seems to fall spitefully on the innocent Amalia. The pretext for the attack is this: he has overheard her talking in her sleep, apparently dreaming of Balli. He asks his friend to stay away from the household so as not to compromise the spinster sister. Emilio has thus destroyed the sole plea-

sure of the person he claims to love—for whose sake he has forbidden himself to marry. The consequences are horrible. Absorbed as he is in his reconciliation with Angiolina, he fails to notice in the following weeks how much Amalia is suffering from her ever greater isolation. By the time Emilio grasps the depth of her feeling for Balli and the brutality with which he has cast her into a cloister, it is too late. The delicate Amalia, unbalanced by the alcohol she has been imbibing in secret, enters a gruesome delirium that ends with her death.

Emilio has brought down his household. He has lost his gray but devoted sister, and in the meantime the second phase of his adventure with Angiolina proves as torturous as the first. The terrible negligence of Emilio reaches bottom when, on the night that his sister lies dying, he obdurately decides that he must slip out for a last meeting with Angiolina. He imagines that with perfect, cold dignity he can dismiss from his life the woman who in his eyes has brought disaster on his house. He is mistaken, as usual. Before he can frame any reproach for Angiolina he loses control of himself because he suspects from her fine dress that she is engaged this night on another mission of infidelity. He ends by screaming insults and hurling stones after her as she runs out of his sight. It is a revealing scene: with utter irresponsibility Emilio has abandoned his sister again, since he cannot restrain his desire to have one more interview, however painful, with Angiolina. Furthermore, he means to blame his lover for having brought him to grief, yet his violent outburst shows unequivocally whose intemperance has led to the catastrophe. Amalia and Angiolina both depart in innocence, the first dying as a helpless victim of circumstances far more powerful than she, the second exiting blameless by reason of her complete obliviousness to the damage she has done. Only Emilio has been both conscious and reckless.

One of the most impressive qualities of *As a Man Grows Older*—and one of the reasons for which it has been judged superior to Svevo's first novel—is its coherence of purpose. From the opening pages we are immersed in Emilio's self-deception. Obsessively he fights Angiolina's hold over him, and with sure vengeance his passion for her returns every time he smugly concludes that he has thrown off the yoke. After their reconciliation, he finally takes her to bed, and it is not just physical satisfaction he anticipates, because he also imagines that the fascination exerted by the object of his fantasies will vanish once he has physically possessed her whom he imagines as a siren. We understand pages prior to Emilio's pained admission that this will not be the case. We may find Svevo's protagonist transparent, while to himself Emilio remains consistently opaque. We follow his hectic course with dread, and the misadventures, so varied in their particulars, strike us as predictable, fated. Given his persistent error, we do not doubt that Emilio's downfall is inevitable.

The narrative of *As a Man Grows Older* changes pace after Amalia's death, and in the final few pages of the novel months and then many years elapse. First there are glimpses of Emilio distraught and dazed, making a pilgrimage to his sister's grave, or anguished by a report that Angiolina has run off to another city with a bank clerk suspected of embezzlement. Eventually all such turmoil recedes, and from the vantage point of middle age Emilio looks back on that superheated season of adventure with an artist's detachment. More than "emotion recollected in tranquillity," however, his memories are a last refusal to accept himself and others as they really are, or were. He cherishes the image of Angiolina, who remains as alluringly beautiful as ever in his mind's eye, but he also endows her with all the suffering innocence of Amalia. Quixotic in his real escapades, Emilio now prefers once again not to learn from brutal experience; instead he cultivates his fantasies even more intensely, standing far removed from the events and making them more perfect in his recollections than they ever were in actuality. The same cruelty as before accompanies this exercise,

for, as the narrator says, by transposing Amalia's virtues onto the image of his mistress, Emilio makes his sister die a second time. In truth this man knows no repentance.

The last lines of *As a Man Grows Older* were much loved by Joyce, who could quote them from memory. They do form a poignant epitaph to unfulfilled desires and a tribute to the hold that the departed exert on the survivor. In this they may recall the ending of Joyce's short story "The Dead" (1914), where Gabriel struggles to comprehend the revelation that his wife's truest love has always been reserved for her childhood sweetheart, now dead. With his own less soaring but equally effective lyricism, Svevo evokes a similar disappointment for Emilio. Even if Svevo's protagonist manages to construct an idealized Angiolina for his album of memories, we understand the wistfulness underlying that invention. Thus the secret force of this ending derives from the pathos summoned up when we see Emilio cultivating in the solitude of his middle age a fantastically beautiful image of a lover he never really had:

> In the idle littérateur's mind, Angiolina underwent a strange metamorphosis. She kept her physical beauty intact, but she also acquired all the qualities of Amalia, who died a second time on her account. She became sad, mournfully still, while her eyes turned clear and intelligent. Emilio saw her before him as though on an altar, and she was the personification of meditation and grief. He loved her eternally, if love is admiration and desire. She represented everything noble that he had imagined and seen in that period. . . . That tall, magnificent symbol sometimes came back to life, becoming the woman he had known as a lover, though she always kept her sad reflectiveness. Yes, Angiolina reflects and weeps! She meditates, as if the secret of the universe and of her own existence had been explained to her; she cries as if in all the world she had never found a single one of those companions sent down to her as gifts from God.
> (*Opera omnia*, 2:390)

Svevo first came into serious contact with Freudian ideas around 1908 through conversations with a friend of his wife's family, Edoardo Weiss, who later became a leading practitioner of psychoanalysis in Italy. No doubt Svevo's interest in Freud was also whetted by the experience of his brother-in-law Bruno Veneziani, an aspiring concert pianist who traveled to Vienna in 1910 to be analyzed by the master himself. The analysis did not proceed well, and upon his return to Trieste Bruno announced that Freud had found his neuroses incurable. The incident evidently percolated through Svevo's fantasy, emerging more than a decade later in his third and last novel, *The Confessions of Zeno.* Here we have a protagonist, Zeno Cosini, whose psychoanalytic treatment has left him doubtful as to whether his disorders can ever be healed—or whether they are disorders at all. As we might expect from a writer so attached to the anti-heroic, Svevo in this book takes a doubtful view of the therapeutic value of Freudian analysis. The plot of psychoanalysis, if one can call it that, has too many heroic dimensions: the tormented patient saved by the intervention of the wizard-like doctor; the unbalanced sufferer rescued from himself and righted; the patient's internal demons exorcised to create a healthy being and a tranquil ending. Svevo's plots contain much more skepticism about the capacity of humans to be satisfied and successful, and usually he is inclined to smile at the wizards of the world—doctors, scientists, social theorists—when they claim to have the key to human well-being.

The clash between the psychoanalytic world view and Svevo's doubt first appears in a playful device at the start of the tale. Borrowing a time-honored convention of the novel, the author represents his book as a manuscript found and published by an editor. But the purported editor is none other than Zeno's psychoanalyst, who warns in a preface that the reader should not be alarmed to encounter in the pages that follow a hostility directed toward him by the patient (the writer of the confessions). Such animosity, he maintains, can be readily accounted for by psychoanaly-sis, which expects the analysand's resistance, describing it as an evasive action taken to avoid the unsettling truths brought to light by the analyst. Seemingly, the psychoanalytic point of view has the upper hand at this moment, for these prefatory comments furnish the reader with a way of regarding ironically all that comes after, especially Zeno's jeers at analysis itself. If he accuses psychoanalysis of being absurd and useless, that only testifies to his inability to accept the painful but correct conclusions it has offered him. Yet the scientific impartiality conveyed by the introduction crumbles when, in his closing words, the analyst-editor reveals that his patient has abandoned the cure and that, as a way of getting revenge for this defection, he has decided to publish his former charge's autobiography in hopes that it will wound him. Needless to say, such an admission lowers the credibility of the psychoanalyst. He now appears at least as emotional and contradictory as he claims the patient to be. Thus Svevo pokes fun at the pretensions of analysis to explain human behavior in a rational manner and to control it for the benefit of man. The reader approaches Zeno's confessions forewarned as much about the physician as about the patient.

Zeno's case history opens with his campaign to quit smoking. As in the other two novels, these confessions begin on a comical note, with facetious adventures. The search for a way of ridding himself of his nicotine dependency takes Svevo's hero through a series of doctors and therapies, all failures. Zeno himself constantly makes plans to give up cigarettes, writing an infinity of resolutions to himself and picking dates and times that appeal to him as propitious moments for shedding his loathed habit. But his will is too weak. He feels that if he could swear off tobacco he would prove himself a determined, forceful man, though by the time he formulates this conviction his weakness has been demonstrated so repeatedly that his continued attempts to liberate himself seem only humorous. The contest is unequal: temptation routs Zeno's paltry resolve every time.

This quest for self-control reaches a pinnacle of absurdity when Zeno has himself committed to a sanitorium where he will be deprived of cigarettes—and then promptly bribes his custodian to let him out so that he can go smoke again. The human mind, he says, resembles a master and his slave locked in perpetual combat: the master is always ordering the slave to do this or that, and the slave is always inventing the means to evade those dictates. Zeno concludes that his nature and probably all human natures are out of control. Who could conceive of a permanent harmony between master and slave?

Furthermore, he is tempted to believe that we are better off not dwelling on the master's inability to preserve his authority. The beatific ones in life are those who do not worry themselves over the irreconcilability of an impulse or desire that flings them in one direction and a sense of duty or guilt that tugs them in another. Thus Zeno admires and envies his father, who accepts the standard bourgeois morality but who also has apparently philandered without compunction. The secret of this peace of mind lies in remaining unconscious of the inconsistency between the beliefs and the deeds. Pangs of conscience attack those who analyze their own behavior; and the more obsessive the self-study, the more grievous the twitches. The title of the novel in Italian implies this process, for, literally translated, *La coscienza di Zeno* means "Zeno's Consciousness" or "Zeno's Conscience," an ambiguity Svevo seems to exploit in the novel.

The pains that attend consciousness emerge even in the silliest ways for Zeno. Chatting with an old friend afflicted with rheumatism, he hears the sick man, who has evidently spent much time researching his illness, describe how every step taken involves the movement of fifty-four muscles. This statistic overwhelms Zeno. Without any awareness of the complexity of walking, he had never encountered problems in putting one foot forward, then the next. But now that he is cognizant of the fifty-four separate flexes that contribute to each step, he starts to limp painfully.

The longest episode in Zeno's recitation of his life story is dedicated to his marriage. This section brings us to the heart of the novel's analysis, offering the by now familiar portrait of the incompetent protagonist whom others manipulate with ease while he himself remains incapable of asserting his will. Yet the conclusions of this tale are somewhat different from those Svevo arrives at in his earlier two novels. At first sight Zeno seems to cut a sorry figure, outwitted at every turn, obliged to marry the woman he did not want, and denied the one he desired most. But as the years go by his lot appears more fortunate; Svevo's last novel mitigates at least the personal fate of his inept anti-hero, making him neither exit with the suicide of Alfonso Nitti nor drift into the sad delusions of Emilio Brentani, but survive and even prosper in an odd way. In exchange, however, Svevo's pessimism develops on a cosmic level, and the contentment that is granted to Zeno himself is more than outweighed by the vision of universal cataclysm with which the novel finishes.

Forlorn after his father's death, which leaves him comfortably well-off but alone in the world, Zeno resolves to marry. He embarks on this enterprise with an ingenuousness that invites others to take advantage of him, as indeed they promptly do. Zeno's attentions focus on the daughters of a businessman whom he has visited in hopes of gaining wisdom about the management of his affairs. Giovanni is a crafty animal, a hard-boiled fellow, flattered to be asked for advice but also ready to mock the younger man's gullibility. Unlike himself, Zeno's future father-in-law is an eminently practical man. He has given all four of his daughters names beginning with the letter "A" so that their monogrammed clothing can be handed down without alteration from one sister to the next. To Zeno, however, this curious alphabetical uniformity—Ada, Augusta, Alberta, and Anna—has a mystical significance. His name, after all, starts with a "Z," and surely it would be an auspicious union if the omega could join with the alpha.

The mishaps commence when Zeno picks Ada, the most beautiful of the sisters, as the object of his quest. Ada is a level-headed character, and she seems to have accepted her father's sensible notion that a prospective husband should shine above all with the bourgeois qualities of seriousness and diligence. Zeno, who cannot help exposing his insecurities and foibles to the parlor audience in Giovanni's home, soon finds himself treated with impatience and disdain by Ada. What is an earnest young woman to think of a man who cut short a business trip to England because a cat scratched him? Zeno labors to explain that the feline's antipathy had an emblematic value, persuading him that Britannia would not be hospitable to his endeavors, but such excuses cannot win Ada's esteem. This suitor is too bizarre and frivolous for her. Moreover, as Zeno discovers to his distress, Ada has another beau, one both debonair and serious-minded. Guido Speier is the usual foil for Svevo's inept personages: self-confident while his opposite number is plagued by doubts, and perfectly, smoothly natural in contrast to the hyperconscious, self-inhibiting Zeno. Guido plays the violin brilliantly, with apparent effortlessness, while Zeno, who studies the score exhaustively, can only summon stilted sounds from his instrument. His rival speaks fluently and convincingly of commerce, whereas Zeno's inheritance, as it turns out, has been entrusted to an administrator because his father never believed him decisive enough to manage a business himself. In short, Guido has all the marks of the capable, successful entrepreneur, while poor Zeno, besieged by a thousand uncoordinated ideas and impulses, can only fumble nervously and foolishly. Ada's decision is a foregone conclusion.

Ultimately, after further misadventures that are among the best comic scenes in Svevo's works, Zeno consoles himself for his failure to win his first choice by marrying the plainest of the daughters, Augusta, who is cross-eyed. He wonders whether Giovanni and his wife have not maneuvered him into this matrimony; after all, he is a man of some substance, and with four daughters to marry, it is a coup for the parents to find even a half-plausible match for their ugly duckling.

By this point Svevo seems to have led his protagonist into the same frustration to which Alfonso Nitti and Emilio Brentani are condemned; like theirs, Zeno's beloved has eluded his embrace as well. Easily duped and too uncertain to impose his will on the world, he finds himself controlled and exploited by others. But the sad fate that Svevo assigns to the principal characters of his first two novels is not applied in Zeno's case. *A Life* brings a callow youth to self-destruction before he can reach maturity; *As a Man Grows Older* takes the protagonist through his disappointments and errors to the renunciation and withdrawal of a lonely middle age. *The Confessions of Zeno*, however, encompasses the many stages of a man's development, and instead of leaving the title character to founder in his immaturity or grow bitter and remote at his failures, Svevo's last novel grants him consolations that come with a life fully lived, from youth to old age.

Zeno's salvation is precisely that "consciousness" or "conscience" of the novel's title which initially seems such an impediment to his pleasures, preventing him from enjoying a cigarette in peace or even walking normally, then tripping him up during his courtship of Ada—for he is the suitor hampered by awkward self-consciousness, while Guido sails lightheartedly past to triumph. But Guido's carefree days are numbered. Having married, he enters business with the same blithe self-assurance that had enchanted his bride and her family. But things quickly go sour. In fact, Guido's admired boldness conceals a total incompetence, and he soon dissipates a fortune in idiotically bad transactions, even drawing funds from Ada's dowry into the ruin.

Moreover, Guido's suave courtship, so winning in comparison to Zeno's gaffes, comes back to torment Ada when she sees the same techniques reworked for the benefit of the pretty secretary her husband has hired. The worst is that Guido has no guilt to trouble him in his extramarital passion. When Ada must go away for a lengthy medical treatment, he casually suggests that the secretary take her place in running the household, which now includes twins. His wife suffers excruciating jealousy, but Guido remains as unthinking as ever.

Zeno's self-reflexive consciousness no longer appears such a pathetic hobble. After all, it is the source of moral qualms as well as painful inhibitions. True, Zeno also takes a lover, but unlike Guido he feels guilt at betraying his wife, and then more guilt because he knows he cannot devote himself properly to the lover! This sort of indecisiveness keeps him from doing the harm that Guido unhesitatingly inflicts on Ada. As his in-laws gradually recognize, the unpromising Zeno has turned out to be a better husband than Ada's brilliant catch. He even tries to help Guido out of his financial morass, but that is a difficult task because his brother-in-law has no capacity for mending his ways. Trying to blackmail Ada into rescuing him by handing over a part of her dowry, Guido threatens suicide. The first time he uses the ploy with excellent results. But the second time Ada refuses to take him seriously, and the not especially potent dose of poison her husband swallows kills him because the doctor is summoned too late, when the gravity of the situation can no longer be denied. Guido goes to his grave unreformed, still fancying that he can manipulate others at will. In the meantime Zeno, once scorned because he was too clumsy to manipulate those around him, now is praised for his virtuous character. His ineptitude has become a noble trait.

Many years pass, and we find an old Zeno stretched out on the divan in his psychoanalyst's study. All of the preceding episodes—from his inability to control his smoking to his traumatic parting with his father and his unsatisfied passion for Ada—still lie heavy on his breast. But the psychoanalyst's method of unburdening him only makes Zeno sarcastic. His smoking habit (according to this turn-of-the-century doctor) is not harmful in itself but torments Zeno simply because it has become a subconscious focus for his guilt at having competed with his father. An inner moral system keeps punishing the son for his supposed transgressions against the father, and once this unconscious mechanism has been exposed, it can be shrugged off and there will be no more guilt feelings attached to lighting up a cigarette. Zeno understands the game that psychoanalysis wishes him to play. He promises to mull over the physician's insight, and at their next session he announces that he has smoked a great deal and no longer feels remorse at every puff. The doctor beams ecstatically because his therapy has succeeded. But really Zeno cannot absorb this retraining; he says that every time he leaves the analyst's study he shakes it off, just as a dog emerging from the water shakes the moisture from its coat.

And no wonder. Svevo represents psychoanalysis as the abandonment of scruples. The consciousness that bedevils Zeno is to be explained away as a medieval torture mechanism that the mind has devised for itself and that it can with equal ease discard. The patient resists this perception. He does not want to be cured. In his preface the analyst warns the reader that Zeno resisted the insights offered him. Indeed he did, but it is not clear that such a refusal is a bad thing in Svevo's eyes. After all, Guido is the novel's best example of the unfettered consciousness, and his is not a pretty fate.

Zeno takes another cure at the end of the book, and it is as problematic as the outcome of his psychoanalytic treatment. On the outbreak of World War I he is left stranded in Trieste, and for the first time in his life he has a free hand to run his own business affairs. His management is a triumph: he simply buys anything that is offered, waits till wartime scarcities make the article valuable, then resells it at a profit. Crowing at his success, Zeno says that he must write to his analyst, who has taken refuge in Switzerland, to show him how he has overcome his commercial inhibitions as well. Now he bursts with strength and health.

Zeno's irony does not escape us. The war has allowed him to turn a handsome profit, but he does not have to tell us that Armageddon constitutes a somewhat drastic remedy for his previous inability to succeed in business. Psychoanalysis aimed at disposing of his guilt and leaving him free, just as World War I destroys his native city and permits him to make a healthy profit. Extrapolating from the little bruise on mankind's face that is the world war, Zeno ends his narrative with a vision of a total cure for the whole, sickly planet: certain diseased individuals will invent and deploy the ultimate weapon, and its explosion will efface once and for all the illnesses of the human race.

SVEVO'S MODERNIST PESSIMISM

An intellectual historian would have no difficulty in situating Svevo among the wave of the European intelligentsia which, in the second half of the nineteenth century, began to question optimistic views of man's behavior and fate and to emphasize instead the irrational and tragic in human events. Just when scientific advances, social theories, and political programs were offering the vision of an ever brighter tomorrow, this generation arrived with its doubts, wondering whether man and his institutions were as perfectable as some dreamed.

Svevo delights in parodying the leading versions of the positive outlook on life of his day. When he focuses on psychoanalysis in *The Confessions of Zeno,* he attributes to its therapeutic claims a foolish confidence in the patient's ability to dispose of haunting problems.

Analysis is naive enough, in Zeno's opinion, to believe that Sophocles had diagnosed the one and only problem ever to face the human being: Oedipus' desire to kill his father and sleep with his mother. His analyst, Zeno ironically notes, is probably the only person in the world who, upon hearing that his patient longs to sleep with two beautiful women, asks himself why this should be so. But even worse than the naiveté of analysis, in Zeno's judgment, is its conviction that guilty feelings constitute a mere sickness to be treated and overcome. (How superficial a reading of Freud this represents may be determined by studying works such as *Totem and Taboo* [1918] or *Civilization and Its Discontents* [1930].) Here scientifically justified optimism passes beyond ludicrousness and becomes dangerously wrong-headed as well.

Socialism is another therapeutic measure for mankind that Svevo casts in a dubious light. In both *As a Man Grows Older* and *The Confessions of Zeno* the protagonist dreamily endorses socialist doctrine without convincing anyone, including himself, that it is practicable. Emilio explains to the lower-class Angiolina that the capitalist system and bourgeois morality are responsible for throttling their happiness, preventing them from loving each other freely, obliging her to sell herself to many men. Warming to his subject he speaks in glowing terms of class struggle and the liberty for all that will follow the overthrow of capitalism. Angiolina, however, listens with skepticism and finally retorts that the idea of socialist equality strikes her as silly: workers are so greedy and lazy that a harmonious sharing of the pie is unthinkable. This reply discountenances Emilio, but since he never really surrenders his illusions, it is no surprise that his socialist fantasy returns at the novel's close, where it is attributed, like Amalia's suffering, to the idealized and completely unreal figure of Angiolina. Ultimately, Svevo seems to consign the socialist rationalization of human drives to the realm of never-to-be-fulfilled yearning.

In *The Confessions of Zeno* much the same discussion takes place. Zeno imagines that his love life, which includes a wife, a mistress, and a disappointed passion for Ada, would be simplified if socialist ideals prevailed. Relationships would be unfettered, without jealousy or guilt. But though he nobly pledges himself to live by these terms, Zeno's usual weakness subverts his intentions, and he soon falls back into the throes of an irrational jealousy. In this novel the socialist remedy is no more persuasively presented than the psychoanalytic one.

As Gramsci notes in his *Quaderni dal carcere* (*Prison Notebooks*, 1947), Svevo had written a piece for the socialist-reformist magazine *Critica sociale* in the late 1890's. This curious fable, entitled "La tribù" ("The Tribe"), imagines in some far-off Eastern state a civilization that leaps over all the miseries of capitalist development and arrives directly at a socialist paradise. Europeans and the European-trained are forbidden entrance to this nation, for they are fatally infected with capitalist ideas and can never shake them off. Having devised the implements of their own torture, the Europeans are powerless to undo history, forget capitalism, and be saved. Svevo's tale has its ambiguities. It does envision a socialist state, yet that garden of Eden is displaced to a distant, fantastic zone. In a similar fashion the novelist places Emilio's and Zeno's longings for free love and harmony in the realm of wishful thinking, however tempting and beautiful those ideals may be. We probably conclude that Svevo, in common with a sizable part of his generation of Italian artists and intellectuals, admired socialism. (Even D'Annunzio in his youth had proclaimed himself a socialist.) But there is no mistaking his fatalism about its program's chances for success in perfecting society.

Svevo also exercised his irony on a third theory from the repertory of nineteenth-century positivism, Darwinism. As modern historians of science and cultural critics have shown, Darwin's ideas were interpreted in a great variety of ways in the late 1800's, as everything from justification for racism (the stronger races supposedly destroy the weaker ones in the struggle for survival) to a humanist vision of progress (through his own efforts man evolves toward an ever-better state). Svevo takes a bitter look at the Darwinian struggle for survival in *A Life,* considering it not through the eyes of the powerful and the triumphant as his contemporary D'Annunzio did, but from the viewpoint of the weak man, Alfonso Nitti, who, despite his momentary pretense to be a Superman, cannot bring himself to exploit others in the manner that his mentors urge. In *The Confessions of Zeno* Darwinism figures again, most significantly in the final pages where Zeno sardonically shows mankind evolving, not according to a healthy natural selection as animals do, but along the lines of a perverse process that favors an ever-increasing sickness and self-destructiveness. Finally, Svevo takes a more humorous but equally deprecatory stance in a little essay called "L'uomo e la teoria darvinia" (Man and Darwinian Theory, n.d.). Among other jokes, he hypothesizes that the most amorphous creatures are the best candidates for successful adaptation in the future, since they have not already gotten themselves stuck in one narrow evolutionary channel. Being so undeveloped and vaguely defined himself, Svevo adds tongue-in-cheek, he is clearly in line to be raised to a superior status in the coming evolution of humanity. Whether wearing his tragic or his comic mask, Svevo looks askance at Darwinsm, or rather at those who are only too eager to identify themselves with the strong and healthy heroes of the struggle that Darwin envisions as a basic natural law.

Thus we can see the how Svevo partakes of the modernist conception of a world in fragments, without system. There is no orderly, balanced development in the lives he recounts but only a muddling through—at best. Sometimes to the accompaniment of laughter, at other moments with anguish, he unfolds tales that never end in success and satisfaction and never follow that ascending development for man forecast by the optimistic. His protagonist, as the critic Giacomo Debenedetti perceives in an essay of 1929, "Svevo e Schmitz," is that type from Jewish popular wisdom whom we know as the schlemiel: timid, harassed, unable to find his way through the maze. Debenedetti expresses irritation at the perpetual incapacities of Svevo's characters, but it is also possible to appreciate them for not incarnating a facile optimism, not adopting a confident and, at worst, predatory demeanor. A moral integrity does attach to their weakness, and that must suffice if we are to appreciate Svevo's anti-heroes.

Selected Bibliography

EDITIONS

INDIVIDUAL WORKS

Una vita. Trieste, 1892.
Senilità. Trieste, 1898.
La coscienza di Zeno. Bologna, 1923.

COLLECTED WORKS

Opere. Edited by Bruno Maier. Milan, 1954. Contains *Una vita, Senilità, La coscienza di Zeno,* and *La novella del buon vecchio e della bella fanciulla ed altri scritti.*
Opera omnia. 4 vols. Edited by Bruno Maier. Milan, 1966–1969. Contains *Epistolario, Romanzi, Racconti, saggi, e pagine sparse,* and *Commedie.*

TRANSLATIONS

A Life. Translated by Archibald Colquhoun. New York, 1963.
As a Man Grows Older. Translated by Beryl De Zoete. Introduction by Stanislaus Joyce. New York, 1932.
The Confessions of Zeno. Translated by Beryl De Zoete. Introduction by Renato Poggioli. New York, 1948.

BIOGRAPHICAL AND CRITICAL STUDIES

Biasin, Gian Paolo. "Strategia dell'antieroe." In *Il vento di Debussy.* Bologna, 1985.
Bon, Adrian. *Come leggere "La coscienza di Zeno" di Italo Svevo.* Milan, 1977.
Camerino, Giuseppe A. *Italo Svevo.* Turin, 1981.
Contini, Gabriella. *Il romanzo inevitabile: Temi e tecniche narrative nella "Coscienza di Zeno."* Milan, 1983.
Debenedetti, Giacomo. "Svevo e Schmitz." In *Saggi 1922–1966.* Edited by Franco Contorbia. Milan, 1982.
Fonda, Carlo. *Svevo e Freud: Proposte di interpretazione della "Coscienza di Zeno."* Ravenna, 1978.
Freccero, John. "Zeno's Last Cigarette." In *From "Verismo" to Experimentalism,* edited by Sergio Pacifici. Bloomington, Ind., 1969.
Furbank, P. N. *Italo Svevo: The Man and the Writer.* London, 1966.
Gramsci, Antonio. "La 'scoperta' di Italo Svevo." In *Letteratura e vita nazionale.* Rome, 1977.
Lebowitz, Naomi. *Italo Svevo.* New Brunswick, N.J., 1978.
Lucente, Gregory L. "The Genre of Literary Confession and the Mode of Psychological Realism: The Self-consciousness of *Zeno.*" In *Beautiful Fables: Self-consciousness in Italian Narrative from Manzoni to Calvino.* Baltimore, 1986.
Luti, Giorgio. *Italo Svevo e altri studi sulla litteratura italiana del primo Novecento.* Milan, 1961.
Moloney, Brian. *Italo Svevo: A Critical Introduction.* Edinburgh, 1974.
Montale, Eugenio. "Italo Svevo in the Centenary of His Birth." In *The Second Life of Art: Selected Essays of Eugenio Montale,* translated and edited by Jonathan Galassi. New York, 1982.
"Omaggio a Italo Svevo." *Solaria,* vol. 4, nos. 3 and 4 (1929).
Pacifici, Sergio. "Italo Svevo's Anti-Heroes." In *The Modern Italian Novel from Manzoni to Svevo.* Carbondale, Ill., 1967.
Palumbo, Matteo. *La coscienza di Svevo.* Naples, 1976.
Saccone, Eduardo. *Il poeta travestito: Otto scritti su Svevo.* Pisa, 1977.

ITALO SVEVO

Staley, T. F., ed. *Essays on Italo Svevo.* Tulsa, Okla., 1969.

Svevo, Livia Veneziani. *Vita di mio marito.* Trieste, 1958.

Tessari, Roberto. "Svevo e Pirandello: Guarigione ironica e sofferenza umoristica della 'malattia' industriale." In *Il mito della macchina: Letteratura e industria nel primo Novecento italiano.* Milan, 1973.

Zampa, Giorgio, ed. *Carteggio Svevo-Montale, con gli scritti di Montale su Svevo.* Milan, 1976.

JARED M. BECKER

ARTHUR SCHNITZLER
(1862–1931)

IMMEDIATELY AFTER the appearance of his novella *Leutnant Gustl* (translated as *None But the Brave*) in 1900, in which he portrays all the shortcomings of an aggressive soldier of the empire, Arthur Schnitzler was viciously reviled in Vienna by the forces of reaction. This was hardly the first time; indeed, he weathered a storm of vilification throughout most of his career. This fact is astonishing because he was not intrinsically a political writer. When he did touch a social issue, as in *Das Märchen* (The Fairy Tale, 1891), *Freiwild* (*Free Game*, 1896), and *Professor Bernhardi* (1912), he did so more by accident than by design. This tendency is also true of *None But the Brave,* in which his tangible purpose transcended exposure of the military's hollow code of honor. The furor he engendered, improbable as it seems, stemmed from his probing into the underlying motives of his fictional characters. When he undertook a literary theme of social consequence, he treated it as a means to inquire into individual egoism as an indicator of a universal problem.

Schnitzler's world was so completely the unexplored country of the psyche that he and his Viennese contemporary Sigmund Freud are often mentioned in the same breath. In an often-cited letter, the father of psychoanalysis congratulated Schnitzler on his sixtieth birthday, claiming that he had considered the author his double in psychological exploration and as a consequence had avoided approaching him. This letter led shortly to their first meeting. Schnitzler's notoriety, however, derived not from a lurid treatment of sexuality and perversion, but from a thoughtful and frank discussion of the struggle within all of us to cope with the fundamental problems of love and faith. If anything, the manner in which he treats sexuality is mild and discreet. He intuitively felt that the most effective and permanent moral indictment is couched in aesthetic terms. As a consequence, his work is still fresh and vital despite our distance from the "dying empire" of Austria around World War I. From before 1900 until 1925, no writer was more talked about, and no dramatist had more plays performed on the stages of Germany and Austria than did Schnitzler. Less than two decades later, however, his name had all but disappeared into an oblivion that has lasted until very recently. The reasons for his literary demise lie in the course of his life and his literary career.

The oldest of four children, three of whom survived childhood, Schnitzler was born to a Jewish family in 1862 in Vienna. His father, Johann Schnitzler, was one of the most renowned laryngologists in Europe. His mother, Louise Markbreiter, was the daughter of a well-situated and famous physician, Philipp Markbreiter, who founded the *Wiener medizinische Presse,* a medical journal that Johann Schnitzler took over as managing editor immediately after his marriage. The pursuit of medicine was an established tradition in the Schnitzler family, which insisted that the children follow suit; Arthur and his younger brother Julius did just that, and his sister married a doctor.

Although Schnitzler studied and practiced medicine only as a concession to his father, he profited immensely from this profession after he abandoned it—as soon as he was able to support himself as a writer. As an assistant physician in the psychiatric clinic of the renowned Theodor Meynert, for a time he was an editor of the *Internationale klinische Rundschau* and published one article in this journal, "Über die funktionelle Aphonie und deren Behandlung durch Hypnose und Suggestion" (On the Function of Aphonia and Its Treatment by Hypnosis and Suggestion). His experience with hypnosis bore literary fruit in two plays, *Anatol* (1893) and "Paracelsus" (1898). Contact with patients in his consulting chambers sharpened his eye for the vagaries of human personality, and his direct involvement in a dispute at the polyclinic that his father had established, provided background for two other works, *Free Game* and *Professor Bernhardi*. The affair was trivial in the extreme, despite its ugly overtones. Schnitzler was in charge of the preparations for a polyclinic-sponsored ball, and when the organizational coffee party was announced in an anti-Semitic tabloid by an employee of the polyclinic, Schnitzler expressed his disapproval of this employee in a board meeting. Challenged to a duel, Schnitzler ignored and thus dismissed the foolish matter, which was then hushed up, but he never forgot its true significance. The mood of the drama *Free Game,* written seven years later, recapitulates this confrontation.

The author enjoyed the manifold advantages of a privileged upbringing, one of which was education by private tutors beginning when he was three. Among his father's guests and patients were richly varied personalities and intellectuals, even noblemen, and, more importantly, actors from the legitimate stage. The Burgtheater, Vienna's citadel of dramatic art, provided another school. In his father's private theater loge he began to acquire his sense of the stage very early in life.

The first seventeen years of his life flowed imperturbably, unmarked by any real crises. He went through public school without traumatic experiences, but he certainly did not look back on it later with nostalgia; in fact he harbored a permanent dislike for formal education. This antipathy carried over to his studies at the university; he passed all his courses there, but often just barely. His early attempts at literary expression, a number of poems written when he was in his middle teens, revealed little promise in lyric poetry. Unlike his friend and contemporary Hugo von Hofmannsthal, who was astonishingly precocious, Schnitzler did not possess genuine talent in this medium, as his late verse dramas confirm. What revealed the consummate artist in him were his compulsive need to create, his sheer industry, and his vivid imagination. Shortly after his eighteenth birthday he had written twenty-three complete dramas and had begun thirteen others.

Young Schnitzler possessed sharp insight into human weakness and saw through his father's bourgeois pretensions, stress on creature comforts, and uncritical view of his established world. Johann Schnitzler and his snobbery earned Schnitzler's reflective disdain when Johann objected to his daughter's marriage to a poor medical student, for Johann himself had been in the same situation as a young man when he had asked for the hand of Louise Markbreiter. Schnitzler's next step was to turn his jaundiced eye on society itself. At the age of eighteen, when he published an essay, "Über den Patriotismus" (On Patriotism) in the newspaper *Der freie Landesbote* (The Free Rural Messenger), he argued against the high-flown phrases of chauvinistic fervor.

By the time he began studying medicine at the University of Vienna, he had established a pattern in his life that persisted throughout his extensive period of bachelorhood. Besides composing waltzes and poems, he became a devout habitué of the opera, theater, concert hall, café, pool hall, and racetrack. Sometimes he bet too heavily at the races, coming close to financial ruin on at least one occasion. These gambling experiences paid off many years later in the story *Spiel im Morgengrauen* (*Daybreak*, 1926), in which the hero's losses at cards result in suicide. His most serious amusement, however, was attending dances and pursuing flirtations—serious because his relations with the opposite sex were tempestuous, compelling, and overwhelming. For many years this extremely handsome man was a womanizer, and the likelihood of his marrying seemed slim until his actual wedding day late in life. His continual success with women made him wary of committing himself on a permanent basis, for he earnestly doubted women's constancy. In reality, his own self-doubt caused him to hold out until his forty-first year, when he married Olga Gussmann, twenty years his junior. He was obsessed by the idea that no woman would remain faithful to him for more than two years.

Another reason for prolonging his bachelorhood was that he saw no need to settle into marriage. All his domestic needs were taken care of by his mother, with whom he lived more than half his life, so he had the best of both worlds. There were many women in his life, including the actresses Mizi Gluemer and Adele Sandrock, both of whom performed in his plays. Very important in his early adulthood was Olga Waissnix. Although she represented a hopeless love, being already married, she understood young Schnitzler and his artistic aspirations as few others did, effectively lending him encouragement before success came his way. Their intense feeling for each other lasted until her untimely death in 1897 and is fully documented in their long-standing correspondence. She was followed by, among others, Jeanette Heger, who became his first steady amour and with whom, as he painstakingly recorded in his diary, he had had 465 sexual unions after only eighteen months of their relationship.

With Marie Reinhard he found perhaps his deepest relationship before his marriage. He saw in her someone worthy of marriage (this was her first affair), but he still could not bring himself to marry, even though he knew the social stigma and burden of guilt she bore as his mistress. Schnitzler was eventually severely shaken by the tragic outcome of this relationship. In 1897 their child was stillborn after Marie had endured racking birth pangs, and a year and a half later she died with surprising suddenness from a ruptured appendix. Her calming influence on his artistic temperament and the shock of her death forced him to reevaluate his situation and to consider seriously the one-sided nature of his relationships with women. Her precipitate death was one reason he finally considered marriage.

Schnitzler represents a supreme paradox in his relations with women. An extremely undemonstrative man, he could give way emotionally only to his wife and children or to his female partners. Even with his own brother and sister he had difficulty communicating his feelings. Only such an event as a death in the family breached the wall of his reserve and allowed him to reveal the deep affection within. In all his life there were only a scarce few whom he addressed by the familiar *du*. He sought female companionship with a sense of urgency, but he was without a doubt a difficult and irritating man to live with. His marriage to Olga Gussmann, although literarily rewarding because of her perceptive criticism of his newly created works, was often stormy, as had been his earlier love affairs, in which he had irrationally tormented his lovers with accusations. He knew he was a pronounced hypochondriac and possessed an inflexible sense of justice, and he was easily consumed by jealousy. His rigid insistence on justice became a virtue in his artistic works, unwilling as he was to compromise the most minute aesthetic point, but it certainly did not lead to peace and contentment in his private life. When his wife Olga broke with him to pursue her own life as a concert singer, he adamantly refused to take her back after the quick failure of her career. In his works he was very tolerant and compassionate when he portrayed women exploited by patriarchal society, but in his private life he adhered to the double standard. When Mizi Gluemer deceived him, he was so bitter that he was unable to forgive her, completely dismissing from his mind the fact that he had been unfaithful to her at the same time.

While a student in 1882 Schnitzler volunteered for the army for one year as an officer doctor, presumably more from vanity than from patriotism. Besides a break from his university studies, which did not appeal to him, he gained the right to wear a uniform, which improved his chances for sexual conquests. His service also inexorably strengthened his negative view of the military's narrowly rigid code.

Schnitzler never left the city of his birth for very long except for ten weeks in London and seven in Paris. His name, like that of Johann Strauss, was closely associated with Vienna, more so than that of any writer of the modern age. At the beginning of the last decade of the nineteenth century there emerged a literary circle that provided a label for the newspapers' cultural sections, and later for literary histories: "Young Vienna." Initially there were, besides Schnitzler, only minor figures who did not succeed in making a reputation. As time went by, however, the leading literati of the day, Hofmannsthal, Richard Beer-Hofmann, Herman Bahr, Felix Salten, and others, met to talk over their new works; among them was the quarrelsome Karl Kraus, who later became known for his venomous attacks on this group, especially on Schnitzler. Also called the Griensteidl Society after the café where they often met, Young Vienna was less an organization than a casual gathering of friends who profited by discussing their ideas or by reading their works aloud at a member's home. Indeed, had it been a real society Schnitzler would probably not have been a member at all, so averse was he to joining a group of any kind.

Schnitzler's first literary success came from novelettes published in journals and newspapers. These apprentice forays, which presaged the consummate storytelling to come, share an elegance of mood and an immersion in Schnitzler's world solely on his terms. In 1886 "Er wartet auf den vazierenden Gott" (He Is Waiting for the Itinerant God) appeared in the *Deutsche Wochenschrift*. This short tale shows the author's ironic insight into the literary pose of the dilettante and reveals that he is aware of the pretense that often existed in his own café atmosphere. "Der Andere" (The Other Man, 1889) stands out as the most significant of these early attempts. This story treats an infidelity that the bereaved husband discovers only after seeing another man kneeling at his wife's grave. It examines the jealousy, pain, and ambivalence that follow when an illusion collapses. In form "Der Andere" anticipates Schnitzler's first stream-of-consciousness narrative, *None But the Brave*. Although in "Der Andere" the hero's thoughts do not tumble forth in the same associative way to form a truly complete interior monologue, it is nevertheless an impressive foreshadowing.

There is at times an anecdotal quality to these early works, which are more in the nature of vignettes. Schnitzler explores the healing power of death for the survivors, how death tests their level of tolerance and their ability to forgive, and how it forces them to reevaluate their past behavior. In another major theme of this period, illicit love spiced with the element of risk becomes a compelling enticement, but passion of this kind must of necessity clash with reality.

Schnitzler also wrote a number of short philosophical sketches or parables, one of which grew to considerable length. Two from this early period are revealing for their ingenuity. The hero of "Die drei Elixire" (The Three Elixirs, 1894) reflects Schnitzler's own attitude toward the opposite sex. Consumed with jealousy over his sweetheart's past amours, he travels to the Orient and brings back the first of the elixirs referred to in the title, which will furnish the certitude he craves. By slipping it into her glass, he discovers through her confession her previous amorous entanglements. Embittered by these revelations, he abruptly leaves her and the women of his subsequent affairs. The second elixir he obtains enables him to cancel the memory of past love affairs in the mind of his beloved, but he is only content for a short while, for his own role in her life could likewise be obliterated. The third elixir will grant him mastery of the future, but the next morning his sweetheart does not respond to his kisses, for she is dead. The only complete certainty about existence comes with death. The other parable, "Um eine Stund" (For One Hour, 1899), is very close to the story line of Fritz Lang's German film classic of 1921, *Der müde Tod* (*Destiny*), in which a man pleads with the angel who collects the dying to extend the life of his beloved.

None of Schnitzler's short narrative efforts before the turn of the century can be called a sustained character study. However, in 1894 he produced a long and involved story, *Sterben* (*Dying*), that was at the same time a convincing analysis of his hero's agony. This work chronicles the step-by-step dissolution of love under the pressure of the hero's fear of certain death. Granted only one year to live, the consumptive Felix extracts a promise from his beloved Marie to follow him in death. As his health wanes her hold on life becomes stronger, and she refuses to renew her pledge to die with him. His adamant insistence, fueled by his fear of death, leads to a widening estrangement and finally to hate in place of love. Marie, in the throes of first love, pledged her word, but time brings moderation and clarity, and the will to live triumphs. Interestingly, the male hero is found wanting in moral qualities, while Marie is projected as a tower of strength and character. It required an author who was also a physician possessing firsthand experience with dying patients to write such a profound analysis of the fear of death and its consequences. With the publication of *Dying*,

Schnitzler established his literary reputation and his name became known outside the German-speaking world. It was his first work to be translated—into French.

Unfortunately for him his growing esteem as an artist came too late for his father, who died in 1893, never having known the exceptional talent of his son. Schnitzler keenly felt the loss, but his father's death was a positive factor in his creative life, for his father could no longer inhibit the free unfolding of his genius. Earlier Schnitzler's father had been extremely upset by the appearance of several of his early novelettes and a scene from the play *Anatol* in the magazine *An der schönen blauen Donau*. He was sorely afraid that his son would not be taken seriously as a doctor if potential patients learned that he dabbled in literature. (*Anatol* had been preceded by "Alkandis Lied" [Alkandi's Song, 1890], a one-act dramatic poem involving the theme of infidelity and set in the exotic Orient. Although it has never been performed and directly reflects the youth of the author, "Alkandis Lied" is notable for a remarkably sophisticated rendering of a dream and its consequences for the dreamer's waking life.)

In 1891 *Anatol* became Schnitzler's first performed work when one scene was staged in a private performance in Vienna. *Anatol* has turned out to be one of his most durable and one of his most controversial works. It consists of a sequence of seven dialogues or scenes loosely strung together; they premiered at different times and places. It was not until 1910 that as many as five of the seven were performed together. In 1899 the Berlin censors banned the scene "The Wedding Morning" on moral grounds. On the morning of the hero's wedding, Max, his friend and best man, comes to Anatol's apartment to discover him after a night of love with a former amour, the actress Ilona. When she learns of his impending wedding, she is beside herself, but is consoled by Max's remark that it is not she who will be deceived, but the bride-to-be, for Anatol can always come back to her. Love is only a cynical game for Anatol, and his marriage will not put an end to his affairs. This scene more than the others led to the mislabeling of Schnitzler as a self-indulgent and immoral writer. Three decades later, in 1932, the prestigious Burgtheater, the arbiter of dramatic taste and art in Austria, added *Anatol* to its repertoire.

Anatol introduced both the quintessence of Schnitzler and the false image of him as a frivolous man of letters. Critics immediately identified the author with his hero. They were certainly aided in their view by the knowledge that he had earlier signed the pseudonym Anatol to a number of his poems in order to conceal his literary activity from his father. But this identification tallies only superficially. Although it is true that Schnitzler was a hedonistic man-about-town caught up in a number of casual love affairs, he was not dissolute, and he continuously examined his life and experiences for artistic purposes. His invention, Anatol, is cut essentially from different cloth; although charming, Anatol is a weak and amorphous personality whose sentimental side leaves him open to ridicule. Also, he is neither intellectual nor creative, except when he "creatively" deceives himself.

Initially *Anatol* harvested mainly invective, for Schnitzler touched a nerve in society by daring to discuss openly the hypocrisy of the accepted Victorian moral code behind which excess prevailed. However, in addition to its shock value, it also stamped Schnitzler as a decadent as well as an immoralist, and henceforth any work of his drew automatic responses from many a conservative critic. Curiously, however, the stereotype of decadence was due more to Hofmannsthal's inappropriate prologue to this play, in which the Venetian rococo world of Canaletto, the 1760's, is described as a formal garden now neglected. Critics repeatedly cited one line especially, "early ripened, sad and fragile," that helped to mold the long-term view of both *Anatol* and his creator. Other works of Hofmannsthal, his melancholic "Ballad of Outward Life" and his poem "Some, It's True," which includes the line "Weariness of long-forgotten races I can-

not brush off my eyelids," could conceivably support a case for the decadence of the time, but they reflect the pessimism of the poet, not of Schnitzler or of his hero, so energetic in the pursuit of love. Still, the damage had been done. So eager were critics to label *Anatol* decadent or trivial that they missed its psychological subtlety and its universal comic relevance. Typical of its appeal is the following remark by Anatol, almost Wildean in its paradoxical force: "I ask every woman: 'Did you love anyone before me?' And every woman asks me: 'Will you love anyone after me?' We always want to be their first love; they always want us to be their last."

Das Märchen, Schnitzler's next dramatic work, is the literary harvest of his relationship with Mizi Gluemer. The great intensity of his affection for her was countered by his knowledge of her past as a "fallen" woman, and some of his obsessive attitudes appear in this full-length drama, which premiered in Vienna in 1893. Although both hero and author understand that, considering the lives they themselves lead, they hardly have the right to condemn a woman for having had previous lovers, they still remain prisoners of convention and of the prevailing social morality. Still, the work itself announces a new attitude toward women, especially actresses, and toward the double standard by airing a problem that many were aware of but few discussed.

Many people saw in the play a glorification of free love, and thus Schnitzler's first opening night in the legitimate theater resulted in a failure and a scandal that drew brutal aspersions. In retrospect it is difficult to believe that the criticism of that time could be both so personal and so vehement over something so innocuous. One anonymous critic wrote: "One is amazed at the terrible moral degeneration that issues from this work. We implore Mr. Schnitzler to regard us as hypocrites and Pharisees; in return, he will allow us to look upon him as something else, something that every text of natural history specifically describes." The "something else" was a pig.

At this time two people who had a positive impact on his outlook and artistic aspirations entered Schnitzler's life. Otto Brahm, an indefatigable fighter for avant-garde drama and the promoter of Henrik Ibsen, Gerhart Hauptmann, and other modern talents, became both a lifelong support in his theater in Berlin and a true friend until the very end. Schnitzler also found Marie Reinhard. Their brief relationship was characterized by self-torments that his unsteady nature manufactured. Around the same time Schnitzler wrote *Liebelei* (*Light-o-Love*, 1896). This represented an impressive breakthrough, being his first drama staged at the prestigious Burgtheater, his first full-blown success, and his first play, which has become more famous with the passage of time, to reach an international audience. It was also daring and unheard-of to present a young unmarried woman engaged in an affair as a heroine on the stage of the Burgtheater. However, fears of another scandal, of a storm of outrage to accompany this work as well, were not realized. A true emancipation and revolution took place with Schnitzler's dramatic triumph. The ossified concepts of an older generation were giving way to new ideas. Young girls from the suburbs saw themselves on the stage where before had stood only costumed historical figures declaiming in verse. The wholesome Christine Weiring, one of his most memorable heroines, finds herself deeply in love with Fritz Lobheimer, who is soon to die in a duel over his affair with a married woman. When the fatal news reaches her, Christine realizes how little her affection for him was requited and goes off, ostensibly to take her own life. This ending is the weakest aspect of the work, for it is not quite credible that she, depicted as a very strong character, would throw her life away for the superficial Lobheimer. The ending also places the work on the border between drama and melodrama, even though most critics view it as a genuine tragedy of love.

Light-o-Love had one negative impact, for it stamped Schnitzler for all time as the creator of "the sweet young thing" (*das süsse Mädel*), the lower-class girl from the suburbs who enters into an affair with a man of higher social standing. Christine Weiring established a stereotype for the rest of Schnitzler's literary career, much to his annoyance. So often was every unmarried woman of his later works described as a "sweet young thing" that he drafted his own critique of the reviewers and even struck back in his burlesque of 1905, "Zum grossen Wurstel" (The Big Wurstel Puppet Theater), when the puppet Liesl states:

> Just because I am a simple girl,
> And Vienna's the scene of the plot,
> They call me *süsses Mädel*,
> Whether I am or not.
> (*Gesammelte Werke: Die dramatischen Werke*, 1:875)

Despite Christine, the *süsse Mädel* concept fails to do justice to the intention of the author. Schnitzler had originally entitled the work "Das arme Mädel" (The Poor Girl) to emphasize Christine's identity as an exploited woman from a background of poverty.

Two years later Schnitzler's most tendentious piece, *Free Game,* gave rise to more controversy. The free game (perhaps better translated as "fair game") in this drama are the actresses of a small-town theater (who are treated practically as prostitutes by the military officers stationed there) and a young man who will not let himself be provoked into fighting a duel. The convalescent Paul Rönning rejects the prevailing dueling code as senseless, especially since he, a civilian, would be up against Karinski, an aggressive officer well-versed in firearms. His rejection does not save him, however; the enraged Karinski, his honor at stake, shoots him to death. In essence the dueling code, under the guise of preserving honor, can justify legalized murder or can inflict a pitiless social penalty on those unfortunate enough to be implicated.

At first Viennese directors refused to stage the play, which was not faring well in the press. Schnitzler was forced to wait two years after its premiere in Berlin under Otto Brahm before it was staged there. In the meantime, identified by his enemies, especially anti-Semites, with his dramatic hero, he had to submit to many personal attacks and was abused as a coward. Military officers ostentatiously walked out of the first performance in Breslau, but a little later the military in Prague demonstrated in favor of the play's message. By 1905, when the work was revived in Vienna, the mood had swung completely over to Schnitzler's side; there was enthusiastic applause following the hero's anti-dueling monologue. In *Free Game* Schnitzler adroitly questioned a social institution and by doing so laid it to rest for all time, thus superannuating his own drama. Because it had addressed the problem so successfully, it shortly became an out-of-date museum piece.

Reigen (*Hands Around,* 1900), which the author wrote within two months in 1897, epitomizes Schnitzler and his art even more than *Anatol,* which it echoed in style. Here ten people in pairs are presented onstage, the prostitute with the soldier, the soldier with the chambermaid, and so on up the social ladder and down again until, at the end, a member of the nobility, a count, is found in the arms of the prostitute of the beginning. *Hands Around* is regarded as one of the finest series of dialogues ever written, each a masterpiece of nuance covering the spectrum of human emotions, social attitudes, and class-conscious hypocrisies. Each dialogue or scene of cohabitation contains incisive social satire as well as an element of the danse macabre. Schnitzler demonstrates that caste distinctions are artificial and that all members of society are equal before the power of Eros. Although this drama is suffused with typical Schnitzlerian restraint (there is no inclination to lasciviousness or titillation, for the stage is darkened when each pair embraces in passion), fashioning a stage presentation around the sexual act precluded its being performed for nearly twenty-five years.

Schnitzler's next drama, *Das Vermächtnis* (*The Legacy,* 1899), which revolves around an illegitimate child, derives its inspiration from his relationship with Marie Reinhard. This three-act drama, premiered by Otto Brahm in Berlin in 1897, is a one-sided exposé of bourgeois hypocrisy and is one of Schnitzler's weaker efforts. Fatally injured in an accident, a dying young man asks his parents to look after the woman he has been living with and their young child, his "legacy." They do so, but on their own timeserving terms. When the child itself dies, they let the mother, Toni, know how unwelcome she is. The young, unhappy Toni goes away, perhaps to her death. As the leading figure she is more victim than heroine, which is why the drama did not stand the test of time despite some memorable characterizations and an initial favorable public reception. Once again Schnitzler was targeted as a dramatist who sanctioned free love, but this time the criticism was relatively mild.

Schnitzler's next three plays, one-act works, premiered together at the Burgtheater in 1899: "Paracelsus" (1898), "Der grüne Kakadu" ("The Green Cockatoo"), and "Die Gefährtin" ("His Helpmate"). They are discrete in time and place, but they all interweave illusion with reality in such a way as to mock stiff reliance on smug common sense as a sole guideline. The Renaissance figure Paracelsus, the father of chemotherapy, is portrayed as a man outside narrow bourgeois society who, by employing hypnosis, obtains a measure of revenge on his adversaries and at the same time provides them with a brief moment of insight. Cyprian, complacently sure of his wife Justina's affections since their marriage thirteen years earlier, begins to doubt when she reveals in a trance her earlier love for Paracelsus and her rejection of another suitor, Junker Anselm. Her unveiled subconscious memory, however, blends and confuses the two experiences. Paracelsus' last words in this verse drama have become a favorite citation among critics, who have applied it indiscriminately to the author himself: "Certainty is

96

nowhere. . . . We are always playing, and wise is he who knows that." For his critics, this statement reinforced the stereotype of Schnitzler as an author who was not serious, who continually played frivolous games, as if he himself had spoken these words, not his fictional creation.

"The Green Cockatoo" is Schnitzler's most spectacular work, theatrically speaking. As the Bastille is about to be assaulted at the beginning of the French Revolution, members of the aristocracy visit a disreputable tavern, the Green Cockatoo, where actors perform on a stage. The aristocrats cannot wholly grasp whether what they see, a preview of the coming political turmoil, is theater or life. Nor can the distinction be completely drawn by the audience of Schnitzler's play. So interlaced is the illusory with the real that the effect is a true tour de force. This work offended some members of the Austrian imperial court who consequently closed it down after only eight performances. When Schnitzler persisted in squarely confronting the arbitrary evasions of the court theater officials and in reclaiming his contractual rights to the play, he made more powerful enemies and became persona non grata then and for the future.

The third part of the premiered trilogy, "His Helpmate," harkens back to the early novella "Der Witwer" (The Widower, 1894), in which a man learns that his deceased wife's lover did not take the affair seriously. In the play Professor Pilgram had known of his wife's infidelity with his assistant, but had tolerated it because of her youth. His tolerance receives a severe jolt when, after firing his assistant, he finds out that his wife had been playing a game of instinctual gratification. Only then does he realize how little he had known the woman closest to him in his life.

The one-act play was Schnitzler's most successful genre and became his trademark. In a letter to Otto Brahm dated 1 October 1905, he acknowledged its hegemony in his creative output, stating that this type of presentation "combined into a cycle is a form that lies deep within my nature." This preference naturally accorded with a mentality that concentrated on the substratum of human motivation, but because of these concise dramas as well as the brief novellas, he was in time disparaged as a miniaturist. Such reproach overlooks the fact that he still wrote impressively on a monumental scale; more than half his dramatic efforts were full-evening presentations, and his later tales, besides his two novels, came close to epic length.

Schnitzler wrote one more play before the nineteenth century ended: *Der Schleier der Beatrice* (The Veil of Beatrice, 1901). This work had a long period of gestation. Originally conceived in a contemporary setting, it turned into a costume verse presentation of the Italian Renaissance. It is perhaps Schnitzler's least understood work and remains a riddle to this day, with critics evenly divided. Some appreciate its beauty and consider it one of the most significant creations of the time; others find it overly complicated and too cold and distant. Even Otto Brahm was "more captivated than warmed." Max Lorenz's review of 1901 has received special attention: "Schnitzler wanted to become Shakespeare, but in the attempt only ceased being Schnitzler." At its first performance in Berlin in 1903 there were both applause and hissing after each act, and reviewers were either lavish or severely critical in their praise. When it was produced at the Burgtheater in 1925, favorable notices completely vindicated Schnitzler. Nevertheless, it is an uneven work, partially handicapped by imperfectly mastered verse and by a diffusion of focus. Beatrice Nardi embodies the childlike and the elemental as she is awakened to love, but she emerges unscathed from her adventures because she is governed by her natural instincts. She is torn between the man of action, the Duke of Bologna, and the man of contemplation, the poet Filippo Loschi. At her wedding banquet she rushes from the duke to spend an hour of love with Filippo, who urges her to commit suicide with him. He kills himself, but she, magnetized by life, reneges on her promise and flees, forgetting her veil. The mood is one of nervous splendor, for Bologna and its inhabitants are doomed by the besieging army of Cesare Borgia. Thus the dramatic tensions are played out in a setting of urgency.

Schnitzler's difficulties with *Der Schleier der Beatrice* were not confined to its content or to the critics' reactions. A serious altercation took place between him and the director of the Burgtheater, Paul Schlenther, who arbitrarily broke his written promise to stage the play there. The director's despotic conduct, very likely a residuum of the animosity engendered by "The Green Cockatoo," led Schnitzler to issue an ultimatum: either perform it or reject it. This was followed by an outright rejection of the drama, which in turn resulted in a public protest by the playwright and six friends and critics over such high-handed action. Schlenther then claimed that his original letter to Schnitzler had not constituted an acceptance of the play. Schnitzler's reply, which was published in a number of newspapers, struck at the root of the controversy with telling effect. He asked how it was possible for a director to relinquish the performing rights to a work that he had never accepted. Schnitzler dealt with the whole matter in an impersonal way, only to find himself the target of vituperative ad hominem attacks. Arch-conservative newspapers intervened to claim a conspiracy of the Jewish press and writers of Vienna. Schnitzler's challenge to Schlenther's authority exacted a price: banishment. It was five years before he saw another première of his work at the Burgtheater. In addition, as the author learned later, Schlenther's rancor blocked his nomination for the Grillparzer Prize for *Der Schleier der Beatrice*.

A pantomime, "Der Schleier der Pierrette" (The Veil of Pierrette, 1910), which formed the earliest conception of this play, was to have a life of its own. Set to music by Ernst von Dohnanyi, it enjoyed a great success at the Dresden Opera in 1910. When it was produced in New York in 1928, the theater critic Robert Littell called it "not only the best pantomime I have yet seen, but also one of the most competent and imaginative items in a very remarkable New York theatrical season."

In 1899 Olga Gussmann entered Schnitzler's life. An aspiring actress using the name Dina Marius, this ambitious eighteen-year-old woman, half Schnitzler's age, engineered their meeting. Within a short span she became someone he could confide in, and, above all, someone to talk to in depth about his literary works. Then she began living with him, bore him a son, and shortly thereafter became his wife.

In the first year of the new century Schnitzler wrote several of his best prose works. One of them, *None But the Brave,* stands out as a milestone of German literature, the first stream-of-consciousness narrative written in this language. Among Schnitzler's finest works, it was composed within the short span of six days. It also stood out for the impact it had on Schnitzler's enemies. Its hero, Lieutenant Gustl, is given a dressing down in the opera foyer by a suburban baker for intemperately blurting out his hostility, and Gustl now believes his honor is at stake. Since this civilian is not worthy of dueling, Gustl can gain no satisfaction and feels irreparably disgraced, even if the matter does not reach the ears of his commanding officer. Because he knows what has happened and perceives his own dishonor, he feels his only course of action is suicide. What emerges from the thought associations that cascade from Gustl is a portrait of a distressingly uninviting young man, a peculiarly blinkered individual, anti-Semitic, hateful, and loveless. This officer is hardly a gentleman.

The critical reactions to this portrayal were enormous and also one-sided, since Schnitzler did not stoop to defend his works or explain or correct the misconceptions they engendered in the public. The rage of the conservatives, military, and anti-Semites toward Schnitzler was now unequaled. Several times he was unofficially subpoenaed to appear before a disciplinary officers' court to answer charges that he had defamed the honor of the Austrian army. He refused, declaring that he did not concede that a military court had any jurisdiction over his literary works. The furor and personal vilification in the right-wing press subsided only after he was stripped of his reserve commission in the army.

Although this work unequivocally serves as a sharp indictment of the military caste mentality and its archaic dueling code, it is much more than a socially conceived piece of art. The ingenious use of the interior monologue would be misplaced, in part, were that all there was to it. What Schnitzler depicts here is the first dissection of a specific personality type in German—if not in all—literature: the psychopath or sociopath. Only much later was this type defined clinically when the field of psychiatry developed into a branch of institutionalized healing. In the young Lieutenant Gustl, Schnitzler lays bare an individual who lacks a conscience and consequently those attributes which define one as a social being. Because his feelings are only surface deep, he can register neither the joy of human affection nor the pain of tragic loss. The author marvelously weaves the hero's aggression into his thoughts, depicting his inability to love or to transcend his own ego. Emotionally Gustl can never understand either the outrage he may and often does commit or its aftermath, when regret or remorse are appropriate. The act of love is for him simply mechanical. He is further characterized by an appalling deficiency in basic responses to the most fundamental expressions of feelings and personal values. As a result, both his hate and love are haphazard. All these descriptive traits are admirably summed up in the last aggressive thought he utters, "I'll make mincemeat out of you!," for Gustl does not take his own life. He is not allowed to commit suicide because it would lend a tragic and redeeming aura to the conclusion. His life is not worthy of that, considering how little value is placed on it. Ironically he is reprieved early the next morning when, after roaming the streets all night, he learns

that the baker has suddenly died of a heart attack. Thus his final reaction reveals how threadbare his sense of honor is, for he no longer thinks of ending his own life.

In contrast to *None But the Brave*, "Der blinde Geronimo und sein Bruder" ("Blind Geronimo and His Brother," 1900) is a deceptively simple story, effortlessly told but rich in nuance. After having accidentally caused his brother's blindness in childhood, Carlo devotes his whole life to him. For many years, day in and day out, they have eked out a precarious existence by begging in the tourist region of the Alps where Italy, Switzerland, and Austria come together. After a complete stranger plays a trick on Geronimo, telling him he had given Carlo a twenty-franc coin when in reality he had donated only a few cents, their monotonous life is disrupted when Geronimo's long-slumbering resentment erupts. In order to disprove Geronimo's claim that he is a thief, Carlo actually steals a twenty-franc piece. The content of his entire life rests on this theft, for his existence is as dependent on his brother's as Geronimo's is on his. Will a man who literally and figuratively cannot see understand his brother's sacrifice? Schnitzler's resolution is both moving and beautiful. In this work of noble simplicity the author demonstrates an extreme sensitivity for the right tone and mood of the two beggars as they inarticulately grope their way through their conflict. His humanity bridges the spiritual and intellectual distance separating him from the prosaic world of poverty.

Frau Berta Garlan (*Bertha Garlan*, 1901) is the author's longest prose narrative of this period, falling just short of novel length, and was inspired by the fate of his youthful love Fanny Reich. This woman, caught up in a loveless marriage and then living as a widow with her child in a provincial town, saw her life slip by uneventfully. Schnitzler rebuffed her attempts to renew their old acquaintance. When her fictional counterpart in Vienna, Bertha Garlan, recrosses the path of her former sweetheart, Emil Lindbach, who has in the meantime become a famous violinist, the outcome is nearly the same as it was for Fanny Reich. A night of passion is followed by Emil's cold, unconscionable rejection. Bertha's traumatic escapade is contrasted to the adulterous experience of her neighbor, Frau Rupius, which ends tragically. At the end Bertha attains a kind of bitter clarity:

> Bertha divined what an enormous wrong had been wrought against the world in that the longing for pleasure was placed in a woman just as in a man; and that with women that longing is a sin, demanding expiation, if the yearning for pleasure is not at the same time a yearning for motherhood.
>
> (*Gesammelte Werke: Die erzählenden Schriften,* 1962, 1:513)

Bertha Garlan's insight shows how far ahead of his time Schnitzler was. More importantly, the psychology and humanity of a woman as seen from her inner perspective are astonishingly illuminated in a way that is both dispassionate and compassionate.

A pathological counterpart to Bertha Garlan's analysis of a woman's erotic wish fulfillments is to be found in another long novella written thirteen years later, *Frau Beate und ihr Sohn* (Frau Beate and Her Son, translated as *Beatrice,* 1913). This heroine is also a widow with a child, but this time the libidinal fixation has as its object the seventeen-year-old son, Hugo. Both mother and son are stimulated by sexual temptations—Hugo with a woman his mother's age and Beate with a comrade of her son—until their incestuous desires, consummated in a boat, are followed, in a kind of atonement, by a watery death. Despite its steamy atmosphere this story is told with great delicacy, stressing the psychological responses of the heroine. For some admirers of Schnitzler's art, however, this work was completely unacceptable from a moral standpoint.

Other novellas followed in the next few years, but only one is exceptional, "Die Fremde" ("The Stranger," 1902), Schnitzler's most pessimistic work. It conveys the blackest despair by the artlessly simple method of contrasting a psychotic with a neurotic. The effect of hopelessness is further enhanced by a sober chronicle style in the manner of a case history. Although the title refers to the schizophrenic Katerina, it is not her involvement with reality, or lack of it, that concerns the reader, but rather Albert Webeling's feeble defense against his death wish. The brief account of their mechanical and emotionless honeymoon is in its horror among the strangest on record in literature. Katerina does not live in a connective world where one attempts to build a future on the present. Therefore, it is Albert who commits suicide whereas she continues to live in her delusional world.

A cycle of four one-act plays published under the collective title *Lebendige Stunden* (*Living Hours,* 1901–1902) was written in the years 1900 and 1901. The first, the title-piece of the collection, concerns an aesthetic son who selfishly takes for granted his mother's sacrifice in suicide since it will enable him to create "living hours" in his calling as a poet. When reproached for his disdain of the last period of her life, *her* living hours, he responds: "Living hours? They do not live longer that the last person who remembers them. It is not the worst profession to make such hours endure beyond their time." Which is the more important, life or art? This question is raised by the mother's companion, who resents the son's attitude. "Die Frau mit dem Dolche" ("The Lady with the Dagger," 1902), the second play, employs a flashback technique from the present to the Renaissance. A painter receives the inspiration to complete his masterpiece when his wife kills his rival with a dagger. In "Die letzten Masken" ("Last Masks," 1902) the dying journalist Rademacher rehearses his revenge on his erstwhile friend and competitor Weihgast, a successful poet, but when Weihgast appears, Rademacher cannot bring himself to tell Weihgast that he has had an affair with his wife. In the face of death, such petty ego gratification seems both idle and futile. The best of the four, "Literatur"

("Literature," 1902), is one of Schnitzler's most amusing farces. Two literary hacks, Klemens and Margarete, use their love affair for literary purposes, undercutting and compromising both the genuineness of their feelings and the pathos of their art. This last play of the cycle was often staged independently of the other three.

Between 1902 and 1904 Schnitzler wrote *Marionetten* (Marionettes), which consists of three one-act plays: "Der Puppenspieler" (The Puppeteer, 1903), "Der tapfere Cassian" ("Gallant Cassian," 1904), and "Zum grossen Wurstel" (The Big Wurstel Puppet Theater). In the first, the puppeteer is the poet Georg Merklin, who manipulates real people as if he were operating the strings of a marionette. When the result surprises him, he retreats into the shell of his own personality. "Gallant Cassian" is a puppet play whose shy, introverted hero, suddenly blessed with luck at dice, presumes too much and pays with his winnings, his beloved, and his life. The sudden shift in fortune is enhanced by the broad exaggeration of the puppet stage. In 1909 this play was set to music by the composer Oscar Strauss. More complex, the burlesque "Zum grossen Wurstel" reminds one of "The Green Cockatoo" with its theater within a theater. Schnitzler uses the naiveté of the children's puppet stage to satirize his own works and his critics. Figures from his earlier dramas appear onstage. At the end of this highly original masterpiece a mysterious figure cloaked in blue cuts through all the marionette strings with one stroke of his sword, and the puppets fall lifeless to the ground. Here Schnitzler, himself personified, makes his entrance on the stage as the lord of fictional creation.

Schnitzler broke new ground in 1903 with his drama *Der einsame Weg* (*The Lonely Way*, 1904). The play introduces a new kind of hero for him, one who mercilessly feels his emptiness and is incapable of playing a game, like Anatol, to soften its impact, or, like Filippo Loschi, of making the grand gesture. This drama marked the first of Schnitzler's cre-

ations of characters who cherish no illusions. Originally entitled "Die Egoisten" (The Egoists), this work presents people whose indolence in emotional commitment is lifelong and who cannot respond as complete human beings. A study in the pathology of loneliness, it is mired deep in despair. There are actually two parallel plots. In the main plot Felix Wegrat learns that the painter Julian Fichtner, a former lover of his mother, is his real father, not the man who raised him. Felix rejects Julian, who has lived selfishly for himself and his art. The other dramatic action centers on the poet Stephan von Sala, Schnitzler's most consistently alienated character. A figure cruelly aware of his shortcomings, Stephan embodies a central facet of Schnitzler's outlook: the knowledge that most people fail to make real contact with another human being. He has an affair with Felix's half sister Johanna. When he learns that she has ended her life for his sake, he too commits suicide. Also central to the plot is another lonely figure, the actress Irene Herms. She has also lived for fulfillment in her career, having denied her deep maternal instincts. Now, too late for motherhood, she faces a future based only on nostalgia. *The Lonely Way* reflects the peculiar existence of the person of exceptional talent, for whom every effort to achieve artistic perfection leads away from a binding human commitment. If this drama is not staged with subtlety and consummate actors, it can make a mockery of the author's art, as so many productions, including its premiere in Berlin, have demonstrated. The wealth of nuances in *The Lonely Way* has not yet been exhausted, and this play should consequently assume more significance among Schnitzler's dramatic works.

In 1904 *Zwischenspiel* (*Intermezzo*, 1906) premiered at the Burgtheater. It revolves around the conductor Amadeus Adams and his opera-singer spouse Cäcelie. Given their independent natures, they are unable to save their relationship. Having grown apart, they still remain close friends until even this friendship is destroyed by their yielding to passion with each other. Although subtitled "A Comedy in Three Acts," the play is nevertheless more elegiac than funny. The author himself was critical of this play, but it still remained in the repertoire until 1919. Although it must be catalogued among his weaker dramas, it earned him the Grillparzer Prize for the best play of 1908.

Schnitzler's next play, *Der Ruf des Lebens* (The Call of Life, 1906), contains three acts. Each act is a stage in the life of the heroine, but they are so disconnected that her character cannot unify the play. Moral objections were again raised, especially because the heroine is not held accountable for murdering her cruel and demanding father, who was suffocating her call to life. This time, however, the actors themselves at the premiere in Berlin took issue with the content of the work. Most of the critics were hostile, in some instances unexpectedly so. Schnitzler had never before incurred such vehement opposition, although the play was successful for a short while when it was performed four years later at the Volkstheater in Vienna. In *Der Ruf des Lebens* Schnitzler stepped outside the subtly shaded presentation of life he had hitherto adhered to, and resorted to something like melodrama.

Shortly after the failure of *Der Ruf des Lebens*, when Schnitzler's spirits were at their lowest ebb, he suddenly returned to an earlier plan for a one-act play, and, within three weeks, completed his most cheerful comedy, *Komtesse Mizzi oder der Familientag* (*Countess Mizzi; or, The Family Reunion*, 1908). Light and sparkling, it is a gentle ridicule of society that centers on the nobility. That a countess could have an illegitimate child and several lovers was not very surprising to anyone at that time, but to have this presented on the stage was. Some people thought Schnitzler had taken leave of his senses in treating this theme, but times had changed. The few noblemen who took offense did not exert wide influence. It was the author's intention not to attack aristocrats per se, but to portray them for the sake of a comic situation.

Der Weg ins Freie (*The Road to the Open*), Schnitzler's most extensive work and a product of four years' creative labor, appeared in 1908. The uproar this novel caused came not so much from the general public as from his Jewish friends and acquaintances, who saw themselves portrayed in it. Many of them, to Schnitzler's chagrin and dismay, did not understand the play. Hofmannsthal detested the work for its indiscreet use of private lives. He was probably referring to the main plot of the story, the love affair between the hero, Georg Wergenthin, and Anna Rosner, which undeniably mirrored Schnitzler's relationship with Marie Reinhard. The novel depicts the Jewish artist and the Christian woman of the lower middle class, her pregnancy and his elaborate efforts to pass over it in silence and set up house for her, her agony in giving birth to a stillborn child, and his unwillingness to marry her. It would, however, be too facile to claim that this novel is a cathartic exposé of Schnitzler's private struggle with his own emotional and artistic natures; on the contrary, it confirms that he was an extremely private person who had no real intention of placing his personal life on public display.

The title itself is also misleading. Contrary to expectations that the hero will overcome the barriers restricting his creative freedom and clarify for himself his role as an artist, he is at the end no further along the way to the independence he seeks, ill-defined and vague as it is, than he was at the beginning. The main plot also presents some problems, for Schnitzler refuses to let his hero step forward and appear as a character of flesh and blood. Georg Wergenthin is only a pale emanation of Schnitzler, the man constantly in the middle of a literary storm and the vigorous critic of his society. Schnitzler is so neutral and objective that he never annotates or comments and consequently does not convey the complex nature of his character. The hero's main concern, the relationship with Anna Rosner and what to do with her, only superficially reflects Schnitzler's relationship with Marie Reinhard and other facts of his autobiography. In Anna Rosner the author has created a curious monument to the woman whose sudden tragic death in 1899 caused him to write to Hofmannsthal that he was dominated by an immense indifference to everything that seemed to him to be the substance of life. Georg's love for Anna Rosner dies because of his own listlessness. So unattractive is the portrayal of his behavior to Anna that Schnitzler seems to be flagellating himself in print for his role in Marie Reinhard's life.

Schnitzler deals with what it means to be Jewish, but interestingly, the hero himself does not suffer an identity crisis. Schnitzler leaves it to the subsidiary figures to address the problem of Jewish identity. The hero's particular personal situation, despite the title, really serves as a means to advance concepts of art, views on politics, and most compellingly, attitudes of and about the Jews in Austrian society at the turn of the century. *The Road to the Open* therefore is a valuable and important document for posterity in understanding the social atmosphere of Vienna at this time. Schnitzler presents the entire spectrum of Jewish attitudes, except for religiously orthodox Jews and the Jewish proletariat, and singles out typical representatives of Jewish society. Oskar Ehrenburg, modeled after the father of Zionism, Theodor Herzl, forms a contrast to his son, who would convert to Christianity if doing so would not cost him his inheritance. In the Golowski family the young generation belongs to the radicals: Leo is politically rabid, and his sister Therese speaks for the social democrats. The Jewish artists consider their Jewishness from a psychological point of view. Both the Eisslers are examples of successful assimilation. Old Eissler is a famous composer of waltzes and thus "old Viennese" par excellence; his son is such a charming cavalier that his Jewishness is almost nonexistent. Among the writers, Heinrich Berman can never forget that he is Jewish, but Edmund Nürnberger is indifferent.

Jewish attitudes to Gentiles are analyzed as well. The characters individually react to the social pressures they experience as members of a minority, sometimes with hypocrisy, sometimes even anti-Semitically in order to ingratiate themselves. To attack another Jew could make them acceptable, as Schnitzler had seen when Jewish critics attacked his works. Foremost as an example of the opportunistic Jew was the Thersites-like Kraus, who always had an unkind word for Schnitzler.

For Schnitzler the character of the person in question determined whether he was Jewish in a positive or negative sense. He refused to stereotype people, least of all Jews. He frequently felt Jewish only to the extent that anti-Semites continuously reminded him of it. In fact, he resisted all preconceived modes of thinking: he refused to acknowledge ties or traditions. He felt that he had a right to decide every issue and to evaluate every social institution or convention for himself. Characteristically, he wrote, as recorded in *Aphorismen und Betrachtungen* (Aphorisms and Observations, 1967): "I love my fatherland not because it is my fatherland, but because I find it beautiful." Schnitzler was one of history's first world citizens, as his personal "confession" in the same work attests: "I feel no solidarity with anyone because he happens to belong to the same nation, class, race, or family as I do. . . . I have fellow citizens in every nation, comrades in every class, and brothers who have no inkling of my existence."

The years 1909 to 1912 saw the pinnacle of Schnitzler's popularity as well as some impressive artistic achievements. In the short-story genre he produced two miniature masterpieces, "Der Tod des Junggesellen" ("The Death of a Bachelor," 1908) and "Das Tagebuch der Redegonda" ("Redegonda's Diary," 1911). In the first work the final shaft of the deceased is barbed. Three nameless friends, a doctor, a merchant, and a poet, answer the summons of the dying bachelor but arrive after his death. They learn from his letter that he had at one time or another made love to each of their wives. This tale is replete with ironies.

The work focuses on how each friend reacts to the infidelity of his wife. Each reveals his own ambivalent character and attitudes, but the bachelor himself is likewise shown to be imbued with conflicting feelings. In his immaturity he is like the stranger in "Blind Geronimo and His Brother." He was obviously no real friend to the three; his malicious gibe from his deathbed had been designed seven years earlier, but he places the incriminating letter in his room where it might have been overlooked. In fact, it is discovered only by accident. That he is a bachelor is crucial: he has only physically possessed his friends' wives; he has not shared a life with any of them.

"Redegonda's Diary" is a mystery story in capsule form. Like the silent film classic of 1919 *The Cabinet of Dr. Caligari,* this tale is told from the perspective of a man in a delusional state. The riddle inherent in the plot exists as a challenge to the readers. This work is not a joke, as has been claimed by a number of critics, for Dr. Wehwald, the deluded narrator, presents the reader with all the clues needed to decipher the puzzle. If the readers first accept the appearance and disappearance of the hero as simply the frame to set the stage for the latter's subjective first-person impressions, then they will be able to see through the contradictions of the tale. A concise masterpiece, "Redegonda's Diary" epitomizes Schnitzler's narrative art with its perfect harmony of form and content. Two other stories of this period, "Die Hirtenflöte" ("The Shepherd's Pipe," 1911) and "Der Mörder" ("The Murderer," 1911), are less noteworthy, despite their reputation. In "The Shepherd's Pipe" we are confronted by a parable extended almost to book length, and, although the crammed adventures of the heroine, Dionysia, rivet the reader, they are accumulated only, and mechanically at that, to contrast with her husband's tolerant but sapless life of contemplation. "The Murderer" is memorable for the ingenuity of its plot, but because it is related from the cold and distant vantage point of the hero, the reader is only superficially involved.

Schnitzler's greatest moment in the theater took place in 1909 with *Der junge Medardus* (Young Medardus, 1910). This is his longest and most ambitious drama, containing five acts and a prologue and painted on a broad historical canvas with a huge cast: sixty-eight individual roles and masses of citizens and soldiers. So monumental is the effort needed to produce this drama that only a few theaters then existing could stage it. Set during the Napoleonic wars, it appeared in time for the hundredth anniversary of the Battle of Aspern. The hero Medardus plans to assassinate Napoleon, whose forces occupy Vienna, in order to gain revenge on the French for the death of his father. Medardus also plans to avenge the suicides of his sister and her lover François, the heir to the French throne, who had taken their lives because the duke of Valois would not permit François to marry a commoner. By seducing Hélène, the duke's daughter, Medardus can disgrace both her and her family. However, the Schnitzlerian hero Medardus cannot control his own nature, and his counterfeit affection for Hélène turns into genuine love. In the denouement Medardus stabs Hélène, thinking that she has cast him aside for Napoleon, although she actually was on her way to assassinate Napoleon. Thus the heroism of the protagonist contains a question mark, as is to be expected in a work by Schnitzler.

Behind the melodramatic plot Schnitzler has fashioned characters and scenes of memorable intensity. He re-creates history by means of a vast panorama full of pageantry that includes every layer of Viennese society. The result was not only a national drama without equal but also a resounding triumph. So sensational was its effect that on opening night at the Burgtheater he received thirty curtain calls. Even the voices on the right were momentarily stilled or came out with friendly reviews.

Another significant success, which brought twenty-four curtain calls for the dramatist on opening night, was the premiere of *Das weite Land* (*Undiscovered Country*, 1911) in 1910.

On the same night this play was performed for the first time in nine cities in Germany and Austria. For many the work was thematically too advanced, and, although fascinated by its theatrical effect, they felt uncomfortable with what they saw. Schnitzler was once again identified with the morality practiced by his major character. Nevertheless, the play has become one of his most frequently performed works since World War II. The undiscovered country of the title is the landscape of the soul, where totally incompatible impulses dwell. The protagonist, Friedrich Hofreiter, in whom one does find something of the author himself, is another egoist. Here we see a withering, overpowering, self-possessed cock of the walk who pursues love affairs diligently. He will not let his age of forty-two stand in his way; he plays the game of seduction as if he were twenty. He even urges a similar attitude on his wife, Genia, but when he learns that she has actually taken a lover, he forces a duel and kills his young rival. He effects this drastic solution not because his honor is at stake, but simply on account of his personal vanity. Ironically he also destroys, without realizing it, something of himself.

This is a classic confrontation between age and youth. Hofreiter is brazen in his hypocritical exploration of the dueling code of honor. So dominating is his personality that he, although an unsympathetic figure, wrests admiration from the audience. From behind the facade of sophisticated dialogue Friedrich Hofreiter projects the contradictions of his complex personality. In this cultured and cultivated protagonist Schnitzler has handed down a powerful aesthetic indictment of the morally flawed wealthy middle class of Austria before World War I. The author labeled this drama a tragicomedy, which, at first glance, does not appear to characterize this work. Despite the third act, which abounds with real humor and takes place in a resort hotel in the Alps—an entirely different setting from the rest of the play—the comic aspects are essentially submerged in the shocking finale. Nevertheless, the brutal destruction of the young Otto von Aigner, the lover of Genia, is undercut as a tragedy by the play's comic ambience and by the stress on the emptiness of this particular class's games. In a curious fashion, then, the designation of the play as a tragicomedy precisely describes the vanity of this antebellum world.

The ultimate success in Austria of Schnitzler's next drama, *Professor Bernhardi*, was delayed for six years until censorship ended with the fall of the monarchy in 1918, but Otto Brahm's production of this work in Berlin in 1912 was enthusiastically received, and the play became an international triumph before it could appear on the stage in Vienna. Although *Professor Bernhardi* is labeled a comedy in five acts and is funny in places, the theme is hardly comical and there are tragically unpleasant overtones throughout. A young girl at the point of certain death is free of pain and believes she will recover. A Catholic nurse summons a priest without the permission of the clinic's leading physician, Professor Bernhardi. The latter, who is a Jew, places a higher value on her dying in peace and contentment than on her being granted final absolution. He refuses to allow the priest to see the patient, but the sister of mercy manages to inform her of her fate, thus hastening her death. When the incident publicly surfaces, it becomes a cause célèbre. Patronage of the clinic dries up, and Professor Bernhardi is suspended, brought to trial, and sentenced to a short term in prison. Politics and anti-Semitism play a decisive role.

Although Professor Bernhardi acts in line with his principles, he has no desire to be a martyr or to stand in the limelight. When he is rehabilitated at the end, he wants only to be left alone and to continue his work. Professor Bernhardi is frequently regarded as a monument to the author's own father, but this dramatic hero stands equally for the uncompromising, if reticent, attitudes of Schnitzler himself. The Austria of the author's time is mirrored with precision in this drama. The thirteen members of the clinic's administrative board represent a racial, religious, and ideological cross section of that society. Schnitzler again examines the conservative, clerical, and anti-Semitic Habsburg social order as it was. Yet no one could call this play a chronicle of decadence, for the fears Schnitzler presents here have been borne out by history and were thus truly prophetic. Even in Austria today, three-quarters of a century after its origin, *Professor Bernhardi* possesses the power to excite passions.

On his fiftieth birthday in 1912, Schnitzler could see his plays being performed on the stages of the three most prestigious theaters in Vienna, rehearsals of five of his works taking place in Berlin, and his dramas being simultaneously presented in twenty other cities in Germany and Austria. The great theatrical triumph of *Professor Bernhardi* in Berlin, however, was overshadowed by the death of Otto Brahm, professionally the best friend Schnitzler ever had.

World War I, which marked the end of an era, also ended Schnitzler's overpowering dominance in the theater, where, by sheer ingenuity and prolificacy, he had virtually silenced his critics. Henceforth he achieved only sporadic and ambivalent success, although his particular brand of individualism stood out uniquely during this time. When hostilities broke out, he was asked to write a patriotic play. He flatly refused. Nothing was further from his mind, nor was he interested in doing this throughout the war. Opportunism reigned and war fever affected almost all minds except Schnitzler's. Even Hofmannsthal lent his voice in praise of the great conflict. Schnitzler kept still. His private thoughts on the war, expressed in "Und einmal wird der Friede wieder kommen" ("Someday Peace Will Return")— included in *Aphorismen und Betrachtungen*— which did not reach print until 1939, could not have been published during the war, so contrary were they to the nationalistic mood. His wife was painfully embarrassed by his absolute refusal to support the war in any way. He would not even practice his calling as a doctor to help the war effort. Creatively he refused to swim with the tide, writing on prewar themes.

In 1915 his *Komödie der Worte* (*Comedies of Words*), three one-act plays, were staged. As the title suggests, words used to communicate can also mislead, both consciously and unconsciously, or can create barriers to understanding. "Stunde des Erkennens" ("Hour of Recognition"), the darkest part of the trilogy, describes a relationship as an exercise in futility when suspicion takes hold of a partner. A man, believing that his wife is unfaithful, becomes so bitter that he harbors resentment for ten years, only to discover that his belief is groundless. Words that were not uttered cause the ultimate harm. In "Grosse Szene" ("The Great Scene"), another play in the trilogy, the actor Herbot is such a consummate performer that he cannot always distinguish between a role and real life. The illusion he creates on the stage carries over into his personal life, but the deception of his own marriage cannot be undone, despite his virtuoso performance for his wife, his paramour, and her fiancé. Schnitzler was extremely proud of this work, considering it among the best one-act plays in world literature.

"Das Bacchusfest" ("The Festival of Bacchus"), also from the *Comedies of Words* trilogy, is attractive for its scintillating dialogue. This time words are used by the poet Felix Staufner to forestall his wife's running off with another man. He wins her back by narrating the plot of his new play, "The Festival of Bacchus," which alludes to their own situation. Here the word in art impinges on that in life. Despite their initial popularity, these one-act works soon earned disparagement and then severe opprobrium. That a drawing-room conversation takes place in the middle of the great slaughter of the war incensed Schnitzler's critics, causing them to doubt the author's loyalty to his country. Still, while Schnitzler seemed to stick his head in the sand, he did so consciously and without illusions. He had never before pursued a course because it was fashionable, and to avoid explicit commentary on the war, he continued to portray that which is timeless in people.

One other dramatic work was staged during the war, *Fink und Fliederbusch* (Fink and Fliederbusch, 1917), his only comedy without a love interest. In its paradoxical dichotomies it approaches Shavian and absurdist drama. A journalist writes reactionary articles for a conservative daily under the name Fink and for a liberal column for a democratic newspaper under the byline Fliederbusch. The debate within himself heats up until he is pressured into fighting a duel with himself. At the end, in typically Schnitzlerian fashion, it is not certain who he is or where he stands. In turning his satire on journalists and their hypocrisy, such as the theater reviewer who writes plays and then ensures their success by reviewing them favorably, Schnitzler once again unleashed a storm, albeit within a restricted circle. His revenge on his detractors in the newspapers was hardly appreciated, and the reviews were mainly negative.

From 1918 until his death Schnitzler's art shifted from dramatic to narrative productions. He wrote only four plays in this period, and in each instance the setting was the past, two being set before World War I and the others in an even earlier period. *Die Schwestern oder Casanova in Spa* (The Sisters or Casanova in the Spa) appeared in 1919. Here Schnitzler again sides with his women figures, three who desire Casanova in his prime; he creates women characters who, like men, are emancipated, not discriminated against by the double standard of morality. This verse comedy raises the question of which woman is deceived when young Casanova unwittingly enjoys passion with another woman than the one expecting to meet with him. Never was Schnitzler more playful than in this unproblematic comedy. Its premiere earned much applause, but a revival in 1923 was its last performance.

The other period piece, also in verse, is *Der Gang zum Weiher* (The Walk to the Pond). It was tentatively completed in 1921, appeared first in book form in 1926, and opened on the Burgtheater's stage in 1931. Many regard it as Schnitzler's greatest dramatic failure. An ambitious five-act drama, it is an obscure and brittle work with too many unpoetic lines of poetry; hardly anyone liked it except its author. As an expression of Schnitzler's own loneliness, waning influence, and advancing age, it seems to drown in pessimism and disillusionment, but it also takes a flinty-eyed look at expedient politics, patriotic phrases, and martial hysteria. Resignation in the face of reality is the key to *Der Gang zum Weiher*. It is no accident that the hero, Sylvester Thorn, is an aging poet who is no match for his young, impetuous rival, Konrad von Ursenbeck. The latter is a firebrand who urges war as the best political solution. Unlike Friedrich Hofreiter and Casanova, who gain respite from the toll of age by fighting back, Sylvester Thorn harbors no illusions, knows that he has lost to youth, and takes his lonely walk to the pond to end his life.

The heroine, Leonilda, is more captivating. When contrasted to Fanny Theren, the fallen woman of *Das Märchen*, Leonilda shows what a long way Schnitzler's leading female figures had come. She is totally unconcerned with the dictates of basic conventions or the possibility of incurring a social penalty for her behavior. In *Der Gang zum Weiher* Schnitzler indirectly speaks for the future emancipated woman despite the play's setting in a Ruritanian land. This drama had a short life on the stage, and many critics wrote off Schnitzler as belonging to the world of the past. However, when it premiered it was discovered that this piece, removed in time, had the power to address the present. It showed that the theater is not restricted to what is topical. In his last theatrical premiere Schnitzler celebrated a personal triumph when he received several curtain calls for *Der Gang zum Weiher*.

Komödie der Verführung (Comedy of Seduction, 1924) is Schnitzler's least fathomable work. There is an ethereal and fabulous quality about it that transcends its fundamental realism and lends it a timeless and modern air. Three women, an aristocrat, a patrician, and a petty bourgeoise, play out their fateful roles after being seduced by Max von Reisenberg. Although Max serves as a catalyst in awakening the true feelings of each woman, he is really superfluous and has no lasting significance as a personality in the lives of these three emancipated women. He is an Anatol whose time has passed. One woman chooses suicide, another opts for unmarried motherhood, and the third goes her own way, bent on pleasure. Schnitzler psychologically treats the sexual quest of each, analyzing their thoughts much as he had previously delved into the motives of his male characters. Once again he places his figures in a setting of impending catastrophe, the eve of World War I, as an intensifier of human emotions. Significantly, the heroine who commits suicide is Countess Aurelie. Premiered in 1924 at the Burgtheater, it was met with a lukewarm response. The new age was too impatient for the mood and nuance of prewar Vienna.

Im Spiel der Sommerlüfte (In the Play of the Summer Breezes, 1930) also conjured up the past world that the author knew so well; again Schnitzler travels back to the time before World War I. Presenting flirtations in the summer breezes, the play is his most innocuous work. The characters pleasantly divert the audience as they play games that have no lasting consequences. Critics who took issue with this play as merely reflecting a long-dead world forgot that, as in a work by Anton Chekhov, atmosphere and characterization can make effective theater. When it was first performed in 1931 at the Volkstheater, Schnitzler was called before the curtain by sustained cheers of approval. Many a theatergoer undoubtedly realized that this work would probably be his last.

While his power to command on the stage was waning, Schnitzler refined his narrative technique and composed truly readable and imaginative masterpieces of fiction. These late prose works are detailed studies of an individual's deepest concerns and his struggles to assert himself fully with dignity within the limits of his personality. Carefully wrought, they captivate the reader as they reach a rare pinnacle of psychological awareness. In merit, with their superb blending of content and form, they match any of his earlier works. Beginning with *Doktor Gräsler, Badearzt* (*Dr. Graesler, Resort Physician*) in 1917, they are full-scale character studies. This work delves into the mentality of a middle-aged bachelor who, as he practices medicine, also practices casuistry with his emotions. Both haunted and crippled by his sister's suicide, Dr. Graesler is a man of limited volition at best, who procrastinates so interminably in his courtship of Sabine that she finally rejects him. After reading his sister's love letters, which reveal her promiscuity, after experiencing a superstitious dream, and after cathartically shedding tears, he is prepared to accept life on more equal terms and is ready to drift into marriage with his housekeeper. The long road to the altar for Emil Graesler is paved with shocks of recognition. However, ultimately he marries another caretaker of his house, who thus replaces the sister of his bachelor life. This work has been viewed as a product of Schnitzler's own acute sense of having grown old, but it is a tale less about aging than about a man battling to resolve his inner conflict.

Another man in a mid-life crisis who tries to reconcile his life is the hero of *Casanovas Heimfahrt* (*Casanova's Homecoming*, 1918). In Casanova we have the complete antipode of Dr. Graesler, one who is willing to go to any lengths to uphold his legendary reputation as a lover of women. Casanova makes love to Marcolina by stealth, taking the place of the young man she is expecting in her dark room, but his victory is Pyrrhic: he is repelled by her at dawn. Then, after dispatching his rival in a duel by sword, he must flee, one step ahead of the law, to a precarious life in his native

Venice, where he is politically persona non grata. Nevertheless, he remains undaunted, vigorously taking his chances in the ever-changing vicissitudes of life. What arrests our attention so completely in this work is the fullness of life that it displays. Casanova's colossal selfishness is set off against his open generosity; he views love as a taking, but also as a gift on his part. In this dramatized episode of his life we are presented with a synoptic view of the entire past of a man who loved and lived both instinctually and intellectually and who was constantly defiant in the face of adversity. The ultimate portrait of this hero resembles a mysterious kaleidoscope that reflects diversified forms of life and vibrantly sets forth the contradictions of the human personality.

Although it was a great critical success, *Casanova's Homecoming* offended many people, even causing an uproar over its immorality and a trial in the United States, with the author as the defendant in absentia. But Schnitzler neither condemns nor condones his hero in this story; he does not take sides. If we come to admire Casanova at the end, it is because he genuinely stands up to life without regret or a trace of self-pity.

In his next story, *Fräulein Else* (1924), Schnitzler takes up the stream-of-consciousness technique he had employed in *None But the Brave,* only this time more penetratingly in that he reaches into the mental infrastructure of his protagonist, thus allowing unconscious material to mingle with the flow of rational thought. Fräulein Else is the nineteen-year-old daughter of a Jewish lawyer in Vienna who, at a vacation resort in the Alps, receives an urgent telegram from her mother to try to save her father from being imprisoned for embezzlement. She is to ask his business friend, the art dealer von Dorsday, also vacationing there, for the money needed to rescue her father. Von Dorsday is willing to advance the money, but only if she will agree to appear before him in the nude. The extortionate demands of her mother and von Dorsday exert powerful psy-

chic pressures that the defenseless, immature girl cannot withstand and that trigger an open expression of her inner conflict. She does not go to von Dorsday's room; instead, she reveals herself naked to the startled hotel guests gathered in the salon. Later, after fainting and being taken to her room, she ends her life by taking poison.

Indirectly, but unknown to Else herself, her interior monologue establishes her strong erotic attachment to her own father. Her confused sexual longings force her to turn a shameful, degrading request she cannot avoid into something infinitely worse, but because of unconscious pressure the choice is not hers to make. Baring herself to a crowd of people instead of only to von Dorsday is her way of cushioning the shock of the inevitable act. Von Dorsday is too close in age to her father, so too personal a confrontation with this father-substitute would have threatened to unleash intolerable psychic forces. She subconsciously takes a way out that is less painful, but that is more damaging from a social viewpoint. Von Dorsday's strange demand elicits an equally perverse exhibitionistic response in Else, but the unlikely coincidence of two opposing desires dovetailing so neatly is overshadowed by the masterful flow of the story. This work was rightly a great success; it was praised by the critics and sold well in the bookstores.

Traumnovelle (Rhapsody), a story of 1925, is as complex as *Casanova's Homecoming* in its minute depiction of psychic processes. The various translations of this title, *Fridolin and Albertine, Pierrette,* and sometimes simply *Rhapsody,* miss the mark, for it was surely the intention of the German *Traumnovelle* (Dream Novella) to focus on the wavering line separating reality from a dreamlike apprehension of life. Schnitzler contrasts the erotic dream of Albertine with the mysterious experiences of her husband, Fridolin. Bent on fulfillment, with the help of a disreputable friend Fridolin risks attending a meeting of a secret society where masked women dance naked with the men and interlopers are killed. He escapes the place with his life only because one woman he meets there sacrifices herself for him. Determined to track her down, he becomes convinced that a woman reported dead is the same one who saved him, but his efforts do not produce the certainty he seeks. Eventually in his associations he confuses this enigmatic woman with the personality of his own wife. The crisis in their marriage is resolved when they confess their experiences to one another: Fridolin's dreamlike adventure in reality and Albertine's vivid lifelike dream in which her husband is sacrificed. They become acutely conscious of the relationship between love and death and become aware that not all yearnings, including the temptation to adultery, can be stilled. Fridolin's actual adventures assume the highest priority in the plot of the story and, laced with subjective perception, take on the elements of an intricate dream. The German title of this work refers as much to these mysterious events as it does to the actual dream of his wife. The fusion of unconscious longings with a descent into the underworld produces an exciting and compelling story. *Rhapsody* was acknowledged as a masterpiece by both critics and readers.

Daybreak, which appeared the following year, is a fast-paced tale about gambling that in effect condenses a whole lifetime into a span of a few hours. Lieutenant Willi Kasda sits down at the gaming table to raise enough money to rescue his former comrade Bogner from financial ruin, but he only incurs his own heavy burden of debt. Desperate in the face of permanent disgrace, he goes in vain to his uncle Robert and then to Robert's former wife Leopoldine, once a lowly flower seller but now a rich woman by dint of her business enterprise. Willi had once spent a night with her and then had forgotten her, not realizing that her affection for him was genuine. She promises to send him news in the evening, but instead she comes herself to spend the night in his room. At dawn she goes away, leaving behind a fraction of the sum he needs, only enough to rescue Bogner; in so doing she

seeks revenge for the money he paid her for love many years ago. Seeing no way out, Willi shoots himself. Too late, Willi's uncle arrives with the money Leopoldine has advanced to save him. The title, literally translated as "Play at the Break of Day," is regarded as referring to the feverish gambling until dawn, but it could equally allude to the game of love between Willi and Leopoldine. The story has, in effect, a disguised incest theme, with the uncle's former wife representing the tabooed object of affection. At the end Robert's suspicions about the relationship are awakened but then dispersed by the hero's orderly. Be that as it may, the hero's tribulations are memorably recorded and fascinate the reader.

Therese: Chronik eines Frauenlebens (Theresa: The Chronicle of a Woman's Life), a novel that appeared in 1928, is a chronicle of a woman's Gethsemane, beginning in her sixteenth year. Theresa courageously fights her way through life unaided, gradually but inexorably losing ground in the struggle, until she meets a tragic and violent end. She is killed by her own illegitimate son, the antisocial Franz, who had grown up on a farm in the care of primitive-thinking foster parents. In this, his most naturalistic work, Schnitzler objectively anatomizes the career of a person who is defeated both by her own emotional commitments and by the chance forces of society. Her life exemplifies the haphazard drift that normally characterizes an individual's quest for inner fulfillment. She is exploited many times over by the men in her life and by the various families she works for as a governess. Entirely worn down at one point, she entertains for a brief moment the idea of becoming a prostitute. The novel has consequently been praised for its social message, but the social aspect of this work is of less significance than the delineation of the heroine's struggle to solve fundamental problems of her personal life. Schnitzler demonstrates that Therese, like all of us, does not automatically gain self-protective insight in a human relationship and thus cannot always make judicious decisions when her own interests are at stake. The last in a gallery of Schnitzler's sympathetic women figures, Theresa is portrayed with compassion and objectivity. Although it was not the intention of the author to target the social exploitation of women, he still produced in *Theresa* a work that could serve as a model for the feminist literature of recent times.

For sheer brilliance it would be difficult to match Schnitzler's final work, *Flucht in die Finsternis* (*Flight into Darkness*, 1931), in which he carefully surveys the inner landscape of a man suffering from paranoia. Robert is obsessed with his fear that he may become insane and demands that his brother Otto, a doctor, kill him painlessly should madness take hold of him. As time goes by, Robert is tormented by a greater anxiety: he becomes more and more convinced that Otto, without foundation, considers him to be mad and plans to do away with him. The more strenuous his efforts to forestall the realization of his fears, the greater the rift with reality becomes, until his unchecked persecution complex leads him to strike back fatally at his brother. Schnitzler weaves a luxuriant tapestry of motives and influences in his depiction of Robert's developing psychosis. He shows Robert lucidly interpreting the people and events that affect his life except at crucial moments when he places an unusual stress on a harmless occurrence or remark. In a manner worthy of a psychiatrist, Schnitzler presents many levels of reality. It is immensely ironic that Schnitzler's last work should bear this title, for in a few short years after its appearance there occurred in the world he knew so well a deliberate flight away from reason and light.

The postwar period in Schnitzler's life, except for a few good moments, was marked by personal loss and tragedy. He never really felt at home in the new Austria; he ceased to address it in his plays and instead turned increasingly to the past. He did not understand many of the new attitudes and had only contempt for the current trends in politics, especially Marxism. Nor could he reconcile himself to the then-popular literary fashion of expressionism. The dissolution of his marriage changed his life for the worse, and in a sense he never recovered from it. As early as 1913 Olga Schnitzler had tried to pursue a separate career as a concert singer; the break became certain in 1918 and legally final in 1921. Henceforth, deep abiding loneliness characterized his personal life, despite the number of liaisons he entered into. An even greater trauma was the suicide of his eighteen-year-old daughter Lili in Venice in 1928. She had shown signs of instability several years previously and had been married only slightly more than a year to a young Italian army officer, an unswerving follower of Benito Mussolini, when she took her life after a domestic quarrel. Schnitzler had doted on her excessively. His grief was correspondingly intense, and he aged rapidly thereafter. He lived to witness the divorce of his other child, Heinrich, but not to see Heinrich's happy second marriage or to enjoy the role of grandfather to Heinrich's children. (Heinrich Schnitzler had debuted as an actor at age eighteen, and later became a director of a theater and of his father's plays, a professor of German literature in the United States, and finally executor of the family estate.) Other shocks to Schnitzler were the passing away of many old friends and acquaintances, including Hofmannsthal and Georg Brandes.

Another tribulation was the uproar surrounding the staging of *Hands Around* in 1920. Although the controversy contributed to his worldwide renown and helped him financially, as did increasing sales of his prose fiction, through the rough economic period of the 1920's, the outcry was both sensational and painful. The play was roundly condemned as pornographic by many critics and injected new life into the stereotype of Schnitzler as an immoral writer. It led to the arrest and eventual trial of the entire original Berlin cast. In Leipzig theatergoers had to sign a statement that they were there of their own free will.

Organized demonstrations interrupted performances in Munich and Vienna. In Vienna it became a matter of daily controversy in the press, a bookstore displaying the work was smashed, and physical violence almost broke out in Parliament. Later, stink bombs were thrown, seats demolished, and members of the audience assaulted. In retrospect, the hue and cry appears ludicrous although more widespread than all the earlier scandals attached to Schnitzler. When revived in 1922, *Hands Around* caused scarcely a ripple in opposition circles. Even so, Schnitzler was thoroughly weary of the whole affair and, despairing of its being interpreted correctly, withdrew the play, which remained out of circulation until 1982, when Henrich Schnitzler resurrected it.

The growing radicalization of society and the systematic defamation of his person helped to make him feel that he had been consigned to history, especially since reactionary critics claimed that his art was passé. He was also disconsolately aware that many of his works would not be fully appreciated during his lifetime. When he died of a cerebral hemorrhage on 21 October 1931, he was spared the sight of the triumph of his enemies and of the literary and cultural interregnum to follow.

Schnitzler's contributions to literature are impressive. He was an incomparable innovator in literary technique and psychological exploration, intuitively arriving at some concepts that Freud acknowledged he discovered only through clinical research. He was among the first in literature to deal with mental illness and pathological attitudes from a modern clinical point of view. He was also a pioneering author who broke new ground in capturing the feminist point of view, offering for the first time in Austria a revealing look at the subservient role of women. At a time when a woman was often considered merely a doll, he portrayed female figures who were fully animated by their instincts and heroic in confronting adversity. He thereby anticipated liberating attitudes that occurred many years in the future. His sense of society was unmatched, like a daguerreotype, accurately capturing its image without illusion. As early as his first drama he was simultaneously the chronicler of his time and ahead of it. His themes, more protean than has been acknowledged, center on love and death, specifically on the interior chemistry of a relationship and on the shattering and healing effect of death. They possess a universal quality that transcends the time of their expression. His interest in death was not morbid fascination, but a means to express a psychological universality. In his view, man's fate lies within. Schnitzler's introspection, illuminating to this day, should consequently be compared to the almost unbearably dogmatic naturalism of German literature and to the naive morality of later socialist writers.

As a writer of comedy, Schnitzler has no peer in German literature. Comedy is certainly not the genre made famous by German playwrights. The literature of France, England, and Italy is well stocked with comedies, but there existed only a handful in all German literature up to Schnitzler's time; before he appeared, not one German dramatist had produced more than two comic works of real merit for the stage. Some of Schnitzler's comedies are the only examples in the first half of this century that can still play today as vital and intellectual theater experiences. A master of situation and dialogue, he is the only successful creator of the comedy of manners in all of German literature.

Hofmannsthal understood the true stature of Schnitzler the dramatist:

> Schnitzler's dramas are consummate works for the theater, designed to captivate, to engross, to entertain, and in an ingenious manner to surprise; they are fully satisfying to the spectator in performance, and yet capable subsequently of continuing to preoccupy one's feelings and thoughts; their plot and dialogue mutually reinforce each other; the characters are brilliantly conceived; each lives his own life but nevertheless serves only the totality. When one sees these plays performed, one has the feeling that their

creator is at home on the stage and has no other ambition than to produce effective theater.

(*Gesammelte Werke in Einzelausgaben, Prosa IV* [Frankfurt, 1955], p. 99)

Another writer who made the taboo subject of sexuality the focal point of his works was D. H. Lawrence. Unlike Lawrence, Schnitzler focused not on sex itself but on the intimate relations of his characters and thus unmasked their attitudes, prejudices and fears. Lawrence, identified with free love, immorality, and permissiveness, was also famous for using "four-letter words." Not so Schnitzler; he was surprisingly discreet and never wrote salaciously. His understanding was based on intuition, not on theory, and there was no hint of repressed sexuality on his part. Nor was there a self-conscious tone, nor an angry sense of wanting to prove something, nor a measure of scorn and rejection of his society. Schnitzler daringly but temperately presented the fundamental problem of his society: how to express one's need for love without resorting to hypocrisy or risking social ostracism. Although he was remarkably free of a moralizing polemical tone, the reaction by the guardians of morality was an automatic response of condemnation. He was paradoxically the most vigorous force and the greatest influence in the theater of his age, and at the same time the most unwanted and the most deprecated.

Why did Schnitzler's star, which had blazed so brightly in the ascendant, sink so quickly after his death? The most persistent explanation given for his fall from favor is that the society he had described so personally had been eclipsed as well. Many critics have maintained ex cathedra, and also in passing, that Vienna at the turn of the century was decadent, and they have stereotypically applied the label "fin de siècle" to the author's work. To do justice to Schnitzler, it is necessary to put to rest a cliché that has maligned him. To a great extent the designation of decadence has resulted from confusing literature with politics. That Habsburg Austria was politically underdeveloped does not imply that its literature reflected its reactionary climate. In a sense imperial Austria was, as an ancien régime, a dying culture, but Schnitzler's continual row with the censors and prevailing attitudes hardly shows that he accepted it uncritically. That his works exasperated so many is the best evidence that his position was poles apart from a world described as decadent.

Another untenable restriction implicit in the term "end of an age" is that the intellectual hub alone was in a state of decay. It is certainly odd to claim that only the capital, Vienna, from which new cultural forces radiated, and not the empire itself or the republic that followed, was dying. World War I is invoked as the line of demarcation for the transparent reason that it meant the end of the monarchy, but this fin de siècle label that is attached to Franz Josef's Austria is essentially a retrospective convenience to assist historians, literary and otherwise, to organize the past. World War I removed Austria from European supremacy, abolishing the monarchy and reducing a great heterogeneous European power to a country one-third its former size. Before the war there was imperial Austria, but afterward only a balkanized state. If personal aspirations had been altered by the great upheaval, they had to be manifested as a diminution, not as an increase, of vigor and élan. However, the citizens of antebellum Austria could not have foreseen the consequences of World War I and behaved, as does every person within his time, with ambitions unchecked and the search for meaning of life undiminished. This so-called period of decadence served as the brightest beacon of German culture, representing in effect a flowering of life and letters. How strange to consider that era decadent and, by associative extension, inferior, when the period that followed in the 1930's was barbaric and provincial.

The case for Schnitzler's decadence rests in the main on *Anatol, Hands Around,* and *Light-o-Love,* three early plays that clung to his name then and still do tenaciously today. But works of greater merit and maturity followed, and he still made his mark in postwar literature, especially in fiction. In his often-cited letter to Jakob Wasserman of 3 November 1924 Schnitzler responded articulately to the label "passé" that critics had pinned on him. He claimed that nothing had changed in his society except that there were fewer inhibitions on the expression of villainy and dishonesty: the types he had often portrayed were still in existence.

It was not decadence at all, but virulent and lingering anti-Semitism, that was the root cause of Schnitzler's relegation to near oblivion after his death. The voice of reason was drowned by the rising tide of reaction and racial hatred in Austria even before the National Socialists and the Anschluss. In the anti-Semitic press, which apodictically promulgated a new unsentimental ideology, Schnitzler was contemptuously dismissed as the representative of refined Jewish decadence. He was singled out more than any other writer because he had been most prominent and had antagonized the most people. Almost alone in his time, he dared to treat openly the anti-Semitism rife in his society. Because no criticism was tolerated, he became in effect a nonperson in the society in which he had lived. Since he had not been a fighter for social progress, but had pursued his lonely calling undeterred by the ferment in society, his name was not revived by the West during the struggle against Fascism, and after World War II he was still given short shrift by critics in Germany and Austria. As late as 1968 he was perfunctorily dismissed in a study of world drama as a clever but superficial writer of comedy. More often than not his neglect in the critical world is characterized by simple omission or an extremely brief description in passing that treats him as a literary curiosity.

Certainly Schnitzler's name was not and will not be championed in East Germany and Marxist societies in which the utopian ideology of class struggle refuses to admit that there are human problems besides exploitation by the economic ruling class. Marxist dogma will continue to persist in categorically rejecting unconscious motivation as a viable force in human behavior. Schnitzler was naturally skeptical of social reformers, considering the more utopian the more suspect, and his open contempt for political leftists after World War I further discouraged his acceptance by socialists.

For a long time Schnitzler remained a literary polestar for only a select few who could think beyond the cultural moment. Recently, however, the term "Schnitzler renaissance" has been employed in diverse critical remarks about the author, beginning with the hundredth anniversary of his birth. By the 1970's revivals of his plays and increased activity in secondary literature amounted to a rediscovery and a realization that his literary range of themes and interests went far beyond the clichés of "the sweet young thing," preoccupation with sex, and fin de siècle fatalism. Nevertheless, this new appreciation has yet to reach a large number of his works; his rehabilitation has therefore a long way to go. Schnitzler will continue to fascinate, but the course and extent of his renaissance, given the nature of his art and the widespread prejudices of society, are difficult to predict.

Selected Bibliography

EDITIONS

INDIVIDUAL WORKS

NOVELS AND STORIES

"Er wartet auf den vazierenden Gott." Vienna, 1886.
"Der Andere." Vienna, 1889.
"Die drei Elixire." Munich, 1894.
Sterben. Berlin, 1894.
"Der Witwer." Vienna, 1894.
"Um eine Stunde." Vienna, 1899.
Leutnant Gustl. Vienna, 1900.
"Der blinde Geronimo und sein Bruder." Vienna, 1900.

ARTHUR SCHNITZLER

Frau Berta Garlan. Berlin, 1901.
"Die Fremde." Vienna, 1902.
Der Weg ins Freie. Berlin, 1908.
"Der Tod des Junggesellen." Vienna, 1908.
"Das Tagebuch der Redegonda." Munich and Leipzig, 1911.
"Der Mörder." Vienna, 1911.
"Die Hirtenflöte." Berlin, 1911.
Frau Beate und ihr Sohn. Berlin, 1913.
Doktor Gräsler, Badearzt. Berlin, 1917.
Casanovas Heimfahrt. Berlin, 1918.
Fräulein Else. Berlin, 1924.
Traumnovelle. Berlin, 1925–1926.
Spiel im Morgengrauen. Berlin, 1926–1927.
Therese: Chronik eines Frauenlebens. Berlin, 1928.
Flucht in die Finsternis. Berlin, 1931.

PLAYS

"Alkandis Lied." Vienna, 1890.
Anatol. Berlin, 1893.
Das Märchen. Dresden and Leipzig, 1894.
Liebelei. Berlin, 1896.
Freiwild. Berlin, 1898.
Das Vermächtnis. Berlin, 1899.
"Paracelsus." Berlin, 1898.
"Die Gefährtin." Berlin, 1899.
"Der grüne Kakadu." Berlin, 1899.
Reigen. Vienna and Leipzig, 1900.
Der Schleier der Beatrice. Berlin, 1901.
Lebendige Stunden. Berlin, 1901–1902. Includes "Lebendige Stunden," "Die Frau mit dem Dolche," "Die letzten Masken," and "Literatur."
Marionetten. Berlin, 1903–1905. Includes "Der Puppenspieler," "Der tapfere Cassian," and "Zum grossen Wurstel."
Der einsame Weg. Berlin, 1904.
Der Ruf des Lebens. Berlin, 1906.
Zwischenspiel. Berlin, 1906.
Komtesse Mizzi oder der Familientag. Vienna, 1908.
Der junge Medardus. Berlin, 1910.
"Der Schleier der Pierrette." Leipzig, 1910.
Das weite Land. Berlin, 1911.
Professor Bernhardi. Berlin, 1912.
Komödie der Worte. Berlin, 1915. Includes "Stunde des Erkennens," "Grosse Szene," and "Das Bacchusfest."
Fink und Fliederbusch. Berlin, 1917.
Die Schwestern oder Casanova in Spa. Berlin, 1919.
Der Gang zum Weiher. Berlin, 1926.
Komödie der Verführung. Berlin, 1924.
Im Spiel der Sommerlüfte. Berlin, 1930.

SHORT STORY COLLECTIONS

Die Frau des Weisen. Berlin, 1898.
Die griechische Tänzerin. Vienna and Leipzig, 1905.
Dämmerseelen. Berlin, 1907.
Masken und Wunder. Berlin, 1912.
Die griechische Tänzerin, und andere Novellen. Berlin, 1914.
Die dreifache Warnung. Leipzig, 1924.
Traum und Schicksal. Berlin, 1931.
Die kleine Komödie. Berlin, 1932.
Ausgewählte Erzählungen. Frankfurt, 1950.

DRAFTS, PROJECTS, AND FRAGMENTS

Das Wort: Tragikomödie in fünf Akten. Fragment. Edited by Kurt Begel. Frankfurt, 1966.
Aphorismen und Betrachtungen. Edited by Robert O. Weiss. Frankfurt, 1967.
Roman-Fragment. Edited by Reinhard Urbach. *Literatur und Kritik* 13:135–183 (1967).
Frühe Gedichte. Edited by Herbert Lederer. Berlin, 1969.
Zug der Schatten: Drama in neun Bildern. Unfinished. Edited by Françoise Derré. Frankfurt, 1970.
Ritterlichkeit: Fragment aus dem Nachlass. Edited by Rena R. Schlein. Bonn, 1975.
Entworfenes und Verworfenes. Edited by Reinhard Urbach. Frankfurt, 1977.
Jugend in Wien: Eine Autobiographie. Edited by Therese Nickl and Heinrich Schnitzler. Vienna, Munich, and Zurich, 1981.

COLLECTED WORKS

Gesammelte Werke in zwei Abteilungen: Die erzählenden Schriften. 3 vols. Berlin, 1912. *Die Theaterstücke.* 4 vols. Berlin, 1912.
Gesammelte Werke in zwei Abteilungen: Die erzählenden Schriften. 4 vols. Berlin, 1922. *Die Theaterstücke.* 5 vols. Berlin, 1922.
Gesammelte Schriften. 2 vols. Berlin, 1928.

MODERN EDITIONS

COLLECTED WORKS

Gesammelte Werke: Die erzählenden Schriften. 2 vols. Frankfurt, 1961.
Gesammelte Werke: Die dramatischen Werke. 2 vols. Frankfurt, 1962.

CORRESPONDENCE

"Arthur Schnitzler an Marie Reinhard (1896)." Edited by Therese Nickl. *Modern Austrian Literature* 10:23–68 (1977).

ARTHUR SCHNITZLER

Der Briefwechsel Arthur Schnitzler—Otto Brahm. Edited by Oskar Seidlin. Tübingen, 1975.

Hugo von Hofmannsthal—Arthur Schnitzler: Briefwechsel. Edited by Therese Nickl and Heinrich Schnitzler. Frankfurt, 1964.

"Vier unveröffentlichte Briefe Arthur Schnitzlers an den Psychoanalytiker Theodor Reik." Edited by Bernd Urgan. *Modern Austrian Literature* 19: 236–247 (1975).

TRANSLATIONS

Anatol. Translated by Grace Isabel Colbron. In *Sixteen Famous European Plays.* New York, 1943.

Beatrice. Translated by Agnes Jacques. New York, 1926.

Bertha Garlan. Translated by Agnes Jacques. New York, 1918.

"Blind Geronimo and His Brother." Translated by Eric Sutton. In *Little Novels.* New York, 1929.

Casanova's Homecoming. Translated by Eden and Cedar Paul. New York, 1948.

Comedies of Words. Translated by Pierre Loving. Cincinnati, 1917. Includes "Hour of Recognition," "The Great Scene," and "The Festival of Bacchus."

Countess Mizzie, or The Family Reunion. Translated by Edwin Björkman. New York, 1946.

Daybreak. Translated by William A. Drake. New York, 1927.

"The Death of a Bachelor." Translated by Eric Sutton. In *Little Novels.* New York, 1929.

Doktor Graesler. Translated by E. C. Slade. In *Vienna 1900: Games with Love and Death.* New York, 1974.

Dying. Translated by Frederick Eisemann. In *The Little Comedy and Other Stories.* New York, 1977.

Flight into Darkness. Translated by William A. Drake. New York, 1931.

Fräulein Else. Translated by Robert A. Simon. In *Viennese Novelettes.* New York, 1974.

Free Game. Translated by Paul H. Grumann. Boston, 1913.

"Gallant Cassian." Translated by Moritz A. Jagendorf. *Poet Lore* 33:507–520 (1922).

"The Green Cockatoo." Translated by Horace Samuel. In *The Green Cockatoo.* London, 1913.

Hands Around. Translated by Keene Wallis. New York, 1929.

"His Helpmate." Translated by Pierre Loving. In *Comedies of Words.* Cincinnati, 1917.

Intermezzo. Translated by Edwin Björkman. Boston, 1913.

The Legacy. Translated by Mary L. Stephenson. Boston, 1911.

Light-o-love. Translated by Bayard Quincy Morgan. Chicago, 1912.

"Literature." Translated by Pierre Loving. In *Comedies of Words.* Cincinnati, 1917.

Living Hours. Translated by Helen Tracy Porter. *Poet Lore* 17:36–45 (1906).

The Lonely Way. Translated by Edwin Björkman. Boston, 1904.

"The Murderer." Translated by Eric Sutton. In *Little Novels.* New York, 1929.

None But the Brave. Translated by Richard L. Simon. In *Viennese Novelettes.* New York, 1974.

"Paracelsus." Translated by Horace Samuel. In *The Green Cockatoo.* London, 1913.

Professor Bernhardi. Translated by Louis Borell and Ronald Adams. London, 1936.

"Redegonda's Diary." Translated by Eric Sutton. In *Little Novels.* New York, 1929.

Rhapsody: A Dream Novel. Translated by Otto P. Schinnerer. New York, 1927.

The Road to the Open. Translated by Horace Samuel. New York, 1923.

"The Shepherd's Pipe." Translated by O. F. Theis. In *The Shepherd's Pipe and Other Stories.* New York, 1922.

Someday Peace Will Return: Notes on War and Peace. Translated by Robert O. Weiss. New York, 1972.

"The Stranger." Translated by Eric Sutton. In *Little Novels.* New York, 1929.

Theresa: The Chronicle of a Woman's Life. Translated by William A. Drake. New York, 1928.

Undiscovered Country. Translated by Tom Stoppard. London and Boston, 1980.

BIOGRAPHICAL AND CRITICAL STUDIES

Cook, William K. "Arthur Schnitzler's 'Der blinde Geronimo und sein Bruder': A Critical Discussion." *Modern Austrian Literature* 5:120–137 (1973).

Derré, Françoise. *L'Oeuvre d'Arthur Schnitzler; Imagerie viennoise et problèmes humains.* Paris, 1966.

Garland, H. B. "Arthur Schnitzler." *German Men of Letters* 48:57–75 (1964).

Lindken, Hans-Ulrich. *Interpretationen zu Arthur Schnitzler*. Munich, 1970.

Liptzin, Sol. *Arthur Schnitzler*. New York, 1932.

Reichert, Herbert W., and Herman Salinger, eds. *Studies in Arthur Schnitzler: Centennial Commemorative Volume*. University of North Carolina Studies in Germanic Languages and Literature, no. 42. Chapel Hill, N.C., 1963.

Rey, William H. *Arthur Schnitzler: Die späte Prosa als Gipfel seines Schaffens*. Berlin, 1968.

Schinnerer, Otto P. "The Early Works of Arthur Schnitzler." *Germanic Review* 4:153–197 (1929).

Schnitzler, Heinrich, Christian Brandstätter, and Reinhard Urbach. *Arthur Schnitzler: Sein Leben, Sein Werk, Seine Zeit*. Frankfurt, 1981.

Schorske, Carl E. "Politics and the Psyche in *Fin de Siècle* Vienna: Schnitzler and Hofmannsthal." *American History Review* 66:930–946 (1961).

Swales, Martin. *Arthur Schnitzler: A Critical Study*. Oxford, 1971.

Wagner, Renate. *Arthur Schnitzler: Eine Biographie*. Vienna, Munich, Zurich, and New York, 1981.

BIBLIOGRAPHIES

Allen, Richard H. *An Annotated Arthur Schnitzler Bibliography: Editions and Criticism in German, French, and English, 1879–1965*. University of North Carolina Studies in Germanic Languages and Literature, no. 56. Chapel Hill, N.C., 1966.

Berlin, Jeffrey B. *An Annotated Arthur Schnitzler Bibliography, 1965–1977*. Munich, 1978. Includes an essay entitled "The Meaning of the Schnitzler Renaissance."

JAMES R. McWILLIAMS

MAURICE MAETERLINCK
(1862–1949)

MAURICE MAETERLINCK WAS a man of paradoxes. Tall, heavyset, and robust, the picture of assurance and strength, he was shy, reserved, and sensitive, ill at ease with people and incommunicative. He carried in him a heritage of both Flemish mysticism and Flemish sensuality, yet he was a Fleming who spoke and wrote in French. He chose to live more than fifty of his eighty-six years in France, yet never renounced his Belgian citizenship. A writer whose poems and lyrical prose have inspired literally dozens of composers, Maeterlinck himself neither understood nor liked music. An agnostic who lost his faith before he was twenty, he spent most of his life in search of God. Winner of the Nobel Prize for Literature by the age of forty-nine and a figure of international stature, Maeterlinck had slipped into such obscurity by the time of his death that the Belgian man of letters Valère Gille could observe, "Belgium is in mourning—and doesn't know it."

Maurice-Polydore-Marie-Bernard Maeterlinck was born in Ghent on 29 August 1862, the first child of Polydore-Jacques-Marie-Bernard Maeterlinck and his wife, Mathilde-Colette-Françoise Van den Bossche. Both parents were of old Flemish stock, wealthy, conservative, Catholic, and French-speaking. Mathilde Maeterlinck's father was a lawyer; Polydore, although trained as a notary, did not practice. He lived on the income from land and investments and devoted his time and energies to a variety

of interests, including horticulture and the raising of bees. The family was eventually completed by a daughter, Marie, and two more sons, Ernest and Oscar.

Maeterlinck remembered his father as an essentially fair and kind man who masked his timidity—and reacted to his overly strict upbringing—by being authoritarian to the point of tyranny within his own family. The death of Oscar at twenty-one brought about a brief emotional rapprochement between Maeterlinck and his father, but the two men never enjoyed a close relationship, and the son's literary pursuits remained totally incomprehensible to his father. Mme Maeterlinck, more overtly loving and indulgent, on several occasions helped Maurice with money to pay the costs of printing his early works, but she too found his literary aspirations beyond her. For them, as for most of the affluent bourgeois of nineteenth-century Ghent, the joys of the table and conventional pleasures and comforts were far more attractive than intellectual and aesthetic satisfactions. Although they did not share their son's love of literature, all his life he shared their love of good food and wine.

Maeterlinck's childhood and youth were spent in and near Ghent. He was born in a house on Peperstraat (rue du Poivre) in the old city, not far from the Cathedral of St. Bavon. When he was three, his father had built on the boulevard Frère-Orban a large, imposing house that remained the family home, though, for the most part, only in winter. From May to September each year the family lived in a country home near Oostacker, a village a few miles north of the city on the east bank of the canal linking Ghent to Terneuzen, Holland. The grounds of the summer home extended to the canal, on which the adventurous young Maurice had more than one brush with disaster. An impressive supply of gymnastic equipment kept the children active and encouraged the enjoyment of vigorous physical exercise that characterized Maeterlinck most of his life. It was at Oostacker also that Polydore Maeterlinck conducted his experiments in hybridization of fruit trees and flowers, raised his bees, and engaged in woodworking. The mysteries of hothouse and hive fascinated the children, as did the sight of boats on the canal, moving behind hedges and trees as though in the garden itself. The flat, marshy meadows stretched north and west to the misty horizon, beyond which lay other mysteries, other unknowns: the estuary of the Scheldt, the island of Walcheren, and the sea.

To judge by *Bulles bleues* (Blue Bubbles, 1938), the memoirs written by Maeterlinck in America during World War II and published a year before his death, most of his memories of the summers at Oostacker were happy ones. His memories of grandparents, aunts, uncles, and cousins show, not surprisingly, a mixture of feelings that range from affection to dislike. Recollections of his school days, however, are generally somber.

Maeterlinck's formal education began when he was six, at a convent school in Ghent that accepted boys as pupils up to the age of seven. His training there was largely religious, with a bit of arithmetic. Among the prints of religious paintings that decorated the classroom walls was one of Pieter Brueghel the Elder's *Massacre of the Innocents,* a picture that impressed itself vividly on his memory and inspired his first short story. After the convent school Maeterlinck entered the Institut Central, a private school where he stayed five years. In *Bulles bleues* he claims to remember only one thing from that time: a rule of style given by a composition teacher, never to repeat a word on the same page. His father eventually became dissatisfied with the quality of education at the Institut Central and, when Maeterlinck was twelve, enrolled him as a day boarder at the Jesuit Collège Sainte-Barbe, also in Ghent.

Although in retrospect Maeterlinck saw the Jesuit fathers who taught him there as intellectually solid, patient, devoted, and selfless, he recalled those in charge of the boys outside the classroom as "insufferable, limited, and vexatious." In *Bulles bleues* he remarks:

> Without bearing any ill will toward the good Fathers, I must acknowledge that I endured among them the most unpleasant moments of my life. They had a strange liking for dirt and ugliness that could only upset a little boy as clean as I was, and one as fond of good lines and beautiful colors, of flowers and tall trees.
>
> (p. 84)

With even stronger feeling he recalls his distress at the priests' obsessive preoccupation with carnal sin and divine retribution—the only subject, seemingly, of the sermons that the boys heard—and at the atmosphere of mutual suspicion and tale-bearing that a few of the priests encouraged.

Maeterlinck was a competent student, outstanding only in French composition. He continued to cultivate his interest in sports and learned to fence, another activity he enjoyed long after he left school. He credits his father's blunt skepticism with freeing him early from the fear of hell and purgatory that the Jesuits tried to inculcate in him. "Though at heart," Maeterlinck adds in *Bulles bleues,* "he was not so sure himself about the eternal flames and, since one can never be sure what will happen, from time to time he invited the parish priest to dinner." Yet, for all his resistance to the spiritual teachings of the Jesuit fathers, it can hardly be said that he escaped their influence. The gloomy atmosphere and the obsession with death and punishment that clouded so many of his days at the Collège Sainte-Barbe, as well as the dreary, gray city outside its walls, must surely have contributed significantly to the morbidity of Maeterlinck's early plays and to his lifelong absorption with the mystery of human existence and its end.

During his last years at the Collège Sainte-Barbe Maeterlinck developed a close friendship with two schoolmates, like him aspiring writers: Charles Van Lerberghe and Grégoire Le Roy. The 1880's were a period of great artistic ferment in Belgium as well as France, and the three friends threw themselves into it wholeheartedly. Maeterlinck had, at his parents' insistence, begun studying law at the University of Ghent in the autumn of 1881 but, finding his studies tedious and unchallenging, he gave more and more of his time to writing and to involvement in the literary "renaissance" then gathering momentum. He claims to have written hundreds, even thousands, of poems during these university years, imitating successively François Coppée, the popular "Poet of the Humble," and three adherents of the Parnassian or art-for-art's-sake movement—Théodore de Banville, Leconte de Lisle, and José María de Heredia—before moving eventually in the direction of Charles Baudelaire, Paul Verlaine, and Stéphane Mallarmé.

Several literary reviews were founded in Belgium at this time, one of the first being *La jeune Belgique.* Maeterlinck subscribed to this magazine, which numbered among its contributors Georges Rodenbach and Emile Verhaeren, both rising poets who, like Maeterlinck and his friends, had been classmates at the Collège Sainte-Barbe. In November 1883, *La jeune Belgique* carried Maeterlinck's first published poem, "Dans les joncs" ("In the Rushes"). It was a conventional little work, but its fate was better than that of a second poem he submitted, which the editor rejected as "supremely bad." The other leading journals were *L'Art moderne,* founded about the same time as *La jeune Belgique,* and *La Wallonie.*

L'Art moderne at first stressed social and political concerns with respect to the arts, in contrast to the art-for-art's-sake orientation of *La jeune Belgique; La Wallonie* became the chief periodical in Belgium devoted to the symbolist movement, and some of Maeterlinck's chansons later appeared in its pages.

Maeterlinck completed his studies and, in June 1885, received his doctorate in law. He was then admitted to the bar and had his name officially added to the register of lawyers of the Court of Appeals in Ghent. Instead of beginning a practice, however, he persuaded his parents to subsidize a visit to Paris, ostensibly to let him observe firsthand the skills and eloquence of French lawyers. He went to Paris in October, accompanied by Le Roy. The two young men settled in modest rooms on the rue de Seine, and were joined there sometime later by Van Lerberghe. In *Bulles bleues* Maeterlinck notes that four or five visits to the Palais de Justice were sufficient to convince him that the ways of justice in Paris were no less picayune and quibbling than those he had observed in Brussels, and he "never again set foot in those majestic halls." Rather, he now felt free to visit more congenial milieux. Before long he and Le Roy began to frequent a brasserie in Montmartre where they regularly met a number of young and obscure writers, among them the meridional poet Paul Roux, who later became famous under the name Saint-Pol Roux.

In the spring of 1886 Maeterlinck was also introduced to Verlaine, but for him, as for his young cohorts, the greatest experiences were the evenings when they were joined in the crowded brasserie by Villiers de l'Isle-Adam. The Breton writer, author of the tragedy *Axël* (1890) and *Contes cruels* (*Cruel Tales,* 1883), was then in his fifties and just finishing his novel *L'Eve future* (*Tomorrow's Eve,* 1886). In *Bulles bleues* Maeterlinck described him quite simply as "the most indisputable genius of the time, whom life had mistreated like a criminal." Villiers talked of literature, but for the most part he recited passages from his writings—completed, still in progress, or yet to be committed to paper—in a "white, cottony, muffled voice that already seemed a voice from beyond the grave." In later years Maeterlinck was able to see the flaws and weaknesses that marred Villiers's work, but all his life he felt gratitude for the inexplicable good fortune that introduced him just then to the man "who was to orient and determine [his] destiny." Never in his life, Maeterlinck said, had he met another man who "so clearly and irrevocably gave the impression of genius" as Villiers. After escorting Villiers home on those evenings, the young men would leave "the tireless magician and inexhaustible visionary" at his door, feeling stunned or revitalized as though they had been with "a giant from another world."

Not surprisingly, the fruit of this intense and enthusiastic literary activity was a new magazine, *La pléiade: Revue littéraire, artistique, musicale et dramatique.* De Banville was the review's nominal sponsor, and the names of Van Lerberghe, Le Roy, and Maeterlinck—his first name given its Flemish spelling, Mooris—appeared with the others on the title page. It lasted through only six issues, but *La pléiade* gave Maeterlinck his first publications in France. His story "Le massacre des innocents" was printed in the May issue, and a half dozen poems, later collected in *Serres chaudes* (*Hot-Houses,* 1889), followed in June. The story evokes the biblical account (Matthew 2:16) of the slaughter in Bethlehem, by Herod's order, of all male children two years old or less. Like Brueghel, Maeterlinck placed the event in sixteenth-century Flanders, which was then under the bloody rule of the Spanish duke of Alba. He tells the story in an objective, visual manner that recalls Brueghel in its precise observation of detail, and he even builds his narrative on the activities of the various groups of people in the painting. Rather than seeking to involve readers emotionally, Maeterlinck keeps them at a distance, then leaves them at the end to contemplate the cruel fate allowed to befall the innocent. Vil-

liers reportedly praised the story but advised Maeterlinck to abandon literary realism and turn to symbolism—a change of direction that his heady months among the symbolist and "decadent" writers in Paris most probably would have brought about alone. His reflective nature could hardly have been left untouched by the symbolists' preoccupation with the great mysteries of life and destiny; his sensitive imagination was inevitably stimulated by the idea of expressing through suggestion and evocation the feelings and thoughts that defied direct expression in words.

Shortly after Maeterlinck, Van Lerberghe, and Le Roy returned to Ghent in the summer of 1886, Rodenbach, whom they had seen in Paris, published an article about them called "Trois nouveaux poètes" (Three New Poets) in *La jeune Belgique.* He described Maeterlinck as "beardless, with short hair, protruding forehead, clear, distinct eyes, with a straightforward gaze, his face harshly set . . . a real Flemish face, with undertones of reverie and colorful sensibility. At heart a taciturn person who is very reserved, but whose friendship must be reliable." Such was the young man who reluctantly left Paris to embark on a legal career in Belgium, fulfilling his father's wishes though not his own. He practiced law in Ghent rather halfheartedly for about three years. The work failed to inspire him and he found the courtroom uncongenial because of the extreme discomfort he experienced when required to speak in public, a problem he faced all his life. Much of the legal work he had came to him through friends and family connections, and his father supplemented his meager income with an allowance. He continued to live in the family home and to spend summers in Oostacker, keeping fit by boating, bicycling, skating, and other outdoor activities, according to the season.

His inner life, however, was less stagnant and aimless than his outer life might seem to be. During these years he began reading the medieval Flemish mystic known in Belgium as Ruysbroeck the Admirable and in Holland as

Jan van Ruusbroec. The founder, in the fourteenth century, of an Augustinian abbey at Groenendaal, near Brussels, Ruysbroeck was the author of a number of tracts for his fellow religious, one of which, *The Adornment of Spiritual Marriage,* Maeterlinck translated into French. While reading in connection with his work on Ruysbroeck, Maeterlinck discovered the writings of Ralph Waldo Emerson and the German mystic poet and novelist Novalis. Apparently it was in the late 1880's, too, that he became interested in Dante Gabriel Rossetti and the English Pre-Raphaelite Brotherhood; among projects he considered then were translations of Rossetti and a study of the Flemish Primitive and Pre-Raphaelite painters, although neither of these ideas bore fruit. He saw Villiers de l'Isle-Adam again in 1888, when the Breton writer delivered a lecture at the Cercle Artistique et Littéraire in Ghent, of which Maeterlinck was a member. In June 1889, Maeterlinck's second story, "Onirologie" (Oneirology), was published in *La revue générale,* a Brussels review; at about the same time *Hot-Houses* was printed at his own expense in Ghent.

"Onirologie," as its name reveals, is a story that has to do with dreams. The principal character, who lives in the United States, knows nothing about his origins or background. He has a strange dream, filled with mysterious, unfamiliar landscapes and frightening visions and sensations. Subsequently learning that he was born in Utrecht, he goes to Holland and in that city is stunned to discover the place he had seen in his dream. As he invites the reader to meditate on inexplicable fate at the end of "Le massacre des innocents," and as Edgar Allan Poe might also have done, Maeterlinck here leaves the reader to elucidate the mystery.

The influence of Poe and Nathaniel Hawthorne is clearly evident in "Onirologie," and scholars have traced details of the story to other sources as well. Such obvious borrowings from other writers are hardly rare in the works of young poets, novelists, and playwrights who are still seeking their own voice. No one was more aware of this than Maeterlinck, and no writer more readily acknowledged his debts or did so with such disarming candor. Of his poetry, for example, he wrote to the French dramatist and critic Octave Mirbeau, "In *Serres chaudes* you will find only Verlaine, Rimbaud, Laforgue, and—for which I have been criticized—Walt Whitman, and almost nothing of myself. . . . You are wrong to consider me a great poet. I am only a child, groping in the dark, . . . grasping at whatever I encounter" (from an unpublished letter, quoted by M. Postic). The poems of *Hot-Houses* indeed reveal these influences, and others as well: Baudelairean *spleen,* languor, and longing for the ideal; the full panoply of symbolist imagery—swans, lilies, withered flowers; water frozen, stagnant, or rising in a pure, fresh jet; moonlight and mists; correspondences between outer and inner, physical and spiritual worlds. Yet, behind the facade of conventional, and to some extent assumed, dissatisfaction and melancholy, the Maeterlinck of these years is evident: a young poet who finds his inner life at once nurtured and stifled by the hothouse of isolation that separates him from the materialistic, monotonously predictable outer world he loathes; a young man who has lost his religious faith, but is not yet ready or willing to abandon the search for God.

Written over a period of four or five years, the thirty-six poems in *Hot-Houses* do not form a sequence. Most of them use conventional meters and rhyme, but seven are written in unrhymed free verse, then still a considerable novelty in French poetry and the only likely evidence of Whitman's influence. The unity of the volume emerges from themes, images, and the consistently subjective viewpoint. The central image of the hothouse is echoed in many related ones, such as the aquarium and diving bell, that evoke a closed, claustrophobic, over-luxuriant, and unnatural world. A pervasive sense of immobility and constriction contrasts with the urge to move, to

123

escape, to live unfettered in rain, snow, and sun. Prayers of aspiration toward God are mingled with expressions of hopeless disillusionment. Freedom is seen only in fantasy; nothing can be fulfilled.

A final point of interest in *Hot-Houses* is the anticipation of characteristics of Maeterlinck's first play, *La Princesse Maleine* (*Princess Maleine,* 1889), and his other symbolist dramas. With respect to language, we already find in the poems Maeterlinck's typical use of repeated words, sounds, and images to create emotional rather than purely musical effect and to suggest litany and incantation. Particularly in the poems in free verse, thematic kinships have been pointed out: solitude, disorientation, imprisonment, cruelty, illness, and death. Strange, jarring juxtapositions of images—which for Maeterlinck represented "things not in their place"—foreshadow similar ominous sensations evoked in the plays of something vaguely, but seriously, amiss.

Four months after the appearance of "Onirologie" in *La revue générale,* the same periodical published an article by Maeterlinck about Ruysbroeck. (The article was subsequently revised to serve as an introduction to his translation of *The Adornment of Spiritual Marriage,* which was published two years later.) By the end of 1899 *Princess Maleine* was running serially in Brussels in another magazine, *La société nouvelle,* and had been printed in Ghent (an edition of thirty copies) by Maeterlinck and his friends. Verhaeren praised the play in *L'Art moderne* in late November, as he had hailed the appearance of *Hot-Houses* some months earlier. Other critics wrote glowingly of both Maeterlinck and his play in *La pléiade* (Brussels), *La jeune Belgique,* and *La Wallonie;* the last-named also published Maeterlinck's second play, *L'Intruse* (*The Intruder*), in January 1890.

No doubt partly because of this critical interest, Maeterlinck risked another edition—this time 150 copies—of *Princess Maleine,* but only about fifteen were sold. He sent inscribed copies to a few friends, and one with his compliments to Mallarmé in Paris. The French poet had delivered a lecture on the recently deceased Villiers de l'Isle-Adam in Ghent the previous February, and Maeterlinck had met him then—whether for the first or second time is not known. Mallarmé acknowledged the gift promptly, "in a few words chiseled like jewels," and that, Maeterlinck assumed, was the end of it. Mallarmé, however, impressed by the play, had passed it on to a dramatist friend, who in turn gave it to the popular French novelist and playwright Octave Mirbeau. On 24 August 1890, the Paris newspaper *Le figaro* carried on its front page, under a two-column head reading "Maurice Maeterlinck," a wildly enthusiastic review signed by Mirbeau. He called *Princess Maleine* the greatest work of genius of the time, comparable only to Shakespeare, perhaps greater, and yet the creation of a totally unknown author. Other critics, and a disconcerted Maeterlinck himself, promptly challenged Mirbeau's evaluation, but the article ensured that the young author was no longer unknown. Maeterlinck henceforth was an international figure.

Much of the plot and most of the characters of *Princess Maleine* are drawn from a fairy tale by the Brothers Grimm, "Jungfrau Maleen" ("Maid Maleen"). Maeterlinck sets the action in a misty, legendary Holland and begins with a scene reminiscent of the first scene of *Hamlet.* At night two officers discuss the threat of a storm, the red moon, the ominous reappearance of a comet, and a rain of stars. In the lighted castle of King Marcellus of Ysselmonde some distance away, the celebration of the betrothal of Marcellus' daughter, Princess Maleine, to Prince Hjalmar is interrupted by fighting. Maleine, weeping, runs out into the garden, and moments later King Hjalmar, the father of Maleine's fiancé, bursts forth, cursing King Marcellus for "doing a monstrous thing," calling for his horse, and vowing a war of vengeance. When King Marcellus later asks Maleine to marry the Duke of Burgundy, who has loved her for a long time, she refuses. "You still love Hjalmar?" "Yes, Sire!" "You will give him up?" "No, Sire!" Faced with her refusal and imminent war, Marcellus has her immured in a tower in the midst of a wood, alone except for her nurse, an earthy character inspired by Juliet's nurse.

When Maleine and her nurse eventually escape from the tower, they find Maleine's parents dead and the kingdom of Ysselmonde laid waste by the war. Maleine seeks Hjalmar, only to discover that, believing her dead, the indecisive prince has become engaged to Uglyane, daughter of the evil Queen Anne of Jutland. The old king, Hjalmar's father, is now senile and besotted with love for Anne; she, in turn, has designs on both him and his son. Maleine becomes a lady-in-waiting to Uglyane and, arranging a rendezvous with the prince in the name of Uglyane, reveals herself to him. When Prince Hjalmar affirms his determination to marry Maleine, Queen Anne attempts to poison her. Failing in this, she strangles Maleine in the presence of the helpless old king while a violent storm rages outside. When Hjalmar discovers what has happened, he stabs the queen and then kills himself. The old king remains, reduced to a state of idiocy, and the play ends with a chorus of nuns intoning the Miserere to the tolling of bells as they transport the bodies to their final rest. The bells and singing cease, nightingales are heard outdoors, and then a rooster hails the dawn as the curtain falls.

In the Grimms' earlier fairy tale there is no wicked queen. Maid Maleen substitutes, in disguise, for the ugly fiancée and is married to the prince. When the truth is discovered, the ugly princess is repudiated, and the lovers are happily united forever. Maeterlinck's changes are significant, of course, because they allow the tragic development of the situation and, consequently, the expression of his pessimistic view of life. More than anything else, *Princess Maleine* is a statement of Maeterlinck's belief in man's helplessness before the hostility of fate and the injustice of death.

The play is not tragic in the traditional sense, as has often been pointed out, because the characters do not resist or transcend their destiny. Their perceptions are intuitive, not intellectual; their responses are instinctive rather than rational. Yet though they remain shadowy and undeveloped, they achieve sufficient reality to engage concern and sympathy. The characters seem to dwindle in size with their increasing awareness of the vast, invisible forces that so arbitrarily determine their fate. Maeterlinck conveys this awareness powerfully, through suggestion alone. Without analysis or explanation, the inner drama is projected; the characters emerge as symbols of humanity, and their situation is seen as symbolic of the human condition. This is Maeterlinck's originality and his real achievement in the play. For this reason, rather than because of the obvious borrowings from Shakespeare or even because of the sometimes adroit, sometimes excessive use of conventional signs and symbols, *Princess Maleine* deserves to be called the first symbolist drama. In this fact we find its true importance, not in Mirbeau's exaggerated claims for it. The struggle for public acceptance of symbolist poetry had largely been won by 1890; *Princess Maleine* was a specifically theatrical challenge to the concrete, explicit naturalism then dominating the stage.

Maeterlinck's next play, *The Intruder,* was published in January 1890, less than two months after *Princess Maleine.* It already shows markedly greater assurance in the handling of symbols, clearer focus, and tighter structure; it is also more personal and original. The time of the action is the present, but the setting is an old castle, in a room dimly illuminated by stained-glass windows with a tall Flemish clock standing in one corner. A father, his three daughters, his brother, and his aged father-in-law await the arrival of the father's sister, a nun. In rooms on either side are the girls' mother, who is ill, and their baby brother, born a few weeks earlier. The old man, who is blind, has forebodings that all is not well with his daughter. The father tells him that the doctor has assured them she is recovering and invites the old man to go with him into the bedroom and see her, but he refuses. The uncle expresses pity for the grandfather's unease, attributing it to his blindness: "Not to know where you are, where you've come from or are going to . . . and always that darkness, that darkness. . . . I'd rather not be alive."

As time passes, the blind man's fears intensify and begin to disquiet the others. The daughters notice a strange silence outdoors and see the swans in the pond swim away in fear. The grandfather's hearing, sharpened by the loss of his sight, detects familiar sounds that seem suddenly strange and ominous, and he claims to hear sounds that the others do not hear at all. The lamp, for lack of oil, suddenly goes out, leaving only eerie moonlight shining through the window. The clock, which has marked the hours of their waiting, strikes midnight. The infant begins to wail offstage, and a black-robed nun emerges from the mother's room, silently making the sign of the cross. The family members realize now that the visitor they had awaited, whose arrival they had sensed but not seen, was Death. As they go silently into the mother's room, her old father, left alone, cries out in anguish: "Where have you gone? They have left me all alone!"

Apart from being shorter, *The Intruder* differs most obviously from *Princess Maleine* in its simplicity and realism. Although there is some stylization of characters and language, there are no echoes of Shakespeare, no abrupt changes of scene, no fairy-tale atmosphere or characters. The setting in an old château and the modern dress suggest timelessness rather than remoteness. The ordinariness of the situation draws the spectator into the play at the same time that it augments the mysterious elements by contrast. Even the things that cause alarm or unease are not, for the most part, unusual in themselves.

To call attention to the unspoken drama behind the spoken words and silences, Maeterlinck juxtaposes pairs of opposites—the natural and the supernatural, the rational and

the intuitive, the visible and the invisible. The real or implied conflicts between these opposites provide the dramatic tension as well. The father and the uncle are people of the everyday world; they seek and find natural, rational explanations for the things that trouble the daughters and, most of all, the grandfather. By his age and blindness, the grandfather is cut off from the ordinary, visible world and has a heightened sensitivity to invisible, spiritual realities. He responds directly and emotionally to them; he does not try to rationalize or explain. The phenomena that the father and uncle easily explain and dismiss trouble him because he perceives them differently. The other men, who see only random, insignificant occurrences, lack the blind man's spiritual vision, which enables him to apprehend the swans' fear, the sound of a door closing, the dimming of the lamp as related manifestations of an invisible presence. Only the audience sees from both points of view. When at the end of the play the others leave the grandfather and enter the room of the dead mother, he is suddenly terrified and disoriented at finding himself back in a world he no longer knows. Alone, unable to see, literally standing between the impenetrable mysteries of the beginning and the ending of life, the grandfather embodies the description given of him by the uncle—the image of the human condition.

Like *The Intruder,* and published in the same year, Maeterlinck's third play, *Les aveugles* (*The Blind,* 1890), is in one act. Twelve blind people—six men and six women—who live on an island have been taken out for a walk by an old priest. He has left them in a forest, and they are waiting for his return, seated in two groups, facing each other and some distance apart. Unknown to them, the priest is not far away; he has been visible to the audience, leaning motionless against a tree upstage center, since the curtain rose. The blind people become increasingly distressed and frightened as they wait. Finally the dog from the hospice in which they live appears and leads them to the priest, who they discover is dead. They think they hear footsteps in the dead leaves, but their queries are answered by silence. Other sounds disturb them. Snow begins to fall, and the baby of one of the women starts to cry. Bewildered, not knowing where to go, the blind turn here and there until the woman holding the baby says, "The steps have stopped among us! . . . Who are you?" The silence is broken only by the baby's continuing cry and an old woman's plea: "Have pity on us!"

The blind people are differentiated according to the nature of their blindness. Some were born blind; some once had sight and dimly remember it; one can see a faint line of light between his eyelids. Their attitudes vary also: one man is resigned to his condition; a young girl who once could see hopes to regain her sight; some prefer to stay inside, others to go out and feel the change in their surroundings. One young woman, the mother of the baby, is mad as well as blind. Yet none of the characters is given a name, either in the cast listing or in the play. They are identified only as "Oldest Blind Man," "Young Blind Girl," and so on. The lack of names may suggest an attempt to broaden the symbolism, but it also serves to underscore the eventual realization that each of them is alone. Never having seen one another, they do not really know each other. And ultimately the differences among them pale in the light of what they have in common.

The symbolism in *The Blind* is more systematic and unified than in the earlier plays, and its significance is clear. Whether one views the priest as a representative of the church, religion, or religious faith, the meaning is the same. Deprived of their guide, people can only grope in the darkness, ask questions that can have no answers, know only that the beginning of new life—symbolized in both *The Intruder* and *The Blind* by a baby—accompanies the end of the old.

Maeterlinck makes extensive use of sounds in this play, along with constant references to hearing, listening, and not listening. The dialogue is composed of his characteristic short phrases and frequent repetitions. Judgment as to the effectiveness of these by now familiar devices would seem to be largely a matter of taste, since critical opinions range from calling this play Maeterlinck's most realistic to finding it contrived and excessively dependent on gimmickry. Although the artifice is occasionally too obvious, the play is marked by emotional power and sure control of dramatic tension—an achievement all the more remarkable since there is essentially no action at all in the play. In *The Intruder* Maeterlinck reduces external action to the minimum; here internal movement is almost nonexistent as well. Only the discovery that the priest is dead can be called action, and even then it is only the realization of something that has been there all along. The situation of the characters does not change from beginning to end of the play; at best they gain only a slightly keener awareness of their lot before the curtain falls. Maeterlinck has sometimes been called the creator of static theater. Whether or not that is so, *The Blind* is an astonishing anticipation of Samuel Beckett's "actionless" plays *Waiting for Godot* (1952) and *Endgame* (1957), written more than sixty years later.

Late in 1890 Maeterlinck wrote *Les sept princesses* (*The Seven Princesses*, 1891), the last, he said, of his "little trilogy of death." It is clearly related to the two preceding plays by form—a single act—as well as by subject. It returns, however, to the fairy-tale world of *Princess Maleine*; in the stage directions, Maeterlinck describes the scene revealed when the curtain rises:

A spacious hall of marble, with laurel, lavender, and lilies in porcelain vases. A flight of seven white marble steps divides the whole wall lengthwise, and seven princesses, in white gowns and with bare arms, lie sleeping on these steps, which are furnished with cushions of pale silk. . . . At the back of the hall, a door with powerful bolts. To the right and left of this door large windows whose panes reach down to the level of the floor. Behind these windows, a terrace. . . . Between huge willows, a gloomy canal without a bend, on the horizon of which a large ship approaches.

The action takes place on the terrace and is seen through the windows; inside, the princesses lie sleeping until the very end. After an absence of seven years, Prince Marcellus returns to claim the hand of Princess Ursule, whom he loves. He finds the old king and queen, his grandparents, on the terrace, anxiously watching the sleeping princesses. Unable to enter through the door, which is bolted on the inside, Marcellus must take an underground passage that leads through vaults that contain his ancestors' tombs. As he prepares to descend, the ship moves out to sea again to the accompaniment of a sailors' chant. Marcellus enters the room by lifting a marble slab in the floor; six of the princesses awake then, but he discovers that Ursule has died in her sleep.

The Seven Princesses is a puzzling and, on the whole, unsatisfactory play. Its dialogue is perhaps the most irritatingly trivial and repetitious to be found in Maeterlinck's work. Symbolism hangs heavily over every aspect of the play, yet remains obscure. If the willow-lined canal and the ship in the background evoke the landscape of Oostacker, the wall and great windows separating the princesses from those outside recall the transparent barriers in *Hot-Houses*. Some critics have related the play to a passage in the writings of the German philosopher Arthur Schopenhauer, where he likens the world of ideas to a fortress without doors that can be entered only through a subterranean passageway. Others have compared it to the legend of Orpheus and Eurydice or to a Pre-Raphaelite painting. Still others read it as an allegory of the conflict between the real world and the ideal world, or of love, even after it passes through death, failing to attain its ideal fulfillment. Maeterlinck added a further dash of mystery to his little play in 1901 when, without explanation, he omitted it from the collected edition of his plays.

After the furor attendant on Mirbeau's article about *Princess Maleine* had subsided, Maeterlinck's life settled again into the ordered existence he preferred. He joined the Civic Guard of Ghent and rented a small apartment in Brussels, although he retained his quarters in the family homes in Ghent and Oostacker. He generally wrote in the morning and devoted his afternoons to walking or other physical activity. He made brief trips, to England in the autumn of 1890 and to Cologne for the pre-Lenten carnival in 1891. During these same years he experienced bouts of depression, which were aggravated, if not caused, by concerns about his future, worries about his health (luckily unfounded), and the death of his brother Oscar on 20 May 1891.

In September 1891 Maeterlinck was somewhat grudgingly nominated by the official committee to receive the government's Triennial Prize for Dramatic Literature. Learning this in advance and remembering previous slights to other writers, Maeterlinck publicly declined the prize. A considerable controversy ensued, which was revived three years later when the committee declared him ineligible for the award on the basis of his earlier refusal.

The day after Oscar died, one of Maeterlinck's plays was publicly performed for the first time. *The Intruder* was included in a special benefit matinee program in Paris at the Théâtre d'Art, an avant-garde theater recently founded by the youthful poet Paul Fort. Response was mixed, but generally favorable. The young producer Aurélien Lugné-Poë had been among those who persuaded Fort to include *The Intruder* on the program. Maeterlinck met him the following December when Lugné-Poë played the oldest blind man in a production of *The Blind*, also mounted at the Théâtre d'Art. This performance was unfortunately broken up by a too easily distracted dog, but Maeterlinck was sufficiently impressed to suggest that Lugné-Poë produce *Pelléas et Mélisande* (*Pelléas and Mélisande*, 1892), which he was then writing. When the Théâtre d'Art brought its production of *The Intruder* to Brussels in March 1892, Lugné-Poë visited Maeterlinck in Ghent, and thus began a professional and friendly relationship that lasted many years. The performance of *The Intruder* was less happy. Confusion and the mishandling of stage effects—such as raising instead of dimming the light—again produced unintentional comedy.

Pelléas and Mélisande was completed in the spring of 1892, but a year passed before it reached the stage in a single matinee performance on 17 May 1893, at the Théâtre des Bouffes-Parisiens. Maeterlinck dedicated the play to Octave Mirbeau, and it was probably at the time of this Paris performance that the two men actually met for the first time.

The situation in *Pelléas and Mélisande* resembles the story of Paolo and Francesca, in which a young woman falls in love with her brother-in-law. Golaud, grandson of Arkel, the king of Allemonde, gets lost while hunting a wild boar and comes upon a beautiful young girl weeping beside a fountain in a wood. She will tell him only her name, Mélisande, and that a sparkling object in the depths of the fountain is a crown that had been given to her. Golaud marries her and, with some trepidation as to his grandfather's approval, brings her home to the family's dark, gloomy castle close to the sea. There she and Golaud's younger half brother Pelléas fall in love, both of them either unwilling or unable for some time to acknowledge, even to each other, what has happened. Pelléas' father, who has been ill, finally takes a turn for the better; Pelléas, in an attempt to avert the destiny he foresees, prepares to leave. At one last moonlight meeting by a fountain in the wood, Pelléas and Mélisande admit their love for each other and kiss for the first time. Golaud, who has become increasingly suspicious, catches them together, kills Pelléas, and pursues Mélisande. The next morning she and Golaud are found in front of the castle gates. Golaud has wounded her slightly and tried to kill himself, but it is Mélisande who dies, after giving birth to a daughter. She dies, not from the wound, "which would not have killed a bird," but because "she was born without reason . . . to die; and she dies without reason."

Pelléas and Mélisande is Maeterlinck's masterpiece. Although we may be reminded of *Princess Maleine* by the dreamlike atmosphere, the heavy presence of illness and death, and similarities of detail, we are really in a different world. The characters in *Pelléas and Mélisande* are, like those in the earlier plays, remote and mysterious, but they are more complex and their emotions are more specifically evoked. As a result, they possess a greater degree of psychological reality and individuality. Mélisande is as shy, instinctive, and inarticulate as a little creature of the wild. Innocent, fearful, yet direct, she gives her love to Pelléas fully and unhesitatingly, in keeping with her nature. Yet her actions give glimpses into her soul. In her first full scene with Pelléas she plays with her wedding ring and drops it in the Fountain of the Blind. The symbolism is obvious, but it is soundly based on psychological truth. Pelléas is aware of the power of his love for Mélisande and, more than she, afraid of where it might lead. His indecision about whether to visit his dying friend or to stay with his seriously ill father reflects and complicates the ambivalence in his feelings for Mélisande. Golaud, understanding neither them nor himself completely, is driven by his jealousy to appalling cruelty toward Mélisande; he wants desperately to believe in her innocence, but his suffering is so acute that he cannot make himself believe. No character in this play is comparable to the malevolent Queen Anne of Jutland; indeed, no character truly has base motives—not even Golaud, who can no more help himself than can Pelléas and Mélisande. The characters' fundamental goodness—or at least their instinct to be honorable—is not challenged on moral grounds either. The social and religious implications of illicit love are simply not at issue.

Although there is violence in this play, it does not dominate as it does in *Princess Maleine*. Rather, a grave melancholy overhangs this story of a passion as all-consuming as the tragic love of Tristan and Iseut. Arkel, the old and nearly blind king, articulates it best. After a long experience of life he is moved only by pity and compassion for the suffering of others. "If I were God," he says after the harrowing confrontation between Golaud and Mélisande, "I would have pity on the hearts of men." And when Mélisande dies in the final scene, he laments, "But the sadness, Golaud . . . but the sadness of everything we see!"

The action seems less arbitrary than in the earlier plays. Events unfold naturally and coherently, without contrivance yet without sacrificing their apparently random occurrence. Nothing is prolonged unnecessarily; the drama behind the events moves steadily. In the dialogue Maeterlinck's characteristic short, repeated phrases and non sequiturs are less common than in most of his plays and are therefore less obtrusive and used with more telling effect. In the love scenes particularly his easy lyricism achieves new heights of expressivity. The ebb and flow of emotions is simply and perfectly reflected in the tone and rhythm of the language.

Symbols are everywhere, of course, but are more varied and more subtly used than in the earlier plays: the action in the scene of the wedding ring; the setting of the scenes in the grotto and underground vaults; the ever-present water—in fountains, in the sea, in tears; Mélisande's hair, which Pelléas caresses in sensuous rapture and which Golaud pulls to punish and shame her. W. D. Halls suggests that Mélisande herself is the symbol of love, which illuminates life for a time but cannot prevent inevitable suffering and death. The centrality of love is perhaps this play's most important departure from the earlier ones. In them the dominant emotions, for players and spectators alike, are fear and terror, sometimes horror. Here love is both the dominant emotion and the chief motivating force. The love of Hjalmar and Maleine is almost incidental in the relentless destruction wrought by a hostile fate; the love of Pélleas and Mélisande over-

powers them and ultimately reveals itself as the instrument of destiny.

Lugné-Poë's Paris production of *Pelléas and Mélisande* was visually stunning, with costumes inspired by Flemish Primitive and Pre-Raphaelite paintings and stark settings full of shadows cast by overhead lights. The play was performed behind a gauze curtain to heighten the atmosphere of mystery and remoteness. The audience received the play well, although critics were divided. Among those present was a Brussels theater director who arranged for two performances there early the following month. After the first of them Van Lerberghe wrote to a friend that all Maeterlinck's supporters were present, but "the bourgeois" were out in force also, laughing, jeering, and otherwise disrupting the performance. The Belgian critics were also harsh. Toward the end of the year Lugné-Poë and Maeterlinck took the production to Rotterdam and The Hague, where it enjoyed considerable success. Nearly five years later, in the summer of 1898, Maeterlinck and Van Lerberghe went to London to attend the first full-scale production in English, starring Mrs. Patrick Campbell as Mélisande. Some of the costumes were designed by the Pre-Raphaelite artist Sir Edward Burne-Jones, and incidental music had been composed by Gabriel Fauré. The whole occasion was a critical and popular triumph and must surely have been enormously gratifying to Maeterlinck as he remembered his early struggles for recognition in his homeland.

In 1894 Maeterlinck published three plays that he called "dramas for marionnettes": *Alladine et Palomides* (*Alladine and Palomides*), *Intérieur* (*Interior*; also translated as *Home*), and *La mort de Tintagiles* (*The Death of Tintagiles*). The idea of having his plays performed by nonhuman "actors" had intrigued Maeterlinck from the time he was writing *Princess Maleine*, and he explains his feelings in a short preface. First of all, he believes that having the "actors" move only in response to manipulation from behind the scenes would symbolize perfectly his concept of man as the plaything of invisible forces beyond his comprehension. On another level he finds that the physical presence of an actor becomes an obstacle between the spectator and the character created by the author. He follows Charles Lamb in holding that too strong an appearance of reality on the stage produces an immediate discomfort that destroys the pleasure, the "sublime emotions," one experiences in reading and seeing characters only in imagination. "The theater is the place where the majority of masterpieces die," Maeterlinck asserts, "because the representation of a masterpiece by means of accidental and human elements is antinomical. All masterpieces are symbols, and a symbol cannot withstand the active presence of man." In performance, he adds, "the mystic density of the work of art disappears." It is interesting to note that one of Maeterlinck's plays was actually performed by marionettes. In 1891 Les Marionnettes de Ranson (Ranson's Marionettes) performed *The Seven Princesses;* the setting was designed by Paul Sérusier and the marionettes were created by Maurice Denis. Both these men were artists associated with the Nabis, a short-lived movement in early-twentieth-century painting, inspired by Paul Gauguin, that held pictures to be arrangements of color on a flat surface and eschewed attempts at rendering three dimensions in two. The most important of the Nabis were Édouard Vuillard and Pierre Bonnard.

Alladine and Palomides is a play that Maeterlinck himself dismissed, perhaps too readily, as "a decoction of *Pelléas.*" Although a slight and rather artificial work, it nonetheless contains some lovely pages, and its female characters are particularly interesting. Alladine symbolizes passionate, sensual love—albeit she is one of Maeterlinck's innocent, half-child heroines; Astolaine represents ideal love. Astolaine, the sole surviving daughter (of seven) of King Ablamore, is betrothed to the young knight Palomides. The old king has fallen in love with an exquisite Greek slave, Alladine, and plans to marry her following the marriage of his daughter. When Palomides arrives, he and Alladine fall in love as suddenly and as completely as Pelléas and Mélisande. Palomides tells the truth to Astolaine, who releases him from his promise. It is not his choice, she says, but the will of fate, and she loves him all the more. "I love you too," Palomides responds, "more than the one I love." The king, however, is enraged by what to him is betrayal of both his daughter and himself. He has Alladine and Palomides sealed in the vaults under the castle. Astolaine and Palomides' sisters rescue them, but too late. Palomides and Alladine die, each alone in a separate room, each calling faintly to the other. Death still triumphs, even over ideal love.

Interior is the most perfect of Maeterlinck's static dramas and the one in which he pushes his use of silence to its limits, again foreshadowing practices of such twentieth-century dramatists as Beckett and Harold Pinter. Two essays in *Le trésor des humbles* (*The Treasure of the Humble,* 1896) elucidate this play particularly well, although the ideas they contain underlie all his symbolist plays. In the first essay, "Le silence," Maeterlinck states:

> Those who are able to speak the most profoundly feel most keenly that words never express the real and individual relationships between two people. If I speak to you now of the most serious things—of love, death, or destiny—I do not actually touch death, love, or destiny; whatever my efforts, there will always remain between us a truth that is not spoken . . . and yet this truth that had no voice will have lived for an instant between us. . . . This truth is *our truth* about death, destiny or love; and we have only been able to grasp it in silence.
>
> (p. 22)

This idea of the inadequacy of words to convey subjective truth, which can be reached only through silence, parallels the view we have already noted with respect to human actors as obstacles in the communication between the dramatic poet and the spectator. In the ninth essay in *The Treasure of the Humble*—"Le

Tragique quotidien" ("The Tragical in Daily Life")—Maeterlinck discusses another related idea: "There is an everyday tragedy which is more real, profound, and consistent with our true existence than the tragedy of extraordinary events. . . . The true tragedy in life—normal, deep, and general tragedy—begins only at the moment when what we call adventures, sorrows, and dangers are past." It is one of these quiet, everyday tragedies, perceived and communicated in silence, that forms the basis of *Interior.*

When the curtain rises, the spectators find themselves looking at the back of a house from its garden. Large windows reveal the lighted room inside, where a father, mother, two daughters, and a sleeping baby present a picture of quiet contentment. In the garden an old man who knows the family and a stranger are talking quietly as they await the moment when one or both of them must knock at the door and tell the parents that their third daughter has drowned. A group of peasants bring the body up from the river. The old man goes to the front door (visible through the windows) and delivers the tragic news. His telling, like the family's reactions, is only seen, not heard. The windows separating the two observers (and the audience) from the family are reminiscent of those in *The Seven Princesses,* and the situation vaguely recalls that of *The Intruder.* Here, however, simplicity and ordinariness are complete. There are no exotic fairy-tale touches, no reliance even on stage effects. The words of the observers and the feelings they express are the symbols that point to the real drama, which is played out in silence.

The Death of Tintagiles is written in five acts so compressed that the whole play is shorter than *The Intruder* or *The Blind.* The setting again is a dark castle on an island. Although only a little boy, Prince Tintagiles has been brought to the island to forestall any possible future rivalry for the throne of his grandmother. She is a queen of awesome power, never seen in the play, but clearly a symbol of death. Tintagiles' two sisters, Ygraine and Bellangére,

are determined to keep him from the queen's clutches. During the first night they clasp him in their arms as they sleep, but the queen's three veiled servants manage to free him. The sisters awake, and Ygraine pursues them to the queen's tower. There a massive iron door blocks her way. Tintagiles calls faintly for help from behind it, but all Ygraine's frantic efforts to open it fail. The sound of his little body falling is heard through the door. Ygraine pleads with the queen, who does not answer. After a long silence, Ygraine finally screams in frustration and anger, "Monster! Monster! I spit on you!" and collapses in sobs.

This little drama is perhaps the most despairing of all Maeterlinck's plays. Death is inexorable in its destruction, even of the most innocent. Yet unlike all the characters in the previous plays, Ygraine does not submit to destiny passively. Her resistance is ultimately futile, but she fights back and heaps scorn on her enemy.

The next few years brought many changes in Maeterlinck's life and career. For two years he wrote nothing more for the theater. In 1894 he wrote a preface, "Ralph Waldo Emerson," for a French translation (ascribed to I. Will) of seven essays by the American philosopher. The following year he published his own translation into French of two works by Novalis: *Les disciples à Saïs* (The Disciples at Saïs) and *Fragments* (Fragments). In January 1895 he met Georgette Leblanc, who became his companion for more than two decades. In 1896 he compiled some new and some previously printed short pieces in *The Treasure of the Humble,* the first of his twenty-three volumes of essays. And in 1897 he left Belgium to establish permanent residence in France.

Georgette Leblanc was a French opera singer and actress, in her mid-twenties when she met Maeterlinck. Her memoirs, *Souvenirs (1895–1918)* (*Souvenirs: My Life with Maeterlinck,* 1931), describe how she read by chance Maeterlinck's preface to Emerson's essays and determined to meet him: "All night long I had read and reread Maeterlinck's preface. By morning I was sure that in all the universe he was the one man I could love." According to the memoirs, she reoriented her life with the intention of meeting Maeterlinck, going so far as to cancel her contract with the Opéra-Comique in Paris for a far less lucrative one at the Théâtre de la Monnaie in Brussels. After some months in Belgium she managed, through a friend, to arrange a meeting at an after-theater party. She recalls her impressions of Maeterlinck on that occasion:

> His face had a troubled expression which time and the exercise of life have concealed. It disclosed that excessive sensitiveness which remains always his fundamental quality. . . . His physique has the heavy squareness of a Flemish peasant. . . . He was then less handsome than in his maturity. The bone structure was too apparent. But his look, blue and brief, caught one's attention and held it. On the whole he charmed by a certain awkwardness, by a whole world of hidden emotions and fears which passed wavelike behind his features and constantly modified them. All of this in disaccord with his physical strength created his personality.
>
> (*Souvenirs: My Life with Maeterlinck,*
> translated by Janet Flanner; pp. 10–11)

Following their meeting in Brussels, Maeterlinck invited Leblanc to visit him in Ghent. The day was considerably less than a success, in part because of rainy weather, but she met his parents, and they did deepen their acquaintance. Among other things he told her that he customarily had several mistresses at once. Leblanc comments: "It was a pastime like any other. But as for happiness, it didn't exist outside of pleasure and a good constitution. . . . I dreamed of offering him both that love and that happiness." Maeterlinck subsequently visited Leblanc at her apartment in Brussels, and they made excursions together to several places in Belgium and southern Holland, including the island of Walcheren, the "land beyond the horizon" of his childhood summers in Oostacker. Maeterlinck also did

some traveling on his own. He attended a successful performance of *Interior* in Paris in March 1895 by the Théâtre de l'Oeuvre, Lugné-Poë's successor to the Théâtre d'Art, after which he accompanied the troupe on a tour of *Pelléas and Mélisande* that took them to Liège, Rotterdam, and The Hague. He then crossed with them to England for a week of repertory in London that included *The Intruder* and *Pelléas.* Response in England was unenthusiastic, but Maeterlinck had occasion to meet George Bernard Shaw and William Butler Yeats, among other English writers.

Through these and later separations, usually for professional reasons, Maeterlinck and Leblanc continued corresponding and seeing each other when they could. Maeterlinck proposed in 1896, but marriage was impossible for them. At the age of seventeen, Georgette had been married in Spain; the union could be ended only by a papal dispensation. More important, however, were her ideas on marriage: "Had I been asked to cross Brussels in short skirts and flat heels it would not have seemed more unprecedented or useless," she wrote in *Souvenirs,* adding, "At his first word he read on my face such bewilderment that he did not continue. Besides he immediately shared my view." They agreed instead on a pact that each remained at liberty to dissolve at any time. It was understood also that they would move to Paris, where she would find more theatrical opportunities and their open liaison would be less likely to create scandal than it would in Belgium. The move to Paris was not accomplished until the spring of 1897, though they spent some time together in the Vendée during the summer of 1896. There Maeterlinck finished *Aglavaine et Sélysette* (*Aglavaine and Sélysette,* 1896), the play he had begun after the publication of *The Treasure of the Humble.* It was the first of his works inspired by his love for Leblanc.

The subjects of the essays in *The Treasure of the Humble* seem at first glance diverse and random. Abridgments of prefaces he had written—the one on Emerson that had impressed

Leblanc, as well as those for his translations of Ruysbroeck and Novalis—are included, along with his well-known essay on silence, others on "mystical morality," tragedy, women, the soul, and destiny. One of the earliest to be written, "Les avertis" ("The Predestined"), was inspired by the death of his brother. The volume is unified, however, by the recurrence of several themes and ideas and by the relationships that emerge among them. If there is a single underlying thread, it is Maeterlinck's concept of the soul—the essential, deepest self, which is encountered in silence rather than speech, and which can communicate directly with other souls across time and space. He explores, in sustained oppositions, mind and soul, consciousness and the subconscious, intelligence and intuition. In "La morale mystique" ("Mystical Morality"), he affirms the purity of the soul, which remains undefiled by the acts of the body; in "The Predestined" and "Sur les femmes" ("On Women"), as in his plays, he ascribes extra sensitivity and prescience to women and children because their natural gift of intuition exceeds that of men. The essay "L'Étoile" ("The Star"), first published in 1894, is as pessimistic as anything in the plays: "There is no destiny of joy, there is no happy star," Maeterlinck asserts. But elsewhere, especially in the essays written last, glimmerings of hope and optimism reflect a perceptible shift from a preoccupation with death to an exploration of the possibilities of life.

Like *The Treasure of the Humble,* some of Maeterlinck's subsequent volumes of essays collected pieces written and published before, but more of these volumes were conceived as wholes, exploring many aspects of a single topic. Yet Maeterlinck's manner of working and the essential characteristics of his writing did not change with the genre of the work or the passing of time. Only rarely do his essays give the impression of rigorous logic or carefully organized structure. They are most often meditations that follow the free movement of his thought. He liked to note his ideas on bits of paper as they came to his mind and pin them to the wall, taking them down later for reflection, development, and rewriting. He was sometimes accused of imprecision and inconsistency, or of obscurity in expression, charges of which he was not totally innocent. At the same time it is well to remember both the nature of his subjects and his approach to them. Although concerned with reality in its most everyday forms, Maeterlinck strove chiefly to illuminate its relation to the great mysteries of existence, the eternal and, often, the inexpressible. He was neither scientist nor philosopher, although he shared their interests. He was a poet and a mystic. Language, style, and imagery were his tools; he spoke to feelings rather than to reason. The introspection that he cultivated and encouraged was concerned less with understanding human behavior than with seeking glimpses of the meaning of existence.

The beauty of the soul is the subject of "La beauté intérieure" ("Interior Beauty"), the final essay in *The Treasure of the Humble.* Maeterlinck touched on this theme in the character of Astolaine in *Alladine and Palomides;* in *Aglavaine and Sélysette* it is central. A young couple, Méléandre and Sélysette, have been happily married for four years. They live in an old castle with Sélysette's grandmother. Aglavaine, Sélysette's recently widowed sister-in-law, comes to live with them. In contrast to Sélysette, one of Maeterlinck's typical innocent and fragile heroines, Aglavaine is "not like other women . . . ; [she has] a stranger, more spiritual beauty; a beauty that reveals her soul, never conceals it." Sélysette's instinctive fears are promptly realized: Méléandre and Aglavaine fall passionately in love within a week. Because their love is on such an exalted plane, they cannot bear to make Sélysette suffer, and Aglavaine prepares to leave. Sélysette, in her love for both of them, commits suicide by jumping from a tower. As she dies, however, she says it was an accident, in order to free them from guilt. Her final words are: "Put your hand over both my eyes, Aglavaine. . . . You must close them as you opened them. I fell by leaning too far." The noble, spiritual love to which Aglavaine and Méléandre aspired has been surpassed by Sélysette's sacrificial love. Neither Maeterlinck nor Leblanc was happy with the play, which Maeterlinck had originally intended to end with the triumph of Aglavaine. Yet, despite its ending, the play shows a fundamental change hinted at in *The Death of Tintagiles.* The characters are not completely passive; moreover, they change. Their "eyes are opened" and they—especially Sélysette—affirm their liberty to choose and act.

Maeterlinck's only other publication in 1896 was *Douze chansons (Twelve Songs)*, a group of poems reminiscent of folk songs and medieval in color. Several of them had been published before, and the collection included Mélisande's song, "Les trois soeurs aveugles" ("The Three Blind Sisters"), from the play. Three more poems—two of them songs used in later plays—were added when Maeterlinck reissued *Songs* and *Hot-Houses* in a single volume in 1900.

Maeterlinck and Leblanc settled in Paris in the spring of 1897. Since their apartment on the rue Pergolèse was small, they also rented a study a few blocks away so that Maeterlinck could work undisturbed by her musical practicing. They spent the summer in a villa in Normandy; throughout his life Maeterlinck followed his father's pattern of winters in the city, summers in the country. He resumed his customary routine also, with mornings given to work (at this time on *La sagesse et la destinée* [*Wisdom and Destiny*, 1898]) and afternoons reserved for bicycling or walking. When they returned to Paris in the autumn, an active social life began—another change for the quiet, reclusive author. In addition to Maeterlinck's expatriate friends and such longtime acquaintances as Mirbeau and Fort, they entertained many of the most prominent figures in the world of the arts. Mallarmé, the novelists Maurice Barrès, Jules Renard, André Gide, Colette, and Anatole France, and the sculptor Auguste Rodin all enjoyed their hospitality. Oscar Wilde also dined with them in the

spring of 1898, but Maeterlinck found him "a superficial personality" and did not pursue further acquaintance.

Wisdom and Destiny was published simultaneously in Paris, London, and New York in the autumn of 1898. Coming only a few months after the enthusiastic reception of *Pelléas and Mélisande* in London, this event firmly established Maeterlinck's international literary reputation. By now his work's were regularly translated into German as well as English; as his popularity grew, publication in London, New York, and Berlin frequently preceded the appearance of his books in Belgium and France.

The evolution in Maeterlinck's thought noticeable in the last plays and in some of the essays in *The Treasure of the Humble* is completed in *Wisdom and Destiny.* His early pessimism is replaced by hope and a distinct, if not total, optimism. The change is due in large part to the presence and influence of Leblanc in his life, but, as was true with his "conversion" to symbolism, the literary climate of the time and his own psychological and emotional needs no doubt contributed also. Eclectic as always in his search for ideas, Maeterlinck here draws on a characteristic variety of writers, ranging from Thomas Carlyle to Blaise Pascal, but the predominant influence is that of Marcus Aurelius, the Stoic Roman emperor. While Marcus Aurelius chose reason as his guide, however, Maeterlinck sees wisdom as the highest power and the only one that can, if not overcome destiny, at least help man to deal with it. He finds wisdom not in the absence of passions but in the purification of those we have. He explores the nature of happiness and of love, the role of sacrifice—"few things still bear the name of sacrifice for a soul whose devotion, pity, and abnegation are no longer the necessary roots but the invisible flowers"—and the place of death in the natural order. Again he considers the connections between inner and outer life and reaffirms his belief that the essential truths of human destiny are to be found in the simplest lives: "The last word will never go to the exceptional, and what we call the sublime ought only to be a more lucid and penetrating awareness of what is most normal."

This book caused the first serious rift between Maeterlinck and Leblanc. She too pinned to the study wall ideas that Maeterlinck sometimes used, and she frequently helped him, in conversation, to elucidate his thought. Hurt by his failure to acknowledge her contribution, she asked for coauthorship of *Wisdom and Destiny.* Although Maeterlinck eventually compromised on a long dedicatory acknowledgment, the wound remained.

Maeterlinck's next book was *La vie des abeilles* (*The Life of the Bee,* 1901). His interest in bees dated from boyhood, and he records here his own observations and experiments. The book has been commended for its scientific accuracy, but, not surprisingly, Maeterlinck's purpose goes beyond that. His beautifully lucid study is interspersed with comparisons between human society and that of the bee, usually to the detriment of the former. The bee is depicted as a model of adaptability and responsible social behavior, and Maeterlinck ascribes to it intelligence as well as instinct. Considering the "destiny" of the bee—to make honey—he suggests another parallel:

> No being that I know of has been designed to produce, like us, that strange fluid that we call thought. . . . Bees do not know if they will eat the honey they harvest. Like them we do not know who will benefit from the spiritual power we bring into the universe. As they go from flower to flower and gather more honey than they or their children need, let us also go from reality to reality, seeking everything that may nourish that incomprehensible flame.
>
> (pp. 312–313)

In 1902 Maeterlinck published three plays. Two of them—*Ariane et Barbe-Bleue, ou la délivrance inutile* (Ariadne and Bluebeard; or, The Useless Recognition, translated as *Ardiane* [*sic*] *and Barbe Bleue*) and *Soeur Béatrice* (*Sister Beatrice*)—were written as opera librettos; the third was *Monna Vanna.* Maeterlinck wrote all three as vehicles for Leblanc.

The first of these plays is an adaptation of the Bluebeard story. The sixth wife, Ariane, does not believe Bluebeard has killed his first five wives and determines to learn his secret. When her husband gives her six silver keys and a gold one, which he explicitly tells her not to use, as in the story she disobeys. Behind the forbidden seventh door she finds imprisoned the other wives, whose names are those of Maeterlinck's early heroines: Mélisande, Alladine, Ygraine, Bellangère, and Sélysette. A revolt of his peasants puts Bluebeard, bound, at the mercy of Ariane. She frees him, then invites the other wives to leave with her. They all choose to remain and Ariane leaves accompanied only by her nurse. Intended for Edvard Grieg, the libretto was rejected by the Norwegian composer and set instead by Paul Dukas. His opera was successfully produced at the Opéra-Comique in May 1907, with Leblanc enjoying a personal triumph as Ariane.

Sister Beatrice recounts the ancient legend of a nun who escapes from her convent with a lover, but is replaced there by the Virgin Mary so that her absence is never known. Written for the composer Gabriel Fabre, who died before completing his score, *Sister Beatrice* was performed as a play in Paris in 1915. Two other composers later set it to music. Maeterlinck dismissed both these plays as of no importance in his development as a dramatist, but they illustrate again the changes wrought by his love for Leblanc. Like *Monna Vanna,* which followed them, they celebrate love; and Ariane and Monna Vanna are both strong, independent women obviously modeled on the actress.

By coincidence 1902, the year that saw the publication of Maeterlinck's two opera librettos, was also the year in which Claude Debussy completed his setting of *Pelléas and Mélisande.* Maeterlinck had given Debussy permission to use the play in 1893 in a letter that also generously gave him complete authority over performances of the opera. Leblanc alleges in her memoirs that Debussy had agreed with Maeterlinck that she should create the role of Mélisande but then offered the part to the young Scottish soprano Mary Garden. Angry exchanges ensued, with Maeterlinck threatening violence and challenging Debussy to a duel. All this, followed by a vitriolic letter to *Le figaro* when Maeterlinck learned that he had forfeited all control over the opera, brought much delight to scandalmongers but little credit to him. Years later Maeterlinck admitted that the wrong had all been on his side. Later still—breaking a vow never to attend the opera—he saw Mary Garden in the role she had created and wrote her a most gracious, appreciative letter.

Leblanc was strong-willed, ambitious, temperamental, and, by all accounts, very hard to work with. Her clash with Debussy was not the only time that Maeterlinck intervened on her behalf—indeed not even the only one in 1902. She had decided that *Monna Vanna* was to be her debut role in the spoken theater. In getting her way she trod on many toes; Maeterlinck owed much to the director, Lugné-Poë, who ignored affronts from both of them and remained loyal to Maeterlinck despite his low opinion of Leblanc and her acting ability. In the end the play was a success, and eventually Leblanc performed in it throughout Europe.

Monna Vanna is a historical drama set in fifteenth-century Italy. Florentine troops led by a Venetian mercenary, Prinzivalle, are besieging the city of Pisa. Guido Colonna, the Pisan commander, sends his father to bargain with Prinzivalle, as the people of Pisa are starving. He returns with the message that Prinzivalle will lift the siege if Guido sends his wife, Monna Vanna, to spend the night with him. Outraged, Guido refuses the offer, but Monna Vanna says she will do it for the sake of the city. In Prinzivalle's tent she discovers that he has known and loved her since she was a child of twelve. He declares his love ardently but does not touch her. When at dawn Prinzivalle's life is threatened by enemies among the Florentines, Monna Vanna takes him back to Pisa. She tells her husband the truth, but he refuses to believe her and imprisons Prinzivalle. Appalled at her husband's distrust,

Vanna says she has lied and that Prinzivalle did violate her. She obtains the key to his cell on the pretext of wanting to impose her personal vengeance, but the escape of Monna Vanna and Prinzivalle is implied.

In the preface to the 1901 edition of his collected plays Maeterlinck indicates a change in his ideas on the theater. He states that he now believes the dramatist must bring his view of the world to the level of real, everyday life, to show in what ways, circumstances, and forms the "superior powers" act on human destiny. All this Maeterlinck attempts to do in *Monna Vanna,* if not with total success. The characters are the most articulate he has yet drawn; the action is clear and concrete; and the meaning of the play is left in no doubt. The moral question it poses—is the life of a city more important than a wife's honor?—receives an unqualified answer, accompanied by a strong affirmation of the power and primacy of love. Despite its strength and its popularity, however, the play was neither unflawed nor universally admired. Its dialogue, while often reaching lyrical heights, is also frequently unnatural and reveals little attempt at individual characterization. A number of Maeterlinck's friends found *Monna Vanna* inferior to his earlier works; Shaw confessed to thinking the play "an overrated abortion." In 1903 the Belgian government awarded Maeterlinck its Triennial Prize for Dramatic Literature for *Monna Vanna;* this time, despite continuing rancor toward his homeland, he accepted the honor.

The next five years saw the publication of one more play and three volumes of essays. *Joyzelle* (1903), an elaborate allegory of the power of love, is an inflated reworking of Shakespeare's *The Tempest* with Arthurian echoes (Merlin is one of the protagonists); it was a resounding flop when produced with Leblanc in the title role. *Le temple enseveli* (*The Buried Temple,* 1902) and *Le double jardin* (*The Double Garden,* 1904) collect a number of Maeterlinck's recent essays. *The Buried Temple* contains six quite lengthy essays, most notably "La justice" ("Justice"), a study of justice—"not legal justice, but that imprecise but effective justice, ungraspable but inevitable, which approves or disapproves, rewards or punishes all the acts of our lives." *The Double Garden* is composed of sixteen shorter essays, most of which are lighter in tone and substance than those in the preceding volume. The most popular is "Sur la mort d'un petit chien" ("On the Death of a Little Dog"), the dog being Maeterlinck's young bulldog, Pelléas. The others range in topic from the pleasures of the automobile to universal suffrage (which he favors), from the modern theater to wildflowers.

The title essay of *L'Intelligence des fleurs* (*The Intelligence of the Flowers*, 1907) develops the idea that flowers can be said to have intelligence. This claim is attested to, Maeterlinck avers, by their methods of self-protection and propagation of the species, methods comparable to the ways in which the bee fulfills its destiny of producing honey. He again draws analogies with man, whose purpose in life he now defines as the accumulation and transmission of knowledge. Human intelligence, he holds, is a manifestation of a greater, universal intelligence whose goals, like man's, are happiness and the conquest of death. The remaining essays deal with a great variety of subjects. Immortality, politics, social justice, and revolution fall under his scrutiny, and he declares that "in all social progress the greatest task, and the only difficult one, is to destroy the past."

Maeterlinck's father died in October 1904. Never having felt close to him, Maeterlinck did not seem to feel the loss acutely, but his inheritance assured him a substantial supplement to the income from his writing and enabled him to buy a villa at Grasse early in 1906. Henceforth he spent his winters in southern France, rather than in Paris, and his summers as usual in Normandy. The failure of *Joyzelle* in 1903 and the absence of any important new publication for several years produced a temporary decline in Maeterlinck's literary reputation, but he did not seem distressed and happily withdrew to the reclusive life he preferred.

While his outlook was at its most optimistic, Maeterlinck wrote the play that was in every respect his greatest and most lasting success, and that the majority of critics rank with, or close to, *Pelléas and Mélisande* at the summit of his artistic achievement, *L'Oiseau bleu* (*The Blue Bird*, 1909). Written for the most part during the summer of 1905, it was first staged in Moscow in 1908 by the great actor-director Konstantin Stanislavsky.

The night before Christmas two poor children, Tyltyl and Mytyl, get up from their beds to watch the celebration across the street in the home of some rich children. Suddenly an ugly fairy, who is named Bérylune and resembles their neighbor Mme Berlingot, appears and asks them to go find the Blue Bird for her daughter, "who is very ill and would like to be happy." To help them in their search, she gives them a magic hat adorned with a diamond that will let them see the essence of things. When Tyltyl puts on the hat and turns the diamond, everything is transformed: Bérylune becomes ravishingly beautiful, the humble home glows like jewels, the pet animals begin to talk, and the souls of all the things in the room are freed. Accompanied by Tylô the dog and Tylette the cat and the "souls" of Bread, Sugar, Fire, Water, and Light, the children leave through the window to begin their search. The first stop is at the palace of Bérylune; then by themselves the children visit the Land of Memory. There, "where there is nothing more to fear and death is meaningless," they have a joyful reunion with their grandparents and dead brothers and sisters. Their search and adventures continue— through the Palace of Night, the Forest, the Cemetery, the Palace of Happiness, and the Kingdom of the Future—but they fail to catch the Blue Bird. When they awaken the next morning, all is familiar but everything looks newer and more beautiful. Tyltyl finds that his pet turtledove has turned blue during the night, and he gives it to Mme Berlingot for her crippled daughter. The gift restores her ability to walk, but when the daughter comes to ask Tyltyl how to feed the bird, it escapes. Tyltyl consoles her: he will catch it again. He turns to the audience and asks anyone who finds it to return it to him because "we will need it later on in order to be happy."

To the classic quest narrative Maeterlinck has added allegories and symbols that bedeck it with light and color like a magical Christmas tree. *The Blue Bird* is a work for children and for the child in everyone. The symbolism does not need ponderous analysis; its message is clear and cheering. If the secrets of the universe are beyond our grasp, happiness is not. We need not seek it in the Forest, in the Palace of Happiness, or in the luminous blue halls of the future. It is within our reach every day if we know how to look. Should we lose it for a while, we can find it again, for ourselves and others. The fairy-tale atmosphere is sustained with poetry, charm, and a welcome spicing of humor through all the play's six acts and twelve scenes. Maeterlinck was always much concerned with the visual aspects of his plays, but never more than here. He describes the elaborate stage effects in great detail; when he describes settings and costumes he evokes familiar illustrations for the stories of Charles Perrault—the seventeenth-century author of *Cinderella, Puss-in-Boots,* and *Tom Thumb*—and the Brothers Grimm, as well as the "Anglo-Greek" style of the popular British illustrator Walter Crane. The dialogue that in his symbolist plays sometimes jars on the lips of adults is perfectly in place and in tune in *The Blue Bird.* Its faultless naturalness and simplicity fit the characters and offer an ideal context for the play's visual splendors.

Stanislavsky was just the man needed to realize Maeterlinck's intentions with this work on the stage. His production amazed and delighted both author and public. Leblanc, having observed Stanislavsky, supervised rehearsals for the Paris production, in which she played the role of Light. It reached the Théâtre

Réjane in March 1911, a year and a half after the opening of the long-running London production. During rehearsals in Paris an eighteen-year-old actress, who doubled in two small roles, asked Maeterlinck for his autograph. Thus the writer met Renée Dahon, who became his wife eight years later.

The Nobel Prize for Literature was awarded to Maeterlinck in 1911 "because of his many-sided literary activity and especially for his dramatic works, which are distinguished by imaginative richness and poetic idealism, which sometimes in the veiled form of the legend play reveal deep emotional inspiration, and also appeal, in a mysterious way, to the reader's feelings and imagination." The recognition came well after Maeterlinck had passed the high point of his creative powers.

The years after 1906 were not productive ones. Although eye trouble and periodic depression caused interruptions, a more fundamental reason was that the well of inspiration seemed to be running dry. As early as the summer of 1907 Leblanc had written her brother, "Maurice still cannot work. . . . I feel that he is at a difficult turning. It also seems to me that he needs a new direction." Earlier that year he had completed a drama about the French Revolution, *Marie-Victoire* (1927), but, dissatisfied with it, withheld it from publication for twenty years. In 1908 he wrote *Marie-Magdeleine* (*Mary Magdalene,* 1913). A weak play—neither performed nor published in France until five years later—it is chiefly of interest as the last play he wrote for Leblanc. As in its predecessors, the central theme is love, which here finds its expression in self-sacrifice. During the summer of 1909 Maeterlinck undertook a translation into French of *Macbeth,* which enjoyed an unusual and enthusiastically received production that August.

Two years before, feeling a need for change, Maeterlinck and Leblanc gave up their summer home at Gruchet Saint-Siméon and leased the abandoned Benedictine Abbaye de Saint-Wandrille, near Rouen. Partly in ruins and located on extensive wooded grounds through which a trout stream passed, the abbey entranced both of them. Leblanc describes it in loving detail in her memoirs, recalling how Maeterlinck, when kept by the Norman rains from his customary outdoor exercise, would "put on roller skates and skate the length of the halls at top speed, his pipe in his mouth, a book under his arm and his dog behind him." It was her idea to stage *Macbeth* in the abbey and its grounds, moving cast and spectators from place to place as scene changes were called for. The audience was limited to sixty, and the production was a triumph. The following summer an equally successful performance of *Pelléas and Mélisande* was given, with Leblanc as Mélisande. Her plans for future years, however, fell victim to Maeterlinck's intense dislike of the distraction from his work and invasion of his privacy.

The Belgian government, which in 1910 had again given its Triennial Prize in Literature to Maeterlinck for *The Blue Bird,* organized a gala in his honor after he received the Nobel Prize. A performance at the Théâtre de la Monnaie in Brussels that included the first act of *Pelléas* and the reading of an excerpt from *The Life of the Bee* was followed, the next day, by conferral of the insignia of Grand Officier de l'Ordre de Léopold. In the years remaining before World War I Maeterlinck did little writing, but enjoyed his new winter residence on a hill overlooking Nice—he named it "Villa des Abeilles"—and his new pastimes, boxing and motorcycling.

Two other deaths early in the century had affected Maeterlinck much more deeply than the loss of his father in 1904. His friend Van Lerberghe died early in 1907 and his mother in June 1911, after an extended illness. These events surely contributed to Maeterlinck's renewed concern with the problem of death. His next essay, *La mort (Death),* written in 1910–1911, was published then only in English. After it appeared, much amplified, in French two years later, the Catholic church put Maeterlinck's name on the Index, thereby censuring those of his works considered to contain heretical ideas.

Death (in its revised version translated as *Our Eternity,* 1913) sets forth the reasoned beliefs about death that Maeterlinck held at that time. Although they are necessarily provisional, in light of his insistence that answers to the great enigmas are ultimately unknowable, they did not significantly change in the course of thirty-six years of further reflection. Outside of religion—which he rejects, along with belief in reincarnation or metempsychosis—he sees only four "imaginable solutions" to the problem of what happens after death. "Total annihilation," he argues, "is impossible. We are the prisoners of an infinity without outlet, in which nothing perishes and everything is dispersed, but nothing is lost." Survival with our present consciousness, or with no consciousness at all, he finds equally implausible. The only explanation he can accept is survival in a "universal consciousness." But while he concludes that truth is undiscoverable, there is reason to continue the search: "For if we do not know where truth is, we nevertheless learn where it is not." And there could be a worse fate: "If there were no more insoluble questions nor impenetrable riddles, infinity would not be infinite; and then we should forever have to curse the fate that placed us in a universe proportionate to our intelligence."

When the war engulfed Belgium and moved on into France, Maeterlinck and Leblanc left Saint-Wandrille, where they were staying, and settled at Villa des Abeilles for the duration. The reports of atrocities perpetrated in Belgium by the invading forces abruptly changed Maeterlinck's heretofore sympathetic regard for German cultural values and his ambivalent attitude toward his own country. Denied military service because of his age, he plunged into propaganda work for the Allied cause. Overcoming his fear of public speaking, he spoke on behalf of his country in England, Italy, and Spain and published articles in France, England, and America about heroism and the horrors of war, patriotism and the dreadful suffering imposed on his native land. His articles and speeches were collected in a volume published in 1916 called *Les débris de la guerre* (*The Wrack of the Storm*); reprinted in it also for its singular relevance was his story "The Massacre of the Innocents."

In 1917, in Nice, Maeterlinck again turned to playwriting. First came two propaganda plays, a two-act "sketch" entitled *Le sel de la vie* (The Salt of Life) and a full-length drama set in Flanders, *Le bourgmestre de Stilmonde* (*The Burgomaster of Stilemonde* [*sic*], 1919). The latter was translated and performed in Spanish in Buenos Aires in 1918; after the war it was given in Spain, England, and America but never in France. Its simple plot concerns a Flemish village taken over by German soldiers, one of whom is the burgomaster's son-in-law. When a German officer is shot, the burgomaster's old gardener, Claus, is accused. Convinced of Claus's innocence, the burgomaster "confesses" and is executed by the Germans. Although the play is a work of some substance and dramatic power, its propagandistic intent overshadows its literary and dramatic worth.

Maeterlinck's next play, *Les fiançailles* (*The Betrothal*, 1922), is a sequel to *The Blue Bird*; it depicts the grown-up Tyltyl's search for the woman destined to be his wife. Produced with success in New York and London— although never in France—*The Betrothal* anticipates in its subject the next major change in Maeterlinck's life: his marriage to Renée Dahon.

After meeting Dahon in 1911, Maeterlinck and Leblanc had made her their protégée, even inviting her to live with them for a while. Meanwhile they saw less and less of each other and their own relationship disintegrated because of personal and professional conflicts. Finally, in December 1918, when Leblanc was in Paris and Maeterlinck in Nice, he sent her a telegram accusing her of infidelity and announcing the end of their relationship. He refused to see her or to answer her letters, and

on 15 February 1919, at the age of fifty-six, he married Dahon.

For a year or two after the war Maeterlinck remained in the spotlight. The universities of Brussels and Glasgow conferred honorary doctorates on him, and the Belgian government raised his rank from Grand Officier to Grand Croix de l'Ordre de Léopold. In December 1919 he and his wife sailed to New York. His first visit to the United States began with the premiere of an opera by the distinguished French conductor Albert Wolff based on *The Blue Bird*; it was given at the Metropolitan Opera House, where Wolff was then conducting, as a benefit for Belgian and French war orphans. A lecture tour arranged for the month of January was hampered by Maeterlinck's inability to pronounce English intelligibly. In February 1920, at the invitation of the movie producer Sam Goldwyn, the Maeterlincks made a much-publicized crossing of the United States by private train. In California Maeterlinck wrote three scripts for Goldwyn— never filmed—and gave several more lectures. During these months Maeterlinck was often amazed and generally disoriented by the pace and pattern of life in America, particularly by what he perceived as the lack of privacy. He liked Americans for their friendliness, enthusiasm, and generosity, but was shocked by their ignorance and lack of a cultural tradition. He returned to France in May with much relief and little regret.

In 1917 Maeterlinck had published essays on clairvoyance, mental telepathy, apparitions, and similar paranormal phenomena in *L'Hôte inconnu* (*The Unknown Guest*). The "unknown guest" is intuition, which, he believed, if properly trained, could liberate the power of the subconscious. In *Le grand secret* (*The Great Secret*, 1921), Maeterlinck undertakes a study of occultism, from the ancient religions and cults of the Orient, India, and Egypt to nineteenth-century theosophy. His main conclusion is that God is unknowable. But, since modern man needs a new religion, he suggested that one based on total agnosticism, like the Vedic religion, might be compatible with reason.

Between 1921 and 1925 Maeterlinck published nothing, partly for reasons of health, partly because of extensive travel with his wife. During these years, too, he began increasingly to withdraw from public concerns and public involvement, seeking instead quiet and privacy. In 1930 the Maeterlincks bought a large house overlooking the Baie des Anges at Nice. They named it Orlamonde, an allusion to the song sung by Bluebeard's imprisoned wives. Here the writer's daily routine rarely varied: writing in the morning, a walk or a drive in the afternoon, reading and conversation in the evening, with substantial meals always punctually served. In 1932 Maeterlinck received the highest honor that Belgium could confer: he was made a count. In 1935 he wrote a play for his wife, *La Princesse Isabelle* (Princess Isabelle, 1935). Set in contemporary Flanders, it has a bit of the poetic charm of his early plays and a happy ending. Mme Maeterlinck left her self-imposed retirement from the stage to appear in it for a short run in Paris.

In all, Maeterlinck published ten plays after World War I, three of which had been written earlier. One of his most sympathetic critics, Alex Pasquier, regretfully observes, however, that comparing any of them with the earlier plays "is fatal." *Le miracle de Saint-Antoine* (*The Miracle of St. Anthony*, 1919), Maeterlinck's only true comedy, stands out for its high spirits and its evocation of Flemish characters, but it did not succeed on the stage. Three plays that he wrote during World War II—*L'Abbé Sétubal* (Father Setubal, 1959), *Les trois justiciers* (The Three Justiciaries, 1959), and *Le jugement dernier* (The Last Judgment, 1959)—were published posthumously. They are of particular interest because of their return to mysticism and a treatment of religious themes that approaches Christian orthodoxy.

Between 1926 and 1932 Maeterlinck published three more volumes of natural history: *La vie des termites* (*The Life of the White Ant,* 1926), *La vie des fourmis* (*The Life of the Ant,* 1930), and *L'Araignée de verre* (The Glass Spider, translated as *Pigeons and Spiders,* 1932). Rather than model societies, however, Maeterlinck now finds in the insect world evidences of God's failure. Man being his least perfect creation, the writer wonders if the dark world of the termite is a foreshadowing of what awaits man; his pessimism could hardly be more complete.

The same years saw three more volumes of "scientific" inquiry into the universe. *La vie de l'espace* (*The Life of Space,* 1928) studies the dimensions of space and time; *La grande féerie* (*The Magic of the Stars,* 1929) examines the mysteries of astronomy and identifies God with the universe; finally, *La grande loi* (*The Supreme Law,* 1933) considers the laws of universal attraction and relativity. Maeterlinck's "great inquiry," in the end, left him where he began: the mysteries were still unsolved; agnosticism remained. His final essays led him no further. Called his "Pascalian Series" because the fragmentary form and unsystematic organization are reminiscent of Pascal's *Pensées,* they compose six volumes: *Avant le grand silence* (*Before the Great Silence,* 1934), *Le sablier* (*The Hour Glass,* 1936), *L'Ombre des ailes* (The Shadow of Wings, 1936), *Devant Dieu* (Before God, 1937), *La grande porte* (The Great Door, 1939), and *L'Autre monde, ou le cadran stellaire* (*The Great Beyond,* 1942). In these books he reviews all the thinkers he has studied and all his own thought. He can only conclude again that he can know nothing.

The Maeterlincks left France in 1939 for Portugal, and in 1940 they moved to the United States, where they divided their time principally between New York and Florida. The flurry of public attention upon their arrival was brief; most of their exile was spent quietly. In the last years Maeterlinck fell victim to a series of incapacitating illnesses, a new and depressing experience for one accustomed to robust health. The Maeterlincks returned to France in 1947, and the following year Maeterlinck's last book appeared. *Bulles bleues* is subtitled "Happy Memories" and recaptures his youth and young manhood in Flanders. The serene prose, the quiet humor, the relaxed candor reveal again the zest for life that neither pessimism nor despair could eradicate. Maeterlinck died of a heart attack at Orlamonde on 6 May 1949. At his request there was no service, and his body was cremated.

It is commonplace among critics to remark that, had Maeterlinck died at fifty, his literary reputation would not have suffered. Whatever merit they may have, it is true that no essays or plays he wrote in the second half of his life measure up to his earlier works. His most original contributions belong to his symbolist period, as does his one certain masterpiece. His greatest popular successes belong to his "second period," the first ten years or so with Leblanc. From this fact emerges another paradox: although he lived and wrote through the entire first half of the twentieth century, the essential Maeterlinck belongs to the nineteenth, in spirit as well as chronology.

Maeterlinck's place in literary history is assured by his creation of the symbolist drama; although he anticipated later writers, his actual literary influence is so slight as to be negligible. His influence is more apparent in the composers he inspired than in the few writers who imitated him. And, considering the rarity of productions of Maeterlinck's plays, we may be grateful to have Debussy's *Pelléas and Mélisande* or Dukas's *Ariane* rather than none at all.

During his lifetime Maeterlinck was always better appreciated in England and America than in France or Belgium. As his international reputation has withered, Maeterlinck's prestige in Belgium has grown, so that now it is in his native land that he is most avidly studied and warmly appreciated.

Selected Bibliography

EDITIONS

INDIVIDUAL WORKS

PLAYS

La Princesse Maleine. Ghent, 1889.

Les aveugles (précédés de L'Intruse). Brussels, 1890.

Les sept princesses. Brussels, 1891.

Pelléas et Mélisande. Brussels, 1892.

Alladine et Palomides: Intérieur. La mort de Tintagiles. Trois petits drames pour marionnettes. Brussels, 1894.

Aglavaine et Sélysette. Paris, 1896.

Ariane et Barbe-Bleue, ou la délivrance inutile. In *Théâtre,* III. Brussels and Paris, 1902.

Soeur Béatrice. In *Théâtre,* vol. 3. Brussels and Paris, 1902.

Monna Vanna. Paris, 1902.

Joyzelle. Paris, 1903.

L'Oiseau bleu. Paris, 1909.

Marie-Magdeleine. Paris, 1913.

Le miracle de Saint-Antoine. Paris, 1919.

Le bourgmestre de Stilmonde. Paris, 1919.

Les fiançailles. Paris, 1922.

Le malheur passe. Paris, 1925.

La puissance des morts. Paris, 1926.

Marie-Victoire. Paris, 1927.

Berniquel. Paris, 1929.

Juda de Kérioth. Paris, 1929.

La Princesse Isabelle. Paris, 1935.

Jeanne d'Arc. Monaco, 1948.

Théâtre inédit: L'Abbé Sétubal. Les trois justiciers. Le jugement dernier. Paris, 1959.

POEMS AND STORIES

Serres chaudes, poèmes. Paris, 1889.

Douze chansons de Maurice Maeterlinck. Paris, 1896.

Deux contes: La massacre des innocents. Onirologie. Paris, 1918.

ESSAYS AND PREFACES

Preface to Ralph Waldo Emerson, *Sept Essais.* Brussels, 1894.

Le trésor des humbles. Paris, 1896.

Preface to Camille Mauclair, *Jules Laforgue.* Paris, 1896.

MAURICE MAETERLINCK

La sagesse et la destinée. Paris, 1898.
La vie des abeilles. Paris, 1901.
Le temple enseveli. Paris, 1902.
Le double jardin. Paris, 1904.
L'Intelligence des fleurs. Paris, 1907.
La mort. Paris, 1913.
Les débris de la guerre. Paris, 1916.
L'Hôte inconnu. Paris, 1917.
Preface to Paul Fort, *Ballades françaises: Si peau d'ane m'était conté.* Paris, 1917.
Les sentiers dans la montagne. Paris, 1919.
Le grand secret. Paris, 1921.
Preface to *Les epîtres de Sénèque.* Lyon, 1921.
La vie des termites. Paris, 1926.
La vie de l'espace. Paris, 1928.
La grande féerie. Paris, 1929.
La vie des fourmis. Paris, 1930.
L'Araignée de verre. Paris, 1932.
La grande loi. Paris, 1933.
Avant le grand silence. Paris, 1934.
Le sablier. Paris, 1936.
L'Ombre des ailes. Paris, 1936.
Devant Dieu. Paris, 1937.
La grande porte. Paris, 1939.
L'Autre monde, ou le cadran stellaire. New York, 1942.

COLLECTED WORKS

Serres chaudes, suivies de quinze chansons. Brussels and 1900.
Théâtre. Introduction by Maeterlinck. 3 vols. Brussels and Paris, 1901–1902.
Morceaux choisis. Introduction by Georgette Leblanc. Paris, 1910.
Serres chaudes. Quinze chansons. Nouveaux poèmes. Introduction by Louis Piérard. Paris and Brussels, 1947.

MODERN EDITIONS

INDIVIDUAL WORKS

Insectes et Fleurs. Paris, 1954. Contains *La vie des abeilles, La vie des termites, L'Araignée de verre, L'Intelligence des fleurs,* and "Les pigeons."
Intérieur. Pelléas et Mélisande. L'Oiseau bleu. Introduction by Pierre-Aimé Touchard. Paris, 1956.
Les meilleures pages. Preface by Alex Pasquier. Brussels, 1958.
Pelléas et Mélisande. Preface by Henri Ronse. Paris, 1983.

COLLECTED WORKS

Poésies complètes: Serres chaudes. Quinze chansons. Neuf chansons de la trentaine. Treize chansons de l'âge mûr. Edited by Joseph Hanse. Brussels, 1965.
Théâtre complet. Introduction by Martine de Rougemont. Geneva, 1979.
Serres chaudes. Quinze chansons. La princesse Maleine. Introduction by Paul Gorceix. Paris, 1983.

MEMOIRS

Bulles bleues: Souvenirs heureux. Monaco, 1948.

TRANSLATIONS BY MAETERLINCK

L'Ornement des noces spirituelles de Ruysbroeck l'Admirable. Brussels and Paris, 1891.
Annabella ('Tis Pity She's a Whore): Drame en cinq actes de John Ford. Paris, 1895.
Les disciples à Saïs et les Fragments de Novalis. Brussels and Paris, 1895.
Shakespeare, la tragédie de Macbeth. Paris, 1909.

TRANSLATIONS

Note: Except for the poems in *Bulles bleues,* and a very few minor plays, everything Maeterlinck wrote was translated almost as soon as it was written. The following are currently in print:
Aglavaine and Selysette. Translated by Alfred Sutro. New York, 1911.
Alladine and Palomides. Translated by Alfred Sutro. New York, 1908.
Before the Great Silence. Translated by Bernard Miall. New York, 1936.
The Betrothal. Translated by Alexander Teixeira de Mattos. New York, 1918.
The Blind. Translated by Alba Amoia. In *An Anthology of Modern Belgian Theatre,* edited by Alba Amoia, Bettina L. Knapp, and Nadine Dormoy-Savage. Troy, N.Y., 1982.
The Blue Bird. Translated by Alexander Teixeira de Mattos. New York, 1907.
The Burgomaster of Stilemonde [*sic*]. Translated by Alexander Teixeira de Mattos. New York, 1911.
The Buried Temple. Translated by Alfred Sutro. New York, 1902.
The Cloud That Lifted and The Power of the Dead. Translated by F. M. Atkinson. New York, 1923.

Death. Translated by Alexander Teixeira de Mattos. New York, 1911.

The Double Garden. Translated by Alexander Teixeira de Mattos. New York, 1904.

The Great Beyond. Translated by Marta K. Neufeld and Renee Spodhem. New York, 1947.

The Great Secret. Translated by Bernard Miall. New York, 1922.

The Hour Glass. Translated by Bernard Miall. New York, 1936.

The Intelligence of the Flowers. Translated by Alexander Teixeira de Mattos. New York, 1907.

Interior: A Play. Translated by William Archer. New York, 1908.

The Intruder. Translated by Bettina L. Knapp. In *An Anthology of Modern Belgian Theatre*, edited by Alba Amoia, Bettina L. Knapp, and Nadine Dormoy-Savage. Troy, N.Y., 1982.

The Intruder, and Other Plays. Translated by Richard Hovey. New York, 1911. Includes *The Blind, The Seven Princesses*, and *The Death of Tintagiles*.

Joyzelle. Monna Vanna. Translated by Alexander Teixeira de Mattos and Alfred Sutro. New York, 1907.

The Life of Space. Translated by Bernard Miall. New York, 1928.

The Life of the Ant. Translated by Bernard Miall. New York, 1930.

The Life of the Bee. Translated by Alfred Sutro. New York, 1901.

The Life of the White Ant. Translated by Alfred Sutro. New York, 1927.

The Magic of the Stars. Translated by Alfred Sutro. New York, 1930.

Mary Magdalene. Translated by Alexander Teixeira de Mattos. New York, 1910.

"The Massacre of the Innocents." Translated by Alexander Teixeira de Mattos. In *The Wrack of the Storm*. New York, 1916.

The Measure of the Hours. Translated by Alexander Teixeira de Mattos. New York, 1907.

The Miracle of Saint Anthony. Translated by Alexander Teixeira de Mattos. New York, 1918.

Mountain Paths. Translated by Alexander Teixeira de Mattos. New York, 1919.

On Emerson, and Other Essays. Translated by Montrose J. Moses. New York, 1912.

Our Eternity. Translated by Alexander Teixeira de Mattos. New York, 1913.

Pelleas and Melisande. Translated by Alba Amoia. In *An Anthology of Modern Belgian Theatre*, edited by Alba Amoia, Bettina L. Knapp, and Nadine Dormoy-Savage. Troy, N.Y., 1982.

Pelléas and Mélisande, and Other Plays. Translated by Richard Hovey. New York, 1896. Includes *Alladine and Palomides* and *Home*.

Pigeons and Spiders. Translated by Bernard Miall. New York, 1936.

Plays of Maurice Maeterlinck. 2 vols. Translated by Richard Hovey. Chicago, 1895. Volume 1 contains *Princess Maleine, The Intruder, The Blind*, and *The Seven Princesses*. Volume 2 contains *Alladine and Palomides, Pelléas and Mélisande*, and *The Death of Tintagiles*.

Poems: Hot-Houses, Fifteen Songs. Translated by Bernard Miall. New York, 1915.

Princess Maleine. Translated by Richard Hovey. New York, 1894.

Sister Beatrice and Ardiane [sic] *and Barbe Bleue*. Translated by Bernard Miall. New York, 1901.

The Supreme Law. Translated by K. S. Shelvankar. New York, 1935.

The Treasure of the Humble. Translated by Alfred Sutro. New York, 1897.

Twelve Songs by Maurice Maeterlinck. Translated by Martin Schütze. Chicago, 1902.

The Unknown Guest. Translated by Alexander Teixeira de Mattos. New York, 1914.

Wisdom and Destiny. Translated by Alfred Sutro. New York, 1898.

The Wrack of the Storm. Translated by Alexander Teixeira de Mattos. New York, 1916.

BIOGRAPHICAL AND CRITICAL STUDIES

Artaud, Antonin. "Maurice Maeterlinck." In *Oeuvres complètes*, vol. I. Paris, 1956.

Bithell, Jethro. *Contemporary Belgian Literature*. New York, 1916.

————. *Life and Writings of Maurice Maeterlinck*. New York and London, 1913.

Brucher, Roger. *Maurice Maeterlinck: L'Oeuvre et son audience—Essai de bibliographie, 1883–1960*. Brussels, 1972.

Daniels, May. *The French Drama of the Unspoken*. Edinburgh, 1953.

Doneux, Guy. *Maurice Maeterlinck: Une poésie, une sagesse, un homme*. Brussels, 1961.

Halls, W. D. *Maurice Maeterlinck: A Study of his Life and Thought*. Oxford, 1960.

Hanse, Joseph, and Robert Vivier, eds. *Maurice Maeterlinck, 1862–1949.* Brussels, 1962.

Harry, Gérard. *Maurice Maeterlinck: A Biographical Study, with Two Essays by Maurice Maeterlinck.* Translated by Alfred Allinson. London, 1910.

Knapp, Bettina. *Maurice Maeterlinck.* Boston, 1975.

Leblanc, Georgette. *Souvenirs (1895–1918).* Paris, 1931. Translated by Janet Flanner as *Souvenirs: My Life with Maeterlinck.* New York, 1932.

Pasquier, Alex. *Maurice Maeterlinck.* Brussels, 1963.

Postic, Marcel. *Maeterlinck et le symbolisme.* Paris, 1970.

Sabetier, Robert. *Histoire de la poésie française. La poésie du dix-neuvième siècle, deuxième partie: Naissance de la poésie moderne.* Paris, 1977.

Symons, Arthur. "Maeterlinck as a Mystic." In *The Symbolist Movement in Literature.* New York, 1908.

Taylor, Una Ashworth. *Maurice Maeterlinck: A Critical Study.* Port Washington, N.Y., 1968.

Terrasson, René. *Pelléas et Mélisande, ou l'initiation.* Paris, 1982.

BIBLIOGRAPHIES

Since 1955 La Fondation Maeterlinck in Ghent has published regularly in its *Annales* current scholarship and bibliographical information on Maeterlinck.

RICHARD S. STOWE

GERHART HAUPTMANN

(1862–1946)

TOTALING NEARLY FOURTEEN thousand pages, the Centenary Edition of Gerhart Robert Hauptmann's collected works comprises eleven volumes. The collection includes dramas, novels, autobiographical writings, novellas, poetry, speeches and newspaper articles, fragments, and verse epics written between 1879 and the author's death in 1946. His works speak of individuals caught between poles of light and darkness, intellect and eros, social structures and freedom, and of humanity's painful struggle toward a better world. His characters, who sense that there is no way out of a loneliness imposed by forces beyond their grasp, react by seeking a solution at the boundaries of the intellect, where the magical, the mystical, the unsettling, the unknowable, and insanity itself often wait.

An idealist, Hauptmann saw himself in the tradition of Plato, Arthur Schopenhauer, Johann Wolfgang von Goethe, and the German romantics, who saw existence as basically dualistic; and he followed Friedrich Nietzsche and Friedrich Schelling in seeing man's nature as divided between Dionysian and Apollonian forces—subjectivity and objectivity, chaos and order. Hauptmann was a "religious" man, a term he defined as thinking about the infinite rather than the finite aspect of existence. He studied the major religions and philosophies and observed his fellow man in order to find a common ground, a fundamental basis from which to interpret reality for a

humanity divided into unrelated entities and adrift without a fixed course. On his sixtieth birthday he spoke before the University of Berlin of "The Way to Humanity":

> Mankind must rise ever further, and we Germans must rise and lead. We have teachers; we have leaders in the present and past whose duties must now begin. With the living dead, in rank and file, I see the true path of glory of future German literature, which will stride with a higher goal in mind. Let us hope, let us hope therefore for it and that it goes beyond progress! And to this end let that come about for us all which the poet Novalis longed for: a new, divine world inspiration.
>
> (6: 768)[1]

Hauptmann saw beyond perceived reality to a place where a new humanity had broken its social, political, intellectual, and spiritual chains in order to enjoy once again its divine heritage.

The turn of the century was a time of political and cultural change throughout Europe, including Germany. Socialism and the problems of the working class were paramount in the minds of young writers. The view of reality termed naturalism seemed to them a proper program for implementing the changes that needed to be made in the attitudes of

[1]Unless otherwise noted, all quotations are taken from the eleven-volume *Sämtliche Werke*, edited by Hans-Egon Hass and Martin Machatzke [Berlin 1962–1974].

middle-class Germans. They sought to make society aware of the positivistic, anti-metaphysical view of man espoused in the new socialistic thought, and of man's behavior as determined by environment *and* inheritance rather than by the latter alone. They were convinced that such a revolutionary approach to art (that is, a reflection of real life) would allow mankind to be viewed in a new light that would lead to social change. These young reformers' beliefs are summed up in Arno Holz's formula: art equals nature minus *X* (*X* being the talent of the artist and his means of reproduction). As Holz explained, "Art has the tendency to return to nature; it becomes so according to the degree of its prerequisites of reproduction and its implementation." Leo Tolstoy, Émile Zola, and Henrik Ibsen, among many others, had led the fight to improve conditions for the average man—or they had, at the very least, shown the terrible ravages of external social forces on him. Hauptmann and his fellow members of the secret literary organization Durch (Through) strongly felt themselves to be part of the new movement of social compassion. Important members of this group were Bruno Wille and Wilhelm Bölsche, editors of the journal *The Free Stage,* and Julius and Heinrich Hart, editors of *The German Monthly Papers.* But Otto von Bismarck's government was also interested in these young firebrands, and in 1887 many of them appeared before the court during the Breslau socialist trials; Hauptmann was called as a witness, and denied any official affiliation with the socialist movement.

The struggle toward the goal of a "new humanity" produced works that are highly descriptive of everyday life while also subtly suggesting a tempting, if ill-defined, existence beyond our perception. Such a work is Hauptmann's *Bahnwärter Thiel: Novellistische Studie aus dem märkischen Kiefernforst (Flagman Thiel,* 1888). His best-known and still most widely read and interpreted short novel, *Flagman Thiel* depicts a common working-man's struggle between Eros and spirituality.

Thiel is a simple man who marries the shrewish and brutally passionate Lene after the untimely death of his beloved first wife, Minna. He soon discovers that Lene treats Tobias, the son of his first marriage, cruelly while favoring her own newly born child. Unable to bring himself to confront Lene because of his enslavement in the "iron net" of Eros, as the narrator terms it, he seeks refuge in his isolated keeper's hut, which lies quite a distance from the house along the railroad tracks. Here he has a vision one day of Minna carrying a bloody bundle toward him on the tracks.

One day, unexpectedly, Lene insists upon accompanying him to his hut, his "shrine" to Minna, where she intends to plant potatoes. Upon arrival, Lene insists that Tobias stay with her to watch the baby rather than go with Thiel. Busy preparing the ground, she allows Tobias to wander off. Soon, a trainman comes from the railroad tracks carrying the dying boy, now a bloody bundle of rags that recalls Thiel's vision. Only half conscious of his actions now, Thiel finds himself contemplating Lene's murder as revenge for her negligence in Tobias' death. He senses he is going insane but is unable to struggle against the "red fog" that overcomes his senses. While Tobias' body is being returned by train to Thiel's hut, he retreats further into himself and must be led home. At this point guilt transforms Lene into the caring wife she had not been; she watches over her unconscious husband, bathing his forehead, anxiously awaiting some improvement. The events of the day take their toll, and Lene falls asleep. When the men return from the tracks to the Thiel home with the child's corpse, they find her skull split by a hatchet, her face disfigured beyond recognition. Thiel is discovered the next morning sitting between the rails at the very spot where Tobias died. Bound hand and foot, the gatekeeper is taken into custody, but his insanity is evident, and he is removed to the insanity ward of the charity hospital.

Flagman Thiel illustrates a good deal of the naturalist credo: Thiel belongs to the working class, his character is determined by both genetic and external social factors, and he is a victim of forces he is not equipped to understand. Also according to naturalist techniques, nature and causal relationships in the story are scientifically rendered in detailed, accurate, objective descriptions. Even here during the heyday of naturalism, however, there was a strong, undeniable romantic-mystical-mythological undercurrent in *Thiel*, as in most of Hauptmann's works. The opposing forces of nature and the new industrial society appear in symbolic, and therefore unnaturalistic, form. Nature is represented by the sun, the forest, the moon, deer, and other animals; threatening society is represented by the train, which acts as the objective symbol of irrationality and appears at points of tension, as does Thiel's Lene, once referred to as "a machine." These symbols form a tight complex that underscores the totality of man's experience of reality.

Flagman Thiel attracted primarily the attention of the literary avant-garde readers of *Gesellschaft* (Society), the naturalist organ that published the story. On the other hand, *Vor Sonnenaufgang, Soziales Drama* (*Before Daybreak,* 1889) created an instant public scandal when first performed on 20 October 1889 at the Lessing Theater in Berlin. It was a production of the Free Stage Society, a private group of enthusiasts that was formed to produce plays that were censored by the conservative Prussian regime. Theodor Fontane, the grand old man of German literature and an admirer of the young idealists, characterized the play's author in a letter to his daughter as "a real captain [*Hauptmann*] of that black gang of realists . . . an Ibsen totally devoid of cliché." A member of the society was less kind. During the premiere Dr. Isidor Kastan, a physician and journalist as well as leader of the conservative opposition to the new naturalist theater, outraged by the alchoholic father's incestuous fumblings after his daughter in act 2, screamed, "Are we in the theater or a bordello!" And at the call for a midwife in act 5, he swung a set of forceps over his head,

threatening to throw them onto the stage. The audience was thrown into tumult; the actors were jeered and constantly interrupted, but the play somehow carried on. The next day Berlin's newspapers had a field day: they termed the Free Stage "a smutty men's club" and "a distillery theater"; Hauptmann was decried as "the most immoral playwright of the century." The depiction of "real" life had come to the German stage, an event that was all the more exciting due to the strict enforcement of the Socialist Laws, which prohibited the performance of any uncensored, and therefore unauthorized, version of a play with "social" content.

Designed to be viewed as if four walls were present, not the three of traditional Aristotelian theater, the play is organized by a simple plot. One day, Alfred Loth, social reformer and teetotaler, appears in the village of Witzdorf to visit his old school friend Hoffmann, who has married the daughter of a Silesian farmer named Krause who has recently become wealthy by the discovery of coal on his property. A tragic love affair between Loth and the farmer's younger daughter Helene develops. Loth warns her inadvertently at the beginning of the relationship that he could never marry a woman with tainted genes; in fact her father is an alcoholic, as is her married sister. When Loth discovers that Helene is the daughter of an alcoholic, he leaves her, and she commits suicide.

On the surface the play appears to be a showcase of naturalism, providing a stark, dispassionate depiction of reality, presenting an audience with the information necessary to arouse a desire to change the materialistic view, as represented by the newly rich farmers, and pointing out through the ironic portrayal of the dogmatic Loth the need for more compassion in the social structure. However, while the goals of the young Hauptmann cannnot be completely separated from those of his idealistic colleagues, there is a deeper level to his work of this period, one that parallels his lifelong penchant for description. From 1885

149

to 1890 he wrote his "Jesus-Studien" (Jesus Studies), unpublished fragments that are comments on the New Testament. These contain a very personal vision of a human Christ and his struggle with the practical problems of delivering the Good Word of a new kingdom; Hauptmann once called Jesus "the first socialist." In the studies he concentrates at one point on the parable of the sower—"The Sower" was to have been the original title of *Before Daybreak*. The correspondence between the points of the parable and the play's moral structure are striking. Christ tells the multitude of a sower who cast seed upon the ground, some of which the birds ate, some of which fell upon stony places and grew poorly for lack of soil and was then parched by the rising sun, some of which landed among thorns and was choked, and some of which fell onto fertile soil and was fruitful (Matthew 13:3–8). In Hauptmann's play, Loth is the sower, an ironic Christ figure. Helene's consciousness, formed more by the desperation of her demeaning life at home and her desire to flee it than by real love of Loth, and Witzdorf itself, where all social order has broken down, are the unprepared acre upon which the seeds of selflessness cannot grow. The Krause family represents the thorns among which the seed has fallen, but their material riches hinder them from accepting the gift of selflessness and love. The symbol of the rising sun in both the parable and the play emphasizes the destructiveness of illumination on that which is unready to accept such a gift. As it is in a Christianity practiced without social compassion, utopia is truly beyond the grasp of both Loth and the people of Witzdorf.

Other "family tragedies" quickly followed *Before Daybreak*. Pen and notebook in hand, Hauptmann gathered material from the lives of family and friends to produce *Das Friedensfest* (*The Reconciliation*, 1890) and *Einsame Menschen* (*Lonely Lives*, 1891). The former contains conversations with Frank Wedekind, contemporary playwright and friend prior to the play's performance, about the relationship of Wedekind's quarrelsome and eccentric father, the model for the older Scholz, with his family. Hauptmann recorded these "secrets" while visiting Wedekind and his family in Zürich in 1888. While the play's title in German means "festival of peace," the play itself is anything but peaceful. Wilhelm Scholz returns like the prodigal son to celebrate Christmas with his family and to seek reconciliation with his father, whom he has not seen since striking him six years earlier. The "spring magic" of redemption comes in act 2, and Wilhelm falls unconscious in a paroxysm of joy after having shed his pent-up feelings of guilt. He and his older brother, Robert, a cynic, rejoice in the discovery that their father has loved them all along. But in a storm of passion brought on by alcohol, Robert suddenly denounces the celebration as "a children's comedy," whereupon his father just as suddenly begins once more to regard the entire family as his enemy. Again, as at the outset, each member of the family wallows in his private emotional hell, and the audience realizes how thin the veneer of love and understanding is, how certain the continuation of the cycle of suffering.

Lonely Lives, Hauptmann's favorite among the dramas of his youth, has its origin in his brother Carl's marital difficulties, but the author admits that although the main character, Johannes Vockerat, acts like Carl, he is actually more like himself. And Johannes' wife Käthe, he adds, resembles his wife, Marie Thienemann, more than she does his sister-in-law, Martha. As Hauptmann's writing became increasingly personal, it also became more popular. But while giving him the wider exposure he so much desired, it also angered those of his friends and family who felt betrayed by him.

Josepha Krzyzanowska, an irresistible young intellectual who visited Carl first in Zürich and then in Berlin, and who almost drove Carl and Martha to divorce due to Carl's infatuation with her, comes alive as Anna in this play, so aptly called by one critic "Nervous People." When

Johannes Vockerat finds that Anna Mahr is more interesting and desirable than either his wife or his pseudo-scientific Darwinian studies, the Vockerat clan gathers to force him back to happiness. But Anna has only precipitated a long-standing problem; Johannes has always been unable to decide between middle-class security and innovative living. When Anna is asked to leave for the sake of the family, Johannes feels he has no choice but to end his life. Käthe and Johannes, these "nervous people" or "modern people," suffer in a marriage built on the opposing moral values of two generations: the "stultifying" Christian and the "natural" Darwinian. Unable to find comfort in either, they are consigned to the limbo of irresolution. Johannes' death solves nothing; he simply exchanges existential isolation for nothingness.

Hauptmann had not existed in a literary vacuum before his triumph of 1889; he had experienced private and public successes—and failures—that directed him steadily toward a career as a writer. He never finished the gymnasium (high school), and when he left in 1878 he described the event as a "release from prison." His Uncle Schubert in Lederose (Silesia) invited him to take up the practical study of farming there. After one year the harsh working and living conditions gave the rather delicate young man lung damage that plagued him until 1904. The lessons he learned in pietism and his youthful love for Anna Grundmann (recorded in the verse epic *Anna*, 1921) also stayed with him and reappeared often in his works.

In 1880 he studied art at the Royal Art and Trade School in Breslau, having given himself over to a desire to sculpt. He was expelled for "poor behavior and unsatisfactory industry." Professor Robert Haertel then befriended Hauptmann, gave him private lessons, and the following year persuaded the academy to allow its former student to declaim his poem "Hermannslied" (The Lay of Herman) before it in an assembly. Hauptmann was readmitted to the academy. The poem had been a product of his stay in Lederose, and it expressed the

pan-Germanic feelings, so important throughout his life, to which he and his "blood brothers" Carl Hauptmann and Alfred Ploetz, the influential eugenicist, had sworn allegiance under a sacred oak in Breslau in 1878.

In 1881 he became engaged to Marie Thienemann, whose memory is preserved in the verse epics *Die blaue Blume* (The Blue Flower, 1927) and "Mary" (1936). Now supported financially by his fiancée, he enrolled in 1882 at the University of Jena, where he studied history. During this period he, Ploetz, Carl, Ferdinand Simon (son-in-law of the socialist leader August Bebel and later a physician), Otto Pringsheim (later an important economist), Max Müller (the musician), and Henrich Lux (the influential writer on Icarian communism) formed the utopian "Pacific Society," whose aim it was to study the American utopian colonies and eventually settle there. Ploetz actually visited the French Icarian colonies founded by Étienne Cabet in Texas and Illinois in 1848 and sadly reported back that these attempts at communal living had all failed. This news, coupled with the shock of having been suspected of a socialist plot to overthrow the government in 1887, no doubt contributed to Hauptmann's internalization of the quest for the utopia he had sought in the practical world. He would now concentrate his efforts toward utopian reform in literature, thus avoiding any further overt political trauma.

In 1883 Hauptmann went to Rome to study sculpture. He returned to Germany in 1884, ill with typhus and distraught because a fellow sculptor had destroyed his works in a fit of insanity. For two semesters he studied at the University of Berlin, where he heard lectures by some of Europe's most influential scholars: Ernst Robert Curtius, renowned literary critic and expert on the German-Latin Middle Ages; Emil Du Bois–Reymond, noted Swiss physiologist and opponent of vitalism; Heinrich von Treitschke, famous historian and advocate of Prussian hegemony; and Paul Deussen, editor of the 1911 Schopenhauer edition and translator of Hindu scriptures, both of which Hauptmann later studied. After he was told in the winter of 1884–1885 that he would die in six months if his bohemian life-style continued, Marie arrived to help him mend his ways. They married in March and moved to Erkner, a suburb of Berlin, where he began the "Jesus-Studien," and where his sons Ivo, Eckart, and Klaus were born in 1886, 1887, and 1889, respectively.

Hauptmann credited the move to Erkner with literally saving his life. Here his literary career began in earnest, having been interrupted only briefly by his earlier passionate attraction to sculpting and painting. He did, however, sculpt and paint throughout his life. He began observing and taking notes on the everyday events around him. His first work is the novella *Fasching: Eine Studie* (Fasching: A Study, 1887), in which he depicts in minute detail the events leading up to the tragic drowning death of the sailmaker Kielblock and his wife and child on their return from a Shrovetide ball. The tale is based on the actual drowning death of the boatwright Zieb and his family in the Flakensee (a lake near Erkner) on 13 February 1887. *Fasching* was influenced by his reading of the author and radical firebrand of social reform Georg Büchner, particularly by Büchner's novella *Lenz* (1839); Hauptmann found his interest in psychological realism mirrored in *Lenz*. *Fasching*, while representative of the naturalist style and philosophy, allows us a glimpse into Hauptmann's literary future: descriptions of actions, psychological motivations, and nature may be accurate, but they play against a romantic background of demonic nature that lends the story a non-naturalistic profundity not found in the programmatic works of the naturalist writers and theorists Arno Holz and Johannes Schlaf, who together wrote *Papa Hamlet* (1889) and *Die Familie Selicke* (The Selicke Family, 1890).

The world of myth and visionary experience are never far removed from Hauptmann's consciousness. When he decided in 1887 to visit the area of his birth, the Sudeten Mountains—

Marie had departed for the sickbed of her sister Frida—he fell under the spell of the region's legends, history, and tradition of mysticism. The fervency, youthful naiveté, and exuberance found in his first collection of poetry, *Das bunte Buch. Gedichte* (The Book of Many Colors: Poems, 1888), then gave way to what Hauptmann called the "quiet, earnest, and promising path" that led to works such as *Die Weber* (The Weavers, 1892), and in a more ecstatic but no less profound way to *Hanneles Himmelfahrt* (The Assumption of Hannele, 1894).

The Weavers stirred controversy even before its first performance. This most frequently printed and read of Hauptmann's plays appeared in both a dialect and a standard German version, neither of which was allowed on the public stage until 25 September 1894 due to official Prussian censorship (its private premiere was arranged by the Free Stage Society in Berlin on 26 February 1893). The Prussian Upper Administrative Court explained that its decision to ban this play about the revolt of Silesian weavers in 1844 was based on the "risk of public disorder" rather than "risk of damage to the public morality." The "risk" in question rested on serious political considerations, for the revolt of 1844 had threatened to undermine the stability of a Prussian rule founded on an intent to foster industrial progress without regard for the worker. Bismarck's government knew that conditions were once again right for a challenge to authority: the poverty and misery of life in the Berlin of 1892 were overwhelming, and the government still reacted to all change with oppression and violence. The first two stanzas of the song that the rebellious weavers sing in act 2 evoke the strong sense of injustice felt not only in 1892 but also in the revolt of 1848, the result of many years of similar social oppression, when poets such as Heinrich Heine, Ferdinand Freiligrath, Hermann Püttmann, Georg Weerth, and Ludwig Pfau recorded their sympathy with the weavers in similar poems:

Here in this place is a tribunal
far worse than secret trials,
where no verdict is needed
to take a life so quickly.
Here a man is slowly tormented,
here the torture chamber,
here are counted so many sighs
as witness of the misery.

(2:375)

The suffering of the Silesian weavers became a rallying point, a symbol, for man's inhumanity to man and struck deeply into both conservative and liberal consciences. Hauptmann rekindled feelings of social compassion for the disenfranchised worker, the victim of greed, at a time when the labor movement was gaining strength. This made his play look suspiciously political, which it does seem to be, but a closer examination of it shows clearly that the problem of man's relationship to the chaotic forces that rule his existence is also addressed.

In *The Weavers*, hunger has driven the Silesian weavers of Peterswaldau and Langenbielau to revolt against the exploitative capitalist mill owner, Dreissiger. In five acts we witness the effects of their own desperation on the "group protagonist," the weavers. The younger and older generations are portrayed as antagonists, both of whom are victims of a middle-class society that is organized against their welfare. When the young people take to the streets, indiscriminately burning and pillaging, soldiers are summoned and the uprising is brutally suppressed. There are no victors, as the open ending of the play suggests.

Fontane viewed the fifth act of *The Weavers* as an artificial addition because it appeared to negate the revolutionary tone set by the first four. But in being both revolutionary and antirevolutionary, he concludes, the piece speaks to the consciences of both sides. In the naturalistic style, *The Weavers* provides no solution to problems; rather, it seeks to expose them in depth and allow the audience to decide. Even though four of its five acts deal with the suffering of the weavers and the apparent righteousness of their struggle against capitalist

greed and religious and social hypocrisy, the moral force of the fifth act's "hero," Old Hilse, balances the mass hero of the first four acts. Hilse refuses to move from his loom by the window and join the rampaging mob: "My heavenly father set me here. Ain't that right, mother? And here we'll stay and do what we have to, even if the snow burns." A bullet strikes him through the window, and he falls dead over his loom. Is this divine retribution for his unwillingness to change with the times, or perhaps a metaphor for a topsy-turvy, amoral existence that ends quite unresolved in ironic coincidence? Whatever the answer, the death of this brave, staunch old man is deeply affecting, while the easy, even joyful, willingness of the young weavers to take life is shocking. As art *The Weavers* is balanced and effective; as propaganda it is neither. Art, not politics, was Hauptmann's religion.

Among the three most important and enduring German comedies are Gotthold Ephraim Lessing's *Minna von Barnhelm* (1767), Heinrich von Kleist's *Der zerbrochene Krug* (*The Broken Jug*, 1811), and Hauptmann's *Der Biberpelz* (*The Beaver Coat*, 1893). Subtitled "A Comedy of Thieves," the latter was originally to have been a political attack à la Molière entitled "The Hypochondriac: Fear of the Police Under the Socialist Laws." But Hauptmann's brief and unpleasant contact with the Prussian legal system in 1887 and his general disinclination toward public political involvement probably decided him against such a course of political commitment.

Written in Erkner, the play brings to life characters Hauptmann had actually observed and situations in which he had participated. The hub of this comedy is the theft of the pensioner Krüger's new beaver coat by Mother Wolff, who combines Silesian cunning with Berlin wit and outsmarts the pompous, arrogant district police magistrate von Wehrhahn. The character of Dr. Fleischer, the young, idealistic social democrat, serves to introduce the author's political sentiments into situations, while suggesting the lack of deeper understanding of the well-meaning but too theoretically oriented democratic spirit. The play's comedic appeal is based on puns, use of dialect, and the many misunderstandings brought about by Krüger's deafness, as well as strong contrasts such as that between Mother Wolff's low social position and her obvious, and profound, understanding of society's inner workings, as well as more immediately apparent contrasts such as the juxtaposition of Wehrhahn's authority and his falsetto voice. If the poverty of the Wolff family is not itself funny—if, for example, their elder daughter has become decadent before her time due to a system without compassion—and if the sociopolitical realities of an oppressive time are clearly and accurately portrayed in *The Beaver Coat,* we can still rejoice with Mother Wolff at the defeat of Wehrhahn ("rooster").

The Beaver Coat is a perfect fable for the time. The character of Dr. Fleischer expresses the democratic, social reformist outlook of many of Germany's young intellectuals during the political turmoil of the "Septennatskampf" of 1887, the struggle of conservatives against liberals to maintain a peacetime army for a period of seven years. When the conservatives lost this bid, parliament was dissolved and new elections were called. Using the fear of war, Bismarck's conservatives convinced the people to vote for them and a strengthened army. The immediate result was a reduction in social expenditure, which gave rise to a stronger liberal opposition. This undertone of political turmoil is not overtly expressed in *The Beaver Coat* but rather takes form in the struggle between Wehrhahn and Fleischer. The latter is patterned after Hauptmann himself and, perhaps, Wilhelm Liebknecht, who founded the Socialist Workers' Party in 1869, whom he had closely observed and admired during the socialist trials. Wehrhahn's zeal for spying on and persecuting those, like Fleischer, who have not recognized "the highest values of the nation" is boundless. He is a stereotype of the Prussian bureaucrat, a product of increasing Prussian militarism and the accompanying anti-civilian attitude nurtured by expansionist military victories of 1864, 1866, and 1870.

Of the three main characters—Fleischer, the democrat; Wehrhahn, the royalist bureaucrat; and Mother Wolff, the thief, poacher, and victim of social injustice—only Mother Wolff achieves her goal in the comedy. Wehrhahn is stymied in his effort to catch the thief, both by his own blind arrogance, which makes him overestimate his abilities, and by her native wit and superior knowledge of human nature. Fleischer is left to dangle under the light of official scrutiny and suspicion. But this is not really an open ending in the programmatic naturalistic manner, for the central theme, the nature of social injustice, has been resolved: Mother Wolff now has the money she has gained through theft, but in the getting of it she has been reduced in symbolic stature. With the sale of the coat, she may be able to reach her vaguely stated goal of financial security, but she has sacrificed her superiority to the "system" as a woman defending her brood. She has outsmarted herself to become a capitalist like those who oppress her.

That Mother Wolff has transformed herself becomes clear in *Der rote Hahn* (The Red Rooster, 1901), in which Hauptmann develops her character to its logical conclusion. Here the widowed Mrs. Wolff, now married to Fielitz the shoemaker and police informer, stretches her cunning to the breaking point by setting her house afire to collect the insurance, which she plans to invest in her son-in-law's business. Here she is no longer the victim of injustice; she is a genuine criminal with whom we cannot sympathize. *Der rote Hahn* was a failure on the stage because it seemed to many to be merely Hauptmann's copy of an earlier, successful work whose sociopolitical values had been watered down. The great critic Alfred Kerr summed up the objections: "One says, there is a great deal in this piece, but it does not come out! The other says, there is a lot in this piece, why can't you detect it! Which party will win? One thing is certain: this important tragicomedy had little effect on us all."

A sudden change took place in Hauptmann's approach to theater in 1894 with the performance of his neoromantic "dream poem" *The Assumption of Hannele.* The stark realism and strident social reformist stance of *Before Sunrise, The Weavers,* and *The Beaver Coat* give way in this play to the delicate beauty and sometimes maudlin compassion of the art nouveau movement, as typified, for instance, in the drawings of Aubrey Beardsley. Like Hugo von Hofmannsthal's *Der Tor und der Tod* (*Death and the Fool,* 1899) and Oscar Wilde's *The Happy Prince* (1888), Hauptmann's play shows how no person, however confused in spirit or lowly of stature, is outside of the plan of existence. Instead of depicting actual revolt, inner rebellion, and victimization in a clearly understood format, Hauptmann presents the "fever vision" of the poor orphan Hannele Mattern, who is starving. Society is never directly indicted for its lack of compassion for her hunger, loneliness, and abuse by a drunken father, but when she ascends to heaven in the final scene of act 2, surrounded by a chorus of angels singing, "Rock-a-bye baby, to Heaven we go," the years of her suffering are compressed into a moment of epiphany: somewhere, someone cares for the weak and helpless. Who, we cannot say, for it is not clear whether Hannele has dreamed this ascendance, or whether there might indeed be a place of higher reward beyond her poorhouse existence. Good has triumphed over evil, but not in this life.

Not all eyes were tearful, however. Loyal critics who had followed Hauptmann's development were disappointed, even scandalized, that he should wander from the path of social activism and write a "blasphemous" piece that, they reasoned, hypocritically mysticized real poverty and thereby lent moral support to the idea of a superior upper class. According to Paul Schlenther, theater director, critic, and Hauptmann admirer, "the sanctimonious wanted to blame it [*Hannele*] on the social

democrats, the social democrats on the sanctimonious." One thing is clear: Hauptmann had given expression to the second, the mystical, side of his personality, which sensed a dual, Platonic scheme of things. The "mystical" plane is accessible not through reason and observation, but only through intuition, dream, and vision. When Hannele dreams, we experience with her the world she has created out of snatches of Grimm's fairy tales, Bible verses and characters, nursery rhymes, and most importantly, her own desire to taste the positive side of life that has been denied her by a society without compassion. So it really does not matter whether our "poor little match girl" has actually died and gone to a heaven where her bleak life will be fulfilled in the light and where she will marry the Christlike figure who resembles her earthly teacher, Mr. Gottwald, or whether she deludes herself with the sweet illusion of fulfillment; the fact remains that Hauptmann here posits the existence of "another" reality, one that forces us to see the social problems of *Hannele* in a different light.

In 1893 Hauptmann had dedicated *Hannele* to his wife, Marie, with the words: "Children pick red clover, carefully pluck the blossoms, and suck on the pale, fine shafts. Their tongues enjoy a faint sweetness. If you only extract so much from my poem, I will not be ashamed of my gift." But by 1894 their marriage had reached a point of crisis because of Hauptmann's deepening romantic involvement with Margarete Marschalk, whom he had met when she was seventeen years old at the gala following the premiere of *Hannele* in Berlin in 1893. Their attraction grew, aided by a mutual love of music, and Hauptmann soon found himself dividing time between Marie and Margarete. When he explained his feelings to Marie in 1893, she refused to understand, and early in 1894 Marie fled with her three sons to their old friend Ploetz in Meriden, Connecticut. *Hannele* was to have its French premiere in Paris that January, but Hauptmann, in great emotional turmoil, followed Marie on the steamer *Elbe* and did not see the performance. The novel *Atlantis* (*Atlantis*, 1912) records the crossing, though it includes a shipwreck as its central event. Critics found it to be one of Hauptmann's most uneven works. Shortly after it appeared, however, the *Titanic* sank, and the poet's "mystical" proclivities, by then well developed, invited a view of both novel and author as prophetic.

In May the family returned together to Germany, but July found Hauptmann living alone in an apartment in Berlin-Grunewald, from where he took a second research trip to Bavaria to study the history surrounding Florian Geyer, the aristocrat who sided with the peasants in the revolt of 1525. The marital split widened; Hauptmann agreed to try to save the marriage by spending time alone in Zürich, where he hoped to distance himself from Margarete, but the attempt proved unsuccessful. In 1900 Margarete bore him a son out of wedlock, and in the same year Hauptmann had two homes built, one for himself and Margarete in Agnetendorf and another in Dresden for Marie and the children; divorce and remarriage to Margarete in 1904 followed. Hauptmann never overcame feelings of guilt at having "abandoned" dependent and melancholic Marie, and undertones of these feelings are suggested in the struggle between wife, husband, and lover in *Die versunkene Glocke* (*The Sunken Bell*, 1896).

Florian Geyer (1896) and *The Sunken Bell* were published in that order. Two more different but nevertheless intimately related dramas can scarcely be imagined. The first deals with the peasant revolt of 1525, in which Geyer, actually a quite minor figure in the revolt, found the brutality of the aristocracy intolerable and strove for the equality of classes that Martin Luther's misunderstood epistle "Freedom of a Christian" appeared to proclaim; Luther meant that each Christian was spiritually, not politically, free. Hauptmann portrays Geyer as an idealistic hero, the incarnation of revolution as it should be. Against the egotism and opportunism of the other nobles, Hauptmann sets Geyer's boundless but simple ide-

alism, which proclaimed discipline, the obligation to uphold one's word of honor, and the hard consequences that await those who disobey these elementary rules for the preservation of order in Germany. Geyer dies at the end of the play, a victim of his own tragic belief in the honor of others.

Hauptmann wrote the play in an artificial language meant to evoke the sixteenth century, a period of great social activity. The language and the length make *Florian Geyer* difficult to perform and often tedious to listen to or read (the original script was over three hundred pages long and included more than seventy roles). It is often criticized for being epic rather than dramatic, but in its weakness lies its strength, for it is in the epic mode that the author captures the hero's sublime German idealism and conveys the essence of the broad events of the time. Hauptmann went not only to history books for background but also to Luther; to Thomas Murner, a preacher, humanist, poet, and opponent of Luther; to Ulrich von Hutten, a humanist and proponent of a strong, united German empire; to Andreas Gryphius, a baroque author called the German Shakespeare; and to other literary and religious figures of the sixteenth and seventeenth centuries in order to anchor his production firmly in national tradition. The play was instantly unsuccessful—many actually booed during its premiere on 4 January 1896 in Berlin. Hauptmann wrote, somewhat bitterly and in a depressed mood, for he had been sure of its success, "German national sentiment is like a cracked bell: I hit it with a hammer but it did not resound." But by 1917 and World War I *Florian Geyer* had come to represent the epitome of the German spirit in adversity, which, like the heart of Geyer himself, was seen as containing a "burning righteousness." Directly after the war, the betrayal of Geyer assumed the mystical, national overtones of the stab-in-the-back motif that appears as early as the twelfth-century Germanic *Nibelungenlied* (*Lay of the Nibelungs*), a work that depicted the Germanic spirit in its struggle with the psychological and political forces of fifth-century Germany, a time when a bloody revenge and brutality were common. In 1944 the piece was honored by the Nazis as a true "people's drama" because of its appeal for German unity. The Eighth SS Cavalry Division even bore the play's name. Hauptmann had indeed struck a responsive cultural chord, while at the same time inadvertently providing propaganda for an extreme view. This was not the last time he accomplished either.

In *The Sunken Bell, Florian Geyer's* larger-than-life idealism is transferred to the bell-founder Heinrich, whose dual calling, and the struggle this implies, is represented by his profession: he is both craftsman and conduit to the world of ideality; he is an artist. In the fairy-tale quality of the nymph or wood spirit Rautendelein and the loyalty and steadfastness of Heinrich's wife, Magda, the love conflict of the author's life, his love for Margarete Marschalk and feelings of loyalty toward his first wife, Marie, is reflected. Caught between the real and the utopian, Heinrich thrashes about in his pursuit of equilibrium. He wishes to forge past the restrictions of Christian social ethics to a natural religion, symbolized by the sun, that would free the "chosen" one to follow natural inclinations. But Heinrich is also unsure he is a chosen artist. Looking back on *The Sunken Bell* in his autobiographical *Buch der Leidenschaft* (Book of Passion, 1930), Hauptmann writes, "I recall that we [members of the Pacific Society] would not countenance marriage, also that we fought against the Christian denial of the world, with its contempt for the body and natural drives, as destructive insanity." Hauptmann had read and studied many of Friedrich Nietzsche's writings, including *The Birth of Tragedy* (1872), *Thoughts Out of Season* (1873), and *Genealogy of Morals* (1887). In *Buch der Leidenschaft,* as in the play, Hauptmann is attracted to a positive, personally liberating reevaluation of the intellectual's relationship to society, here reflected in the institution of marriage.

The Wilhelminian social order, modeled after that of Queen Victoria in its strict observance of outward morality and narrowness of intellectual view, had reaffirmed early-nineteenth-century values of home and hearth, again placing the artist outside of respectability. In 1896 Kaiser Wilhelm II went so far as to exert his influence against awarding the Schiller Prize to the too "political" *Hannele,* although the Imperial Academy of Sciences in Vienna recognized the work with the Grillparzer Prize in the same year. In spite of such royal treatment, Hauptmann considered himself an exemplary patriot whose duty was to portray his beloved German people as if it were a personality, a dear friend: "So I must become a kind of accumulator of the needs, hopes, and wishes of humanity and especially of the German people, charged with its suffering, hoping, desiring, loving, and dynamic power."

Heinrich dies in Rautendelein's arms at the end of his tortured yet glorious search for a relationship to the ideal, symbolized by the nymph. A return to the smothering reality of normal life with wife Magda would have meant the end of his artistic life. But even though he must die, the utterance of his single dying word, *Sonnenglockenklang* (bell sound of the sun), expresses the hope of a place for those like him in a dualistic universe. This hope also seems to express Hauptmann's yearning for an ever-closer relationship with Marschalk.

From January to May of 1897 Hauptmann and Marschalk traveled in Italy. A stopover in Rovio provided a great deal of material for the later novella *Der Ketzer von Soana (The Heretic of Soana,* 1918). In November he began one of his most enduring plays, *Fuhrmann Henschel (Drayman Henschel,* 1899), which represents a departure from fairy- and folktale sources and a return to his native Silesia for inspiration. A friend, Moritz Heimann, had described to him the content of fellow Silesian Hermann Stehr's novella *Der Graveur (The Engraver,* 1898). With enthusiasm Hauptmann set to work to rival Stehr's depiction of Silesian village life. Hauptmann later said of the play:

"My so-called naturalism was in reality only a return to the natural, the traditional. As we recently experienced in Hirschberg, even the simple peasants of Agnetendorf can play my 'Drayman Henschel' very well. They are simply playing themselves. Abstraction is an inherited evil of German literature."

Drayman Henschel is the story of a man's struggle with fate and the destruction that must result, since the sensitive Henschel is trapped between his powerful inclination toward the spiritual and his equally strong lust for life. While ill, his wife imagines that her husband might take up with their servant girl, Hanne. She therefore extracts the promise that he will not marry the girl if she dies. But Henschel is no match for the egotistical, lusty, domineering Hanne Schäl, who soon has him in her net: Henschel, who convinces himself and allows himself to be convinced of the need for a mother for his sickly daughter, marries Hanne. His daughter dies soon afterward, and soon Hanne's true character shows through: she deceives him with the waiter Georg and threatens to leave Henschel if he does not accept her illegitimate child as his own. In a verbal exchange with a former employee Henschel learns of his wife's infidelity. He confronts her, and she runs from him. Remembering now the promise to his first wife, he feels pangs of conscience that are manifested in visions of a reproachful spouse. Like Lene in *Flagman Thiel,* who is also a second wife, Hanne becomes fearful of losing her husband. When his friend Wermelskirch arrives to cheer Henschel up, the latter disappears into the next room, where he commits suicide.

In the "ghost" of Henschel's wife, returned to haunt him for breaking a sacred promise, the author represents the Silesian proclivity toward mysticism, a simple dualistic belief in a reality beyond that breaks through at moments of stress. But *Drayman Henschel* is more than a mere tribute to a tribal and traditional peculiarity; it is also the first of many works that reflect Hauptmann's interest in Platonic dualism—in particular, man's intermediate position between opposing forces such as good and evil, light and dark, Dionysian and Christian. The working principle behind Platonic idealism is, as Hauptmann discovered during his studies of that philosopher in 1894, that the world is understandable not through logic but rather through intuition.

Hauptmann called his diaries and notebooks a "humus" for his works. The "humus effect" becomes clear in a notebook entry of 1898 in which he records his feelings while watching at his father's deathbed: "Life contains everything, even death, but death is the gentlest form of life. . . . There is nothing that has been more maliciously slandered than death—unless it has been life!" This entry illustrates how Hauptmann first observed life, then recorded his observations in a notebook or diary, and finally used it in his works, as we see below. The death of his good friend Hugo Ernst Schmidt and his older brother Georg in 1899 further contributed to the feeling of personal suffering out of which grew the drama *Michael Kramer* (1900). Kramer's words at the bier of his son Arnold at the end of act 4 record the personal aspect of the work and its relationship to these deaths, expressing Hauptmann's own sense of the gentleness of death:

> I am of the opinion . . . one shouldn't be afraid in this world. Love, it is said, is as strong as death. But just turn that sentence around: death is also as gentle as love. . . . —Listen, death has been slandered. That is the most malicious deception in the world! Death is the gentlest form of life: the masterpiece of eternal love.
>
> (1:1173)

When James Joyce translated *Michael Kramer* in 1901, he recognized death and the symbolism of death as the philosophical foundation of the play. A typical fin-de-siècle subject, the life and suffering of the artist serves in this play as a backdrop for Hauptmann's more general probing into the mystery of existence. Michael Kramer's final cries of anguish are those of one lost in a reality he does not understand. The shallowness of a coquette and the brutal playfulness of the "good citizens" in a tavern frequented by his talented but lazy and unstable son Arnold have driven that young man to suicide by drowning. Kramer is powerless to prevent this fatality, because he lacks compassion for the ugly, misshapen social outcast Arnold and because he fears his own artistic inadequacy. This inadequacy is called to mind by his son's greater talent for describing the suffering of life with a few quick sketches or strokes; the older Kramer has been working in vain for years on the "definitive" depiction of the suffering of Christ. Arnold's death is an epiphany for his father, for with it he gains sudden and brief insight into the relationship of death and life: death is not a negative aspect of existence but rather a positive and gentle form of life itself; in death, Arnold is transfigured. Great suffering, as with Christ or with Ludwig van Beethoven, to whose death mask Kramer speaks his final words, has the power to unite seeming opposites, but Kramer's insight is merely a glimpse into the underlying unity of all things; man is still not capable of fathoming the underlying structure of existence. Kramer asks:

> Where should we land, what are we drifting toward? We small creatures, abandoned in Enormity. As if we knew where we were going. . . . It has nothing to do with earthly festivals! It isn't the heaven of the clergy! It's not this and not that, but what. . . . What will it be when it's finished???

(1:1173)

Kramer's words reflect the intellectual atmosphere of the turn of the century. Rainer Maria Rilke, perhaps the greatest German poet of the twentieth century, attended the dress rehearsal of the play in 1900. He called it Hauptmann's greatest to date but stated that it would probably be decades before it was properly understood. Hauptmann was indeed ahead of his time in portraying man and artist caught in the midst of the cultural change and the accompanying psychological stress brought on by a burgeoning middle-class economy and its anti-intellectual values. This is typified by Arnold's conflict as an artist, directly before his suicide, with the brutally unfeeling "gentleman" of the middle class in the tavern in act 2.

In 1901 Hauptmann moved into the Haus Wiesenstein near Agnetendorf in Silesia, which was his permanent residence until death. His health had frequently been impaired since youth, and between 1901 and the summer of 1904, in which year his divorce seemed to account for at least part of his recovery, he devoted himself to writing and to becoming reacquainted with the Silesia of his youth and of tradition. He was also called as a jurist in nearby Hirschberg (April 1903) for the hearing of a charge of child murder and perjury against the twenty-five-year-old agricultural worker and waitress Hedwig Otte. By September the play Rose Bernd (Rose Bernd, 1903) was finished, and by October it was performed in Berlin.

Rose Bernd owes its existence to the court case. Its literary parentage is, however, twofold. On one hand the play is in the great tradition of German middle-class tragedy (Lessing's Miss Sara Sampson [Lucy Sampson; or, the Unhappy Heiress, 1755]; Friedrich von Schiller's Kabale und Liebe [Love and Intrigue, 1784]) and on the other in that of the child-murder drama (Heinrich Leopold Wagner's Die Kindermörderin [The Child Murderess, 1776]; Goethe's Urfaust [1775] and Faust [1808]. Rose Bernd contains the best from both traditions: it is a drama both about the individual pitted against a cruel and unjust social system and culture and about the murder of an infant. The themes blend in Rose's action, forced by a system, both in the community and at home, that provides few alternatives to the innocent of spirit but less pure, in society's eyes, of virtue. "The flesh has its own spirit," Wedekind said, and so it is with Rose Bernd, who, like Thiel and Henschel, cannot deny her natural sexuality. She is indeed exploited by the virulent Flamm, a local landowner, but hers is for the most part a willing submission.

Unfortunately for Rose, her rendezvous with Flamm at the beginning of act 1 is observed by Arthur Streckmann, a notorious philanderer. He threatens to reveal the relationship if she does not submit to him. One day in summer while Rose is bringing lunch to her father and Keil, her betrothed, in the field, Streckmann appears and renews his overtures to Rose, who is by now firmly held in the net of exploitation and eros woven by those who wish to bend her to their wills. Incensed by Streckmann's coarse allusions to their relationship—he has had his way with Rose during a visit in which she wished only to beg him to forget he had seen her rendezvous with Flamm—Keil struggles with him. Streckmann seriously injures Keil's eye. By fall the court case that Bernd has filed against Streckmann on behalf of his future son-in-law has come due. During the course of the hearing Rose denies having had sexual relations with either Streckmann or Flamm, both of whom have sworn to these relations before the court. Flamm then overhears Rose's perjury in a conversation between Rose and his crippled wife. He distances himself from Rose; his wife, who now knows all, generously renews her offer to take care of both Rose and her expected child. But it is too late for kindness in small measure to help Rose. Between the fourth and fifth acts she strangles her child.

When she reappears in act 5, she is changed: her suffering has given her insight into the human condition. Having just returned from the fields, where she has killed and left her baby, she is confronted by her father and accused of having perjured herself before the court. But Rose's attention is now directed inward, to the image of the tiny, dead body she has left in the field. She is distraught and reacts hysterically to her father's accusation: "That's nothing at all. Nothing. . . . Something is lying there! That's something! It's lying near a willow! That's something! I don't care about the other. There I looked earnestly at the stars. And I screamed and

called out earnestly! No heavenly Father stirred." The gendarme arrives with a document for Rose to sign, and she, near madness at the thought of being separated from her child, cries forth her deed in staccato. Bernd now sees beyond his own pious ambitions to the truth. The drama ends with his words: "The girl . . . how she must have suffered." Just as Rose's baby died of strangulation, so Rose was robbed by the narrow, village bourgeois attitude of any chance to grow beyond the "small chamber," as she calls it, of their vision of the moral world. With Rose Bernd's fervent cries to be with her dead child again, Hauptmann inversely invokes the mythological image of the Greek Demeter, who recalls the life she has given forth. He has in effect integrated action and characters from the traditional classical theater into the milieu of a modern Germany in the throes of social change. (Not coincidentally relevant to the moral tone of the play, Marschalk bore Hauptmann a son, Benvenuto, out of wedlock in 1900.)

After his marriage to Margarete in 1904 Hauptmann became even more productive than usual, working on, among other plays, *Gabriel Schillings Flucht* (The Flight of Gabriel Schilling, 1912), *Die Jungfern vom Bischofsberg* (*The Maidens of the Mount*, 1907), *Das Hirtenlied* (*The Song of the Herdsman*, 1921), and *Und Pippa tanzt!* (*And Pippa Dances!*, 1906). The year 1905 was full of honors and excitement for the forty-three-year-old author. He received the Grillparzer Prize for the third time; Oxford University awarded him the Honorary Doctor of Letters (in conjunction with the presentation, he visited Stratford-upon-Avon, where he broke a reed from the riverbank to commemorate his visit; it was thereafter kept in a place of honor at Haus Wiesenstein); he visited George Bernard Shaw; and Hugo von Hofmannsthal visited him, describing him as "an unbelievably good, actually touching person." The intellectual mood of Europe was equally ebullient: Pablo Picasso had begun his "pink period"; the expressionist group of artists known as *Die*

Brücke (the Bridge, including Ernst Kirchner, Erich Heckel, Karl Schmidt-Rottluff, Emil Nolde, Otto Mueller, and others), had been formed in Dresden; Henri Matisse had founded his school of fauvism in Paris; revolution had become open in Russia; and Albert Einstein had published his *Special Theory of Relativity* (1905).

On a more personal level, Hauptmann had fallen passionately in love with the sixteen-year-old actress Ida Orloff, who had appeared as Hannele in a new production and who later played Rautendelein and Pippa. Orloff influenced his literary productivity more than any other woman, perhaps any person, in his long life. She served as a model for Pippa, for Gersuind in *Kaiser Karls Geisel* (*Emperor Charles's Hostage*, 1908), for Ingigerd in *Atlantis* (1912), for Melitta in *Phantom* (1923), for Mignon, Siri, and Wanda in works of the same names (published in 1947, 1967, and 1928, respectively), and for Ludowike in *The Maidens of the Mount.* Hauptmann's personal contact with Orloff broke off with her engagement to Karl Satter in 1907. The complex relationship she had with Hauptmann, with its erotic overtones and idealistic moods, comes alive onstage in *And Pippa Dances!*

Hauptmann claimed never to have read Robert Browning's "Pippa Passes" (1841); the two pieces do indeed appear to have only an ethereal quality in common. The playwright describes Pippa as "a symbolization of the inner search, . . . the outer fable of the piece is merely an excuse"; he suggests that the play was "a poetic attempt at liberation" from the passion that bound "a forty-three-year-old man to a girl of seventeen." Although the Orloff experience certainly influenced *Pippa,* it does not further shape the themes.

The work represents a true glimpse into Hauptmann's personality. As early as 1894 he had conceived of the main character, Wann (When), who appears under other names and in other works throughout the author's life, from the fragmentary "Der Mutter Fluch" (The Mother's Curse, begun in 1894) to the fragmentary novel left unfinished at his death, *Der neue Christophorus* (The New Christopher, 1943). Wann has been called an ideal image of the author himself, who, as a character, looks down from the isolated, snowy ridge of the Sudeten Mountains (that is, Agnetendorf) and intervenes in the affairs of men; he is gifted with magical powers and with insight into the secrets of creation. As Hauptmann describes him, "He is tall, broad-shouldered, and his powerful head is surrounded by flowing white hair. His beardless, stern face is, so to speak, covered with runes. . . . His garments consist of a robe of coarse linen with wide sleeves that reaches to the knee." In Wann we see a mixture of elements from Germanic mythology, alchemy (which Hauptmann studied), and traditional Christianity; he is magician and Christ, master and servant, a syncretistic portrait of intellect. The play's other main characters, the director of the glassworks, who appears only in act 1 (*Pippa* is subtitled "A Glassworks Fairy Tale"), Michel Hellriegel, Huhn, and Pippa, represent respectively reason, imagination, sexual drive, and that spark of life at whose bidding all dance.

The outer fable of the play is simple: During a card game at Wende's tavern in the foothills of the mountains, Tagliazoni, an Italian glassblower, is caught cheating, and when his companions stab him to death, his daughter Pippa is kidnapped by the old giant Huhn, also a glassblower, and taken to his hut in the high forest. The director has attempted, unsuccessfully, to protect Pippa from Huhn. Michel Hellriegel, a traveling journeyman, follows them and gains entry while Huhn searches for Pippa's suspected rescuers. Michel's playing a few notes on his ocarina causes Pippa to dance; Pippa and Hellriegel escape the half-wild Huhn and find themselves high on a mountain, where Wann invites them into his Faustian study. While they are in this strange house, Huhn again appears and struggles with Wann; the giant falls moaning into Pippa's arms. After recovering from his struggle with the demons of his soul, he is invited to dance with Wann, who has warned Pippa against this. But Michel is obsessed by the desire to see Pippa dance again. He plays his ocarina; Huhn thumps time with his fists. Pippa falls dead to the floor and Huhn cries, as he had in the forest, "Jumalai!" (Joy to all!) and joins her in death. At his dying words, Huhn crushes the Venetian wineglass he holds in his great hands. Michel, now blind, is led by Wann to the door and shown the way to the Golden Stair of Venice, Hauptmann's symbol of art, and wanders off into the snow, tapping his way slowly forward.

Intellect (Wann) has shown imagination (Michel) the way to fulfillment of the artistic vision represented by the glassworks. With Michel's blindness comes the inner vision (*myein,* in Greek) of the mystic seer. Suffering has brought him to where he can see the city of Venice, his vision of the artistic ideal, but in return it demands much of the whole person, represented by these different characters: the taming of the irrational erotic impulse as symbolized by the death of Huhn, and with it the loss of much of the artist's joy in the creative process, as represented by Pippa's death. Wann lives on, but with the loss of Huhn and Michel Hellriegel there is a loss to the whole character Hauptmann attempted to create out of the fragmentary elements of his own intellect. After the intensely personal experience of dealing with the inner relationships of his artistic temperament, it is little wonder that the author's spirit of intellectual discovery, active and eclectic in the most trying of personal times, stands ready to break new ground.

Hauptmann's trip to Greece in the spring of 1907 is recorded in his *Griechischer Frühling* (Grecian Spring, 1908). He visited Patras, Olympia, Corinth, Argos, Athens, Eleusis, Delphi, and Sparta with wife Margarete, sons Ivo and Benvenuto, and his friend the painter Ludwig von Hofmann. Always drawn by religion and its symbols, the gods, Hauptmann developed a special interest in Dionysus and Demeter, whose respective cult cities are Athens and Eleusis. Dionysus became for him the representation of the creative, artistic, irrational impulse in opposition to the intellect; Demeter seemed to embody suffering humanity. These concepts appear fused with their Christian and pagan counterparts in such works as *Die Insel der grossen Mutter* (*The Island of the Great Mother,* 1924), *Till Eulenspiegel* (1928), and *Der neue Christophorus.* Alert to indications of the innate cultural truth of mythology, the author found in this trip material from another, earlier attempt by man to fathom the ultimate meaning of existence. This insight, combined with his knowledge of Christianity and his study of Buddhism from as early as 1901, began to give Hauptmann's works a less descriptive, more ethereal cast; and after his visit to Delphi, tragedy took on the bloodier quality of Greek antiquity. Perhaps more importantly, the trip reinforced Hauptmann's longing to find a synthesis between the Christian (spiritual) and the Greek (physical) views of life.

Der Narr in Christo Emanuel Quint (*The Fool in Christ: Emanuel Quint,* 1910) was no doubt influenced by Hauptmann's "Jesus-Studien" of 1885–1890 and by thoughts about a planned "social drama" to be called "Jesus of Nazareth." The novel is an attempt to show what would happen if a Christlike figure were to return to the godless world; it was also to be, as Hauptmann wrote, "a criticism of the hypocrisy of Christianity, a mirror of the times, but also much more." This important work sold only eighteen thousand copies; it was praised as "wonderful" by Shaw and characterized by Wedekind as a novel "only a professor of literature has to read to the end." It illustrates what many have called Hauptmann's Silesian proclivity toward mysticism, some hints of which had already appeared in *Drayman Henschel, Hannele,* and *Pippa.* With particular regard to his view of Christ as recorded in the diary of his 1897 trip to Italy, he writes:

From that moment on . . . in which I pieced together my Christ from the patchwork of the

Bible, I have tried twenty or more times unsuccessfully to portray him. . . . No spring unfolds without the "Son of Man" being resurrected for me. I see him walking in my—in our world. I follow him with glances; I recognize him in the strangest situations, opposing all of the hostile, hypocritical forces of time. But he disappears again.

(*Gerhart Hauptmann.*
Italienische Reise 1897, p. 47)

Four years later, however, Hauptmann was able to depict the personal, human figure that had so long eluded him. In *The Fool in Christ: Emanuel Quint,* he is portrayed as a man of inner strength, permeated with a love of mankind, who wishes to transform through love those he encounters. For Quint suffering is not an option; it is a necessity if love is to be lasting. But his eight modern disciples are unable to understand the Master's words, "God is spirit," so they call for a concrete sign that will prove that Quint is the Son of Man. Convinced that his teaching has been in vain, Quint resolves to conduct a last test of humanity by going from door to door, country to country, asking to be admitted to the households of a suffering humanity that is either unwilling or unable to recognize its savior. Quint dies, accidentally, in a snowstorm near the Gotthard Pass. Six months later his frozen body is discovered. There is no possibility of resurrection for the modern Christ, since his power to project a personal, human love onto the tattered screen of the modern soul is broken. The spirit within man is dead. As Quint says, "The world is nothing more than a prison of the Enemy." The death of love-compassion-selflessness (they are identical for Schopenhauer, whose works Hauptmann had previously studied) entails the death of the soul.

Quint's teaching is one of selflessness, and as such it cannot compete with the physical glory of an industrial society enamored of both its material wealth and its supposed progress toward utopia here on earth. He, like Johannes Vockerat in *Lonely Lives* and Old Hilse in *The Weavers,* dies having accomplished nothing

regarding the betterment of the human spirit. Solitary suffering produces only individual salvation. Years later in *Der neue Christophorus,* Hauptmann grapples with a "practical" solution to this problem.

Silesian life, folk legend, and scientific achievement interested Hauptmann greatly. He felt himself a part of the great tradition that includes such thinkers as Jacob Boehme, a Silesian mystic; Angelus Silesius, a Silesian mystical poet; and by way of influence on the first, Paracelsus, the Swiss physician and theosophist. Boehme he viewed as the "German Socrates" and Silesia as the "Attica of Germany." Due to the inordinate attention paid to his relationship to the sixteenth-century mystic, it is important to note that no direct, verifiable, significant transfer of material can be documented. Rather, the widely scattered, often epigrammatic material from Boehme that Hauptmann so often quotes, and misquotes, in his notebooks reveals him as a companion of the spirit, a member of the same tradition of idealism, a fellow German, and a man of similar attitude concerning the existence of a Platonic reality. It was Boehme, not Hauptmann, who was lost in the inner mystical vision.

The landscape of Silesia itself produced a deep and lasting effect on Hauptmann's view of reality. As he explains in an article on the Sudeten Mountains from a Berlin newspaper, dated Christmas Day 1941:

They look back on millennia of a superhuman-tragic existence. And when one speaks of the impetuous sky of the Sudeten Mountains, and the eternal-dramatic clouds, with which this or that god shrouds himself—often lightning and thundering, then sending forth storms, mowing the forests like grass—these things the flat-landers are unfamiliar with. It is a close, threatening greatness that extends into eternity and into the Boundless, forcing a personal relationship. This extra-human language became commonplace for me and it filled the emptiness under whose spell I had fallen.

(2:779–780)

In complete accordance with Hauptmann's sense of dualism, of seeing life as opposing forces of light and darkness, good and evil, real and supernatural, Dionysus and Christ, he was as comfortable in the bustle and avant-garde atmosphere of Berlin as he was in his bucolic Silesian countryside. Out of a close acquaintanceship with this city over the years came the play *Die Ratten: Berliner Tragiko-mödie* (*The Rats,* 1911). It is perhaps the bitterest, most ironic, and most complex of Hauptmann's dramas, in large part because of its two thematic focal points, the social and the moral. It not only shows a rotting social structure, undermined by the "rats" of dissent against Bismarckian social and military "Realpolitik," it also provides still another glimpse into his personal life. Among the nine versions of *The Rats* that exist, the author includes, for example, a series of remarks and dreams of his wife, Margarete; and when his three-day-old son Erasmus died in May of 1910, he added the motif of the death of the infant child of Frau John, the main character.

Hauptmann spoke of the play as "consisting of the opposition of two worlds" and as having these worlds as its "point of departure." He refers to the worlds of the middle and lower classes of Berlin, but in a deeper sense, the work is concerned with human existence as a middle kingdom between unknowable realms of light and darkness. In this twilight existence, reflected in and reinforced by the play's upstairs-downstairs action in the house and its opposing moods of comedy and tragedy, we glimpse only vague shadows of forces that manipulate the players. They are trapped in a world of shadow where moral, or human values cannot be sharply discerned.

Harro Hassenreuter, ex–theater director, and Frau John, wife of a manual laborer, oppose one another in developmental lines that seldom touch. Hers is the tragic role; his is that of the pompous, tragicomedic blusterer. One day Frau John discovers that the servant girl Pauline Piperkarcka is pregnant but does not wish to keep the child. Having lost her own infant son years before, she convinces Pauline to bear the child and give it to her to raise. She then assures her husband that the child is theirs, born during one of his working absences in Hamburg. The tragedy of a suffering mother comes to a climax when Pauline, in a fit of conscience, confesses to the police that she has given her child to Frau John. When Frau John learns of this from her husband, she exhibits signs of nervousness and accuses him of a lack of trust.

In the meantime Frau John's criminal brother Bruno arrives for a visit. She knows he has seen Pauline and attempts to extract information from him. He explains that he has asked Pauline to leave Frau John in peace with regard to the child so that everything will be all right, and adds that when she protested, he murdered her. Now at the threshold of insanity, afraid of losing both freedom and her child, Frau John cries, "I'm no murderer; I didn't want that!" Withdrawing from the world, she falls asleep on the sofa; when Walburga, Hassenreuter's daughter, and Erich Spitta, her affianced private tutor, arrive, they wonder at the strange behavior of the otherwise energetic woman. When her husband tells all about the Bruno affair in the course of the conversation, suspicion falls on Frau John regarding the child's identity. Her archenemy Frau Knobbe—a woman she considers beneath her socially—confirms the facts. Unable to live with the idea of losing her little Adalbert, she dashes from the house and dies in the traffic below, a suicide. The atmosphere of the "bloody" Greek tragedy Hauptmann had experienced in Greece finds expression in the death of Frau John, a true *mater dolorosa,* a suffering Demeter, beside whose depth of human emotion Hassenreuter's hypocritical bourgeois moral precepts pale to comedic insignificance.

The "comedic" action of *The Rats,* firmly rooted in irony, is carried by the conflicts between the young Spitta, a former student of theology who aspires to an acting career, and both Hassenreuter's absurdly conservative Bismarckian political views and outdated concepts of dramaturgy and Pastor Spitta's morally bankrupt, socially stagnant views on church and religion. Erich Spitta represents in part a younger Hauptmann, but in a wider sense also an entire generation of artists vexed by the oppressive and decadent sociopolitical system of the late 1880's. Hassenreuter expresses this underlying theme of corruption in a tirade to Spitta about the travesty of a growing anti-classical (anti-Goethean) theater in act 3:

> These rats [naturalists] are starting in politics—a plague of rats—to undermine our splendid new unified German Empire. They are cheating us of the reward of our efforts! and in the garden of German art—a plague of rats!—they are eating away at the roots of the tree of idealism: they want to drag the Crown through the dirt.
>
> (2:779–780)

The unwillingness to adapt to changing social attitudes and needs inherent in Hassenreuter's outlook precludes the introduction of the new, the invigorating: sooner or later the social structure, like that of the lives of the people in the converted barracks where the play takes place, must collapse of its own internal weaknesses. The absurdity of a "practical Christianity" in our age is illustrated after Frau John's dash from the room, when young Spitta asks, "Don't you think that a truly tragic fate was at work here?" and receives Hassenreuter's superficial and ironic reply: "Tragedy is not bound to class. I have always told you that." Hollow words of a society without compassion, for Hassenreuter had his chance to practice what he termed "practical Christianity," but reconsidered his offer to adopt the orphaned John baby because of the time and expense it would involve.

At the height of his fame and recognition as the greatest of living German writers, Hauptmann received the Nobel Prize for Literature in 1912. But only one year later he lived through the fiasco of his *Festspiel in deutschen Reimen* (*Commemorative Masque*, 1913). In the form of a review of German history during Germany's heroic struggle to free itself from Napoleon, he presented the public with an unpopular, and unwelcome, portrayal of motives that were most naturally equated with, and in contrast to, the prevailing patriotic fervor of prewar Europe. Princes and monarchs appear in the piece as puppets of a "Theater Director," and the house of Hohenzollern, whose jubilee the play was to celebrate, is hardly mentioned. The production was banned by royal decree in June 1913. The royal house refused to state its reasons. According to a Breslau newspaper, both the kaiser and the crown prince felt insulted by the piece, and although it is quite probable that a perceived insult to the personal honor of the house was responsible for the ban, it is likely that the presentation's closing lines, illustrative of the author's real view of Germany's role in modern Europe and in peace as opposed to war, constituted his greatest "blunder":

> [Germany's purpose] is the deed of peace, not that of war!
> The good turn! Never the misdeed!
> Is not the naked murder of war a far different thing?
>
> (2:1003)

A positive aspect of Hauptmann's work with the dramaturgical side of the *Commemorative Masque* was the interest in stage production that it awakened in him. In ensuing years he directed many of his own plays, with the thought of reconciling the literary ideal of the pieces with the technical realities of the stage. A voracious reader and man of unquenchable curiosity concerning underlying motivations, Hauptmann not only worked with the practicalities of theater production but also became increasingly attracted to the coincidences of philosophical thought present in major cultures and religions. His preoccupation with religious thought and Eastern religions began in earnest with his "Jesus-Studien" and continued with a close reading of Schopenhauer's *The World as Will and Representation* (1818)—particularly the fourth book, which deals with suffering—and, as early as 1901, with a fascination with Buddhism that drew him into serious consideration of Hinduism, Taoism, Tibetan Buddhism, Confucianism, Gnosticism, alchemy, and the writing of Jacob Boehme as repositories of human wisdom and of the central features of mankind's utopian struggle toward a better world. Reflections of these interests are found in his drama *Indipohdi* (*Indipohdi*, 1920), which he himself directed in 1922 in Dresden.

C. F. W. Behl recorded many of the events in Hauptmann's private life between 1932 and the writer's death. He reports that Hauptmann viewed *Indipohdi* as his "final farewell piece," in which the "basic atmosphere" is one of a world God has created and then forgotten, leaving man not with free will but rather with an inescapable destiny. Only in suicide has he a free choice.

In this play Prospero, a European prince who has been deposed by his own son, seeks refuge from fate on a Pacific island where he is received as "the white savior." Like Shakespeare's character of the same name, he is a sorcerer. But although he controls "shadows" and "illusions," fate controls him. He has escaped the wrath of his son only to become further entangled in fate's inexorable plan, for his son, Ormann, is then shipwrecked on that very island, and the scenario of deposition again plays itself out. Prospero claims his option of suicide to escape fate's web. Beneath this facade, however, lies a more elemental struggle: Prospero's development toward spiritual harmony. He, like the Buddha, has left the courtly world and worldly power to seek himself in isolation, symbolized by the actual begging bowl before his door.

"Pleasure is the root of suffering." Hauptmann often underlined this dictum of Buddhism in his copy of Karl Eugen Neumann's German translation of the Buddhist scriptures. This profound recognition of the illusion of all existence, all joy, comes to life in Prospero's complaint, "Awful creation, which incubates suffering from the egg of happiness." With such a perception he is prepared to meet his fate. But still there remains within him a spark of sensuality, which manifests itself in his love for Tehura, the high priestess. Prospero's sacrifice must, however, be accomplished alone, and he realizes that the perceived world he has so carefully constructed is actually an illusion created by suffering. He must relieve suffering through death.

The external events leading to Prospero's dramatic leap into the volcano are classically simple. Ormann lands upon the island. Pyrrha, Prospero's daughter, falls in love with this mirror image of herself. Ormann and Pyrrha rise against their father, who sees in this act a fulfillment of the fate he had sought to escape: his own blood has once again risen up against him. Although initially successful, Ormann is captured and prepared for sacrifice to the volcano, god of the island. Prospero realizes that only his own sacrifice can save his son: fate must be appeased. And more: self-sacrifice will restore the control of reality he relinquished when he became a sorcerer.

Act 5 shows a Prospero to whom existence has been partially laid bare on the way up the slope of the volcano with his beloved Tehura. They are reaching toward nothingness. No longer subject, he believes, to the illusions of perception, he moves toward redemption. The "magic" he had practiced did not free his will from the illusion of existence and give him control over his own fate. Indeed, the "magic" *was* the illusion. Having now recognized this, he is able to see the folly in any attempt to separate his personal will, Schopenhauer's *principium individuationis*, from the fabric that fate—some unknown force—weaves about man. The nothingness toward which Prospero now returns, and for which he yearns, is the "whole" out of which he has been separated by the illusion of magical control.

In many ways an allegory of Hauptmann's lifelong struggle as an artist to understand his own and man's place in the cosmic scheme and to control and create reality through the written word (*logos*), *Indipohdi* (which means "no one knows") is also a recognition of the impossibility of such a task, as well as of the immorality of an individual trying to receive redemption alone. As Hauptmann later wrote in *Der neue Christophorus,* "I could never feel redeemed unless the whole of humanity were redeemed with me."

Two works that illustrate the serious and the playful sides of Hauptmann's "pagan" nature are *The Heretic of Soana* and *The Island of the Great Mother.* For all its bittersweet beauty and praise of eroticism, the former work reveals the negative consequences of total submission to the primal urge: isolation and the relinquishing of free will. Eros, a subject Hauptmann had dealt with in *Flagman Thiel, Atlantis,* and *And Pippa Dances!,* again displays its enigmatic nature. Franceso, a young village priest struggling toward sexual enlightenment, succumbs to the power of Eros, the oldest god. He renounces the priesthood and with it the church's distorted view of mystical reality, which is devoid of the erotic feelings he has recently experienced in nature and himself. His involvement with Agata Scarabota eventually forces the couple to seek refuge on Mt. Generoso, stronghold of Eros. It is significant that the intensity of erotic feeling that washes over the lovers can exist only beyond the boundaries of organized society and religion. Accordingly, Francesco's transformation possesses meaning only for him. He may feel "changed, intensified, free" after acknowledging the power of Eros over him, but he is also an outcast, incapable of "creating" beyond the narrow limits imposed by it. He, unlike Dante or Shakespeare, does not control his visions; rather, they control him. At the end of Francesco's tale, as told by a third-person narrator, he is indeed a "totally lifeless sacrifice of Eros."

We might well view *The Heretic of Soana* as the first part of an experiment to ascertain man's chances of spiritual survival in the revealed realm of Eros. Part 2 takes place in the novel *The Island of the Great Mother,* in which we observe Eros' Puck-like ability to lead astray those who deem themselves most able to comprehend him.

In *The Island of the Great Mother* Hauptmann divides Eros into its male and female counterparts, pits them against one another, and stands back to observe. The true irony of the work lies, however, in the fact that the spirit of the *magna mater* (Great Mother), the mystical, erotic force of nature that rules all male and female relationships, remains in control on the island, regardless of the measures either the men or the women take to secure their supposed independent sociopolitical futures. Their artificially constructed "Mother-Mysterium" is a cult that deifies female superiority in mystical thinking. The opposing male society of the Thinking Hand, forced by the women to take refuge on the far side of the island, stresses the practical, creative nature of the male. When, however, Eros asserts himself at the end of the novel, the factions are reunited in orgiastic reconciliation. To demonstrate what he believes to be the true content of reality, Hauptmann contrasts the "lower" (physical) island with the "upper" or Platonic island, thus providing the reader with an overall perspective of both physical and spiritual events.

At the conclusion of the novel the futility of a one-sided attempt to fathom the content of cosmic, and therefore human, relationships is illustrated in the death of Laurence Hobemma, the female theosophist who had devoted herself to unraveling the mystery of woman's true place in humankind's development. When her body is found, her open eyes face the rising sun, which is the controlling symbol of the novel. In concert with Dante's use of it in the *Inferno,* Hauptmann further broadens it into a symbol of hope for a better, if inscrutable, future for mankind in the struggle to grasp the complexities of a dualistic existence. Hobemma's attempt to justify existence in purely feminine terms has led to death. Phaon, the only male survivor of the shipwreck that had landed the participants on the island, is the father of the entire younger generation and must now depart from the island in search of the unifying principle of existence. Just as Hauptmann has borrowed philosophical concepts, characters, and symbols from Plato, Herbert Spencer, and the legend of Sappho, so now he extracts the essence from Dante's ascent from Hell to Purgatory, from spiritual darkness to the light of hope. Phaon is "called" by the sun to leave his creations. As if in a dream, he finds himself afloat upon the sea with his young lover, Diodata. Sails filled with the "breezes of freedom," they depart toward a new and perhaps hopeful beginning. Looking back on the island, he thinks, "How terrible that we remain eternally separated from our dearest creatures. The torture of this insight is so great and is so terribly intensified by any attempt to end this separation that only flight remains to ease it."

The Island of the Great Mother displays in tropical abundance Hauptmann's acquaintance with gnostic, Hindu, Buddhist, Greek, and many other sources. But it is in essence a satirical, somewhat superficial, often tongue-in-cheek look at the human condition. However, in *Des grossen Kampffliegers, Landfahrers, Gauklers und Magiers Till Eulenspiegel Abenteuer, Streiche, Gaukeleien, Gesichte und Träume* (The Adventures, Pranks, Tricks, Visions and Dreams of the Great Combat Pilot, Traveler, Showman and Magician Till Eulenspiegel, to give the work its full title), Hauptmann borrows the satirical cloak of the legendary fourteenth-century trickster and folk hero to cover with saving humor his own earnest and Germany's sometimes desperate journey through the postwar experience. He prefaced the work with St. Augustine's phrase, "This life is nothing but a human comedy which leads from temptation to temptation."

Krafft Christian Tesdorpf, whom Hauptmann met while the pilot was convalescing from combat wounds on Hiddensee, an island off the North German coast, served as a model for Till Eulenspiegel. With Tesdorpf's adventures as pilot, tea planter, and explorer Hauptmann combined the events of his personal intellectual development to form a journey

through his own consciousness, giving a fascinating glimpse into his syncretistic use of sources.

In many ways a "novel of education" in hexameter, this modern Ship of Fools allows us to follow Hauptmann's process of intellectual maturation through its most difficult years. Of the work's eighteen adventures, the fourteenth, which is described as "Till's most bitter, most difficult, most depressing, and also most dangerous," provides the most profound glimpse into the artist's struggle for identity. In it Till (i.e., Hauptmann) comes face to face with the forces of chaos that could destroy his soul and lead to insanity, the worst fear of the artist. Till arrives at Wittenberg, city of Luther, to find it in full bacchanalian revelry. He meets proponents of Leninism, as well as Mahatma Gandhi, Francis of Assisi, bishops, jesters, "the Moloch of the Masses," and the gnostic Helene, who bears the suffering of mankind. When the council begins, Till attempts to establish unity among these opposing factions, but he is unsuccessful. In an outburst of compassion for his German people, who so often slaughter each other for this or that ideal, Till cries to Hetairos, the inner guide, to rescue him from impending insanity. Upon awakening from this apparent dream—"Is life a dream?" Till later asks—he exclaims to his female companion:

Listen, Gule! Life has proven to be a middle kingdom between
material and spirit! But know, I am
fed up, having had so long, like now, to bob between heaven and earth.
And so I'll scram, but the How, dear child, remains a secret.

(4:844)

By the end of the verse epic, adventure eighteen, Till has decided that life has handed him enough disappointment; he is ready to depart. On a hiking tour of Switzerland, he spends a night, his last, in the "Our Savior" hostel, where he meets a Christ figure who invites him to visit him soon "at home" if Till wishes to hear more of his life story. Next day, Till stumbles and falls over a cliff. Clinging to a branch, suspended between heaven and earth, he resigns himself joyously to letting go and falls cheerfully to his death below. The laughter of the prankster can still, as in the folk legend, be heard about his tombstone, which bears the inscription "MILES FATI" (Soldier of Fate), a fitting epitaph for the end of an era of personal, political, and intellectual uncertainty. As Hauptmann later told Behl: "[Till] was a kind defense against the sadness and nightmarish problems of the present. I slipped into Till and always felt happy when I was Till. Through him and with him I enjoyed the times—in spite of everything. . . . Today I could not write a single line of *Till*."

From 1918 until his death in 1946 Hauptmann retreated more into himself, only occasionally, as in a May-December tale of romantic tragedy, *Vor Sonnenuntergang* (*Before Sunset,* 1932), appearing again as the German "naturalist," describer and recorder of everyday human conflicts. His character the Pater, in part his alter ego, states in this regard in *Der neue Christophorus:*

> *Antahkarana* in Sanskrit means inner activity; that is, on the other hand, thinking. So I gave myself over to inner activity. I know no other way of serving my fellow men than to strengthen the mustard seed of my faith: so I went beyond the Faust idea and became at home in a world that the religious writings of the Indians call magical.
>
> (10:880)

Works such as *Der Neue Christophorus* and *Der grosse Traum* (The Great Dream, 1942) are the result.

Hauptmann maintained that *Der grosse Traum,* like all of his works, began with a dream. That work was to be "the dream of all dreams," the one piece he had written that would outlive all other works. This verse epic was so important to him that, with the New Testament, he had it laid in his coffin. His self-proclaimed "legacy of life," *Der grosse Traum* consists of twenty-two cantos of irregular length and consciously employs the Dantean tercet as its basic lyric form. It is not, however, an attempt to copy or vie with the great Italian, but rather a personal approach to the search for harmony between the poles of denying and submitting to the world. Hauptmann uses the lyric form to express the inexpressible, to give form to the dream vision of life:

> I am basically a cheerful person but I had experienced in dream as a child the horror of our tiny human existence in the immense cosmos. The dream has always been for me a terrible and great source of knowledge. This has nothing to do with Freudianism! I have nothing more final to say than I wrote in *Der grosse Traum.* I do not care if fat commentaries are written about it. This poetry is for me a personal experience.
>
> (C. F. W. Behl, *Zwiesprache mit Gerhart Hauptmann,* p. 104)

"Fat commentaries" are indeed required to gain even a broad sense of this most complex of epics. Basically, Hauptmann has cast gnostic, Buddhist, Greek, and very modern, sometimes bitingly political, thought and commentary in a Dantean mold. He has Satanael, the oldest of God's sons (Christ's older brother), guide the narrator through the dream of life in search of the meaning of existence, the "core of reality." Here, as in *The Island of the Great Mother* and *Der neue Christophorus,* he is confronted with the Icarian dilemma: how to escape the bonds of an intellectually and spiritually insufficient reality without courting destruction. Hauptmann as narrator descends to the chthonian mystery, experiences the "paradise of suffering" of the City of the Dead, and then ascends to the chaos of life. After experiencing hell on earth, the poet is admitted to the "Valley of the Good," where he encounters the Great Mother, who has been hinted at but never seen in so many of his works. She explains that reason may probe the mystery of existence, but the core of truth must remain undiscovered if it is to offer comfort to the searcher. Abruptly *Der grosse Traum* ends:

"Come again," said my little mother silently,
"as often as you wish and want. True to
the early lap, you will be a child of heaven,
even if through hells, the great dream leads."

(4:1083)

A utopian vision ended, the narrator has been shown the symbolic significance of life, even though the symbols do not correspond unerringly to a fixed vision. As the narrator proclaims:

Dream is everything, but not everything dream.
The new eye is born to see,
no eyelid closes against the inner space.

(4:1083)

The other great testimony and legacy of Hauptmann's life is *Der neue Christophorus,* which he began as "Merlin" in 1917 and worked on until shortly before his death. As complex in form, style, and content as *Der grosse Traum,* this novel-like fragment is composed in *Konvolute* (sheaves, or a rambling diary form in which the author can jump quickly from subject to subject) instead of chapters, a technique that allowed the author greater inner freedom and the ability to go from the fantastic to the mystical, according to Behl. This device reflected Hauptmann's working habits at the time. He conceived of the work as a type of spiritual diary and therefore worked on its spasmodically, with no fixed format regarding direction or goal. *Der neue Christophorus* takes us on a mythopoeic journey, beginning with the birth of the boy Erdmann (man of earth) in the grave of his mother. Pater Christophorus arrives and assumes responsibility for the child. He then carries this child of hope across the stream of spiritual rebirth, becoming himself a new St. Christopher. Erdmann embodies a new mythology for mankind that will bring redemption to all. Amalgamating Buddhist, Hindu, Gnostic, Taoist, Christian, Greek, and Islamic teachings, and the thought of Jacob Boehme, Plato, Schopenhauer, and many others in a veritable feast of influence, Hauptmann proclaims

faith, the basis of all these belief systems, to be the foundation of our visible reality. Pater Christophorus–Hauptmann asserts:

I am a poet and not a prophet. I grasp the world poetically, not with the fanaticism of the self-righteous. Nevertheless I stand where a German philosopher [Boehme] recorded his main insight . . . : "If we observe the visible world with its being and observe the lives of its creatures, we find in them the simile of the invisible spiritual world which is hidden in the visible world, like the soul in the body. And we see that the hidden God is near to all and is through all and is hidden in invisible being."

(10:823)

Erdmann is to become Christlike by sacrificing himself for his fellow man to forge yet another rung in the ladder of human evolution, which men must climb to become like gods. Hauptmann never planned to end the novel, and in explanation of this he often quoted Goethe's remark that "everything that a person takes up seriously is unending." But Erdmann, the character Hauptmann intended to represent the progress of the child called "culture," is to point mankind forward on its road, to rescue it from its own apathy and teach it its place in a tradition as old as the cosmos. With his death and the consequent establishment of the new myth, powerful strides can be made toward a world where "love of humanity, peace, and harmonious patience" reign. As Hauptmann wrote in the 1943 introduction to the fragment: "If this work is granted time for conclusion, an embodiment of the German individual would have to stand at the end, and beyond this, in the present and pointing to the future, the new human being." All of mankind, all religions, all "social" thought—and all thought for Hauptmann is social—stands behind Erdmann–Pater Christophorus–Hauptmann's vision of a union of the human spirit with its own divine essence. In the world of myth, created by the poet through the power of the word (*logos*), lies modern man's chance for a renewed consciousness, the requisite of a physical, political, and social utopia.

GERHART HAUPTMANN

While *Till Eulenspiegel, Der grosse Traum,* and *Der neue Christophorus* record Hauptmann's inner visions, his mystical insights and artistic development, his perception of the World War II years are expressed in terms of the tragedy of ancient Greece. His *Atriden-Tetralogie* (Atridae Tetralogy) consists of the plays *Iphigenie in Delphi* (Iphigenia at Delphi, 1941), *Iphigenie in Aulis* (Iphigenia at Aulis, 1944), *Agamemnons Tod* (The Death of Agamemnon, 1948), and *Elektra* (Electra, 1948). It was inspired by Euripides' *Iphigenia at Aulis,* Goethe's *Iphigenia auf Tauris* (1779), Heinrich von Kleist's *Penthesilea* (1808), the author's own early attempts in his *Florian Geyer* and *Hamlet in Wittenberg* (Hamlet at Wittenberg, published in 1935 after nine years of Shakespeare studies), and peripherally by the Richard Strauss and Hugo von Hofmannsthal opera *Elektra* (1909), as well as by Eugene O'Neill's reworking of Aeschylus in *Mourning Becomes Electra* (1931). Again, however, this is no attempt to rival other literary masterpieces; Hauptmann's tetralogy deals with the Atridae family (descendants of King Atreus of Mycenae, father of Agamemnon) and their struggle against destiny.

The tetralogy forms the second high point in Hauptmann's dramatic career and is considered one of his great masterpieces. Erwin Piscator, who staged the Berlin production of the plays, claims them to be Hauptmann's "last words to the German people" and further asserts that they are "political" drama. In essence they concern Hauptmann's unique mystical interpretation of human history, while at the same time providing a very personal view of the Greek gods and their relationship to mankind. They are, in sum, a thin veil for the expression of deepest horror by a humanist and idealist at the barbarity and brutalizing effect of war on a people and a world. As Piscator later stated:

Was there in the time during which Hitler had covered the world with war and death a more convincing, probative parable that attempted to understand the disaster that had emanated from Germany than this ancient myth? Didn't this ancient vision of a family in its death-rage represent the madness of a people, of the German people?

("Gerhart Hauptmanns *Atriden-Tetralogie,"* in Schrimpf, ed., *Gerhart Hauptmann,* p. 319)

This interpretation is perhaps one-sided regarding such a culmination of Hauptmann's artistic-dramatic skills, but Piscator's assessment does evoke the atmosphere of doom, destruction, and lurking uncertainty that pervades the plays. And it expresses poetically the playwright's waning optimism concerning mankind's peaceful progress toward utopia. In one of his last newspaper addresses to the German people, in April 1945, he wrote, the bombing of Dresden still fresh in his mind: "I am almost eighty-three years old and stand before God with my legacy, which is unfortunately powerless and comes only from the heart: it is the wish that God would love, purify and refine mankind more to its own good than he has up to now."

Hauptmann died on 6 June 1946 in Haus Wiesenstein in Agnetendorf. He was about to resettle in Berlin—Silesia had become a Polish province—at the invitation of Soviet military authorities, who honored him as a proletarian writer. The last of the "poet princes," Hauptmann was an artist who lived for his art, was his art, regardless of the decades of turmoil through which he lived. In the sixty-odd years of his literary production he wrote in almost every literary style. Critics like to decry his departure from "the path of truth" (naturalism); they criticize him for "switching" from symbolism to romanticism, from classicism to mysticism, and so on. What such detractors have failed to understand is that Hauptmann felt bound by no style, no philosophy, no single allegiance or influence; his was the way of humanity, and where it took him, he went with faith, hope, and the fervent desire that the literary result would serve as a beacon for the oppressed of mind or spirit, as a guide to Germany and the world in the path toward human spiritual evolution. "Man is the measure of all things," Hauptmann quotes Protagoras in *Der neue Christophorus;* he believed this and was in this sense a true realist, following man through the labyrinth of his total being. For his progression beyond the materialism of his youth he was called "extremely overrated, artificially pompous," a writer who lost the "passion of great art"; but he never stopped delving ever deeper into man's intellectual past to contribute to the future of his beloved humanity. Gustav Leuteritz wrote in the Berlin newspaper *Tägliche Rundschau* of 15 November 1946:

> When generals die, one pins their decorations to a velvet cushion. When we took leave of Hauptmann, there stood next to his coffin, under the burning candelabras, a small table on which lay in respectful rows eighteen volumes: the great critical edition of 1946, the immortal witness to his protean spirit, the artist's deed of peace.

Selected Bibliography

EDITIONS

INDIVIDUAL WORKS

Promethidenlos. Berlin, 1885.
Fasching. Berlin, 1887.
Das bunte Buch. Gedichte. Beerfelden, 1888.
Bahnwärter Thiel. Berlin, 1888.
Vor Sonnenaufgang. Berlin, 1889.
Das Friedensfest. Berlin, 1890.
Einsame Menschen. Berlin, 1891.
Die Weber. Berlin, 1892.
Der Biberpelz. Berlin, 1893.
Hanneles Himmelfahrt. Berlin, 1894.
Florian Geyer. Berlin, 1896.
Die versunkene Glocke. Berlin, 1896.
Fuhrmann Henschel. Berlin, 1898.
Michael Kramer. Berlin, 1900.
Der rote Hahn. Berlin, 1901.
Rose Bernd. Berlin, 1903.
Und Pippa tanzt! Berlin, 1906.
Kaiser Karls Geisel. Berlin, 1908.
Griechischer Frühling. Berlin, 1908.
Der Narr in Christo Emanuel Quint. Berlin, 1910.
Die Ratten. Berlin, 1911.

Atlantis. Berlin, 1912.
Gabriel Schillings Flucht. Berlin, 1912.
Festspiel in deutschen Reimen. Berlin, 1913.
Der Ketzer von Soana. Berlin, 1918.
Anna. Berlin, 1921.
Indipohdi. Berlin, 1921.
Phantom. Berlin, 1923.
Die Insel der grossen Mutter. Berlin, 1924.
Die blaue Blume. Berlin, 1927.
Des grossen Kampffliegers, Landfahrers, Gauklers, und Magiers Till Eulenspiegels Abenteuer, Streiche, Gaukeleien, Gesichte, und Träume. Berlin, 1928.
Wanda. Berlin, 1928.
Buch der Leidenschaft. Berlin, 1930.
Vor Sonnenuntergang. Berlin, 1932.
Hamlet in Wittenberg. Berlin, 1935.
Das Abenteuer meiner Jugend. Berlin, 1937.
Iphigenie in Delphi. Berlin, 1941.
Der grosse Traum. Berlin, 1942.
Der neue Christophorus. Weimar, 1943.
Iphigenie in Aulis. Berlin, 1944.
Mignon. Berlin, 1947.
Agamemnons Tod. Berlin, 1948.
Elektra. Berlin, 1948.

COLLECTED WORKS

Das Gesammelte Werk: Ausgabe letzter Hand zum 80. Geburtstag des Dichters. 17 vols. Berlin, 1942.
Gesammelte Werke. 8 vols. Edited by Hans Mayer. Berlin, 1962.
Die Kunst des Dramas. Edited by Martin Machatzke. Frankfurt, 1963.
Die grossen Dramen. Berlin, 1965.
Die grossen Beichten. Berlin, 1966.
Die grossen Erzählungen. Berlin, 1967.
Die grossen Romane. Berlin, 1968.
Das dramatische Werk. 4 vols. Berlin, 1974.
Sämtliche Werke: Centenar-Ausgabe zum hundertsten Geburtstag des Dichters. 11 vols. Edited by Hans-Egon Hass and Martin Machatzke. Frankfurt and Berlin, 1962–1974.
Das dramatische Werk. 8 vols. Edited by Hans-Egon Hass and Martin Machatzke. Frankfurt, 1977.
Das erzählerische Werk. 10 vols. Edited by Ulrich Lauterbach. Frankfurt, 1981–1983.

JOURNALS AND CORRESPONDENCE

Gerhart Hauptmann. Diarium 1917–1933. Edited by Martin Machatzke. Frankfurt, 1980.

GERHART HAUPTMANN

Gerhart Hauptmann und Ida Orloff. Dokumentation einer dichterischen Leidenschaft. Frankfurt, 1969.

Gerhart Hauptmann: Italienische Reise 1897. Berlin, 1976.

Gerhart Hauptmann—Ludwig von Hofmann Briefwechsel 1894–1944. Edited by Herta Hesse-Frielinghaus. Bonn, 1983.

Gerhart Hauptmann Notizkalendar 1889–1891. Edited by Martin Machatzke. Frankfurt, 1982.

Gerhart Hauptmann—Otto Brahm Briefwechsel. Edited by Peter Sprengel. Tübingen, 1985.

Gerhart Hauptmann Tagebuch 1892–1894. Edited by Martin Machatzke. Frankfurt, 1985.

TRANSLATIONS

And Pippa Dances! Translated by Mary Harned. Boston, 1907.

The Assumption of Hannele. Translated by G. S. Bryan. Boston, 1909.

Atlantis. Translated by Adele and Thomas Seltzer. London, 1912.

Before Sunset. Translated by John Reich. New York, 1948 (microfilm of typewritten copy).

The Dramatic Works of Gerhart Hauptmann. Numerous translators. 9 vols. Edited by Ludwig Lewisohn. New York, 1913–1929.

Flagman Thiel. Translated by Adele Seltzer. In *Great German Short Novels and Stories.* New York, 1952.

The Fool in Christ: Emanuel Quint. Translated by Thomas Seltzer. New York, 1976.

Gerhart Hauptmann's "Before Daybreak": A Translation and an Introduction. Translated by Peter Bauland. Chapel Hill, N.C., 1978.

Gerhart Hauptmann: Three Plays—The Weavers, Hannele, The Beaver Coat. Translated by Horst Frenz and Miles Waggoner. New York, 1977.

The Heretic of Soana. Translated by Bayard Q. Morgan. New York, 1958.

The Island of the Great Mother; or, The Miracle of Île des Dames: A Story from the Utopian Archipelago. Translated by Willa and Edwin Muir. New York, 1925.

Lonely Lives: A Drama. Translated by Mary Morison. London, 1898.

Michael Kramer. Translated by Ludwig Lewisohn. New York, 1911.

Phantom. Translated by Bayard Q. Morgan. New York, 1922.

The Rats. Translated by Ludwig Lewisohn. New York, 1929.

The Reconciliation. Translated by Roy Temple House. Boston, 1910.

The Sunken Bell. Translated by Charles Henry Meltzer. New York, 1930.

The Weavers. Translated by Frank Marcus. London, 1980.

BIOGRAPHICAL AND CRITICAL STUDIES

Amrine, Frederick. "Hauptmann's *Vor Sonnenuntergang*: A New *King Lear*?" *Colloquia Germanica* 13:220–232 (1980).

Bachman, Charles R. "Life into Art: Gerhart Hauptmann and *Michael Kramer.*" *German Quarterly* 42:381–392 (1969).

Batley, E. M. "Functional Idealism in Gerhart Hauptmann's *Einsame Menschen*: An Interpretation." *German Life and Letters* 23:243–254 (1970).

Behl, C. F. W. *Zwiesprache mit Gerhart Hauptmann: Tagebuchblätter.* Munich, 1949.

Berger, Paul. *Gerhart Hauptmanns "Ratten": Interpretation eines Dramas.* Winterthur, 1961.

Clouser, Robin A. "The Spiritual Malaise of a Modern Hercules: Hauptmann's *Bahnwärter Thiel.*" *Germanic Review* 55:98–108 (1980).

Coupe, W. A. "An Ambiguous Hero: In Defence of Alfred Loth." *German Life and Letters* 31:13–22 (1976).

Cowen, Ray C. *Hauptmann-Kommentar zum dramatischen Werk.* Munich, 1980.

————. *Hauptmann-Kommentar zum dramatischen Werk.* Munich, 1981.

Daiber, Hans. *Gerhart Hauptmann oder der letzte Klassiker.* Vienna, 1971.

Dithmar, Reinhard. "Komik und Moral: Das Lustspiel im Unterricht am Beispiel von Gerhart Hauptmanns Diebskomödie *Der Biberpelz.*" *Der Deutschunterricht* 20:22–34 (1968).

Dobie, Ann B. "Riot, Revolution, and *The Weavers.*" *Modern Drama* 12:165–172 (1969).

Francke, Arno. "Wanderer zwischen den Welten: Mystisches Schwärmertum bei Gerhart Hauptmann." *Schlesien* 16:92–95 (1971).

Guthke, Karl S. "Alfred Kerr und Gerhart Hauptmann." *Monatshefte* 54:230–290 (1962).

————. *Gerhart Hauptmann: Weltbild im Werk.* Munich, 1980.

———— and H. M. Wolff. *Das Leid im Werke Gerhart Hauptmanns: Fünf Studien.* Berkeley, 1958.

Hildebrandt, Klaus. *Naturalistische Dramen Gerhart Hauptmanns: Die Weber, Rose Bernd, Die Ratten—Thematik, Entstehung, Gestaltungsprinzipien, Struktur.* Munich, 1983.

Hilscher, Eberhard. *Gerhart Hauptmann.* Berlin, 1969.

Hoefert, Sigfrid. *Gerhart Hauptmann.* Stuttgart, 1974.

Knight, K. G., and F. Norman, eds. *Hauptmann Centenary Lectures.* London, 1964.

Krogmann, Willy. "Gerhart Hauptmanns *Versunkene Glocke.*" *Zeitschrift für deutsche Philologie,* 79:350–361 (1960).

Ley, Ralph. "The Shattering of the Construct: Gerhart Hauptmann and His *Ketzer.*" In *Perspectives and Personalities,* edited by Ralph Ley, Joanna M. Ratych, and Kenneth Hughes. Heidelberg, 1978.

McCormick, E. Allen. "Rautendelein and the Thematic Imagery of the *Versunkene Glocke.*" *Monatshefte* 54:322–336 (1962).

———. "Gerhart Hauptmann's *Und Pippa Tanzt!*" In *Theatrum mundi.* Munich, 1980.

Martini, Fritz. "Gerhart Hauptmanns *Der Biberpelz*: Gedanken zum Bautypus einer naturalistischen Komödie." In *Wissenschaft als Dialog: Studien zur Literatur und Kunst seit der Jahrhundertwende—Wolfdietrich Rasch zum 65. Geburtstag,* edited by Renate von Heydebrand and Klaus Günther. Stuttgart, 1969.

Maurer, Warren R. *Gerhart Hauptmann.* Boston, 1982.

Mauser, Wolfram. "Gerhart Hauptmann's *Biberpelz*: Eine Komödie der Opposition?" *Michigan Germanic Studies* 1:215–233 (1974).

Meinert, Dietrich. *Hellenismus und Christentum in Gerhart Hauptmanns Atriden-Tetralogie.* Cape Town, 1964.

Philip Mellen. "Gerhart Hauptmann's *Einsame Menschen*: Christ in Crisis." *Germanic Notes* 11:41–44 (1980).

———. "Gerhart Hauptmann's Vor Sonnenaufgang and the Parable of the Sower." *Monatshefte* 74:139–144 (1982).

———. *Gerhart Hauptmann: Religious Syncretism and Eastern Religions.* Bern, 1984.

Muller, Siegfried H. *Gerhart Hauptmann and Goethe.* New York, 1949.

Osborne, John. "Hauptmann's Family Tragedy *Das Friedensfest.*" *Forum of Modern Language Studies* 4:223–233 (1968).

Piscator, Erwin. "Gerhart Hauptmanns Atriden-Tetralogie." In *Gerhart Hauptmann,* edited by Hans J. Schrimpf. Darmstadt, 1976.

Post, Klaus D. *Gerhart Hauptmann: "Bahnwärter Thiel"—Text, Materielien, Kommentar.* Munich, 1979.

Promies, Wolfgang. "Aspekte des närrischen in Hauptmanns *Till Eulenspiegel.*" *Revue de Littérature comparée* 37:550–580 (1963).

Reichart, Walter A. "Grundbegriffe im dramatischen Schaffen Gerhart Hauptmanns." *Publications of the Modern Language Association of America* 82:142–151 (1967).

———. *Gerhart-Hauptmann-Bibliographie.* Bad Hamburg, 1969.

Requardt, Walter, and Martin Machatzke. *Gerhart Hauptmann und Erkner: Studien zum Berliner Frühwerk.* Berlin, 1978.

Rey, William H. "Der offene Schluss der *Weber*: Zur Aktualität Gerhart Hauptmanns in unserer Zeit." *German Quarterly* 55:141–163 (1982).

Schlenther, Paul. *Gerhart Hauptmann: Sein Lebensgang und seine Dichtung.* Berlin, 1898.

Schrimpf, Hans J., ed. *Gerhart Hauptmann.* Darmstadt, 1976.

Schwab-Felisch, Hans. *Gerhart Hauptmann: "Die Weber."* Frankfurt, 1967.

Sinden, Margaret, *Gerhart Hauptmann: The Prose Plays.* New York, 1975.

Sprengel, Peter. *Gerhart Hauptmann: Epoche, Werk, Wirkung.* Munich, 1984.

Usmiani, Renate. "Towards an Interpretation of Hauptmann's *House of Atreus.*" *Modern Drama* 12:286–297 (1970).

Voigt, Felix A. *Gerhart Hauptmann und die Antike.* Berlin, 1965.

Wahr, Fred B. "Comments on Hauptmann's *Der Grosse Traum.*" *Germanic Review* 27:42–54 (1953).

———. "Hauptmann and Bachofen." *Monatshefte* 42:153–159 (1950).

Wiese, Benno von. "Wirklichkeit und Drama in Gerhart Hauptmanns Tragikomödie *Die Ratten.*" *Jahrbuch der Deutschen Schiller-Gesellschaft* 6:311–325 (1962).

PHILIP MELLEN

GABRIELE D'ANNUNZIO

(1863–1938)

IF, ACCORDING TO André Gide's quip, France's greatest poet is "Victor Hugo, alas!" modern Italy's is Gabriele D'Annunzio—except that most people attach a similar or stronger expletive. For virtuoso technique, there have not been many Italian writers, at least not since the days of the Neapolitan Giambattista Marino in the seventeenth century, who have been able to match D'Annunzio as a master of literary razzle-dazzle. His reputation, however, has declined sharply since his death. Although few figures in the history of Italian literature have enjoyed a more enthusiastic reception by the public and the critical establishment during their lifetimes than D'Annunzio did, perhaps none has then fallen to comparable depths of critical silence and supposed "unreadability." Nonetheless, D'Annunzio, like sin or taxes—or the historical fact of Italian Fascism—will not go away. Like it (or him) or not, D'Annunzio was the dominant influence on Italian literature in the first part of this century; his presence still looms behind much of today's Italian prose, poetry, and hortatory discourse. But D'Annunzio was more than a writer. He was a public figure who impressed himself on the collective consciousness not only because of his poetry, novels, plays, speeches, and memoirs, but also because he articulated an ideology especially congenial to the Italian middle classes at the beginning of the industrial era in Italy, and kept himself in the public eye through his theatrical displays of prowess as a man of action and spectacular lover.

Not only did D'Annunzio's narratives spawn a host of popular novels in which the more lurid aspects of his explorations of erotic behavior were aped and inflated; not only did his poetry lead by reaction to the deliberately understated writing of the "crepuscular" poets and such minimalists as Giuseppe Ungaretti; Italian social life in the twentieth century was also lastingly affected by D'Annunzio's example. In such different areas of linguistic and social activity as the dialogue adopted in the early Italian cinema, epistolary style, the rhetoric of seduction, modes of dress, and ways of composing a speech or an article for the popular or scholarly press, D'Annunzio's massive and noisy example was the inevitable model.

Given his overwhelming commercial success at the turn of the century and the later flow into the murky waters of Fascist rhetoric of expressive modalities that he had invented, it is not surprising that new generations of intellectuals from the Fascist and post-Fascist eras should view D'Annunzio and his works with some hostility. Beginning with the consolidation of the Fascist regime in the late 1920's and continuing up to the years immediately following World War II, D'Annunzio came more and more to be viewed in Italy first as a grotesque parody of his earlier self and of current establishment values, then as a distasteful reminder of a hateful and repudiated regime. It is only now, some fifty years after his death and nearly as many since the demise of the political system with which he was sometimes unfairly identified, that a measured appraisal of his work can perhaps begin. In his last years D'Annunzio found himself consigned by Mussolini to the gilded cage of Il Vittoriale degli Italiani (the triumph of the Italians), where he lived out his days as an ideological mummy sealed off from everyday life. Until recently, much D'Annunzio criticism has similarly embalmed his writings in the malodorous fluids of the political views they seem to adopt. Only in very recent times has the critical silence surrounding D'Annunzio noticed by Gianfranco Contini in 1968 begun to be breached and his texts to be reexamined in the light of such issues as the relation of writing to corporeality and the body, the role of the unconscious in ideology, and the importance of rhetoric in material and cultural production.

D'Annunzio was born on 12 March 1863 in the provincial town of Pescara in the Abruzzi of southeastern Italy. He was the son of *galantuomini,* members of the emergent southern middle class in the newly united Kingdom of Italy. Although the family of this future prince of Montenevoso (a title bestowed on him in 1924 by King Victor Emanuel at the suggestion of Benito Mussolini) was a far from aristocratic one, D'Annunzio's circumstances as a child were comfortable, especially as long as his father, Francesco Paolo, was still in possession of the family fortune that he had inherited from an adoptive uncle and that he later squandered so spectacularly. Nonetheless, as Francesco Paolo himself was shrewd enough to realize, a town like Pescara could provide only limited educational and social opportunities for someone of Gabriele's promise. Accordingly, when only about eleven years old, the young D'Annunzio was packed off to the academically rigorous and socially prestigious Cicognini boarding school at Prato, near Florence. Here he received an excellent education,

distinguishing himself for his quick wit, taste for pranks, and impatience with institutional discipline, as well as for the hard work and academic ability that consistently put him at the head of his class. At the Cicognini D'Annunzio came into contact with the Greek and Latin poetry that became such an important part of his intellectual and literary makeup, and he exchanged his native Abruzzi speech patterns for the Tuscan dialect that he used with great skill and evident relish for the rest of his life.

D'Annunzio was only sixteen and still a schoolboy when he published his first volume of verse, the *Primo vere* (First Spring) of 1879. A second edition that was, as he put it, "corrected with pen and fire," was issued the following year just after someone—almost certainly the poet himself—had spread the rumor of the tragically immature (but commercially opportune) death of its author. The poetry contained in *Primo vere* is modeled ostentatiously on that of the *Odi barbare* (Barbarous Odes, 1877) of Giosuè Carducci. In these poems Carducci, Italy's leading poet of the time (and in 1906 the winner of the Nobel Prize for Literature), had broken with the Italian metrical tradition of syllabic and stress organized verse by writing poetry in Italian based on Greek and Latin quantitative meters. In following Carducci's lead, therefore, D'Annunzio was attempting to insert himself into the renovation of Italian poetry and culture begun by the older poet. At one point he even considered calling his own volume "Odi arcibarbarissime" (Extra-super-barbarian Odes), though it is not entirely clear whether such a title would have suggested that his own work fell short of or went beyond that of his predecessor.

If the poems of *Primo vere* follow Carducci in form, in content they are much more steamily sensual than their usually austere models. In addition, the sharp plasticity of Carducci's best work is replaced in the D'Annunzio volume by a taste for the resolution of poetic tensions in music, a poetic strategy that D'Annunzio developed further in later years. These early poems, however, brim with youthful exuberance and have a surprising air of mastery about them. In these first poetic attempts D'Annunzio was both choosing to ally himself with what was newest in Italian poetry and keeping a sharp eye on his image in a public forum where charisma (or at least so he believed) was as important an attribute for a poet as verbal ability.

A certain measure of fame did in fact arrive with D'Annunzio's next volume of verse, *Canto novo* (New Song), published in 1882. After the failure of the sonnets commemorating his grandmother gathered in *In memoriam* (1880), D'Annunzio returned in this new volume to the "barbarous" metrics and poetic modalities of *Primo vere*. Like most of D'Annunzio's poetry of the 1880's *Canto novo* was later reorganized and substantially reworked into a "definitive" edition (in this case in 1896), and the lack of modern editions of the original version has sometimes made critical comment on this work difficult. It is clear, however, that the dominant theme of both the 1882 and the 1896 versions of this volume is that of metamorphosis. In these poems the animal, vegetable, and human realms are made to interpenetrate in a joyous affirmation of the biological unity of all of nature. In this second volume of verse by D'Annunzio a distinct physical background for the poems has also taken shape, the primitive Abruzzi landscape of the poet's childhood, drenched by the sun and washed by the sea: "Thàlatta! Thàlatta!" (The sea! The sea!) the poet exclaims excitedly—and in Greek—at one point early in the volume. Against this rough landscape powerful emotion is unleashed in an atmosphere of sharp sensation and vivid color: for example, vermilion sunsets against the deep blue sea sparkling like amber and topaz. The love celebrated in these lyrics is no longer derived from books but is instead the result of lived experience, the poet's encounter with Giselda or "Elda" Zucconi, to whom the volume was dedicated in its first (though not subsequent) editions. But the most enduring love in this volume is love for poetry, in particular for the difficult Greek and Latin forms that the poet is proud he has been able to tame in this second but now more assured and individualistic homage to Carducci. D'Annunzio's delight in this task is an important aspect of this collection, an element in that life-affirming and irrepressible joy that Giuseppe Antonio Borgese identifies as the dominant note in D'Annunzio's early poetry, a joy not just in making verses but

> l'immensa gioia di vivere,
> d'essere forte, d'essere giovine,
> di mordere i frutti terrestri
> con saldi e bianchi denti voraci.

> the immense joy of living,
> of being strong, of being young,
> of biting into the fruits of the earth
> with healthy white voracious teeth.
> ("Canto dell'ospite")

Many of the poems of the original edition of *Canto novo* were written at the same time as D'Annunzio's "veristic" or realistic short stories, and they share the latter's preoccupation with the often desperate lives of poor peasants, fishermen, and social outcasts. In some of these poems (all expunged from later versions of the volume), there are clear references, if not to social protest, at least to what was known at the time as *la questione sociale*. This is also the last time such issues arise in D'Annunzio's writing.

In his next volume of verse the poet turned away from the undeveloped Abruzzi with its attendant social and economic woes and focused on the sophisticated Rome where he was then making a living as a journalist and developing a reputation as a social lion and flamboyant seducer of women. It is at this point that art and life began to merge into a single process for D'Annunzio; from this point on he treated all that he did in the "text" of life primarily as material for his writing.

His first book of poetry from this period was *Intermezzo di rime* (Intermezzo of Rhyme,

177

1884; revised and published as *Intermezzo* in 1894). The poems in this volume are in traditional rhymed forms rather than in the quantitative meters of *Primo vere* and *Canto novo*. Always an omnivorous reader, D'Annunzio had gone beyond Italy and Carducci to find new models for his poetry in such French poets as Charles Baudelaire and Guy de Maupassant. Although part of his intent in doing this was to de-provincialize Italian poetry by inserting it into a more European context, D'Annunzio caused a scandal with this new work, which was greeted by certain critics as the "pornographic" offspring of a "swinish and impudent" writer. The uproar over *Intermezzo di rime* boosted sales and inflated D'Annunzio's reputation both as poet and as expert in what the work's "Preludio" calls "all the beautiful impure things."

Most of the poems in the volume are on sexual topics, among them a series of sonnets ("Le adultere") on great adulteresses of history, studies of the female nude, and an account of the thirteenth labor of Hercules—a feat whose nature can easily be imagined. But of all the poems in the collection, "Il peccato di maggio" (May Sin) is even today the most scandalous—not so much for what the poem says as for its surprisingly frank autobiographical content. In this work of self-aggrandizement, the author-narrator's seduction of a character clearly meant to represent the woman who became D'Annunzio's wife is described in unusually graphic language. The assertion that "the ripe apples of her breasts" are "fed by the bluest veins that run in human paradises" seems a clear allusion to the aristocratic blood of Duchess Maria Hardouin di Gallese, who a few months after the *peccato* that is so glowingly described in this poem became D'Annunzio's wife and nine months from that fateful May—but only six months after their marriage—gave birth to their son, Mario. Aside from its place in the history of D'Annunzio as consummate cad, "Peccato di maggio" also marks the first treatment in his poetry of the amorous stroll or *passeggiata*, a

theme that plays an important role in D'Annunzio's later work in both prose and verse.

D'Annunzio's next book of poetry is divided into two parts. First published in 1886, it was known in its first version as *Isaotta Guttadàuro e altre poesie* (Isaotta Guttadàuro and Other Poems) and in the revised edition of 1890 as *L'Isottèo—La Chimera* (Isottèo—The Chimera). In the first part of this collection D'Annunzio set himself a virtuoso task: to reproduce the language and situations of Italian pre-Renaissance poetry—the literary equivalent of the Pre-Raphaelite painting popular in the 1880's. As in those paintings, there are many glimpses in these poems of the beautiful faces of what Enzo Palmieri, in an annotated version of *L'Isottèo—La Chimera,* has called D'Annunzio's "impassioned and mysterious muses . . . the faces of women not loved in vain." More importantly, in their evocations of past moments of Italian cultural supremacy as a reminder and stimulus to the present, the *Isaotta/Isottèo* poems also show that D'Annunzio's attitude to the past is becoming increasingly nationalistic. At the same time, the impossible wealth and luxury of that past as depicted in the sensual surfaces of these poems is an almost wholly imagined reality not unlike that created by the unhistorically "barbaric" and equally unreal "veristic" stories of these same years. The D'Annunzio of these works was interested not in history but in art, which in both the prose and the poetry of these years was represented more and more as the supreme value in life. As he says in the conclusion to *Isottèo:*

> *O poeta, divina è la Parola;*
> *ne la pura Bellezza il ciel ripose*
> *ogni nostra letizia; e il Verso è tutto.*

> O poet, the Word is divine;
> in pure Beauty heaven has placed
> all our happiness; and the Line of verse is
>   everything.

Many of the poems in the second half of *Isaotta Guttadàuro ed altre poesie,* the "other poems" that later became *La Chimera,* have a contemporary setting. Among them are some of D'Annunzio's most successful texts, the musical and charming *romanze* (romances) and *rondò* (rondels) that have often been anthologized. In them the voice of the poet is a lighthearted one, intent on capturing a moment of pleasure that is often erotic but might just as well derive from the fall of light against the tawny architecture of the Roman squares, fountains, and palaces through which the poet moves with confident urbanity. The epigraph from Gustave Flaubert at the beginning of *La Chimera* is an invitation to fame, to artistic mastery, and above all to sensual delight. And although the Chimera lurks in the background of these texts, threatening pain and destruction as the price of love, she too is *bellissima* (very beautiful), and the labyrinths she inhabits are filled with roses.

These are poems of pleasure, whether in Papal Rome or in the country, in modern times, in the Renaissance, or in the days of Christ, a Christ whose son Eleabani (a character in the poem who doubles as D'Annunzio's persona) here proclaims a holiness that is not of the spirit but of the flesh. In this and other poems in this volume the sacred is evoked not from piety but for the power of religious emotion to intensify the thrills of the profane. In "Donna Francesca," for example, the pleasure of sexual conquest is deepened by the poet's surprising the title character at her prayers, slowly undoing her hair, and then consummating his religious and erotic rite on the altar of her bed. In these poems such shocking (or at least titillating) material is always presented, if not in good taste, at least with great elegance. By this time D'Annunzio was master of a variety of poetic forms, able to draw at will from the Greek and Latin classics, Renaissance literature, or the contemporary French and Italian traditions to find the necessary drapery for the carnal indulgences his verses evoke.

The elegance and preciosity of *Isottèo—La Chimera* and its insistence on the supremacy of the aesthetic make it a work that might well have been composed by Andrea Sperelli, the hero of D'Annunzio's first novel, *Il piacere* (*The Child of Pleasure,* 1889). By the time he began to compose this text, D'Annunzio was already a practiced writer of prose, much of it racy journalistic work that he produced during the 1880's for such fashionable Roman papers as the *Cronaca bizantina, Tribuna,* and *Capitan Fracassa.* By this time he had also written several short stories, works that were radically different in subject and tone from his society reporting. Just as in his early poetry D'Annunzio had turned to the successful Carducci for a model, in these short stories he followed the lead of the newest and most important current in Italian prose fiction of the time: the verismo movement, especially the stories and novels of its greatest exponent, the Sicilian Giovanni Verga. Although other influences (Maupassant, Émile Zola) can be traced in these early stories, it is Verga and other native *veristi* who were the principal models for D'Annunzio's three collections of short fiction: *Terra vergine* (Virgin Land, 1882), *Il libro delle vergini* (The Book of the Virgins, 1884), and *San Pantaleone* (1886; revised and republished in 1902 as *Le novelle della Pescara* [*Tales of My Native Town*]).

In these stories and sketches D'Annunzio's native Abruzzi, like Verga's Sicily, is treated as a privileged zone of existence where human life can be observed in its rawest and thus most authentic form. Like Verga's, D'Annunzio's attitude toward his characters and their actions is impassive and "scientifically" objective, though he is notably lacking in Verga's compassion for those who stumble and fall in the Darwinian struggle for life. For D'Annunzio it is the struggle itself and the resulting revelations of the true meaning of human nature that matter—not the heroic dignity of the primitive protagonists in this often losing battle. D'Annunzio's characters in these stories of carnality, blood, and primitive closed-mindedness are rarely dignified or heroic. Many of them are physically repellent, the stronger devoted to their own pleasure at any cost, the weaker prey to sexual and other passions as destructive as they are irresistible. Abruzzi folklore, as presented here, is little more than brutal superstition, while village religion is anachronistic, cruel, and comfortless.

Many of D'Annunzio's short stories are tales of failure, descriptions of crucial encounters with the limits of life and desire as they are set by the human condition itself. The nature and extent of these limits were of great interest to D'Annunzio throughout his career, possibly because he spent much of his life combating constraints on his own life and conduct—if not those of the human condition itself, then the more mundane social, financial, and legal restrictions in which he frequently found himself entangled. Even in these early stories D'Annunzio is fascinated with the idea of the "exceptional man" who is able to go beyond the limits of normal existence. We can see glimmerings of D'Annunzio's later idea of the Superman, for example, in "Il duca d'Ofena" (The Duke of Ofena), who gathers his lover's body in his arms and strides defiantly into the flames of his burning palace, thus depriving the rebels who have set it afire of the satisfaction of having the pair's corpses in their power. Similarly, in "Dalfino" the title character avoids punishment for murdering his rival by swimming dolphinlike out to sea to what will certainly be his death but is at least a fate that he has chosen rather than one inflicted upon him by the state.

Despite references in these and other stories to peasant rebellions and legal and other conflicts between village life and the institutions of the new Italian nation, in his tales of Abruzzi life D'Annunzio is not really interested in social issues. It has been pointed out that the often bestial "primitives" who appear in these tales are as remote from the real social and economic realities of late-nineteenth-century Italy as are Paul Gauguin's South Sea islanders or the enigmatic savages of Henri Rousseau. But in his reduction of human life to an animal-like striving, not so much for survival as for mastery over others, and in his fascination with superior individuals who are able by force of will and superiority of style to vanquish physical and conventional contingencies, D'Annunzio looked ahead to important components of his own future political and artistic ideology and to currents that became increasingly important in European thought and life in the years to come.

When D'Annunzio turned to novel-writing, the first work he produced was quite different from these naturalistic early stories. *The Child of Pleasure* was written in five months in 1888 and published the following year. It is an account of two love affairs in the life of the dashing man-about-Rome Count Andrea Sperelli, a character modeled in part on D'Annunzio himself. Sperelli's first amorous encounter is with Elena Muti, a beautiful and sensually enthusiastic Roman duchess. When Elena leaves him for a financially expedient marriage, Andrea, who is recuperating from a duel, initiates a second love affair with the frostily beautiful Maria Ferres. Although successful in seducing Maria and thus able to create a third, ideal mistress in his mind's eye by thinking about the sexy Elena while making love to her more spiritual successor, Andrea ruins everything by pronouncing Elena's name during just such a moment. At the end of the book he finds himself abandoned by both women, alone and disconsolate in a Rome that is sinking into a vulgar cultural miasma in which cultural and artistic values are slowly perishing along with Andrea's illusions.

Stylistically, *The Child of Pleasure* is a tour de force and a successful one at that. Not only is it one of D'Annunzio's most structurally coherent novels, but its carefully cadenced poetic prose also often rises to real lyric heights, as in the work's initial paragraph, which describes a golden December evening in the Piazza di Spagna. A good bit of this opening page, in fact, comes from a passage in *La Chimera*, and the entire novel is peppered with intertextual allusions to works by D'Annunzio and other writers, sculptors, and painters. As Arturo Mazzarella has pointed out, one result of this tendency to compare everything—not only the many art objects that crowd these pages but also the settings and characters—to great works of art is that these things become reified, and consequently reality is reduced to little more than a precious but lifeless museum. If this is so, there can be little doubt that Andrea Sperelli is the most vital and interesting exhibit in this collection. In addition to his skills as a lover, horseman, and swordsman, his abilities as poet and engraver, and his trained eye as collector of bric-a-brac and objets d'art as well as of women, this "last descendant of an intellectual race" is convinced that he has been able to make his life itself into a work of art. In D'Annunzio's time Sperelli provided an attractive model for bourgeois readers eager to emulate the mannerisms of an Italian aristocracy that was beginning to fade in economic importance but was allied with the bourgeoisie in the struggle to discredit working-class aspirations to social and economic parity. Throughout this novel the erotic is identified with the rare and the costly and seems to be reserved for the rich and/or aristocratic. Not only, for example, does Andrea take great pleasure in riding with Elena in an expensive carriage where the latest in heaters keeps her "tiny ducal feet" warm, his satisfaction at being with her in a place of comfort and intimacy is increased by the glimpses he catches of "obscure people" suffering in the chill and muddy streets outside the carriage windows.

But if D'Annunzio's polemic against all that is vulgar sometimes seems to include the bourgeoisie in the mob that was his principal target, his criticism did not disqualify this text for success with middle-class readers masochistically willing to endure a modicum of class excoriation along with the other titillations the novel provided. There were plenty of these, including a sickroom seduction and an episode of lovemaking in which every pore of Elena's body is described as a jealous mouth competing ardently for Andrea's attention. For all this, Andrea is a remarkably passive lover. Elena, as a "belle dame sans merci," dominates him easily; it is she, for example, who initiates their sickbed coupling.

The elaborate and self-conscious seductions like this one, which constitute the center of interest of this novel, take place against the background of events in the Roman society world of the time. Among these were the many auction sales resulting from the breaking up of great households of the time, an activity that provided such novelists as Verga and later De Roberto and Giuseppe di Lampedusa with material for significant historical meditation. In D'Annunzio's case the end of an era signaled by these sales meant more than the replacement of one class with another; it signified a disastrous decline of all that was most precious in Italian civilization. Andrea Sperelli is deeply offended by this crumbling of artistic values because in him "the aesthetic sense" is so powerful "that it had taken over for the moral sense." When Andrea employs this aesthetic sense in a quest for an erotic ideal that he believes to be latent in a world emptied of both historical and aesthetic significance, he ends up as a defeated anachronism. Although D'Annunzio himself called Andrea a "monster," the protagonist's failure at this book's conclusion can be seen as a result of his inability to adopt the even more "monstrous" attitudes toward good and evil typical of the protagonists of some of D'Annunzio's later novels.

Problems of good and evil are very much at the heart of D'Annunzio's next two novels: *Giovanni Episcopo* (*Episcopo & Company*) and *L'Innocente* (*The Intruder*). Both of them were published in 1892, and both deal with guilt and with attempts to justify the crime of murder. *Episcopo & Company* is much the shorter of the two; it was composed in January of 1891, just after D'Annunzio had finished his military service. Stylistically, both *Episcopo & Company* and *The Intruder* represent a break with the lyric and sometimes purple prose of *The Child of Pleasure*. In an important dedicatory letter to the Neapolitan novelist and woman of letters Matilde Serao at the beginning of *Episcopo & Company*, D'Annunzio expresses "shame and rage" at certain passages in his earlier novel and asserts that in this new work he will "study people and things DIRECTLY and without intermediaries." As part of this program for greater stylistic verisimilitude and immediacy, both of the new texts are first-person confessions and adopt a more flat and conversational tone than that employed in the sometimes stylistically overblown *The Child of Pleasure.*

Episcopo & Company was heavily influenced by the writings of Feodor Dostoevsky, French translations of whose novels had begun to appear in the 1880's. It tells the story of a man morbidly lacking in willpower and constantly humiliated by the mean-spirited people with whom he lives and works. Set among the lowest social stratum of the same Rome where Andrea Sperelli occupied the most exalted heights, the novel describes an "underground man" who is in many ways Andrea's exact opposite. But even though he is more developed psychologically than any of D'Annunzio's previous characters, Giovanni Episcopo does not have the spiritual depths of the Christlike characters of Dostoevsky's fiction. While he does suffer, he does not do so for noble motives, and his spiritual anguish ennobles neither himself nor others. His disastrous marriage to the promiscuous and sadistic Ginevra, for example, is contracted not because he has any desire to save her from a life of disgrace but because he too is dominated by the same physical lust that he finds so deplorable an element in human relations in general. When, at the end of the story, Giovanni kills his rival, the sinister bully Giulio Wanzer, the violence of the act itself provides the resolution of the narrative tensions that have been established, and there is little suggestion that Giovanni will achieve any sort of Dostoevskian redemption.

This short novel marks an important stage in D'Annunzio's career: for the first time characters that he has created speak in a voice at least somewhat different from the author's. Thus D'Annunzio follows the artistic dictum set out in this work's dedicatory letter: "o rinnovarsi o morire" (either renew oneself or die), a motto that fits all of his production from this time forward. With *Episcopo & Company* D'Annunzio abandoned the "veristic" objectives of his earlier studies of destructive passion by probing for the first time into the depths of a character's psychological life. Thus this is not a naturalistic work, even if its clinical interest in causation and pathology is typical of that movement and plays an important role in D'Annunzio's other novel of 1892, *The Intruder.*

The Intruder was written in the spring and summer of 1891, just after *Episcopo & Company*. Found "highly immoral" and turned down for publication by Treves in Milan, it first appeared in installments in Serao and Scarfoglio's *Corriere di Napoli* and then in a volume by the Neapolitan editor Ferdinando Bideri in 1892. An important film by Luchino Visconti, also called *L'Innocente*, was made from the novel in 1979. The hero of *The Intruder* is another of D'Annunzio's self-styled "exceptional men." Like Andrea Sperelli, Tullio Hermil is a Victorian playboy "constantly unfaithful to a constantly faithful woman." The woman involved is Giuliana, his long-suffering, beautiful, and—and here lies the story—almost constantly faithful wife. Others in Tullio's family include his doting mother, two adoring daughters, and a devoted brother who oversees the agricultural enterprises that help support the family. Tullio is the father in this group, his only rivals to the title of principal authority figure being his bachelor brother Federico, the faithful peasant retainer Giovanni da Scordio, and the family doctor, who sees to Giuliana's gynecological maladies but is unable to save her newborn son from being murdered at the novel's conclusion by the jealous Tullio.

Much of the book's action centers on the intrusion into this family of the illegitimate child, at once the "innocent" of the Italian title and the "intruder" of the English title. This child has been conceived by Giuliana in a "single moment of weakness" with Filippo Arborio, a Roman rake and successful writer. Arborio is also a familiar D'Annunzian character, and he is so much Tullio's alter ego, is so indistinguishable from Tullio, that at least one critic has defended Giuliana's "weakness" as not being adultery at all, since Filippo is so much like Tullio that she can scarcely be expected to tell them apart.

Whatever Giuliana's guilt in this matter (and it may also be that she is the book's "innocent"), Tullio is certainly guilty of both infanticide and long-standing cruelty to his wife. His consciousness of his guilt is the subject of the lengthy and intense conversations he has with himself in the course of the novel. As in *Episcopo & Company,* which is also a confessional monologue, this work reveals considerable interest in pathological states and in the causal relations between crime and madness. For if *Episcopo & Company* is principally a story of lust, *The Intruder* is a tale of pain in both a medical and a moral sense. Once again there are many sickbed scenes, with Giuliana convalescent throughout the story and with Tullio also in a kind of limited moral recovery from his erotic excesses with "the other woman," Teresa Raffo. Although it might be said that the moral torment he suffers provides Tullio with an ethical dimension lacking in Andrea Sperelli, his decision to forgive Giuliana but kill her child marks the limits of his moral achievements. For this reason some critics have concluded that the novel is a failure because of D'Annunzio's inability to understand the Dostoevskian and Christian notion of redemption. Another reading of the work, however, claims that, despite the ostentatiously amoral contentions that so shocked early readers, *The Intruder* is little more than a reaffirmation of conventional middle-class morality. In this view Tullio's reaction to his wife's unfaithfulness is not unlike the "crime of honor" committed by Compar Alfio when he discovers Santuzza's unfaithfulness in Verga's 1880 story

(and Pietro Mascagni's 1890 opera) *Cavalleria rusticana.* In D'Annunzio's tale of middle-class chivalry, adultery is wrong, but it is especially wrong for women. Those women who do insist on sexual independence are swiftly punished for "moments of weakness" by gynecological infections and the eventual loss of their children.

Security lies only within the family circle, whose members—especially the mother and the deceased sister, who here has the significant name Costanza—take on the status of secular saints as a suitable reward for their unflagging support of their frequently transgressing men. In this charmed circle an intruder of any sort must be resented as "different" and "other," just as non-Italians are seen as "other" in D'Annunzio's later and more overtly racist fiction and political declamations. For all its pretensions to unconventionality and wickedness, *The Intruder* is a study of what might be called a "Laius complex," in which a father is unable to bear the competition for his wife's affection represented by her baby, whether conceived within the bounds of marriage or not. When this infant intruder is eliminated—and especially when, as here, he is snuffed out with the mother's connivance—the Laius figure is reassured that the mother's love for him is whole and undiluted, and the psychological tension of his story finds release.

Sexual warfare becomes even more important in D'Annunzio's next novel, *Trionfo della morte (Triumph of Death,* 1894). Written in stages over several periods of his life, *Triumph of Death* is the most composite of D'Annunzio's novels. Part of it was published as *L'Invincibile* (The Invincible) in the *Tribuna illustrata* while D'Annunzio was doing his military service. After his return and during the "Russian" period of *Episcopo & Company* and *The Intruder,* he took it up again, completing it after his crucial encounters with Barbara Leoni, with the philosophy of Friedrich Nietzsche, and—though this was less decisive than the first two—with the music of Richard Wagner. *Triumph of Death* is also autobiographical: D'Annunzio's financial and other troubles with his father are reflected in those of Giorgio Aurispa with his father, and Giorgio's steamy relationship with Ippolita Sanzio is based uncomfortably closely on D'Annunzio's equally warm affair with Leoni; D'Annunzio even incorporated some of his letters to her into the text of the novel.

Triumph of Death is once again the story of a failure, or rather a series of failures. As it begins, Giorgio is seeking to give some meaning to his life and to establish a more psychologically satisfying relationship with his mistress, Ippolita. When family concerns take him on a visit to his relatives in the Abruzzi, Giorgio recognizes how different he has become from the other members of his family and realizes that he can no longer be of much use to them in resolving their existential problems or financial difficulties. When he then slips away with Ippolita for an extended country idyll, their unrestrained lovemaking is tainted by his awareness of Ippolita's unyielding otherness even at those moments when she gives herself to him most unreservedly. Painfully aware of his alienation from both his family and his mistress, Giorgio begins to think of Ippolita as *la nemica* (the enemy) and to view her as a threat to his own existence.

While in the country with Ippolita, Giorgio is struck by the vigorous beauty and wholesome religious practices of the peasants who live around them, people from whose stock he has himself sprung and whose authenticity and vitality he finds characteristic of a superior race that he longs to emulate. But when he and Ippolita join a pilgrimage to a rustic sanctuary at Casalbordino, his admiration for the simple people of the region quickly turns to repulsion. In a famous episode Giorgio and Ippolita are set upon by a grotesque assemblage of filthy and ignorant beggars and invalids abjectly seeking a miraculous cure from menacing powers they hold in superstitious awe. This is not the sturdy pre-Christian peasant religion that Giorgio had imagined earlier, nor are these the superior beings he had

thought to find in this rustic setting. Casalbordino thus marks the end of his populist and racist notions of identification with the people of his native region.

Furthermore, Giorgio is by now increasingly repelled by Ippolita, whose sterility he rather unkindly associates with impurity, further imagining her womb to be "a burning furnace" where "every seed must perish." In such circumstances sexual contact with Ippolita becomes increasingly distressing. Finally, after a scene in which he is either unwilling or unable to satisfy her sexual demands except by a digital proxy that initially induces orgasmic convulsions but then causes uncontrollable laughter, Giorgio hurls both himself and a struggling and unwilling Ippolita off a cliff in a final *Liebestod* inspired by (even if not quite congruent with) that at the conclusion of Wagner's *Tristan und Isolde* (1857–1859). Death the invincible has triumphed over this character's unsuccessful attempts to establish communication with an entity beyond the limits of his own ego—whether with a family or some other collectivity, a religion or an ideology—or even simple communion with another human being.

The impotence that dogs Giorgio Aurispa in *Triumph of Death* is ideological as well as sexual and existential. In his next novel D'Annunzio took steps to fill the ideological void that lurks in the background of all his early fiction and into which Giorgio could be said to plunge at the end of *Triumph of Death*. In *Le vergini delle rocce* (*Maidens of the Rocks*, 1896) the sterility that dominates the previous text is replaced by an obsession with fertility, as the aimlessness of Giorgio Aurispa gives way to Claudio Cantelmo's threefold mission to realize in himself "the perfect fullness of the Latin type," to "gather the purest essence of the universe into a single and supreme work of art," and, finally, to sire a superior human being "worthy of aspiring to the actuation of increasingly elevated possibilities." Claudio not only wants to become a Nietzschean Superman and a superior artist; he also wants to be the father of the future king of Rome, a kind of "Superbambino." To accomplish this, Claudio must have a wife, and *Maidens of the Rocks* is the story of his attempts to find a woman worthy of this lofty task. But although he seems about to select one of the three daughters of a noble but decadent family at whose moldering estate much of the novel takes place, by its closing pages Claudio has not decided which of the three "virgins of the rocks" is to be his mate.

Even if this novel lacks closure and ends with a sharp sense of the same failure that characterizes D'Annunzio's earlier novels, there is much in this book that is new and important. For one thing, the chaste and marriage-bent Claudio is D'Annunzio's first positive hero, at least in the realm of sexual conduct. For another, in this work D'Annunzio transcends his conceptualization of the female sex as being divided into sterile and impure (but immensely desirable) women on the one hand and sacred mothers (and sometimes sisters) on the other. For the first time in D'Annunzio's fiction a novel's hero is able to imagine a single individual as both woman and mother, even if he is still too bewildered to decide which of the three sisters might best serve him in this role.

Even more important than this change in the dominant psychosexual value system of the book is the decisive presence in it of the thought of Nietzsche, whose works D'Annunzio had read in French translation during this period. Nietzsche's thought, as transformed by D'Annunzio's artistic and therefore less than philologically rigorous approach, had already been important for *Triumph of Death*. With *Maidens of the Rocks* it became a crucial part of his ideology and determined much of his thinking on art and living from that time forward. D'Annunzio's program for the superior man is racist and aesthetic as well as elitist: his *Superuomo* must be Italian and an artist as well as a dominator. For D'Annunzio, the world itself is the creation of a few superior and artistically gifted minds. In volume 2 of

Proze di romanzi, he describes the world as "the representation of the sensibility and thought of a few superior men who have created and then increased and decorated it, . . . a magnificent gift granted by the few to the many, from the free to the slaves, from those who think and feel to those who must work for a living." Although significantly different from Nietzsche's own metaphysical and ethical views, D'Annunzio's articulation of this elitist view of the universe was not out of line with Italian social and political history in this period, which saw not only the formation of the Italian socialist movement but also a turn to the right in Italian politics, especially under Francesco Crispi, with anti-socialist policies at home and increasingly imperialistic tendencies abroad.

But *Maidens of the Rocks* is something more than "a novel of political nostalgia par excellence," as Richard Drake has called it, in which the conservative forces in the country could find a justification for their own anti-democratic views. It is true that in this work the state is described as "an institution perfectly adapted to favoring the gradual elevation of a privileged class toward an ideal form of existence" and toward "a new realm of force" that will "dominate the multitudes." However, what gives D'Annunzio's proto-Fascism a unique coloring is that he yokes this concept of political force exercised by a racially determined elite to an equally fervid devotion to the cult of beauty. Claudio is inspired by his heroic ancestors "for the beautiful wounds that they opened, the beautiful fires that they set, the beautiful cups that they emptied, the beautiful clothes that they wore, the beautiful horses that they broke, the beautiful women that they enjoyed, for all their slaughters, their intoxications, their magnificent gestures, and their lusts."

As Emanuella Scarano Lugnani has noted, D'Annunzio's tendency "to transpose exquisitely aesthetic categories onto an ethical plane" has important consequences for the book's style. In *Maidens of the Rocks* earlier attempts at psychological investigation and moralistic justifications have been abandoned for an almost complete reliance on style as bearer of the work's message. Although we do not see him create the "Superbambino" and future king of Rome, the aesthetic Superman who is the first-person narrator of this book has fathered a Superstyle that enables him to master an otherwise opaque, resistant, and offensively crass and materialistic world. In the intensely rhetorical and lyrical prose of *Maidens of the Rocks,* naturalism is turned inside out and transformed into a kind of "anti-realism." With its submersion of plot, characterization, and verisimilitude in the boiling reagent of D'Annunzio's most emphatic and heated writing, the nineteenth-century novel breaks up under the impact of a new oratorical and apocalyptic mode. The novels and other prose works that D'Annunzio wrote from this time forward abandoned the conventions of nineteenth-century prose narrative in favor of new narrative forms more consonant with the age of modernism.

Il fuoco (The Flame of Life, 1900) might qualify as the "supreme work of art" that Claudio dreamed of creating in *Maidens of the Rocks;* it certainly continues the anti-novelistic tendencies apparent in that book. It was completed and published during a period when its author was creating some of his most enduring poetry and had launched his project for an Italian national theater. Although famous for its detailed and sometimes crudely indiscreet (and not entirely accurate) descriptions of D'Annunzio's love affair with Eleonora Duse, the novel also expands on D'Annunzio's theory of the Superman and contains rich descriptions of Venice and the surrounding territory in the autumn both of the year and of that city's glory as an artistic and imperial power. Stelio Effrena, the hero of this work, is a successful, even impossibly successful, poet and orator. His companion, "Perdita" or "la Foscarina," is a celebrated actress much older than he (in reality Duse was only five years older than her lover), and her physical decline parallels the waning of the year and of Venice's fading glory.

When *The Flame of Life* was first published, Duse's friends and many admirers were outraged by the way D'Annunzio treated her in it. For her part, the actress announced that she knew the book and had authorized its printing, judging the pain it caused her to be of less importance than its contribution as "a masterpiece of Italian literature." "Besides," she continued, "I am forty years old . . . and in love!"

As in most of D'Annunzio's novels, there is very little real action in this work. Like *Maidens of the Rocks, The Flame of Life* is based on thematic repetitions and variations, a technique similar to that of the leitmotifs in the operas of Wagner, who makes a cameo appearance in the novel and whose Bayreuth Festspieltheater D'Annunzio hoped to eclipse by establishing the Italian national theater he describes in these pages. In its highly declamatory prose and its preoccupation with problems of the theater, *The Flame of Life* marks the transition between D'Annunzio's novels of the early and middle 1890's and the plays that follow. There is also further development in it of D'Annunzio's attitudes toward women and political activism.

In *Flame of Life* woman's role is once again to serve ("Servire! Servire!" is Foscarina's cry to Stelio), but this service is now for the sake of artistic expression by the Artist-Superman, with women "perfect and nearly divine instruments of his fictions." Just as Duse turned over portions of her salary to support D'Annunzio's efforts in the theater, Foscarina happily submits her will to his creative needs, content to be "a ring for his finger, a glove, a piece of clothing, a word to be spoken or not, a wine to be drunk or poured onto the ground." Like the ideal spouse of *Maidens of the Rocks,* Foscarina is to be a breeder, though the aim of her creative collaboration with the Superman is "Supertheater" rather than a "Superbambino." Like many of the female characters in D'Annunzio's previous novels, Foscarina too is impure. In her career as an actress, she has been possessed and spiritually smudged by the multitudes for whom she has performed. Although it is partly this impurity that attracts him to her, Stelio does not fail to punish Foscarina for it. In a famous episode in a hedge maze at Stra in the Venetian hinterland, he hides from the increasingly disoriented actress until she is beside herself with terror and frustration and collapses in tears to the ground.

If dominance of this adoring woman is a relatively easy feat, Stelio is also able to master the harder trick of dominating large crowds of listeners by the force of his invective. In D'Annunzio's earlier novels crowds are always shunned as vulgar and anti-aesthetic. But for Stelio the crowd is a challenge, and stirring a multitude to action is an important way for him to exhibit his credentials as an "exceptional man." "It seems to me," he says in a phrase suggestive of much twentieth-century messianic political rhetoric, "that the spoken word, straightforwardly directed at a multitude, should have as its purpose nothing but action, even violent action." What D'Annunzio sought and found in the theater of his time was the means and opportunity to stir people to action. In this project he was surpassing Duse/Foscarina by mastering the forces that had dominated and sullied her. His mastery over the actress herself, therefore, constituted control both of a woman and of an essential mediating element in his quest for further control of a mass audience.

For the D'Annunzio of this period, not only was the theater a superior kind of politics, but politics was little more than theater played out before a different kind of audience. It is thus not surprising to find that during the time when D'Annunzio was busiest writing plays, he also ran for office. Once elected, furthermore, his flair for the dramatic did not abandon him and, after being seated in parliament in 1897, the poet suddenly and dramatically changed sides, moving from extreme right to extreme left, proclaiming as he did so that as "a man of intellect" he was thereby "choosing life." One way for the "exceptional man" to master reality—the enduring problem in D'An-

nunzio's system—is through mastery of an entity larger than himself, whether through the writing of plays with successful orations of the sort described at the beginning of *The Flame of Life*, or through political activity of a more conventional sort. With this novel D'Annunzio moved away from literature in the usual sense and toward action, though this road took him through the theater first.

Forse che sì forse che no (Maybe Yes, Maybe No, 1910) was D'Annunzio's last full-length novel; it was written after his experiments in the theater and his very successful lyric poetry of the late 1890's and early 1900's. By the time he wrote this work, Duse had been replaced in D'Annunzio's affections by a procession of other women, among them Alessandra di Rudinì, Giuseppina Mancini, and Natalia de Goloubeff—three exceptional women whose sometimes extravagant behavior and distressing tendencies to madness left their mark on D'Annunzio's depiction of Isabella Inghirami's powerful eroticism and ultimate insanity in this novel.

In *Forse che sì forse che no*, for the first and perhaps only time in D'Annunzio's fiction, the action moves forward briskly, without the descriptive prolixity of his previous work; instead of the usual dialectic between the exceptional man and his female antagonist, there are five well-realized characters. By the time D'Annunzio wrote this book, not only had he grown as a writer, but certain kinds of dangerous physical activity had also become an essential element in his life. He now knew, for example, how to drive an automobile and how to fly an airplane, two skills shared by his newest "exceptional man," Paolo Tarsis. Unlike D'Annunzio's previous heroes, Paolo is not a writer or aesthete. Of middle-class rather than aristocratic origins, he does not feel out of place in the modern world, whose transportation and communication devices—this is perhaps the first European novel in which a telephone call figures importantly in the plot— he dominates as readily and effortlessly as he does women. Paolo is also unusual among

D'Annunzio's heroes in that he does not demonstrate his prowess only in isolation, but has a comrade, Giulio Cambiaso, with whom he shares adventures all over the world and even beneath the sea in an early submarine.

In this book the aesthetic qualities of previous heroes are still present, but they are concentrated in a lesser figure: Aldo Lunati, Isabella's irresistibly beautiful but somewhat passive younger brother, who is her partner in incest. Paolo, who is repelled and at the same time sadistically and violently attracted to Isabella when he learns of her morbid attachment to her brother, is an early aviator who sees flying as a way to transcend both his own human weaknesses and the terrestrial world of betrayal, lust, and pain in which Isabella plays such an important part. Thus, at the end of his story, the extended solo flight he successfully completes not only frees him from the "sewer" of human relations in which he has been floundering but also restores him to the world of nature, which is presented for the first time in this novel not as a resistant material to be conquered but as the essential medium of Paolo's accomplishment. For her part, Isabella is a more inventive and strong-willed match for her lover than is Ippolita Sanzio of *Triumph of Death,* as is clear from the book's opening episode, in which Isabella explicitly defies both Paolo and the threat of death in the racing car he is recklessly piloting.

Unlike her potentially ardent but still innocent younger sister, Vana, Isabella is an "austere science" of sexual practice. In her frenetic and sometimes violent masochism ("Know me . . . seek me . . . reach me . . . kill me") Isabella seeks neither happiness nor balance but a state of disequilibrium that will allow her to attain a new kind of understanding, her goal being "to reach the bottom of the abyss, or is it the subterranean temple?" Her incest with her brother recalls episodes in earlier novels by D'Annunzio, in which love for a sister is contemplated for its erotic piquancy but is not given the negative valence that attaches to it here. Once again, woman, especially when "foaming with voluptuousness," is a force that limits the hero's aspirations and autonomy, though now—thanks to the airplane—he need not jump off a cliff to get away from her. The opposition between purity and impurity in *Forse che sì forse che no* once again has woman occupying the impure pole, but for the first time the opposite pole of this dialectic is located in the untrammeled skies, a region accessible only to the male heroes of a technological civilization. In this last novel by D'Annunzio the freedom that the hero has been seeking seems finally attainable through the technological power of a new industrial nation managed by a race of modern supermen. The text thus represents a turning-away from the politics of nostalgia to a more up-to-date nationalism of the sort that was beginning to emerge throughout Europe on the eve of World War I.

From a technical point of view, this is perhaps D'Annunzio's best-constructed novel, moving forward with the precision of a finely tuned internal combustion engine. Its lexicological delight in precise technological vocabulary on the one hand and effective natural imagery on the other makes it one of D'Annunzio's richer prose texts. But its preoccupation with action is the element that shows most clearly the direction that D'Annunzio's thought took next.

Throughout the 1890's D'Annunzio was writing poetry as well as fiction. In 1892 he published *Elegie romane* (Roman Elegies) and in 1893 *Poema paradisiaco* (Paradisiacal Poem). During the same period he also brought out new and revised editions of some of his earlier verse collections: in 1890 a new edition of *L'Isottèo—La Chimera,* in 1894 a revised *Intermezzo di rime* with the shortened title *Intermezzo,* and in 1896 a new edition of *Canto novo.* Throughout the decade the same restless experimentation that characterized his activity in fiction can be seen in D'Annunzio's poetry as well. *Elegie romane* and *Poema paradisiaco,* although different in form and tonality, are both attempts, in a voice that was more and more distinctly D'Annunzio's own, to move beyond the poetry of the 1880's. *Elegie romane* consists of twenty-four poems arranged into four books of six poems each, plus a concluding *congedo* or envoi poem. All of the texts in it, though of varying lengths, are in the same form: the quantitative elegiac couplets employed by Carducci in the *Odi barbare* and by D'Annunzio himself in *Primo vere*. What is new about *Elegie romane* is its organization of poems written on a variety of occasions into a single coherent narrative.

Book 1 of the volume describes the poet's condition of satisfied desire with his lady, the same Barbara Leoni who appears as Ippolita Sanzio in *Triumph of Death*. In "Il vespro" (Evening), for example, we see him walking ecstatically through the streets of Rome after an afternoon of love with her, a *passeggiata* that is repeated in many other poems of this collection as the poet and his "chosen one" explore the fountains, villas, parks, and churches of papal Rome and the surrounding countryside. However, already by book 2, the poet's love for the goddesslike creature of these poems has begun to disintegrate, and his sadness changes first to desperation and then to homicidal fantasies. In "Villa Chigi," when the disconsolate lovers wander through a forest punctuated by the sounds of wood-chopping and the smoking pyres of the charcoal burners, the poet has a vision of his partner dismembered by a woodsman's ax, "lifting her suppliant hands from the red / lake and saying with her eyes: 'I never hurt you.'" A similar fantasy is articulated in "In un mattino di primavera" (Spring Morning), in which the poet imagines awakening to find his lady dead on the pillow beside him.

In book 3 these morbid fantasies give way to an evocation of such familiar Roman landmarks as Saint Peter's Cathedral, the Tiber River, the Pincio Park, and the Villa Medici, as the poet, who is now alone, attempts to console himself at the end of his love affair. In book 4 he has moved to a kind of exile in Naples, a situation he compares to that of Ovid in Pontus

(though the Roman poet did not flee the capital because of bad debts, as D'Annunzio did). But even in that sunny city and with a successor located for the superseded Roman goddess,

Tutto pareami quivi solitudine,
vacuità, tristezza, immobile tedio, nel muto
lume, sotto i muti chiari lontani cieli.

Everything seemed solitude,
vacuousness, sadness, immobile tedium, in the soundless
light, beneath the silent clear distant skies.
("Nella Certosa di San Martino di Napoli")

Throughout this volume, the classical forms and elegiac tonality plus the sharply etched settings of baroque Rome and Naples give the melancholy story of detachment, sadness, and loss that the poems recount a classical seriousness and dignity of a kind that had not been seen before in D'Annunzio's poetry.

Although D'Annunzio's next book also organizes occasional poems into a unified narrative, in *Poema paradisiaco* he abandons the quantitative forms of *Elegie romane*, thus making a definitive break with this kind of prosody. In language, too, *Poema paradisiaco* represents an important departure from all of D'Annunzio's previous poetry. The texts included in this volume employ a much more restrained and colloquial diction than D'Annunzio had ever used previously. These are poems meant to be murmured instead of declaimed. In addition—and this is not without irony since the compositions in this volume are in some ways his most offhand and least overtly ambitious texts—this collection is among the volumes by D'Annunzio that have exerted the greatest influence on later Italian poetry.

Poema paradisiaco is usually described as belonging to D'Annunzio's period of *bontà* or "goodness." In it the scene has shifted away from the big cities to the provincial Abruzzi, where the poet has returned to his childhood home and the family circle of his sister and mother. Instead of the fancy mistresses of previous volumes, the women whom he encounters here are simpler but also wearier, more melancholy and enigmatic. In Enrico Thovez's words, in this volume

> the earlier, all too accessible lovers have become enclosed gardens, parks of intangible delight. . . . The pliant and lightly clad panthers have become austere veiled figures with long necks bent like dying lilies, hands that are diaphanous and pure like the communion host, and eyes full of shadows and mystery, pale like the waters of the underworld.
>
> (p.181)

In "Climene," for example, the title character is dressed in white satin, with a broad felt hat shading a weary face and eyes "long and transparent as topazes . . . moist with an unshed tear." When she speaks it is to murmur the name "Alceste" as a "dry leaf rustles / entangled on the ground by the hem of her dress." "La passeggiata" (The Stroll) begins:

> *Voi non mi amate ed io non vi amo. Pure*
> *qualche dolcezza è ne la nostra vita*
> *da ieri: una dolcezza indefinita*
> *che vela un poco, sembra, le sventure*
> *nostre e le fa, sembra, quasi lontane.*

> You don't love me and I don't love you. Still
> there is some sweetness in our life
> since yesterday: an indefinite sweetness
> that veils, it seems, our misfortunes
> and makes them, it seems, almost remote.

It is evident throughout this volume, in such texts as "Il buon messaggio" (Good News), "Nuovo messaggio" (More News), and "Consolazione" (Consolation), that the poet himself is aware that his embrace of goodness, simplicity, and childhood innocence stems more from disgust (or at least temporary satiation) with his former life than from a sincere desire for a new way of living. What quickly proved to be a transient point of view is expressed, however, in ways that were new and that had enduring effects on D'Annunzio's later poetry and prose.

As can be seen from the extracts quoted above, in the *Poema paradisiaco* the conversational vocabulary as well as the looser and more informal syntax, with its frequent enjambments and interruptions and consequent fragmentation of the poetic line, create a different sort of discourse in which—never mind how "fictitiously" or how "sincerely"—a more intimate and mysterious level of the poet's psychological life comes to the surface. It was both the technical qualities of this work and its sometimes self-deceiving and self-serving introspective content that made it of interest to such later—and different, both from D'Annunzio and from each other—poets as Guido Gozzano and Eugenio Montale.

Contemporary with *Poema paradisiaco*, and in fact published together with it in the early editions, are the *Odi navali* (Naval Odes, 1892). There are eight of these, all on maritime themes and with such titles as "La nave" (The Ship), "A una torpediniera nell'Adriatico" (To a Torpedo Boat in the Adriatic), and "Per la morte dell'Ammiraglio di Saint-Bon" (On the Death of Admiral Saint-Bon). Of mostly documentary interest today, *Odi navali* demonstrate how in the same period of his life D'Annunzio could produce both the psychologically intimate work of *Poema paradisiaco* and these quite different declamatory texts. They also foreshadow the bellicose political writing of his later years.

By far the most ambitious of D'Annunzio's poetic projects toward the turn of the century—indeed, in his entire career—was that of *Laudi* (Praises) or, to give them their full title, *Laudi del cielo del mare della terra e degli eroi* (Praises of the Sky, of the Sea, of the Earth, and of the Heroes). This work was planned to occupy seven volumes, one for each of the daughters of Atlas, who were metamorphosed into the seven stars of the Pleiades. Of the volumes projected, however, D'Annunzio published only four: *Maia* in 1903, *Elettra* and *Alcyone* in 1904, and *Merope* in 1912.

Maia serves as prologue to the entire project. A long poem of more than eight thousand lines of varying length organized into twenty-one-line stanzas, it was written quickly and was intended as a single piece of narration. *Maia* aspires to be a "total poem" (as D'Annunzio called it) on the role of the D'Annunzian Superman in the modern world. In its first section this *Laus vitae*, or "Praise of Life," describes a trip to Greece based on D'Annunzio's own yacht trip there with his friend Edoardo Scarfoglio in 1895. Fortified by mystic encounters with Dionysius and Aphrodite and in emulation of Ulysses, the hero of the poem sets out to "pick the world like an apple" and squeeze it to "satisfy [his] perennial thirst." In his voyage, first to Greece and then to the cities of modern Italy, "Everything [is] dared / Everything attempted," though evidently not successfully, since the poet cries, "Oh why is not human power / as infinite as desire?" and goes on to note how "that which was not accomplished / I dreamed; / and so great was my ardor / that the dream was the same as the act."

In addition to its evocation of classical Greece and the world of mythology, in its later sections the poem describes the squalor, degradation, and ferocious class struggles of the modern city, as well as the technology and activities of a new age whose heroes are the colonizing merchants of industrialized Italy. The mythical Greek past thus lives on as a stimulus to the domination and eventual mastery of both the forces of nature and the inferior races of a world in which "Pan is not dead" and the Tenth Muse is Energy. In line with this message the poem itself is expansionist in form, moving forward in pulsing rhythms and ample syntactical units that make use of frequent repetition and anaphora. A difficult work because of its often arcane vocabulary and learned allusions, *Maia* has never had many readers. It is of interest, however, for the political ideology it espouses, whether this is understood as a generic and murky socialism or an apology for anti-democratic aggression and racist imperialism. In this sense *Maia* prefigures Italian Fascist thought itself, which in its early years also mixed the proclamation of egalitarian ideals with a politics of aggression and violence.

In 1904 D'Annunzio published two more collections of his *Laudi: Elettra* and *Alcyone*. Although different from each other in conception and quality, the two works first appeared in a single volume. Unlike the prolix but narratively and stylistically coherent *Maia, Elettra* is a collection of occasional lyrics, many of which had already been published elsewhere. The dominant theme of the volume is that of praise for the great man and of hope that he will soon return to restore Italy to its ancient glory. In it there are poems to Giuseppe Garibaldi, Giuseppe Verdi, Dante Alighieri, and Vincenzo Bellini among the Italians, and to Hugo and Nietzsche among the non-Italians. The volume also contains nearly sixty sonnets called "La città del silenzio" (The City of Silence), on smaller Italian cities of great prominence during the Middle Ages and Renaissance where the clamor, the passion, and the achievements of bygone ages have now been replaced by deserted streets and silence. In his invectives against the present and his encomia to great Italians of the past whom he hopes that future citizens will be able to emulate, D'Annunzio assumes a position taken earlier by Carducci; and he seems throughout the work to be proposing himself as the older poet's successor as national bard.

In the volume's concluding poem, "Canto augurale per la nazione eletta" (Auspicious Song for the Chosen Nation), his political program for curing the nation's ills is made explicit. In this text the plow and the prow of a military ship are symbols of Italian efforts in labor and war; the eagle that brushes the plowman's forehead and then comes to rest in a shipyard is an augury of future victories, when the ship will be launched "to domination of the world." After ten stanzas that all end with the refrain "Italia, Italia!" the poem concludes with a vision of the "Latin sea covered with slaughter," all to the glory of Italy,

> *fiore di tutte le stirpi,*
> *aroma di tutta la terra,*

Italia, Italia,
sacra alla nuova Aurora
con l'aratro e la prora!

flower of all the races,
fragrance of all of the earth,
Italy, Italy,
consecrated to the new dawn
with the plow and the prow!

Although some of the sonnets to the "cities of silence" in *Elettra* have been widely anthologized, the rhetorical overemphasis of much of this volume has led some to view it as a work of political propaganda in which this writer's earlier elitist and aesthetic positions have degenerated into a jingoism as mindless as it was widely shared by the middle and ruling classes of his day.

The other volume of poems published with *Elettra* in 1904 was *Alcyone,* far and away the most successful of all the *Laudi* and probably D'Annunzio's best book of poetry. *Alcyone* is made up of eighty-eight lyrics in different poetic forms composed between 1899 and 1903 and then carefully arranged for this collection. The tone of the poetry is usually described as aulic or stately, and the texts in it employ a large number of technical, rare, or archaic words, some of which D'Annunzio drew from specialized lexicons and dictionaries that he consulted for this purpose. D'Annunzio himself was very pleased with this third installment of his *Laudi.* In letters to his publisher he speaks of how the poems in it were "born in his soul as spontaneously as froth on the waves" and of how in the book he had finally found "certain things he had sought in vain for a very long time." It is his last important book of poetry.

At its simplest level, *Alcyone* is an idealized vacation diary. *Maia* describes a yacht trip to Greece, *Elettra* imaginary encounters with great men of the past. In similar fashion, *Alcyone* describes a prolonged period of evasion from the duties of ordinary life, a moment of pause or *tregua* (the title of the first poem in

the collection) when the D'Annunzian Superman is on vacation, with no responsibilities except to immerse himself in physical sensations of sun, sand, and sea, as well as in intellectual memories of a glorious historical and mythological past. In this volume the poet abandons himself to a world of sensation and memory, a world he makes no effort to comprehend but whose beauty he seeks to capture in the aristocratic activity of poetic creation. Tuscan geography, first in Florence and Fiesole and then at the mouth of the Arno and surrounding territory, takes on an ever denser historical and mythical significance as the poet exalts and redeems this countryside from its otherwise trivial and time-bound condition as a point in real space and ordinary history accessible to anyone with enough time and money for a seaside holiday.

For D'Annunzio the Tuscan seashore is not just a popular spot for a vacation, but a magical site reminiscent of ancient Greece and a place where the gods of antiquity return to earth. Where *Canto novo* was a celebration of the senses and of the natural world understood in a physiological and thus positivistic fashion, *Alcyone* views that same world from the mystic and thus anti-positivistic because pseudo-religious perspective of a worshiper of the nature deity Pan. D'Annunzio attempts in this book to revive the ancient and sensually vital world of pagan myth, though at its conclusion he reveals that the only viable relation for the modern imagination with the world of classical mythology is that of a tourist wandering in the broken temples of a past stripped of meaning and vitality. Even in this case, however, the poet possesses supreme power as someone who, by naming the natural and potentially mythological world, allows its otherwise mute and nonexistent being to find articulate form. In this volume the word itself has become an instrument of domination, a mastery not so much of other people—the sexual conquest of women or oratorical domination of crowds described in his novels—as of the physical, biological, and botanical universe. Giorgio Bàrberi Squarotti has described how in *Alcyone*

> natural objects are a function of the word that the poet gives them, the landscape is as if displaced and disquieted by a desire for speech denied to hills, river, moon, rain, and trees, but granted to the poet who thus resolves the drama of silence imposed on objects and allows them to clarify themselves, to make themselves manifest, to tell how and why they exist and what their deepest secret is.
>
> (p.145)

In this activity of giving a name to chaos, the poet of *Alcyone* is a new Orpheus who not only animates nature through his song but also merges in Pan-like dissolution with the world he is creating.

After the opening poem, in which the poet asks the "Despot" of ambition for a "pause" in his ordinary activities, and a second introductory poem to "Il fanciullo," or "the lad" of poetry, the book opens with an evocation of the landscapes of Florence and the surrounding hills in late spring, where the promise of summer is everywhere. The poetic model for much of the writing here is that of the Franciscan *laude* or hymn of praise. In "Lungo l'Affrico" (Along the Affrico) the sky after a rainstorm is mirrored in puddles as earth and heaven reflect each other, the poet himself merges into the scene he is observing, and

> *Tutta la terra pare*
> *argilla offerta all'opera d'amore,*
> *un nunzio il grido, e il vespero che muore*
> *un'alba certa.*

> The entire earth seems
> clay proffered to a labor of love,
> the [swallow's] cry a harbinger, and the
>   dying evening
> a certain dawn.

In "La sera fiesolana" (Fiesole Evening), there is a similar interpenetration of psychological and natural states as the poet and his lady watch the evening fall, and he compares the words he whispers to her with the effects of the time of day on the landscape:

> *Dolci le mie parole ne la sera*
> *ti sien come la pioggia che bruiva*
> *tepida e fuggitiva,*
> *commiato lacrimoso della primavera,*
> *su i gelsi e su gli olmi e su le viti*
> *e su i pini dai novelli rosei diti*
> *che giocano con l'aura che si perde,*
> *e su 'l grano che non è biondo ancora*
> *e non è verde,*
> *e su 'l fieno che già patì la falce*
> *e trascolora,*
> *e su gli olivi, su i fratelli olivi*
> *che fan di santità pallidi i clivi*
> *e sorridenti.*

> Let my words in the evening
> be gentle as the rain that rustled
> tepid and fleetingly
> spring's teary goodbye,
> on the mulberry trees, the elms, the grapevines,
> and on the pines with their new pink fingers
> that play with the dying breeze,
> and on the wheat that is not yet blond
> but is not green,
> and on the hay that has endured the sickle
> and changes color,
> and on the olives, on the brother olives
> that render the hillsides
> wan and smiling with sanctity.

Similar attempts to recapture perceptual virginity for his readers through tightly focused descriptions of natural objects in verses that, like those just quoted, have evident biblical echoes can be seen in such other poems of this section as "L'ulivo" (The Olive Tree) and "La spiga" (The Ear of Wheat).

But with "Furit aestus" (Summer Rages), the mood changes sharply as June gives way to July and the gentle Florentine hills are replaced by the erotically charged seascape of the Tuscan coast near Pisa. In the first of four *Ditirambi* (dithyrambs) that introduce new sections of the volume, D'Annunzio describes the threshing of wheat in the broiling July sun. In "Bocca d'Arno" (Mouth of the Arno) the mouth of the river is compared to that of a beloved woman, while in "La pioggia nel pineto" (Rain in the Pine Grove) both the speaker and his companion, Ermione (the poetic character inspired by Eleonora Duse who appears throughout these poems), merge into a landscape that, like them, is transfigured by a rhythmic rain whose musicality the onomatopoetic verse captures with great efficacy. After the delicately beautiful "Innanzi l'alba" (Before the Dawn), "Meriggio" (Midday) describes the total submission of the poet to the natural forces of sun, sea, and landscape—to a point where

> *Non ho più nome nè sorte*
> *tra gli uomini; ma il mio nome*
> *è Meriggio. In tutto io vivo*
> *tacito come la Morte.*
>
> *E la mia vita è divina.*
>
> I have neither name nor fate
> among men; but my name
> is Midday. I live in everything
> silent as Death.
>
> And my life is godlike.

The next dithyramb tells the story of Glaucus, the fisherman who ingested a magical weed and was changed into a sea god. He is the first of many characters in this part of the poem to undergo physical metamorphoses in passages often inspired by Ovid. Like the speaker of "Meriggio," Glaucus too wants to cast off his present identity in order to return to the godlike state he enjoyed beneath the sea but now seems to have lost irrevocably: "O gods of the deep," he cries at the end of the poem, "call back the exile / restore his godhead to him!"

Part 4 of *Alcyone* is preceded by a poem titled "Stabat nuda aestas" (Summer Stood Naked); its dithyramb describes the chase and capture of Summer, which has been transformed into a beautiful woman whom the poet seizes and forces to submit to his will. But despite this conquest, the season is beginning

to decline, and the poems in this concluding part of the volume are increasingly melancholy. After a final dithyramb on the last days and death of Icarus, the poet dreams seven "Sogne di terre longane" (Dreams of Distant Lands,) all of which begin with the word *Settembre* (September) and describe voyages away from the now desolate seashore where the poet stands in the flotsam, bereft of his lover and alone once more in the dying season. Throughout the volume it is the landscape rather than the poet that changes, and at its conclusion he seems little altered by all that has happened. *Alcyone* ends on a note of emptiness and loss: loss of the summer, which has come to its inevitable conclusion; loss of Ermione, who has gone back to her life "beyond the serene rivers, / beyond the green hills / beyond the blue mountains"; loss above all of the gods who have abandoned the hills and the sea, creatures of myth that the brittle and erudite images of this poetry could not prevent from finally fading.

During this same productive period, from the 1890's to World War I, when D'Annunzio was composing the poems that were eventually collected in *Alcyone,* he was also busy writing for the theater. That D'Annunzio would write for the stage at some time in his career seems inevitable, given the theatrical nature of both the man and his work. Throughout his life this author seems to have demanded the immediate response to his art that only an audience, whether in the theater or gathered in a square beneath a balcony, can supply. Even when he was alone, working in the silence of his study on such texts as *Notturno* (Nocturne, 1921) or *Libro segreto* (Secret Book, 1935), D'Annunzio always felt that he was on stage in some way or other. It is also significant that his activity in the theater dates from the same years as his early political activism. When he ran for parliament in 1897, D'Annunzio was compelled to use his verbal abilities to control an undifferentiated and collective audience different from the elite at which he had directed the prose and poetry of his earlier years. Although the eventual "Deputy of Beauty" (as he came to be known during the electoral campaign of 1897) was not an effective member of the Italian lawmaking body (and partly for this reason was not reelected when he stood again in 1900), his plays of the late 1890's and afterward are a kind of political performance in the same way that his political gestures later in his career were always strongly theatrical.

If D'Annunzio's political propensities were one factor turning him toward the theater, another was his friendship, business partnership, and romance with Eleonora Duse. Duse, by universal consent Italy's greatest actress of the period, starred in most of D'Annunzio's early plays, many of which were conceived and written expressly for her. Not only did this actress make D'Annunzio's work the center of her repertory during her tours of Europe and North America, she was also generous in sharing performance profits with her lover, and she stuck by him and his work despite the controversy the plays often stirred and the financial setbacks they both suffered when their productions flopped. Without her, it seems safe to say, D'Annunzio's theater would have been less extensive and of lesser quality than it was.

The first of D'Annunzio's plays is *La città morta* (*The Dead City,* 1898). Although it is clearly this work that Stelio Effrena salutes in *The Flame of Life* as a forerunner of a new kind of Italian theater, the play is in many ways a conventional treatment of middle-class marriage and jealousy. It is set in Greece among a group of archaeologists who have discovered the tomb and treasure of the Atrides, much as Heinrich Schliemann had done shortly before the play was produced. The leader of this archaeological expedition is Leonardo, who has come to Greece with his sister, Bianca Maria. Accompanying them are a married couple, the poet Alessandro and his blind wife, Anna, the latter being the role Duse interpreted in the original production. The play's conflict develops when Alessandro and Bianca

Maria discover that they are in love. When Anna, the familiar victim figure, becomes aware of their love, she tries to clear the way for their union by committing suicide. But Leonardo is also incestually in love with his sister, and when he learns of her passion for Alessandro, he murders her rather than give her up to his friend and rival.

Although its plot is based on the standard love triangles of conventional drama of the day, *The Dead City* enunciates a number of concerns that are important in all of D'Annunzio's plays. To begin with, it deals with violent passion in a context heavy with literary allusion (Bianca Maria is reading aloud from Sophocles as the curtain rises). When faced with these devastating passions, it is the women in this early play who are willing to sacrifice themselves while the male characters are exceptional beings whose intellectual and artistic superiority puts them beyond conventional notions of right and wrong. But since neither of the Superman characters in this work is an especially decisive individual, the action tends to languish, and the women characters stand out as more interesting than the men. Although written in prose, the language of this first play by D'Annunzio is so lyrical and literary that the dialogue, though possibly appropriate for the kinds of issues raised by ancient Greek tragedy, is simply not believable in the mouths of what are supposed to be young Italian intellectuals at the turn of the twentieth century. The violent passions that they express, therefore, appear today as little more than excessive posturing.

In two shorter works of these same years, *Sogno d'un mattino di primavera* (Dream of a Spring Morning, 1897) and *Sogno d'un tramonto d'autunno* (Dream of an Autumn Sunset, 1898), D'Annunzio uses similarly lyric language to treat themes of lust and violence in plots drawn in the first case from the Italian Renaissance and in the second from the history of Venice. With *La Gioconda* (*Gioconda*) and *La gloria* (*Glory*), both published in 1899, D'Annunzio returns to contemporary subjects.

In the first he examines the claims of art and the artist to superiority over ordinary experience and individuals. Again it is the woman character who is called on for a sacrifice: Lucio Settala's wife not only turns over her artist-husband to his mistress, the Gioconda of the title, but she also sacrifices her beautiful hands to his art when she allows them to be crushed in the fall of one of his statues.

La gloria is one of D'Annunzio's most politically explicit plays. Although the Ruggero Flamma who appears in it is based on the historical figure of Francesco Crispi, many have seen in D'Annunzio's portrait of this dictator an extraordinary foreshadowing of Mussolini and the "Mussolinian style" in politics. The most interesting character in the play, however, is not the dictator but the Superwoman or *Superfemmina* who is the power behind his office and who, among other things, utters the phrase later taken up by Mussolini: "Chi si arresta è perduto" (Whoever stops is lost). Far from sacrificing herself for the male characters, Elena Comnèna makes it clear that she will let nothing stand between her and the object of her desires, be they political or sexual. When her first lover, Cesare Bronte, has been replaced both in her bed and at the head of the nation by Flamma, whose star then also begins to fade, "la Comnèna" is quick to abandon him too, stabbing him and then tossing his body to an angry crowd at the final curtain.

With his next play D'Annunzio turned from contemporary subject matter to an episode from Italian medieval history that had already been made famous by Dante. *Francesca da Rimini* (1902) was D'Annunzio's first play in verse; it was later made into an opera with music by Riccardo Zandonai. In D'Annunzio's own account this text is "a poem of blood and lust," a first example of what his critics, who are here thinking especially of the play's frequently archaic vocabulary and syntax, have described as his "fake antique" style. In retelling the story of Paolo and Francesca in a plot that makes abundant use of the Italian chronicles of the Malatesta family, D'Annunzio is trying to make his highly charged poetic dialogue acceptable to audiences who had whistled at it in plays with modern settings. In an important sense the real hero of this play—which once again revels in jealousy, incest, murder, war, and bloodshed, and whose characters are once again exceptional beings—is the deliberately archaic and immensely rich and detailed language itself.

A similarly stylized language is featured in *La figlia di Iorio* (*The Daughter of Jorio*, 1904). The most frequently performed and successful of D'Annunzio's works for the theater, *The Daughter of Jorio* is set among Abruzzi peasants. Partly because D'Annunzio's audiences had only the vaguest and most stereotypical notions of this region and its inhabitants, it was hoped that the language of the characters would be accepted as sufficiently realistic for the play to be taken seriously. In *The Daughter of Jorio* the outsider and transgressor of conventional law is the shepherd Aligi, whose artistic inclinations and dreamy temperament have placed him at the margins of the archaic peasant society in which he lives. When Mila di Codro, the daughter of Jorio of the title, seeks refuge from a mob of drunken, sun-crazed reapers bent on sexually assaulting her, Aligi gives her sanctuary at the family hearth. Aligi's lack of solidarity with the men of the village is a transgression of the prevailing patriarchal social code and leads to the downfall of both characters, as Aligi first leaves the village along with Mila and then engages in a duel to the death with his father for possession of her. After Aligi kills his father, he is saved from execution as a parricide when Mila claims that she has bewitched him. As the play ends, the daughter of Jorio leaps into the awaiting funeral pyre exclaiming, "La fiamma è bella! La fiamma è bella!" (The flame is beautiful). Although *The Daughter of Jorio* can be read on one level as a story about the most conventional of middle-class problems (the reconciliation of the artistic temperament in an uncomprehending family, how to stave off an unsuitable marriage, the struggles of father and son for sexual dominance, male promiscuity versus female faithfulness), in this work D'Annunzio elevates these themes to mythic and thus universal significance.

In his next two works, however, the playwright returned to more familiar, contemporary settings. *La fiaccola sotto il moggio* (The Light Under the Bushel, 1905) is set in the Abruzzi, but not among peasants. It, too, is a story of family passion and jealousy, this time the hatred of a daughter for a stepmother who has been elevated from servant status and is now ruling the household. At the play's conclusion this usurper is killed by the daughter, who then herself dies from snakebites she has purposely incurred by plunging her arm into a bag of poisonous serpents provided her by her stepmother's father. One of the more frequently produced of D'Annunzio's plays, *La fiaccola sotto il moggio* features a clash between two powerful female characters that results in their mutual destruction but that offers little in the way of tragic insight.

Più che l'amore (More than Love, 1907) is the story of an African explorer during the time of Italy's colonial adventures. Unable to finance the additional trip to Africa that means "more than love" to him, Corrado Brando murders a moneylender in a gratuitous act that he feels is justified by his status as an exceptional individual. But Corrado is no Raskolnikov. When compared to the soul-searching that wracks Dostoevsky's philosophical hero in the Russian writer's novel *Crime and Punishment* (1866), his heroic gesturing seems shabby, egocentric, and ill-conceived, his crime the result of nothing more exalted than simple greed, and his seduction and abandonment of Maria Vesta an act of callow insensitivity rather than of tragic desperation. It is not surprising that *Più che l'amore* was one of D'Annunzio's biggest failures in the theater.

With his next work, *La nave* (The Ship, 1908), the playwright had the good sense to place the action further back in time than ever before—to sixth-century Venice, the period of

that city's struggle with the Byzantine Empire for control of the eastern Mediterranean. The heroine of this work, Basiliola Faledro, is perhaps the most extravagantly *Superfemmina* (and outrageously proto-"camp") of all D'Annunzio's female creations for the stage. The plot drips once again with jealousy, lust, and political ambition. In the early years of the Venetian state power is equally divided between church and state, institutions headed in this instance by two brothers, Marco and Sergio Gràtico. Basiliola is the leader of a rival faction, and her own brothers have had both their eyes and their tongues torn out by the Gràtico forces. In revenge for this Basiliola manages to get both Gràticos to fall in love with her and then incites them to a public duel in which Marco kills Sergio as the drunken Venetian populace cheers him on. Horrified at what he has done, Marco decides to launch the warship of the play's title and sail away to foreign conquests in far-flung lands of the Adriatic, there to engage in heroic deeds that will serve both to expiate his sin and to augment Venetian glory. His eyes now opened to Basiliola's perfidy, Marco has her seized and is about to fasten her to the prow of the ship as a living figurehead when she breaks free and flings herself defiantly into the flames that burn on an altar in Saint Mark's Square.

After *La nave*, D'Annunzio wrote one more play in Italian, *Fedra* (Phaedra, 1909), in which the Phaedra story is retold in a modern context as influenced once again by Nietzsche and by ideas of the exceptional individual. He also brought out three plays in French: *Le martyre de Saint Sébastien* (The Martyrdom of St. Sebastian, 1911), produced in Paris in 1911 with Ida Rubinstein as the saint and with music by Claude Debussy; *La Pisanelle ou la mort parfumée* (Pisanella, or Perfumed Death, 1913), in which the heroine meets her death by being smothered in roses; and *Le chèvrefeuille* (*The Honeysuckle*, 1914), a French version of the play known in Italian as *Il ferro* (Iron, 1914). In these same years D'Annunzio collaborated on the script for the movie *Cabiria*

(1914) and sketched out an opera libretto on the thirteenth-century Children's Crusade for music by Giacomo Puccini. Although this project was never completed, a film based on D'Annunzio's work on this subject was issued in 1916.

In considering D'Annunzio's theater in general, we see that many of his plays suffer from a lack of dramatic action. Despite their often lush linguistic textures, too many of D'Annunzio's tragedies read (and act) like the last scenes of works in which all the action occurs in the earlier acts. Despite the violence often unleashed—even wallowed in—on D'Annunzio's stage, his tragedies rarely provide his audiences with tragic insight or leave them with a heightened sense of the nature of the human dilemma. Despite their aspirations to metaphysical status, D'Annunzio's plays are primarily political gestures and further examples of his "anti-realism" on both the artistic and political levels.

In the frequently adulatory writing about him during his lifetime, D'Annunzio was often referred to as a "poet-hero," "poet-warrior," or "poet-soldier." Beginning around the time of World War I, energetic and visible political activism became an important component in this writer's life and career. This activism is in many ways D'Annunzio's most flamboyant work of art and the part of his artistic production that was most enthusiastically received by public opinion of the time. Like writers elsewhere in Europe before and after World War I, D'Annunzio seemed to be seeking in violent and often dangerous political action an authentication of both himself and his writing.

His career as activist, soldier, and political leader began not in Italy but in France, where in 1910 he went into what he called "exile" but was really refuge from his Italian creditors. It was in France in 1912, after the outbreak of the Turco-Italian war, that he wrote the truculent political poems of *Le canzoni della gesta d'oltremare* (Songs of the Deed Beyond the Seas), published in 1912 with *Merope* in the fourth

volume of the *Laudi*. When Germany invaded France and World War I began in earnest, D'Annunzio churned out a flurry of articles and speeches on the necessity for Italy to intervene in the war on the side of France and of "civilization." Invited in May 1915 to give a speech at Quarto, near Genoa, commemorating Garibaldi's "Thousand" volunteers in the struggle for Italian unification a half century earlier, D'Annunzio made the event into a triumphal return and gave an impassioned address urging Italian intervention in the current conflict. When Italy did join the fighting, D'Annunzio, even though he was fifty-two years old, signed up and was accepted for active duty. Already familiar with airplanes from the days of *Forse che sì forse che no,* he flew a number of missions behind enemy lines. In the celebrated "flight over Vienna," he bombarded the Austrian capital with red, white, and green leaflets inviting its citizens to surrender. Leaflets were also left during the Beffa di Buccari, a torpedo-boat excursion, in which D'Annunzio participated, into Buccari harbor near the Adriatic port of Fiume on the Dalmatian coast, where an Austrian ship was torpedoed and sunk.

But the most famous of all these heroic excursions (D'Annunzio was decorated several times during the war—usually, it seems, at his own insistence) came after the conclusion of the war. In September 1919, with hostilities at an end but the status of certain territories belonging to the conquered belligerents still uncertain, D'Annunzio, at the head of a group of legionaires, marched to Fiume on the Istrian coast south of Trieste and seized the city, declaring it Italian and himself its new governor. As *Comandante,* he remained in possession of Fiume until January 1921, a modern-day Sancho Panza governing his island, though without the blessing of his superiors that Cervantes' fictional figure enjoyed. While in Fiume, D'Annunzio helped write a utopian and libertarian constitution for the city, made almost daily public speeches to his legionaires and the assembled populace, and did his best to translate his literary ideals into political realities. In the process he invented much of what later became the mottoes and rituals of Mussolini's Fascism, although with the March on Rome of 1922 it was not D'Annunzio the *Comandante* but Mussolini the *Duce* who emerged as the leader of Fascist Italy.

The volumes of mostly autobiographical prose D'Annunzio produced in France during his "exile" and in Italy before and after Fiume vary a good deal in content and structure. The work in this group of writings has a more subdued tone and less complex syntax, contains fewer erudite allusions and less arcane vocabulary, and places less emphasis on the exceptional man than does his earlier writing of whatever sort. The late works thus represent a new direction for D'Annunzio's fiction. Throughout them there is a greater sense of the fragility of existence and an increased sensitivity to the evanescence and the limitations of even the most dramatic and violent human action. For the D'Annunzio of this period writing was no longer a means for dominating either the reader or a crowd that he wished to stir to political action. His works of these last years of his life are deeply concerned with his own most intimate psychology and are devoted to exploring his memories and to meditating on the world around him. "Life," he wrote in 1916, "is not an abstraction . . . but a kind of diffused sensuality, a knowledge available to all of the senses, a substance good to smell, to feel, and to eat." The goal of these late writings is to establish contact with this mysterious but still sensually attractive entity and in the attempt to determine the limits of writing as a way of knowing rather than as a mode of doing.

The first of the autobiographical writings in this group is *Solus ad solam* (One [masculine] to One [feminine], published posthumously in 1939). This self-styled "book of pain and madness, of desperation and of love," is in diary form, with entries running from 8 September to 5 October 1908; it was not published until a

year after the poet's death. In these journal notations to the woman whose story is the subject of the book, D'Annunzio examines his painful and ultimately destructive love affair with Countess Giuseppina Mancini. Although it is now clear that at some point the poet edited his account of the dramatic events that led to this woman's desperation, semi-public degradation, and temporary madness, this earliest of his confessional texts is a first example of the presentation to the reading public of a private, sometimes even shameful, series of events in the poet's intimate life. In his treatment of this material (which he never authorized for publication though he did use part of it in the concluding sections of *Forse che sì forse che no*), D'Annunzio is concerned both with justifying his behavior with Countess Mancini and with lamenting the diminution of their passion due to the ineluctable passage of time and the vulgarity and incomprehension of the world in which they are forced to live and love.

Contemplazione della morte (Contemplation of Death, 1912) was inspired by the deaths of two people to whom D'Annunzio felt particularly close: the contemporary Italian poet Giovanni Pascoli, and his French landlord at Arcachon, Adolphe Bermond, an ardent Christian and, in D'Annunzio's eyes, an unusually admirable person. Written in France and first published in installments in the *Corriere della sera, Contemplazione della morte* is a first-person, diarylike work organized into four dated sections. Its main subject is the writer's examination of his own consciousness as thoughts of his friends blend with memories of the past and with reflections on art, religion, and the end of existence. Here D'Annunzio ponders "the ashes of dreams" that lie on his tongue," on which he must either chew or choke to death.

La Leda senza cigno (Leda Without the Swan) was written and published in *Corriere della sera* in 1913 and then in a volume with a long *licenza* or envoi in 1916. It is a short story rather than a memoir like *Solus ad solam* or *Contemplazione della morte.* Like *Contempla-*

zione della morte, La Leda senza cigno was written on the Atlantic coast of France at Arcachon; the desolate landscape of this region is an important element of the physical and psychological "Aspects of the Unknown" (as *La Leda senza cigno* is subtitled) that D'Annunzio investigates in this work. Once again, the style is subdued as D'Annunzio attempts to capture "a certain interior nakedness, the absence of images and melodies in which the soul may imitate that dawn transparency when day and night interpenetrate." *La Leda senza cigno* concerns a beautiful but vampirelike woman whose surface attractiveness conceals a dangerous inner reality that both fascinates and terrifies the narrator. At the end of his story, Desiderio Moriar manages to escape destruction at this woman's hands. However, since he has not succeeded in breaching her inner reality, the *Sconosciuta,* or unknown woman, remains as elusive as a statue of Leda and the swan that he remembers from the Florence Bargello but that has since been broken and was only a copy of a lost Leonardo da Vinci original in the first place. Art, it would seem, is by its nature little more than a palimpsest of an infinitely receding and finally ungraspable reality that disappears into erasure the more it is contemplated.

Notturno (Nocturne) is probably the most celebrated of this group of autobiographical writings; it was certainly the most commercially successful. This text owes its existence to an accident that D'Annunzio supposedly suffered when a fighter airplane in which he was riding during the war made a forced landing, causing him to strike his forehead against the machine-gun mount. As a result of this injury, the poet not only permanently lost the use of his right eye but was also temporarily confined to bed, immobile and with both eyes bandaged. In these circumstances, between February and April 1916, he wrote *Notturno,* inscribing its individual sentences on "more than ten thousand" narrow strips of paper that were then deciphered and transcribed by his daughter Renata and then—after additional editing by the poet—published in a volume in 1921.

Much of *Notturno* is devoted to a consideration of the physical and existential act of its own composition. The pause in the poet's physical activities that it represents came at a crucial time in D'Annunzio's life. By 1916 *Alcyone* was behind him, and the springs of poetry—or at least poetry of that sort—had run dry. By 1921 his role as political activist had come to an end as well, as had his project for establishing a national Italian theater capable of vying with that of Wagner. In addition, the last of his grand love affairs was over, and D'Annunzio was more and more alone. Moreover, particularly when compared to the aviators he had come to know during the war, the *Comandante* was by this time an old man. It was partly in response to these unpleasant facts that, with this text, D'Annunzio threw himself into a final period of literary experimentation. What has been called his "nocturnal" prose (as distinct from the "solar" poetry of such volumes as *Alcyone*) represents his last cycle of experiments with new literary forms and unexplored expressive modalities. In the volume that provided the name for this final phase of expression, death is again the obsessive presence.

In *Notturno* there are several descriptions of the corpses of young comrades of the narrator who have perished in action. The decay of these young bodies forcibly reminds the poet of his own status as a possibly unworthy and certainly decrepit survivor not only of the violent actions in which he participated but also of the times themselves that have shaped the lives and deaths of these young men. In this text D'Annunzio's rhetorical machinery is set to whirring in a low key that is reminiscent of *Poema paradisiaco,* except that here the expressive restraint seems the well-deserved point of arrival of long stylistic labor rather than simple intertextual mimicry. The melancholy sensations and evanescent memories from different periods of its author's life of this prose nocturne give its text a musical quality whose restrained and tentative harmonies are radically unlike the resounding oratory of the earlier works. At the same time that it traces the progress of D'Annunzio's infirmity and convalescence and its own composition, *Notturno* is a further meditation on the efficacy of writing as a hedge against the darkness that D'Annunzio felt to be steadily closing in upon him.

The largely short sketches collected as *Le faville del maglio* (Sparks from the Forge) had for the most part already appeared in the Milanese newspaper *Corriere della sera.* Written over a period extending from 1896 to the middle and late 1920's, they were collected, edited, and in some cases rewritten by D'Annunzio during the 1920's and then published in two volumes: *Il venturiero senza ventura e altri studii del vivere inimitabile* (The Luckless Adventurer and Other Studies in Inimitable Living) in 1924, and *Il compagno degli occhi senza cigli e altre studii del vivere inimitabile* (The Comrade with Eyebrowless Eyes and Other Studies in Inimitable Living) in 1928. All of the *Faville del maglio* are reminiscences of D'Annunzio's childhood, especially his student days at the Cicognini boarding school. In addition to their documentary and artistic value, the sketches in these volumes are historically important as the first of many works of childhood memoirs that became popular in Italy under Fascism and afterward.

D'Annunzio's last book, *Libro segreto* (Secret Book) or, to give it its full title, *Cento e cento e cento e cento pagine del libro segreto di Gabriele D'Annunzio tentato di morire* (A Hundred and a Hundred and a Hundred and a Hundred Pages of the Secret Book of Gabriele D'Annunzio Tempted by Death), was published in 1935. In some ways little more than the random jottings of an insomniac old man still in thrall to dreams of sexual, artistic, and political super-potency, the *Libro segreto* is of considerable interest for D'Annunzio's dry-eyed consideration of the temptations of suicide, the inadequacy of art to render "the black abyss of the heart," and the brief time remaining for him "to sing a new *Canto novo* and

delude [him]self that [he is] happy." The book ends with these desolate verses:

> *Tutta la vita è senza mutamento*
> *Ha un solo volto la malinconia.*
> *Il pensiero ha per cima la follia.*
> *E l'amore è legato a tradimento.*

> All of life is monotony.
> Melancholy has just one face.
> Madness is thought's highest place.
> And love is bound to treachery.

In addition to the works already discussed, D'Annunzio left a large number of speeches and political correspondence and a vast number of letters of all sorts that even today remain mostly unpublished.

Like many creators of a strong and distinctive style, D'Annunzio is easy to parody. In the writings of his last years—especially the political messages he fired off with embarrassing regularity to the popular press—it seems almost as though he was unable to resist this temptation himself. And now that the simple-minded Fascism of his times no longer seems much of a threat, D'Annunzio's dreams of political, sexual, and artistic domination can easily be dismissed as compensatory fantasies born of a personal impotence not unlike that of the historical condition of the nation whose spokesman he pretended to be. At the same time D'Annunzio was not just an excessively emphatic writer about power. Like the romantics who preceded him and whose final, exasperated epigone he in many ways was, D'Annunzio's most enduring subject was always himself, in all of his depths, falsehoods, and contradictions. A narcissist before he was a Superman, D'Annunzio never wavered from his scrutiny of himself—whether this self-analysis is conveyed in the astute ventriloquism with which he wrote his early prose and verse, in the deft harmonies of his mature poetry, in the frequent bombast of the novels and plays, or in the involuted sincerity of his final reminiscences.

In considering the portrait of himself that

D'Annunzio has left us, certain not entirely flattering contradictions stand out. For all his belief in the superiority of Italian culture, for example, D'Annunzio had no affection for the Italian people and could barely stand to be touched by them. So, too, his literary and artistic connoisseurship was clearly more instrumental than philological, quickly exhausted once the objects of his attention had been subsumed into his own writing. In addition, for all his renown as a seducer, it is the women, not the men, in D'Annunzio's texts who are the more fully realized and stronger characters—"la belle dame" who is "sans merci" and to whose power the Superman succumbs.

Nonetheless, what remains of this writer, when stripped of his racial and cultural pretensions and his belief in his invincible virility, is something more than the "ashes" and emptiness of the last works. The exuberance that sustains so much of D'Annunzio's work, from his brash early poems to the somber tonalities of the final reminiscences, is a part of the joy he took in writing not only as a means of domination and a weapon to brandish before the more terrifying aspects of existence but also as a way of celebrating the pleasures of the cosmos and of living in it. Even in his last years, face to face with ultimate mysteries that he was neither foolish nor dishonest enough to claim he had mastered, D'Annunzio held tight to the written word as the best means he knew for defining himself and as the surest way to squeeze a few drops of pleasure from an otherwise arid and reluctant but nonetheless seductive universe.

Selected Bibliography

EDITIONS

Note: The dates in the following entries (which by no means constitute a complete account of D'Annunzio's publishing record) are of first appearances in a volume and do not take into account either dates of performance or of publication in periodicals.

INDIVIDUAL WORKS

POETRY

Primo vere. Chieti, 1879; rev. ed., Lanciano, 1880.
In memoriam. Pistoia, 1880.
Canto novo. Rome, 1882; rev. ed., Milan, 1896.
Intermezzo di rime. Rome, 1884. Revised as *Intermezzo,* Naples, 1894.
Isaotta Guttadàuro ed altre poesie. Rome, 1886. Revised as *L'Isottèo—La Chimera (1885–1888).* Milan, 1890.
Odi navali. Naples, 1892. Augmented edition published in first edition of *Poema paradisiaco.* Milan, 1893.
Poema paradisiaco—Odi navali—1891–1893. Milan, 1893. Includes augmented edition of *Odi navali.*
Elegie romane (1887–1891). Bologna, 1892.
Laudi del cielo del mare della terra e degli eroi, Vol. 1. Maia. Milan, 1903.
Laudi del cielo del mare della terra e degli eroi, Vol. 2. Elettra—Alcyone. Milan, 1904.
Le canzoni della gesta d'oltremare. Laudi del cielo del mare della terra e degli eroi. Libro IV. Merope. Milan, 1912.

NOVELS AND SHORT STORIES

Terra vergine. Rome, 1882; rev. ed., 1884.
Il libro delle vergini. Rome, 1884.
San Pantaleone. Florence, 1886. Revised as *Le novelle della Pescara.* Milan, 1902.
Il piacere. Milan, 1889.
Giovanni Episcopo. Naples, 1892.
L'Innocente. Naples, 1892.
Trionfo della morte. Milan, 1894.
Le vergini delle rocce. Milan, 1896.
Il fuoco. Milan, 1900.
Forse che sì forse che no. Milan, 1910; rev. ed., 1932.
La Leda senza cigno. Racconto seguito da una licenza. Milan, 1916.

PLAYS

Sogno d'un mattino di primavera. Rome, 1897.
La città morta. Milan, 1898.
Sogno d'un tramonto d'autunno. Milan, 1898.
La Gioconda. Milan, 1899.
La gloria. Milan, 1899.
Francesca da Rimini. Milan, 1902.
La figlia di Iorio. Milan, 1904.
La fiaccola sotto il moggio. Milan, 1905.
Più che l'amore. Milan, 1907.

GABRIELE D'ANNUNZIO

La nave. Milan, 1908.
Fedra. Milan, 1909.
Le martyre de Saint Sébastien. Paris, 1911.
La crociata degli innocenti. Milan, 1911.
La Pisanelle ou la mort parfumée. Paris, 1913.
Cabiria. Turin, 1914.
Il ferro. Milan, 1914.

AUTOBIOGRAPHICAL WRITINGS

Contemplazione della morte. Milan, 1912.
Notturno. Milan, 1921.
Le faville del maglio. vol. 1. Il venturiero senza ventura e altri studii del vivere inimitabile. Milan, 1924.
Le faville del maglio, vol. 2. Il compagno dagli occhi senza cigli e altri studii del vivere inimitabile. Milan, 1928.
Cento e cento e cento e cento pagine del libro segreto di Gabriele D'Annunzio tentato di morire. Milan, 1935.

POSTHUMOUS AND COLLECTED WORKS

Opera omnia. 49 vols. Milan, 1927–1936.
Solus ad solam. Florence, 1939.
Tutte le opere. 9 vols. Milan, 1939–1950.
Poesie complete. Edited by Enzo Palmieri. 8 vols. Bologna, 1941–1959.
Taccuini. Milan, 1965.
Altri taccuini. Milan, 1976.
Poesie. Edited by Federico Roncoroni. Milan, 1978.
Prose. Edited by Federico Roncoroni. Milan, 1983.
Versi d'amore e di gloria. Edited by Annamaria Andreoli and Niva Lorenzini. 2 vols. Milan, 1982–1984.
Lettere a Giselda Zucconi. Edited by Ivanos Ciani. Pescara, 1985.

TRANSLATIONS

The Child of Pleasure. Translated by G. H. Harding. New York, 1898.
The Daughter of Jorio. Translated by C. Porter, A. Henry, and P. Isola. Boston, 1907.
The Dead City. Translated by A. Symons. London, 1900.
Episcopo & Company. Translated by M. L. Jones. Chicago, 1896.
The Flame of Life. Translated by Gustavo Tosti. Boston, 1900.
Francesca da Rimini. Translated by A. Symons. London, 1902.

Gioconda. Translated by A. Symons. New York, 1901.
The Honeysuckle. Translated by C. Sartoris and G. Enthoren. London, 1915.
The Intruder. Translated by A. Hornblow. Boston, 1897.
Maidens of the Rocks. Translated by A. H. Antona and G. Antona. Boston, 1898.
Tales of My Native Town. Translated by R. Mantellini. New York, 1920.
Triumph of Death. Translated by A. Hornblow. Boston, 1896.

BIOGRAPHICAL AND CRITICAL STUDIES

Alatri, Paolo. *Gabriele D'Annunzio.* Turin, 1983.
Bàrberi Squarotti, Giorgio. *Invito alla lettura di Gabriele D'Annunzio.* Milan, 1982.
Borgese, Giuseppe Antonio. *Gabriele D'Annunzio.* Milan, 1983.
Chiara, Piero. *Vita di Gabriele D'Annunzio.* Milan, 1978.
Contini, Gianfranco, compiler. *Letteratura dell' Italia unita.* Florence, 1968.
De Michelis, Eurialo. *Tutto D'Annunzio.* Milan, 1960.
Drake, Richard. *Byzantium for Rome.* Chapel Hill, N.C., 1980.
Goudet, Jacques. *D'Annunzio romanziere.* Florence, 1976.
Jullian, Philippe. *D'Annunzio.* Translated by Stephen Hardman. New York, 1973.
Klopp, Charles. *Gabriele D'Annunzio.* Boston, 1988.
Ledeen, Michael A. *The First Duce: D'Annunzio at Fiume.* Baltimore, 1977.
Luti, Giorgio. *La cenere dei sogni.* Pisa, 1973.
Mazzarella, Arturo. *Il piacere e la morte.* Naples, 1983.
Mutterle, Anco Marzio. *Gabriele D'Annunzio.* Florence, 1982.
Petronio, Giuseppe. *D'Annunzio.* Palermo, 1977.
Rhodes, Anthony. *The Poet as Superman.* London, 1959.
Ricciardi, Mario. *Coscienza e struttura nella prosa di D'Annunzio.* Turin, 1970.
Scarano Lugnani, Emanuella. *Il Novecento.* Vol. 9. Bari, 1976.
Thovez, Enrico. *Il pastore, il gregge, e la zampogna.* Naples, 1910.

CHARLES KLOPP

CONSTANTINE CAVAFY
(1863–1933)

CONSTANTINE CAVAFY CRAVED recognition on a worldwide scale. That he should now enjoy it is ironic considering his assumption that fate always frustrates our hopes for fame. It is also improbable, since he never published in the normal manner, merely distributing his poems gratis to a select circle of Greek admirers.[1] Even during his lifetime, however, a small group of English-speaking readers began to find his work original and impressive. Here again we encounter irony, for this repute was occasioned by the very agent Cavafy so mistrusted—the strange fate that, sending E. M. Forster to Alexandria in World War I, brought about Cavafy's first appearance in English translation when Forster included a version of "Apoleipein o theos Antonion" ("The God Abandons Antony," 1910) in his *Alexandria: A History and a Guide* (1922) and supplemented this with a wry essay published in the following year in *Pharos and Pharillon* about this singular "Greek gentleman in a straw hat, standing absolutely motionless at a slight angle to the universe."

Since then, Cavafy has enjoyed ever-growing esteem among writers and critics. He has even reached the general reading public as the shadowy "old poet" of Lawrence Durrell's *Alexandria Quartet* (1957–1960), where he epitomizes

the dappled spirit of Alexandria with its weariness, worn sophistication, and priapic intrigue. What Durrell helps specialists and the broader public alike to realize is that we are touched by Cavafy because we are all now somewhat "Alexandrian."

Fate, far from frustrating Cavafy's desire for worldwide fame, has been posthumously good to him; but in the process it has played another ironic trick: it has made him respectable. Although many of his poems are veiled enough to be suitable for schoolgirls, when correctly interpreted they are almost all openly or covertly scandalous, for they either deny, ridicule, or (worst of all) ignore the three bulwarks of respectable bourgeois society: Christianity, patriotism, and heterosexual love. His near-canonization has gone furthest in Greece itself, in a kind of twisted fulfillment of the sentiments that Cavafy expressed under the significant title "Poly spanios" ("Very Seldom," 1911). In this poem we see an exhausted and stooped old man who nevertheless still has a share in youth:

> Young men recite his verses now.
> His visions pass across their animated eyes.
> Their healthy voluptuous minds,
> their shapely tight-knit bodies
> are moved by his revelations of the beautiful.

It is easy enough to understand how these lines of wish fulfillment with their benignly

---

[1]For this reason, the dates given in this essay are dates of composition rather than publication. Although some of Cavafy's poems exist in several versions, only the composition dates of final versions are given here.

homosexual overtones can be sentimentalized by schoolmasters into an inoffensive poem on the incorruptibility of art. And it is also easy enough to forget, when in 1963 on the centenary of Cavafy's birth we hear a Greek schoolgirl characterize him as "the beloved poet of youth," that fifty years previously his own sister forbade her daughter to read Uncle Costas' disreputable verses. Nor is it any less ironic that another feature of canonization during the centenary observances should have been a speech in which Cavafy's verse was flanked by excerpts from Thucydides and Saint Paul. Thucydides (representing patriotism: the glory of the classic tradition) makes a strange bedfellow for an author who so studiously ignored everything that Greek chauvinists idolize. Paul is equally incompatible, representing as he does the religion that extirpated or at least forced underground the pagan gods Cavafy so studiously cultivated. But the fact that young girls can now read Cavafy without scandalizing their parents indicates that Athens, London, Paris, and New York feel an affinity for this previously disreputable figure, accepting him as the spokesman of a Western tradition that, lacking vital, new drives or a solid moral or religious understructure, has become effete, weary, cynical, eclectic, and, by consequence, tolerant.

Cavafy's sophisticated modernity is all the more astonishing because it seems to issue from nowhere, or at best from some backwater. While Marcel Proust, Thomas Mann, T. S. Eliot, Virginia Woolf, Joseph Conrad, André Gide—all at the center of things and fortified to a greater or lesser extent with the writings of professional philosophers—were giving us their carefully elaborated artistic visions of *Homo europaeus,* together with implied attitudes toward time, memory, the afterlife, morality, God, and absolute truth, here was Cavafy doing the same thing as though naively, by instinct. He is of course the very opposite of a naive, instinctive poet; yet, because of a fateful crossing of psychological disposition,

personal circumstances both economic and social, and the fact that he was a Greek living in Alexandria, he did not need philosophers or acquaintance with literary trends in order to evoke *Homo europaeus:* all he needed was to write about himself, having first discovered how to remove every sentimental element from this personal indulgence.

The method he found led him to Alexandrian history. If this sounds paradoxical, it is but one such facet of this most paradoxical of men. Obsessively the subjective poet of self, he was at the same time largely detached and objective—an anti-lyrical lyricist. Although modern to the core, he remained oblivious to contemporary affairs, preferring to lose himself in remote periods of history. Proudly conscious of his identity as a Greek and of the part played by Greece in Western civilization, he nevertheless largely ignored the great figures: Homer, the dramatists, Pericles, Socrates, Plato, Aristotle. In his personal life he was a monkish, antisocial recluse who nevertheless craved, and received, the constant adulation of a circle of disciples. By day a fastidious aristocrat conscious of his social position, sensitive about any slights, and crushed if he failed to be invited to the dinner parties of Alexandria's respectable moneyed class, by night he lived a dissolute life in the city's slums, giving himself over with deliberate recklessness to the purchased fulfillment of what he himself termed "love that is sterile and rejected." Perhaps most paradoxical of all is that this aristocrat and bohemian, with his exclusively urban mentality, spent so many years as a petit bourgeois official in the Egyptian government's Ministry of Irrigation.

He was truly a man with a stance at a slight angle to the universe—a stance, however, that becomes understandable when we know a little more about his life and background: about his psychological disposition and his social and economic circumstances, about Alexandria itself, and about the specific technical problems Cavafy had to work out before his artistry could become distinctive. For although his poems are neither syntactically difficult nor outwardly cryptic and although they are therefore "available" to the average reader who comes to them without a panoply of scholarship, part of Cavafy's modernity is that he does require this scholarship. Perhaps this is simply a result of his astonishing egocentricity: he is saying, in effect, "My poems are me, and if you wish to read them the way they should be read, you will have to know all about me, and that means knowing all about my life in Alexandria, my aristocratic ancestors, my city's glory and decline, and the other things that interest me, such as the defunct dynasties of Byzantium and Syria and the encroachment of Christian asceticism on the splendid paganism of the Hellenistic kingdoms of the East."

To begin, then, with Cavafy's life in Alexandria: After his fortieth year—that is, from the time he began to develop his mature poetic style—outwardly his existence was uneventful, perhaps because his most exciting activity was writing poetry. The thirty succeeding years, those that produced the poems comprising his canon, were spent entirely in Alexandria, except for a trip to a hospital in Athens just before his death. A major characteristic of this Alexandrian period is a spiritual as well as physical identification between the poet and his birthplace. "I polis" ("The City," 1894), although a very early poem and one that deals most basically not with Alexandria but with Cavafy's anguish over his homosexuality, is prophetic on a literal level, and it gives a good idea of just what Alexandria came to mean to him, in both his writing and his personal life. The poet vows he will "go to another land . . . another sea." In Alexandria his every effort is doomed:

Wherever I cast my glance, wherever I stare,
I see my life's black ruins here
where I passed so many years in loss and waste.

Another city will be found, he tells himself at first—a better one. But then he realizes the truth: "You will find no new lands, you will find no other seas":

The city will follow you. You will patrol
the same streets, in the same districts grow
    old,
turn white in these same houses.
. . . .
for you there is no vessel, road for you there
    is none.
Here in this tiny corner, such harm you have
    done
your life, the loss spreads over the entire
    world.

Even during his lifetime, Cavafy's identification with his city was recognized; he was considered *the* poet of Alexandria and enjoyed a certain notoriety as such. Forster and Durrell give us some idea of his peculiar renown among his fellow Alexandrians, and this picture is confirmed and enlarged by many Greeks who knew him and have recorded their impressions. All seem to agree on at least two points: his eccentricity and his extraordinary powers as a conversationalist. Timos Malanos, his earliest biographer, says Cavafy was always acting, that his appearance, gestures, and tone of voice were so strange that mimicking him became a favorite Alexandrian pastime. But this does not mean he was an object of ridicule; on the contrary, he attracted a circle of loyal young disciples whom he met regularly at a café. His powers of repartee are proved by the fact that so many of these companions habitually recorded everything he said: an entire circle of Mediterranean Boswells. Cavafy, with his almost pathological need to be admired, must have played his role with gusto, enthralling his auditors in the way Forster so well describes:

He may be prevailed upon to begin a sentence—an immense complicated yet shapely sentence, full of parentheses that never get mixed and of reservations that really do resolve; a sentence that moves with logic to its foreseen end, yet to an end that is always more vivid and thrilling than one foresaw. . . . It deals with the tricky behaviour of the Emperor Alexius Comnenus in 1096, or with olives, their possibilities and price, or with the fortunes of friends, or George Eliot, or the dialects of the interior of Asia Minor. It is delivered with equal ease in Greek, English, or French.

(*Pharos and Pharillon*, pp. 91–92)

An equally charming picture, part truth, part wish fulfillment, is given in the final stanza of Cavafy's poem "Irodis Attikos" ("Herodes Atticus," 1911). Here we see perhaps one more habitual topic at the poet's café table, and we are offered a Cavafian definition of consummate bliss:

How many young lads in Alexandria now,
in Antioch and Beirut
(the future orators that Hellenism is readying)
when they gather at the choice tables
where the talk is sometimes of lovely philosophy
and sometimes of their exquisite love affairs,
suddenly, absorbed, fall silent?
They leave their glasses untouched beside them
and reflect on Herodes' good fortune
—what other philosopher was granted so
    much?—
that in his wants and actions
the Greeks (the Greeks!) should follow him,
neither judging nor discussing,
not even choosing anymore, just following.

Much of the legend that has grown up around this eccentric poet centers on his flat at 10 rue Lepsius. His niece Hariklea Valieri records that when his relatives, scandalized by the neighborhood, implored him to leave, he rose, went to the window, drew back the curtains, and said, "Where else could I be better situated than here, amidst these three centers of existence: a brothel, a church which forgives, and a hospital where you die?" Favored visitors were admitted to this sanctum, with its subdued light, the ornate Oriental furniture that Cavafy had brought from his family's baronial mansion, and the three diamonds embedded in the sitting-room wall. If the guest was young and handsome, an addi-

tional candle would be lighted, but the host always sat in shadow: hypersensitive about his aging, he could not bear to let his wrinkles be seen or to have anyone insinuate that *he* was no longer young and handsome. Cavafy could not contemplate old age with equanimity. In "I psyches ton geronton" ("The Souls of Old Men," 1898), he views the senescent as enduring a wretched, burdensome life while at the same time "they tremble they might lose it"—these

bewildered contradictory
souls that sit comicotragically
in their ancient, their ruined hides.

If to philosophize is to learn to die, Cavafy was never a philosopher, and those who see Stoic overtones in some of his poems overlook the fact that on his deathbed he wept. Cavafy was not a philosopher; he was a voluptuary, and for a voluptuary (especially one who disbelieves in an afterlife) the irreparable disaster is old age, while the sole consolation, the sole drug to narcotize this "wound from a hideous knife" as Cavafy terms it, is reverie—reverie about foregone pleasure, foregone vigor. In most cases such reverie is dissipated and lost; in Cavafy's it was solidified into poetry.

It is to the past, therefore—first to Cavafy's youthful years before the poems were written and then beyond that time to the glory and decline of his family—that we must turn for the "events" of his largely uneventful life. In the poet's youth we have the homosexual assignations in the slums of Constantinople and Alexandria; these, with their exultation and frustration, are repeatedly described in the poetry, sometimes in a veiled manner, sometimes openly. Here is Cavafy by night. By day we have the dandified scion of a once-great house, struggling to maintain a dignified position that he himself knows has been lost forever. Conflict between the nocturnal and diurnal selves, inevitable at first, is recorded in "Omnyei" ("He Resolves," 1905), a poem whose autobiographical nature is confirmed by notes found among the poet's papers after his death:

Every so often he resolves to begin a better life.
But when the night comes with its own advice,
with its compromises and promises;
when it comes with its own fleshly
power that desires and seeks—then, lost,
he goes again to the same fatal pleasure.

But this situation, although superficially one of irresolvable conflict, contained its own resolution, and in so doing provided the "method" of Cavafy's poetry. For Cavafy's genius perceived that his sexual decadence was congruent with his and his family's decline and that this personal misfortune was in turn congruent with the decline of the local Greek community as a whole; furthermore, he saw that his situation bore analogy to the ups and downs of Greek fortunes in Alexandria over a period of two millennia, to the decline of Hellenism as a civilizing force in numerous other cultural centers, and (implicitly) to the weary decadence of contemporary European civilization in general. Cavafy now had at his fingertips an expanding series of equivalent situations, any one of which could be used poetically to symbolize any, or all, of the others. By placing his personal dilemma in this huge perspective embracing family and race and by learning to view everything with an attitude of resignation, he was able to resolve his personal troubles without sentimentalizing them.

The best evidence of family decline is a descendant obsessed with family glory. Cavafy betrays this obsession in "Genealogia" ("Genealogy"), a monograph that he wrote sporadically between 1882 and 1909 and finally abandoned in 1911 (this date, as we shall see, may be significant). Here he dwells with pathetic insistence on the glories of both his paternal and maternal ancestors. Among these, on his father's side, were the governor of a city in Moldavia, a chief priest of the church at Antioch, a head physician of St. George's Hospital in London, and an entire branch of Italian nobility; on his mother's side were a prince of Samos, two wives of high-level Belgian diplomats, and a wealthy philanthropist whose "splendid funeral" Cavafy especially mentions.

Status, respectability, and cosmopolitanism seem the common ingredients of the family tradition, and these mark the poet's own childhood as well. According to the same document, his father's export business was the largest in Egypt from about 1851 to 1870, with branches in London, Liverpool, Manchester, Constantinople, Cairo, and elsewhere. The Cavafy mansion, in the town's most aristocratic neighborhood, maintained a French tutor, an English nanny, four or five Greek menservants, an Italian coachman, and an Egyptian groom. But this affluence did not last; the fortunes of Cavafy and Sons roughly paralleled those of the Greek community in general.

To understand what happened, we must know a few facts. Modern Egypt dates from the French occupation of 1798–1801, when Napoleon drove out the Turks and brought French scientists, engineers, and historians in his wake. Under the rule of Mohammed Ali (effectively in command ca. 1810–1840) new seed and methods were introduced, making Egypt into a great producer of cotton. A revitalized Alexandria became the country's export center, and Ali, mistrusting the Egyptians, gave concessions to foreigners, encouraging in particular a Greek monopoly of foreign trade. The Greeks prospered to such an extent that by the 1850's, soon after the founding of Cavafy and Sons, they controlled the commercial life of Cairo, Khartoum, and Alexandria. In 1845 there were two thousand Greeks in Alexandria; in 1900, twenty thousand; in 1907, twenty-six thousand. The researches of Stratis Tsirkas, updated by Alexander Kitroeff, have shown that the original Francophile Greek plutocracy, including Cavafy's father, declined in the 1870's and 1880's owing to increased British influence in Egypt. This group was replaced by a nouveau riche class of Anglophile Greek merchants, who in turn suffered from the financial crisis of 1907, the growing antagonism toward all Europeans, the founding of the nationalist movement in 1919, the agreement to end extraterritoriality in 1937, the revolution against King Farouk in 1952, and finally the expulsion of the Greek community by Gamal Abdel Nasser in the early 1960's. For us the important thing is to realize that Cavafy, as Tsirkas puts it, "emerges from the atmosphere of the Greek community of the Middle East at the moment it was traveling the road of its bankruptcy and liquidation."

Without the demise of Cavafy and Sons we would not have had the poet as we know him, if only for the fact that after Cavafy's father died, leaving only a meager estate, his widow was forced by circumstances to take her children to live in England. This sojourn, which lasted for seven of Cavafy's most formative years, put the definitive stamp on the poet's cosmopolitanism. It is essential to remember in any consideration of his artistic development that he knew and loved English literature (as well as French), habitually conversed in English with his brothers, spoke Greek with a British accent, and began his poetic career with translations and imitations of English and French verse. However, the other side of the coin is equally important: although he could very well have continued in this imitative way, or even have written exclusively in the English or French languages (as did Yannis Papadiamantopoulos, who became famous as the "French" poet Jean Moréas), he did not. The lure of Greek greatness and decline, and above all the magic of the Greek tongue, proved too compelling.

Cavafy returned to Alexandria at the age of sixteen. Subsequently, he went to Constantinople for three years, a period about which we know very little but which he always deemed the freest and "most beautiful" of his life. At twenty-two the young poet came back to Alexandria, this time to stay. Cultured, sophisticated, proud to the point of arrogant snobbery, and saddled with what Durrell likes to call "tendencies," he was forced by a malevo-

lent fortune to go each morning to the office in order to "sit among insignificant functionaries," as he put it. We see him behind the mask of a Sidonian actor in "Theatron tis Sidonos (400 M. Ch.)" ("Theater of Sidon [A.D. 400]," 1923), a poem that may serve as a convenient illustration of how Cavafy linked his personal situation with the general decline of Hellenism:

Son of an esteemed citizen,   first of all a
    handsome
young man of the theater,   pleasing in diverse
    ways,
now and then I compose   in the Greek language
    excessively daring verses. . . .

We also learn the important fact that these verses, being about "the choicest gratification, leading / to love that is sterile and rejected," are of course circulated most secretly in order to keep them from "dun-clad discussers of morals."

The personal situation in this poem is presented through a ruse. The historical mask and the pose of scholarly accuracy in time and place enable Cavafy to distance and objectify what is in fact a personal indulgence. Then, beyond this, the poet employs historicity to draw us into the expanding series of equivalent situations, thus weighting his poem with meaning not apparent in the bare prose sense.

The extent of the personal indulgence becomes clear when we remember that the poem's "excessively daring verses" are of course Cavafy's own disreputable work and that in circulating them most secretly the handsome Sidonian is following Cavafy's own practice. This practice was to issue his poems singly or grouped in folders that he circulated among select friends. No book of his was ever published during his lifetime.

The element of "Theater of Sidon (A.D. 400)" that draws us into the equivalent situation and thus links Cavafy's personal troubles with the general decline of Hellenism is the all-important date included in the title. Cavafy expects us to remember A.D. 400 as the time when triumphant Christianity was forcing Greek paganism in Sidon, Alexandria, and the rest of the Hellenistic world to breathe its last breath. The poem in its larger implications, therefore, is one of many in which Cavafy laments the historical retreat of the pagan way of life (which he continually identifies with "the choicest gratification") before the taboos and respectability of Christianity. By means of this equivalent situation the verses express his own predicament as a latter-day pagan still in a hostile environment of sexual restrictions unknown, he would have us believe, to pre-Christian Greeks.

As the years passed and Cavafy's sensual desires came to be frustrated by creeping old age as well as Christian morality and bourgeois respectability, the poet found increasing solace in reveries of a bygone period of freedom and fulfillment—probably those three beautiful years in Constantinople. In the same way, his historical reveries were directed to Hellenism's zenith as well as its nadir. But in neither the personal nor the historical case was he willing to sentimentalize; he saw the frustration and failure along with the exultation. Just as his own vigor and youth had succumbed to decrepitude, so the various Hellenistic centers had undergone the same process, and the method by which he could recapture in poetry the soars and swoops of his personal history was to evoke the history of his people—in particular the vicissitudes of that people in Alexandria.

The best way to gain acquaintance with Cavafy, therefore, is to follow the entire history of Alexandria as he displays it in his poems. In his view the city was at its most dazzling during the early period of pagan Greek rule, roughly from 300 to 200 B.C. When the Romans intruded, the dimming began. They eventually won complete control, and then came Christianity's turn to intrude. The Greek spirit was almost entirely snuffed out when Rome itself turned Christian. Finally, the Arab conquest

in the seventh century brought total blackness. Such, in capsule, is Cavafy's view.

At this point it may be well to remember that Cleopatra was not an Egyptian but a Greek and that Alexandria, though a meeting ground of Greeks, Jews, Egyptians, Syrians, and others, was dominated by Greek culture and was originally ruled by Macedonian monarchs whose blood from first to last was as purely Greek (since they generally married their brothers or sisters) as that of the dynasty's founder, Ptolemy. This first Ptolemy determined to make his capital city the world center of culture—"I doxa ton Ptolemaion" ("The Glory of the Ptolemies," 1911):

> the mentor city, the Hellenic world's acme
> wisest in all the arts, in all philosophy.

The instrument for effecting these glorious cultural aims was the Mouseion, "the great intellectual achievement of the dynasty," as Forster writes in *Alexandria: A History and a Guide.* Not only did the Mouseion

> mould the literature and science of its day, but it has left a permanent impress upon thought. . . . It was essentially a court institution, under palace control, and knew both the advantages and disadvantages of royal patronage. In some ways it resembled a modern university, but the scholars and scientists and literary men whom it supported were under no obligation to teach; they had only to pursue their studies to the greater glory of the Ptolemies.
>
> (p. 17)

These studies resulted in the calendar we still use today; the determination of the earth's diameter; the astronomical calculations that were codified by Claudius Ptolemy (also an Alexandrian, but one who lived after the fall of the dynasty whose name he shared); the *Elements* of Euclid; the beginning of literary scholarship; and—most important in connection with Cavafy—a school of epigrammatic poetry that influenced him in attitude, subject matter, and technique. Callimachus, Meleager,

Crinagoras, Rhianus, Aratus, and the others whose works have come down to us wrote, as Forster says, "when the heroic age of Greece was over, when liberty was lost and possibly honour too." The literature they developed

> was disillusioned, and we may be glad that it was not embittered also. It had strength of a kind, for it saw that out of the wreck of traditional hopes three good things remained—namely the decorative surface of the universe, the delights of study, and the delights of love, and that of these three the best was love.
>
> (p. 29)

Cavafy's indebtedness to this school of epigrammists cannot be too often stressed. We need only add one additional genre cultivated in this lustrous period, 300–200 B.C.—the "mime," little scenes from everyday urban life, dramatized in dialogue—and we have precedents for every aspect of Cavafy's poetic manner. Forster's list of characteristics is remarkably applicable: disillusionment that lacks bitterness, obsession with the wreck of traditional hopes, complete absence of the heroic spirit, love of study, and a hedonism that cultivates the delights of love. We must subtract only the interest in the decorative surface of the universe (Cavafy's urban mentality was deliberately oblivious to nature) and put in its place one further delight and consolation, that of poetry itself—or, to be more exact, of *Greek* poetry.

Since it was the instrument for making Alexandria the summit of pan-Hellenism, the Mouseion was bound to suffer once the Hellenic world began to capitulate to the superior strength of Rome. By 200 B.C. the Ptolemies were already under Rome's "protection," a situation that eventually led not only to the dynasty's famous end, when Cleopatra applied her asp, but also (and of far greater consequence) to Julius Caesar's accidental burning of the Mouseion together with its extraordinary library. Once established as Egypt's protector, Rome found pretexts for further intervention owing to internal dissension among the Ptole-

mies themselves, so that by the time of Ptolemy VI (ca. 150 B.C.), the rulers of Egypt, as well as other Hellenistic monarchs, had become mere puppets. Indeed, when this Ptolemy was expelled from Alexandria by his brother, he was obliged to go begging to Rome in order to ask the Senate to reinstate him. The Romans settled the dispute wisely—in their own interests—by dividing the kingdom and thus further weakening it. Cavafy treats the incident in two poems. In "I dysareskeia tou Selefkidou" ("The Displeasure of Selefkidis," 1910) he follows his source, the historian Diodorus Siculus, and recounts the meeting between Ptolemy and Demetrios Selefkidis, himself a hostage in Rome at the time; in "Presveis ap' tin Alexandreia" ("Envoys from Alexandria," 1915), departing from history, he conveys the decline of Greece most piquantly by inventing a futile embassy to the Delphic Oracle, which itself has been overshadowed by the rival "oracle" in Rome. He has ambassadors from Alexandria arrive at Delphi bearing extraordinary gifts from "the rival Ptolemaic kings." The Delphic priests, having accepted these treasures, are understandably uneasy:

> How
> most astutely to arrange which of the pair—
> of such a pair—should be displeased, will require
> their fullest expertise.

But suddenly the ambassadors say farewell; they have no further need for a decision. The priests are relieved but also bewildered:

> For grave news reached the envoys the day before; of this they're unaware.
> The oracle was given in Rome; the partition took place there.

The end of the dynasty is known to every schoolboy, but chiefly from the Roman point of view. The official Augustan version, propagated by Vergil, is that Mark Antony unmanned himself by capitulating to Cleopatra's infinite variety and languid Oriental debauchery and that Octavian's naval triumph at Actium in 31 B.C. signified the triumph, as C. M. Bowra puts it, of "the upright spirit of Rome over the corrupting influences of the East." Cavafy, in some of his most memorably ironic poems, treats the leading figures and events in an altogether different way.

Regarding Octavian's triumph over Antony, in "Endimo tis Mikras Asias" ("In a Township in Asia Minor," 1926), he sees that, at least from the vantage point of the average contemporaneous Greek, one Roman ruler was much the same as another—all were nuisances to be placated with rhetoric and tolerated insofar as they recognized the cultural superiority of Greece.

> The news about Actium, the outcome of the
>   naval engagement there,
> was most assuredly unforeseen.
> But we have no need to compose a new
>   document.
> Let only the name be changed. There in the
> concluding lines, instead of "Having delivered
>   the Romans
> from pernicious Octavian,
> that travesty of Caesar,"
> now we shall put, "Having delivered
>   the Romans
> from pernicious Antony."
> The entire text is beautifully suitable.

Hereupon follows the panegyric. The victor is praised as "unsurpassed in every martial deed" and as "admirable for civil achievement," but above all as "the well-disposed venerator of Hellenic customs," whose deeds are therefore worthy of being extensively narrated

> in the Greek language, both in verse and prose;
> in *the Greek language* which is the bearer of fame.

"And so forth and so on," the poem continues. Yes, "everything is splendidly suitable."

A second poem—one of several effective superimpositions of speech rhythms and prosaic tone upon the decorous form of couplets rhymed as often as not in homonyms—likewise views the event with irony, but with an

irony that takes an entirely new turn. If we may judge by repeated elaborations of this theme in other poems, Cavafy here is not just inventing a stratagem on the part of Cleopatra's representatives to keep the populace from knowing the truth about Actium; he is suggesting that the people themselves, through this lie, are vainly trying to preserve their own pathetically impossible hopes in the face of brutal reality. Once again the title includes an all-important date. "To 31 P. Ch. stin Alexandreia" ("31 B.C. in Alexandria," 1924) opens as a peddler reaches the city

>   from his tiny
> village near the purlieu, still grimy
> from the journey's dust. "Incense!" he cries
> through the streets, and "Gum! Finest oil! Dyes
>
> for the hair!" But with the great noisy herd
> and the music and parades, how can he be heard?
>
> The throngs push him, drag him, pound him with
>   their fists;
> and when at last, perfectly confused, he asks
>   "What madness is this?"
>
> he too is tossed the gigantic palace yarn
> —that Antony, in Greece, has won.

This theme of vain hopes out of keeping with the hidden plans of destiny is paramount in "Alexandrinoi vasileis" ("Alexandrian Kings," 1910), a third poem dealing with the fall of the dynasty. It is characteristic of Cavafy's eccentricity that he should ignore Cleopatra and instead treat Caesarion, the queen's illegitimate son by Julius Caesar. The poet assumes that his readers will know this boy's tragic fortune: to be murdered in his teens by order of Octavian after the suicides of Cleopatra and Antony. Caesarion's death ended the Ptolemaic dynasty; but in this poem, set just three years before Actium, Antony and Cleopatra advance preposterous claims for all three of the royal heirs (the two youngest were sired by Antony), investing them with the rule of dominions most of which had yet to be conquered. Cavafy emphasizes the pathetic ostentation of the ceremony of investment and departs from his source, Plutarch, in making it not the Romans but the Alexandrians themselves who "knew of course what all this was worth." Still, he has them enjoy the show, for this is an age in which glitter seems self-justifying. Like their cousins in the township in Asia Minor, the Alexandrians (including Hellenized Egyptians and Jews) are largely devoid of illusion; yet they still deliberately wish to perpetuate the final illusion of Greek hegemony, whether it be cultural or political:

Alexander: they named him king of
Armenia, Media, and the Parthians.
Ptolemy: they named him king of
Cilicia, Syria, and Phoenicia.
Caesarion stood more to the front,
dressed in pinkish silk,
a posy of hyacinths on his breast
his belt a double row of sapphires and amethysts,
his sandals laced with white ribbons
embroidered with rose-tinted pearls.

Caesarion received the greatest designation of the three: "him they named King of Kings." The Alexandrians knew of course that these were simply "the words of play-actors," but the atmosphere was just right—fine weather, the courtiers' impressive grandeur, Caesarion's "grace and beauty"—and people kept hurrying to the festival,

    and they grew enthusiastic, and cheered
    in Greek, in Egyptian, and some in Hebrew,
    enchanted by the lovely spectacle—
    though they knew of course what all this was
        worth,
    what hollow words were these kingships.

According to Malanos, Cavafy remarked in connection with this poem that he dressed Caesarion in pinkish silk "because in those days a yard of such silk cost the equivalent of several thousand of today's drachmas." The statement is characteristic of Cavafy's antiquarian mind; like the old writers of the Mouseion, he was a scholar as well as a poet. But,

again like his prototypes, he did not allow his scholarship to keep him from stretching facts or departing from them entirely. The difference is that they, being on salary, departed from truth in order to flatter their royal employers and retain their jobs; Cavafy did so in order to give freer rein to his imagination. His antiquarianism is never an end in itself but rather an aid toward the imaginative expression of personal and social problems that are perennial and thus modern. If he was a historian, a recorder of Alexandrian events and personages, this was because he found in them the imaginative sheathing for a substance that is personal and contemporary.

This paradoxical linkage between the antiquarian verifying every detail and the romancer making out of history what he liked can be seen in "Kaisarion" ("Caesarion," 1914), a companion poem to "Alexandrian Kings." In addition, "Caesarion" indicates how Cavafy's imagination was triggered by small, insignificant details around which a poem could be built. In this case it was Plutarch's statement that as Octavian (called C. Julius Caesar Octavianus before he ascended the throne as Augustus) was deliberating what to do with his young Alexandrian rival, Caesarion, a subordinate said to him, "Too many Caesars is not good," whereupon C. Julius Caesar Octavianus put the rival Caesar to death. This poem is also an example of Cavafy's habitual method of weaving homosexual suggestions into historical context and of making the finished work deal most basically with his own frustrations based on fear of persecution by "the rabble." The poem begins by describing its origins:

    In part to verify chronology,
    in part to while away the hour,
    last night I took up an anthology
    of Ptolemaic inscriptions to explore.
    . . . .
    When I succeeded in verifying the chronology,
    I would have dropped the book, had not a
        small
    insignificant mention of King Caesarion
    immediately attracted my attention.

The young king with his "ill-defined fascination" is now made exceedingly handsome and sensitive by the poet's imagination, all the more freely because "in history but few / lines are found" about him. "My art," says the poet, addressing the vision he has created, "bequeaths a dreamlike / winsome beauty to your face":

So completely did I imagine you
that late last night as my lamp was
waning—I purposely let it wane—
I thought you came into my room.
You stood before me, it seemed, as you must have
    been
in conquered Alexandria,
pale and weary, an idealist in your grief,
still hoping they'd have mercy on you,
the rabble, who kept whispering their "Too many
    Caesars."

In a further consideration of the dynasty's fall Cavafy turns to Antony, using him as a vehicle for a poem that is really about Alexandria itself. "The God Abandons Antony" is the chief evidence advanced by those who wish to characterize Cavafy as a stoic counseling brave, realistic acceptance of disastrous reality:

When suddenly at midnight hour
an unseen troupe is heard to pass
with exquisite music and with cries—
do not uselessly lament your fortune
giving way at last, your projects that have failed,
. . . .
Above all, do not be deceived; do not say it was
a dream, that your hearing had been mistaken;
do not stoop to futile hopes like these.

But although this poem does seem to insist that false hopes must be rejected in favor of stoic acceptance, it is actually a hedonistic paeon that refuses to admit that pleasure, too, is illusory and vain. The emphasis is not on stoic acceptance of death, but rather on the serenity derived from accepting pleasure as a self-justifying good: "As if long ago prepared, as a man of courage, / as it becomes you who deserved such a city" (i.e., who deserved the hedonistic life), you must

listen as a final pleasure to the sounds,
the exquisite instruments of the mystical troupe,
and bid farewell to her, the Alexandria you are
    losing.

For Antony in this poem we can read Cavafy the voluptuary, trying to confront his own aging. But despite the loss of pleasure, life went on for him; and so it did as well for Alexandria after the deposition of the Ptolemies. Indeed, the city continued to be a great cultural center for many centuries, though the character of its achievement changed. Instead of the dainty and often obscene epigrams of Callimachus and his school, heavily esoteric philosophy began to appear; then, with the coming of Christianity, doctrinal disputes concerning the nature of Christ became prevalent; and finally, in a complete turnabout, ascetic monks uncompromisingly rejected not only pagan license but also art, philosophy, and learning in any form whatsoever.

Philosophy in those days gravitated toward theology, not toward semantics as it does today. Residents of Alexandria—whether Jews, pagan Greeks, or Christians—were interested in God, and being both Alexandrians and of a philosophical temperament that was "mystical rather than scientific," as Forster writes, "as soon as they hit on an explanation of the universe that was comforting, they did not stop to consider whether it might be true." Philo, living at the time of Christ, represents the culmination of the Jewish school at Alexandria. Writing in Greek and building his philosophical system upon the Greek concept of the *logos*, he is also a splendid indication of how irresistible Hellenistic culture was for Jews as well as other barbarians. But obviously the clash of religious and cultural loyalties caused tensions, such as those experienced by Ianthe in Cavafy's poem "Ton Evraion (50 M. Ch.)" ("Of the Jews [A.D. 50]," 1912). Painter

215

and discus thrower, Hellenized Ianthe is nevertheless close to the synagogue. His "most precious days," he says, are when he abandons beautiful Hellenism and becomes the man he should "always like / to remain: son of the Jews, of the holy Jews." "Exceedingly fervent his declaration," comments the poet with sarcasm; in reality, Ianthe

> remained nothing of the sort.
> In him, Alexandria's hedonism and art
> had a devoted child.

Like their Jewish colleagues, the Greek philosophers of Alexandria viewed God's nature in a mystical rather than a scientific way. Because these Neoplatonists followed Plato in considering the flesh ephemeral and sensual pleasure therefore vain, they were not likely to find a disciple in Cavafy. Nevertheless Ammonios Sakkas, founder of the Neoplatonic school and reputed teacher of Longinus and Plotinus, appears in a delightfully sardonic poem called "Apo tin scholin tou perionymou philosophou" ("From the School of the Renowned Philosopher," 1921) that is really not about philosophy at all. The protagonist has been Sakkas' pupil for two years. Growing weary both of philosophy and of Sakkas, he enters politics, only to abandon this calling because his superior is an "idiot" surrounded by "solemn-looking official blockheads" whose Greek is "thrice barbarous." Next, his curiosity is attracted somewhat by the church; he'll be baptized "and be taken as a Christian." But the thought that his parents, who are "ostentatious pagans," will assuredly cut off his allowance makes him quickly change his mind. Forced to do something, he becomes a client of Alexandria's "every secret den of debauchery." His good looks aid him in this regard; he can be sure that his beauty will endure "for ten more years" at least:

> After that,
> perhaps he would go to Sakkas again.
> And if the old man had died in the meantime,

he'd go to some other philosopher or sophist—
someone suitable can always be found.

Or, finally, he might even return to
politics, laudably recalling
his family traditions,
patriotic duty, and other such blather.

The handsome young man of this poem is a type who haunts Cavafy's work. Sophisticated and bored, he tends to interpret his own deficient moral vigor as a lack of savoir faire in others. Embroiled in the rivalry between Christianity and paganism, he is hardly the type to embrace either faith except for convenience or personal advantage, a characteristic he seems to have shared with many of his fellow Alexandrians. For they were of an eclectic temper from the start. Their local cult, custom-made by the first Ptolemy to suit their needs, combined the two Egyptian deities Osiris and Apis to form Serapis, who was then dressed in Greek robes and depicted with a Zeus-like face and beard. Already accustomed to a multiplicity of gods in hypostatic union, the Alexandrians found it easy enough at first to assimilate one more—Christ—especially since in his role as intermediary between humans and God the Father he spoke to the problem of God's inaccessibility, which had already been occupying both the Jewish and Neoplatonic philosophers of the city. At this early stage, therefore, just as it was natural for the poem's handsome young student to be attracted a little by the church, so too was it natural for him to be more curious than fervent, seeing Christianity as a complement to his existing practice rather than as a challenge. Apropos of this situation, Forster quotes a letter written by a visitor to Alexandria in 134 who observed that "those who worship Serapis are Christians, and those who call themselves bishops of Christ are devoted to Serapis!"

But although the theological and philosophical difficulties occasioned by the multiplicity of gods were at first solvable, the political problem was more refractory. It led to thoroughgoing persecution of Alexandrian Christians by Diocletian and other Roman emperors, which in turn led to equally thoroughgoing persecution of Alexandrian pagans once Christianity became the official religion under Constantine. Both phases of this persecution helped the adherents of Christianity to overcome their lack of fervor; by the fourth century the theological differences had grown fully as refractory as the political ones had been before. When Christianity became not only official but compulsory by decree of Theodosius in 392, paganism was doomed. Shortly before this, the ascetics who had fled Alexandrian lechery to settle in the desert had banded together in order to return in triumph. These monks destroyed the great temple of Serapis, the Serapeum, together with the library housed there—an even greater collection than the one destroyed earlier by Julius Caesar. Forming the nucleus of what became the native Egyptian, or Coptic, church, they grew powerful in temporal as well as eternal matters and, hating everything Greek, made Egypt a particularly vulnerable portion of the Byzantine Empire. As a result Alexandria fell to the Mohammedans in 641, eight centuries earlier than either Athens or Constantinople.

From Cavafy's point of view this is a frightfully distressing story, but one he could identify with and, as with each of his other forms of anguish, could transmute into poetry. Was he not, just like the earlier Alexandrians, a pagan who allowed himself to be taken for a Christian and who, at the same time, tended to be tolerant and eclectic by nature rather than militantly narrow in his allegiances? It is characteristic of his fickleness that, although his work at times seems defiantly anti-ascetic, there are several poems in which he envies men of affairs who at the eleventh hour don the monk's habit; similarly that on his deathbed, after being scandalized by the appearance of a priest to administer the last rites, he consented. Like his poetic personae, Cavafy was incapable of being a narrowly heroic devotee of any cause, even the anti-Christian one. What was natural to him, and what therefore interested him poetically,

was compromise, dilemma, self-delusion, indecision, bewilderment: the true, weak, and "human" reactions of the average person caught between antagonistic loyalties. An example is the dilemma of the son in "Ierefs tou Serapiou" ("Priest of the Serapeum," 1926) who laments his father, that "good old man / who always loved me the same." This bereaved son is a convert pledged to honor Christian precepts. He affirms to his new Savior:

> all who deny thee
> I abhor. But now I lament.
> I mourn my father, O Christ,
> even though he was (dreadful to admit)
> a priest at the accursed Serapeum.

The pagan-Christian conflict is a perfect sheathing for Cavafy's obsessive concerns because it lends itself not only to the theme of irreconcilable personal dilemma but also to the related problems of art and homosexuality. The hostility displayed by Christianity's "dun-clad discussers of morals" to Greek poetry (and especially to "excessively daring verses" about "love that is sterile and rejected") we have already seen implied in "Theater of Sidon (A.D. 400)." It is clear that Cavafy identifies pagan Greece with art and homosexuality. These two in their turn are connected to each other not simply because each is related to Greek paganism but also because according to Cavafy's personal aesthetic theory it is homosexuality that constitutes poetry's muse. In "I archi ton" ("Their Beginning," 1915) the two male lovers rise from bed, dress "hurriedly, without a word," and depart "separately, furtively," as though they suspect that something about them betrays "what kind of bed they'd lain in, a little while before."

> But how the artist's life has gained!
> Tomorrow, the next day or years afterward will be
>   written
> the powerful verses that here had their beginning.

The connection is explained in "Ki akoumpisa kai plagiasa stes klines ton" ("And I Leaned and Lay on Their Beds," 1915), one of the erotic poems that Cavafy suppressed. Here he recounts how he avoided the heterosexual hall when visiting a brothel and proceeded to "the secret rooms / considered shameful even to name." But not shameful to him, he continues, because what kind of poet would he be if he took his pleasure "in the commonplace hall"?

Paganism, homosexuality, and art being linked in Cavafy's mind, the pagan-Christian conflict is open to a great variety of treatments. As always, Cavafy is a master at extracting diversity of nuance from similar predicaments. The two poems that follow illustrate this, the first being governed by irony, the second by pathos. The predicament of Myrtias, the protagonist of the first poem, is parallel to that of the young Jewish lad already encountered, though he lives at a later date; and we may conjecture how likely he is to keep his spirit as ascetic as before when he is confronted by "Ta epikindyna" ("Things That Are Dangerous," 1911). Myrtias vows:

> I shall not fear my passions like a coward.
> My body I shall devote to sensual gratification,

especially to "the most daring erotic desires." This he will do "without / the slightest fear,"

> because when I will it
> (and I shall have the power to will it, fortified
> as I'll be with theory and study)
> at the crucial moments I shall rediscover
> my spirit, as before, ascetic.

The second poem, "I arrostia tou Kleitou" ("Kleitos' Illness," 1926), again links the pagan-Christian conflict with homosexuality, but in a subordinated and altogether different way. Bowra says of this poem:

> The pathos of the sick young man is left behind and replaced by a different pathos, more complex and more profound, of his old nurse, whose desire to save him makes her forsake her adopted religion and even so to no avail. The situation

expands and develops and invites a greater variety of response than its opening suggests.

(p. 53)

The opening announces Kleitos' illness:

> Kleitos, an engaging young man
> about twenty-three years old,
> with superior upbringing and a
> rare knowledge of Greek,
> Kleitos is gravely ill.

The cause is a fever that decimated Alexandria, but it is also something else: Kleitos is "vexed because his friend, a young actor, / had ceased to love him or want him." His parents tremble for his life, as does an old servant woman, a pagan who accepted baptism when she "entered service / in this house of conspicuous Christians." Remembering an idol she "worshiped when a child," secretly

> she takes some patties, and wine, and
> honey;
> she sets them before the idol; she chants the
> supplication,
> odds and ends, whatever passages she can
> recall—not realizing
> (the fool) how little the black demon cares
> whether a Christian is cured or not.

From the preceding poems we see that Cavafy is able to evoke the psychological condition of Alexandrians at each stage of the incursion of Christianity upon the city's ancient traditions: first, the easy skepticism of those who could be bishops of Christ and at the same time devotees of Serapis; second, the gentle anguish of people who saw that a decision had to be made and who lived at a time when it still could be made either way; lastly, the bitterness of would-be pagans unlucky enough to be born in the period after 400, when the decision was made for them by the imperial court. Although Cavafy's usual tone is an irony that precludes bitterness, a poem like "Eige etelefta" ("If Dead Indeed," 1920) unmasks his dismay at Alexandria's decline.

The protagonist here is musing on the fate of Apollonius of Tyana, who can be taken as typifying the pagan Greek philosophers. No one seems to know what became of Apollonius, though there are numerous stories. Could he he have been translated to the heavens? And yet there was "his miraculous / supernatural apparition / to a young student at Tyana":

Perhaps it is still too soon for his return,
his second appearance in the world;
or perhaps, transformed, he roams
among us unrecognized. But appear again he
    shall,
just as before, teaching us the right; and then,
    surely,
he shall restore the worship of our gods,
and our seemly Greek rites.

The poem ends with a mention of Emperor Justin; this is Cavafy's method of indicating that the action takes place in the period 518–527, when the battle to preserve Greek religion and culture had been decisively lost and when only a little more than a century remained before the final debacle, the Arab conquest. The musing protagonist is "one of the few pagans, / the very few, who had remained." But otherwise he is an insignificant, cowardly man who outwardly

played the Christian and went to church.
It was the period when Justin the Elder
reigned in extreme piety
and Alexandria, a god-fearing city,
abhorred all wretched idolaters.

This poem with its bitterly ironic conclusion brings to an end Cavafy's historical survey of Alexandria, a survey that has taken us from the glories of the initial Ptolemies in the third century B.C. to the beginnings of Roman intervention in the second century, the extinction of the dynasty with the death of Caesarion near the end of the first, the domination by pagan Rome from 30 B.C. to the reign of Constantine the Great in the fourth century, and finally to the dismal period when, with Christianity the compulsory religion, Alexandria as "the mentor city, the Hellenic world's acme"—this glorious Alexandria—was no more.

It is obvious that Cavafy possessed in the individual events of Alexandrian history a treasury of analogues to his own psychological, economic, and social condition. What needs to be emphasized once again is that each event must be viewed in relation to the city's history as a whole. When Cavafy records a low-water mark in Alexandria's fortunes, we are meant to recall the surging glory of the Ptolemies; conversely, just as his description of Caesarion's splendid investiture tacitly recalls the boy's impending and ignominious death, so in describing any phase of Alexandrian splendor Cavafy tacitly asks us to remember that this great center of empire, with its palaces, its Pharos, its fabulous libraries and wealth, was fated to become an Arab fishing village of four thousand inhabitants.

And not only Alexandria. As suggested earlier, Cavafy's treasury contains an expanding series of equivalent situations, and his larger concern is the fate of Hellenism in general rather than the decline of any particular center of Greek culture. Thus the Alexandrian poems are but one cycle. Others treat the demise of the Seleucid dynasty, the hopeless efforts of the Achaean League to hold off the advancing Roman legions, and the miserable condition of the later Byzantine emperors. Identical themes run through all these poems: Hellenism as a great cultural force, the Greek language as the preferred speech of subject peoples, the often absurd efforts of non-Greeks to ape their cultural betters—in short, pride of race (which must be distinguished from pride of country: in the latter sense Cavafy is the least patriotic of poets). And accompanying all this pride in Greek achievements is the ever-present knowledge, whether tacit or expressed, of eventual frustration and decline.

The pendulum swing between prosperity and adversity expanded temporally as well as spatially, repeating itself, as we have seen, in

Cavafy's lifetime, and not only in his family's business or in the fortunes of the rest of Alexandria's Greek community but also in the Greek world at large. Mainland Greece, though liberated by the Revolution of 1821 from four centuries of Turkish rule, long remained a puppet state controlled by its "protectors," the Great Powers; furthermore, it remained a state whose irredentist dreams were smashed toward the middle of Cavafy's creative period by the disastrous campaign of 1921–1922 in Asia Minor that deprived the Greek people of a territory they had occupied since Homeric times. In looking at the full spectrum of Greek affairs Cavafy naturally concluded that history runs in ever-recurring cycles, always in the same pattern of advance and decline, from which there is no escape. Thus it is hardly surprising that his attitude toward this situation should have been colored not solely by irony, whether bitter or not, but also by resignation: everything is fated to turn out as it does, and we must learn to accept what we cannot control. This seems to be Stoicism pure and simple; but despite the fact that many poems do counsel acceptance of fate, nowhere in Cavafy do we see the central Stoic doctrine that man should be free from passion—from grief or joy. Quite the contrary. It is misleading, in short, to attribute Cavafy's resignation to a conscious espousal of philosophical doctrine. We ought rather to ascribe it to psychological and cultural factors. Resignation was Cavafy's way of coming to terms with his homosexuality; furthermore, it was the predictably Greek response of this Hellene to the "fated" conjunction in him of his sexual orientation, traditional Greek attitudes about the malevolent role of the gods in human affairs, and the recurring pattern of prosperity and liquidation governing Greek commercial and intellectual life in Alexandria and elsewhere. Little wonder, with the wheel of fortune revolving so inexorably, that Cavafy should have been one of the early singers of "Monotonia" ("Monotony," 1898), that particular facet of resignation which pervades modernist literature:

One monotonous day follows another
identically monotonous. The same things
will happen to us again and again,
the same moments come and go.

Here we begin to see Cavafy's artistic problem. Since the fatalism underlying this ennui was for him not a pan-European emotion but rather a traditional Greek attitude bound up with his own Greekness, his first task after his student days was to keep himself from overabsorbing Western European approaches and thus deliquescing into sophisticated but non-individualized cosmopolitanism. Next, once Greece had won out over England and France, he had to avoid hackneyed approaches to the Greek experience—in particular the approach of mythologizing. This meant going against almost everyone: Homer, the foreign romantics he had cultivated in his youth, and even the leading Greek poets of his own time, who, encouraged by both Western example and "nationalistic" fervor, found the old-time gods and heroes as obligatory a subject as Henry Wadsworth Longfellow did the American Indians.

It is nevertheless true that Cavafy left in his canon some early poems with subject matter drawn from the heroic age. Characteristically, his emphasis here as elsewhere is overwhelmingly on the futility of man's hopes in the face of the whimsy or outright malevolence of the gods. In the few poems derived from Homer Cavafy chooses subjects such as the dilemma of Achilles' immortal horses, weeping for the death of Patroclus although by rights they should be above involvement with pathetic human beings, the toys of fate. Whatever period he drew from, he pared away what was irrelevant or stereotyped and extracted what he needed to give outward shape to his own preoccupations. As Bowra states, "With careful skill he would probe a subject until he found in it some final, insoluble conflict, and then he would present this in an individual dramatic crisis."

But these early poems, though expressing preoccupations central to all of Cavafy's work, do not achieve this individual dramatic crisis; derivative and remote, they fail to escape the Pentelic bloodlessness of so much latter-day mythologizing. Cavafy eventually realized that the Olympians can be nothing more than decorative for us, so exclusively have we viewed them as symmetry on pediments in museums or read in urnal poems about their non-kinetic élan (as in John Keats's "Ode on a Grecian Urn," 1820). Fortunately, he abandoned the gods, and by one of those paradoxes that seem to haunt him, he conquered remoteness by turning to subject matter infinitely more remote to most of us than Homer. This subject matter, in turn, lent itself to new methods of presentation and resulted in the irony and the individual dramatic crises that enabled Cavafy to treat the mythological themes of fate and resignation in an original, effective way.

Three poems on these themes illustrate varying approaches and varying degrees of success. First, there is the didacticism of "Teleiomena" ("Finalities," 1910)—like an unadorned Ludwig van Beethoven statement to be submitted elsewhere to numerous variations, some perfunctory, others startling and brilliant:

> With fear and suspicion,
> agitated minds and frightened eyes,
> we desperately plan how
> to shun the certain danger
> that so horribly threatens us.
> Yet we are mistaken; this danger is not on its
>   way.
> The messages were false
> (or else we did not hear them, or failed to
>   understand them well).
> Another disaster, one we never imagined,
> suddenly, torrentially, overwhelms us,
> and unprepared—no time now—we are swept
>   away.

Second, in one of the Homeric poems, "Troes" ("Trojans," 1900), Cavafy employs the worn method of didacticism mixed with evocation by means of simile; after stating a proposition, he illustrates it from the heroic age, reminding us of the parallel between that age and our own.

> In our efforts we're like victims of misfortune;
> in our efforts we're like the Trojans.

This explicitness he eventually forsook; nevertheless, the poem shows the mature Cavafian touch in expanding the Trojans' predicament until it becomes the universal condition of mankind. "We succeed a bit," have "high hopes,"

> But something always comes out and stops us.
> Achilles, before us in the trench,
> comes out and intimidates us with great shouting.

In the third and last poem, "Perimenontas tous varvarous" ("Waiting for the Barbarians," 1898), the equation between history and our own time remains unstated; simile gives way to metaphor. The same theme of fate—the discrepancy between our hopes and brutal reality—is here treated not from a positive and tragic point of view ("something always comes out and stops us"), but from a negative one that lends itself to irony and even comedy: our hopes will never be realized, there is no solution, no answer; we latter-day Alexandrians of the twentieth century, not being of a heroic age, cannot even redeem ourselves with splendid deaths as the Trojans did, but must simply go on living as before, weary and disillusioned, seeking solutions that either do not exist or, if they do exist, do not come. The sentiment of resignation—the response of the older Greeks to the irresponsible caprice of the gods—is presented in a new way that makes it, instead of decorative and remote, evocative, near, and unrelentingly honest. Cavafy saw long before the creator of Godot that we must go on waiting; no solution will be provided or indeed is possible; the barbarians, even if they did come, would be but a new species of Alexandrian:

> What are we waiting for, gathered in the
>   marketplace?

The barbarians are to arrive today.

. . . .

Why should this uneasiness commence all at
    once,
this confusion? (How grave the faces have
    become.)
Why are the streets and squares rapidly emptying
and everyone returning home most thoughtfully?

    Because it is nighttime and the barbarians
      did not come.
    And several men arrived from the frontier;
    they said there are no barbarians any longer.

And now what will become of us without
    barbarians?
Those people were some sort of a solution.

Like all of Cavafy's most successful poems,
"Waiting for the Barbarians" presents an individual dramatic crisis with immediacy, accom-
plishing this not only because the author and
his didactic explanations have been refined
out of existence but also because of such
factors as the careful details of scene and
costume that make the poem visually evocative, and, above all, because of the author's
psychological insight into his characters. We
see in them what we know too well in ourselves: the propensity of people to believe that
a cataclysm can be therapeutic and consequently their readiness to throw themselves, as
Bowra puts it, "into causes which are, on a
wider view, entirely inimical to their interests."
But Cavafy's psychological insight into others
derives, as we might suspect, from his insight
into his own problems; in his personal life he
knew full well the fatal attraction of an inimical "cause." Thus the poem's political situation is a dramatic projection of Cavafy's personal situation, and the governing attitude of
resignation is none other than the attitude that
enabled Cavafy finally to make peace with his
homosexuality.

The qualification "finally" is important, for
Cavafy's acceptance came only after a struggle.
It is characteristic that the nature of the opposing forces in this personal struggle should
be seen in a comment by Kimon Friar on the

political significance of "Waiting for the Barbarians." The poem, writes Friar, "is deeply
moving to those who understand the secret
temptation in the hearts of free men to cast off
their responsibilities and yield themselves to
directing power." Cavafy's personal struggle
was the same: moral responsibility versus the
temptation of abandonment to the directing
power of fate. We are reminded that any division of the poet's work into personal-imper-
sonal or didactic-historical-erotic is false: each
of the modes implicitly includes the others.

The progression toward fatalistic abandonment is evident both in the openly erotic poems
and in the veiled "political" and "didactic"
ones that seemingly have nothing to do with
Cavafy's personal problems. Among early examples of the second category is "Che fece . . .
il gran rifiuto" (1899),[2] which extols moral decision, or at least regards it as a possibility.
Next comes an intermediary stage in which
Cavafy praises those who, trapped by circumstance, still dutifully and freely (and thus with
dignity) choose to do what necessity requires.
Finally, there is the complete (yet ironically
viewed) fatalism of a poem like "As fronti-
zan" ("They Should Have Taken Care," 1930),
in which the protagonist blames the gods for
his own deficiencies in moral fiber. "I've been
reduced practically to vagrancy," he complains. The "fatal city" of Antioch has devoured
his funds, but he is still "young and in perfect
health," with an "admirable mastery of Greek,"
not to mention inside information on both military and civil affairs. Thus he considers himself "qualified in the fullest" to serve his "beloved homeland Syria." His intention is to be
useful in whatever position he is placed. But if
he is thwarted by those in power, he'll not be
the one to blame:

I'll apply first to Zabinas,
and if that moron does not appreciate me

---

[2]This poem retains its Italian title in English translation. The Italian is from Dante Alighieri's *Inferno* 3.60 and
means "who mock . . . the great refusal." Cavafy deliberately omits "per viltà" (from cowardice).

I'll go to his rival, Grypus.
And if that blockhead, if he too does not engage
    me
I go straight to Hyrcanus.

One of the three, at any rate, will want me.

And my conscience is clear
regarding the indifference of my choice.
All three harm Syria equally.

But, ruined man that I am, how can I be
    blamed?
Poor me, I'm just trying to make ends meet.
The almighty gods should have taken care
to create a fourth who was good.
To him, gladly, I would have gone.

The same gradual development toward fatalistic abandonment occurs in the openly sexual poems. In 1905 in "He Resolves" Cavafy could still write, "Every so often he resolves to begin a better life," though even here the poet admits that such resolutions are in vain. Henceforth they cease entirely, giving way to an increasing defiance of the bourgeois demand for moral responsibility and an increasingly frank avowal of the poet's outlawed tendencies. If we look for the reason, we find over and over again the sentiment of resignation, a yielding to the "directing power" of fate. Homosexuals are destined to be as they are. In "Meres tou 1896" ("Days of 1896," 1925), for example, the protagonist's erotic bent, one "condemned and strictly forbidden," is "innate for all that"; in "Iasi tafos" ("Tomb of Iasis," 1917) personal beauty constitutes a mixed blessing and curse that dooms one to dissipations that are fatal in more than one sense of the word:

> since everyone considered me so much a
>   Hermes and Narcissus,
> abuses corrupted and destroyed me.

Cavafy came to terms with his sexuality through the attitude of resignation. Having done this, he began to broadcast his sexuality more openly and defiantly—possibly abetted by various contributory factors such as the system of publication by broadsheet, the general relaxation of moral censure after World War I, and his retirement in 1922 from the Ministry of Irrigation. Perhaps we have here simply the exhibitionism of an aging reprobate (most of the poems Cavafy admitted into his canon were written after his fiftieth year). In any case, at some point he began to turn his back on the bourgeois world of his ancestors and decided to give himself over, poetically now as well as physically, to the way of life so out of keeping with his dignified pedigree. The abandonment of "Genealogy" in 1911 may help us to date the beginning of this change; it is perhaps no coincidence that he eventually grouped all the early verses together under the heading "Before 1911" while assigning each of the later poems to a definite year, thereby establishing 1911—when he was forty-eight years old—as the beginning of his maturity.

But from a literary point of view the most interesting and important reason for Cavafy's increasing frankness was an aesthetic one: the poet's conviction that debauchery formed the source of his art. We have already seen this conviction in "And I Leaned and Lay on Their Beds" and "Their Beginning." Another poem, "Noisis" ("Understanding," 1915), attempts a retrospective analysis of Cavafy's failure to control his fleshly desires. During the years of his youth he did not understand why his "repentances were never constant." But now he sees the meaning of those years:

> In the debauchery of my youth
> my poetry's intent took form,
> my art's domain was planned.

The question is whether Cavafy's debauchery was unconsciously cultivated for the sake of poetry, as this poem retrospectively argues, or whether, as in "Idoni" ("To Sensual Pleasure," 1913), his poetry was cultivated to preserve the memory of past debauchery: "My life's delight and chrism: memory of the hours / I found and held sensuality as I wished it." Whatever the case, the fact remains that Cavafy's life grew more and more a "recherche du temps perdu" as he aged. Memory became as exciting as the remembered occasion. Action and contemplation coalesced; to remember was to act, and to fix the remembered incident in poetry was to forestall the incident's corruption:

> Try to keep them, poet,
> no matter how few can be retained:
> the visions of your love-life.
> Insert them half-hidden in your phrases.
> Try to hold them, poet,
> when they are roused in your mind
> at night, or in noontime brightness.

The final aspect of Cavafy's artistic problem now becomes evident. He had first to maintain his Greekness and avoid aping Western European modes. He then had to guard against a hackneyed mythological approach to the Greek experience. Finally, he had to discover how to indulge the memory of his own anguished homosexual assignations and yet avoid repulsive sentimentality. It is all somewhat the same problem, for he was able to treat his deviation without sentimentality by eschewing the worn-out language, imagery, and tone of nineteenth-century romanticism and by cultivating instead the dramatic, ironical evocation of Hellenistic history, which in turn enabled him to express so much more than his homosexuality. The secret to the actual mechanics of this non-sentimental indulgence seems to be revealed in the fourth line of "Otan diegeirontai" ("When They Are Roused," 1913), the poem just quoted, "Insert them half-hidden in your phrases:" in other words, *semi*-confession achieved first by objectifying the visions of his loving—placing them in dramatic contexts in which they are attributed to other personages real or imagined, contemporary or historical—and second by maintaining a balance between caution and reckless abandonment.

This second consideration is of great interest, for just as Cavafy moved from the necessity for moral decision to the resigned acceptance of his sexuality as fated, so the poetry moves from extreme caution to extreme openness and self-indulgence. Here we have a yardstick for judgment: does Cavafy achieve his goal of "half-hidden" confession, or does he err through either an excess or a deficiency of frankness?

In the early poems he tended to suppress any direct revelation of the nature of his personal anguish; he veiled his trouble by using neutral symbols such as "Teichi" ("Walls," 1896):

> Without pity, without shame, without
>   consideration
> they have built all about me great high walls.
>
> And now here I sit in desperation.
> I think of nothing else: this fate galls
>
> my mind, for I had so many things to do
>   outside.
> Oh, when the walls were built, how did I not
>   take note?
>
> But no sign or sound of builders by me was
>   descried.
> Imperceptibly, they excluded me from the
>   world without.

On the other hand, in many of the later poems in which he returns to the lyrical, nondramatic expression of "Walls," his use of the first person, originally an inhibitor leading him to excessive caution, now has the reverse effect. Even though some of these poems are outwardly narrative in form or vaguely dramatic in conception, they are energized by self-indulgence, so that the incident recorded is laden with an emotion out of proportion to the event. "Na meinei" ("To Remain," 1918) is an example. The narrator and his lover are hidden behind the wooden partition of a deserted tavern at half past one in the morning. No one would have seen them, but in any case they had grown so excited that they "gave little thought to precautions":

> Our clothes came half-unbuttoned—they were
>   few,
> since a gorgeous month of July was ablaze.
> Fleshly enjoyment between

half-unbuttoned clothes;
flesh's swift denuding, of which the image
has come across twenty-six years
to remain now in this poem.

Although some of these first-person erotic poems lack the perspective needed to save them from sentimentality, most show remarkable control; it would be misleading to dwell on Cavafy's lapses into excessive emotion. Given the basically subjective nature of his poetic concerns, the remarkable thing is that he so frequently did achieve a delicate equilibrium between fear and recklessness, control and abandon, while also avoiding the extremes of bitter aloofness on the one side and sentimental indulgence on the other. As Durrell has Balthazar say in *Justine* (1957), the old poet's "exquisite balance of irony and tenderness would have put him among the saints had he been a religious man." That his control lapses as infrequently as it does is testimony to the fact that he was his own best critic. Not only did he consciously realize that his natural pitfall would be "to [overdo] the effect and [strain] the sentiment, both fatal accidents in art," as he says in a letter; he also had the integrity to suppress those poems he considered unworthy. The extent of this suppression may indicate a pathological fear of disapproval; but whatever the motives, the astonishing fact remains that in 1910 at the age of forty-seven he allowed his private audience to see only twenty-one of the approximately 220 poems he had written up to then. Even after he had developed his mature style and was completing up to seventy poems a year, he sanctioned sometimes as few as four or five, putting away or destroying the rest.

All this attests to Cavafy's extraordinary craftsmanship. It is true that he exercised freedom in versification and diction, cultivated speech rhythms, and favored economy, flatness, and anticlimax in defiance of the expansive rhetorical style then in vogue in Greece. But everything was deliberate, every "non-poetic" or "anti-poetic" element being introduced for a specific poetic effect. There is evidence not just internally in the poems themselves but also externally in Cavafy's letters and self-commentaries that he counted syllables, was proud of his ingenuity in rhyming, took great care with punctuation because he considered it vital to a poem's meaning, and used specific vowels to produce specific effects. Rewriting constantly, he always strove for the exact cadence, the *mot juste.*

Regarding the latter, a whole literature of controversy has grown up. Why did Cavafy employ such odd diction? his critics ask. Why such an inconsistent hodgepodge of purist Greek and offhand colloquialism? Why, for instance, do we find the demotic (i.e. spoken, colloquial, "improper") *adérfia* instead of *adélfia* (brothers) in the first stanza of "Alexandrian Kings," while in the second stanza the "proper" form of the accusative, *vasiléa* (king), is used instead of the demotic *vasiliá*? Or why in one place does Cavafy prefer the modern grammar of *mes stes phráseis sou* (in your phrases), employing the accusative after "in," whereas elsewhere for the same pattern he prefers the ancient Greek dative: *en glóssi ellinikí* (in the Greek language), and this only three lines from an "incorrect" spelling of the verb "to go"?

Further examples are given by Rae Dalven in the notes to her volume of translations. She shows how Cavafy's "first consideration was not whether an expression or construction was purist or demotic, but whether it served his poetic purpose." Cavafy himself once summed the matter up when he remarked: "Of course we should write in the demotic. But . . . the artisan of words [he is playing on the root sense of the Greek term for "man of letters"] has the duty to combine what is beautiful with what is alive." His eclectic mentality prevented him from being a doctrinaire partisan of either the demotic or the purist cause; he saw the Greek language, from ancient to modern times, as one diverse but unified entity full of riches for the poet, and he refused to accept the arbitrary exaltation of one period or style as an inflexible standard.

To this might be added some further considerations. It seems, in the first place, that Cavafy merely wrote as he spoke, in the motley argot of one who indulged in palimpsests by day and pederasts by night. Beyond this, additional purisms and archaisms (so hopelessly lost in translation) were introduced to give flavor and authenticity to the historical poems. The private joy of a poet-scholar following in the tradition of the Mouseion, these archaisms often serve the added purpose of conveying meaning through allusion. For example, the dun-clad discussers of morals in "Theater of Sidon (A.D. 400)" are obviously meant to be Christians. This is never stated directly, but the archaic expression translated as "dun-clad" was a regular epithet for Christians in the Byzantine chronicles Cavafy knew so well. Rather an obscure allusion, it is true, but in the poet's defense it must be noted that he did not introduce such expressions indiscriminately. He rigorously excluded anachronisms from his poems, and he always valued intelligibility over donnish erudition. Édouard Roditi notes that when Cavafy wished to employ a word that might fail to be understood, he would "engage in apparently idle conversations with a number of friends or strangers. In the course of these talks, he would skillfully find occasion to use the doubtful word: if it was always properly understood, Cavafy then knew that he could use it in his poem."

The precision evident here is perhaps the chief overall characteristic of the poems themselves. Cavafy deliberately strove for originality, for an unquestionably individualistic style. Turning his back on worn-out modes, he chose as models for what he needed the ancient Alexandrian epigrammists and writers of mime. In them he found frugality, terseness, realism, dramatic objectivity, and scholarly exactitude in the realm of technique, while in the realm of theme he found disillusion, weary paganism, and obsession with thwarted hopes and wilting senses. The extraordinary things are that in turning to the past for both the method and content of his poems he avoided a sterile antiquarianism, and that in cultivating the paradox implicit in the situations he treats he kept himself from the triviality of valuing paradox for its own sake. To call him either antiquated or trivial would be completely to misunderstand his work. On the contrary, he always strikes through to fundamentals of the human situation, doing so in a manner that is consistently and importantly modern.

Nikos Kazantzakis wrote of him that he should have been "a fifteenth-century Florentine, a cardinal, secret adviser to the Pope, negotiating the most diabolic, intricate and scandalous affairs." The truth of this serves only to indicate Cavafy's modernity all the more, for like so many twentieth-century poets he was a spiritual anachronism: out of place in his own age and seeking—with the frustration and failure inevitable in such a search—for a tradition that like the great sea would both buoy him up and nourish him. Although there is scarcely a hint of the metaphysical or theological in his work, the very absence of such considerations is a factor in the Cavafian predicament. It may be surprising to know that Cavafy repeatedly lamented his inability to accept Christianity; he especially regretted that he could not believe in an afterlife. Out of this inability, of course, came his fear of death; and out of his overall rejection of the supernatural came his attempt to salvage some meaning for a humanity whose existence now seemed meaningless.

The meaning he found was, paradoxically, the meaningless revolutions of the wheel of fortune. Experience that is incomplete, conflicts that remain unresolved, plans and achievements that go awry, love that bears no fruit—these, whether in history or in one's own intimate past, must now be considered meaningful in themselves. There is no longer a goal by which life is to be justified: life must be its own justification. Yes, we continue to aspire and plan, but when, like Antony, we are abandoned by the gods, we must realize that the sheer pleasure and intensity of living is the only good.

Changing the metaphor, Cavafy tells us in the final stanza of "Ithaki" ("Ithaca," 1910) that the journey, not the destination, is what constitutes our reward. True, arrival in Ithaca is your "destined end":

> But do not hasten the journey in the least.
> Better it continue many years
> and you anchor at the isle an old man,
> rich with all you gained along the way,
> not expecting Ithaca to grant you riches.
>
> Ithaca granted you the lovely voyage.
> Without her you would never have departed on
>   your way.
> She has nothing else to grant you any more.
>
> And though you find her squalid, Ithaca did not
>   cheat you.
> So wise have you become, so experienced,
> you already will have realized what they mean:
>   these Ithacas.

Acceptance of the process itself in contradistinction to the goal (for we now have many Ithacas, not one) is what constituted Cavafy's own freedom and enabled him to be animated and yea-saying where another in his circumstances might have shriveled like Shakespeare's Jaques into despondency.

But for all its vitality, this outlook is still basically tragic. Although affirmative in spirit, it is at the same time rigorously pessimistic, for it denies as illusory all the comforts invented by humankind: eternity, order, decorum, absolute good, morality, justice. If to declare "Yes" to necessity is our only salvation, we are indeed pitiable creatures; yet we achieve a modicum of dignity by contemplating our predicament honestly and accepting it with fortitude.

That is precisely what Cavafy did, and this psychological as well as historical honesty— this refusal to ignore, veil, or romanticize—is a further aspect of his modernity. Unable to look upward to heaven for his answers, he looked backward into history and inward into his own psyche. What he found in both places was awful: cowardice, disillusion, sordidness, contradiction, paradox. This he exposed bravely in his poetry and in so doing stripped naked his own being—that superlatively paradoxical being of a priapic monk whose slight angle to the universe may be shared by more people than we would like to admit.

Selected Bibliography

EDITIONS

Poiimata. Alexandria, 1935.
Kavafika aftoscholia. Edited by G. Lechonitis. Alexandria, 1942; repr., Athens, 1977.
"I genealogia tou Kavafi." *Nea Estia* 43:622–629 (1948).
Poiimata. Athens, 1952.
Anekdota peza kimena. Edited by M. Peridis. Athens, 1963.
Peza. Edited by G. Paputsakis. Athens, 1963.
Poiimata, A (1896–1918), Poiimata, B (1919–1933). Edited by G. Savidis. Athens, 1963.
Anekdota poiimata 1882–1923. Edited by G. Savidis. Athens, 1968.
"The Unpublished Drafts of Five Poems on Julian the Apostate by C. P. Cavafy." Edited by R. Lavagnini. *Byzantine and Modern Greek Studies* 7:55–88 (1981).

TRANSLATIONS

Collected Poems. Translated by Edmund Keeley and Philip Sherrard. Edited by George Savidis. Princeton, 1975.
The Complete Poems of Cavafy. Translated by Rae Dalven. New York, 1976.
"The Early C. P. Cavafy." Translated by John Cavafy. *St. Andrews Review* (Fall–Winter 1974).
Passions and Ancient Days. Translated by Edmund Keeley and George Savidis. New York, 1971.
The Poems of C. P. Cavafy. Translated by John Mavrogordato. London, 1951.
Selected Poems. Translated by Edmund Keeley and Philip Sherrard. Princeton, 1972.

BIOGRAPHICAL AND CRITICAL STUDIES

Alexiou, M. "Eroticism and Poetry." *Journal of the Hellenic Diaspora* 10:45–65 (1983).
Beaton, R. "C. P. Cavafy: Irony and Hellenism." *Slavonic and East European Studies* 59:516–528 (1981).

————. "The History Man." *Journal of the Hellenic Diaspora* 10:23–44 (Spring–Summer 1983).

Bien, P. "Cavafy's Three-Phase Development into Detachment." *Journal of the Hellenic Diaspora* 10:117–136 (Spring–Summer 1983).

Bowersock, G. M. "The Julian Poems of C. P. Cavafy." *Byzantine and Modern Greek Studies* 7:89–104 (1981).

Bowra, C. M. "Constantine Cavafy and the Greek Past." In *The Creative Experiment*. London, 1949.

Caires, V. "Originality and Eroticism: Constantine Cavafy and the Alexandrian Epigram." *Byzantine and Modern Greek Studies* 6:131–156 (1980).

Capri-Karka, C. *Love and the Symbolic Journey in the Poetry of Cavafy, Eliot, and Seferis*. New York, 1982.

Chartis nos. 5/6 (April 1983). Special issues dedicated to Cavafy.

Dallas, Y. *Kavafis kai istoria*. Athens, 1974.

Epitheorisi Technis 18:547–742 (December 1963). Special issue dedicated to Cavafy.

Forster, E. M. *Alexandria, a History and a Guide*. Alexandria, Egypt, 1922.

————. "The Poetry of C. P. Cavafy." In *Pharos and Pharillon*. Richmond, England, 1923.

————. "The Complete Poems of C. P. Cavafy." In *Two Cheers for Democracy*. London and New York, 1951.

Friar, Kimon. "One of the Great." *New Republic*, 26 January 1953.

Golffing, F. "The Alexandrian Mind: Notes Toward a Definition." *Partisan Review* 22:73–82 (Winter 1955).

Grand Street nos. 2/3 (Spring 1983). Special issue dedicated to Cavafy.

Haas, Diana. "Cavafy's Reading Notes on Gibbon's *Decline and Fall*." *Folia Neohellenica* 4:25–96 (1982).

I Lexi no. 23 (March–April 1983). Special issue dedicated to Cavafy.

Journal of the Hellenistic Diaspora 10 (Spring–Summer 1983). Special issue dedicated to Cavafy.

Kazantzakis, Nikos. "Cavafy." In *Journeying*. Boston, 1975.

Keeley, Edmund. *Cavafy's Alexandria: Study of a Myth in Progress*. Cambridge, Mass., 1976.

————. "Cavafy's Voice and Context." *Grand Street* nos. 2/3:157–77 (Spring 1983).

Kitroeff, Alexander. "The Alexandria We Have Lost." *Journal of the Hellenistic Diaspora* 10:11–21 (Spring–Summer 1983).

Lagoudis, P. *Alexandria Still: Forster, Durrell and Cavafy*. Princeton, N.J., 1977.

Liddell, R. *Cavafy: A Critical Biography*. London, 1974.

Malanos, T. *O poiitis K. P. Kavafis*. Athens, 1957.

The Mind and Art of C. P. Cavafy: Essays on His Life and Work. Athens, 1983.

Nea Estia 14 (15 July 1933). Special issue dedicated to Cavafy.

Nea Estia 74 (1 November 1963). Special issue dedicated to Cavafy.

Panayotopoulos, I. M. "K. P. Kavafis." In *Ta prosopa ke ta kimena*, vol. 4. Athens, 1982.

Papanoutsos, E. P. *Palamas, Kavafis, Sikelianos: Tria meletimata*. Athens, 1949.

Peri, M. "Kritiki episkopisi ton kavafikon metafraseon." *Mandatoforos* no. 18:5–34 (November 1981) and no. 19:4–37 (April 1982).

Peridis, M. *O vios kai to ergo tou Konst. Kavafi*. Athens, 1948.

Roditi, E. "Cavafis and the Permanence of Greek History." *Poetry* 81:389–392 (1953).

Sareyannis, I. A. *Scholia ston Kavafi*. Edited by Z. Lorenzatos. Athens, 1964.

Savadis, G. P. "To arheio K. P. Kavafi." *Nea Estia* 74:1539–1547 (1963).

————. *I kavafikes ekdoseis (1891–1932)*. Athens, 1966.

———— et al. *Kyklos Kavafi*. Athens, 1983.

Seferis, G. "Cavafi and Eliot: A Comparison." In *On the Greek Style: Selected Essays on Poetry and Hellenism*. Boston, 1966.

Sherrard, P. "Constantine Cavafis." In *The Marble Threshing Floor*. London, 1956.

Spender, Stephen. "Cavafy: The Historic and the Erotic." *New York Review of Books*, 15 June 1972.

Tsirkas, Stratis. *O Kavafis kai i epochi tou*. Athens, 1958.

————. *O politikos Kavafis*. Athens, 1971.

Valieri, Hariklea. "O theios mou o Kostas." *Tachidromos*, 27 April 1963.

Vayenas, N. "The Language of Irony: Towards a Definition of the Poetry of Cavafy." *Byzantine and Modern Greek Studies* 5:43–56 (1979).

Yourcenar, Marguerite, and Constantin Dimaras. *Présentation critique de Constantin Cavafy*. Paris, 1958.

PETER BIEN

FRANK WEDEKIND
(1864–1918)

THE HISTORY OF German drama is unthinkable without the name of Frank Wedekind, yet there have been few critics willing to rank him among the greatest of modern dramatists. Rarely—and often poorly—translated, he remains virtually unknown outside Germany, but even there his reputation has fluctuated widely. This is not simply because the overall quality of his work is irregular; it is rather because the nature of that work has always raised more questions than it has answered: questions about its structural and formal eccentricities, about its ambivalent meanings, about the relationship of the playwright to his audience, about the appropriate way to present his works onstage. To be sure, Wedekind's contributions to sexual enlightenment and the development of a modern sense of morality have long been acknowledged, as has his remarkable influence on subsequent playwrights; but fundamental questions still remain concerning his method, his intentions, and above all about his place in the history of drama and the theater.

For Bertolt Brecht, Wedekind's importance did not lie so much in his dramatic or theatrical achievements as in his contribution to a new moral attitude. Wedekind, he wrote, was "one of the great educators of the new Europe" whose "greatest work was his personality." He had taught a whole generation to regard the social and moral world from a perspective other than that of the preceding century. Wede-

kind accomplished this through a great variety of works: essays, polemics, short stories, lyric poetry, and pantomimes as well as through contributions to the satiric magazine *Simplicissimus,* or as the star attraction of Die Elf Scharfrichter (The Eleven Executioners), a satiric cabaret at the turn of the century.

Brecht's reference to Wedekind's personality as his "greatest work" came undoubtedly from thinking of the image the man created for himself as "the terror of the bourgeoisie" (*Bürgerschreck*). As "the martyr of his profession" appearing in his own plays, he tried also to discredit literary and theatrical censorship. Never a great actor, Wedekind had an original style that helped to break the stranglehold of naturalism on the German stage and led to the so-called epic approach espoused notably by Brecht.

Wedekind's public persona generated a legend in which the man and the playwright both tend to disappear behind sensational images. For this Wedekind himself is at least partly responsible, and during his lifetime he compounded the confusion by frequently appearing in key roles of his own work, thereby encouraging an identification between art and life that, in his own mind at least, was intended only as a means to an end. But it is important to realize that Wedekind only meant to point to something general or abstract outside of himself. His dramaturgic procedures are likewise indirect and ambivalent: the tone of any particular work is intermittently parodic, grotesque, or tragicomic. Conventions are used only to be destroyed. Even Wedekind's vaunted *Humor* (the German term transcends the English meaning), arising from the contrast of extreme attitudes, serves to depersonalize any self-reference.

JUVENILIA

Benjamin Franklin Wedekind was born on 24 July 1864 in Hanover, the second of six children. His father, Friedrich Wilhelm Wedekind, a gynecologist, and mother, born Emilie Kammerer, a sometime actress and singer, twenty-four years younger than her husband, had recently returned to Germany after a long period of residence in San Francisco. Dr. Wedekind had settled there after years of restless wandering throughout Europe and the Middle East and acquired a small fortune in real estate during the heady years of the Gold Rush; Emilie had moved to that city after concertizing up and down the coast of South America. Although the birth announcement in St. Aegidius' church says that "the child is expected to return with his parents to California unbaptized," Friedrich Wilhelm had determined that all his children should have a German upbringing. The father named the child born in America, Armin, after a Germanic hero, Hermann the Cheruscan, and the first child born in Germany after an American champion of freedom and individual enterprise. This boy was called "Franklin" throughout the first two decades of his life.

Very concerned that his sons should not become cannon fodder for the Prussian army, Dr. Wedekind took pains to establish their American citizenship. Franklin was represented as the offspring of naturalized parents and registered in school as "from San Francisco." But the German—and later the Swiss—authorities did not accept this declaration, so that the question of Wedekind's true nationality caused him considerable trouble throughout his life; it has never been settled decisively. To say that Wedekind had "an American heritage," as some scholars maintain, is stretching the truth, for even though Wedekind makes frequent reference to America and its peculiar ways, this part of his background provided him with no more than a stock of slogans, names, and ideas. He simply used the country as a locale, much as Brecht later focused on Chicago. It was not a personal experience he reworked into art, merely another element for allegorical constructions.

Franklin began school in Hanover, and by the time he was eight the family had been augmented by the births of Wilhelm Lincoln in 1866, Frieda Marianne Erika in 1868, and Donald Lenzelin in 1871. The following year Dr. Wedekind abruptly moved the growing clan to Switzerland. While on a business trip, on the spur of the moment and without consulting his wife, he purchased Lenzburg Castle in Aargau, one of Switzerland's most venerable monuments. A second girl, Emilie, named after her mother, was born there in 1876. Thus the children all grew up as quasi-Swiss in a medieval romantic setting, which remained their home until Friedrich Wilhelm's unexpected death in 1888.

Lenzburg left ambivalent marks on Wedekind's mind and emotions. On the one hand, a "long and happy childhood" there helped form his idea of happiness—"the golden sunny joy of youth, innocent pleasure, laughing play and sweetly serious dreams." On the other hand, adolescence brought the knowledge that even paradise is not invulnerable to evil: the same place that had brought him such joy also caused him much disillusionment and pain. The chief cause was the deterioration of his parents' marriage, probably inevitable given the diversity in their ages, interests, and outlooks. They decided to go their separate ways, each dealing with the children on his or her own terms. The father withdrew to his own quarters in the castle, becoming a remote paterfamilias and indifferent lord of the manor whose power lay only over the purse strings.

For Franklin, the collapse of his parents' marriage signified the failure of love and the irreversible decline of sexual potency; he began to wonder whether sex and love were compatible with each other and whether the institution of marriage could accommodate either. As his garden of delights turned into a rank bed of weeds, he even began to reflect on his own possible responsibility for the loss of this Eden.

School became another cause of suffering. The freedom the children enjoyed at the castle clashed harshly with the discipline imposed in the classroom. A desultory pupil, though adequately trained at the local schools and given a first-rate education at the Realschule (high school) in nearby Aarau, Wedekind grew occasionally rebellious as well. His school poems and essays—like *Frühlingserwachen* (*Spring's Awakening*, 1891) a few years later—show no charity toward either Aarau, "a stereotype edition of a small provincial town," or its renowned educational institution; for him they were the epitome of bourgeois philistinism and the embodiment of everything he despised in the narrow-minded bourgeoisie around him. Wedekind's image of German *Spiessbürgertum* (Babbitry) was molded at the outset by what he had first encountered in Switzerland.

School moreover interfered with his writing. Franklin's earliest known poem dates from 1875, but by 1877, in the revealing "De scriptore" (Concerning the Writer), he had already begun to think of the difficulties of pursuing his favorite occupation and to plan how to cope with them. As he saw it, the poet is a man of uniquely unconventional experience whose work the philistine always misunderstands and attributes to mere laziness. In this conflict with authority, the only recourse is to invent figures in one's imagination (*im Geiste*) that are more sympathetic to one's endeavor.

Writers whose juvenilia have literary merit are rare and Franklin is not a notable exception. He tried his hand at all the conventional literary genres, lyric poetry predominating. The themes are mainly erotic, reflecting his preoccupation with sex, or rather with the lack of it, and with imagining the results if he were lucky enough to experience it. The tone ranges from ecstatic to despairing, their mode conventional to grotesque, with a preference for the parodic: convention juxtaposed with a light obscenity. The poems have no single literary model, unless it be Heinrich Heine, but Horace, Ovid, Christoph Martin Wieland, and Johann Wolfgang von Goethe are among the prominent influences.

One piece of juvenilia alone is uniquely Wedekindian: the fragment called "Felix und Galathea" (written in 1881, published in 1908), intended originally to provide Franklin's schoolmates with something they could perform at one of their end-of-semester celebrations. A mock idyll in mixed verse forms, it deals wittily with two prime sexual anxieties of the male adolescent. One is the fear of not being able to control one's sexual urges. The inexperienced and clumsy shepherd lad, Felix, tries to make contact with the not-so-innocent and not unwilling shepherd lass, Galathea, but fails ignominiously when neither of the youngsters can deal with pent-up emotion. The second part of the story reveals the opposite fear: that sexual union might force one into an "ideal" marriage. Here Felix and Galathea are depicted as living in wondrous bliss awaiting the fulfillment of their love through the birth of a child. Franklin's parody of the bourgeois romance is clever though heavy-handed. It shows precociousness, not only in daring to broach such a subject but also in devising an amusing and irreproachable way to express it. The work also contains a hilarious satire of philistine adult male behavior: a chorus of impotent old men warn the "innocent" Galathea of Felix's vicious intentions, all the while smacking their lips in voyeuristic anticipation of what they hope will come to pass.

TAKING ISSUE WITH NATURALISM

After graduating from Aarau almost a year behind schedule in 1884, Franklin spent a semester in Lausanne studying painting and French before joining his brother Armin at the University of Munich. His ostensible purpose was to study law according to his father's wishes; actually, he spent most of his time savoring the city's cultural and literary attractions, trying out its ways of life both high and low, making his first serious attempts at becoming a writer. The opera impressed him more than the theater, and he rejected the prevailing literary avant-garde (the so-called Munich naturalist school) as a misguided attempt to capture reality. After meeting Michael Georg Conrad, the leading light of "this sterile poets-of-depravity" movement, he wrote: "As we know, nature herself is not always beautiful—the Lord help us!—not even always a source of enjoyment, and when one quashes every spark of intellect in her and then tears off every shred of the poor creature's clothing, a lot of things are bound to come to view that won't be very edifying for our convalescing human hearts."

Franklin's two years in Munich were not very productive. The only notable fruit of the period is *Der Schnellmaler, oder Kunst und Mammon* (The Sketch Artist, or Art and Mammon, written in 1886, published in 1889), subtitled pretentiously "a great tragicomic original farce in three acts." The plot revolves around a young painter, Fridolin Wald (F.W.), who is looking for success and social recognition so that he can marry Johanna, the daughter of a wealthy factory owner, Pankratius Knapp. But his work has not helped him to this goal and he has been forced to earn his living making quick sketches to entertain society. His would-be father-in-law despises him for it, and Wald's conscience will not permit him to elope with the girl without being able to support her. He sinks into despair when a rival appears for Johanna's hand, the chemist Dr. Steiner, inventor of "potato sugar," who has already gained Knapp's admiration for his business acumen and enterprising spirit. Fridolin's friends believe he has only two choices: to join the business world and win over Knapp,

or admit defeat and join the pessimists who already know that this world holds no values worth fighting for.

The play is typical of Wedekind's early work. It presents a crisis in which the protagonist must choose between two courses of action. It is also typical that he makes this choice in accordance with his nature or disposition rather than as the result of argument or circumstances. And so Fridolin, a *Weltschmerzler* already haunted by visions of death (and a parody of the Byronic hero), opts for suicide. He is saved at the last minute in spite of himself, and the play comes to a happy end, not accidentally, though literally by a series of accidents: the poison Fridolin thinks will kill him turns out to be sugar water; Dr. Steiner is exposed as a con man; and the director of the Royal Art Collection, Baron von Bernolt, turns out to be eager to purchase the young painter's "Prometheus Unbound." Significantly, it is an aristocrat, not a bourgeois, who finds a way to reconcile art and mammon.

The baron closes the play by saying: "It's gradually dawning on me that my role in this affair is that of a quite ordinary deus ex machina. But I must plead with you to take it seriously; after all, we're not standing on the stage here." With this, Wedekind wants it understood that his comedy was meant to be a piece without literary pretensions, a latter-day child of the Viennese folk theater, its conventions exaggerated and revitalized. Wedekind may also be said to have exorcised his tendency toward pessimism by mocking his protagonist–alter ego, thereby making fun of the naturalist attempt to depict "real life" onstage. But violating current dramatic expectations did not recommend the work to theater managers, and it is no wonder that *Der Schnellmaler* did not, as he fondly hoped, "pave the way" for his debut as playwright on the Munich stage.

Dr. Wedekind eventually got wind of Franklin's goings-on in Munich and a long-standing dispute over his professional future came to a head in the fall of 1886. During one violent quarrel the son forgot himself and struck his father. Financial support ceased and Wedekind was compelled to seek his own living. He found a post near Zurich as head of advertising and public relations for the spice firm of Maggi and Co.; but the job, he complained, "confines me in a dark stall to keep me producing as much milk as possible." After six weeks he could take no more, although later he liked to boast that his insights into the business world and the capitalist system derived from his stint with this firm. Work for Maggi did not keep him from literary activity; he wrote feverishly, concentrating on shorter prose fiction, in the belief this would provide the quickest route to fame and fortune. But narrative was not Franklin's strong point, and even he did not feel proud of these productions; not one was accepted for publication. His financial situation grew more precarious, yet he refused to be discouraged, comforting himself with the thought that he was still "standing on my own two feet. . . . I must continue to be an egoist in order to get ahead on my own. I'm confident about reaching my goal, for I'm carrying it within me and it goes far beyond just writing novellas."

The sole dramatic work of the Zurich period, a comedy entitled *Elins Erweckung* (Elin's Awakening, written in 1887; some scenes published in 1894, the whole fragment in 1921), shows more promise than achievement, though here Franklin was more in his element. The work touches on characteristic themes and, as the title suggests, anticipates *Spring's Awakening* in a striking manner. Franklin's sketches for the play, which remained a fragment, show that it would take issue with current attitudes to sex and marriage, contrast conventional morality with one more firmly rooted in nature, and outline the possibility for a better kind of relationship between men and women, founded on sexual emancipation. The choice of themes, like the decision to cast his work in verse, shows the persistent wish to offer his generation an alternative to the stage naturalism of most contemporaries.

Elins Erweckung proceeds episodically. Elias (the name Elin appears only in the title), a probationer in theology, is about to undergo his final test, preaching a sermon on Easter Sunday. He rehearses this in front of his friend Oskar, who offers a devastating critique of it as morally dishonest and reproves his inflated manner of delivery. But the sermon is the least of Elias's present worries. He is tormented, first, by recurrent sexual dreams that seem to him dirty, sacrilegious, even criminal, and next, by the likelihood of having to marry Nettchen Schimmelpfennig, a good Christian spinster who has taken care of him during his years of study with the tacit understanding that her reward will be a permanent union.

Elias is afraid to abandon the conventional views he acquired at school, home, and church, whereas his friend Oskar, a student of medicine, looks on the phenomena of life scientifically, indeed, materialistically and cynically. To him Elias' sexual nightmares are perfectly normal, a part of growing up; marriage would certainly relieve his suffering, but it is not the only way to solve the problem. Elias' doubts and guilt are nothing but the result of hypertrophied morality. Oskar urges Elias to turn his back on the life he has led so far, since it has only bound and weakened him, and to launch out boldly, for the world badly needs rebels and outlaws, men and women ready to fight for the future of mankind.

Elias' conversion to Oskar's views comes only after the appearance of Ella, a young "martyr of civilization," who is trying to escape from the lustful Count Schweinitz. Elias rescues her and she in turn relieves him of the burden of sexual need by her easy response to him. The fragment breaks off there without hinting at the future of their relationship. The original sketch suggests that they will form a marriage on the basis of a more natural morality than the accepted code, and that Elias, free now of Christian dogma, will preach a new gospel proclaiming the value of unencumbered sexual love.

The revaluation of values Wedekind implies in *Elins Erweckung* is particularly clear in the contrast between Ella and her lecherous pursuer. According to convention, Ella the prostitute is an immoral creature, an outcast from society, whereas the aristocrat Schweinitz, who is justified in his behavior by the social order, is a moral man. Wedekind inverts this judgment; the honest, open person, the generous giver of herself, is morally above the self-indulgent hypocrite who is ready to use force to have his way with a dispossessed woman. The play combines the ethical message with a religious one: Elias as a true Christian believed that God had created man in his own image; he now believes in a deity who is an image of the best to be found in human beings.

The only other noteworthy works of the Zurich period are two feuilletons published in the *Neue Zürcher Zeitung*. With "Zirkusgedanken" (Circus Thoughts) and "Der Witz und seine Sippe" (Wit and Its Kindred), both in 1887, Wedekind declared his Weltanschauung and his aesthetic position. The circus piece is the most significant of several that Wedekind devoted to the subject during these years. In Zurich, he had become a regular visitor at the famous Circus Herzog, fell in love (at a distance) with its star performer, and argued that this popular entertainment not only allowed forms of expression banned from "higher" culture, but also offered, in the words of Robert Jones, a "visual allegory of a practical wisdom to which his contemporaries might well pay some attention." Later in life he claimed, without any truth, that in the years 1887–1888 he had traveled around Europe with the Circus Herzog as secretary and general factotum.

"Zirkusgedanken" advances the principle of elasticity, by which Wedekind means the ability to get on one's feet after a setback, to persist in one's course no matter what stands in the way. He cites the circus horse who does not falter in a dangerous steeplechase as an example of the "practical wisdom" most needed by us "children of the nineteenth century," whose lives have become "a fruitless race for happiness." This calls for "a continuous overcoming of obstacles," and elasticity is the means for succeeding in our headlong will to live, just as egoism is its necessary ethical component.

Wedekind next turns to tightrope dancers and trapeze artists in order to make an allegorical distinction between two types of behavior. The highwire artist, concentrating on keeping her balance, is a "real-practical idealist"; the trapeze artist, supported from above, is an "abstract-exalted idealist." According to this rather tenuous distinction the "abstract-exalted idealist" tries to impose his ideas on reality, and, if he fails, loses the justification for his existence. The "real-practical idealist" modifies his ideas according to circumstances, so as to maintain his equilibrium. That obviously is the only course for those who want to go on living; and it is art's function to communicate this wisdom through allegory.

In his second feuilleton, Wedekind defines the principle of his dramaturgy. The main subject is *Humor* rather than wit, and humor in German includes the ability to perceive and rise above contradictory views of the human situation. In this sense *Humor* is indeed related to wit, which brings opposites together. Both wit and humor, according to Wedekind, "lift one above the world onto the elevated level of tranquil objectivity."

Humor is Wedekind's characteristic artistic method. He insisted that this quality was present in all his works and also governed his attitude toward existence. Here is what he says of the mimic effect *Humor* exercises on those inured to it:

The mouth would like to laugh and the eye to weep, but since each prevents the other from carrying out its intention, the lips succeed only in bringing forth a gentle smile while the eyebrows rise almost unnoticed at both ends. The conflict so generated has a much more moving effect than either of the extremes (laughter or tears) would have; it also proves much more favorable to artistic representation.

(9:319)[1]

It is clear that Wedekind, without saying so, is defining the nature of tragicomedy, a term he applied only later to his own dramatic output: "I always thought of my plays as tragicomedies . . . but of course I didn't choose to designate any of them with this term because I thought that doing so would display an abysmal lack of humor."

Wedekind earned little from his journalism and it did not lead the way, as he had hoped, to a steady job. By the fall of 1887, with barely enough money to buy the necessities of life, he no longer had any illusions about self-support through free-lancing and his spirits began to sink. He wrote to his mother that "Europe, if you permit me to say so, is thoroughly repugnant to me," and he contemplated immigrating to America as his brother Willy had done. At this point the family persuaded Franklin and his father to reconcile. A compromise was reached: Franklin agreed to resume his law studies, this time in Zurich, but was allowed to continue writing on the side.

Zurich in the 1880's was a lively intellectual city. An influx of writers, artists, and scholars had left Germany to escape Bismarck's anti-Socialist legislation. Wedekind met several of these temporary exiles, in particular the small circle around Carl and Gerhart Hauptmann, which called itself "Young Germany." Wedekind soon found himself on the fringes of a movement whose ideas he often shared, though he was out of sympathy with its methods. The Young Germans met frequently to read aloud and discuss their latest theories and works. Wedekind's contribution was usually an erotic poem sung to the accompaniment of his guitar or a passage from one of his plays in progress, none of which met with much enthusiasm from his listeners. His rela-

tions with Gerhart Hauptmann were notably ambivalent, for each sensed the other as the antipode to himself. Wedekind was especially troubled by this reverse image of his nature, returning to the contrast throughout the years and trying to justify his own accomplishments by comparison with Hauptmann's.

In October 1888 Franklin's father died suddenly, freeing the son from imposed restraints and providing him with sufficient means to do as he liked. His portion of the inheritance was estimated at some 20,000 Swiss francs, not counting his share from the sale of the castle and of his father's eccentric collection of paintings, coins, and bric-a-brac. Franklin decided to move to Berlin, the current center of German literary life and, as he thought, the real crossroads of European intellectual developments. Unfortunately, he was not allowed to stay long enough to enjoy the city's enormous variety, for the German authorities refused to honor the Swiss attestation of his American citizenship. He did renew his acquaintance with the repatriated Hauptmann brothers and through them was introduced to still another group of the naturalist avant-garde, the so-called "Friedrichshagen Circle," which was bent upon changing the world through an art based on scientific and sociological principles. The Friedrichshagen approach was essentially passive, emphasizing scrupulously exact observation and recording of external circumstances. By contrast, the naturalist group around M. G. Conrad in Munich called for the artist's personal engagement with social problems and for using the truth it had discovered for practical reforms. Wedekind had little sympathy with either enterprise. He did approve of the naturalists' search for truth and desire to redress injustice, but he could not accept their premises or mimetic assumptions. The plays he had written so far all show dependence on nineteenth-century dramatic conventions, but Wedekind had already resolved that his work should aim not at imitating external reality but at revealing truths as yet undiscovered or unacknowledged.

[1]All quotations, unless otherwise indicated, are taken from the nine-volume edition of *Gesammelte Werke* (Munich, 1912–1921).

235

Unable to stay in Berlin, Wedekind returned to Munich and remained there for the next two years—an extraordinarily productive period for him. The Conrad group included almost every major creative talent in Munich, and Wedekind became a member of Conrad's Gesellschaft für Modernes Leben (Society for Modern Life) when it was founded in 1890. This did not change his attitude toward the movement, and, what proved more important, Wedekind threw himself into the life of the city's lower culture, hoping it would bring him the clues he needed for his work. Crucial in this connection is his friendship with W. W. Rudinoff (pseudonym for Willi Morgenstern), then at the beginning of a remarkable career as one of Europe's most talented entertainers—a man of many parts, at home in many languages and every sort of company. Rudinoff was the first great personality Wedekind had encountered and he was overwhelmed by the savoir faire and immense vitality of this monumental dilettante. He deeply admired the man's unpretentiousness, his indifference to fame, and the almost religious zeal with which he dedicated himself to his work. Rudinoff responded by taking Wedekind under his wing and introducing him to his own circle, which included circus performers and many bohemians. These became Wedekind's closest friends and associates over the next few years.

The first product of this Munich period, *Kinder und Narren* (Children and Fools, 1891), later revised and retitled *Die junge Welt* (The New Generation, 1897), sums up Wedekind's views of the naturalistic avant-garde. A series of young girls at boarding school, impatient at their upbringing, vow not to marry until they have secured the right to develop their individuality, their human dignity. Their male friends oppose this stance: "We men are born fighters; the whole world is our battlefield, and you women are the paradise for us within this world, unceasingly bubbling over with crystal-bright water for our refreshment." By the end of the play, the girls have abandoned their cause, the men have tempered their egoism, and both have stumbled through trial and error to mate with a suitable partner.

Wedekind had Henrik Ibsen's *Comedy of Love* (1862) in mind when writing this play; less obviously, he was also thinking of *A Doll's House* (1879), whose feminist theme had been a subject of discussion in his parents' house. What was a modern woman to do? Wedekind was opposed to both the conventional notion of woman as a glorified "house animal" and the naturalist avant-garde notion of the "male woman." Neither allowed woman to realize her potential. Yet his play offers little by way of substitute, and perhaps the problem had no great interest for Wedekind in any event. His real contribution in *Kinder und Narren* lies in demonstrating how opinion determines conduct. The would-be progressive generation of the 1880's, as Wedekind saw it, was afflicted with a theorizing sickness that undermined its purpose and well-being. The more the figures of the play analyze themselves and their friends, the greater the confusion about their situation.

Wedekind also charges artists of his generation with standing away from life as observers and analysts: they produce opinions but provide no insight into the universal nature of things. Hence Wedekind's motto for the play: "Realism is a pedantic governess; it has made you forget human beings. Turn back to nature." Wedekind caricaturizes the poet in the play, Meier, as a man who always carries a notebook with him, even into the privacy of his bedroom, a habit which has brought his marriage to near ruin.

It is usually assumed that Wedekind meant the poet to be a caricature of Gerhart Hauptmann, who had used in his *Das Friedensfest* (A Family Reconciliation, translated as *The Coming of Peace,* 1890) intimate family secrets that Wedekind had confessed to him in Zurich. But Wedekind's satire was directed rather at the practices of an entire generation. When Meier at the end of the play is close to madness, he fulfills Wedekind's prophecy of 1886 about naturalist artists in general: They "begin with too much zeal" and end up "by going crazy." Typically, Wedekind models his figures on real-life persons and then presents them as representatives of an idea. In *Die junge Welt,* the revised version of the play, Wedekind also rejects naturalism's optimistic assumption that knowledge results in improvement by arousing people to change their behavior.

Kinder und Narren has never secured a place in the German repertoire. Critics have rightly charged Wedekind with undertaking too much and producing too little, and the less charitable among them have noted that for all its anti-naturalist stance, it depends more heavily on naturalistic techniques than any other Wedekind play. The dramatic figures are undermotivated psychologically; they are puppets more than creatures of flesh and blood. Wedekind was in fact working toward a drama in which the interplay of forces and the realignment of relationships would replace plot and the depiction of characters.

All these features appear in *Spring's Awakening,* subtitled "A Children's Tragedy," the major work of Wedekind's Munich period and his first undisputed masterpiece. The playwright has taken his own advice to "go back to nature" and give direct expression to feelings aroused by personal experience. Yet this "nature" does not mean human emotions, but elemental force, the libido or drive of life, the instinctual and irrational, eros and sex. As for the human beings Wedekind depicts, they are dramatic figures encountering this force in the crucial passage from childhood to adulthood.

Wedekind's choice of puberty as his subject was epoch-making. Few before him had ventured into this territory. A note jotted down early during work on the play is instructive: "The male as well as the female [figures] are all at the age of about fourteen years. The slender stalk has shot up, the buds, heavy with sap, threaten to crush it, the petals have not yet unfolded but the calyx stands open and permissive." Apart from the obvious sexual imagery, this description points to a state of exquisite ambivalence, expectancy coupled with uncertainty. At stake is the question of survival: whether those who are passing from one stage of development to another will mature successfully.

The finished play also puts the matter in a social and moral context, nature within a human framework. The question now becomes, will development occur according to the adolescent's own inclinations, or according to the patterns society has established for it? In the final scene Wedekind sums up these claims as obligation (the demand for social conformity) and desire (the individual's need to realize himself in his own way). Wedekind's answer is that maturity is best served not by choosing one course over the other, but by balancing these claims according to individual need.

Spring's Awakening lacks a clearly-defined plot and has no central protagonist; the action takes place in a series of loosely connected scenes. Five adolescents are singled out for special attention. Of these, two do not survive to adulthood: Wendla Bergmann's ignorance of sex leads to pregnancy and fatal abortion; Moritz Stiefel, no less ignorant, commits suicide out of fear of life and shame at disappointing his parents' expectations. By contrast, Ilse, a *fille de joie,* and Hänschen Rilow decide to ignore adult demands and go their own ways. Between these opposite pairs stands the young Melchior Gabor, who insists on choosing his own path to freedom but also wants to do justice to the moral code. He is sent to reform school for his pains. (He is the one who gets Wendla with child and writes the essay on cohabitation for Moritz that causes him to be expelled from school.) Melchior is saved from suicide only because the mysterious Masked Gentleman convinces him that the advantages of going on living, however doubtful, outweigh the emptiness of nonexistence.

Wedekind's indictment of the way adolescents are reared begins with the family. Wendla urges her mother to give her the facts about procreation, but Mrs. Bergmann cannot bring herself to say what she knows. She lacks the language with which to discuss sex. Not only can Mrs. Bergmann not change her inhibitions, she also cannot free herself from the tyranny of public opinion. To keep Wendla from having a child out of wedlock, she arranges for an abortion that proves fatal. As for Moritz Stiefel's father, a mean man of petit bourgeois pretensions, he pushes the child beyond his abilities, thereby driving his son to kill himself when he is not promoted. At his funeral the distraught father, not seeing his own responsibility for the event, cries out: "The boy was not mine! I didn't like what I saw in him from the very beginning!"

Melchior Gabor is also betrayed by his parents, while his parents' self-righteous belief is that *he* has betrayed *them*. When the father, a jurist, discovers that his son has transgressed, he sees this as a manifestation of "moral insanity" and sends the boy to a reformatory. Mrs. Gabor's views seem to be directly opposed to her husband's. A liberal, enlightened woman, she has always trusted her son's "sunny" disposition and good judgment: "You're old enough, Melchior, to know what is good and what is not good for you. Do whatever you feel is right." Yet when confronted with the fact of Melchior's wrongdoing, Mrs. Gabor immediately pulls back. Her son has violated her trust; she agrees that he belongs in a reform school.

Wedekind's exposure of the family in *Spring's Awakening* is matched by his attack upon the German school system. In his day the gymnasium was still the acknowledged guardian of humanistic education, its lofty ideal to train mind and body in harmony, its social purpose to prepare youngsters for enlightened citizenship and productive service to their country. The school Wedekind depicts in this play is an outrageous parody of the ideal. The curriculum is directed solely at the mind, with no reference to the body and its needs; the courses cram information into the pupils' heads without showing its pertinence to the business of living. The teachers are narrowminded pedagogues who squabble over trifles and ignore their pupils' concerns. They fit the malicious nicknames Wedekind has invented for them: Bonebreaker, Flykiller, Starveling, and Calflove, led by the Rector Sunstroke, a pedant in thought and word.

At Moritz Stiefel's funeral, the rector says: "Suicide, as the crassest conceivable transgression *against* the moral order of the universe, is also the greatest conceivable proof *for* the moral order inasmuch as the man who murders himself saves the moral order the necessity of passing judgment on him and simultaneously confirms its very existence." Wedekind had perceived the link between conventionalized language and denatured humanity from the very outset of his career. As early as 1885 he wrote: "I still believe that all this slavish consideration for others, the many empty phrases and mutual untruths one has to exchange with others nowadays . . . , is largely to blame for the fact that our world has lost its naiveté; nobody is able to think or feel naturally anymore."

But Wedekind should not be misunderstood. He had only a minor interest in pointing the finger of blame, and he did not aim at causal analysis or reform, although Wedekind did tell one critic that he hoped his work "might help educators, parents, and teachers to arrive at a more humane and rational judgment of puberty." Nor does *Spring's Awakening* look to the abolition of the institutions it criticizes, for the status quo was not about to change. Moritz, returning from beyond the grave to persuade Melchior to join him in death, suggests that the inherited morality will go on forever, blocking any chance of improvement: "We [the dead] watch parents put children into the world so that they can say to them: 'How lucky you are to have parents like us!' And we see the children grow up and do the same!"

Wedekind in fact seems to think that childrearing, whether well- or ill-intentioned, strict or permissive, does not by itself determine how the adolescent responds to his "crisis." Melchior knows all anybody can know about sex, yet he blunders into a fateful offense against Wendla's freedom; Wendla herself has been protected against harm, yet she brings about her own undoing. There is no way to avoid the sufferings of puberty; it is a cruel time of danger as well as opportunity.

Wedekind seems to have assumed a kind of biological determinism here. The play indicates that one's ability to cope with crisis rests to a large extent on an internal disposition. By nature inclined to accept and carry out what others determine for them, youngsters like Wendla and Moritz are doomed to conformity. When they fail to meet society's demands, they fall by the wayside. Ilse and Hänschen, on the other hand, seem equipped by nature to survive misfortune. Impious, even frivolous in their egoistic disregard for the consequences of what they do, they are moved primarily by instinct and physical need, bent on pleasure, living according to the inner law of their nature.

Fascinated as he was by such a possibility, Wedekind stops short of recommending the free pursuit of eros as universally valid. Ilse knows she will eventually end "in the garbage dump"; Hänschen regards his dalliance with another boy as only a passing phase in their development.

What Wedekind sees beyond and beside their way is a third possible attitude—that of the person who, though eager to experience life, still feels answerable to conscience for his acts. Throughout the play, Melchior Gabor is torn between convention and freedom, between intellect and sensuality, between obligation and desire. These incompatibles are indeed irreconcilable. Melchior must therefore decide whether living is worth the candle. In the final scene he faces a choice between life and death: his dead friend Moritz beckons from the grave, but the Masked Gentleman (probably a projection of Melchior's own deepest wishes) promises him adventure and experience; like Mephisto in *Faust,* he offers the chance to "get acquainted with everything of interest the world has to offer." Melchior refuses to forgo what he has not yet lived through, despite all uncertainty.

The question of morality still remains. Once again the Masked Gentleman comes to the rescue with a definition of morality tailored to Melchior's needs: "By morality I understand the real product of two imaginary factors. The imaginary factors are Obligation and Desire. The product is called morality and its reality cannot be denied." According to this definition, morality is no longer an immutable set of rules divinely ordained; it becomes dynamic, the result of adjustment between social demands and personal inclinations; it belongs to this world, no metaphysics involved.

It would be difficult to overestimate the importance of *Spring's Awakening*. The play incorporates most of Wedekind's concerns so far and refines his dramatic technique. In the Zurich essay his principle of representation was defined as "the plastic-allegorical," by which performers live out the idea they stand for, and Wedekind's treatment of Moritz illustrates the method. This figure dreams of a headless queen who, like himself, longs for a stronger-minded guide; loses his own head (figuratively) in a crisis; and later enacts the truth about his incapacity for life by blowing out his brains. At the end, when Moritz appears to Melchior with his head tucked under his arm, still seeking a mentor, we see the consistency of Moritz's allegorical role as that of a death-oriented temperament.

Spring's Awakening has further significance as a stumbling block in Wedekind's career. Published in a small edition in 1891 at the playwright's expense, the work circulated only among his circle of friends and the literary coteries of Munich and Berlin. Censorship made a production in a state-supported theater impossible, and the few private stages of the time, which might have risked presentation before an invited audience, considered the subject too hot to handle. Thus *Spring's Awakening* joined *Der Schnellmaler* and *Kinder und Narren* as still another curiosity in Wedekind's library of unperformed and largely unread plays. If anything, the book edition harmed his future, for it alerted the censors to this subversive author—obviously "a purveyor of pornography," the charge that was leveled at him for years whenever he presented a new work for publication or performance.

TESTING THE VITALIST IDEAL

After Zurich and Munich and Berlin, then, Wedekind found himself eager to break out of German provincialism. He turned to Paris and lived there (and briefly in London) for the next four years. His aim was to achieve a way of life totally free from the social and moral restraints that had governed his youth; his professional goal was to intensify the search for a "great and powerful art" that would rejuvenate contemporary German literature and theater by reaching down to the fundamentals of human existence. Alwa Schön's passionate declaration in *Die Büchse der Pandora* (*Pandora's Box*, 1904) echoes Wedekind's own convictions:

> The curse that plagues modern literature is that we're much too literary. We don't talk about any other problems besides those our scholars and scientists call attention to. Our horizons are determined by the special-interest groups we belong to. To get back on the track of a great and powerful art we need to associate as much as possible with people who have never read a book in their lives and whose actions are governed by simple animal instincts.

(3:125–126)

Wedekind knew of two spheres in which he could find the alternative, anti-bourgeois ways of life he was looking for: one was the fringe world of lowbrow popular entertainment that he had already known so well in Munich; the other was the underworld of free love and prostitution. Wedekind devoted his first years in Paris almost exclusively to these socially risky areas of experience, ignoring the opera, concert halls, and theaters favored by the respectable and making no effort to get in touch with the men and women who were remaking French literary history. He rarely attended art exhibitions; he did not even visit (or at least comment on) famous sites and monuments, as though inspection of these would compromise his anti-bourgeois mission. Like many Parisians of the time, Wedekind believed the true centers of the city's culture were its palaces of pleasure—the nightclubs, circuses, and music halls, which offered high-quality entertainment unmatched in any other European metropolis. Here Wedekind found the model he had been looking for: a sensual world, exuding elemental emotions, teeming with bodies bent on display, always aiming at effect, ready to join with other bodies in untroubled enjoyment.

Although the circus had interested Wedekind since his years in Zurich, only in Paris did it begin to permeate his life and work to a degree unprecedented among modern German writers. To begin with it provided an alternative to the contemporary theater Wedekind rejected. All its prevailing forms were obsessed with words—with "literature," which concealed instead of revealing the truth about human behavior; and all, with the possible exception of the French boulevard pieces, assumed that the purpose of art was to produce works of universal validity and lasting value.

The circus, on the other hand, offered a critique of established values and suggested alternatives; it was the living antithesis of bourgeois rigidity, complacency, steadfastness, devotion to permanence. Wedekind relished the circus's emphasis on sheer physicality, its display, its flaunting of the human body. In an age of frock coats and corsets, men and women were prisoners of moral prudishness as well as of fashion. By contrast, the scanty costumes of circus performers signaled freedom—both of limb, the better to bring off acrobatic feats, and of spirit, showing pride and freedom in the physical. Wedekind was convinced that the body mirrors the soul—he liked to say that a person's nature could be read from his walk. He found perfection in a man or woman in the complete correspondence between one's outer physical and inner spiritual being; or, as he put it, fulfillment of the spirit was dependent on fulfillment of the flesh.

Another virtue of the circus was its power to rejuvenate an adult's weary, disillusioned way of life by treating everything as though it were a game. The world had grown too serious, too intellectual and self-conscious; the circus had kept its naiveté, "the ineffable childlikeness" of life, the surrender to "innocent pleasure, laughing play, and sweetly serious dreams" that for Wedekind still constituted the very essence of happiness.

Wedekind's praise of "elasticity" has already been noted; without it, he thought, man would surely perish in the race of life: "Each of us takes a fall now and then. But the man who lacks elasticity is running on his Achilles' heel; one accident and he remains lying where he fell, while the wild chase goes heedlessly past him, yapping and yelling" its way to the finish. Along with elasticity Wedekind recommended equilibrium—another circus skill. By this he meant composure in the face of unfavorable circumstances, the maintenance of physical and moral well-being, the end for which elasticity was the means. His image for the perfect equilibrist was the tightrope dancer already described in "Zirkusgedanken," forced to "secure her balance every moment anew."

To Wedekind, moreover, the circus, music halls, nightclubs, and the like formed the natural habitat of the anti-bourgeois. In meeting such people he was greatly assisted by his old Munich friend Rudinoff, now fulfilling a series of engagements in Paris. He also found what he was looking for among the many young women who were trying to snatch a few moments of pleasure by making themselves available to affluent males. These women were not vulgar prostitutes; the Parisian cocotte at the turn of the century did expect some material reward for her services—a good meal, a place to sleep, a trinket or article of clothing, some pocket money—but she offered more than mere sex: companionship for lonely hours, a companion at the cabarets, sympathetic listening. The women Wedekind got acquainted with afforded him these satisfactions; he chose them not solely out of curiosity about sex, but also (and ultimately more important for his work) in order to discover the "essential nature" of the opposite sex. Wedekind "studied" a wide variety of women during the Paris years, being careful to treat them as persons rather than as sex-objects. His diaries tell of some dozen women who drifted in and out of his life, partners in sex to be sure, but also informants on the elusive nature of women and on the fundamentals of male-female relations. Wedekind's search went beyond mere direct experience to include reading in literature, science, and the history of those institutions (marriage, prostitution, hetaerism) affecting the status of women.

The four years in Paris were among the happiest in Wedekind's life. They also brought moments of misery, when the euphoria of living as he wished wore off in the face of its limitations: his inheritance was soon spent, forcing him to turn home and even to depend on strangers for basic needs. The departure of his closest German companions caused bouts of loneliness; his health began to deteriorate from sexual excesses and irregular habits; he fretted about the slow progress of his career and often felt too weary to pursue the work under way. Despite such ups and downs, Wedekind could boast of some remarkable accomplishments. He finished a comedy, *Der Liebestrank* (The Love Potion, written in 1892, published in 1899), and his "monster tragedy," *Pandora's Box*, which became the basis for his later *Lulu* plays; he wrote the first act of a dramatic idyll, *Das Sonnenspektrum* (*The Solar Spectrum*, written in 1894, published in 1921) and sketched a sexual utopia entitled "Abhandlung Eden" (A Treatise on Eden); he completed four dance poems or pantomimes, finished several shorter works of prose fiction, began his only novel, *Mine-Haha* (written in 1895, published in 1901), and wrote several poems and ballads that he set to his own music or to adapted melodies.

All these works arose from the original impulse to create "a great and powerful art" that would inject new zest into German life and letters, but they are by no means exclusively utopian in nature. They also take stock of possibilities and probe relentlessly into the limitations and perversions to which the ideal might be subjected. Most of the works show a certain ambiguity, a recognition of complex realities that barred the way to realization and thwarted the idealist's mission.

The eight narrative pieces published in 1897 under the title *Die Fürstin Russalka* (*Princess Russalka*) do not show Wedekind to be a great writer of short fiction, but they do deserve to be better known, and at least one of them ranks among the best tales in modern German literature. The central theme in most of these stories is the unhappy consequences of society's insistence on suppressing the libido. *Princess Russalka,* for example, having been brought up with no knowledge of the biological basis of sex, is full of inhibitions and anxieties. She enters a marriage that remains childless, suffers the indignity of adultery, abandons her religion, and adopts the life of an emancipated woman until saved through the understanding and long-suffering of a second husband. In "Der greise Freier" (The Senile Suitor), a young girl is prevented by her piety from marrying the man of her choice. Nearly hysterical from the resulting strain on her nervous system, and haunted by the fear of being coupled with an old man, she is on the verge of suicide when her sister arranges a secret meeting with the girl's would-be lover. Despite fulfillment, the shock and strain of this illicit affair brings about her death. "Rabbi Esra," which, recast, became one of Wedekind's most notable stage successes, recounts the struggles of an elderly Jew to reconcile the claims of spiritual and of sensual love. Finally giving himself to a beautiful woman who satisfies his physical needs, he discovers that spiritual contentment soon follows. But

certainly the best of these early tales is the much-anthologized "Der Brand von Egliswyl" (The Conflagration at Egliswyl), the story of a robust farmhand whose prowess with the girls is cut short by his infatuation with a cruel flirt. The girl drives him to despair and frustration. When she finally does yield, he finds himself impotent. Enraged by such humiliation he sets fire to the whole village, but instead of admiring him for this substitute show of ardent masculinity, the girl turns him over to the authorities.

Most of these pieces are cast as framework stories, a form often favored by German nineteenth-century writers: a first-person narrator looks back to relate or confess the events that have led to his or her present situation. Wedekind subtly alters moods and diction according to the circumstances within the story and often closes with a brief, stunning account of the impact the narrator's tale has made on the fictitious listener. The theme of Eros creates correspondences among the stories and the plays of the period, and some figures appear in both series. Unlike the dramas, however, the short fictions are never ironic and present no stylistic difficulties. Occasionally they reveal a touch of sentimentality, a trait the young Wedekind otherwise avoids.

The four pantomimes of the 1890's (later called dance poems) incorporate the substance of his concerns during the Paris-London period. All the great circuses of the 1890's included pantomimes as a regular part of their attractions, and the form attracted Wedekind as a way of getting an audience for his work and replenishing his rapidly vanishing finances. Neither wish came true, although a French version of *Die Flöhe, oder der Schmerzenstanz* (The Fleas, or the Dance of Pain, written in 1892, published in 1897) was accepted, but never staged, by the Folies Bergère.

Wedekind regarded pantomime as a promising way of revitalizing the stage. Here was theater in its most elemental guise: a visual and aural manifestation of extraordinary sensuous appeal, an action without words and hence without intellectuality, conveyed by body language, in which the actor-dancer-mime comes into his own by displaying his ability to tell a story through movement. The form was open to stylistic experiments while free from the demand for stylistic unity. And even though meant primarily to entertain, pantomime recommended itself as the best medium for expressing matters that could not be expressed in words, in particular the truths about sexual behavior that had been sharpened by Wedekind's Paris experience.

In composing such works for a German public, Wedekind had little help from his native tradition apart from Heine's sporadic attempts with the genre in midcentury. Wedekind's own work was thus a pioneering effort. So was his preoccupation with the dance, a folk form only then beginning to attract the attention of serious artists; it was perhaps induced by Nietzsche's call for a Dionysian art, which he associated with the rhythms of the dancing human body. Exactly how and when Wedekind's pantomimes came to be written is not known. They do not fall into a sequence or show progression though their relation to the circus is closer in some than in others. Most depend on fairy-tale elements—transformations, magical events, stock figures, familiar folk symbols—corresponding to states of mind; all compare animals and human beings, a favorite Wedekind technique, indicative of the libido; all contain sudden shifts of mood, draw contrasts between activities, deal in extreme situations, flaunt incongruities, and exaggerate or fall into general tomfoolery.

Die Flöhe, oder der Schmerzenstanz is the story of a queen modeled after Maria Leszczyńska, the wife of Louis XV of France, who loses her daughter (Adelaide) to a mysterious beggar woman and eventually recovers the girl in the form of a huge flea. Loss and recovery depend on the (changed) attitude of the queen, who has refused to have her palm read by the beggar, displaying a fear of the future and fear of contact with "the lower orders." Adelaide is magically restored to her mother, however, after the queen has learned to accept the presence of a flea on her person and to love it despite its animal nature.

The "dance of pain" in the subtitle refers to the trained fleas (also symbolizing libido) in a traveling circus that refuse to perform decorously as trained, and instead escape into the skirts of the queen's ladies-in-waiting. This unaccustomed invasion of privacy, after a night of painful itching and scratching, gives way to a Dionysian dance of joy. The queen herself sleeps through the commotion, but finally awakes to find a huge flea resting between her legs too. When the director of the circus (no doubt the beggar woman in another guise) insists on reclaiming his star performer, the queen objects, draws him to her bosom, and smothers "the ugly little animal with kisses on its forehead, cheeks, and mouth." With this acceptance of the animalic, the queen is able to enjoy sexual fulfillment once more, symbolized by the child's restoration to her.

The social message of *Der Flöhe* is that the cure for the bourgeois world lies in valuing the impulses that come from a "lower" order of society—the circus world, no less! The queen, incidentally, learns that her daughter not only has profited from her experience as a performer in the circus, but "has lost nothing of either her human charm or her refinement as a prince's daughter."

Wedekind also mocks the upper class's attitudes toward sex. The women in the pantomime see it as a torture, a "sacrifice" they have to go through; they submit unwillingly to the sneaky, brutal little beasts from the outside. And this outrage must also be reconciled with their sense of piety. The males, on the other hand, behave like young men who have been starved too long, and perform a wild victory dance after achieving their goal, leaping around "like cannibals who have just consumed a magnificent feast," congratulating each other on their conquests, and relating in mimic detail the charms of the ladies they have just enjoyed.

243

After comedy comes melodrama; after the triumph of sexual vitality, the nightmare of sexual excess. Wedekind's *Der Mückenprinz* (The Prince of Gnats, probably written in 1893, published in 1897), which his biographer found "embarrassingly cynical," focuses relentlessly on the perversion of libidinal energy by the privileged, egoistic young males of Wedekind's own class. It is an allegory of the sexual behavior prevalent in the male-oriented, male-dominated society of Wedekind's own time.

The pantomime opens on an Eden-like landscape in which the mating dance of two gnats ends in delicate coupling. This represents sexual behavior in its natural state. The situation changes radically with the appearance of a human being, the self-centered Prince Leonor, who immediately kills the female gnat (Arethusa) and imprisons the male (Tutos) in an enormous cage from which he is forced to observe what follows, namely a series of sexual indignities, each more disgraceful than the last. Leonor first violates then discards a peasant girl; he flirts with her companions; he courts and then marries a magician's daughter (Ada) but grows tired of her; he commits adultery with a lady of the court, infecting her with a disease that then breaks out in himself; he mistreats his unfortunate spouse, first trying to get her to betray him with another man and then subjecting her to public humiliation. All these actions are accompanied by the release and reimprisonment of the incarcerated Tutos, representing the prince's alter ego, the kind of man who, unlike Leonor, derives pleasure from the act of pleasing others. Only in the last episode does the prince get his comeuppance and his patient wife her revenge: Ada's magician-father unleashes a swarm of gnats who sting Leonor to death, after which the ill-used Tutos is transformed into a human being, a Prince of Gnats worthy of the title.

The best-known of Wedekind's pantomimes is *Die Kaiserin von Neufundland* (The Empress of Newfoundland, probably written in 1894, published in 1897), a tragicomedy or, to coin a term, a tragic farce. Its theme, the perversion of human need through human excess, is illustrated by the empress's unhappy obsession with sex. To put it differently, the pantomime depicts a search for self-fulfillment that leads to self-destruction. The work echoes the theme of *Der Mückenprinz* and may again reflect the author's own torments. But in the second treatment of the theme, again an allegory, we also find a social commentary on the role of sex in determining the relation of male and female in marriage. Sex is of course complicated by class, money, and the struggle for psychological domination. In this sense, *Die Kaiserin von Neufundland* is Wedekind's first attempt to deal with what has come to be called sexual politics.

The pantomime begins with the Empress Felissa facing a dilemma. She has been told by her doctors that her health demands that she marry or she will die. Though indignant at this assault on her individuality, Felissa chooses the lesser of two evils and consents to interview some suitors for her hand. The first, a poet named Pustekohl (a parody of the young Gerhart Hauptmann), woos her by reading from his latest manuscript and is laughed out of court. The second, the pugnacious megalomaniac Napoleon, frightens and then angers the empress. When he threatens to commit suicide if rejected, she ostentatiously thanks heaven to be rid of him. The third, Alwa Adison (Thomas A. Edison), lulls her to sleep with his interminable calculations and his promises of enormous wealth through future inventions. Only the fourth suitor, the weight lifter Holthoff, "the strongest man in the world," stirs Felissa's emotions, and after a demonstration of his remarkable strength, she loads him with jewelry, places her crown on his head, and "snuggles her half-naked body tenderly into his arms."

Felissa's choice of a circus performer over some of the greatest achievers in Western civilization seems at first glance to confirm Wedekind's familiar denigration of intellect in favor of the body, or his thesis that fulfillment of the spirit rests on fulfillment of the flesh. But the real point lies elsewhere. Wedekind's story illustrates the destructive effect of sexual obsession. The empress, infatuated by Holthoff's physical prowess, eggs him on to greater and more prolonged demonstrations of his potency, as symbolized by his lifting ever-larger weights and holding them aloft for a longer and longer time. Infatuation turns to ecstasy and ecstasy to madness. In the end, Felissa begs her lover to end her misery with a blow from one of his weights. Exhausted by his own exertions, Holthoff is unable to do this, and the empress strangles herself with a strand of her own hair.

The pantomime describes a relationship Wedekind sees as typical—an ill-matched pair whose attempts to meet each other's desires or needs brings out the worst in them, distorts their individual virtues, and exhausts their peculiar resources, while also inverting their relative social and psychological positions. The infatuated empress loses her throne and worldly possessions; the circus strongman comes to act like a king, using up the fortune Felissa has given him. Both have lost all vestiges of human dignity: Felissa grovels for mercy and a small sign of affection; Holthoff, depleted by overindulgence, is a physical and moral wreck.

The humor in this wretched situation resides in the manner of presentation—exaggeration and incongruity blend the tragic and the ridiculous. Adding to the grim fun, although this is universally overlooked by the critics, is the parodic way in which Wedekind exposes what he considers fundamental in human relations, especially in modern marriage. He shows that the root of attraction is raw sensuality, that the coupling grows out of self-interest and is sustained only by self-advantage, that even without a contractual obligation both partners must be prepared to pay for what they get, that the female's submissiveness is only a ploy to get what she craves and the male's assertiveness no more than a means of maintaining confidence in his own manliness.

Wedekind is also sure that relations founded on a quid pro quo are ultimately self-defeating, a kind of negative competition in which demand and output vie with each other; they upset the balance within the person and between the two sexes.

Bethel (probably written in 1893, published in 1921) is the most ambitious of Wedekind's pantomimes, both in inventive range and what it calls for in presentation. Unlike the three others, it owes little to the fairy tale, and depends exclusively on the circus. The action takes full advantage of the arena as a setting: huge stage properties, masses of performers, space for constant movement. In the last act Wedekind introduces the famous German clown figure *der dumme August* (Stupid Augustus). The work offers spectacle on a large scale—rowdy, vulgar, farcical action, a series of events charged with sensuality and brimming over with vital energy. The pantomime has been faulted for its unflattering (indeed, erroneous) picture of America, especially since Wedekind's bizarre images helped to create the mythology later exploited by German playwrights, notably Brecht. But this misses the point. *Bethel* contains a no less damaging portrait of German conditions, and Wedekind's attention is still concentrated on the socio-psychological concerns that occupied his Paris years.

The central question in *Bethel* is whether the virtues of seemingly incompatible spheres of existence are transferable from one to the other—specifically, whether the spirit of the circus world can penetrate the stuffy atmosphere of the bourgeois world and rejuvenate it. The two worlds depicted are Germany and America, opposites that are meant to be taken allegorically as standing for the contrast between old and new. The qualities opposed are system versus anarchy, moribund culture versus raw nature, gravity versus gaiety, convention versus adventure, and rigidity versus defiance of authority. This combat is never represented literally as the circus world versus the bourgeois, but the audience is shown what

Wedekind means by the arena setting and the striking juxtaposition of qualities associated with each sphere, particularly through the behavior of the uninhibited Leona and the tomfoolery of the clown figure, Stupid Augustus. Thus Leona wears a tararaboomdeeay costume and is given to dancing the cancan, symbols that contemporary audiences would easily interpret as freedom from restraint, defiance of moral or social expectations, letting oneself go in Dionysian excitement. The dance, with its high kicks and lifting of the skirt, would signal an invitation to sexual adventure.

Bethel, then, tells the same tale as the rest of Wedekind's pantomimes: release and channeling of the libido; it is the source of creative energy, the catalyst for restoring life to society. The point is driven home once more by Wedekind's equating of animal and human. Bethel is a trotting horse and her human counterpart is the rambunctious Leona. What happens to Bethel also happens in an inversely complementary way to Leona; the fate of the animal parallels the fate of the woman. The one significant difference is that Bethel behaves unselfconsciously, doing what comes naturally, whereas Leona, in the specifically human situation, must always overcome the obstacles that would hinder the free expression of her true nature.

The story of *Bethel* is too complicated to summarize: it involves horse-racing in Europe and prizefighting in America, alternating journeys between the Old World and the New, attacks by wild Indians and gigantic mosquitoes, and similar nonsense. More important, it tells of a struggle that is also a quest for identity: the New World striving for recognition, the Old World laboring to distinguish between true and false, trying to determine what is valid for it. The action culminates in a fantastic trial that exposes the Old World's inability to solve the problem, yet brings the rediscovery of its native comic spirit in the person of Stupid Augustus, who, quite appropriately, falls in love with the irrepressible

Leona. In the final scene, the courtroom is dismantled, Leona climbs on the judge's bench to dance a boisterous cancan, and the entire assembly joins in homage to Bethel, the libidinal power that reconciles all differences.

Der Liebestrank, also known under the title *Fritz Schwigerling,* is the first play Wedekind finished in Paris. It is an attempt to apply the principles of the circus to a dramatic work; in Wedekind's own words, it was conceived as "defense and justification of bodily art opposed to intellectual art." The explanation is helpful, but has done little to change the general view of the play as a charming but inconsequential entertainment. Yet a closer look reveals considerable depth and unexpected pleasures.

The story is laid in Russia. Prince Rogoschin, an aging roué, invites a one-time circus virtuoso, Fritz Schwigerling, to his country estate, ostensibly to tutor his children, actually to enlist Schwigerling's assistance in securing the favors of his ward, Katharina, who has so far successfully resisted him. Believing Schwigerling to be a gypsy and therefore practiced in magic, the prince wants him to brew a love potion that will make Katharina fall into his arms. To ensure that Schwigerling will not fail him, the prince puts him under lock and key until the job is done. Forced to choose between freedom and making potions—"Who in the world wouldn't practice magic under such circumstances?"—Schwigerling concocts a vile liquor, warning the prince that its efficacy depends on the drinker's not thinking of a bear while consuming it. Rogoschin naturally does exactly what he is not supposed to do, and the potion fails in its purpose. Schwigerling then persuades the prince to seclude himself in his chamber and drink boiling-hot tea until he has sweated out the unwanted images that keep coming into his mind. Meanwhile, Schwigerling plots escape, and with the help of the prince's wife, Lisaweta (who reveals herself as Schwigerling's long-lost but never-forgotten first wife, Cordelia), he runs away from his predicament, taking with him

Katharina and Coelestin, the prince's man-servant (now disclosed as an old friend from the circus in Paris).

Criticism of the play has concentrated on the clash between Schwigerling and Rogoschin over the principles for bringing up the prince's children. The prince wants them to be able to "speak their piece in society" and "play a role in their circle like the one their father played as a young lieutenant in Moscow." Hence they are to develop savoir faire and learn as many languages as possible. Schwigerling agrees with these aims but interprets them in his own way. The boys are to "feel absolutely at home" everywhere, not simply in the haunts of the aristocracy. Their savoir faire should be designed to serve in difficult as well as harmless situations. Schwigerling promises the prince that *his* pupils will know how to get out of every predicament. But prince and tutor disagree on method. Rogoschin, ruled by family tradition, misinterprets what he has seen in the circus and puts his trust in force: "I was brought up with the whip, and my father was brought up with the whip. The reason I chose you as tutor was that you as a former animal trainer know how to handle that instrument." Schwigerling assures the prince that he has never found use for the whip—"I give you my word that I've taught a pig everything that can be taught a halfway talented pig: dancing on a tightrope, calculating the course of the planets," without any whip. But the prince remains adamant: "A pig, sir, might put up with that, but we're not dealing with pigs here!"

The debate recalls the educational indictments in *Spring's Awakening:* the prince's principles would destroy his children's individuality and turn them into exact replicas of himself. Schwigerling's method is intended to "tickle the children's ambition and awaken their self-confidence. . . . I want to loosen their limbs until the spirit pervades them, until freedom and joy tremble in every vein." He is positively poetical about the virtues of circus training:

> We evaluate an artiste according to her grace, her temperament, her—soul, if you'll permit me the expression. . . . The decisive thing is always and only the human being, spiritual *and* physical beauty, the beauty of motion and the beauty of form. . . . The spirit, the soul, which lies dormant in the beautiful organization, must appear in perfect, rhythmically metrical form.
>
> (2:219)

All this is familiar to the reader of "Zirkusgedanken," but it is important to realize that the original situation and the later one are not the same. The question arises whether the sentiments re-expressed by the author still apply. Wedekind would not be Wedekind if he did not subject his own thoughts to the test in a later context. In *Der Liebestrank,* his self-interrogation is whether the grand ideas he held about the circus and its virtues can in fact be realized in the larger social world. In *Bethel* he found room for optimism; in this play the outcome seems rather more doubtful.

As bearer of the ideal, Schwigerling is at the heart of the question, and here it soon becomes obvious that the playwright has undercut his protagonist. Schwigerling's pedagogy is derived from training animals, not human beings; it disregards the social context in which upbringing has to take place. Besides, Schwigerling has had no previous experience as a teacher, and shows no natural gift when dealing with Rogoschin's browbeaten boys. In the first scene he breaks the whip and gives half of it to each youngster; in another, he gives some elementary instruction in fencing (which they have already had) and in Italian (which they cannot understand). Schwigerling the tutor is in fact a fake; he has taken the job *faute de mieux* after a falling-out with his circus director, and with typical bravado convinces himself that he can handle it. He has tried everything else, why not a professorship in modern philology? "One can enjoy the quiet and take care of one's body until the sun breaks through again somewhere on the horizon! Then out I go again with refreshed energies!" He manages to fool the prince about his skills, but to those who know him he is a living distortion of the grace and pride he extols: his old friend Coelestin pooh-poohs his *je ne sais quoi,* and Katharina scoffs at his teaching, decidedly unimpressed with his so-called educational principles. When he finally gains her trust, it is not because he has taught her how to overcome the limitations of Rogoschin's world, but because only he can help her to escape back into his own circensian heaven. Even Schwigerling's vaunted elasticity, which by his own long-winded testimony has served him so well through the years, has gone a little slack in his present surroundings. Faced with an emergency—how to assist (or frustrate) the prince's wooing of Katharina—Schwigerling shows poverty of invention; the love potion is the prince's idea, the tea-sweating strategy comes from the princess.

Schwigerling's inadequacy supports doubts as to whether the virtues of the circus can actually provide a cure for the degeneration of society. Can they be effective or even survive in that hostile social environment? Certainly Schwigerling himself succumbs at a crucial point. Encountering his first wife again and gradually falling in love with Katharina, he "grasps at his heart" and cries, "If only someone could explain what's happening inside me!" The onslaught to his equilibrium comes from all sides: he has witnessed the prince's vain obsession with Katharina, observed Coelestin's longing for a spiritual love in his worshiping of the remote Lisaweta, experienced Katharina's demonic urge to satisfy desire by destroying everything around her, and discovered his own susceptibility to the past when the princess turns out to be his first great love. Wedekind's splendidly parodistic recognition scene points to the debilitating effect of an attempted return to innocence. No wonder the princess tells him "to see to it, my lad, that you get back to your free and happy element."

Der Liebestrank shows the playwright's development of his peculiar method of juxtaposing dramatic figures of allegorical importance.

Schwigerling's relation with the play's two main female figures is a case in point. He is poised, so to speak, between past and future, between the older woman who once made him a man and the younger who might revitalize his dormant sexual powers, between nostalgia and expectation. Katharina is without sentimentality or perhaps even sentiment: "There is no such thing as love, neither of an earthly nor a heavenly kind." She is afraid of nothing, least of all the prince; and like her pet vulture, Kama, she is prepared to consume anyone and anything in order to appease the hunger in her soul. Her sole weakness is ignorance, and it is only in this respect that Schwigerling can help her. Self-interest makes allies of an ill-matched pair: he gets his opportunity to educate a human being, but in the circus arena, where he is at home; she discovers belatedly that this sphere has always been her destiny: "I'll be ruined forever in body and soul within six months if I'm prevented from doing what providence has created for me in every muscle and fiber of my being." Biological determinism, which was implied in *Spring's Awakening,* here comes into its own.

Lisaweta, by contrast, looks back on, not forward to, the circus. Her career there is over and done with. A trapeze artist in her youth, forced to perform "the paphlagonian diver's leap night after night" until her ribs were broken; trained then to be a belly dancer and exhibited on every stage of the Union; slated finally, after her beauty had faded, to be tattooed from head to foot and displayed "at the Philadelphia World's Fair as a captive of the Indians," Lisaweta escaped only because Prince Rogoschin bought her "for the monstrous sum of 150,000 dollars as the Virgin of the Colorado River" and took her to Russia to become the mother of his children and manager of his household. Wedekind does not seem to deplore this fate, for he makes it clear that the princess has had her day of glory: she basks now in the comfort of the spirit after excelling in the skills of the body.

In a formal sense, *Der Liebestrank* also

embodies the circus's essential principles: the play is a farce (*Schwank*), the story of a prank successfully brought off. The target is the family, representing Wedekind's attempt to get back at the institution whose moral structure was diametrically opposite to the one he had decided on for himself. Other playwrights were also attacking the family, but none (in Germany at least) with the weapons of ridicule; this is Wedekind's innovation. Typically, he so distorts the facts of real life that they are not readily recognizable. Here is a husband who purchases a wife and then neglects her, a father who forces his household to jump to the blasts of a whistle and terrifies his children, a guardian whose lust for his ward turns her into a caricature of a young girl seeking her place in life, and a mother and wife who is not allowed to take part in her sons' upbringing— a family, in short, in which no one treats another in the way the institution prescribes.

Katharina in *Der Liebestrank* is another variant of the female type that had long been taking shape in Wedekind's mind. The child prostitute Ella in *Elins Erweckung,* the horseback rider Ännchen Tartini in the poem of that name, Ilse in *Spring's Awakening*—all belong to such a type; Lulu is to be its culmination. Wedekind saw in these figures the essence of the female sex. These women exist to give pleasure—sensual, body-centered, governed by the instinct of their sex, their lives are devoted to loving; they desire only to be desired and to satisfy the desires of others; their raison d'être is to foster that intimacy between male and female that only sexual intercourse provides.

Plagued by curiosity about girls even before adolescence, Wedekind had concluded by the time of his first stay in Munich that it was "simply impossible" for a man to understand the nature of a woman: "We men are just as incapable of finding our way into the inner life of a woman as we would be into that of a baboon. The female is a different product of nature, governed by other principles and con-

ditions of existence, and for that reason alone will always remain a *terra incognita* for us. We can tread on her territory and swim in her waters, but we can never really know her."

Wedekind's search had little or nothing to do with individuality: "I'm not looking for X; I'm looking for the Female. It's welcome to me in any form. Someday the veil must be torn." And he insisted that love had no part in the quest. On the contrary, love interferes with the discovery of essence because it drags in incidentals: emotions, sentiments, playing by the rules. On this account, he regretted that the woman with whom he was then having an affair had fallen in love with him: "Sad, but true. When I hear her talk so enthusiastically, I suspect that my way of speaking might be the humble cause of stirring her emotions. The Spirit [*Geist*] has gained the upper hand and now I'll have to pay the devil for it."

Defining the nature of the female leads Wedekind to define the nature of the male, and thereby their difference. The obvious difference was sexual, so he spent much of his mental energy reflecting on the particular ways in which men and women respond to sexual experience. In *Spring's Awakening* Moritz Stiefel, who can only imagine what he has never experienced, thinks:

> A girl takes her pleasure the way the gods do. . . . She keeps herself free from bitterness until the last moment and then feels all Heaven break loose over her. But she fears Hell even at the moment when she becomes aware of the paradise unfolding for her. Her feelings are as fresh as the water flowing from a rock. . . . The satisfaction a man feels at such a moment seems to me flat and stale by comparison.
>
> (2:124)

To which Melchior, who might have been expected to defend the male outlook, replies only, "I don't like to think about it." Here Wedekind may have been debating with himself, for he had already decided enviously that in the matter of sex, the advantage, whether measured by capability or degree of enjoyment, lay mostly on the female side.

This continuing inquiry doubtless accounts for Wedekind's consorting with the cocottes and prostitutes of Paris. They came closest to representing his idea of female sexuality, and even when they fell short of embodying this, they could still supply the kind of knowledge he was looking for. His dealings with such women also suggested that another anti-bourgeois institution besides the circus might enable a woman to realize the potentialities of her sex. He was thinking of the bordello and in Paris he devoted several short tales and poems to the subject. The boldest product of this preoccupation is *The Solar Spectrum,* a series of dialogues subtitled "An Idyll of the Modern World." It describes the escape of a young girl, Elise, from her prudish family life into a brothel, where she hopes to find a way of life that will save her from neurosis and fulfill her nature as one born to give joy through sensual pleasure.

But *The Solar Spectrum* is ambiguous enough to cast doubt on Wedekind's faith in the vitalist ideal. The work exists only as a fragment, and the author's outline for it gives conflicting clues about his intentions. A mocking irony pervades the whole, insinuating that nothing he depicts should be taken at face value. What is Wedekind's own view of the events described?

The difficulties begin with the subtitle. The bordello as scene of an idyll? The oxymoron was undoubtedly intended. Certainly "idyll" accurately describes the establishment depicted in *The Solar Spectrum*: it is a quiet place, in a park-like setting. The girls radiate harmony and beauty. Clad only in loose, diaphanous garments, with colors chosen to match the hues of the solar spectrum, together they form "a beauteous rainbow," "a flow of silent music." Men enter the place as though into a paradise, where they can forget responsibility, receive gratification without fear of consequences, indulge themselves sexually without pangs of conscience, repair damaged

egos, and build up sexual confidence, knowing that the girls will gracefully cater to their whims.

This idyllic arrangement is bolstered by the establishment's official "philosophy." The madam advertises her house as "a temple of joy and health"; she professes democratic principles (all ranks and classes are admitted so long as they maintain decorum); she ensures the smooth exchange of favors with strict rules and regulations. Ordinary concerns of the workaday world are banished: no politics, no morality, no rivalry; everything is subordinated to the pursuit of pleasure. The girls have been taught that "there is just one way to be happy in this world, and that is to do everything one can to make others as happy as possible." So that there should be no doubt about the Eden-like scene, Wedekind adapts the traditional idyll form: a place apart from the world, a static situation, episodes without development. The action consists only of variations on a pre-existing state.

The ruling principle throughout is the aesthetic. In addition to physical beauty on every hand, the bordello sponsors regular visits from the poet Eoban, who graces the establishment with his songs and entertains the girls by articulating their feelings. Wedekind's notes for unwritten episodes show that the girls write and act in their own playlets. The house physician, moreover, recommends that a copy of a famous contemporary painting, Kaulbach's *Who Buys the Gods of Love?*, be hung in the reception room. He links the artistic with the erotic even more closely by persuading the madam to employ the inexperienced Elise: "She'll soon find out where her strength lies. It's the same as with our poet Eoban. You can't dictate to him either how he should write. True art has to develop out of itself. Everything else, no matter how nicely it agrees with rules, is nothing but prostitution." In short, art equals sex; the artist who deals in words is the counterpart of the artist whose medium is love.

The male visitors rationalize their bordello experience as a means of achieving some higher value, a truly creative type of activity. Theophil, for example, claims that he has been inspired by the sensual delights of the brothel to write a new opera; Adalbert says he has learned there what love is and will use his new knowledge in a drama; Peter dreams of marriage with his favorite partner and thinks she will teach him the fine manners he needs in order to climb up the social ladder; and Theodor cherishes the memories he will take with him when he marries a woman from the aristocracy. None of these men hint that their real reason for visiting the place is the simple desire for sexual gratification. Motives are prettified and sex not even mentioned by them, although it is the subtext of every conversation.

Wedekind obviously wanted above all to take aim at those who willfully ignored fundamental realities—sexual drive, extramarital relationships, social abuses. He may also have aimed his irony at the aestheticizing tendency of the new literary generation, the so-called aesthetic or *l'art pour l'art* movement, which he found especially despicable because it dodged the reality of sexuality by creating an aesthetic illusion about it.

Wedekind likewise exposes another truth behind appearances, by making it clear that the bordello is not, as it seems, a place of peace and harmony, but suffers from the same discord and contradictions that afflict all human communities. The girls squabble and envy those who seem to enjoy greater advantages than they; the madam, who professes to treat them all alike, has her favorites and treats the others to verbal abuse. Besides, sickness and disease are common, death strikes without warning, medical aid is called for to cure the girls and minister to madam's bouts of depression. Unpleasant reminders of the world outside appear with every client, and even Eoban sings of ways of life that the girls, suspended as they are between chastity and marriage, will never be able to experience. The play ends with a poem confirming this unhappy fact, causing a flood of tears in a place where only happiness is supposed to dwell.

Wedekind leaves no doubt that this putative idyll exists only for men and can be sustained only by the exploitation of women. His attention to this fact has somehow gone unnoticed. The girls' freedom and individuality have been reduced to meet the specific function they perform within the group; they exist solely as marketable objects. The madam is an entrepreneur interested only in the continuing prosperity of her business. She may say, "If I had my way I'd let everyone take his pleasure free of charge," but her actions speak louder than words. When the death of her favorite touches her feelings, these quickly give way to cynical thoughts as to how the loss will affect her enterprise. And when she does accept a replacement, it is only because she is persuaded that the new girl is a true "professional" who will amply compensate for the one who has just died.

The bordello in some respects parallels the "normal" family. The patriarchal system is matched by the matriarchy ruled over by the madam in *The Solar Spectrum*. And Wedekind hints at some other complementary features, notably in his amusing treatment of virginity, where he inverts the usual expectations. For marriage, the purity of the female is required; for the brothel, extensive sexual experience. Wedekind ridicules both these attitudes when he has the new girl, Elise, show up as still virginal and then, by the force of her natural urge alone, bring about her own defloration.

We have noted Wedekind's earnest delving into the nature of sexual experience and its variation in men and women. The question is now posed here in the play's opening episode. For Franziska, sex is never boring—"The more one makes love, the more one would like to make love." A man can only wish this were so for him. Gregor says to her, "I envy you. If I had been born a pretty girl, I would probably have chosen your profession too." Male surfeit and female insatiability are illustrated throughout the play. The men have to rest in the afternoon to perform in the evening. As the house physician caustically remarks, "It's not fair that they have to pay for their pleasure, given the extreme modesty of their demands."

The males in *The Solar Spectrum* are preoccupied with sex, yet it is not the core of their existence; it is rather the prelude to something else that is to give life significance. They find it refreshing, but it demands an expenditure of energy and is soon forgotten. For the girls, the gratifying of male desire is as important as it is obvious. One of Eoban's most popular songs, "Ilse," tells how a girl who has been practicing her art since the age of fourteen would rather die than discover she is no longer capable of pleasing a man. But the business is without illusion. Schneewittchen speaks for the group when she indignantly rejects Adalbert's claim upon her feelings as well as her body: "He thinks I have to fall in love with him because he's slept with me four nights in a row. But I've not been hired to *love* him, and one should never do more than one's paid for." None feel regret as to how it all began. They think poorly of their first experience. Franziska: "I must say, I was actually disappointed." Schneewittchen: "I had imagined it to be much more beautiful." Scharolta: "I was here for a whole year before I felt anything. I just pretended." Yet those who have also made sex their profession come closest to fulfilling their destiny as women. At least that is the male view expressed in *The Solar Spectrum*.

Clearly, Wedekind was still trying to solve the mystery that seemed forever to elude him. He was sure of only one thing: in the matter of sexual relations men know little of what actually goes on, deceive themselves about female response, and claim credit where it is not due. Elise's entering the bordello by choice and her self-defloration prove that men are superfluous: women can find their natural sexuality on their own. Two other episodes show that men have little or no control over what actually happens in a sexual encounter. The superconfident Edgar is sure that *he* will be the one who chooses "the most beautiful girl," but he is told by the madam in advance—correctly, as it turns out—on whom his choice will actually

fall; she may not know *him* but she does know her girls. In another episode, planned but not written, the girls present a skit called "The Key of Salomis" (a metaphor for the phallus). It purports to show "the art of seducing any girl in ten to twenty minutes." What it actually shows is that this art, in the words of Artur Kutscher, "rests less on the man's skills than on the woman's eagerness to provide them both with pleasure."

The culminating work of Wedekind's Paris-London years is the pair of *Lulu* dramas. The most complicated and most original among his plays, this double drama occupied his attention off and on for over twenty years. Throughout the 1890's he was at work on a "Schauertragödie" (Horror Tragedy), completed in 1895 under the title "Die Büchse der Pandora: Eine Monstertragödie" (Pandora's Box: A Monstertragedy). It was never published. In that same year he divided the work into two: the four-act *Erdgeist* (*Earth Spirit*) and the three-act *Pandora's Box,* the latter not published until 1902. It is these two versions of the *Lulu* material that have occupied many scholars and critics. Prologues were added to each play at later dates, and in 1913 Wedekind put together again what he had split by composing a new five-act play under the title *Lulu.*

Many of the changes Wedekind undertook in his original one-act were made to circumvent the censor, others by the wish to help audiences to understand his intentions, while still others arose from ambiguities in his conception of the central figure. Lulu is on one level a mortal woman like any other, alternately triumphant and then defeated by the men she encounters. She also exists allegorically as the embodiment of an instinctual and amoral force that every man has to cope with in himself and that also threatens the foundations of society. Furthermore, as the titles suggest, Lulu is a mythological figure, analogous to such archetypes as the Greek Helena and the Hebrew Lilith. In calling his first play *Earth Spirit* Wedekind may be saying that Lulu represents the motive force that energizes all earthly activity—the principle of desire. In naming his second play *Pandora's Box* he may be saying that Lulu contains all the gifts the gods have bestowed on men, equivocal as these may be: it is not the gifts but their use that brings happiness or unhappiness. And when man tries to break into that box—here again a sexual analogy—it is always because he hopes that he will find his greatest joy within. Despite these uncertainties about Lulu, the dramatic action is straightforward— a series of encounters between Lulu and the male figures who try to possess or use her according to their own image of her. The main difference between the two plays is that in *Earth Spirit* Lulu dominates, resists, and triumphs over those who try to exploit her, whereas in *Pandora's Box* she gradually loses her freedom and finally falls into the hands of Jack the Ripper.

Wedekind uses different types of structure for these plays. In *Earth Spirit* it is theme and variation—one basic event recurs in each of the four acts: Lulu is linked with a man who dies after discovering that her reality differs from his image of her. Her first husband, Dr. Goll, succumbs to a heart attack when he discovers her in a compromising situation with a younger man. Her second husband, the painter Walter Schwarz, slits his throat on learning about her promiscuous affairs. A would-be suitor, Prince Escerny, retreats in confusion when she rejects his offer to throw himself at her feet. Her third husband, Dr. Ludwig Schön, is shot by Lulu in self-defense when he tries to force her to commit suicide.

This succession of deaths has led to much misunderstanding about the play and its protagonist. Lulu has been seen as a femme fatale, a destroyer of men. This interpretation does not hold water. Lulu plays an entirely passive role in *Earth Spirit;* her actions are reactions to the imposition of others' wills. Amoral, indifferent to bourgeois norms, Lulu is unaware of the implications of what she does; she lives only to be desired, to give and receive pleasure. And as someone who lives for love, embodying the vitalist principle, Lulu is by nature incapable of killing; she does not cause death; she is only the occasion for it, and when it comes she recoils from it uncomprehendingly. The men who are destroyed through knowing Lulu bring about their own destruction, because they are unable to sustain the illusions they have created of her for egoistic ends. As Alfred Polgar astutely wrote in 1905, she is "the *hetaira* out of organic necessity." Her tragedy arises not from her own nature, but from the men's "mania to master that which cannot be mastered, their ridiculous efforts to have a woman realize the dream *for* them which the woman's beauty has aroused *in* them."

The point is best seen in the episode with Dr. Schön, the only man Lulu ever professes to love, no doubt because he comes closest to understanding what she has to offer the world and also has the necessary (Wedekind would say, brutal) intelligence to be her guide. But Wedekind typically makes potentiality turn into perversity, and Schön fails to accept Lulu's challenge to his judgment and becomes her chief enemy. Their relation begins with his rescue, many years earlier, of the child Lulu from her life in the streets. He takes her into his home and provides her with a solid bourgeois upbringing. Schön in time perverts this paternal role and makes Lulu his mistress. He compounds the outrage by simultaneously pursuing marriage with a woman of rank. Irritated by his sexual enslavement to Lulu, wary of her uncertain origins, and fearful of her indifference to conventional morality, Schön tries to marry her off to someone else, hoping to keep her at a distance, yet still available to himself as need arises. He arranges the ill-fated match with Dr. Goll and the even more disastrous marriage with the gullible Schwarz. Finally, after failing to couple Lulu with Prince Escerny, he succumbs to her himself as the fourth in the fatal series of male self-deceivers.

Earth Spirit criticizes, in the person of Dr.

Schön, the so-called *Gewaltmensch* (man of power) who believes he can control events and manipulate human beings for his own purposes. (Schön is the influential editor of a widely distributed newspaper.) Yet the target in *Earth Spirit* is neither marriage and social types nor the uneven struggle between Lulu and Schön; it is rather the devious and ultimately futile ways in which the male figures try to cope with the force exerted upon them by the female. She—the female—is something different from them, not of their own making, and perpetually eluding their control. Lulu stands for the male's confrontation with a separate order of existence, not comprehensible to his limited, predominantly rational, approach to life. In sum, Lulu represents the quintessence of female sexuality as seen from, and in confrontation with, the male point of view.

The difficulty of writing such a play was obvious: how to represent something that defied comprehension and transcended its concrete manifestations and yet behaved like a dramatis persona. Wedekind's solution was brilliant but also ambiguous, giving rise to further confusion about his intentions. One device was to present Lulu negatively, showing what she is not. Still another was to keep her wrapped in mystery, a mystery not only for others but also for herself. In one striking scene of *Earth Spirit,* Schwarz's interrogation over Goll's dead body, Lulu is unable to answer any of his questions; her sole reply is a desperate "I don't know." By a third stratagem, Lulu is shown only through her effect on others, or through others' view of her, the result being that she exists only partially, relatively, in only one dimension.

Wedekind underscores the fact by having each of the men call her by a different name. Dr. Goll, for example, calls Lulu "Nelli," a name that recalls the heroine of a nineteenth-century domestic drama, a child-bride, perhaps, carefully guarded by her husband and expected to fuss over him. Impotent himself, Goll attempts to make the irrepressible Lulu into a work of art that he can show off to others. He has her portrait painted and trains her as a dancer, while keeping watch to ensure that others will not tempt her to escape his control. This very love of art is what makes him drop his guard for a moment and let Lulu get involved in the compromising game with Schwarz, the painter. This brings on the old man's fatal heart attack.

To Schwarz, Lulu is known as "Eve," the female prototype, created by God to be man's helpmate, who became his temptress, causing his loss of innocence and of paradise. As Eve, Lulu suggests male superiority and male anxiety: the creature has been formed out of his substance but is entirely unlike himself. Schwarz's blindness as to Eve's nature and that of his own feelings is the cause of his undoing. When faced at last with reality, he commits suicide.

Finally, Dr. Schön (and later his son Alwa) call Lulu "Mignon" after Goethe's remarkable figure, whose name reminds us of Schön's saving the orphan girl from walking the streets. It also suggests an unpossessible object of desire: she is not of this world and longs for release from it.

Having answered to so many different names, that of "Lulu" seems to her "positively antediluvian." Yet there is one figure in *Earth Spirit* who always calls her by it, and he remains one of Wedekind's most intriguing creations. Schigolch, the old beggar out of *Elins Erweckung,* turns up twice in the later play, totally unmotivated unless it be to take advantage of Lulu's momentary good fortune. The links between these two are suggestive but obscure. Both bear unconventional names, hinting at a common origin in some primitive or elemental state of being. Even if Schigolch is not her father, as Lulu claims and he denies, some relation between them has existed since her birth, one that occasionally skirts the erotic and incestuous. Even at his age he feels faintly those stirrings that Lulu awakens in all males. But he differs from the other four men in treating Lulu as an individual in her own right. He is in fact cynical about her, takes her as she appears, accepts whatever truth she embodies from moment to moment—all this without forgetting that Lulu is a woman, subject to the laws of nature, and destined to go the way of all flesh. "We're nothing but degeneration and decay," he reminds her, and then, crassly, "Your admirers aren't going to preserve you in ethyl alcohol, you know. It's called 'beautiful Melusine' as long as it's still alive and kicking. But afterwards? They wouldn't take it as a gift at the zoo. They'd be afraid their precious beasts would get stomach cramps."

Schigolch's warning is carried out in *Pandora's Box,* which traces the fulfillment of Lulu's destiny in decline and death. In dramatic terms, this second *Lulu* drama follows the first as in a chronicle depicting the fall of the central figure after his or her rise to power and glory. It also resembles the revenge play, in which an injury done to an individual or to the moral order must be compensated by punishment. Yet these patterns do not adequately describe *Pandora's Box* and may even mislead if relied on for clues to its meaning. After all, the "society" in which Lulu suffers her fall is not the same as that in which she triumphed, and her "avenger" is himself an outcast who flouts its moral expectations. In addition, long before she meets her death at the hands of Jack the Ripper, she has become a different person, a perversion of her former self, not just a victim of mortality but a transgressor against the laws of her own being. For all these reasons, Lulu's end must be seen as inherent in what she is, the logical consequence of her own acts.

This question of Lulu's "true self" is particularly intriguing. Despite her mystery, it is plain that the Lulu of *Pandora's Box* behaves in untypical ways. She now practices deception. Thus she escapes from prison disguised as another woman and repeats the trick during her long flight from the law. She lies again and again to both friends and foes. She pretends in order to get rid of an unwanted hanger-on, and she betrays her most faithful admirer to secure

her own safety. Is this the "real" Lulu showing her true colors? The question is misplaced. Lulu has always been seen as both angel and devil, as child and seductress; and despite her protestations that she need never pretend to be anything but herself, she is in fact a dissembler by nature. Lulu's course in *Pandora's Box* is but the underside, the conscious, deliberate counterpart, of her previous behavior. In *Earth Spirit* she acts immediately, instinctively, openly, as a person at one with herself; in *Pandora's Box* she has become intentional, self-aware, aiming at specific ends. In a word, the second Lulu is afflicted with self-consciousness.

The turning point in her life occurs in the last scene of *Earth Spirit,* when she kills Ludwig Schön. The action, to be sure, springs from the instinct of self-preservation, but it also signifies a new self-awareness. Lulu realizes for the first time that death is not just something that happens to others; it is a threat to her as well. Because of the argument that precedes her act, Lulu cannot help becoming conscious of its enormity and of what she has lost by it: "I have shot him . . . the only man I ever loved!" Violence is out of character for her; it runs counter to her habitual passivity. With this killing Lulu steps across the line that has always separated her from society; she thereby forfeits her inviolability and becomes vulnerable.

To put it differently, in *Pandora's Box,* Lulu's relation to society has altered. The men she meets now are no less eager to exploit her—indeed, they are caricatures of the males in the earlier play. Rodrigo Quast, for example, the strongman from the circus who wants to train Lulu as an aerialist in order to live off her earnings, recalls Dr. Goll and his efforts to train her as a dancer. The difference is that she has been reduced from artist to *artiste,* from one who expresses herself to one who makes money for others. The change is from an activity natural to her personality to one that is wholly external. It shows in her diminished power to please, her loss of freshness, her inability to command respect; she is no longer unique, unfathomable, self-confident, and at one with herself. The men have now begun to doubt that she can make their dreams come true. Rodrigo questions her stamina for the feats he has planned for her; Alwa Schön, who has had some success with a play based on her early career, wonders whether she could be used in a sequel now. Only the Marquis Casti-Piani, a procurer and police spy who is entirely impervious to Lulu's sexuality, thinks he knows how to handle her: she belongs in a brothel. He tells her brutally:

> What you offer is a selection of choice delicacies, but once a man has frittered away his time with them he's hungrier than ever. You've been at this loving business much too long. . . . When a healthy young man falls into your hands you ruin his entire nervous system. All the more reason why you're so suited for the place I have in mind for you.
>
> (3:148)

Lulu manages to escape the brothel, but does sink into prostitution, driven to it by the need to keep herself and her little troupe (the parasitic Schigolch and Alwa, who has become unable to work owing to frustration and disease) from starving.

Once again the question arises, What does Lulu stand for? To herself Lulu remains a mystery; to the men in touch with her she is an everlasting paradox as well as a threat to their existence. Men have only two responses to such power: to control or to annihilate it. In *Earth Spirit* Wedekind records men's failure to control the Lulu principle; in *Pandora's Box* they destroy it.

The men Lulu lures to her attic room in London severally recall the figures she was involved with at the height of her career. The last, Jack the Ripper (echoing Dr. Schön's remark "That was a tough job!"), is the only one equal to bringing her unhappy course to an end. This recapitulation of figures is another example of the theme-and-variation technique typical of Wedekind's early work. The action intensifies as it goes on. At first angered at her humiliating situation, Lulu gradually warms to the contact with her customers until the encounter with Jack actually makes her eager for his favors. She does not die easily.

That Lulu should be mutilated by him has seemed to some critics unnecessary and unduly moralistic, as though the playwright were set on a sensational conclusion. Yet Jack belongs to the very earliest conception of the play. The reasons for this are instructive. Jack was a contemporary fact, like Nietzsche or the cholera epidemic, both mentioned in the plays—proof that the action is rooted in historical reality. He is thus a reminder that Lulu, even though she is a figure larger than life, is also a very mortal individual. Jack, moreover, acts solely for the pleasure of destroying what makes Lulu a source of pleasure. To make this fact stand out, Wedekind decided to drop the "motives" he had attributed to Jack in earlier versions, such as a wish to make a contribution to science by adding Lulu's genitalia to a collection he hopes to sell to the London Medical Society (!).

Much has been made of the words Lulu utters after her escape from prison: "While I was there I dreamed once, for a couple of nights, that I'd fallen into the hands of a sex maniac [*Lustmörder*]." Critics have assumed that these words express a wish for the end Lulu finally meets. If so, Wedekind makes little of it. What he saw as inevitable was the real point: Lulu, who was born to give pleasure, must live and die discharging that function. The result is *Lustmord*: pleasure coexistent with destruction, sensuality in the abstract. The whole human being has been reduced to the single part that is the source of what is both highest and lowest in human experience.

Any discussion of the *Lulu* dramas must include a word on Lulu's portrait. It is being painted at the beginning of *Earth Spirit* and is reintroduced in the last scene of *Pandora's Box*. The painting depicts Lulu in a Pierrot costume, and is present in every act except one, where its role is played (at the theater) by Lulu herself.

The painting is a unifying device, establishing her presence even when she is not there.

It also draws attention to the subject of art. The painter Schwarz lives "from palette to mouth," totally dependent on wealthy patrons who pay him and "call the tune." Dr. Goll continually badgers the painter as to how the portrait should look, offering also his views on contemporary art. Wedekind here and elsewhere in the play expresses his disgust at the increasing commercialization of art, its status as "a luxury article for the bourgeoisie."

One may note in passing the contrast between Wedekind's use of Lulu's portrait and Oscar Wilde's use of the portrait of Dorian Gray. In the latter, it is the portrait that records change, the shocking effect of Dorian's decay, while in Wedekind's work the portrait remains the same while the reality changes.

This disparity makes one reflect on the relation between life and art. Wedekind suggests through various speeches in the play that each of the men gazing at the portrait has turned to art as a substitute for the reality he unconsciously feels unable to cope with. The notion of art as illusion, and a substitute for a reality that is too hot to handle, recalls the main theme of *The Solar Spectrum*.

In addition to all that has been said, the two *Lulu* dramas constitute an effort to revitalize modern society with a new kind of art. This had been Wedekind's motive in going to Paris. The result appears negative. For if Lulu represents the revivifying force, then the failure of those around her to take advantage of it is an expression of extreme pessimism on Wedekind's part. The play does not even show a struggle between forces but depicts a steady decline. Pandora, the bearer of gifts, offers a hope that in the end remains within her tantalizing box.

SOCIETY AS VICTOR

By 1895 Wedekind had realized that his hopes of revitalizing the German theater from France were not going to succeed and that his chances of getting *Pandora's Box* published or produced from abroad were slim. He decided to return to Germany and seek his fortune anew on home ground. His first stop was Berlin, where he renewed acquaintance with the circle around Gerhart Hauptmann, by now a celebrity, and tried to persuade various theatrical organizations, which had been formed expressly to present modern works, to mount a production of *Earth Spirit*. Rebuffed again, Wedekind withdrew to Switzerland and spent the next few months eking out a living by giving public readings of scenes from Ibsen and other contemporary playwrights.

Early in 1896 Wedekind was invited by the publisher Albert Langen, whom he had met in Paris, to join a new satirical weekly based in Munich, to be called *Simplicissimus*. It was planned to oppose political and religious conservatism in German life, mainly by means of cartoons and short prose pieces. During the first year and a half, Wedekind became its most prolific contributor, with some fifteen poems, three short stories, six feature "interviews," and numerous cartoon captions. Though he always protested that his work for *Simplicissimus* was a waste of time, he was in no position to spurn the job—and it did introduce his name to a wide public. It also left him time for serious writing. Best of all, Langen agreed to publish any of Wedekind's works that the journal's lawyers thought would get by the censors.

The first volume to appear on this basis was *Princess Russalka*, an anthology of shorter pieces in diverse genres: eight prose fictions, a collection of eighty-four lyric poems, and three pantomimes (but not the rambunctious *Bethel*). *Princess Russalka* showed a side of Wedekind not previously known to his tiny public, but the collection did little to further his career. Only the poems drew favorable notice, and though they are intrinsically not very important, they later encouraged the development of the so-called lyric grotesques favored by Brecht and other social satirists of the mid twenties.

In early 1898 the Literary Society in Leipzig produced *Earth Spirit,* with Wedekind playing the role of Dr. Schön. Success in Leipzig led to another production in Munich, and Wedekind was soon invited to join the city's leading theater, the Schauspielhaus, in the triple role of director, actor, and dramaturge (in charge of selecting plays and editing texts). The very night of his acting debut, however, Wedekind learned that he was about to be arrested on charges of lèse majesté for a poem in *Simplicissimus.* He slipped away to Zurich and later to Paris. When it became clear that he would not be forgiven soon, he surrendered to the authorities and was sentenced to seven months' imprisonment. His time in jail was well spent, for there he finished a new play, *Der Marquis von Keith* (*The Marquis of Keith,* first published under this title in 1901), and revised his novel, *Mine-Haha, oder über die körperliche Erziehung der jungen Mädchen* (Mine-Haha, or On the Physical Education of Young Girls, 1895–1899).

Next came a one-act play, *Der Kammersänger* (The Court Singer, translated as *The Tenor,* 1899), presented in Berlin during his imprisonment and then produced on several stages throughout the country, with Wedekind often playing the role of Professor Dühring. The plot is simple: a famous tenor, Oskar Gerardo, has just completed an engagement at the local opera house and is about to go to Brussels, when he is thrice interrupted in his hotel room—by an admiring teenager who offers him flowers and "herself" in an overflow of adolescent enthusiasm; by an aging composer, Professor Eugen Dühring, who begs the singer to make his new opera "marketable" by taking over the title role; and by a married woman with whom he has had a brief fling and who now wants to run away with him.

From the first, audiences have taken the work as autobiography, and Wedekind himself seemed to encourage this identification. Dühring, he admitted, was modeled on himself "as I appeared vis-à-vis the theater at age thirty-three." But Wedekind's main intention was to show the degrading position of the artist under modern capitalism. The unhappy Dühring believes that art is a calling sanctioned by an all-powerful divinity "whose creatures willingly sacrifice themselves to it." He has unswervingly pursued a creative course no one else recognizes: he is not "marketable." Gerardo has also made art his life, but has observed all the rules for success. He is the accommodator par excellence, and not to be moved from his hard-won position by appeals to the heart. Every move Gerardo makes is governed either by considerations of contract or by the decisions of his manager and the expectations of his public. According to Gerardo, Dühring has overestimated the value of art: "We artists are nothing but a luxury article of the bourgeoisie, who compete among themselves to see which of them can pay us more."

Similarly, when Gerardo rejects Helene Marowa's offer to abandon her husband and children for him, it is out of prudence: "My contract forbids me to either marry or travel in the company of women." He even denounces the force that has drawn them together: "Love is a bourgeois virtue! . . . When two people get together, they know exactly what they can expect from each other. They don't need love for that!"

Wedekind later professed to dislike the play—"the worst of my works"—but it has been performed more frequently than any of his other plays, and it gave him a firm place in the German repertoire. Its economical dramaturgy, its fast-moving dialogue with occasional flashes of aphoristic brilliance, the presence of familiar character types, and the careful build-up of tension in the three episodes have all contributed to the play's popularity.

For his next major work, *The Marquis of Keith,* Wedekind drew upon the circumstances surrounding the founding of the Deutsches Theater in Munich in 1896. The model for his title figure was Willy Grétor, a notorious art dealer and forger who had befriended him during his last months in Paris.

The slightly crippled marquis is the bastard

son of a gypsy and a village schoolmaster. Determined to rise in the world, he has succeeded by means both fair and foul, and now is one of the most talked-about men in Munich. Somewhere along the way he has acquired his title, taken a mistress, the widowed Countess Werdenfels, and seduced a fifteen-year-old girl, Molly Griesinger, who has become his common-law wife and now runs his household.

In Munich, this egoist brimming with energy and self-confidence is working on his most ambitious project to date: the construction of a gigantic amusement palace (*Feenpalast*) in which art and business will flourish by mutual support. The trouble with this dream is that Keith has no money to make it come true. He has to turn to the capitalists in Munich society, brewers and restaurateurs and building contractors. By the time the play opens, Keith has won over all the supporters he needs except for Consul Casimir, the richest and most powerful man in town.

At this point Keith is visited by an old boyhood friend, Ernst Scholz, an all-around failure. He now wants Keith to teach him how to enjoy life, and because Scholz is prepared to pay handsomely for such bizarre instruction, Keith takes him on. Wedekind's constructivist (allegorical-critical) method is still at work here. The encounter of the men, wrote Wedekind is "the interplay between a Don Quixote of pleasure [Keith] and a Don Quixote of morality [Scholz]." The secondary figures are similarly aligned: Molly, Keith's common-law wife, is a counterpart to Scholz; Anna, Keith's mistress, who is wooed by Scholz but eventually won by Casimir, is a counterpart to Keith. The plot is designed to show how Keith's pursuit of fame and fortune is bound to fail; Keith is successively abandoned by all those he has tried to exploit. Bourgeois principles defeat his attempt to manipulate bourgeois people in his own interest. The final blow is given by Consul Casimir when he discovers that Keith has forged the consul's name on a telegram supporting Keith's project. The consul demands that Keith turn over the *Feenpalast* plan to him

and leave the city. Keith weighs suicide, then decides that the 10,000 marks Casimir offers is enough for a fresh start elsewhere. "Life is just a playground slide," a climb up only to come down again. Individualist and visionary, Keith has tried to beat the bourgeois world at its own game and found himself beaten by it instead.

The Marquis of Keith marks a change in Wedekind's technique. The allegorical-constructivist method is present, but the structure of the work is neither the open form of *Spring's Awakening* nor the cyclical episodic movement of the two *Lulu* plays. It resembles rather a conventional five-act structure. But the conventions of so-called classical drama are employed outrageously and parody the contemporary French and German practice. The language of the play reveals what Wedekind is up to, for the dialogue does not in fact imitate conversation but amounts to a contest of wit or a monologue interrupted by another's remarks. Throughout, there are aphorisms of almost Wilde-like brilliance, in effect stylizing the language on a high rhetorical plane.

Wedekind's hope that the public would respond favorably to *The Marquis of Keith* was disappointed. The element of parody bewildered the audience and perhaps the performers also. As Wedekind explained it, the players had been trained to act in a naturalistic style and could not cope with the abstract, analytical, and allegorical mode. Wedekind consequently turned his attention more and more to acting. Altogether untrained, he played only sporadically until about 1904. Then he decided to take acting lessons, an experience he found "liberating" because, as he put it, it opened up "new dramatic dimensions." He accepted more frequent engagements, and after his marriage to the actress Tilly Newes, the two appeared regularly together in productions of his work. In 1910 Wedekind published *Schauspielkunst: Ein Glossarium* (A Commentary on the Art of Acting, 1910), in which he took issue with current theatrical styles and proposed alternatives. The commentary makes a notable contribution to reform of the theater arts.

By most accounts, Wedekind showed only moderate competence as an actor. Critics faulted him for awkwardness, stiff, puppetlike movements, and overblown mannerisms, but they agreed that his presence commanded the stage and that his interpretation of his own roles made them not just comprehensible but unforgettable. According to Leopold Jessner in 1914, "The day on which Wedekind began to roam the land was the beginning of a new era"; that is, he pioneered the type of performance later associated with Brecht and the "estrangement" school of acting. Wedekind soon involved himself in another development—the renovation of the theater itself as an institution. To provide an alternative to the highbrow conservatism of established stages and to the lowbrow excesses of the popular *varietés* (vaudeville), a few daring members of the avant-garde conceived the new "literary cabaret."

The cabaret originated in France. Wedekind and others brought knowledge of it to Germany in the late 1890's. About the same time, the notion of a literary art concerned with everyday, practical matters—in O. J. Bierbaum's phrase, *eine angewandte Kunst* (applied art)—had taken strong hold on the avant-garde imagination. Bierbaum's publication of *Deutsche Chansons* (German Songs, 1900) illustrated the kind of poetry he had in mind, and Wedekind was represented in it by nine lyrics. The first literary cabaret to succeed was Die Elf Scharfrichter (The Eleven Executioners) in Munich. The audiences were purposely kept small to ensure an intimate atmosphere and reduce overhead; the artists who created the numbers also performed them, and the programs offered a great variety: poetry recitations, songs, sketches, marionette plays, parodies, monologues, pantomimes. The "Executioners" appeared in appropriate costume and stage names to underscore "the sharpness of their judgments" and "the decisiveness of their execution."

Wedekind's participation was sought by all the new literary cabarets. The notoriety of his *Simplicissimus* prison term was a powerful drawing card; and his satiric talents had become known, thanks to Bierbaum's anthology. The belief that he practiced what he preached in the area of sexual freedom added a valuable note of eroticism to the cabaret's socio-political criticism. But Wedekind at first declined to join the movement; he could not see himself appearing as a "buffoon and clown . . . when I'm not allowed to open my mouth [on the legitimate stage] with the best I have to say."

He finally succumbed to Die Elf Scharfrichter because of a desperate need for money. His only stipulation was that his appearances take place under his own name; the other "Executioners" kept their identities hidden. "Why a pseudonym?" he asked. "When one does a thing like this it's not to hide oneself but to get oneself known." From three nights a week, he soon was appearing every night by popular demand, singing one of his ballads and accompanying himself on the guitar. His deadpan renditions, his cold gaze fixed on the audience, and the sound of his harsh voice matching his words created a somewhat sinister atmosphere. He seemed to implicate the listeners in the questionable goings-on he was singing about. He acquired an immense popularity through his ballads, through the recitation of his "Rabbi Esra," and through the staging of his pantomime *Die Kaiserin von Neufundland* by the group.

Die Elf Scharfrichter brought Wedekind more money than he had ever earned before. Now he no longer needed to beg from his family and friends. He also gained a following through people who went to his plays because they had heard him sing. Wedekind wrote nothing new for the cabaret, drawing solely on the works already created in Paris. The cabaret also left its mark on the plays written after this time, beginning with *König Nicolo, oder So ist das Leben* (King Nicolo, or Such Is Life, 1902), which incorporates song and dance numbers.

It was the success of *King Nicolo* that led Wedekind to give up the cabaret. The play was his first to meet with unqualified acceptance on a state-supported stage. Those who knew his work could hardly believe that the new play was by the man who had writen the *Lulu* dramas and *The Marquis of Keith*. *King Nicolo* deals with the replacement of the king of Umbria by a former butcher, Pietro Folchi. Accused of debauchery and of disregard for his subjects, Nicolo is banished by Folchi under pain of death. But he cannot bear to leave the land he has ruled over; he escapes with his daughter, Alma, and wanders in disguise throughout the country trying to find employment among the common people. Failing at every turn, Nicolo curses the king (meaning himself), who prevents him "from becoming a human being like any other." The words are overheard and interpreted as a reference to the new monarch, and Nicolo (now known as Gigi Ludovicus) is brought to trial, accused of lèse majesté, sentenced to prison, then banished a second time. Nicolo assumes yet another disguise and goes with the ever-faithful Alma to the yearly midnight gathering of social outcasts and vagrants, seeking employment with a theatrical troupe. He auditions as a tragedian in a play about a monarch unrecognized as such by his own people, but his acting only arouses raucous laughter. Still, one producer sees possibilities in Nicolo's "caricature" and hires him to be the leading man in a new royal farce. Equipped with still another name, Epaminondas Alexandrion, the former king tours the country with great success and eventually performs before King Pietro. Seeing both truth and danger in Nicolo's portrayal of a king who is humbled and degraded by the force of his own nature, Pietro orders him to give up his profession and become the king's jester. Still unrecognized, Nicolo spends his last years at court, hoping that the romance that blossoms between the king's son and his own daughter will lead to marriage, thereby assuring Alma of her rightful place in the kingdom. When Pietro objects

to the match and orders the jester to forbid it, Nicolo risks death and banishment for a third time by declaring his true identity. Though unconvinced—the jester seems to have gone mad—King Pietro is moved by so much passion, cancels Nicolo's sentence, and agrees to his son's union with Alma. When the jester-king finally expires from the strain of his tribulations, Pietro has him buried in the royal vault—"whoever he might be," for "history must not say of me that I made a jester out of a king."

At first glance, *King Nicolo* seems an anomaly. The fictitious historical setting and its trappings—costumes, pageantry, crowd scenes—do not occur elsewhere in Wedekind's work, and other devices, such as songs and a play-within-the-play, indicate that Wedekind wanted to reach a wide audience. Nor had he been so openly autobiographical before. Some critics have found the play a mere confessional drama. Sol Gittleman writes, "One need only substitute *Dichter* [poet] for *König* [king] to recognize Wedekind's personal lament over his own artistic situation." This interpretation restricts the meaning of the play and obscures the author's true purpose, however.

The prologue, spoken by the actors who portray Nicolo and Alma, gives important clues. The play is about human dignity, its nature and vulnerability in an invariably hostile environment.

The prologue also enjoins, "No laughter, please!" and the play, despite many potentially comic scenes, does leave an impression of unrelieved seriousness, excluding all *Humor*. In contrast to Wedekind's usual procedures, there was no confrontation of extreme opposing attitudes and therefore no way for an audience to arrive at a balanced position with respect to them. Wedekind himself came to regret the "five long acts of complaining."

Still, his attempt to coach the audience in the prologue was intended to make the point that the theme of a serious play concerns everybody; in this instance it affirms that all mankind is alike in being governed by the two opposite forces incarnated in the figure now addressing them—"a little king and a big fool." It is because one tries to be the former that one becomes the latter, to the loss of one's human dignity. One must keep up the inner "king" without becoming a great "fool" in the process. That process, which entails self-discovery, begins early in the play, when Nicolo realizes that he alone is responsible for losing his throne; after all, a king must present to his people "the image of their own good fortune" lest he rob them of their justification for existence.

The agent of Nicolo's ultimate self-revelation is his own daughter, Alma, in her disguise as clown. She stands for that aspect of the self which is objectified in some form of independent existence—offspring, creation, or other work that permits the self to see what it conceals or ignores. In this play-within-the-play she tells the king that she is also his "daimon," his "dream." It thus becomes clear that he has let his kingly powers tempt him to indulge instinctual desires, an offense against his nobler self.

Wedekind believed he had hit here upon a universal dilemma. Every man is a "king" by virtue of being unique and separate from other men, and also a "fool" by imagining he can use his powers on others for his benefit alone. Yet without the assurance of being a "king" one loses sense of one's own worth and one's dignity. All this being true, Nicolo is happiest in prison, where there is no need to maintain dignity and one can give oneself over to dreams.

In the final scenes of the play Nicolo has given up hope of regaining any position—powerless, he is a mere adviser who can be disregarded at will. His only "dignity" consists in the opportunity he has to further the union between Alma and young prince Filipo, which would ensure continuity to his royal line. His outburst, followed by the revelation about his identity, brings about his death, and that self-sacrifice for the sake of his child (she who has come from him but is independent of him)

shows dignity beyond anything he had been able to conceive before.

TAKING STOCK

With *Karl Hetmann, der Zwergriese* (Karl Hetmann, the Pygmy-Giant, first published in 1904 under the title *Hidalla, oder Sein und Haben* [Hidalla, or Debit and Credit]). Wedekind enters yet another phase. In the first part of his career Wedekind had put his art at the service of vitalism, charging it with the rejuvenation of society by advocating the release of libidinal forces pent up within a moribund culture. This first phase ends with the *Lulu* dramas, which show that society did not want his message that art is powerless.

In the second phase the plays abandon confrontation in favor of showing a great dilemma—the impossibility of being both part of and apart from the social matrix. The figures in these later plays wonder how to maintain some measure of human dignity in the face of that predicament.

The third phase is marked by a shift from biological and psychological determinants to the sociological. All the themes of the preceding dramas appear once more but the analysis and self-criticism are more thoroughgoing. Matters formerly implicit are now made explicit and are openly discussed by the characters of the play. As to tone and mode, they include parody as before and add to it paradox.

At the center of *Karl Hetmann* are an idea and its propounder. It is as if Wedekind were trying to account for his failure as a prophet of utopian ideals. He now sees the fruitlessness of the effort as due no less to himself than to his opponents. The traditional drama of ideas does not question the merits of what it celebrates; the idea remains inviolate even at the cost of destroying the individual who represents it. But in Wedekind's new play the idea—or rather, the complex of ideas—promulgated by Karl Hetmann is presented from the start as untenable, a bizarre mixture of early Wedekind vitalist principles, perverted Nietzscheanism, and contemporary cult eugenics. Hetmann has founded an International Society for the Propagation of Human Thoroughbreds to which only rich and beautiful members of the bourgeois white race are admitted. The men and women members are free from moral and marital obligations and none may deny sexual favors to any other member who requests them. Ironically, Hetmann himself is barred from membership because he is a "deformed, homely creature . . . , toothless, with thinning hair and oversized eyes flashing with passion." He has to content himself being general secretary in his own organization.

Wedekind now proceeds to show that the intellectualization of an instinctual impulse when it takes obsessive hold of those who formulate it is the fundamental cause of the personal and social evils depicted in the play. Hetmann is afraid that his ideas cannot stand on their own without concrete realization. He therefore chooses a stunningly handsome young man, Morosini, to serve as Grand Master of the society. Morosini protests that he is a "completely ordinary everyday person," a total failure so far, a "pygmy-giant" in the ways of the world. Morosini's true character as a man-on-the-make comes out later, when he betrays the cause by selling himself to one of the two rich women bidding for his hand in marriage.

Hetmann's second false step is to ask a businessman, the publisher Rudolf Launhart (whose real-life model was Albert Langen), to be his propaganda agent for the organization. Whether Hetmann knows from the beginning that Launhart is a scoundrel is less important than his own eagerness to seek a sponsor and use the media to enlist the public's interest. Hetmann gradually falls under Launhart's control, while the businessman profits at the prophet's expense. Nor does Hetmann's unhappy experience with Launhart ever persuade him to break off the association; even after discovering Launhart's duplicity, even after serving a term in jail thanks to Launhart's maneu-

vering (shades of the *Simplicissimus* affair), Hetmann continues to depend on the man who has tricked him. At the very end, Hetmann is used by Launhart once more, for the book he has written (entitled "Hidalla, or the Morality of Beauty") falls into Launhart's hands and will be printed by him after Hetmann's suicide.

Wedekind's critique of Hetmann is matched by an even more biting critique of the capitalist and his moral system. Launhart is portrayed as a capitalist living off the money and talents of other people, his sole motive the lust for profit, a schemer whose plans are financed and carried out by unsuspecting dupes.

Hetmann's decline into ridicule is in three stages. First the alliance with Launhart to force the state to take up *Lebensreform* (life-reform) ends when a compromising manuscript of Hetmann's "Lovelife in Bourgeois Society in Comparison with That of Our Domestic Animals" gets into the censor's hands as the result of Launhart's chicanery. Hetmann is imprisoned and the organization falls apart.

Hetmann sets about rebuilding the society from scratch. He plans to insult "the mob," as he calls the world, by attacking premarital virginity; they will counterattack, making him a martyr, and his death will entrench the cause. Once again his own associates contribute to his downfall. He is denounced by his own Grand Master as mad and carted off for observation at an asylum.

At the asylum, Hetmann is declared perfectly sane. He decides on still another course: to withdraw from public life and write an in-depth study of his own doctrines. Disillusioned and wanting only freedom, he still cannot understand why as a "moral human being" he has always been in hopeless conflict with the moral world:

I don't complain about my fate because I haven't succeeded where no one else would have succeeded either. But since it has become apparent that everything in this world can't be any different from the way it already is, I've been bored beyond all measure. Children amuse them selves playing pirates and prisoners. . . . But what are we grown-ups supposed to play?

(4:329)

Hetmann now lacks the will to break through his lethargy, and Nemesis finally arrives in the person of Mr. Cotrelly, who introduces himself as the bearer of an important proposal—an offer to join the circus in the role of Stupid Augustus, the misfit who, as Cotrelly defines him, "falls over every obstacle, always chooses the right moment to come too late . . . [and is] always trying to help people who already know what to do ten times better than he does."

The realization that he has become a laughable figure in the eyes of the world is the last straw. Hetmann disappears into the alcove of his tiny room and hangs himself in a characteristic Wedekind conclusion. Others in his work also perish as a result of ridicule. Wedekind had hit upon a potent modern way to register the depths of human suffering; it is a fate harsher than death.

Another peculiarly Wedekind touch is the circus director's description of his conversation with Hetmann as a soliloquy (Selbstgespräch). Like the Masked Gentleman in *Spring's Awakening,* the device enables the protagonist to take stock of his situation and reach a conclusion. It is also Wedekind's way of revealing the position he himself had arrived at during the preceding years. His enthusiasm had turned stale; the world as circus had lost meaning for him as a place to play the thankless role of Stupid Augustus, the clown who continues to perform his risible actions without ever altering his routine or changing the situation around him.

But *Karl Hetmann* has a subplot that bears upon Wedekind's change of vision: Hetmann's relation with Fanny Kettler, who is the most attractive female figure in Wedekind's work. Fanny is unpretentious, beautiful, intelligent—a prime example of the type of human being Hetmann's society was intended to breed. The physical and the spiritual are at one in Fanny, her inner life is as immaculate

as her outward appearance, and she is a rarity among Wedekind's women in being able to love without sentimentality and not solely out of sexual desire. And she loves Hetmann. At the beginning of the play he sees her as "a crippled soul" because she cannot bring herself to yield to another member of the society as the rules require. Later he calls her "a robust soul" for not abandoning him, and at the end, when his own powers have waned, he praises her as "one of the most splendid children of mankind ever created by nature." Yet he still refuses to return her love, fearing that their union would mean the end of the cause, which justifies his entire existence: "I'm not like those people who abandon their dreams and expectations when they get to be thirty years old! I'm forty now and my dreams are more childlike, my expectations more demanding, my hopes more glorious than ever before!" On another occasion, answering her entreaty for his love he says: "Am I supposed to couple my monstrous, repulsively misbegotten form with your luminous beauty? Am I supposed to abandon everything that brings me knowledge, strength, elasticity, and self-confidence merely in order to hold you in my arms?" So Hetmann cheats himself out of the very thing he longs for by his adherence to an *idea* of that reality.

During his work on *Karl Hetmann,* depressed by lack of success and fear of having reached a dead end, Wedekind contemplated giving up writing entirely. "I'm through with literature," he wrote to a friend. "It's not likely that I'd be able to overcome the public's stubborn aversion to me in the next ten years, even with the most strenuous efforts, and what then would I have had from life? I tell myself every day with great relief that from now on literature can go to the devil as far as I'm concerned!" In 1905 his unexpected success in playing the role of Hetmann brought an immediate change of heart: "Right after the performance I sat down and wrote my one-act play *Totentanz* (Dance of Death)." It was later renamed and published as *Tod und Teufel* (*Death and the Devil,* 1905) to avoid confusion with August Strindberg's already-famous drama.

Death and the Devil, subtitled "A Dance of Death in Three Scenes," is the most schematic and abstract of Wedekind's works. The setting is a brothel, the subject prostitution; the figures are not persons but attitudes. The play brings together a young woman from the upper classes, Elfriede von Malchus, who is a member of the International Society for Prevention of the White Slave Trade, and who has come to the brothel to rescue one of her family's former servants from a life of degradation; the Marquis Casti Piani, a procurer (taken from the *Lulu* dramas), who is responsible for the girl's presence here; Lisiska, the girl herself; and her client, Herr König, who says he has come for "refreshment" and an "exchange of pleasures" with a bona fide "daughter of joy."

The reformer and the procurer debate the merits of prostitution, with the odd result that she admits he has won the argument and enthusiastically offers herself to him in marriage. Next, Casti Piani arranges a demonstration of his claim that sensual pleasure is "the only ray of light in our earthly existence." Reformer and procurer together secretly observe the rendezvous between Lisiska and Herr König and discover to their chagrin that their ideas about the trade were mistaken. In the final scene, Elfriede and Casti Piani both abandon their earlier views: she now wants to become a prostitute herself, a martyr to the life-in-death, death-in-life existence to which her sex has been condemned; he, having received unshakable proof that his justification of prostitution is false, sees no reason to go on living and commits suicide.

In Casti Piani's original opinion, bourgeois marriage is often no better than unacknowledged "white slavery"; reformers like Elfriede should cease their efforts to raise the moral status of so-called daughters of joy and try to elevate the moral status of joy itself. "Human life," he tells her bitterly, "is death ten times over before one actually dies." The only antidote to its pain and anxiety is sensual pleasure.

Besides, says Casti Piani, "your mission against prostitution is no less a substitute for your sensuality than my trafficking in young girls is a substitute for mine—if, indeed, you can imagine my having any sensuality at all." Both reformer and procurer have committed themselves to a mere idea. Wedekind, having shown again the underlying similarity within apparent opposites, goes on to blame the idea mongers for prescribing modes of conduct for the rest of the world, in the name of an illusory morality and promise of happiness.

The figures in *Death and the Devil* learn about themselves through their unlikely discussions, while the audience discovers the assumptions that lie beneath their words and conduct. Thus Elfriede yields to Casti Piani in argument, then bursts out: "Marry me, and you will find out what supreme sacrifice a woman in her immeasurable love is capable of!" But what Elfriede really wants, whether she knows it or not, is to enhance her self-esteem by subordinating her wishes to her husband's, and even adding the bait of money: "Aren't you enticed by the fact that marrying me will suddenly put sixty thousand marks in cash at your disposal?!"

Casti Piani tells her he is indifferent to what she calls love, and that her bourgeois origins have denied her what he values—nobility of breeding, tender emotions, a sense of shame; she lacks "any feeling whatsoever for the effect of her caresses." Bourgeois marriage is just a cultural arrangement like any other and all "cultural arrangements exist to be overcome." Casti Piani repeats his dedication to sensuality, but is in fact no longer capable of experiencing what he praises; his pleasures are vicarious, existing only in his mind.

Still, he persuades Elfriede to join him in the voyeurism of watching a "typical" meeting between prostitute and customer. What they witness differs radically from what they (or the bulk of the audience) might expect. The scene is written in verse, suggesting an idyllic episode, but the words belie the poetic mood. Lisiska's young customer chose her because he

265

saw "a ray of innocent bliss" in her eyes. What he actually finds is a girl who has left respectability out of desperate sexual appetite. Even so, she has never obtained the satisfaction she craves; worse, her appetite has grown by what it fed on until it has become "unquenchable desire . . . a hellish drive in which nothing of joy remains." She feigns joy in König's embrace; actually she feels disgust for him and her own body, together with a longing to be mistreated—not for penance and punishment, but in the hope that abuse would someday bring about her death. *Death and the Devil* leaves no doubt that sexual reality differs entirely from what eager young men are apt to think of it.

Casti Piani and Elfriede also draw divergent conclusions from what they have seen. Elfriede finds she has misunderstood sexual desire and the place of public resort set up for it. But she mistakes prostitution as "a self-sacrifice and martyrdom" of an almost sacred nature. Hence her decision to become a prostitute and unite with the long-suffering members of her sex.

In Casti Piani's response, Wedekind gives us not ridicule but tragic irony. When the procurer sees that sex does not bring joy after all, the basis of his existence is destroyed: "What shall I still do in the world if even sensual pleasure is nothing but hellish butchery like everything else in human existence?" Seeing also the absurdity of Elfriede's falling for the illusion he himself has just rejected, he shoots himself. Wedekind's own view of the play hinged upon the Casti Piani figure. As he wrote: "The universal theme I proposed to treat through my protagonist was . . . the cynic who with inner necessity perishes of his own cynicism . . . the confirmed pessimist who falls a victim to his own pessimism." Thus Casti Piani embodies not only elements of several immediately preceding dramatic figures, but a fair share of the tendencies to which Wedekind himself was also vulnerable.

Wedekind's immediately following plays show a falling-off in creative power. Whether he no longer had anything original to say, as some critics assert, or whether he came under external pressures he had not experienced before is not easy to determine. In any event, after 1906 Wedekind's life changed radically: he now had a wife and family to care for; he was continually away from home to act in his own works; and the enormous success of *Spring's Awakening* in Max Reinhardt's production of November 1906 had created a demand for new plays by him.

He somehow found time to turn out at least one play a year and each, in its way, contributed to his further development. The focus on himself in these works, indeed, the caricatures of himself, have often been taken as evidence that he was writing mere confessionals, and the references to social questions were regarded as proof that dramatic objectivity had succumbed to a *Tendenz* that he had once repudiated. Neither opinion does full justice to Wedekind or his new plays.

The first of these new works, *Musik,* subtitled "Ein Sittengemälde" (Music: A Moral Portrait, 1907), may well have exercised more influence on subsequent dramatists than any other of his plays. The plot is deliberately banal. A young Swiss girl with the impossible name of Klara Hühnerwadel has come to Munich to be trained as a Wagnerian singer. She attracts the attention of a famous voice teacher, Professor Josef Reissner, who persuades her to take private lessons and stay as a non-paying guest with his family. The result is an unwanted pregnancy. On Reissner's advice, Klara has an abortion, and when it turns out that she will be indicted in a criminal action that would involve the professor and his family, she obeys his demand and flees the country. When Klara returns, again on Reissner's orders, she is imprisoned for eight months. Released, she goes back to live with the Reissners and again becomes pregnant. Determined at last to go her own way and make her own decisions, Klara gives birth to her child in isolation but soon loses it through illness. In the final scene her mother reclaims her errant daughter, who by this time is close to madness. She is convinced that she has forfeited her right to human sympathy and become a laughingstock: "People get cramps from laughing when they hear the story of my sufferings."

Musik reads like a hackneyed petit bourgeois calamity. Wedekind did in fact model the play on a well-known Munich scandal. In his own circle many resented his exploitation of the affair and were put off by his flippant treatment of it. He only made matters worse by joking about the play: "Its underlying purpose is to attack the ever-increasing study of music."

Most people realized he had been pulling their legs, but they did not see that he had also misled them when he professed to be aiming at the abolition of Paragraph 218 of the Civil Law, the anti-abortion clause. The women's rights movement in particular took him seriously, citing his earlier views on the right of a woman to dispose of the fruit of her body. Actually, Wedekind had always strongly opposed the suffrage movement. It is therefore most unlikely that his play illustrates or was ever intended to point out the evils of Paragraph 218.

Wedekind's later comments on *Musik* are more plausible. What he had written, he said in 1911, was a parody: "We have parody music by Offenbach of high artistic caliber; why shouldn't an artistically respectable parodistic drama also be possible?" He did not go on to say so, but the object of the parody was the many versions of the "tragedy" of the ruined girl, which constitute a veritable subgenre of German literature. Two works in particular were in the current repertoire: Friedrich Hebbel's *Maria Magdalena* (1844), whose heroine is also called Klara, and Hauptmann's recent *Rose Bernd* (1903). Plays about the unwed mother in German were invariably cast in the tragic mode, these youthful victims of circumstance presented so as to arouse compassion. But Wedekind leaves no doubt that Klara brings on her "fate" through her own stupidity. She is depicted as totally unfit for a high

career in music. She is a half-hysterical woman paralyzed by guilt and shame.

Nor do the other figures rate any better. Her seducer is presented as a consummate egoist, outwardly self-confident but inwardly a coward, out to take advantage of her without incurring responsibilities himself. Reissner's wife, Ilse, an indecisive, over-reactive woman, is so lacking in substance that even her best intentions lead to misfortune. As for the writer Franz Lindekuh, a strongly critical caricature of Wedekind himself, he is depicted as both fool and villain. He lends the money to send Klara out of the country and later threatens to expose her second pregnancy to the press in order to destroy Reissner. In short, he intervenes so as to force events in the direction he thinks they ought to go. He is another of Wedekind's "idealists," an intellectual moralist who tries to impose his ideas on others. Reissner's outburst against Lindekuh in act 3 is a high point of the play:

"You run around day in and day out with a murderously unsatisfied, insatiable moral hunger. Morally speaking, you're a monomaniac! You're a Don Quixote who hasn't the least idea what the world is all about, but you still expect life to accommodate itself to your crazy obsessions and then you become a dangerous wild animal when things don't turn out as you expect!"

(5:80)

Wedekind managed his exposé in a way that subsequent dramatists were eager to imitate: his figures condemn themselves through their characteristic speech and behavior. Thus when the prison director hands Klara over to the Reissners after her term in jail, he congratulates her on having such "self-sacrificing and loyal friends; it seldom happens that anyone in deep misery can count on people like these!" Klara's mother, also, mistaking Lindekuh for the father of Klara's child, reproaches him for making the girl so "abysmally unhappy," and thanks the Reissners profusely "for all you have done for my daughter."

The banalities of the dialogue depend for

their effectiveness on actors who can "play double" and also on audiences who can keep aloof from the action. These are requirements of the epic or dialectic theater, of course, and Wedekind anticipates both their presuppositions and devices. The title and subtitle of the play certainly tell us to look for ironies throughout. Klara fails to make "music," for example, however that word may be interpreted, and the "moral portrait" hardly conceals the ubiquitous immorality on all sides.

The dramaturgy of *Musik* is unusually innovative and supportive of Wedekind's intentions. He calls the play a "chronicle," thereby signifying that the work is not the enactment of a conflict, but a history of events. As such it "distances" the viewers from what is actually depicted and induces them to reflect on what such events might portend. Wedekind also casts his chronicle in the form of a *Moritat,* a type of ballad once sung by wandering singers whose subjects were gruesome or sensational events; these ballads were frequently printed, often with illustrations. Accordingly, each of the four acts in *Musik* is introduced by a hackneyed phrase describing the unlucky circumstances that follow.

Neither Wedekind's ingenious technique nor his well-aimed barbs have been able to dispel reservations about the play. The sticking point remains the mocking treatment of misfortune, the feeling that Wedekind is asking people to laugh at something that is no laughing matter. Yet this demand occurs in all tragicomedy. Some things in life do not permit a clear-cut response and should perhaps be greeted with mixed emotions. As the doctor in *Musik* puts it: "That's the unfortunate experience I have with so many unfortunate cases—that the misfortune begins to seem ridiculous precisely at its most unfortunate moment!" We have it from Wedekind's widow that cases in which "tragic occurrences sometimes take a turn toward the grotesque absolutely fascinated Frank." The parody resulting from this original fascination was another product of Wedekind's

principle that no telling criticism of society could possibly be made if it simply reproduced the dramatic forms that society had already created for expressing them.

Apart from performances in Wedekind's lifetime by the husband-and-wife team, *Die Zensur: Eine Theodizee in einem Akt* (Censorship: A Theodicy in One Act, 1908), has rarely been produced. The play presents a writer in crisis. Walter Buridan feels ready to complete the masterwork he has planned for a lifetime, but is held back by insecurities. He is afraid that if he leaves the beautiful and sensual Kadidja, his mistress of eighteen months, even for the short time needed to finish his manuscript, he will lose her. He hesitates also out of fear that another play of his may run afoul of the censors and never reach the public for which it is intended. In the opening scene Buridan tries inconclusively to persuade Kadidja to give him "the little time I need for intellectual concentration." In the second, he vainly tries to convince Dr. Cajetan Prantl, the current censor, of the high moral bearing of the works he has produced so far. In the last scene he rebukes Kadidja, whose unexpected appearance during the interview with Prantl only confirms the censor's lack of belief in Buridan's sincerity. Deeply wounded by her lover's reproach, Kadidja leaps to her death from the balcony of their room.

The Wedekinds' success with *Die Zensur* derived in part from what was perceived as a shameless but fascinating parade in public of their private affairs. The parallels are striking—up to a point—and Wedekind no doubt counted on attracting attention in this risky way. But this use of biographical material proved counterproductive. Audiences at first missed the point that personal details can be raised to a level of generality to exemplify a typical moral process. They also missed the opportunity to learn something about Wedekind's artistic philosophy, for the play is almost meta-dramatic in spelling it out. The masterpiece Buridan hopes to produce is twice defined in the play. He puts it to Prantl almost exactly as he had put it to Kadidja:

> Since earliest childhood I have tried to reconcile the veneration for beauty that nature arouses in us with the veneration demanded of us by the eternal laws of the universe. But we take no joy in the beauty of universal laws and we have no respect for the laws of universal beauty. The goal I've sacrificed my life for . . . is the reuniting of the sacred and the beautiful as the divine object of our pious devotion.
>
> (5:131)

This is a version of the "two souls in one breast" theme of Goethe's *Faust*. Wedekind's hero longs equally for beauty, physicality, and sensuality on the one hand and spirit and intellect on the other, and cannot choose between them. Hence his name, that of the French philosopher Jean Buridan (*ca.* 1300–1358), who denied the freedom of the will by telling the story of a donkey who starved to death because it could not bring itself to choose between two equally appetizing bundles of hay.

But it is not simply Buridan's reluctance to choose between one or the other sphere that seals his fate; it is also the refusal of those who represent the two choices to recognize each other's sphere as legitimate. Kadidja sees no value in her lover's occupation; it is too "intellectual," a rejection of life for the sake of art. That he should neglect her even briefly seems a rejection of her being.

Prantl also thinks little of Buridan's writing, but not because it is too intellectual; to him it is too sensual. When Buridan speaks of beauty, Prantl thinks, he really means the circus and debauchery, which must lead politically to a union of church and brothel in a utopian socialistic state. The writer's job is surely to entertain and afford pleasure by excluding matters that are the provenance of other social institutions. What business has Buridan to try to map out a new morality?

The argument in the play sums up the objections urged against Wedekind's dramatic work and his rejoinders. It presents at the same time the causes of Wedekind's difficulties—his insecurity, self-deception, indecision, perversity, and inability to control chance by calculation. Buridan loses his case against the censor, but it is also clear that Prantl's principles are self-condemning and castigate contemporary censorship for its insistence that moral matters be judged by the biased officials of church and state. In effect, Wedekind forces his audiences to reconsider the institution of censorship itself. The final twist is that Buridan turns censor himself—toward Kadidja. She breaks in on his interview with Prantl and brings home to the writer that it is what she stands for that is responsible for the censoring of his work.

Students of Wedekind should go to the play for its many suggestions about his purpose and method in playwriting, as well as for ideas developed in his essays and notes but only hinted at in the play itself. The subtitle of the play, "Eine Theodizee in einem Akt," points to Wedekind's concern with the role of morality in art and religion. But in the play the cause of "evil" is not God but the playwright himself. So "theodicy" should perhaps be taken to mean rationalizing rather than justifying the literary creation Wedekind has in mind. In any event, Buridan's words to Prantl are clear as to the author's own views: "Can you," he asks the censor, "cite anything in my works whose ultimate purpose is not to glorify and give artistic form to the eternal order which all of us must acknowledge in humility?" And again: "In none of my works did I ever show the Good as Bad or the Bad as Good. I have never falsified the consequences that arise from the actions of human beings. I have always and everywhere simply shown these consequences in their inexorable necessity."

Still trying to meet the public demand for new works, Wedekind next wrote a *pièce á clef,* a nineteenth-century genre still favored in the early twentieth century. The figures and story of *Oaha* (1908), later published as *Till Eulen-*

spiegel (1916), rehearse the *Simplicissimus* affair of over a decade earlier. Wedekind had already used some of the material in the Launhart portion of *Karl Hetmann;* in the new play it sustains the entire plot. There is only more divergence: the publisher, here renamed Georg Sterner, is at odds with the staff of his satiric journal and eventually has to hand it over to them.

Obviously, Wedekind's memories of that period still rankled. He still wanted to get back at the publicist Albert Langen, with whom he had been bound in such a love-hate relationship over the years. In *Oaha* the Langen figure, Sterner, is doomed by his folly and arrogance and misjudgment of his employees' abilities.

The economic setting is also the reverse of what we saw in *Karl Hetmann:* Wedekind there depicts an individualistically centered capitalistic enterprise, while in *Oaha* capitalism is replaced by a socialistic enterprise. The journal *Till Eulenspiegel* is managed by a group of artists who share the burden of work and the profits equally. Wedekind forgoes any political or economic critique in favor of a socio-psychological satire. His targets are not so much the real-life figures as the traits of certain types. Wedekind wants us to see that the "Albert Langen" in *Oaha* is an inferior version of the type, for he creates a contrasting figure, Harry Gadolfi, whose model is the art forger Willy Grétor (earlier, Wedekind's referent for the marquis of Keith). Gadolfi is described as "superior in effectiveness to all other persons" in the play, especially Sterner, who comes off by comparison as a rank amateur. "If you were a born deceiver," says Bouterweck, the Wedekind figure in the play, "I'd know how to deal with you. But you deceive people simply because you're too stupid to act in an honest way."

Since Sterner's business is the dissemination of wit, Wedekind's sampling of what the editor finds witty turns into an exposé of public taste in general; more specifically, of what Wedekind considered the lack of humor in Germany during the Wilhelmine era. The high point in *Oaha* is the scene in which Sterner and his colleagues confer about ways to improve the wit content of *Till Eulenspiegel.* Dr. Kilian, whose model is the playwright Ludwig Thoma, lists the qualities necessary for a successful witticist:

> In the first place, the creature we hire . . . must not feel either love or hate for anything in the world. In the second place, that creature must be panic-stricken at the very thought of having to think. . . . It dare not have any idea of how one thing might be related to other things in the world. It must just juxtapose distantly related things in an intimate relation and then let the reader's imagination run wild.
>
> (5:181)

But among the humorless producers of this humor magazine, Sterner is the one most lacking in the quality they supposedly represent. He laughs uproariously at remarks that leave others cold; he delights in practical jokes that do no more than discomfit someone else. His ultimate coup is the hiring of Oaha, a deaf-and-dumb cretin from the Swiss countryside, to supply the captions for the cartoons of the graphic artists on the staff. His reason: "The more vulgar a person's emotional life, the more brilliant his wit."

Wedekind never quite fulfills the potentialities of his theme, so that the attack on contemporary *Humorlosigkeit* (lack of humor) remains a disjointed series of clever ideas. The individual characters—or caricatures—are for the most part entertaining, especially the parody of the Lulu figure, under the name Wanda Washington, an American who falls madly in love with Sterner and pursues him "like the devil incarnate." Two years earlier, she had been at the point of entering a brothel in Venice but could not because "my papers were not in order." And she sighs: "How I envied those simple girls from the country whose papers are always so perfectly right!"

For Wedekind devotees who can recognize the real-life models because they are familiar with the details of the *Simplicissimus* affair, *Oaha* can yield a fair amount of pleasure. Others are apt to conclude that this is one of Wedekind's weakest productions.

NEW DIRECTIONS

After completing *Oaha,* Wedekind felt disturbed by critical charges that his last four plays had proved him "artistically dead," "completely sterile." He resolved on a radical change of subject matter and a corresponding readjustment of technique. The result was a series of one-act playlets, "three pictures from family life," which were intended to express his deepest sentiments about "the inner necessities on which marriage and family life are based." He then rearranged, shortened, and recast the trio to shape a single work with the title *Schloss Wetterstein: Drama in Drei Akten* (*Castle Wetterstein: Drama in Three Acts,* 1912). As Wedekind expected, the new play raised the censor's hackles; it was not released for production in Germany until after the abolition of censorship in 1919.

The central figures of *Castle Wetterstein* are Leonore von Gystrow, her second husband, Rüdiger von Wetterstein, and her daughter by her first marriage, Effie. The action stretches over a period of years from the founding of the new family until its dissolution with Effie's death. Each act depicts the struggle for power between a man and a woman: in the first act this occurs within a conventional bourgeois marriage; next, within a partnership in which husband and wife have pledged mutual independence; and last, in the nexus of prostitution. Each institution represented is tested and found wanting. At the same time, each central figure, whose conduct "follows the rules," is shown as helpless in the grip of one or the other socio-moral scheme.

Castle Wetterstein otherwise disregards the conventions of the family drama. In particular, Wedekind avoids the familiar in favor of extravagant personalities in extreme situations. The recently widowed Leonore is wooed by the man who has murdered her husband and eventually accepts him; she then rescues her new husband from death and despair by throwing herself into the arms of a man she despises; lastly, her daughter Effie helps a man commit suicide so as to secure money for her lover but becomes a suicide herself when she is made to lose her belief in herself—all these improbable or impossible actions are meant to keep audiences from mistaking the situations for reality or from feeling genuine emotions about unreal situations. Instead, attention should concentrate on the underlying theory of the social and moral mechanisms involved. Part 1, cast as a comedy, with the supertitle "In allen Sätteln gerecht" (Ready for Anything), centers on Rüdiger von Wetterstein, who, in a delicious parody of Richard III, woos and wins the hand of his victim's widow. She thinks of herself as a champion of respectable marriage; he is determined to win her for a new type of free-love relationship. He has planned the break-up of his as well as her marriage and rigged the duel that ends Major von Gystrow's life. Though Wedekind gives "psychological" reasons for Rüdiger's triumph, Leonore is eventually won over by the type of relationship he proposes in place of bourgeois conventionality: an equal partnership. "You're not supposed to belong to me!" he tells her at one point. "You belong to yourself! Marriage is made for human beings, not human beings for marriage! Your happiness, your freedom to develop—these should be the most sacred goals of our life together!"

The point of the scene is to expose Leonore's ardent championship of bourgeois marriage and its supposed virtues. The arrangement is revealed as untenable or outmoded or moribund, easily discarded under the onslaught of determined opposition. In spite of her protestations, Leonore is revealed as a self-deceiver, an unwitting actress, who holds to norms she has never taken the trouble to question. Her susceptibility to mere words is obvious when she tells Rüdiger: "One can forgive a person anything, allow him anything, as long as he is able to express the kind of things you can!"

But wars won by words can be lost the same way and Rüdiger relies too much on phraseology. A bad omen is the presence of the ebullient Effie, who finds it somewhat difficult to accept Rüdiger as her "father" and gives signs of being less conventional and more libidinous than her mother.

Part 2, described as a drama and supertitled "Mit allen Hunden gehetzt" (Beset Upon on All Sides, or "Wily as a Fox") puts the free-love marriage to the test. The arrangement has led to a stalemate. Rüdiger, a spineless failure in the real world, is no match for his rival in business, who also wants to steal his wife. He turns to the unbridled Effie in hopes of rekindling his last spark of manhood.

The situation is this: A certain Meinrad Luckner has taken a fancy to Leonore and maneuvered Rüdiger to the brink of bankruptcy. He is ready to save him only if she will yield herself. That she despises Luckner only whets his lust: "There's nothing more terrible for me than when a woman finds me personally attractive."

The dilemma facing Rüdiger and Leonore by Luckner's intrusion—who is to be sacrificed for the other's sake—marks the collapse of their equal-marriage scheme. Rüdiger confesses he is too weak to do away with himself and lets it be seen that he expects Leonore to make the sacrifice. She, on her side, is afraid that he will eventually despise her for her adulterous sacrifice or succumb to the sensuality of the omnipresent Effie.

One way out of the dilemma is suggested by Effie, who by now has shed her first husband and virtually become a prostitute herself. Let Leonore throw herself at Luckner's feet, professing passion—her acting with such shamelessness will discomfit the astonished Luckner, and they will be rid of their problems. Effie is right! The disoriented Luckner kills himself in Leonore's presence. The Wettersteins are now free. But both their characters are damaged in each other's eyes as well as in their own. And Effie and her stepfather, as if compelled by a force beyond their control, take advantage of Leonore's disgrace to have a brief affair.

The last act takes place many years later in Castle Wetterstein, Rüdiger's ancestral home, though it is now owned by Karl Salzmann, an entrepreneur who has turned it into a high-class bordello. Everything in it—walls, furniture, curtains—is snow-white. Outside is an indescribably beautiful landscape—nature's counterpoint against a culture of opposite hue.

Described as a tragedy and supertitled "Mit allen Wassern gewaschen" (Too Clever by Half), this part of the trilogy centers on Effie. She lives at Wetterstein like a queen holding court; her minions are a defrocked priest turned philosopher, an anarchical physicist working on a bomb, a bard who specializes in parody, Effie's "agent," Salzmann, and her personal physician, Dr. Scharlach, who has been experimenting to find the secret of her being. All are nihilists at odds with society. Effie's parents also live at the castle, comfortably provided for by a lifetime pension through Effie's "earnings." This noble courtesan also supports her lover, a prince whose tiny principality would revert to the emperor if it were not for the money she continues to supply.

The interrelations here follow the principles of prostitution. Effie is a one-dimensional creature—pure libidinal energy, comparable to Lulu. All the men she comes in contact with call her by a different name. Effie is clearly the last vestige of the vitalistic idea Wedekind had once so fervently promoted and later found so difficult to drop even after it had proved untenable; in her that idea is given its quietus—she and her type are repudiated once for all.

Wedekind's change of mind is expressed in the medical diagnosis that Effie's vaunted sensuality is pathological: "You said . . . that my insatiability in loving was due to chronic digestive disturbances? . . . And that this moist gleam in my eyes, the ease with which I arouse desire, are caused by some affliction of the liver?" The news is devastating. Her belief in the "naturalness" of her behavior is shattered.

She nevertheless resolves to go through with her latest commission, for she needs the 100,000 marks promised for the job: it is to assist an Argentinian multimillionaire, Mr. Chagnaral Tschamper, to die while enjoying a naked woman. The challenge for Effie is heightened by danger: it has been rumored that Tschamper has made the same request before and yet has always survived in perfect health; the deaths resulting from his encounters have always been those of the prostitutes who take him on.

Effie is confident of her power to carry out the assignment successfully; Tschamper, though, is determined to have her carry it out in *his* sense, which is diametrically opposite to what she assumes. The nakedness he has in mind is not of the body but of the soul; the goal of this exposure is not *his* death but that of the woman who bares herself to him. Effie, needing the money to provide for her prince-lover, is in no position to object to Tschamper's instructions and is gradually led by him from frustration to shame to desire and finally to utter desperation.

Tschamper forbids her to undress, thereby preventing her from using her physical beauty as a means of controlling the situation. Next, he insists on directing her attention to the saddest events in her past, awakening her long-dormant conscience. When Tschamper's soul-probing forces her to recall the father she herself had scarcely known, and he then takes on the role himself, reproaching her for not fulfilling the obligations a daughter owes to a father, Effie breaks into tears. She begins to regard Tschamper as a father figure reincarnated and, in one of those reversals familiar in Wedekind's work, begs him to marry her. She says what only the males have said earlier in the play: "Did ever man and woman find one another better matched than you and I?" And then, in good bourgeois fashion: "You need a woman who can satisfy your hunger for great emotions; you need a woman who will show you that she is ready to sacrifice everything for you." But when Tschamper taunts her with the

thought that he might indeed drink the poison ostensibly prepared for him, she seizes the cup and expires in torment. As he watches her writhing at his feet, enjoying his psychological *Lustmord* (death-lust), Tschamper gloats: "It's strange how much power a man has over the life and death of a woman. And you're not the last." Then, disclosing the source of his power, he says: "Prostitutes, unlike other children, never feel superior to their parents."

It is sometimes said that *Castle Wetterstein* lacks a theme—which is not quite the same as saying it lacks unity. Wedekind was scolded for not providing what the family-drama formula had led his critics to expect. But his intention was to test, by example, three of the most prevalent types of arrangements for the relations between men and women. He shows that each is inherently flawed, doing more harm than good to those who depend on them for support. Money and sexual politics are other matters treated in this play, along with one additonal concern of deepest importance, both to Wedekind and his contemporaries: call it the lack of belief or, more precisely, the absence of anything one could believe in. The preoccupation appeared in his work soon after he came to see that vitalism could not fulfill his expectations. It haunts all the succeeding plays like a persistent ghost. In *Castle Wetterstein* Effie's loss is the most severe, for after Dr. Scharlach's reductionist diagnosis of the one virtue she truly believed in, Effie says:

Erloschen ist des Lebens Flammenpracht,
Nur freudlos düstre Kohlen blieben übrig.
Verkaufs-Entsühnung, Dirnen-Heiligung,
Wie albern, wie entsetzlich schal mir das
Jetzt klingt! Und doch kehr ich nicht um.
  Jetzt kommen
Verfall und Niedergang. Sie sollen aufrecht
Und stolz mich finden, wie das Glück mich sah.
                                        (6:62)

Life's glorious flame is quite extinguished,
And nothing's left but dark and cheerless ashes.
Expiation through venal love, the whore's

Sanctification, how shockingly stale it sounds
To me now. Yet I shan't turn back. Corruption
Approaches and declines. But they'll find me
Upright and proud as my good fortune found me.
(Fawcett and Spender trans., p. 251)

One can hear Wedekind's own voice in this lament. And even if his age had not yet come to such a realization, he himself had grown to see that the libidinal route to salvation, precisely because of its susceptibility to perversion, was not the way to go. In the light of this conclusion, those who scan his career will find his accommodation to bourgeois society in the works to come much more understandable.

Der Stein der Weisen, oder Laute, Armbrust, und Peitsche (The Philosopher's Stone, or Lute, Crossbow, and Whip, 1909) is a minor work that deserves to be better known. In it, Wedekind uses verse throughout the play and creates an imaginative world with only minimal reference to historical or social factors. Again, the form owes little to tradition, a fact Wedekind draws attention to in the unusual subtitle, "Eine Geisterbeschwörung" (A Summoning of Spirits). The situation is a projection of Wedekind's own, and it is handled for the playwright's own benefit—the "summoning" is also an "exorcising" of spirits. One might say that biographically, *Der Stein der Weisen* grew out of the mid-life crisis of a man who had reluctantly given up his bachelor freedom and found the potency that had been his pride vanishing in domesticity.

Basilius Valentius, a necromancer, has withdrawn from society in order to fashion a private world. Possessing the philosopher's stone, the mandragora, and the mirror of Solomon, he has the means to make nature do his bidding; he can also enforce his will on others without damage to himself, using a lute (the power of song), a crossbow (the word or wit), and a whip (the power of discipline). Despite this arsenal, Basil hesitates to use it. The weapons have become for this somewhat disillusioned old

man a means of self-protection, not of action. After long experience he sees the world as consisting of nothing but danger and death. It is a place where "desires are never stilled," love is attained only through cunning, and fame and riches only by those who never search for them. Human happiness may be attained occasionally, but its limits are narrow: "It lies between boredom and fatigue. For the man who is bored any task is a pleasure; for the one who is fatigued, any pleasure becomes a burden."

Unlike Faust, of whom we are reminded, this brooding magician is not yet entirely dissatisfied with his lot, and he has no wish to experience what he may have missed earlier. Not so his *famulus*, Leonhard, a young man who—in a reversal of Goethe's figure—complains that his master is keeping him a slave for his own purposes, robbing him of his youth. In a sudden burst of insight arising from his own healthy instincts, he accuses the old man of hoarding his powers and suppressing his libido because "the need for love is always pestering you. And because you don't know whom to turn to, you torture yourself horribly."

Basil is annoyed but not offended; he is touched somewhat more by the visit of an old school chum, Father Porphyrion, a Dominican friar, who hopes to save his friend from persecution and death by making him abjure his heathen ways. Father Porphyrion thinks Basil is in league with the Devil, but to the magician it is the priest who plays the role of Mephistopheles in trying to tempt him back to a belief in such idols as God and the church, which he has long since renounced. Basil is not in the least upset by the prospect of being burned at the stake as a heretic; but he is taken aback when Porphyrion charges him with arrogance and pride in assuming that his wisdom has been employed for the good of mankind and that his power puts him in the same class as God himself. These charges strike close to home. And once again the theme of frustrated love is sounded, this time by Basil himself, who accuses Porphyrion (much as Leonhard had done) of shackling his potential for life precisely because he no longer experiences the joys of love: "What you have stammered and raged at me, what has clouded your understanding, has all been collecting in that cistern you call a brain, simply because you haven't loved a girl for years!"

The erotic theme develops in an innovative fashion: Basil interviews three figures—four, if Leonhard is included—who successively bring him enlightenment. Since Wedekind stipulates that all four roles are to be played by the same person (an actress), it seems clear they represent different aspects of Basil-Wedekind's nature, or different phases of his development. They stand for aspirations and activities he has come to neglect or is no longer capable of. Basil's outlook is gradually undermined, and the outcome differs from what either Father Porphyrion hopes or Basil expects.

Kunz von Blutenburg is the first visitor, a dissolute and rapacious adventurer traveling in the guise of a student. Kunz is eager to become "one of the world's most famous men" and counts on Basil to help him achieve his goal. But Kunz's primary aim is to have a good time, especially in bed, and with the kind of exotic women other men don't consort with—a succubus above all! Basil is shocked when he learns that these longed-for orgies are *not* for the sake of knowledge and to round out experience, nor out of pleasure in the perennial battle of the sexes either, but solely in order to give vent to his own surcharged feelings. This coarse manifestation of ego unnerves Basil, perhaps because it recalls his own past. At any rate, he thinks of his former loves and the songs he composed for them. So stimulated, Basil longs for a succubus himself and accordingly conjures up the figure of Lamia.

Lamia's visit does two things: She destroys the illusion that Basil has ever known a "real" woman; his loves have all just been "pretty painted creatures of his imagination." And she makes him turn upside down his notion of the relation between the sexes: the man is not superior to the woman, but the woman to the man. The price Lamia demands for dallying with him is marriage, and with it, all the possessions he has so carefully accumulated for his security. When Lamia also insists that he overlook her sexual activities, be dependent on her, and ignore anything she might do in private, when in addition she demands that he wear the chastity girdle meant for her while she dons the magic girdle he has reserved for himself, Basil decides he has had enough of haggling for her favors and dismisses her. As so often happens in Wedekind, the hope of satisfying a longing turns into the fear that fulfillment will prove a nightmare.

Basil is prepared to change his view of women, whom he had previously considered a breed apart, but he has not changed his taste. Since his aggressiveness (Kunz), his sensualism (Lamia), and his ability to train disciples (Leonhard) have all turned against him, there is no one left but Guendolin, "my treasure, my companion in battle, my sense of humor!" It is she Basil conjures up next.

Yet it soon becomes clear that he and humor have long since parted company. Irritated, Basil uses his whip to try to force Guendolin to his will. But she has only truth to give him about his actual place in the scheme of things: he has been nothing but "an angry philosopher wandering through life, studying the joys of others because you yourself are on such strained terms with God. That's why you write such unbearably lurid books on life, laughter, and loving." Basil is blind to the essence of humor because he has used it apart from the human beings who are its source. For him it has only been an idea; in reality it is a response to circumstances. The episode recalls Wedekind's own analysis (and condemnation) of himself immediately after his release from prison: "Life doesn't like anyone who takes life too seriously. . . . No one knows this better than I, who am so caught up in concepts, ideas, points of view, principles, intentions, purposes, fears, and hopes that I never get around to *myself.*"

Similarly, Basil realizes that Guendolin has through his own doing actually become alienated from him: "You are my complete opposite!" She persuades him to give up his crossbow (wit) as well as the philosopher's stone that has always protected him from attack, and then turns the weapon on him: "Thousands have already perished for lack of humor, all because the world has spoiled their sense of humor for them." It was a harsh judgment for an author to make of himself.

Wedekind's reawakened interest in the Faust-legend culminates in *Franziska: Ein Modernes Mysterium in fünf Akten* (Franziska: A Modern Mystery Play in Five Acts, 1912). The possibilities of a female Faust had attracted him ever since his Paris days, and the public interest in women's rights seemed to invite a contribution to the subject. Franziska Eberhardt yearns to "escape" and enjoy the "freedom of movement" and "pleasures in living" hitherto reserved for men. Rejecting the first suitor for her hand, whom she herself has seduced in order to lose her virginity, Franziska explains: "If we were to marry, in the next ten years I would only learn who you are . . . and continue to remain a stranger to myself."

A Mephisto figure soon arrives to fulfill her longing. He is a down-and-outer from outside Franziska's narrow circle. Announcing himself pretentiously as a *Sternenlenker* (charioteer of the stars), he claims that he can "form a star of the first magnitude out of any mortal." Yet this boasting fellow bears the plebeian name Veit Kunz and is currently employed as an insurance agent, that is, someone who deals in security. He has been a singing coach, acrobat, journalist, con man, detective, and much else. Now Kunz promises Franziska "the best opportunities for developing all your talents and gifts in the most productive, most perfect, most extensive manner."

Connoisseurs of Wedekind at once recognize the type and understand the reasons why Franziska accepts his offer. The Mephisto figure tells the Faust figure only what she wants to hear and is already prepared to act out.

Wedekind makes Veit Kunz a self-seeker who sees in Franziska opportunity to obtain comfort, certainty, security, and self-assurance. She, however, is out for the opposite—possibility, freedom, self-development. Wedekind naturally sees to it that neither gets what he or she is looking for; both revert to their basic natures as a result of the fateful encounter.

A continuing parody of Goethe's play emerges as Kunz and Franziska's odyssey parallels that of Faust and Mephisto. Wedekind's version of the prologue is a conversation between mother and daughter that is also a parody of a parody, Wedekind's own *Spring's Awakening*. The pact Franziska makes with Veit Kunz is completely in the spirit of the legend: he will help her toward her goal of independence for two years and then can claim her as his own. Wedekind adds some intriguing touches: Franziska believes that things may not work out just as he thinks; he insists that they will, because the "laws of nature," which ordain that a woman always eventually winds up as the slave of a man, are in his favor. The rest of the play tests both these assumptions.

The first episode brings the pair to a nightclub in Berlin—the equivalent of Goethe's Auerbach's Tavern. Franziska, disguised as a man, learns what the "Little World" is like. It is a place where people sell themselves to make a living, a place of raw emotions, gigantic egos, perverse family relationships, and violent behavior. And Franziska-Franz also experiences the first consequences of her assumed sexual role: a girl falls in love with "him," which makes her boyfriend jealous; he is subsequently killed accidentally.

The next episode, matching the Gretchen story in *Faust,* also results in tragedy. Franz-Franziska has married Sophie, a young woman of the upper class; the marriage has not been consummated because they misunderstand each other, always citing the wrong reasons for their lack of rapport. The ironic situation was intended to depict "the worst possible conventional bourgeois marriage," that is, an arrangement made impossible because it is based on false presuppositions and bound to traditional ways of thinking about the way such a relationship must be. Sophie is eventually driven mad by a suspicion that his neglect of her is due to an affair with another woman. All ends tragically with Sophie's suicide when she learns that the "man" she has married is in fact a woman.

Franziska seems to fall ever more under Veit Kunz's control, but she is also beginning to question his manipulation of her and is coming ever closer to a true view of her situation. That the realization of her true nature is due to Kunz is made plain when we learn that this male-in-disguise has become his mistress and is now bearing his child.

The development toward self-knowledge is confirmed in the next episodes, which correspond to Goethe's imperial court scene and the classical Walpurgis Night. The pageantry, song, and interplay between pretense and reality here have contributed much to the work's popularity onstage. The scenes are also intellectually demanding, recapitulating as they do some favorite Wedekind themes and pointing beyond the play itself to ideas found only in his essays and notebooks.

At the court of the duke of Rotenburg the lovers find total confusion: the ducal marriage is about to break up in rancor and the duke has lost the support of his people and his ministers. Veit Kunz plans to save the situation by using Franziska's talent for acting: disguised as a genie or daemon, she will inspire the duke with self-confidence. She does this reluctantly, and a trumped-up séance with the duke leaves her with a bad conscience, questioning the propriety and purpose of the actions Kunz has led her to perform.

What Veit Kunz wants to effect during the two years of the pact is the development of all Franziska's talents for his future benefit. These are voluptuousness, thirst for power, an easygoing temperament, passion for games, love of pleasure, and "the most glorious of all, immeasurable self-conceit." The flaw in this calculation is that he sees Franziska one-

sidedly, egoistically; the qualities he finds in her are those he would like for himself and he has not foreseen that what he is trying to do may in fact produce a person different from the one he aims at creating.

The last parallel to Goethe's *Faust* shows Veit Kunz at the height of his powers, producing one of his own works before an audience of five thousand. It is a mystery play dealing with God's visit to the underworld "in order to rescue the spiritual heroes of the past from the growing threat of forgetfulness." The climax shows Helen of Troy and Christ comparing their missions in history. The roles are played by Franziska and Veit Kunz. For him it is the height of his intellectual, artistic, and social success, obtained by exploiting the potential he has detected in his female Faust. She decides to rebel and defeat his prophecies about her. She accomplishes this by falling in love with another actor, Ralf Breitenbach, who exudes sheer sexual energy. But her rebellion against the artist who wants to re-create her personality according to his own lights threatens to turn tragic. Finding that he has lost the Mephisto wager, Veit Kunz tries—unsuccessfully—to commit suicide. The tragedy is averted by humor when Kunz is told that the end of the relationship is inevitable: "Have you ever known a man who knew his own wife? Or vice versa? . . . It's a logical impossibility."

The final episode of *Franziska* brings us full circle. Franziska has accepted the role that nature has assigned her sex and dotes on the four-year-old Veit-Ralf. She is visited by both her former lovers, each offering to act as her future protector—Breitenbach, as he says, in place of her mother, Veit Kunz in place of her former patron, the deceased Hohenkemnath—although both refuse to assume the responsibilities of being a father to the child. She rejects them both.

Audiences have been sharply divided about *Franziska*. Some value it as a spectacle and clever parody, others think it the work of a turncoat, the betrayal of a lifetime's striving. The detractors are particularly incensed at Fran-

FRANK WEDEKIND

ziska's settling down in domestic bliss; it seems a bourgeois happy ending difficult to distinguish from *Kitsch*. And indeed, Karl Almer, the man who wants to marry Franziska, talks in a vein not very different from her mother's in the prologue: "The world, you know, is really not as abominable as some birds of ill-omen try again and again to make us believe." Almer has faith in goodness and believes that the threat to it comes only from wanting too much, from "those who don't know the limits of their talents and the limits of the world."

Yet we should not draw hasty conclusions about the author's intentions. Franziska does accept and enjoy her maternal role, and apparently will take Almer as stepfather for her child, but that outcome is not wholly conventional. Both parties realize that the important thing is that there be equal well-being on both sides, that both always be conscious of "what we can be for each other."

As always with Wedekind, the connection between art and biography is discernible below the surface of the work. After five years of an often turbulent marriage, he had found (or at least could envisage) a possible way of accommodating to its difficulties. As for the spectator, Wedekind wants him or her to feel doubt about the bourgeois idyll. When Franziska wonders why Almer, who is painting a mother and child, has put a wreath of roses around them, he explains that it was probably in memory of "some Madonna or other" (nostalgia for a lost ideal, perhaps), or perhaps "as a small concession to public taste."

THE FINAL PHASE

Wedekind's final phase brought forth three plays that may be considered as a unit if only because they have all vanished from the German stage entirely. They are also alike in being based on familiar literary material, instead of his own imagination: *Simson, oder Scham und Eifersucht* (Samson, or Shame and Jealousy, 1913–1914) goes back to the Hebrew legend; *Bismarck* (1916) draws on recent German history, and *Herakles* (1917) on Greek mythology. In all three works the problem is greatness, or how to establish a heroic identity and maintain dignity in the teeth both of a hostile world and of one's self-destructive impulses. Apart from *Bismarck,* whose form anticipates the modern documentary drama by incorporating historical records, Wedekind in these late works uses verse, song, and epic-like structures. In each play a single, strong-minded individual and his conduct dominates the sequence of episodes; there is no "matching" opponent as in the earlier works, hence no occasion for the humor principle.

Whether the growing popularity of expressionist drama or the countertrend to neoclassic forms was the cause, Wedekind's last plays occasioned a decline in his reputation as a creative force in the theater. Yet ironically his achievements as a playwright were by now generally acknowledged, and a great public celebration on his fiftieth birthday elicited respectful tributes from Germany's leading writers and members of the theater. Nevertheless, the generation that had looked to him for inspiration, if not leadership, now saw in his work a repudiation of his political and moral tenets; the one-time "terror of the bourgeoisie" had turned into a bourgeois himself. Except for his continuing fight against censorship, Wedekind no longer campaigned against hypocrisy and complacency.

Without going into detail, one may distinguish three main tendencies in the last plays. First, all three pay scant attention to the deeds usually associated with the central figure; the action concentrates on the last stage of a great career, in particular on moments of crisis, of defeat or near defeat, or self-doubt or humiliation. The action is internal, leading to the discovery of an inner strength.

Second, this inner process suggests what the hero has lacked to qualify for true greatness so far—the peculiarly human (*menschlich*) orientation needed to justify heroism. Samson, for example, is made to see that his exercise of manly power has been egoistic; the fateful encounter with Delilah makes him undergo the shame and jealousy that he had once attributed solely to the weaker sex. Besides, as a singer and poet (a Wedekind invention) Samson recapitulates all the possible stages of an artist's relation to his audiences. Only when blinded does Samson, like Oedipus, perceive the truth of his situation, and only his patient acceptance of it allows him to recover the physical power that now reflects his inner strength.

Bismarck, as Wedekind sees him, is a powerful egoist with only one goal: the unification of his country. Significantly, the German people play no part whatever in the economy of the work. The drama here lies in Bismarck's struggle against the temptation to give up when appreciation of his efforts is denied him. Inner strength in this case grows with learning to persist and endure. The testing of Wedekind's Herakles is closer to Samson's: he must realize that despite the twelve labors successfully performed, he has not yet been able to tame his own urge to sex and violence. His task is overcoming self in order to find the better self within. In the words of Hans-Jochen Irmer, he learns that happiness lies "in the mutual elimination of power [*gegenseitige Entmachtung*], in love, in a free exchange of bodies and souls, in the victory of a uniquely human life over a dictatorial or slavish existence."

As is his wont, Wedekind adopts a critical stance toward his protagonists. Samson wants to rid the world of shame and jealousy, but can think of no way other than destroying the Philistine world. Bismarck's dream of unity culminates in a war he tried his best to avoid, which casts a retrospective doubt over the quality of his greatness if not over his actual accomplishment. Even Herakles fails. He contemplates the one deed that might most benefit mankind—to free Prometheus and join him in performing what neither can do alone—but he cannot devise a concrete way to carry out the program. The much-feted, much-maligned Wedekind of these last years must have felt the irony of this ending—Herakles, who has fought against the gods, is in the end received by the Olympians and given a conspicuous place among the stars.

Frank Wedekind's death on 9 March 1918, a few months before his fifty-fourth birthday, came as a great shock. He had suffered several minor illnesses during his life, none serious enough to interrupt his regular work, and his acting schedule, which took him year in, year out to all the major German-speaking stages throughout Europe, had created the impression of indomitable energy and indestructibility. Yet the war years left Wedekind exhausted and world-weary. The fight with publishers and against censorship had taken their toll; marriage with Tilly Newes was emotionally draining; he was plagued by fears of impotence and shaken by the charges about his loss of creativity. An appendectomy in 1915 was not entirely successful—the wound refused to heal; an operation two years later for a hernia resulting from the earlier surgery worsened his condition. When Wedekind himself insisted on another, purely cosmetic, incision to correct the damage previously done and he rose from his bed too soon in order to fulfill his acting engagements, the strain was too much. His funeral in Munich turned into an occasion for displaying the divided feelings he had always aroused in his countrymen. More theater than drama, it recalled the extreme type of situation Wedekind favored in his playwriting and was a fitting recognition of the effect a remarkable personality had exercised on the life of his time.

Selected Bibliography

EDITIONS

INDIVIDUAL WORKS

PLAYS

Der Schnellmaler, oder Kunst und Mammon. Zurich, 1889.
Kinder und Narren. Munich, 1891.

Frühlingserwachen. Zurich, 1891.

Elins Erweckung. Munich, 1894. (Two scenes.)

Der Erdgeist. Munich, 1895.

Die junge Welt. Berlin, 1897. Revised version of *Kinder und Narren.*

Der Kammersänger. Munich, 1899.

Der Liebestrank. Munich, 1899.

Der Marquis von Keith. Munich, 1901.

Die Büchse der Pandora. Munich, 1902; Berlin, 1904.

König Nicolo oder So ist das Leben. Munich, 1902.

Hidalla oder Sein und Haben. Munich, 1904.

Tod und Teufel (Totentanz). Vienna, 1905; Munich, 1906.

Musik: Ein Sittengemälde. Munich, 1907.

Die Zensur: Eine Theodizee in einem Akt. Berlin, 1908.

Felix und Galatea. Berlin, 1908.

Oaha: Satire der Satire. Berlin, 1908.

Der Stein der Weisen. Berlin, 1909.

Karl Hetmann, der Zwergriese (Hidalla). Munich, 1911. Revised version of *Hidalla, oder Sein und Haben.*

Schloss Wetterstein: Drama in drei Acten. Munich, 1912.

Franziska: Ein Modernes Mysterium in funf Akten. Munich, 1912.

Simson, oder Scham und Eifersucht. Munich, 1914.

Bismarck. Munich, 1916.

Till Eulenspiegel. Munich, 1916. Revised version of *Oaha.*

Herakles. Munich, 1917.

Bethel. Munich, 1921.

Das Sonnenspektrum. Munich, 1921.

OTHER WRITINGS

"Der Witz und seine Sippe" and "Zirkusgedanken." Both published in *Neue Zürcher Zeitung,* 4–6 May and 29–30 June 1887.

Die Fürstin Russalka. Munich, 1897. An anthology including the following works: *Seelenergüsse* (includes "Der Brand von Egliswyl," "Rabbi Esra," "Der greise Freier," "Die Fürstin Russalka," "Das Opferlamm," "Die Liebe auf den ersten Blick," "Bei den Hallen," and "Ich langweile mich"), *Die Jahreszeiten; Theater* (includes *Der Schmerzenstanz [Die Flöhe, oder der Schmerzenstanz], Der Mückenprinz,* and *Die Kaiserin von Neufundland*).

Mine-Haha, oder über die körperliche Erziehung von jungen Mädchen. Munich, 1901.

Schauspielkunst: Ein Glossarium. Munich, 1910.

Die Tagebücher: Ein erotisches Leben. Frankfurt am Main, 1986.

COLLECTED WORKS

Gesammelte Werke. 9 vols. Edited by Artur Kutscher and Joachim Friedenthal. Munich, 1912–1921. Works appearing here for the first time are *Das Sonnenspektrum,* the complete *Elins Erweckung,* and *Bethel.*

Ausgewählte Werke. 5 vols. Edited by Fritz Strich. Berlin, 1923.

Gesammelte Briefe. 2 vols. Edited by Fritz Strich. Munich, 1924.

Prosa, Dramen, Verse. 2 vols. Selected by Hansgeorg Maier. Munich, 1954, 1964.

Werke. 3 vols. Edited by Manfred Hahn. Berlin and Weimar, 1969.

Stücke. Afterword by Bertel F. Sinhuber. Munich, 1970.

TRANSLATIONS

Five Tragedies of Sex. Edited and translated by F. Fawcett and S. Spender. London, 1952. Includes *Spring's Awakening, Earth Spirit, Pandora's Box,* and *Death and the Devil.*

King Nicolo, or Such Is Life. Translated by Martin Esslin. In *The Genius of the German Theater,* edited by Martin Esslin. New York, 1968.

Lulu: A Sex Tragedy. Adapted from Wedekind's *Earth Spirit* and *Pandora's Box* by Peter Barnes. Translated by Charlotte Beck. London, 1971.

Lulu and Other Sex Tragedies. Edited and translated by F. Fawcett and S. Spender. London, 1973. Includes *Earth Spirit, Pandora's Box, Death and the Devil,* and *Castle Wetterstein.*

The Lulu Plays. Edited and translated by C. R. Mueller. Greenwich, Conn., 1967. Includes *Earth Spirit, Pandora's Box,* and *Death and the Devil.* (The latter is not a *Lulu* play.)

The Marquis of Keith. Translated by B. Gottlieb. In *From the Modern Repertoire,* edited by E. R. Bentley. Bloomington, Ind., 1952.

———. Translated by C. R. Mueller. In *Masterpieces of the Modern German Theatre: Five Plays,* edited by R. W. Corrigan. New York, 1967.

Princess Russalka. Translated by Frederick Eisemann. Boston, 1919. Includes the essay "On Eroticism" and eight short stories: "Princess Russalka," "The Grisly Suitor," "I Am Bored,"

FRANK WEDEKIND

"The Burning of Egliswyl," "Les Halles," "The Victim," "The Inoculation," and "Rabbi Esra."

The Solar Spectrum, Those Who Buy the Gods of Love, "An Idyll from Modern Life." Translated by D. Faehl and E. Vaughn. *Tulane Drama Review* 4:108–138 (1959).

Spring's Awakening. Translated by Eric Bentley. In *The Modern Theatre,* edited by Eric Bentley, vol. 6. New York, 1955–1960.

Spring Awakening. Translated by Tom Osborn. London, 1969.

Such Is Life. Translated by F. Ziegler. In *Modern Continental Plays,* edited by S. M. Tucker. New York, 1929.

The Tenor. Translated by S. Tridon. *Golden Book Magazine* 5:65–73 (1927).

Tragedies of Sex. Edited and translated by S. A. Eliot. New York and London, 1923. Includes *Spring's Awakening, Earth Spirit, Pandora's Box,* and *Damnation! (Damnation!* is an alternate title for *Death and the Devil.*)

BIOGRAPHICAL AND CRITICAL STUDIES

Best, Alan. *Frank Wedekind.* London, 1975. Includes bibliography of works in English.

Boa, Elizabeth. *The Sexual Circus: Wedekind's Theatre of Subversion.* Oxford, 1987.

Chick, Edson M. *Dances of Death: Wedekind, Brecht, Dürrenmatt, and the Satiric Tradition.* Columbia, S.C., 1984.

Emerich, Wilhelm. "Die Lulu-Tragödie." In *Das deutsche Drama vom Barock bis zur Gegenwart: Interpretationen,* edited by Benno von Weise. 2 vols. Düsseldorf, 2:207–228 (1958).

Gittleman, Sol. *Frank Wedekind.* New York, 1969.

Höger, Alfons. *Frank Wedekind: Der Konstruktivismus als schöpferische Methode.* Königstein, 1979.

————. *Hetärismus und bürgerliche Gesellschaft im Frühwerk Frank Wedekinds.* Copenhagen and Munich, 1981.

Irmer, Hans-Jochen. *Der Theaterdichter Frank Wedekind: Werk und Wirkung.* Berlin, 1975.

Jelavich, Peter. "Art and Mammon in Wilhelmine Germany: The Case of Frank Wedekind." *Central European History* 12:203–236 (1979).

————. *Munich and Theatrical Modernism: Politics, Playwriting, and Performances, 1890–1914.* Cambridge and London, 1985.

Jones, Robert A. *Art and Entertainment: German Literature and the Circus, 1890–1933.* Heidelberg, 1985.

Klotz, Volker. *Dramaturgie des Publikums.* Munich, 1976.

Kutscher, Artur. *Frank Wedekind: Sein Leben und seine Werke.* 3 vols. Munich, 1922–1931.

Maclean, Hector. "Wedekind's *Der Marquis von Keith*: An Interpretation Based on the Faust and Circus Motifs." *Germanic Review* 43:163–187 (1968).

Natan, Alex. "Frank Wedekind." In *German Men of Letters,* vol. 2, edited by A. Natan. London, 1963.

Polgar, Alfred. Cited by Karl Kraus in *"Die Büchse der Pandora,"* in *Literatur and Lüge.* Vienna and Leipzig, 1929.

Rothe, Friedrich. *Frank Wedekind's Dramen: Jugendstil und Lebensphilosophie.* Stuttgart, 1968.

Seehaus, Günter. *Frank Wedekind in Selbstzeugnissen und Bilddokumenten.* Reinbek, 1974.

————. *Frank Wedekind und das Theater.* Munich, 1964.

Shaw, Leroy R. *The Playwright and Historical Change: Dramatic Strategies in Brecht, Hauptmann, Kaiser, and Wedekind.* Madison, Wis., 1970.

Wagener, Hans. *Frank Wedekind.* Berlin, 1979.

Wedekind, Tilly. *Lulu: Die Rolle meines Lebens.* Munich, 1969.

LEROY R. SHAW

MIGUEL DE UNAMUNO
(1864–1936)

MIGUEL DE UNAMUNO Y JUGO, one of Spain's most polygraphic writers and also one of its most important intellectual figures in the early twentieth century, was born on 29 September 1864, in the Basque city of Bilbao. His first clear memory is one of special significance for a man who read widely in eight languages, became a professor of classical Greek at the University of Salamanca, and devoted some attention to the bearing that language has upon thought and personality. The living room in the house in Bilbao was off limits to the children, but young Unamuno spied one day on his father entertaining a certain M. Legorgeux. The indelible impression of surprise and mystery created by the fact that both men were speaking a foreign language constitutes Unamuno's earliest memory: "So people can understand each other in a way different from us! At the early age of six, the mystery of language caught my attention."[1]

On both the paternal and the maternal (Jugo) side, Unamuno's roots were Basque as far back as could be traced. His father, who had prospered tolerably well in his youth in Mexico, upon returning to Spain opened a bakery in Bilbao, married a niece considerably younger, and, soon after his conversation in French with

M. Legorgeux, died. Doña Salomé, Unamuno's mother, lived until 1908, and her traditional religious beliefs and conservative nature along with those of Concepción Lizárraga, whom Unamuno married in 1891, contributed to the web of matriarchy in Unamuno's life, a situation he found congenial on an everyday basis but against which he rebelled intellectually and politically.

The Basque national character is rooted in separateness. Of unknown ethnic and linguistic origins, the Basques have long enjoyed a reputation as fierce individualists with a disposition to violence in order to preserve their way of life. Undoubtedly, Unamuno's own celebrated individualism, his refusal to be stereotyped ("Put me under miscellaneous," he once said), his unusual conviction of his uniqueness—all these well-known features drew something from his ethnic background. The Basques are unique in Europe, and Unamuno was especially aware of this. His doctoral dissertation at the University of Madrid studied the problem of the origins of the Basque people, and his pride in his Basque roots never wavered.

Four years after the death of his father, Unamuno lived through the Carlist bombardment of Bilbao. The first shell fell a few houses from his own on 21 February 1874, and the event removed him roughly from childhood and signaled the beginning of what he called "the thread of my history."

---

[1]All quotations from Unamuno's works are from *Obras completas,* edited by Manuel García Blanco, 9 vols., 1966–1971. Citations below quoted material refer to volumes and pages of this edition.

The two Carlist wars muddied an already confused nineteenth century in the Iberian Peninsula. Fernando VII died at the end of 1833, and the Carlists refused to recognize his daughter Isabell II, proposing instead the younger brother of Fernando, Carlos Isidro, whence the term *carlista*. This action precipitated the First Carlist War (1833–1840). Carlist strength came from Navarre, rural Catalonia and Aragon, and the Basque provinces, and drew upon provincial distrust of Madrid, ultraconservative dogmatic Catholicism, and, in line with a practice of the French branch of the Bourbon family, denial of the right of succession to female heirs. The Carlist army got to the outskirts of Madrid but was unable to mount a successful attack. The overthrow of the Bourbon monarchy in 1868 provoked the so-called Second Carlist War (1872–1876) and saw a new pretender, Carlos VII, take the field. This time the Carlists set up a government and issued currency, but the revolt remained confined to the north, and with the Bourbons restored to the throne, the troops of Alfonso XII put down the Carlists for good.

The Carlists set siege to Bilbao in 1873, and the city was not liberated until 2 May 1874, when liberal soldiers arrived to bring relief. Although Miguel and his friends played with the still warm shell fragments and boasted loudly of how close the explosions had come, the siege quickly turned serious, and the *bilbaínos* resorted to a diet of rats and cats to stay alive. Unamuno's membership in a pious and conservative Carlist family did not prevent him from understanding the Bourbon viewpoint. It is significant that the "thread of his history" begins in this fratricidal strife, for his sense of the Cain and Abel aspect of Spanish history became especially strong, and he explored this civil rancor on the personal level in his striking novel *Abel Sánchez* (1917). His memories of the Carlist siege form the basis of his first novel, *Paz en la guerra* (*Peace in War,* 1897).

Unamuno's participation as a ten-year-old in this fractious episode of Spanish history was counterbalanced by what was in many ways the uneventful and peaceful existence of a traditional middle-class childhood in a provincial nineteenth-century city. Bilbao in the 1870's counted a population of only eighteen thousand, and the young man was soon free of the town to walk along the River Nervión and to explore the green and pleasant countryside. Unamuno's fondness for nature, which resembles at certain moments that of the English romantics, had its formation in these early years. Later he turned into an indefatigable walker and excursionist and wrote endless articles on his journies across Spain and Portugal, which were published in *De mi país* (Of My Land, 1903). Inspiration for much of his early poetry, such as the volume *Poesías* (Poems, 1907) also springs from these long walks in nature. During his life he constantly sought and found solace in the rocks and hills of Spain.

Miguel de Unamuno was also a devoutly Catholic youth. He attended mass daily, was named secretary of the executive committee of the Brotherhood of San Luis (St. Aloysius) of Gonzaga, and felt distinct, if naive, longings for what he termed sainthood. A certain mystical bent did indeed characterize his youth. Some of this was sublimated in his description of nature in *Peace in War*, and some of it is present in his long poem that contemplates and meditates upon a Diego Velázquez painting of Christ on the Cross: *El Cristo de Velázquez* (*The Christ of Velázquez,* 1920). At the same time, a definite evangelical sense informed his early Christianity. Opening the Bible by chance one day, he came across the passage: "Go ye forth and preach the gospel." It took some time to suppress the notion that he should obey this injunction. In his adult life he converted his pen into a pulpit and bestowed upon his vast written work all the urgency and devotion of a minister spreading the word. Nevertheless, as he confessed in his recollections of those years, his mystical visions were soon diminished by the sensual attractions of his sweetheart, Concha Lizárraga.

Sensitive, impressionable, given to long bouts of reading, a product of the petty bourgeoisie of Bilbao, Unamuno set off to study philosophy and letters at the University of Madrid in the fall of 1880. The indifferent high school student at the Instituto in Bilbao blossomed overnight into an outstanding university performer, who consistently earned the highest marks in his classes. Living in a pension in what he termed the anthill of Madrid, keeping much to himself, he discovered the strong intellectual bent of his character, his need for ideas and books.

Two events during his four years at the University of Madrid had a profound effect on his life. While still a high school student, he had come across a book in his father's library by the fervent and shrewd nineteenth-century Catholic apologist Jaime Balmes and thus learned indirectly of Immanuel Kant, Johann Gottlieb Fichte, René Descartes, and G. W. F. Hegel. Excited by this contact, he purchased an inexpensive notebook and proposed to draw up a system of philosophy very symmetrical and bristling with formulas. In Madrid direct exposure to philosophy reawakened this interest. Displaying what became a firm tenet of his intellectual life—that works should be read in their original language—he learned German and became enamored of "stupendous Hegel," and then taught himself English in order to take possession in the original of Herbert Spencer's logical positivism. Both philosophers left a strong impression on the young university student's mind. Hegel's use of dialectics to point out that contradiction could be a fruitful collision of ideas, leading in turn to a higher truth, is a lesson that Unamuno never forgot and that he applied in his works. Spencer's drive to systematize and his penchant for constructing typologies, which eventually led to the development of sociology, satisfied Unamuno's own youthful desire for classification and structure. As Unamuno gradually began to realize that there were mysteries in the world outside of systems, a variety of feelings that logical positivism was inadequate to deal with, he shook off Spencer's influence. Hegel's presence remained. In fact, as he later recalled, he had read Spencer in a Hegelian manner.

The second event proved even more formative. Once in Madrid, his custom of hearing mass every day began to waver. One Sunday he asked himself what it would mean to stop going to mass altogether and, to his surprise, he discovered that to do so would be an act of no consequence. This rupture with the forms and rituals of his faith bespeaks two important points: the inroads that his reading in philosophy had made on the simple, unquestioning faith of his childhood and an impatience with what he perceived to be the mechanical manner in which many of his fellow Catholics went through the outward aspects of their faith (someone intoning prayers without feeling in church is a common scene in his novels). This lapse emphatically did not mean that in the long run Unamuno ceased to be a religious person. On the contrary, by the turn of the century he devoted his considerable energy and intelligence to the enterprise of conducting an impassioned inquiry into what it meant to be a religious individual in an increasingly secular society.

Back in Bilbao with his doctorate, Unamuno became a fretful private tutor of Latin. His students lacked motivation, and their teacher chafed at the humdrum routine that offered little scope for his energy and talents. Except for the presence in it of his future wife, the atmosphere of his native city began to oppress him. In 1889 one of his uncles financed the Grand Tour for Unamuno, and off he went to France, Switzerland, and Italy. His travel diary and scattered articles reveal no special effect from his journies (he loved Florence and was impressed by the heritage of Dante, although the Apennines reminded him of his native mountains), but they show that a great deal of the time he missed Concha. In his erudition Unamuno eventually became the most cosmopolitan of Spaniards, and for a few years he was an exponent of the need to Europeanize his country, but unlike many of his fellow writers and artists, he did not make the obligatory annual pilgrimage to Paris or Rome. An energetic traveler in the Iberian Peninsula, he left his country again only to visit the Italian front in 1917, spend six years in exile in France, and go to England to receive an honorary degree in 1936 from Oxford.

Concepción Lizárraga became his wife on 31 January 1891. Born in Guernica two months before Unamuno, she met her future husband when they were both fourteen years old. Since they were childhood sweethearts, it soon became taken for granted that they would marry. She was a sturdy, blond, commonsensical woman, a faithful Roman Catholic, the perfect foil for his intense, nervous, intellectual temperament. He laughingly remarked that her tastes in literature were "down to earth" and obvious. But that was no problem for her husband, for he sought in her not intellectual stimulation (there was plenty of that in his books and his own fertile mind), but rather a domestic escort, a mother to his children, and, in moments of anguish, a maternal figure for him. Overcome one day in 1897 by his fear of death, he wept on her shoulders, and she comforted him as one of her children, a scene that he recounted in his letters and used in his novels. She is the model for the long-suffering, understanding wife who appears in several of his pieces of fiction. She bore him nine children and died on 15 May 1934, two and a half years before he did.

Unlike many artists and writers, Unamuno thrived on domesticity. In the land of Don Juan he was an unswerving monogamist, indeed something of a prude about sexual matters. No small irony resides in the fact that despite the unorthodox nature of his faith theirs was the ideal Christian marriage: the wife, a perfect helpmate; the husband, hardworking, loyal, and a good provider.

Six months after their marriage, Unamuno sat for the national examinations (*oposiciones*) that enabled him to become a professor (*catedrático*) at a Spanish university. The chair in classical Greek at Salamanca was open, and the young groom was successful in obtaining it.

The great University of Salamanca, established in 1218 and during Spain's heyday an important seat of European learning, was a community of twelve thousand when the young Basque couple arrived; its intellectual reputation long ago tarnished, it had become, in the words of Thomas Carlyle, a fortress of ignorance. The new professor chose not to disappear into this stronghold of the past, nor even to lose himself in a life of Hellenistic scholarship. When one of his colleagues made the suggestion that he edit and publish some Greek manuscripts in the library of the Escorial, Unamuno declined. Recalling the incident in 1905, he made two points: erudition was too often a form of retreat from the world, and scholarship was not the type of activity that could satisfy his spirit. In a society as problematic as Spain's, he said, individual talent should not be wasted in establishing new readings of Greek manuscripts. His own ambition would not be realized by having his name appear on some international list of authorities on obscure philological matters: "I know more than enough Greek to put my students in contact with the language of Plato."

Such was the academic nonconformist who arrived in the sleepy little town on the banks of the river Tormes, where, except for six years' exile in France, he spent the rest of his life. Townspeople wondered about his religion, or lack thereof; they might also have questioned his politics. In the fall of 1894, Unamuno began to collaborate in a new Bilbao weekly entitled *La lucha de clases* (Class Struggle). He sent an open letter to the director that was published in Bilbao and Madrid, and Spanish Socialists welcomed the recently appointed professor of Greek into their party. Unamuno's statement bubbled with characteristic enthusiasm. For some time, he said, he had been persuaded that the "pure Socialism" initiated by Karl Marx was the only viable idea around. He stressed that the key contemporary social struggle was between those who work so that others may eat and those who live off the sweat of others' brows. Socialism was, he said in a phrase that would have disturbed Marx, the religion of humanity. Pablo Iglesias, the founder of the Spanish Socialist party, came to speak at Salamanca and was introduced by Unamuno.

The Socialist party appears to be the only political party he ever joined. It certainly represented one of his first ventures into the mine field of applied ethics, the movement from ideas to action. Unamuno let his membership in the Socialist party lapse early in 1897. As time went on, he became less enchanted with the tenets of socialism, and an issue involving the imprisonment of the director of *La Lucha de Clases* added to his doubts. The editor Valentín Hernández was thrown in jail when *La Lucha de Clases* printed an unsigned article severely criticizing the army. The article may have been written by Unamuno, but he did not acknowledge this fact. Meanwhile, Hernández, as editor, willingly accepted responsibility.

Although Unamuno collaborated enthusiastically for three years in the columns of *La Lucha de Clases,* his knowledge of Marx was probably never very profound. Indeed, his basic attraction to the movement seemed to smack of literary association. He was not unaware of socialism's appeal to the likes of Leo Tolstoy and Henrik Ibsen. At the same time there is no reason to doubt his compassion for the plight of Spain's proletariat, one of the most downtrodden in Europe, nor his belief that capitalism one day would have to bring about a more equitable distribution of income and goods. Whether he would have been able to accept Vladimir Lenin's contention that acknowledgement of the class struggle also meant recognition of the eventual dictatorship of the proletariat is a moot question. From today's perspective, he seems to have been largely an armchair Socialist.

In the fall of 1897, his religious crisis in the spring of that year still fresh in his memory, he confided to Juan Arzadun, a Basque friend, that he felt more Socialist than ever before and again said that he believed that the socialization of the means of production was inevitable. But there was, he stated, a greater ill than economic inequity. To his friend he made what became an incessant declaration in his work: socialism does nothing about answering the question of why we die. For once the social problem is solved, we are still left with the following riddle: Is life worth living if death is its only end?

From February to June of 1895 Unamuno contributed monthly essays to the Madrid review *La España Moderna* (Modern Spain). The series appeared under the general title of *En torno al casticismo* (On Authentic Tradition), and it met with a profound silence. Then came the disastrous six-month war with the United States in 1898. Spain's loss of the last of its once numerous colonies in the New World suddenly catapulted the nation's attention to what came to be known as the Spanish problem. Unamuno reissued his essays in book form in 1902, at which time they joined a list of other distinguished musings on the Spanish plight. Subsequently, *En torno al casticismo* has taken its place as a threshold to the Unamuno oeuvre. Fondness for citation, dense and sometimes illogical argument, the tendency to revert to a linguistic point of view in his discussions, a strong empathy for the landscape of Castile, an awareness of Europe: here are themes and methods that became recognizeable features of Unamuno's work.

The adjective *castizo* means chaste and pure. When applied to certain customs, sayings, food, and actions, it came to mean "truly Spanish" (as Spanish as eating roast chestnuts in winter or drinking a cold barley and almond beverage [*horchata*] in the summer). In the mouths of the traditionalists *castizo* bestowed ultimate approval; to the liberals it was a label associated with a provincial mentality. Europe, rationalism, Charles Darwin were not *castizo*. Pío Baroja's style was not *castizo*, but the nineteenth-century novelist Juan Valera's was.

Understanding of *casticismo,* says Unamuno, depends on obtaining a clear idea of the meaning of the word "tradition." Beginning a lifelong habit of resorting to etymologies as a starting point in his arguments, he points out that "tradition" derives from the Latin *tradere,* which means "to hand over," to pass something from one point to another. History, however, is not merely the vast kaleidiscope implied by a constantly changing series of movements. Underneath the daily handing over is a sediment of nonchange, an eternal tradition, says Unamuno, in one of his many paradoxes. This eternal tradition reveals the flimsiness of basing approval on the concept of *castizo,* which is rooted too much in the flux of ideas.

This notion of nonchange Unamuno called *intrahistoria* (intrahistory), and he uses the sea as a metaphor to explain it:

> The waves of history, with their noise and foam . . . roll over an immensely deep and silent ocean where the sun never reaches. Everything in the newspapers . . . is only the surface of the sea [and newspaper accounts] say nothing about the silent life of millions of people with no history who all day everyday get up at the sun's bidding to pursue their hard tasks. . . . Upon this silent humanity stand those who make noise in history.
>
> (1:793)

The term *intrahistoria* has enjoyed a certain currency. Some commentators have linked it to Jung's notion of the collective unconscious, but Unamuno meant nothing more mysterious than did the French historian Jules Michelet, who had insisted that people were more important than leaders and that the best of history was *underneath* in obscure depths. It is the French historians of the *Annales* school (Fernand Braudel and E. Le Roy Ladurie) who have given countenance to Unamuno's idea. Their concern with daily life in the village outside the raging battles, with private emotions and the effects of events on common people represents a fruitful application of Unamuno's *intrahistoria.*

What is, then, Spain's eternal tradition, and is it any different from that of humanity in general? The answer leads Unamuno to a discussion of national character in which he focuses on Castile, the geographical and political center of the nation, and implies, via the concept of determinism, that a great deal of the Castilian character is shaped by the austere nature of the landscape in which the Castilians live. Unamuno's evocation of the central meseta brims with poetry. *En torno al casticismo* introduces landscape as a literary theme in the writings of the Generation of '98:

> How beautiful the settled sadness of this ocean full of stones and sky! In its contrasts of light and shadow, it is a uniform and monotonous landscape, with distinct colors and few nuances. . . . There is a lack of gentle transition. . . . This landscape does not arouse voluptuous feelings of *joie de vivre,* nor does it suggest concupiscent emotions of comfort . . . there are no folds of earth that beckon like a nest.
>
> (1.809)

The Spaniards who people this lunar landscape are themselves lacking in gentle transitions and subtle nuances. Silent, taciturn, tenacious, they created a Castilian school of painting harsh in its realism and a popular music monotonous to an extreme. Reading in William James's *Principles of Psychology* (1890), Unamuno came across the observation that images in the mind are surrounded by a halo or penumbra, a fringe that forms part of the image's context. Unamuno chose the Spanish word *nimbo* (nimbus) to express the same notion, and he said that in the extreme climate and landscape of Castile, people, ideas, and culture carry no nimbus. Sequentiality, like rosary beads, dominates Castilian thought. Subtlety, gradation, and a sense of mystery find little place in it. Proceeding along the lines of the French determinist Hippolyte Taine, Unamuno seeks to explain literature by reference to national character. The theater of

288

Pedro Calderón de la Barca serves as his prime example. The presentation of hieratic assumptions and categorical ideas precludes a nimbus, such as the deep psychological truths that the characters of Shakespeare wear.

Unamuno, echoing Giambattista Vico and Johann Gottfried von Herder, justifies this excursion into literature as a means of elucidating national character by pointing out the intimate connection between language and the temperament of a people. In a passage that foreshadows major concerns of twentieth-century linguistics and philosophy, he writes: "Language is the receptacle of a people's experience, and the sediment of its thoughts. In the deep folds of its metaphors (and metaphors compose the immense majority of words), the collective spirit of a people slowly leaves its mark."

Since Hippocrates, writers have been boldly asserting that climate and topography determine physical and temperamental attributes of a people. As technology begins to control certain aspects of nature, this notion seems less imposing, but whether we agree with the tenets of determinism or with Unamuno's particular interpretation, these passages introduced abiding themes into Spanish literature at the turn of the century: landscape and the influence of Castile on the national character. *En torno al casticismo* was a germinal work.

Having laid bare the eternal tradition of the Spanish people, Unamuno recommends that the discussion of *lo castizo* be set aside and that the country open its doors and windows to the influence of the rest of the world. For the Iberian Peninsula, this means that the winds of Europe should blow across the Pyrenees and refresh the stagnant Spanish air. Don Quixote symbolizes the Spanish tendency to live in a world of fantasy, and the Don should give up his outlandish notion of reintroducing chivalry into the modern world and assume once more his original non-mythic name: Alonso Quijano. Unamuno's concluding observation echoes the cry of the Europeanizers against *casticismo*. In a few years he completely changed his mind,

but in 1895 that was the final word in this pivotal book in the Unamuno canon.

Summering in the Basque provinces in 1896, Unamuno put the finishing touches on *Peace in War*, which he published the following year. Its inspiration is drawn from Unamuno's experiences in the 1874 Carlist siege of Bilbao. When compared to the conventions that obtained in the nineteenth century, Unamuno's first work of fiction reveals a few irregularities, some of which may be chalked up to the fact that this was his first sally into what he called "the lists of the novel." Its interest in history and its roster of historical characters invite the reader to consider it as a historical novel (there is nothing in it that cannot be documented, claims the neophyte novelist). But set too close to the present moment (the Second Carlist War ended in 1876) and placed in a country still suffering severe stress from unresolved social conflicts, *Peace in War* does not exude the romantic attraction of distance to be found in those of Sir Walter Scott's novels that have a medieval setting. Nor has Unamuno made any effort to provide the characters drawn from history with any depth of presentation.

The protagonists in the forefront of the novel are composites of Unamuno himself, his family, and his friends. Even they are wooden. We do not learn until one of the closing scenes, and then only through the memory of a minor protagonist, that Ignacio, arguably the hero of the novel, was sturdy, ungainly, and heavy of step. In future novels Unamuno turns this defect into a virtue, pointedly refusing to describe the physical features of his fictional inventions, creating what he called the naked novel. But in this first effort none of the book's personages, from generals to schoolboys, makes a very vivid impression.

Ignacio, the son of a devout Carlist couple who own a candy shop in the district of Bilbao (where the novelist himself was born), and the skeptical, orphaned Pachico Zabaldibe represent different sides of Unamuno. Ignacio's desire to escape from Bilbao to discover how things really are and to flee from the dour and fatalistic stereotyping of provincial life ("What is imbibed with your mother's milk escapes only in the coffin") signals one aspect of the restless young Miguel. Pachico's timid temperament, his sensitive, mystical bent, and his voracious reading are characteristics that even more closely resemble the author. The novel is refreshingly frank about the adolescent sexual drive of Ignacio (the ritual of sin and confession); the provincial eccentricities come to life; and the harrowing features of the siege are well done. Ignacio finally joins the Carlist troops and is killed in one of the last battles, and his crushed parents retire to a small village to make, with Catholic resignation, their way out of the world their son has already abandoned. Pachico, like the author, continues reading and looking for answers.

Peace in War nicely illustrates the concept of intrahistory. The names of the Carlist leaders, the battles, and the political maneuvers have been, indeed, scattered like the most fragile spume. But the novel provides an enduring impression of the daily lives of the *bilbaínos:* the boys playing with the still warm shells, the uncle's pornography collection, a village wedding, the dignified dying of people in the substratum of history: "Of all that war, what would remain? thought Pachico. Dry notices, a few lines in histories yet to be written, a brief reference to one of many civil wars."

Shells explode, people march off to war, and partisans brawl over their cause. Yet much of the novel describes the state signified in its first word: the warm routine of life, daily discussions over hot chocolate, the romance of reading, and above all the abiding comfort of nature. At the end of the novel Pachico contemplates the mountains and realizes that life is a combination of peace and war, that in the breast of peace one can fabricate war, and that one can take refuge in some kind of peace in the midst of war. This became the dialectic of Unamuno's own life.

In the first week of January 1896 Unamuno's third son, Raimundo Jenaro, was born. Within a few months, the boy suffered an attack of menengitis, one of his hands became paralyzed, and his head enlarged with the symptoms of hydrocephalus. He died in 1902.

By March of 1897 the burden of his son's illness caused Unamuno to break down. His conviction that Raimundo's suffering was a form of punishment visited upon him by God, as well as his own long-standing fear of death, provoked what has come to be known as his religious crisis. Reason suggested that death was the extinction of the spirit, that nothingness awaited—and Unamuno found himself crushed by this vision of *la nada.* He stared at his son, drew sketches of him, and writhed at the helplessness of his own febrile mind in the face of this biological mandate. Finally, one night he broke down in his wife's arms, and she comforted him with the words, "My child, my child!" Unable to sleep, he slipped out of the house and appeared unannounced at the door of the Dominican monastery. For three days neither his family nor the university knew of his whereabouts. At last he took refuge in Alcalá de Henares with an old friend, Father Juan José de Lecanda. It was Holy Week.

While with Father Lecanda, he began a diary, the first entry of which is dated 14 April. The diary, discovered in 1957 and published in 1970 as *Diario íntimo* (Intimate Diary), is our source for Unamuno's spiritual agony. In it he copied a sentence from Frederick William Faber, the English Anglican priest whose conversion to Roman Catholicism had created a stir: "A year from now I will either be a Catholic or a madman." Neither eventuality proved true, but it was a close call. Every fiber of Unamuno's being longed to return to the comfort of his faith, to the explanation that Raimundo's illness and suffering were part of God's will, that eternal peace in heaven awaited the Christian at the end of life. He pored over the New Testament and reread Father Faber, but on the morning of Easter Sunday when the faithful awoke to the glad tidings of the Resurrection, he said simply that he could not be numbered in their ranks.

In the last resort reason denied him reentry

into his faith. The pages of his diary are awash with religious sentiments and with pristine statements from his Catholic upbringing, but he was unable to make the blind leap into the arms of faith. Several entries indicate that he felt he might be going mad, and eventually he discussed the temptation of suicide. He excoriates his egoism as a form of illness and deplores his sense of himself as an actor. Above all, he sees intellectualism as the enemy, a terrible madness and a kind of vanity.

The diary records no solution. The struggle that it depicts turned out to be a way of life for Unamuno. He returned home ready to carry on for thirty-nine years a running battle between the tenets of reason that denied him the comfort of faith and his own profound need to construct a belief that would do away with his crushing sense of nihilism. Once more within the cocoon of his family, reacting to the needs of the university, his fear of madness departed, but the struggle between despair and belief, reason and faith, continued without truce and, as he said later in "Mi religión" ("My Religion," 1910), without any hope of victory.

By the turn of the century, Miguel de Unamuno was a name to be reckoned with in Spanish intellectual life. *Peace in War* did not lack for readers, but most of all his numerous articles in leading journals on a wide range of issues were provoking discussion and reaction. With wit, an acerbity often marred by a tendency to preachiness, a fondness for paradox, and a tolerant attitude toward contradictions in his arguments, Unamuno was beginning to attract national attention. He held forth on such topics as educational reform, the purity of the Castilian language, true patriotism, and, of course, the battle between science and faith. A brief essay in 1896 entitled "Civilización y cultura" (Civilization and Culture) contains insights into the continuity of culture, the difficulty of distinguishing between the individual's sphere of influence and that of the environment, and the question of why civilization has to be viewed in linear terms such as progress or retrogression. Cer-

tain readers might beg for further development of his points, others chafe at an apparent thinness, but no one could deny the vivacity of a writer familiar with Carlyle, Vico, and George Eliot, and one just starting to learn Danish in order to grapple with Søren Kierkegaard.

En torno el casticismo had bestowed sympathetic attention on the obscure subjects who people the depths of intrahistory, but all along Miguel de Unamuno had nursed a desire to join the movement of the waves on the sea's surface. Even before he acquired a modicum of fame, an occasional letter includes an outburst of anger at his lack of recognition. On the heels of his religious crisis he began to see one undeniable proof of immortality: individuals live on in memory. Notoriety might widen the circle, as could politics and war, but art had a long radius and a wide audience. For centuries after their disappearance into dust, Shakespeare, Dante, and Cervantes lived on in their readers. Unamuno noted in an essay of November 1898 entitled "La vida es sueño" (Life Is a Dream) that in a secular age the tendency was to seek a simulacrum of immortality among the shadows that wander the Elysian Fields. He descries this as a parody of what immortality should be, but it is increasingly clear that by 1900 the urge to fame had become a permanent spur in his life. Who can deny the telling insight in the closing lines of this untitled entry for 9 March 1929, in his rhymed journal *Cancionero* (Songbook, published posthumously in 1953):

> *Aquí os dejo mi alma—libro,*
> *hombre—mundo verdadero.*
> *Cuando vibres todo entero*
> *soy yo, lector, que en ti vibro.*
>
> I bequeath you my soul in this book,
> a true world for me.
> When you shudder, dear reader,
> it is I trembling in you.
>   (6:1188)

The spiritual crisis of 1897 resulted in another ploy for which Unamuno is famous; he went public with his agony and turned his religious problems into the stuff of literature. Several times in his diary, he deplored his theatricality, and he was bothered by a constant awareness that everything he did was calculated to attract attention, including the diary. After 1897 he apparently decided to accept this aspect of his personality and to use it for his own ends. He became increasingly and openly aware of his reading public. Also, it had become clear to Unamuno that in Spain his religious situation was not to be the subject of a meaningful dialogue with another individual, especially a priest. Father Lecanda seemed too ready to confide Unamuno's plight to whoever would listen, and a certain Father Arintero at Salamanca grew impatient with what he considered to be Unamuno's Lutheran tendencies. In any event, these are some of the reasons behind Unamuno's decision to make his doubts and agonies the theme of several novels and many poems and essays and to turn literature into a confessional. He remained impervious to what his critics objected to as egoism; after all, Friedrich Nietzsche was no less subjective and emotional, nor for that matter was Kierkegaard.

One of the first occasions for this confessional mode presented itself in 1898 when he spoke to the Ateneo, a private club and library in Madrid, on the topic of Nicodemus the Pharisee. The audience grew uncomfortable at what it sensed were personal confidences from this tall Basque with the reedy voice. Nicodemus confessed his faith to Jesus only at night; thus he symbolizes the compromising and hypocritical intellectual, unable or unwilling to declare his faith in full daylight. Unamuno, who knew full well how reason could undermine faith, devoted the rest of his talk to pointing out how faith could be creative and could provide access to areas of reality where logic could not reach.

In an age beginning to drift toward impersonality, Unamuno found it necessary to make a case for the importance of the individual. The essay "¡Adentro!" ("Go Within!," 1900) is a seminal effort in this vein. By casting it in the form of a letter to himself, Unamuno continued with the public confession he had begun in the Ateneo. The writer of the letter (Unamuno) assures the addressee (Unamuno) that the recent radical sense of nothingness that had been bothering him (a reference to the crisis of 1897, whose reverberations never entirely ceased) can best be vanquished by a drive to excel, to achieve as much as possible. Do not settle for second best, he tells himself; do not succumb to the fatalism of so many proverbs. A bird in the hand is not necessarily worth two in the bush; go after those in the bush, and in the process wings might be grown. On one level this is a pep talk to fortify his combative nature, but it is also an admonition to continue searching for answers to the spiritual quandary in which he found himself. He goes on: you have chosen writing as your form of action in the world; think, then, not in terms of a Spanish audience but of a universal one. The city with its bustle and belittling demands is not necessarily the best platform from which to reach this universal audience. The apparent lack of dialogue in the country can be remedied by the vigor of daily writing, better done free of the mindless chatter of the city. (At about this time Unamuno had considered competing for a chair of Spanish literature at the University of Madrid, but at the last moment changed his mind. Salamanca remained his pulpit from which to reach the world.)

Unamuno next describes a view of individual development that startlingly anticipates an idea associated with existentialism:

> One thing in your letter I don't like . . . is your insistence on drawing up a plan for your life. Forget about a plan, you're not a building. Plans don't make life, instead life draws up a plan in the process of living. Don't persist in regulating your actions by means of your thoughts; let the latter inform, deform, and transform the former. . . . Your life is a continuous development in time . . . you will discover yourself by the way you act.
> (1:948)

Unamuno here uncovers one of the themes of existentialism as expounded later in the century by Jean-Paul Sartre: thrown into the world, the individual has total responsibility for his or her actions; there is no preconceived plan but only the task of realizing oneself. For plan, substitute "dogma" or "doctrine," and Unamuno's finding becomes even more vital. Individuals should not be bent by inflexible outside schemes; bloodless dogma should not dry up the sap of personal truth.

Such a view of individual responsibility emphasizes, in Unamuno's eyes, the importance of each one of us. Don't think yourself superior, he admonishes himself, for we are all superior in the sense that each one of us is unique and irreplaceable. This point, which is made again with vehemence in *Del sentimiento trágico de la vida en los hombres y los pueblos* (*The Tragic Sense of Life*, 1913), can be taken as representing a strong measure of romantic egotism. But it can also be understood as a reaction to the author's distress over the ultimate extinction that faces him and all of mankind. To snuff out a mind and, in the case of artists, intellectuals, and scientists, a storehouse of wisdom and insight as well is, as Unamuno later says, the ultimate injustice. Seen from this point of view, the observation gains in humanism what it loses in fanciful thinking.

Bristling with paradox and contradiction, "Go Within!" attracts because of its spirit. Read as Unamuno's response to his sense of nihilism rather than, as many have done incorrectly, a recipe for ethical conduct, it is a compelling statement. It is one of a triptych of essays published in the same year under the simple title *Tres ensayos* (Three Essays, 1900). The other two are "La fe" (Faith) and "La ideocracia" (Ideocracy), the latter an attack on the stultifying effect of ideology. Taken together, they represent a clear statement of the Unamuno platform. The essay on faith views the problem with some of the dynamism of "Go Within!" Faith, proclaims Unamuno, contrary to the catechism definition as belief in what we do not see, is, instead, an act of creation, of taking what we do see and converting it into faith. The early Christian community, still surrounded by the aroma of Christ, accepted what it saw as faith. With the development of sophistication in the Christian religion, faith lost its spontaneous nature and became a problem of belief. Maintain faith, then, says Unamuno, having recourse to a typical tautology, in faith itself.

In the first year of the new century, a fairly clear idea emerged of where Unamuno was heading and of what he proposed to do. For several decades the prevailing dogma about the world and man's situation in it had been one of scientific determinism. Darwin had been read, rightly or wrongly, as destroying the revelation of our divine origins related in the book of Genesis. Taine and Spencer had strengthened the grounds for believing that man was a mere automaton, a lump of clay pushed and pulled by the environment and even educated by unthinking responses to behavior patterns. Writing his Socialist articles in the last decade of the nineteenth century, rebelling against the narrowness of the Catholic Church, Unamuno had been content with this orientation, even excited by it. But the tragedy of his encephaletic son devasted this acceptance of the prevailing ideology.

His intense plea for the ratification of faith was to a large extent an effort to allow the individual a measure of freedom to make choices in the materialistic scheme of things. Unamuno's egotism, for which he was long criticized, was the inevitable result of the crusade he led to rescue the human spirit from the grasp of materialism. The position in the essay "Go Within!" is one that was also recognized at around the same time by William James, a writer whom Unamuno had read: the individual, the man of flesh and blood, as Unamuno called him, is ultimately the source of everything we know; there is no revelation but through human beings. That is why, by striking out for the territory "within," we not only learn about ourselves but about all others as well.

By 1900 Unamuno's basic religious ideas had also taken shape. Like Kierkegaard he rejected dogma and institutions and insisted that belief is a form of suffering. From William James's "The Will to Believe" (1896) he drew the notion that faith has a way of preceding fact and introducing it. In 1900 he also became the rector of the University of Salamanca. His base was solid; his audience was growing. Already he was a name in Latin America; some of his essays on socialism had been translated into German; and he soon made his way into French and English.

At this point Unamuno the man begs for attention. After all, he earned a slice of his fame by insisting that the man of flesh and blood should be the starting point of philosophy, and intrahistory stresses the value of knowing more about such matters. Relatively tall, bearded, with a pronounced aquiline nose and owl-like eyes accentuated by a pair of gold-rimmed glasses, he commanded attention by what he called his "civil uniform," a dark blue suit with a black vest that fitted close to his neck and gave him the appearance of an Anglican clergyman. When these articles of clothing wore out, he replaced them with identical pieces. Parsimonious and puritanical, he was an incessant talker, and when he first arrived in Salamanca, one acquaintance remarked, people avoided him like the plague. Seated at a café table, nervously playing with bread crumbs in his fingers, he held a monologue on any subject in the world. As an outlet for this same nervousness, he got into the habit of creating birds by intricately folding pieces of paper. Some of these graceful creatures are still preserved in his study at Salamanca. Unlike many monologuists, he also listened, for his novels are full of anecdotes he obviously heard from friends. But, above all, he was a reader. He left a library of four thousand volumes, all of them ferociously marked up. His interests included literature, history, languages, philosophy, psychology, politics, and above all religion. He liked to read several different books at once; on one occasion, he was working his way through the unusual combination of Tacitus, Gustave Flaubert's letters, Francis Parkman, and Adolf von Harnack.

Unamuno's second novel, *Amor y pedagogía* (Love and Education), appeared in 1902. In satirizing the baleful effects of a thoughtless application of the notions of scientific determinism to the upbringing of a child, Unamuno spoke partly from his own experience, for science could not cure his son's encephalitis nor quell the emotional chaos in which the father floundered.

Avito Carrascal scientifically selects a wife with the view in mind of her bearing him a genius. While she is pregnant, he reads her a biography of Newton, takes her to museums and to the opera, and insists that she consume large quantities of kidney beans (*alubias,*) which he has heard are a better source of nourishment than meat. His wife suffers from indigestion and a frustrated desire to read pious magazines. A son is born, is given the name Apolodoro, and despite all his father's efforts turns out to be an average child, with no special ability in math or philosophy, the product of a Catholic middle-class background that his father's plans have been unable to modify. Apolodoro unscientifically falls in love, loses his girl to another man, and, under the influence of Hildebrando F. Menaguti, a caricature of an effete modernist poet, commits suicide. So much for the capacity of a scientific education.

Excellent stretches of dialogue and a tone of sharp humor make the novel readable, but the characters are not rounded. Each one exists by virtue of a defect or an obsession, a device that Unamuno perfects in *Abel Sánchez.* No physical descriptions are given; there is no sense of time and place.

Amor y pedagogía moves away from the conventions of the nineteenth-century novel: strongly delineated characters and a richly described social setting. It also makes a significant departure from conventional form. Unamuno tells the reader that he has added a prologue and an epilogue not clearly related to the novel because his publishers thought the manuscript too short. By writing the prologue and the epilogue to enlarge the book, Unamuno was forced to take a look at the creative process. In the prologue he recognizes that his characters are puppets for his ideas, and that he does not know how to create women. It may be observed that this need, imposed by a reality outside of the creative process—the demand to fill pages in order that the publisher can produce a book of a certain size—unwittingly gave him a new viewpoint on a work of fiction. In the face of such a necessity Unamuno gradually realized how contingent could be the structure of a novel. Thus a blend of forces external and internal begin in 1902 to suggest the fragility of form and to raise the possibility of authorial intervention (the prologue is delivered in a voice other than the author's, allowing the author to talk about himself), a presence that becomes imposing in a decade with the appearance of *Niebla* (*Mist,* 1914).

Unamuno's reading and interpretation of Miguel de Cervantes Saavedra's *Don Quixote* (1605, 1615) serve as an excellent means of following the change in his philosophical outlook. It also aids in understanding the unusual view of literature that he was in the process of developing.

During the years surrounding the writing of *En torno al casticismo,* Unamuno stated loudly and clearly that Spain suffered from a surfeit of quixotism, for which the only cure was a radical one: let Don Quixote die so that Alonso Quijano may be reborn. Alonso Quijano's sanity was destroyed by the voracious reading of books of chivalry; on his deathbed he renounces his madness and says that he should be called Alonso Quijano the Good. Unamuno commends Cervantes' unromantic conclusion, for it means the end of chimeras and tilting at windmills, a return to the reality of life and the serious business of getting on with practical things, not heretofore a notable Spanish trait.

A dramatic about-face in Unamuno's attitude toward this great novel occurred after the religious crisis of 1897. The first indications

may be seen in a 1905 essay entitled "Sobre la lectura e interpretación del 'Quijote' " ("On the Reading and Interpretation of 'Don Quixote' "). Unamuno registers his anger at two kinds of readers: those who confess they have never been able to get through the novel and those who read it pretty much the same way a priest says mass, without any feeling. The former pass for cultivated men, but they are hypocrites, for they do not know what is, in effect, the Spanish bible. The latter are pedants, boringly involved in establishing the meaning of various passages. At this point Unamuno makes a revolutionary observation for the year 1905. Even if we assume that we can decipher Cervantes' meaning and can discern that he indeed intended to put an end to the reading of books of chivalry, Cervantes' intention has little to do with what the rest of us see in the book. Such a statement was greeted with groans by those dedicated to set interpretations of the novel, but in light of today's more tolerant notions of authorial intent, which many critics believe can only be imperfectly known, and of our dynamic idea of reader involvement in a text, it seems startlingly contemporary. In any event, no one, avers Unamuno, reads the novel for its poetry and universal truth. The reign of Don Quixote has yet to be born in Spain.

With the publication, also in 1905, of *La vida de Don Quijote y Sancho* (*The Life of Don Quixote and Sancho,*) Unamuno became, in contradiction to his earlier opinion, an apostle of quixotism. His preface to the second edition (1914) reiterates his quarrel with meaning. The novel *Don Quixote* belongs to everyone. Some will be concerned with interpreting the book's meaning for its time and place and the intentions Cervantes had in writing it, but I am concerned now, he wrote, only with the meaning that I give to it, and in addition I reserve the right to quarrel with the way Cervantes handled certain matters. And that meaning, given the message of the essays that appeared in 1900, is predictable: the Don is the ultimate spiritual figure; his struggle against the harsh reality of

Spain, doomed from the outset, is the agony of Unamuno in search of a faith in which he can believe. Don Quixote's stubborn bravery, his refusal to admit defeat until the end when Cervantes sends him home to die in his bed like a good citizen, is exactly the model Unamuno needs to sustain the tribulations of his own life, devastated by a loss of faith and the realization that death is the final end.

Dulcinea, Don Quixote's ideal love, symbolizes perfectly what Unamuno feels about faith. Chaste and continent, the Don loves Dulcinea without expecting to be loved in return; in other words, he has faith in faith. His deeds of glory are for her benefit; she gives him a reason for living. Throughout the book's chronicle of misadventure and defeat, Don Quixote is never disloyal to his absent, unattainable, ideal mistress. Flat on his back in one of the final chapters, with the sword of the Knight of the White Moon pressing on his throat, Don Quixote agrees to renounce chivalry, but not Dulcinea. His conqueror allows him to arise, content that the fragile fifty-year-old man has agreed to return home, unconcerned that his devotion to an ideal has not been compromised.

His comments on the famous adventure of the windmills illustrate how Unamuno takes possession of the text. The knight was right, declares Unamuno; fear blinded Sancho's eyes and made him see windmills instead of his master's giants. Today, Unamuno continues, these windmills are giants in the form of locomotives, turbines, steamships, machine guns, instruments for performing ovariotomies; in other words, they stand for all the so-called advances made possible by science. Don Quixote once more rolls in the dust and, says Unamuno, that is what giants (read technology) can do to us—break our lances; but if we are of the material of the Knight of La Mancha, they cannot break our hearts. There are more than enough oaks to repair our lances, and we continue our struggle to right the wrongs of this world, including our battle against the dispiriting dictates of reason.

When it was pointed out to Unamuno that Spain was woefully lacking in the products of technology, he replied testily, "Que inventen ellos" (Let others invent); Spain will supply the spiritual questers.

He is especially hard on Sancho. The famous helmet of Mambrino, in reality a barber's basin that the knight chooses to regard as the enchanted helmet of Mambrino, gives rise in the novel to much discussion and eventual altercation. During the course of these events it becomes apparent that Cervantes is allowing his protoganists their own points of view. For some of them it is a barber's basin; others, mockingly, side with Don Quixote. Sancho proposes a compromise; call it, he says, a "basin-helmet." This bit of guile infuriates Unamuno. No, Sancho, runs his admonishment, it is either a basin or a helmet; there is no "basin-helmet" worth a damn.

One other figure in history never wavered in his faith, suffered the torment of doubters, was mocked and beaten, and kept his sights fastened on an ideal. Unamuno can easily convert the Knight of the Sad Countenance into a Christ figure and refer to him worshipfully as Our Lord Don Quixote. Cervantes' hero thus joins Feodor Dostoyevsky's Prince Myshkin in *The Idiot* (1869) and Benito Pérez Galdós' Nazarín in the novel *Nazarín* (1895) as fictional representations of Christ-like characters. Unamuno's impassioned gloss, therefore, extends the romantic reaction to Cervantes' classic: it is the saddest book ever written, said Lord Byron, because it makes us laugh at the defeat of ideals.

The Life of Don Quixote and Sancho certainly rescues Cervantes' novel from the dry-as-dust commentary of the philologists. It also raises fascinating issues about the role of the reader and anticipates, to a certain extent, what is now called reader-response criticism. Several times in the book, Unamuno dismisses Cervantes as an author who lacked a clear idea of what he was about. The implication is that Don Quixote is more important than Cervantes. The implication is also that a literary text exists in its own right, free and apart from its author, awaiting all kinds of readers, including those as impudent and daring as Unamuno. We are here only a step or two away from Jorge Luis Borges' intrusion upon Cervantes, an accidental author, whose text Pierre Menard attempts to relive by writing *Don Quixote* all over again in the twentieth century. What in Unamuno is a deadly serious imposing of his ideas and personality upon an established text is, in the case of Borges, a tour de force about the palimpsestic nature of all texts.

In a letter to Federico de Onís, a former student who became a leading professor of Spanish in the United States and in the process inculcated many of his students with the spirit of Don Miguel, Unamuno voiced his annoyance at being termed a philosopher; what I am, he said, is a poet. In joining together the role of poet and philosopher, Unamuno functioned in a tradition suggested by Nietzsche and continued by Martin Heidegger, who thought the poet especially capable of speaking about philosophical problems.

In 1907, at the age of forty-three, Unamuno published his first book of poems, *Poesías.* During his lifetime he received little recognition as a poet, and even today his lack of balance and his weakness for hackneyed phrases make his position in the history of Spanish poetry somewhat problematical. The critical consensus is that his poetry must be valued for its sheer humanity.

Part of the reason that Unamuno's contemporaries failed to appreciate his poetry is due to his literary tastes. In an age that read the French symbolists Paul Verlaine and Stéphane Mallarmé and reacted with interest to Rubén Darío's *modernismo* (an amalgamation of romanticism and symbolism coming out of Latin America), Unamuno drew inspiration from Alfred, Lord Tennyson, Robert Browning, John Milton, Giosuè Carducci, Giacomo Leopardi, and Dante. Such reading imposed an "old-fashioned" note on his verse and led one critic to remark that Unamuno was the great

nineteenth-century poet Spain never had, an ironic reference both to him as anachronistic in the twentieth century and to Spain's modest nineteenth-century output in poetry.

He expressed his poetic credo in a predictably combative register. Imagery clouds emotion; music, the great injunction of Verlaine, soothes: poetry cannot be direct and disturbing if it obscures itself with images and lulls the reader to sleep with music. Language should pelt the reader. *Fábrica* (factory), *escarbar* (to scrape), *crujir* (to crackle), *costra* (scab), and *desollar* (to flay) are samples of the non-poetic words he uses, as though addicted, in his first book. Family, religion, *patria,* and the great theme of death were, likewise, not topics calculated to appeal to the readers of Mallarmé and Darío.

In a series of three long, free-verse poems that he calls *salmos* (psalms), Unamuno expresses the essence of his religious anguish. The first psalm is a clear example:

¿Dónde estás, mi Señor; acaso existes?
¿Eres tú creación de mi congoja,
o lo soy tuya?
. . . .
¿Tú, Señor, nos hiciste
para que a ti te hagamos,
o es que te hacemos
para que Tú nos hagas?
. . . .
Tú me abrirás la puerta cuando muera,
la puerta de la muerte,
y entonces la verdad veré de lleno,
sabré si Tú eres
o dormiré en tu tumba.

Where art thou, my Lord, dost thou indeed exist?
Art thou creation of my anguish,
or am I thine?
. . . .
Hast thou, Lord, made us
so that we may make thee,
or do we make thee
so that Thou mayest fashion us?
. . . .
Thou shalt open the door when I die,
the door of death,

and then I shall see the truth in full.
I shall know if Thou art,
or I shall sleep in thy tomb.

(6.217–220)

This poem points out what might be termed the humanistic origins of the concept of God. All deities are born within the human breast, William Blake had said. Nietzsche's aphorism in its taut paradoxical tone is even more remindful of Unamuno: "What? Is man merely a mistake of God's? Or God a mistake of man's?" If, as Unamuno feared might be the case, death is absolute, then both God and Unamuno die together.

Unamuno published half a dozen more books of poetry, and he left many moving descriptions in verse of Castilian plains, anguished Spanish Christs in small village churches, the towers of Salamanca, and one much-anthologized portrait of a Castilian cemetery, presided over in wind and rain by a cross, forgotten by all but the grazing sheep, a final poignant example of intrahistory. Literally hundreds of his poems return to the tragic sense of life, as does this verse without a title from *Romancero del destierro* (Ballads of Exile, 1928):

> El cuerpo canta;
> la sangre aúlla;
> la tierra charla;
> la mar murmura;
> el cielo calla
> y el hombre escucha.
>
> Body sings;
> blood howls;
> earth chatters;
> sea murmers;
> heaven is quiet
> and man listens.

(6.773)

Finally, there is the example of his rhymed journal, *Cancionero.* Begun in exile, its basic purpose is to fix in words Unamuno's gradual decline. It consists of 1,755 poems written from 26 February 1928 until 28 December 1936, three days before his death. The *Cancionero* includes some of his worst poetry and some of his best. It is a remarkable record of the fall of a great personality and a chronicle of what Unamuno saw, felt, and read in a nine-year period, including reflections on such disparate topics as the caves of Altamira and the novel *Moby Dick.*

"What is this Unamuno's religion?" The question supposedly came from some Chilean friends, and Unamuno set about answering it in an essay dated 7 November 1907 and published in 1910 as the lead piece in *Mi religión y otros ensayos* (My Religion and Other Essays). It is one of the clearest statements of his agonistic position with regard to matters of faith and religion.

The question is not answerable in a straightforward way, as Unamuno's readers know. But the rector of the University of Salamanca proposes to explore what it means to raise such an issue. It is the type of question, unfortunately, that tends to be asked by people with lazy minds. They are looking for solutions and pigeonholes because they are uncomfortable with a skeptical position and an open universe. Still, in the face of this query posed persistently to Unamuno in Spain and by his followers abroad, there is a kind of response:

> My religion is to seek truth in life and to put some life in truth, with the knowledge that I shall not find what I seek while I am alive. My religion is to struggle incessantly and tirelessly with mystery. My religion is to wrestle with God from break of day until nightfall, as it is reported Jacob did. . . . I reject the notion that we cannot know. In any event, I want to climb the inaccessible peaks.

(3.260)

If Unamuno told his readers that he was a Catholic or a Calvinist, they could heave a sigh of relief and insert him into the proper cubicle. But such an act of classification would vitiate his individuality. There are no sects, only believers, or, to put it more aptly, there are no opinions, only opinionizers. This last observation takes Unamuno another step in the direction of existentialism, for what he implies is that existence precedes essence, that the individual arrives on the scene and produces an idea (or opinion) and that, therefore, it will be well to begin by scrutinizing what individuality means before debating abstract ideas and opinions.

Nowhere in this moving little essay does Unamuno deny the existence of God. Since no one has convinced him rationally of God's existence or of his nonexistence, Unamuno must decide to deal with the question in terms of mystery. Ultimately a problem of knowing wherefore we live and die, the mystery cannot be ignored; it transcends everyday living. I expect very little, he wrote, of a culture that does not have a religious sense, just as I cannot conceive of a cultivated person who does not cry out at the injustice of life without immortality.

There is no solution, but a consolation of sorts does exist: the daily struggle without hope of victory nurtures the spirit and prevents it from collapsing into the miasma of despair. So-called Christian existentialists like Gabriel Marcel and Karl Jaspers have confirmed that religion for modern man is often based on struggle, doubt, and argument with mystery, so once again the irascible sage of Salamanca was out of step only with his own time and place.

The Tragic Sense of Life, the book for which Unamuno is best known, has been translated into Italian, French, German, Czechoslovak, Latvian, Japanese, and English. Thousands have been moved by its compassion for the human predicament and its angry contest with death. One such reader is exemplary: the medical doctor Fauré Beaulieu, who, in the carnage of the trenches of World War I, wrought its first French translation in 1917.

Man, declares Unamuno in the famous opening chapter, is an end, not a means. Philosophy exists to explain human individuals, and the point of departure of any philosophical system should be *el hombre de carne*

y hueso (the man of flesh and bone), "the man who is born, suffers and dies—above all dies; the man who eats and drinks and plays and sleeps and thinks and wills."

This point of departure is rich in implications of existentialism. Unamuno later on in this book proposes the revision of a long-standing dictum in the history of philosophy. Descartes' celebrated maxim *Cogito, ergo sum* (I think, therefore, I am) should be, says Unamuno, reversed: I am, therefore, I think. The primary reality, in other words, is not that I think, but that I exist. With this assertion Unamuno establishes the primacy of human existence over cognition, preceding by more than a decade Heidegger's declaration that cognition is only a mode of existence. Further down the road was Sartre, who in *Existentialism and Humanism* (1946) explains: "What do we mean that existence precedes essence? We mean that man first of all exists, encounters himself, surges up in the world—and defines himself afterward." Or, as Unamuno put it in 1900, plans don't make life; life makes plans.

For Unamuno too much of philosophy has been concerned with abstractions. He pleads that we take into account the man of flesh and blood who was Kant, the concrete individual who was Kierkegaard, who struggled and suffered in the battle to overcome his doubts about Christianity. "And what a man he was!" interjects Unamuno approvingly. The concept of humanity itself is an abstraction. Even science with its turbines and astronomy owes its existence to the consciousness of concrete individuals.

A philosophy rooted in existence has only one vital theme, that of personal destiny, the immortality of the soul. Philosophy began as a means of explaining death and should return once again to this paramount task. For, shouts Unamuno in a burst of feeling rarely equaled in intensity in twentieth-century philosophy:

I do not want to die—no; I neither want to die, nor do I want to want to die; I want to live forever and ever and ever. I want this "I" to live—this poor "I" that I am and that I feel myself to be here and now, and therefore the problem of the duration of my soul tortures me.

(7.136)

Unamuno supposedly once said that a heaven of abstract ideas was not acceptable; should he ever get to eternal paradise, he would expect to be wearing his shoes spattered with the mud of Salamanca. The anecdote points up his insistence on the continuation of the "I" that he knows. In the face of such apparent egotism, some reader is sure to growl, Who are you? To the universe nothing, to myself everything, is Unamuno's reply. And along the same lines comes the well-known statement "Otro yo no puede darse" (Another I cannot be found). In "Go Within!" he had already proclaimed the uniqueness of each individual. Today this insistence on the specialness of each one of us has less of an egotistical cast than it did for Unamuno's first readers. A certain countenance from an unexpected source—science—is part of the reason for this shift in reaction. The neural complex is so staggering and the gene pool so huge and subject to such infinite modification that a statistical case could be made for the uniqueness of the combination of all these variables in the human body.

If all things, including the vast accomplishments of science, spring from human consciousness, what of God? Unamuno faces the issue squarely, but he does not reach either Nietzsche's conclusion (God is dead) or that of the atheistic existentialists Sartre and Albert Camus. He recognizes that "it is the furious longing to give finality to the Universe . . . that has led us to believe in God, to wish that God may exist, to create God." But he is not content with this one-sided, perhaps pragmatic, interpretation. Whether there is a God who created us poses a question he does not wish to abandon. To discuss it, he plays on the Spanish verbs *creer* (to believe) and *crear* (to create); there is, after all, the difference of only one vowel between these two key words. "Creer en Dios" is, to a certain extent, "crear a Dios,"

even though He may have created us first. A whole chapter discusses this interplay, first posited in "Salmo I" of *Poesías.* The quandary is a painful one, for if Unamuno denies the existence of God, then he denies the duration of his soul, at least within the terms stipulated by Christianity. In the last analysis what he proposes is a symbiotic relationship between the individual and God: "God and man, in effect, mutually create one another; God creates or reveals himself in man and man creates himself in God." (This mutual dependence also characterizes the vision of a lowercase god experienced by the poet Juan Ramón Jiménez in his last years.)

In a chapter entitled "El problema práctico" (The Practical Question) Unamuno tackles the problem of how to live on a day-to-day basis with the knowledge of the tragic sense of life. Perhaps because emotions are essentially impractical or perhaps because, as in the case of all existentialists, the ethics of conduct prove intractable to a convincing solution, it is one of the most disappointing parts of the book. In the face of possible total extinction we must, he counsels, live and do our work passionately well, to the point where we become irreplaceable to others. He relates the story of the village shoemaker who plied his trade with such care and perfection that upon his death the entire village felt lessened. "Vivir apasionadamente bien" (to live in a passionately moral manner) seems a quixotic solution, but that, for Unamuno, is high praise, for the book concludes by reiterating the spiritual mission of Our Lord Don Quixote in European civilization.

The Tragic Sense of Life, which was placed by the Vatican on the Index of Forbidden Books in 1957, has a kind of unity that logically trained minds are loath to recognize. Expecting a system, they find none; looking for the conventions of expository prose, they encounter a rambling gloss on numerous authors. But logic cannot dismiss the passion that informs this book; its ethos is one that has affected every reader at one time or another. And it is an honest book in the sense meant by

Nietzsche when he said, "I mistrust all system-atizers and I avoid them. The will to a system is a lack of integrity."

Unamuno successfully forced his ideas and style upon the novel, but he was notably unable to do the same with the theater. The crackling dialogue of some of the novels turns declama-tory or trails off into strange abstractions when carried to the stage. Ideas overwhelm plot, and the lack of character development sustained by the novels is fatal for the plays. Endemic themes are the problem of personality and the conundrum of faith in a secular age.

La esfinge (The Sphinx), written in the fate-ful year 1898, but not produced until 1909 and unpublished until 1959, creates in Angel the counterpart of Unamuno, an indecisive intel-lectual unable to perform effectively in politi-cal life. *La venda* (The Blindfold, written in 1899, published in 1913, produced in 1921) dra-matizes the problem of faith. A young woman, blind all her life, is cured by medical interven-tion, but in order to find the house of her father to tell him the good news, she must close her eyes and follow the path of her blindness once more. *El hermano Juan* (Brother Juan, written in 1929, published in 1934) skewers the Don Juan legend, for Unamuno's puritanical streak made him a bitter enemy of this Hispanic myth. His most successful play is probably *El otro* (*The Other,* written in 1926, and published and produced in 1932), in which a split personality is effectively handled. Cosme and Damián are identical twins. One kills the other, but wives and friends are not sure who the survivor is. The play continues to explore the strange de-pendency encased in relationships of hatred, as portrayed in *Abel Sánchez,* and it also an-alyzes the topic of the subject split into antag-onistic roles, a situation that occupied Una-muno from his diary until the end of his life.

Unamuno's reputation as a novelist has increased since his death. *Mist* is recognized as a landmark in the development of the self-conscious novel. *Abel Sánchez* stands as a chilling portrait of an obsession. *Cómo se hace una novela* (*How to Make a Novel,* 1927)

finishes the deconstruction of the novel form begun in *Mist* and lays bare the autobiograph-ical basis underlying most works of fiction. *San Manuel Bueno, mártir* (*Saint Emmanuel the Good, Martyr,* 1931) brings to fiction a moving presentation of the tragic sense of life and serves as a fitting finale to Unamuno's writing career. These *nivolas,* as Unamuno called them, playing on the words *novela* (novel) and *niebla* (mist), must now be reck-oned with in any assessment of twentieth-century literature. Their anticipation of cer-tain techniques of Luigi Pirandello and Borges alone validates this assumption.

Critics, notably Geoffrey Ribbans and Paul Olson, have tended to divide Unamuno's nov-els into three groups: first the historical novel *Peace in War;* then the two *nivolas Anor y pedagogía* and *Mist,* which have in common many features, including a protagonist who fails to achieve the status of an autonomous personality; and finally the novels of passion, including *Abel Sánchez, Tres novelas ejem-plares y un prólogo* (*Three Exemplary Novels and a Prologue,* 1920), *La tía Tula* (*Aunt Ger-trude,* 1921), and presumably *Saint Emmanuel the Good, Martyr.* The formulation of such categories is made difficult by the fact that Unamuno, when talking of his novels, in-cluded *The Life of Don Quixote and Sancho* as well as *How to Make a Novel,* the first of which, Olson argues, is a commentary, and the second an autobiographical account of Una-muno in exile thinking about writing a novel. For the purposes of our discussion, we shall consider the latter as a novel.

Not long after composing *Peace in War,* Unamuno became aware of the fact that the conventional novel style would not suit him. Referring to biology, he came up with a pair of terms that broadly distinguished two ways of writing. An oviparous writer carefully collects notes, reads documents, makes outlines, and then hatches the work. A viviparous writer gets an idea in his head, massages it, and finally sits down to write, guided by the original idea, but with no other plan—accepting "lo que salga" (whatever comes out). This is the manner of writing, said Unamuno in 1904, that best suited his way of being. The premium here on spontaneity and vitality in writing corresponds to the insistence in "Go Within!" that plans and scaffoldings should not be imposed upon life. In Unamuno's scheme of things it was quite natural that he should become a viviparous writer.

In the middle of a novel itself—chapter 17 of *Mist,* to be precise—Unamuno has his characters carry on a discussion about the nature of a novel and come up with the now classic definition of a *nivola.* Víctor Goti is writing a novel. In answer to Augusto Pérez' question "What's it about?" he replies, "It doesn't have any plot, or better still, the plot will unfold. The plot will develop itself." For, Víctor goes on, that's the way life is: there's no plot. Indeed, some of the characters in Víctor's proposed novel will not even have any character, a direct reference to his friend Augusto Pérez. Víctor plans to put in lots of dialogue because, as he says, people like conversation. When Augusto points out that it can't be called a *novela* (novel), Víctor decides to call it a *nivola. Mist* and *Amor y pedagogía* are the two prime examples of *nivolas,* but excellent dialogues characterize all of Unamuno's works, and most of his novels are decidedly viviparous in that they lack a sense of an outside shaping structure.

Another characteristic of the Unamuno novel, already noticeable in *Peace in War,* is the striking lack of novelistic detail. The richly described settings of a novel by Charles Dickens, the loving verbal sketches of faces and clothing in Galdós—none of these are features of Unamuno's novels. If we cannot remember the physical appearance of any of his characters, the reason is that the author, apart from a bare detail such as San Manuel's blue eyes, never tells us how they look. Variously referred to as skeletal or naked novels, these tales outside of time and place depend for their unity and impact on the presence of a single passion: Joaquin's envy in *Abel Sánchez,* the

desire for motherhood in *Aunt Gertrude.* They are ahistorical novels, in a sense, examples of intrahistory, treating as they do the depths of sameness of the human passions (desire, envy, greed) unruffled by the waves of history.

The fact that *Mist* circulates in eleven languages constitutes ample proof of the international reputation it enjoys. The boldness with which it challenges the traditional themes and structure of the realistic novel and its profound as well as humorous approach to metaphysical questions make it a landmark novel of the twentieth century. It occupies a pivotal position in Unamuno's novelistic output as well, not only for its experimental tone but also because it served to stimulate him in the writing of further novels and short stories.

The framing apparatus of prologue, postprologue, and epilogue introduces the problematic nature of the chief protagonist's reality and alerts the reader to the fact that a series of planes describing relationships among author, characters, and readers is about to be drawn. At the insistence of Unamuno, Víctor Goti writes a prologue to introduce the sorrowful case of his friend Augusto Pérez, taking in the process a few swipes at Unamuno (calling him too clever, a monomaniac) and raising doubts about the veracity of the novel's conclusion. Unamuno huffily counters with a postprologue that accuses Goti of indiscretion and warns him that, should Unamuno so desire, he could see to it that Goti suffers the same fate as Augusto Pérez: extinction at the hands of Unamuno the author. Since Goti disputes the outcome of the novel, the reader sees at once the clever dialectic between reality inside and outside of the text, as well as the question of free will unfolding on the level of the relationship between an author and his *entes de ficción* (literary characters). The ruse, of course, adds to the reader's sense of the authenticity of what he or she is reading, and in this case it worked so well that zealous librarians for the British Museum and the University of Salamanca made a special entry in their catalogues for Víctor Goti, which is preserved to this day.

In the first scene Augusto Pérez appears in his doorway, hand outstretched in a gesture typical of the Roman emperor for whom he is named. Actually, he is only checking the weather. He has no destination in mind and decides he will follow the first dog that comes along. Instead, an attractive woman passes by, and he sets out after her. Eugenia is a beautiful, cool, intelligent piano teacher, and Augusto falls in love, or thinks he does. Eventually, he loses her to another man. There are two additional women in Augusto's life: his cook Ludivina, who represents a regression to the stage of maternal dependency, and Rosario, the laundress, who suggests the possibility of a mature sexual relationship.

Augusto Pérez, however, is not destined to have a mature relationship with anyone, because his flabby willpower and his continual impression that he is drifting along in a dream raises doubts about his very existence: "I end up by doubting my own existence and imagining, from the point of view of someone looking at me, that I am a dream, a character in fiction." Lonely, unconnected, unloved, Augusto ponders suicide. But before taking the final step, he decides to travel to Salamanca to visit Unamuno, who has written an essay on the subject. This encounter between the author and his creature is an historical moment in the history of literature, antedating by seven years Luigi Pirandello's *Six Characters in Search of an Author,* in which characters in a play search out the playwright in order to discuss his plans for them.

There is an enigmatic smile on author Unamuno's face as he ushers into his study in Salamanca the figment of his imagination. Augusto is horrified to learn that Unamuno knows the most intimate details of his life, and thus Augusto's worst fears are realized: he is an *ente de ficción.* They fall to arguing vehemently about whether Augusto, existing only as a creature of Unamuno's, has the freedom to commit suicide. Augusto reminds his creator of the fact that he has often said that Don Quixote is more real than Cervantes; if so, why

is this not true for Augusto Pérez? As for the discussion heats up, Unamuno suddenly delivers a cruel blow: Augusto does not have permission to commit suicide, but Unamuno is free to kill him whenever he chooses. Augusto, discovering an appetite for life, turns angrily to Unamuno and shouts: "You too, my lord and creator, you too will die and return to nothingness." As the shaken Augusto departs, Unamuno wipes away a furtive tear.

The novel concludes on a ludicrous note when Augusto, terrified by his impending death at the hands of God Unamuno, begins to overeat (*Edo, ergo sum*) and sends a telegram to Unamuno saying, "You got your way." The doctor ascribes his death to a heart attack, thus laying the ground for the enigma of Augusto's demise, referred to by Goti in the prologue and raising, of course, the question about the veracity of the text in general, the existence of Augusto Pérez, and, certainly, the existence of the Unamuno who appeared in chapter 31.

The encounter between author and character, a simulacrum of the relationship that obtains between God and humankind, testifies to the persistence of Unamuno's principal theme. But it is only one of the numerous riches contained in *Mist.* Searchingly present is a profound ontological question. "What need is there for being?" Augusto asks his dog, Orfeo, in anticipation of a similar question posed by Heidegger in 1931. Many guises of love appear, but whatever aspect they present—devotion, eros, deceit, conjugal routine—they cannot overcome the strong suggestion that intimacy is difficult.

Finally, there are the themes that spring out of literature. What is the nature of literary characters, and what is the nature of the novel itself? The pervasive discussion in the waning years of this century about self-consciousness in art (a poem aware that it is a poem, a novel talking about itself) was given a large boost by Unamuno's *Mist.* In addition, the character of Augusto Pérez may be viewed as a step in what has been termed the demise of the character in fiction. Augusto's tenuousness, his sense of existing in a mist, confirms the conviction held by some recent French writers that the stable ego of the typical nineteenth-century novel was a delusion. Several decades after Augusto's inglorious death, Alain Robbe-Grillet and Nathalie Sarraute denied literary characters any depth of presentation, and Roland Barthes in *Elements of Semiology* (1967) announced that the concept of character was obsolete.

Discussed with subtlety, imbued with the author's usual passion, and laced with a robust sense of humor, these are some of the elements that weave in and out of this seminal novel. The person who hates with a consuming passion depends totally on the existence of the object of hatred for the validation of his or her own life. This is the stark psychological lesson portrayed in *Abel Sánchez*, Unamuno's most impressive "naked novel."

Joaquín Montenegro and Abel Sánchez, so runs the opening sentence of this retelling of the Cain and Abel story, cannot remember a time when they did not know each other. Unamuno thus establishes their symbiotic relationship in the novel's first words. Insouciant, popular, and talented, Abel becomes a painter of distinction, marries Joaquín's girlfriend, takes on in middle age a series of mistresses, and, on the limited occasions when he is aware of it, shows no concern for the passion of envy that is consuming his friend and of which he is the source. Joaquín, although an accomplished, hard-working doctor, is antipathetic; his dream of attaining glory through achievement in science turns into the pinched reality of a small town medical practice.

Unbeknownst to everyone except his wife and daughter, Joaquín constructs his entire life in response to his "enemy," Abel. Even as a child, Joaquín would pick a fight, if only on the pretense that Abel gave in too easily. Abelín, Abel's son, is neglected by his father and comes under the influence of Joaquín, who encourages him to become a doctor. Joaquín then perversely desires a commingling of their bloods and pleads with his daughter Joaqui-

nita to marry Abelín. From this union comes a son Joaquín, who is attracted to his grandfather Abel's paints and palettes. Joaquín once more sees himself foiled by Abel's charm and popularity and makes as if to throttle his old friend, who, suffering from heart disease, dies on the spot. Shortly afterward, Joaquín too breathes his last, having been deprived of the reason for his existence.

Told in long, vivid patches of dialogue, interspersed with bleak confessions excerpted from Joaquín's journal, the portrait of envy and rancor is unsettling. With unfailing paranoia, Joaquín interprets every action in terms of his consuming hatred for Abel. He is truly a dark individual, whose passion we remember when all else about the novel is forgotten.

Unamuno's own life was gradually becoming embroiled in the passion of politics. Outspoken in his belief that the antiquated Spanish educational system needed reform and recently involved in a dispute over the makeup of the university senate, Unamuno returned from vacationing in Portugal in the summer of 1914 to find himself summarily dismissed as rector of the University of Salamanca. In the ensuing years Unamuno's verbal assaults on the government of Primo de Rivera reached such a volume that the dictator could not ignore them. Much against his will, Rivera exiled Unamuno to the Canary Islands and then allowed him to escape to Paris. There Unamuno lived unhappily for a few months and then finally settled in Hendaye, near the Spanish border, where he could keep an intellectual and nostalgic eye on Spain. His position symbolized the plight of intellectual dissent in Spanish society, which is the effect he wished to achieve, but his victory was at the cost of spiritual turmoil and suffering, for Unamuno was a homebody, and he spent much time in despair over his uprooted state. Finally, with the fall of the dictatorship he returned to Spain in 1930, converted into a popular hero.

How to Make a Novel was begun in a Paris pension in the summer of 1925 and finished in

Hendaye, within sight of the Spanish Basque country, in May 1927. Written in the misery of exile in the city then considered to be the cultural capital of the world, this epitome of a self-conscious novel ("a novel about reading a novel," as Unamuno observed) commands increasing attention on the part of those convinced that literature is best understood as a creative intertwining of reading and writing that does not fit neatly into such prearranged categories as the novel, history, or essay.

The usual framing apparatus, consisting this time of prologue, portrait, and commentary on the portrait, carries out its expected function—that of playing, as in *Mist,* with the veracity of the text. However, in the case of the present text its history is so unusual that it makes one think that reality itself is a literary ploy. Unamuno wrote *How to Make a Novel* in Spanish, and his friend Jean Cassou translated it into French for publication in the *Mercure de France.* Meanwhile, Unamuno forgot to ask Cassou for the original manuscript so that, while in Hendaye, he could prepare the Spanish version. As a result, he "retranslated" his novel from French into his native language.

Unamuno defends this inconvenient, even quirky, recourse with what was then a striking statement. He has, he says, no wish to recover the original text, for words, once they are written down, are dead. Having been fixed on the page, their vitality is sapped; they are locked into position, immutable. This observation proved to be remarkably prescient in its similarities with key pronouncements in current critical theory. Jacques Derrida's notion that writing brings death comes to mind, and the statement by Paul Ricoeur that to read a book is to consider its author already dead (to meet him or her in the flesh provides a kind of disturbance) also develops the notion, clearly present in Unamuno, that there are two kinds of texts: an oral, living one; and a written, dead one.

Naturally, when the reader comes along, words may return to life, but they are not fully resurrected, argues Unamuno, unless the reader devours the text. Unamuno uses the verb "to eat" and equates it with Christians eating the Word made flesh in the rite of Holy Communion. There are readers who only read, but they do not (and here terms from reader-response criticism fit in nicely with Unamuno's line of thought) "appropriate" and "actualize" the text. They do not read with intensity, participate in the text, argue with it, and, in a sense, "recreate" it. When Unamuno asserts that by rereading a text the author "recreates" it, which is the process at work in Unamuno's "retranslation" of *How to Make a Novel,* he is providing a concept that Juan Ramón Jiménez employed, down to the very terminology, to explain his practice of rewriting vast amounts of his poetry, as well as foreshadowing some of the major ideas of such critics as Wolfgang Iser and Stanley Fish.

Jean Cassou's pen portrait of Unamuno, which is part of the novel's frame, is glossed by Unamuno, who remarks in the process that writing, in effect, is nothing but commentaries upon commentaries: Dante glosses the Bible; Cervantes, books of chivalry. Everything is books and reading, avers Unamuno, anticipating by nearly two decades Borges' short story "The Library of Babel" (1941).

With the firm conviction that "what is truly novelistic is how the novel is made," Unamuno turns at last to the novel itself and sets us down in front of the white, terribly blank pages that face all writers. Their vacancy reminds him of *la nada,* but at the same time they offer a means of vanquishing nothingness. *Scribo, ergo sum* is Unamuno's final gloss on Descartes' maxim: by writing, he can perpetuate himself, and thus writing comes to be the equivalent of living.

In this novel that he discusses and dissects while he is writing it, he invents a protagonist: U. Jugo de La Raza, who is obviously Unamuno himself. This gives rise to a disquisition that seeks to establish the autobiographical bedrock not only of fiction (an assertion for which there existed numerous precedents, from Flaubert's "I am Emma Bovary!" to Unamuno's claim that all characters are their creator) but of all writing. Historians, like novelists, impose their point of view; historical figures are possessed by writers and acquire that curious existence dubbed "textual" that so fascinated the author of *Mist*. Once again, Unamuno makes a significant starting point with regard to an influential idea: the subjective base of narration as explored in general by certain narratologists and, in the field of history, by Hayden White.

What of U. Jugo de La Raza? He stumbles across a book in the bookstalls along the Seine and, browsing in it, discovers the warning that when the reader reaches the end of the book, he will die. In actuality, this book is Honoré de Balzac's *La peau de chagrin* (*The Fatal Skin*, 1831), in which a magic piece of leather grants its owner's wishes, but with every wish granted shrinks in size, as does the life span of the owner. Unamuno's enduring theme thus resurfaces. The book is a metaphor for life, but no matter how slowly it is read—even syllable by syllable—it still comes to a close. In the case of U. Jugo de La Raza, says the narrator, I will not give you the end.

In November 1930, his exile over and back once more in Salamanca, Unamuno finished the short novel *Saint Emmanuel the Good, Martyr*, which he published the following year. In it, he once said, he had put all he knew about the tragic sense of life. The novel has been read and interpreted in this light, but its literary values should not be overlooked. In no other work of fiction by Unamuno are point of view, tone, and characterization, the latter albeit still on the stark side, so well brought off. Furthermore, with the reappearance of intrahistory in the novel comes a sense of acceptance that generates a calm unusual in Unamuno's writings. Paradoxically, this note of quietude in the midst of struggle may be attributed to the weight of sixty-plus years on the author's shoulders. *Saint Emmanuel the Good, Martyr* is a book written in the autumn of life.

In the village of Valverde de Lucerna lives a tall, slender, erect priest with piercing blue eyes and a commanding voice. A manly man who chops wood and helps round up stray cattle, he nevertheless has such compassion for the villagers that the narrator refers to him as a matriarchal man (*un varón matriarcal*). His energy is matched by his tolerance. Unlike most village priests, he is not concerned with condemning people as liberals, masons, or heretics. Instead, he inveighs against envy and gossip.

Yet there is something amiss. First of all, one notices the incessant activity. "He was always occupied," says the narrator, "sometimes even occupied in search of occupations." In bits and pieces the reader discovers the priest's secret: he does not believe in hell (Unamuno confesses in his diary that this was one of his first problems with the church). Manuel tells the narrator Angela that heaven is in Valverde's lake. Finally, Angela notices that Manuel's splendid voice, which leads the congregation in the recital of the Credo, always grows silent upon reaching the phrase: "I believe in the resurrection of the flesh and life everlasting." His voice disappears into that of his people, who finish the Credo for him.

Angela, who is half in love with Don Manuel, always seems to be on the outside of his secret, unwilling to admit it fully to herself. It is her brother Lázaro, recently returned from America, who learns the full nature of the priest's suffering. The village awaits with confidence the conversion of the unbeliever Lázaro, which takes place one Sunday in full view of everyone; but the priest has pleaded with Lázaro to feign conversion in order to protect the peace and happiness of his charges.

Angela is horrified, and the reader gradually learns that Father Manuel has lived his exemplary religious life so that people in the village will have something to cling to, for, he says to Lázaro, they could not face the truth—the truth being that they will live, suffer, and die with no hope of immortality. If religion is the opium of the people, cries Don Manuel, echoing Marx's famous cry, then let us give them more opium.

Critics have tried to account for this apparent about-face in Unamuno, who had proclaimed at least since 1910 that the only answer to doubt was an agonistic stance. In one sense there is no need for an explanation, for Father Manuel's agony is real, he resists suicide by ministering to his flock, he lives life with passionate dedication, and, when he dies, he leaves a great vacuum in the heart of Valverde de Lucerna. On the other hand, it is more difficult to answer the charge of alleged hypocrisy leveled at Don Manuel's creator or to suppress dismay at the pious fraud that is carried out. Is Unamuno's agonistic recipe for living only for the select few?

By casting Manuel as a Christ figure, Unamuno heightens the tragedy of faith enacted in this work. Manuel's name in Hebrew means "God is with us," a fact that every villager could easily witness; the priest's voice in the pulpit becomes especially emotional when he repeats the words of Christ on the Cross, "My God, my God, why hast thou forsaken me?"; when he offers the communion wafer to the unbelieving Lázaro, the cock crows three times (an allusion to Peter's betrayal of Christ); and he says to Angela, "Pray for our Lord Jesus Christ," meaning pray that He exists, and pray for me.

Father Manuel finds an ambivalent kind of peace strolling along the shores of the village lake, watching the snowflakes disappear into the water in winter, and studying the mountain's reflection on its blue surface. The ambivalence derives from the fact that the lake has a suicidal pull for him. One day, he sees a shepherdess standing on the mountainside and singing a folk song. She is, he exclaims suddenly, part of nature and not of history. Valverde de Lucerna continues its unheralded existence in the folds of intrahistory, its tranquillity zealously protected by the unbelieving priest.

The narrator, Angela Carballino, who outlives Father Manuel, writes her memoirs at the age of sixty. Part of the narration's attraction derives from the fact that everything is presented indirectly to the reader. Don Manuel is described in the dialogue of others; his secret is never directly revealed to the narrator. This contributes to a misty, dreamlike atmosphere. The fictional devices, including extensive use of the verb in its imperfect tense, underline the problem of being and, of course, of immortality. Says Unamuno in the inevitable postprologue, perhaps we shall all one day escape history and be sheltered in some divine novel.

History yet had some reckoning with Unamuno. Upon his return from exile, he became embroiled in Spanish politics. In 1936, dismayed by the Republican government's inability to keep order, he lent his support to the Franco rebellion but eventually turned away in disgust from the Fascists when he witnessed their acts of atrocity in Salamanca and saw Franco accepting help from Hitler and Mussolini. Still, he kept his peace until the celebration of Columbus Day on 12 October 1936 at the University of Salamanca. General Millán Astray, organizer of the Spanish Foreign Legion, gave a speech accusing one-half of the Spanish population of treason, and shouted, "Long live death." Unamuno rose in reply but was soon shouted down by the general's cry of "Death to intelligence." The rector of the university retorted, "You will conquer but you will not convince." Perhaps only the presence of Franco's wife kept Unamuno from being mobbed by the pro-Fascist audience. He was deposed of his rectorship (it had been restored to him by the Republican government) and placed under house arrest.

On the afternoon of 31 December 1936 he sat in his living room talking with a visitor, a former teacher turned nationalist soldier. Each man had his feet under the table, where a brazier gave forth warmth. Unamuno suddenly turned pale and stopped talking. The brazier began to smoke; it was Unamuno's slipper. A stroke answered for him at last his enduring question.

Unamuno's weaknesses—a tendency to dwell on one or two themes, his unwillingness to put forth a system, a certain superficiality and self-righteousness—are counterbalanced by obvious strengths. In an age of increasing specialization he was one of the last writers to feel comfortable in several different genres. He has to be counted as a forerunner of Christian existentialism and of current notions about reading and writing. Waiting to be mined from his vast work is a fairly coherent theory about language, a conviction expressed in different parts of his work that the human individual defines himself and is defined by words. In any event, he continues to achieve his goal as a writer: he unsettles his readers and causes them to react as people of flesh and blood to what he has written. His spirit is indeed sheltered in his work.

Selected Bibliography

EDITIONS

INDIVIDUAL WORKS

NOVELS
Paz en la querra. Madrid, 1897.
Amor y pedagogía. Barcelona, 1902.
Niebla: Nivola. Madrid, 1914.
Abel Sánchez: Historia de una pasión. Madrid, 1917.
Tres novelas ejemplares y un prólogo. Madrid, 1920.
La tía Tula. Madrid, 1921.
Cómo se hace una novela. Buenos Aires, 1927.
San Manuel Bueno, mártir, y tres historias más. Madrid, 1931.

SHORT STORY COLLECTIONS
El espejo de la muerte. Madrid, 1913.

POETRY
Poesías. Bilbao, 1907.
Rosario de sonetos líricos. Madrid, 1911.
El Cristo de Velázquez: Poema. Madrid, 1920.
Rimas de dentro. Valladolid, 1923.
Teresa: Rimas de un poeta desconocido. Madrid, 1923.
De Fuerteventura a París: Diario íntimo de confinamiento y destierro vertido en sonetos. Paris, 1925.
Romancero del destierro. Buenos Aires, 1928.

Antología poética. Edited by José María de Cossío. Buenos Aires, 1946.
Cancionero: Diario poético. Edited by Federico de Onís. Buenos Aires, 1953.

DRAMA
El otro: Misterio en tres jornadas y un prólogo. Madrid, 1932.
El hermano Juan o el mundo es teatro: Vieja comedia nueva. Madrid, 1934.
La esfinge. In *Teatro completo.* Edited by Manuel García Blanco. Madrid, 1959.

ESSAYS
En torno al casticismo. Barcelona, 1902. Originally published as a series of essays appearing in *La España moderna,* February–June 1895.
Tres ensayos. Madrid, 1900. Includes "¡Adentro!," "La ideocracia," and "La fe."
De mi país: Descripciones, relatos y artículos de costumbre. Madrid, 1903.
Vida de Don Quijote y Sancho según Miguel de Cervantes Saavedra, explicada y comentada. Madrid, 1905.
Mi religión y otros ensayos. Madrid, 1910.
Por tierras de Portugal y España. Madrid, 1911.
Soliloquios y conversaciones. Madrid, 1911.
Contra esto y aquello. Madrid, 1912.
Del sentimiento trágico de la vida en los hombres y los pueblos. Madrid, 1913.
Andanzas y visiones españolas. Madrid, 1922.
La agonía del cristianismo. Madrid, 1931.
Autodiálogos. Madrid, 1959.

COLLECTED WORKS
Obras completas. Edited by Manuel García Blanco. 16 vols. Madrid, 1959–1964.
————. Edited by Manuel García Blanco. 9 vols. Madrid, 1966–1971.

MEMOIRS
Diario íntimo. Madrid, 1970.
Recuerdos de niñez y mocedad. Madrid, 1908.

TRANSLATIONS
Abel Sánchez and Other Stories. Translated by Anthony Kerrigan. Chicago, 1956. Includes *The Madness of Dr. Montarco* and *Saint Emmanuel the Good, Martyr.*

The Agony of Christianity. Translated by Pierre Loving. New York, 1928.

The Christ of Velázquez. Translated by Eleanor L. Turnbull. Baltimore, 1951.

Essays and Soliloquies. Translated by J. E. Crawford Flitch. New York, 1925.

The Last Poems of Miguel de Unamuno. Translated by Edita Mas-López. Rutherford, N.J., 1974.

The Life of Don Quijote and Sancho of Miguel de Cervantes Saavedra. Translated by Homer P. Earle. New York, 1927.

Mist, a Tragicomic Novel. Translated by Warner Fite. New York, 1928.

Perplexities and Paradoxes. Translated by Stuart Gross. New York, 1945.

Poems. Translated by Eleanor L. Turnbull. Baltimore, 1952.

San Manuel Bueno, mártir. Translated by Francisco Segura and Jean Pérez. London, 1957.

————. Comparative and critical edition with annotated English translation by Mario J. and María Valdés. Chapel Hill, N.C., 1973.

Selected Works of Miguel de Unamuno. Translated, edited, and annotated by Anthony Kerrigan, Allen Lacy, and Martin Nozick. 7 vols. Princeton, N.J., 1967–1984. Contents are as follows:

    Vol. 1. *Peace in War: A Novel.*

    Vol. 2. *The Private World: Selections from the Diario íntimo and Selected Letters 1890–1936.*

    Vol. 3. *Our Lord Don Quixote: The Life of Don Quixote and Sancho with Related Essays.*

    Vol. 4. *The Tragic Sense of Life in Men and Nations.*

    Vol. 5. *The Agony of Christianity and Essays on Faith.*

    Vol. 6. *Novela / Nivola.* Contains *Mist, Abel Sánchez,* and *How to Make a Novel.*

    Vol. 7. *Ficciones: Four Stories and a Play.* Contains *Tía Tula; San Manuel Bueno, mártir; The Novel of Don Sandalio, Chessplayer; The Madness of Dr. Montarco;* and *The Other.*

Three Exemplary Novels and a Prologue. Translated by Ángel Flores. New York, 1930.

The Tragic Sense of Life in Men and Peoples. Translated by J. E. Crawford Flitch. London, 1921.

BIOGRAPHICAL AND CRITICAL WORKS

Barea, Arturo. *Unamuno.* Translated by Ilsa Barea. New Haven, Conn., 1952.

Batchelor, R. E. *Unamuno—Novelist: A European Perspective.* Oxford, 1972.

Blanco Aguinana, Carlos. *El Unamuno contemplativo.* Mexico, 1959; 2d ed., Barcelona, 1975.

————. "Unamuno's *Niebla:* Existence and the Game of Fiction." *Modern Language Notes* 79: 188–205 (1964).

Earle, Peter G. "Unamuno and the Theme of History." *Hispanic Review* 32:319–339 (1964).

Ferrater Mora, José. *Unamuno: A Philosophy of Tragedy.* Translated by Philip Silver. Berkeley, 1962.

Gullón, Ricardo. *Autobiografías de Unamuno.* Madrid, 1964.

Ilie, Paul. *Unamuno: An Existentialist View of Self and Society.* Madison, Wis., 1967.

Krause, Anna. "Unamuno and Tennyson." *Comparative Literature* 8:122–135 (1956).

Lacy, Allen. *Miguel de Unamuno: The Rhetoric of Existence.* The Hague and Paris, 1967.

López-Morillas, Juan. "Unamuno and Pascal: Notes on the Concept of Agony." *PMLA* 65:998–1010 (1950).

Mackay, John A. "Miguel de Unamuno." In *Christianity and Existentialism,* edited by Carl Michalson. New York, 1956.

Marías, Julián. *Miguel de Unamuno.* Translated by Frances M. López-Morillas. Cambridge, Mass., 1966.

Nozick, Martin. *Miguel de Unamuno.* Princeton, N.J., 1971.

Olson, Paul R. "Unamuno's Lacquered Boxes: *Cómo se hace una novela* and the Ontology of Writing." *Revista hispánica moderna* 36:186–199 (1970–1971).

————. *"Niebla": A Critical Guide.* London, 1984.

Pérez de la Dehesa, Rafael. *Política y sociedad en el primer Unamuno, 1894–1904.* Madrid, 1966.

Portillo, Luis. "Unamuno's Last Lecture." In *The Golden Horizon,* edited by Cyril Connolly. London, 1953.

Ribbans, Geoffrey. *Niebla y soledad.* Madrid, 1971.

Round, N. G. *Unamuno: Abel Sánchez.* London, 1974.

Rubio Barcia, José, and M. A. Zeitlin. *Unamuno: Creator and Creation.* Berkeley, Calif., 1967.

Rudd, Margaret. *The Lone Heretic.* Austin, Tex., 1963.

Salcedo, Emilio. *Vida de Don Miguel.* Madrid, 1970.

Sánchez Barbudo, Antonio. *Estudios sobre Galdós, Unamuno, y Machado.* Madrid, 1968.

Turner, David G. *Unamuno's Webs of Fatality.* London, 1974.

Valdés, Mario J. *Death in the Literature of Unamuno.* Urbana, Ill., 1966.

————, and María Elena de Valdés. *An Unamuno Source Book: A Catalogue of Readings and Acquisitions.* Toronto, 1973.

Wyers, Frances. *Miguel de Unamuno: The Contrary Self.* London, 1976.

Young, Howard T. *The Victorious Expression—A Study of Four Contemporary Spanish Poets: Miguel de Unamuno, Antonio Machado, Juan Ramón Jiménez, Federico García Lorca.* Madison, Wis., 1964.

Zubizarreta, Antonio. *Unamuno en su nivola.* Madrid, 1960.

HOWARD T. YOUNG

BENEDETTO CROCE
(1866–1952)

A T THE BEGINNING of his autobiography, published in 1918 with the title *Contributo alla critica di me stesso* (A Contribution to the Criticism of Myself, translated as *An Autobiography*), Benedetto Croce comments, "My family life suffered an abrupt interruption and a major upset with the Casamicciola earthquake of 1883, in which I lost my parents and my only sister, and I myself remained buried under the rubble for several hours, injured in several parts of my body." This description of a traumatic event in the life of an adolescent, an event of the type that has long-standing consequences on the development of the person-to-be, resembles a passage in the *Autobiografia* (1728) of Giambattista Vico, Croce's favorite philosopher. Written in the third person, Vico's autobiography starts with the narration of the following event:

> Giambattista Vico was born in Naples in 1670 from honest parents, who left a good name for themselves. The father was good-humored, the mother quite melancholic, and both personalities shaped the character of their son. As an infant he was restless and full of spirits. But at the age of seven, falling headlong down the stairway from a high floor, he remained for five hours motionless and out of his senses. He fractured the right side of his cranium, but the skin was not cut. The fracture caused a large tumor and the boy suffered a substantial loss of blood from the trauma. The surgeon, considering the fracture and the long period of unconscious-

ness, predicted that he would either die or survive as an idiot.

> (Giambattista Vico, *Autobiografia*, edited by M. Fubini [Torino, 1965], p. 3)

One cannot help reading into Croce's lines a romantic attempt to identify with his intellectual mentor. If autobiography is almost always narcissistic, Croce's complacency here is a search for confirmation in Vico's page. His autobiography is without doubt Croce's attempt to affirm his own excellence in intellectual achievement reached despite the most contrary conditions. It reads like an acknowledgment of self-worth reaped against all possible odds in a field not usually recognized by the majority. To be exceptional in the transaction of daily business is rare enough, but to be exceptional in the pursuit of knowledge despite extremely adverse conditions borders on the heroic and the legendary.

In Italy during his lifetime, and possibly even after, Croce became somewhat of a legend. He was perceived by many as the only light of reason left in a country overwhelmed by Fascist madness. He was as untouchable as an intellectual can be under a dictatorship. Benito Mussolini, fearing the renown Croce enjoyed outside of Italy, allowed him to speak and write without censorship, although his works contained thinly disguised attacks on the regime. Croce liked this privileged position and probably thought it was owed to him. He had a concept of the role of the philosopher in society that recalls that of the nineteenth-century German idealists: that the man of knowledge should stand high above the general public and instruct it; that the philosopher is ultimately a guide to the world.

This may not be enough to qualify Croce as the last of the philosophers of the past nor as one of the pioneers in the twentieth-century revolution in the theory of knowledge. But what does tend to qualify him as such is his belief that philosophy is the field of knowledge capable of offering a unified picture of the world—his belief that the human mind, properly trained and educated, could develop an omni-comprehensive vision of all fields of human endeavor and behavior. In trying to substitute history for religion or, as he often said, to secularize religion, he maintained that a proper understanding of the course of human experience would teach man the reason and meaning of his existence. In history properly understood, and not in God, would man find an explanation for his being.

In order to understand man and his history, Croce studied and wrote on philosophy, ethics, economics, aesthetics, literature, art, history, politics, and education. Because he was so engrossed in understanding how these fields of knowledge came into being and developed, and especially how they could contribute to the future development and betterment of the human condition, Croce either remained totally blind to or rejected most contemporary intellectual movements. The concept of the avant-garde was alien to him. The idea of revolution and abrupt change, whether political or intellectual, artistic or moral, an idea so dear to modern experience, increasingly became the object of his attacks.

Like Horace, Croce always fought for the middle way; he preferred slow evolution and careful inquiry over change and experimentation. But no matter how contrary his views are to those of the present age, Croce is nonetheless considered a towering figure in the twentieth-century intellectual landscape. Ludwig

Wittgenstein and Martin Heidegger may well be the thinkers who puzzle and exercise the ingenuity of contemporary students of philosophy, but Croce is the one who will be read by those looking for a unified, albeit somewhat obsolete, system of thought. His *Estetica come scienza dell'espressione e linguistica generale* (Aesthetic as Science of Expression and General Linguistic, 1902), despite its sharp distinction between the world of the "real" and the world of "artistic expression," contains interesting insights into the nature of artistic creation. His writings on the theory of history, while generally and correctly considered by most to be very much in line with nineteenth-century ideas on the subject, anticipated and influenced many current developments.

Above all, the passion that exudes from every one of his printed pages is captivating. For Croce the life of his mind was synonymous with existence. Thinking and writing were his only way of being. In his belief that man's weaknesses are vindicated by reason and clarity of vision lies the true import of Croce's intellectual legacy.

THE ROMAN EXPERIENCE AND THE FIRST WRITINGS: ART, HISTORY, AND POLITICS

Following the Casamicciola earthquake and the loss of his parents in 1883, Benedetto Croce and his younger brother, Alfonso, were assigned to the care of their uncle Silvio Spaventa and were moved to Rome. This was a major change for young Benedetto. From the quiet life of the southern Italian province he was abruptly projected into the lively atmosphere of the nation's capital. In the house of Spaventa, a high-ranking politician, he met other politicians, professors, and journalists. Among them was a professor of philosophy who left a permanent mark on Croce's intellectual formation. He was Antonio Labriola, who, when Croce started attending his lectures at the University of Rome, was developing a strong sympathy for the philosophy of Karl Marx, in whom Croce too became interested. Philosophy, though, was for the time being just an avocation for Croce. As a matriculated student he attended the school of law.

In 1886 Croce returned to Naples, and in the following years he dedicated himself entirely to historical studies and wrote several essays on the Neapolitan history of the past three centuries. He also traveled extensively through Germany, Spain, France, and England. Although he later described this period of travel and study as a phase in which he was totally "projected toward the outside world," it was through his interest in the past that he developed a desire to understand better the nature and the philosophical meaning of historical thinking. It was precisely at this time that Croce read, along with many other Italian and German philosophers, Vico's *Scienza nuova* (*New Science*, 1725–1730), which remained the book he referred to most often throughout his life. *New Science* was a pathbreaking attempt to understand all fields of human activity, including art and religion, within the framework of history. Vico was to remain for Croce the first thinker ever to establish the relativism of human knowledge and experience; for Vico, and thus for Croce, everything is to be best understood within its proper historical framework. His shift in interest toward an understanding of the nature of history led Croce to write his first major essay. Croce's description of this intellectual experience in his autobiography contains the nucleus of his future thinking:

After many meditations and a whole series of temporary solutions, in February or March 1893, having intensely meditated for an entire day, in the evening I drafted an essay with the title of "La storia ridotta sotto il concetto generale dell'arte" [History Reduced to the General Concept of Art], which was a sort of revelation to myself. In fact it not only gave me the joy of clearly seeing certain concepts which were previously confused, and the logical cause of some philosophical errors,

but I was also amazed by the passion and enthusiasm with which I wrote it.

(*Filosofia, Poesia, Storia*, p. 1149)

In "La storia ridotta sotto il concetto generale dell'arte" (this is the title of two lectures delivered by Croce at the Academia Pontiniana of Naples, 1893–1894; the lectures were revised and published as *Il concetto della storia nelle sue relazione col concetto dell'arte* [The Idea of History and Its Relationship with the Idea of Art, 1896]) Croce lays the foundations of the major philosophical subjects that he further develops in independent treatises during the years to come. They involve the nature of art, history, and logical thinking. Beginning his treatise with the question "Is history an art or a science," Croce proceeds to attack the prevailing opinion of some of the major contemporary German historians, such as Gustav Droysen and Ernst Bernheim, that history is indeed a science. Croce's criticism in the treatise deals in the first place with the question of aesthetics, and after a review of different contemporary points of view on the nature of artistic expression, he adheres to the Hegelian assumption that art is, albeit in a unique way, a representation of reality:

In art all human and natural reality—be it beautiful or ugly depending on the point of view—becomes beautiful because it is perceived as a *reality* in the wide sense, which needs to be expressed in its entirety. All characters, all actions, all objects, as they enter into the realm of art, lose (artistically speaking) those qualifications which are typical to them in real life, and are judged only according to the way in which they are represented artistically.

(pp. 26–27)

Art, Croce concludes, is a way in which reality can be expressed. And is history not also a manner in which we represent the world? Science, the philosopher continues, is of a different nature and should not be confused with culture and knowledge in general. The goal of science is to discover the general principles and laws that govern the world of nature, while history narrates single and individual cases or chains of events; the two should not be confused. Nor should history be confused with the theory or the philosophy of history, as they are expressed in the works of Vico, Johann Herder, and G. W. F. Hegel. While the former deals with particular and individual cases, the philosophy of history tries to establish general rules about the pattern of human action through time. The philosophy of history, about the legitimacy of which Croce is at this preliminary stage of his philosophical development still uncertain, can also be considered the science of history. But history itself, Croce insists, is something different.

In trying to establish the peculiar nature of history after having denied it any relationship to science, Croce writes:

> In the presence of an object—or a character, or an action, or an event—the human mind cannot but have one of two possible reactions. It can either wonder what the object is, or it can represent it in its concrete appearance. It can either *understand it,* or simply *see it.* It can, in sum, submit the object to a *scientific* process, or to an *artistic* one. There is no other choice.
>
> (p. 39)

However, it would be simplistic, Croce continues, to conclude that if history is not a science it falls entirely into the realm of art. In fact, while it is true that both art and history represent reality without offering a scientific account of it, there are different ways in which representation comes into being. Art represents what is emotionally *interesting* and tries to touch on all subjects and points of views capable of arousing a feeling. On the other hand, history represents what is factually interesting and what has actually happened. In other words, history is "that sort of artistic production which has as its object of representation what has really happened," and unlike art, it cannot fall into falsehood and the imaginary.

Il concetto della storia nelle sue relazione col concetto dell'arte represents a major step in Croce's intellectual development. On the one hand, it seems to indicate the conclusion of a period in which the young thinker was totally dedicated to scholarship. On the other, as it indicates Croce's need to confront culture from a more general perspective, it appears to be a major philosophical revelation. The essay contains in embryonic form all the philosophical problems to which Croce later dedicates the major body of his philosophical system. There is no doubt that this is the work in which Croce's need to develop a complete classification of all fields of human knowledge reaches its full consciousness.

In 1895 Croce received from his former professor and friend Antonio Labriola the first of his writings on Marxism, *In memoria del "Manifesto dei communisti"* (In Memory of the *Communist Manifesto*). Labriola was by this time an official Socialist and was in regular correspondence with Friedrich Engels. He looked to Croce for help in order to get his work published. Croce did not disappoint Labriola's ambitions. He agreed to publish the *Manifesto* and, later, the other Marxist writings of the professor (which were being published in France at about the same time in Georges Sorel's journal *Le devenir social*) and became himself highly interested in what he called "the philosophy of historical materialism." A great deal has been said and written about Croce's interest in Marxism between 1895 and 1900, and Croce himself, discussing the matter many years later in the *Contributo alla critica di me stesso,* deals with this intellectual phase in an ambivalent manner. On the one side, he admits that Marxism led him to the study of economics, a science that from then on he considered essential to the proper understanding of historical events. On the other, he recognizes that Marxism became for him a kind of blinding religion, a ready-made system through which all reality could be easily understood and explained. The most positive aspect of Croce's burning passion for

314

the philosophy of Marx was a rejuvenating effect that helped destroy many of his acquired beliefs and ideas, such as his "abstract moralism." In the *Contributo* Croce looked back critically at his infatuation for Marx and said that it led him to believe that the course of history, which according to Marx leads inevitably to a Socialist order, has the right to bring with it and to annihilate individuals. It was naive, he added, to believe that Socialism could lead to the palingenesis of humanity.

Croce's meditations on Marx at the time he was publishing Labriola's works led him also to write several essays on Marxism. These writings were later collected and published in 1900 in a volume entitled *Materialismo storico ed economia marxistica* (*Historical Materialism and the Economics of Karl Marx*), which includes essays that both criticize and attempt to place in a historical context what Croce had earlier believed was a totally new and revolutionary philosophy. Moreover the criticism, which is developed on several philosophical levels and takes different angles, including, at times, outright attacks, are an indication of the brevity of Croce's love affair with Marxism.

In the first and most important essay of his collection, "Sulla forma scientifica del materialismo storico" (Concerning the Scientific Form of Historical Materialism), Croce attempts an explanation of this new and "fashionable subject." Using many of the conceptual themes of *Il concetto della storia,* Croce attempts to prove that historical materialism, as it is expounded by Marx and interpreted in Italy by Labriola, constitutes not a new philosophy of history but rather an addition of new elements to our ability to understand history itself. He again repeats that inasmuch as a philosophy of history presupposes "the reduction to concepts of the course of history," historical materialism, with its interest in observing particular and contingent economic factors, can never amount to a totalizing view of the course of human events. Croce adds that Marx claimed that Hegel, the quintessential philosopher of history, set "history in the

mind, and that it must be turned upside down so that it may stand on its feet." But Marx's relationship to Hegel is for Croce merely developmental—it was mainly through the works of Hegel that Marx was initiated into philosophy. Croce perceives Marx's frequent references to Hegel as a philosophical stepping-stone, a search for a point of departure on the part of an ambitious new thinker. In reality, Croce adds, historical materialism is not an attempt to rewrite Hegel's philosophy of history from another point of view; Hegel's "Idea" is not turned upside down by stating that human ideas are a reflection of material reality. What Marx said, Croce continues, is that in order to understand history, one must observe and study special material elements such as "land, natural production, and livestock." Marx did not conclude that the complex of these phenomena leads to an all-encompassing view of human destiny. Even the Marxist ideas of progress and historical necessity are for Croce relegated to circumstances and specifics. They are a way of interpreting certain aspects of human history and can in no way be identified with fate and destiny, which are metaphysical and transcendental concepts.

Therefore, if the final legacy of historical materialism is but a call to observe material conditions when studying historical events, what, Croce asks, is its relationship to Socialism? It is precisely on this point that Croce mounts his strongest attack on the self-proclaimed Socialist Antonio Labriola. In fact Labriola had claimed that a materialistic view of history would necessarily point to Socialism as the natural outcome of the evolution of history. According to Croce this conclusion is one that contradicts Labriola's very idea that materialism is not a philosophy of history: "Once established that historical materialism is devoid of any remnants of finality and of providential values, it can support neither Socialism nor any other political system." At its best, Croce believes, historical materialism, which is neither a philosophical system nor a method through which one can study history, adds a new point of view to historical studies. It is a call to look at specific facts rather than abstract ideas, to observe human action in its actual development without any need to make a single event comply to an abstract design. What historical materialism is, Croce concludes, and the way in which it should be more appropriately viewed and named, is "a realistic view of history."

It may well be that Croce's passion for Marxism and his subsequent sudden rejection of it could be given a psychological explanation. The former might be the consequence of the young intellectual's enthusiasm for a new and revolutionary philosophy, and the latter might be the outcome of a meditation on the consequences of Socialism on the part of an upper-class southern Italian with inherited wealth. Croce may well have repeated this same pattern later on, at the beginning of Fascism, when, fearing the turmoil and anarchy provoked by the left, he refused to speak up against it. Only later, when the dictatorship had a firm grip on the country, did Croce distance himself from it. Croce did, however, admit to positive influences coming from his Marxist experience. Among them, and most important, Croce recognized the crucial role that Marxism played in helping him do away with traditional morality and in calling attention to economic factors in the study of history.

THE SHAPING OF A PHILOSOPHICAL SYSTEM

The Marxist interlude and other historical investigations sidetracked Croce and forced him to postpone a philosophical project aimed at further investigating the nature of art, logic, ethics, economics, and history. Between 1902 and 1917, though, Croce was able to publish, among other works, four volumes that constitute the core of his philosophical thinking and amount to a philosophical system, which he called "la filosofia dello spirito" (the philosophy of spirit). They are *Aesthetic as Science of Expression and General Linguistic, Logica come scienza del concetto puro* (*Logic as the Science of the Pure Concept*, 1909), *Filosofia della pratica: Economica ed etica* (*Philosophy of the Practical: Economic and Ethic*, 1908), and *Teoria e storia della storiografia* (*History: Its Theory and Practice*, 1917). These four books, along with other works on the same subjects, written to clarify obscure points and to answer criticism, and the articles he wrote over many decades for the journal *La critica* (which he founded in 1902 with the philosopher Giovanni Gentile), made Croce one of the leading philosophers of the first half of the twentieth century.

While Croce's philosophical system is divided into four main areas of inquiry, art, logic, history, and ethics are not to be considered as totally separate areas. They have their own specific realms of activity, but Croce is always ready to insist that these four areas have a dialectical relationship with one another, that one cannot exist without the other. If indeed man's artistic inclinations should be understood and studied independently from his logical, historical, and ethical needs, for Croce logic, history, and ethics are not possible without those inclinations. Similarly, if logic is the science of pure concepts, the science of the conceptual instruments through which we understand the world and make generalizations about the many changing ways in which the world presents itself to the mind, these concepts are nevertheless historically determined. The philosophies of Immanuel Kant and Hegel, for example, could have come into being only at the time in which Kant and Hegel wrote, and they reflect the intellectual needs relevant in their times, such as the need to explain the scientific process. Kant and Hegel and their philosophies were historically determined, a product of a set of historical conditions. To philosophize is for Croce equal to writing the history of philosophy, a history that takes into account the philosophical tradition and adapts it to the needs of the contemporary world. These needs also include contemporary ethical needs. In turn, Croce adds—and here lies the clue to the proper understanding of Croce's dialectical system— a philosophy will also influence the way in which art, history, and ethics express themselves at any point in time. This is true even if art as a form of human expression is prelogical and preconceptual, and even if it is art that creates the "representations" that constitute the background that makes logical thinking possible.

What then is Croce's system? What is his logic? According to Robin G. Collingwood, one of Croce's most interesting and careful students, "his logic is the theory of thought." "To think" is for Croce "to make judgments," including judgments on art, history, and ethics. In order to define what a logical judgment is, Croce finds himself criticizing the traditional philosophical position, which distinguishes between abstract and universal judgments and individual and practical judgments. His goal is to take philosophy out of the traditional dualist impasse in which it has often been caught. Judgment, Croce adds, should be neither metaphysical and independent of reality nor empirical and tied to particular observations of reality. The Kantian classification of judgments as either a priori (abstract) or a posteriori (concrete) is what Croce sets out to attack. Judgment, Croce says, should include both. In order to prove this point Croce begins by saying that "if man does not speak, he does not think," and that to "think is at the same time to speak." Just the same, language must be clearly distinguished from thought. Language belongs to the realm of "intuition" and results in "expression" and "representation." But logical knowledge "goes beyond simple representation. The latter [representation] consists of individuality and of multiplicity; the former [logic] consists of the universality of the individuality, of the unity of multiplicity; one is intuition, the other is a concept." But by establishing that the origin of concepts lies in language, or in intuition, also defined as expression and representation,

Croce is able to save the realistic part of what is, in its true nature, an abstract logical construction. The example of the concept of "perpetual motion" is, in this respect, highly illuminating. Croce writes:

> Perpetual motion is a kind of motion that is thought of as taking place without finding obstacles. It can never be confused with that type of motion that occurs when there is this or that obstacle. And this is clear. But such a conceptual fiction, if it is entirely separated from its representation, reaches the realm of the void, where it is impossible to survive; or, out of the metaphor, it gains universality by losing its contact with reality. . . . Perpetual motion does not take place in the real world, because motion takes place under certain conditions and therefore amidst obstacles. A thought with nothing real is not a thought; and that concept is not a concept, but a conceptual fiction.
>
> (*Logica come scienza del concetto puro*, 1909, pp. 19–20)

Thought, instead, occurs by means of "pure concepts" (a term that Croce prefers to the platonic one of "Idea") and not by means of "conceptual fictions," also called, for the sake of brevity, "pseudo-concepts." A "pure concept" is distinct from a "pseudo-concept" in that the former is simultaneously universal and concrete. It is universal because it goes beyond single representations, and it is concrete because it can be verified with one or more of the single representations that make it possible. A pseudo-concept pretends instead to detach itself from the realm of single and individual representations but is unable to do so. In order to clarify his argument Croce goes on to give some examples of what is and what is not a pure concept. Such examples indicate the ultimate goals of his philosophy. He claims, for instance, that "tragic form" is not a pure concept and that it is impossible to establish a theory of tragedy because through the study of literary genres one easily learns that the term "tragic form" is not a concept as it is referred to a limited number of artistic representations that in reality have few similarities among them. The aim of thought is instead that of showing connections and similarities that are really universal, and that apply to a vast body of things that previously appeared to have no relation among themselves.

It is interesting to note that from the establishing of his most theoretical principles down to his examples Croce constantly refers to the question of the nature of artistic expression. His interest in the nature of art led him, in fact, to devote one of his major works to the subject of aesthetics. *Il concetto della storia* has as its primary goal the intent of establishing what is the real nature of art so that it may be distinguished from that of history.

Language, Croce says, is one form of art, and art partakes of the nature of language. Language and art are the first two means through which man, both throughout his history and within his own life cycle, learns to express himself. The *Logic* is the second volume of Croce's "filosofia dello spirito." It is not by chance that the first installment of his philosophical corpus, the *Aesthetic as Science of Expression and General Linguistic,* was precisely an inquiry into the nature of art and of language, art's twin companion. Croce's *Aesthetic* is the author's most studied book, the one for which he is still best known. Along with other subsequent volumes on the nature of art aimed at clarifying and perfecting his theory, the *Aesthetic,* divided as it is into a theoretical and a historical section, was received as a broad attempt to reform romantic aesthetics and to establish a new and path-breaking theory. Croce's reform was, from most points of view, a real success. Although his attempts to translate the ideas of the *Aesthetic* into his own literary criticism put him at times in very controversial positions, as when he criticized Dante and other major Italian writers for mixing poetry and literature with subjects, such as philosophy and history, that are alien to it, his philosophy of art remains even now a theory that any serious philosopher of art must take into consideration. Sec-

ond only to the names of Plato, Kant, and Hegel, the name of Croce appears with the greatest frequency in contemporary studies on the nature of art. This is especially noteworthy if one considers that contemporary aesthetics, dealing mainly with the many twentieth-century avant-garde experiences, touches on intellectual complexities of which Croce was in great part unaware.

"Knowledge has two forms," Croce writes at the beginning of the *Aesthetic*; "it is either intuitive knowledge or logical knowledge; knowledge through fantasy or knowledge through the intellect; knowledge of individual things or knowledge of universals; of single things or of their relations; in other words it produces either images or concepts." It should be clearly understood, Croce adds, that the first form of knowledge, the one that is based on intuition and that perceives reality through fantasy, is totally independent of the second, and it is this first form of knowledge that pertains to the realm of artistic expression and production. Through this distinction Croce brings art outside the world of logical thinking. Intuitive thinking comes before conceptual thinking. While the latter is based on the former, the former has a field and a realm all its own. It is a form or an aspect of the spirit that constantly claims its own independence. At any time or stage of human development and of history, before thinking logically and applying his scientific capabilities to understand and transform the outside world, man feels a need to express himself artistically. Even in the most evolved stages of human history, when our intellectual and scientific abilities are most highly developed, the intuitive and expressive needs press their urge and claim their independence. Artistic expression, while changing in form according to the needs of the times, remains forever a permanent aspect of human nature:

A work of art may well be full of philosophical concepts; it can have more, and more profound ones, than a philosophical dissertation, which in turn can be abounding with descriptions and intuitions. But, despite all these concepts, the end result of a work of art is an intuition; and despite all those intuitions, the end result of a philosophical dissertation is a concept.

(*Estetica come scienza dell'espressione e linguistica generale,* 1922, p. 5)

By firmly basing the nature of art in intuition and in the expression of intuitions, Croce reaches some important theoretical conclusions. In the first place he is able to affirm that art, or expression, is "a form of consciousness" and that therefore it is unchanging. One cannot speak of a history of art or of an artistic development nor of artistic progress in the same way in which one speaks of historical progress. If indeed literary critics speak, for example, of artistic decadence at the end of the Italian Renaissance, what they are really saying is that at that time Italian art became unable to renew itself and was simply satisfied with imitating the forms it had previously developed. Had the Italians been able to express their political decadence, Italian art would not have, as critics like to put it, "decayed." The renewal came instead outside of Italy, with Cervantes in Spain and Shakespeare in England, two artists able to develop new kinds of literary creations. However, Cervantes and Shakespeare did not "progress" over the Italians; they simply opened a new artistic cycle. The nature of art, precisely because it is art and not science, has the specific characteristic of not bearing, within its system, comparisons among works of art composed in different periods:

Not only is the art of the savages, insofar as it expresses the impressions of the savage man, not inferior, as art, to the art of more civilized peoples, but every individual, or rather, every moment of the spiritual life of an individual, has its own artistic world; and all of these worlds bear, from an artistic point of view, no comparison with one another.

(p. 150)

From a more philosophical point of view, to base artistic expression on intuition enables Croce to place aesthetics outside the strictures of the Aristotelian, classical, and neoclassical concept of imitation or mimesis. Stating that through the idea of mimesis one is unable to separate and distinguish artistic expression from scientific and historical knowledge, Croce goes on to say that not until the eighteenth century did philosophy become fully aware of the nature of aesthetic expression. The philosopher who for Croce set the basis for all future discussion on aesthetics, and who, with few errors, discovered aesthetics as a branch of philosophy, was Giambattista Vico.

Vico remains today one of the most controversial and difficult-to-interpret figures in the history of Western thought. Vico, considered by some a historian, by others a philosopher, and by others still an anthropologist, an aesthetician, and, more simply, a rhetorician in the Ciceronian and Renaissance sense of the word, was claimed by scholars coming from many different fields of the humanities (including Croce) as their own. Coming indeed from the rhetorical tradition and writing in the secluded and intellectually depleted environment that was the city of Naples at the beginning of the eighteenth century, in his *New Science* Vico set out to write a rhetoric of human expression. He also enriched his treatise with elements derived from his lifelong studies in history, philology, economics, law, religion, and any other area of knowledge on which he was able to set his omnivorous mind. The end result is a highly complex and almost cabalistic treatise that defies classification and that appears to be both a history and a philosophy of human activity. When Croce interpreted Vico's work and tried to make him the father of modern aesthetics, he emphasized the philosophical aspect over the historical one, disregarding the fact that in the *New Science* the two remain, at least at the conscious level, indistinguishable. Croce approaches Vico's history of mankind not as a history— that is, not as a historical account of the stages, both intellectual and material, experienced by man since his first appearance on earth—but rather as a philosophy. In other words, for Croce Vico's stages are not chronological but contemporary, not developmental but synchronical aspects of the human spirit. "The truth is," Croce writes, "that his [Vico's] philosophy of history, his ideal history, his *New Science Concerning the Common Nature of Nations,* does not deal with concrete and empirical history, which evolves through time; and it is not history, but a science of the Ideal, a Philosophy of the Spirit." Whether it is wrong or right, this interpretation of Vico's thought leads Croce to affirm that for Vico artistic expression is a common characteristic of mankind in every age and stage of its development. Artistic expression is indeed for Vico the typical manner of expression in the early stages of human development and at the initial stages of every new historical cycle. Lacking more sophisticated and intellectual ways in which to communicate, early man condenses in poetry and art all of his knowledge, which at a later, more developed time he is able to expound in the language of science and philosophy. Croce interprets Vico literally when he states that for Vico artistic expression is the form of expression of "a period in the history of humanity." He may instead be stretching Vico's thought to make it identify with his own when he says that Vico's "is an ideal history, the periods of which are not contingent but are forms of the spirit," and that therefore art is "a moment of the ideal history of the spirit, a form of consciousness." Insofar as for Croce Vico's historical stages are not chronological parts of human development but instead exist all at the same time to compose the various forms of the spirit, Croce's view of artistic expression as based on intuition seems to agree with Vico's view of art as the first and primary form of human expression.

For the very same reason that Croce makes Vico the father of modern aesthetics, he condemns Hegel's view, which he considers tainted by a Platonic flaw. Just as Plato had seen art, or poetry, as a more primitive and mythological form of expression, Hegel, Croce says, deems art as no longer sufficient to satisfy the needs of intellectual understanding in a modern and developed cultural age. For Hegel, therefore, art is destined to disappear. This point of view, according to Croce, is the natural consequence of the stress that Hegel places on the cognitive aspect of art: "Art having been placed in the sphere of the absolute Spirit, next to Religion and Philosophy, how can it survive with such powerful and invading companions, and especially with Philosophy, which, in the Hegelian system, rests at the top of the entire spiritual development?" By contrast, Croce's anti-Hegelian argument on the subject of art, supported as it is by some Vichian elements, helps us understand the final meaning of his *Aesthetic.* The fact that art does not die, that every age, whether primitive or developed, is able to produce its own distinctive artistic masterpieces, indicates that its origin is a permanent and unchanging aspect of the human spirit, which is intuition. If, as Vico states, primitive man is able to express himself only poetically and artistically, it does not necessarily mean that this inclination will disappear once more advanced systems of understanding are developed. Art, Croce concludes, is a perennial human need, an ever-living aspect of culture. Primitive man may well have been only poetically inclined, but historical evolution and growth do not cancel the past. Rather, they subsume the past into the present.

History is ever-present, and the past lives in the present. Nothing in human experience is ever canceled. This constant precept in all of Croce's writings is the subject of the fourth volume of the "filosofia dello spirito," *History: Its Theory and Practice.* The main goal of this book is not, as it may initially seem, to define what history is and how it can be identified in opposition to other intellectual and creative pursuits such as philosophy and art. The book has instead the intention of proving that history, as well as a historical approach to the understanding of the world, is equal to a philosophy. To think historically is equal to adhering to a philosophical view based on history. While in his essay Croce discusses in some detail various technical aspects of historiography and describes such particuliarities as chronology and periodization and the various rhetorical means used in the writing of history, he is quick to add that these are only those practical aspects that constitute the substratum of the craft. They do not help in defining what history is. History, Croce writes, is to think of the past as if it were the present, to make the past live again in our present times, because it is the past that makes the understanding of the present possible:

> When the development of culture in my historical moment (and it would be superfluous to add: of myself as an individual) opens before me the question of the Attic Civilization, of the philosophy of Plato, or of a special aspect of the Attic living conditions, that problem becomes as close to my being as the history of a business matter I am involved in, or of a love affair, or of an incumbent danger; and I study it with the same anxiety, and am bothered by the same unhappiness until I am able to solve it. Hellenic life, in that case, is present in me; and it stimulates me and it torments me, just as seeing an enemy, or my loved one, or the dear son who causes me so much worry.
>
> (*Teoria e storia della storiografia*, 1927, p. 5)

Just as philosophy coincides with the history of philosophy and is the history of what "is eternally present," so philosophy coincides with history. The identification of history and philosophy does not contradict Croce's earlier position on the subject as expressed in *Il concetto della storia,* and should not be confused with Croce's denial of the Hegelian and romantic faith in the philosophy of history, which he considered nothing but the application of the abstract concept of predetermined development to the raw facts of history. Where in the earlier study he was interested in estab-

lishing the differences and similarities between history and art, in his *History* he develops his analysis to include historical events in the realm of universal thinking:

> History is thought and, as such, thought about the universal, and of the universal in its concrete aspects, and therefore always determined in its particular aspects. There is no fact, as small as it may seem, that can be understood (or conceived or qualified) as other than in the universal. In its most simple form, which is its essential form, history expresses itself in judgments, which are an inseparable synthesis of the individual and the universal.
>
> (p. 48)

The same dialectical principle that creates the simultaneous relationship of unity and of distinction between history and thought is applied by Croce in *Philosophy of the Practical: Economic and Ethic* to establish a rapport between thought and action. *Philosophy of the Practical* is Croce's essay on ethics, and it is also probably Croce's weakest philosophical work among the four that compose the "filosofia dello spirito." The weakness stems from Croce's treatment of moral issues in an abstract philosophical manner, just as he deals elsewhere with art, logic, or history. The result is that no clear view is obtained of how "the proper action" and "good and evil" can clearly be defined. On the contrary, such concepts, while not being described in themselves or in terms of what they mean, are analyzed in the context of Croce's larger philosophical system. Consequently, "the proper action" and "good and evil," the constant themes of moral philosophers, become simply a part of the course of human history and human thought, having a necessity of their own and a raison d'être simply by virtue of the fact that they are permanent aspects of existence.

After having established in the first pages of the essay that thought and action are inseparable, that "will is thought that translates itself into action," and that no action is possible without prior thought and knowledge, Croce proceeds to say that "good" is the consequence of proper thought and that "evil" is "non-thought" or wrong thinking. Evil can either be perceived as such and therefore not enacted, or it may not be realized and understood and may therefore be put into action. In both cases, however, evil fulfills somewhat of a positive role as it dialectically contrasts "good" and corrects another evil:

> When the slanderer understands the idea, or better, the impulse that possesses him and compels him to slander, he is taken aback and refrains from slandering; and in such a case he is not a slanderer but an honest man who resists a temptation (no other definition of the honest man can be provided except this one that he resists temptations). But if he instead slanders, that means that the refraining force was not, or is not, there anymore, and that his evil words are no longer a malignant act, but simply represent his need to vent his feelings and to amuse himself or to respond to an evil that he has suffered; that is, they are no longer an evil but a good.
>
> (*Filosofia della practica*, 1932, pp. 128–129)

The question of the presence of evil as a reality of everyday life is paramount to the understanding of Croce's ideas on liberty, which obviously include his ideas on free will and free action. Given the fact that to will is to act, or, more precisely, that since will is thought man can will only what he is able to do, Croce concludes that man is necessarily free. It is a relativistic view of freedom with colorings of Stoicism, as it believes that since man can think only what he can do, he feels no constraints to his freedom. The word "freedom," he adds, must be understood not in its most universal and abstract meaning, but as something historically determined. In each phase of human history and in each moment of life, man finds himself conditioned by exterior and necessary facts. It is by freely acting within these conditions that human freedom expresses itself, since it is through free action that man is able to change and modify the present situation. There can be no freedom without necessity, since free will and action can take place only in contingent and real situations that are bound by necessity.

It should be quite clear that Croce's *Philosophy of the Practical* is not a treatise on ethics in the normative sense. It does not attempt to define what good is, and even less to indicate how it can be attained. More than a guide to the pursuit of the good life and of happiness in the tradition of the utilitarian treatises on morality, the *Philosophy of the Practical* is a philosophical meditation on how the man of wisdom, and only he, can find, if not happiness, peace of mind in the human condition. Croce's morality evokes that of the Stoics. Although it tries to justify self-interest as the positive driving force behind economic development and progress, Croce seems to conclude that the ultimate ethical form is the volition of the universal, the universal being the ultimate truth of Croce's philosophical system:

> The moral individual is conscious of working for the Totality. The most dissimilar actions conforming to moral duty are conforming to Life, and would be contrary to duty and therefore immoral if instead of promoting Life, they were to depress it and mortify it. Where it seems that facts show the contrary, it is the interpretation of the facts which is wrong, because it uses as a criterion for life not that true life the good of which is served, as is known, also by dying—by dying as an individual, as a group, a social class, or a people.
>
> (p. 293)

In the end morality is achieved through knowledge and through the consciousness of being, as individuals, part of a whole that contains, and confronts us with, all aspects of human existence, good and evil. The final message of Croce's ethical treatise may be summarized in the classical dictum "Know thyself."

CROCE, HEGEL, AND VICO

Croce often claimed to have rejuvenated nineteenth-century idealistic philosophy by adding to it a more realistic and concrete point of view. A sharp critic of the English philosophical tradition and of its nineteenth-century developments in pragmatism, utilitarianism, and psychologism, Croce nevertheless believed that idealism, while representing the most mature and advanced achievement in the history of Western philosophy, was caught in a dualistic deadlock. If idealism, the major representative of which Croce believed to be Hegel, developed a vision of the spirit and of the mind as those human functions capable of giving a totalizing view of the world, it was also the philosophy that believed that philosophical and spiritual thinking should encompass all mental activities. As a consequence of this, Croce concluded, idealism was unable to understand and account for mental activities that are prelogical and prephilosophical, intuitive rather than rational. As the ideal and the absolute confidence in philosophy became Hegel's only realities, they also became, for Croce, his major philosophical error.

While Croce's attempt to correct the excesses of idealism was carried out in the four volumes of the "filosofia dello spirito," at about the same time he wrote two essays on Hegel and Vico in which he assessed the import of their philosophies and identified the parts of their thinking that were still viable at his own time. It goes without saying that the act of writing on these two thinkers and not on others was in itself a statement. While he always refused to be called a Hegelian or a Vichian and asserted in line with his philosophy that he was Hegelian and Vichian to the same extent that he was a follower and an interpreter of all the other philosophical schools of the Western tradition, there is little doubt that Croce saw in Vico and in Hegel the mentors of his philosophical system.

In the essay on Hegel, first published in 1906 with the title *Ciò che è vivo e ciò che è morto nella filosofia di Hegel* (*What Is Living and What Is Dead of the Philosophy of Hegel*) and then in 1913 in an amplified version under the title *Saggio sullo Hegel* (Essay on Hegel), Croce claimed that Hegel's thought was a work "of

mature thinking, the result of a long philosophical incubation." According to Croce, the major achievement of Hegel's thought was that he wrote a philosophy of philosophy, also called a logic of philosophy. In other words, Hegel considered one of the major objects of his philosophical system to be the mental process through which philosophy itself is produced. What really counts in Hegel's legacy, Croce says, along with some important discoveries in his study of reality, is that he made thinking the object of his thought. In this respect the theory of dialectics was Hegel's major discovery. Trying to define the nature of Hegel's dialectics, Croce says that in any investigation of reality aimed at defining what reality is, the philosopher finds himself in the difficult position of having to deal with concepts radically opposed to one another, concepts such as "true" and "false," "good" and "evil," "beautiful" and "ugly," "positive" and "negative," "life" and "death," and so on. The problem that Hegel posed, and brilliantly solved, is the following: How can we reach a unifying assessment of the real world that is capable of accounting for a reality made of such real and opposite concepts? Or are there always two different realities, the unified vision being unreachable?

The solution to the problem lies in the assumption that reality is not immobile but is constantly evolving, and that it is by the dialectics of such opposite concepts that evolution itself becomes possible. Describing Hegel's finding, Croce writes:

> The opposites are opposed to one another, but are not opposed in respect to unity; the true and concrete unity is nothing but unity, a synthesis of opposites: it is not immobility, it is movement; it is not stable but evolutionary. The philosophical concept is a concrete universal; and therefore it is the thought of reality as united and divided at the same time.
>
> (*Saggio sullo Hegel*, 1913, p. 15)

The secret of Hegel's dialectic, Croce goes on to say, lies in the assumption that the two opposites are in fact two "moments" of a process—the "thesis" and the "antithesis"—both of which are resolved in a third "moment," called "synthesis"; the concept of "being" cannot exist and cannot be defined without its opposing "moment," that of "nonbeing." In turn both are resolved in their synthesis, which is "becoming" and which includes and solves the two previous opposite "moments." Indeed, one could not think of the living process, the human process, without including in it the two separate elements of "being" and "nonbeing," of life and death. The same is to be said of other opposites, like true and false, good and evil, and so on. Thinking is indeed a unifying process, a process that conceives of the idea—the idea of the world—as the synthesis of a series of opposites that find their solution in the principle of "becoming."

Unfortunately, Croce goes on to say in the more critical part of his essay on Hegel, the German philosopher turned his major discovery into his major weakness when he attributed to the dialectical principle all aspects of humanity, thus making philosophy the only field of spiritual activity toward which man naturally tends. Next to "opposite" concepts, Croce says, which are solved in the unity provided by dialectics, man's spiritual activity also proceeds through "distinct" concepts, and Hegel was wrong to put "opposite" and "distinct" concepts on the same level. By doing this he was unable to account for certain spiritual expressions, such as art and history, as permanent productions of the human soul:

> Truth does not have with falsehood the same relationship that it has with goodness; beauty does not have with ugliness the same relationship that it has with philosophical truth. Life without death and death without life are two opposing false concepts; their truth is life, which is a relationship between life and death, of itself and its opposite. But truth without goodness and goodness without truth are not two false concepts that are solved in a third concept: they are false conceptions that are solved in a relationship of degrees.

(pp. 63–64)

The extension of Hegel's mistaken conception to the world of art particularly bothers Croce. In fact, Hegel maintains that art has its antithesis in philosophy and that it is therefore bound to disappear once philosophical thought reaches its full development. On the contrary, Croce says, art is an aspect of spiritual activity that comes into being prior to philosophical thought and independently of it. While art enables philosophy to develop, it always maintains intact its position within the life of the spirit. The relationship between art and philosophy is for Croce not a dialectical one, since each occupies a different degree in the human soul. It is therefore wrong to assume, as Hegel does, that the full development of the human spirit to a stage of total consciousness is bound to make art, thought of as a lower rather than different form of understanding, totally obsolete. According to Croce, this erroneous point of view finds its origin in Hegel's philosophy of history, which sees the past as a dialectical and evolutionary process and which applies a priori concepts to the stages of human development: "Before researching the facts [of history], Hegel already knows what they should be; he knows them in advance, as one knows the philosophical truths that the spirit is able to find in its universal being without deriving them from contingent facts."

In the end, while praising Hegel for the discovery of dialectics and the development of philosophy into a science that studies not only the world but also the way the mind functions while philosophically understanding the world, Croce is unable to subscribe to the Hegelian position that philosophical thinking can subsume all other aspects of the life of the spirit. Because he made a religion of philosophy, and despite his many philosophical breakthroughs, Hegel remains for Croce still in line with the traditional philosophical school. In fact, his absolute faith in philosophy, his reference to philosophy as the only system of understanding, reminds Croce of ancient metaphysics. The only difference is that in Hegel the religious concept of God is renamed with the more philosophical title Logos.

Vico, Croce thought, is a good antidote to Hegel's mistakes in the same way that Hegel can be seen as completing philosophical problems that Vico left unsolved. In recent years Vico's work has enjoyed a great revival of interest. This revival, while it can in part be attributed to Croce's rediscovery of Vico, has also greatly modified Croce's point of view on the author of the *New Science*. Indeed Croce has been more and more accused of turning Vico into a precursor of idealistic and Hegelian philosophy and ultimately of his own. Instead, for modern scholars Vico is hardly a philosopher at all, but a theorist of human culture and a precursor of anthropology. While many of the contemporary anti-Crocean views on Vico are probably correct, one must acknowledge that differences in point of view are a natural consequence of the great complexity of Vico's work. Croce himself was well aware of these complexities when in his essay on Vico, *La filosofia di Giambattista Vico* (*The Philosophy of Giambattista Vico,* 1911), he wrote, "Philosophy, history, and empirical science are in him [Vico] from time to time converted into one another and . . . produce those perplexities, misunderstandings, exaggerations, and falsifications that often disturb the readers of the *New Science.*"

When Croce approached and interpreted Vico's text, he freely assumed that these "perplexities" were outright mistakes of which Vico was not aware, and he took the liberty of clarifying and correcting them. While doing this Croce took the position that he was correctly interpreting Vico's thought and that he was saying what Vico wanted to say but could not find the words for. As a result, philosophy, history, and natural science, which in Vico are "converted into one another," become, in Croce's interpretation, three different aspects of Hegelian "moments" of Vico's "new philosophy of the spirit." From this point of departure Croce felt free to make Vico the founder of modern aesthetics, although Vico himself

never used the word "aesthetics" and instead referred to "sapienza poetica" (poetic wisdom) as the original form of thought and knowledge used by man in the first developments of culture. By taking this view, Croce forced Vico to disagree with Hegel and to agree with him in the assumption that art is a permanent aspect of human expression, one coincident with the intuitive moment of the cognitive process. On the contrary, it should be noted that one recent scholar of Vico, Michael Mooney, in *Vico in the Tradition of Rhetoric* (Princeton, N.J., 1985), has seen in Vico's "poetic wisdom" a "form of knowledge" that "does not mark, as he [Croce] . . . held, the boundary between arts and sciences. Not only does Vico maintain, with Bacon his mentor, the traditional understanding of 'arts,' but also assigns a 'poetic' origin to the entire cycle of learning—sciences as well as art." Quite contrary to Croce's interpretation, in other words, "poetry" for Vico would have been the first form through which culture expressed itself and would have encompassed all other forms of knowledge, the arts and the philosophical and natural sciences. In future developments, man would find more advanced and logical forms of expression, and, while the poetic moment as the moment of fantasy and creativity would still remain alive, logical knowledge would constitute an advancement, as in Hegel, over poetic wisdom.

In trying to make Vico the predecessor of his own philosophy, Croce was able on the one hand to revive an interest in his thought and on the other hand substantially to distort it. Croce turned Vico into himself when he assumed that, unlike Hegel, Vico did not develop a philosophy of history. He believed that Vico's universal history, divided in various developmental and recurring cycles, was intended as a metaphor for how man understands the world, the cycles being just contemporary moments of the spirit.

A different interpretation might be given of Croce's forcing Vico's thought to comply with his own. It could be argued that this does not necessarily constitute an obvious and blatant example of Croce's lack of interpretative skills and of his inability to penetrate the work of another thinker by means of textual criticism. After all, Croce was not a critic but a philosopher, and indeed he was a philosopher who claimed over and over again that the writing of philosophy is a constant rewriting of the history of philosophy in order to extract from the past what is relevant to the present. In this context his essay on Vico could be the most revealing single example of Croce's method. He wrote on Vico with the same goal he had in mind when he wrote on Hegel: in order to find out what, for Croce, was still "living" of Vico's thought. To approach the past programmatically through the present may be considered by some an overt act of misinterpretation, but by others it may be considered the most honest intellectual endeavor. Whether conscious or not, the act of critically evaluating texts lost in the fog of history, with the historical and intellectual conditions under which they were written often impossible to reconstruct in their entirety, is an act always influenced by the personality of the evaluator. Croce claimed that as much as the critic may—and should—try to uncover the background of a work of the past, he will never be able to do so entirely. When writing about another author, one necessarily also writes about oneself. Historical interpretation, Croce seems to conclude, is similar to the process that takes place in psychoanalysis, where the search for the events that shaped one's youth is always selective and favors those events that can best explain one's present. History and the history of philosophy are the psychoanalysis of culture.

CROCE AS PUBLIC FIGURE, AND THE LATER WORKS

By the end of the second decade of the century and following almost thirty years of extremely intense work and philosophical production, Croce had become a public figure in Italy and abroad. He was recognized as one of the leading thinkers of his time, and some of his major works, such as the *Aesthetic,* were being translated into foreign languages and receiving vast acclaim. As is common in Italy, where intellectuals and artists of special distinction acquire the standing of national prophets, Croce's fame was such that it compelled him into public national life. The Italian political situation at the beginning of the 1920's was one of deep turmoil. Coming out of World War I politically victorious but economically destroyed, the country faced a social unrest that many feared would lead to a Socialist revolution. The traditional political parties represented in the Italian parliament found it increasingly difficult to handle the discontent of growing masses of unemployed and of young war veterans unable to re-enter the mainstream of society. In this situation the new party of Mussolini, who preached nationalism along with strong opposition to Socialism and Communism and who did not look down on violence as a means of political advancement, became in the eyes of many the only way out of what was perceived by everyone as a serious political crisis. Shortly before the Fascist March on Rome of 1922, Croce was offered, and accepted in 1920, the position of minister of education. In that role he started a major reform of the Italian educational system and remained in office until the middle of 1921, when Prime Minister Giovanni Giolitti's government was deposed. Croce then returned to Naples and watched from a distance the development of the political situation that led to the Fascist dictatorship.

A great deal has been said and written about Croce's initially ambiguous attitude toward Fascism. Croce himself admitted that in the years when Mussolini imposed his stronghold over Italy he took a waiting position. He probably felt that Fascism was the only way to avert a revolution; he said that he believed that Fascism would be just a passing phenomenon:

With the resignation of the Giolitti government I returned to my studies, from which I was not removed even during the first stages of Fascism, which I considered, I must admit rather superficially, as a postwar phenomenon, with aspects of youthful and patriotic reaction that would disappear without doing any evil and maybe leaving behind something good. I could not believe that Italy would allow her freedom to be taken away, a freedom that had cost her so much effort and blood and that men of my generation considered a permanent acquisition.

(*Contributo alla critica di me stesso,*
in *Filosofia, poesia, storia,* p. 1172)

Mussolini, on his part, had an ambivalent attitude towards intellectuals. On the one hand, he officially proclaimed that they were useless members of society; on the other, he suffered from the inferiority complex of the uneducated toward the educated, and he tried to organize them and make them supporters of the regime. Following this policy, in 1924 Mussolini offered Croce the directorship of the ministry of education. Croce turned the offer down and in the following year published *Il manifesto degli intellettuali antifascisti* (Manifesto of the Anti-Fascist Intellectuals), which was subscribed by several hundred signatures. With this *Manifesto* Croce officially distanced himself from the Fascist dictatorship and took a firm stand of opposition that remained unchanged until the end of his life. While it contains a sharp attack on the Fascist ideology, Croce's *Manifesto* is again a revelation of his philosophical credo. It is in fact very much in line with his theory of good and evil since it assumes that while Fascism is indeed an evil, it may at the end result in a higher good:

The present political struggle in Italy will bring about, by means of contrast, the revival and a better understanding in our people of liberal methods and institutions and will make such methods better loved and respected. And maybe one day, looking serenely at our past, we will be able to judge that the trying times we are now going through, painful and grueling as they are, are but a stage that Italy had to experience in order to strengthen its national life, complete its

political development, and feel more strongly its duty as a civilized people.

(*Filosofia, poesia, storia,* p. 1060)

Croce reappeared on the public scene again in 1943, when he was instrumental in rebuilding the Liberal Party, and later, when he participated in the political events of the postwar period. He was minister at large in the first Italian democratic government of 1944 and was active in collaborating with the Allied forces in the struggle to liberate Italy from the German occupation.

Through his entire life Croce never abandoned his work, which he pursued with the tenacity of a missionary. Following the establishment of his philosophical system before 1920, Croce kept on writing on his favorite subjects, logic, history, aesthetics, literature, and ethics, trying to redefine and amplify the scope of his philosophical system. He also wrote some important historical essays, such as *Storia d'Italia dal 1871 al 1915* (*History of Italy, 1871–1915,* 1928) and *Storia d'Europa nel secolo XIX* (*History of Europe in the Nineteenth Century,* 1930), which were also very well received. His monumental amount of work, along with the publication of his journal *La critica* from 1903 to 1944 and then *Quaderni della critica* from 1945 on, make of Croce the quintessential philosopher, the man who dedicates his entire life to the production and diffusion of his thought. He believed with the faith and the tenacity of the saint and the mystic that the light of reason could, and *should,* win over the darkness of irrationality. He took upon himself the duty and the responsibility of revealing the road to a better understanding of the world.

While somewhat surprising, the fact that Croce's name is not mentioned even once in Bertrand Russell's *A History of Western Philosophy* (1945) dramatically points to the differences between two radically distinct schools of thought. Unlike Russell, and the English pragmatic school in general, Croce did not believe that the role of philosophy and logic was simply to study that which is understandable in the world. Croce had a higher vision of the mission of philosophy, a vision that stemmed first of all from the need to understand the self and what it means to be human. Croce's struggle to understand the world originated in his soul and in the need to find, if not happiness, at least some peace of mind amidst the confusion and the corruption of external reality, as he himself indicates in the *Contributo alla critica di me stesso:*

> And even now sometimes darkness fogs over my intellect; but the acute anguish from which I suffered so much during my youth is at this point a chronic anguish, which from being violent and savage has become domesticated and tamed.... Now I know its symptoms, its remedies, and its course, and I have therefore acquired the peace of mind that maturity brings to those who, and this should be clear, have worked hard to become mature.

(p. 1171)

Selected Bibliography

EDITIONS

The dates in parentheses give the last edition of the work to appear before Croce's death. These are given because during his lifetime he kept republishing his work, almost always with modifications.

INDIVIDUAL WORKS

HISTORY

I teatri di Napoli dal Rinascimento alla fine del secolo decimottavo. In *Archivio storico perle provincie Napoletane.* Naples, 1889–1891. (Bari, 1916, 1947.)

La rivoluzione napoletana del 1799. Rome, 1897. (Bari, 1948.)

Saggi sulla letteratura italiana del Seicento. Bari, 1911. (Bari, 1948.)

Le Spagna nella vita italiana durante la Rinascenze. Bari, 1917. (Bari, 1949.)

Storie e leggende Napoletane. Bari, 1919. (Bari, 1948.)

PHILOSOPHY AND LITERARY CRITICISM

Materialismo storico ed economia marxistica. Palermo, 1900. (Bari, 1946.)

Estetica come scienza dell'espressione e linguistica generale. Palermo, 1902. (Bari, 1922, 1950.)

Logica come scienza del concetto puro. Bari, 1909. (Bari, 1947.)

Filosofia della pratica, economica ed etica. Bari, 1909. (Bari, 1932, 1950.)

La filosofia di Giambattista Vico. Bari, 1911. (Bari, 1947.)

Problemi di estetica e contributi all storia delléstetica italiana. Bari, 1911. (Bari, 1949.)

Saggio sulla Hegel séguito da altri scritti di storia della filosofia. Bari, 1913. (Bari, 1948.)

Cultura e vita morale: Intermezzi politici. Bari, 1914. (Bari, 1926.)

Teoria e storia della storiografia. Bari, 1917. (Bari, 1927, 1948.)

Primi saggi. Bari, 1919. (Bari, 1928.) Includes "La storia ridotta sotto il concetto generale dell'arte."

Goethe. Bari, 1919. (Bari, 1946.)

Una famiglia di patrioti con altri saggi storici e critici. Bari, 1919. (Bari, 1949.)

Conversazioni critiche: Prima e seconda serie. Bari, 1919. (Bari, 1950.)

L'Italia dal 1914 al 1918. In *Pagine sulla guerra,* vol. 2. Naples, 1919. (Bari, 1950.)

Ariosto, Shakespeare, e Corneille. Bari, 1920. (Bari, 1950.)

Storia della storiografia italiana nel secolo decimono. 2 vols. Bari, 1921. (Bari, 1947.)

Le poesia di Dante. Bari, 1921. (Bari, 1948.)

Nuovi saggi di estetica. Bari, 1929. (Bari, 1948.)

Etica e politica. Bari, 1931. (Bari, 1945.)

La letteratura della nuova Italia: Saggi critici. 6 vols. 1914–1940. (Bari, 1957–1968.)

OTHER WRITINGS

Il concetto della storia nelle sue relazioni col concetto dell'arte. Rome, 1896.

Contributo alla critica di me stesso. Naples, 1918.

Storia del Regno di Napoli. Bari, 1925.

Uomini e cose della vecchia Italia. 2 vols. Bari, 1927. (Bari, 1943.)

Storia d'Italia dal 1871 al 1915. Bari, 1928. (Bari, 1947.)

Nuovi saggi sulla letteratura italiana del Seicento. Bari, 1931. (Bari, 1949.)

Storia d'Europa nel secolo decimonovo. Bari, 1932. (Bari, 1948.)

Conversazioni critiche: Terza e quarta serie. Bari, 1932.

Storia della'età barocca in Italia. Bari, 1933. (Bari, 1946.)

Poesia popolare e poesia d'arte: Studi sulla poesia italiana dal Tre al Cinquecento. Bari, 1933. (Bari, 1946.)

Ultimi saggi. Bari, 1935. (Bari, 1948.)

La poesia. Bari, 1936. (Bari, 1946.)

Vite di avventure, di fede, e di passione. Bari, 1936. (Bari, 1947.)

La storia come pensiero e come azione. Bari, 1938. (Bari, 1943.)

Conversazioni critiche: Quinta serie. Bari, 1939.

Il carattere della filosofia moderna. Bari, 1941. (Bari, 1945.)

Poesia antica e moderna: Interpretazioni. Bari, 1941. (Bari, 1943.)

Discorsi di varia filosofia. 2 vols. Bari, 1945.

Filosofia e storiografia: Saggi. Bari, 1949.

La letteratura italiana del Settecento: Note critiche. Bari, 1949.

Varieta di storia civile e letteraria. 2 vols. Bari, 1949–1950. Volume 1 was first published separately (Bari, 1935).

Storiografia e idealità morale. Bari, 1950.

Letture di poesia. Bari, 1950.

Filosofia, poesia, storia. Milan and Naples, 1951. Includes Contributo alla critica di me stesso and Il manifesto degli intellectuali antifascisti.

Poeti e scrittori del pieno e del tardo Rinascimento. 3 vols. Bari, 1945–1952.

TRANSLATIONS

Aesthetic as Science of Expression and General Linguistic. Translated by D. Ainsle. London, 1967.

An Autobiography. Translated by R. G. Collingwood. Oxford, 1927.

The Breviary of Aesthetic. Translated by D. Ainsle. Houston, Tex., 1961.

Guide to Aesthetics. Translated by P. Romanell. Indianapolis, Ind., 1965.

Historical Materialism and the Economics of Karl Marx. Translated by C. M. Meredith. London, 1966.

History as the Story of Liberty. Translated by S. Sprigge. London, 1962.

History: Its Theory and Practice. Translated by D. Ainsle. New York, 1960.

History of Europe in the Nineteenth Century. Translated by H. Furst. London, 1953.

A History of Italy, 1871–1915. Translated by C. M. Ady. New York, 1963.

Logic as the Science of the Pure Concept. Translated by D. Ainsle. London, 1917.

The Philosophy of Giambattista Vico. Translated by R. G. Collingwood. New York, 1964.

Philosophy of the Practical: Economic and Ethic. Translated by D. Ainsle. London, 1913.

Philosophy, Poetry, History: An Anthology of Essays. Translated by S. Sprigge. London and New York, 1966.

What Is Living and What Is Dead of the Philosophy of Hegel. Translated by D. Ainsle. New York, 1969.

BIOGRAPHICAL AND CRITICAL STUDIES

Agazzi, Emilio. Il giovane Croce e il Marxismo. Torino, 1962.

Brown, M. E. Neo-Idealistic Aesthetics: Croce—Gentile—Collingwood. Detroit, 1966.

Carr, H. W. The Philosophy of Benedetto Croce: The Problem of Art and History. New York, 1969.

Collingwood, Robin G. The Idea of History. Oxford, 1946.

De Gennaro, A. A. The Philosophy of Benedetto Croce: An Introduction. New York, 1968.

Dodds, A. E. The Romantic Theory of Poetry: An Examination in the Light of Croce's Aesthetic. New York, 1962.

Gramsci, A. Il materialismo storico e la filosofia di B. Croce. Torino, 1948.

Jacobitti, E. E. Revolutionary Humanism and Historicism in Modern Italy. New Haven, Conn., 1981.

Nicolini, F. Croce. Torino, 1962.

Palmer, L. M., and H. S. Harris, eds. Thought, Action, and Intuition as a Symposium on the Philosophy of Benedetto Croce. New York, 1975.

Sartori, G. Stato e politica nel pensiero di B. Croce. Naples, 1966.

Sprigge, C. J. Benedetto Croce, Man and Thinker. New Haven, Conn., 1952.

MANFREDI PICCOLOMINI

RAMÓN DEL VALLE-INCLÁN
(1866–1936)

IDIOSYNCRASY HAS CHARACTERIZED the lives of many noted writers. Indeed, interest in some of these individuals is sustained more by their colorful behavior than by their literary achievements. During his lifetime, it was the unfortunate lot of Ramón del Valle-Inclán to be viewed largely as an eccentric because he cultivated an individuality that was forceful and unyielding, argumentative and cynical, founded as it was on a subjective approach to ethics, aesthetics, and metaphysics. He was not alone among his contemporaries in creating a distinctive personal life-style, however. Jacinto Benavente y Martínez, Miguel de Unamuno, Azorín (José Martínez Ruiz), Pío Baroja y Nessi, Antonio Machado, and others who are grouped with Valle-Inclán in the Generation of '98 possessed an arrogant individualism (*egolatría*, as Unamuno termed it) that went to the extreme of ferocity. These men from different provinces of Spain came together in turn-of-the-century Madrid and began to issue their dissimilar works. Despite the divergence of their writings they came to know of each other through the periodicals in which they published; and they became acquainted in the *tertulias* (social-literary-political gatherings) convened daily in the cafés of the capital. Yet neither of these concurrences suffices to explain their grouping as a generation. The reason Azorín coined the generation concept is that these writers shared a vociferous concern about "the problem of Spain": the erosion of

national prestige and power since the seventeenth century. It was the ignominious defeat of Spain by the United States in 1898 that catalyzed Valle-Inclán and his generation into a formidable voice of dissent. In their opinion the crisis of the times demanded a complete reassessment of national and personal values.

For his part Valle-Inclán met this demand decisively. His attitude toward life and art was marked by renunciation of mercenary occupations; disdain for pettiness and hypocrisy, aloofness from the mainstream of politics, religion, and literature; dissatisfaction with the social order; impatience with the self-serving nature of public and elite institutions; passionate reaction to injustice; personal purification through privation and fasting; independence on all levels; and Aristotelian "just pride." Although he realized that perfection could never be achieved in the human context, he knew as well that unless the attempt was made life would have little meaning. Recognizing this, he carefully molded everything that concerned him so that the totality he sought, in the Aristotelian sense, might be approached in the course of his lifetime.

On 28 October 1866 the maritime village of Villanueva de Arosa in Galicia, a northwestern province of Spain, witnessed the birth of the child who ultimately brought it renown. He was the scion of two once-prominent families fallen into penury and forced to live meagerly in their ancestral homes. Baptized a Catholic with the name Ramón José Simón Valle y Peña, he was the second of five children of a man who earned his living as a coastguardsman but whose literary ambition led him to write poetry, work occasionally as a journalist on his own newspaper, cultivate the friendship of prominent regional writers, and expand the impressive library of his illustrious ancestors. As a young man Valle himself began to write poems and stories, but, seeing the literary hardships endured by his father, he complied with his father's decision that he should study law at the university in Santiago de Compostela. While there he published several pieces, nonetheless, and a literary career began to hold some appeal for him. When his father died in 1890 Valle abandoned his studies and his narrow native environment to begin his adventurous public life. After a brief stay in Madrid, he journeyed to Mexico and supported himself as a journalist. There the fledgling writer and adventurer took a definitive step in creating his public image. He adopted a literary pseudonym impressive in its *hidalgo* tonality, rich in noble cadences and sonority, and expressive of high aspirations founded on the glories of a past in which his ancestors occupied places of honor. He emerged from his Mexican sojourn as Don Ramón del Valle-Inclán.

Once more in Galicia, he complemented his new name with a radical change in appearance—flowing hair and beard, large spectacles, sarape, and wide-brimmed hat. This bohemian façade became his trademark on the streets of Madrid, causing him to be dubbed "the son of Jules Verne," and remained with him the rest of his career. His impoverishment—he had abandoned journalism to pursue his art—eventually affected his health; his body refused any but the smallest amounts of simple foods, and he was forced periodically to remain in bed because of internal problems, some of which required surgery. Yet his dignity never succumbed under the stress of poverty and disease. He bore his situation stoically, adopting the theory that fasting and suffering were the means to creativity and mysticism.

Valle-Inclán became a stalwart member of several literary *tertulias.* The daily gatherings became the focus of his public life, and in them he earned the laurels of aesthetician, critic, wit, raconteur, political analyst, and guru. His influence on contemporaries through this forum was vast, as many have acknowledged. To the painters, writers, and others who gathered around his table (among them Pablo Picasso, Federico García Lorca, Rubén Darío, José Gutiérrez Solana, Gregorio Martínez Sierra, Ignacio Zuloaga, Diego Rivera, and Henri Matisse), Valle-Inclán was the standard-bearer of the tenet "art for art's sake" and an instigator of their imaginations. He became as influential in his circle as Samuel Johnson had been in his; he lacked only a Boswell to capture for posterity the pronouncements that his listeners claim were of greater import than the impressive works he left behind.

The countless anecdotes fabricated by friends and columnists attest to the decorative social manner that Valle-Inclán cultivated: he told calculated and outrageous lies of an autobiographical nature, made ironic and cynical pronouncements on all subjects, exhibited notorious behavior in public places (which included shouting during performances of plays he disliked and which brought him before magistrates on several occasions), and used robust language that was often elusive in its archaic intellectuality and Galician articulation. In 1899, during an argument with his friend the journalist Manuel Bueno, he was struck by the man's cane on his left wrist. The blow drove the cuff link into the flesh and gangrene set in a few days later. The arm had to be amputated. He later forgave Bueno and they remained lifelong friends. Valle-Inclán entertained his public on the stage of life; the loss of his arm as the result of the altercation deprived him of the proper stage he had sought in his brief career as an actor. His friends celebrated the notoriety and verve of "this grand Don Ramón of the billy-goat beard," as Darío immortalized him in a poem. It was only after Valle-Inclán's death on 5 January 1936 that his writings began to receive the attention they deserved, his controversial public figure no longer obscuring their merits.

Insofar as it is possible to describe the creative foundation of an author who produced twenty-four plays, twelve novels, seven collections of stories, three books of poetry, and assorted other titles, not to mention numerous translations and adaptations from the French, Italian, and Portuguese, it can be said that Valle-Inclán's literature, like his life, was conceived and crystallized under self-imposed aesthetic concepts. The full exposition of his ideas on creativity is found in *La lámpara maravillosa* (*The Lamp of Marvels,* 1916), subtitled "Ejercicios espirituales" (Spiritual Exercises). In this apologia Valle-Inclán fully develops the travails of the artist in rising above his humanity and in breaking the bondage of the body to set his creative spirit free in order to reach the heights of beauty. In Valle-Inclán's version of the agon, the artist becomes a mystic through a threefold aesthetic initiation: "There are three transits through which the soul passes before it is initiated into the mystery of Eternal Beauty. The first transit, painful love; the second transit, joyful love; the third transit, love with renunciation and quietude." Serving his apprenticeship by reading the teachings of the heterodox Spanish mystic Miguel de Molinos (1628–1691) and the Italian Cabalist Giovanni Pico della Mirandola (1463–1494), Valle-Inclán underwent the process of mystical-aesthetic initiation described in *The Lamp of Marvels.* His commitment to the search for creative fulfillment is visible in the concerted effort he made to actualize aesthetic principles in his literature—an effort that can be traced back to the stories issued in Spanish and Mexican periodicals prior to 1895. These early works display their author's dedication to stylistic perfection, the first hallmark of his aesthetic stance, for, he believed, "literary men will live in future anthologies because of a well-written page. Beauty resides only in form. Whoever fails to carve and polish his style will be no

more than a poor writer." This approach informed all his writings.

In 1895 he published his first book, *Femeninas: Seis historias amorosas* (On Females: Six Love Stories, 1895), which contains six tales whose protagonists are amorous Latin women. The work shows the earliest polarity in Valle-Inclán's literature: a belated romanticism that paid homage to José Zorrilla, author of *Don Juan Tenorio* (1844) and one of the idols of the emergent writer. Valle-Inclán's second book, *Epitalamio: Historia de amores* (A Tale of Love, 1897), marked the beginning of the author's dedication to the totality of creation; in it he integrated content and design to achieve an artistic whole. This personal attention to the physical aspect of his books, specifically the illustrations, was a second characteristic of Valle-Inclán's aestheticism.

While *Femeninas* passed largely unnoticed, *Epitalamio* caught the attention of several prominent critics. Clarín (Leopold Alas), who devoted an entire newspaper column in *Madrid cómico* to the slim volume, concluded that its author was a man of imagination capable of achieving a personal style but regretted that the work looked back to innovations of an earlier era namely, romanticism. Navarro Ledesma also pointed to this rearward view in a derogatory way, noting that Valle-Inclán was an exotic writer whose work contained "an excess of intellectual elegance or decadent refinement." But as Azorín noted years later, these critics did not realize that the past was merely a springboard, not a rut, for Valle-Inclán. The validity of this observation is evidenced by the author's revisions of his first books and by the way he changed their original format when they were included in his collected works, of which there were many different editions in his lifetime.

Although he had adapted Carlos Arniches' play *La cara de Dios* (The Face of God, 1900) into a novel, Valle-Inclán achieved his first literary success as a novelist with the publication of *Sonatas: Memorias del Marqués de Bradomín* (*The Pleasant Memoirs of the Mar-*

quis de Bradomín: Four Sonatas, 1902–1905). This series of four modernist novels relates the sensual life of the protagonist in autobiographical episodes allied to the four seasons. The splendid if anachronistic figure of the marquis recounts his amorous exploits from the spring of his youth to the winter of his old age; in the process he adds to the classic concept of Don Juan, who was affected solely by passion and death, the sensibility needed to appreciate his surroundings and to reminisce about the women whose lives he has indelibly touched. Bradomín moves within society only as it permits or condones, not with the satanic fury that compels Don Juan to shatter its commandments. He samples life with the gusto of the wine-taster whereas Don Juan downs one draught, finds it wanting, and then seeks desperately after another. Bradomín lives the more fully. Perhaps his is a life of delusion, but he enjoys the multifaceted experience nonetheless.

Sonata de primavera (Spring Sonata), first in the series, presents the voluptuary who was the young Bradomín. In this novel he is a papal knight with the mission of conferring the cardinal's biretta upon Estefano Gaetani, the bishop of Betulia. To that end Bradomín sets out for the Gaetani palace but arrives to find the old cleric at the point of death. Upon Gaetani's demise Bradomín's thoughts turn to María Rosario, one of the five daughters of the princess, the dead man's sister. With demonic purpose he seeks to snatch the girl from God's grasp as she is about to enter convent life. The marquis begins systematically to seduce the girl by speaking into her ear and attempting to kiss her hand. The virginal María Rosario resists the advances, although the torture of love is evident on her face and in her nervous hands. Later, driven by his passion, Bradomín enters her room through a window; yet when she faints he does no more than place her upon the bed and contemplate her innocent body. The act of breaching her bedroom, however harmless, causes complications in the household, and witchcraft is invoked against

the seducer. But Bradomín scoffs and continues his erotic game on other occasions. A final attempt to convert the girl to his pagan love fails only because of the accidental death of María Rosario's youngest sister, whom she had left unattended because of Bradomín's overtures. Half-crazed with the fever of denied passion, María Rosario turns on her adversary and blames him for the death. Bradomín departs in great melancholy. He has seduced not the body of María Rosario but her mind. And she will remain always before him to torture him with what might have been and to condemn him to remorse, although not to the point that he abandons his sybaritic life.

In *Sonata de estio* (Summer Sonata) Bradomín is discovered aboard a British frigate bound for the tropics. The need to escape from reminders of a recently terminated love affair with Lili is taking him to Mexico, where a long-neglected family estate awaits his possession. Recurring visions of Lili's beauty are interspersed with sobering sights such as the distasteful foreign faces of his shipmates ("The Anglo-Saxon race is the most contemptible on earth"). But the disdain, born of the boredom of a lengthy sea voyage, is dispelled upon his arrival in Mexico. The vibrancy and color of the tropics seduce the sensibilities of the marquis. He becomes further enmeshed in the web of sensuality by La Niña Chole, the Creole beauty of whom he becomes enamored when he sees her posed, like Salammbô, against some temple ruins. Destiny brings her ever closer to Bradomín until the two pledge their love despite her incestuous involvement with a notorious general, who is both her husband and father. When the lovers' escape is discovered by the general, he pursues them with his men. Bradomín, his life spared by La Niña Chole's intercession, watches inertly as she is taken away by the man to whom she belongs. His act of confrontation and conquest is a fine statement of *machismo* on the part of the general. But that night a shot is heard nearby, and Bradomín's reproachful thoughts are interrupted by the news that the general is dead. Suspecting the truth, Bradomín rushes out to find La Niña Chole waiting to give herself to her new king. The marquis accepts her love with a magnanimous forgiveness of her inconstancies to him.

Sonata de otoño (Autumn Sonata) is set in the Brandeso palace in Galicia, home of a noblewoman who years before had forsaken husband and daughters to become Bradomín's paramour. Two years before the novel opens, religious scruples have driven Concha to disavow her passion and to implore the marquis never to return to her side. Bradomín honors the request. But now, after two years of silence, Concha writes him of her grave illness and expresses a longing to see him once more before her death. Recalling their trysts and the ironic religiosity of his mistress praying her rosary before giving herself to his caresses, Bradomín sets out for her palace. His arrival animates the languishing woman, and they talk endlessly of their intimate past. Then, despite her feeble attempt to interpose her illness as an excuse, Bradomín seduces her again. The renaissance of love restores Concha's spirits, if not her body. But Bradomín is exalted by the new experience of possessing the fragile and funereal beauty of his mistress. He makes love to her incessantly although there is no doubt that death waits at the end of her ecstasy. And, as is fitting, Concha dies in the arms of her lover. Although tempted by the corpse's beauty, Bradomín does not succumb to necrophilia. Instead, he goes to the room of his cousin Isabel to enlist her aid in returning Concha's body to her own bed. But his effort ends in a grotesque twist: as he attempts to awaken his cousin, he is seduced by her beauty, postpones his mission, and makes love to the willing Isabel. He never reveals Concha's death to Isabel but tends to the corpse himself. He retires to a sleepless night, haunted by the accusing eyes of the crucified Christ he has passed while carrying the body of Concha. In the morning Bradomín is saddened by the loss of the woman who most loved and admired him; as he recalls in his memoirs: "I cried like an ancient god seeing his cult extinguished!"

Sonata de invierno (Winter Sonata) takes place in the Basque and Navarre regions of Spain, particularly in the city of Estella, where court is held by Don Carlos, the pretender to the Spanish throne from whom the Carlist movement derived its name. Don Carlos claimed the right of succession upon the death of his brother, Fernando VII, in 1833. But Fernando had revoked the Salic Law, which guaranteed Don Carlos the throne as the only male heir, and had replaced it with the Pragmatic Sanction, which made possible the ascension of his daughter Isabel. While most liberal elements supported the regency of María Cristina for the infant queen, the conservatives sided with Don Carlos. The result was the First Carlist War (1833–1839), a civil war which brought into being the Quadruple Alliance (Spain, England, France, and Portugal). It is this conflict that Valle-Inclán uses as the backdrop to his novel.

Sonata de invierno narrates the final season in the romantic life of Bradomín. Now grown old, the marquis recognizes that he is fated to be alone since all the great loves of his past have preceded him in death. He finds, ironically, that after having loved many and often he has entered old age unloved. His eyes fill with tears as he combs the white hair that had once been the proud mane of the romantic lion. He exits to engage in his last military battle. As he rides out, a musket ball smashes into his left arm, heralding the end of his adventurous career. Interned at a nearby convent, Bradomín watches with a clinical eye as the arm is amputated and finds in the loss a possible gain: the advantage of sympathy that women will shower upon him. Testing his new attitude, Bradomín begins the seduction of the young girl who is caring for him. He comes to suspect that the novice is his daughter, but this does not deter him; the possibility of an incestuous relationship adds spice to his desire, especially when it appears to be his last opportunity for love. He extracts words of love from the fascinated girl, but her ordeal leads her to "confess" to the mother superior. Bradomín is ordered to leave the convent he has desecrated. As he has done so many times before, the marquis departs in a melancholy mood. But now he lacks the certainty that other intrigues await him. Defeated but dignified in his acceptance of fate, Bradomín leaves Estella. He knows that he has become old and pitiable; he knows that his only future lies in recalling his past by compiling his memoirs.

The four *Sonatas,* published between 1902 and 1905, are exemplary of the artistry of Valle-Inclán in his first novelistic period. On the one hand, the series of novels brought to fruition those stylistic and aesthetic elements first manifested in earlier works, among them the use of three adjectives of differing tonality to describe the physical, moral, and intellectual aspects of a character, and the revival of archaic words. On the other hand, the four books were freed from the anarchic tendencies, youthful bravado, and archaic penchant that marred many of Valle-Inclán's first stories. The tenets that guided this new maturity were those of modernism, a Hispanic movement that had its birth in the poetry of the Nicaraguan Darío and that sought to convey the exotic through vivid imagery and metaphor. Through the skillful application of the modernist aesthetic, what Ortega y Gasset has termed "phraseological chemistry," Valle-Inclán created for himself the singular style that made him the exemplary prose writer of the movement. On a par with the poetry of Darío stands the early prose of Valle-Inclán: both are bulwarks of modernism.

Another modernist work, *Flor de santidad* (Flower of Sanctity, 1904), is the most underrated of Valle-Inclán's novels yet one of the best. Its powerful plot, played out against the mountainous landscape of Galicia, restates the author's theme of folk superstitions. In the mind of Adega, the country girl who is the novel's protagonist, a deep sense of piety is transformed into sensuality when, convinced that the pilgrim before her is Christ, she gives herself to him. In her action there is no sacrilege or pride; rather, she sees herself as another virginal girl chosen by God to fulfill his plan. In that scheme, she believes, she has been selected to be the mother of Christ's son. Holy enthusiasm urges her to publish the tale and to reveal her pregnancy to the people of her village. But the superstitious villagers conclude that Adega has been seduced by the devil's emissary. In the end, pregnant and deserted upon the death of the all-too-human pilgrim, she permits herself to be exorcised in a mass for the possessed and to be presented nude to the seven waves of the sea required to cleanse her. Unlike the raving women who accompany her through the unsavory proceedings, Adega remains calm and pensive. The holy visions that followed her sexual initiation, along with the messianic hope she harbors, sustain her and raise her above social convention. Led by ignorance to accept a common sexual act as divinely instigated, Adega acquires an unshakable, if mistaken, faith. Her devotion makes her heroic.

Subsequent novels show a trend away from the erotic themes of the *Sonatas* and *Flor de santidad* and a new literary concern with politico-historical topics. Valle-Inclán's interest in this area had begun while he was a student and intensified in Madrid at the *tertulias.* To his friends who became political figures (among them Manuel Azaña, president of the Second Republic, and Ramiro de Maeztu, ambassador to England), Valle-Inclán was a shrewd analyst who effectively synthesized history and detailed the application of such international ideologies as anarchism and Marxism in Spain. He himself ran twice for elective office but, because of his indifference toward campaigning, lost in both cases. Always the individualist, he could not be readily placed in one camp or another. In his first years as a journalist and bohemian, he admired the cause of anarchy because it represented the autonomy and authority of the individual; during his Carlist period, he was attracted by the latent power of the classic king; when he declared himself a Socialist, it was because the Spanish working classes were led by strong men like Alejandro Lerroux; his Marxism was founded on the authority and order that Vladimir Lenin had forged out of the chaos of the Russian Revolution. It was the same with his fascism. The Roman figure of Benito Mussolini draining the Pontine Marshes, leading his people toward the recovery of lost prestige, and raising out of the ruins a new imperial Rome satisfied Valle-Inclán's concept of the hero and led him to admire Mussolini, although he foresaw Mussolini's failure because of his inability to rise above personal ambition. From the start of his public career, then, Valle-Inclán demonstrated only a partial affinity to whatever ideology he favored. His larger outlook had as its premise the concept of enlightened authoritarian rule. Historical evidence, he believed, showed that the only possible way of achieving humanitarian goals was to have the ideal imposed upon society by a disciplined and selfless ruler, be he monarch, president, or dictator. These Machiavellian views are reflected in those novels that study politics in action, though his works, when dealing with politics, do so in terms of the past rather than the present.

The theme of Carlism, given its first ample treatment by Valle-Inclán in *Sonata de invierno,* reappears in the play *Voces de gesta* (Epic Voices, 1912) and in a series of novels collected under the title *La guerra carlista* (The Carlist War). The latter, a trilogy, began with *Los cruzados de la causa* (The Crusaders of the Cause, 1908), whose Galician setting removed the action from the battlefields of the war. Bradomín and his uncle, Don Juan Manuel Montenegro, act together again, this time to accomplish the former's secret mission on behalf of the Carlist cause. The plot centers on three actions—the government's search of a convent that contains a cache of rebel arms; the induction into the army of a young man and his subsequent death, resulting from the desertion of his post at the convent when conviction and duty come into conflict; and

the conveyance of the weapons away from the convent by the Carlist supporters.

The novel, replete with movement and suspense, lacks expert treatment of its subject. Valle-Inclán was to gain this expertise when, after the publication of *Los cruzados de la causa,* he made the first of many trips to the strongholds of Carlism. Accompanied by politically prominent friends who lived in the area, Valle-Inclán crisscrossed the Carlist country and became intimate not only with the geographical setting in which the cause flourished and bled but also with many of the generals and nobles who had distinguished themselves in its service. The sequels to the first novel show the mastery of detail, history, and landscape that Valle-Inclán achieved during this sojourn.

Consequently, perhaps, *El resplandor de la hoguera* (The Splendor of the Bonfire, 1909) is less a plotted novel than a sequence of episodes occurring amidst the hostilities. And although only one battle scene is described, the presence of war is pervasive. Everywhere in the work there is evidence of the bloody and frustrated history of Carlism. Everywhere, too, is visible the impartiality of the author in recounting events or depicting characters. Valle-Inclán wrote the novel without recourse to the fatiguing series of occurrences, outcomes, and dates that usually typify accounts of wars. He penetrated to the core, and the result is a view of the war as seen through the medium of selected characters and events. The vision and its presentation are poetic in that the view is impressionistic rather than purely historical and the narration given in prose replete with poetic insight. Rather than make a protagonist act out his role with the war as a backdrop, the author brought the war itself into the foreground and made the human beings involved in it part of the overall scheme of things. Similarly, when he later viewed World War I from the French lines as a correspondent, Valle-Inclán recorded a series of aesthetic impressions that he later collected in the slim volume titled *La media noche: Visión estelar de un momento de guerra* (Midnight: A Stellar Vision of a Moment of War, 1917).

The third novel in the series, however, has a historical protagonist of imposing stature in Manual Santa Cruz, a controversial priest whom the author treats with deep psychological and sociological insight. The ferocious warrior-priest, who was more a bandit than a patriot in the eyes of both government and Carlist forces, is portrayed in *Gerifaltes de antaño* (The Ancient Gyrfalcons, 1909) with a sympathy born of the recognition of his legendary viability. The cruel, despotic man is interpreted in the novel as a fanatic with a holy cause—his ideal—that makes him inflexible. In his willful dedication, he emerges in epic proportions.

Upon publication, *La guerra carlista* was compared with the *Episodios nacionales* (National Episodes, 1879–1898) of Benito Pérez Galdós and with some novels by Baroja. But Valle-Inclán's conception and treatment were vastly different. While Galdós approached reality with the historian's prudent attention to particulars of nineteenth-century Spain, Valle-Inclán selected only those aspects indispensable to his impressionistic interpretation. The external and precise depictions of the *Episodios nacionales* occupy a pole opposite to the internal and diffused portraiture of *La guerra carlista*. But this is not to contrast the two authors' abilities or preparations for the task. Valle-Inclán was no less versed in the history of the period than Galdós. However, the latter's scholarship is evident on every page, while Valle-Inclán's interpretative technique disguises his equally learned basis. Valle-Inclán has written history with the touch of an artist. He has gone beyond mere externals into that realm that Unamuno designated *intrahistoria,* history's roots in individuals. Baroja, on the other hand, did not have in him either the historian who was Galdós or the aesthetician who was Valle-Inclán. He dealt with the Carlist struggle simply because he had an interest in a remote ancestor who had been involved in it. His concern, therefore, was founded on a personal premise, and he could not tolerate any but a similar reason for involvement. Since neither Valle-Inclán nor Galdós possessed credentials of that nature, Baroja disapproved of both as historians of Carlism. But despite this characteristic objection, *La guerra carlista* is a vivid evocation of an important period. The series also consoled its author, who would have derived great personal satisfaction had he been able to participate in the intrigues of that recent past. More than aesthetic gratification, however, the works he dedicated to the cause brought him the honor of wearing the highest Carlist decoration.

Since the Bourbon hierarchy in Europe had supported Isabel's claim to the Spanish throne, Valle-Inclán's Carlist affiliation led him to an anti-Bourbon stance. The author submitted the oppressive and unenlightened government of Isabel to literary scrutiny in the cynical play *Farsa y licencia de la reina castiza* (The Farce of the Noble Queen, 1922) and in a new series of novels. The latter was an ambitious project in which Valle-Inclán set out to record the social and political events leading up to the Revolution of 1868, which deposed the queen, and the subsequent instability at home and in the colonies. The series, titled *El ruedo ibérico* (The Iberian Cycle), was to be divided into three parts, each consisting of three novels. However, Valle-Inclán lived to publish only two works in the first series, leaving the third near completion.

El ruedo ibérico treats the Spanish people's confrontation with the possibility of a bloody upheaval like the French Revolution. That such an event did not take place was a mixed blessing, in Valle-Inclán's opinion, for Spain's inability to annihilate its oppressors paved the road for future social and political disquiet. This tragic flaw in the character of nineteenth-century Spain led Valle-Inclán to mock everyone and everything responsible for this period of debacle, from those who did not comply with the duty that their positions of trust imposed on them, to the masses, who failed to take the opportunity for self-determination. *La corte de los milagros* (The Court of Miracles, 1927) looks at the moments immediately preceding Isabel's exile. The opening episode, in which the papal nuncio vests the queen with the Order of the Golden Rose for her services to the church, serves as sarcastic contrast to Isabel's concupiscent and vulgar life. Throughout the novel Valle-Inclán draws an unflattering portrait of the queen and her unsavory courtiers, pointing out their laissez-faire attitude toward social problems and their immersion in personal gratification at the cost of national dignity and empire. In *¡Viva mi dueño!* (Hurrah to the Hilt!, 1928), the second novel, the important scenes deal with various revolutionary groups that prepare the overthrow of the Isabeline regime after the death of Ramón María Narváez, prime minister and pillar of the monarchy. The opposition is further detailed in *Baza de espadas* (Intervention of Swords), published posthumously in 1958, wherein Republicans and Carlists, progressives and conservatives, plot out their intrigues from the city of Cádiz against a decadent political superstructure.

Valle-Inclán oversees the actions of his characters from an aesthetic height that they themselves cannot attain. In so doing, he adheres to a long-held maxim: "There are three ways to view characters in literature: from the knees, like Homer with his heroes; face to face, like Shakespeare with his; and by looking down on them, like Cervantes who, at every instance, believes himself more sane than Don Quijote." Valle-Inclán, one-armed like Cervantes, adopted the same aesthetic position, as the major figures in the series make clear. The Duke of Cádiz, Don Francisco de Asís de Borbón, cousin of Isabel II by nature and her husband by political expediency, is caricatured with harsh and depreciative strokes as an ineffectual man who is unable to emerge from the massive shadow of his wife or to assert himself in front of her lovers and courtiers. He is a puppet in the hands of his confessor and his barber, just as the queen is maneuvered by her religious confidante and

by an opportunistic nun, à la Rasputin. Valle-Inclán treats these regal personages as overstuffed puppets whose sawdust is trickling out of their seams. These figures make histrionic gestures and grimaces that proclaim the absurdity of a once mighty nation now ruled by such fragile, unethical, and half-witted buffoons.

Church and state alike are targets of Valle-Inclán's ire, as neither possesses the heroic base that characterized its past. The warrior-priests of the Crusades have been replaced by Tartuffians, while the knights who regained Spain from the Moors and led her to world domination have given way to foreign-bred snobs. The pharisaical pride of the Catholic church and the philistine bravado of the state in nineteenth-century Spain demeaned all sociopolitical endeavors and required of an ethical author the verbal flogging that Valle-Inclán gave these institutions. Only the masses elicit any sympathy in *El ruedo ibérico*. The inequities he had witnessed in Spain and abroad led Valle-Inclán to espouse the most drastic social reforms, especially after the successful establishment of the Communist regime in Russia. In this series of novels, as in much of his work, there is a strong defense of the masses in their quest for equity.

The theme of revolution is manifest also in *Tirano Banderas* (Banderas the Tyrant, translated as *The Tyrant*, 1926), which achieved a clamorous success totally unexpected by an author accustomed to public tepidity. The novel's first two editions were exhausted immediately, and critical opinion was lavish in its praise throughout Spain and Latin America as well as in those countries where translations appeared, including the United States. Critics were unanimous in commending *The Tyrant* as Valle-Inclán's best novel, and many ranked it among the greatest in Spanish literature. Indeed, *The Tyrant* is at the evolutionary apex of Valle-Inclán's novelistic production, representing his greatest achievement in style, plot, and characterization. This novel is an amalgam of many strains of Latin American history, language, and culture. Mexico, Cuba, and Argentina, especially, are the sources for the synthetic format since these were the countries of the Western Hemisphere that Valle-Inclán knew from firsthand experience. The information from this reconnaissance was translated into the vitality of the novel. But the author's approach goes beyond interpretative realism or authenticity. The work demonstrates once more Valle-Inclán's superior viewpoint, through which he poses society before what he called "the deforming mathematics of the concave mirror," making his characters like freaks in a carnival sideshow. The novel augments this aesthetic position with the background of a fair against which the characters act out their grotesque roles.

The Tyrant relates a moment in the history of Tierra Firme, a fictional Latin American nation whose very name is a mockery in light of the instability that characterizes its political structure. Tierra Firme is a hothouse of corruption on all levels. With sociological insight dramatized by sarcasm, Valle-Inclán unmasks hypocrisy and points accusingly at the fierce cruelty inherent in both the powerful and the downtrodden. The novel is highly democratic in that there are no individualized heroes; the novelist sees the whole social order he depicts as suspect and seeks to portray shades of degeneracy by depicting representative types.

Santos Banderas, the tyrant of the title, has been given a Christian name, meaning "holy" or "saint," that is ironic in the context of his demonic actions, and a family name, meaning "flag," that implies patriotism when in reality his dictatorial practices have strictly personal ends. The savage antics of Banderas are made possible by the acquiescence of a corrupt army and the vested interests of native and foreign businessmen. The diplomatic corps, too, especially that which represents Spain, approves of his behavior in fact but feigns disaffection in public. Even Santos Banderas must be sympathized with in the face of the hypocrisy that surrounds him.

On the antagonistic side stand the masses with their eternal plight. Their leader is Filomeno Cuevas, a rancher of Creole stock who has raised an army of Indians and other small ranchers to combat the Banderas regime. The revolution, then, is led by an amateur with no knowledge of military tactics. But the naiveté of his plan is complemented by courage and faith. The self-reliance of Cuevas, however, leads to an intense pride that corrodes his heroic possibilities; he is only too human. Likewise, the brutalities committed by the rebels lessen the likelihood of admiration for their cause. In its attempt to restore the ideals that distinguished the rebellion against Spain, the new uprising wends its way through many grotesqueries that involve the aloof as well as the participants, often tragically. Further, there is no evidence that the overthrow of the tyrant will remedy anything. But as the novel evolves the suspicion increases that the allure of power will affect the ideals of the revolution.

The themes of *The Tyrant,* often developed independently, are framed in powerful episodes that prepare for the climax of the novel. Fatally, everything is drawn together in the life of Santos Banderas. As the revolution comes to the doors of his stronghold, a former monastery, the tyrant loses control over his troops. In increasing numbers they desert to the rebels. Finally, recognizing that his power is at an end, Banderas acts resolutely for the last time. He goes to his daughter's chamber and looks at her without emotion. There is no compassion in his heart for the suffering the girl might undergo at the hands of his enemies; instead, there is the selfish dread that if she lives she will be used to mock her father. This he cannot tolerate, and he ends her life with fifteen knife thrusts. After the deed, with bloody dagger in hand, Santos Banderas stands defiantly at the window, facing the advancing rebel forces. He is cut down immediately by their rifle fire. In a matter-of-fact manner that caps the grotesqueness of the novel, the final lines detail the beheading and quartering of the dictator's corpse. The parts are distributed to the capital and four other cities, there to be displayed in public places. Ironically, these remnants of tyranny would in time become the relics that would sanctify the false patriot and thereby make literal the names of Santos Banderas.

Although his most successful writings were novels, Valle-Inclán's best work was done for the theater. He stated periodically that his works were not intended for the stage, but those denials stemmed from moments of ire at the theater's commercialism. His plays were refused production or given limited engagements too often for him not to feel bitter toward the theatrical establishment. And yet throughout his career he always sought out the theater, as actor, playwright, translator, or director; on several occasions he served as artistic director of theatrical troupes with which his wife, the actress Josefina Blanco, was associated. While these activities were not continuous, his participation in the theater was extensive and may be divided formally into three periods (1898–1899, 1903–1913, 1920–1936) during which his enthusiasm eclipsed the intermittent negativity.

For Valle-Inclán the theater was a setting for freedom: freedom of the playwright to articulate his ideas with artistic integrity, of the public to accept or reject these ideas audibly according to how much it was or was not entertained, and of the critic to comment candidly on the play's merits or faults. In vitalizing the first freedom, Valle-Inclán often encountered indifferent audiences who preferred the euphuistic melodramas of José Echegaray and the confectionary comedies of the brothers Serafín and Joaquín Alvarez Quintero. Audience and management alike failed to recognize that Valle-Inclán's plays were important steps for a dramaturgy moribund since the Siglo de Oro, Spain's Golden Age in politics, literature and the other arts (1492–1680), except for the brief life of romanticism. In exercising his right as a critic, Valle-Inclán found that his vociferousness in the theater was not appreciated when he damned a play and that at times he had to succumb to the greater authority of a

magistrate when he was carted off to face charges of disrupting the peace. Nonetheless, despite its shortcomings, it was the theater that held the promise of best fulfilling the aesthetic he espoused, and Valle-Inclán wrote for it with expectation of personal success as a dramatist.

As a playwright, he believed that the audience must be moved intellectually as well as emotionally. To achieve this dual end, he made his characters inferior to their creator and chose to oversee their activities in the style of the puppeteer; the audience too, he thought, should stand above and beyond the play's characters. Only through this alienating tactic could there be objectivity. The theater could aspire then to be both a museum and a laboratory, a place in which experience and experimentation would function jointly. To implement the museum concept, Valle-Inclán looked to the great theater of Spain's past and found in it an atmosphere that suited his needs. He savored the history and themes, traditions and superstitions, archaic names and language that its plots featured. These aspects served as a springboard for his own experimentation.

The first of Valle-Inclán's plays was *Cenizas* (Ashes, 1899), a three-act melodrama later revised and published as *El yermo de las almas* (The Barrenness of Souls) in 1908. In its definitive form, this work demonstrates a conjunction of characters, themes, and plots that had appeared earlier in stories, announcing an evolution of prose fiction into drama that was typical of much of Valle-Inclán's work. The melodrama of frustrated love presents a fallen wife who escapes with a passionate artist only to have conscience, religion, and her mother torment her into an operatic death. Like many subsequent works, the play attacks those traditional forces—religious suppression, hypocrisy, regard for reputation, and their entourage of civilized vices—that dash the illicit but sincere love of two unimportant human beings against their breakers. It is a play of emotion rising out of frustration, "Episodios de la vida íntima" (Episodes of the Intimate Life), as

Valle-Inclán chose to subtitle it. Love endures the many and separate adversities, but the individuals involved are crushed trying to preserve love's meaning against the conspiracy subverting it.

Valle-Inclán's next ventures into dramatic writing consisted of two vignettes published in 1903 and 1905 respectively. *Tragedia de ensueño* (Dream Tragedy) casts a compassionate glance at a human being whose life has been distorted by the ironic and cruel machinations of fate. The tragedy lies not in the cumulative deaths of an old woman's seven sons and their children, but in the irony that this centenarian must live on, alone, without understanding the reason for her endurance. In *Comedia de ensueño* (The *Dream Comedy*) the search for the ideal, in this case redemption, is presented in an allegorical setting reminiscent of *The Arabian Nights,* with attendant exoticism and mystery. The captain of a band of thieves returns to his mountain cave bearing a ring-laden hand he has severed from a princess; as he displays his prize, however, a stray dog enters the cave and absconds with it. The captain sets out on horseback, risking sanity and life in a search that fate has decreed futile. In these small works, Valle-Inclán already treats the absurdity of man's existence, a theme he pursued in longer plays of a later period.

In *El Marqués de Bradomín* (The Marquis de Bradomín, 1907), a three-act play, the protagonist of the *Sonatas* is depicted as a theologian and confessor of love rather than the erotic scoundrel that he was in the novels. Bradomín does not appear until the second act, and then his visits to the castle of his childhood sweetheart, Concha, are brief and full of the uneasiness of a long separation. Yet it is he and not any other of the many characters—noble, ecclesiastic, or folk—who dominates the entire drama. There are three moments in which his dramatic importance is particularly emphasized. In the first act, his impending arrival after years of absence gives rise to an intensity that peaks in the second

act. There, his presence motivates the dialogue to eloquence as the lovers meet. In the third act, his departure creates a void that, in turn, gives way to a deeply pathetic mood. Interlaced with these moments of dramatic impetus are episodes of varying import and hue: sequences in which beggars are arrayed against the backdrop of field and castle in compositions that possess all the vicious humor, candor, and folk quality of a canvas painted by the elder Brueghel.

The interaction of nobility and populace evidenced in *El Marqués de Bradomín* became a cornerstone of the playwright's work. The theme is at the core of *Las comedias bárbaras* (Barbaric Plays), dramatic biographies of distorted lives ruled by medieval traditions, pagan superstitions, and animal passions. The plots of the three plays center on Don Juan Manuel Montenegro, no longer the passing figure that he was in earlier writings but fully developed as the last of the feudal lords. The playwright makes Don Juan Manuel the only remaining pillar of a social order around whom are arrayed the dependents—his sons, mistresses, wife, servants, serfs, and countless beggars—in various horizontal and diagonal positions, as if in a painting. These people, with their fears, hatreds, and peculiarities, are contrasted with the decadent assurance of the protagonist. But ironically, it is these weaker beings who share in his dethronement, for in standing by during his fight with his sons they contribute by omission to his fall.

Cara de Plata (Silver Face), although not published until 1922, heads the trilogy and gives the first impression of Don Juan Manuel Montenegro: strong, *simpático,* romantic, and somewhat of an idealist. He is not yet the cruel husband of *Aguila de blasón* (The Emblazoned Eagle, 1907) nor the pathetic old man of *Romance de lobos* (Wolf Song, 1908). In *Cara de Plata* he is the robust *hidalgo* entrenched in his feudal traditions, a stance that prompts the drama's social explicitness. The plot shows the interplay of classes on many levels as indignation rises and develops into hostility when the law upholds the right of Don Juan Manuel to stop the unauthorized crossing of his lands, thus severing the most direct access to the market for peasants and others. Also inconvenienced is the abbot, who is prevented from traversing the owner's bridge by Cara de Plata, one of Don Juan Manuel's sons, in a show of justice to a group of peasants previously denied access. But while these only murmur and complain, accepting the bitter ruling of the powerful court, the abbot seeks vengeance for the public affront to his dignity and status, a vanity that ultimately reveals his corrupt nature. He savors the possibility of revenge when he learns that his niece, Isabelita, is living incestuously with her godfather, Don Juan Manuel. Enveloped by the miasmatic custody exercised by her lover, Isabelita has been initiated into the torture of loving love's warlock. The perplexity of her condition is visible in the final act, when, as the abbot arrives to retrieve the errant girl, she finds she cannot loose the bonds that tie her to a profane love. Don Juan Manuel gloats over his new victory. This is the second unbearable insult to the abbot, who cannot accept the rebuke by turning the other cheek. He threatens his adversary with excommunication and damnation—worthless anathemas in the presence of the Devil's own disciple.

Intense pride burns in both men—in the one as the outgrowth of his heritage and self-sufficiency and in the other as the substitute for moral rectitude and faith. And so it is that in the final moments of the drama, as the priest faces Don Juan Manuel in a last attempt to overthrow the court order, he is again defeated, this time in front of a great public gathered to watch the struggle between the representatives of church and state. His inability to defend the faith and his discrediting at the hands of the feudal lord reduce the abbot to a mere charlatan. Left without the chalice and the Sacred Species he has blasphemed openly, the abbot retreats in panic. Cara de Plata reacts to this conflict with shocked disbelief. Since he does not know about the abbot's own sacrilegious acts, to him Don Juan Manuel's blasphemy seems ghastly and irreparable. This provides one reason for the son's loss of respect for his progenitor; the second and most important reason is his discovery that his father has seduced Isabelita, the woman Cara de Plata loves. Left without Isabelita's love because she has chosen his father, and having lost all respect for Don Juan Manuel, Cara de Plata mounts his horse and rides off. Like the bandit captain in *The Dream Comedy,* he searches for redemption, unaware of the tortures to be endured before such mercy might be found. Don Juan Manuel has lived many more years and has still to find his own redemption; his son has ahead of him that elusive search which shaped his father into a cynical egocentric, a search that will cease only with the end of his time.

Aguila de blasón, written in five acts, is conceived in terms of Don Juan Manuel's legendary stature, in which are mixed ravenous passion, personal magnetism, and animal instinctiveness. Fierce against his enemies, a law unto himself, and disdainful of those who show him love, Don Juan Manuel is the personification of self-indulgence. His rampant unfaithfulness and sardonic disregard for his wife's feelings, his demonic possession of Isabelita in a strange bond of sexual and menial servitude, and his lordly demands on the miller's eager wife, acceded to by her husband when his rent is waived, combine to highlight the protagonist's hyperactive libido. Don Juan Manuel is incapable of experiencing a sincere emotion; nothing touches him deeply or long unless it is an affront to his seignorial dignity. Even Isabelita's attempted suicide by drowning has only a tepid effect on the aging *hidalgo,* and there is no more than remorse in his compliance with his wife's demand that he leave the ancestral house as a punishment for the most blatant of his seductions. He departs in the company of his grotesque buffoon and the miller's wife. In the end, Don Juan Manuel is pathetic rather than tragic, for his life lacks the momentous recognition that defined the hero of classical tragedy. Only another absurdity in a world full of figures without focus, Don Juan Manuel declines in stature; his proud eagle stance has become the four-legged pose of the wild beast.

Romance de lobos is the three-act conclusion to the *Comedias bárbaras*. Immediately, it creates an unholy aura of superstition and witchcraft as a drunken Don Juan Manuel, riding alone after the celebration of a local festival, encounters (envisions?) an unearthly funeral procession near a roadside cemetery. Through this experience he discovers that his wife, Dona María, is dying and sets out for her estate to seek pardon for his nefarious acts against their marriage. On the way he meets a band of beggars and, befriending them in a rare moment of humility undoubtedly inspired by his recent unnerving experience, he persuades them to accompany him. The unusual group hurry to their various destinies. On arriving, Don Juan Manuel is met with the news of a double tragedy: his wife has died, and five of their sons have despoiled the ancestral castle. Prostrate with grief at not being able to seek his wife's forgiveness, Don Juan Manuel labels himself her murderer. But his belated remorse is meaningless since expiation is no longer possible. Recognizing this, he abandons the estate to his rapacious sons and prepares to die. He retires to a cave near the sea to await his end.

This refusal to face life is not to be permanent, however. The anguished cries of a mother and her children who have been mistreated by the reigning sons, coupled with the growing complaints of other beggars, renew Don Juan Manuel's interest in resuming his rightful place so that justice may be administered again. Gathering the beggars about him as a motley army and inspiring them with revolutionary zeal, the former feudal lord storms the castle gates. He faces his sons with characteristic pride and passion. But weakened by his penitence, he cannot match the strength of his son Mauro. He falls from Mauro's single blow, dealt with the force of Freudian release. There is a stunned silence until one of the beggars, a gigantic leper, fanatically attacks Mauro. Both fall into the flames of the hearth, but only the leper rises. The chorus of incensed poor proclaim the dead Don Juan Manuel as their father while the real sons of the old *hidalgo*, incapable of any but egotistic emotions, curse their lot and the likely result of their murderous act.

The mixed ending proposes no solutions. The wolves have fought among themselves, and two have died. Yet other wolves and other victims remain to fulfill nature's cruel requirements for balance. Don Juan Manuel, once the invincible beast, became too human in his personal remorse and social compassion to survive the expectations of the masses and the onslaught of his untamed offspring. Unaccustomed to his chosen role as leader of the poor, Don Juan Manuel is not effective in redressing wrongs. Since there is no future for him in his avocation, he must die. His demise augurs the fall of the old order. Later, Valle-Inclán's prognostication took on new meaning with the rise of Communism.

If the *Comedias bárbaras* posit that the human condition is often convulsive regardless of one's social status, *Voces de gesta* proposes that disillusionment is no less a constituent of life's absurdity. Although its setting is not defined and its period not stated, this *Tragedia pastoril en tres actos* (Pastoral Tragedy in Three Acts) is a further treatment of Carlism; it expresses lyrically the brave but futile efforts of a people (personified in the shepherdess Ginebra) to restore Carlino to his rightful throne. In the end, her vengeance executed, the blind Ginebra presents her king a trophy—the head of his adversary. The triumph uncovers not the resurgence of hope that she had come to expect in the uncrowned monarch but rather a lack of will that keynotes his political pessimism. The specter of death that Carlino has become wanders alone into the mountains stoically. Ginebra is no longer the symbol of a people striving on behalf of its rightful king because he is no longer a king striving and suffering for his people. The unanimity of the cause has become the single purpose of mere individuals—Carlino and Ginebra. In pointing to this shift, Valle-Inclán traced the reality of the Carlist movement: by the time this work appeared in 1912, Don Carlos, grandson of the original claimant, had abandoned Spain and his hopes to die in Italy in 1909, and the movement had become less a possibility than a historical memento. The epic voices that characterized Carlism at its inception had become disgruntled murmurs of no political consequence; there were no more Carlist wars. Valle-Inclán's verse tragedy is a suitable epitaph for Carlism in the wake of apathy among its upper- and lower-class supporters.

The theme of the interplay between nobility and populace has other expressions in Valle-Inclán's dramas. *Cuento de abril* (April Tale, 1910) versifies the plight of a haughty Infante (prince) of Castile who travels to Provençe to woo a gentle princess and, unable to wrest her love from a sentimental troubador, returns to his kingdom perplexed over the girl's choice. In this instance a commoner overcomes the social barriers, and his instrument is love. The same goal is attempted but not reached in the farce *La Marquesa Rosalinda* (The Marchioness Rosalinda, 1913), whose central plot pivots on another commoner. Arlequín occupies the apexes of two triangles—the one completed by the Marchioness Rosalinda and her husband, the Marquis d'Olbray, the other by Colombina and her husband, Pierrot. By his amorous involvement with both women, representing the upper and lower sectors of society respectively, Arlequín directly engenders all the action or otherwise motivates it. Finally, after many intrigues, the jealousy of Colombina and the enticements of Rosalinda are cast aside by the disillusioned Arlequín. He sets out from the court with his comedians, a sad but wiser man for having barely emerged unscathed from his foray into the upper social stratum.

Another who seeks to venture into that realm where royalty dwells is the protagonist of *Farsa de la enamorada del rey* (The Farce of the Girl Who Loved the King, 1920), a poetic drama in three acts set in the eighteenth century. Here two traditions—folk and courtly—are depicted on parallel planes, coexisting but mutually exclusive. Each has run on its own course until the tavern girl Mari-Justina's romantic inclination for the elderly king inspires the possibility of a union. When the young girl sees the monarch face to face, however, romantic ideals vanish and love retreats. But the monarch understands only too well and magnanimously unites Mari-Justina and Lotario, the minstrel who has loved her in vain. He also rewards Lotario's self-sacrifice in giving way to the king for the sake of the girl's happiness; he names Lotario adviser to the throne. When the king raises the poet to the high post and dismisses his previous counselors (hypocrites all), an ideal is satisfied: the kingdom has been placed under the best of plebeian influences, that of the poet. The Aristotelian dream, which Valle-Inclán shared but could not see fulfilled in his own life, becomes an accomplished and salutary fact in this play.

While *La enamorada del rey* traces the high aspirations of a common girl, *La reina castiza* portrays a highborn character's descent to the lowest vulgarity. In this caricatural play Isabel II is treated with a venomous candor that surpasses that of *La corte de los milagros.* The play, like the novel, is a tirade against the Bourbon monarchy and the queen who was its embodiment in Spain. Valle-Inclán interprets the reign of Isabel as an absurd moment in Spanish history in which cardboard figures abounded. Of these, the queen was the most grotesque. The play portrays her as totally amoral in her notorious affairs with men from all social levels, affairs that often benefit them but never damage her because she purchases respectability by means of royal appointments.

The high-spiritedness of most of these plays belies this author's deep concern with the social and political inequities that marked European life in the period of World War I. The times were too severe for reality to be relegated to a secondary role, and Valle-Inclán recognized the need to write about anguish and frustration, both of which he knew intimately. As a poet, he had already made his statement in *La pipa de kif* (The Pipe of Kif, 1919). He found it necessary to state his concern also in his dramas. He did so through a group of plays designated *Esperpentos,* an archaic term, referring to unpleasant sights, that Valle-Inclán restored and applied to absurd or disjointed persons or situations. In these sui generis dramatizations of life's grotesqueness, man's psyche and environment are explored, and the findings are amplified and deformed as if in a concave funhouse mirror. The result is a distortion that accentuates the absurdity of human existence.

In *Luces de bohemia* (*Lights of Bohemia,* 1924) the process first takes dramatic form. This is a drama in fifteen scenes that traces the final hours in the bitter life of Máximo Estrella, a poet blinded by syphilis who has struggled for recognition only to witness the deterioration of hope. His life moves steadily toward its pathetic denouement while the grotesqueries of existence become increasingly visible in the incidence of irony, cynicism, baseness, lewdness, opportunism, mockery, and alienation. The dissonance of life becomes the reality of Máximo Estrella.

Lacking funds with which to support his family after the loss of his newspaper column, Max proposes collective suicide to his wife but postpones the idea because of their daughter's youth and his own lingering hope. As he has done before, he sets out to seek fortune on the streets of Madrid. In the company of Don Latino, an opportunist who poses as a friend, Max embarks on a mission that takes him throughout the city: to the bookshop of Zaratustra, where he argues in vain for a better price for his books and discusses the state of Spain; to a tavern containing an array of low-life types that seem to have stepped out of the works of Miguel de Cervantes, Francisco Quevedo, and Francisco Goya; through streets full of rioting workers; to a bakery where he obtains a lottery ticket

with the money from the sale of his cape and where he encounters other modernists whom he joins in their political tirades, only to be arrested as a drunkard. In a dark dungeon he holds a conversation with another prisoner, an anarchist, discoursing on the decadence of the Spanish political system until that very evil itself enters the cell in the person of an official summoning the youth to his death as Max sits by helplessly. The angry modernists, meanwhile, appear in the offices of a sympathetic newspaper to ask the editor's assistance in their protest against the jailing of their friend. The corruption of the police is emphasized when a single telephone call to the ministry results in the order to free Max. Before leaving his captors, however, the blind poet bursts into the office of an official, a friend from the happier past. Demanding an apology for his arrest, he receives instead a few bills and the promise of a monthly income. Ironically, the money is to be taken from the police fund.

Unwisely, but in typical fashion, Max squanders the money he has just received and spends the rest of the night on the streets of the capital with Don Latino at his side. As dawn approaches and dampness penetrates to his bones, Max returns to his own street. In a gruesome voice he speaks of burials to a bemused Don Latino. Resignedly, Max lies down on his portal to die while his cynical companion, tiring of what he thinks is a macabre joke, takes Max's wallet for safekeeping. Soon, the body of Máximo Estrella is discovered by his neighbors. His death has left two women to mourn in the company of the modernists and a drunken Don Latino. But a new figure enters the scene. Basilio Soulinake declares authoritatively that Max is not dead but only in a cataleptic seizure. The concierge contradicts him, and the ridiculous argument is carried on over the corpse and in the presence of his family. The finality of this proof causes Max's daughter to beat her head against the floor. The burial accomplished, two philosophic gravediggers rest from their task while the somber figures of Bradomín and

Darío pay their last respects. In the meantime, the drunken Don Latino has returned to the tavern, where he squanders the prize money won by Max's lottery ticket. The news that two women have committed suicide interrupts the festivities in the tavern; there is no doubt that they are Max's widow and daughter. The final irony is that the prize money stolen by Don Latino could have prevented all the deaths had the characters been more patient and not resigned themselves to death.

This work is the dramatized biography of the flamboyant bohemian Alejandro Sawa, who was born in 1862 and died under conditions not unlike those described by Valle-Inclán. The unheralded life and degrading death of Sawa verified the absurdity of existence for the dramatist, and he created *Lights of Bohemia* in that cast. A further irony is that in the play Max fathoms this absurdity and founds the definition of the new genre *Esperpento* on it:

> Our tragedy is not real tragedy. . . . [It is] an *Esperpento*. . . . Classic heroes reflected in concave mirrors create the *Esperpento*. The tragic sense of Spanish life can be re-created only through an aesthetic that is systematically deformed. . . . The most beautiful images, when seen in a concave mirror, become absurd. . . . My present aesthetic is to transform classic norms through the mathematics of the concave mirror.
>
> (*Obras completas*, 1944, pp. 597–599)

In expressing these precepts and defying the aesthetics that society holds sacred, Máximo Estrella becomes the symbol of the individual confronting traditional values and structures that he finds inadequate, even corrosive. But his ideality does not effect a change because society at large has accepted what it has inherited. Máximo Estrella and his real-life counterpart defied tradition and society; as a consequence they forfeited their lives.

In Valle-Inclán's drama, the bitterness of *Lights of Bohemia* is never repeated in the same harsh tone. But there are other plays that portray the range of human frailty and social vices with the satirical gusto and planned distortion of the *Esperpento*. *Divinas palabras* (*Divine Words*, 1920) is exemplary in this regard. In this play Valle-Inclán's interpretation of rural Galicia's reality (sorrow, drudgery, death) encompasses the grotesque, both in situation and in characterization. This tragicomedy shows that the bucolic, too, can be seen in the distortive mirror. *Divine Words* is a tale of sexuality told in terms of repression and license with the added spice of farcical elements. The play is populated by assorted types: beggars, hucksters, peasants, a blind man, a pilgrim, a soldier, an innkeeper, a troupe of children, and a seamstress. With these very human characters in bold relief despite their minor roles, the playwright proceeds to delineate the moral depravity to which they and the principals have fallen.

The play opens with the sexton Pedro Gailo outside the village church; his righteousness is seen immediately as he soliloquizes on the vagrancy of those he observes. The entrance of Lucero and his mistress Poca Pena gives a focus to his words. The two sit on the curb arguing over the fate of their illegitimate child, and when Lucero strikes his woman, the sexton intervenes. The nomad receives the tongue-lashing with an amused look. Although the conflict between the two men has been established over a woman, its roots go deeper, for Pedro Gailo recognizes in Lucero all the social and moral vices he despises yet secretly longs to emulate. Lucero, with his animal magnetism, amorality, paternal laxity, and inherent cruelty, is the antithesis of Pedro Gailo. The difference will be underscored when Lucero makes the sexton a cuckold.

Mari-Gaila, wife of Pedro Gailo and the third of the leading characters, appears in the third scene accompanied by her daughter. She learns of her sister-in-law's sudden death, and as if triggered automatically, she throws out her arms and with an ancient, tragic rhythm begins a plaintive monologue. The women around her echo the chant. After the brief ritual mourning, the practical Mari-Gaila establishes her claim to the dead woman's chief possession: her idiot child. The hydrocephalic dwarf had been carted about by his mother as a prop for her begging, and Mari-Gaila is anxious to inherit the grotesque Laureano. Desire for monetary gain motivates a counter-claim as well. The dead woman's sister and Mari-Gaila face each other; the struggle seems inconclusive until a minor official intervenes, like Solomon, to suggest a shared ownership of the idiot, each to have him for three days with Sunday as a day of rest. The agreement is celebrated with liquor, and even the dwarf is given his portion after he performs his freak-ish sounds and makes grotesque faces.

At the fair where she goes to display Laureano's unusually prominent genitals, Mari-Gaila meets Lucero and promises to see him later. The tryst is held in a deserted shack on the beach. Meanwhile, disturbed by taunts about his wife's dishonorable behavior, Pedro Gailo returns home in a drunken stupor and sharpens a butcher's knife. His daughter tries to deter his plan of killing her mother but succeeds only in stirring an incestuous lust in him. Afraid of his intent but resolved to overcome him, Simoniña grapples with her father as he caresses her body. But the girl subdues him and puts him to bed, retiring to a safe corner where she awaits her errant mother. Mari-Gaila and Lucero stroll through the fair like two innocent lovers, an old beggar having been entrusted with the dwarf so that the illicit pair may be together. However, Mari-Gaila pays for her momentary pleasure when she returns and finds that Laureano has died in an epileptic fit brought on by an excessive amount of alcohol that some men had forced on him. Her daughter is elected to sneak the cart containing the body to its co-owner who discovers the horrible sight of Laureano being devoured by two hogs the following morning.

Ultimately, Pedro Gailo accepts the responsibility for the dwarf's burial. Lucero returns to witness the preparations, and soon he is again mocking the sexton with his wife. But this time their intimacy is witnessed by a group of field hands. Lucero flees alone, but Mari-Gaila isn't fleet enough. Dogs and men chase her as she flees half-naked; then, in an attempt to satisfy the lust of her pursuers, she stops and removes the rest of her clothing. The men place her in a cart and wheel her into the village where bells announce an important occurrence. As the townspeople gather, Pedro Gailo watches from the belfry. The shock of what he sees makes him fall from his perch. He recovers in time to greet his wife with book and candle—which, along with the bell, were the priestly instruments of exorcism—while the neighbors hurl insults and stones at Mari-Gaila. The sexton utters the words Christ spoke in defense of the prostitute in the Gospel, but it isn't until he utters the divine words in Latin, the mystery of which has a magical effect, that the crowd disperses. Pedro Gailo completes the apotheosis by leading the repentant adulteress through the cemetery into the church. The trajectory symbolizes both their rebirths into proper Christianity.

Divine Words is one of the masterworks of Valle-Inclán. Not only does it give evidence of the playwright's control of dramatic form and dialogue but it also becomes universal in its sensitive treatment of the human condition, achieved through such finely drawn characters as Pedro Gailo and Mari-Gaila. In Lucero he has created a memorable satyr—half-human, half-satanic—who, despite his erotic nature, has nothing in common with the finesse of a Bradomín; Lucero is the embodiment of the paganism that lies beneath the veneer of civilized man, more so than Arlequín in *La Marquesa Rosalinda* or Don Juan Manuel Montenegro in the *Comedias bárbaras*.

Among other plays that treat the theme of rural Galicia are three small works. In *La rosa de papel* (The Paper Rose, 1924) a drunken Simeón Julepe is hammering at his forge while his wife Floriana lies dying in the same room. Her pleas for peace at her last moments have no immediate effect on the insensate man, but he finally starts to leave to avoid her whimpering. Before doing so, however, he attempts to discover where his wife has hidden the money she has saved for their three children. Frustrated in his efforts, he leaves the dying woman alone. But after her death, he uncovers the cache in a grotesque scene in which the cadaver is displaced while the search is made. His avarice transforms the tragedy of human death into a burlesque. The infernal attitude of the husband before the demise of his wife and his subsequent stupor after a visit to the tavern annotate the alienation of love and, indeed, of all emotion in his life. Julepe's final manifestations of love, as he addresses and embraces the corpse, are not the result of a belated realization of how much he loved his wife; rather, they are blind offerings in a ritual mourning, made all the more grotesque by the man's inebriation. His physical awkwardness, reflecting the instability of his spirit, causes the fire that consumes man and wife at the end of the drama.

Sacrilegio: Auto para silvetas (Sacrilege: A Play for Silhouettes, 1924), the second work, is set in a thieves' lair reminiscent of the one in *Dream Comedy*. Although the piece is designated a play of shadows, light (or its absence) plays an important role in creating atmosphere and in defining the characters. Identity is diffused by the half-light of the torch, by the darkness of blindfolded eyes, and by the falsification of names and voices. It is fitting that identification be hindered in this manner, for, as Dante has indicated, thieves lose their identities as punishment for depriving others of property (an extension of identity). But Valle-Inclán takes his plot a step further. Frasquito, one of the thieves, has been sentenced by his companions to die for his avarice. Despite the condemnation, Frasquito treats his former cohorts with contempt. Being a practical man and realizing that there is no reprieve from his sentence, he asks only that he be permitted a last sexual fling and that a priest be called to hear his confession. The thieves take advantage of Frasquito's deafness and his temporary inability to see (because of being blindfolded) to discuss the two requests, concluding that

only the second will be granted, if sacrilegiously. Instead of bringing a real priest, one of the group poses as a monk. Blindfolded and deaf, Frasquito does not recognize the impostor. He begins his confession, and his sincerity moves the thieves. But before his words can soften their hearts, their leader silences the penitent with a blast from his rifle. The play ends immediately.

The termination of Frasquito's life is shocking. However, even more horribly shocking is the realization that by killing him when he did the leader of the band deprived Frasquito of redemption. His soul will be damned for all eternity. Or will it? The answer, if there is one, centers on the question of faith. Frasquito confessed his sins with real repentance to one he believed was a priest; his sorrow was evident and moving, as the reaction of the thieves attests. Does it matter that Padre Veritas was an impostor? Does it matter that Frasquito did not receive absolution, even under these fictitious circumstances? Is sorrow sufficient, or does sanctification by a duly instituted authority have to be given? These are the crucial questions posed by the sudden death of the thief. They are moot ones, except in the context of faith. The play ends with an irony characteristic of Valle-Inclán: by executing Frasquito the leader has "saved" his horde of thieves from reform and redemption; in effect, he may have condemned them all, including himself. Which is the sacrilege?

In the third of the plays, *Ligazón: Auto para silvetas* (Blood Pact: A Play for Silhouettes, 1926), the dramatist again employs light and darkness to give his characters the quality of silhouettes. Against the brilliance of the moon, profiles acquire an aura of unreality. The static luminosity of heavenly bodies and the reflection of their light on objects contrast with the dynamic shadows of characters in the night landscape, set blackly against the moon. In this visual sensuality words seem discordant echoes. The characters speak of marital arrangements, of passion, of love's prostitution, of demonic pacts, of death, but it is action (movement and gesture) that paces the play. The sensual girl who is the protagonist of the piece refuses to sell herself to a rich old man and binds herself instead to a knife-sharpener in a ritual blood pact. In the unholy union of two bloods a victim is needed; and in the darkness of the setting the unfortunate old suitor is sacrificed by the pair. The Devil has received his due.

Macabre plays of avarice, lust, and death, *La rosa de papel, Sacrilegio,* and *Ligazón* are powerful pieces worthy of the Grand Guignol theater in Paris in their dramatic effects and interpretations of humanity's baseness. They remind mankind that it possesses terrible demonic tendencies and that these may rise from the caverns of the subconscious at any time to affect the course of life, either for individuals or for a large segment of society.

Yet another thematic vein was explored in *Los cuernos de Don Friolera* (Don Friolera's Horns, 1925), *Las galas del difunto* (The Corpse's Regalia, 1926), and *La hija del capitán* (The Captain's Daughter, 1927), three plays collected in *Martes de Carnaval* (Shrove Tuesday, 1930). These three *Esperpentos* are strongly anti-militaristic, deriving their inspiration from the abuses and corruption of the Primo de Rivera regime together with the foreign fiascos of Spanish arms. Although the dictator had been forced into a French exile in 1929, a military figure still controlled the Spanish government when the anthology was published, and so it was not anticlimactic. The collection's provocative title predicted that the excesses of carnival would be followed by the privation of Ash Wednesday. The outlandish masks of the revelers were, in effect, replaced by somber faces in the Lenten period that followed Primo de Rivera's exile and culminated in civil war.

Los cuernos de Don Friolera is the best of these three *Esperpentos.* In it the plot of the cuckold provides the framework for a satire that exposes the inanity of social conventions and debunks the type of drama that thrives on hackneyed themes. Thus the play is both a social and a theatrical document: the prologue and epilogue that frame the twelve scenes of the *Esperpento* make clear Valle-Inclán's attitude on the second point while the play proper discloses his social commentary.

As the prologue commences Don Estrafalario and Don Manolito, peripatetic intellectuals, are seen conversing against the active background of a fair. Through the former Valle-Inclán expresses his theory on laughter with statements that parallel those of his contemporary Henri Bergson: "Tears and laughter arise from the contemplation of elements which are on a par with us. . . . We reserve our mockery for that which relates to us. . . . My aesthetic requires the surpassing of pain and laughter, as in the case of dead men telling each other tales of the living." The treatment of emotions on the stage was a serious concern for Valle-Inclán, and he vehemently opposed those writers who, like Echegaray, abused the comic and the tragic muse in order to achieve a momentary reaction from the audience. The sublimation of emotion, as Don Estrafalario states, represents a first step in preparing the audience for objectivity. It is this process that *Los cuernos de Don Friolera* implements.

The first step, as the prologue indicates, is to eclipse reality. This is done through a puppet show presented at the fair before an expectant crowd that includes Don Estrafalario and Don Manolito. The fantasy of the show unfolds as the cuckold Friolera, indifferent to the infidelity of his mistress, is goaded into killing her as a point of honor. The prodding of the puppeteer brings on the indignation that leads to the execution. But before Friolera can be imprisoned by the same society that demanded his act of ablution, he is told by the puppeteer how to revive his victim. The playlet ends on this burlesque note. This plot is paralleled in the play proper, as well as in a third interpretation narrated in the epilogue. However, each version contains variants, and together they provide three views of the theme: fantasy, reality, legend.

In the middle version, Lieutenant Astete is

troubled not so much by his wife's infidelity as by the strict military code that demands that the cuckold salve his honor and that of his regiment with the blood of both wife and lover. After much indecision, the pressure of his superiors forces him to act. As his wife and daughter prepare to flee from the imminent danger under cover of darkness, Astete fires his pistol. He soon discovers that he has killed his daughter. His commanding officer honors his request to intern himself in a sanitarium. In the epilogue, a blind man sings a romance in which the cuckold has become a folk hero. Don Manolito and Don Estrafalario, sitting in a jail cell accused as anarchists, listen to the epic; the latter expresses his preference for the fantasy of the puppet show.

This and all the *Esperpentos* make caricatures of the characters. This dehumanization destroys all possibility of attachment or sympathy. But it is not the dramatist who creates the grotesqueness that the *Esperpento* contains; he merely takes a superior position, like the puppeteer, and surveys the activities below. What he observes is that modern man is unable to cope with his burden:

> Life—its events, sorrows, loves—is ever the same, fatally. What changes are the characters, the protagonists, of life. Those roles were previously played by gods and heroes. . . . Today, destiny is the same, fate is the same, greatness is the same, pain is the same . . . but the shoulders are different, minuscule for the support of that great weight. Out of that stems contrast, disproportion, the ridiculous.
>
> (as quoted in *La vida altiva de Valle-Inclán*, p. 114)

Valle-Inclán has given Friolera the same tragic base that Shakespeare gave Othello, but he has purposely taken away his greatness and humanity to create the *Esperpento*. Similarly, Máximo Estrella has been exiled from any pity because Valle-Inclán has consciously excluded the nobility of the tragic hero from his composition. In both cases, as in all the *Esperpentos*, it is impossible for an audience to experience a catharsis, for it is the playwright's desire to estrange emotions so that reason may prevail. In achieving this plateau, Valle-Inclán anticipated the alienatory theater of Bertolt Brecht.

Rather than encourage empathetic response in his audiences, as did classic tragedy, Valle-Inclán opted to foster their objective exploration of the enigma of human existence. This approach was more appropriate to the times, he believed. The *Esperpento* concerns itself with sociopolitical injustice, the instability of interpersonal relationships, the oppressive reliance on tradition, the subservience of the populace to superstitions (including religion), and the implausibility of selflessness in contemporary life. Because it attains its goals so admirably, the *Esperpento* is the apogee of the playwright's efforts and helps establish him as a major figure in Spanish drama; because it views life in an absurdist mode, the *Esperpento* marks Valle-Inclán as the precursor of Samuel Beckett and Eugène Ionesco.

Selected Bibliography

EDITIONS

INDIVIDUAL WORKS

PROSE

Femeninas: Seis historias amorosas. Pontevedra, 1895.
Epitalamio: Historia de amores. Madrid, 1897.
La cara de Dios. Madrid, 1900.
Sonata de otoño: Memorias del Marqués de Bradomín. Madrid, 1902.
Jardín umbrío. Madrid, 1903.
Sonata de estío: Memorias del Marqués de Bradomín. Madrid, 1903.
Corte de amor. Madrid, 1903.
Sonata de primavera: Memorias del Marqués de Bradomín. Madrid, 1904.
Flor de santidad: Historia milenaria. Madrid, 1904.
Sonata de invierno: Memorias del Marqués de Bradomín. Madrid, 1905.

Los cruzados de la causa: La guerra Carlista, I. Madrid, 1908.

El resplandor de la hoguera: La guerra Carlista, II. Madrid, 1909.

Gerifaltes de antaño: La guerra Carlista, III. Madrid, 1909.

La lámpara maravillosa. Ejercicios espirituales. Madrid, 1916.

La media noche: Visíon estelar de un momento de guerra. Madrid, 1917.

Tiranos Banderas. Novela de Tierra Caliente. Madrid, 1926.

La corte de los milagros: El ruedo ibérico, I. Madrid, 1927.

¡Viva mi dueño!: El ruedo ibérico, II. Madrid, 1928.

Baza de espadas: El ruedo ibérico, III. Barcelona, 1958.

DRAMA

Cenizas: Drama en tres actos. Madrid, 1899.

El Marqués de Bradomín: Coloquios románticos. Madrid, 1907.

Aguila de blasón: Comedia bárbara. Barcelona, 1907.

Romance de lobos: Comedia bárbara. Madrid, 1908.

El yermo de las almas: Episodios de la vida íntima. Madrid, 1908.

Cuento de abril. Madrid, 1910.

Voces de gesta: Tragedia pastoríl. Madrid, 1912.

La Marquesa Rosalinda: Farsa sentimental y grotesca. Madrid, 1913.

El embrujado: Tragedia de Tierras de Salnés. Madrid, 1913.

Divinas palabras: Tragicomedia de aldea. Madrid, 1920.

Farsa de la enamorada del rey. Madrid, 1920.

Farsa y licencia de la reina castiza. Madrid, 1922.

Cara de Plata: Comedia bárbara. Madrid, 1923.

Luces de bohemia. Madrid, 1924.

Los cuernos de don Friolera: Esperpento. Madrid, 1925.

Tablado de marionetas para educación de príncipes. Madrid, 1926. Contains the plays *La enamorada del rey, La cabeza del dragón,* and *La reina castiza.*

Retablo de la avaricia, la lujuria, y la muerte. Madrid, 1927. Contains the plays *Ligazón, La rosa de papel, El embrujado, La cabeza del Bautista,* and *Sacrilegio.*

Martes de Carnaval: Esperpentos. Madrid, 1930.

Contains the plays *Las galas del difunto, Los cuernos de don Friolera,* and *La hija del capitán.*

POETRY

Aromas de leyenda: Versos. Madrid, 1907.

La pipa de kif. Madrid, 1919.

El pasajero: Claves líricas. Madrid, 1920.

Claves líricas: Versos. Madrid, 1930.

COLLECTED WORKS

Opera Omnia de Don Ramón del Valle-Inclán. Madrid, 1941–1943; Madrid, 1954. This series of individual volumes of Valle-Inclán's works, never completed, was begun by Editorial Rúa Nueva in 1941–1943, and subsequently expanded by Editorial Plenitud in 1954.

Obras completas de Don Ramón del Valle-Inclán. 2 vols. Madrid, 1944; 2d ed., 1952; 3d ed., 1954. First edition published by Talleres Tipográficos de Rivadeneyra, subsequent editions by Editorial Plenitud.

TRANSLATIONS

Divine Words. Translated by Edwin Williams. In *Modern Spanish Theater,* edited by George Wellworth and Michael Benedikt. New York, 1968.

The Dragon's Head: A Fantastic Farce. Translated by May Heywood Broun. In *Poet Lore Plays,* series 2. Boston, 1919.

The Dream Comedy. Translated by Murray Paskin and Robert O'Brien. *La voz* 6:7–9 (1961).

"The Golden Rose." Translated by Warre B. Wells. In *Great Spanish Short Stories,* edited by Julian G. Gorkin. Boston, 1932.

The Lamp of Marvels. Translated by Robert Lime. West Stockbridge, Mass., 1986.

Lights of Bohemia. Translated by Edwin Williams. In *Modern Spanish Theater,* edited by George Wellworth and Michael Benedikt. New York, 1968.

"My Sister Antonia." Translated by Harriet de Onís. In *Spanish Stories and Tales,* edited by Harriet de Onís. New York, 1956.

The Pleasant Memoirs of the Marquis de Bradomin: Four Sonatas. Translated by May Heywood Broun and T. Walsh. New York, 1924.

The Tyrant: A Novel of Warm Lands. Translated by Margarita Pavitt. New York, 1929.

Valle-Inclán: Autobiography, Aesthetics, Aphorisms. Edited and translated by Robert Lima. Privately published, Monaca, Pa., 1966.

RAMÓN DEL VALLE-INCLÁN

BIOGRAPHICAL AND CRITICAL STUDIES

Balseiro, José A. *Blasco Ibáñez, Unamuno, Valle-Inclán, y Baroja: Cuatro individualistas de España.* Chapel Hill, N.C., 1949.

Casares, Julio. *Crítica profana: Valle-Inclán, Azorín, Ricardo León.* Madrid, 1916.

Díaz-Plaja, Guillermo. *Las estéticas de Valle-Inclán.* Madrid, 1965.

Fernandez Almagro, Melchor. *Vida y literatura de Valle-Inclán.* Madrid, 1966.

Fichter, William L. *Publicaciones periodisticas de Don Ramón del Valle-Inclán anteriores a 1895.* Mexico, 1952.

Gómez de la Serna, Ramón. *Don Ramón María del Valle-Inclán.* Buenos Aires, 1944.

Gómez Marín, José A. *La idea de sociedad en Valle-Inclán.* Madrid, 1967.

González López, Emilio. *El arte dramático de Valle-Inclán: Del decadentismo al expresionismo.* New York, 1967.

Gullón, Ricardo, ed. *Valle-Inclán Centennial Studies.* Austin, Texas, 1968.

Lado, María Dolores. *Las guerras carlistas y el reinado isabelino en la obra de Ramón del Valle-Inclán.* Gainesville, Fla., 1965.

Lima, Robert. *Ramón del Valle-Inclán.* New York, 1972.

————— and Dru Dougherty. *Dos ensayos sobre teatro español de los veinte.* Murcia, 1984.

Madrid, Francisco. *La vida altiva de Valle-Inclán.* Buenos Aires, 1943.

March, María E. *Forma e idea de los Esperpentos de Valle-Inclán.* Madrid, 1967.

Paz-Andrade, Valentín. *La anunciación de Valle-Inclán.* Buenos Aires, 1967.

Risco, Antonio. *La estética de Valle-Inclán en los Esperpentos y en "El ruedo ibérico."* Madrid, 1966.

—————. *El demiurgo y su mundo: Hacia un nuevo enfoque de la obra de Valle-Inclán.* Madrid, 1977.

Sender, Ramón J. *Valle-Inclán y la dificultad de la tragedia.* Madrid, 1966.

Speratti Piñero, Emma S. *La elaboración artística en "Tirano Banderas."* Mexico, 1957.

—————. *De "Sonata de otoño" al Esperpento: Aspectos del arte de Valle-Inclán.* London, 1968.

Umbral, Francisco. *Valle-Inclán.* Madrid, 1969.

Ynduráin, Francisco. *Valle-Inclán: Tres estudios.* Santander, 1969.

Zahareas, Anthony, ed. *Ramón del Valle-Inclán: An Appraisal of His Life and Works.* New York, 1968.

Zamora Vicente, Alonso. *Las "Sonatas" de Valle-Inclán.* Madrid, 1955.

—————. *La realidad esperpéntica (Aproximación a "Luces de Bohemia").* Madrid, 1969.

BIBLIOGRAPHIES

Lima, Robert. *An Annotated Bibliography of Ramón del Valle-Inclán.* University Park, Pa., 1972.

Rubia Barcia, José. *A Bibliography and Iconography of Valle-Inclán (1866–1936).* Berkeley, Calif., 1960.

ROBERT LIMA

VICENTE BLASCO IBÁÑEZ

(1867–1928)

EXCEPT FOR MIGUEL de Cervantes, Vicente Blasco Ibáñez is probably the most widely read Spanish novelist, both at home and abroad. Certainly he was one of the most prolific writers his country ever produced (his works run to thirty-six volumes), a result of his extraordinarily dynamic and energetic nature and of his determination to show both the positive and negative aspects of Spain to his countrymen and to the world.

Blasco has yet to receive a balanced judgment by literary critics. Most offer exaggerated praise or scorn for his works; many have ignored him altogether. For years most Spanish critics denied the value of his novels due to rejection of his radical political ideas, envy of his financial success, or a low opinion of his literary origins. (Blasco did not participate in some of the stylistic renovations of the so-called Generation of '98, adhering instead to many of the realistic–naturalistic practices of the nineteenth century, thought by many to be out of date.) But while Blasco's passionate attacks on the Spanish political scene and eventual millionaire status led to ostracism and exile from his Spanish contemporaries, such English-speaking critics as William Dean Howells, Havelock Ellis, Walter Starkie, Gerald Brenan, A. Grove Day, and Edgar Knowlson, Jr., have offered a more balanced perspective.

Certainly there are significant defects in some of Blasco's work. One must discriminate carefully between the hits and the misses.

Without question his early Valencian novels represent his greatest achievement, revealing a powerful double legacy that cannot be ignored: a pictorial, concrete, at times poetic style of strength and beauty, and a striking portrayal of human action. Later in his career, as Blasco strayed further and further from the format and the setting he knew best, the aesthetic value of his novels declined dramatically. While a definitive study of his total literary production remains to be done, recent analyses of individual novels have at least offered glimpses into the genuine artistry of his best works.

Blasco was born in a room over a corner grocery in Valencia on 29 January 1867. From his parents he inherited the vigor of the Aragonese peasants, and from an impoverished childhood he gained the spirit of struggle and defiance. During his early years this lad of sturdy build, brown eyes, and curly hair could be seen walking the beach of nearby Cabañal or talking to fishermen and sailors more often than sitting at his desk in school. By the age of fourteen he had written a cloak-and-dagger novel, by fifteen he had published a short story in Valencian dialect, and by sixteen he had run away from the University of Valencia to Madrid. There, while doing secretarial work for the aging writer Manuel Fernández y González, he gained the inspiration for his first series of lengthy writings—a dozen romances that he later repudiated. By age seventeen he had published a poem advocating chopping off all the crowned heads of Europe, starting with Spain.

The death of Alfonso XII in 1885 marked the young writer's start as Republican conspirator and frequent political prisoner. After completing his law degree in 1888 and his first forced exile in France (brought on by increasingly anticlerical speeches), in 1891 Blasco married his cousin María Blasco del Cacho, who endured his tempestuous nature and stormy career and bore him five children before their separation just prior to the outbreak of World War I. On 12 November 1894 he released the first issue of *El pueblo,* a newspaper that he ran virtually single-handedly and in which many of his best works appeared in serial form. It was into this enterprise that he poured all his energy and stamina, as well as the entirety of his inheritance from his parents.

Blasco proved a born leader of crowds, self-assured, fluent in his oratory, with a booming voice whose warmth quickly dispelled any cold first impression that might have been caused by his pointed beard, moustache, and aquiline nose. As time passed he grew increasingly impulsive and impatient to eliminate the stupidity, ignorance, and laziness around him. Anti-religious in a city venerated as the repository of the Holy Grail and republican in a region noted for its conservative monarchism, he never shirked his iconoclastic stance.

Nevertheless his election as the Valencian representative to the Cortes (the Spanish parliament) in 1898 was the first of many political achievements. To growing political fame was added an international literary reputation with the French translation of *La barraca* (*The Cabin,* 1898) in 1901. In 1904 he abandoned his home at La Malvarrosa on the Valencian shore and took up residence in Madrid and other Spanish cities.

In 1909 and 1910 Blasco made two trips to Argentina, first to give lectures and subsequently to supervise the development of some new settlements. There he remained, fighting harsh climates and jungle dangers, until economic difficulties led him back to Europe just prior to World War I. Shortly afterward he launched into a campaign to help the Allies, in the form of nine volumes of *Historia de la guerra europea de 1914* (History of the European War, 1914–1919), speeches throughout neutral Spain, and several novels, of which *Los cuatro jinetes del Apocalipsis* (*The Four Horsemen of the Apocalypse,* 1916) had the greatest political and financial impact. When unexpected wealth poured in from this work's reprints, translations, and film rights, he moved to the French Riviera, where he wrote most of his last novels.

By 1925 Blasco had undertaken a triumphant tour of the United States, composed lengthy travel literature based on a six-month luxury-liner trip around the world, and received news of the death of his wife. Within months he married Elena Ortúzar, the daughter of a well-known Chilean general, and soon thereafter, in failing health, he retired to his Riviera home to churn out his final writings. The night before his sixty-first birthday, weakened by pneumonia, diabetes, and overwork, he died uttering the words "my garden, my garden," a reflection of his ardent desire to have his Menton garden resemble those of his beloved Valencia. In his will he bequeathed his home to "all the writers of the world" and insisted that he not be buried in a non-Republican Spain. On 29 October 1933, two years after the proclamation of the Second Republic, his body arrived in Valencia amid the impassioned eulogies of those who had scorned him years before. Over forty-seven years later, as renovations were undertaken on the Blasco home at La Malvarrosa, the first international symposium on his works was held, and a determination to rectify the ignorance of his finer literary talents was voiced.

Blasco was a man of action first and a writer second. His works bear a profound and constant autobiographical stamp—the mark of a rebel, a revolutionary journalist, a colonizer, a sailor, a fighter for the cause of peasants, fishermen, and slum dwellers, and an exile who attacked his government yet remained loyal to Spanish traditions, as reflected in his tireless efforts to glorify his country's imperial past and to combat anti-Spanish feeling. It is with at least some justification that he is remembered by many of his countrymen more for his life than for his writings.

Following Blasco's first romances, five phases can be discerned in the writer's career: (1) His Valencian works, *Arroz y tartana* (Rice and Carriage, translated as *The Three Roses*, 1895), which he considered his first novel, through *Cañas y barro* (*Reeds and Mud*, 1902), and including two collections of stories, *Cuentos valencianos* (Valencian Tales, 1896) and *La condenada* (The Condemned Woman, 1900). Within this group, three works can be considered the novelist's masterpieces: *Flor de Mayo* (*The Mayflower*, 1896), *The Cabin*, and *Reeds and Mud*. (2) Novels of social protest, written between 1903 and 1905 and dealing with the church (*La catedral* [*The Shadow of the Cathedral*, 1903], set in Toledo, and *El intruso* [*The Intruder*, 1904], set in the Basque provinces) or with exploitation of the vineyard and big-city workers (*La bodega* [*The Fruit of the Vine*, 1905] and *La horda* [*The Mob*, 1905], set in Jerez de la Frontera and Madrid, respectively). "Art," the author explains, "should not be simply a mere manifestation of beauty. Art should be on the side of the needy defending forcefully those who are hungry for justice." Nevertheless, interminable didactic monologues, long ideological question-and-answer dialectics, and overtly symbolic characterization lessen the aesthetic worth of these works. (3) Psychological novels, in which the author stresses character development within specific settings: *La maja desnuda* (The Naked Maja, translated as *Woman Triumphant*, 1906), Madrid; *La voluntad de vivir* (The Will to Live, 1907), the Madrid and Paris aristocracy; *Sangre y arena* (*Blood and Sand*, 1958; also in translation under the title *The Blood in the Arena*), bullfighting in Sevilla and Madrid;

Los muertos mandan (*The Dead Command*, 1909), the Balearic Islands; and *Luna Benamor* (*Luna Benamor*, 1909), Gibraltar. While some of these works are admirable for their characterization and for their descriptions of landscape and local customs, they are inferior to the Valencian writings. (4) Cosmopolitan and war novels, including *Los argonautas* (The Argonauts, 1914), a detailed account of a transatlantic journey, envisioned as the first in a series of works dealing with Latin America, and several novels written to defend the Allied cause: *The Four Horsemen of the Apocalypse*, *Mare Nostrum* (*Our Sea*, 1918), *Los enemigos de la mujer* (*The Enemies of Women*, 1919), *La tierra de todos* (*The Temptress*, 1921), and *La reina Calafia* (*Queen Calafia*, 1923). These proved as popular as they were lacking in profound artistic merit. (5) Historical novels of Spanish glorification, ranging from the account of Pope Benedict XIII's life to the voyages of Columbus and a love story set in Monte Carlo.

In some ways Blasco is a transitional figure between the age of the realistic novel (1870–1900) and the Generation of '98, a group of early-twentieth-century writers concerned above all with Spain's social problems. Works like *The Fruit of the Vine* and *The Mob* demonstrate his participation in their preoccupation with Spanish social issues, and most of his works, particularly in his early periods, reveal the extraordinary sensitivity to landscape that Pío Baroja's generation displayed. His regionalistic *costumbrismo* (a term referring to the nineteenth-century romantics' attempts to capture local customs and mores) and his use of descriptive detail are techniques that relate Blasco to the earlier generation of Benito Pérez Galdós and José María Pereda.

It was Blasco who introduced the *pueblo*, the common people, rather than the middle class, as a frequent source of the novel's protagonist, a character who struggles heroically against his environment and his own animal instincts. A convincing narrative action of sharp contrasts, a pictorial, concrete, sensual,

357

often impressionistic realism of strength and beauty, and an admirable tightness and unity of plot are the features that set the Valencian novels apart as his most accomplished works.

Blasco was not a contemplative man, and his themes, while relevant and often powerful, are not complex or subtle. Likewise his modes of characterization, his third phase notwithstanding, are a far cry from the probing, individualizing approach of most of the late-nineteenth-century realists. His figures lack depth, are often excessively masculine and melodramatic, and seldom rise above mere types. They can be divided into two classes: good and bad. These opposites are inevitably caught up in an eternal struggle with each other or with nature. There are few inner battles of conscience, few motivations besides those of glory, power, sexual gratification, or material survival. Nevertheless, Blasco's main type—the man of action, passion, animal instinct, and rebellion—is a graphic and powerful creation, made convincing by the sheer force of his portrayal if not by any unique identity. Batiste (*The Cabin*), Retor (*The Mayflower*), Toni (*Reeds and Mud*), and, in later novels, Sánchez Morueta (*The Intruder*), Gallardo (*Blood and Sand*), Centauro (*The Four Horsemen of the Apocalypse*), Ferragut (*Our Sea*), and Renovales (*Woman Triumphant*) are such characters, presented in deliberate (albeit artificial) contrast to their opposites, who are weak and lazy types like Tonet (*The Mayflower*) and the other Tonet (*Reeds and Mud*). Blasco's women are also one-sided: they are either oppressed and overworked domestics, conventional society figures, or women of action and conquest. The last group would include Dolores (*The Mayflower*), Neleta (*Reeds and Mud*), Leonora (*Entre naranjos* [Among the Orange Trees, translated as *The Torrent*, 1900]), Doña Sol (*Blood and Sand*), and La Marquesita (*The Fruit of the Vine*). Finally, one should note that even if Blasco did not create great characters, he did succeed in capturing dramatically the heterogeneity of the masses. One striking example of this skill is Pimentó of *The Cabin,* who represents the people of the region around the Valencian *huerta* (an agricultural region, consisting in Valencia of rice fields and orange groves).

Although Blasco has often been referred to as "the Spanish Zola," he rejected the naturalists' pseudo-scientific, analytical approach and emphasis on crude detail, ultimately mitigated the impression of fatalistic determinism through his admiration of man's will to fight and a suggestion of optimism, and, finally, often presented a lighter, less objective, and more poetic tone than is the norm in Émile Zola's novels. Nevertheless, there are many moments when a strong measure of pessimism and philosophical determinism or the use of unpleasant language and description demonstrate the influence of French naturalism.

Finally, one should not forget that Blasco produced some of the finest Spanish short stories of the modern era. One has only to look at the moving portrait of the protagonist of "Dimoni" ("Demon") in *Cuentos valencianos* to realize the author's skill in this genre. John B. Dalbor, the only critic to have undertaken detailed studies of these pieces, believes that many of the stories are in fact superior to the author's novels and that the very best of these are to be found in the collections *Cuentos valencianos, The Condemned Woman,* and *El préstamo de la difunta* (The Dead Woman's Loan, 1920).

The analyses that follow will concentrate primarily on the Valencian novels. It is here that Blasco's descriptive power—tumultuous, exuberant, dramatic, and exact—is most evident, a talent that sprang from a keen and rapid sense of observation and an uncanny ability to improvise.

THE MAYFLOWER

The Mayflower is the second of Blasco's six Valencian works and the first of his trilogy on the life of elemental man in this region (along with *The Cabin* and *Reeds and Mud*). Emilio

Gascó Contell, Rafael Sosa, and others have judged this work one of the finest presentations of the life of seafaring people ever written in Spain. Paul Smith concurs and offers an analysis of the novel's relationship to *Reeds and Mud,* demonstrating clearly the obvious coincidences in plot and characterization between the two works and indicating that *The Mayflower* shows the possible influence of and (probably unconscious) borrowings from Zola's *Le ventre de Paris* (*Savage Paris,* 1873; Tía Picores resembles Mère Mehudin) and *L'Assommoir* (1877; e.g., the ear-tearing episode); from the nineteenth-century Spanish novelist Palacio Valdés' *José* (1885); from the Italian novelist Giovanni Verga's *I malavoglia* (*The House by the Medlar Tree,* 1881); from Pereda's *Sotileza* (1884); and from earlier stories by Blasco himself.

The setting of *The Mayflower* is the fishing village of Cabañal on the Costa de Azahar near Valencia. The description of regional scenes and customs and many of the characters are typically drawn from firsthand observation. As a boy Blasco had watched the oxen pull the fishing boats onto the beach in Cabañal. He had once been marooned during a fierce storm on a small island in the Gulf of Valencia, and he himself had made a contraband trip to Algiers in 1895, similar to the one that takes place in the novel.

The plot of *The Mayflower* concerns the struggles of the poor fishermen of the Valencia area. Pascualet, called El Retor (The Rector) because of his benign clerical appearance, corresponds to Batiste in *The Cabin* and Toni in *Reeds and Mud,* as he works and saves so that someday he can afford his own boat and free himself from the demands of another captain. His spendthrift brother, Tonet (much like Pimentó and Tonet in the other novels), is lazy and hates manual labor. When their father is killed at sea, their mother, Tona, cleverly converts her husband's boat into a beach tavern, where she earns a meager but adequate living for the family. El Retor goes to sea as an apprentice, but Tonet turns to drink and

women until he leaves for service in the navy. By this time a third child, Roseta, has been born of Tona's affair with a passing customs guard. When Tonet returns to find that his brother has married the seductive Dolores, he soon agrees to marry Rosario, who has waited for him for many years. Soon, unknown to El Retor, Tonet renews his previous youthful encounters with Dolores, and battles between the sisters-in-law increase in frequency and intensity despite the attempts at reconciliation managed by the ancient village matriarch, Tía Picores. A boy is born to El Retor and Dolores who is actually Tonet's child.

After years of hard work and saving and after a tense smuggling adventure to Algiers that results in considerable profit, El Retor is able to arrange for the building of the finest vessel ever seen in the village, named the *Mayflower* after the brand of tobacco that had been smuggled into Spain on the earlier trip. Prior to the ship's second sailing, Rosario reveals to El Retor that for years his brother has had an affair with Dolores and that his son is really Tonet's offspring. After a night of shock and humiliation and after refusing for the moment to avenge the affront by his brother, El Retor sets sail in one of the worst storms ever to hit the coast of Cabañal. In a suspenseful and tumultuous final chapter, El Retor confronts his brother on board the *Mayflower,* extracts a confession from him, and then refuses to give him the boat's only life jacket. Instead he puts it on Tonet's son and tosses him overboard. The lad is thrown upon the rocks, and the ship is ripped apart by the fury of the wind. Dolores and Rosario, watching the action from the shore, mourn their loss, and old Tía Picores shouts a final condemnation of the wealthy people of Valencia, who have exploited the fisherfolk and are ultimately responsible for the deaths the women have witnessed.

Although many aspects of plot and characterization (elements that were later incorporated into *Reeds and Mud* and *The Cabin*) are simple and lack profound inspiration, the novel excels in its rendering of milieu, its descriptions, and the sheer force of its action.

Blasco's usual viewpoint is one of neutrality and omniscience and indicates clearly the influence of the French naturalists. The suffering and hardships of the fisherfolk of Cabañal are viewed with a frankness and objectivity that one could not often find in the Spanish realistic novels of a decade or two earlier.

As is the case with the other Valencian novels, Blasco frequently transports the reader through the minds of the various characters and gives intimate glimpses into the emotions, knowledge, ignorance, and opinions of those characters. This omniscience is especially evident at moments of crisis, as when the narrator says, "Christ, what a joke! . . . It was Rosario, his sister-in-law! Was she coming in search of her husband?" Blasco does not rely simply on a presentation of exterior circumstances to explain his characters' struggle against the forces of their milieu.

Nevertheless, Blasco is not consistently objective in his approach. Occasionally he does in fact make his own opinions very evident. He calls Tonet "that rascal" and "another scamp"; Dolores' father, Paella, is "a bad man," "an old drunk"; Dolores appears as "a beautiful snake who could easily drop some men to take up with others"; and Tona's brother-in-law Tío Mariano is depicted as "greedy and cruel." The author's undisguised irony and sarcasm fall upon Tonet, referred to as "a gem" of the family whose "pretty genius" is shown when he finds out about the marriage of Dolores and Pascualo; Dolores, described as a wonderful woman and a true mother for the misguided Tonet; and many others, including a whole crowd of "grotesque huge figures" involved in the Good Friday procession, the "height of caricature." Blasco also reveals his emotional involvement at several points in the novel, such as in the moving (if somewhat melodramatic) lament by Tona when El Retor is about to set out to sea: "Pascual embraced the old woman, kissing her swollen eyes, which were also weeping. . . . "My son, my son!" groaned Tona

as she embraced El Retor, in whom she could see an astonishing resurrection of his father"; or in her final lament over the body of little Pascualet: "The grandmother struggled with her hands to bring back to life that little head whose eyes had closed forever."

On a slightly deeper level Blasco demonstrates his control of the story by creating a progressively dominant tone of fatalism, if not a total philosophical acceptance of it. Such a tone is conveyed, for example, by his use of foreshadowing, evident from the very beginning in the phrases "the puddles . . . red like rivulets of blood" and "the carriages were like black coffins." Later Blasco adds that the men go to sea "as if a fatal force were dragging them," and on the night before the final outing El Retor observes that "with his experience as a sailor, the weather did not seem good." But it is Tona who, as a kind of Greek dramatic chorus, constantly reminds us that we can expect the worst. It is she who sees her son as the image of her dead husband while El Retor prepares to go to sea, she who expresses the thought that "the damn sea was drawing them in to do away with the family."

The use of situational irony is a second way in which Blasco reveals his manipulation of the novel's fatalistic atmosphere. When he perishes at sea, old Tío Pascualo's boat becomes a temporary coffin; afterward the salvaged vessel brings in more money than before, as a tavern. Tona naively gives Martínez money for his "trip to Huelva," and Rosario's idolizing of Tonet contributes to his unfaithfulness, since she does not want to cause a quarrel with him when he first visits Dolores. El Retor, ignorant of the truth about his "son," thinks Tonet has "an outstanding nature. One had to recognize that he loved him and also his wife Dolores and Pasqualet very much." El Retor chides a woman who has been beaten after cheating on her husband, saying, "How thankful people like him were to God for having been given the pleasure and the luck of possessing an honest wife and a peaceful home!"

Finally, *The Mayflower* displays its author's

humor, as exemplified by the scenes in which Tona makes fun of Martínez's accent, and the women mourn for the figure of the Virgin Mary while still looking to "see if it had more adornments than the year before." More explicit is the case of the priest Don Santiago, who, knowing that El Retor is willing to pay for whatever is necessary for the blessing of his new boat, decides to wear his best vestment, one that "was not too appropriate for the ceremony, yet he would wear it for him, for the Retor was a good Christian and knew how to get along well with other people." His confused yet spirited ritual, sprinkled with extra "amens" and the approving nods of El Retor, is a delightful change of pace for the reader, culminating in the author's description of how the priest "began the ascent, catching the floundering cape underneath his feet on every rung. And the vestment of white and gold caught the afternoon sun and gleamed afar like the shell of a bright climbing scarab."

It is not simply in his perspective that Blasco mixes the objective, or neutral, with the subjective, or biased. He creates a similar balance in the language of the work. His style, in the most general terms, is natural and spontaneous, at times distinctly colloquial (even when it is clear that the author, and not one of the characters, is talking). The realistic exactness and vividness of the writer's language are conspicuous: "The Retor's ruddy face had turned pale as death, and he kept biting nervously at his fingers, those blunt, bony, calloused fingers of a fisherman."

During moments of narrative action the movement of syntactically short, expressive phrases generates a feeling of excitement and intensity:

A mediodía cambió el tiempo. Sopló el viento de Levante, tan terrible en el golfo de Valencia; el mar se erizó levemente; avanzó el huracán, arrugando la tersa superficie, que tomaba un color lívido, y un tropel de nubes se aglomeró en el horizonte, cubriendo al sol. En la playa fue grande la alarma.

Toward noon the weather changed. An easterly wind came up, the dread Levante, that can blow so wickedly in the gulf of Valencia. The sea at first was lightly wrinkled; but as the hurricane advanced the placid looking-glass gave way to a livid menacing chop, and piles of clouds came racing up from the horizon and blotted out the sun. Great was the alarm along shore.

(*Obras completas* 1:406)

At times the use of reiteration heightens dramatically the effect of movement:

El mar, mugiendo en la densa lobrequez; los cañares de la playa, doblándose a impulsos del vendaval, como cabelleras de gigantes enterrados; las olas, avanzando, cual si quisieran tragarse la Tierra, y una legión de sombríos demonios, agitándose, mudos e incansables, sacando fardos de la barca, que se deshacía por instantes, pescándolos en las espumosas aguas para enviarlos como pelotas a la playa.

Darkness, everywhere, and a sea bellowing in the gloom, the reeds and shore grass bent low under the gale, the breakers tumbling in as though bent on swallowing up the land, while a legion of dark-skinned men, with their clothes off, tugged at great bales in the hold of the vessel that was rapidly going to pieces and fished them out from the foaming waters and dragged them up on the beach, where they disappeared mysteriously.

(*Obras completas* 1:440)

Indeed, Blasco's descriptive passages—fresh, graphic, colorful, often highly sensuous—stand as the author's most significant artistic contribution to literature. For this reason it seems logical that he dedicated the novel to his childhood friend Joaquín Sorolla, the artist whose use of vivid transcription and dazzling colors is reflected in the novelist's prose. Although proportionately there is not as much description of nature in *The Mayflower* as there is in *Reeds and Mud* (the opening pages relate the awakening of the town rather than of the countryside, as they do in *Reeds and Mud* and *The Cabin*), nevertheless in many impressive, lyrical passages a vivid plasticity and an appeal to the senses predominate. For example, passages occur within a strictly visual framework: "The sea was catching the ashen brightness of the nocturnal sky, and boats and buildings stood out in dark outlines of indigo against a vast background of nickel gray."

Blasco's use of colors—reds, yellows, whites, and blues to depict scenes of tranquillity, and grays, blacks, or maroons to create an atmosphere of gloom or danger—suggests an impressionistic technique seen throughout his Valencian novels:

> El cielo, inundado de luz, era de un azul blanquecino. Como copos de espuma caídos al azar, bogaban por él algunos jirones de vapor, y de la arena ardiente surgía un vaho que envolvía los objetos lejanos, haciendo temblar sus contornos.

> The sky, overflowing with sunlight, had a whitish sheen. A few silver clouds were lazily drifting along like handfuls of foam scattered haphazardly over the expanse of heaven; and from the heated sands a damp radiation was shimmering, giving tremulous, hazy outlines to objects in the distance.
>
> (Obras completas 1:423)

Among the examples of vivid visual description are the many graphic delineations of the characters themselves:

> La siñá Tona estaba muy vieja. . . . Bajo la luz cruda y azulada de la luna, veíase su cabeza escasa de pelos. Los pocos que conservaba, tirantes y blancuzcos, formaban como un enrejado sutil sobre la sonrosada calvicie. El rostro, arrugado, tenía las mejillas fláccidas y colgantes; y sus ojos negros, de los que tanto se había hablado en la playa, asomaban ahora, tristes y mates, por entre las abotagadas carnosidades que pretendían sepultarlos.

> Siñá Tona was getting very old. . . . The raw bluish light of the moon made evident that the hair on her head had thinned, leaving a scant network of taut gray locks over her sunburned scalp. The wrinkles now sank deep into her emaciated face while her cheeks hung loose and baggy, and her black eyes, once the talk of the whole shore, peered sad and faded from the folds of skin that drooped about them.
>
> (Obras completas 1:433)

Some descriptions have a specifically auditory appeal. Others appeal predominantly to the sense of smell, such as the clothes of the fisherwomen, which give an odor "not only of the salty environment of the sea, but like the smell of the muddy ditches," or Rosario's basket, which "reeked, mixing its rotten smell with the perfume of cheap chocolate that was emitted from the nearest kitchen."

We are thus immersed in a series of sensuous descriptions of Cabañal and of the sea. We envision the dawn after a night of rain, we hear the distant whistle of the first trains leaving Valencia, and we smell the wet earth of the village streets and the strong odors of the local fish market. Moreover, the descriptions of rotting fish are but a mild indication of the naturalistic elements that Blasco incorporated into some of his most intense transcriptions of realistic detail:

> Algo blando y viscoso que les hizo gritar con instintivo horror. . . . Sacaron un cuerpo hinchado, verdoso, con el vientre enorme próximo a estellar. La cabeza era una masa repugnante. Todo el cuerpo estaba destrozado por las mordeduras de los voraces pececillos, que, no queriendo soltar su presa, erizábanse sobre el cadáver, comunicándole espulzantes estremecimientos.

> Something soft and glutinous made them scream with horror. . . . They drew out a corpse, swollen, green, the belly inflated to the point of bursting. The decaying flesh was gnawed away in places by hungry little fishes, some of which, loath to let go their prey, were still clinging to it by their teeth, wriggling their tails and giving an appearance of disgusting life to the horrible mass.
>
> (Obras completas 1:408b)

As in the later Valencian novels, many of Blasco's descriptions here are "costumbristic" in their descriptions of daily, even trivial, picturesque habits and customs. Just as much of the enjoyment of reading Baroja's trilogy on the País Vasco derives from the reader's immersion in the author's native region, so here the charm of the novel is in large part the result of the lively depictions of local traditions and ways of life. Among the costumbristic descriptions in *The Mayflower* are those of the weighing and selling of fish, life aboard the ship of Tío Borrasca, the activities in the village as El Retor and Tonet walk to see Tío Mariano, the Café de Carabina, Tonet's memories of life in Algiers, the transformation of the Cabañal beach during the summer, Tonet's guitar songs, Tío Batiste's superstitions, and, most prominent of all, the rituals associated with the Good Friday procession and the embarcation and return of the village fleet (in which Blasco makes a rare authorial intrusion to explain the customs involved).

A more precise examination of the components of Blasco's descriptions reveals that he frequently uses animals as the vehicles of his imagery. Dolores has "a robust breast" and "powerful female jaws of solid, bony construction"; the men of the village are described as "flocks of workers" and the people salvaging the cargo of a sunken ship are "a swarm of black ants"; likewise Tona's children are "seagulls," a squadron of French ships are "large animals," Tío Paella calls his prostitutes "my herd," Don Santiago is "a crawling insect," El Retor appears in the Holy Week scene as "a caged bear," and the people in the procession are "a large ball of black cockroaches." Blasco's intention is to emphasize man's similarity to the brute force and primitive irrationality of animals, to demonstrate that the pressures of environment and heredity have reduced man to a sub-human level.

Other objects besides humans are likened to animals as well. The ship *Garbosa* is repeatedly described as an old horse. Frequently the sea is likened to a raging, moaning beast, an image that relates to the theme of man's vulnerability to exploitation and dominance by

the natural forces around him. Personification, a frequent technique in *The Mayflower,* is usually linked with the harsh life of the fishermen: "tired of having worked all night long, the gas factory ejected the last of its deadly fumes"; the dilapidated carriages move to market "in a lazy row, swinging, leaning toward one side, as if they had lost their sense of balance." The sea, especially, takes on human characteristics: "it spit out furious surf"; "the sea . . . that hypocrite"; "a good friend who gets angry at times." Likewise personified are the church bells, the gas meters, fish, the sun, the *Garbosa,* and seagulls.

Blasco's favorite device is the simile, of which there are over seventy instances in *The Mayflower.* These are used either to intensify the macabre and grotesque or to create moments of more purely descriptive delineation; for example, "the thunder crashed, as though a huge piece of canvas had been ripped asunder."

Blasco's language, then, is at times indisputably subjective, even poetic, and is the result of an artistic consciousness that is clearly visible, despite the fact that he might have been rushed or exhausted during the writing of the novel, when he often stayed awake for days at a time to prepare an installment for his journal, *El pueblo.* The writer's use of symbolism is likewise indicative of his conscious artistry. The symbolic aspects of *The Mayflower* lend unity and depth to the novel. In general these elements center around the man-sea relationship or the leitmotif of man's bestiality. The ship's name, the *Mayflower,* itself must be considered in light of its symbolic (ironic) connotations, in juxtaposition to the American Pilgrims' vessel. Similarly, old Pascualo's boat is seen as a "crib" used by Tona to raise a new generation of fishermen (who, in turn, will also be sacrificed to the sea). Both boats—as opposed to the Pilgrims' *Mayflower*—are elements in a greater scheme, the battle against a seemingly predestined destruction. For this reason Blasco describes the fishing vessels as soldiers and, at various points, as caskets on the waves. The sea itself is, of course, the most significant symbol of the force of destiny, weighing mercilessly upon the lives of the villagers of Cabañal. Thus the death of the child in the sea at the end represents a kind of symbolic sacrifice to an angry god. Because of the expiatory significance of such a sacrifice, a somewhat similar act was inserted by Blasco in all three novels of the Valencian trilogy. (Toni throws his child into the lake in *Reeds and Mud,* and Pascualet, Batiste's youngest son in *The Cabin,* dies from a fever that he contracts when hostile schoolmates throw him into an irrigation ditch.)

Finally, the artistry of Blasco's style is evident in the skillful use of contrasts. These are basically descriptive, as in this case of different odors:

> *La báscula estaba ocupada por unos panaderos de las afueras, guapos mozos, con las cejas enharinadas, cuadrado mandil y brazos arremangados, que descargaban sacos de pan caliente y oloroso, esparciendo una fragancia de vida vegetal en el ambiente nauseabundo del pescado.*

> The scale was occupied by some bakers from the surroundings; they were handsome boys, with flour-stained eyebrows, with their square aprons and rolled-up sleeves, who unloaded sacks of warm, odorous bread, emitting a vegetal fragrance of life in the nauseous fishy environment.
>
> (*Obras completas* 1:398)

Similarly, descriptions of the sea (at one point tranquil, later stormy) intensify the contrast between the outbound and return trips of the *Garbosa.*

Blasco also employs the use of contrast for the presentation of character: the different reactions in Dolores' mind to El Retor and Tonet during the Good Friday procession; the scene at home between Tonet and Roseta after the procession as compared to that of El Retor and Dolores; the uses made by El Retor and Tonet of the money earned on the contraband

trip ("while he [El Retor] was putting body and soul into his new enterprise, Tonet, with his share in the booty, was enjoying one of his seasons of prosperity"); El Retor's and Roseta's different ideas about men; and the varying rapidity with which time seems to pass in El Retor's mind during the long monologue near the end of the novel.

Finally, contrasting situations are integrated skillfully into the plot. The economic circumstances and marital stability of Roseta's and Tonet's relationship are shown to deteriorate in comparison with the apparent situation of El Retor and Dolores; the success of the contraband expedition is contrasted to the tragic outcome of the final outing on the *Mayflower;* and lastly, the consequences of the ship's two sallies are meant to stand in ironic juxtaposition, especially evident when, before the second venture, El Retor thinks that "there was a good chance for the luck to hold."

Thus, Blasco's style—his rich, vivid descriptions, his use of imagery, light, movement, and contrast—represents the most significant aspect of the novel's artistry. On the other hand, one cannot consider his characterizational techniques unique or memorable. Although the novelist based many of his characters on real-life models from Cabañal, they are, in general, deliberately "flat" (to use E. M. Forster's term), since the concept of naturalistic predestination precludes any substantial change in their psychological development. Blasco was more interested in developing a rapid, suspenseful plot line for his daily readers than he was in creating any kind of depth in his personages. As a result most of the characters merely represent particular dominant passions or vices. Blasco was content to present an initial outline in a few quick strokes and then to allow the villagers to explain themselves, at least superficially, through a series of indirect transcriptions of their thoughts.

Although no one character can be termed the "protagonist," El Retor emerges after the fourth chapter as the main focus of the plot, subject to the influence of all the other figures. (Tonet is the most important secondary figure.) Thus the older brother is affected by Tona's maternal sentiments, by Dolores' and Tonet's relationship, by Tío Mariano's enthusiasm for contraband, by Roseta's warnings, and by the treachery and deception of the sea (as a significant character in itself). Only Tía Picores seems not to form a part of this sphere of influence.

A slightly different general view of the characters might comprise three classifications: (1) the main figures, grouped as two sets of opposing interests: El Retor and Tonet, Rosario (El Retor's counterpart) and Dolores (Tonet's counterpart); (2) minor figures, such as Tona, Tía Picores, Roseta, Tío Mariano, Don Santiago, Tío Batiste, and Martínez; and (3) the villagers. The actions of the characters can be visualized as taking place within two planes of conflict: man against man (e.g., El Retor and Tonet) and man grappling with his environment. From about the middle of the work, the sea attains the status of a character, as revealed through the increasing use of personification (a treacherous cat to Tonet, a good friend to El Retor, a fighter striking blows against the *Garbosa,* and so forth).

El Retor, the first of Blasco's strong heroes, is trustworthy, naive, hardworking, money-conscious, stubborn, serious yet likeable, and generally easygoing. In his perseverance he is repeatedly likened to his father and follows a similar life in response to his natural instincts and the pressures of the sea. Foremost among these instincts is his pride, evident even as a child, when he first has his own clothes and takes care of Tonet, and later, when he sees himself as a mighty provider and a kind of father to the *Garbosa* ("he attended, like a dutiful father, to the agonized moans that came from the *Garbosa*'s joints"). His helping of Tona and Tonet is due more to his need to feel successful than to a sincere desire to aid his family. He is furious at his brother not so much because of Tonet's clandestine affair with Dolores but because he himself has been

the object of ridicule. When his pride is wounded, he can become a violent "other self," "a beast that began to roar and claw inside him at the thought of being deceived." His last escape to the sea is motivated not only by feelings of vengeance or suicide but also by a need to escape ridicule, "to get away from those who . . . might make fun of him."

Although Blasco's treatment of El Retor is by no means profound, in the last two chapters of the novel the reader observes a significant introspective glimpse of a kind almost unique in the author's Valencian works. Through a long interior monologue suggestive of Miguel de Unamuno's later portraits of inner conflict and uncertainty, El Retor is forced to confront his loss of dignity, reverts to the vengeful, animalistic side of his nature, feels shame when he realizes that his shouts might be overheard, fails to follow through on his plan for revenge, and, too late, near the very end of the novel, regains a sense of justice and a realization of his own sins. The sequence of mental ramblings is memorable and suggests that without the pressures of time and the force of his own tumultuous nature, Blasco might have created psychological portraits of considerable depth. As it is, El Retor appears as a kindly, naive animal, momentarily enraged when his feelings are hurt.

Tonet, like his brother, is generally an unchanging, "flat" character, the opposite of El Retor: pleasure-loving, unrepentant, lazy, self-centered, given to drink, and lacking in any kind of spiritual affection for Dolores. Instead, he revels in the illicit, animalistic nature of their relationship: "This criminal pleasure . . . made them constrain their bodies, shuddering their flesh with pure animal vibrations, as if the disgracefulness of the passion increased the intensity of the pleasure." Like El Retor he is described in animalistic terms (as a seagull, "a child of feline shrewdness," "a sly cat," and one who "could swim like a fish," suggesting once more the influence of the environment. Unlike his counterpart in *Reeds and Mud,* he is not the victim of the wiles of any woman and, as a more unscrupulous person, feels no guilt whatever for his actions.

The minor characters of *The Mayflower* are more obvious embodiments of particular sentiments or weaknesses. Most appear to blend in naturalistic fashion into the atmosphere around them. Dolores is the female counterpart of Tonet, sensuous, self-centered, and immoral. As the offspring of Tío Paella, an alcoholic carriage driver who delivers prostitutes to local clientele, she demonstrates more clearly than most characters the naturalists' concept of hereditary influences. Rosario, El Retor's counterpart, is constant and loyal, struggling to protect her own interests but weakly falling victim to Tonet's cruelty and indifference. Tona, although she clearly represents a chorus-like voice of fate, as demonstrated by her increasingly strong warnings against the sea to El Retor, is nevertheless a slightly more rounded character; she is resourceful and astute, selfless and loving toward her sons and Martínez, but she reveals weakness in her indulgent favoritism toward Tonet, her naiveté and lack of judgment concerning Martínez, her materialism, and her almost cruel indifference to the emotional needs of Roseta. Because of this lack of attention Roseta learns to be independent and strong and comes to love solitude. She is a good person who works hard and is sensitive to the feelings of others (e.g., she has no desire to hurt El Retor by revealing what she knows concerning Dolores, although she shares her mother's hatred for men in general).

One of the interesting features of the novel is the way Blasco develops the entire *pueblo* as a kind of mass character, accustomed to the hell of life's struggle and to the constant challenge of death and reacting as a single entity to external stimuli (e.g., the simultaneous actions of the villagers in the market at the arrival of the police).

Old Tía Picores deserves separate mention. Sharp-tongued and prideful yet generous and understanding, as in her actions toward Dolores and Rosario, she stands apart from the rest of the characters as the typical "old wise one" seen in Blasco's other Valencian works (compare Tío Tomba in *The Cabin* and Tío Paloma in *Reeds and Mud*). Usually this character appears at critical moments in the action and offers advice that is subsequently ignored. Tía Picores, along with Tona and, to a minor degree, Tío Batiste, represents the oracle of things to come. The fact that her counsel is not heeded is the source of her frustration and a direct cause of the novel's fatal conclusion. Significantly, Tía Picores appears in three symmetrically spaced scenes: in chapter 1 as mediator between the women, in a similar role in chapter 5 during the Good Friday procession, and as the oracle and voice of the author in chapter 10. In the last scene, one of Blasco's most powerful and impressive conclusions, it becomes clear that she is the spokeswoman for the town's latent resentment against the exploitation of the fisherfolk by people of the city (a role assumed by her counterparts in *Reeds and Mud* and *The Cabin* as well). Her function in *The Mayflower* (as opposed to that of other characters) is related not to plot development but rather to her role as an unsuccessful mediator between other characters and as an instrument for thematic declaration.

The development of character, then, is again not of paramount importance in the novel. Characterization, in fact, supports theme. The animalization and consequent lack of depth of the characters, for example, serve to reinforce the central thematic statement of the work, that man's struggle against the bestiality of his own instincts and the powerful forces of nature is a futile one. *The Mayflower* thus demonstrates the fullness of Blasco's acceptance of the naturalists' deterministic philosophy. Although the ending does not constitute a cry of despair on the part of the author, it is obvious that we are left with little or no hope for the future (as compared to *Reeds and Mud,* where we know that Toni will continue to work and develop his land). Here the sea controls all. The sea reaches out for the ships "as if a fatal destiny were pulling them."

Within the double framework of men against men and men against the environment, Blasco seems to imply that what matters is to continue living, to have the courage to resist fiercely the forces of destiny and the pressures of society. Man must accustom himself to struggling and to bending. With respect to the double framework itself, it is important to note that the two levels are inextricably related: El Retor dies at the end (resolving the theme of man against the environment), partially as a result of the influence of Tonet (man against man), who causes him to venture out too far into the storm.

Other thematic concerns are evident. Excessive human pride is condemned; it causes many of El Retor's problems, and the sailors follow him to the sea at the end "because of the egotistical rivalry." Thus it is that Tona thinks that kindness is "the natural condition of insignificant human beings." On the other hand, Blasco clearly admires the hard work, determination, and bravery of many of the fishermen. Though he does not deride religious values themselves, the author wryly parodies and ridicules the hypocritical or ludicrous nature of many of the Holy Week practices of the region. The costumes make the youth appear as black cockroaches, those representing the Jews are like cheaply dressed actors from some medieval play, the soldiers seem like waddling insects, and the uniforms of some look as if they were "ripped from a burial casket."

More important is the theme of the villagers' exploitation by the people of the city: "These people, made brutal by danger and perhaps sentenced to death, went to sea so that others could see sweet-smelling red molluscs on their white tablecloths." Through Tía Picores' final diatribe, Blasco also curses the irresponsible well-to-do who have indirectly brought about the tragic events by forcing the people of Cabañal to live in a vicious environment of fear and hatred. The wealthy bourgeoisie buy their fish for next to nothing, and the villagers who cannot survive are preyed upon by loan sharks such as Tío Mariano. The resultant decadent social atmosphere stifles the emergence of a healthy society. There is no childhood education or meaningful home training. No government agency aids the families of men lost at sea. The rich boat-owners stay home, while the poor rent their ships and receive only a small portion of the catch. There is no official protection against the upper class's forcing the villagers to sell their fish at reduced prices. When Picores faces inland at the end, the suggestion is that the sea is not the only guilty party in the fishermen's life of hardship.

Finally, a minor theme or leitmotif is the recurring criticism by the women of their husbands' oppression of them, the notion that "men were either scamps or brutes." This indictment is expressed by Tía Picores, through Tonet's treatment of Rosario, by Tona, by Roseta, and by El Retor himself in a drunken conversation with Roseta toward the end of the novel. The treatment of the women must ultimately be seen as the result of environmental pressures, which tended to encourage the expression of animalistic instincts.

As in his other Valencian novels, Blasco's main purpose here seems not to have been the expression of theme. Instead, *The Mayflower* is a vehicle for forceful, sensitive description and for a relatively objective depiction of the savage struggle within and around the people of the region. The framework for these descriptions and for this topical presentation of conflict is a narrative structure that is consciously and deliberately calculated and simple, yet fascinating in its detail.

The novel is constructed upon two main lines of action: El Retor's attempts to escape from poverty and material hardship, and the adulterous relationship between Tonet and Dolores. These two narrative threads approach each other in a clear fashion during the contraband episode (e.g., Tonet's musings about Algiers in terms of the women he has known there) and converge in a simultaneous resolution during the novel's final, climactic action, when El Retor tries to face Tonet's treachery and the force of nature together.

With respect to the divisions and chronology of the plot line, Blasco follows a pattern displayed in other works: three expository chapters, consisting of an episodic introduction (much like the first scene in *Reeds and Mud* or the delivery of milk in *The Cabin*) and two chapters of retrospective background. After this, the main action develops as a linear, basically causal progression, the result specifically of the adultery. Whether this pattern came from the influence of the works of González (whose novels Blasco had read) or stemmed from a newspaperman's desire to maintain reader interest between installments, the author evidently took great pains to develop a plot line with increasing appeal and an accumulation of elements designed to heighten suspense in particular episodes (for example, as the *Garbosa* sets sail, "Ay, may heaven help them, and not send a storm!"). Nevertheless, the careful reader is aware early in the story (perhaps at the time of the weddings) that the general outcome is inevitable.

In the next-to-last chapters of both *The Mayflower* and *The Three Roses*, Blasco records the inner experience of the main characters—El Retor and Juanito—as they undergo similar emotional crises, although the introspective musings of the former are more profound. In *The Mayflower* the final tragedy is extended and presented in more detail than in the final chapters of *The Three Roses*. In comparison with *Reeds and Mud* (and, to an extent, *The Three Roses*), there is no real denouement, an omission that further intensifies the final impact of the characters' death.

The plot divisions themselves can thus be divided into two sections: exposition and rising action. In the former, chapter 1 provides an episodic introduction (in medias res) through minor characters, and chapters 2 and 3 provide retrospective narration (twenty years earlier), progressing to present time, concentrated primarily on the perspective of Tona as a preparation for the presentation of El Retor and Tonet. The rising action involves development of El Retor and Tonet and a progressive

intensification of the plot from plans for the contraband trip through Rosario's revelation of the truth about the lovers (the causal "climax") to the final narrative climax itself.

The pace of the action, especially after the plans for the construction of the boat in chapter 6, is increasingly rapid until the end, although the passing of the hours is subjectively felt by El Retor as slower during the marvelous pages of his interior monologue.

The novel's four main costumbristic "digressions"—like those of *Reeds and Mud* and *The Cabin*—are in fact integral to the plot line and to the unity of the work's structure as a whole: 1) The opening market scene serves as a backdrop to the later violence of both man and nature. 2) The Good Friday procession, which demonstrates the progressive relation and opposition between the two men, relates symbolically to the other main break in the action, the contraband trip. Tonet and El Retor are compared in Dolores' eyes (Tonet, the captain of the "Jews," the anti-Christ, appears superior to El Retor); the meeting of the Jews and the Virgin corresponds ironically to the meeting between Rosario and Dolores; the mothers' weeping at the Virgin's grief, while not entirely sincere, foreshadows their laments when their sons set out against the dangers of the sea; and finally, Tonet and El Retor are to leave on Holy Saturday and will return (victorious) on the day commemorating Christ's victory over death. 3) In the smuggling expedition itself the two men are more directly involved, and their rivalry becomes even more apparent. The episode relates directly to Blasco's thematic concerns insofar as it demonstrates the only way the poor fishermen can hope to make any kind of sizable profit. 4) The blessing of the boats represents symbolically the "rites of manhood" for El Retor, the introduction of primitive man in a hostile, savage environment. The extra blessings (and Tona's warnings) serve as an ironic preparation for the final disaster at sea, just as the traditional taunts foreshadow ironically the subsequent revelation to El Retor about Dolores and Tonet's love affair.

It is no mere coincidence that these costumbristic scenes are spaced evenly through the narrative (chapters 1, 5, 6, and 8). In this way interest is maintained for the readers of *El pueblo* at the same time that important plot development is introduced. A similar arrangement can be found in *Reeds and Mud* (e.g., the lottery that brings Tonet into contact with Cañamèl) and *The Cabin* (e.g., the school scenes, which lead to the child's being thrown into the drainage ditch afterwards).

Another way in which Blasco has unified the structure of the novel is by using parallel or corresponding scenes. Besides those already mentioned in the analysis of style, these include: Dolores and Rosario's fight over the location to sell fish in chapter 1 and their later dispute over the best place from which to witness the procession in chapter 5; El Retor's ironic comments to Roseta in chapter 8 concerning the man deceived by his wife and the scene in which he is told by Rosario of his own deception; El Retor's argument with Roseta over the role of men and his agreement (while drunk) with her at a later point; the fight between the women at the beginning (with Picores as a mediator) and the fight between the men at the end (where Picores cannot intercede and can only deliver a final condemnation of the circumstances that caused the tragedy); the death of old Pascualo in chapter 2 and the death of his son El Retor in chapter 10.

The structure of the novel, consequently, is carefully designed both as a unified, artistic whole and as a series of suspenseful points of interest or stimuli, which served to maintain the readers' attention throughout the work's serialization in *El pueblo.* Despite the overtly manipulative aspect of the narrative organization, the action itself appears fresh, vital, and spontaneous.

All these general properties of the novel—perspective, style, characterization, theme, structure—are intrinsically interrelated to give *The Mayflower* its extraordinary artistic unity. Hence the theme concerning nature and destiny is reinforced by particular facets of style (personification, vividness of description, naturalistic delineation, symbolism), as well as by the ways in which the characters are presented (their domination by the sea; Tona and others as the voice of fate; the very flatness of the characters themselves, suggesting that individual development is impaired by the environment; the conflict of man against man as a reflection of that of man against nature; Picores as the wise one who recognizes the exploitation by the rich of Valencia). Similarly, the many animalistic similes and metaphors relate characterization to the thematic statement concerning mankind's primitive, environmentally controlled nature. The causality inherent in the rising action of the work's structure and the circular elements of the plot line (the fight between the women at the start and between the men at the end; old Pascualo, who defies the sea at the start, and El Retor, who does so at the end) also reinforce the presentation of deterministic circumstances. The costumbristic descriptions of local customs, an integral aspect of Blasco's stylistic technique, serve as a structural element (i.e., in their spacing throughout the novel and as a change of narrative pace) as well as a means of delineating characters (e.g., Tonet opposed to El Retor). And contrasts in style relate to oppositions among the characters and to structural parallels of corresponding scenes (e.g., the success and failure of the two *Mayflower* outings). Characterization and theme are naturally reinforced by Blasco's technique of intrusion into the thoughts of the villagers themselves.

The unity of *The Mayflower*, like that of the other Valencian novels, derives above all from the fact that the author wrote with a clear, paramount goal: to capture in words a people and a region, to present rather than evaluate a particular environment. The expressive, powerful descriptions of the village of Cabañal and the landscape or seascape around it and the vigorous and often dramatic depiction of its inhabitants' primitive and difficult existence—these are the narrative manifestations of this purpose and represent those aspects of the work that are of greatest artistic value.

Despite the reading public's relative unawareness of this novel, it is an important work displaying Blasco's greatest talents. At the very least he deserved the honor bestowed upon him when the inhabitants of the real Cabañal changed the name of the street where he had lived so that it would bear the words "Flor de Mayo."

THE CABIN

The Cabin was Blasco's first universally acclaimed masterpiece. It developed as an extended version of a short story—originally entitled "Venganza moruna" (Moorish Vengeance)—that he composed during four days in 1895 while hiding out from the police, who held a warrant for his arrest for participating in an anti–Cuban war demonstration. The original version was never published; the final version, augmented primarily by the addition of landscape description and costumbristic delineation of local customs, appeared serially in *El pueblo* between 6 and 18 November 1898. Seven hundred copies of the work were published immediately thereafter by the author's friend Francisco Sempere, and within two years a French translation and two Spanish editions had established Blasco as one of the foremost young European writers of the day. The novel is the one Valencian piece that has received relatively thorough critical appraisal. Since most of these studies—particularly those of Richard Cardwell and Vernon Chamberlin—are intelligently thought out and easily accessible, this essay will refrain from detailed examination of some of the work's best-known attributes. Instead, it will simply summarize the features that make *The Cabin* (along with *Reeds and Mud*) one of Blasco's two best literary achievements, expanding upon or correcting past critical views when necessary for an adequate picture of the novel's overall artistry.

In the most general terms, *The Cabin* typifies the expression of Blasco's two most significant talents: descriptive or costumbristic elaboration and the presentation of man's courageous struggle to combat a hopeless situation. To these he added a new emphasis, one that became central in later periods of his career: a protest against social injustice. This last element, surely, is what lends an extra measure of universality to the work and has contributed to its popularity outside Spain.

The plot is extremely simple, lacking any kind of secondary complications and moving without distraction toward the final tragedy. In the village of Alboraya, in the *huerta* region north of Valencia, Tío Barret is evicted by a usurious landlord, whom Barret then kills in a burst of anger. For ten years the villagers, by scaring away potential tenants, prevent anyone from working the land as revenge for Barret's fate and as a warning to other landowners against mistreatment of the *huertanos*. Nevertheless Batiste and his family arrive to restore the property and its shack. Pimentó, the village bully and loafer and a local warden for the rationing of irrigation use, causes Batiste to lose his water rights. Meanwhile other members of the family suffer: his daughter Roseta's romance with the butcher's apprentice is destroyed, and his three boys must fight their way home from school each day. The youngest son is thrown into a slimy irrigation ditch, and this eventually leads to his death. At this point the villagers seem to repent of their actions and take charge of the funeral. Soon, however, Batiste is lured into a tavern fight with Pimentó, which leads to their shooting each other. On the night Pimentó dies from his wounds, Batiste awakens to find the cabin on fire. As the shack burns, the villagers leave the family to their plight.

The Cabin, Blasco was fond of saying, was inspired just as much as his other novels by real events, experiences, and people. His childhood visits to his sister's local wet-nurse had led him to notice one particular desolate, unkept farm, surrounded by well-tended, developed fields; a serious drought in 1879 and the subsequent persecution of the peasants by the landlords when the farmers claimed they could not pay rent were events he remembered well; Eduardo Betoret-París confirms that the description of the Copa tavern, the Tribunal de las Aguas, the Fuente de la Reina, and the many other local sketches are all authentic depictions of actual places or ways of life; and finally, many of the characters—in particular, Pimentó—had counterparts in real life.

The combination of natural simplicity and rich, pictorial expressiveness that became the hallmark of Blasco's style is very much in evidence in *The Cabin*. The opening description of the arrival of dawn, Blasco's well-known "poem of the *huerta*" is the most striking example of the novel's graphic and dynamic visual and auditory powers:

Desperezóse la inmensa vega bajo el resplandor azulado del amanecer. . . . Los últimos ruiseñores . . . lanzaban el gorjeo final como si les hiriese la luz del alba con sus reflejos de acero. De las techumbres de paja de las barracas salían las bandadas de gorriones como un tropel de pilluelos perseguidos, y las copas de los árboles empezaban a estremecerse bajo los primeros jugueteos de estos granujas del espacio, que todo lo alborotaban con el roce de sus blusas de plumas. . . . Despertaba la huerta, sus bostezos eran cada vez más ruidosos. Rodaba el canto del gallo de barraca en barraca. Los campanarios de los pueblecitos devolvían con ruidoso badajeo el toque de misa primera que sonaba a lo lejos, en las torres de Valencia, esfumadas por la distancia. De los corrales salía un discordante concierto animal: relinchos de caballos, mugidos de vacas, cloquear de gallinas, balidos de corderos, ronquidos de cerdos; un despertar ruidoso de bestias que, al sentir la fresca caricia del alba cargada de acre perfume de vegetación, deseaban correr por los campos.

El espacio se empapaba de luz; disolvíanse las sombras, como tragadas por los abiertos surcos y las masas de follaje. En la indecisa neblina del amanecer iban fijando sus contornos húmedos y brillantes las filas de moreras y frutales, las ondulantes líneas de cañas, los grandes cuadros de hortalizas, semejantes a enormes pañuelos verdes, y la tierra roja cuidadosamente labrada. . . . Ya era de día completamente.

The vast plain stretched out under the blue spendor of dawn. . . . The last nightingales . . . poured forth their final warble, as if the light of dawn wounded them with its steely reflections. Flocks of sparrows arose like crowds of pursued urchins from the thatched roofs of the farmhouses, and the tops of the trees trembled at the first assault of these gamins of the air, who stirred up everything with the flurry of the feathers. . . . The *huerta* was awaking, and its yawnings were growing ever noisier. The crowing of the cock was carried on from farmhouse to farmhouse; the bells of the village were answering, with noisy peals, the ringing of the first mass which floated from the towers of Valencia, blue and hazy in the distance. From the corrals came a discordant animal-concert: the whinnying of horses, the lowing of gentle cows, the clucking of hens, the bleating of lambs, the grunting of pigs; all the noisy awakening of creatures who, upon feeling the first caress of dawn, permeated with pungent perfume of vegetation, long to be off and running about the fields.

Space became saturated with light; the shadows dissolved as though swallowed up by the open furrows and the masses of foliage. In the hazy mist of dawn, humid and shining rows of mulberry trees, waving lines of canebrake, large, square beds of garden vegetables like enormous green handkerchiefs, and the carefully tilled red earth became more sharply defined. . . . The day had now completely dawned.

(*Obras completas* 1:481–482)

The dynamic use of movement in such passages and the vigorous nature of the narrative as a whole (particularly in the final chapter) have led several critics to comment on the cinematographic qualities of the novel.

In *The Cabin* nature does not overpower and control man in the way that it does in *Reeds and Mud*. Blasco's theme relates more to man's inhumanity to man, and the physical environment therefore does not receive the constant emphasis to be found in his later masterpiece. Nevertheless, the author reaffirms his brand of "external" regionalism in frequent and often magnificent depictions of landscape and customs. Most striking are those passages that present the beauty and happiness of the *huerta* in ironic contrast to the vicissitudes of Batiste's struggle:

Se arrojó en un surco llorando como un niño, pensando que la tierra sería en adelante su cama eterna y su único oficio mendigar en los caminos.

Le despertaron los primeros rayos del sol hiriendo sus ojos y el alegre parloteo de los pájaros que saltaban cerca de su cabeza, aprovechando para su almuerzo los restos de la destrucción nocturna.

And casting himself down upon a furrow, he wept like a child, thinking that the earth henceforth would be his real bed, and his only occupation begging in the streets.

He was awakened by the first rays of the sun striking his eyes and the joyful twitter of the birds that hopped around his head, availing themselves of remnants of the nocturnal destruction for their breakfast.

(*Obras completas* 1:493)

La vega desperezándose voluptuosa bajo el beso del sol primaveral, envolvía al muertecito con su aliento oloroso, lo acompañaba hasta la tumba, cubriéndolo con impalpable mortaja de perfumes.

The plain, stretching out voluptuously under the kiss of the springtime sun, enveloped the dead child with its fragrance, accompanied him to the tomb, and covered him with an imperceptible shroud of perfumes.

(*Obras completas* I:541)

The appeal to the senses, plays of light and color, consistent use of the imperfect tense, fragmentary syntax, forceful, plastic exactness of detail, mixing of dream and reality (e.g., Batiste's nightmare) and rapid, vivid imagery—these and other aspects of Blasco's im-

pressionistic techniques are exhibited in some of the novel's most beautiful, poetic passages:

Tras los árboles y las casas que cerraban el horizonte asomaba el sol como enorme oblea roja, lanzando horizontales agujas de oro que obligaban a taparse los ojos. Las montañas del fondo y las torres de la ciudad iban tomando un tinte sonrosado; las nubecillas que bogaban por el cielo coloreábanse como madejas de seda carmesí; las acequias y los charcos del camino parecían poblarse de peces de fuego. Sonaba en el interior de las barracas el arrastre de la escoba, el chocar de la loza, todos los ruidos de la limpieza matinal.

The sun, rising like an enormous red wafer from behind the trees and houses that hid the horizon, shot forth blinding needles of gold. The mountains in the background and the towers of the city took on a rosy tint; the little clouds that floated in the sky grew red like crimson silk; the canals and the pools that bordered the road seemed to become filled with fiery fish; the swishing of the broom, the rattle of china, and all the sounds of the morning's cleaning came from within the cabins.

(*Obras completas* 1:483)

At other moments, as a support to the work's deterministic theme, crude elements of Zolaesque naturalistic language are meant to startle the reader:

Cansada la hoz de encontrar obstáculos, había derribado de un solo golpe una de las manos crispadas. Quedó colgando de los tendones y la piel, y el rojo muñón arrojó la sangre con fuerza, salpicando a Barret, que rugió al recibir en el rostro la caliente rociada.

Vaciló el viejo sobre sus piernas, pero antes de caer al suelo, la hoz partió horizontalmente contra su cuello, y . . . ¡zas!, cortando la complicada envoltura de pañuelos, abrió una profunda hendidura, separando casi la cabeza del tronco.

Cayó don Salvador en la acequia; sus piernas quedaron en el ribazo, agitadas por un pataleo fúnebre de res degollada. Y mientras tanto, la cabeza, hundida en el barro, soltaba toda su sangre por la profunda brecha y las aguas se teñían de rojo, siguiendo su manso curso con un murmullo plácido que alegraba el solemne silencio de la tarde.

The sickle, tired of encountering obstacles, had lopped off one of the clenched hands at a blow. It remained hanging by the tendons and the skin, and from the red stump blood spurted violently, spattering Barret, who roared as the hot stream struck his face.

The old man staggered on his legs, but before he fell to the ground the sickle cut horizontally across his neck, and . . . *zas!* severed the complicated folds of the neckerchief, opening a deep gash which almost separated the head from the trunk.

Don Salvador fell into the canal; his legs remained on the sloping bank, twitching, like a slaughtered steer giving its last kicks. And meanwhile his head, sunken into the mire, poured out all of his blood through the deep breach, and the waters, following their peaceful course with a tranquil murmur which enlivened the solemn silence of the afternoon, became tinged with red.

(Obras completas 1:495)

In general Blasco's imagery (numerous metaphors and some one hundred and thirty similes) is particularly striking, serving often to intensify the sensory (especially visual) effect of important moments: "groups of graceful spinning-mill girls passed by, marching with an even step, swinging with jaunty grace their right arms, which cut the air like strong oars"; the lines of peasants on the way to work are "rows of movable black dots, strung out like rosary beads of ants"; and the candles that cast light on Pimentó's body are "yellowish tears of light." Besides the sensory images, relating to the impressionist's desire to vivify colors, sensations, and forms, there is a second kind of simile in *The Cabin,* one that suggests a more fanciful realm. This type is exemplified in the description of the dying Pascualet: "his little brown face seemed to be darkened by a mysterious sadness as though the wings of death cast their shadow on it"; or in the news of Batiste's arrival: "a trembling of

alarm, of surprise, of indignation, it ran on through all the plain as though centuries had not elapsed, and the reports were being spread that an Algerian galley was about to land upon the beach, seeking a cargo of white flesh." The numerous repetitions of contrary-to-fact clauses with *como si* ("as though") serve to reinforce the feeling that supernatural forces control the peasants' destiny, "as though" fate were determined to curse the events of the region.

There are two interrelated kinds of imagery that predominate in *The Cabin* and that increase in frequency as the dramatic action intensifies. First, and of particular thematic importance, are Blasco's typical expressions of animalization. As in *The Mayflower,* both inanimate objects and characters are compared to animals. The bestial nature of man is everywhere evident, from the visions in Roseta's dream to Batiste's increasingly animalistic outbursts. Secondly, images of redness occur from the outset (see the final words of the description of dawn cited earlier) and are particularly significant as reinforcements in presenting the farmers' primitive ferocity and brutality. From the soil that stains the irrigation ditches to the blood spilled by Barret, the facade of the Tribunal building, and the atmosphere of the Copa tavern—the color red reappears as a kind of *sudario rojo* (red shroud) looming over the action of the story. The two dominant images thus complement each other and underline the dehumanization and self-destruction that can come about under the influence of alcohol or in cases of social injustice, hatred, or revenge.

The major costumbristic descriptions of *The Cabin,* while less numerous than in *The Three Roses* or *Reeds and Mud,* are nevertheless extremely significant, both as fascinating and expertly drawn verbal paintings in themselves and as supports for the characterization or the plot development. Five such scenes seem to stand out: (1) the Tribunal de las Aguas, an important link in the chain of developing relations between Batiste and

Pimentó; (2) Don Joaquín's schoolroom, inserted as a humorous change of pace but significant also in the teacher's voicing of Blasco's thematic concerns and as a prelude to Pascualet's death; (3) the scene in the tavern, leading to the drinking contest and renewed hostilities between the two central characters; (4) the marketplace, where Batiste buys a new horse; and (5) Pascualet's funeral. Other such scenes or elements include Pepeta's milk delivery, the silk factory, the Fuente de la Reina, the peasants' hair salon, the custom of long engagements and rigid fatherly control, the usury of the landowners, and the superstitions of Tío Tomba. Sociological studies of the Valencian region confirm the authenticity of these passages as well as other aspects of the novel's characterization and the snatches of local dialect. Nevertheless Blasco the regionalist, attuned particularly to pictorial beauty and to the observation of external reality, confessed to his biographer Camille Pitollet that he was not a "scientific" observer like Zola but that he assimilated imaginatively, rather than documenting empirically, the background for his novels.

It is important to realize, then, that the *costumbrismo* of *The Cabin* is carefully integrated into the fabric of the narrative and is not meant simply as gratuitous, exotic, or picturesque regionalistic elaboration. Finally, we should note that in contrast to the descriptions of local mores of the early 1800's, Blasco's sketches are more concerned with historical and socioeconomic factors; for this reason the idyllic tranquillity of these scenes (the calm of the Fuente, the ritual of the horse-buying, the peaceful atmosphere of Pascualet's funeral) soon collapses into violence.

The author's use of perspective does not—his fame as "the Spanish Zola" again notwithstanding—reflect a totally naturalistic desire for objectivity. For all the claims to impersonality, Blasco's use of humor (e.g., Don Joaquín consoles himself with the thought that he alone in the region wears a tie), the frequent instances of crude irony (e.g., the happy music

played at the funeral), and open authorial identification with the characters are evident deviations from Zola's perspective. In fact, one of the novel's primary flaws relates to the confusion brought about by Blasco's divided sympathies: at first he awakens our support for the tenant farmer in Tío Barret's struggle, only to switch our allegiance to Batiste (following the latter's defiance of the Tribunal's order) in his fight against the superstitions and prejudices of the other farmers. In general Blasco demonstrates more sympathy for the farmers than he does for the common folk of *The Mayflower* or *Reeds and Mud*. Richard Cardwell offers ample proof of the streak of sentimentality that intrudes upon the work's objectivity: "the trite interpolation of human aspiration into the song of the sparrows" at the start, "similar anthropomorphic sentiments in the mind of the cow," the naiveté in the picture of the Barret girls as "angels of God," "overdone and emasculated bourgeois Romanticism" in the account of the horse's death, and "the vision of angels ascending" after Pascualet's passing away.

More often, however, Blasco does maintain a relatively objective stance. This is most evident in his choice of authorial "position." As in the other Valencian novels, instances of omniscient comment (concerning justice, the social function of property, etc.) are far outweighed by the Zolaesque "indirect free style"—descriptive reporting of the thoughts and speech of his characters.

Turning to characterization, we note again Blasco's tendency to create one-sided, superficial figures whose significance is to be found more in their actions or their representational, stereotypic roles as regional types than in any kind of individualistic, psychological profundity. Batiste's dream is the closest thing to the more interesting character reveries found at the end of *The Three Roses* and *The Mayflower*. In great part the figures of *The Cabin* are projections of the primitiveness (and Moorish history) of the region, happy when water is plentiful, miserable in times of drought. There is no attempt at detailed physical description of their appearance or of personalized dialogue, as exhibited in the earlier novels of Benito Pérez Galdós—no hint of the dualistic complexity of environmental immersion plus a higher, cultured spirituality, as found occasionally in Emilia Pardo Bazán. In some instances, such as in Barret's ravings in chapter 2, the treatment of characters sinks to melodrama.

Basically the narrative is constructed around the struggle between Batiste and Pimentó, hero versus antihero, with little attention to subtlety of motivation. Love, never an important factor in Blasco's Valencian novels, is almost totally absent here. Finally, by way of general comment on characterization, we note that *The Cabin* exemplifies well the author's rejection of static, single portraits, and his preference instead for presenting his characters through a dynamic (albeit superficial) series of partial glimpses, most importantly in the case of Batiste.

Batiste himself, developed from the same uncomplicated mold as El Retor of *The Mayflower* or Toni of *Reeds and Mud,* represents the forces of stoic labor and unrelenting struggle. He comes also to symbolize the right of free choice in one's work, the instinct for self-preservation, and the voice of paternal sentiment. Unreflective and blindly oblivious to the warnings of reality, he never breaks from Blasco's pattern. He is capable of deep family love and loyalty but nevertheless degenerates into animalistic savagery as the superior forces of the environment gain control of his behavior. Most of the chapters end with the fear or the symptoms of this disintegration: Pimentó's mocking echo of the Tribunal sentence, the stealing of irrigation, the attack on Batiste's horse, the fight in the tavern, and the final breakdown at the end.

Pimentó appears as a behavioristic representation of the collective psychology of the region, with its prejudices, vengeful impulses, and cowardly fears when confronted with the possibility of open conflict. He is lazy, egotis-

tical, unscrupulous, and hypocritical (as revealed during Pascualet's funeral)—the cowardly bully afraid to stand up to Batiste's rifle when the latter disobeys the Tribunal.

The secondary characters are even more one-dimensional. Tío Tomba ("tomb"), like the Theban prophet Tiresias, is an aged, blind man with the gift of prophecy. Like Don Eugenio of *The Three Roses,* Tía Picores of *The Mayflower,* or Tío Paloma of *Reeds and Mud,* he is the "old wise one," leading the "chorus" in expressing the inexorability of defeat. Of the women, only Pepeta, as a victim of circumstances, and Roseta, in her relationship with Tonet, are slightly humanized. The children— Pascualet, Roseta, and Batiste—are also marginal figures but, like La Borda of *Reeds and Mud,* reveal Blasco's capacity for poignant tenderness and sympathy.

Rather than an investigation of the psychological complexity of the inhabitants of the Valencia region, *The Cabin* is an attempt at social statement encased within a lyrical, descriptive framework. The most evident element of this thematic content is the condemnation of the landlords' exploitation of the peasant farmers. Written amid the widespread prejudices and dissensions of the year when Spain lost her colonies in the war with the United States, the novel can be viewed also as a criticism of any kind of blind hatred, ostracism, and revenge among neighbors and an expression of the need to discard the oppressive weight of outmoded traditions. In brief, the story represents a rejection of man's inhumanity to man.

Despite the confusion caused by Blasco's change of sympathies (initially he appears to admire worker solidarity; later he espouses the right of individual rebellion), other social themes are evident. Don Joaquín, for example, voices the author's plea for improved rural education in order to combat narrow parochialism, social deprivation, and loss of emotional control. The evils of usury and alcoholism are also clearly condemned, and the reader senses the author's conviction that the land should belong to those who till it.

375

Nevertheless, *The Cabin* is not a socially revolutionary novel. No solutions are offered, and Batiste, despite his loyalty to family and his will to struggle, is not dynamic enough for us to conclude that specific remedies may be possible.

With regard to personal, psychological traits, Blasco condemns excess pride (e.g., in both Batiste and Pimentó), hypocrisy, and self-delusion (Batiste consistently ignores the signs of warning, both within himself and from without), and extols the virtues of hard work, fortitude, and family loyalty. Most importantly, man must learn to control his more violent, animalistic tendencies.

On a somewhat more transcendent level of thematic expression *The Cabin* exhibits a diffuse, somewhat inconsistent, but nevertheless undeniable naturalistic pessimism. The critics, we might note, are divided about the extent of determinism operative in the novel. Hayward Keniston and Lawrence Kiddle say in their introduction to a Spanish-language edition of *The Cabin* (*La barraca* [New York, 1960]) that

> the final defeat of Batiste should not be interpreted as proof of the pessimism of the author. Blasco is pessimistic about the role that society and its traditions play in thwarting the individual, but he is optimistic about the capacity for courageous struggle found in a human being. Batiste and his family must leave their farm, but they are not beaten. They will carry on in some other place because, like Don Quixote, they do not recognize defeat. They leave behind them sobering experience of a senseless struggle that brought death to the child, Pascualet, and to the man, Pimentó. It will be harder in the future to unite the community against a newcomer. That is Batiste's victory.

(p. xv)

It is true that *The Cabin* is not as naturalistic in theme as *Reeds and Mud*. Nature itself does not seem to crush the peasants as it does in the later work. Indeed, there does appear to be a sense of idealism, of man's potential for work and for goodness. But Cardwell is nearer the mark when he suggests that a feeling of somber pessimism is more prevailing—what Sherman Eoff terms "a fateful overtone of transcendent implications." This thesis is supported by several factors: (1) there are some moments when the region itself (e.g., its heat) is felt as a distinctive, primordial power, indifferent to and controlling man's actions; (2) a cyclical structure suggests the futility of man's efforts; (3) mankind is seen as unable to control its own savage instincts; (4) there are frequent reminders of the link between the peasants and the vengeful ways of their Moorish ancestors; and (5) the use of leitmotifs (e.g., fire, Tío Tomba's warnings) and of foreshadowing, the animal and color imagery, the frequent repetition of such words as "damnation," "devil," "chill," "funereal," "executioner," etc., and the occasional passages of naturalistic description create an atmosphere of deterministic inevitability. Blasco's pessimism is surely a "dynamic" one, since continued struggle is extolled; but most readers will sense very little hope at the novel's conclusion.

The general structure of the work certainly contributes to this feeling. A sense of inexorability is fostered by the fact that many of the events of the plot form a causal chain: for example, the arrival of Batiste's family leads to the derision of his children at school, which in turn leads to Pascualet's death, the hope engendered by the apparently sympathetic attitude of the peasants when they attend the funeral, Batiste's subsequent readiness to join others at the tavern, the fight there with Pimentó, and, finally, the concluding tragic events. The plot, we have said, can be seen to form a single line of action without secondary complications, which includes a series of climactic moments within an overall crescendo of intensity. Built into this pattern are a number of deceptive pauses (dawn breaking over the region, the Tribunal, the love affair of Roseta and Tonet, the schoolroom scene, the marketplace, the burial), all of which suggest momentary hope only to collapse in tragedy.

The progression of encounters between Batiste and Pimentò also adds to the feeling of inevitability: their first meeting (chapter 3), Pimentó's mocking echo of the Tribunal sentence (chapter 4), the wounding of Batiste's horse (chapter 8), the fight in the tavern (chapter 9), and the final conflict (chapter 10).

As previously suggested, the circularity of plot further reinforces the deterministic theme. Batiste's story is in many ways a repetition of Tío Barret's tragedy: ill-fortune, exploitation, and the power of human instinct serve to break a hardworking tenant peasant and force him from his land. Both men steal water, both react with a strong emotional identification with the soil, and both lose their horses, borrow from the landlords, take up a gun in anger, and fall prey to the effects of alcohol. Barret's eviction, in turn, repeats that of the Moors centuries earlier. Structural circularity is suggested also by similarities between the beginning and ending of the novel: (1) Batiste's family arrives "smelling of hunger, in desperate flight, as if disgrace pursued the family, trampling on their heels" and leaves with "hunger trampling their heels behind them"; (2) a description of dawn over a ruined cabin occi   . the start and at the end; and (3) flames restore the lands at first and then destroy them afterward. Thus, as Cardwell points out, "life becomes a meaningless habit. Man's toil and aspiration come to nothing."

The chapter arrangement is similar to most of the other Valencian novels, except for the fact that, like *The Mayflower*, there is no real epilogue or denouement. Chapters 1–3 provide exposition and introduce the initial conflict: chapter 1 introduces the major characters in medias res; chapter 2 retrospectively narrates the tragedy of Tío Barret; and the transitional chapter 3 includes Tío Tomba's prophecy, introduces Batiste as the "central consciousness" (broken only in chapters 5 and 6), and begins the main action.

In the rising action of the remainder of the novel, the next four chapters are devoted to the family's problems: Batiste's in chapter 4 (the Tribunal and Batiste's defiance); Roseta's in chapter 5 (the initial flashback to chapter 4; the quarrel at the Fuente and Roseta's tragedy); the children's in chapter 6 (Don Joaquín's school—comic relief—leading to Pascualet's tragedy); and the horse's in chapter 7 (the initial flashback; the death of the horse; the wounding of the new horse; the death of Pascualet; the warning of Tío Tomba).

The last three chapters complete the rising action: chapter 8 depicts the funeral (momentary peace); chapter 9 describes hope from the harvest and the fight in the tavern; and chapter 10 includes the warnings of Tío Tomba and the final defeat.

The plot thus exhibits an extraordinary organic unity brought about by the use of leitmotifs (particularly Tío Tomba's reappearances and reminders of the weight of the past), foreshadowing, imagery, careful integration of costumbristic passages into the action, the constant presence of regional landscape, and the causal link between many of the events. Yet each chapter also reveals a certain unified aesthetic autonomy (no doubt necessary because of the installment form in which the novel appeared), mirroring the pattern of inexorability displayed by the whole: an expository presentation of circumstances, a simple, rising action, and a forceful climax or moment of suspense. Except for chapter 8, which deceptively offers the reader hope for a happy resolution and thus heightens the effect of the final disaster, each chapter of the main action ends by highlighting the opposition of the peasants to Batiste's family.

The Cabin does exhibit weakness in its use of perspective, its occasional melodrama and naive sentimentality, and the superficiality of its characterization. Nevertheless, it exemplifies well Blasco's greatest artistic achievements: a careful, tightly woven structure, the forceful presentation of man's capacity to struggle against misfortune, and, above all, a magnificently drawn picture of local landscape and customs. In addition, the powerful social themes help the work to transcend regional depiction to embrace universal concerns. Certainly it is appropriate that many still refer to Blasco as "the author of *The Cabin.*"

REEDS AND MUD

"It is the novel," said Blasco to Pitollet, "that gives me a most grateful remembrance, the one I composed most solidly, and the one I feel is the most well rounded." Of the novels written before the Spanish Civil War, *Reeds and Mud* probably represents the most thorough adaptation in Spain of the tenets of French naturalism. The scene is set between 1890 and 1900 in the swamp-lake region of the Albufera near Valencia, an area well known throughout the country for its rice fields and bird game. Blasco's intimate knowledge of the region has been well documented, and the scenes and characters depicted once again sprang from the author's own acute powers of observation.

The narrative itself is constructed on three levels: (1) the story of three generations (the old fisherman Tío Paloma, his hardworking son, Toni, and his rebellious, irresponsible grandson, Tonet); (2) the lush, all-pervading atmosphere of the Albufera; and (3) a constant, transcendent feeling of the power of destiny, the irrevocable pressures of an abstract, deterministic force. The plot, demonstrating the sharp singleness of effect that one generally finds in a good short story, traces the love affair between Tonet and Neleta from childhood to disaster years later. While the lad is away at war, Neleta marries a sickly but rich tavern owner, Cañamél, in order to escape her impoverished existence. The subsequent illicit love affair between Tonet and Neleta leads to a series of events in which man is shown to be defenseless against the destructive forces of nature and animal instinct. Tonet suffers an emotional breakdown. Before Cañamél dies he writes a will stating that Neleta cannot retain their property if she remarries or associates in an intimate way with another man. After Ne-

leta gives birth to Tonet's child she refuses to see her lover openly and orders him to abandon the child in the city across the lake in order to escape further suspicion of having violated the terms of the will. Instead fear, remorse, and accidents of fate lead Tonet to throw the infant into the lake. When a dog later discovers the baby's corpse, Tonet seeks escape in suicide.

The plot, then, is one of savage actions and strong emotions. Nevertheless, despite the striking and at times shocking turns of events, Blasco restrains from authorial involvement or comment more than in any other Valencian novel.

Reeds and Mud represents one of the first Spanish novels to utilize fully the naturalistic method of authorial neutrality. Our final impression is one of having been exposed to a set of circumstances and incidents without being asked to approve or disapprove and without ascertaining completely the author's feelings with regard to his characters or action. The closest Blasco comes to revealing his own emotions occurs during the poignant closing of the novel.

The writer's particular use of perspective is, in fact, one of the most prominent and significant aspects of his realism. At least five techniques are utilized to create a realistic and objective impression. First, the author's view (and ours) is again almost always within one character or (as at the beginning) within the people as a whole, and we share completely the knowledge, opinions, ignorance, and emotions of that perspective. When Tonet returns from the war, for example, he is referred to as "the son of Tío Toni," not by his name, because at that moment we are within the people's point of view, and they cannot remember exactly what he was called. Dialogue is reported indirectly through the same technique, and there are frequent stylistic changes that accommodate shifts in point of view. Consider, for instance, the manner in which Cañamél's hopes and agitation are reflected in the use of short, abrupt phrases: "He was ready to follow their advice to the letter: he would keep moving about, so that he could get rid of that fat which enwrapped his body and stifled his lungs; he would visit the baths they had recommended; he would obey Neleta, who knew more than he."

Second, Blasco often places the reader in the position of a newly-arrived and hence ignorant onlooker, revealing what is going on only later in a scene, as in the case of the old man's search for an otter or the manner in which we ascertain why Neleta has left for Ruzate toward the end of the novel. At times the reader's view of an incident is at first that of the present moment but soon jumps to the past for full background detail and explanation, eventually reaching again the original point in time. The episode of the Fiesta del Niño Jesús represents the moment when this technique is used most extensively. Third, Blasco frequently utilizes the shifting points of view to reveal more than one outlook concerning the same incident. Thus we witness twice the episode where Neleta opens her window when Tonet whistles from the street below; there are parallel passages presenting the thoughts of the two lovers concerning the possibility of marriage; and the stories about Carlos IV and the visit of royalty to the area centuries before are revealed first through the point of view of Tío Paloma and later through that of Tonet. Fourth, at times we learn later of things that had happened during a previously described scene, occurrences about which we were originally unaware. We realize after the fact, for example, that Tonet has slipped out during the "pre-hunting" party.

Finally, Blasco's technique of shifting points of view relates directly to the force of the novel's occasional humor. The most noticeable elements of this humor are the juvenile enthusiasm of Don Joaquín (a well-to-do Valencian who hires local guides for excursions on the lake) during the hunting incident and the simultaneous "religious love affair" of his guide, Sangonera, with the three dinner pots; the latter's "anti-work" philosophy; Cañamél's

scorn for the doctor's advice against his drinking because "he could not despise the villagers"; and the priest who watches to see who will spit on his church floor and who believes that the question of morals "resided in the stomach." Typically, such scenes offer no subtlety, no refined sense of irony to the reader, but serve primarily (especially in the case of the hunting incident) as comic relief, as a variation in tone from the sense of misery and doom that otherwise pervades most of the novel. Humor here provides a sharp contrast to the action and thus serves to make the plot more forceful and striking. Of particular importance is the fact that the author places the hunting episode between two of the most lugubrious and unpleasant incidents in the novel.

The realism and forceful objectivity that result from these shifting points of view are strengthened by the writer's descriptive techniques. *Reeds and Mud,* more than anything else, stands as a series of descriptive passages, revealing the freshness, the spontaneity, the richness, and the sensual power that constitute Blasco's most significant artistic contribution to literature. With only a few exceptions (for example, the description of the tavern), there are no passages of extended, minute detail. Yet the beauty or destructiveness of nature comes alive before us.

Within these descriptions certain elements stand out. Prominent among these is, typically, the graphic appeal to our senses—as, for example, that of smell, more important here than in any novel of Blasco: "An unbearable stench rose about the vessel. Its planks had become saturated with the odor of the eel-baskets and the grime of hundreds of passengers: a nauseating mixture of gelatinous skins, scales of fish bred in the mud, dirty feet, and filthy clothes." In contrast to the smell of fish or human sweat are the many visual depictions:

La dehesa estaba florida y perfumada como un jardín. Los matorrales, bajo la caricia de un sol que parecía de verano, se cubrían de flores, y por encima de ellos brillaban los insectos, como botones de oro. . . . Los pinos, retorcidos y

379

seculares, se movían con majestuoso rumor, y bajo las bóvedas que formaban sus copas exten-díase una dulce penumbra semejante a la de las naves de una catedral inmensa. De cuando en cuando, al través de dos troncos, se filtraba un rayo del sol como si entrase por un ventanal.

The Dehesa was in blossom, and as fragrant as a garden. . . . The bushes, under the caress of a sun that was as warm as in summer, were full of flowers, and above them insects shone bright as gold. . . . The twisted, ageless pines stirred with a stately murmur, and under the vaults formed by their wide tops a soft shade prevailed, like the shadows in the naves of an immense cathedral. From time to time a sunbeam fell between tree trunks, as if coming in through a window.

(*Obras completas* 1:839)

More frequently, we are engulfed in the sounds of the Albufera: "The song of the cuckoo broke the silence; the frogs of a nearby pool, which had stopped croaking as the children arrived, recovered their confidence and returned to their singsong; the persistent, bothersome mosquitoes buzzed about their heads, their wings gleaming a little in the dark twilight."

Blasco's descriptions are again more dynamic than static. Objects "move" or "move themselves" (reflexive verbs are frequent) rather than being moved by exterior forces. Commentators on his style seem to have overlooked the fact that occasional passages are constructed in chains, with one element building and related to the following, in order to suggest movement. The novelist blends subject and style, to convey, for example, the sensation that objects are seen from the boat gliding across the water:

Las bandas de ánades agitaban sus alas en torno de la proa, que enturbiaba el espejo del canal, donde se reflejaban, invertidas, las barrancas del pueblo, las negras barcas amarradas a los viveros, con techos de paja a ras del agua, ador-nados en los extremos con cruces de madera, como si quisieran colocar las anquilas de su seno bajo la divina protección.

The flock of ducks fluttered around the bow, which itself clouded the mirror of the canal, on which one could see reflected, inversely, the ravine below the village, the black boats tied at the waterline to the thatched fishponds, decorated at their peaks with wooden crosses, as if they wanted to place the eels within the divine protection of their innermost recesses.

(*Obras completas* 1:819)

As with the other Valencian novels, the reader is frequently struck by the exactness of detail or vivid plasticity of the author's style, of which prominent examples are the description of the progressive increase of the moon's light or the portraits of Cañamél, Paloma, and Neleta. Blasco's impressionism is equally visible in *Reeds and Mud,* reflecting the painter's sye; Miguel Ángel Escalante describes this as an "impressionist tendency to reveal through light the depth and clarity of a vibrant air from the sun's heat, which makes the outlines of objects seen at a distance shimmer."

At other moments Blasco's descriptions are unmistakably naturalistic. The candor and unpleasantness of Zolaesque descriptions are present in such scenes as the depiction of decaying fish, Cañamél's tic and his sickness, the priest's administration of last rites to Sangonera, "soiling his cassock with vomit," and the reaction of the boy who "expelled around him nauseous streams of liquids and half-chewed solids." Most famous of all is the scene in which the dog returns with the body of the dead child:

Un lío de trapos y en él algo lívido y gelatinoso erizado de sanguijuelas: una cabecita hinchada, deforme, negruzca, con las cuencas vacías y colgando de una de ellas un globo de un ojo: todo tan repugnante, tan hediondo, que parecía ente-nebrecer repentinamente el agua y el espacio, haciendo que en pleno sol cayese la noche sobre el lago.

A bundle of rags, and inside something livid and gelatinous, squirming with leeches: a swollen infant's head, deformed, blackish, with its eye sockets empty, and the ball of the eye hanging from one of them: all of it so repellent, so ill-smelling, that it seemed of a sudden to darken the water and the surrounding landscape, causing night to fall over the lake in the midst of bright day.

(*Obras completas* 1:922)

Finally, many of Blasco's descriptions are again costumbristic. Foremost among such scenes are the opening boat ride, the lottery, the recounting of the legend of the snake Sancha, the raffling of the largest eel, the Fiesta del Niño Jesús, the hunting expeditions, and many minor descriptions of cooking, Sunday processions, tavern games of *truque,* the village archival system, life in nearby Catarroja, vegetation, and bird and animal life. In addition the past history of the region is again presented and blended into the narrative. However, the deterministic theme, the creation of the man of will (Toni), and the structural relationship between the major costumbristic scenes and the novel as a whole serve to raise the work above a strictly regionalistic level.

As seen from the previous examples of descriptive techniques, Blasco's style again demonstrates a combination of simplicity and rich expressiveness. Certain stylistic elements again serve to raise the language occasionally to the somewhat poetic level seen in other novels: the frequent use of the imperfect (and conditional) tense to render a feeling of timelessness and pictorial vitality, the use of adjectives before their nouns (for example, "por la tarde regresaba al Palmar, con su blanducha y desbordante obesidad rendida por el diario viaje" [in the afternoon she would return to Palmar, her soft, billowy, obese body exhausted by the daily journey]), and frequent vivid imagery, particularly similes. Weeds are "como viscosos tenáculos" (like viscous tentacles); clouds are "como vedijas de blanco lana" (like curls of white wool). Not surprisingly, the characters are constantly likened to animals: Paloma to a bird or fish, the children to eels, or the whole family to "flies on the lake."

Typically, *Reeds and Mud* is a novel of situation, not of character. No figures are presented in depth and none really stands out as a protagonist (a label that might be more accurately applied to the Albufera as a whole). Three levels of characters emerge in the course of the novel: (1) Tonet and Neleta as the main stimulus to the action, Paloma, Toni, and Cañamèl as supporting types, and Sangonera and La Borda as counterfoils; (2) minor figures, such as Don Joaquín, La Samaruca, and the priest; and (3) the whole commenting, gossiping chorus of villagers. Paloma, Toni, and Tonet stand in part as representatives of the past, present, and future, respectively. Most personages, with the exception of La Borda, lack any kind of psychological depth, and all seem to represent dominant passions or vices: laziness (Tonet), drunkenness (Sangonera), avarice (Neleta), the will to work and struggle (Toni), and hatred for the changing times (Paloma).

Within the framework of these few dominating traits, the characters are developed in only a very limited fashion. Tonet is a victim of his own weaknesses: his indifference, his laziness, his hypocrisy, his yearning for adventure, and (under the influence of Neleta) his greed. Caught between the philosophies of his father and grandfather, he is unable to shake off his inertia and irresoluteness and make any decision regarding his life. His suicide, rather than a punishment, should be looked on as a final act of cowardice and self-pity, an escape from facing the future.

Neleta represents feminine avarice as well as the force and fecundity of nature herself (hence her comparison with the serpent Sancha). Constant references to her eyes suggest her role as a crafty, egoistical cat figure. She is individualized only by her sexual frustration and an occasional suggestion of real affection for Tonet.

Tonet's companion Sangonera is a memorable type, at the same time comic and pathetic, a kind of nineteenth-century hippie. His love for nature, his plea that man return to a simple way of life, and his refusal to work because labor violates God's commandments suggest that Blasco has put some of Jean-Jacques Rousseau's perspectives to work in this character's creation. His only concern in life is to have enough to eat and drink, and it is ironic that gluttony is the cause of his death. He, unlike Neleta, dislikes greed; in contrast to Tonet he maintains faith in divine grace; and he alone is happy to the end. In short, he is a modern version of the seventeenth-century *gracioso,* the comic "servant" who nevertheless is able to utter some very wise convictions.

Tonet's grandfather Tío Paloma represents the old way: its customs, its sense of humor, its honesty; as such he is one of the most prominent victims of the novel. His slyness (for example, in avoiding the authorities when he wants to hunt) and his pride (shown by his not wanting anyone to find Tonet's body) are only slight suggestions of individuality.

Toni, Tonet's father, like Batiste of *The Cabin* or El Retor of *The Mayflower,* represents hard work, self-denial, constancy, the undying spirit of struggle. He is one of the few characters who demonstrates generosity and love (as evidenced by his final insistence on seeing his son's body). Cañamél is unidimensionally greedy and corrupt. La Borda, the servant girl in Tonet's house, is love and self-sacrifice incarnate, slaving humbly and uncomplainingly for Toni and Tonet. Only she demonstrates Blasco's occasional capacity for tenderness, as shown in the novel's powerful and touching conclusion:

> *Y mientras el lamento del tío Toni rasgaba como un alarido de desesperación el silencio del amanecer, la Borda, viendo de espaldas a su padre, inclinóse al borde de la fosa y besó la lívida cabeza con un beso ardiente, de inmensa pasión, de amor sin esperanza, osando, ante el misterio de la muerte, revelar por primera vez el secreto de su vida.*

And while Tío Toni's lamentations rent the silence of the dawn like a howl of despair, La Borda, seeing that her father had turned his back, bent over the edge of the grave and kissed the livid head with an ardent kiss, a kiss of immense passion, of hopeless love, daring, in the face of the mystery of death, to reveal for the first time the secret of her life.

(Obras completas 1:927)

More important than the attempt to convey a profound level of psychological development is the very fact of the characters' downfall. This in turn brings us to a discussion of theme, and more particularly, to the question of naturalistic intent.

Reeds and Mud illustrates the fullness of Blasco's acceptance of the naturalists' deterministic philosophy. Man's struggle against the bestiality of his own instincts and the powerful forces of nature is again shown to be a futile one. The death of Paloma's other sons before the novel begins, Cañamél's malaria (a result of the environment), and Tonet's victimization by Neleta's greed are forceful indications of man's inability to combat these forces. Sangonera's alcoholism and Don Joaquín's sudden "pleasure of destruction in shooting birds" illustrate the constant suggestion of man's animalism. The author himself suggests at one point (through Neleta's thoughts) that "the Devil, who doubtless had his hand in this, had considered it better to have obstacles arise in difficult moments."

The use of ironic circumstances again appears repeatedly to emphasize the message that man's efforts seem meager indeed compared to the force of destiny. Tonet is buried in the land that was to serve as the basis for his and his father's future prosperity; Cañamél's will thwarts Neleta's greedy ambitions; Sangonera, whose only concern in life has been to assure himself enough to eat and drink, is killed by his own gluttony; Cañamél's dog finds the corpse of the child (which leads to the destruction of the lovers' relationship through the subsequent suicide of Tonet); and the beauty and impassivity of nature are presented in sharp contrast to the violence and anguish of the suicide scene.

Nevertheless, even in this, Blasco's most Zolaesque work, certain factors would tend to negate the possibility of an entirely naturalistic interpretation. The strengths of both Paloma and Toni are exalted. Heredity is not shown to be a significant force, since all three generations differ greatly. Furthermore, despite the causality of the novel's structural components, the plot of *Reeds and Mud* lacks the strict logic of *The Cabin*. Tonet's suicide, for example, is not really necessary, since there would be no way to identify the body of the child; sheer coincidence helps to bring about the denouement in that, if the child had not been born *that* night, Tonet would not have seen the hunters around his boat and felt compelled to kill the infant rather than take it to its destination; the suicide, in turn, would not have taken place. The deterministic logic evident in many of the French naturalistic novels is not so predominant here. What we do have is a graphic representation of the hardships of life in the Albufera (lack of nutrition, death of the newborn, malaria, etc.), along with a recognition of a certain bestiality native to the human species. The sins of Adam and the serpent are constant, as reflected in the story of the boy and the snake Sancha, and later in that of Tonet and Neleta.

The naturalistic elements of the novel's theme would seem to relate directly to the work's structure, a pattern that again is meant to reflect the inevitability of the denouement (and here there *is* one chapter of denouement following the climax). What we have, in broadest outline, is a now-familiar pattern: three expository chapters, consisting of one episodic introduction (similar to the milk delivery scene in *The Cabin* or the initial market scene of *The Three Roses* and *The Mayflower*) together with two sections of retrospective narration. This is followed by the action proper, a causal plot line building directly to a clear climactic point in the penultimate chapter. The main action and subsequent epilogue (denouement) are in turn built upon the movement between three central points in the plot: adultery, infanticide, and suicide. The narrative structure may thus be outlined as follows:

In the exposition chapter 1 is an episodic introduction, presented in medias res; chapters 2 and 3 provide retrospective narration, progressing from past to present time, presenting family background and general background, in particular of the generations of Tonet, Sangonera, and Neleta. In the rising action, chapter 4 initiates the "plot" proper with the lottery; chapter 5 develops the love affair between Tonet and Neleta, leading to adultery (the start of the central complication); chapter 6 depicts the Fiesta del Niño Jesús, leading to Cañamél's break with Tonet; chapter 7 develops the relationship between Tonet and Sangonera and describes Neleta's increasing difficulties and Cañamél's death and will; chapter 8 includes the discovery of Neleta's pregnancy, the hunting excursion, and the infanticide; and chapter 9 includes Don Joaquín and the hunting scene, Sangonera's sickness and death, the second hunt, and the discovery of the corpse (the climax of the action). Chapter 10 constitutes the epilogue: Tonet's suicide and burial.

What is remarkable about the novel's structure, however, is again its complete unity—a compactness and careful interweaving of interrelated elements that, in view of Blasco's impetuous, tumultuous nature, can only surprise us. The plot is built upon a fairly strict chain of causal links. Thus the child's birth during the time of the hunting excursion leads to the frustration of Tonet's original plans and the subsequent abandonment of the infant in the lake. This in turn causes Sangonera's death, since the latter had taken Tonet's place in the hunt and had devoured all of Don Joaquín's food. In order to erase some of the bad memories of Sangonera during the first outing, Don Joaquín is taken out a second time, which leads to the discovery of the corpse and the subsequent suicide of Tonet.

Then, too, all four major costumbristic scenes are again made integral to the causal plot line. Thus the lottery brings about Tonet's good fortune and leads to the relationship with Cañamél, which in turn serves to encourage the love affair between the boy and Neleta. Similarly, the fiesta causes Tonet's ejection from the tavern (perhaps a factor contributing to Neleta's subsequent coldness toward him), and the hunting excursion provides the occasion for the climax and denouement. The psychological and regionalistic elements of the plot are thus carefully blended to function within a single, uninterrupted crescendo, as in the treatment of pressures in Tonet's life. The chain of events in turn reflects the thematic emphasis upon environmental and deterministic forces.

A series of parallels or corresponding elements serves to lend further unity to the work: the two scenes involving Tonet and Neleta (once as children symbolically "lost" in the woods, and later in the boat), the explicit relationship between the Sancha myth at the beginning (about a snake who accidentally crushes her human companion in an embrace) and Neleta's situation at the end, the hunting scenes, both of which lead to the death of a major character, the lottery and fiesta episodes, the mention of hunting events at the start and the bird-shooting at the end, and the grotesque parallels between Neleta's pregnant state and Sangonera's later sickness.

Certain leitmotifs add to the compact nature of the work's structure. Primary among these are the periodic return to Toni's struggle with the land and the constant presence of the lake itself, the scene of all the novel's major narrative incidents. The repetition of certain images, particularly those relating to man's animalistic nature, serves a similar function.

Finally, Blasco's very skillful use of timing and contrast contributes significantly to the overall effect of the story. The reader notes, for example, how every chapter within the main action again ends with a highly dramatic action or revelation, inciting the reader to continue without pause: Tonet's moving into the tavern (chapter 4), the adultery (chapter 5), Tonet's ejection from the tavern (chapter 6), Cañamél's will (chapter 7), the infanticide (chapter 8), the discovery of the body (chapter

9), and the very poignant lament of La Borda (chapter 10).

Blasco's manipulation of contrasts is, typically, equally forceful. Note for example the striking difference in tone between the humor of the first hunting scene (where a clear parallel to Don Quixote and Sancho is suggested) and the two deaths that surround it. By the insertion of this moment of comic relief, the reader is lulled into suspecting that the pressures of the environment (or of destiny) may not win out after all. But he is thrown back into the world of harsh reality with the grotesque description of Sangonera's death. On a broader scale the contrast between the beauty and tranquillity of nature and the bestial savagery of man's predicament is again present at moments throughout the novel.

We began our analysis by stating that the novel combines three levels of reality: the story of three generations (and in particular of Tonet), the constant presence and influence of the Albufera, and the transcending, symbolic world of deterministic pressures. Just as these planes of action are brought into artistic harmony, so the major aspects of style, characterization, theme, and structure function together to produce a natural and balanced whole. The near-flawless causality inherent in the work's structure serves to support the deterministic theme. The stylistic contrasts between impressionistic description and savage action lead the reader to a similar awareness. The constant presence of verbs in the imperfect or conditional tense enhances our recognition of the intemporality of nature, as well as of man's inability to mitigate a basically animalistic temperament. The costumbristic descriptions again serve to clarify the structure of the novel as well as to aid in the delineation of characters.

Above all, the unity of *Reeds and Mud* derives from the fact that Blasco wrote with the clear purpose of presenting the people, customs, and environment of a region without recourse to moralizing. His artistry is again seen to stem from the rapid, expressive, picto-

OTHER NOVELS

Finally, let us glance briefly at a few representative works from Blasco's later periods.

The Mob is the fourth and last of the novels of social protest. In large part it is a descriptive work, containing excellent impressionistic passages as the reader is led through the slums of the Madrid environs and meets the ragpickers, writers, bricklayers, poachers, gypsies, and juvenile delinquents who constitute the mob. The setting, complete with naturalistic depictions of those who exist by eating the garbage of the rich, is the closest of Blasco's works to Pío Baroja's trilogy *La lucha por la vida* (*The Struggle for Life,* 1904). The story concerns a writer, Isidro Maltrana, who manages to escape from the worst of this impoverished world to become a journalist of sorts. He marries, and his wife dies shortly after giving birth to a son. Her body is then used for dissection in the medical school, the final punishment for Maltrana's having abandoned those of his social class. A spark of optimism occurs at the end, however, as the protagonist, who until now has been a weak-willed individual, swears his determination to work hard and provide his son with a decent life. Blasco concludes the work with a threat for those who do not concern themselves with the poor: one day the impoverished mob will rise as a plague to control the city and obtain their just reward.

The Dead Command, Blasco's most effective psychological novel, is set in the islands of Mallorca and Ibiza and traces the shifting attitude of the hero, Jaime Febrer, toward the forces of tradition. In the first part, when old prejudices prevent the penniless aristocrat from restoring his fortune through marriage to a rich *chueta* (a descendant of fifteenth-century converted Jews), Jaime concludes that "the dead still command." After seeking refuge in Ibiza and fighting for the right to marry a peasant girl, the protagonist finally realizes that life and, above all, love command more than the weight of dead tradition.

While the thematic concerns are interesting (relating to social problems of the islands and the need to conquer the past and control one's environment through struggle, love, and marriage), the real value of the work lies in the excellent regional sketches, especially in the pictorial art of the second part, through which we view local dances, courting customs, and brilliant descriptions of landscape and sea. In the last analysis, the novel achieves artistic merit through those elements that are central in Blasco's Valencian period.

Finally, popular opinion suggests the need to dwell briefly on the author's most successful novel, *The Four Horsemen of the Apocalypse.* Here the protagonist, Julio Desnoyers, is an elegant young Argentine whose father, a Frenchman, emigrated to Argentina because he disapproved of the Franco-Prussian War (1870–1871). After making his fortune in South America, the elder Desnoyers brings his family to Paris. Julio decides to marry Margarita Laurier, a frivolous divorcée, but the outbreak of World War I produces a profound change in the thinking of both. Margarita abandons her interest in fashion and social activities and dedicates herself to the wounded soldiers as a nurse. Julio enlists and sacrifices his life fighting the Germans.

The title derives from the Book of Revelations, which describes the four scourges of Plague, War, Hunger, and Death—forces that, the elder Desnoyers tells us, will walk the earth again. His daughter, Chichi, however, feels that the deaths of the soldiers will serve to stimulate the thoughts of those who live on.

The novel was written as an instrument of propaganda for the Allied cause. Its major weakness is, in fact, the heavy-handed and exaggerated condemnation not only of the German military establishment but also of the entirety of the German people and cultural system. An extraordinarily detailed and vivid account of the Battle of the Marne is the novel's most positive achievement.

Part of the reason that the work has become one of Spain's all-time best-sellers is due to the two motion pictures based on its story produced in Hollywood—a Rudolph Valentino film in 1921 and a World War II adaptation in 1962.

Blasco's works are, to say the least, uneven. While his later novels will no doubt continue to be read for years to come, it is the qualities of his early masterpieces that earn him a significant place in the history of modern Spanish literature: the magnificent, rich descriptions of land and sea and of regional life around Valencia and the powerful portrait of the individual struggling on against overwhelming internal and external obstacles. When adequate studies of his novels are produced and more acceptable translations of his best works finally appear, the world will know this.

Selected Bibliography

EDITIONS

INDIVIDUAL WORKS

NOVELS

Arroz y tartana. Valencia, 1895.
Flor de Mayo. Valencia, 1896.
La barraca. Valencia, 1898.
Entre naranjos. Valencia, 1900.
Sónnica la cortesana. Valencia, 1901.
Cañas y barro. Valencia, 1902.
La catedral. Valencia, 1903.
El intruso. Valencia, 1904.
La bodega. Valencia, 1905.
La horda. Valencia, 1905.
La maja desnuda. Valencia, 1906.
La voluntad de vivir. Valencia, 1907.
Sangre y arena. Valencia, 1908.
Los muertos mandan. Valencia, 1909.
Luna Benamor. Valencia, 1909.
Los argonautas. Valencia, 1914.

Los cuatro jinetes del Apocalipsis. Valencia, 1916.
Mare nostrum. Valencia, 1918.
Los enemigos de la mujer. Valencia, 1919.
La tierra de todos. Valencia, 1921.
El paraíso de las mujeres. Valencia, 1922.
La reina Calafia. Valencia, 1923.
El papa del mar. Valencia, 1925.
A los pies de Venus. Valencia, 1926.
En busca del Gran Kan (Cristóbal Colón). Valencia, 1929.
El caballero de la Virgen. Valencia, 1929.
El fantasma de las alas de oro. Valencia, 1930.

SHORT STORY COLLECTIONS

Cuentos valencianos. Valencia, 1896.
La condenada. Valencia, 1900.
El préstamo de la difunta. Valencia, 1921.
Novelas de la costa azul. Valencia, 1924.
Novelas de amor y de muerte. Valencia, 1927.

PLAYS

El juez. Valencia, 1894.

NONFICTION

Historia de la revolución española (desde la guerra de la independencia a la restauración a Sagunto), 1808–1874. 3 vols. Barcelona, 1892; Madrid, 1930.
París: Impresiones de un emigrado. Valencia, 1893.
En el país del arte (tres meses en Italia). Valencia, 1896.
Oriente. Valencia, 1907.
Argentina y sus grandezas. Madrid, 1910.
El militarismo mejicano. Valencia, 1920.
Historia de la guerra europea de 1914. 9 vols. Valencia, 1914–1921.
Una nación secuestrada (el terror militarista en España): Alfonso XIII desenmascarado. Paris, 1924.
La vuelta al mundo de un novelista. 3 vols. Valencia, 1924–1925.
Lo que será la república española (al país y al ejército). Paris, 1925.
Estudios literarios. Valencia, 1934.
Discursos literarios. Valencia, 1966.

COLLECTED WORKS

Obras completas, 3 vols. Madrid, 1958.

VICENTE BLASCO IBÁÑEZ

TRANSLATIONS

NOVELS

Blood and Sand. Translated by Frances Partridge. New York, 1958.

The Blood of the Arena. Translated by Frances Douglas. Chicago, 1911.

The Borgias; or, At the Feet of Venus. Translated by Arthur Livingston. New York, 1930.

The Cabin. Translated by Francis Haffkine Snow and Beatrice M. Mekota. New York, 1917.

The Dead Command. Translated by Frances Douglas. New York, 1919.

The Enemies of Women. Translated by I. Brown. New York, 1920.

The Four Horsemen of the Apocalypse. Translated by Charlotte Brewster Jordan. New York, 1918.

The Fruit of the Vine. Translated by Isaac Goldberg. New York, 1919.

The Intruder. Translated by W. A. Gillespie. New York, 1928.

Knight of the Virgin. Translated by Arthur Livingston. New York, 1930.

Luna Benamor. Translated by Isaac Goldberg. Boston, 1919.

The Mayflower. Translated by Arthur Livingston. New York, 1921.

The Mob. Translated by Mariano Joaquín Lorente. New York, 1927.

Our Sea. Translated by Charlotte Brewster Jordan. New York, 1919.

The Phantom with Wings of Gold. Translated by Arthur Livingston. New York, 1931.

The Pope of the Sea. Translated by Arthur Livingston. New York, 1927.

Queen Calafia. No translator cited. New York, 1924.

Reeds and Mud. Translated by Isaac Goldberg. New York, 1928.

The Shadow of the Cathedral. Translated by W. A. Gillespie. New York, 1909.

Sónnica the Courtesan. Translated by Frances Douglas. New York, 1912.

The Temptress. Translated by Leo Ongley. New York, 1923.

The Three Roses. Translated by Stuart Edgar Grummon. New York, 1932.

The Torrent. Translated by Isaac Goldberg and Arthur Livingston. New York, 1921.

Unknown Lands: The Story of Columbus. Translated by Arthur Livingston. New York, 1929.

Woman Triumphant. Translated by Hayward Keniston. New York, 1920.

SHORT STORIES

The Last Lion and Other Tales. Translated by Isaac Goldberg. Boston, 1919.

The Old Woman of the Movies. Various translators. New York, 1925.

NONFICTION

Alfonso XIII Unmasked!!!: The Military Terror of Spain. Translated by Arthur Livingston and Leo Ongley. New York, 1926.

In the Land of Art. Translated by Frances Douglas. New York, 1923.

Mexico in Revolution. Translated by José Padín and Arthur Livingston. New York, 1920.

A Novelist's Tour of the World. Translated by Leo Ongley and Arthur Livingston. New York, 1926.

BIOGRAPHICAL AND CRITICAL WORKS

Betoret-París, Eduardo. *El costumbrismo regional en la obra de Blasco Ibáñez.* Valencia, 1958.

Cardwell, Richard A. *Blasco Ibáñez: La barraca.* Critical Guides to Spanish Texts series. London, 1973.

Chamberlin, Vernon. "Las imágenes animalistas y el color rojo en *La barraca." Duquesne Hispanic Review* 6:23–36 (1967).

Dalbor, John B. "The Short Stories of Vicente Blasco Ibáñez." Ph.D. dissertation. University of Michigan, 1961.

Day, A. Grove, and Edgar C. Knowlton, Jr. *V. Blasco Ibáñez.* New York, 1972.

Eoff, Sherman H. *The Modern Spanish Novel.* New York, 1961.

Escalante, Miguel Ángel. "Notas sobre el estilo de Vicente Blasco Ibáñez." *Cultura* 2 (1951).

Gascó Contell, Emilio. *Genio y figura de Blasco Ibáñez: Agitador, aventurero, y novelista.* Madrid, 1957.

León Roca, J. L. *Vicente Blasco Ibáñez.* Valencia, 1967.

Medina, Jeremy T. "The Artistry of Blasco Ibáñez's *Canas y barro. Hispania* 60:275–284 (1977).

———. *Spanish Realism: The Theory and Practice of a Concept in the Nineteenth Century.* Potomac, Md., 1979.

———. "The Artistry of Blasco Ibanez's *Flor de Mayo." Hispania* 65:197–208 (1982).

————. *The Valencian Novels of Vicente Blasco Ibáñez.* Valencia, 1984.

Pitollet, Camille. *Vicente Blasco Ibáñez: Sus novelas y la novela du su vida.* Valencia, 1921.

————. "Vicente Blasco Ibáñez: A Critical Survey of the Novels from 1894 to 1909." Ph.D. dissertation. University of California, Berkeley, 1964.

————. "On Blasco Ibáñez's *Flor de Mayo.*" *Symposium* 24:55–68 (1970).

————. *Vicente Blasco Ibáñez: Una nueva introducción a su vida y obra.* Santiago, 1972.

————. *Vicente Blasco Ibáñez: An Annotated Bibliography.* London, 1976.

Sosa, Rafael. *Vicente Blasco Ibáñez a través de sus cuentos y novelas valencianos.* Madrid, 1974.

Swain, James Q. *Vicente Blasco Ibáñez: General Study—Special Emphasis on Realistic Techniques.* Knoxville, Tenn., 1959.

Tortosa, Pilar. *La mejor novela de V. Blasco Ibáñez: Su vida.* Valencia, 1977.

JEREMY T. MEDINA

LUIGI PIRANDELLO
(1867–1936)

IN PLAYS AND short stories, novels and essays, occasional writings and poetry, reviews, letters, lectures, and interviews—whether speaking in his own voice or in the voices of hundreds of fictional characters—Luigi Pirandello expressed a profoundly original view of the world and man's place in it and left a lasting mark on the history of drama. Considered the most seminal dramatist of our time, he has also been recognized as a cause of and witness to an entire revolution in man's attitude toward the world. Acutely sensitive to the inner contradictions in all beliefs, to the impossibility of separating appearance from reality or, in his own terms, of distinguishing the mask from the face, he gave wide currency to a number of concepts that became pervasive in twentieth-century thought. For him the human personality is mutable, unstable, and discontinuous, truth is indeterminate and contradictory, the world in constant flux, the meaning of words unreliable, man's desire to communicate—to have his "reasons" understood—constantly frustrated and constantly renewed. The art that results from these psychological and epistemological postulates, to which he gave the name of *umorismo* (humorism), cannot reproduce a reality that does not exist and so ends up ceaselessly reflecting upon itself; such an art is but an imitation of an imitation, holding up the mirror not to life, which resists the artist's search for a form to encompass it,

but to the fiction-fashioning process itself. Few writers have had as strong a sense as Pirandello's of the difficulties inherent in "consisting," in being, whether in the form of the individual seeking his identity or of the work—the quintessential work, which is the play not only as text but as performance—almost anthropomorphically striving for its own internal coherence.

Pirandello was born in 1867 during a cholera epidemic that forced his family to leave Girgenti and seek refuge in a farmhouse situated a few miles farther west along Sicily's southern coast, in a region known as Caos (in the local dialect *Càvusu,* from the Greek *Xáos*). This circumstance permitted him later to write in an autobiographical fragment composed with his usual talent for effect: "I am, then, the child of Chaos."

Girgenti—or Agrigento, the ancient name that was restored to it in 1927—was originally the Greek city of Akragas, destroyed by the Carthaginians, conquered by the Romans, and in the ninth century vanquished by the Arabs. In contrast to the western "Greek" shore of the island and the northern "Norman" shore, the region of Agrigento continues even today to bear the deepest imprint in all Sicily of Arabic culture. In his novel *I vecchi ei giovani* (*The Old and the Young,* 1909) Pirandello recalls the narrow, ill-smelling alleys, the women seated on their doorsteps day in and day out, the guttural sounds of their speech and the anxiety of their frightened, flashing eyes, and the many idlers walking up and down the main street with unchanging step, more like automatons than living beings: "The Akragas of the Greeks, the Agrigentum of the Romans, had ended up in the Kerkent of the Mohammedans, and the mark of the Arabs had remained indelible in the souls and customs of the people: taciturn apathy, suspicious mistrust, and jealousy." The Arabic heritage is seen here in a rigidly formal and immobile social structure, with its accompanying reticence and secretiveness, its private, allusive language, and its blocking of the individual's psyche, presenting the perennial danger of a sudden irremediable explosion. The conflict between self and role that plays such an important part in Pirandello's view of an unchanging human condition thus appeared in his first environment as a datum of his experience.

When Pirandello was born, Giuseppe Garibaldi's 1860 expedition to liberate southern Italy from Bourbon rule was still a recent event, and Rome had not yet become the capital of the new nation. Pirandello's family, on both sides, was deeply involved in the struggle for Sicilian independence. The Ricci Gramittos, his mother's family, were professional men from Porto Empedocle (Girgenti's industrial district) whom the government had come to suspect during the revolutionary movements of 1848; Pirandello's grandfather, a combative lawyer of separatist conviction, had had to join other Sicilian exiles in Malta, where he died a young man. His father's family, on the other hand, were relative newcomers to Sicily, having emigrated from northern Italy in the mid-eighteenth century; they were businessmen, trading in the major Sicilian products of citrus fruits and sulfur. Pirandello's father did join Garibaldi's expeditionary force, but more out of a spirit of adventure and personal engagement than because of any tradition of political action or idealism such as that of the Ricci Gramittos. At the time of

Pirandello's birth, his father was managing the family's sulfur mines at Porto Empedocle and becoming involved in occasionally violent clashes with the powerful sulfur Mafia. Memories of the hopeful and passionate days of the Risorgimento (the struggle for Italian independence), which imbue the pages of *The Old and the Young* with nostalgia and with indignation at the political scandals of the new Italy, were kept alive by his mother rather than his father—an indication of a divergence in temperament as well as background within a typically tense family situation dominated by an authoritarian and irascible paterfamilias.

Pirandello became acquainted at first hand with the environment of his father's activities when he spent the summer of 1886 working with him at Porto Empedocle. The intolerable realities of life under the harsh rays of the southern sun, with the continuous creaking of loaded trucks, the ceaseless activity of barefoot men and beasts of burden, the open sewers on the beach, and men standing waist-deep in water and yet ravaged by thirst, are masterfully chronicled in *The Old and the Young.* "They all seem to have gone mad down there," Pirandello comments in revulsion, "turned into animals by the mean, ferocious fight for gain!" Acquaintance with the struggle for economic survival in the sulfur industry convinced Pirandello that he could not follow in his father's footsteps, that his life's work must lie elsewhere, and at the end of the summer he returned to Palermo, where he had completed his secondary education and now began to study law at the university. An unwilling law student, he soon obtained his father's permission to change fields and in 1887 transferred to the University of Rome to study literature.

As with most Sicilians, Pirandello's ties with Sicily remained strong throughout his life, but he never again lived there for any length of time. Yet the island's history, landscapes, and social and psychological situations continued to appear in his works to the very end: sometimes in their undisguised, documentary reality and sometimes in an attenuated, generalized form, as no more than a glow or a coloring pointing back to something once experienced. Pirandello wrote some stories set in Porto Empedocle, Agrigento, or Palermo, and others set in unidentified locales that still vividly recall Sicilian places, circumstances, and attitudes: a lonely country road along a cemetery wall in *All'uscita* (*At the Exit,* 1926), a square in front of a village church in *Sagra del Signore della nave* (*The Festival of Our Lord of the Ship,* 1925), a witch's den, a seaport café, and a princely garden in *La favola del figlio cambiato* (The Story of the Changeling, 1933), and a solitary run-down villa "on the boundary line between myth and reality" in *I giganti della montagna* (*The Mountain Giants,* 1938).

Pirandello was expelled from the University of Rome because of an act of classroom insubordination, and on the advice of one of his professors in 1889 he went to the University of Bonn in Germany. Bonn was famous for its tradition in the study of philosophy, but in the last decades of the nineteenth century it was also the home of a new discipline, romance philology. Pirandello earned his doctorate in philology in 1891 with a dissertation on the sound system of his native dialect of the province of Girgenti. During the time spent in Bonn he also began to work (as part of a course on the aesthetics of the comic and the tragic given by Theodor Lipps) on three Tuscan comic writers of the thirteenth century, which led to a scholarly essay published in 1896, "Un preteso poeta umorista del secolo XIII" (A So-Called Humorist Poet of the Thirteenth Century), an important step on the way to his formulation of the concept of "humorism," the cornerstone of his art. In Bonn he composed a collection of poetry, *Pasqua di Gea* (Gaea's Easter, 1891), and *Elegie renane* (Rhenish Elegies, 1895), inspired by Johann Wolfgang von Goethe's *Roman Elegies* (1795), which he translated into Italian in 1896. He also contributed a number of articles on literary subjects to a Florentine periodical, which marked the beginning of a prolific journalistic career. Recent research is continuing to show how fruitful the Bonn years were in his formation. Virtually bypassing Italy, they provided the young Sicilian with a first contact with Europe, a relationship that was resumed and intensified almost thirty years later, when his success as a playwright made him an international figure more at home abroad than in his native land.

Upon his return from Bonn, supported by a monthly check from his father, Pirandello settled down in Rome, plunging into its vibrant and stimulating artistic and intellectual life. In 1894 he married the daughter of one of his father's business associates; by 1899 he was the father of three children. (His older son became a writer, his younger one a painter, and his daughter married a Chilean diplomat, following him to South America in 1922 and leaving a great emptiness in her father's life.) Pirandello published his first short story at the age of seventeen, but it was only when his mentor, the Sicilian critic and novelist Luigi Capuana, urged him to turn his energies to prose that he abandoned poetry and began the series of stories that he later conceived of as a corpus of 365 tales, *Novelle per un anno* (Stories for a Year), one for each day of the calendar year. By 1919 he had published fifteen collections of these stories, many with titles that underline the crookedness of the world: *Amori senza amore* (Loveless Love Affairs, 1894), *Beffe della vita e della morte* (Tricks of Life and Death, 1902), *Quand'ero matto . . .* (When I Was Crazy . . . , 1902), *Un cavallo nella luna* (Horse in the Moon, 1918), and *Il carnevale dei morti* (Dead Men's Carnival, 1919). He had also written six of his seven novels, published two books of essays on literary and aesthetic problems, and had about twenty plays produced (a few of them in Sicilian dialect). His personal life was seriously disrupted in 1903, when a disaster in a mine in which his father's capital and his wife's dowry were invested cut off his income. He was forced to turn his writing from pleasurable dilettantism to a financially profitable activity and to compete for a permanent position at the teachers' college where he had been teaching grammar, composition, and style since 1898. The disaster also had an effect on his wife's mental stability: in 1919, after many troubled years, suffering from acute paranoia and unable to continue living even a semi-normal life, she had to be institutionalized, a final blow to what had started out as a relatively happy family life.

In a 1934 interview Pirandello declared that his was "a war theater," that "the war [World War I] had revealed the theater" to him: "When passions were let loose, I had my characters suffer those passions onstage." Thus Pirandello was aware—or became aware in retrospect—that his theater grew out of a definite historical period, that it shared the sense of crisis that other works of European literature were expressing at the time, and that the war (and not only his personal experiences) affected the creation of his fictional characters and the manner in which their stories were told. In a similar vein, though with no reference to Pirandello, the German critic Walter Benjamin wrote in his 1936 essay "Der Erzähler" ("The Storyteller") of the end of a narrative tradition, of men returned from the battlefield no longer able to communicate experience, and of "the tiny, fragile human body" standing alone under the open sky "in a field of force, of destructive torrents and explosions." The descriptive and narrative props were gone and the character had broken loose—a situation that Pirandello had anticipated in his 1899 article "L'azione parlata" ("Spoken Action"), in which he used a stanza from a poem by the German romantic Heinrich Heine to signify the transition in ancient Greek literature from epic narrative to tragedy:

> Every night in the castle of Blaye
> One can hear strange noises,
> Quiverings, creakings, rustlings.
> Suddenly the figures in the tapestries

> Begin to move.
> The ghostly troubadour and his lady
> Flex their sleeping muscles,
> Leap from the wall,
> And walk through the halls.

But what in this early article had the limited resonance of a plea for "spoken" dramatic dialogue to replace the florid, literary, "written" language favored by the poetic drama of the time, in the changed climate of the postwar period and in the context of discussions of a "new theater" for Italy could be read as a resolute turning away from narrative in favor of drama.

Pirandello had written some plays and projected others as far back as his adolescence. Of this early activity only a number of titles, genre designations, and indications as to content have come down to us. The titles are suggestive, hinting at a first tentative statement of ideas to be worked out more fully later: among them are "Fatti che or son parole" (Deeds That Have Now Become Words), "Provando la commedia" (Rehearsing the Play), and "Armeggiamenti" (Maneuverings). The genre designations range from "tragedy," "play," and "dramatic scenes" to "one-act drama," "play in three acts," and "play in the vernacular, in seven scenes," pointing not only to the young playwright's versatility but to his concern with the formal aspects of his work. Particularly interesting is his description in an 1886 letter to his sister Lina of "Gli uccelli dell'alto" (The Birds on High), the cranes, those "poor, crazy birds" that almost never rest and are scoffed at by the chickens and the roosters, "bourgeois birds scratching about in the mud":

> Just imagine, in the first act I force the spectators in the theater to become actors in my play, and move the action from the stage to the orchestra. I've introduced a scene for the choruses, as in ancient Greek drama, so as to show the difference between life as it is [normally] lived and as it is lived by those birds of mine on high.
>
> (*Epistolario familiare giovanile* *[1886–1898]*, pp. 9–10)

Two of his early plays eventually were produced: *L'epilogo* (The Epilogue), later retitled *La morsa* (*The Vise*, 1926), and *Il nibbio* (The Kite [the predatory bird]), also known as *Se non così . . .* (*If Not Thus . . .*), later retitled *La ragione degli altri* (Other People's Reasons, 1921).

Pirandello's youthful experiments with writing for the theater were obscured by other interests during his student years at Bonn and in the first twenty or so years of his life in Rome. As a result the impression was created—and for a long time sustained in Pirandello scholarship—that he disdained the theater until he experienced a sudden conversion to it just prior to *Sei personaggi in cerca d'autore* (*Six Characters in Search of an Author,* 1921). Actually his attraction to the theater was never completely dormant, as attested to, among other evidence, by two of his novels, published respectively in 1911 and 1915. The protagonist of *Suo marito* (Her Husband) is a playwright, and two works attributed to her and discussed at some length are actually Pirandello's own *If Not Thus . . .* and *La nuova colonia* (The New Colony, 1928). The second novel, *Si gira . . .* (*Shoot!*), is set in the world of cinema, the newly emerging art medium with which Pirandello was making his first contacts. In 1910 he saw his *The Vise* and *Lumìe di Sicilia* (*Sicilian Limes,* 1920), both one-acts, staged by the company of his fellow Sicilian Nino Martoglio, who later collaborated with him in writing two other plays, this time in dialect. Another one-act play, *Il dovere del medico* (*The Doctor's Duty,* 1926), was performed by another small company in 1913, and the following year the full-length *If Not Thus . . .* had its premiere with a leading company at one of Milan's principal playhouses. Pirandello attributed the failure of *If Not Thus . . .* to the miscasting of the two female roles and the consequent misrepresentation of the play's meaning. This setback, together with Pirandello's meeting with the extraordinary Sicilian actor Angelo Musco (according to the theatrical innovator Edward

Gordon Craig, "the greatest actor in the world"), temporarily deflected Pirandello from theater in Italian. It threw him instead into the intense, passionate, authentic, original world of the Sicilian dialect theater, which represented a much-acclaimed although marginal alternative to traditional theater. Pirandello wrote three plays for Musco in dialect—*Pensaci, Giacomino!* (*Think It Over, Giacomino!,* 1918), *Il berretto a sonagli* (*Cap and Bells,* 1920), and *Liolà* (*Liolà,* 1917)—and he collaborated with him and Martoglio on perhaps the most popular hit of those years, *L'aria del continente* (The Air of the Continent, 1915), a satire on the Sicilian's itch to get away from his island in order to enjoy the temptations (the carefree love affairs) of continental Italy.

Still caught up in the excitement and the controversies (Musco was an unreliable producer) of this first heady brush with theatrical life, Pirandello achieved success in the legitimate theater with *Così è (se vi pare)* (*Right You Are [If You Think So],* 1918), first performed in 1917 and considered his major contribution to the "theater of the grotesque." This was the name given to an innovative type of tragicomic drama in Italy, which, in reaction against naturalism, portrayed men as helpless puppets driven by blind, unknowable forces and exposed social prejudices by revealing the human face—the face that laughs and weeps— beneath the mask of convention. Its two most characteristic works are Luigi Chiarelli's *La maschera e il volto* (The Mask and the Face, 1916) and Rosso di San Secondo's *Marionette, che passione!* (Marionettes, What Passions They Feel!, 1918), whose very titles announce the new thematics.

Between *Right You Are (If You Think So)* and *Six Characters* Pirandello wrote three plays that can be called *grotteschi* as far as subject matter and point of view are concerned, but that were strongly influenced in their structure by the personality of the great actor Ruggero Ruggeri, for whom they were written. In Ruggeri, one of the last undisputed stars in the Italian theatrical tradition, whose acting was distinguished by an analytical, philosophical turn of mind and by the lyricism of his delivery, Pirandello found the interpreter best able to identify with his typical male character: an eccentric, introverted, and suffering reasoner, whose lines might easily have been muffed by less intelligent and accomplished actors. Thus Pirandello wrote *Il piacere dell'onestà* (*The Pleasure of Honesty*, 1918), *Il giuoco delle parti* (*The Rules of the Game*, 1919), and *Tutto per bene* (*All as It Should Be*, 1920) as well as the slightly later *Enrico IV* (*Henry IV*, 1922) for Ruggeri—all plays centered on dominating male protagonists whose ontological and existential identities are at issue: who are these people and how are they to be judged? Concurrently Pirandello was still involved with his earlier, regional works, turning plays that had originally been written in dialect into Italian, adding new ones—*La giara* (*The Jar*, 1925), which he wrote in Sicilian, and *La patente* (*The License*, 1920), for which he prepared two versions, one in dialect and one in Italian—and, because of its Sicilian subject matter and setting, translating Euripides' *Cyclops* into Sicilian. To this same period also belong a number of other plays: *Ma non è una cosa seria* (*It's Only a Joke*, 1919), *L'uomo, la bestia, e la virtù* (*Man, Beast, and Virtue*, 1922), *Come prima, meglio di prima* (*Florian's Wife*, 1921), and *La signora Morli, una e due* (*Mrs. Morli, One and Two*, 1922), in all of which the male protagonist does not have the same dominating role as in those mentioned earlier.

Six Characters, virtually booed off the stage at its premiere in Rome in 1921 but by the end of the following year a worldwide success through performances in London and New York, ushered in a new period in Pirandello's career. During the next two or three years his plays—*Six Characters* especially, but also *The Pleasure of Honesty, Right You Are (If You Think So), Man, Beast, and Virtue,* and *Florian's Wife*—were played in translation in Paris, and Vienna, Cracow, Prague, Athens, Barcelona, Berlin, and Buenos Aires. On the occasion of his first visit to the United States,

in 1923, New York's Fulton Theater was temporarily renamed "Pirandello's Theater." His more and more frequent contacts with theatrical life, as well as his desire to have greater control over the performance of his plays, awakened in him the desire to try his hand at directing and producing. By 1925 he had his own company, the Teatro d'Arte di Roma, financed with the help of the Italian government. He had joined the Fascist Party the year before, partly out of patriotism (also the source of his interventionism during World War I), partly because of his congenital rebelliousness against established institutions, and partly because he hoped that the new regime would support the arts and recognize the propaganda value of a strong and prestigious Italian avant-garde theater.

The Teatro d'Arte played not only in Rome but on tour as well. With his troupe Pirandello performed in Italian in the principal cities of Italy, as well as in London, Paris, Berlin, Dresden, Cologne, Bonn, Budapest, Vienna, and Prague, and in Argentina and Brazil. The appeal of his theater was such that some of his later plays had their premieres (in translation) outside of Italy: *Diana e la Tuda* (*Diana and Tuda*, 1927) in Zurich, *Lazzaro* (*Lazarus*, 1929) in Huddersfield, England, *Questa sera si recita a soggetto* (*Tonight We Improvise*, 1930) in Königsberg, Germany, *Sogno (ma forse no)* (*I'm Dreaming, But Am I?*, 1936) in Lisbon, *Quando si è qualcuno* (*When Someone Is Somebody,* 1933) in Buenos Aires, *Non si sa come* (*One Doesn't Know How,* 1935) in Prague, and *La favola del figlio cambiaro* in Braunschweig, Germany. For the Teatro d'Arte Pirandello hired a newly discovered young actress, Marta Abba, who became his muse. For her he wrote a number of plays whose principal protagonist is a woman: *L'amica delle mogli* (*The Wives' Friend,* 1927), *Diana and Tuda, The New Colony, Trovarsi* (*To Find Oneself,* 1932), and the famous *Come tu mi vuoi* (*As You Desire Me,* 1930), immortalized in the 1932 screen version with Greta Garbo.

Beset by financial difficulties, the Teatro

d'Arte folded in 1928. Shortly thereafter Pirandello left for Germany to work on a film version of *Six Characters* that was, however, never produced. For some time Berlin was more congenial to him than Rome, and two plays he wrote at that time reflect how deeply he was influenced by his second German experience: *As You Desire Me* and *Tonight We Improvise* (with *Six Characters* and *Ciascuno a suo mode* [*Each in His Own Way,* 1924] the third of his theatrical trilogy). In 1930 he went to Hollywood for the production of *As You Desire Me;* in the same year the first Italian sound film was made, *La canzone dell'amore* (Song of Love), based on one of his short stories. He was one of the first to be appointed to the newly founded Royal Italian Academy, and in 1934 he presided at an international meeting sponsored by it, "On Dramatic Theatre." On this occasion he directed a memorable performance of Gabriele D'Annunzio's *La figlia di Jorio* (*The Daughter of Jorio,* 1904), with Abba and Ruggeri in the leading roles. In the same year he was awarded the Nobel Prize. Meanwhile the publication of his work, in new collections and editions, was continuing, as was his involvement with theater and film. He died in 1936, leaving his last play, *The Mountain Giants,* unfinished.

An oeuvre such as Pirandello's, extending over a long period of exceptionally intense creative activity, reflecting experimentation with the full range of literary genres, composed of both a number of very well-known and much-discussed plays and many others familiar only to the specialist, beset by the problems of transmission inherent in works for the theater, and characterized by the repeated use of the same material in several different works, presents more than the usual challenge for an essay of moderate length such as this. To avoid the survey format of short commentaries on a great number of separate texts, the discussion will center on two important concepts that inform Pirandello's thought and have had wide currency in the critical

literature: "the character without author" and "the theater within the theater." Before turning to these, however, some attention should be given to *L'umorismo* (*On Humor*), the booklength essay he published in 1908 as one of the two scholarly works (*Arte e scienza* [Art and Science, 1908] being the other) on which he staked his claim to a permanent teaching post.

In *On Humor* Pirandello sets out to answer a question that had been posed to him in his student days in Bonn. Considered from the perspective of comparative literature, what exactly is the meaning of "humorist" when applied to a writer and of "humorism" as a frame of mind reflected in a particular vision of the world and in the manner in which that vision is expressed in art? Pirandello's introductory examination of the term and of the related questions as to whether humorism is exclusively a modern (i.e., a romantic) phenomenon and whether it can be said to exist in Italy or is predominantly Nordic, brings up a cluster of words (fantasy, caprice, burlesque, melancholy, irony) and examples (ranging from Jonathan Swift and Laurence Sterne to Miguel de Cervantes, Jean Paul Richter, Lodovico Ariosto, and Alessandro Manzoni) that show that humorism is doubtless connected with the comic but that its comic aspects are tempered by a contrasting feeling. In the second, theoretical part of the essay, the purpose of which is to characterize humorism without specific reference to the temporal and spatial contexts in which it occurs, we find the often-quoted vignette of "an old lady, her hair dyed, all sticky with some vile ointment, clumsily made-up and adorned in youthful finery." At first sight she induces scornful laughter, but when it becomes known *why* she is so inappropriately decked out—perhaps it is to hold the love of a much younger husband—the laughter gives way to a different feeling. This "feeling of the opposite" (*sentimento del contrario*), of *why* a thing is incongruous and therefore liable to elicit derision, which follows upon the "recognition of the opposite" (*avvertimento del contrario*), awareness of the fact that something *is* incongruous, is the spring of humorism. Elsewhere in the essay, as also in the earlier "Un critico fantastico" (A Whimsical Critic)—a contradiction in terms if we assume that criticism is the result of rational thinking—Pirandello expresses the same idea not with a story but in figurative language. Humorism, he writes, is "a double-faced herm that laughs on one side about the tears it sheds on the other." The condition of the humorist is to be constantly "off-key, like a violin and a double bass at one and the same time." Reflection is "a little demon that takes apart the mechanism of the image, of the puppet put together by feeling"; it is "a mirror of icy water not only in which the flame of feeling looks at itself but into which it plunges, extinguishing itself." Restlessly shifting between reflection and feeling, intelligence and sentiment, humorism is "the phenomenon of doubling in the act of artistic conception"— the very opposite, that is, of firm belief and objective fact on which naturalism and positivism had rested hardly a generation earlier.

If the concept of humor to which Pirandello gave a unique and personal meaning is one key to his fictional world, the concept of "the character without author" is another. Many writers, especially nineteenth-century novelists, deemed the characters in their works to be more alive and compelling than the persons of flesh and blood among whom they actually lived. Like these writers, Pirandello felt "haunted" or "visited" by his characters, but he managed to make more of the phenomenon than anyone else. What is a Character? he asks in *Six Characters* and elsewhere. Where does he or it come from? What rights does he or it have? Indeed, what *life* does he or it have? The capitalization of "Character" and the uncertainty as to whether the pronoun should refer to a person or a thing are here intended to point to the paradoxical answers these questions may receive. Characters, after all, are not persons, even though they may be so true to life as to be mistaken for such. Nor should characters—fictional creations of authors—be

thought of as having a life outside the work of which they are part, although again they have been known to travel, as it were, from one work to another (not necessarily even by the same author) or to continue living, having new adventures, after the last page of the book is finished or the last line on stage spoken. Yet this is precisely the fate of some of Pirandello's characters, who exist even prior to the creative act of their author and take on a concreteness, a physicality, that overwhelms him, forcing him to defend himself against their intrusiveness, to which, however, he almost always eventually succumbs.

At the time of the novel *Il fu Mattia Pascal* (*The Late Mattia Pascal*, 1904) and of the short story "La casa del Granella" ("The Haunted House"), theosophy and spiritism, both pseudoscientific theories concerning the life of the human personality after physical death, appeared to hold an answer for Pirandello. In a passage from the first edition of the novel, later omitted, he seemed to have found an explanation for the vividness with which some imagined characters assert themselves:

> I have just now read in a book [reputedly C. W. Leadbeater and A. Besant's *Thought-Forms*, 1905] that our thoughts and desires become embodied in a plastic essence in the invisible world that surrounds them, and forthwith take on the shape of living beings. . . . And these beings, as soon as they are formed, are no longer under the control of their generating maker but enjoy a life of their own, whose duration depends on the intensity of the generating thought and desire.
>
> (chap. 5)

Later, as the subject for *Six Characters* began to take shape (early references go back as far as 1917), it was not so much the origin of the character that intrigued Pirandello as the pressures of the character, once it was fully formed, upon him. For instance, Dr. Fileno, in the short story "La tragedia di un personaggio" ("The Tragedy of a Character," also translated as "A Character in Distress"), is a character who has broken loose from his setting. He had been encountered in a mediocre novel by the story's first-person narrator, like Pirandello himself an author. Sensing this author's response to his personality from the unsubstantial world in which he exists, Dr. Fileno begs him for the immortality that being a character in a first-rate book, in a classic, would give him. But the author rejects the plea: Dr. Fileno, whose claim to fame is that he is the inventor of a remedy for all ills, "The Philosophy of Remoteness," should apply that remedy to himself! In perspective—viewed, that is, through the "wrong" end of the telescope—his predicament of being a living character in a dead book would become bearable. And so Dr. Fileno remains the medium through which Pirandello's message is transmitted rather than becoming the suffering character onstage.

Similar and yet different is the situation portrayed in "Colloquii coi personaggi" (Dialogues with the Characters), written during the war, on the eve of the spectacular switch in genres from narrative to drama that was about to take place in Pirandello's work. The piece is perhaps more autobiography than story, but the fictionalization is at times quite evident. As in the preface to *Six Characters* (written five years after the play in an attempt to explain it), there is in "Colloquii coi personaggi" an objective barrier—a fictional waiting room—between Pirandello and the Characters pressing to be heard. In the author's study, as in the lawyer's office in "The Haunted House," each petitioner must wait his turn. Because of the extraordinary circumstances involving the lives of millions of people, audiences have been suspended. But it is to no avail, for the characters now come to the author not as strangers imposing themselves on him but as extensions of himself sharing his anxieties and his sufferings:

> In the darkness that gathered slow and tired at the end of those long sultry summer afternoons . . . I had for the past few days no longer felt alone. There was something teeming in the darkness, in a corner of my room. Shadows in the shadow, that sorrowfully shared my troubles, my longing, my disappointments, and my sudden moods—all my feelings, from which they had perhaps been born or were just beginning to be born. They looked at me, they watched me. They would look at me until finally, against my will, I would be forced to turn to them. With whom could I communicate at a moment like that, except with them? And I approached that corner and forced myself to look at them one by one, those shadows born of my passion, and I began to speak to them quietly.
>
> (*Opere,* 1957, 2:1131)

Before reaching these particular characters, however—those epitomized in the character onstage caught at the moment of crisis—Pirandello had already dealt repeatedly with the predicament and its underlying causes. On the one hand, his perspective is cultural-historical, expressed in images of the diminution of man: man is no longer a king in his palace but, as Pirandello wrote to a sister in 1886, a spider in its web, a snail in its shell, a mollusk in its conch; and to view the world from sidereal distances, as he wrote to another sister in 1887, is to see it shrunken to the size of a lemon. On the other hand, his perspective is existential or philosophical: in the preface to *Six Characters,* he summarizes the causes of his anguish—of man's anguish—as "the deception of mutual understanding founded on the empty abstraction of words, the multiple personality of everyone corresponding to the possibility of being to be found in each of us, and finally the inherent tragic conflict between life, which is continually moving, and form, which fixes it, immutable."

Mattia Pascal is the first major character created by Pirandello. He appears in a novel built around the narrative topos of the man who survives his own death. No situation is at once less true to life and more susceptible to adventurous developments. In the second part of the book Mattia lives the extraordinary and exhilarating experience of a man who has escaped from the constraints of his past life and is free to make a new one for himself. He is the typical voyager without baggage, the stranger in life, and in this sense an optimistic version of the later, tragic protagonist of *Henry IV*. Because of the essential lightness of *The Late Mattia Pascal,* it is perhaps not easy to see at once a kinship between the nameless emperor whose mask hides no face and the small-town librarian, momentarily so disengaged that he can forge his own personality, choose a name and a background, a place of birth and an education, his occupation, and his leisure to create himself, as it were, without so much as a by-your-leave to his author. Of course, there is disgust, rebellion, and even hatred at the core of Mattia's experience. He runs away from home because he has been the victim of fraud and stupidity, of the overriding egotism of his mother-in-law, and because death has deprived him of the only two beings he loved, his mother and his infant daughter. There is later also great sadness in the defeat of his dream of freedom, a defeat that builds up step by step, inexorably, and culminates in his willing acceptance of the very institutions he had at first denied. For Adriano Meis—Mattia's new assumed identity—the moments of growing self-knowledge are small epiphanies, episodes of the plot treated by Pirandello with a mixture of amusement and pathos: Adriano realizes that without legal status he cannot own a puppy, which must be licensed, that for fear of his being unmasked his conversation is limited to the most superficial banalities, that he must not fall in love with a trusting, innocent girl unless he is ready to end up by hurting her, and that he cannot bring the man who robbed him to justice nor challenge the man who insulted him to a duel. He is immobilized, frozen in his non-being, in his "life after death," as effectively as he had been in the coercion and inauthenticity of his original, normal life.

There is anguish in *The Late Mattia Pascal.* Reflection on his state turns Adriano into a spectator of his own life and thus prevents him from living. But there is also the buoyancy of self-affirmation, for Adriano-Mattia's decisive choice is a conscious one. When Adriano leaves his hat and walking stick on the bridge across the Tiber in the simulation of his second suicide (the first suicide had been perceived as such by accident, not by his design), he is no longer running away. With a strong assertion of the will, he turns toward responsibility, intending both to right the wrong he has done as Adriano (permitting a girl to fall in love with his fictitious self) and to seek compensation for the wrongs done to him as Mattia. He will return home to his wife and mother-in-law, no longer to suffer indignities at their hands, but to rebel against them and find some acceptable and realistic modus vivendi. A trick of fate intervenes. In the two years of his absence, his wife, for whom time has *not* stood still, has remarried, and she is now the mother of another's child. Effectively removed from his old life and from his life as Adriano Meis, Mattia now assumes the new personality that has been created for him. In still another change he becomes the living, late Mattia Pascal.

His old friend and fellow librarian Don Eligio may summarize the moral of the tale as proving "the impossibility of living outside of the law and outside of those peculiarities, sad or happy as they may be, which determine what we are." But this conclusion understandably makes no sense to the late Mattia. The lesson *he* learns is a different one. He learns it on the eve of his second suicide in an encounter with his shadow, and it is the lesson of compassion, the end result of a humoristic view of the world. In the rage that wells up in him at the realization that he has not played a trick on life but life has played a trick on him, he catches sight of his shadow on the pavement and in a fit of anger raises his foot to trample it:

> But no, I . . . I could not stamp upon my shadow. Who was more of a shadow of the two of us? I or it? Two shadows! There, there on the ground; and anyone could step on it, crush my head, crush my heart, and I would keep silent, my shadow would be silent. . . . But yes! That is how

it was! That shadow was the symbol, the ghost of my life: it was I, there on the ground, exposed to the mercy of other men's feet. . . . But that shadow had a heart and was unable to love; it had money and anyone could rob it from it; it had a head, but only to think and realize that it was the head of a shadow, and not the shadow of a head. . . . And at that I felt it to be a living thing, and I felt sorrow for it, as though the horse and the wheels of the wagon and the feet of the passersby had actually torn it asunder. And I could not leave it there any longer, laid bare there, on the ground.

(chap. 15)

In this traditional romantic image of the dissociation of the personality, of the *Doppelgänger*, Pirandello's personal touch lies in the revelation of grief. The pain Mattia feels for his objectified self and the fact that sympathy and sorrow have taken the place of hatred and rage make possible the sublimation, the ascetic overcoming of self, with which the book ends. Mattia's decision to write the story of his strange adventure—that is, the substitution of art for life—clinches his acceptance of his new role as survivor of himself and places a second reconciliation, a further denial of tragedy, beside the one expressed by Don Eligio. Thus, in spite of the pessimistic "philosophy" of *lanterninosofia* developed in its pages (in the great surrounding darkness created by uncertainty and the loss of faith, men can survive only by the light of the little private lanterns of their illusions), *The Late Mattia Pascal* remains in the area of the comic. The more obvious reason is simply the very considerable space given to the grotesque and the farcical, from the story of the double illegitimate paternity of Mattia (an episode Pirandello later developed in *Liolà*) to the tremendous scenes that enliven Mattia's married life, from the pathetic but ridiculous figure of the ex–piano teacher at Adriano's boardinghouse in Rome to the wonderful double-talk that takes place at the séances held there. The mixture of seriousness and laughter has generally disturbed readers, and the novel is by and large considered slight, improbable, and

lacking in humanity. Pirandello remained fond of it, however, and in 1921 wrote a spirited defense of the rights of the imagination, which has become an appendix to the book. He compares his critics to zoologists who study man as a species of two-legged animal but deny the designation of man to someone who happens to have a wooden leg or a glass eye. And he defends the humanness of his fictional reasoners, their everlasting questioning and worrying, because "man reasons or is irrational—which comes to the same thing—when he suffers."

As a first-person narrative and chronicle of a rather exceptional personal experience and in the flexibility with which the action moves back and forth, *Shoot!* (later titled *Quaderni di Serafino Gubbio operatore* [The Notebooks of Serafino Gubbio, Cameraman, 1925]) has points of contact with *The Late Mattia Pascal*. But while the latter's circular movement is quite simple—the beginning and the end meet in Mattia's decision to write the story of his life—*Shoot!*, being both a story and a stream-of-consciousness commentary on that story, has a more complex structure. As its later title implies, the novel is divided into notebooks, with the same characters appearing at different moments and in different settings, thus creating the kaleidoscopic effect of life unstructured by any unifying temporal, spatial, or causal concept. In lieu of such a concept, there is Serafino's observant eye, that is, both his physical eyes and the lens of the camera through which he films a movie being produced at that place of converging destinies— both real and fictional—the Kosmograph Studios in Rome. In the final scene, a magnificent concretization of multiple metaphors as well as the culminating action, the movie plot and the fictional real-life plot merge. In a spectacular scene, typical of what the nascent grand-scale movie industry favored in those days, a real tiger is slated to be killed in the make-believe jungle where a group of make-believe Englishmen are on a make-believe safari. The star, Varia Nestoroff, mysterious Russian and merciless destroyer of men, suddenly finds herself caught between two lovers: a discarded one, now turned actor, and the present one, a fiery Sicilian. As the rivalry between the two lovers escalates, an exchange of roles puts the rejected lover instead of the present one into the tiger's cage. Maddened by Nestoroff's ostentatious flirting with the present favorite, he shoots not the tiger—as the script calls for—but her, and is in turn torn to pieces by the beast. All the time, Serafino, who like a detective has pieced together the preceding action—thus giving us the novel—continues filming the scene, his hand regulating the movement of the camera automatically. At the end, when the tiger is shot and Serafino dragged back from the cage, his grasp on the crank is so strong that he cannot let go: "I did not moan, I did not cry. The terror had silenced my voice forever."

Serafino's silence has symbolic significance: the shock of real life is too strong for a first-person narrator such as Serafino. Indeed, one of the themes of the novel is the mechanization of modern life. Serafino writes in the first notebook:

> Man, who was once a poet and deified his own feelings to worship them, has now discarded them as useless and dangerous impediments. Having turned wise and industrious, he has begun to build his new gods in iron and steel and has become their servant and their slave. Long live the machine that mechanizes life!
>
> (notebook 1, chap. 3)

A sentiment such as this is nothing new in Pirandello. Some of the early short stories— "Il fumo" ("Fumes"), "Lumíe di Sicilia" ("Sicilian Limes"), "La balia" ("The Wet-Nurse")— had already given an ironic interpretation of civilization and progress by setting up familiar antitheses that carry an unmistakable value judgment: rural life as against city life, genuineness as against artifice, order as against confusion, and innocence as against corruption. But in *Shoot!* criticism of the machine does not lead to its rejection. Serafino is and

remains a cameraman, proudly perfecting the minuscule area of craftsmanship that is left to him. Described from the beginning as "a hand that turns the crank," he specifies to an idler who questions him: "I, dear sir, do not always turn the crank in the same way. Sometimes I do it more rapidly, sometimes more slowly, as the circumstances require it." And with the sudden intuition of the direction that modern consciousness and art were taking, he adds: "I have no doubt, however, that with time, sir, they will succeed in doing without me."

This reduction of man to thing goes further than Pirandello's earlier view of man as spider, snail, or mollusk—living organisms, after all, still belonging to the animal kingdom on however humble a scale. And it goes further than the identification of man with a puppet (the principal point of reference is a passage in *The Late Mattia Pascal* that describes Sophocles' *Electra* performed in a marionette theater), for the puppet is after all still an image— albeit a rough wooden one—of man. But while the puppet gesticulates, its strings pulled by the God-artist puppeteer who transmits something of himself to it, the camera, a mechanical and not a human agent, impassively records. We have reached the dehumanization of art— and yet it is this very point that leads A. Leone De Castris, the critic who has written most acutely about the emergence of the Pirandellian character, to conclude that *Shoot!* mirrors the development of Pirandello's own human sympathy "from relative pity to absolute compassion, from sorrowful commentary to inanimate silence [*silenzio di cosa*] . . . from a human to a divine feeling, from narrative pity to the high and invisible pity of the tragic poet"—a development reflected in the sequence of Pirandello's fictional representations from Mattia Pascal's pity for his shadow to "Henry IV's" wide-eyed, horrified stare. In the sixth notebook, after Serafino has heard the story of Varia Nestoroff's life, with its mixture of self-degradation and aggression against others, he is seized with disgust at the rising tide of despicable actions and emotions revealed:

> Insanity, crime, or foolishness. Things fit for the movies! Here it is: this woman in front of me with her copper-colored hair. And over there, on those six canvases [painted by another lover of Nesto-roff, whom she has driven to suicide] the bright, luminous dream of a youth who could not come to terms with life. And now, the woman fallen from that dream, fallen from art into the movies. Come then, get the camera ready! Will there be a drama here? Here is the protagonist. Get set, shoot!
>
> (*Opere*, 1973, 2:690–691)

Beginning almost simultaneously with the publication of *Shoot!*, a number of converging factors—among them dramas to be impassively recorded and suffering reasoners who have pushed to the center of the stage—made possible Pirandello's rapid production of a wide variety of theatrical compositions. The first group of memorable stage characters arrived speaking in dialect. They have their fictional roots in Pirandello's Sicilian short stories, where, by the way, they speak in standard Italian. Pirandello derived *Think It Over, Giacomino!* from the story by the same name, *Cap and Bells* from "La verità" ("Sicilian Honor") and "Certi obblighi" ("A Wronged Husband"), and *Liolà* in part from an episode in *The Late Mattia Pascal*. The three protagonists are the mild-mannered but intransigent Professor Toti, the hard-pressed Ciampa, and the exuberant Liolà. Each is faced with a dilemma, and since we are in the realm of comedy, each succeeds in solving his dilemma. The solutions, as is customary in Pirandello, are unconventional but satisfactory to protagonist and audience alike (although some of the early reviewers decried the flouting of ordinary morality).

Professor Toti, a septuagenarian, saves his marriage to the teen-aged Lillina, thus insuring that she will receive the government pension for the sake of which—as a kind of revenge for having been an underpaid civil servant—he had married her on the eve of his retirement. At the same time, putting aside the stance of the wronged husband, he succeeds in saving the family that Lillina and her young lover, Giacomino, already have on the way.

Liolà, the lighthearted village Don Giovanni, is already the father of three illegitimate children—his goldfinches, he calls them, dancing and singing with them across the stage—and he is about to become the father of two more in an intrigue intended to right the wrong that one of the two women involved was about to do to the other.

And Ciampa, the only dark, tragic, that is, potentially violent figure of the three, averts the irreparable act of the betrayed husband against his rival, by inducing the accusing wife (the rival's) to act temporarily insane, in this way relieving him of the need to save his honor in the manner customary to his environment.

In the immediately following plays—*Right You Are (If You Think So)*, *The Pleasure of Honesty*, *The Rules of the Game*, and *All for the Best*, to name the major ones—the characters lose their ethnic characteristics as southerners but maintain their basic psychological trait: the drive to expound their often specious reasons, to make themselves understood at all costs, and to reveal themselves in naked isolation onstage. Leonardo Sciascia, the critic who has most intimately and intelligently understood the underlying Sicilian component of Pirandello's world, speaks of "a current of dialectics . . . present beneath the surface conformism of the Sicilian." Pirandello's central fictional character was at first the village philosopher—or madman—driven by an aspiration for absolutes. But the closer Pirandello moved to this character, the less he saw the external facts of his life—his circumstances, dress, legal identity—and the more he discerned his features—the grimace, the distraught look, the discomposed gesturing, and the "lean and hungry" quality that warns of the presence of distress and imminent revolt against established values. Eventually the local and historical reality that originally conditioned the character was completely subsumed under the universalized representation of anguish.

The shift in emphasis can be illustrated with a few examples. Rosario Chiarchiaro in *The License,* for instance, makes his entrance speaking in dialect and wearing a bizarre costume he has himself devised so as to give concrete expression to the role of bearer of the evil eye that public opinion has assigned to him. Although the pity he evokes from the one judge who is above convention (and from the reader) is timeless in nature, the situation is thinkable only in terms of a specific superstition operating in a specific locale. Ciampa in *Cap and Bells* also appears onstage speaking in dialect, in a situation created by a particular sexual ethic that has its fixed rules of conduct. Again, the reader's sympathy for his plea on behalf of being as opposed to seeming knows no boundaries of time or space, such as the elements of the plot do. Angelo Baldovino in *The Pleasure of Honesty,* instead, reveals nothing of his background. He is presented as a failure, but the causes of his failure remain generic, barely hinted at by a family friend who selects him as the nominal husband for a girl who is, and plans to remain, the mistress of someone else. Called upon to play the role of a respectable man in order to save appearances for "his wife" and her lover, Baldovino, with the wonted intransigence of the Pirandellian reasoner, insists on giving a perfect performance. It soon becomes obvious that the two norms of conduct cannot coexist, that being excludes seeming. Baldovino's behavior exposes the dishonesty and hypocrisy of those who had thought to use him for their own ends. He wins the love of his wife. The final dialogue is the result of an inner transformation that has come about through Baldovino's having actually lived the abstract principle of honesty and having thus proved its superiority as the basis for establishing viable human relationships. The action takes place completely on a psychological level, in the experiencing consciousness of those involved.

Right You Are (If You Think So) is in some respects not substantially different from *The Pleasure of Honesty.* The small-town gossips who want to find out the truth—that is, the objective, documentable facts of the lives of a family of newcomers in their midst—may be misled, and the audience with them, by a suggestion of specific historical time and place: the earthquake that wiped out the town from which the Ponzas have come really occurred in 1915, and the extreme pettiness of the bureaucratic milieu in which Ponza works as a harried clerk at the mercy of his superiors is unmistakably pre–World War I. But just as in *The Pleasure of Honesty, The Rules of the Game,* and *All for the Best,* the action has but little to do with these external circumstances, this almost fake verisimilitude. Like Baldovino, Ponza reveals very little of his background. The stage directions at his first appearance specify that he is dark, heavyset, and dressed completely in black, with a thick black moustache. He clenches and unclenches his hands, speaks with difficulty and ill-contained violence, and maintains a hard, fixed, somber stare. Obviously Pirandello presents him as wearing the mask of his anguish and not the dress of his social condition. In his manner and gesture is contained the outcome—the epilogue—of the drama through which he has lived.

But if like every other Pirandellian character Ponza is "caught in a situation," he is nevertheless used differently by the author. Unlike Baldovino or "Henry IV" or Martino Lori (in *All for the Best*) or Ersilia Drei (in *To Clothe the Naked*), Ponza does not live through an experience onstage. True, he comes forth to defend himself, to give his version of why he keeps his wife and his mother-in-law from seeing one another. Through Laudisi, Pirandello's spokesman in the play, he pleads for each man's right to his "phantom" (the illusion men create about themselves and about one another and in which they live "in perfect harmony, pacified"). But he does not change in the course of the play. What he knows at the end he already knew at the beginning; he has simply suffered more. And objectively, as a character created by Pirandello to a certain end, he has served—together with Signora Frola, Laudisi, and the veiled woman of the final scene—to demonstrate a truth, to teach a lesson. The same separation between the story that is told and the purpose to which it is told later appears in the trilogy of the theater within the theater. And in these plays, as in *Right You Are*, the separation confuses the issue for the spectator, who is asked to give up the deeply cherished expectation of being told a story through to the very end. But while from one point of view there is separation between story and purpose in the trilogy, there is no real clash between them: the character plays himself as character in the making—that is, he dramatizes himself in his role of character— and the intellectual, discursive content of the play is completely absorbed into the fiction itself. That is not quite so in the parable of *Right You Are*. Here the characters are simply themselves, stand-ins for real-life people, but as in all allegory they are embedded in something else. This something else, the message that truth is relative, is transmitted effectively; the situation through which it is dramatized— which one of two people is the crazy one?—is a comedic set piece; there is even an overt plea for compassion, an appeal to the finer sentiments, at the end. What is missing is the tremendous and unequivocal pressure of life onstage that we find elsewhere in Pirandello.

Henry IV gives us this pressure in its fullest tragic impact. Its protagonist is the self-aware and passionate Pirandellian hero caught at the moment of his greatest distress. His "phantom" is the most fragile of all, the most self-contained and lonely one, and it is about to be snatched from him. "Henry" (who only imagines himself to be Henry IV and has in fact no name) does not only *seem* mad to the frivolous, uncompassionate, and uncomprehending crowd that presses—and has always pressed—in upon him; he has actually *been* mad. He had plumbed the abyss of incommu-

nicability when one day, "looking into a pair of eyes . . . like a beggar before a door he will never be able to enter," he had realized that, even if he were to get in, it would be not as himself with his inner world as he sees and feels it but as a stranger to himself, as "the other one [the owner of the pair of eyes] sees and feels in his own impenetrable world." Compassion, which is meaningful in the microcosm of *Right You Are*, where Ponza, his wife, and his mother-in-law support one another by reciprocally creating the life-giving illusion of form, has no place in *Henry IV*. "Henry" is already all form and nothing but form. It is a form no one has given him and no one can share with him, except—by a supreme irony—the play-actors who are hired to sham his court.

These play-actors have an important role in revealing the meaning of the tragedy to the audience. It is they who first introduce "Henry" in a scene that lulls the audience into a false calm. While waiting for the "Emperor" and instructing the latest recruit, the latest "Secret Counselor," in his duties, they step in and out of their roles, triggering a laughter in the spectators that signals the happy recognition that all is as it should be: a wealthy madman may permit himself the luxury of building a castle for his folly ("Henry" has been living in his make-believe environment since the day, twenty years earlier, when he was thrown from his horse while wearing the costume of the German emperor Henry IV), but the men he employs to second that folly have their feet on the ground and enter into the deception knowingly, thus vindicating the accepted superiority of the sane man over the madman.

But when "Henry" is discussed by other characters in the course of arrangements for a "shock treatment" that is supposed to cure his delusion and fling him into the present, he bears the marks not of the madman but of the exceptional individual, the lucid, observant, critical mind that "has understood the game." Even before the accident, we are told, "Henry" was different: Donna Matilda, with whom he had been in love, speaks of him as "a bit strange . . . fanatical . . . eccentric"; Belcredi, who had been his rival and is now Matilda's lover, gives a perceptive analysis of his "lucid overexcitement," in which spontaneity and immediate reflection on that spontaneity—living and watching oneself live—appeared to be at constant war with one another. There follows the evocation of the moment after the accident, when the merrymakers suddenly became aware that, while they were play-acting their roles in the pageant, "Henry" was in earnest, the *mask* of the emperor had become his *face:* "I shall never forget that scene, all our made-up faces, so hideous and so vulgar, before the terrible mask of his face, that was no longer a mask, but madness personified!" The audience is thus prepared for the first appearance of Henry IV and for the scene that follows, in which—in a manner of speaking—both Henrys find themselves onstage together. "Henry" *is* Henry IV, and because of this all the others are forced into their supporting roles; but "Henry" is also suspiciously like himself, that is, he "philosophizes," reasons, in a manner appropriate both to his fictional self and to his real self (*if* we with Donna Matilda and Belcredi could be absolutely certain that he does have a real self). The scene dramatizes the confrontation between sanity and madness that "Henry" later describes in his "Secret Counselors": "Do you know what it means to find yourself face to face with a madman—with someone who shakes the foundations of everything you have built up in yourself and around you, your logic, the logic of all your constructions?"

We have moved then from the initial reassurance that the world of the sane is superior to the world of the insane to the disquieting thought that the unstable, inconstant structure that the madman gives the world may invalidate the solid and logical construction of the sane, of the perfect conformist. But if to be watched and judged by the heightened, half-disfiguring, and thereby half-configuring, intelligence of the psychotic is disturbing and unsettling, to be watched and judged by a coolly composed and intentional madness—that is, by the intelligence that has understood the game and can no longer bear to have anything to do with it—is simply intolerable. This is essentially what happens in *Henry IV* when it is revealed that, though "Henry" had been ill for twelve years, he had one day awakened as from a dream and had then decided—rationally decided—to remain fixed in his madness. There is no doubt that this is the high point of the play, the heavy center of Pirandello's tragic message. "Henry's" tragic insight occurs not at the end, when in a surge of form-shattering life he kills Belcredi; rather, it occurred eight years earlier, when he suddenly opened his eyes again

> and I was terrified, for I knew at once that it was not only my hair that had turned gray, but that everything had turned gray, that everything had collapsed and was ended. And I would be arriving, with the hunger of a wolf, at a banquet that had already been cleared away.
>
> (act 3)

As always in Pirandello, in *Henry IV* the game has already been played out before the action onstage begins; we are set before an epilogue. What "Henry" had with his superior wisdom and in strong self-renunciation composed is ruthlessly destroyed by the stupid meddling of a doctor more interested in the cure than in the patient, by a vapid, flighty middle-aged woman in search of sensation, and by that incarnation of evil, Belcredi, the man who originally precipitated the accident through one of those practical jokes (he had pricked "Henry's" horse during the cavalcade) that respectable society at all levels—the society of the well adjusted—condones and laughs at. *Henry IV* can be understood fully only if the minor figures are taken into account, for they stand concretely for all of the gradations in the inability of the average man to accept otherness. And "Henry's" tragedy is not simply that he *is* other, but that he has understood his otherness and has found that in the corrupt, egotistic, and foolish world around him there is no place for it. His exclusion is therefore doubly definitive: the sword thrust at the end of the play underscores and embodies the intuition of his tremendous aloneness: "This," he says at one point, indicating the costume he was wearing, ". . . is for me the evident, voluntary caricature of that other constant and continuous masquerade of which we are the involuntary clowns, when, without knowing it, we mask ourselves to appear as what we think we are."

Henry IV is Pirandello's highest achievement. Its intellectual content is absorbed completely and expressed completely—without leaving any residues—through the representation onstage. It is the play in which the famous "ideas"—though they are all present as in an exemplary compendium—intrude the least and that best shows how all along it is not the mask but the face behind it that concerns Pirandello. Its many-sidedness will continue to elicit critical attention for as long as the experience of man's encounter with non-being, with the void, has any intellectual or emotional resonance. In *Henry IV* Pirandello gives permanent life to the kind of character he elsewhere portrays as stillborn. "Henry" has the rich, autonomous being-in-art that makes him the center of a confluence of meanings, including some, as the Father in *Six Characters* says, never intended by the author. "Henry"—and there is a host of similarly successful characters in Pirandello—takes his place beside Francesca of the *Inferno*, Sancho Panza of *Don Quixote*, and Don Abbondio of *I promessi sposi* (*The Betrothed*, 1840), to cite only those named by Pirandello himself, as the living character who can scoff even at death because he survives his author, who is lowered to the status of mere instrument in his creation.

In 1933, when Pirandello reordered his collected plays for a new edition, he joined together *Six Characters, Each in His Own Way*, and *Tonight We Improvise* in the first volume. He thus gave pride of place to the play that won him international fame and linked it to two others to form a trilogy, in spite of the fact that the three had been written independently of one another and at different times within a period of almost ten years. In retrospect he had discovered that they had a theme in common: the dramatization of theatrical life itself. These plays not only tell a story—and from the traditional point of view of the well-made play they tell it badly—but they reflect upon the meaning of telling that story and on the particular way in which it is told. They lay bare what usually is prior and external to the work, revealing something of its history, of the difficulties the author encountered in achieving it, of the kind of work he had in mind, possibly even of its place in the development of the genre. These plays are "framed," as it were, not by the proscenium arch, but by the reflections on the art of drama itself in which whatever plot-action is left lies embedded. They can be subsumed into the category of the play-within-the-play, although in that perspective, too, they show their strong originality, for in them the "inner" play is not a cameo piece inserted in the "outer" play but part and parcel of it.

Pirandello prefixed an introductory statement to the 1933 edition in which he wrote that in the three plays "are represented all possible conflicts of the complex of elements that constitutes theater." Not only does the action spill over from the stage—where hitherto in the history of drama it had virtually always been confined—but the three plays exemplify three different kinds of conflict that arise in making theater: the conflict between the Characters and the persons assigned to interpret them, between the spectators on the one hand and the author and actors on the other, and between the actors who have become Characters and their director. (The capitalization is again intended to underline the specific, unusual value given by Pirandello to what is by other writers treated as an ordinary fictional invention.) In all three cases—whether the play is to be made by an author who refuses his responsibility, is to be improvised from a scenario in commedia dell'arte style, or already exists as a text but cannot be performed because of the rebellion of spectators and actors—the play, not the evening's performance, remains uncompleted. Repeated, then, for the spectator is the shock felt by the affronted Rome audience in 1921 when, upon entering the theater for the premiere of *Six Characters,* it found the unset stage—the empty workaday stage—displayed to full public view with the various stagehands, actors, prompter, manager, and director going about their preparatory business unperturbed. By the 1930's, however, the novelty of this situation had somewhat worn off; but by that time, too, Pirandello had learned to exploit the total resources of theater and stage.

The invention of *Six Characters*—its story line—is from one point of view of the utmost simplicity. A strange family one day appears in a theater and introduces itself to an acting company gathered together for a rehearsal. They claim to have been thought up by an author who later abandoned the work in which they were to appear. These six, then, exist solely as Characters, the kind of characters we have already seen importuning Pirandello in his study and in unguarded moments while he is reading or just musing. Finding the setting for their interrupted fictional existence ready, they demand to be given a chance to exhibit the drama that is in them. The Father and the Daughter especially insist that their unwritten drama is a hundred times more worthy of being performed than the play on the program (Pirandello's own *The Rules of the Game!*). The manager and the actors are at first intrigued, not by the Characters, whom they don't understand, but by their story, whose dramatic possibilities they at once recognize. When they try to "compose" the story, however, adapting it to the creation of the illusion of reality onstage, they fail miserably. The manager is a poor substitute for an author, a mere secretary who can write only under dictation, a "translator" who interprets but cannot create. As for the actors, they are hemmed in by the most traditional forms of stage practice: they can think only in stereotypes, and, having no notion of ensemble work, fall to bickering about the relative importance of their respective parts. As a consequence, the Characters' aspiration to life-through-art again fails, and they leave the stage "unrealized," their shadows projected against the backdrop, each in its characteristic stylized and "fixed" gesture. The two younger children, who in the course of the action have died, are not with them.

This is one way of telling the story of *Six Characters.* There is another one as well, more in keeping with what is normally expected in art that imitates life. It deals not with the Characters, but with the content of their lives. Here we encounter Pirandello's familiar social nihilism. The Father is an eccentric who has applied the yardstick of his rationalism to life. Having become aware in the early days of his marriage that there was greater compatibility between his wife and his secretary than between his wife and himself, he had made it possible for the two to leave together and set up their own—though illegitimate—family. In time the second "husband" has died and the wife, now nothing but a Mother, has to provide for her family through the meager living she makes by sewing for a dressmaker who keeps a brothel on the side. The Father, who has lost sight of his wife's second family over the years, comes to Madame Pace's, the dressmaker's establishment, and there by chance meets his stepdaughter. The Mother arrives just in time to prevent the quasi-incest, and the Father, horrified at the result of his original benevolent action, reunites the whole family (including the son from his marriage) in his own house. The tensions that result from the cohabitation of the two separate and related families—the destructive resentment of the Daughter, the icy disdain of the Son, the Father's sense of guilt, and the Mother's grief— lead to the tragic death of the two children: the Girl accidentally drowns in a pool in the garden and the Boy shoots himself, both victims of the neglectful Mother, who is completely taken up by her desire to regain the Son's affections. As the result of this accumulation of disasters, the Daughter (the children's sister and not the Father's daughter) leaves home. Thus the original family is reconstituted: Father, Mother, and Son, "ourselves alienated from one another by the disappearance of that alien family," as the Father puts it in lines later cut from the play, "alienated and utterly desolated—the revenge of the Demon of Experiment that I carry in me."

The only two scenes of this story that the Characters to some extent succeed in acting out are what is openly labeled "The Scene" in act 2—the encounter at Madam Pace's—and the garden scene, which remains, however, even more embryonic. The reason for these failed efforts goes back to the squabbling that erupts each time narrative is about to be turned into drama: the Characters insist on absolute verisimilitude (even if this involves constant changes in stage sets); the director thinks of the conventional form the play must take (children are a nuisance onstage and the proprieties must be respected); and the actors instinctively translate the Characters' experiences into set pieces of repertory (an old man who enters a brothel is supposed to be played "with the self-possessed, roguish air of an elder Don Juan"). All of this creates comic situations of immediate appeal to the audience. Unlike the Six, who are tragic if for no other reason than because they feel their predicament, manager and actors are characters of comedy. They are eager to preserve their sense of dignity, considering themselves great artists and not simple craftsmen. The audience identifies with them in their patronizing humoring and more often intolerant rebuffing of the Characters, in what Thomas Hobbes calls "the sudden glory" of abruptly perceiving one's superiority to others, however little justified that might be. But because of the play's dynamic movement the identification does not hold. Again and again the language of the Characters—especially that of the Father,

which in its ratiocination is the furthest from that of the actors—is the stronger one, engulfing and drowning out the more trivial, commonsense language of the actors and manager.

Three bodies of material can be said to constitute distinct structural elements in *Six Characters:* the story of the Characters' lives—i.e., the narrative content; the attempt on the part of manager and actors to turn the story into a play—i.e., the playwright's technical expertise and his grasp of theatrical practice; and Pirandello's own telling of the story within his representation of the Company's attempt to give it shape—i.e., the making of this particular play and its intended meaning. We have spoken briefly of the first two. Pirandello himself dealt with the third not only implicitly in the play but explicitly, fully, and lucidly in the preface to a new edition he wrote five years after the premiere. In that intervening time *Six Characters* had been performed and reviewed probably hundreds of times, in the most varied productions, in Italian and in translation, directed by Pirandello himself and by other directors, Georges Pitoëff and Max Reinhardt among them. That Pirandello was not satisfied by the original disposition into the single space of the stage of the three bodies of material just mentioned is reflected in the changes he made in the text. That he realized that the meaning of the play still eluded audiences is revealed in the preface, which, if it were possible given its length, should be "performed" together with the play, being in essence no different from the long "lecture" on the work of art in general and on the unusual show about to begin delivered by the character Dr. Hinkfuss in act 1 of *Tonight We Improvise.*

In the preface Pirandello returns to the very beginning, to the emergence of "the character without author," in order to show how he as one author solved the problem by letting a group of restless, homeless Characters loose on a stage and sitting back to watch what would happen:

What had to happen happened, and the result was a mixture of tragic and comic, of fantasy and realism, in a completely new and extremely complex humoristic situation: a drama that seeks at all costs to represent itself by means of its characters, breathing, speaking, self-propelling, who carry it within them and suffer it; and the comedy of the vain attempt at this sudden theatrical realization.

(*Opere,* 1958, 4:38)

It comes as no surprise that Pirandello's answer to "what happened" once he set the play-within-the-play—or, better, the drama-within-a-comedy—in motion refers not to the first of the linked terms but to the second, not to the substance of the plot of the inner story but to the shaping of the work, the artifact created by the outer story. In choosing as the genre designation for his play *commedia da fare* (comedy to be composed), which we read on the title page of the 1921 edition, Pirandello underlined his awareness of the comparative importance that he, as author, must give to its two indissolubly joined parts. For, as portrayed in the preface, *Six Characters* is not primarily (as it would appear to be according to the introductory statement to the trilogy) the representation of the conflict between Characters and the persons assigned to interpret them in the theater; instead, it is the representation of the author's creative act, which takes place in the mind and is externalized (or concretized and "personified") through the medium of the stage. Such is the meaning, Pirandello specifies, of the sudden appearance of a seventh Character, Madame Pace, who does not arrive at the theater with the others but "materializes" when the action calls for her presence:

A break occurred, a sudden change in the level of reality of the scene, for a character can be born in this way only in the poet's imagination, not on a stage. Without anyone having noticed it, I all of a sudden changed the scene: I gathered it up again into my own imagination without, however, removing it from before the eyes of the spectators.

That is, I showed them, instead of the stage, my imagination in the act of creating—my imagination in the form of this same stage.

(*Opere,* 1958, 4:44)

Nevertheless, when all is said and done, it is not only the transcending of art as representation that gives *Six Characters* its special impact, but the pathos of the Character's, of the Father's, crying out for the certainty that only history—that which is over—and art—that which is perpetually becoming—can give. "Il piacere della storia" (the pleasure of history), "Henry" calls it when he describes it to his "counselors": "Fixed forever, you could rest in it, admiring how every effect follows obediently upon its cause, with perfect logic, and every event takes place precisely and coherently in each of its particulars." This is the structure, the meaning, that man seeks in his own life, according to Pirandello, and it is no accident that the simple-minded, hired "counselors" recognize it as such and exclaim over its beauty. For in *Six Characters,* as Francis Fergusson puts it so well, Pirandello's intuition is not only that there is an analogy between his problem as an artist and the problem of the Characters who are also seeking form and meaning, but that there is a further analogy between the quest of the tormented Character and the desire of all men to know their destiny once and for all, to rest in their meaning. There are thus not only two levels in the play, as we have said, but three, with the two stories, the two plots, both lighting up the ultimate, most abstract, and universal concept, that of life in search of its authentic form. The Father's distress is both the guilt he feels because of the circumstances of the story he acts out—his drama—and the anguish he feels as an unfinished Character. There is no separation between these two realities of his, as there is no separation between the double reality of the children, walkons who have no speech as far as the theater is concerned, but persons who have a fate as far as life is concerned. "Fiction? Reality? Fiction! Reality!" are the words that actors and Characters are left shouting at one another when the Boy's gun is turned against himself. And because the spectator is left with the same doubt—which the last brilliant theatrical device of omitting the children's shadows from the final pantomime underscores—this play, which could have been but another fictional treatment of the problem of the artist, is also a complex, many-layered metaphor of the human condition.

The changes that took place in *Six Characters* between the first and definitive edition consisted in excisions, additions, and transpositions. From the point of view of theater history the most important innovations are those that enlarge the acting space. Thus the addition of a flight of steps on either side of the stage made it possible for the actors to move freely between the stage and the orchestra. The Characters, who had originally used the door onstage for their entrance, now come up from the auditorium, and their progress down the aisle is watched with fascination by both the actors onstage and the audience in the theater. At other points, when he wants to judge the effect of a particular action, the manager uses the steps to move from stage to orchestra and back again. The two areas traditionally kept separate, the territory of the audience and the territory of the performance, thus begin to merge. But in *Six Characters* the merging does not affect the audience itself; the spectators remain outside the action and are not put onstage. This subsequent step was taken in the second play of the trilogy, *Each in His Own Way.*

Six Characters departs from convention by not being divided into acts and scenes, although the performance is actually interrupted twice, once without the curtain being lowered but with the principal characters moving to confer offstage, the second time through the accidental lowering of the curtain. *Each in His Own Way* is divided into two acts and two choral interludes (crowd scenes); in addition, the final version of the play begins with a kind

of prelude, a busy scene taking place outside the theater, for which Pirandello sketched the scenario. This scene sets the stage, as it were, warning that the performance is most probably going to be interrupted by Amelia Moreno and Baron Nuti, she a famous and notorious actress, he her current lover. They have found out that Pirandello has turned their story (actually derived from the novel *Shoot!*) into a play portraying them under fictitious names and are indignant about it. They are among the news hawkers and spectators milling about before the performance. Both are surrounded by friends trying to convince them to leave, both are nervously pacing about, agitatedly claiming that there is no intention of creating a scandal. Their impromptu scenes give substance to the notice printed on the billboards (a parallel to the footnote that follows the cast of characters in *Six Characters*) to the effect that it is impossible to foretell the number of acts in this play "because of the probable incidents that will perhaps cut short the whole performance."

If the prelude were missing—as indeed it originally was—the first act of *Each in His Own Way* would present no unusual features, for it is more or less routine Pirandello, this time on the theme of consciousness. A reception is taking place in the elegant palace of Donna Livia Palegari, and, first from snatches of conversation and then from the more and more excited participation of some of the guests, it is learned that she is deeply concerned over a scandal in which her son, Doro, appears to be implicated. The evening before he had come to the defense of the reputation of Delia Morello (i.e., Amelia Moreno in the fictitious real-life story already alluded to in the prelude), who has driven two of her lovers to suicide. A duel is to be fought between Doro and the man who has attacked her, impugning her motives and disagreeing with Doro on how they are to be interpreted. Before the end of the act, however, their roles have been exchanged and Delia herself has contributed to the confusion by accepting the two contrasting views of her past actions as both equally possible. But no sooner has the curtain come down on Doro's exasperated questioning of why he should fight a duel "for something no one understands, neither I, nor he—nor even she! she herself!" than it is raised again, showing the stage not set as drawing-room but as that part of the theater lobby which leads to the orchestra and, farther down, to the stage door. The suspense that had been generated by the initial skirmishes of the action of the inner story is now replaced by a continuation of the expectation and bewilderment generated in the prelude. And the same happens again in the second interlude, when the lobby is again onstage after another episode of the Morello-Rocca story has been enacted in act 2 (Michele Rocca being Baron Nuti transposed into this comédie à clef).

In the stage directions for the first choral interlude Pirandello calls attention to the conceptual implications of these shifts in scene. The portrayal of the theater lobby and of the public, he writes, pushes what had in act 1 appeared in the foreground onstage onto a secondary plane, the plane of fiction. Later in the interlude, the discovery that the play being shown has "a key" and that Moreno and Nuti are in the audience establishes a first plane of reality, closer to life. Finally, in the second choral interlude the three planes of reality—the real persons of the lived drama, the fictitious persons (the characters) of the play being given, and the spectators as represented onstage—come into conflict with one another, with the result that the performance is cut short. It is interesting to note that of this complicated intellectual framework—"a mirror that has gone crazy," one of the fictional critics in the first interlude calls it—the aspect that has had the greatest appeal is the unusual placing of the mirror before the audience. The shock of recognition that any fictionalization of life can provoke is centered here on the immediate experience of being *in* the theater and of seeing that experience reproduced at once, without any interruption, onstage. The scene that is acted out, however, especially in the first interlude, is even more specific than that, for the spectators seen streaming out for the intermission and forming into groups to discuss the play express the same varied, contrasting, and heated opinions that Pirandello's plays, beginning with *Six Characters,* normally elicited. If in the theater-within-the-theater trilogy the drama tends to become a discussion on the drama more than elsewhere in Pirandello, *Each in His Own Way* offers a special version of this recurrent phenomenon: Pirandello's dramaturgy is here attacked and defended directly as part of an action onstage, rather than being presented reflectively in a preface (as in the case of *Six Characters*) or in discussions with the audience (a format Pirandello was particularly fond of, especially for performances abroad).

Like *Six Characters* and *Each in His Own Way, Tonight We Improvise* also has a narrative precedent. The story of the inner play was first told by Pirandello in 1910 in "Leonora, addio!," a title taken from an aria in Giuseppe Verdi's popular opera *La forza del destino* (1861). The textual background, then, comes from melodrama, and the genre reference is to another—and in Italy much-loved—theatrical medium. Dr. Hinkfuss, the play's director, carries a copy of the story with him onstage, the raw material (though in its own medium already perfectly formed) from which he will draw the evening's entertainment. As in *Six Characters,* so in *Tonight We Improvise* the major premise, the *donnée* on which the represented fiction is built, is that it is possible to produce a play without having a written text. This, of course, is what happened in commedia dell'arte, where in the acting companies the actor was also author and the author actor. In fact, the billboard that announces *Tonight We Improvise,* the programs and the flyers and the publicity, carry no author's name and no cast of characters. For the audience *everything* will be a surprise, not just some isolated and hinted-at episodes. Dr. Hinkfuss, the only performer whose identity is known from the beginning, introduces the actors, each one in his generic role: the Leading Actor, the Leading Actress, the Character Actress, and the old Character Actor. He also provides a very brief summary. The story is set in Sicily, in an unidentified city of the interior, "where passions are strong, smolder for a long time, and then flare up violently"—actually almost the blueprint of Pirandello's dramatic action in general. It is the story of a family, La Croce by name, rent asunder by the quintessential Sicilian passion, jealousy.

In format *Tonight We Improvise* is even further removed from the conventional three-act play than its predecessors in the trilogy. Dr. Hinkfuss announces that he has divided the subject matter into many short scenes (we might call them frames, borrowing the term from still another representational medium), with brief pauses in between, sometimes no longer than to permit the lowering of the lights. The acting space has been dramatically expanded, for an improvised action can arise almost anywhere, onstage but among the audience as well, in a box left empty on purpose, or in the lobby spontaneously during intermission. But the intentional mobility of this play, its rapid transitions, its indeterminacies among character, actor, and person, its cinematic qualities, its setting up of veritable *trompe-l'oeil* scenes, its sheer inventiveness, in short—all of which Dr. Hinkfuss promises in his address to the audience—are unexpectedly heightened at the very beginning by the protest the actors have organized offstage. Already invested with their parts for the evening's performance, they have lost their identities as actors (i.e., as persons) and refuse to go through the formality of the introductions. Their spokesman is the Leading Actor, whose lines express the doubling that runs like a red thread through all of Pirandello's work:

> Mr. So-and-So [he says to Dr. Hinkfuss, supplying his own name] no longer exists. Having given his word to improvise this evening, in order to have those lines on his lips that must rise from the depth of the Character he represents, with the action that accompanies them and every appropriate gesture, Mr. So-and-So must *live* the Character, *be* Rico Verri [i.e., the role that is his for the evening]. So much so that I don't know whether he will be able to adjust to all the tricks and surprises and little games of light and shadow that you have prepared to amuse the audience.
>
> (*Opere,* 1958, 1:216)

A few seconds after this dignified speech, a loud slap is heard from behind the curtain, greeted by the indignant lines of the old Character Actor, who did not expect to receive such slaps "for real."

Thus the action is engaged at once on both a serious and a burlesque level. The burlesque predominates in the initial portrayal of culturally conditioned tensions in the La Croce family. Signora Ignazia dreams of the "Continent," that is, of Italy beyond the Strait of Messina, with the greater freedom from social constraints to be found there. She tries to build an enclave where she and her four daughters can enjoy some "continental" fun, entertaining the aviation officers from a nearby airfield at musical soirées and going to the theater with them. The serious takes over with the marriage of one of the daughters to Rico Verri, the "different" one among the group of fun-loving young men. Sequestered by him in their home, cut off from all communication, especially communication with her family, whom Rico has known to be a disruptive influence, Mommina has only the memory of her love for music left. In the final scene she shows her little daughters "what the theater is" by evoking for them what they have never known: the hall, the boxes, ladies and gentlemen all dressed up, the great chandelier hanging from the ceiling, lights and movement, and then the curtains that open, the singers stepping to the ramp, the staged fiction beginning to unfold, and the music welling up from the orchestra pit while the voices of the singers soar over the audience. Mommina, too, had once sung those arias, but in the effort to sing them again for her children, she dies. Is it Mommina who dies? Or is it the Leading Actress? For a moment there is doubt, just long enough to drive the conclusion home: if the actor must *live* his role, he must also die; if he only relives it, gives new life to it every evening, then he must have a written part! It is an open ending, inviting the drama and the discussion of the drama to go on.

There is one aspect of Pirandello's work that almost completely eludes clarification through the concepts of "humorism," "character without author," and "theater within the theater." It is exemplified, for instance, in the two one-act plays, *At the Exit* and *L'uomo dal fiore in bocca* (*The Man with the Flower in His Mouth,* 1926), in *The Mountain Giants* and *La favola del figlio combiato,* and in a number of the late short stories. It shows a Pirandello who has left his ritualistic beginnings far behind and is now more at home with the surreal and the fantastic.

At the Exit is a dialogue between apparitions, "a profane mystery" in Pirandello's genre designation of it, in which "Appearances" and "Aspects of Life" meet on a country road against the backdrop of a cemetery wall. In its dreamlike sequence of scenes death is represented as the slow cessation of all desires: the shadow of a little boy persists just long enough for him to eat the pomegranate he had longed for before death. *The Man with the Flower in His Mouth* is almost exclusively a monologue in which the attachment to life of a man whose death from cancer is imminent is likewise expressed in an epiphany of insignificant things that by their very ordinariness, by their mere existing, provide the necessary anchor to life. In the most famous passage of the play the man evokes shop clerks lovingly attentive to the minutest detail of making a package in a heightening of reality that bears no trace of deformation or grotesqueness, only of a consuming yearning for life.

If in *The Mountain Giants* there are themes that take us back to *Six Characters,* the frame of reference is different, no longer that of the individual whose experience is universalized but that of society itself. *The Mountain Giants*

is one of Pirandello's three "myths" (the other two are *The New Colony* and *Lazarus*): the "myth" of art. The remains of an acting company, decimated and impoverished by its determination to perform a play that it can find no audience for, arrives one night at an abandoned villa high in the mountains. The villa is inhabited by a strange group of outcasts who have sought refuge there; their leader is an erstwhile magician, Crotone, who can make things happen, but only for those who understand fantasy. "We are here at the edges of life," he explains. "At a simple command barriers falls. The invisible appears. Phantasms emerge out of the air. . . ." And in fact, in the eerie night light thoughts, dreams, and wishes materialize, and each member of the company discovers that he is both the body asleep in bed and the "spirit" abroad in the magic of the place. Crotone invites the actors to give up their useless quest for an audience and share with him and his companions the absolute freedom of living in the imagination alone: "Here we are outside the limits of the natural and the possible. . . . For us it is enough to imagine something and it comes to life by itself." But the actors are incapable of understanding what is offered them. They insist on *performing* their fantasy world; that is, they are unable to sacrifice their own personalities and the sense of their indispensability to the work of art to the created thing itself. So they issue forth again and bring their play to the wedding festivities of the "Giants," a race of exceptional men in the valley who are busy exploiting the natural resources of their environment in the interest of material progress. Their play, Pirandello's own *La favola del figlio cambiato,* a fairy tale, has no meaning for the revelers, and in the Giants' drunken frenzy the leading lady and her two supporting actors are savagely mauled to death. In spite of its fragmentary state (the last act is missing) *The Mountain Giants* is powerful theater. In the figure of Crotone Pirandello has created another projection of himself as the self-effacing artist completely tensed to the perception of the abundant life that swirls about him. But it is now no longer simply case histories that are told him, no longer simply characters that burst in upon him or onto his stage; he now receives knowledge of "other beings of which men in their normal state have no perception," the nonhuman inhabitants of the world, the spirits of nature that live in the rocks and the woods, in the fire and in the air. In other words, we are back at the very origins of art, in man's myth-making capacity.

Art has one of its roots in the unconscious, and the manifestations of the unconscious always play an important part in Pirandello's work. We have seen that in the early years, at the time of *The Late Mattia Pascal,* for instance, they appear in the more primitive form of the supernatural. In the stories of his last period the unconscious is taken purely and simply as a psychological or metaphysical dimension, not a force to be controlled but an instrument and a source of knowledge. These stories, like the late plays, are dreams, or myths, or allegories. In "Soffio" (A Breath, 1931), for instance, the protagonist discovers that he has the power of life and death over other men, and step by step he comes to realize that he himself is Death. In "Cinci" (1932) a boy kills another boy and then forgets about it, as though not he but someone else in him had committed the murder. In "Il chiodo" (The Nail, 1936) another boy also kills—in a completely absurd act—simply because he had found a nail on the street and the nail "had wanted" to be used. "Di sera, un geranio" (In the Evening, a Geranium, 1934) takes up the mood of *At the Exit* and evokes the evanescence of consciousness that accompanies death. And finally, in "Una giornata" ("A Day Goes By," 1936), it is Pirandello himself who takes leave from life (he died a year later) in an allegorical vision that equates the whole course of a man's existence to the length of a day beginning in the pre-dawn darkness and ending in the same darkness seventy years later.

In the mid 1920's, when "philosophical" in-terpretations of his work became more and more the fashion, Pirandello himself more than once pointed out what a more balanced and inclusive point of view should be: "My works are born of living images, the inexhaustible and perennial source of art. . . . A work of mine is never a concept that seeks expression through images, but an image . . . that, feeding on the intellectual efforts of the mind, by itself takes on a universal meaning through the intimate coherence of art alone." It should come as no surprise that the key to Pirandello's poetic universe is thus ultimately in the images that held meaning for him—the stage being itself but one of those images. The dramatic concepts and the theatrical devices he popularized and often invented made of him a major determining force in the modern theater. But by virtue of his total oeuvre he belongs among the prime poetic imaginations of the early part of this century: Marcel Proust, James Joyce, Franz Kafka, Robert Musil, Thomas Mann. As for the commitment of the artist to his work, Pirandello is an example of well-nigh total dedication to the intuited embryonic life that seeks liberation through the gift of artistic form.

Selected Bibliography

EDITIONS

INDIVIDUAL WORKS

POETRY
Mal giocondo. Palermo, 1889.
Pasqua di Gea. Milan, 1891.
Pier Gudrò. Rome, 1894.
Elegie renane. Rome, 1895.
Zampogna. Rome, 1901.
Scamandro. Rome, 1909.
Fuori di chiave. Genoa, 1912.

PLAYS
Liolà. Sicilian text with facing Italian translation, Rome, 1917; Italian text, Florence, 1928.
Pensaci, Giacomino! Milan, 1918; rev. ed., Florence, 1925.

LUIGI PIRANDELLO

Cosí è (se vi pare). Milan, 1918; rev. ed., Florence, 1925.

Il piacere dell'onestà. Milan, 1918; rev. ed., Florence, 1925.

Il giuoco delle parti. Milan, 1919; rev. ed., Florence, 1925.

Ma non è una cosa seria. Milan, 1919; rev. ed., Florence, 1925.

Lumíe di Sicilia. Milan, 1920.

Il berretto a sonagli. Milan, 1920; rev. ed., Florence, 1925.

La patente. Milan, 1920.

Tutto per bene. Florence, 1920.

L'innesto. Milan, 1921; rev. ed., Florence, 1925.

La ragione degli altri. Milan, 1921; rev. ed., Florence, 1925.

Come prima, meglio di prima. Florence, 1921.

Sei personaggi in cerca d'autore. Florence, 1921; 4th rev. ed., Florence, 1925.

Enrico IV. Florence, 1922.

L'uomo, la bestia, e la virtù. Florence, 1922.

La signora Morli, una e due. Florence, 1922.

Vestire gli ignudi. Florence, 1923.

La vita che ti diedi. Florence, 1924.

Ciascuno a suo modo. Florence, 1924.

Sagra del Signore della nave, L'altro figlio, La giara. Florence, 1925.

L'imbecille, Lumíe di Sicilia, Cecè, La patente. Florence, 1926.

All'uscita, Il dovere del medico, La morsa, L'uomo dal fiore in bocca. Florence, 1926.

Diana e la Tuda. Florence, 1927.

L'amica delle mogli. Florence, 1927.

La nuova colonia. Florence, 1928.

O di uno o di nessuno. Florence, 1929.

Lazzaro. Milan, 1929.

Questa sera si recita a soggetto. Milan, 1930.

Come tu mi vuoi. Milan, 1930.

Trovarsi. Milan, 1932.

Quando si è qualcuno. Milan, 1933.

La favola del figlio cambiato. Milan, 1933. Text with music.

Non si sa come. Milan, 1935.

Sogno (ma forse no). Milan, 1936.

I giganti della montagna. Milan, 1938.

ESSAYS

Laute und Lautentwickelung der Mundart von Girgenti. Halle, 1891.

Arte e scienza. Rome, 1908.

L'umorismo. Lanciano, 1908; 2d enlarged ed., Florence, 1920.

NOVELS

Il turno. Catania, 1902.

Il fu Mattia Pascal. Rome, 1904; rev. ed., Milan, 1918; with appendix, Florence, 1921.

L'esclusa. Milan, 1908; rev. ed., Florence, 1927.

I vecchi e i giovani. Rome, 1909; rev. ed., Milan, 1931.

Suo marito. Florence, 1911; rev. ed. with title *Giustino Roncella nato Boggiòlo*, Milan, 1953.

Si gira. . . . Rome, 1915; with title *Quaderni di Serafino Gubbio operatore*, Florence, 1925.

Uno, nessuno e centomila. Florence, 1926.

SHORT STORY COLLECTIONS

Amori senza amore. Rome, 1894.

Beffe della morte e della vita. Florence, 1902.

Quand'ero matto. . . . Turin, 1902; rev. ed., Milan, 1919.

Beffe della morte e della vita. Seconda serie. Florence, 1903.

Bianche e nere. Turin, 1904.

Erma bifronte. Milan, 1906.

La vita nuda. Milan, 1910.

Terzetti. Milan, 1912.

Le due maschere. Florence, 1914; rev. ed., Milan, 1920.

La trappola. Milan, 1915.

Erba nel nostro orto. Milan, 1915.

E domani, lunedi. . . . Milan, 1917.

Un cavallo nella luna. Milan, 1918.

Berecche e la guerra. Milan, 1919; new collection with same title, Milan, 1934.

Il carnevale dei morti. Florence, 1919.

Tu ridi. Milan, 1920.

Scialle nero. Florence, 1922; rev. ed., Milan, 1938.

La rallegrata. Florence, 1922.

L'uomo solo. Florence, 1922.

La mosca. Florence, 1923.

In silenzio. Florence, 1923.

Tutt'e tre. Florence, 1924.

Dal naso al cielo. Florence, 1925.

Donna Mimma. Florence, 1925.

Il vecchio Dio. Florence, 1926.

La giara. Florence, 1928.

Il viaggio. Florence, 1928.

Candelora. Florence, 1928.

Una giornata. Milan, 1937.

414

LUIGI PIRANDELLO

COLLECTED WORKS

Opere di Luigi Pirandello. 6 vols. Edited by Corrado Alvaro, Silvio D'Amico, and Manlio Lo Vecchio-Musti. Milan, 1956–1960. Vols. 1 and 2: *Novelle per un anno;* vol. 3: *Tutti i romanzi;* vols. 4 and 5: *Maschere nude;* vol. 6: *Saggi, poesie, scritti vari.*
—————. 5 vols. Edited by Giovanni Macchia, Mario Costanzo, and Alessandro d'Amico. Milan, 1973–. Vols. 1 and 2: *Tutti i romanzi;* vols. 3 and 4: *Novelle per un anno;* vol. 5: *Maschere nude.*

TRANSLATIONS BY PIRANDELLO

Elegie romane di Goethe. Livorno, 1896.

CORRESPONDENCE

Epistolario familiare giovanile (1886–1898). Edited by Elio Providenti. Florence, 1986.

TRANSLATIONS

As You Desire Me. Translated by Samuel Putnam. New York, 1931, 1948.
Better Think Twice About It and Twelve Other Stories. Translated by Arthur and Henrie Mayne. London, 1933; New York, 1934.
Collected Plays. 2 vols. Various translators. New York, 1986–1987.
Diana and Tuda. Translated by Marta Abba. New York, 1950.
Each in His Own Way and Two Other Plays. Translated by Arthur Livingston. New York and London, 1924. Includes *The Pleasure of Honesty* and *Naked.*
Henry IV. All for the Best. Right You Are (If You Think So). No translator cited. Harmondsworth, 1960.
Horse in the Moon: Twelve Short Stories. Translated by Samuel Putnam. New York, 1932.
The Late Mattia Pascal. New York and London, 1923. Translated by Arthur Livingston. New translation by William Weaver. New York, 1964.
The Medals and Other Stories. No translator cited. New York, 1939. American edition of *A Character in Distress.* London, 1938.
The Merry-Go-Round of Love and Selected Stories. Translated by Lily Duplaix. New York, 1964.
The Mountain Giants and Other Plays. Translated by Marta Abba. New York, 1958. Includes *The New Colony* and *When Someone Is Somebody.*
Naked Masks. Translated by Eric Bentley, Gerardo Guerrieri, Arthur Livingston, and Edward Storer. New York, 1952. Contains *Liolà, It is So (If You Think So), Henry IV, Six Characters in Search of an Author,* and *Each in His Own Way.*
The Naked Truth and Eleven Other Stories. Translated by Arthur and Henrie Mayne. New York and London, 1934.
No One Knows How. Translated by Marta Abba. New York, 1949.
The Old and the Young. Translated by C. K. Scott Moncrieff. New York and London, 1928.
On Humor. Translated by Antonio Illiano and Daniel P. Testa. Chapel Hill, N.C., 1974.
One-Act Plays. Translated by Elisabeth Abbott, Arthur Livingston, and Blanche Valentine. New York, 1928. Contains *The Doctor's Duty, The Vise, The Man with the Flower in His Mouth,* and *Sicilian Limes.*
One, None, and a Hundred Thousand. Translated by Samuel Putnam. New York, 1933.
The Outcast. Translated by Leo Ongley. New York and London, 1925; new ed., New York, 1935.
Pirandello's One-Act Plays. Translated by Willaim Murray. New York, 1964. Contains *The Vise, Sicilian Limes, The Doctor's Duty, The License, At the Exit, The Man with the Flower in His Mouth, The Festival of Our Lord of the Ship,* and *I'm Dreaming, But Am I?*
Right You Are. Translated by Eric Bentley. New York, 1954.
The Rules of the Game. The Life I Gave You. Lazarus. Translated by Robert Rietty and Frederick May. Harmondsworth, 1959.
Shoot! Translated by C. K. Scott Moncrieff. New York, 1926; London, 1927, new ed., 1930.
Short Stories. Translated by Lily Duplaix. New York, 1959.
Short Stories. Translated by Frederick May. New York, London, and Toronto, 1965.
Sicilian Comedies: Cap and Bells—Man, Beast, and Virtue. Translated by Norman A. Bailey and Roger W. Olive. New York, 1983.
Six Characters in Search of an Author. Translated by Frederick May. London, 1954.
Tales of Madness. Translated by Giovanni Bussino. Boston, 1984.
Tales of Suicide. Translated by Giovanni Bussino. Boston, 1987.
Three Plays. Translated by Edward Storer and Arthur Livingston. New York, 1922; London, 1923. Contains *Six Characters in Search of an*

Author, Henry IV, and *Right You Are! (If You Think So)*.

To Clothe the Naked and Two Other Plays. Translated by William Murray. New York, 1962.

To Find Oneself. Translated by Marta Abba. New York, 1943.

Tonight We Improvise. Translated by Samuel Putnam. New York, 1932, 1960.

The Wives' Friend. Translated by Marta Abba. New York, 1949.

BIOGRAPHICAL AND CRITICAL STUDIES

Alonge, Roberto et al. *Pirandello e il teatro.* Palermo, 1985.

Atti del Congresso internazionale di studi pirandelliani. Florence, 1967.

Barilli, Renato. *Pirandello: Una rivoluzione culturale.* Milan, 1986.

Bentley, Eric. *The Pirandello Commentaries.* Lincoln, Neb., 1985.

Borsellino, Nino. *Ritratto di Pirandello.* Bari, 1983.

Bragaglia, Leonardo. *Interpreti pirandelliani.* Rome, 1969.

Büdel, Oscar. *Pirandello.* New York and London, 1966.

Cambon, Glauco, ed. *Pirandello: A Collection of Critical Essays.* Englewood Cliffs, N.J., 1967.

Fergusson, Francis. *The Idea of a Theater.* Princeton, 1949.

Giudice, Gaspare. *Luigi Pirandello.* Turin, 1963. *Pirandello: A Biography.* Translated by Alastair Hamilton. New York, London, and Toronto, 1975.

Illiano, Antonio. *Metapsichica e letteratura in Pirandello.* Florence, 1982.

Leone De Castris, Arcangelo. *Storia di Pirandello.* Bari, 1962.

Licastro, Emanuele. *Luigi Pirandello dalle novelle alle commedie.* Verona, 1974.

Macchia, Giovanni. *Pirandello e la stanza della tortura.* Milan, 1981.

Milioto, Stefano, and Enzo Scrivano. *Pirandello e la cultura del suo tempo.* Palermo, 1984.

Muscarà, Sarah Zappulla. *Pirandello dialettale.* Palermo, 1983.

Oliver, Roger W. *Dreams of Passion: The Theater of Luigi Pirandello.* New York, 1979.

Pennica, Gilda, ed. *Pirandello e la Germania.* Palermo, 1984.

Ragusa, Olga. *Luigi Pirandello: An Approach to His Theatre.* Edinburgh, 1980.

Rauhut, Franz. *Der junge Pirandello oder das Werden eines existentiellen Geistes.* Munich, 1964.

Sciascia, Leonardo. *Pirandello e la Sicilia.* Caltanissetta and Rome, 1961.

Valency, Maurice. *The End of the World: An Introduction to Contemporary Drama.* New York and Oxford, 1980.

Vincentini, Claudio. *L'estetica di Pirandello.* Milan, 1970.

BIBLIOGRAPHIES

Barbina, Alfredo. *Bibliografia della critica pirandelliana, (1889–1961).* Florence, 1967.

Donati, Corrado. *Bibliografia della critica pirandelliana (1962–1981).* Florence, 1986.

OLGA RAGUSA

MAXIM GORKY
(1868–1936)

MAXIM GORKY BELONGS to that category of writers whose reputation far exceeds any active literary interest in them. Revered and monumentalized in the Soviet Union, Gorky still remains well known throughout the world, but there is little evidence to suggest that he is much read anymore. In his own time, and especially between his first and only visit to the United States in 1906 and his death in Moscow in 1936, his fame equaled that of Leo Tolstoy or Anton Chekhov. The rapidity with which his works were translated into other languages, including English, clearly indicates the kind of interest Gorky once evoked. But it is likely that the Soviet monumentalization of him (with all its patent distortions) has in some way had a negative impact on his literary reputation abroad. Then, too, as time has enabled readers to see Gorky's works at a greater remove from the circumstances in which they arose, their deficiencies have become all the more obvious. Critics are now less willing to excuse them on the grounds of Gorky's liberalism, compassion, and extraordinary service to his fellow writers and to Russian culture in general from the Revolution up until his death. There has always been so much to admire in Gorky the man, so much to be attracted to, that it was not hard to forgive his flaws as a writer. But as Gorky's personal esteem grew by leaps and bounds, his works seem to have receded in importance, as if the man had become more important than his writings. As with other literary "giants" who are more admired than read, the tendency now is to focus so much on flaws and shortcomings in his work that genuine literary achievements are overlooked.

Gorky is probably thought of today primarily as a dramatist on the strength of his most famous play, the once-sensational and drearily naturalistic *Na dne* (*The Lower Depths,* 1902), which remains the most frequently performed of any of his works for the stage. In the English-speaking world Gorky's reputation as a dramatist first and foremost was strengthened by the generally successful revivals of a few of his plays by the English Royal Shakespeare Company in the 1970's. New productions of *Dachniki* (Summer Folk, 1904) and *Vragi* (*Enemies,* 1906) in both England and America were accompanied by new translations. American productions of such lesser-known plays as *Deti solntsa* (*Children of the Sun,* 1905) and *Egor Bulychov i drugie* (*Yegor Bulychov and Others,* 1932) were also mounted. Curiously, Gorky's first staged play, and one of his best, *Meshchane* (*The Petty Bourgeois,* 1901), is still among the least known of his dramatic works in terms of English-language productions, although it has been translated.

Gorky was also a prolific prose writer, and in this regard he is now primarily remembered as the author of the often-anthologized short story "Dvadtsat' shest' i odna" ("Twenty-Six Men and a Girl," 1911–1912), perhaps his best work of short fiction, and of the weak novel *Mat'* (*Mother*, 1906), which is about the Russian Revolution of 1905. This work has been adulated out of all proportion in the Soviet Union, both because of its subject and because of Vladimir Lenin's enthusiasm for it. But Gorky's best prose writing is too often overlooked and deserves more serious attention. Of his fiction, such early stories as "Makar Chudra" (1892) and "Chelkash" (1895) and his first novel, *Foma Gordeev* (1899), all of which have been published in English translation under these titles, are good and deserve to be read. Apart from these works and "Twenty-Six Men and a Girl," however, as time goes on Gorky is becoming more and more appreciated for his literary reminiscences, which include the autobiographical trilogy *Detstvo* (*Childhood*, 1913), *V liudiakh* (*My Apprenticeship*, 1916), and *Moi universitetii* (*My Universities*, 1923)—of which the first and last are the most interesting and the most successful artistically—and his vivid, sensitive, and often incisive recollections of such fellow writers as Chekhov, Tolstoy, and Leonid Andreev.

There is, then, more of enduring value in Gorky's literary legacy than is thought to be the case nowadays, particularly in the West. But before reviewing his career as a writer, let us first consider the salient facts of his exceptionally colorful life so that we can better appreciate the monumentalization of Gorky that has taken place in his own country.

LIFE

Gorky was born Aleksei Maksimovich Peshkov on 28 March 1868 in the Volga city of Nizhny Novgorod (renamed Gorky after his death), which is situated some 225 miles east of Moscow. The family was lower-middle-class, his mother belonging to a family of textile dyers and his father being an upholsterer who later became a wharf manager. Gorky's father died in 1871, when the future writer was barely four years old. Unable to care for her son herself, his mother gave him over to the care of her parents. Gorky's stay with them ended not long after his mother's death in 1878, when he was driven out of his grandparents' home at the age of eleven by his tyrannical and brutal grandfather, who thought that the time had come for the boy to begin providing for himself.

For the next fourteen years Gorky traveled widely in Russia working at a variety of menial jobs—bootblack, errand boy, bird catcher, dishwasher on board a Volga paddleboat, assistant in an icon-making shop, stevedore, bakery employee, Caspian Sea fishery worker, railway night watchman—all of which brought him into contact with an extraordinary variety of people and places and provided material for much of his later writing, fictional as well as autobiographical.

For all its adventurousness and freedom, Gorky's early life was hard and frustrating. When a thirst for knowledge prompted a vigorous program of self-education, the young Gorky dreamed of entering a university and set out for the city of Kazan for that purpose. But he failed to gain admittance and had to content himself with informal learning through his own efforts and through contacts with students and other educated people. Disappointment over his failure to enter the University of Kazan, the death of his much-loved grandmother, an unsuccessful romance, and a sense of aimlessness about his own life led Gorky to attempt suicide in 1887. Although he fired a pistol at where he thought his heart was, he succeeded only in damaging his left lung, which left him with impaired pulmonary function that may have eventually contributed to his death.

Further frustrations came soon after his bungled suicide. By this time an ardent admirer of the Populist movement in Russia and of Tolstoyism, Gorky made a special trip to visit Tolstoy at his estate, Yasnaya Polyana. But Tolstoy's wife mistook him for a tramp, fed him some rolls and coffee in the kitchen, and refused to allow him to see her husband. A noble effort to rescue a Cossack adulteress who was being dragged naked down a village street tied to a horse cost him a severe beating at the hands of infuriated Cossacks and landed him in the hospital. Rejected for military service because of his damaged lung, Gorky tried to volunteer as an army engineer but was turned down as politically unreliable. About this time, while still in Nizhny Novgorod, Gorky sought out the well-known Populist writer Vladimir Korolenko in order to show him his first as yet unpublished writings. Although Korolenko was friendly and encouraging, Gorky was so stung by his criticisms that he tore up his manuscript and swore that he would never try writing again. (The vow, of course, was soon broken.) Not long afterward, he fell in love with a married woman named Olga Kaminskaia, with whom he lived for a while before leaving Nizhny Novgorod for the Georgian capital of Tiflis. It was in Tiflis that his first story, "Makar Chudra," was published in 1892. Between 1892 and 1894 Gorky was back in Nizhny Novgorod, living with Olga in a bathhouse, the target of considerable gossip. By 1895 his relationship with Olga soured, and Gorky left her, this time reappearing in the town of Samara to work again on a newspaper, *Samarskaia gazeta.*

In 1895 Korolenko, with whom Gorky had kept in touch, arranged for the publication of the young writer's story "Chelkash" in his own magazine, *Russkoe bogatstvo* (Wealth of Russia). This was the first work published by Gorky under his pseudonym "Maxim Gorky" (or Max the Bitter). The following year, Gorky married a young proofreader on *Samarskaia gazeta* named Ekaterina Pavlovna Volzhina, a Populist radical who bore him a son named Maxim and a daughter named Katya.

Gorky's first literary success came in 1898, when his collection *Ocherki i rasskazy* (Stories and Sketches) was published. The book was very well received and sold over one hundred thousand copies, an extraordinary number for Russia at the time. Political notoriety began to

parallel his growing literary fame. The year of the publication of *Ocherki i rasskazy,* Gorky, who was flirting with Marxism, was arrested on a charge of having given seditious readings and was imprisoned in Tiflis. A fellow journalist's intercession brought about his release and permission to return to live in Nizhny "under surveillance," an edict that remained in force until the Revolution. But Gorky ran afoul of the police again in 1901 and was exiled to the central Russian town of Arzamas.

By then, however, Gorky's literary celebrity assured him a high degree of visibility, one that spurred him to greater political activism and at the same time forced the tsarist authorities to deal with him cautiously. Riding the wave of acclaim that attended the publication of *Ocherki i rasskazy,* Gorky initiated a friendship with Chekhov that lasted until the latter's death in 1904. It was through Chekhov that Gorky was at last introduced to Tolstoy, with whom he enjoyed at best an ambivalent relationship. Tolstoy's egomania and coarseness offended Gorky, while Tolstoy found few of Gorky's works to his liking (as he never hesitated to tell Gorky). It was while in the Crimea, where he had gone to recuperate from a bout with tuberculosis, that Gorky had begun nurturing his friendship with Chekhov and Tolstoy, who happened to be there at the same time, and where a visit by the touring Moscow Art Theater in 1900 inspired him to try his hand at playwriting. The first dramatic work he began was *The Lower Depths,* but he dropped it to write *The Petty Bourgeois,* returning to complete the first play only in 1902.

Gorky published his first novel, *Foma Gordeev,* in 1899. The following year he joined the *Znanie* (Knowledge) group of liberal and socially aware writers and artists in Moscow. With Gorky's encouragement the group launched a serious cooperative publishing enterprise under the same name. Gorky was personally responsible for bringing into *Znanie* such writers as Andreev, "Skitalets" (Stepan Petrov), Aleksandr Kuprin, Aleksandr Serafimovich, and the great singer Fedor Chaliapin, who by this time was a good friend of his.

The great success of *The Lower Depths* in its first Moscow production in December 1902, just a few years after the publishing triumph of *Ocherki i rasskazy,* secured Gorky's literary reputation in Russia and for the first time brought him international fame. As Gorky's income began growing from royalties, he became an important contributor to the Social Democratic Party, from which Lenin's Bolsheviks eventually emerged.

The Revolution of 1905 found Gorky in the thick of political conflict. Besides actually participating in the organization of the workers' march on the Winter Palace in St. Petersburg led by the activist priest Father Gapon, Gorky also joined a delegation of intellectuals to the Minister of the Interior to plead for restraint. The plea proved of no avail. When the workers' march was mercilessly suppressed in what has become known as "Bloody Sunday," Gorky helped Father Gapon to leave Russia in disguise.

Within a few days of Gapon's flight Gorky was arrested and imprisoned in the Peter and Paul Fortress, where he managed to write the play *Children of the Sun.* Gorky's literary fame was immensely valuable at this time. Western pressure on the tsarist authorities, as well as financial support from the left-leaning industrialist Savva Morozov, won him his freedom. But hardly was he out of prison in early March when Gorky again threw himself into political activism. With a fresh warrant for his arrest hanging over his head, Gorky left Russia in late May 1905; he fled first to Finland and thence to Germany.

What followed was one of the most bizarre episodes in Gorky's life. Widespread enthusiasm in the West for the cause of the Russian workers, which was accompanied by sharpening anti-tsarist sentiment, made a fund-raising trip to the United States by Gorky—then the hottest Russian literary property—seem like a sound idea. Much fanfare attended the writer's arrival in America, where elaborate plans for a variety of receptions and public functions had been made. But everything turned sour when the Imperial Russian Embassy in Washington leaked the news that the woman Gorky was traveling with was not his wife but an actress of the Moscow Art Theater named Maria Fedorovna Andreeva, who was, in fact, his mistress. Puritanical America recoiled in horror at the news, and a storm of protest swept across the land. Gorky suddenly found himself attacked in print and then ordered to leave his hotel in New York. Planned affairs were hastily dismantled, and in the worst cut of all, a literary dinner at which he was to be the featured guest—which Mark Twain and William Dean Howells had arranged—was canceled, and Twain refused to meet Gorky. With his American visit turned into a shambles, Gorky retreated in shock and dismay to the Staten Island and Adirondack residences of an American friend. It was there that his anger and frustration vented themselves in a frenzy of writing. His negative impressions of America were incorporated in "Moi interv'iu" (My Interviews, 1906) and "V Amerike" (In America, 1906). He also wrote the huge revolutionary novel *Mother* at this time. Before finally leaving the United States in September 1906, Gorky also managed to finish his anticapitalist play *Enemies,* which the great German stage director Max Reinhardt successfully produced the following year at his Kleines Theater in Berlin.

After his departure from America, Gorky settled on the island of Capri, where he remained until an amnesty for political exiles in 1913 on the occasion of the three-hundredth anniversary of the Romanov dynasty made it possible for him to return to Russia.

While on Capri, Gorky kept up an active literary career. Among the many stories he wrote during this period was his famous "Twenty-Six Men and a Girl." He also wrote two more novels, the quite good (though not well known) *Gorodok Okurov* (The Little Town of Okurov, 1909), which is set in an unpleasant provincial town on the eve of the 1905 Revolution, and the longer, and considerably weaker, *Zhizn' Matveia Kozhemiakina* (*The Life of Matvei Kozhemyakin*, 1910–1911), which also has an Okurov setting. Additionally, he wrote a play about a strong mother, possibly inspired by *Mother*, entitled *Vassa Zheleznova* (1910), which was awarded the Griboedov Prize in Moscow in 1912. He also wrote the religiously inspired *Ispoved'* (*The Confession*, 1908), with which Lenin, whom Gorky had moved closer to politically, expressed his displeasure.

Even in Italian exile, Gorky's political activity showed no signs of abating. He attended the Fifth Congress of the Russian Social Democratic Party in London in 1907, though he never actually became a member of the party, and, together with the revolutionaries Aleksandr Bogdanov and Anatoly Lunacharskii, he established a school for revolutionary Russian workers on Capri. There was a steady stream of visitors to Gorky's villa, most of them Russian political activists of every stamp and hue. Overcoming his antipathy to Gorky's *The Confession* and his discomfort with the religio-philosophical views of Bogdanov and Lunacharskii, Lenin himself finally consented to pay Gorky a visit on Capri.

Once back in Russia in 1913, Gorky complemented his own writing with several new publishing ventures, the most important of which was the newspaper *Novaia zhizn'* (New Life), which came to enjoy a wide following, especially among the country's intelligentsia. Politics was as much a part of his life as ever, but as Russia became embroiled in World War I and then in the February Revolution of 1917, he found himself in trouble with both the right and the left. Conservatives were angered by his anti-war views and subjected him to a campaign of vilification in which he was attacked as pro-German and Bolshevik. Among left-wing factions his growing disenchantment with Lenin and the Bolsheviks, whom Gorky upset by his opposition to another uprising after the February 1917 upheaval, caused him difficulties with many of his former admirers and political allies. The suc-

cessful Bolshevik coup d'état in October 1917 and Lenin's postrevolutionary policies only widened the rift. At one point Gorky went so far as to liken Lenin to a chemist working in a laboratory, "with the difference that the chemist employs dead matter with results valuable for life, whereas Lenin works on living material and leads the revolution to perdition."

Although *Novaia zhizn'* was forced to close because of its hostility toward the Bolsheviks, Gorky did become reconciled with Lenin. During the civil war that lasted until 1921, Gorky fought vigorously to preserve Russian culture in one of its darkest hours. He created, for example, a Commission for the Protection of Monuments that not only waged a campaign to save priceless works of art from wanton desecration and destruction during a time of chaos but also provided people with jobs, food rations, and lodgings. Concerned about the plight of artists and intellectuals in a politically polarized and strife-torn Russia, he established a Committee for the Improvement of Living Conditions for Scholars as well as an Institute of World Literature. The Institute proved to be one of Gorky's more successful undertakings. With offices in Petrograd (the former St. Petersburg) and Moscow it launched an impressive program of translation of world classics into Russian and served as a veritable haven for many writers whose lot otherwise would have been precarious. With Gorky's organizations, above all the Institute, as a kind of protective umbrella, artists and intellectuals could count not only on employment and the satisfaction of at least basic material needs but also on Gorky's support when difficulties with the new regime developed.

Gorky's reconciliation with Lenin did not, however, resolve his feud with Grigori Zinoviev, the head of the Comintern and a member of the ruling Politburo, whose repressive measures were repugnant to Gorky and indeed threatened several writers then enjoying the protection of Gorky's organizations. As relations between the two men worsened, Lenin, who would naturally have had to back Zinoviev, suggested that it would be best for Gorky to leave the Soviet Union for a while, ostensibly for reasons of health.

Acceding to Lenin's suggestion, Gorky left Russia in 1921 and spent the next three years traveling extensively around Europe. It was during this period that he put to paper his reminiscences of Chekhov, Tolstoy, and Andreev and also wrote a film scenario based on the life of the seventeenth-century Cossack revolutionary Sten'ka Razin, "Stepan Razin: Narodnyi bunt v moskovskom gosuderstve 1666–1668" (Stepan Razin: A Popular Uprising in Muscovy 1666–1668). This scenario was never produced.

In April 1924 Gorky returned to his beloved Italy, settling this time in Sorrento, where his villa became a kind of mecca for Russian émigrés and exiles. Despite the heavy demands on his time, he was able to write *My Universities*, the third part of his autobiographical trilogy, and to make considerable progress on the four-volume novel *Zhizn' Klima Samgina* (*The Life of Klim Samgin*, 1927–1936), a painfully bleak picture of the Russian intelligentsia from the 1880s to Lenin's arrival at the Finland Station in 1917.

In the Soviet Union, meanwhile, Josef Stalin, who had come to power after Lenin's death, began a campaign to entice Gorky back to his homeland, presumably in recognition of the writer's enormous prestige and in the belief that his presence in the Soviet Union would be of great benefit in the international arena. In 1928 Gorky's home town of Nizhny Novgorod was officially renamed Gorky. Yielding to the increasing pressure on him to return to the Soviet Union, not the least of which was exerted by his legal wife, who visited Sorrento frequently, Gorky made two trips back in the summers of 1928 and 1929, as if testing the waters. Wherever he went, the red carpet was rolled out for him. By 1931 he had made up his mind; he would return home for good. That same year he gave up his residence in Sorrento and settled in a house in Moscow given to him, along with a villa in the suburbs, by the Soviet

government. Gorky remained alive until 18 June 1936. In the last five years of his life, while in the Soviet Union, he kept up a busy pace of work. He returned to playwriting after a fifteen-year hiatus and completed a loosely related trilogy of plays: *Somov i drugie* (Somov and Others, 1930–1931, which he had actually begun in Sorrento before returning to Russia), *Yegor Bulychov and Others*, and *Dostigaev i drugie* (Dostigaev and Others, 1931–1932), of which the middle work is beyond doubt the best and is in fact one of Gorky's more worthwhile contributions to Russian drama.

Although he was catered to by the regime and provided with funds for a variety of literary endeavors, it seems doubtful that Gorky's last years in the Soviet Union were happy. Because of his stature, he could no longer escape involvement in purely propagandistic projects that were intended to glorify the Soviet state and yet were bound to compromise his own personal integrity. The most notorious of these was the collection of articles by thirty-four leading Soviet writers, headed by Gorky, praising the building of the White Sea-Baltic Canal in the early 1930's. The construction was an impressive feat of engineering, but the labor was performed by convicts who ran the gamut from murderers to a large number of political prisoners of the regime. Besides glorifying the new Soviet program of industrialization as exemplified by the canal, the volume, *Belomorsko-Baltyskii Kanal imeni Stalina* (*The White Sea-Baltic Canal in the Name of Stalin*), which was published with much fanfare in 1934, also highly praised the "rehabilitation" of the prisoners to which work on the great project contributed. The volume was translated into a number of languages, including English, and was widely distributed in a massive propaganda campaign to convince the world not only of the success of Soviet modernization but also of the humane, positive nature of the growing network of Soviet labor camps. Gorky's important role in the organization and publication of the volume hardly reflects to his credit, but there is no evidence that he ever resisted taking part in it or that he ever regarded it as a source of embarrassment.

When the Union of Soviet Writers was created in 1934—further evidence of the regime's ability to exercise tighter control over cultural life—Gorky was named the head of it, a position that strengthened his ability to assist writers who had fallen out of grace with the authorities or who were still struggling to maintain a semblance of artistic autonomy. But 1934 also brought great personal tragedy to Gorky. Late that year his son Maxim, on whom he had long doted, died suddenly at the age of thirty-seven, ostensibly of pneumonia and related complications. Although it is impossible to know precisely for what reason or reasons he died, it has long been believed that Gorky's son fell victim to Stalin's growing campaign to eliminate all "opponents," real or imaginary. A staunch Communist, young Maxim's crime may have been no more than a certain outspokenness and sense of humor that managed to offend someone in a high place.

Broken by his son's death and feeling more and more estranged from Soviet society under Stalin's ruthless dictatorship, about which he could no longer have had any illusions, Gorky sought to travel again to the West. He applied for a passport in 1935 and again in 1936, but on both occasions he was refused, possibly because of Stalin's fear that the world-famous writer might choose to remain in the West or might speak out against the regime once there. On the eve of the great purges this was a gamble Stalin doubtless felt he could not afford to take. Gorky's death came on the night of June 18. The official medical reason was influenza, lung failure, and heart disease. An impressive state funeral was held, and his ashes were buried in the Kremlin wall, between those of Lenin's wife and Lenin's sister. At the last of the purge trials in 1938, the two doctors who had treated Gorky and several former prominent Soviet officials—including Genrikh Iagoda, who once headed the security police—

confessed that they were part of a "Trotskyite conspiracy" to murder Gorky as well as his son. There seems little reason to doubt that Gorky was done away with on command and that the command originated with Stalin, despite the "confessions" at the trial in 1938.

SHORT STORIES

Gorky began his literary career with the short story, and it was in that genre that he did some of his best work. Always a strongly autobiographical writer, Gorky found inspiration for his early works in his youthful years as a tramp who traveled far and wide in Russia and held a variety of odd jobs. All of this experience brought him into contact with a motley collection of people who, when he introduced them on the pages of his fiction, at once attracted attention for their novelty. Possessed of a keen power of observation that shows through especially in his stories and reminiscences, Gorky brought to his early fiction a romanticism revealed in his preference for unusual, out-of-the-ordinary characters and, above all, for the tramps and vagabonds he met in his travels; they left an indelible impression on him because of their independence of spirit and their yearning for freedom.

"Makar Chudra," his first story, published in 1892, in some respects sets the pattern for a number of Gorky's later works. For example, the narrative is in the first person, and the narrator is obviously a stand-in for the young Gorky. Further, the story is made up almost wholly of a tale told to the tramp-author-narrator by a colorful character whom he has encountered along the way, in this instance the old gypsy Makar Chudra. And the story-within-the-story has a decidedly romantic character—in "Makar Chudra" it is about the passionate romance between two gypsies, Loiko Zobar and the beautiful Radda. Fiercely proud, each seeks domination over the other. Radda demands that as the price of her consent to marriage Zobar must bow at her feet before the whole camp and then kiss her right hand. Zobar agrees, but when the time comes he plunges a knife into her breast. Summoning up her last bit of strength, Radda pulls the dagger from her and says, "Farewell, Zobar. I knew you would do this." Only then, when she has died at his feet, does Zobar fulfill her wish, throwing himself on the ground and pressing his lips to her feet. At this point, also doing what he must, Radda's father Danilo approaches Zobar from the back and stabs him to death.

"Starukha Izergil' " ("Old Izergil," 1894), one of Gorky's best known stories, is cast in a similar mold. The location this time is the shore of the sea near Akkerman in Bessarabia; the narrator of the three stories-within-a-story is the old Moldavian woman Izergil. Two of the stories she tells are folk legends. One is about Larra, the son of a woman and an eagle, who is condemned to eternal wandering for his murder of a girl of his mother's tribe who rejects his love. The other is about the brave and selfless Danko, who is chosen to lead his tribe to safety through a great forest and who, when they begin to falter and turn on him, out of love for them rips open his breast, tears out his heart, and holds it high above his head as a beacon. The heart shines and illuminates their way to safety. When the tribe is at last out of the forest, Danko drops dead, but his brave heart continues to flame beside his dead body. The middle story is one that Izergil tells about her own love affairs. Beautiful and proud in her youth, she never lacked for lovers, whom she discarded when she grew tired of them. But at the age of forty she met a Pole and fell in love for the first time. She wanted to marry him, but her beauty had by that time faded, and the Pole rejected her. Izergil's own story thus relates to that of Radda and Zobar in "Makar Chudra" and of Larra in her first tale. Like these, it is an admonition on the inescapability of punishment for unbridled youthful arrogance. By contrast, Izergil's character Danko is introduced as a new model of behavior, the

self-sacrificing hero whose strength is displayed not in trampling on the weaker but in guiding and protecting them even if, as in the story, they are small-minded, cowardly, and ungrateful.

That Gorky could see himself in such a role as Danko's is apparent from his story "Moi sputnik" ("My Travelling Companion"), which was also written in 1894. Here Gorky's narrator meets a young Georgian prince, Shakro Ptadze, on the Odessa docks where the narrator is working. In order to help his new friend, from whom someone has stolen all his money and valuables and who is having trouble fending for himself, the narrator agrees to walk with him from Odessa to Tiflis, the Georgian capital. In their travels the narrator discovers unpleasant traits about his companion, traits such as worship of might, arrogance, and self-indulgence that Gorky had previously identified with people whom he found undeniably attractive. But now, as if reversing his former attitude, Gorky has his narrator experience distaste for these traits as embodied in the young Georgian and at the same time has him assume a role in his relationship with the prince analagous to that of Danko and his tribe in old Izergil's last tale.

When they reach Tiflis at last, after many adventures and hardships, the Georgian, despite his promise to look after his traveling companion once they reach his native city, abandons him. The narrator concludes his story with the observation that the sojourn with Shakro taught him that the "wisdom of life is always more profound and all-embracing than the wisdom of men." Gratified by his own sense of superiority over the Georgian, both in morality and in courage, Gorky's narrator suggests that what he learned from Shakro Ptadze was that arrogance, selfishness, and a lack of morality often mask weakness in the face of adversity. For all his bluster and bragging, the Georgian is virtually helpless without the narrator and demonstrates his innate weakness nowhere more obviously than when he abandons his friend once inside the safety and security of his own city.

Whatever other attitudes toward life may be revealed in such stories as "Makar Chudra," "Old Izergil," and "My Travelling Companion," the stories certainly reflect Gorky's admiration of strength, his love of freedom, his attraction to highly individualistic, unusual people, and his strong moral sense—all themes which inform much of his subsequent fiction.

In two of his best stories, "Chelkash" and "Konovalov" (1897), Gorky's attitude toward the freedom-loving outlaw and vagabond seems to undergo a change similar to the reversal of his feelings about the strong and willful. "Chelkash," like other works by Gorky, is built around a pair of contrasting characters, in this case the bold, clever, and hard-drinking thief Chelkash, a familiar figure around the docks of the city in which the story is set, and a poor peasant boy named Gavrila. The boy agrees to assist Chelkash on a night-time theft at sea. When the job is over, his greed for the more than five hundred rubles Chelkash has made that night is nearly palpable. Chelkash agrees to give him forty for his help, but all the boy can talk about is what he would do with all the money if it were his. When they reach shore, Gavrila flings himself at Chelkash's feet and begs him for the money. With pity and loathing for the "greedy slave," Chelkash tosses him the money. Overcome with joy, Gavrila confesses that he even contemplated killing Chelkash for the money. Hearing this, Chelkash can feel only contempt for Gavrila and demands the money back. Gavrila refuses, the two fight, and Chelkash retrieves the money; but as he starts to leave, Gavrila throws a rock at Chelkash's head and knocks him down. In terror the boy runs away. Later, filled with remorse, he returns, tries to help Chelkash get up, and begs for forgiveness. When Chelkash discovers that Gavrila did not take the money from him, he peels off a hundred-ruble note for himself and gives the rest to the boy. Reluctant at first to take the money, Gavrila finally acquiesces and the two

part as friends. To Chelkash, there is nothing to forgive Gavrila for; he understands him only too well, saying, "Today you get me; tomorrow I get you."

Although unappealing, Chelkash is still one of Gorky's more romantically conceived outlaw figures: he is fiercely independent and individualistic, a man who thumbs his nose at society and lives by his own laws and who can only look with contempt at the demeaning lust for money and servility of people like the peasant Gavrila. Capable of his own kind of nobility, Chelkash finally gives the boy most of the money when the latter partially redeems himself by returning to help Chelkash after felling him with a rock.

Another of Gorky's sympathetically drawn vagabonds, Konovalov, in the story of the same name, differs from the writer's other tramp figures, especially Chelkash, in that he is aware of the aimlessness and loneliness of his life. As he confides to the narrator at one point,

> You see, every once in a while I feel so miserable I just can't bear to go on living. It's as if I was the only creature in the whole wide world, as if there wasn't another living thing but me anywhere on earth. And at such times I hate everybody, myself and everyone else. I wouldn't give a damn if everybody died. It must be some sickness in me. That's what started me drinking.
>
> (*Selected Stories,* translated by Bernard Isaacs et al.; p. 238)

The strength and rugged individualism of a number of Gorky's tramps and vagabonds is also characteristic of Konovalov. No matter how much the narrator, a fellow employee at a bakery, tries to convince him that environment and circumstances could have much to do with the way his life has turned out, he refuses to accept the notion that anyone or anything but he himself is to blame for his state. Eventually, the narrator and Konovalov part company, and some time later the narrator learns from a newspaper that Konovalov, aged forty, has hanged himself in the local jail, where he had been taken on a charge of vagrancy. The prison authorities noted that he was a "quiet, peaceable, contemplative man. His suicide, according to the report of the prison doctor, is to be attributed to melancholia."

An issue that looms large in Gorky's work is the apparent need that people living in misery and wretchedness have for comforting illusions to sustain them and to keep alive within them at least a semblance of hope. The best of Gorky's stories on this theme is probably his best known, "Twenty-Six Men and a Girl." The basement bakery setting is the same as that of "Konovalov" and reflects Gorky's own experiences as a worker in a pretzel bakery in Kazan from 1884 to 1887.

Again using the first person and identifying himself as one of twenty-six men working there, the narrator paints a grim picture of the basement bakery, which he likens to a dungeon ("And so we lived, twenty-six men, in the basement of a big stone building, and the burden of life was so heavy that one would think the three stories of the house were built on our shoulders"). They often sing to cheer themselves up, but what brings the greatest joy to their otherwise miserable lives is the daily visit of the sixteen-year-old Tania, a housemaid who works on the first floor of the same building. The men worship her, for as the narrator declares, "Though drudgery was turning us into dumb oxen, we were still human beings, and like all human beings, could not live without an object of worship." An ex-soldier, a handsome dandy who comes to work in the same employer's nearby bun bakery, becomes the catalyst for the shattering of their illusion. The newcomer boasts of his great attraction for women and of how no woman can resist him. As if to silence the dandy's boasting, one of the bakers suggests that at least with one local girl, Tania, he would not have his way. The ex-soldier says that all he needs is a fortnight and she will succumb to his charms just as all the others have done. The challenge to the dandy now whets the bakers' curiosity: will Tania resist him or not? "From now on," writes the narra-tor, "a new exciting interest had been added to our lives, something we had never known before."

One day, the ex-soldier enters the bakery and tells the men to go out into a passageway and peep through cracks in a wooden wall into a yard. Soon Tania enters the yard and disappears through the door of a cellar there. After a while, the ex-soldier follows her in. He is the first to emerge, followed by Tania, whose eyes "shone with joy and happiness, and her lips smiled. And she walked as though in a dream, swaying with unsteady gait. . . ." The sight of this being more than they can bear, the bakers rush into the yard to confront her with her transgression and revile her mercilessly. Tania has at this point become the fallen idol, to be insulted and jeered at. At last, she regains her composure and takes leave of them, hurling abuse at them as she does so, but still straight, beautiful, and proud. Of course, Tania visits them no more, and to the narrator it is as if the sun never again peered into their damp, stony dungeon.

NOVELS

Although they are important for the development of his thought, Gorky's novels are, on the whole, among the least successful of his literary works. As a writer, Gorky's greatest liability was his use of characters primarily as vehicles for ideas, and this practice came through more clearly when he moved beyond the romantic world of his early stories. It is already evident in *Goremyka Pavel* (*Orphan Paul*, 1894), his first attempt at a novel, and it became more obvious as time went on. An immensely sincere writer with deeply held convictions and a highly developed sense of morality, Gorky was as passionate a foe of social injustice in his writings as in his life.

Without exception Gorky's novels, even more than his stories and plays, were made to serve as vehicles for his social and political views. Had he been a greater literary artist, the integration of plot, character, and viewpoint might have been effected in a more natural and convincing way. As it is, however, this is seldom the case, and as a result the works suffer from tendentiousness and the too obvious use of characters as bearers of ideas. Gorky was able to compensate for these faults, at least partially, by his gift for narrative and dialogue and his ability to create sometimes strikingly vivid, believable characters. To be sure, Gorky is almost always *readable,* but in the worst of his works prolixity and burdensome biases compromise even this virtue.

Gorky's first novel, *Orphan Paul,* was published serially in 1894 in the Nizhny Novgorod journal *Volgar'.* It adumbrates certain characteristic features of Gorky's later and longer fictional works. The focus is almost always on a single major character, and the novel traces his or her life from birth or early childhood either to a point of catastrophe in mid-life or to death. Every one of Gorky's novels carries an indictment of contemporary Russian society. The usual targets are social injustice and political repression, the former seen as the result of capitalism and bourgeois philistinism and the latter as the result of an antiquated tsardom that has long since lost contact with the people and seeks only to preserve its vested interests. The major character of the novel is either an embodiment or victim of social and/or political evil or, more commonly, a person whose life at some point reaches a crisis in which he rebels against society. Those who embody the system, which in Gorky's judgment bears responsibility for human misery and injustice, as well as those who defy it in some form or other are usually broken or destroyed at the end.

In *Orphan Paul,* for example, the titular character is an orphan whose life is followed from birth to the time when he is imprisoned and sentenced to penal labor for the murder of a prostitute. The murder has a social dimension to it in that both Paul and the prostitute, who love each other, are victims of what Gorky regards as a morally bankrupt social order that has so marginalized and humiliated them that they are unable to establish a lasting, fulfilling relationship. When it becomes obvious that despite the affection between them their relationship is still unsatisfying, the prostitute resumes her previous way of life despite Paul's strenuous objections. Although she is the only person with whom he has known tenderness and compassion, Paul chooses to kill her rather than constantly to imagine her being with other men. The murder is conceived by Gorky as more than an act of violence directed at a single individual. Rather, it is the release on Paul's part of all the bitterness, anger, and frustration that he harbors toward society as a whole and toward the evil in life that he regards as ultimately responsible for the loss of the only thing that he has ever held dear. The novel promises more than it delivers. Writing about a complex and sensitive relationship between two injured people whom he wants to portray as victims of a repugnant social order, Gorky allows his own anger to take command of the narrative and lead it into exaggeration and melodramatics.

After *Orphan Paul,* Gorky wrote seven more novels: *Foma Gordeev, Troe (The Three of Them,* 1901), *Mother, The Confession, The Life of Matvei Kozhemyakin, Delo Artamonovykh (The Artamonov Business,* 1925), and the four-volume *The Life of Klim Samgin.*

Gorky's views as well as his literary techniques lend themselves to easy summary. A man who admired strength and action and who had almost a reverence for physical activity, for toil, Gorky was utterly contemptuous of the Russian intelligentsia, which he excoriated for its propensity to "philosophize" and for its irresoluteness. Only the writer was spared his contempt, and that was because Gorky himself was one. Becoming a *writer,* indeed a writer of national and international celebrity, particularly in view of his background and lack of formal education, was without doubt the most important thing in Gorky's life. As he himself once wrote, "It is to books that I owe everything that is good in me.

Even in my youth I realized that art is more generous than people are. I am a book-lover; each one of them seems a miracle to me, and the author a magician. I am unable to speak of books otherwise than with the deepest emotion and a joyous enthusiasm. That may seem ridiculous but it is the truth. It will probably be said that this is the enthusiasm of a barbarian; let people say what they will—I am beyond cure" (quoted in the Introduction to *Selected Stories*).

Given his strong moral sense and his outrage at social injustice, it stands to reason that Gorky would regard his literary gift as a great responsibility and would use literature for educative purposes. In fact, doing so was to him a mission from which he could not turn away. Because of his exalted view of literature, of the writer, and of the enormous role the writer could play in social change, Gorky almost always depicts literary figures in his works in sympathetic terms. This attitude also explains his great protectiveness toward writers in the immediate post-revolutionary period, when so many were threatened politically and had difficulty acquiring the basic necessities of life.

Nowhere is Gorky more devastating in his assault on the intelligentsia than in his last novel, *The Life of Klim Samgin,* which he worked on (and indeed never completely finished) from 1925 to the year of his death, 1936. This bleak, dreadfully overlong work is an attempt at a comprehensive view of the Russian intelligentsia from the mid-1870's to the Revolution of 1917. As usual for Gorky, it is built around a single representative character, in this case the liberal intellectual lawyer Klim Samgin. Also typical of Gorky's style, the novel covers a large part of the central character's life, here forty years.

Gorky's literary strategy, epic in conception, is to uncover Samgin's (and hence the intelligentsia's) weakness of will and irresoluteness by examining both his attitudes toward the great events of his time and his personal relationships with other characters, who are meant to represent divergent ideological camps. Although he fancies himself a progressive in his political views, Samgin keeps a healthy distance from the 1905 Revolution and finds himself increasingly more ill-disposed toward the political left as the Revolution of 1917 draws near. Despite his liberal pronouncements and his curiosity about the events taking place around him, Samgin in fact has no strong political views. When he is killed during the Revolution of 1917, it is an accident; by this time wholly unreceptive to the idea of a revolutionary transformation of Russia, he is still too incapable of resolute action to cast his lot with the pro-tsarist forces. What motivates him, above all, is what Gorky regarded as endemic to the bourgeois of the time: economic well-being, hypocrisy, an exaggerated sense of his own importance, conservativism, and a basic reluctance to take a political stand. Had Gorky been able to scale down his ambitions for the novel and had he found some redeeming features in his central figure to relieve the overwhelmingly negative portrait, *The Life of Klim Samgin* might have been a more artistically significant and convincing picture of the ambiguities and conflicts within the ranks of the intelligentsia during one of the most momentous periods of Russian history. Unfortunately, as Gorky wrote the work, it is little more than a fitfully intriguing but on the whole painfully overdrawn and relentless indictment.

Gorky's contempt for the petit bourgeoisie almost rivaled his attitude toward the intelligentsia, and in a number of works he sought to expose the greed, arrogance, and moral vacuity of the commercial class. To a great extent his views were shaped by his personal observations in the home of his grandparents and by his experiences in his years as a vagabond. This subject was closer to him, and this fact stood him in better stead when he came to write such novels about the world of merchant Russia as *Foma Gordeev, The Life of Matvei Kozhemyakin,* and *The Artamonov Business.* Although not without their flaws, two of these works, *Foma Gordeev* and *The Artamonov Business,* are Gorky's most successful novels.

Like the rest of Gorky's novels *Foma Gordeev* pivots on a single major character whose life it traces over the span of a number of years, building toward a culminating action of a defiant or rebellious nature that takes place close to the end of the novel. Gorky's subject is the Russian merchant class, toward whom he had feelings that can best be described as ambivalent. He admired the energy, the drive, and the strength of will of the merchants, but he disliked their materialism, hedonism, insensitivity, selfishness, and lack of moral principle. Although these traits are distributed over several characters in the novel who represent the class, they are most vividly embodied in the figures of Foma Gordeev's father, Ignat, and Iakov Maiakin, his father's best friend and the owner of a rope works. While not oblivious to the defects of the type, Gorky felt a certain natural affinity with men like Ignat Gordeev— a man of peasant origin who through industry, iron will, and determination worked his way up from being a Volga barge hauler to being a wealthy ship owner—and he made this man the most appealing and sympathetic character in the novel. Ignat is dynamic, vital, proud, and life-loving, traits that Gorky always admired. Maiakin, on the other hand, is entirely unsympathetic, a merchant of the old school whose family has had wealth for generations and who is conservative, authoritarian, even tyrannical, self-righteous, contemptuous of weakness, and an ardent defender of his class and its privileges. Ignat Gordeev and Iakov Maiakin are among Gorky's best literary portraits, recognizable as types yet true to life and convincing.

The generational aspect of Gorky's novels has a distinct ideological motivation, well exemplified in *Foma Gordeev.* Invariably, Gorky's children, while they bear the traits of their parents, especially their fathers, are weaker: they are less decisive, less a part of the society in which they grow up, more restless, even physically less impressive. What Gorky seems to be trying to show is the steady, irreversible disintegration of bourgeois Russia. Inheritors of their fathers' businesses and wealth, the sons lack the same motivation and drive. Their values change, as indeed society itself changes, and they become either indifferent to mercantile life or rebellious against everything for which their fathers stand. In any case, the family business invariably suffers an irreversible decline and the children either then destroy themselves in some way or are destroyed by the very society against which they explode in rebellion. Those who survive (more often daughters than sons) are usually the ones who have accepted the inevitability of social upheaval and are willing to move with the times.

In *Foma Gordeev* the rebel is Ignat's beloved son Foma. No longer able to accept the values of his class and live by its norms of behavior, Foma's path runs steadily downward until everything that has been building up in him over a period of time bursts forth in the novel's culminating scene. It takes place during a party aboard the new steamer belonging to the wealthy Volga ship owner Il'ia Efimovich Kononov. All the prominent citizens of the town, the cream of the local merchants, are aboard. Foma is present in response to an invitation by his godfather, Maiakin. At one point during the celebration Maiakin gets up and makes a speech of high praise for the merchant class, at the same time heaping abuse on all those who do not share its values, especially the liberal intelligentsia:

> We love to work. We have a real cult of life—that is we worship life—but they don't. They love talk, we love action. And behold, fellow merchants, the proof of our culture, of our love of development: the Volga! Our beloved Mother Volga! Every drop of her water speaks in our defence and refutes their slander. Only a hundred years have gone by since the day when Peter the Great launched his flat-bottomed boats on her waters, and today, gentlemen, thousands of steamers are plying between her ports. Who built them? The Russian peasant, a totally unlettered man. Who

owns all these huge steamers and barges? We do. Who invented them? We did. Everything here is ours. Everything was born of our minds, of our daring, of our love of action. No one has ever helped us. . . . Which are the best towns on the Volga? The ones that have the most merchants. Whose are the best houses in the towns? The merchants' houses. Who gives most help to the poor? The merchants. We donate hundreds of thousands of rubles to charity, collecting it kopeck by kopeck. Who builds the churches? We do. Who contributes most to the State? We do. Gentlemen, we alone do things for the love of the work, for love of making life better. We alone love life and order. . . . Fellow merchants! You are the salt of the earth; no others are as hard-working and energetic as you are; all that has been done has been done by you, and there is no limit to what you can still do, and therefore I drink this toast to you: I love and respect you deeply, and with all my heart I say: Long live the gallant, hard-working merchants of Russia! May they prosper to the glory of our motherland!

(Wettlin trans., 1956; p. 249)

Maiakin's speech becomes the catalyst of Foma's explosion. Hardly does Maiakin conclude when Foma launches into a bitter tirade against everything Maiakin stands for and has just finished praising to the skies, sparing neither the merchants as a class nor specific members of the entourage on board. The denouement is predictable. Foma is packed off to a mental hospital. When he returns to the Volga town years later, he is a broken, bent man, barely recognizable as Ignat Gordeev's son.

In *The Artamonov Business,* which is set in the period between the Russo-Japanese War of 1904–1905 and the coming to power of the Bolsheviks, the Artamonovs are a family of textile manufacturers. The father, Il'ia, like Ignat Gordeev, is originally of a serf family. Similar in other respects to Gordeev senior, he is crude, oafish, direct, and strong willed. Following his death, his son Petr takes over the family business. Portrayed as a symbol of his class, Petr is a study in moral degeneration. He becomes estranged from people,

ceases to enjoy family life, begins having affairs with girls in his mill, and comes to rely more and more heavily on drink. Before long his life is little more than aimless debauchery. The basic pattern of *Foma Gordeev* is thus repeated. The sons do not measure up to their fathers, and the essential rottenness of bourgeois life eventually produces either rebellion or moral decay. That Petr is capable even of murder is demonstrated by his assault on the clerk Nikonov's stepson Pavel, an unattractive child toward whom Petr's dislike grows in proportion to his increasingly rebellious son's friendship with him. The less Petr is able to exercise his authority over his son, the more he transfers his frustration to Nikonov's stepson. One evening, Artamonov comes upon the boy masturbating in the bathhouse. Terrified at being caught in the act, Pavel throws himself at Artamonov's feet. Then,

with real enjoyment, Artamonov kicked the boy in the chest with his right foot—then halted: the boy cracked, uttered a feeble cry, and rolled over on to his side. For a moment Artamonov felt that the kick had cleared out of his heart some foul rags, which had long nauseated him. . . . The boy lay with one arm thrown forward, the other bent under his knee; one leg seemed much shorter than his other, as if he had slyly crawled up to Artamonov; but this outstretched arm was unnaturally, terribly long. Artamonov staggered, then steadied himself with one hand on the door jamb, took off his cap and with the lining wiped his forehead; it had all at once flooded with sweat. . . . "Up y'get, I won't tell anyone," he whispered. But he was already aware that he had killed the boy, his eyes on the little trickle of dark, dusty blood which was winding out from under the cheek pressed to the boards.

(Brown trans., p. 139)

Gorky often likes to show the breadth of bourgeois family disintegration by introducing more than a single child. Thus, Petr Artamonov has two brothers: Nikita, a hunchback who becomes a monk, and Aleksei, an adopted son of Il'ia Artamonov, who is the virtual opposite of Petr—amiable, better liked in their town, and more interested in trying to do things with and for it. The contrast between the brothers conforms to a pattern in Gorky's novels and plays that has roots in European naturalism. The disintegration of the merchant family begins with the second generation and expresses itself not only in alienation, restlessness, and moral degeneration but also in physical weakness or deformity, the latter functioning as symbolic of genetic deterioration. The relative "positiveness" of Aleksei is easily explained by the fact that he is not a natural son of Il'ia Artamonov.

Again, as elsewhere in Gorky, it is only from the third generation that redemption can be expected, and this redemption almost always takes the form of aroused social consciousness and progressive political engagement. The hope of the Artamonovs lies, therefore, with Petr's son Il'ia (tellingly named for his grandfather as if meant to represent the renewal of the line). As the novel progresses, Il'ia turns on his father and accuses his textile plant of having murdered a whole cemetery of people. From being a student, Il'ia advances to become a teacher and a revolutionary, thus representing Gorky's view that each succeeding generation in Russia is less able to sustain the old ways, becomes less resistant to change. As the children become better educated, better read, and more in touch with events around them, the likelihood is greater of their adopting more liberal views, experiencing a greater sense of solidarity with workers, and becoming more receptive to the ideas of socialism. A serious weakness in Gorky's writing, however, is that while such a development is forecast, it is never really portrayed, and while characters representative of the future, such as Il'ia, are introduced, they are such light or marginal presences that they lack any real substance as characters.

One of the more interesting figures in *The Artamonov Business* is the family worker Tikhon Vialov (the name connotes silence and flabbiness of spirit). A detached individual who seems very knowing and cunning, he emerges in the course of the novel as a kind of moral judgment on the Artamonovs. After disappearing for a certain period of time, he returns near the end of the novel in the company of Bolsheviks. Although he does not seem to have any great affection for them, he has chosen to throw in his lot with them since they are riding a tidal wave of victory and Vialov is not one to be on the wrong side. In confrontation with the very ill and now much slower Petr Artamonov, Vialov tells him,

"You call me a fool, but I saw the truth before anybody else. Now you see how it's all turned about. I said it would be universal penal servitude—and now they've got it. Swept it all away like dust with a rag; like sweeping away shavings. That's how it stands, Mr. Peter. I tell you. Satan used the tool—and you helped him. And all to what purpose? One long chain of wrong, no counting it. I watched it all; marveled—and when would be the stop to it? Now you've got your stop! And all you did, cast in lead."

(Brown trans., p. 338)

As the novel draws to a close, the Artamonovs have lost everything, including their living quarters. In a grim scene at the end, Petr's wife Natal'ia is even forced to forage for a piece of bread and a cucumber to feed him. Unyielding as ever, he stubbornly refuses to eat the food and hurls it away. Characteristically, Vialov picks it up, dusts it off, and consumes it.

Although it is wise not to confuse an author with his literary characters, Vialov's words about the October Revolution of 1917 seem to reflect Gorky's own disenchantment with the Bolsheviks. If he is not unhappy about the passing of the Artamonovs and everything they are meant to stand for in the novel, Gorky is also barely able to conceal his disappointment over the course Russia was being thrust on in the aftermath of the Revolution. That *The Artamonov Business* was written in the West in the 1920's after Gorky left the Soviet Union on Lenin's advice "for reasons of health" lends greater credence to this interpretation.

Gorky's novels *The Three of Them* and *The Life of Matvei Kozhemyakin* are weaker treatments of material dealt with more effectively in *Foma Gordeev* and *The Artamonov Business.* Written soon after *Foma Gordeev, The Three of Them* is about yet another member of the merchant class originally of humble origins (in this case an urban slum) who at a certain point becomes aware of the moral and spiritual bankruptcy of his class and dramatically rebels against it.

The similarity with the story of Foma Gordeev is striking. What is different in the case of Ilya Lunev, the central figure of *The Three of Them,* is a dark Ibsenian secret in his past, the murder of a moneylender, an incident that has frequently been compared to the murder Raskolnikov commits in Feodor Dostoevsky's *Crime and Punishment* (1866). Lunev's murder is motivated by a sense of outrage over the moneylender's exploitation of people, but just like Raskolnikov he steals money almost as an afterthought in the wake of a murder unrelated to theft. In a grim irony the money he steals becomes the foundation of the business he starts in order to achieve the fulfillment of his dream of middle-class respectability. In time he grows to loathe the circumstances in which he launched his career not so much because of the murder he committed—which in his own mind he is able to justify morally—but because in a weak moment he stole tainted money that he then used to begin his climb up the social ladder.

This dark secret in his past sets the stage for Lunev's rebellion against bourgeois society. The "three" of the title refers to Lunev himself and his two close friends Iakov Filimonov and Pavel Grachev, who are also of modest backgrounds. A further reflection of the influence of European naturalism on Gorky is that both characters are studies in human misery, unsuccessful in life and physically ill at the same time, Filimonov with an incurable case of consumption and Grachev suffering from venereal disease. Both Filimonov and Grachev are introduced into the novel to provide a contrast with Lunev's materially successful life. The more Lunev witnesses the growing disparity between his friends' misery and his own good fortune, the deeper grows his sense of anguish and remorse over the way he began his career.

Lunev's relations with his friends and his secret interlock in the novel's climax. His indignation over the smugness and self-righteousness of the bourgeoisie and over social injustice reaches the boiling point at the trial of Grachev's defiant mistress, the prostitute Vera Kapitonovna, who has been charged with stealing a merchant's wallet. Among the judges are prominent citizens (including Iakov Filimonov's despotic father) whose private lives conceal reprehensible crimes known to Lunev. At a party at the house of the shopkeeper Avtonomov to which he goes after the trial, Lunev explodes in a denunciatory scene reminiscent of Foma Gordeev's attack on the prominent citizens assembled on Kononov's boat. Besides railing against the Avtonomovs for everything the middle class has now come to represent in his eyes, he also discloses secrets he knows about them. He then makes a public confession of his own crime both to show that he is no better than they are and at the same time to shock them. The police are summoned to arrest him, but rather than face trial before the same corrupt judges who sat in judgment of Grachev's mistress, he kills himself by running headlong into a stone wall.

In *The Life of Matvei Kozhemyakin,* another overly long novel, Gorky shifts the emphasis from an individual to a town. Outwardly, the novel resembles others by Gorky in its basic *Bildungsroman* structure: the life of the central character, Matvei Kozhemyakin, is traced from his birth to his death in his mid-fifties. Like Foma Gordeev and Petr Artamonov, Kozhemyakin is the son of a self-made merchant, and like them he resists following in his father's footsteps. But the greatest presence in the novel is not Kozhemyakin, a failed would-be radical, or the "progressives" Evgeniia Mansurova, a Populist, and Mark Vasilev, a Marxist, but the small provincial town of Okurov in which Kozhemyakin grows up. The name of the town has since become all but synonymous with the obscurantism, backwardness, indifference, and brutality of pre-revolutionary provincial Russia that, in Gorky's view, shaped the outlook of the masses and made it impossible for them to bring about a dynamic transformation of the country. The novel closes with the death of Kozhemyakin in the revolutionary year of 1905, and there is no doubt that Gorky intended to suggest that the Russian revolutionary movement died that same year with the failure of the workers' protests and uprising. Much of that failure Gorky ascribed to the pervasive influence of towns just like Okurov, whose stifling qualities had a crippling effect on the will.

Two of Gorky's better-known if weaker novels, *Mother* and *The Confession,* link the writer's social and religious views. Based on the Revolution of 1905, *Mother,* for all its good intentions as inspirational literature and for all the abiding Soviet enthusiasm for it as a forerunner of socialist realism, is an abject failure. The novel focuses on the efforts of a group of dedicated and earnest Social Democratic revolutionaries to rouse factory workers and peasants to rebel in the years immediately preceding the 1905 Revolution. The revolutionaries are all exemplary, the defenders of the social and political status quo are all etched in venom, and the workers and peasants whom the revolutionaries try to rouse to political action are backward, uncomprehending, and ultimately unsupportive. The "heroes" of the work are the leader of the revolutionary group, Pavel Vlasov, and his mother, Pelageia Nilovna Vlasova. When the novel culminates in the trial of the jailed revolutionaries, Vlasov has his moment of glory. He rises before the entire court and delivers a stirring declaration of the Socialist faith and the inevitable final victory of the revolutionaries. Here is an excerpt from his address:

"We are revolutionaries and will go on being revolutionaries as long as some people do nothing but give orders and others do nothing but work. We are against the society whose interests you judges have been ordered to defend; we are its uncompromising enemies, and yours too, and no reconciliation between us is possible until we have won our fight. And we workers are sure to win!"

(Wettlin trans., 1962, p. 322)

The court sentences all the revolutionaries, including Vlasov, to exile. As the novel nears its end, Vlasov's mother, Pelageia, resolves to continue her son's work by distributing copies of his courtroom speech, which other revolutionaries have run off on a hectograph machine. Eventually, she too is arrested and brutally taken into custody.

The best-developed character in the novel, the mother is made to undergo an interesting transformation. Originally a devout Orthodox Christian who fatalistically accepts everything that happens as God's will, she comes to share her son's political outlook and acknowledges the need actively to oppose evil. No longer a practicing Christian in an institutional sense, she in fact rejects the church in favor of the wisdom of the anticlerical peasant Rybin, who believes that organized religion has falsified God and that therefore man must create God anew for himself. In a decisive turning point in her transformation she dreams that she sees a priest call for the arrest of her son and his fellow revolutionaries. No longer content to revere God in heaven, the mother, like Rybin, wants to work actively to realize the kingdom of God on earth. She comes to understand that this is indeed what the revolutionaries are committed to and that it is among them that the true meaning of Christianity can be found, rather than in the churches. As Gorky writes:

Quite unconsciously she began to pray less, but to think more about Christ and about the people who, without ever mentioning His name, without seeming to know about Him, lived, or so she

433

thought, according to His precepts and in His manner, seeing the earth as the kingdom of the poor and striving to divide its riches equally among all.

(Wettlin trans., p. 220)

Although he repudiated organized religion as condoning social inequality and political repression, Gorky sought a way to reconcile his socialist views with Christian ideals. This quest for a new faith, as it were, became particularly intense in the first years following the defeat of the 1905 Revolution, a time when a number of the Russian intelligentsia were turning to religion and spirituality for solace. Gorky's attitudes toward the church, traditional Christianity, and what is often referred to as "god building" (*bogostroitel'stvo* in Russian) come through clearly in *Mother.* His next novel, *The Confession,* is more in the nature of a fictionalization of that quest.

In style reminiscent of a parable, this work features, as Gorky's persona, the abandoned and illegitimate boy Matvei—another in the long line of wanderer-narrator figures who goes back to Gorky's earliest stories—who recounts his spiritual journey across Russia in search of a new faith. As he grows up in the care of different people, both lay and clerical, Matvei gains firsthand knowledge of greed, corruption, hypocrisy, and cynicism. His experiences with the established church through its priests and monks leave him with feelings of dismay and loathing. Even marriage and the birth of a child, who soon dies, (his wife also dying in childbirth) fail to overcome his frustration and bitterness over human misery and injustice, before which the church and traditional Christianity only stand silent. But on the way to Siberia he meets a pilgrim, an unfrocked priest, who strengthens his soul and shows him the true path to God—the people, the masses, "the one and eternal source of the creation of God." Although this "God creator," "in rags, filthy, always drunk, who was beaten and flogged," is so repulsive that Matvei can only regard him as a blas-

phemer, his association with a community of such "God creators" in a Siberian factory convinces him of the wisdom of his spiritual mentor's words.

His new faith in the god-building energy of the people is confirmed at the end of the novel, when he beholds a miracle of faith healing at a procession marking the return of the miracle-working icon of the Holy Virgin to the monastery of the Seven Seas in Kazan'. The pleas of the father of a young girl unable to walk are answered by a multitude of the faithful, whose collective will, as they urge the girl to walk and pray for her to be able to do so, cause the girl to rise from inside her carriage and walk. Exulting in the girl's triumph, Matvei at last understands that the master of the earth, his mother, is the people, the "all-powerful immortal people." It is, then, the people who are God, the creator of miracles, and there shall be no other: and he prays to them as "my God, the creator of all gods, which you weave out of the beauty of your soul and the labor and agony of your seeking." The last paragraph of the novel delineates in unambiguous terms the basis of Matvei's, and Gorky's, new faith:

And always do I return there where people free the souls of their neighbors from the prison of darkness and superstition, bring them together, reveal to them their secret countenance, and help them to recognize the strength of their own wills and teach them the one and true path to a general union for the sake of a great cause, the universal building of God.

(*Polnoe sobranie sochinenii,* 9:390)

THE PLAYS

It may be fair to say that, at least in the English-speaking world, Gorky is today thought of primarily as a dramatist on the strength of the international fame of *The Lower Depths* and of the Royal Shakespeare Company revivals of the 1970's.

Gorky's career as a dramatist began in the spring of 1900, when Chekhov urged him to visit him at his place in Yalta and at the same time take in performances of the Moscow Art Theater, which toured there in May. Tremendously impressed by Chekhov, whom he greatly admired as a fiction writer and playwright, Gorky determined to make a name for himself in the drama, just as he had in the short story. Although never wholly comfortable with dramatic form, Gorky worked hard at playwriting and at the outset of this new phase of his literary career was encouraged by an understanding and always sympathetic Chekhov.

In all, Gorky wrote over a dozen plays. These include *The Petty Bourgeois, The Lower Depths, Dachniki, Varvary* (*Barbarians*, 1905), *Children of the Sun, Enemies, Poslednye* (The Last Ones, 1908), *Chudaki* (*Queer People*, 1910), the first version of *Vassa Zheleznova, Zykovy* (*The Zykovs*, 1913), *Fal'shivaia moneta* (The Counterfeit Coin, 1913), *Starik* (The Old Man, 1915; revised 1922), *Somov i drugie, Yegor Bulychov and Others, Dostigaev i drugie,* and the revised version of *Vassa Zheleznova.*

With the exception only of *Yegor Bulychov,* Gorky's best plays (and, to be sure, most of them) were written before the Revolution. Indeed, a fifteen-year hiatus between the writing of *Starik* in 1915 and *Somov i drugie,* begun in 1930, suggests that Gorky's adjustment to a Sovietized Russian society after the Revolution and his permanent resettlement in the U.S.S.R. in 1931 proved infelicitous to his dramatic writing. The sole exception was *Yegor Bulychov* which, significantly, is set in the pre-revolutionary period with which Gorky was always more comfortable as a literary setting.

The world of Gorky's drama is much the same as that of his novels. In *The Petty Bourgeois,* for example, certainly one of his best plays, conflict between parents and children is used once again to expose the ignorance, materialism, greed, and spiritual emptiness of the bourgeois. The only ray of hope in an otherwise somber family portrait is the character of Nil, a worker and foster son of the

Bessemyonovs, in whose home most of the play's action occurs. Nil, whose name is meant to suggest *nothing* and to impart the sense of a man without a past, coming from nowhere, and hence unburdened by the past, is a worker who represents Gorky's attempt at the beginning of the new century to delineate the new Russian hero of proletarian origin. Although with his first plays Gorky demonstrated an ability to write good dialogue and showed considerable skill at portraying groups in convincing terms—in an interesting departure from his novels, where his emphasis is much more on the individual figure—his didacticism proved a largely unsurmountable obstacle. *The Petty Bourgeois* is a case in point. From Gorky's point of view, the most important character in the work is Nil, but as a dramatic portrait Nil is a complete failure, an abstraction, an idealization, a cardboard poster of the worker as Gorky envisaged him, but too schematic to be believable.

The extraordinary international success of *The Lower Depths* owed much to the novelty of the play's setting and characters—a basement flophouse filled with a variety of social dropouts and has-beens. Into this dreary, dark world of misery and degradation comes the mysterious figure of Luka, another of Gorky's "holy" wanderers, a character inspired in part by Tolstoy. Luka's presence in the play initiates yet another inquiry into the moral rightness of the "comforting" or "healing" lie. Luka tells the human wrecks he finds in the flophouse whatever he thinks they need to hear to maintain the illusion that things may yet turn out all right for them. Although Gorky uses the figure of Satin, a murderer, to denounce Luka and the "comforting" lie, his own position seems to be slightly ambiguous. To be sure, Gorky regarded the type of comfort freely dispensed by Luka as worthy only of slaves and masters and as a way of maintaining the status quo—accept things as they are as the will of God and hope and pray that someday life will be better. But Luka is not drawn in completely negative terms. Gorky is careful to have even Satin acknowledge that Luka's motivation is sincere and that he just wants to instill some hope in people who have lost it completely. But the "comforting" lie, in Gorky's opinion, in which the state, the propertied classes, and the church collude, was a social evil that he was passionately devoted to eradicating. The American playwright Eugene O'Neill had a different approach to the "comforting" lie and wrote his own play, *The Iceman Cometh* (1946), partly as a reply to Gorky's *The Lower Depths.*

Dachniki, which is Gorky's most obvious (and not too successful) imitation of Chekhovian technique, addresses a familiar subject, the philistinism of the Russian bourgeoisie and intelligentsia. In the setting of a rustic summer vacation house characters representing a variety of the contemporary intelligentsia moan and groan about the emptiness, cruelty, and meaninglessness of life. The only positive figure in the play is the woman doctor Mariya L'vovna, through whom Gorky articulates his belief that the malaise of the intelligentsia is attributable to their isolation from the people. Echoes of Chekhov's *The Seagull* (1898) and also Ivan Turgenev's famous play *A Month in the Country* (1850) abound, from the play's setting to such characters as a Trigorin-like writer named Shalimov. In the play's final lines the latter sums up both his own feelings and those of most of the other characters. Alluding to the character Ryumin's failed suicide attempt, he says: "It's all so unimportant, old fellow. Everything. People as well as events. Pour me out a glass of wine. So utterly meaningless, old fellow."

Despite Shalimov's world-weariness, Gorky has great faith in the ability of the writer to change society, and he spells this out in the second act of *Dachniki* in Mariya L'vovna's words to the effect that

> we live in a country where only the writer can voice the truth, only the writer can judge impartially the vices of his people and struggle in behalf of their interests. . . . He alone can do

this, and this alone is what the Russian writer ought to do.

Gorky's remaining pre-revolutionary plays deal, for the most part, with issues already raised in *The Petty Bourgeois, The Lower Depths,* and *Dachniki.*

The title of *Barbarians* is ironic and refers to the engineers who come to construct a railway through a provincial town and show nothing but disdain for the people of the area, whom they regard as "barbarians." In their haughtiness and contempt, however, it is the engineers, as representatives of the intelligentsia, who are revealed as the real "barbarians." The play was intended to show the wide gap between the intelligentsia and the common people and the unfitness of the intelligentsia for leadership, but it relies heavily for plot on a distracting, melodramatically conceived romantic intrigue with patently obvious Chekhovian touches.

While incarcerated in the Peter and Paul Fortress in St. Petersburg for his role in the 1905 Revolution, Gorky, in a month's time, wrote the play *Children of the Sun.* Less tendentious than most of his other plays, it is devoted to the young Populist intelligentsia ("the children of the sun"), toward whom Gorky had a certain sympathy. The Populists are shown as well-intentioned but, by virtue of their education and social background, unprepared to cope with the ignorance, superstitiousness, and brutality of the peasants among whom they have voluntarily placed themselves. However, despite the setbacks they experience, the young people remain confident and positive in their outlook.

Enemies, written in 1906 and clearly inspired by the 1905 Revolution, shifts the focus from tensions between the intelligentsia and the common folk to those between ruthless factory owners and workers demanding improved conditions. This play also has a heavy dose of melodrama. When the despotic factory owner Skrobotov is murdered, his relatively more liberal partner Burdin agrees to reopen a closed factory and fire a despised foreman on the condition that the workers turn over Skrobotov's murderer. The workers agree, but they surrender to the police not the real murderer but a younger, less valuable member of their group who agrees to the deception. The plan fails, however, and at the end the police come to arrest not only the actual murderer but a cell of Socialist agitators led by a Tolstoyan apostle of nonviolence. As in his novels, the hope of any future reconciliation between the classes lies with the younger generation, and so in *Enemies* Gorky introduces the figure of Burdin's niece Nadia, who has compassion for the workers and pleads their cause. Although obvious in meaning, *Enemies* is one of Gorky's better-constructed plays and has been successfully staged in the West.

Poslednye, also dating from 1906, is dramatically weaker and ideologically overburdened as compared to *Enemies.* The play has as its subject the alleged attempt by a young terrorist on the life of an unsavory police chief. The work was rejected by the censors and, like *Enemies,* remained unproduced until after the Revolution.

With *Queer People,* Gorky left the direct treatment of politics aside for the moment and returned to the theme of the spiritual malaise of the intelligentsia. As in *Children of the Sun,* his treatment is less strident than usual, although the play is diffuse, theatrically unexciting, and too obviously Chekhovian in the manner of its depiction of personal relationships. The play's most interesting character is the writer Mastakov, who while shown as a weakwilled philanderer nevertheless has an infectious zest for life and a love for Russia and the Russian people that redeems him. Despite his deficiencies of character, Mastakov, as a writer capable of inspiring others with his love of life and country, becomes the sole member of the intelligentsia depicted at all favorably in the play.

Like the novel *Mother, Vassa Zheleznova,* which Gorky wrote after *Queer People,* is another portrait of a strong Russian mother. This time, the mother is not associated with the revolutionary cause but is the wife of a businessman named Zakhar Zheleznov (*zheleznyi* in Russian is the adjectival form of the word meaning "iron"). As her husband approaches death, Vassa stops at almost nothing to keep the family business and fortune intact. Ruthless and iron-willed, she is a sometimes effective character study of a strong woman driven by what she regards as an honorable motive— the preservation of her family and its prosperity—but her methods are anything but honorable. As early as *The Lower Depths,* Gorky evinced his interest in naturalist drama, but his enthusiasm for this type of playwriting went beyond all bounds in *Vassa Zheleznova.* Deformity, illegitimacy, serious illness, physical and emotional cruelty, dissoluteness, licentiousness, infanticide, and suicide color the play in the darkest shades of naturalism and make the work more of a morbid literary curiosity among Gorky's plays rather than anything seriously deserving of production.

Of Gorky's other pre-revolutionary plays, *The Zykovs, Fal'shivaia moneta,* and *Starik,* the best of the three, without a doubt, is *The Zykovs.* Concentrating, as in *Vassa Zheleznova,* on a character study within a "family drama," here Gorky again returns to the world of the Russian merchant class. The central figure of the play is the timber merchant Antipa Zykov, of the same lower-bourgeois social origins as Vassa Zheleznova and a man cut from much the same cloth as she: strong of will and indifferent to the rights and sensitivities of others. A widower, Zykov appropriates his sickly son Mikhail's intended, Pavla, for himself, on the grounds that the young, healthy woman would be a more fitting wife for him than for his son, whom he despises, just as Vassa Zheleznova despises her own weak sons. Zykov and Pavla marry, but the relationship proves unsatisfactory and Pavla drifts back into a relationship with Mikhail. Despairing over the chain of events, Mikhail attempts suicide. Zykov is shocked, and eventually he and his son reconcile. Now aware that Pavla will never be right either for him or for his son, Zykov sends her packing.

Although interest in the play centers on Zykov himself, in a sense the true "hero" of the work is Antipa's sister Sof'ia, a woman as strong and determined as her brother and the one who holds family and business together when Antipa's attention is distracted by the relationship with Mikhail and Pavla. Sof'ia, however, is Antipa's moral superior: modest, principled, self-sacrificing, and unwilling to trade principle for easy gratification. But whatever the differences between them, Antipa and Sof'ia represent the kind of positive, self-assertive attitude toward life that Gorky admired so much in contrast to the passivity, insecurity, and weakness of both Mikhail and Pavla. It is these antithetical ways of responding to life's challenges, which Gorky explores through two interrelated but contrasting sets of characters, that he has placed at the center of *The Zykovs.* Its superficial similarities as a "family drama" with *Vassa Zheleznova* notwithstanding, it is a very different type of play.

Starik, which followed *The Zykovs* by two years and is a much weaker work, was the last play Gorky wrote before the Revolution. The pressure on him to write plays with a Soviet content and his patent inability to do so resulted in a fifteen-year hiatus in his playwriting. Although his interest in drama and theater remained high, he completed no new play during this long period. His return to dramatic writing came only in 1930, when he began work on *Somov i drugie,* which he finished in 1931, about the time that he returned to the Soviet Union for good.

Of the four plays Gorky wrote during the 1930's, *Somov* is the weakest of the group; interestingly, it is the only one set in the Soviet period. It was as if on the eve of his return to Russia, Gorky felt a need to demonstrate that he could deal with the new Soviet society in his fiction and that he could contribute to the creation of a new Soviet theatrical repertoire with plays on postrevolutionary, Soviet subjects. Dealing with the unsuccessful attempts

on the part of the enemies of the new Soviet state in Russia to crush it by supporting external intervention after the Revolution, the play is clumsy, its sole virtue being that it convinced Gorky to refrain from further efforts to write Soviet plays.

Yegor Bulychov and Others, by far the best of his plays of the 1930's, shows how Gorky managed to find a compromise in his playwriting between works with a specific Soviet content, which by now he knew that he could not write with any measure of success, and works with a prerevolutionary setting, which he was now more reluctant to write for political reasons. What Gorky did with *Yegor Bulychov* and *Dostigaev i drugie* was to return to his old "family drama" with a strong hero or heroine but to advance the chronology of the play to the revolutionary period. The already proven formula of a "family drama" and a commanding central dramatic portrait offered familiar ground. But the revolutionary setting enabled Gorky to give his later plays an undeniable relevance for the Soviet period, both chronologically and ideologically. After all, much Soviet drama of the 1920's and 1930's was located in the same revolutionary and civil war years of 1917 to 1921.

Beginning at the end of 1916 during the war against Germany, *Yegor Bulychov* also includes as background events the murder of Rasputin and the abdication of Tsar Nicholas II. The ending of the play is especially dramatic. As the dying Bulychov, a timber merchant, laments his doom, the sounds of a rebellious crowd in the streets below herald the imminent revolution. The play's end is obviously symbolic: Bulychov's death is the death of the old Russia he represents, the Russia of tradesmen, property owners, and capital. Like the destruction of the cherry orchard in Chekhov's play, it marks the irrevocable passing of a way of life. Although *Yegor Bulychov* has several interesting characters, the others are all overshadowed by Bulychov. One of Gorky's most successful dramatic portraits, Bulychov, as a member of a social class about to be swept from the stage of Russian history, evokes considerable compassion. The portrait is more complex than what we generally find in Gorky's plays. Stripped of illusions about life and man and already dying of cancer at the beginning of the play, Bulychov rebels against profiteering in wartime Russia, against the predators he sees all around him, and against the church's exploitation of the ignorance and superstition of the people. Bulychov is also not unaware of social injustice, but he remains a conservative and traditionalist whose social consciousness has expanded only up to a particular point. In the end, Bulychov goes down to his defeat railing against both man and disease as predators but only partially understanding the great transformation that has already begun to take place around him.

Although it is a sequel to *Yegor Bulychov* and superficially resembles it, *Dostigaev* is different in certain major respects. The titular character, who lacks the stature of Bulychov, serves as a collective portrait of the bourgeoisie and capitalists who tried to assume political power in Russia in the short period of the Provisional Government between July and October 1917, after the February Revolution of 1917. Dostigaev is a clever schemer whose goal is survival, who senses the political winds changing and sees that power is passing into the hands of the Bolsheviks. Less concentrated and more crowded a play than *Yegor Bulychov, Dostigaev* also relies more heavily on melodrama, and it lapses at times into contrivance. At the end of the play, a disillusioned Dostigaev resists the attempt of local reactionaries to enlist him in a campaign to oppose what they believe to be an impending Bolshevik takeover in their town. As the local leader of the notorious Black Hundreds and his henchmen are about to leave Dostigaev, they are arrested by the Bolsheviks. Dostigaev himself is placed under at least temporary house arrest, but the play's conclusion is open-ended. Since he has refused to throw in his lot with the reactionaries and since it is revealed that

his wife was the one who summoned the Bolsheviks, Dostigaev's ability to survive may have saved him once again.

Gorky's last work for the stage was an extensive revision of his earlier *Vassa Zheleznova.* In the new "Soviet" version, he makes up for the absence of the theme of class conflict in the original play by introducing an entirely new character, Vassa Zheleznova's daughter-in-law Rachel, a Jew, an ardent Socialist revolutionary, and her mother-in-law's ideological antagonist. The 1935 version of the play also paints its central figure in somewhat less demonic and more tragic terms. Hardly does Vassa, now an old and lonely woman, die (an event that does not occur in the 1910 version) than her sinister brother Prokhov races to steal the contents of her safe with the aim of dispossessing her heirs.

MEMOIRS

As a writer Gorky was a fine, indeed keen observer of the life around him, with an ability to create compelling narrative and natural dialogue. He was at his best when writing about what he had experienced firsthand, when he drew on his own full life. He was at his weakest, however, when he invented things and manipulated incident and character for the sake of his ideological positions. Sometimes his art as a storyteller and his social outlook come together effortlessly, as in several of his short stories, in a novel such as *The Artamonov Business,* or in a play such as *Yegor Bulychov.* Too much of the time, unfortunately, tendentiousness overpowers art, and the results are disappointing.

Where Gorky is rarely disappointing is in his memoirs and reminiscences, which, when all is said and done, may prove the most appealing and enduring of his many works. Gorky's memoir writing falls into two major categories: autobiography and literary portraits.

Gorky's autobiography consists of three

large works: *Childhood, My Apprenticeship,* and *My Universities.* The first, *Childhood,* was written in 1912–1913 and appeared in the newspaper *Russkoe Slovo* (Russian Word) between 25 August 1913 and 30 January 1914. *My Apprenticeship* was written in 1914 and appeared in the same newspaper from 1 November to 6 December 1915. *My Universities* dates from 1922 and was first published in the famous literary magazine *Krasnaia Nov'* (Red Virgin Soil) from March to July 1923. Certain episodes of *My Universities* are dealt with at greater length in separate sketches. In "An Incident from the Life of Makar," which was published in the *Znanie* miscellany for 1912, he takes up in greater detail the reasons behind his attempted suicide in December 1887; "Khoziain" ("The Boss"), written in 1912 and published in the journal *Sovremennik* (The Contemporary) in March, April, and May 1913, contains a literary portrait of the master baker for whom Gorky worked during most of the time that he was in Kazan between the ages of sixteen and twenty. Gorky also continued his autobiographical writing in such sketches as "Storozh" ("The Watchman"), "Vremia Korolenko" ("The Days of Korolenko"), "O vrede filosofii" ("On the Harm of Philosophy"), "O pervoi liubvi" ("First Love"), and "V. G. Korolenko," all of which were written in 1922 and 1923 and which he originally intended including in *My Universities* (these can be found in volume 16 of his collected works [Moscow, 1973]). The sketches cover the period between when *My Universities* stops and the publication of his first literary work. This expanded version of *My Universities* was to be titled "Sredi intelligentsii" (Among the Intelligentsia), but his plan for the revision of the volume was never carried out.

Childhood, the first and best part of Gorky's autobiographical trilogy, traces his life from the age of three to the age of eleven. It begins with the death of his father at the age of thirty-one in 1871 in Astrakhan. It ends with the death of his mother at the age of thirty-seven in 1878 in Nizhny Novgorod and with

Gorky's subsequent expulsion at the age of eleven from the home of his grandparents, where his mother had taken him to live following the death of his father.

Childhood, then, is a record of those early years with his maternal grandparents, the Kashirins. Aside from the vivid and detailed portraits Gorky draws of every member of the household, but above all of his grandparents, Vasili and Akulina Kashirin, the work is also a superb evocation of a time of great change in Russian society. With knowledge, insight, and a splendid eye for detail Gorky presents a graphic picture of the economic and social impact of the emancipation of the serfs and the reforms of the 1860's on such small businessmen as his grandfather, whose once prosperous textile dyeing plant suffered a sharp reversal of fortunes that shattered the integrity of the family and left it in severe financial hardship. It is much the same process of eco-nomic dislocation and consequent social change that Gorky depicted in the disintegration of a middle-class family in *The Artamonov Business.*

Two factors give *Childhood* its great feeling of authenticity and at the same time convey an extraordinary literary sensibility: its absence of any of the tendentiousness and contrivance of much of Gorky's fiction and drama and its examination of a process of far-reaching socioeconomic change through a study of the reactions of various members of a family in whose midst Gorky lived as a young boy and whom he observed keenly at close range. Gorky is especially masterly in his delineation of the psychological differences between his grandparents. As his fortunes decline and his authority begins to crumble, Grandfather Kashirin, an old-fashioned domestic tyrant, becomes ill-tempered, self-pitying, and forlorn. Grandmother Kashirin is woven of different cloth. Her outlook on life is shaped by her religious convictions; she is far less concerned with material well-being than her husband and far more sensitive and responsive to the needs of those around her. Anything but passive, despite her religious fatalism, she demonstrates courage and conviction on more than one occasion; in adversity she emerges as the real backbone of the family. Gorky is careful, however, to avoid sentimentalizing the woman by portraying her as saint like—just as he avoids depicting Grandfather Kashirin in wholly negative terms. All the portraits in the family gallery have strengths and weaknesses, virtues and vices that Gorky captures with an unerring eye for revealing detail and psychological truth.

My Apprenticeship covers the period from the end of 1879, when Gorky began working in a Nizhny Novgorod shoestore, to June 1884, when he left for the city of Kazan and its university. During most of this time Gorky lived with his grandmother's sister, Matrena Sergeeva. Moderately prosperous, the Sergeev family seems to have embodied virtually every negative trait of the Russian middle class of the period and doubtless determined Gorky's later attitude toward this stratum of society. In their materialism, worship of power, and self-righteousness the Sergeevs filled Gorky with disgust and provided the prototypes for much of his fiction.

Although *My Ap~~e iceship* presents an interesting picture o. a family and provides insights into the formation of Gorky's social views, it is on the whole less successful than *Childhood.* It is a longer, more diffuse work and is especially lacking in the absence of a central character or characters of the strength and fascination of the Kashirin grandparents. Much of *My Apprenticeship* is taken up with Gorky's account of the different jobs he held during this period, among them work on Volga river boats and in an icon-painting shop; this focus also diminishes the relative importance of the family setting. Nevertheless, the memoir has its share of interesting figures—apart from the members of the Sergeev family—such as the handsome widow who becomes the object of the young Gorky's romantic fantasy and whom he dubs "Queen Margot"; the washerwoman Natal'ia Kozlovskaya, who in some ways reminded him of Grandmother Kashirin; and his coworkers in Madame Salabanova's icon-painting shop, above all the talented craftsman Zhikarev and his grotesquely huge mistress.

My Universities covers Gorky's life from the age of sixteen to twenty—from June 1884 to September 1888. Gorky left Nizhny Novgorod with the intention of enrolling in the University of Kazan. But he was denied admission and then spent the next four years in the city in the company of a wide variety of people, contact with whom served Gorky as a practical school of life and supplanted the formal learning of the university to which he had no access.

More engrossing than *My Apprenticeship* and almost on the same level as *Childhood, My Universities* is above all a record of the growth of Gorky's mind and the expansion of his horizons. Although undivided into chapters, unlike the memoirs that preceded it, *My Universities* falls naturally into two parts. The first is set in Kazan and is primarily devoted to the life Gorky developed after failing to gain admission to the university. These experiences included, among others, frequent trips to the Volga wharves, where he hobnobbed with stevedores, tramps, and thieves; contact with the *gimnaziia* students who used to gather in the empty lot by the home of the Evreinov family with whom Gorky boarded; acquaintance with the residents of the slum dwelling, the "Marusovka," that he moved to next and with the grocery store keeper Andrei Derenkov, who owned Kazan's "finest library of rare and forbidden literature, a collection used by students from the city's numerous educational institutions and by various other revolutionary-minded people" and whose home was a gathering place for students from the university and theological academy; employment at Vasili Semenov's pretzel bakery, where he collected the material for such stories as "Twenty-Six Men and a Girl" and "Konovalov"; and visits to the "Crazy House," where the psychiatrist V. M. Bekhterev delivered lectures and demonstrated patients.

Sharpening social convictions accompanied the expansion of Gorky's intellect. He became sympathetic toward the cause of revolution as a way of trying to rectify Russia's wrongs, and he grew more and more ill-disposed toward what he came to regard as the passivity of Christian teaching and of Tolstoyism. One of the more vivid encounters described in *My Universities* is with the "Tolstoyan" Klopskii, toward whom he developed only loathing. The more Gorky read and the more he observed the injustices and contradictions in the life around him, the more troubled in spirit he became. He wrote:

> It was then that I realized my weariness of soul, first sensed the caustic mold eating at my heart. From that time on, my state of mind grew steadily worse. I began to see myself with the eyes of a bystander—cold eyes, alien and hostile. In almost every human soul, I began to sense a bristling and unordered cohabitation of contradictions—contradictions not only of word and deed, but also of emotions, the fitful play of which particularly oppressed me.
>
> (*My Apprenticeship, My Universities,* translated by Margaret Wettlin, p. 419)

It was in this state of mind that Gorky tried, and failed, to take his own life in December 1887. The suicide attempt terminates the Kazan part of *My Universities.*

The second part of the memoir is set in the village of Krasnovidovo, farther down the Volga, where Gorky went to work in the shop of the man he calls "Khokhol," who had spent ten years in Siberian exile. "Khokhol's" real name was Mikhail Romas. A Populist, Romas became Gorky's true mentor during this period, and from him and his circle of Populist friends Gorky gained deeper knowledge of and sympathy for revolutionary ideology. The time spent in Krasnovidovo was one of healing and learning for Gorky. When he left, mostly out of disgust with what he saw of the world of the peasantry, among whom Romas and his group had tried to organize a fruitgrowers' cooperative, he sailed with a friend to Samara as a stowaway on a passenger boat. *My Universities* closes with Gorky traveling even further, to the shores of the Caspian Sea, where he disembarked and found work at a Kalmyk fishery.

Gorky's other major body of memoirs consists principally of literary portraits of such writers as Chekhov, Tolstoy, and Andreev. By sheer chance, Chekhov, Tolstoy, and Gorky all happened to be in the Crimea for their health from the fall of 1901 through the spring of 1902. It was in this period that Gorky had the opportunity to meet his most famous peers and to form impressions of them that remained with him the rest of his life. It is these impressions, often remarkable for their insights and acute psychological observations rather than for their literary judgments or analyses, to which the reminiscences are devoted.

Chekhov, who took a serious interest in Gorky and encouraged him early in his writing career, was clearly Gorky's favorite. What Gorky admired most in him was his profound contempt for vulgarity and his art of exposing it everywhere. To Gorky, this quality seemed to spring from the ardent desire to see simplicity, beauty, and harmony in man. "Beautifully simple himself," wrote Gorky, "he loved everything simple, genuine, sincere, and he had a peculiar way of making other people simple." About Chekhov's stories, Gorky observed that

> one feels oneself in a melancholy day of late autumn, when the air is transparent and the outline of naked trees, narrow houses, greyish people, is sharp. Everything is strange, lonely, motionless, helpless. The horizon, blue and empty, melts into the pale sky, and its breath is terribly cold upon the earth, which is covered with frozen mud. The author's mind, like the autumn sun, shows up in hard outline the monotonous roads, the crooked streets, the little squalid houses in which tiny, miserable people are stifled by boredom and laziness and fill the houses with an unintelligible, drowsy bustle.
>
> (*Reminiscences of Tolstoy, Chekhov, and Andreyev,* translated by S. S. Koteliansky, Leonard Woolf, and Katherine Mansfield, pp. 109–110)

442

Gorky's attitude toward Tolstoy was one of ambivalence, at best. Although he was unsympathetic toward the philosophy of Tolstoyism, he recognized Tolstoy's greatness, even his genius. But he was cool to Tolstoy's monstrous ego and was offended by the writer's aristocratic arrogance, which Gorky saw lurking just beneath the surface of his cultivated simplicity and directness. Gorky observed:

> All his life he feared death and hated death . . . must he die? The whole world, all the earth, looks toward him; from China, India, America, from everywhere, living, throbbing threads stretch out to him; his soul is for all and ever. Why should not Nature make an exception to her law, give to one man physical immortality—why not?
> (Koteliansky, Woolf, Mansfield trans., p. 50)

Gorky was also taken aback by the disparity between Tolstoy's background and culture and the crude manner in which he often expressed himself. Tolstoy also liked talking about women, which offended a certain prudishness in Gorky, and it was frequently in the context of such conversations that Tolstoy was at his coarsest. As Gorky recalls:

> Of women he talks readily and much, like a French novelist, but always with the coarseness of a Russian peasant. Formerly it used to affect me unpleasantly. Today in the Almond Park he asked Anton Chekhov:
> "You whored a great deal when you were young?" Anton Pavlovich, with a confused smile, and pulling at his little beard, muttered something inaudible, and Leo Nikolaevich, looking at the sea, confessed:
> "I was an indefatigable ————."
> He said this penitently, using at the end of the sentence a salty peasant word. And I noticed for the first time how simply he used the word, as though he knew no more fitting one to use. All those kinds of words, coming from his shaggy lips, sound simple and natural and lose their soldierly coarseness and filth. I remember my first meeting with him and his talk about *Varen'ka Olesova* [by Gorky, published in 1898] and "Twenty-Six Men and a Girl." From the ordinary point of view what he said was a string of inde-

cent words. I was perplexed by it and even offended. I thought that he considered me incapable of understanding any other kind of language. I understand now: it was silly to have felt offended.
> (Koteliansky, Woolf, Mansfield trans., p. 25)

Gorky felt driven to confess in his reminiscence that in Tolstoy "there is much which at times roused in me a feeling very like hatred, and this hatred fell upon my soul with crushing weight." But while admitting that, as he saw him, "his disproportionately overgrown individuality is a monstrous phenomenon, almost ugly," Gorky's recognition of Tolstoy's greatness prompted him to compare him to a legendary Russian folk hero, the knight Sviatogor, whose weight the earth could not support. To Gorky Tolstoy indeed seemed "godlike."

Gorky had a longer, closer, and more complex relationship with Andreev than with either Chekhov or Tolstoy. Consequently, the reminiscence of Andreev is the longest of any. There were great differences between the two writers, but also an affection, even a sense of camaraderie that kept them close for ten years. Eventually, radically divergent political attitudes, especially after the Revolution and the coming to power of the Bolsheviks, brought the relationship to an end. Andreev eventually emigrated to Finland, where he died in bitterness, an uncompromising foe of the Bolsheviks. Speaking of the differences between them, Gorky wrote:

> Equally irreconcilably did we differ in our views on man, the source of thought, its furnace. To me man is always the conqueror, even when he is mortally wounded and dying. Splendid is his longing to know himself and to know Nature: and although his life is a torment, he is ever widening its bounds, creating with his thoughts wise science, marvellous art. I felt that I did sincerely and actively love man—him who is at present alive and working side by side with me, and him, too, the sensible, the good, the strong, who will follow after in the future. To Andreev man appeared poor in spirit, a creature interwoven of irreconcilable contradictions of instinct

and intellect, for ever deprived of the possibility of attaining inner harmony. All his works are "vanity of vanities," decay and self-deception. And above all he is the slave of death and all his life long he walks, dragging its chain.

(Koteliansky, Woolf, Mansfield trans., p. 161)

Despite Andreev's turn-of-the-century morbidity and fascination with death, his personal laziness, his excessive fondness for drink, and his unconcealed ambition, Gorky was genuinely fond of him and admired both his intellect and his talent. When World War I, then the Revolution, and finally Andreev's emigration and anti-Bolshevik writings ended Gorky's friendship with the man he refers to in his reminiscence as "my sole friend in literary circles," the sense of loss was deep. "Differences of outlook," wrote Gorky, "ought not to affect sympathies, and I never gave theories and opinions a decisive role in my relations with people." Referring to Andreev's hostility toward him over his return to the Soviet Union and his cooperation with the Bolsheviks, Gorky notes that "Leonid Nikolaevich felt otherwise." But in the spirit of their long friendship, Gorky magnanimously expresses his forgiveness in these words: "But I don't blame him for this; for he was what he wished to be and could not help being—a man of rare originality, rare talent and manly enough in his seekings after truth."

The compassion, sensitivity, and decency that inform Gorky's literary portraits characterize virtually all of his writings. His passionate desire for social justice in Russia coupled with an exalted sense of the mission of the Russian writer made it impossible for him to remain outside of his country once the obstacles to his return were removed by the amnesty of 1913. Gorky had a keen sense of Russianness, of identification with the Russian people, and it is essentially in the service of that people that he placed his considerable talent. When misunderstandings with Lenin and disappointment in policies of the Bolsheviks all but mandated another period of separation from his homeland in 1921, Gorky yearned to return to the new Soviet state in order to help it achieve the social and cultural goals in which he believed. Gorky was tireless in his efforts in behalf of the dignity of the individual and the creative autonomy of the artist. If his humanitarian struggle was ultimately doomed by Stalinist repression, it must nevertheless be recognized for its fundamental sincerity and nobility.

Although Gorky is often denigrated as a writer because of his tendentiousness and the reformist zeal that on occasion made him oblivious to the demands of artistic excellence, there is much in his work that can be read with interest and pleasure. His stories seethe with a restless yearning for romantic adventure and demonstrate a keen eye for the unusual and colorful. Taken together, the best of his plays represent a theatrically vivid picture of the Russian bourgeoisie and intelligentsia at a critical juncture in history. Despite their artistic unevenness, his novels offer a view of Russian society that for sheer scope was unparalleled in the works of any other Russian writer of his time. Gorky's interest in the world around him and his remarkable powers of observation are brilliantly reflected in his memoirs and reminiscences, which demonstrate the writing skill Gorky was capable of when not burdened by ideology. Whatever his weaknesses as a writer, Gorky's extraordinary literary output—especially when viewed in the context of one of the most engrossing lives of any Russian writer in history—demands a fairness of evaluation commensurate with Gorky's own stature as a human being.

Selected Bibliography

EDITIONS

INDIVIDUAL WORKS

SHORT STORIES
"Makar Chudra." Tiflis, 1892.
"Moi sputnik." Samara, 1894.

MAXIM GORKY

"Starukha Izergil'." Samara, 1895.

"Chelkash." St. Petersburg, 1895.

"Konovalov." St. Petersburg, 1897.

"Dvadtsat' shest' i odna." St. Petersburg, 1911–1912.

Sluchai iz zhizni Makara, Rozhdenie cheloveka (Dva rasskaza). St. Petersburg and Berlin, 1912.

"Khoziain." In *Sovremennik* (March–May 1913).

PLAYS

Meshchane. St. Petersburg, 1901.

Na dne. Munich, 1902.

Dachniki. Berlin, 1904.

Deti solntsa. St. Petersburg, 1905.

Varvary. Stuttgart, 1905.

Vragi. Stuttgart, 1906.

Poslednye. Berlin, 1908.

Chudaki. Berlin, 1910.

Vassa Zheleznova. St. Petersburg, 1910; Moscow, 1936.

Zykovy. Berlin. 1913.

Fal'shivaia moneta. Berlin, 1913.

Starik. Berlin, 1915, 1922.

Somov i drugie. Moscow, 1930–1931.

Dostigaev i drugie. Moscow, 1931–1932.

Egor Bulychov i drugie. Berlin, 1932, 1933. These are the publication dates of two separate versions of the play.

NOVELS

Goremyka Pavel. Nizhny Novgorod, 1894.

Foma Gordeev. St. Petersburg, 1899.

Troe. St. Petersburg, 1901.

Mat'. Berlin, 1907; Moscow, 1917. This novel was first published in English as *Mother* (New York, 1906–1907).

Ispoved'. Berlin and St. Petersburg, 1908.

Gorodok Okurov. St. Petersburg, 1909.

Zhizn' Matveia Kozhemiakina. Berlin, 1910–1911.

Delo Artamonovykh. Berlin, 1925.

Zhizn' Klima Samgina. Berlin, 1927–1936.

OTHER WRITINGS

A. P. Chekhov. St. Petersburg, 1905; Berlin, 1923.

"Moi interv'iu." St. Petersburg, 1906.

"V Amerike." Stuttgart, 1906.

Lev Tolstoi. Petrograd, 1919.

Leonid Andreev. Berlin, 1919, 1923.

COLLECTED WORKS

Ocherki i rasskazy. Edited by S. Dorovatovskii and A. Churuskin. 3 vols. St. Petersburg, 1898–1899.

Sobranie sochinenii. 30 vols. Moscow, 1949–1955.

Sobranie sochinenii. 18 vols. Moscow, 1960–1963.

Polnoe sobranie sochinenii. 25 vols. Moscow, 1968–1976.

MEMOIRS

Detstvo. Moscow, 1913–1914.

V liudiakh. Moscow, 1916.

Moi universettii. Berlin, 1923.

TRANSLATIONS

Articles and Pamphlets. Moscow, 1950. Contains *My Interviews* and *In America.*

The Artamonov Business. Translated by Alec Brown. New York and London, 1948.

The Autobiography of Maxim Gorky. New York, 1962. Contains *Childhood, My Apprenticeship,* and *My Universities.*

Best Short Stories of Maxim Gorki. Edited by Avrahm Yarmolinsky and Baroness Moura Budberg. New York, 1947; reprinted 1973.

Childhood. Translated by Margaret Wettlin. Moscow, 1973.

Children of the Sun. Translated by John Wolfe. In *Poet Lore* 17 (1906).

The Confession. Translated by Rose Strunsky. New York, 1916.

Enemies. Translated by Kitty Hunter-Blair and Jeremy Brooks. New York, 1972.

Foma Gordeyev. Translated by by Margaret Wettlin. London, 1956; Westport, Conn., 1974. Based on the edition published by Foreign Languages Publishing House (Moscow, 1955).

Letters of Gorky and Andreev 1899–1912. Edited by Peter Yershov. Translated by Lydia Weston. New York, 1958.

The Life of Klim Samgin. 4 vols. Translated by Alexander Bakshy and Bernard Guilbert Guerney. New York, 1930–1938. Vol. 1: *Bystander;* vol. 2: *The Magnet;* vol. 3: *Other Fires;* vol 4: *The Specter.*

The Life of Matvei Kozhemyakin. Translated by Margaret Wettlin. Moscow, 1961.

Literary Portraits. Translated by Ivy Litvinov. Moscow, n.d. Contains memoirs of Leo Tolstoy, Sofia Tolstoy, Anton Chekhov, Vladimir Korolenko,

Mikhail Kotsubinsky, Nikolai Garin-Mikhailovsky, and Mikhail Prishvin.

The Lower Depths and Other Plays. Translated by Alexander Bakshy with Paul S. Nathan. New Haven, Conn., 1959. Contains *The Lower Depths, Enemies,* and *The Zykovs.*

Mother: A Revolutionary Novel. Translated by Margaret Wettlin. Moscow, 1950; New York, 1962.

My Apprenticeship, My Universities. Translated by Margaret Wettlin. Moscow, 1977.

On Literature: Selected Articles. Translated by Julius Katzer and Ivy Litvinov. Moscow, 1960.

Orphan Paul. Translated by Lily Turner and Mark O. Strever. New York, 1946.

The Petty Bourgeois. Translated by Igor Kosin. Pullman, Wash., 1972.

Plays. Translated by Robert Daglish, Bernard Isaacs, and Margaret Wettlin. Moscow, 1968. Contains *The Lower Depths, Enemies, Yegor Bulychov and Others,* and the revised version of *Vassa Zheleznova.*

Reminiscences of Tolstoy, Chekhov, and Andreyev. Translated by S. S. Koteliansky, Leonard Woolf, and Katherine Mansfield. London, 1968.

Selected Stories. Translated by Bernard Isaacs, Rose Prokofieva, Avril Pyman, and Margaret Wettlin. Moscow, 1981. Contains "Makar Chudra"; "My Traveling Companion"; "Old Izergil"; "Chelkash"; "One Autumn"; "Song of the Falcon"; "Konovalov"; "Twenty-Six Men and a Girl"; "Song of the Stormy Petrel"; "Tales of Italy"; "The Ice Is Moving"; "A Man Is Born"; "The Creepy-Crawlies"; and "First Love."

Seven Plays of Maxim Gorky. Translated by Alexander Bakshy with Paul S. Nathan. New Haven, Conn., 1945. Contains *Barbarians, Yegor Bulychov, Enemies, The Lower Depths, Queer People, Vassa Zheleznova,* and *The Zykovs.*

The Three of Them. Translated by A. Linden. London, 1905.

BIOGRAPHICAL AND CRITICAL STUDIES

Borras, F. M. *Maxim Gorky: The Writer.* Oxford, 1967.

Byalik, Boris. *M. Gor'kii—dramaturg.* Moscow, 1977. This is the second, revised, and augmented edition of this work.

————. *O Gor'kom: Stat'i.* Moscow, 1947.

Kaun, Alexander. *Maxim Gorky and His Russia.* New York, 1931.

Lenobl', Genrikh. *O M. Gor'kom—khudozhnike slova: Sbornik statei.* Moscow, 1957.

Levin, Dan. *Stormy Petrel: The Life and Work of Maxim Gorky.* New York, 1986.

Habermann, Gerhard. *Maksim Gorki.* Translated by Ernestine Schlant. New York, 1971.

Hare, Richard. *Maxim Gorky: Romantic Realist and Conservative Revolutionary.* London, 1962.

Kastorskii, Sergei. *Gor'kii—khudozhnik: Ocherki.* Moscow and Leningrad, 1963.

Muchnic, Helen. *From Gorky to Pasternak: Six Writers in Soviet Russia.* New York, 1979.

Novikov, Vasilii. *Tvorcheskaia laboratoriia Gor'-kogo—dramaturga.* Moscow, 1965.

Rischbieter, Henning. *Maxim Gorki.* Hanover, 1973.

Tager, E. B. *Tvorchestvo Gor'kogo sovetskoi epokhi.* Moscow, 1964.

Weill, Irwin. *Gorky: His Literary Development and Influence on Soviet Intellectual Life.* New York, 1966.

Wolfe, Bertram D. *The Bridge and the Abyss: The Troubled Friendship of Maxim Gorky and V. I. Lenin.* New York, Washington, and London, 1967.

HAROLD B. SEGEL

STEFAN GEORGE

(1868–1933)

FOR FIVE MONTHS in 1968, on the occasion of the one hundredth anniversary of Stefan George's birth, the German Literary Archives in the Schiller Museum at Marbach held a unique exhibition of some five hundred literary and pictorial documents in his honor. Manuscripts and first editions of his own work formed the lesser part of the exhibition; his poetic output was relatively small. The two volumes of the complete edition of 1958 comprise only about six hundred pages of his own poetry and sixty pages of prose writings; the remaining five hundred pages contain translations from other poets (Charles Baudelaire's *Les fleurs du mal* [*Flowers of Evil,* 1857], Shakespeare's *Sonnets* [1607], and selections from Dante Alighieri's *Divine Comedy* [1313–1321] forming the bulk). What made the exhibition unique and what would have pleased George is that it included a great variety of materials stemming from the circle of his friends, the so-called *George-Kreis:* writers, poets, and scholars who had been influenced or trained by him. They and their descendants have had no mean share in preserving the memory of George.

Although George's work lacks facile popular appeal, as does, for instance, Goethe's *Faust II* (1832), he has not suffered such a period of neglect as Goethe did for sixty years after his death. It is true that two brief, ironically contrasting eclipses of George's renown did occur during and after the Hitler years in Germany.

First, some scholars as well as the Nazi cultural manipulators, who presented George as a spiritual forebear of the Third Reich, lost interest and disavowed him by 1935, the year of publication of Arvid Brodersen's *Stefan George: Deutscher und Europäer* (Stefan George: German and European), a monograph that stressed George's concern for Europe as a spiritual entity rather than for a German hegemony. Then, however, with the collapse of the Nazis ten years later, interest in George declined altogether, and critics took him to task for the allegedly clear affinity between his poetry and the tenets of National Socialism. Today the controversy among critics concerning the artistic merits and the political significance of George's work and influence continues unabated, while the study of his poetry is beginning to be part of the West German high school and university curricula.

George was uncompromising in his total rejection of modern society with its class distinctions based on external criteria such as family origin, creed, or race, and with its many sectarian "isms" in politics and aesthetics. What mattered to him were the highest cultural achievements of past ages insofar as they were still alive and capable of meaningful translation into action. He was a humanist who saw the education of select incorruptible young individuals as his mission. He wished to further their highest ethical potential as the path to a cultural rejuvenation of the body-politic. His chief means to this end were art and the informal gathering of persons whom he taught to read great poetry.

One can only speculate on the shape that George's image will take a hundred years from now. It is, however, gradually becoming clear that a dispassionate assessment of the poet's artistic accomplishments has to take into account his social attitudes. In other words, his work and person are not easily separable. Phases and incidents of his personal life are only dimly reflected or evoked in the poetry. He wrote no poems during the last five years of his life; yet, he must have regarded his pedagogic mission as completely embodied in his poetry, as he continued in his direct bid for spiritual power in the informal training of disciples who formed the core of a cultural renewal.

Those who knew and revered him called him "Master"; they agreed that a magic power issued from his person "which inspired fear and reverence and which could only be counterbalanced by love," as the historian Friedrich Wolters (1876–1930) put it. There were others who took an instinctive dislike to what seemed to them a solemn severity and hierarchical pose, a pose that became even more distasteful when it was imitated by some of the disciples. No one denied that George had a commanding presence, a probing glance, an impressive countenance, and a superior intelligence. We are told the young George felt that in a former life he had been a royal personage; in his middle years his bearing led some to take him for a reincarnation of Dante.

During the Wilhelmine era almost all German writers and poets of rank were in some measure critical of the establishment and its imperial ambitions, but no one was more absolute and near-contemptuous in his opposition than George. In examining his poetry his refusal to interact with his society on any terms other than his own has to form part of the discussion.

Ever since George's first publication, *Hymnen* (Odes, 1890; one hundred copies, privately printed), his poetry and his person have been the subject of speculation and controversy. It seemed that, while he shared with the naturalists a disdain for the stale and mediocre level to which German art had sunk since the death of Goethe, his approach was that of the aesthete and practitioner of *l'art pour l'art,* remote from public concerns. This is suggested by "Weihe" (Initiation), first of the *Hymnen:* "Out to the river! . . . rest in the grass, be overwhelmed / By strong primeval scent, shunning disturbing thought." Yet by the end of the decade it became clear that his non-involvement was not mere escape and that a fervent sense of mission lay behind it. A positive approach had to be preceded by a wholesale rejection. George said later to Ernst Robert Curtius, renowned romance scholar and medievalist: "But the nineteenth century is fundamentally corrupt, it must be rejected radically. The idea of progress through science is madness. In all great epochs men knew that knowledge is meant only for the few and can only be communicated step by step." George wanted to bring about a moral and cultural rebirth of Germany and make it the leading nation of Europe in an educative process along the lines of the Platonic Academy. The rebirth had to begin with an elite of young men who themselves would become leaders and educators, but ultimately, as he said to the historian Kurt Breysig in 1916, he demanded "from everybody, be he poor or rich, stupid or clever, that he become different."

The fact that all this was to happen through art (poetry in particular) indicates, on the one hand, how quixotic and problematic was the poet's relation to, and concept of, reality. On the other hand, it stresses the absoluteness of his claim. In Robert Boehringer's *Ewiger Augenblick* (Eternal Moment, 1965) the story is told that once, when George was a little boy, he was left alone in the house. He went and locked all the rooms and buried the keys in the garden: "That way he made himself master of the house." Stefan George wanted to begin at the beginning, a trait not uncommon among Germans, who as a nation have labored so long and so tortuously in their search for identity. Curtius remarked with reference to George that "at the root of every great work of the German mind there is an absolute beginning."

Stefan George lived and died as a freelance poet and writer, if his aloofness from all public office and private employment can be thus described. He was entirely independent of family ties. Although his room at his parents' house in Bingen was always ready for him, he never cared to stay there for great lengths of time. He had no other permanent domicile but stayed for varying periods of time with friends in Berlin, Munich, and Basel, or in a pension in Heidelberg. The only public honor he did not decline was the Goethe Prize of the city of Frankfurt in 1927, awarded when he was sixty. In July 1933 the newly installed Nazi government, through its Ministry of "Culture," founded a German Poets' Academy and wanted George to grace it as its first president. They were willing to put up an annual Stefan George Prize as an emolument for the poet or for anyone he cared to select. His young Jewish friend Ernst Morwitz personally delivered the poet's answer, in which he declined unequivocally. His last sentence is supposed to have read, "It is true, I am the ancestor of every national movement, but how the spirit [Geist] is to enter politics—that I cannot tell you." One month later George left Germany. An old physical ailment struck with redoubled force. He died in Minusio, Switzerland, on 4 December 1933.

Stefan George is said to have begun writing verse when he was a little boy. At the age of seven he invented his own secret language, an experiment he repeated at least twice more before he was twenty. Only two apparently indecipherable lines from the last and most elaborate of these inventions—a kind of streamlined romance language—are preserved. They form the conclusion of his poem "Ursprünge" (Origins, 1904):

> *In einem sange den keiner erfasste*
> *Waren wir heischer und herrscher vom All.*
> *Süss und befeuernd wie Attikas choros*

> *Über die hügel und inseln klang:*
> Co besoso pasoje ptoros
> Co es on hama pasoje boañ

> In incantations which none comprehended
> We were the sovereigns and ruled the All.
> Sweet and impelling as Attica's choros
> Over the islands and hills we sang:
> Co besoso pasoje ptoros
> Co es on hama pasoje boañ

The poet's great-grandfather had emigrated from France (Département de la Moselle) to the right bank of the Rhine (Büdesheim, opposite Bingen). His son Stephan became a vineyard owner and member of the regional parliament. Stephan's grandson was named after him, but the French equivalent of Stefan—Étienne—was the more frequently used alternative by which he was known until he was well over twenty and felt reconciled to being a German; at home French was spoken as much as German. Later, in retrospect, George emphasized that his homeland was that of the Franks, that is, the realm of Charlemagne, and he referred in "Franken" ("Frankish Lands," 1902–1903) to the grandfather's "praise of the ever young / and generous earth whose glory warmed him / and whose anguish, though from a distance, caused him tears."

George was not a child prodigy. His early German verse, which he was careful not to publish until he believed that his stature was established, shows nothing resembling the precocious perfection of the poems of Loris—the nom de plume of the sixteen-year-old Hugo von Hofmannsthal. A certain awkwardness marks George's juvenilia, which he entitled *Die Fibel* (The Primer, 1901). There seems to be some justification in regarding this awkwardness as evidence of a childhood trauma, due to his bilingualism and all it entailed culturally. George said to Curtius, "There was a moment when I was faced with the decision as to whether to become a German poet or a French one." His case is analogous to that of the nineteenth-century Swiss poet Conrad

Ferdinand Meyer, who had been unable to make up his mind to write in German until the Germans covered themselves with military glory and achieved political unification through the war with France in 1870–1871. The factors determining George's decision twenty years later were ironically different: the new German Empire disgusted the sensitive Rhinelander through its materialistic vulgarity and artistic and intellectual mediocrity. The realities of the German scene appeared to him paltry and inimical to creativity. They drove him to travel abroad for nearly two years after he was graduated from the gymnasium in Darmstadt: to London, Switzerland, northern Italy, Paris, Spain, Copenhagen, and finally Paris again.

His sojourn in the French capital and his participation in the famous *mardis soirs* of Stéphane Mallarmé have sometimes been represented as the means by which the symbolist movement spread to the German-speaking world. This is not entirely correct. The work of Baudelaire, Mallarmé, and the symbolists was received by the Germans rather slowly, it is true, but the process began without George and before his Parisian experience. Moreover, it is erroneous to identify George's work and views, except for some aspects of the early poems, with the philosophy of the major symbolist figures. What inspired the young George and made him return to his own country with the firm resolve to be a German poet was the primacy of euphony and formal perfection as it was upheld by his French *confrères* (brothers-in-art); the esteem in which the poet's vocation was held in France; the noble living example of *le Maître,* Mallarmé; and the express blessing and commission with which his French friends sent him off to bring about a renewal of poetry and art in Germany. All this amounted to a reaffirmation of George's own aspiration and will to (spiritual!) power.

The encouragement he had received was decisive. He began to gather like-minded friends about him and founded the review *Blätter für die Kunst* (Pages for Art) not long

afterward. The name of the magazine was evidently borrowed from the French *Écrits pour l'art.* As co-editor he chose Carl August Klein (1867–1952), whom George had met when they were both students at Berlin University in 1889, and as place of publication the German capital, which he loathed but recognized as one of the "great highways." His concept of the "new art," however, differed from symbolist aesthetics. It was not metaphysically oriented; it did not imply that the signs of the phenomenal world have their correspondences in the ideal realm as well as among themselves. In the first issue of the *Blätter* (October 1892) Klein pointed out that literary epochs did not run exactly parallel in the two countries and insisted that George had to seek a path of his own because "the perfection of the 'Parnasse' which we have not yet attained is, as a point of view, already outdated over there." Since an innovator in German poetry, Klein continued, had to direct his efforts against post-romantic egocentricity and sentimental mediocrity as well as against the lusterless, formless products of naturalism, it was, indeed, precision in formulation and adherence to strict formal patterns that distinguished George's work from the outset. Such traits as the mystic, oracular, and reflective tendencies of symbolism are absent.

This does not mean that the calculated compactness of George's work does not have its linguistic obscurities and syntactic complexities, but these are not due to the vague suggestiveness of indecipherable private symbols. The cult of artistic perfection, the erudition that evokes different periods of history or elements of the artistic national heritage and that preceded the symbolist movement in France, were what George saw as the foremost needs of the German poetic language. So he led German metrics back to the rules of classical prosody at a time when the symbolists began to fight for the freedom of verse. In 1894 he wrote, "Free verse means as much as 'white blackness'; let him who cannot move well in rhythm stride along unbound," and "The value of poetry is determined not by meaning (then it would be wisdom or erudition), but by form." He defined form as something not merely external but as "that deeply moving element in rhythm and sound, by which at all times the originators, the Masters, have distinguished themselves from the epigones, the artists of second rank." While this is not a satisfactory definition of "form," it should make clear that for George, at this stage at least, sound came before sense.

It was in Paris that George was introduced to the poetry of Baudelaire and was so profoundly impressed that he began immediately to translate it into German. In 1891 he published 115 of the 151 poems of *Flowers of Evil* as *Die Blumen des Bösen*. The work is remarkable for its bold originality in the euphonious handling of the German language and, especially, for the light that the poet's translation technique throws upon his own conception of poetry. There is justification for saying that in Baudelaire George searched for himself. In so doing he misunderstood Baudelaire in some important aspects. The motive of spleen that permeates the French work from beginning to end is suppressed or eliminated by the translator. The crucial first poem, the apostrophe "To the Reader," is absent from the translation. The title of the first part of *Flowers of Evil*, "Spleen et idéal," is rendered as "Trübsinn und Vergeistigung," which means approximately "Dreariness and Spiritualization." Thus the fundamental dualism of human existence as the French poet saw it is bridged by the activating implication of "spiritualization." Moreover, George practices a kind of censorship in that he omits whole poems or tones down expressions that refer to details of crude physical and erotic realities. He wants to see Baudelaire as the poet of "fervent spirituality."

A closer examination of *Die Blumen des Bösen* shows, furthermore, an extraordinary reduction in the variety and number of Baudelaire's images, due to a shortening of the lines; in place of the original's alexandrines we find iambic pentameter. One of George's maxims

was *rein ellenmässig: die kürze* (in terms of inches simply: brevity). There is a strong tendency in George to fashion the line of verse as a basic unit. Consequently the translation is, by comparison with the original, pithy and apodictic and at times syntactically overcomplicated. Finally, and this is again related to the reduction in length, the comparison shows that the translation—parts of which are indeed brilliantly skillful—often does violence to the images of the original in such a manner that sense is sacrificed for the sake of sound.

In George's work, insistence on formal conciseness serves the purpose of a strict control of emotion. One can sense the poet's urge to challenge and revolutionize but also a deep melancholy and besetting doubt in these lines from the last poem of *Hymnen*, "Die Gärten schliessen" (The Gardens Are Closing):

Heisse monde flohen aus der pforte.
Ward dein hoffen deine habe?
Baust du immer noch auf ihre worte
Pilger mit der hand am stabe?

Torpid months fled through the gate.
Did your hope become possession?
Do you still believe their words?
Pilgrim you, with staff in hand?

One of the tenets on which George took a peremptory stand was that a direct statement of negative values is unpoetic and to be avoided. Under the mask of the lonely pilgrim the poet tried to master his precarious relationship to the world by searching for likeminded friends in his exploration of it. This led, later, to the forming of the *George-Kreis*.

The matter treated in his second book of poetry, *Pilgerfahrten* (Pilgrimages, 1891), recalls some of the physical and geographical details of George's travels; in the case of the poem "Mühle lass die arme still" (Windmill cease to move your arms), for example, we may recognize details that suggest a North German landscape. But the poet uses elements of reality in order imaginatively to present a clash of human and demonic agents. Possibly the poem shows the power of the Catholic church only insecurely defended from stronger dark and unknown forces as they take possession of "young brides of Heaven" who cross a frozen lake after first communion:

Mühle lass die arme still
Da die heide ruhen will.
Teiche auf den tauwind harren
Ihrer pflegen lichte lanzen
Und die kleinen bäume starren
Wie getünchte ginsterpflanzen.

Weisse kinder schleifen leis
Überm see auf blindem eis
Nach dem segentag sie kehren
Heim zum dorf in stillgebeten
DIE beim fernen gott der lehren
DIE schon bei dem naherflehten.

Kam ein pfiff am grund entlang?
Alle lampen flackern bang.
War es nicht als ob es riefe?
Es empfingen ihre bräute
Schwarze knaben aus der tiefe . . .
Glocke läute glocke läute!

Windmill cease to move your arms
Since the heath desires rest.
Ponds expect a thawing wind.
Guarding them are shimmering lances
And the little trees are rigid
Like a white-washed gorse-bush cluster.

Gently gliding white-clad children
Cross the lake on clouded ice
After being blessed they now turn
Toward their village stilly praying
To the distant god of dogma
Or to their adored redeemer.

Did a whistle graze the ground?
Anxious flickering shakes all lights.
Was there not a call from someone?
Youths all black, from deep below,
Fast arose to take their brides . . .
Bell ring out, ring bell, ring out!

The difficulties accompanying the presentation of George's poetic art in translation (especially when analysis and interpretation are

attempted) are well-nigh insurmountable. The English versions given here aim only at communicating the meaning, the meter, and the general tone. The rhyme has been sacrificed, as have other subtleties of euphony. Lines 4 and 14 of the original "Mühle . . ." poem cause one to speculate about the reason for the use of lanzen and lampen. The preciousness of the word "lances," when it refers to "reeds," is probably due not to an expressionistic urge but rather to a need for vowel euphony, while "lamps," which could refer to candles in the children's hands or to the lights on the shore or to both, may very well be used solely to complete the a-e pattern throughout the stanza. (George used a centered dot instead of a comma or a semicolon.)

The book Algabal (1892) followed quickly on Pilgerfahrten. In Algabal, inability to come to terms with the world of man because it falls short of the poetic dream is turned into rebellious opposition to reality; the humility of the pilgrim is transformed into a wish-dream of power and amorality, as embodied in the figure of a solipsistic late Roman emperor. The transition between the two books is the last pilgrim poem, "Die Spange" (The Link):

Ich wollte sie aus kühlem eisen
Und wie ein glatter fester streif
Doch war im schacht auf allen gleisen
So kein metall zum gusse reif.

Nun aber soll sie also sein:
Wie eine grosse fremde dolde
Geformt aus feuerrotem golde
Und reichem blitzendem gestein.

I wanted it of coolest iron
And fashioned like a firm smooth band.
Yet all the mountain's shafts were barren,
Had no such metal for the mold.

Different now it shall be made.
Like a great and wondrous cluster:
Of gold which is as red as fire,
Of richest sparkling precious stones.

George's emperor Algabal is a symbolic figure rather than a historical personage, although it is not difficult to recognize features he has in common with the boy emperor Heliogabalus of the early third century A.D., with literary treatments Heliogabalus received at the hands of French *décadents* and symbolist authors, and with King Ludwig II of Bavaria. The book bears an inscription to Ludwig's memory as addressed to him by his "younger brother," Algabal. Again the poetry does not present factual accounts but conveys the splendor of the artificial, sunless, non- or anti-natural subterranean realm that Algabal has created for himself. Here the deified emperor's power and profligacy are as absolute as his yearning for beauty. However, he is a figure of tragic isolation. The most famous poem of the book is the untitled poem about the great black flower that conveys Algabal's disillusionment with his fantastic schemes that used to (but can no more?) make him forget *Sorge* (care):

Mein garten bedarf nicht luft und nicht wärme
Der garten den ich mir selber erbaut
Und seiner vögel leblose schwärme
Haben noch nie einen frühling geschaut.

Von kohle die stämme·von kohle die äste
Und düstere felder am düsteren rain
Der früchte nimmer gebrochene läste
Glänzen wie lava im pinien-hain.

Ein grauer schein aus verborgener höhle
Verrät nicht wann morgen wann abend naht
Und staubige dünste der mandel-öle
Schweben auf beeten und anger und saat.

Wie zeug ich dich aber im heiligtume
—So fragt ich wenn ich es sinnend durchmass
In kühnen gespinsten der sorge vergass—
Dunkle grosse schwarze blume?

My garden requires no warmth. It is airless,
The garden which I have built as my own,
And the swarms of lifeless birds which it harbors
Have never beheld yet the blossoms of spring.

Of charcoal the tree trunks, of charcoal the
  branches,
And gloomy the fields within borders of gloom.

The boughs are full-laden with fruit never
  gathered
And gleam like lava in groves of pine.

A grayish glow from a hidden hollow
Betrays not when morning or evening nears
And dusty vapors from oil of almond
Hover above the crops and the leas.

But how, in my sanctuary, shall I create thee
—I asked when brooding I walked through this
  realm,
In bold speculations oblivious of care—
Wondrous flower, great and black?
(*Werke: Ausgabe in zwei Bänden*, vol. 1, p. 47)

The symbol of the black flower here is anti-romantic—that is, it is pointedly not a dream symbol like Novalis' blue flower or Baudelaire's "black tulip, blue Dahlia" of the "Pays de Cocagne" (Country of Abundance). Algabal "is concentrating on a complete reversal of the natural which is to culminate in the artificial production of an organic form," as Morwitz has pointed out—that is, in the willed creation of a large flower that possesses a color not found in nature.

The poetry of the *Algabal* cycle is an example of artifice turned into art. However, it does not spring from an "art for art's sake" concept. The poet's distance from reality does not mean that he does not wish to relate to it. While he does not and cannot, at this point, address himself directly in his poetry to the problems of his age, he is delivering a challenge in the guise of an immoralist. George is reported to have said, "*Algabal* is a revolutionary book."

He supervised its printing in Paris in September 1892 and went home to Bingen ill. It is safe to assume that what he lightly referred to as "the weakness of nerves from which each of us suffers a little" was a period of physical exhaustion and inner conflict that he was loath to discuss with anyone.

Great attention was paid by George to the cyclical order of the poems in every one of his works. The preferred order was tripartite and was first used in *Algabal*. The three parts of the book are "Im Unterreich" (In the Subterranean Realm), "Tage" (Days), and "Andenken" (Memories). The four poems of "Im Unter-reich" convey the luxurious and artificial splendor of the emperor's present surround-ings. In the ten poems of the second part some of his actions and reactions are evoked, all ominously pervaded by an atmosphere of crime and menace. All but two of the poems are written in the first-person singular. In the ninth Algabal hears noises of an impending palace revolt by "the herd that forgets to obey" and resolves to anticipate his "Ides of March" by a self-inflicted demise. He does not tell us, needless to say, whether he carried out the resolve; in the next poem he hears the sound of enchanting Syrian music from above ground and wonders whether to chase the musicians away or whether to yield to the temptation to remain among the living. Since this is the end of "Tage," to be followed by "Andenken," all spoken by the emperor in person, the reader has to forgo the satisfaction of hearing the end of the "story." Seven poems form the "Anden-ken," narcissistic reflections of feelings and events from the emperor's youth, such as his elevation to throne and divinity by the victori-ous Roman soldiers who were under the spell of his boyish beauty, his poisoning of two children in their sleep, and an early death wish ("Gloomy comforter, son of the night"). The book has one more poem, "Vogelschau" (Augury). It is outside the Algabal cycle, the lyrical "I" being the poet speaking of the next phase of his work. He sees white swallows fly again "in the wind so cold and clear!" after the exotic parrots and hummingbirds, which "flitted through the wonder-trees / in the forest of tusferi," have vanished. The return to a calmer, cooler poetry is thus augured.

The next two volumes of poetry share a general tone of calmness variously felt as serenity, subdued tension, or delicate melan-choly. One was published privately (two hundred copies) in 1895 under the lengthy threefold title *Die Bücher der Hirten- und Preisgedichte, der Sagen und Sänge und der hängenden Gärten* (The Books of Eclogues

and Eulogies, of Legends and Lays, and of the Hanging Gardens). The other, called *Das Jahr der Seele* (The Year of the Soul), appeared in 1897, published privately in two hundred cop-ies. No sharp chronological dividing line sep-arates the individual poems of the two cycles. The publication of *Das Jahr der Seele* was being planned when *Die Bücher* . . . was at the printer's, as we know from a letter George wrote to his Bingen friend Ida Coblenz some-time in 1895 in which he speaks of a "turning point" in his life and of "looking back upon a whole life which, I feel, is being replaced by an entirely different one. I want to end it with the publication of my *Bücher.*" He then mentions that *Hymnen, Pilgerfahrten,* and *Algabal* are to be in the first volume (it appeared in 1898), that *Die Bücher* . . . are to be in the second (also in 1898), and that "the latest poems" are to be published as *Annum* [*sic*] *animae* or *Das Jahr der Seele* in the third. These were to be regular public editions, available through the book trade. Everything that he had put out hitherto had appeared in private editions of one hundred to two hundred copies, owing to both limited demand and limited funds. Actually *Das Jahr der Seele* had also to be published privately first, and then publicly in 1898.

The short preface to *Die Bücher* . . . implies that the poet intended to put an end to roman-tic historicizing and to glorifying the past in poetry. His books are to contain motifs and reflections of the three great realms of Antiq-uity, the Middle Ages, and the Orient insofar as his modern consciousness produces a live response to them. In his own words, "Of the great realms of our civilization, no more is contained here than what is still alive in some of us."

The craftsmanship practiced to this end is subtle. The poet does not merely evoke the original themes to which his "soul" responds. The motifs, while traceable to erudite sources of previous poetic treatment, are transformed by a modern sensibility. All of the fourteen *Hirtengedichte* are rhymeless, and all but two are non-stanzaic. The meter is predominantly iambic, with five feet in some poems, six in others. Two are in hexameters. No strictly Greek metric patterns are used. The first three poems consist of nine, ten, and ten serene and stately lines respectively and deal with the relationship of two maidens who share the fate of having lost their betrothed on the same day, a loss that marked the beginning of their friendship. They spend each anniversary of the day in reminiscing and walking together to the well to fetch water, until after seven years one of them senses behind her "sister's" quiet happiness a preoccupation with a new "secret": from behind the vine-covered fence she expects someone to come and carry her away. The transfigured simplicity of the theme is ingratiatingly deceptive. The sparse and calmly measured words are certainly similar to some Alcaic or Sapphic strophes. However, the fact that the water pitchers are made of gray clay and that there are two poplars and a pine tree by the well show that the locale is not meant to be identified as Mediterranean. Moreover, one must not overlook the symbolism of the trees: if we take the poplars to stand for the girls, the one pine indicates that the betrothed was one and the same man. Similarly, the young hero of "Tag des Hirten" (The Shepherd's Day) is not simply an untutored ancient shepherd. Enjoying the fine spring weather, he abandons his flock to wander through a cool valley with rushing mountain streams, goes to sleep in the forest, and in the evening climbs a peak to admire the sunset, "crowning . . . himself with holy leaves." In other words, he is rather like an enthusiastic young poet in the vicinity of the Rhine, leaving "the herd" behind to rise above the everyday world.

The poem "Der Herr der Insel" (The Lord of the Island), in the same group and written in blank verse, tells a beautiful fable that allows no optimistic conclusion about the fate and function of the poet in the modern world. The "Lord" of the title is a great bird with purple plumage who "when rising in low and heavy flight . . . looked like a somber cloud." At night he dwells on the beach and attracts the dolphins with his song. Thus he has lived from the beginning of creation and has been seen only by the shipwrecked. When one day "the white sails of men" approach in order to land, he rises and, after surveying his territory once more, opens his great wings and "departs" (i.e., from this life), uttering "subdued notes of pain." The resemblance of this bird to Baudelaire's "Albatross" is evident, but the symbolist's image for the *poète maudit* is that of a pitiful sufferer who is mocked by the sailors as Christ was by the soldiers, whereas the Lord of the Island vanishes without losing an ounce of his dignity. One cannot but be reminded of the report that when Germany lost World War I and there was, for a while, the danger that the Bolshevists might take over the country, George carried poison with him. In 1933, soon after Hitler had come to power, the poet left quietly for Switzerland.

The eleven *Preisgedichte* are addressed to "young men and women of this time," each of whom is given a Greek pseudonym. Two, for instance, are superscribed *An Menippa,* which stands for Ida Coblenz. Among the others addressed are the two young Belgian poets Edmond Rassenfosse and Paul Gérardy; the Frenchman Albert Saint-Paul, who had introduced George to *Flowers of Evil* and to Mallarmé's Tuesday evenings; the Polish poet Waclaw Lieder, some of whose poems George translated into German; and the philosopher-psychologist-graphologist Ludwig Klages, whom the poet had met in Munich. The poems, mostly characterizations, memories, and admonitions, are early evidence of the pedagogical *eros* at work.

The middle book of the volume, the *Sagen und Sänge,* reflects George's knowledge of and feeling for the Middle Ages. The first rather lengthy rhymed poem is "Sporenwache," a title that refers to the prayerful night vigil before the dubbing of a knight. It presents a young nobleman alone in the candle-lit chapel where a valiant ancestor lies buried. Details of the chapel, the tomb, and the knight's attire are authentically pictured. His meditations, told in the first-person singular, reveal the state of his soul before the final heroic dedication: thoughts of a golden-haired maiden cross his mind. He is upset by that tempting vision. Fortunately, his glance lights upon the figure of the Redeemer, who is sitting on the Virgin's lap with outstretched arms, whereupon he vows total allegiance to service in the army of his Lord. It is easy to discern here the poet's respect for, and idealization of, an individual's dedication to a high ethical purpose with a touch of the ascetic. However, George's predilection for ritual and for the solemnity of cult as such is equally important, as is the poet's original touch of ending the poem with a miracle: a covey of winged heads of angels flies up from the altar.

None of the poems of *Sagen und Sänge* should be taken as personal confessions; they are imaginative poetic creations. Thus also the poem "Vom Ritter der sich verliegt" (The Knight Who Lies Idly) exists for its own sake; it is a virtuoso piece of sound images:

> *Hör ich nicht dumpf ein klirren ·*
> *Kämpfer die die rosse schirren?*
> *Bange rufe vom altan ·*
> *Speere schwirren?*
>
> *Drunten schlägt ein tor nur an.*
>
> *Ist es nicht der gäste lache?*
> *Emsig knecht und kastellan*
> *Unter rebenschmuckem dache?*
> *Frohe wache?*
>
> *Wurde nicht in zarte saiten*
> *Ein gedehnter griff getan:*
> *Ahnungsloser schöner zeiten*
> *Scheues gleiten?*
>
> *Drunten schlägt ein tor nur an.*

Do I hear a muffled clatter?
Fighters harnessing their horses?
Anxious calls from balconies?
Lances whirring?

It was but a clanging gate.

Do I hear the guests rejoicing?

Busy servants, castle-stewards
Under vine-decked galleries?
Happy sentries?

Did not someone gently waken
Tender strings to praise the fairest
Distant times which unsuspecting
Shyly glided by?

It was but a clanging gate.

Only the title and the first of the three stanzas rendering the knight's acoustic deceptions have a specifically medieval flavor. A more personal involvement informs the poem "Frauenlob." The title refers to the late medieval poet, and the first of the "Meistersinger," Heinrich von Meissen, who had earned his sobriquet through his varied and unending praise of women in his song. At his funeral a large crowd of women is said to have wept for him and to have poured "choicest wines, flowers, and jewels" into his grave. George presents Frauenlob's devotion to women as ever unrequited; hence the offerings after his death form a bitter contrast. This again expresses the disillusioned and sometimes sentimentalized view that the young poets of the late nineteenth century took of themselves and their lonely position vis-à-vis modern society.

A group of fifteen poems forms the second part of this middle book, under the title *Sänge eines fahrenden Spielmanns* (Songs of a Wandering Minstrel); they include restrained and tender wooing notes sounded by the minstrel who will be satisfied by a loving gesture on the part of the adored lady, or the soliloquy of the highborn girl who threw a ring to the fiddler but is prepared to face reality if he should forget her. One of the finest "songs" consists of three melancholy stanzas in which the minstrel-poet expresses fatherly anxiety in the face of the inexorable realities of life and decides to leave the beloved "child":

> *Sieh mein kind ich gehe.*
> *Denn du darfst nicht kennen*
> *Nicht einmal durch nennen*
> *Menschen müh und wehe.*

Mir ist um dich bange.
Sieh mein kind ich gehe
Dass auf deiner wange
Nicht der duft verwehe.

Würde dich belehren ·
Müsste dich versehren
Und das macht mir wehe.
Sieh mein kind ich gehe.

See, my child, I go now.
For you must not know,
I must never name,
Man's distress and pain.

I am grieving for you
See, my child, I go.
From your cheek the fragrance
Must not blow away.

I would have to speak of
Things which will give hurt,
I would feel much anguish.
See, my child, I go.
(*Werke: Ausgabe in drei Bänden,* vol. 1, p. 95)

The third of the cultural realms that nurtured the poet's soul is the Orient. George knew and loved *The Arabian Nights' Entertainments* from childhood and continued to be fascinated by the Near and Far East all through his life. He knew Christoph Martin Wieland's *Oberon* (1780) and Goethe's *West-östlicher Divan (The West-Eastern Divan,* 1819).

Whereas Wieland's approach to the Orient, in the opening lines of his epic poem *Oberon,* is a learned one—he asks the Muses to saddle the Hippogriff for his "ride to the old land of romances"—George enters directly and swiftly the land that was his own. He rides a magic horse that is like El Borak, the fabled steed the angel Gabriel gave to Muhammad so that he could, even in his lifetime, instantly traverse the seven heavenly spheres to visit Paradise. The short opening poem of the *Hängende Gärten* says:

Wir werden noch einmal zum lande fliegen
Das dir von früh auf eigen war:
Du musst dich an den hals des zelters schmiegen ·

Du drückst an seinen zäumen den rubin
In einer heissen nacht und ohne fahr
Gelangst du hin.

We now shall fly to repossess the land
That was your own from early days:
You must hold closely to the palfrey's neck
And press the magic ruby on the rein.
Then safely faring through one fevered night
You will arrive.

During the time when George was writing this book his acquaintance with Ida Coblenz had developed into friendship. She had reacted to his poetry with remarkable perception and was especially fond of what she called the "Semiramis-Lieder." She said many years later that they were written for her. It would be erroneous to designate this or any other personal experience as the source of these poems, but here the lyrical "I" is obviously not as alone and removed from the world as the lyrical "I" of *Algabal.* Characteristically, the lyrical subject in the *Hängende Gärten* is again a ruler, one who has felt predestined for kingship from his childhood days, as is recalled in the sixth poem, "Kindliches Königtum" (Childhood Kingdom). He remembers vividly the days when "In distant valleys hidden you created / Your state in serried bushes' secrecy . . ." and when "The comrades whom your glance enflamed for you / Felt honored by your coin and grant of lands." The Oriental master-servant relationship appealed to George.

"Kindliches Königtum" contains the earliest occurrence of the word *Staat* (State) in the sense of a group of faithful followers. The idea of devoted service and voluntary submission of the will to the Master's greater insight is at the core of George's later thinking and practice in the gathering of an elite around him. In 1930 Wolters published *Stefan George und die Blätter für die Kunst: Deutsche Geistesgeschichte seit 1890* (Stefan George and Pages for Art: German Intellectual History Since 1890). The presumptuous note in the subtitle is hard to miss.

The *Buch der hängenden Gärten* moves in a

STEFAN GEORGE

purely fairy-tale atmosphere. The returning ruler conquers the enemy's city and enters it in a conciliatory spirit. He then yields to pleasure and luxury and forgets the active life in his splendid palace. The tortuous tensions of Algabal are absent, but the real world seems like a delusion. The mood of the poem that ends the first section (of ten poems), "Friedens-abend" (Peaceful Evening), is reminiscent of the "Knight Who Lies Idly." The succeeding fifteen non-stanzaic love poems of between seven and fourteen lines each are the *Hängende Gärten* proper, although the title is probably meant to suggest a dreamlike state between reality and illusion and is not a direct allusion to the legendary terraced gardens of the famous Babylonian queen. The suspense of longing anxiety and passion is evoked by dense and stately language. There is in at least two poems the suggestion of fever heat in the garden, but this is emotional rather than physical or climatic. A close look at the details of the vegetation reveals that we are not necessarily in a Persian or Arabic landscape. The one mention of palm trees and the white sand outside the city does indeed suggest a southern or eastern climate, but otherwise we have purple-black thorn, "velvet-plumed fern," clumps of centaury, bluebells, silver willows, and fishponds, which clearly include European flora and fauna. The final poem of this section speaks of separation and termination through powerful nature symbols:

Hohe blumen blassen oder brechen ·
Es erblasst und bricht der weiher glas
Und ich trete fehl im morschen gras ·
Palmen mit den spitzen fingern stechen.
Mürber blätter zischendes gewühl
Jagen ruckweis unsichtbare hände
Draussen um des edens fahle wände.
Die nacht ist überwölkt und schwül.

Slender blooms are drab or broken
Drab and broken is the fishponds' glass
And I step amiss in withered grass.
Palms with pointed fingers prick me.
Weary leaves in hissing turmoil

Jerkily are chased by unseen hands
All around our Eden's fallow walls.
The night is overcast and close.

Part 3 of the book deals with the end of the dream kingdom. The ruler finds he is about to lose both his love and his country because he has been neglecting his royal duties. The consequence of the king's practicing "tender airs" is that he lacks the strength to take up arms for defense, and he loses his kingdom to an invader. Finally he decides to end his life by drowning. The cycle closes with one of the finest examples of George's terse poetic sorcery, "Stimmen im Strom" (Voices in the River). It renders the lure of the water, and we hear the waves' promise of blissful dissolution:

Liebende klagende zagende wesen
Nehmt eure zuflucht in unser bereich·
Werdet geniessen und werdet genesen·
Arme und worte umwinden euch weich.

Leiber wie muscheln · korallene lippen
Schwimmen und tönen in schwankem palast·
Haare verschlungen in ästige klippen
Nahend und wieder vom strudel erfasst.

Bläuliche lampen die halb nur erhellen·
Schwebende säulen auf kreisendem schuh—
Geigend erzitternde ziehende wellen
Schaukeln in selig beschauliche ruh.

Müdet euch aber das sinnen das singen·
Fliessender freuden bedächtiger lauf·
Trifft euch ein kuss: und ihr löst euch in ringen
Gleitet als wogen hinab und hinauf.

Lovers lamenting and laden with sorrow
Come and seek comfort in our domain.
Here waits enchantment and here will be healing,
Words will caress you and arms will enfold.

Coral-lined lips among conch-shaped bodies
Swim in the watery palace and sing.
Hair is entwined in the branches of seaweed
Nearing and ever receding again.

Torches creating a faint bluish twilight
Hovering columns encircling the house,
Waters like viols in tremulous motion,
Rock you in blissful contemplative calm.

458

But in the end, song and thought leave you weary
Slow-floating pleasure is stopped by a kiss
And you dissolve into soft undulation,
Glide as a wave up and down in the stream.

The water that entices to death is a variation of streams and fountains that the poet uses elsewhere as a mirror and a means to attain self-knowledge. Here it represents the allurement of death after the victim has attained self-knowledge and felt ultimate despair.

Regarding the whole of George's work from *Hymnen* to *Die Bücher* . . . , we see that a close connection exists between the dream of kingship and the love of woman. Algabal moves in a void, exhibiting no truly human quality as a ruler or as a lover. His incapacity for love and the inhuman aspects of his reign cause his unhappiness and death. The owner of the "hanging gardens," however, is at first a successful ruler and a popular hero, and in love he proves equally successful. His death is the result of the loss of both his kingdom and his love. He falls in love when his power is greatest, and he loses his kingdom because his passion makes him neglectful of his rule, and subsequently he loses his beloved. Both experiences, power and love, are conceived in the same terms; namely, they create relationships of inequality. The autocrat is the master over his slaves; this same power gives him the right to the most beautiful and chaste of women. At the same time the terms of master and servant are to a degree interchangeable. In love the "master" often assumes the attitude of the worshiping servant. This love degenerates quite frequently into servility. Likewise, George's minstrels and knights will do anything for their ladies, no matter how cruel and cold the latter may be. In George's hierarchical thinking the relation between the sexes is based upon an initial plea by one partner and the possibility of a granting by the other. The alternative of a harmonious "give-and-take" hardly exists. Nonetheless *Hängende Gärten* does contain an approximation of a more normal human attitude, both in the ruler's magnanimity toward the conquered and in his brief union with the beloved.

The next volume, *Das Jahr der Seele,* has gone through more editions and has attracted more readers than any other of George's books. It was originally dedicated to Coblenz; but the poet put an abrupt end to his friendship with her when, in 1895, she formed an intimate bond with Richard Dehmel, a poet whom George detested and whom she eventually married. The dedication of the *Jahr* was changed to the poet's sister, whom Ida disliked.

While there are half a dozen poems in the volume which were written in direct response to the Ida experience and while the book as a whole could be seen as a reflection of the experience of woman as a companion, an experience that ended on a note of resignation or even renunciation, the poet's own warning should be heeded. In the preface to the book he insists that "seldom are I and You so much the same soul as in this book." In other words, the book is not to be seen as a latecomer in the illustrious line of German love and nature lyrics from Friedrich Gottlieb Klopstock and Goethe to the romantics and Heinrich Heine. These poems are not personal confessions, nor do they attest to a harmony between the poet and the forces of nature. If there is a dialogue between an I and a You (both of which appear on occasion in the plural), they are both fictitious, although authentic, subjects in the poet's consciousness to whom he has assigned their roles.

Likewise, the natural phenomena we find in the poems are skillfully manipulated. They reflect nature as subjected to human interference. We are in a fenced park with a gate and benches. The beech trees form a shady avenue. And to our surprise, the "year of the soul" consists of only three seasons: fall, winter, and summer. The well-known opening poem is spoken in the form of an invitation, "Come to the park they say is dead . . . ," and the addressed is asked to see how the last flowers of autumn, far from being dead, can easily be shaped into an autumnal image. Whether the

459

colorful remnants of the declining year symbolize individual memories of the poet or the obscure beauties of the *fin de siècle,* there is in any case a restrained joy at the artist's discovery of beauty and at his ability to give it form. In another autumn poem the fruits are said to "knock" on the ground, that is, they do not drop on the ground as nature and wind would have it; rather they knock or tap on the ground with a purpose as a man might rap at a door.

Sad despair begins the winter section, "Waller im Schnee" (Pilgrims in the Snow), but we note again the distance from and the manipulation of nature in the use of language that refers to human crafts, such as weaving and sewing: the snow "flakes" are said to "weave a pale sheet" where the soul would be bedded. In the third part, "Sieg des Sommers" (Summer's Victory), rather tentatively and haltingly the poet fights his way through to a note of affirmation of the joy of living in and for the here and now. Among the symbols for the victorious summer there are "silver tufts" that form the trimming (as of a garment) on the meadow's edge.

In the same volume, following the three seasons of the "year," there is a large group of poems that are expressly occasional or directly addressed to friends, entitled "Überschriften und Widmungen" (Inscriptions and Dedications). The volume's final section contains the thirty-two "Traurige Tänze" (Sad Dances), which form melancholy variations on the themes and motifs evoked in the "seasons" of the soul, including the anguish of poetic creation and the overwhelming force of human longing. Characteristically, the poet does not allow the book to end on a negative note. In the last poem he can discern "the tender-breathing wind of distant land" coming as a "liberator."

It is surprising how quickly George's reputation grew during the second half of the 1890's, despite the apparent inaccessibility of his poetry. Conscious and careful management on the part of the poet is evident. After he had gathered around him a select group of talented young men who shared his tastes and ideas, he decided that the time had come to approach a more general reading public. One means to this end was a number of favorably disposed articles (nine altogether) that appeared in well-known, reputable journals between 1894 and 1900. The authors, to all intents and purposes hand-picked by the poet, included the poets von Hofmannsthal and Karl Wolfskehl and several Berlin University professors. A wide section of the intelligentsia was thus introduced to the "New Poetry."

Moreover, during these years George gradually shifted his point of view from his early cosmopolitanism to a more deliberate identification with German concerns. He saw his work as a continuation of the German literary tradition and regarded his mission as a peculiarly German one and himself as the chosen herald of a revitalized heritage that had lain buried since the early part of the nineteenth century. In 1896 Jean Paul Richter (known as Jean Paul), by then almost forgotten, was enthusiastically acclaimed by George in the *Blätter* as an early proponent of the art-for-art's sake principle and as Germany's "greatest poetic power (not the greatest poet, Goethe is that)." In 1900 George, together with Wolfskehl, published a selection of Jean Paul's work as the first in a three-volume anthology called *Deutsche Dichtung* (German Poetry).

Another remarkable rediscovery took place when the gifted young Norbert von Hellingrath (1888–1916) became acquainted with George and his poetry in 1909 and, almost simultaneously, with the work of Friedrich Hölderlin (1770–1843), one of the greatest lyrical poets of Germany, who had, like Jean Paul, been neglected by the critics and ignored by the nineteenth-century reading public. The whole body of his poetry, which included outstanding translations from ancient Greek authors, had been written between 1794 and 1804 (the rest of his life was clouded by mental illness). In the Stuttgart Public Library Archives, the young Hellingrath discovered Hölderlin's translations of Pindar's Odes into magnificent German. He was able to decipher the extremely difficult handwriting. Boehringer reports that after the publication of the eighth volume of *Blätter für die Kunst* (1908–1909), George averred that the ninth one would not appear until "the gods themselves would send a contribution." In 1910 he was able to open volume 9 with some of Hölderlin's Pindar translations, and the complete edition came out in the same year. Thus began the rehabilitation of the genius of Hölderlin. It continued with further valuable manuscript discoveries and with the new critical edition of his complete works.

George's constant traveling between Berlin, Munich, Frankfurt, Vienna, and Heidelberg demonstrates the care and devotion with which he cultivated multiple personal contacts. The result was the presence of Georgeans in the chief intellectual centers of Germany from around 1900 on. Anticipating the moment when his stature would be recognized, George said bluntly to Hofmannsthal in 1897, "For, as you know, not to seek success is great; to seek and not achieve it, indecent."

Der Teppich des Lebens und die Lieder von Traum und Tod, mit einem Vorspiel (The Tapestry of Life and the Songs of Dream and Death, with a Prelude, 1900) reveals the new didactic stance in all its aspects, especially in the *Vorspiel.* This is a cycle of twenty-four poems of four quatrains each, strictly identical in form. The composition is austere and the diction solemn. It is conceived as an inner dramatic dialogue between the poet and "a naked angel" who is the messenger of *das schöne Leben* (to be paraphrased, perhaps, as "the nobly beautiful life"). The Christian dogma of man's redemption had lost validity for George, and the concept of the tragic life of unredeemed modern man was equally unacceptable. However, the poet became convinced that he was an especially chosen instrument of a spiritual power whose will he carried out when he charged himself with the task of creating a new quality of life. The sudden appearance, in the first poem, of the messenger from *das schöne Leben* suggests that the concept is something the poet had known

before and is not a new revelation; it is his own formulation. God, or a god, as the source of the angel's authority is not mentioned in the *Vorspiel.* The absence of any invocation before the messenger's appearance indicates that he represents the poet's alter ego. The biblical image of Jacob wrestling with the angel is used to express the poet's possessing himself of spiritual power and enthusiasm for his mission: "I will not let you go unless you bless me."

The "beautiful" life is to be lived here and now; it is akin to the Greek *kairos,* the opportune moment that is to be realized in this earthly life or not at all. It is a matter of being, not of becoming. The quality of life to be led by those seized by the ideal is dependent on their aristocratic predisposition or instinctive nobility. The adherent must rise above the currents or conflicts of contemporary life and shun such readily available modes of life as Christianity, the pursuit of scientific-materialistic progress, or even adherence to the "small band" that professes to imitate the ancient Greeks. Although George's love of the south and its clarity of thought and climate never ceased, he now heeds the angel's command to love the "fields and winds" of the homeland.

To learn to live the *schöne Leben* required moral discipline and intense cultivation of personality. The great task of the poet was to impart the message to the circle of his disciples. Within this *Kreis,* careful distinctions of spiritual rank and maturity were made. However, the hierarchic structure was not embodied in anything resembling a dogma or set of rules. It was expected that the disciples would give allegiance to the poet-prophet as unwaveringly as he followed the angelic command; but his guidance was as informal as that of the peripatetic philosophers.

Despite the new focus on his German spiritual ancestors, George did not fail to honor the great luminaries of the Western tradition as a whole. The national and cosmopolitan aspects of his mission were seen as correlative; in fact, George and his followers shared the conviction that a regenerated Germany would lead a European cultural revival. Hence the poets of ancient Greece, Shakespeare, Dante, and Petrarch are apostrophized in the eighteenth poem of the *Vorspiel.*

The opening poem of the central part of the book, "Der Teppich" (The Tapestry), offers a clue to the complexity and difficulty of the task with which George finds himself faced when he attempts to interpret existence. For him the meaning of the pattern is hidden and enigmatic, discernible only at rare moments and only by the elect:

Hier schlingen menschen mit gewächsen tieren
Sich fremd zum bund umrahmt von seidner
   franze
Und blaue sicheln weisse sterne zieren
Und queren sie in dem erstarrten tanze.

Und kahle linien ziehn in reich-gestickten
Und teil um teil ist wirr und gegenwendig
Und keiner ahnt das rätsel der verstrickten . . .
Da eines abends wird das werk lebendig.

Da regen schauernd sich die toten äste
Die wesen eng von strich und kreis umspannet
Und treten klar vor die geknüpften quäste
Die lösung bringend über die ihr sannet!

Sie ist nach willen nicht: ist nicht für jede
Gewohtne stunde: ist kein schatz der gilde.
Sie wird den vielen nie und nie durch rede
Sie wird den seltnen selten im gebilde.

Here men are intertwined with plants and beasts,
Strange, but enframed within a silken fringe,
And azure crescents, milk-white stars adorn
And cut across them in their frozen dance.

And simple lines traverse a rich design
And parts are juxtaposed in crass confusion
And no one disentangles the enigma . . .
Until one evening it springs to life.

In awe the branches, dead so long, now move,
The figures tightly held by strokes and curves
Now clearly step before the knotted tassels,
Presenting the solution which you pondered!

It will not come when bidden, nor observe
A wonted hour: nor be owned by guilds
Or multitudes. No words will give the key.
The chosen who discern the plan are few.

During the late 1890's George was attracted to two men: Klages and Alfred Schuler, who together with Wolfskehl formed the so-called *Kosmische Runde* (Cosmic Round) and who believed that intellectualism (*Geist*) was the soul-destroying evil of modern civilization. Schuler presented himself as the clairvoyant reincarnation of an ancient Roman and lectured on the Eternal City. Klages, philosopher, graphologist, and racist, based his ideas for a return to a Teutonic, primitive, pre-Christian creed on the writings on matriarchy of the Swiss philosopher and anthropologist Johann Jakob Bachofen, for example his *Das Mutterrecht* (Matriliny, or Mother Right, 1861). In the long run George had no use for occultism. The relationship to Klages and Schuler cooled gradually until George precipitated a complete break early in 1904, although Wolfskehl and George remained close friends the rest of their lives.

The so-called Maximin experience of 1904 and its poetic transformation was George's answer to the cosmics. In the spring of 1902 George met an attractive fourteen-year-old boy with a radiant personality and a gift for poetry. His name was Maximilian Kronberger, and he attended the Maximilian-Gymnasium at Munich. We have an account of his friendship with the poet, as recorded by the boy in a sober and businesslike manner in his posthumously published diary. A fatal attack of meningitis put an end to his life in April 1904. It was a terrible blow to George, who, in a letter to a friend, wrote of "the crushing end: I mourn an incomprehensible and early death that almost led me, too, to the last abyss."

The encounter soon underwent a poetic transformation. The impression the boy made on the poet must have been profound, for George and some of his disciples did not hesitate to compare this experience to Dante's encounter with Beatrice and Hölderlin's with Diotima. Maximilian Kronberger was renamed Maximin. A slim volume, *Maximin: Ein Gedenkbuch* (A Memorial Volume), edited by George, containing poems by the Master and members of the circle as well as some of Kronberger's own was published in 1906. The first sentence of George's *Vorrede* (Preface) sets the Dantean tone: "We had just surpassed the midday height of our life and we were anxious as we contemplated the near future." The unselfconscious nobility and natural simplicity of the youth appeared to be a divine embodiment of *das schöne Leben,* by 1906 also referred to as *das neue Leben* (the new life). The death of the youth is seen as tragic but meaningful. During his short earthly existence he had lived the exemplary "beautiful" life. He was transfigured into the god whose re-embodiment appears only "once in every epoch." George saw himself as the divine youth's prophet and thus finally as the sanctified poet and seer of his age. The strange mythological creation of a spiritual son whose servant and "son" George has now become is contained in the twenty-two poems that form the central cycle or ring of the seven parts of the volume entitled *Der siebente Ring* (The Seventh Ring, 1907), George's seventh volume of poetry.

The Maximin myth alienated many of George's admirers and scandalized those who had been indifferent. His Dutch friend, the poet Albert Verwey, was shocked and rejected the apparent deification of the sixteen-year-old Kronberger as an extremely German idea, while admitting that the poetry was a magnificent tour de force. The poet Rudolf Alexander Schröder (1878–1962) protested bitingly against the blasphemous undertaking of creating a "boy mediator." It is true, however, that George never attempted to persuade others to make the deified Maximin a part of their personal beliefs.

One of the facts which shows that the deified Maximin is an abstraction is the organization of the poems in *Der siebente Ring.* The core, that is, the fourth "ring" or group of poems, speaks of the advent, death, and transfiguration of the god. The preceding third group of twenty-one poems forms the antechamber, so to speak, of the sacred central part of the book. It includes two poems that resulted directly from the Maximin experience, some that speak in general terms about love and passion, and eight fervently erotic poems which were actually written before George knew Kronberger, but now appear to be connected with him. The outer rings (the first and seventh), on the other hand, contain far less personal and esoteric matter. The first ring is of quite general import, as its title "Zeitgedichte" (Poems Addressed to Our Age) indicates. The most famous among this group, "Das Zeitgedicht," begins with the stern, sonorous line, "Ich euch gewissen · ich euch stimme . . ." ("I am your conscience, I am your voice . . ."). It is a direct address to the poet's contemporaries in which he calls them to account. He judges that they have wasted their vital strength while he, the poet, knows those things that will endure:

Da ihr aus gift und kot die seele kochtet
Verspriztet ihr der guten säfte rest.
. . . .
Eins das von je war (keiner kennt es) währet
Und blum und jugend lacht und sang erklingt.

Of dung and poison was your soul concocted,
You spilled all that remained of precious sap.
. . . .
What was of old (by no one seen) endures
And youth and flowers laugh and songs abound.

In the poem "Nietzsche" George does not indicate that he owes anything to the philosopher but recognizes a certain kinship in outlook. He sees Friedrich Nietzsche's greatness in his proclaiming the end of an old era. However, he pities him for his failure to formulate and put into practice the way in which the new was to be brought about. When he wrote the poem in 1900, he felt he knew the secret of the new life and defined it as "constraint within a circle of love." An almost literal quotation from Nietzsche's *Versuch einer Selbstkritik* (*Attempt at Self-Criticism,* 1886) concludes the last of the poem's four resounding eight-line stanzas: ". . . this new soul was / Not meant to speak but should have sung instead."

The seventh and last ring is composed of similarly outward-directed, mostly short gnomic poems addressed to contemporaries or praising historic places and personages. The sixth cycle, entitled "Lieder," will be referred to below in connection with a similar group of "Songs" in George's last volume of poetry. Between *Der siebente Ring* and that last volume, however, there was *Der Stern des Bundes* (The Star of the Covenant, 1913), the book that, together with Goethe's *Faust,* German soldiers are said to have carried in their knapsacks as they went to war in 1914.

It is important to realize that the majority of George's poems from after *Der siebente Ring* on are didactic "State" poetry (George and his disciples referred to themselves and the future of the new or regenerated elite as the "State") and that the Maximin myth inspires and directs especially the gnomic poetry of *Der Stern des Bundes,* his most rigidly formal cycle of poems. It has precisely one hundred poems, totaling one thousand lines, and is subdivided into an introduction (nine poems), three "Books" of thirty poems each, and a "Schlusschor" (Final Chorus). However esoteric and cryptic they may appear at first sight, they are poems, not a breviary; that is, their value does not depend on the relative merit of the cult they serve. The first section, "Eingang" (Introit), deals with the god and what he did for and through the poet. Echoes of the biblical creation myth are mingled with classical allusions:

Neblige dünste ballet euch zu formen!
Taucht silberfüsse aus der purpurwelle!
So drang durch unser brünstiges beschwören
Der wehe schrei nach dem lebendigen kerne.

Let misty vapours take on clustered form!
Let silver feet emerge from purple waves!
Thus through our fervent conjurations broke
The woeful cry for living substance.

The *Erstes Buch* (First Book) is about the poet: his past, his work, his manifold functions, and his relationship to his contemporaries, friends ("helpers of yore," before the advent of Maximin), and the cosmic. The *Zweites Buch* (Second Book) treats specifically the poet's insight into the characters and problems of his close friends after Kronberger's death. In each of these poems the poet and the respective friend are engaged in a dialogue. No names are used. The new form of Eros is presented in connection with the idea of *geistige Zeugung* (spiritual procreation). Associations of men who devote themselves to this concept, like the *Kreis,* are held to be more enduringly creative than men and women can be together. After Ida Coblenz only the painter Reinhold Lepsius' wife Sabine had a more than casual acquaintance with George. Some more motherly-sisterly figures enjoyed his confidence in later years, but on the whole women had no part in the "State," and while casual friendships and love affairs were tolerated marriage was practically taboo. The irreparable break between Friedrich Gundolf (1880–1931) and the Master came when Gundolf insisted on marrying Elisabeth Salomon. He had previously been prevented by George from marrying a Swedish girl. George's disapproval of his favorite disciple's choice of marriage partners must be seen in the light of the close personal and working relationship that had developed between the two men from their first meeting in 1899, when Gundolf had begun his studies in German literature. He sought advice and help from the Master on anything he wrote; they collaborated, for instance, on Gundolf's new translation of Shakespeare's dramas that began appearing in 1908. Besides disliking certain ones among Gundolf's girlfriends, George feared not only that marriage would create distance between the two men, but also that Gundolf's career as a brilliant literary critic and university lecturer at Heidelberg would suffer.

The *Drittes Buch* (Third Book) deals, in its first ten poems, with the meaning of spiritual rebirth and with particular aspects of the new nobility of the spirit. No. 6 warns the newly born to beware of romantic yearnings while in female company and to shun the seductiveness of sweet music, for both will sap the strength of the soul. A gradually hardening antagonism toward music, as being inferior to poetry, can be traced in George's development as it ran almost parallel to the rejection of women. At the same time, a number of George's earlier poems attracted some notable composers. Arnold Schönberg, for instance, set the fifteen poems of the middle part of the *Hängende Gärten* to music for voice and piano in 1907–1908.

The next ten poems represent the "laws" of the Georgean "State." No. 11 tells the young to be hard and forward-looking, to be prepared to act, and, if necessary, to use a dagger:

Ihr sollt das morsche aus dem munde spein
Ihr sollt den dolch im lorbeerstrausse tragen

Ye shall spit from your mouth all that is rotten
And carry among laurel leaves the dagger

No. 12 succinctly brands the asking or granting of forgiveness as abominable. The disciple must atone for great wrongs by learning from heroes to throw himself onto his sword and must atone for small ones "silently by deeds." Among the body of George's dedicatory poems there are a few that commemorate young suicide victims.

No. 14 defines the three stages of knowledge or wisdom: inborn, handed-down, and the wisdom that opens the gate to final initiation. However, the third stage is attained only by "those with whom the god has slept." Another version of the same idea is to be found in the twenty-fourth poem: "Ein weiser ist nur wer vom gott aus weiss" (paraphrased: "A wise man is only he whose knowledge stems from the god"). This is a rendering of line 154 of Pindar's second Olympic Ode: "Sophos o polla eidos phya" ("Wise is he who knows much from nature"). It is significant that George says "god" where Pindar has "nature." It is not certain, however, whether he made the change with knowledge of the original or simply took it over from Tycho Mommsen's translation, which Morwitz had brought to his attention. This poem and the rest of the last group of ten

are poems of praise, all based on more or less veiled instances in the poet's experience. The twenty-ninth explains what happens to the disciples when they have reached maturity:

Entlassen seid ihr aus dem innern raum
Der zelle für den kern geballter kräfte
Und trächtiger schauer in das weite land.
Aus jedes aug erriet sich hier sein grad
Aus jedes form die art zukünftigen wagens
Ihr seid im gang getrennt im zweck gesellt.
Euch kreist im blut dreifacher wein der liebe
Die starken heute sind die gestern schönen
Gediehn durch überschattung des Erweckers
Des kraft euch stählt des lächeln euch beglänzt.

You are dismissed now from the inner room,
The cell that breeds the core of potent strength
And pregnant showers. So go forth.
The glance of each will tell his worth and rank,
The form of each his kind of future daring.
By separate paths you reach a common goal.
The threefold wine of love flows in your blood.
The fair of yesterday today are strong,
Have grown through the Arouser's shielding care
Whose smile and strength will radiate through
    you.

The beginning lines of this poem are a typical example of the ever-recurring biological imagery for the growth of the "new life."

George was convinced that the poet's dream was the stuff that life could be made of. On the other hand, he insisted that he *could* have been a man of action. He is reported to have said to Boehringer, "If at the age of twenty I had had 20,000 soldiers, I would have put all the potentates of Europe to flight." On the same occasion he said that he had completely overcome the temptation to let himself be lured into the active life. Breysig has recorded a conversation of 3 November 1916 in which George stated that he would "certainly be able to turn to politics. . . . If, during the war, things should take a turn for the worse, and no better person was available to assume the leadership [i.e., the office of chancellor], he would do it." The problem of the active life versus the poet's is the subject matter of the ninth poem of the first book of the *Stern,* where George alludes to the Greek poet Tyrtaeus, whose songs stimulated the Spartan soldiers to deeds of heroism and thus helped win a battle.

George never wrote or said anything that could be considered war propaganda. However, his thinking was more and more directed toward Germany's national and international problems. He saw far sooner than some of his younger friends (i.e., in the fall of 1916, if not earlier) that World War I was a disaster for his country and that defeat was a possibility. Yet he also believed in the necessity of war and prophesied that "tens of thousands" would have to be killed before the building of a new world could begin and that this might involve everybody in another world war. A poem that was published in 1921 as one of *Drei Gesänge* (Three Cantos) bears the prophetic title "Einem jungen Führer im ersten Weltkrieg" (To a Young Leader in the First World War). A young officer is addressed here as he returns from the war profoundly disillusioned, and the poet tells him not to regard the personal effort and discipline as waste of energy.

Drei Gesänge was incorporated into a group of fifteen longer poems that form the opening section of the last volume of poetry published during the author's lifetime, *Das neue Reich* (The Kingdom Come, 1928). This volume lacks the close cyclical cohesion of earlier volumes. Some of its poems were written as early as 1908, but included also are all those written after *Der Stern des Bundes.* The latter are not numerous but are weighty in some of their pronouncements. The first of the three cantos, entitled "Der Dichter in Zeiten der Wirren" (The Poet in Times of Confusion), is written in three stanzas of thirty lines of blank verse each. It has given rise to much debate concerning the degree to which George can be said to have prepared the advent of National Socialism. The poet compares himself with Cassandra and Jeremiah, who warned their people of impending disaster and refused to dispense easy comfort. Like them he sounds like "coarse metal and is not listened to."

George proceeds to explain his tasks as guardian and spiritual provider for his nation, especially its younger generation. He believes that after having gone "through deepest waste" the chosen ones will one day enable "the heart of the continent to save the world." The purified German youth will "measure men and things with genuine norms" and "bring forth the only helper, the Man" ("Den einzigen der hilft den Mann"), who will then "affix the true symbol on the national banner" and, at the head of his "loyal band," will plant the "New Reich." It is obvious that in this context "New" could easily be read as "Third," even if twelve years later the poet turned away in disgust from the brown reality that must have seemed to him a vulgar travesty of what he wanted.

There is no denying that George's assumption of the role of the prophet, pedagogue, and seer amounts to a monumental pose. There is, however, another, more private and relaxed side of his personality. Correspondingly, there are sections all the way through to the very end of his work that show less formal rigidity than the great cycles of "State" poetry. We find expressions of grief, defeat, and disillusionment in the end sections of *Der Teppich des Lebens*—"Lieder von Traum und Tod" (The Songs of Dream and Death); *Der siebente Ring*—"Lieder" (Songs); and *Das neue Reich*—"Das Lied" (The Song). A poem from the "Lieder" may serve as an example:

> *Im windes-weben*
> *War meine frage*
> *Nur träumerei.*
> *Nur lächeln war*
> *Was du gegeben.*
> *Aus nasser nacht*
> *Ein glanz entfacht—*
> *Nun drängt der mai ·*
> *Nun muss ich gar*
> *Um dein aug und haar*
> *Alle tage*
> *In sehnen leben.*

> In the wind's weaving
> My question was

STEFAN GEORGE

Only a daydream.
Only a smile
Was what you gave.
Upon misty night
Rose lustrous light—
It will be May ·
Now I must live
In yearning
All my days
For your eyes, for your hair.

*(Werke: Ausgabe in
zwei Bänden,* 1:309)

Mistakenly, many commentators (especially the hagiographers) insist that in his later years George adopted the tone, feeling, and form of the simple folk song. George's verdict on this type of the lyric genre had always been severe. In his anthology *Deutsche Dichtung* he deliberately omitted Goethe's and the romantics' refashioned or imitated *Volkslieder,* and in 1902 he remarked to Hofmannsthal that in most cases "their obvious silliness" is but thinly disguised through the interference of those who handed them down. In excluding the folk-song tradition from the realm of high poetry he remained consistent. One poem in particular implies a refutation of George's alleged adoption of the folk-song tone. "Das Wort" (The Word, 1919), in the group "Das Lied" of *Das neue Reich,* manifests its nonsong quality in its structure of rhyming couplets as well as in the title. It is obviously not the musical connotation of *Lied* that explains the placing of this poem under such a group heading, but rather the references in it to the store of motifs, stemming from legend, myth, or folklore, on which the poet draws. In "Das Wort" the poet speaks of his creative task as neither simple nor folklike, but as rather arduous. He has to pay recurrent visits to the "gray Norn" of Teutonic mythology, whom he must ask to give the name for every "new dream or wonder from afar" that he brings to his country. At the bottom of her well she searches for the name. Once it happened that she could not grant his request because she found that no suitable word was "sleeping in the depth":

*So lernt ich traurig den verzicht:
Kein ding sei wo das wort gebricht.*

Thus I learned sadly to forgo:
No thing exists for which there is no word.

The poem is both a supreme glorification of the poet's creative power and an acknowledgment of its limitations. A melancholy admission of ultimate frailty and subjection to unknown demonic forces prevails also in what is probably the last poem George wrote—it has no title:

*In stillste ruh
Besonnenen tags
Bricht jäh ein blick
Der unerahnten schrecks
Die sichre seele stört*

*So wie auf höhn
Der feste stamm
Stolz reglos ragt
Und dann noch spät ein sturm
Ihn bis zum boden beugt:*

*So wie das meer
Mit gellem laut
Mit wildem prall
Noch einmal in die lang
Verlassne muschel stösst.*

Through stillest calm
Of pensive day
Falls suddenly a glance
Which stirs the soul that was secure
With unsuspected fright.

As on the ridge
The tree stands firm
Unmoved and proud
Until quite late the storm
Will bend it to the ground.

As will the sea
With one shrill sound
With one wild leap
Blow once again into
The long deserted shell.

*(Werke: Ausgabe in
zwei Bänden,* 1:468)

In the twenty-second poem of the *Vorspiel* the poet asks the angel if he will have to stand alone to the end. He receives the chilling answer that the disciples "love you, yet are weak and cowardly," and that at the close "only you and I" will remain.

When George died years later in his self-imposed Swiss exile this prophecy was not literally fulfilled; a few close friends, both young and old, were with him. Among them were the two Counts Stauffenberg. Claus Schenk, the younger of the two brothers, was the man who planted the bomb in Hitler's field headquarters on 20 July 1944 and paid for it with his life, as did all the other men of the so-called Kreisau Circle who had plotted to overthrow the Third Reich and failed. The charismatic Percy Gothein (1896–1944), a less known but equally important spiritual descendant of George, also paid the price for resisting tyranny when, on a secret mission for the Kreisau Circle in Holland, he was arrested by the Gestapo and deported to the concentration camp in Neuengamme near Hamburg. He died there on 22 December 1944 "of natural causes," as the official report stated.

Thus there were followers of the poet who demonstrated through their actions the significance of the line in *Der Stern des Bundes* "Does Word precede the Deed or Deed the Word?"—a rhetorical question to which one might supply the answer: "In the beginning was the Word," i.e., the creation of the world and historical events *follow* upon the spoken or written word (be it inspired by god or demon). In Germany and elsewhere courageous attempts to resist Nazi brutality and falsehood have been celebrated as efforts to save the honor of what has been referred to as the "secret Germany" ("Geheimes Deutschland," the title of a George poem of 1928, first published in *Das neue Reich*).

In determining Stefan George's rank as a poet, however, one must not judge his achievements solely by their social and political irradiation and certainly not by the fact that history appears to have ridden roughshod over the dream of the "New Reich." Among modern German poets there were and are very few indeed who would deny that they owe a debt to this consummate expert in the craft of poetry, an inspired, if stern, rejuvenator of the German poetic language.

Selected Bibliography

EDITIONS

INDIVIDUAL WORKS

Hymnen. Berlin, 1890.

Pilgerfahrten. Vienna, 1891.

Algabal. Paris, 1892.

Die Bücher der Hirten- und Preisgedichte, der Sagen und Sänge, und der hängenden Gärten. Berlin, 1895.

Das Jahr der Seele. Berlin, 1897.

Der Teppich des Lebens und die Lieder von Traum und Tod, mit einem Vorspiel. Berlin, 1900.

Die Fibel: Auswahl erster Verse. Berlin, 1901.

Tage und Taten: Aufzeichnungen und Skizzen. Berlin, 1903.

Der siebente Ring. Berlin, 1907.

Der Stern des Bundes. Berlin, 1913.

Der Krieg. Berlin, 1917.

Drei Gesänge. Berlin, 1921.

Das neue Reich. Berlin, 1928.

Phraortes, Graf Bothwell: Zwei dramatische Fragmente aus der Schulzeit. Edited by G. P. Landmann. Düsseldorf and Munich, 1975.

COLLECTED WORKS

Gesamt-Ausgabe der Werke: Endgültige Fassung. 18 in 15 vols (includes three double vols.). Berlin, 1927–1934.

Werke: Ausgabe in zwei Bänden. Edited by Robert Boehringer. 2d ed., Munich and Düsseldorf, 1968; 3d ed., 1976.

Werke: Ausgabe in vier Bänden. Edited by Robert Boehringer. Munich, 1983.

Gedichte. Edited by H. Nalewski. Leipzig, 1987. In paperback.

Sämtliche Werke in 18 Bänden. Edited by G. P. Landmann and U. Oelmann. Vols. 2, 4, 5, 6/7, 10/11, 13/14. Stuttgart, 1982– . In progress.

STEFAN GEORGE

TRANSLATIONS BY GEORGE

Die Blumen des Bösen. Berlin, 1891. George's translation into German of selected poems from Baudelaire's *Les fleurs du mal.*

CORRESPONDENCE

Stefan George—Hugo von Hofmannsthal: Briefwechsel. Edited by Robert Boehringer. 2d enlarged ed., Düsseldorf, 1953.

Stefan George—Friedrich Gundolf: Briefwechsel. Edited by Robert Boehringer and G. P. Landmann. Munich and Düsseldorf, 1962.

Stefan George—Ida Coblenz: Briefwechsel. Edited by G. P. Landmann and E. Höpker-Herberg. Stuttgart, 1983.

WORKS EDITED BY GEORGE

Blätter für die Kunst. Edited by Carl August Klein and Stefan George. 12 vols. Berlin, 1892–1919; repr. in 6 vols. Düsseldorf, 1967.

Deutsche Dichtung. Edited by Stefan George and Karl Wolfskehl. 3 vols. Berlin, 1900–1902.

Maximin: Ein Gedenkbuch. Edited by Stefan George. Berlin, 1907.

TRANSLATIONS

Choix de poèmes. Translated by Maurice Boucher. 2 vols. Paris, 1941 and 1943. Bilingual edition.

Poems: In German and English. Translated by Carol North Valhope and Ernst Morwitz. New York, 1943.

Stefan George in fremden Sprachen: Übersetzungen seiner Gedichte in die europäischen Sprachen ausser den slawischen. Collected and edited by G. P. Landmann. Düsseldorf and Munich, 1973. Translations in thirteen languages.

Stefan George: Selected Poems, in Ukrainian and Other, Mostly Slavic Languages. Edited by I. Kostetzkyi and O. Zujewskyi. 2 vols. Stuttgart, 1971 and 1973.

60 Poemas de Stefan George: Vertidos al español. Translated by Clotilde Schlayer. Düsseldorf and Munich, 1964. Bilingual edition.

The Works of Stefan George. Translated by Carol North Valhope and Ernst Morwitz. Chapel Hill, N. C., 1949; 2d rev. ed., New York, 1966.

BIOGRAPHICAL AND CRITICAL STUDIES

Boehringer, Robert. *Ewiger Augenblick.* 2d ed., Düsseldorf, 1965.

———. *Mein Bild von Stefan George.* 2 vols. 2d enlarged ed., Düsseldorf, 1967.

Breysig, Kurt. *Stefan George: Gespräche, Dokumente.* Amsterdam, 1960.

Brodersen, Arvid. *Stefan George: Deutscher und Europäer.* Berlin, 1935.

Curtius, Ernst Robert. *Essays in European Literature.* Translated by Michael Kowal. Princeton, 1973.

David, Claude. *Stefan George: Son oeuvre poétique.* Lyon and Paris, 1952.

———. *Stefan George: Sein dichterisches Werk.* Translated into German by Alexa Remmen and Karl Thiemer. Munich, 1967.

Emrich, Wilhelm. *Poetische Wirklichkeit: Studien zur Klassik und Moderne.* Wiesbaden, 1979.

Glöckner, Ernst. *Begegnung mit Stefan George: Auszüge aus Briefen und Tagebüchern, 1913–1934.* Edited by F. Adam. Heidelberg, 1972.

Goldsmith, Ulrich K. *Stefan George: A Study of His Early Work.* Boulder, Colo., 1959.

———. "Shakespeare and Stefan George: The Sonnets." In *Theorie und Kritik: Festschrift für Gerhard Loose,* edited by S. Grunwald and B. A. Beatie. Bern and Munich, 1974.

———. "Wilamowitz and the Georgekreis: New Documents." In *Wilamowitz nach 50 Jahren,* edited by W. M. Calder III, H. Flashar, and T. Lindken. Darmstadt, 1985.

Gsteiger, Manfred. "*Die Blumen des Bösen:* Stefan George als Übersetzer Baudelaires." In *Literatur des Übergangs.* Bern, 1963.

Gundolf, Friedrich. *George.* Berlin, 1920.

Hähnel, K.-D. "'In der kunst glauben wir an eine glänzerde wiedergeburt': Stefan Georges Gedichte 'Im windes-weben' und 'Komm in den totgesagten tag und schau.'" *Zeitschrift zur Germanistik* 7:420–434 (1986).

Heftrich, E., P. G. Klussman, and H. J. Schrimpf, eds. *Stefan George Kolloquium.* Köln, 1971.

Helbling, L. [Wolfgang Frommel], C. V. Bock, and K. Kluncker, eds. *Stefan George. Dokumente seiner Wirkung.* Amsterdam, 1974.

Hildebrandt, Kurt. *Erinnerungen an Stefan George und seinen Kreis.* Bonn, 1965.

———. *Das Werk Stefan Georges.* Hamburg, 1960.

Kahler, Erich von. *Stefan George: Grösse und Tragik.* Pfullingen, 1964.

Klett, Ernst. "Stefan George." *Neue Sammlung* 23:42–61 (1982).

Kommerell, Max. *Briefe und Aufzeichnungen, 1919–1944.* Edited by Inge Jens. Olten, 1967.

Landmann, Edith. *Gespräche mit Stefan George.* Düsseldorf, 1963.

Landmann, Georg P., ed. *Der Georgekreis: Eine Auswahl aus seinen Schriften.* Cologne, 1965.

————. *Vorträge über Stefan George: Eine biographische Einführung in sein Werk.* Düsseldorf and Munich, 1974.

————. "Stefan George als moderner Dichter." In *Die Wirkung Stefan Georges auf die Wissenschaft: Eine Symposium,* edited by H.-J. Zimmermann. Heidelberg, 1985.

Lepsius, Sabine. *Stefan George: Geschichte einer Freundschaft.* Berlin, 1935.

————. *Ein Berliner Künstlerleben um die Jahrhundertwende.* Munich, 1972.

Mason, E. C. "Rilke und Stefan George." In *Festschrift H. A. Korff,* edited by J. Müller. Leipzig, 1958.

Metzger, M. M., and E. A. Metzger. *Stefan George.* New York, 1972.

Michels, Gerd. *Die Dante-Übertragungen Stefan Georges: Studien zur Übersetzungstechnik Stefan Georges.* Munich, 1967.

Morwitz, Ernst. *Die Dichtung Stefan Georges.* 2d ed., Godesberg, 1948.

————. *Kommentar zu dem Werk Stefan Georges.* Düsseldorf, 1960; 2d ed., 1969.

————. *Kommentar zu den Prosa-, Drama-, und Jugend-Dichtungen Stefan Georges.* Düsseldorf, 1962.

Poupard, D., and J. E. Person, Jr., eds. *Twentieth-Century Literary Criticism: Excerpts from Criticism of the Work of Novelists, Poets, etc., Who Died Between 1900 and 1960, from the First Published Critical Appraisals to Current Evaluations.* Vol. 14. Detroit, 1984.

Salin, Edgar. *Um Stefan George: Erinnerung und Zeugnis.* 2d ed., Munich, 1954.

Schonauer, Franz. *Stefan George in Selbstzeugnissen und Bilddokumenten.* Hamburg, 1960.

Schultz, H. Stefan. *Studien zur Dichtung Stefan Georges.* Heidelberg, 1967.

Sebba, Gregor. "Das Ärgernis Stefan George." *Colloquia Germanica* 2-3:202–231 (1970).

Seekamp, H.-J., R. C. Ockenden, and M. Keilson. *Stefan George: Leben und Werk—Eine Zeittafel.* Amsterdam, 1972.

Thormaehlen, Ludwig. *Erinnerungen an Stefan George.* Edited by Walther Greischel. Hamburg, 1962.

Winkler, Michael. *Stefan George.* Stuttgart, 1970.

Wolters, Friedrich Wilhelm. *Stefan George und die Blätter für die Kunst: Deutsche Geistesgeschichte seit 1890.* Berlin, 1930.

Wuthenow, Ralph-Rainer, ed. *Dokumente zur Wirkungsgeschichte.* 2 vols. Stuttgart, 1980–1981.

Zeller, Bernhard, ed. *Stefan George, 1868–1968: Der Dichter und sein Kreis.* Munich, 1968.

BIBLIOGRAPHIES AND CONCORDANCES

Bock, Claus V. *Wortkonkordanz zur Dichtung Stefan Georges.* Amsterdam, 1964.

Landmann, Georg P. *Stefan George und sein Kreis: Eine Bibliographie.* Hamburg, 1960; 2d ed., 1976.

ULRICH K. GOLDSMITH

PAUL CLAUDEL
(1868–1955)

ALTHOUGH BORN INTO the family of a civil servant, Paul Claudel did not follow in his father's footsteps. His career as a diplomat led him beyond officialdom and beyond France itself into the appreciation of other lands and cultures; if ever a person had more than one country, it was he. His *Livre de Christophe Colomb* (*The Book of Christopher Columbus*, 1929) is typical of his world outlook. Marcel Proust once said that a work of art enabled one to see the world better; Claudel was for years the official spokesman of his country, but a spokesman who extended his role and invited the world to find in his writings a unique vision.

Speaking with hindsight, one may say that Claudel's first home prepared the elements that governed his life: on 6 August 1868, Paul-Louis-Charles-Marie Claudel was born at the house of his great-uncle, a priest. That house in Villeneuve-sur-Fère-en-Tardenois was a rectory secularized during the French Revolution. Claudel's intellectual life developed along the narrow path between church and state, and his writings record by implication the fact that France in the nineteenth century had become ever more secularized. It was the time of science and positivism triumphant, of the intellectual determinism of Hippolyte Taine and the skepticism of the unfrocked Ernest Renan, the noted orientalist and author of the shocking *Vie de Jésus* (*Life of Jesus*, 1863). French education was no longer a monopoly of the

church; the village priest was no longer the voice of the community. In short, the fragmentation of culture had begun and was being celebrated by many thinkers and writers, Marcel Proust included.

Claudel's father was an unfriendly person, a pupil of the Jesuits, and—like a good many of his classmates—hostile to the church. Claudel's mother was of peasant stock, but could claim an earlier aristocratic ancestry, presumably "right-thinking." It was in that time and place, at war with itself, that Claudel began his spiritual pilgrimage and search for truth. His trilogy of plays *L'Otage* (*The Hostage*, 1911), *Le pain dur* (*Crusts*, 1918), *Le père humilié* (*The Humiliation of the Father*, 1920) presents this struggle between church and state.

Claudel had two sisters, Camille and Louise, with whom he often engaged in lively quarrels. Camille eventually became a gifted sculptor and fell in love with her mentor, Auguste Rodin. After having lived with him for some time, she became insane; Paul accompanied her to the asylum where she spent many years of her life. The father's work and his concern for the development of Camille's talents had led the family to different places of residence and eventually to Paris. Before then, at the lycée of Bar-le-Duc, Claudel may have met the future president of the Republic Raymond Poincaré. At Nogent-sur-Seine, he was tutored by the journalist Colin, and Camille had as a teacher the sculptor Alfred Boucher.

Claudel got his lycée education at the famous Louis-le-Grand, the now secularized Jesuit school, formerly Collège de Clermont. In 1883, being younger than most boys in his class, Paul failed his last year of the *baccalauréat,* although in some subjects he won honors, at the expense of his competitor Romain Rolland. (The official who awarded these honors was Renan.)

Two years later, Claudel passed his finals and took his degree. The great event of 1885 was Victor Hugo's death and burial in the Pantheon among the heroes of France. Claudel witnessed the triumphal cortège that brought out all of Paris, literary and plain people, to crowd the boulevards.

It was in 1886 that Claudel, aged eighteen, discovered the poems of that other wanderer, Arthur Rimbaud. Rimbaud as man and writer was more than a passing influence on Claudel, for here was a modern writer, brought up in the secular world, who had been converted to Catholicism. Rimbaud's life was anything but saintly, but it showed the young Claudel that something existed other than the naturalistic world he had known until then. Toward the end of this pivotal year, Claudel made his first turn toward Christianity: on Christmas Day he attended mass at Notre Dame. He went again to vespers a few hours later and, close to the statue of the Virgin Mary, experienced stirrings of faith. From that moment he became a reader of the Bible. The cathedral itself, that Bible in stone, as Hugo called it, also became a part of Claudel's "reading." He was already familiar with Alban Butler's *Lives of the Saints* (1756–1759, 4 vols.). He now read Pascal, Dante, Bossuet, Aristotle, and others. And then, there was Stéphane Mallarmé.

At that time, Mallarmé was the high priest of the symbolist movement in Paris. Aspiring young writers came to his Tuesday at-homes to hear the master speak of literature and of the great work of universal import he was pondering and hoping to write under the title *Le livre* (The Book). Claudel was one of the group, but not a frequent visitor. Nor was he much of a listener in later life. Although he became a founding member of the *Nouvelle revue française,* his official duties, which required travel, kept him away from the literary coteries so common in Paris to this day.

Before the Mallarmé Tuesdays or the association with the *Nouvelle revue française,* Claudel published anonymously the first version of his first play, *Tête d'Or* (Golden Head, 1890). He had already written works in which one finds the unusual sort of blank verse that was to be his characteristic form; these were *Morceau d'un drame* (Fragment of a Play, 1892) and *L'Endormie* (The Sleeping Woman, 1925). The first lines of *Tête d'Or* depict a character beset by uncertainty, but the reader senses that the language that expresses it is firm, and indeed that here is a new departure in verse. Cébès is speaking:

Here I am,
Imbecile, ignorant,
A new man confronted with unknown things,
And I turn my face toward the Year and the
   rainy arch,
      my heart is filled with boredom!
I know nothing and I can do nothing. What to
   say?
      what to do? For what will I use these
      hands hanging by my side? these feet
      which bear me away as do dreams?
All that one says, and the reason of the wise
   has instructed me
With the wisdom of the tambourine: books
   are drunk,
And there is nothing but myself who looks
   about, and it seems to me
That everything, the foggy air, the newly
   plowed fields,
And the trees, and the clouds overhead
Speak to me with a language more vague
      than the ia! ia! of the sea, saying
"O young being, new! who are you? what are
   you doing?
For what are you waiting, host of these hours
      which are neither day nor shadow,
Nor ox which smells sleep, nor laborer
      lingering at our gray border?"

And I answer: I don't know! and I desire in
    myself
To cry, or cry out
Or laugh, or jump and shake my arms!
"Who I am?"

(first part)

Claudel began his career as a writer with
the observation that one exists. But the words
for it are ambiguous: "Here am I," but also, in
playful French, "I, a voice, here." It is a voice
that cries out: "Here I am. I am a voice, to be
seen and not just to be heard." Appropriately,
Claudel's turned out to be a voice of the
theater, the place for seeing, for vision, par
excellence.

Yet right after this affirmation comes a
questioning, a word of fragmentation. "Here I
am"—a being who is ignorant, in motion, not
at all static, but asking and wondering who
he is. The question implies the presence of
Descartes: "I think, therefore I am." Claudel's
questioning makes the reader expect "Who am
I?" But by using the more colloquial inverted
form "Who I am?" the author seems to converse with the reader. The question resembles
an affirmation. Most of us would answer as
though the question were "What am I?" Claudel's work is an exploration of this difference.
The question is perhaps metaphysical, but the
reader-actor replies in the most material manner. The character Cébès continues his cantata of wonderment:

O things, here,
I offer myself to you!
See me, I need
And I don't know what.

(first part)

Tête d'Or is a play about the will, about one
man's conquest of a kingdom. Claudel, much
like Proust speaking of his "traveler," says that
the land explored is oneself. The conquest is of
that realm and no other.

Simon Agnel, at the start a lamb of a man,
as his last name suggests, becomes the savior
of Europe, the terrible and courageous *Tête*
d'Or. He meets the questioning Cébès as he
himself is about to bury his dead wife. The two
men form an alliance to push back the barbarians who are threatening the kingdom. When
victory is within grasp, Simon loses his friend.
Then comes ambition, a new will to conquer
the world. Agnel pushes on, but falls victim to
his own desire. Bringing death to others, he
ends by succumbing to it.

Well before the two world wars, Claudel
depicted a kind of superman, one who is
doomed to failure by the vastness of his ambition: "My desire / Has been for great things"
(1.148). When he is apparently dead, his soldiers note that in the end he would no longer
know human doubt, because the only thing he
carried within him was his inextinguishable
desire. The former king's daughter, who has
been wandering in the forest, is taken by the
enemy and nailed to a tree. It is to a spot
nearby that the wounded Tête d'Or is brought.
She slowly wakes up after the horrible torture
and the king, hearing her, crawls over and
removes the nails from her hands. Then he
collapses, and it is the freed princess who
leads him to his funeral bed. Tête d'Or does not
cease feeling the great yearning that gives him
hope and breath itself: desire is life. He dies
and the princess says:

A desire lived in him
Still.
I saw him in his mutilated form, having
All forgotten except the paradise of himself,
Exactly like a powerful horse.

(second part)

She understands why Tête d'Or, like the horse,
cries out on encountering something or someone other than himself. Symbolically, she is
the being whom he lacked. He is the tortured
animal in need of her. His last words are that
she shall be queen. That for him is the end
indeed; his words are the counterpart of her
knowledge of his need for her—ultimately of
their need for one another. His power restores
her to what is rightfully hers, but only her
presence calls forth his acknowledgment. Al-

ready, in this first complete play, we note Claudel's need or lack, which forms a part of his lifelong *Art poétique* (*Poetic Art,* 1907).

That "books are drunk" is one of Cébès's observations. It recalls Baudelaire's invitation to get drunk—on wine, poetry, or virtue. In French, the word "book" (*livre*) includes in its spelling the word for the excess that is inebriation: (*l)ivre. Tête d'Or* is thus a preface to Claudel's work, as Baudelaire's "To the Reader" is to his poetry. Like Cébès, the nineteenth-century character—Madame Bovary, or the actor-reader in Baudelaire—falls victim to boredom. Cébès is bored; books are of no use, he cries out for help, for what he truly wants, for that ever-evasive prize, Happiness. Tête d'Or does not promise it, but Cébès's words have moved him; the two men leave the road they had been following; symbolically, there is no longer any road. All that Tête d'Or says is: Follow me!

But Agnel finds himself in the same dire straits. Cébès's call evokes Agnel's, and the pair conclude an alliance in front of a tree that is called the tree of knowledge.

Claudel's joining the diplomatic corps led to his meeting Philippe Berthelot, who became a close friend. Berthelot, a talented, cultivated man, was the son of the great chemist Marcellin Berthelot. This association had one practical result. Claudel, as we saw, had become a believer, and he soon discovered that as an overtly Catholic writer he needed protection against the anticlerical bureaucracy. It was Berthelot who, behind the scenes, saved the diplomat from suffering hardship on account of the poet.

Shortly before leaving France for the first time, Claudel experienced his second moment of vision and made a second communion at Notre Dame. Also before going on this first mission as consular officer in New York, he left with friends a second play, *La ville* (*The City,* 1901), which has eventually published. In it, Paris is the scene in which the antagonism of various groups supplies the action.

The time is less clear than the setting. The city is indeed at the heart of the drama—the city of man, and as we learn from allusions to the New Testament, the city of God as well. For Claudel, time and space juxtaposed define history, which includes any particular action or story. As he puts it:

> What is this mistrust of the past?
> For me, the present appears so enormous
> that nothing ceases to be a part of it?
> What we call history
> Is not a succession of vain images,
>   but the development, as things leaving
>   time cease to belong to it,
> Of order and composition.
> He who reads, when he reads, there is a
>   progress in his reading.
>   (second version, act 3)

It is clear that for the playwright, all is *not* vanity. Language especially, language that participates in the creative act, is of transcendent worth. In the world of *The City,* the secular is not separate from evangelical concerns. The secular city of smoke is a mere shout, whereas that of Christ is "the revelation of the proffered word": "instead of empty dreams / The Truth and the reality of what is." One of the characters utters his own creed, which derives its full poetic force from its structural likeness to the Credo of the Catholic liturgy. Secular citizen *and* believer, he sees the church as "the visible Word," that is, word and act made manifest. The creator is seen in economical terms; despite man's *felix culpa* (happy error), God "does not want to lose anything of his creature but find again his original investment, with interest!" The future ambassador knows finance as well as theology.

Whereas in *Tête d'Or* the absence of God is noticeable, and salvation is to come from the politics of the city and some new species of hero, in *The City* the perspective has changed. Here Claudel has given the power of the gods to a multitude of men called Prometheus. Power is still the matter of the play, but no longer in the form of will and ambition. Nor is it the spirit of the meek and humble that now transforms the polis. Rather, strength is the gift of the believer—hence the use of the Credo toward the end of the play. In the words of Besme, the engineer who knows the weight and measure of things, and of Coeuvre, the poet who knows their artistry, Claudel gives us a glimpse of his outlook, which is as earthly as it is spiritual. Besme acknowledges that through the poet's voice one achieves harmony with the melody of the world: "You explain nothing, O poet, but all things by you become explainable." Coeuvre says that he breathes and brings forth a word. But Besme wonders whether every word is an answer or whether it calls for one: "Who questions you or whom do you answer? / Where is that exchange, that mysterious breathing of which you speak?" At the same time, Coeuvre doubts his own vision and wonders whether he is indeed loved—or does love. As engineer, Besme is the father of the city, and he too is at a point of crisis. The people worship him as they would a god; but he knows that he is the plaything of his emotions and that he will die. He feels the weight of death for all. He thinks he has built a dwelling in which man has managed to live, but all alone. It is a tomb with no exit. He wishes, like Job, that he had never been born. A builder who trusts in power, he discovers the nothingness of things. He finally dies at the hands of his own citizens.

But Claudel's "city" does not end on this note of despair. If joy is denied to Besme, it is granted to Coeuvre's son, Ivors. Having seized control of the city and destroyed it, Avarice leaves things in the hands of a poet's son. Meanwhile, what has become of Coeuvre himself? He is now a priest and bishop and, as such, converts his son to his own belief of what happiness is: "Happiness is not a luxury; it is within us, in ourselves." The poet and priest then explains the restitution of man through Jesus. Nothing that Ivors might do can restore order to society. The play ends with Ivors's own expression of the creed, that is, of his father's vision:

> The gathering of all men is comparable
> to one single man.
> And just as the Christian dedicates to his
> Creator that portion of the world by which
> he lives, so it is that the entire
> Universe was placed in the hands
> Of the Man, so that he would pay
> homage to it.
> (second version, act 3)

For Claudel, society and the land are alike sacred. Coeuvre does not forget that he was once a poet, and the reader wonders whether in this figure the author has not merged the monk he once thought of becoming. Coeuvre recalls to his son, who will lead the city, his former verse, which lacks both rhyme and meter and which may thus characterize the city:

> And I gave to it in the secret of my heart
> this double and reciprocal function
> By which man absorbs life and restores,
> in the supreme act of expiration,
> An intelligible Word.
> And so the life of society is only the double
> side of the giving of thanks or hymn,
> By which humanity absorbs its principle
> and restores its image.
> (second version, act 3)

The father's word calls for an answer from his son, to embody the continuous process of displacement and "restitution," the building of self and city in the image of the Christian God. We have moved far from the incantation of Cébès at the beginning of *Tête d'Or*, where the unknown and the uncertain prevail.

The United States was the first foreign nation visited by the young Claudel as a representative of his government. His responsibilities included cultural and business exchanges in that atypical part of the country, New York City. It was a difficult time for the poet, his salary being that of a very junior civil servant. But he did not waste his opportunities. He started the habit of reading and writing a great deal every day. He read the Greek

475

fathers of the church and he translated Aeschylus. In his prose poems, *Connaissance de l'Est* (*The East I Know,* 1900), he describes New York as the terminal at the end of a trade route. Tracks and wharves surround it. The lower part of Manhattan is "the extremity of this tongue" ("Cities," *The East I Know*). A year later he was in Boston, and in the same prose poem he says:

> Boston is made up of two parts: the new city, pedantic, greedy, like a man who, showing off his riches and his virtue, keeps them for himself . . . ; the little hill of the old city, so like a snail, contains all the twists and turns of commerce, debauchery, and hypocrisy.
>
> ("Cities," *The East I Know*)

While in Boston, he still had very little money and often had to skip one meal each day. But it was there that he wrote his American play, *L'Échange* (The Exchange, 1901). The title itself is indicative; the work suggests Henry James's novels about the meeting of cultures—*The American* (1877) or *The Europeans* (1878). But for Claudel there were three cultures: France, the United States, and a more primitive America, incarnated in the Indian Louis Laine.

There is more in this drama than a new world and the money market, for the rich American, Thomas Nageoire Pollock, and the penniless and landless Louis Laine find that money is the symbol of what may not be shared. The play negates the cooperative vision and affirms a new faith. Pollock would give glory to his god, not the creator, but the god of "lots of fun":

> Above all
> It is good to have money in the bank.
>> Glory be to the Lord who has given the
>> dollar to man
> So that everyone might sell
>> what he has and procure what he desires,
> And that all might live
>> in a decent and comfortable manner. Amen!
>
> (first version, act 1)

In other words, blessed is the man whose godliness consists in the multiplicity of exchanges and not just in possession. Claudel perceived that in American life God and Mammon have formed an alliance. He could have rewritten the Gloria as "In God we trust. Glory to God in the highest . . . and the dollar to men of good will!" That glory is not Being, but Having.

Pollock is married to Lechy Elbernon, and Laine to the young Frenchwoman Marthe, whom he calls his Bitter-Sweet. The other possible exchange that Pollock would like to make is to have Marthe come and live with him. Laine has already enjoyed the favors of Lechy, but Marthe, who is not to be bought because she does not put her trust in money, refuses. Laine, who has made a contract with Pollock, and now has some money, tries to abandon Lechy as well as his wife. Lechy is an actress, less retiring than Marthe, and, having shared Laine with her, is reluctant to give him up. As he tries to leave, she kills him. Pollock's house and the money in it go up in flames. Pollock makes no effort to save either, for he has found peace in talking to Marthe: he is blessed and may live to enjoy yet another exchange.

There is in the play the ground for one more exchange to come. It takes place in *Le partage de midi* (*Break of Noon,* 1906). Pollock wants to make an exchange with Louis and, by so doing, to cancel the contract between man and wife (not, to be sure, husband and wife), for woman is the object of the exchange, however desperately she may want to be no part of any deal. This new exchange takes place out of time: "It is noon and the day is broken in two. / The sun devours the shade of our bodies, marking the time which is no time: Noon." Contract (or alliance) is an image Claudel develops in other plays as well. It is more than a theme; it is at the root of his artistic vision and as such it slowly becomes more and more sharply defined.

Claudel's next diplomatic mission took him to China. He was stationed for a time in

Foochow, then in Shanghai and Hankow. China was then open to foreigners, including French missionaries. With some of these Claudel became friends. On his way back to Europe, he visited the Holy Land and was struck by the traces left on it by the crusaders in the form of monuments—the ruins of castles and forts. His journey to the East is recorded in *Sous le signe du dragon* (Under the Sign of the Dragon, 1948), which was his report to the Foreign Office at the end of his China mission.

Once more in France, Claudel felt he was at a turning point in his life. The heightened sense of his identity, the spiritual journey he had completed, brought him to consider the possibility of entering the Benedictine order and thereby a life of calm and stability. He went first to the monastery at Solesmes and then to the one at Liguge. But the spell of the cloister was short-lived; his spiritual advisers recommended that he not stay. Claudel later came to believe that he lacked the necessary resolve and that if he had determined to remain, he would have been allowed to do so.

Sent back to China, he now went through another difficult period. On board the S.S. *Ernest Simon*, Claudel met a beautiful woman. She was married; he was not. They fell in love and remained together for some five years. From this liaison came the substance of the play last mentioned, *Break of Noon*.

This play is a transmutation of Claudel's own experience and one of the most beautiful plays of the French theater. The title re-echoes Lechy's words in *L'Échange:* noon is "a time out of time, a time that is not time at all." The scene is a steamer on the Indian Ocean, the ship serving as a symbol of motion and voyaging. It also indicates the characters' restlessness, their search for land, a spot where they can drop anchor. One of them speaks with humor of her predicament, using the words of Christ: unlike the birds of the air or the foxes of the field, he had no place to rest his head. She has no place to set up house.

A young couple, Yse, her husband, De Ciz,

and their children are on their way to China. On the ship Yse meets a former friend, Amalric, who now has a plantation in the East. He had courted Yse as a young girl and wants to rekindle his love for her. Mesa, a man of retiring temperament, is a customs official who is returning to China after a failed attempt to carry out what he thought was a religious vocation. All four people are looking for something; they are like adventurers seeking to make a fortune. Fortune itself—chance—has brought them together, but all they seem to own is the great ocean, the ship, and one another. It looks to them as if destiny meant them to share this last possession. This sharing is, of course, an old theatrical device—the sudden, chance meeting of lovers—or so Mesa is tempted to think. For him, love is a comedy poorly acted. He has been called back to China after failing to satisfy the inner voice calling him to a religious life, but he is still hounded by his God.

Mesa falls in love with Yse, and what stands between him and her is his God. He cannot help telling her how beautiful she is, but Mesa has to struggle with his conscience. His question to Yse about Another, whom it is necessary to tolerate within oneself, for he dwells there forever, shows Mesa's troubled soul. The ship making its way to China is not simply a ship of fools. On it, Yse and her society may be tossed about, but the passengers are subject to another movement, from within, and unceasing: "He lives, I live. He thinks and I weigh in my heart His thought."

This state of mind is far removed indeed from that of Cebes at the beginning of *Tête d'Or*. Mesa's voice discloses the presence of God. The image implied is frequent in Claudel, and it is one he shares with Gerard Manley Hopkins, whom he also resembles in other ways. For Hopkins, one's being spells out what it is. For Claudel, it is God who spells out one's being. In the first version of *Break of Noon*, the image of "being read" by God is more in evidence, less theoretical in form, than its later exposition in his *Poetic Art*. Here, one is a book that needs a reader and (we are given to understand) a lover. Mesa wants to be known and read, to be an open book, transparent. This transparency is linked with the language of what is to be read and with the very voice and intonation of the God who "utters" man and spells him out. Mesa, on his side, wants to know all things so that he may be entirely known. This knowledge is always a rebirth or new birth to things and with things. It is for Claudel an extension of the Incarnation, of his own and God's "writing" of the world, whether in poetry or in prose.

De Ciz, Ysé's husband, has had a life of instability. Ysé accuses him of having made her live among savages—one of them the famous Rimbaud. We saw what a profound effect the reading of Rimbaud had on Claudel. Here, on this fictional voyage, Rimbaud is presented in a different light through Ysé's characterization of him as a savage:

> I have never met anyone so stupid! There are magnificent sunsets in Harrar. Ah! as far as sunsets are concerned, we have it over everyone! That's about all one has for distraction. I could be taken aback, and sometimes I would say to him, "Come on, Rimbaud, tell me, don't you find that beautiful?" But he wouldn't answer and would only look at me with his stupid look. The sun first and me afterward.
>
> (version for the stage, act 1)

Rimbaud, obviously, is no longer the means of contact with the Spirit but an idiot. At the same time, for De Ciz, he is a successful businessman. One infers that the object of De Ciz's search is wholly materialistic. Claudel has designed this adventurer as a non-poetic Rimbaud who in the end leaves his beautiful wife for the sake of the El Dorado he conceives China to be. Claudel may be said to be using Rimbaud for the purpose of negation. Rimbaud is no longer the author of the *Illuminations*; his name now means an exclusive concern for what is material—a symbolism that corresponds to the actual facts of Rimbaud's later life as a trader in Africa.

Similarly, the "break" that De Ciz makes is with the better half of himself. What Ysé values is what Rimbaud is no longer able to see. She is fearful of herself, of the weakness in her being that might show up if De Ciz leaves her. By his decision to do just that, the order of Ysé's life is shattered. She knows that she loves Mesa; that is why she feared what would happen if she were free of De Ciz. But once he has made his choice, she turns to her lover and even has him encourage De Ciz in his wanderlust. A child is born to the lovers, but the momentum of separation that has started cannot be stopped. Ysé later leaves Mesa and finds support in the person of Amalric.

Meanwhile, there is revolution in China and the lovers are caught in it. Mesa, who has a safe-conduct, hopes to take Ysé and his child to a safe place; searching for them, he gets into a fight with Amalric and is wounded. The child dies at the hands of Ysé, who flees with Amalric. Soon after, she learns that De Ciz has died. She now leaves Amalric and returns to Mesa, whom she may now love legitimately. The play ends with their marriage in the sight of God.

During the time when Mesa has been left by Ysé, he regains consciousness from his hurt, and the first words he speaks are addressed to God. He wants to know why—why he has suffered at the hands of a woman he loves. His complaint is twofold. He wants to know why this particular woman, and he wants to know why God brought Ysé to him without his own consent. God has taken charge of everything, and that is not fair. God has been the stronger in this partnership made manifest in Man, and God has not respected the agreement. Mesa exclaims, "It's quite clever of you to play the superior with me," and upbraids his all-powerful partner for not keeping the covenant made before the creation of the world. Mesa thus sums up the action of the play, the encounter of a man and a woman. But his grievance goes further: that providential encounter subjects the two to the trial of temptation. Mesa reminds God that he has been stuck on a ship with this beautiful woman for forty days. The number alludes to another temptation, that of Christ in the desert. What *Break of Noon* means to show, therefore, is the struggle of a man with his own passions and with God, not separately but in one mighty combat. Claudel's thought has never been more consistent: if Mesa forms an illegitimate relation with Ysé, the sacrament of marriage is not destroyed; it only becomes hateful. And when Ysé abandons Mesa, she also abandons God in him.

Mesa had wanted to know everything so as to be known by everything. In the full knowledge that he gains of Ysé, the sharing or rebirth has taken place and is expressed in the word "sacrament." With the death of De Ciz, what had been a hateful sacrament becomes a blessed one.

The story of *Break of Noon* is hardly original, but it is revivified and refreshed by Claudel's poetic idiom and his strong sense of drama. In the last scene of the play, Ysé and Mesa stand up, join hands, and slowly raise them upward. That they should now be one is traditional, but their oneness exists in the unity of God, who, for inexplicable reasons, has brought them together. The spectator understands that the tale is not the life of a saint, but a human affair in all senses of the term.

How Claudel handles the deity is the chief interest. In having Mesa complain to God like Job, the dramatist may shock some readers, but it is nothing new in the literature of religion and mysticism. Nor is Claudel influenced only by the Bible and his own faith. He is also influenced by the world, the flesh, and the devil—the devil being the humorous critic inside him.

For Claudel, humor is a part of the rebirth he often portrays in his plays. Mesa and Ysé embody the struggle of believing in someone outside themselves. Mesa's belief in the reality of this Other is inseparable from his love for the married Ysé. In other words, the love of woman and man is just as powerful a force as religion. Claudel seems to say through Mesa

that religion binds and love unbinds the human spirit. For this spirit, to be most free is to be in the flesh.

Claudel broke with his lover in 1904 and returned to France. There he undertook to comfort the poet Francis Jammes in *his* spiritual battle. He then met and married Reine Sainte-Marie-Perrin, the daughter of a famous architect who had designed the towering basilica of Notre Dame de Fourvières in Lyon. Unlike Claudel's family, the Perrins were religious. In their midst Claudel found a haven. The couple were married on 15 March 1906 and immediately made ready to go to China. They spent a few days in Peking and proceeded to Tientsin, where Claudel joined the consular staff. He was now a family man as well as a government official and a poet. His first new work was the ode "L'Espirit et l'eau" ("Water and the Spirit"), the first of the *Cinq grandes odes* (*Five Great Odes,* 1910).

A child was born on 20 January 1907 and named Marie. The third of his odes, the "Magnificat," was a song of thanksgiving for the event. But Claudel tired of Tientsin and appealed to his highly placed friend Philippe Berthelot for help in securing a transfer. He shortly joined his wife and child at the seaside resort of Shan Hai Kwan, where he wrote *Processional pour saluer le siècle nouveau* (Processional with Which to Greet the New Century, 1910).

About this time, Claudel began corresponding with Jacques Rivière, another young intellectual going through a spiritual crisis, and also with an orientalist, Louis Massignon, who was later to become an authority on Islam. Claudel's position under an anticlerical regime was difficult. To publish works inspired by religious zeal exposed him to disfavor among his superiors, and his dismissal of an employee at the consulate proved an occasion for possible retaliation. True, Joan of Arc was just then canonized by the church, but, although she was popular as a national heroine, she was not popular with the government. Claudel continued to publish, but with prudence.

It was during these last days of his service in China that Claudel conceived the idea of founding a sort of fraternity. The doctrine of the Communion of Saints suggested the form. As usual with him, it was to anticipate the heavenly reality by something concrete, something to embody faith through living flesh and bones. His correspondence had put him in touch with several persons who, like himself, had gone through a spiritual crisis. What he envisioned was a society through which, by prayer, correspondence, and cooperation, writers and others could find spiritual support and encouragement.

A new assignment intervened. On 16 August 1909, Claudel left China on the Trans-Siberian Railway, bound for Paris. In France, he spent some time on the estate of his in-laws and renewed his friendships with André Gide, Jacques Rivière, Jacques Copeau, and others. His next posting was to Prague, where at first he lived in discomfort, because his quarters were not ready. But Prague proved beneficial in the end; Claudel came to love its baroque art and enjoy the society of its friendly people.

The year 1911 was spent partly in France, partly in Prague. *L'Annonce faite à Marie* (*The Tidings Brought to Mary*, 1912) was completed in the Perrins' barn at Villeneuve. This is Claudel's best-known and most popular play. Typically, it underwent several reworkings, its source being in fact the earlier play *La jeune fille Violaine* (The Damsel Violaine, 1926).

Claudel had written the first version of *La jeune fille Violaine* before leaving for New York, his first post. The time of the play is some distant past. The owner of a farm, Anne Vercors (a man, despite his name), is about to go on a long journey. He tells his family of his plans quite suddenly, without warning or reason. In the second version, he learns that his brother has died in America. Before leaving, he entrusts his wife and two daughters, Violaine and Bibiane, to Jacquin (Jacques) Uri. Jacquin is Violaine's fiancé, but he is secretly loved by

Bibiane. Jacques loves Violaine, as does also her cousin, Eloi Baubé. Violaine feels affection for Eloi, but her love is for Jacquin.

The drama unfolds through the jealousy and malicious lying of Violaine's sister. Bibiane tells Jacquin that Violaine has been unfaithful to him, and he asks his fiancée for an explanation. Violaine knows that she has done no wrong, and so declines to justify herself: Bibiane's accusing word is met by silence from the accused. The name Violaine is suggestive of the color purple and of violets, as some critics have pointed out, but it also connotes physical violence done to her by her sister; and *viol* means rape. What is taken by force from Violaine is not only her fiancé, for Jacquin, failing to get the assurance he wants, spurns her and chooses Bibiane for his wife; Violaine also has to give up her share of the land and, moreover, is blinded by Bibiane, who flings a handful of burning embers at her.

La jeune fille Violaine is thus another play about sharing. It foreshadows Marthe's fidelity to Louis Laine in *L'Échange:* she could not be seduced by Pollock, who had to use his wiles (and did so successfully) on her husband. Louis was first presented as a sensual being. Vio*laine,* whose name echoes his, participates in a different kind of sharing. Whereas Louis gives himself and takes everything without being challenged, Violaine gives up property, fiancé, and self, although she is questioned about her faithfulness. It is an "exchange" of a different order. Her contract—she is betrothed to Jacquin—is also with herself. Marthe does battle to keep Laine; Violaine lets violence be done to her. It is she who suffers, but, through the faith that Jacquin has denied her, she will have even more to share with him later. Again, like *L'Échange, La jeune fille Violaine* is about trust: a father entrusts his family and land to a young man. That young man breaks trust with his fiancée, and a sister violates her own sister's rights.

In the second version (written in 1901) the father, Anne Vercors, leaves his family so as to care for his dead brother's widow and children in America. One person's absence requires the other's. It is Claudel's way of indicating how trust begets trusts. Because of the father's faithfulness toward his brother, that of his own family is tested. Only so can fidelity be shown—or violence be done. One is reminded of Flannery O'Connor's *The Violent Bear It Away* (1960).

Driven from home, Violaine can take refuge only in the woods. Meanwhile, Bibiane has given birth to a son who, like Violaine, is blind. The holiness of the young girl, who lives in a cave in the forest, and her powers as a worker of miracles have been bruited about the countryside. Sick people from the area come to her for cures. And not even the injury that Bibiane has done to her sister keeps the former from asking the latter for a miracle: Violaine, with Bibiane's blind child, Aubin, in her arms, prays to God

> Have pity on him, Lord! Is there not
>   a desire
> Between the child of man
>   and yourself? and which is stronger than
>   you?
> He calls out to you and, behold,
>   there is your Presence.
> (first version, act 3)

For Claudel, a bond unites the children of men and their God. No need for a Prometheus to steal the fire and give it to men; man's desire is enough, for it is shared by the deity. In the play, this call of the child brings as answer the presence of Violaine's God—there is no call without an answer, and so the child's sight is restored.

Bibiane's ingratitude is expressed later by another act of violence. She tries to kill Violaine in an ambush. Violaine is rescued and brought to the family homestead, where she tells Jacquin all that has happened. Just before her father returns from his peregrinations, she cries out:

> Look, there is their love.
> My father has abandoned me, my mother
> handed me over; and my fiancé
> Has rejected me, and my sister.
> (first version, act 4)

Violaine's words, although filled with sorrow over her fate, also convey her hope. Like the child Aubin, whose sight she helped restore, she utters the cry "*Ita, pater!* I am coming! Take me away from here! / Toward the Lord of life, toward the nourishment of the Bread!"

Anne Vercors, returning, expects to find his family as he left it. But his first questions, "How is my wife? Where is Violaine? And is her husband here?" omit any mention of Bibiane, who has been the agent of mistrust. Before the end of the play, Bibiane confesses her wrongdoing to both father and husband. Jacquin already knows about it from Violaine, but Bibiane's own words are needed for pardon to be granted. The bells of the *Angelus* are heard in the distance, the commemoration of Christ's own Word. Bibiane leaves her corner and comes to sit at the feet of her husband.

The second version of the play shows significant changes. Jacquin Uri becomes Jacques Hury and Violaine's cousin Baubé becomes Pierre de Craon. Bibiane takes the name Mara. Pierre is an engineer, a builder of churches with the personality of a poet. In *The City*, it will be recalled, Besme was an engineer who had come to see that everything was ignorance, with nothing beyond. He could only repeat, "Nothing is." Claudel gives his second engineer the power of a worker in words as well as the faith of a Christian. This is not to say that Pierre has his head in the clouds. When taking leave of Violaine, he finds it difficult to reveal his feeling for her, knowing that she loves Jacques Hury. Claudel takes the opportunity to make him reflect on the birth of speech:

> The word, young girl,
> Is not formed as is a note
>   under the finger of the organist when the
>   foot presses the bellows.
> But with time, obscurely,
> More profound than the heart and the
>   intestines, during meals and walks, during

the silent hours of work, it builds
itself.
Like the spiritual seed in us, like the
seminal capsule,
Until from the bond that ties it the secret
stalk
is released.

(second version, act 1)

Pierre's confession of love becomes, indeed, the occasion for a small treatise on the subject. No matter how sincere he is, his words to Violaine fail to bring the two together, at least not as husband and wife. While imparting his love, Pierre also shares with her the fervor of his faith. She in turn confesses how full of joy she is. She allows him to kiss her on the cheek. Her sister, Mara, embodying the opposite of happiness though in search of it, witnesses this kiss of friendship and, with the reluctant help of her mother, turns it into a kiss of treason. She tells Violaine that she loves Jacques. Thereupon all resistance from the favored sister ends. Against Jacques's accusation Violaine offers no defense.

Her motive is not explained in anything we hear from her. So Jacques appears as the lover who has been deceived. At that point, he is as much the victim of passion as Violaine is of Mara's own. When she throws the hot embers in Violaine's face, Mara cries out:

She gives me all that she has.
The queen! as though I were asking her for a
penny.
Here, Cinderella! Keep this for yourself, stupid!

(second version, act 2)

What makes this version of the play different is that Pierre's discourse on love is, as it were, incarnated in the character of Violaine. Pierre had spoken of generosity and the giving of oneself. Mara succeeds in her treachery, but only because of Violaine's acquiescence and—as Pierre says—because of the time it takes to summon up a response. Ascribed to stupid ignorance by Mara, Violaine's answer is at first, and only on the surface, silence. That response takes as concrete a form in the second version as in the first, but in the second the motive has changed. In addition, Pierre de Craon is more complex, as is his harangue, which Violaine takes to heart. Rimbaud had discovered that "I is another"; recognizing this truth in himself, Claudel has Violaine do the same:

Who then, in us, other than ourselves,
has said *I*? has said this more mature and
foreign I?
So is there with us
Someone? and how long has he been there?
And how must we close our eyes
to see him?

(second version, act 3)

To Mara when she comes to beg for a miracle, Violaine recounts her own life since her exile from her father's house. Physically blind, the young woman can now see with changed vision. She has lost father, mother, eyes, and hands, but she has been given someone else, who lives within her and leads her steps. That other is God: "I expected an answer, but I received in my soul and in my body / More than an answer."

Claudel's world view is everywhere: a call does not go unheeded. God's response becomes a second presence among his creatures, yet another Incarnation. The church dogma states that Jesus takes on human flesh, that he is both God and man. Claudel extends this definition of God by showing that his incarnation is coextensive with many beings. God becomes not only another, but many others, among whom is Violaine. To the aspect of intrigue and treachery that is the condition of woman and man, Claudel would add the aspect of love. In the pardon that Jacques gives at last, he tells Mara that it comes from Violaine in him; it is Violaine, united in them both, who forgives.

When Anne Vercors returns to his family from America, one is curious to learn what knowledge of the New World he has acquired.

482

Between the first and the second versions, Claudel had again lived in the United States, and he puts in the father's mouth the impressions that a Frenchman might have of Americans: "They like sugary things; they eat candy, they drink lemonade." Again, in the States, nothing matures as it should, the land is poorly farmed, Americans are lazy, they don't know how to work, the mechanical spoils their mind as well as their land, the young men are old. Such are the impressions of a first visit. In Claudel they underwent revision as he enlarged his knowledge of the country beyond the precincts of New York and Boston.

As noted earlier, *La jeune fille Violaine* went through another transformation and became *The Tidings Brought to Mary.* It was shown on various stages, with some of France's best actors in the cast; Louis Jouvet starred in the 1947 production at the Théâtre Athénée. In 1948 there appeared a second and definitive version for the theater, and the play won a permanent place in the repertory when adopted by the Comédie-Française in 1955.

In this ultimate redaction of the text, Anne Vercors goes not to America but to the Holy Land. Pierre de Craon is still an engineer, but he has met with disaster. The first time he stayed at the farm, he tried to seduce Violaine, and that very day he contracted leprosy. On a return visit, as he is about to take his leave, he confesses to Violaine what his punishment has been. She is moved by his plight and, feeling in no way repelled by his disease, she gives him a good-bye kiss. Mara witnesses this, and when Jacques confronts Violaine, she shows him that she too is a leper. The leper is the outcast par excellence, and Violaine suffers the full force of the ostracism that medieval society imposed on the victims of the dread affliction.

The new title indicates the schema of the play. As Violaine and Pierre meet in the opening scene, they hear the *Angelus,* that is, the tolling of the church bells that call the faithful to pray in words celebrating Mary's conception of Jesus and her role in their salvation. In the first text of *The Tidings Brought to Mary,* Violaine and Pierre recite the prayer in alternating verses. In the second, adapted for the stage, Claudel has the two hear the *Angelus* being rung at a nearby convent. The chorus sings the *Regina coeli, laetare, laetare* (Queen of heaven, rejoice, rejoice!). Celebrating the Incarnation of Christ at this moment counterpoints the result of the exchange they have just made in a kiss—an exchange that causes their separation both from one another and from all those who come to know of their disease. The *Angelus* tells of the union of God and man in one person; but this particular peal of the bells betokens the opposite, the separation of man and woman.

Mara gives birth to a stillborn child and again seeks a miracle from her sister. The time is now Christmas, and from the belfry the Gloria rings out. As Violaine tells her sister "a child is born unto us," she takes the dead child from Mara and asks her to read the lessons for the Christmas service, one of them being from the Gospel of Saint Luke. The child to be born is Mara's own, thanks to Violaine's intervention. Using the angel Gabriel's words to the shepherds, Violaine tells her sister, " 'And behold I announce to you great joy.' " Once again the *Angelus* is heard, and Violaine tells Mara to listen as the child slowly awakens.

Through this rewriting of the Gospel story, Claudel provides what may be regarded as his medieval miracle play. But it is meant to be something more than a play looking back to the past; it is not just a retelling of the biblical narrative. It looks forward to the present by expressing Claudel's thesis about the spirit and the flesh. The Incarnation is not only a historic occasion to celebrate. In the play the time frame is shattered and the tidings are shown as not solely for Mary. Since they relate to an event taking place within a Body, they continue to require a body. Claudel seems to say that the Incarnation is possible as a present reality; it is present because there is a Violaine. In this theater of the possible, the child does come to life. Mara has given the child flesh, Violaine gives the spirit—by giving her own eyes, as Mara discovers: "Violaine! What does this mean? Her eyes were black / And now they are blue like your own."

The stage affords Claudel the opportunity not only to juxtapose variant portions of the Gospel, but also to make the most of what a play—a show—is for: to make the spectator think he or she is at the center of the action. The world of *The Tidings Brought to Mary* is medieval only in its costuming. The substance of the drama is that there is a Word that must be told, a Word to be announced, a Word to be anchored in flesh and bones. Language becomes body—poetry or prose—but not just poetry or prose, spoken or written. Neither is it the body of God speaking to the body of man, but of God to woman—and only thus to man.

It is in *The Tidings Brought to Mary* that the importance of women in Claudel's work reaches a new peak. In *Tête d'Or,* the princess was symbolic of hope for the ambitious hero. Crucified on the tree, she was the sign that his desire for conquest had come to naught. In the first act the tree is a symbol of the strength of man; in the last it holds a woman who becomes that strength.

Tête d'Or does not rely on any clear biblical source. *The Tidings Brought to Mary* relies heavily on the Gospel narratives, as well as on the cult and tradition of Catholicism. With W. H. Auden, one readily excuses Claudel for having written so well, even when the imagery is foreign to one's contemporary surroundings. Making the Word flesh is not, for Claudel, a lofty idea to commemorate, or even a good thesis for the stage. The mystery is actual and occurs in the words and through the person of Violaine.

Claudel's next assignment, in 1911, took him as consul-general to Frankfurt am Main, where the Germans were friendly—unlike some Catholics in his native country. For *The Tidings Brought to Mary* were not always well received by the devout. Still, among the clergy

he had a champion in the rector of the Catholic Institute, Monsignor Baudrillart, and among the laity there was the poet Charles Péguy, who was newly converted.

During that same year a production of *The Tidings Brought to Mary* was planned. It opened on Christmas Eve and was fairly well received by the audience, but not by the Catholics, who suspected Claudel's orthodoxy. (He also reached Catholic readers through unsigned polemical articles that he wrote in answer to *Le réveil municipal de Clichy,* an anticlerical paper.) He was not neglecting poetry, producing a hymnal known under the title *Corona benignitatis anni Dei* (*Coronal,* 1915) and the first version of *Protée* (Proteus, 1914), a farcical variation on the return of Menelaus to Greece.

After Frankfurt, Claudel was sent to Hamburg; and in the autumn of 1913 two of his friends produced *The Tidings Brought to Mary* at Hellerau in Saxony, where it met with a warmer reception than in Paris. It was another play, *The Hostage,* that first found real favor in the French capital. Then came the war, and Claudel returned to France with his family. Soon, the rapid advance of the German troops caused the French government to move to Bordeaux, and Claudel with it.

On his return, after the Germans had been pushed back, he produced *La nuit de Noël de 1914* (Christmas Night 1914, 1915), a play criticizing the Germans for destroying a small town in Champagne. Those who had been killed Claudel shows as suddenly coming back to life—two soldiers, many small children, and the priest. These are the Innocents of modern times who have been executed to avenge the cutting of a telegraph line.

Although short, the play is at once a prayer and an indictment. That the Germans did not bombard the place on Christmas Day seems to show their respect for the Christian religion, but some French soldiers interpret it as a joke. The play ends with the hour of midnight resounding; there is a cry that the bell is ringing. But the scene underlines the barbarism of war by showing on the stage the traditional Christmas crèche (Nativity scene) during prayers, while the German guns pound out twelve shots on Rheims Cathedral.

Claudel was fond of Germany and the Germans, but he could not refrain from a cutting irony in the priest's sermon: "Lord, thou knowest it is not easy to pray for a German. These are a people so perfectly honest, and virtuous, and certain of doing good, even when they kill children." Claudel adds to his topical play a polemical thrust: Germany is represented by the lovers of darkness—Goethe, Kant, and Nietzsche—while France is represented as the standard-bearer of joy for the world.

In Rome during the war, Claudel represented the French National Office for Foreign Trade. His aim was to recover some of the trade advantages that had earlier fallen into German hands. Claudel found that many in orthodox Rome did not care for his use of the Bible in *Coronal*. He was meeting the response that a "Catholic writer" must be prepared for, whether or not he advertises himself as one. Badgered by criticism and yet tirelessly performing his duties for the French state, he also found time to write: the pope was to be the subject of his next play, *The Humiliation of the Father*.

On 1 January 1917 Claudel was appointed minister plenipotentiary in Rio de Janeiro, with the young composer Darius Milhaud as secretary. There he demonstrated his skill as a diplomat, obtaining for France much-needed military aid and negotiating a treaty of cultural exchange. He was served equally by his keen eye for commercial matters and his poetic gifts. During this Brazilian sojourn, Claudel and Milhaud collaborated outside their office: *L'Homme et son désir* (Man and His Desire, 1917) was the product of a two-page scenario for which Milhaud composed the score.

But the major work that Claudel wrote in Brazil was *La messe là-bas* (The Mass There, 1919). Its many parts correspond to the development and structure of the Latin mass—its Introit, Gloria, Preface, etc. The writing shows

Claudel's poetic art intermingled with his belief. The poet is a witness to the vanity of things: "All things of which one says that they pass, I am your witness that they have passed." But creation for Claudel is also a celebration. Just as for Mallarmé everything existed in order to make a poem or The Book, so things for Claudel have their purpose: "They probably do not pass uselessly, they squeeze out to the very last stanza the Poem." For Claudel, whatever is not God is what could not be. All things serve as witness to God's existence, and do this through the poetry of what is. There used to be World Fairs: now the Europeans have joined in yet another "cooperative," war. In *La messe là-bas* the poet is startled out of his opening reverie by the ringing of the bell that signals the entrance of the priest who is to celebrate mass. The first words of the liturgy are then spoken, the same words that are the first to be spoken in another work, James Joyce's *Ulysses* (1922): "I will go unto the altar of God" (from the Introit).

In the Gloria, Claudel points to the sun as the sign of God's glory. The glory of God is bound up with a witness who is man, hence the sun becomes an object of contemplation:

There is nothing else so beautiful that one can
   look at it other than for a very short time,
Like the verse on paper, which the white
   interrupts from time to time,
And like the idea which, in order to take up again
   the end with all the original force,
Needs other ideas one upon another to prepare it
   and give it that force for one second, which
   bears away all.

Characteristically, to move toward God is not merely to approach him:

Praised be God who has not allowed us to be any
   continuous being!
And who by the Breath that he has placed in this
   vacuum which constitutes us
Has forced us to take a word toward Him and
   open ourselves up fathomlessly.

What God calls forth is poetry, the word that is both speech and direction. Directed discourse is being par excellence, the being who speaks and not, as Claudel playfully puts it in *Le ravissement de Scapin* (The Kidnapping of Scapin, 1952), the rational Descartes or the "thinking reed" of Pascal.

When the priest celebrates the liturgy of the Word as he reads the Gospel and Epistle, what Claudel celebrates at the same time is his own past hearing of those texts, not in one particular place but in the various cities where he has lived and attended mass; Brazil expands into Paris, Boston, China, Prague, Frankfurt, and Hamburg.

In the "Offertory," Claudel takes up the various persons who might go to mass. Among them one, who is attentive, is raised to the level of the universal—the one who cannot be disturbed, or the one who receives his task in the early morning and does it—in this lies his offering to God. Then, there is another, "whose domicile is not to be at home. . . . Only exile teaches him his country." But this exile and all Appearance, and all that is Nothingness— the poet tells us—these too may be somehow returned to God.

At the "Consecration," Rimbaud is invoked. He is still the explorer par excellence. And what he sought is not beyond some mysterious forest or beyond the seas. The object of his desire is at home, shown in the monstrance; it is the accident in substance. Claudel relies here on Scholastic theology to express his belief in the ubiquitous presence of God; God becomes an accessible body. This part of the poem ends with a voice saying, "Rimbaud, did you think you could always flee me?"

The "Pater Noster" shows a father leaving his family and evokes the pain that wife and children must endure as the head of the household goes off to war. France becomes Mount Zion lamenting its lack of a leader, a family in want of a father: "Have pity on us." And strangely mixed with this cry to the eternal Father is that of the earthly. He is such only because he has known woman and she has

known his caress, the benediction of this knowing being the children, a benediction built on man's weakness. In Claudel, woman is no longer the weaker of the sexes.

Communion. Ego sum. Je suis. (I am.) God is in man. God now speaks to man and Claudel restates a main tenet of his poetic art: "If we were not different, there would not be this desire, there would not be this great embrace that exists between husband and wife! / If you were not my son, I would not be today that Father around whose neck the Prodigal Son throws his arms."

The soul is like a woman trying to conceal her lupus from her lover. She is a woman in prison visited by her friend. She cries and, under her clothing, she clutches her identity tag. These are the powerful images that describe the soul's search for God, for communion with him—but how strange! *Lupus* means wolf: the soul is that which devours and is devoured.

Ite, missa est (Go, you are dismissed) is an invitation to wayfaring. The mass has been celebrated. Christian duty has been done, and the harvest is ready. Here, at the end of the ritual, Claudel puts in a few words his whole poetic vision, the basis of his work, which he sees as both flesh and spirit in the materiality of the Word: "Sens, égal de l'arbre qui dure et de la moisson qui dort. / Un monde a l'intérieur de ta pensée jaunir dans le même souffle d'or!" (Sense, so like the enduring tree and the sleeping harvest. / A world within your thought ripens in the same golden breeze!). *Sens,* the imperative of "feel," means, in Claudel's system, direction, movement, creativity, meaning. Feel the world that endures and that has in it possibilities of germination and of birth, since man and woman are equals in creation. Like the tree, they form Claudel's recurrent images. The human pair cannot be hewn down, but are lasting, eternal, filled with the spirit.

In *La messe* Claudel includes the French custom of distributing bread at the church door. This part carries the title "Le pain bénit" (The Holy Bread). In his day the Catholic liturgy ended with a reading from the Gospel of Saint John, the first words of which celebrate the Word. Claudel seizes the opportunity to bring in the great wayfarer and reader Christopher Columbus, who "pacified the unleashed Creation by giving from the ship's stern a reading of the Gospel of Saint John."

Finally, the poet reminds us that in the end is the beginning. The Word and Adam, both creations, are linked. When the poet lifts his head from his work, he hears the same breath or spirit that ruled Paradise before Adam gave form to Eve.

In February 1919 Claudel returned to France by way of New York. In September he was made minister to Denmark. While in that northern country, Claudel also served as the French representative on the international committee for settling the status of the border province of Schleswig. In 1921 he left Denmark to become ambassador to Japan. He and his family were there during the massive earthquake of 1 September 1923 and took an energetic part in helping the victims.

By 1925 Claudel was back in France, at the château of Lutaine, his summer home. There he wrote *Les conversations dans le Loir-et-Cher* (Conversations in the [Department of] Loir-and-Cher, 1935). This volume of table talk is about many things—cathedrals, art, death. The autumn found him in England on a lecture tour during which he met G. K. Chesterton at the French Institute.

Early the following year he was back in Japan, where he helped to found the Maison de France to promote cultural exchange. Claudel was next considered for the post of ambassador to Germany. He saw in the possible friendship of France and Germany the seed of a united Europe—the "United States of Europe." For Claudel was not a chauvinist. But circumstances altered, and in December Claudel was appointed ambassador to the United States. He came to Washington by way of San Francisco. In this country his peasant common sense and strong grasp of business affairs enabled

him to cement friendly relations between France and the United States at a time when France faced the difficulty of paying its war debts. Claudel was once again in France at the signing of the Kellogg-Briand Pact on 27 August 1928.

America inspired him to write *The Book of Christopher Columbus.* The vogue of Max Reinhardt's lavish production *The Miracle* (1911) was a further incitement. But writing suffered many interruptions. Claudel wanted to "learn" the country; he made trips to Chicago, and to the Deep South as far as the Cajun swampland. He came across a town named Sodom, and immediately wanted to send a postcard to his friend André Gide, whom he was trying to convert. This effort failed, as one may read in Gide's *Journals;* but Claudel pursued his self-assigned mission to convert others. His correspondence with Gide, Jacques Copeau, Jacques Rivière, André Suarès, and other friends throws light on the literary life in twentieth-century France.

In March 1933 Claudel was posted as ambassador to Belgium. He was fascinated by Rubens' painting *Christ in the Tomb,* which seemed not just to live but to breathe. Claudel described the Netherlands as "a kind of lung." Land and art are, for the writer, bodies, incarnations of an idea, the translation of self. Claudel's essays on art, especially on the Dutch painters, are gathered in *L'Oeil écoute* (*The Eye Listens,* 1946) and *Autres textes sur l'art* (Other Writings on Art, 1960). Like one of the characters in Proust, he had a love for Vermeer. In Belgium, Claudel felt the soil kindred to his own; for one thing, French was spoken there, and he found many former friends, among them the actress Eve Francis, who had played in *The Hostage.* By way of pilgrimage, he visited the prison where Verlaine had been held. Claudel's term in Brussels ended in 1935.

In the same year he made his first try as candidate to the Académie Française. He then retired to the château of Brangues in the Isère (French Alps). In Belgium he had written

Jeanne d'Arc au bûcher (Joan of Arc at the Stake, 1939), a cantata with narrator, for which Honegger composed the music, for the dancer Ida Rubenstein. He also wrote *La sagesse, ou la parabole du festin* (Wisdom, or the Parable of the Feast, 1939), a second version of what was earlier simply *La parabole du festin.* For this poem the composer was Darius Milhaud. The subject of Joan of Arc a figure of perennial appeal to other writers—Mark Twain, Anatole France, George Bernard Shaw, and Jean Anouilh—was treated by Claudel in the form of an oratorio. Joan and Brother Dominic share the stage. Who is to preside over the trial court? It is a question for mortals, but Claudel goes back to the medieval theater and makes animals speak while men become dumb beasts. It is his way of showing the kind of judgment that Joan faces. Politics and religion must combine in the personality of the judge. The Tiger, the Fox, and the Serpent decline the role; Cauchon (the historical person) accepts, and is made to identify himself in a sort of pun: *"Ego nominor Porcus"* (My name is Cochon [pig]). The two spellings correspond to a long and short o respectively. Using Latin gives dignity to the farm animal now raised to the dignity of judge, while the name itself degrades him. There must be a judge, so let it be the Pig. The chorus sings:

> *Porcus! Porcus! Sit Porcus preaeses noster. Non habemus alium judicem nisi Porcum. Vivat et à jamais vivat Porcus porcorum! Dignus, dignus, dignus est praesidere in nostro praeclaro corpore! Sicut lilium inter spinas ita formosus iste inter cucullos.*

> The pig, the pig! Let the pig be the judge. We have no other judge than Pig. Long live, forever live the Pig of Pigs! He is worthy, worthy to preside over our distinguished body! Like the flower among the thorns, so is he among the layabouts.

> (scene 9)

The words echo those of the mob that shouted, "Let Jesus be crucified," and pro-claimed, "We have no other king but Caesar!": "We have no other judge than Pig!" The character then puts on the mask of a pig. The sheep becomes the assessor, and the ass the clerk of the court: it is a medieval show in which Claudel runs the gamut of language in French and Latin to underscore the plight of Joan.

In 1947 Claudel was received into the Académie Française by François Mauriac. In 1945, after the death of Charles Maurras, who had been expelled from the Académie and given a life sentence for collaboration with the Germans, Claudel had forborne candidacy, to protest against the eulogy accorded Maurras by Jules Romains. This about-face in the members' attitude revolted him. Of course, many could not understand Claudel's support of Francisco Franco, the right-wing dictator of Spain; it was the usual entanglement of politics and literature.

On 17 February 1955 *The Tidings Brought to Mary* was added to the repertory of the Comédie-Française. On 22 February, Claudel died. Unlike Hugo, he was not given burial at the Pantheon; his funeral appropriately took place at Notre Dame.

In addition to plays, writings on art, biblical commentary, and correspondence with writers, actors, and producers, Claudel kept a journal. It was published in 1968–1969.

It would be wrong to classify Claudel as a propagandist for religion who exhibited his soul for the edification of the public. His trilogy (*The Hostage, The Humiliation of the Father,* and *Crusts*) is as much concerned with love and sacrifice as it is with the politics of religion in revolutionary France. And Claudel has another side, that of satire and humor. Protée is amusing, and so are *Le ravissement de Scapin, L'Ours et la lune* (The Bear and the Moon, 1919), and other parodies. Likewise unpolemical are such works as *La femme et son ombre* (Woman and Her Shadow, 1927) and *La lune à la recherche d'elle-même* (The Moon in Search of Herself, 1948).

True, *La sagesse, ou la parabole du festin* re-enacts the drama of the Gospel parable; the

Bible was a frequent source of Claudel's inspiration. In *L'Histoire de Tobie et de Sara* (The Story of Tobit and Sara, 1942) he shows young Sara possessed by demons and in need of the right husband to rescue her. But these are not thesis plays.

Claudel was first and foremost a poet. His utterance was not limited to one form, one theme, or one purpose. His religious faith marked all his writings, but so did his education and his society; they did not limit him: he translated Aeschylus, Coventry Patmore, and the Chinese poets. He even tried his hand at imitations of the Japanese, in *Cent phrases pour éventails* (A Hundred Sentences for Fans, 1927).

In the preface to that work, he distinguishes between the letters of the Western alphabet and the Oriental ideographs. Our letters are a kind of "semantic engine." Thus the letter *I* may be "a dart, the index finger, a tree, a column, the affirmation of the person and of unity." In themselves, words are unstable; they only translate the writer for his reader, furnish a meeting place on the white page. *Le mot,* or the word, acquires its force by motion; it is "an ensemble obtained by successiveness." By contrast, the Oriental characters change the writer's stance. Writing is no longer a horizontal movement but a vertical relation: "The poet is no longer simply the author but, like the painter, he becomes the spectator and critic of his own work; he sees himself in the act of performing it."

Claudel's collection of one hundred poems resembles haiku poetry. They reflect (as does his *Dodoitzu,* 1945) his love of Japan and his adaptation to its culture. They also show conciseness of thought and poetic power. "Encre" (Ink), for example, bears witness to the relation between the material aspect of poetry and the spirit and body of man:

> *Encre*   *sève*
> *de l'esprit*
> *et sang*
> *de la pensée*

> Ink   sap
> of spirit
> and blood
> of my thought

In another poem we are shown air as both a source and a means for the production of poetry:

> *Éventail*   *Je*
> *pulse l'air*
> *dans*
> *un*
> *pays*
> *ficti*
> *f*

> Fan   I
> draw air
> in
> an
> imaginary
> countr
> y

The "I" that breathes is the fount of the fictional or imaginary; as such, it depends on the physical aspect of breath as well as its "inspiration," which means "breathing in."

Mystery informs these poems, and often the tables are turned on the reader's expectation:

> *J'écoute*   *à mon oreille*
> *la voix*
> *de quelqu'un*
> *qui parle*
> *les yeux fermés*

> I listen   at my ear
> the voice
> of someone
> who speaks
> with eyes closed

The *Five Great Odes* were written on different occasions and celebrate either poetry itself (for example, "The Muses") or else some important moment in Claudel's life. The "Magnificat" is a thanksgiving hymn for the birth of Claudel's child. With the tribute to a new life, it acknowledges what the poet's own life has meant. "O the long bitter streets of yesterday and the time when I was alone and one! / The walk through Paris, that long street which goes toward Notre Dame!" Claudel becomes "the young man called by name" of the Bible. Saint Luke's reference to the Virgin Mary's thanksgiving and verses of Mary's own hymn are interspersed in the ode: "My soul magnifies the Lord. . . . My spirit has exulted in my Savior."

Claudel then equates his joy with that of John the Baptist and strives, like Mary, to express his humility. His mind swings on two axes alternatively, that of Old Testament history and his own. God's dealings with Moses and with John continue in his own life. The biblical *Magnificat* celebrates the deity taking on flesh; likewise, Claudel's "Magnificat" finds words to give flesh to feeling. The economy of salvation is paralleled in Claudel's poetic economy: "Let the noise become voice and let the voice in me become Language! / Amidst the universe which stutters, let me prepare my heart as someone who knows what he has to say."

The poet, moreover, has been delivered from the inebriation, the tyranny, of books and ideas. He attacks the verbal gods of his day— truth, progress, humanity, even art and beauty. One recalls the opening of Mallarmé's sonnet: "The flesh is sad and I have read all the books." In this special sense, bookishness is idolatry and breeds boredom; but Mary's words declare: "You have deposed all these powers from their throne." Flesh and language are thus renewed in Claudel's writing.

In the "Magnificat," Claudel recognizes that he was not called to live a monastic life. His world is the earth considered as a palimpsest, a record of layered errors and truths. His world is also his body—not dead to the world but rather alive and performing upon it the alchemy of poetry. Other voices may have called to him—the novel or the history of lands visited. But the voice he now wants to hear (and speak) is that which is limitless and founded in God. The poet wants to be let out of the prison of self and into the will of God: "And here I am his father with You."

Mesa in *Break of Noon* complains that God has not carried out the established plan, but has taken advantage of his superiority. Claudel refines that idea (and implies that God was man well before the Incarnation) by showing that God does share his power. For he puts in man's hands that power which is humility. In so doing, God does not merely remove himself from his works; he vanishes utterly. Claudel uses the word *anéantissez* (annihilate): "And here I have become with you a principle and a beginning."

The ode has a polemical side. Claudel inveighs against the French masters who have wrought destruction, which he defines as bringing things together without giving them unity through the self. His villains are Voltaire, Renan, Michelet, and Hugo—workers with words who disqualified themselves from the life he himself has found in the work of words.

Claudel's poem ends with a series of benedictions, and a representation of the rite that goes by that name. The image of the priest haunts Claudel: "And here I am like a priest." Claudel encounters God serenely in this ritual of benediction. The host in the monstrance being (under the accidents of bread) Christ, the poet-priest takes Christ and, like Mary, incorporates him. The "Magnificat," in keeping with the promise made to Abraham, is a benediction forbidding death. For his tombstone Claudel chose the words "Ici reposent les restes et la semence de Paul Claudel" (Here lie the remains and the seed of Paul Claudel). They imply not an end but a beginning, together with a look backward to the beginning of time and a present that is generative.

Claudel's poetry, it need hardly be said at this point, is marked—some say marred—by his faith and his use of the terms, figures, and ritual of the Catholic church. The spiritual and material shocks that Claudel had suffered in life were bound to surface in his writings.

What, in effect, did writing mean to him? In *Cent phrases pour éventails,* the little "Encre" quoted above may also be read *ancre* (anchor). Likewise, in translating Li Tai Pe in a collection of Chinese poems, Claudel makes the title *Pour encre, poète* (For ink, poet) and suggests that writing is a pleasure. But it is ephemeral as a pleasure, its importance to him being (as we have seen) enormous—religious, metaphysical, symbolic of life, breath, thought, and sexuality.

In another sense, that movable feast of writing and traveling was linked for Claudel with a worldly institution, the church. In "Strasbourg" the cathedral of that city becomes "one great poem" discoursing sacred and profane history. In *Coronal* the poet, Don Rodrigue, paints the likenesses of saints, and Claudel turns to his own use the many ritual commemorations of events in the life of Jesus and Mary, ending with the stations of the cross.

The first station, the place for meditation along this painful journey, tells the reader he is witnessing the end: "It is over." For the finite is to be completed by the divine. Pontius Pilate's *Ecce homo* (Here he is) is glossed as: "We no longer want Jesus Christ with us because he gets in the way." The second station evokes the popular image of carrying one's own cross. In this passage Claudel mingles compassion for Christ with irony. When Jesus falls on the way to Calvary the spectator-poet asks, "How do you like it, this earth that you made?" But the scoffer also feels the fall—Adam's, Christ's, and his own; so the sarcasm and irony turn into a prayer: "Save us from our first sin, which takes us by surprise." Christ's fall, too, takes him by surprise.

In the fifth station, Claudel shows Jesus no longer able to carry his cross. Simon the Cyrenian is called on and is harnessed, like a beast, to the cross to drag it along. The sense is: the work is only fit for beasts of burden. What for Jesus was *Tolle! Tolle!* (Take it up) becomes for the other *Attelle* (Strap it on); Simon must be hitched to it like an animal.

Even so, "he does take it up heftily and walks behind Jesus / So that nothing of the Cross may drag along and be lost." (There is here a hint of the miracle of the loaves and fishes, where the disciples gather up the scraps so that nothing may be lost.)

Earlier in the poem, man received the eucharist as Christ does his cross: "We give him wood for his bread." The imagery should be completed by the reader, who should think of his own fall, made voluntarily, through boredom. For Claudel's spectator uses Jesus' own words, charged with sarcasm for anyone else: "Que fera-t-on du bois mort, si l'on fait ainsi du bois vert?" (What will you do with dead wood, if that is the way you handle the green?), the wood being the cross.

On the cross, Jesus feels thirst. *Sitio,* quotes Claudel in Latin, a language he supposedly did not care for, but of which he makes such pointed use in many of his writings. Then the poet-bystander answers with a sarcasm that echoes the jeering of the crowd in the Gospel account: "Are you speaking to me? Do you still need me and my sins?" But here is more than mockery, and the poet-reader is more than a bystander. He is involved, *engagé,* committed: "Am I the one needed so that all can be consummated?" Jesus' work needs someone else. His cry is a call, perfect only if it is completed by an answer. The Passion of Christ, Claudel implies, can only be if there is compassion.

Plainly, Claudel's religious imagery is anything but that of a traditional Catholic writer. Whether we think of *Break of Noon* or *Le soulier de satin* (*The Satin Slipper,* 1929) we find him as free of all Catholic stereotypes as of the shibboleths of any coterie. *The Satin Slipper* deserves mention by way of conclusion, because it epitomizes the poet's work and life. It is a play about desire. The curtain rises upon the hero with Rodrigue's brother, a Jesuit and a world traveler, tied to a shipwrecked boat. He prays for Rodrigue, who formerly chose the flag of Christ, but who now wants to possess the world and its honors. (The words used allude to Loyola's consideration of the two standards in his *Spiritual Exercises.*) The matter of the play is the discovery of what Rodrigue and Prouhèze really desire since desire takes varying forms.

Claudel uses as a motto for the play the Portuguese proverb "God writes straight with crooked lines." Rodrigue's path toward the novitiate bends, and he takes the road toward being a conquistador and painter. From the first words of Cébès in *Tête d'Or* to Rodrigue's in *The Satin Slipper,* Claudel's road as a writer saw him at times uncertain and struggling: was he to be prophet or poet? Claudel devised his own standard. He found that as a poet he could serve as well as a religious man in an order; he could be Rodrigue *and* his brother. A second motto flanks the Portuguese proverb— Augustine's *Etiam peccata* (Sins also serve). Claudel's poetic art reinterprets the epigraph and says *Etiam verba* (They also serve who sit and write).

Selected Bibliography

EDITIONS

INDIVIDUAL WORKS

POETRY
Connaissance de l'Est. Paris, 1900.
Cinq grandes odes, Processional pour saluer le siècle nouveau. Paris, 1910.
La cantate à trois voix. Paris, 1913.
Corona benignitatis anni Dei. Paris, 1915.
La messe là-bas. Paris, 1919.
Poèmes de guerre. Paris, 1922.
Feuilles de saints. Paris, 1925.
Cent phrases pour éventails. 3 vols. Tokyo, 1927.
Dodoitzu. Paris, 1945.

PLAYS
Tête d'Or (first version). Paris, 1890.
Morceau d'un drame. In *La revue indépendante.* Paris, 1892.
La ville (first version). Paris, 1893.
L'Arbre. Paris, 1901. Contains *L'Échange, Le repos du septiéme jour, Tête d'Or* (second version), *La ville* (second version), and *La jeune fille Violaine* (second version).
Le partage de midi (first version). Paris, 1906. Version for the stage, Paris, 1949.
L'Otage. Paris, 1911.
L'Annonce faite à Marie (first version). Paris, 1912. The definitive version for the theater is in *Théâtre II.* Paris, 1948.
Protée: Drame satyrique en trois actes (first version). Paris, 1914. Second version in *Deux farces lyriques: Protée, L'Ours et la lune.* Paris, 1927.
La nuit de Noël de 1914. Paris, 1915.
L'Homme et son désir. Paris, 1917.
Le pain dur. Paris, 1918.
L'Ours et la lune. Paris, 1919.
Le père humilié. Paris, 1920; rev. ed., Paris, 1945.
L'Endormie. Paris, 1925.
La jeune fille Violaine (first version). Paris, 1926.
La parabole du festin. Paris, 1926.
La femme et son ombre. Published in *L'Oiseau noir dans le soleil levant.* Paris, 1927.
Sous le rempart d'Athènes. Paris, 1927.
Le soulier de satin (first version). 4 vols. Paris, 1929. Version for the stage, Paris, 1944.
Le livre de Christophe Colomb. Paris, 1929.
Jeanne d'Arc au bûcher. Paris, 1939.
La sagesse, ou la parabole du festin. Paris, 1939.
L'Histoire de Tobie et de Sara. Paris, 1942.
La lune à la recherche d'elle-même. Paris, 1948.
Le ravissement de Scapin. In *Opéra.* Paris, 1952. Also in *Théâtre II.* Paris, 1956.
L'Échange (new version). Paris, 1954.
La danse des morts. In *Théâtre II.* Paris, 1956.
Le jet de Pierre. In *Théâtre II.* Paris, 1956.

ESSAYS
Art poétique. Paris, 1907.
Positions et prospositions. 2 vols. Paris, 1928–1934.
Les conversations dans le Loir-et-Cher. Paris, 1935.
Figures et paraboles. Paris, 1936.
Présence et prophétie. Fribourgh, 1942.
L'Oeil écoute. Paris, 1946.
Contacts et circonstances. Paris, 1947.
Discours et remerciements. Paris, 1947.
Accompagnements. Paris, 1949.
Autres textes sur l'art. In *Oeuvres complètes.* Vol. 17. Paris, 1960.

BIBLICAL COMMENTARY
Paul Claudel interroge le "Cantique des Cantiques." Paris and Fribourgh, 1948.

Emmaüs. Paris, 1949.
Introduction à Isaïe dans le mot à mot. Paris, 1974.
Jérémie. Paris, 1974.

OTHER WRITINGS
Sous le signe du dragon. Paris, 1948.

COLLECTED WORKS
Théâtre I. Paris, 1947; 2d ed., 1956.
Théâtre II. Paris, 1948; 2d ed., 1956.
Mémoires improvisés. Paris, 1954.
Oeuvre poétique. Paris, 1957.
Oeuvres en prose. Paris, 1965.
Journal I (1904–1932). Paris, 1968.
Journal II (1933–1955). Paris, 1969.
Oeuvres complètes. 28 vols. Paris, 1950–1986.

TRANSLATIONS BY CLAUDEL

L'Agamemnon d'Eschyle. Foochow, 1896.
"Poèmes de Coventry Patmore." *La nouvelle revue française* (1911–1912)
Les choephores d'Eschyle. Paris, 1920.
Les Euménides d'Eschyle. Paris, 1920.
Li, Po. *Pour encre, poète.* In *Oeuvres complètes.* Paris, 1950–1986.

CORRESPONDENCE

Correspondance, 1904–1938: Paul Claudel et André Suarès. Preface and notes by R. Mallet. Paris, 1951.
Correspondance Paul Claudel—Darius Milhaud (1912–1953). Preface by H. Hoppenot and introduction and notes by J. Petit. In *Cahiers Paul Claudel 8.* Paris, 1967.
The Correspondence Between Paul Claudel and André Gide (1899–1926). Translated by J. Russell. New York, 1952.
Jacques Rivière—Paul Claudel: Correspondance, 1907–1914. Introduction by I. Rivière. Paris, 1926.
Letters from Paul Claudel, My Godfather. Collected by Sr. A. du Sarment. Translated by W. Howard. Westminster, Md., 1964.
"Lettres à Lugné-Poe (1912–1928)." In *Cahiers Paul Claudel 5.* Paris, 1964.
"Lettres de Paul Claudel à Agnès Meyer (1928–1929)." In *Cahiers Canadien Claudel 6.* Ottawa, 1969.
Paul Claudel—Francis Jammes—Gabriel Frizeau:

Correspondance (1897–1938), avec des lettres de Jacques Rivière. Preface and notes by A. Blanchet. Paris, 1952.

TRANSLATIONS

The Book of Christopher Columbus: A Lyrical Drama in Two Parts. Translated by the author with A. Meyer and D. Milhaud. New Haven, Conn., and London, 1930.
Break of Noon. Translated by W. Fowlie. Chicago, 1960.
The City: A Play. Translated by J. S. Newberry. New Haven, Conn., 1920.
Coronal (Corona benignitatis anni Dei). Translated by S. Mary David. New York, 1943.
The East I Know. Translated by T. F. Benet and W. R. Benet. New Haven, Conn., 1914.
The Essence of the Bible. Translated by W. Baskin. New York, 1957.
The Eye Listens. Translated by E. Pell. New York, 1950.
Five Great Odes. Translated by E. Lucie-Smith. London and Chester Springs, Pa., 1967.
The Hostage: A Drama. Translated by P. Chavannes. New Haven, Conn., 1917.
I Believe in God: A Meditation on the Apostles' Creed. Edited by A. du Sarment. Translated by H. Weaver. New York, 1963.
Letters to a Doubter. Translated by H. L. Stuart. New York, 1927.
Lord, Teach Us to Pray. Translated by R. Bethell. New York, 1948.
A Poet Before the Cross. Translated by W. Fowlie. Chicago, 1958.
Poetic Art. Translated by R. Spodheim. New York, 1948.
The Satin Slipper. Translated by J. O'Connor. New York, 1945.
Tête d'Or: A Play in Three Acts. Second version. Translated by J. S. Newberry. New Haven, Conn., 1919.
Three Plays: The Hostage, Crusts, The Humiliation of the Father. Translated by J. Heard. Boston, 1945.
Three Poems of the War. Translated by E. J. O'Brien. New Haven, Conn., 1919.
The Tidings Brought to Mary. Translated by L. M. Sill. New Haven, Conn., and London, 1916.
Two Dramas: Break of Noon, The Tidings Brought to Mary. Translated by W. Fowlie. Chicago, 1960.

Ways and Crossways. Translated by J. O'Connor. New York, 1933.

BIOGRAPHICAL AND CRITICAL STUDIES

Beaumont, E. *The Theme of Beatrice in the Plays of Claudel.* London, 1954.

Berchan, R. *The Inner Stage: An Essay on the Conflict of Vocations in the Early Works of Paul Claudel.* East Lansing, Mich., 1966.

Bulletin de la Société Paul Claudel. 107 nos. Paris, 1958– .

Cahiers canadiens Claudel. 6 vols. Ottawa, 1964– .

Cahiers Paul Claudel. 12 vols. Paris, 1959–.

Chiari, J. *The Poetic Drama of Paul Claudel.* London, 1954.

Claudel Newsletter. 4 vols. Kingston, R.I., 1968.

Claudel Studies. Dallas, 1972.

Études Claudéliennes. Tokyo, 1943.

Ferlita, E. *The Theatre of Pilgrimage.* New York, 1971.

Fowlie, W. *Claudel.* London, 1957.

Freilich, Joan S. *Paul Claudel's "Le soulier de satin": A Stylistic, Structuralist, and Psychoanalytic Interpretation.* Toronto, 1973.

Griffiths, R., ed. *Claudel: A Reappraisal.* London, 1968.

Hellerstein, N. S. "The Theme of the Actor and Its Symbolic Function in Paul Claudel's Works." *Essays in French Literature* 18: 22–28 (1981).

Knapp, B. L. *Paul Claudel.* New York, 1982.

Lesort, P.-A. *Paul Claudel par lui-même.* Paris, 1963.

MacCombie, J. *The Prince and the Genie: A Study of the Influence of Rimbaud on Claudel.* Amherst, Mass., 1972.

Matheson, W. *Claudel and Aeschylus: A Study of Claudel's Translation of the "Oresteia."* Ann Arbor, Mich., 1965.

Mauriac, F. *Réponse au discours de réception de Paul Claudel à l'Académie française.* Paris, 1947.

Maurocordato, A. *Anglo-American Influences in Paul Claudel, I: Coventry Patmore.* Geneva, 1964.

Paul Claudel. 5 vols. Published by *La revue des lettres modernes.* Paris, 1964–1968.

Spitzer, L. "Interpretation of an Ode by Paul Claudel." In *Linguistics and Literary History.* Princeton, N.J., 1948.

———. "A Linguistic and Literary Interpretation of Claudel's *Ballade.*" *The French Review* 16: 134–143 (1942).

Waters, H. A. *Paul Claudel.* New York, 1970.

Wood, M. "The Theme of the Prison in *Le soulier de satin.*" *French Studies* 22:225–238 (1968).

PETER S. ROGERS

ANDRÉ GIDE
(1869–1951)

THROUGHOUT ALL HIS life and work André Gide searched for a plenitude that would balance and satisfy the needs engendered by various aspects of his personality: a persistent inclination toward mysticism and introspection, an ever-present temptation to indulge in pleasures of the flesh, and a need for rational testing and recording of experience. It took Gide the better part of eighty years to achieve some degree of fullness of experience and to reconcile antinomies within himself. He had progeny, he made peace with his God, he experienced the intensities of human existence, and he left behind him his complete works. As he wrote in *Thésée* (*Theseus,* 1946), "For the good of future humanity, I have done my work. I have lived."

If in eighty-two years Gide managed to accomplish so much, it took him at least the first twenty-four to formulate and to see the virtues of plenitude. Formed by the rigorous Protestant ethic, with its penchant for introspection, of his widowed mother and her companion, Anna Shackleton, Gide spent his early life attempting to enforce ascetic principles of behavior; he denied the sensual, the temporal, and the real in favor of the spiritual, the eternal, and the imaginary. He was ideally suited for the symbolist movement, or so it seemed from his first book, *Les cahiers d'André Walter* (The Notebooks of André Walter, translated as *The White Notebook,* 1891). But nothing human can be suppressed successfully, as Gide learned through experience. The more his hero tries to follow the ascetic path, the more he feels tempted by the scenic route; moreover, temptations overcome make him vulnerable to the sins of pride. Made distraught by his own ambivalent nature, by the evanescent world of his mind, by the ambiguity of his relationship with his cousin and intended wife, and by all sensual contact with the world, André Walter dies of brain fever and of the hallucinations he has learned to invoke with ease.

The first important result achieved by the publication of *The White Notebook* was to bring Gide into contact with Parisian literary circles. He met Maurice Barrès and Oscar Wilde, was introduced to most of the prominent symbolists, and frequented Stéphane Mallarmé's Tuesday evenings and José María de Heredia's Saturday afternoons. He decided to make a place for himself in the literary whirl. A first choice was to identify himself as a symbolist. The second was to justify this choice by composing a theory of the symbol, *Le traité du Narcisse* (*Narcissus,* 1891), and a symbolic travelogue, *Le voyage d'Urien* (*Urien's Voyage,* 1893). Although not the account of a real voyage, as the pun in the title suggests ("le voyage du rien" [the voyage of nothing]), the book represents nevertheless a timid step in the direction of a broader experience of life; Gide's imaginary travelers make their way through three landscapes suggest-ting as many responses to life: the sensual ("sur une mer pathétique" [on a sea of emotion]), the introspective ("la mer des Sargasses" [the Sargasso Sea]), and the ascetic ("la mer glaciale" [the Arctic Sea]). The last still best suits Gide's nature, and the second still tempts him, but he has grown enough to consider, however indirectly and negatively, the first and most troubling of his own interior landscapes.

But he evidently did not succeed in convincing himself of the evils of the flesh: he returned to the theme in his next work, *La tentative amoureuse* (*The Lover's Attempt*, 1893). Gide argues here that passion is self-consuming and hence destructive, that desire satisfied produces boredom, self-satisfaction, and complacency, and that the pleasures of the flesh can be addictive and dissolve the will. He presents the case in the form of a journey through the seasons of the year and in the persons of two young lovers, Luc and Rachel. Even before a year passes, both Luc and Gide become impatient with this love affair. Luc abandons Rachel in the hope of finding "new things"; Gide, abandoning both hurriedly, ends the story with similar aspirations.

Gide finished *The Lover's Attempt* during the summer of 1893, at about the time he and Paul-Albert Laurens decided to travel to North Africa to spend the year broadening their experience and fulfilling themselves. So radical a decision to explore the real world was prepared well in advance. For some time Gide had been gathering sufficient energy and arguments to break away from family, country, God, and his own pious impulses. During June 1891 he found in Jules Laforgue's writing a kindred spirit that encouraged him to develop a measure of objectivity flavored with irony; conversations with Wilde provoked a certain boldness in his thought and in the realization of his uniqueness; a visit to Munich in March and April 1892 affirmed his growing independence from his mother, as did the discovery of Johann Wolfgang von Goethe's plays, which he both read and saw there; and another experi-

ment in independent traveling, in Spain during August 1893, further drew the young introspective out of himself and into the world of sensation. Finally, credit for Gide's gradual emergence is also due to the simple and sensual poetry of Francis Jammes and the pleasant summer months spent in the company and on the grounds of the Laurens family at Yport.

The *Journal* (1939) entries of 1893 document Gide's transformation. On 17 March, while visiting relatives at Montpellier just before leaving for Spain, Gide notes, "I love life and prefer sleep not because of its nothingness but because of dreams." A month or so later, Gide writes: "No longer read books by ascetics. Find exaltation elsewhere; admire the difficult joy of equilibrium, the joy of life's plenitude. May each thing offer all possible life it contains. It is a duty to make oneself happy." And, further expressing the attitude that was fully realized by the decision in October to leave for North Africa, Gide claims:

> I know that when I want to partake of those things which I had denied myself because of their beauty, it will not be like a sinner, in secret, with the bitterness of repentance; no, it will be without remorse, with force and joy. Leave the dream world at last and live a full and forceful life.

(1:35)

Throughout the journal from April to October 1893 Gide rejects ever more boldly his former asceticism and pious yearnings for fulfillment in the kingdom of absolutes. He speaks of becoming robust, happy, and normal, of abandoning himself to life, and of putting the various aspects of his personality in equilibrium. He goes even further, seeing happiness and the highest form of originality in the absence of limits and scruples, in accepting, even seeking, all the sorts of experience that the human can possibly undergo. In the following years, after his trip to North Africa, Gide formulated this principle: "I am done with any system of morality that does not allow or teach the most noble, and most beautiful, and the most liberal use and development of our forces." Repeating later on in the 1894 journal entries other statements of this sort, he underscores the consciousness and deliberateness of his search for plenitude.

In North Africa Gide got more than he had bargained for and almost more than he could handle: an attack of tuberculosis and the subsequent slow convalescence in the desert town of Biskra intensified his physical reawakening and immersion in the world of sensations. Yet the first book Gide wrote and published after *The Lover's Attempt* and the first North African sojourn was not an ode to joy, but rather a mad piece of folly, the first sustained example of Gide's humor. *Paludes* (*Marshlands*, 1895) originated in early 1893 but was not composed until the fall of the following year, while Gide was continuing his cure in the cool mountain air of Neuchâtel. Because his reawakening was so recent and because he was anticipating returning to Biskra for the oncoming winter, it is not surprising that the "new" Gide should look back at his past nor that, fortified with newly won objectivity, he should treat this past with avenging irony. But even more interesting is that this first expression of the new Gide contains a sense of the comic that announces in many ways his subsequent work.

Gide himself has characterized his sense of humor as anchored in an inclination toward the bizarre, the illogical, and the unexpected. It expresses the mind's refusal to take seriously a suffocating world, suggesting that Gide's humor serves to mask problems that preoccupy him, enabling him to experiment with possible solutions casually and without the inhibiting effects of stage fright. From 1893 to 1895, when he was struggling both to free himself from his mother's moral influence and to define for himself the role and nature of the artist, he repeated on several occasions that everything in the truly original artist must appear new, that he alone has the key to a special world of his own. He wrote in his journal of this time: "He [the artist] must have

a particular philosophy, aesthetics, ethics; his entire work tends only to result in revealing these. And that is what makes his style. I have also discovered, and this is very important, that he has to have a particular sense of humor."

Not all that is funny in Gide's writing and reported conversations can be classified under one type of humor or be made to fit within the category of his special sense of humor. In the journals, in much of the autobiographical material, and in some of the imaginative works, Gide's jokes range through most of the familiar categories, from low lusty humor to highbrow word and sound plays. Even within the framework of the *soties* (satirical farces), as he came to call his comic works, there is a variety of humor. Nevertheless, a point of view establishes a context of humor in the *soties* that is both peculiarly Gidian and rigorously consistent with the totality of Gide's world. On several occasions Gide uses the adjective *saugrenu* to describe his sense of humor. It means bizarre, absurd, or ridiculous, and tends to describe, in Gide's use, the vigorous but incongruent confrontation of two systems of thought or associations—that is, the confrontation of two or more words, ideas, or events, each of which suggests a frame of reference only apparently related to the others. At the basis of Gide's whimsy there is an eruption of illogic within a context promising logic or at least treated as logically coherent. Because the *saugrenu* operates on two levels, the level of incongruency and the suggested level of congruency, it is closely related to irony; it suggests what might be while falling short of the potential, remaining schematic, incomplete, or stunted.

There are many examples of this type of humor outside of the *soties*, in the *Journal*, in the memoirs, but none so succinct perhaps as two notations from the notebook of the hero of *Marshlands*. The first is "Lane bordered with birthwort," while the second reads, "'Why, dear friend,' said I, 'with a still uncertain sky, have you brought only one umbrella?' 'It's a parasol,' she answered." In the first example a lyrical description clashes with a cacophonous learned term and reveals a rather misguided eagerness for precision. In the second, a basically insignificant question is elevated to a level of serious and earnest inquiry by a vague preciosity of language; it is thereupon met with the same cuteness of formulation, which has a logic all its own, yet does not relate to the reality of the situation except on a purely linguistic level. Angèle, the narrator's interlocutor and companion, is perfectly rigorous in her logic of compromise: in the face of uncertain weather, rather than being caught with no umbrella at all or left carrying two to no avail, she compromises. Her choice is as logical as drizzle. But further rendering the exchange entirely nonsensical, the two major nouns (*ombrelle* and *en-tout-cas*) mean essentially the same thing: "parasol."

In his memoirs, *Si le grain ne meurt* (*If It Die . . .* , 1926), Gide attributes the tone of these notations and his ability to sustain it to a mood he can describe only by the English word "estrangement." Because of his illness and his long-anticipated sensual reawakening in North Africa and because of his eagerness to return after his Swiss convalescence, Gide naturally felt dissociated from his erstwhile self and comrades. He was striving to live in the world, to absorb it and delight in it, while they persisted in rejecting it. But his feelings of estrangement were all too familiar to him and were an integral part of his personality. He confesses to a sort of dissociation from reality and to a disbelief in the reality of the world on numerous occasions throughout his life. Mentioned early in the *Journal* and frequently thereafter in various forms and recalled in *If It Die . . .* in several contexts, his difficulty again crops up at the very end of his life in *Ainsi soit-il ou les jeux sont faits* (*So Be It, or The Chips Are Down*, 1952), and is recorded succinctly in his journal: "I have never been able to *adhere* perfectly to reality." Such a handicap, better described as an inability to possess himself fully, to integrate a sense of self with

emotion, thought, and sensation, explains the structure of his world view, his lifelong search for and idealization of plenitude and equilibrium as well as, eventually, his sense of humor. "What exalts us is the feeling of plenitude," Gide remarked in his journal shortly before his first voyage to North Africa. And in the same entry he articulated the opposite notion: "What makes us laugh is the feeling of atrophy in something capable of fullness. All things have within them the potential for plenitude."

It seems reasonable, on the basis of these and similar remarks made at so important a period in his life, to use them as guides for a discussion of his fiction. In addition to revealing the personal aspirations articulated early in life and maintained to its very end, these remarks suggest aesthetic analogues that, together with the problem of point of view, lie at the core of Gide's fictional technique. Atrophy in a personality fully capable of attaining fullness, traced from either a subjective or an objective point of view, yielded works of art Gide felt obliged to distinguish as either *récits* (tales) or *soties*. Viewed objectively, the results are comic; told from the vantage point of the victim, they are tragic. But in either case they record personality deformations that keep their victims from realizing the full measure of their potential.

SOTIES

The main fault of his protagonist in *Marshlands*, which Gide in the preface called a sickness, is precisely his inability to ignore the stifling, swamplike world he lives in. He sees nothing but mediocrity all about him, in his friends, and in himself as well. But he is trapped in circumstances of his own making. The victim of an obsession that transforms his vision of the world and that in turn increases his feelings of "boredom, monotony, futility," he finds himself caught in an ever-narrowing spiral that brings the isolated fault of his personality to its conclusion in absurdity. The protagonist, potentially a full, round character, is flat, deformed, and atrophied by his obsession.

Gide's *Marshlands* is composed of the daily journal entries of a man of letters and excerpts from the book, "Marshlands," that he is busy writing. In the central episode, a mock symposium sponsored by his friend Angèle, he demonstrates his talent for transforming a variety of stimuli into terms consistent with his obsession. He describes his book in ways most appropriate to his interlocutors: for the physiologist, "Marshlands" is the story of animals whose eyes have atrophied as a result of living in the dark caves; for the critic, he quotes Vergil, and borrows Tityrus as his own hero; for the psychologist, the book is the story of the normal man, the protopersonality everyone takes as the point of departure for his own development; for the moralist, it is a didactic work intended to spur people to action; and for the group as a whole, " 'Marshlands,' at this moment," he says, "is the story of Angèle's reception." He explains that the only way to tell a story so that everyone will understand it is to change its form in line with each new psychological and intellectual orientation. And, in fact, when he describes "Marshlands" to his very active friend Hubert, he recounts Tityrus' adventures—or non-adventures—day by day to the point of boring him. For the calm and delicate Angèle, his account verges at times on the tabloid human-interest story with interspersed discussions of fictional techniques.

Given the narrator's obsession, together with his lucidity and his desire to change, how does he break out of his distasteful situation? He cannot, of course, and every attempt to move, to change his ways, is frustrated, primarily by his own timidity and inertia. Nothing comes of his visits to the hothouses of the Jardin des Plantes except imagery for his book; his voyage to a suburban park aborts as well; he does not even finish his book but begins another with a similar paludal title, "Polders" ("Marshes"). It is not surprising,

then, to discover, alongside the swamp image and the attendant ideas of immobility, images that suggest enclosure and confinement. Nouns such as "door," "gates," "windows," "curtains," "courtyards," and adjectives implying limitations, such as "small," "closed," "narrow," "circular," and so on, abound in the narrator's journal. The more obsessed he becomes, the more desperately he idealizes the contrary: the new, the unexpected, departures, voyages, action, freedom, and, especially, spontaneity.

Stagnancy horrifies him. At Angèle's banquet he informs the hostess that nothing irritates him more than "what goes round and round in place." Like the fan in her apartment, he and his friends are not truly immobile, yet they do no more than move about in place; they are stagnant. Their acts have become habits containing their personalities; they define themselves not by the style of an action, but by the action itself. But it is not only their own "normality" that encourages them along the easy path; everything urges them to lapse into a rut. The narrator proclaims: "And that's just what irritates me: everything outside, laws, customs, even the sidewalks seem to determine our lapses and ensure our monotony." That the narrator himself cannot avoid these setbacks is a point hammered home by the failure of his paltry little trip. He himself incarnates the stagnancy he cannot abide and, further, develops it to its extreme. In effect, Gide's narrator enacts in his own way the principle suggested in one of the "remarkable sentences" listed at the end of the *sotie:* "One must carry out to their conclusion all the ideas one has raised."

The major characters of *Le Prométhée mal enchaîné* (*Prometheus Misbound*, 1899) also bring to some sort of conclusion the ideas they raise, and, as a consequence, at least two of them emerge deformed. Gide's second *sotie* is made up of events that are as bizarre as the moods and futile gestures of his first. One May afternoon on the boulevards of Paris the "miglionnaire" banker, Zeus, delivers unsolicited and randomly a 500-franc bank note to an undistinguished person and, also at random, rewards another's kindness with a vigorous slap in the face. Meanwhile Prometheus, tired of his long sojourn in the Caucasian mountains, sheds his shackles and goes for a walk in Paris. At a café he meets Damocles and Cocles, the recipients of Zeus's largesse, who recount their stories and describe the transformations their lives have undergone since they were singled out. Damocles is obsessed by the sudden and inexplicable receipt of the bank note, while Cocles wins sympathy for his misfortunes. As his misfortunes grow (he loses an eye), Cocles continues to seek the others out, knowing he will profit from the sympathy of others. He receives the directorship of a large foundation to aid the blind. Damocles, on the other hand, cannot explain why he received the money and is tortured by the impossibility of finding its source and of repaying, or at least thanking, the unknown donor. Because of Zeus's gesture each has risen from the anonymous mass of people and has gained an identity. Because Damocles received money and can neither explain nor repay it, he discovers he has scruples; Cocles, unjustly victimized, becomes the underdog who seeks and attracts sympathy. Each nourishes his new identity with his whole being. Prometheus, the man with the eagle, recognizes himself in both the man with one eye and the man with the burden of debt. The eagle functions here as a symbol of an obsession that tyrannizes the person who nurtures it. Prometheus concludes that everyone must possess an identity to which he can devote himself: we must all have an eagle of our own that we can feed with our very substance.

But as Prometheus nourishes his eagle, he diminishes as it flourishes. Similarly, Damocles, so distraught by the dilemma that defines him, finally expends himself on it and dies of brain fever. Pondering these new developments, Prometheus reconsiders the substance of his first lecture, which he delivers near the beginning of the book, and, for Damocles' funeral oration, comes up with a parable that he hopes will clarify the tie between Damocles' death and his own decision to kill his eagle.

The parable has as its principal characters Angèle, Tityrus, and two more Vergilian figures, Meliboeus and Menalcas. Tityrus, surrounded by swamps and inertia, is prodded into activity by Menalcas, "who planted an idea in Tityrus' head and a seed in the swamp before him." The seed grows first into a plant and then into a gigantic oak to which Tityrus devotes himself and around which develops a settlement he eventually administers. Angèle, the librarian, invites the reluctant Tityrus to take a trip to Paris, from which place Meliboeus, the naked, Pan-like, flute-playing free spirit, takes Angèle with him to Rome. Tityrus, thus abandoned, finds himself once again at home, alone, and surrounded by swamps. The audience titters a bit, charmed by the humor in Tityrus' simplicity and circular busyness. But they do not fully grasp Prometheus' apparent reversal of position; the appearance itself of a sense of humor in one who had earlier claimed "an irremediably serious turn of mind" so disconcerts them that they laugh also, from nervousness. Happy that he has been able to please them, Prometheus admits that since Damocles' death he has found the secret of laughter. One cannot help trying to clarify this secret by resorting to Gide's own ideas on similar matters: laughter arises from atrophy and from the objectivity that permits the perception of a stunted growth as caricature.

Prometheus is astounded to discover that Zeus refuses to keep eagles, that he just distributes them. This revelation contradicts his basic precept and undermines his commitment to his own eagle. More damage is done to his original principle when he sees in Damocles the effect of excess devotion to one's eagle. Through Damocles' death Prometheus realizes that death is the limit beyond which one cannot develop an idea in oneself, that developing an idea to such an extreme is costly and prevents knowing other ideas. Prometheus realizes, in short, that unless he is careful, his eagle will end by devouring him completely. Such objectivity affords Prometheus a gauge to measure the excess of his beliefs and the degree of their complicity in Damocles' death. He now realizes that he need not forfeit all control to his eagle—that, although committed to an idea, he need not relinquish his autonomy. Before leaving the Caucasus, he had rid himself of "chains, tendons, straitjackets, parapets, and other scruples" that were petrifying him, and between four and five in autumn, he strolled down the boulevard that goes from the Madeleine to the Opéra; similarly, in his fable Tityrus, feeling that his "occupations, responsibilities, and various scruples held him no more than the great oak," smiled and left, "taking with him the money box and Angèle, and toward evening strolled with her down the boulevard that goes from the Madeleine to the Opéra."

Tityrus, too, discovers laughter when he discovers his freedom. It is neither futile nor tragic that the exercise of his new freedom ultimately leads him nowhere, that he has not progressed, that he returns to the neutral terrain he began on. Although abandoning himself to events, and ideas, and seeds, he does not abdicate his willpower and his control, so that when he needs them he can overcome his eagles and retain the potential to grow. The new Tityrus does not stagnate. "An idea," Gide says in the *Journal*, "continues to be a living force so long as all the nourishment in it is not used up in phenomena." Once it has been used up, it is abandoned. "Was it of no use, then?" his audience asks Prometheus after he has eaten the eagle. He answers: "Don't say that, Cocles! Its flesh has nourished us. When I questioned it, it answered nothing. But I have eaten it without rancor: had it made me suffer less, it would have been less fat; less fat, it would have been less delectable." Prometheus does not entirely reverse his previous position. Everyone must devote himself to his eagle; every idea must be brought to its furthest limit. But there are times when one must go beyond

it, abandon it, or bring it to complete fruition outside of the self; otherwise one endangers one's health and full development. Prometheus survives the story in good health and spirits, feasts upon the eagle, and writes this book with one of its quills.

The work of art, precisely, allows the exceptional man to accomplish what he feels capable of without adverse consequences; it permits him a plenitude and an equilibrium that are, as Gide noted in 1897, "realizable only in the work of art." The mechanics of this procedure were outlined years later by Gide in an often-quoted letter to a critic who, in reviewing *L'Immoraliste* (*The Immoralist*, 1902), identified Gide with his hero: "How many buds we carry in ourselves, dear Scheffer, which bloom only in a book. . . . My recipe for creating a hero is quite simple: take one of these buds, put it in a pot—all alone—soon one has an admirable individual." Gide evidently permitted three unlikely characters to grow in his *sotie* along lines dictated by different approaches to a basic tenet of his early ethical code, which he imagistically synthesized in Prometheus' devotion to his eagle: in *The White Notebook* and in *Narcissus*, Gide formulated this tenet by saying, "We must all manifest, we must all represent"; he later developed it in a pamphlet, "Quelques reflexions sur la littérature et la morale" ("Some Thoughts on Literature and Ethics," published first in 1897 and again in 1899 as an appendix to *Prometheus Misbound*, and ultimately added to the *Journal* as "Literature and Ethics").

In *Les caves du Vatican* (*The Vatican Swindle*, 1914) the preoccupations of the earlier *soties* concerning action, freedom, and personal identity are brought into society. Despite the hubbub and social confusion of *Marshlands*, the prime concern is the point of view of the narrator and diarist. In *Prometheus Misbound*, too, Gide emphasizes the relationship of his caricatures to themselves. In *The Vatican Swindle* he is again concerned with man's relationship to himself and with the nature and function of identity, but here these preoccupations are placed in a social context; people interact with one another, and their actions have social consequences. This slight change in point of view is reflected in the very form of the novel. Like a blown-up philosophical tale in the manner of Voltaire, *The Vatican Swindle* is handled with the traditional narrative tools Gide had previously avoided: the third-person narrative with frequent plunges into the interior world of its characters; intrusion of the author's comments and opinions on the matter at hand; detailed, descriptive passages of places and persons; deliberate excursions into exposition of background and history of events and people; and, more subtly, a multiplicity of tones that coincide with the varieties of subject matter. *The Vatican Swindle* is essentially a traditional novel of adventure simplified and pushed to the extreme of parody.

The novel is divided into five parts, each bearing as its title the name of one of the major figures. Like Damocles and Cocles, each of the figures is so devoted to his eagle that he has atrophied and become one with it: Anthime Armand-Dubois, a behaviorist and mechanistic scientist, a pillar of the Society of Freemasons, and a militant atheist; Julius de Baraglioul, a traditionalist in politics, religion, and aesthetics, and a novelist convinced of the immutability of the novel of psychological analysis, of the consistency of human behavior, and of the inscrutability of the French Academy; Amédée Fleurissoire, a sincere and devoted believer, a manufacturer of religious articles, and a latter-day poor man's Parsifal or Sir Galahad. Even Protos (protagonist of the chapter entitled "Les mille-pattes" ["The Millipedes"], the name of the international organization of outlaws he leads), who is ever-present and constantly changing form and disguises and who advocates freedom and flexibility, is fixed by his need and program to oppose the staid members of the society he lives in. Only Lafcadio is free enough both socially and emotionally to be lawless and

flexible like Prometheus. Although he too is a caricature, he becomes so enviable and attractive that Gide almost filled out his portrait with flesh and bone; at the end of *The Vatican Swindle* he is very nearly a round character, moving about in a two-dimensional world.

The people of *The Vatican Swindle* are divided into two groups, the select minority Protos calls "the subtle ones" and, by far the majority, "the crustaceans." To the first group belong only Protos and Lafcadio. But the qualities that make Lafcadio "a subtle one" serve no goal other than his own enrichment, whereas in Protos, who is as subtle and cunning as the devil himself, they are subservient to his need to dominate and oppose. Lafcadio was formed, without the rigors of family, by his courtesan mother and the talents of her successive lovers. Completely free and spontaneous, a creature of inconsistency, victim only of an insatiable curiosity that prompts him to act, Lafcadio lives heedless of consequences in a manner idealized by his complete opposite, the narrator of *Marshlands*. Capable of any action that tests and reveals him, Lafcadio feels his grip is "large enough to embrace all of humanity, or perhaps to strangle it." So far he has not committed a harmful act, but realizing that the difference between harmful and beneficial is slight for the man of action at the moment of action, he becomes interested in all the unforeseen elements in an act of violence. As a result he hurls Amédée Fleurissoire from the train compartment they are sharing while traveling between Rome and Naples.

The consequences of this act go beyond the exaltation surrounding the event and reach into the calm, lucid moments of his present life. "I lived oblivious," he tells young Geneviève de Baraglioul; "'I killed as though in a dream, a nightmare in which I've been floundering ever since.'" He was oblivious because he was unaware, as Protos informs him later, that one cannot live lawlessly, that even the millipedes have a rigid code and discipline, that one cannot "move out of one society so simply, without immediately falling into another," and that it is inconceivable "that any society can do without laws." Circumstances are so manipulated by Gide that the decision to accept responsibility for Fleurissoire's death depends on Lafcadio alone. At first he threatens to do so; by the end of the book, however, the narrator suggests that he will not give himself up so easily. Lafcadio can, like Prometheus, rise above a situation and continue to exercise his freedom.

This is not so for the crustaceans of the book, nearly all of whom exchange one eagle for another, one fixed identity for another, one society with its system of laws for another just as stringently legalized. Miraculously cured of rheumatism, Anthime becomes a Catholic, only to return to his old ways after Fleurissoire's death; Julius changes aesthetics and psychology based upon the example of gratuitous and inconsistent behavior offered by Lafcadio but reverts when he is elected to the Academy. Even in Fleurissoire a waning, pious fervor promises radical changes whose full development is cut short by Lafcadio's act.

In *The Vatican Swindle* Gide dramatizes the consequences of gratuitous acts as well as those arising from a change in identity. In the latter case he appears to test Prometheus' final hypothesis, concluding that, once atrophied by devotion to an idea, one is so deformed that atrophy remains even if the idea passes. Atrophy, as Gide means it, is the wasting away of a whole organism that results from improper nourishment or exercise of some of its important elements. He exemplifies it by fragmenting the human personality, exaggerating a few distinctive traits, and virtually excluding the rest. Depending upon the manner and the context in which these dominant traits are presented artistically, they become either exaggerations in caricature or tragic flaws.

A constant danger for Gide was too close identification with his characters. Understandably alarmed, he noted in a 1912 journal entry that his puppets in *The Vatican Swindle* were getting out of hand and rounding out

with blood and bones: "They are forcing me to take them more and more seriously." Maintaining his characters at the level of caricature was essential to the free working-out of ideas he considered important. The obvious consequence of getting closer to his characters and treating them sympathetically would have been to undermine the whimsy of the *sotie* and inhibit his freedom. But even more dangerous, this seriousness would have transformed his work from caricature to tragedy. A key device, although not used in the first of the *soties,* is the objective third-person narrative, which gave Gide the distance from his characters that freed his whimsy and enabled him to see the ridiculousness in certain modes of seriousness and ultraserious behavior. Conversely, the first-person narrative presents a case subjectively and without the perspective that establishes some reasonable hierarchy of values. Unless this device is handled ironically, as Gide did in *Marshlands,* it lessens the distance between author or reader and the characters, evokes sympathy, and sets the scene for tragedy.

RÉCITS

Jean Hytier noted that the *soties* are stories in which wisdom bears the mask of folly, while the *récits* reveal the folly under the appearance of wisdom. Essentially, then, the *récit* is the reverse of the *sotie,* distinguished by means of aesthetic devices alone. But the stuff each is made of is the same: deformation of the human personality presented either from the point of view of the victim or from some objective point of view.

All the *récits,* from *The Immoralist* to *Geneviève* (1936), tales recounted in the first person, are what Gide called critical or ironical books. *The Immoralist* is a book of warning, a critique of a certain form of individualism, characterized by a tendency to relinquish self-control to instincts. After the death of his young wife, for which his own selfishness and negligence were largely responsible, Michel finds himself alone, independent, and free. But after three months of abandon, he realizes that "knowing how to liberate oneself is nothing; what is difficult is knowing how to be free." He summons to his side several faithful friends, who sit and listen to him recount his life.

Brought up under the subtle limitations inculcated by his Huguenot mother, he transferred this severity and asceticism, upon her death, to the rigorous task of fashioning himself after his father. At twenty he was so skilled in philology and archaeology that his father farmed out research projects to him. Later, to satisfy his father's deathbed wish, he agreed to marry without quite knowing, at twenty-four, what marriage or life could entail. The first part of the book traces Michel's evolution from a concern with dead things to the discovery of a taste for life, from a vague awareness of his own sentiments to a need for sensation, and from a context of abstraction to a world of concrete things. Although he begins truly to see the world with the help of his wife, it is the severe attack of tuberculosis and subsequent slow convalescence in North Africa that reawaken him to life and to himself. In his search for health he establishes a simple and simplistic code that is finally carried beyond his convalescence: everything healthful and healthy is good while all else is evil. Because his early education and all the conventions of society it perpetuates offer resistance to his self-revelation, he brands them as evil and evolves an antisocial, anti-establishment doctrine that rejects artifice, culture, restraint, and intellect. He relinquishes his will and abandons himself to his instincts in the hope of casting off the new man and reaching the authentic, or "old," man the Bible speaks of.

Like Anthime Armand-Dubois, Michel falls into a system as rigid as the one he would escape. But he does not succeed in changing himself as thoroughly as he thinks. He carries over many intellectual needs: for strategy, for rational justification, and, mostly, for some authority against whom to react. Marceline,

his wife, takes on this last role; she is his last tie to civilization and as such he has to destroy her. Ménalque, his friend and mentor, on the other hand, represents the ideal Michel has set for himself: the lucid, independent, and complete utilization of one's energies. Incapable of carrying out such an ethic, Michel simply abandons himself to sensation, attempting to justify and modify his behavior in reaction to the opposing ideals Ménalque and Marceline represent. Both realize, however, that Michel is eluding their influence. Marceline can do nothing to control her husband's growing selfishness. Ménalque, after noting the inconsistency in Michel's supposed disdain for property and his many possessions, finally urges Michel to keep his "calm happiness of the hearth." The last remark that Ménalque makes about Michel seems to sum up his evaluation of his would-be disciple: "One believes one possesses, and, in fact, one is possessed."

Possessed indeed to the point of dissolution of his willpower, Michel cannot abandon Marceline and live the life he dreams of all alone; he drags her back with him to North Africa, where she finally dies. Thereafter, unable to help himself, he needs others to tear him away from the small Algerian village he has settled in, to give him reasons for living, and to help him "prove to himself that he has not exceeded his rights."

If Michel's eagle is an obsession with sensations to the detriment of intellect and willpower, Alissa's, in *La porte étroite* (*Strait Is the Gate*, 1909), is made of other stuff. Where Michel dissolves willpower and exalts instinct, she denies instinct and tenses her will through continual self-abnegation. Alissa embodies the pious tendencies of young Gide, but allows them to grow independently of Gide's "grain of good sense." She chooses the narrow path of piety leading to God and ultimate self-denial in death. The more she effaces herself, the more she has to prove her worth by further sacrifices. God, of course, does not respond, and Alissa, in a moment of desperate solitude, cries out, "I should like to die now, quickly, before I understand once again that I am alone." Like Michel, Alissa is condemned to bring to conclusion one human tendency. As a consequence of her ascetic piety, she negates not only herself but also Jerome, with whom she could have enjoyed the calm happiness of the hearth. Like Michel, she lacks, as Gide notes in *Journal des faux-monnayeurs* (Journal of "The Counterfeiters," 1926), "the bit of good sense that keeps me from pushing their [the characters'] follies as far as they do." But Alissa lacks even more; beneath her intense piety she has a need to sublimate her fears and intensities into safe and traditionally respected channels. By striving for sanctity, she avoids having to create a personality of her own and to deal with instincts she fears are hers.

Strait Is the Gate is divided into two parts, or, rather, it is composed of two *récits:* Jerome's narrative of events and Alissa's record of her reactions in her journal. Although they represent two independent *récits,* the second narrative, along with Alissa's dialogues and letters quoted in the first part, is by far the more interesting and mc ˃ important. Jerome's narrative exists onl₁ ₐs a preparation and contextual explanation for the spiritual evolution traced in Alissa's journal. Jerome comes off as a rather docile and dependent man in whose literary style is reflected hesitation, self-righteousness, and fondness for constant qualifications. His style is flaccid, picky, Gide said on several occasions, but it is necessarily so. Jerome's narrative puts Alissa's journal and personality in relief by sparing her the need to recount facts and events that would normally weaken the intensity of her emotions and character development. Jerome acts as a possible and ever-ready solution to her dilemma but leaves any decision entirely up to her. His constancy and passivity are part of the décor in Alissa's world and exert upon her no pressure that she cannot easily combat.

Several other characters model for her the consequences of Jerome's offer. Tante Plantier, fertile, buxom, and devoted to her issue, as well as to that of her family, offers earthly wit, wisdom, and sound advice. Alissa's sister, Juliette, also counsels a less stringent path and acts upon her beliefs. Rather than waste her life pining for Jerome, with whom, unbelievably, she is in love, Juliette attempts by force of will to balance her needs and the possibilities of satisfying them. She marries another and settles down to some semblance of happiness.

After her sister's marriage, Alissa finds herself facing the still available Jerome and persists in not yielding. "An absolutely useless heroism," Gide said about her resistance. "Thought of her fiancé invoked in her, immediately, a sort of flush of heroism that was not voluntary, but practically unconscious, irresistible, and spontaneous." But this heroism is not entirely gratuitous. Jerome's presence immediately calls into play Alissa's sense of her own virtue, which is as strong as she fears her propensity to vice demands. In the closely knit world circumscribed by their families and the Protestant parish, only Alissa's mother, Lucile Bucolin, is an intruder. A Creole by birth and a courtesan by temperament, she flaunts herself with great glee in the ascetic environment she married into. While her children are still young and impressionable, she obtrusively takes a lover and finally disappears with him. It is apropos of this tragedy that the local pastor plants the justification of Alissa's and Jerome's withdrawal from life in a sermon based on Christ's words "Strive to enter through the narrow gate" (Luke 13:24). Sensitive to what she fears she inherited from her mother and aware that she resembles her greatly, Alissa early chooses to develop only the spiritual side of her nature, to which she directs all her intensity.

Alissa's choice of the narrow path is also strengthened by the numerous dead-end paths traced by those around her: examples of her unhappy father, of Jerome's widowed mother forever dressed in mourning, and of her lifelong companion, Miss Flora Ashburton, all encourage her to take any involvement other than a spiritual one as weakness or vice. But she is also trapped by a weak Jerome. Instead of helping her to integrate conflicting elements in her personality through his protection and understanding, he follows her lead and plays her game. "It is by being infatuated with his own weakness that man imitates," Ménalque tells Michel in a line eventually deleted from *The Immoralist.* In Alissa's case, it is through fear that she imitates the asceticism prevalent in her milieu, and it is because her intensity is frustrated by Jerome's weakness that she strives to realize what she feels is her noblest part by developing it to its extreme in death.

La symphonie pastorale (*The Pastoral Symphony,* 1919), like the other *récits,* is an ironic book. It criticizes self-deception of a kind to which Gide himself was particularly vulnerable: liberally interpreting the Scriptures to suit one's own needs and weaknesses. The pastor of La Brévine, a small mountain village in the Swiss Jura, recounts the development and education of a blind fifteen-year-old girl he had found two-and-a-half years earlier. Although not deaf, his young charge spent her first years in total silence and darkness because her aunt, whose death provided the occasion for the pastor's recovery of the child, was deaf herself. Moved by charity, the pastor decides to undertake the salvation of this soul lost in darkness, at great moral and physical expense to his wife and his own children. He soothes his disgruntled wife with arguments of charity and promises of help, although, in truth, his first impulse is to cite some of Christ's words. He says, "I kept them back, however, because it seems to me improper to cover my behavior behind the authority of the Holy Scriptures." But this is precisely what he does, increasingly and heedlessly, throughout the book. Moreover, as his wife seems to become more and more peevish toward him and as his own children interest him less, he becomes withdrawn and dependent upon himself to satisfy his intellectual, emotional, and spiritual needs. Because Gertrude, as he calls his charge, needs constant, patient attention and because she proves intelligent and responsive, he begins to fashion her as a complement to his own soul. Like an aging André Walter, he hopes to form the soul of his beloved so like his own that nothing can separate them. But soon love and charity change into something less generous and more earthy. When his wife chides him for spending more time with Gertrude than he ever spends with his own children, he hides behind the parable of the lost sheep. The more intense he becomes, the greater grows his dependence upon the Gospel as a source of sanctions.

But his dependence is selective. In the second notebook, where the narrative, rather than describing past events, yields to day-by-day journal entries, he immediately confesses his discovery of his true feelings after having reread his story. He had not previously realized that love was in question because he had felt no guilt. It is a small step, then, to defend the innocence of those feelings, and it is a step he takes blithely. The second entry of the notebook is laden with irony: "Gertrude's religious instruction has made me reread the Evangile with new eyes. It is more and more apparent to me that a number of notions that make up our Christian faith stem not from Christ's words but from St. Paul's commentaries." He proceeds to reconstruct standards of guilt by defining evil as any obstacle to happiness. The Gospels, he feels, teach principally "a method for attaining a life of happiness." The pastor concludes, "Gertrude's complete happiness, which shines out from her whole being, comes from her ignorance of sin." Moral strictures, he argues, invoking part of St. Paul's letter to the Romans, are dictated not by law but by love: "Nothing is unclean in itself; but it is unclean for anyone who thinks it is unclean" (14:14).

Gertrude's education makes her, in effect, a creature living in an illusory world of goodness, beauty, and eternal happiness. Into his world of harmony, indeed a pastoral symphony in its own way, the pastor allows no intrusion of reality. He rejects his son's interest in Gertrude and forbids him to court her, going so far as to accuse him of wanting to "take advantage of a disabled, innocent, and guileless person." When he is finally convinced of his son's honorable intentions, he can only ask for more time to think of a valid opposition to his proposed plan. "An instinct as sure as the voice of conscience warned me that I had to prevent this marriage at all costs." Later called upon to explain his reasons, he admits that he followed his conscience and not his reason, invoking Gertrude's innocence, impressionability, and lack of prudence. "It is a question of conscience," he concludes lamely.

Since the standard of judgement is his own conscience, his task is to ease this conscience. He immediately takes communion, surprisingly unattended—as though he would rebuke them—at the altar by either his wife or son. The son's abstention is clarified by the subsequent entries in the second notebook and puts into relief the exegetical clash that long interested Gide. His son, the pastor believes, feels doomed as soon as he discovers himself without props or authority to guide him. But Jacques insists upon facing the ever-present reality of sin, evil, and death by supporting St. Paul and accepting the necessity of commandments, threats, and prohibition. "In submission lies happiness," he says, and quotes a verse from Romans that his father had curiously overlooked earlier: "Do not let what you eat cause the ruin of one for whom Christ died" (14:15). The pastor remains absolutely impervious to the meaning of this verse by claiming fidelity to Christ and not to St. Paul; he is closer to Christ when he teaches that sin is only what disrupts the happiness of another "or compromises our very own." The example of his father, Jacques admits late in the book, has in fact guided him to understand the wisdom of converting to Catholicism.

Gertrude herself senses the incompleteness of the world view offered her by the pastor. In a tender scene near the end of the book, she acknowledges that her happiness seems to be based on ignorance. She would prefer lucidity to happiness, would prefer knowing what evil and ugliness there is about her just to be sure that she is not adding any of her own. The subsequent conversation suggests what she has on her mind; she wants reassurance from the pastor that her children will not inherit her blindness, that their love is real and passionate, although guilty. Finally, she admits that, although she ought to feel guilty, she cannot stop loving him. The pastor cannot respond, cannot reassure her one way or the other, cannot do more than wallow in his own lightheadedness. He is now thoroughly prepared to do what he feared Jacques had in mind, to take advantage of weakness, innocence, and ignorance.

The discovery that Gertrude's sight can be restored acts as a catalyst to the pastor's expression of his true feelings for her. Unable to refuse to do for her what must be a boon, he is still reluctant to break the news to her. On several occasions he tries and fails until finally he finds himself alone with her in her room: "I held her close to me for some time. She made no move to resist and, as she raised her face toward mine, our lips met." She enters the hospital the following day. After a successful operation and convalescence, she returns home and attempts suicide. When she sees the family, and especially Amélie, the wife, she realizes immediately that she has usurped the place of another; she sees her sin, her error. Now thoroughly familiar with St. Paul, thanks to Jacques's company during her convalescence, she quotes Romans: "I was once alive apart from the law, but when the commandment came, sin revived and I died" (7:9). She dies, in fact, shortly after, with a reproach on her lips; having seen Jacques she realized that it was he whom she loved and that it was he whom she could have married were it not for the pastor. Jacques, on the other hand, follows through to the end the path diametrically opposed to his father's: he accepts orthodoxy and converts himself and Gertrude to Catholicism.

Like Michel, the pastor, although with different emphases, if not different motives, refuses, at least in theory, to acknowledge any authority other than his own conscience, a conscience he claims thoroughly grounded in the words and example of Christ. In practice, however, he constantly passes off responsibility onto God, Christ, or the Scriptures, finding what he deems authorization for his own passion.

Les faux-monnayeurs (*The Counterfeiters*, 1926), the first and only book of his that Gide dared call a novel, had so long been on his mind that when he began writing it, in June 1919, he decided to record his progress in a special logbook, *Journal des faux-monnayeurs.* His timidity and reluctance with regard to the term "novel" can be explained by the rigor of his concept of the genre. The novel, for Gide, must of necessity present reality as seen from multiple vantage points; it must suggest the profusion and formlessness of the real world, while at the same time demonstrating a number of attempts to come to grips with it either artistically, psychologically, socially, or philosophically, and so that all points of view interact with one another. The first *sotie* and the *récits* present, at most, no more than two points of view whose consistencies of voice are not hindered by any external pressures. The main concern in these works is essentially the interior world of the protagonist—hence the first-person narrative. With *The Vatican Swindle* Gide begins to show an interest in the reciprocal influences of the interior and exterior worlds of a number of protagonists each in conflict with another. Its relation with the more sober *The Counterfeiters* is attested to by Gide's long-standing intention to use Lafcadio as a principal character of the later book; but even more convincing is the absolute identity of tone between the *sotie* and several chapters of the novel recounted in the third person. Particularly revealing is the second chapter, in which the two magistrates, Oscar Molinier and Albéric Profitendieu, stroll home at competitive paces and, puppetlike, parade for one another personalities atrophied not so much by their profession as by their own images of themselves. Both are as much caricatures as Anthime Armand-Dubois or Amédée Fleurissoire.

Significant, too, is the omniscient third-person narrative device used rarely by Gide, although insistently in both *The Vatican Swindle* and *The Counterfeiters.* But in the latter, the ominscient author surpasses the role of a technique or device: he himself becomes a character in the story he has invented not only by reacting to and commenting upon his people but also by illustrating still another point of view and still another attempt, this time successful, to make something of reality, to make a book out of the material the world offers. Like the omniscient author, Édouard is writing a novel also called "The Counterfeiters" and keeping a journal in which he notes all that can be of use for his book. Here he faces the same problems with handling events and incorporating them into meaningful experience suggested by Gide and the omniscient author he plays. Finally, through letters, but mostly through dialogue—since dialogue is an exchange of two or more points of view—reported either by the omniscient author or by Édouard, Gide succeeds in presenting still more points of view and efforts at fashioning a viable approach to reality.

In the novel, then, a number of people speak for themselves and reveal their efforts to reconcile themselves somehow to the world around them. Some have already erected a workable system and have settled themselves into it; for the most part these are members of the older generation: the magistrates; the pastors Azaïs and Vedel, who are Parisian equivalents of the pastor of *The Pastoral Symphony*; La Pérouse, who is painfully discovering the cruel trick God has played on him through the death of his grandson; Passavant, who like Baraglioul plays to the crowd; even Pauline Molinier, who spends the better part of her life covering up the inadequacies and hypocrisy of her husband. For the most part, adolescents or young adults—that is, those undergoing the dynamic process of "becoming"—understandably attract and retain most of the narrator's and Édouard's attention. And still a third group finds a voice in the novel: the young teenagers who are struggling not so much with the world at large as with the immediate social and cultural influences they are undergoing (Boris, George, Ghérandisol, and the vaguely suggested Caloub).

These three groups represent not only three major divisions of society but more significantly three stages in the struggle between atrophy and plenitude, or, in terms consistent with the novel's central image scheme, between the authentic and the counterfeit. The profound subject of the novel is precisely the many ways in which people choose to face the world, alternatives that are completely external to their personality and based on convention, revolt, or a simple lack of common sense. Gide's *Counterfeiters* is, in fact, a catalogue of the various ways in which one can live in a counterfeit life—but, especially, it is a catalogue of the various pressures that tend to divert those striving for plenitude.

In the very center of the novel two significant events take place: Édouard discusses the theory of the novel in general and of his own in particular, and Bernard uncovers a counterfeit coin. The two events are intimately related, especially in regard to the development of Édouard's character. One of his interlocutors finally asks him exactly who are the counterfeiters he proposes to write about. Like his predecessor, the narrator of *Marshlands*, Édouard gets tangled up in the exposition of ideas too close to him and in the description of work in progress. The bad impression he makes upon his friends is only partially atoned for by the narrator's intrusion and explanation of Édouard's thought. Édouard's use of the counterfeiters is purely figurative, we learn. At first the term designated certain of his colleagues:

But the attribution broadened considerably; according as the wind of the spirit blew from Rome or elsewhere, his heroes became either priests or freemasons. If he let his mind go its way, it would soon capsize in abstraction where it would wallow comfortably. Ideas of exchange, devaluation, inflation were little by little overrunning his book as did theories of dress in Carlyle's *Sartor Resartus* where they usurped the character's roles.

(Bussy trans., 1951, p. 176)

Although Édouard's title, "The Counterfeiters," refers to something quite concrete, he thinks of it in figurative and abstract terms. And it is precisely this mode of thinking that his young secretary Bernard objects to. Bernard shows him a false ten-franc piece and urges him to begin not with the idea of the counterfeit but with a fact, a false ten-franc coin, for example. He forces him to admit that such reality, although it does indeed interest him, basically troubles him. In fact, so deep is this trouble that only his diary and the processes of articulation it requires can give any semblance of reality to whatever happens to him. Or at least so he rationalizes in his journal. But he goes on to demonstrate a case in point. Recording the thoughts provoked by the false coin and his subsequent discussion with Bernard, he realizes that we create the drama of our lives by our attempts to impose upon the world our interpretation of it and by the way it resists:

The resistance of facts invites us to transpose our ideal construction onto the world of dreams, of hope, of future life in which our belief is nourished by all our failures in this one. Realists begin with facts and adjust their ideas to them. Bernard is a realist. I am afraid I won't be able to get along with him.

(Bussy trans., p. 189)

That is, unlike Bernard, Édouard will not adjust himself to facts but will adjust them, in his novel and journal, to fit his own ideals. With this admission, Édouard unwittingly classifies himself among the counterfeiters. Like Azaïs, the old pastor, and his son-in-law, Vedel, Édouard has constructed a world for himself frequently unencumbered either by fact or by reality. But even Edouard changes and leaves us with a slight hope; finally settled in a satisfactory relationship with his nephew, Olivier, he manages to write the first thirty pages of his novel.

However ambiguous Édouard's own status might appear at the end of the novel, that of most others who had been in flux throughout the novel seems clear. Those who had reached the final stage of development at the opening have failed and live counterfeit lives. What is worse, however, is that in persisting in their errors they force those around them either to imitate them or to reject their errors in favor of extremes just as false. Because of his fervor, sincerity, and simplicity, the old pastor, Azaïs, forces those he faces into playing roles, acquiescing, and being hypocrites as soon as they feel unable to share his conviction and enthusiasms. The hypocrisy of his son-in-law, Vedel, who continues to effect piety and devotion out of fidelity to an early enthusiasm, thickens the atmosphere of lies that his children have to grow up in. They are all pushed into making some sort of stand with regard to their upbringing; most of the children rebel and cynically project their rebellion into an ethic. An unnamed son leaves for Africa when he feels he cannot handle the rumblings of puberty; Laura goes off to England, marries a colorless French professor, commits adultery, and finds herself bearing her lover's child; Sarah ultimately goes off to England, thus proclaiming her independence after having exercised it promiscuously under the very nose of familial authority; and Armand, sensitive and troubled, becomes intellectually promiscuous and establishes cynicism and hypocrisy as the tenets of his behavior. Rachel alone stays at home; through total self-effacement she undertakes to deal with all the realities her father and grandfather do not acknowledge by keeping the household financially solvent.

Laura, after a bad start, seems to be heading toward a better future; she returns to her husband, who forgives all and promises to treat the child as his own. Under similar circumstances Albéric Profitendieu made a similar promise to Marguerite some nineteen years earlier. When Bernard discovers to his great relief that Profitendieu is not his real father and that he will not have the problem of resisting or submitting to the centripetal forces of heredity and early upbringing, he runs away from home seeking adventures that will enable him better to gauge his true potential. Like Michel, he dares free himself and follow his bent. Unlike his predecessor, however, he enters into a long struggle with himself from which he emerges, if not victorious, at least a bit more mature and endowed with that grain of good sense that so many of Gide's characters lack. Unlike Lafcadio, too, he learns that in this world it is not enough to dare: "He was beginning to understand that other people's happiness is often the price of daring." Learning that Profitendieu is alone and ailing, he returns home, not out of weakness, but out of the affection he had always felt for the man he had long taken for his father; he returns, too, because he has gained a feeling of freedom so profound that it frees him from the constant need to test and prove it. With Bernard and Laura, Olivier Molinier also promises to develop in the direction of authenticity. Unlike his brothers, he manages to escape the baneful influence of his complacent and hypocritical father and his well-meaning though no less hypocritical mother. Adopted by Edouard, his uncle, Olivier will live in an open atmosphere that will permit him to develop fully.

As sensitive and intelligent as his younger brother Olivier, Vincent Molinier falls into Michel's trap of illusory self-development and freedom. He seduces and then abandons Laura, is seduced, in turn, by Lady Griffith, and then exalts himself and her by exercising his will and strength, destroying first his more noble and generous instincts and finally his mistress herself. He abandons himself to his instincts, ignorant of the proviso in Édouard's often-quoted formula: "It is good to follow your bent, provided it moves upwards." George Molinier, although still a teenager, seems at first to have chosen the way of revolt and defiance. Like his classmate Ghérandisol, nephew and protégé of the novel's Protos-like figure, Strouvihou, George is in the process of fashioning himself into a "subtle one" and inadvertently falls into a system as rigid as the one he would escape. Through a suicide pact reserved for only a select few in their class, he and Ghérandisol provoke the suicide of another classmate, the timid and tormented grandson of La Pérouse, Boris. It is only with great effort that he finally comes to his senses and seeks the help of his mother. Ghérandisol, on the other hand, regrets only having lost his sangfroid by uncontrollably shuddering at the sight of the cadaver. Boris is a victim not only of his classmate's cruelty but also of his temperament, his early upbringing, and especially of Sophroniska, a sort of Freudian analyst into whose care Boris has been entrusted. Rigorously following certain psychoanalytic theories, Sophroniska so deforms facts to fit her interpretation of reality that she cannot realize the true causes of Boris' emotional improvement. Of far greater effectiveness for the young boy than her theories is the idyllic relationship between her charge and her daughter, Bronja.

In this one book, into which Gide wanted to pour all that life had shown and taught him, there is a catalogue of various types of counterfeit personalities and of the influences that force them to forsake authenticity. Essentially, the book is a study of the adolescent personality in its struggle and growth toward either a full or an atrophied maturity. But the book also contains aesthetic theories of fiction in the process of maturing in Édouard's mind, which are balanced against the logbook of Gide's own theories. Gide put much of his own thought into the mouth of Édouard; but the latter frequently develops his ideas to a point beyond logic or refuses to anchor them in

reality. Reality bothers him, he tells Bernard during the long discussion of the novel, and for this very reason Bernard is quick to suggest that in his book Édouard begin right off with facts, with counterfeit coins. Although Bernard, the realist, introduces the false coins only in part 3, postponing these real facts forces them to act as concrete catalysts in a rather abstract system. As Édouard thinks first of the counterfeit only in a figurative sense, so, too, Gide's novel presents a series of people either living a lie or in the process of struggling with one. But these lives are viewed as counterfeit—that is, they earn the counterfeit label—only when the reality of the counterfeit coins intrudes into the orderly world of the novel. Similarly, the brutality of Boris' death intrudes into Édouard's consciousness and perception of the world:

> That is why I will not use Boris' suicide in my "The Counterfeiters"; I already have enough difficulty understanding it. And, then, I don't like "news items." They have in them a bit of the peremptory, the undeniable, the brutal, the outrageously real. . . . I allow reality to support my thought as a proof, but not to precede it. I don't like being surprised. I see Boris' suicide as an *indecency* because I didn't expect it.
>
> (Bussy trans., p. 363)

Boris' grandfather, La Pérouse, cannot assimilate this event either; plunged into a mystical despair that makes man the victim of a unified God and Satan, he cannot express his sorrow directly, a sorrow too profound, too "astounding," as Édouard observes, "to allow any steady contemplation."

After *The Counterfeiters*, Gide wrote nothing of the stature of his previous fiction unless it be *Theseus*. One can easily suppose that he literally used himself up on his novel just as he had foreseen in *Journal des faux-monnayeurs*. As he suggests on several occasions in his journal, were it not for an "undeniable diminution" in his creative prowess, his interest in social problems and in communism would not have usurped the place of his personal and moral concerns. But the lessening of his creative powers during the 1930's can be even further explained from another vantage point. Nearly all of his books up to and including *The Counterfeiters* answered a profound psychological need. The work of art provided him with a crutch thanks to which he was able to achieve "an equilibrium beyond time, an artificial health," as he says in the *Journal,* that he felt totally incapable of achieving in living. But as he grew older and more and more reconciled to his homosexuality, the stability obtained by composing works of art was slowly, imperceptibly transferred onto his person; he began to live by maintaining a balance of various contradictory forces of his personality. If, as Gide so often claimed, the spur of every impulse to social reform is an anomaly, an imbalance, a potential atrophy, his own deep-rooted perplexities dissolved as he exorcised the tyrannical potential of each of them. As he became well adjusted, he lost all desire to repeat reforms he had already worked out; by 1926 he had written cathartically of asceticism, of hedonism, and of a sort of romantic imagination; he had written a defense of homosexuality, a case study of himself, in the form of memoirs; and he had written the long-dreamed-of *summa, The Counterfeiters.*

In a journal entry for 19 July 1932 Gide stated, "Each of my books has, up until now, focused upon an uncertainty." A glance back at his work up to *The Counterfeiters* bears out the validity of this insight; supporting it, too, are the many statements Gide made in the *Journal* and elsewhere concerning the answers each of his works provided for his inner needs. In his attempt to achieve a fuller life, without the inhibiting consequences of real action, Gide relied upon his fantasy and made his protagonists act out to the fullest extent possible each of his own temptations. This explains the compensatory violence of a book like *Les nourritures terrestres (The Fruits of the Earth,* 1897), produced at the beginning of his career and certainly representing an epochmaking statement in the Gidian canon. It

explains, too, why in 1927 Gide brought this book out of limbo and republished it; and finally, it explains why in 1935, at the peak of his political fervor, he returned to this same literary style and published *Les nouvelles nourritures (New Fruits of the Earth).*

As Gide knew long before he wrote the 1927 preface, *The Fruits of the Earth* was a book of convalescence, the fruit, as he wrote to Christian Beck—a young poet and philosopher also afflicted with lung problems—in 1907, of his tuberculosis: "There is in its very lyricism the excesses of one who clutches life as something he has almost lost." The scope of this statement should be extended to include the excesses of him who embraces life as something he has long denied himself. There is no fanatic like a new convert, and Gide consciously exorcised the extremes of hedonism and fanaticism in his song on the fruits of the earth. Conscious of the efficacy and psychic stability provided by a "system of compensations," and of the "usefulness of illness," as he noted in his *Journal* in 1896, he abandoned himself to extolling fervor, freedom, and joy. In abandoning himself—at least in literature—he both compensated for the effects of a cloistered youth and adolescence and let these "safe" compensations run their course. In this way he expended his hedonism, but he did not abandon his theory; he continued to praise the fruits of the earth and urged his fictional disciple Nathanaël, no less strongly at the end than at the beginning, to go his way alone, to rely on no one and nothing outside himself, to the point even of abandoning his master and this "manual of evasion."

The Fruits of the Earth has been taken most frequently as a panegyric of hedonism. It is true that those who speak in the "essay" tell of joy encountered and appetites satisfied, but the tone of voice in all cases is unique and uniform. Essentially, it is a hortatory tone, with Ménalque inviting his listeners and the narrator urging his readers and especially his young disciple, Nathanaël, to feed upon the fruits of the earth. In a very real sense, then,

The Fruits of the Earth, like an antidote to *Marshlands,* represents the aspirations of a long-sheltered and ascetic youth toward a full earthly experience and ultimately toward an equilibrium between the pleasures of the senses and those of the soul. But for the young Huguenot even pure hedonism was not easy to achieve without the essential condition so difficult for an introspective intellectual: the suppression of his thought and attendant self-consciousness. It is not surprising that the narrator feels obliged to reject speaking of himself, to defer "the ballad on the different forms of the mind," and to state, "Have you noticed that there is no one in this book? And even I am no more than a vision in it." Similarly, in the 1927 preface, Gide felt it necessary to point out that rather than hedonism his book glorifies destitution and, primarily, stripping oneself of one's ever-hovering intellect. In almost the same way as Gide condemned his own thought on a number of occasions, Ménalque in book 4 chides a comrade, who has wife, children, books, and a study, for expecting "to savor the powerful, total, and immediate sensation of life without forgetting what is extraneous to it. Your habit of thinking is a burden to you; you live in either the past or the future and you perceive nothing spontaneously. We are nothing except in the instantaneousness of life; the entire past dies in it before anything yet to come is born." And this Ménalque affirms after recounting how at fifty he sold "absolutely everything, not wanting to retain anything *personal* on earth; not even the slightest memory of yesteryear."

Book 4, which is nearly entirely devoted to Ménalque's autobiography, picks up and repeats the ideas and themes carefully suggested and developed in the first three books. The central idea developed by Ménalque revolves around his aversion to possessions of any kind for fear of possessing no more than that. Such a fear of property originally kept him from making any choices and ultimately from undertaking any action at all. But he finally understands that "all the drops from this vast divine source are equivalent; that the tiniest suffices to intoxicate us and to reveal the plenitude and totality of God." In effect, destitution provokes our thirst and hunger, incites our fervor, and enables us to receive and enjoy anything in our path. Ménalque rejects everything that might inhibit his receptivity to all sensations in their force and immediacy: he rejects family, institutions, hopes for the future, reliance on the past, everything but the slow, deliberate, and random cultivation of all his senses. He rejects, too, anything that stops challenging him to find and deploy new strengths; when people and things become familiar, he feels, they breed repose and reliance on past accomplishment. It is in this spirit that he concludes: "My heart without any attachment on earth has remained poor, and I will die easily. My happiness is made of fervor. Through all things indistinctly, I have adored intensely."

Fancy is bred not in the eye but in the mind, and therein lies the flaw in Gide's book and its ethics, a flaw that he was well aware of and casually exploits in the book itself. Fervor must be maintained at any price and by any means if the intensity of sensations is to continue as a cultivation of the self. This movement from the search for experience to the search for sensations and for ever-new sensations capable of maintaining fervor eventually degenerates into a frenzied hunt for stimulation. Finally there obtains a loss of the self so complete, a self so detached from past and future, that the narrator feels possessed: "What is called 'meditation' is an impossible constraint for me; I no longer understand the word 'solitude'; to be alone with myself is to be no longer anyone; I am inhabited."

In a letter to Marcel Drouin, his brother-in-law and a friend since adolescence, Gide wrote that he was concerned in *The Fruits of the Earth* with only one side of the coin, with the joy of desire and not the anguish and dissolution that it causes. But this in no way implies he was unaware of the other side; he dealt with it later, contenting himself for the moment with suggesting in the later books of *The Fruits of the Earth* possible outcomes of Ménalque's doctrine that call to mind *Saül* (1903) and *The Immoralist*. He felt that the importance of *The Fruits of the Earth* lay precisely in the full and unfettered exploitation of the sensual side of his personality. Letting it run its course, at least in the work of art, brought him to several other conclusions he later was able to verify in life. In "Le renoncement au voyage" ("Renunciation of Travel," included in *Amyntas,* 1906), Gide realized that his hypersensitivity stemmed mostly from his thirst for sensation so long repressed and not from a permanent physiological state. You cannot go back and find the same intensity of a former naive self, Gide says during his sixth visit to North Africa. And even in book 8 of *The Fruits of the Earth* the narrator nostalgically states the difficulty of becoming once again the young man he was in Biskra: "He who I was, that other one, ah! how could I become him again?"

Thus even in *The Fruits of the Earth,* where Gide planned to sing the joys of the flesh and fruits of the earth in compensation for the austere and cerebral side of his nature, he could not but indicate the deformed figure such a program can produce and by contrast suggest the ideal of equilibrium and plenitude. Here, already, are prefigurations of Michel and Saül, both dispossessed by the will-eroding power of their desires. And at last, even in his last *récit,* the long, happy life of Theseus, which he recounts with a measure of satisfaction and an abundance of detail, Gide cannot help confronting his pragmatic hero with the suffering inspired by Oedipus.

The long road traveled by Gide in search of tranquillity and plenitude is dramatically illustrated by the juxtaposition of these two books, *The Fruits of the Earth* and *Theseus:* the one an initial Dionysiac plunge into sensation doubled by a vague hesitation and anticipation of disaster, and the other no less intense sensually but set in balance by a taut,

springlike willpower, a Corneillian sense of duty and service, and a devotion to a balanced exploitation of all his strengths. Theseus is a child of this earth, physically, intellectually, and emotionally agile; he is socially and sexually wily and adept, yet less given to indulgence of his pleasure than of his strengths and virtues.

The first great lesson Theseus recalls in his memoirs is a reliance on reason; the second is an exercise in strengthening his will. His father, Aegeus, one day told him that his pastoral life would have to come to an end: he was a king's son and would have to become worthy of succeeding his father on the throne. By a ruse, claiming that special weapons for Theseus were hidden by Poseidon beneath a stone, Aegeus succeeds in building up both Theseus' moral and physical strength; in his determination to find the weapons Theseus leaves no stone unturned, beginning even to tear apart the palace terrace. Aegeus gives his arms to Theseus, feeling that his son has amply shown a desire for glory that will not permit them to be used for any but noble end and mankind's happiness. In this manner Theseus developed a code that enabled him to overcome many monsters both within and without his personality; he strengthened his will, which enabled him to "stop living with abandon, however pleasing this freedom might have been." Although always ready for pleasure and never refusing to savor an amorous exploit, he never let himself be saddled by any and quickly went beyond them; in love, as in all else, "I was always less concerned and withheld by what I had accomplished than pulled by what still had to be done; and the more important always seemed to me still to come."

Theseus suggests that the hero is the one with an exceptionally strong will, the strength of which enables him to transcend the normal limits of good and evil and, for the greater glory of himself and future generations, to do, in fact, no evil, or at least to compensate for it. He embodies Gide's ethic in a curiously neo-

Leibnizian form: what is, is good, and what the hero does is good. A constant control and assurance is provided by his sense of duty and the full exploitation of his strengths and aptitudes. The hero ever strives to integrate within his experience the largest possible segment of reality about him, with its and his harmonies and dissonances.

The basis of the *récit* is a series of great encounters from which Theseus derives some personal benefit; two chapters are devoted to his early life and to the formative influences of his father and grandfather; eight chapters are devoted to Theseus' stay in Knossos, his encounters with Daedalus, Minos, and his family, particularly Ariadne, Phaedra, and the Minotaur; the final chapters revolve around the flight from Crete and the founding of Athens; finally, in an epilogue, Gide dramatizes a confrontation between Oedipus and Theseus. The confrontations with Daedalus and later with Oedipus are the key chapters of the narrative. As architect of the labyrinth, Daedalus is especially qualified to explain the subtle nature of his prison as well as to provide Theseus with a plan enabling him to enter the maze, accomplish his deed, and escape with little difficulty. To detain people in his labyrinth, Daedalus explains, it would be more effective to design a structure from which people would not want to escape. With this in mind, he fills the hallways and rooms of the maze with appetizers, incenses, and gases of all sorts that act upon the will: "Each person, following the inclination of his own mind thereupon prepares, loses himself, if you will, in his own private labyrinth." The way to overcome these subtle narcotics is to maintain a taut will, support it with a handmade gas mask, and guide oneself with reels of thread, firmly anchored outside the labyrinth. Daedalus calls this thread "a tangible symbol of duty" and says it is Theseus' bond to his past and to his future; without it, his life would become a hopeless imbroglio and a permanent immersion in the present and in the presence of sensations.

In the last encounter at Colonus, Theseus and Oedipus measure themselves against one another. By beginning the epilogue with an account of his own suffering, Theseus attempts to equate himself with Oedipus. Only in this area does there seem to be a common ground between the two. For Theseus had suceeded in all he had undertaken, whereas Oedipus had failed. "His misfortunes," Theseus writes, "could only enhance his grandeur in my eyes. No doubt I had triumphed everywhere and always, but on a level which, in comparison with Oedipus, seemed to me merely human, inferior, I might say." Here for the first time Theseus catches a glimpse of the infinite and has difficulty understanding. Why had Oedipus accepted defeat by putting out his eyes? Had he not even contributed to it? Oedipus gropes around for an answer likely to reach his interlocutor and convey some sort of meaning to him. He says he put out his eyes to punish them for not having seen the obvious, as an instinctive gesture, as an attempt to see his destiny through to the very end, or to destroy the false picture of the world of appearances in the hope of seeing into the "real, insensible" world beyond that is the realm of God. Theseus admits he does not quite fathom these explanations but does not deny the importance the spiritual world might have for some; yet he cannot accept the opposition Oedipus sets up between their two worlds. As in most of the book, in fact, Theseus' incomprehension and then final acceptance of Oedipus on Attic territory are the fruit of his constant attempt to contain all extremes and maintain them in equilibrium.

Like Theseus, Gide attempted to take into account as much of the world and as many ways of approaching it as possible. Theseus might not understand Oedipus' mystical impulse, but he certainly does make a place for Oedipus in his realms. So, too, Gide himself; but he went beyond each of his characters by balancing within himself both transcendental and terrestrial values. This attitude is evident in his memoirs, his journals, his travelogues, and especially in his criticism, where it becomes an aesthetic criterion. He saw himself as a modern counterpart to the classicists, in whom he valued above all else their modesty and its artistic analogue, litotes, as well as their stiving to take into account and maintain in harmony as much of reality as possible and to express the totality of their age. The limits of art, he said in a lecture titled "Les limites de l'art," written in 1901 ("The Limits of Art," undelivered but published in *Prétextes* [*Pretexts*, 1903]), like the limits of the human personality, are not external or legislatable but exist within the artist and within the human being. As such, they are not simply separate extremes but limits of a continuous extension. That is, Gide clarifies by quoting Pascal, "one knows one's greatness not by being at one extremity, but by touching both at the same time and filling in between them." Echoing this notion in the *Journal* of 1930, Gide remarks flippantly that he is ever conscious of his limits because he never occupies the center of his cage: "My whole being rushes toward the bars." The conclusion of the lecture rephrases an idea very dear to Gide: the artist must submit "to himself as much as possible, as much of nature as possible." This rewords an earlier idea often repeated in the *Journal* and elsewhere that Gide reprinted in capitals in *The Fruits of the Earth:* "Take to oneself as much humanity as possible."

Gide's unending search for harmony, for an equilibrium valuable only if attained with difficulty, lies at the heart of his ethic and aesthetic; works of different types, developing character traits to their extremes, represent less an exclusion by catharsis than an attempt to integrate these traits in the context of his whole personality. "Let's integrate, then," he tells his imaginary correspondent, Angèle, in a letter on classicism appearing in *Incidences* (1924). "Let's integrate. All that classicism refuses to integrate just might turn against it."

Selected Bibliography

EDITIONS

INDIVIDUAL WORKS

PROSE

Les cahiers d'André Walter. Paris, 1891.
Le traité du Narcisse. Paris, 1891.
Le tentative amoureuse. Paris, 1893.
Le voyage d'Urien. Paris, 1893.
Paludes. Paris, 1895.
Les nourritures terrestres. Paris, 1897.
El Hadj. In *Philoctète, Le traité du Narcisse, La tentative amoureuse, El Hadj.* Paris, 1899.
Le Prométhée mal enchaîné. Paris, 1899.
L'Immoraliste. Paris, 1902.
Amyntas. Paris, 1906; new edition, Paris, 1925.
Le retour de l'enfant prodigue. Paris, 1907. Includes *Le traité du Narcisse, La tentative amoureuse, El Hadj, Philoctète,* and *Bethsabé.*
La porte étroite. Paris, 1909.
Isabelle. Paris, 1911.
Les caves du Vatican. Paris, 1914.
La symphonie pastorale. Paris, 1919.
Les faux-monnayeurs. Paris, 1926.
L'École des femmes. Paris, 1929.
Robert. Paris, 1930.
Les nouvelles nourritures. Paris, 1935.
Geneviève. Paris, 1936.
Thésée. New York, 1946.

DRAMA

Philoctète. In *Philoctète, Le traité du Narcisse, La tentative amoureuse, El Hadj.* Paris, 1899.
Le roi Candaule. Paris, 1901.
Saül. Paris, 1903.
Bethsabé. Paris, 1912.
Oedipe. Paris, 1931.
Perséphone. Paris, 1934.
Le treizième arbre. Paris, 1942.
Robert ou l'intérêt général. Neuchâtel and Paris, 1949.

POETRY

Les poésies d'André Walter. Paris, 1892.

LITERARY CRITICISM, SOCIAL CRITICISM, AND TRAVEL WRITING

Prétextes. Paris, 1903.
Oscar Wilde. Paris, 1910.

Nouveaux prétextes. Paris, 1911.
Souvenirs de la cour d'Assises. Paris, 1914.
Dostoïevski. Paris, 1923.
Corydon. Paris, 1924.
Incidences. Paris, 1924.
Voyage au Congo. Paris, 1927.
Le retour du Tchad. Paris, 1928.
Essai sur Montaigne. Paris, 1929.
L'Affaire Redureau suivie de faits divers. Paris, 1930.
La séquestrée de Poitiers. Paris, 1930.
Divers. Paris, 1931.
Retour de l'U.R.S.S. Paris, 1936.
Retouches à mon "Retour de l'U.R.S.S." Paris, 1936.
Attendu que . . . Algiers, 1943.
Interviews imaginaires. Yverdon and Lausanne, 1943.
Littérature engagée. Paris, 1950.

AUTOBIOGRAPHICAL WORKS

Numquid et tu. Paris, 1926.
Si le grain ne meurt. Paris, 1926.
Jeunesse. Neuchâtel, 1945.
Feuillets d'automne. Paris, 1946.
Et nunc manet in te. Neuchatêl, 1951.
Ainsi soit-il ou Les jeux sont faits. Paris, 1952.

COLLECTED WORKS

Oeuvres complètes. Edited by L. Martin-Chauffier. 15 vols. Paris, 1932–1939.
Théâtre. Paris, 1942.
Théâtre complet. Edited by Richard Heyd. 8 vols. Neuchâtel, 1947–1949.
Romans, récits, et soties: Oeuvres lyriques. Edited by Y. Davetet and J. J. Thierry. Paris, 1958.

JOURNALS

Journal 1889–1939. 4 vols. Paris, 1939.
Journal 1939–1949. Souvenirs. Paris, 1954.
Journal des faux-monnayeurs. Paris, 1926.

CORRESPONDENCE

Correspondance André Gide et Dorothy Bussy, Juin 1918–Janvier 1951. 3 vols. Edited by Jean Lambert. Paris, 1979–1982.
Correspondance Francis Jammes et André Gide, 1893–1938. Edited by Robert Mallet. Paris, 1948.
Correspondance Paul Claudel et André Gide, 1899–1926. Edited by Robert Mallet. Paris, 1949.

Correspondance Rainer Maria Rilke et André Gide, 1909–1926. Edited by Renée Lang. Paris, 1952.
Lettres de Charles De Bos et réponses d'André Gide. Paris, 1950.
Marcel Proust. *Lettres à André Gide.* Neuchâtel, 1949.

TRANSLATIONS

Amyntas. Translated by Villiers David. New York, 1958.
The Correspondence Between Paul Claudel and André Gide. Translated by John Russell. New York, 1952.
Corydon. Translated by Hugh Gibb. New York, 1950.
The Counterfeiters. Translated by Dorothy Bussy. New York, 1951. Includes *Journal of the Counterfeiters.*
Dostoevski. Translated by Dorothy Bussy. New York, 1926.
The Fruits of the Earth and New Fruits of the Earth. Translated by Dorothy Bussy. New York, 1949.
If It Die. . . . Translated by Dorothy Bussy. New York, 1935.
The Immoralist. Translated by Dorothy Bussy. New York, 1930.
Isabelle. Translated by Dorothy Bussy. In *Two Symphonies.* New York, 1931.
The Journals of André Gide. 4 vols. Translated by Justin O'Brien. New York, 1947–1951.
The Living Thoughts of Montaigne. Translated by Dorothy Bussy. New York, 1939.
The Lover's Attempt. Translated by Dorothy Bussy. In *The Return of the Prodigal.* London, 1953.
Madeleine. Translated by Justin O'Brien. New York, 1952.
Marshlands and Prometheus Misbound: Two Satires. Translated by George D. Painter. New York, 1953.
My Theater. Translated by Jackson Matthews. New York, 1951.
Narcissus. Translated by Dorothy Bussy. In *The Return of the Prodigal.* London, 1953.
The Pastoral Symphony. Translated by Dorothy Bussy. In *Two Symphonies.* New York, 1931.
Pretexts: Reflections on Literature and Morality. Edited by Justin O'Brien. Translated by Angelo Bertocci et al. New York, 1959.
The Return of the Prodigal. Translated by Dorothy Bussy. London, 1953.

The School for Wives. Translated by Dorothy Bussy. New York, 1950. Includes *Robert* and *Geneviève.*

So Be It, or The Chips Are Down. Translated by Justin O'Brien. New York, 1959.

Strait Is the Gate. Translated by Dorothy Bussy. New York, 1924.

Theseus. In *Two Legends: Oedipus and Theseus,* translated by John Russell. New York, 1959.

Urien's Voyage. Translated by Wade Baskin. New York, 1964.

The Vatican Swindle. Translated by Dorothy Bussy. New York, 1925.

The White Notebook. Translated by Wade Baskin. New York, 1965.

BIOGRAPHICAL AND CRITICAL STUDIES

Brée, Germaine. *André Gide, l'insaisissable protée.* Paris, 1953. Revised and translated by Germaine Brée as *Gide.* New Brunswick, N.J., 1963.

Cordle, Thomas. *André Gide.* New York, 1969.

Delay, Jean. *La jeunesse d'André Gide.* 2 vols. Paris, 1956–1957. Translated by June Guicharnaud as *The Youth of André Gide.* Chicago, 1963. Abridged.

Fayer, H. M. *Gide, Freedom, and Dostoievsky.* Burlington, Vt., 1946.

Guerard, Albert J. *André Gide.* Cambridge, Mass., 1951.

Hytier, Jean. *André Gide.* Algiers, 1938. Translated by Richard Howard. Garden City, N.Y., 1962.

Ireland, G. W. *André Gide.* New York, 1963.

Martin, Claude. *La maturité André Gide: De "Paludes" à "L'Immoraliste" (1895–1902).* Paris, 1977.

Moutote, Daniel. *Le journal de Gide et les problèmes du moi (1889–1925).* Paris, 1968.

O'Brien, Justin. *Portrait of André Gide: A Critical Biography.* New York, 1953.

Rossi, Vinio. *André Gide: The Evolution of an Aesthetic.* New Brunswick, N.J., 1967.

Yale French Studies 7 (1950). Special issue devoted to Gide.

VINIO ROSSI

HEINRICH MANN
(1871–1950)

WELL INTO HIS exile from Germany, Heinrich Mann wrote a brief study of Friedrich Nietzsche. It was typically suave, conveying magisterial judgments in an aphoristic style. But Mann's remarks betrayed a personal animus. When he left Nietzsche and all other writers to history—a work of literature has an indeterminate duration; it develops after the author's death, "he is finishing it from beyond"—Mann was pleading his own case. Alternately claimed and disowned by various parties and schools, he had seen his reputation plummet. His only solace at this point was a vaguely defined hope summoned from a nebulous future. More than political retribution was implicit in his valediction to Germany: "There'll come a day!"

Since the 1940's Heinrich Mann has been known primarily as Thomas Mann's brother. Yet many readers, particularly the radical intellectuals of Weimar, found him the superior Mann. The journalist Kurt Hiller considered him a serious candidate for the presidency of Germany; Ludwig Marcuse dubbed him the Hindenburg of the left. Without any fixed political identity his strength was quite literally his word. It proved a flimsy prop: Adolf Hitler burned his books, and years later the FBI monitored his mail. They may have been his most attentive American readers.

Mann's complicated history gives a particular edge to an oeuvre that claims such disparate advocates as Rainer Maria Rilke, Ber-

tolt Brecht, and Thomas Mann. A critic friend observed of the Manns that Heinrich was wiser and Thomas deeper. In truth Heinrich is not as technically daring as Thomas, nor as willing to submit literary forms to a relentless critique and parody.

A Francophile, he declined to become an essayistic novelist in the German manner; he left intratextual commentary to his brother. Nor is he a linguistic athlete; he agreed with Michel de Montaigne that language should be enriched, not expanded, and he deplored the German weakness for compound words. His style is distinguished by his skillful smuggling of rhetorical and analytical judgments into fictions that generally consist of rapid scene changes and highly charged dialogue. Despite his constant attention to intellectual matters, he never becomes a Shavian Prussian, all dazzling intelligence and no heart. Instead, his penchant for the bizarre, the arcane, and the lewd complicates his most abstruse arguments. In a career of wild swings from aesthetic distance to political engagement he remained *l'homme moyen sensuel* (the average sensual man).

A cultural dialectic was inherent in his name. Luiz Heinrich Mann was born 27 March 1871 in Lübeck, the first child of Thomas Heinrich Mann and his wife Julia de Silva-Bruhns. He had four siblings, Thomas, Carla (his favorite, an actress who committed suicide at twenty-nine), Julia (who killed herself when she was fifty), and Victor. Their father, the scion of a dynasty of merchants, was a community leader and served a term as state senator. Their mother, a Creole, had been born and raised in Brazil. If the father stood for order and stability, the virtues associated with *Bürgertum* (a burghers' culture that predated the solecisms of the bourgeoisie), the mother conveyed a gentler, more sensuous attitude. An amateur musician and writer, she encouraged her sons' artistry while inculcating a pattern of aesthetic "tact" that avoided the sentimental and the histrionic: a sensuous austerity characterizes both sons' work. Heinrich's father opposed his desire to become a writer, although Heinrich insisted that his father had eventually bestowed a final blessing.

It is doubtful that parental reservations could have daunted him. Judging by his autobiographical stories, he was stubborn and combative as a youth. If Thomas Mann's fictional children, particularly Hanno Buddenbrooks, seem to be little neurasthenics, already baffled by events, the child in Heinrich's story "The Violin" questions his victimization. The musical instrument becomes an extension of himself, and when he loses it, "his sense of justice is offended in his own person where it is most vulnerable." The terms are set: the child has a profound, almost visceral sense of injustice. Such a child will always conflate public folly with personal injury.

His schooldays were uneventful; he finished gymnasium and received an *Abitur* (the equivalent of two years of college), unlike his brother, who dropped out before graduating. But he hated the Prussian educational system and later created a devastating portrait of the pedant as tyrant. His early conflicts with employers reflect an irreverence toward authority. While Thomas aimed for a "representative" status, Heinrich was marked as the rebel. (Of course, for the massively ambivalent Mann brothers, such formulas are inadequate. Thomas knew well that he was a most unlikely choice to represent anyone, and both brothers eventually assumed public roles as representatives of the same culture, albeit roles in opposition.)

Heinrich was a diligent if slow student of literature. He later admitted that his early writing efforts did not pay off. When success came, it derived from sustained application rather than from native genius. To that extent, it resembled the concern for craft, for significant details, that Thomas Mann considered the hallmark of German artists since Albrecht Dürer. But unlike Thomas, Heinrich's Germanic industry powered a Gallic temperament. His early models were French writers, among them Stendhal, Gustave Flaubert, Guy de Maupassant, and Paul Bourget. As his essays indicate, he discovered in Flaubert the model of an author who avoids rhetorical commentary in favor of action and dialogue. Flaubert also intuited the new role of mass culture, the tabloid journals, and public occasions that dominated his characters' fantasies. Stendhal, Flaubert, and Maupassant all wrote about young provincials on the make; their male ingenues are both naive and calculating, as are Mann's first heroes. Bourget, the least known of his French mentors, added an uglier element: his cynicism is crossed with racism, and anti-Semitism. In a typical Bourget novel, *Cosmopolis* (1893), the journalist hero is guided through Roman society by an aged reactionary, a Catholic nobleman who continues to lament Henri IV's defeat of the Catholic monarchist French League (he is also pining for Comte de Gobineau, the nineteenth-century racist). In the 1890's, Mann was himself a racist with his own convictions about cultural decline: he wrote several essays filled with vicious caricatures of Jews. Traces of Bourget can be found in his conservative criticism of the period and in his glorifications of the greatly loving woman.

That image of passionate woman, central to all his work, had sources other than French novels. Equally potent was the theater. Both Manns loved opera, but their infatuations were not purely aesthetic. (Thomas wrote of his favorite, Richard Wagner, that as a composer he made a fine writer; and Heinrich admitted that his preference for Giacomo Puccini derived from the Italian's superior politics.) As Nietzsche instructed them, opera was a bourgeois luxury; the later media, radio and films, drawing upon another class base, democratized form and content. Simply put, this meant that a nightclub singer could be as tempting as an operatic soprano. Whatever the musical arena, Mannian theater provides a spectacle of beautiful, sexually obliging women whose performances manifest the *promesse de bonheur* (prospect of a future happiness) that German romantics once sought in high art.

Thomas Mann defines the artist as a person smarter and more sexual than other people, a remark that illuminates both Manns. Sexuality for them was also bisexuality; when explaining to his first wife his use of a female persona, Heinrich noted that "as an artist one is bisexual." But if Thomas' nature was largely homoerotic—as revealed in his diaries or any clearheaded reading of his fiction—Heinrich's was effusively heterosexual. His erotic passages may not arouse a modern reader but they cannot be ignored. In fact some critics condemned the ubiquitous hijinks as vulgar; the young Thomas found them embarrassing.

Yet sexual curiosity is one of Heinrich's most appealing traits. His women suffer from the same jitters as does Madame Bovary; they have urges that find no reflected forms of desire, and their frustrations never fail to move their creator. Both Manns indulge in a literary transvestism, but Thomas does so to dramatize his own desires in disguise, while Heinrich becomes a woman so he can enter her sensuous reality. This allows him to present women as figures more humane and adventurous than their men: they are "the bolder and more clear-sighted sex." He may fairly be considered a proto-feminist, and if his sexual encounters often end in stasis, a standoff between the sexes remains a legitimate topic. As his views of community changed, Mann saw erotic response as a key to politics: thwarted or perverted, it led to fascism; liberated, it enabled a progressive and social happiness. But

he could never assume a disinterested pose. His great words on satire sprang from the kind of intellectual who is an embarrassed patron of burlesque, a voyeur satirizing himself and his obsessions: "No one has ever written good satire without having some sort of affinity with the object of his ridicule. He is either an apostate or one who has been excluded. In satire there is envy or disgust, but always an outraged sense of community."

During the 1890's Mann worked for a Berlin bookseller, moved to Munich with his family after his father's death in 1891, studied art, dabbled in journalism and fiction, and traveled to Italy with his brother. Julia Mann subsidized her son's first publication, *In einer Familie* (Within a Family, 1894), a tepid novel about a Wagnerian who has a brief adulterous fling but returns, chastized, to the moral conventions of matrimony. His early stories tend to be melancholy evocations of "decadence," a fashionable preoccupation that saluted both Nietzsche and French poets and earned him a certain reputation as an expressionist. That a concern with decadence may coincide with right-wing politics (a foregone conclusion in the 1980's) was evident in a series of editorials he wrote for *Das zwanzigste Jahrhundert* (The Twentieth Century), a Munich magazine. At that time he mounted an old burgher's attack on the new bourgeoisie. Claiming that modern commercial Germany had lost its soul, he called for a revival of community and religious belief. (Although he later welcomed the advances of science, he continued to posit the superior virtues of "spirit" or "spirituality," burdening the already overloaded German concept of *Geist* with additional significance.) He displayed a rather Nietzschean affection for war as a force that would bestir the sleepy Germans. His attacks on middle-class pacifism and intellectual tolerance might have been written by conservatives today: he found liberal efforts inimical to law and order and boringly effete.

He did favor the idea of a united Europe but

largely as a means of defense against the East; he considered the Russians bears and barbarians. At his most reactionary he indulged in blatant anti-Semitism. Although he disliked the vulgar forms of Jew-baiting and abhorred violence against them, he regarded the Jews as a spiritually bankrupt group whose spiritual poverty had a materialistic corollary. They did not constitute a class or special rank—at that time, as a burgher's son, he promoted the *Mittelstand* (middle class) as Germany's most durable group—because they were too flighty and mobile, insufficiently grounded, though according to Mann they certainly owned enough property. Mann emphatically disowned these positions later; his first wife was a Jew whose life was broken at Auschwitz. Yet his initial stance, assertive and wrong-headed, can be seen as a prologue to a career jammed with political confusions.

His need for stability sprang from its absence in his own life. In 1904, after *Buddenbrooks* (1901) had made the Mann family history common knowledge, Heinrich contributed a note to his publisher's catalog. After making wisecracks about his clan's literary fate—Hanseatic merchants transformed into artists—he recalls how, nervous and physically ill, he had traveled to Italy in search of an aestheticized homeland. The recognition that he had no home liberated him into the authority of his own style: "Being caught between two races strengthens the weak, makes him single-minded, difficult to influence, obsessed with creating for himself a little world, a homeland that he cannot find elsewhere." So much for *Bürgertum* (nationhood). Forty years later Theodor Adorno defined "homeland" as "the state of having escaped," a Hegelian presence-in-absence, an abstract convoking of exiles. Mann seems to mean something quite similar: his "home" is any place "away from home."

In his study of the Mann brothers Nigel Hamilton cites Heinrich on the homeless author who finds "nowhere" a readership that knows his heart. He will limit his audience to one,

by which at least it gains in intensity. He treads shocking paths, puts the bestial beside beautiful dreams, ideals beside satire, couples tenderness with hostility. The aim is not to amuse others. . . . No, he creates sensations for a single being. He is out to make his own life richer, to improve the bitter task of his own loneliness.

(p. 79)

One may find the self-pity excessive—after all, he had already published several novels—and regard the Nietzschean mask of aesthetic loneliness as coyly self-serving. Unmistakable is the self-regard, the onanistic preoccupation with his own pleasure, dour and isolated as it may be. Still, this act of revelation must have spoken intimately to Thomas Mann, who knew for himself the self-delighting, self-affrighting nature of the literary act.

Dialogue between the brothers may have been that convoluted. Thomas disapproved of Heinrich's plots, tone, and rate of production. (Between 1900 and 1910 Heinrich turned out eight novels, Thomas two.) Although Thomas saluted his brother's narrative skills, saying, "You're one of the few left who tells stories one can take seriously," it is questionable whether a writer who always disdained making things up, insisting that his fictions were drawn from his own experience, could take storytelling seriously. There were political conflicts as well. By 1910 Heinrich had moved to the left. In his major essay of the year, *Geist und Tat* (Spirit and Deed), he announced that literature must become a political forum. He demoted the artist's status by labeling him a worker, claiming that the great man was an outdated German trope. Thomas professed himself baffled by such assertions: "I don't think I understand freedom."

Thomas always moved slowly, as befitted someone who professed himself "belated," doomed to experience tradition solely in an ironic sense. To many readers the precociously Tolstoyan craft of *Buddenbrooks* surpasses anything else in Thomas' canon, much less Heinrich's. But others think that Heinrich's early work, more topical, vivacious, and unfinished—as the journalistic rate of production might guarantee—provides a more useful guide to the era as well as astonishingly prophetic views of Germany's future.

Im Schlaraffenland: Ein Roman unter feinen Leuten (1900) was Heinrich's first important novel. Schlaraffenland is a fairyland; the English translator renames the novel *Berlin: The Land of Cockaigne.* While parallels can be found with French novels, Mann's depiction of a hustling young writer has a special twang. Mann was, of course, an outsider, coming to Berlin from Lübeck. More than that, much of the novel was written in Italy while his political criteria were shifting. Finally, by invoking Germany's most cosmopolitan city with a Gallic sardonicism, he cultivates a tone that will entertain any urbanite. Mann wrote about Berlin of 1893, but the city is recognizably the same place Alfred Döblin and Bertolt Brecht portrayed in the 1920's. It's all there: the greed and back-stabbing, the fads and stunts. Above all, Mann captures a variety of speech styles from aristocratic to working-class and discovers a common denominator in that irreverence sometimes called *Berliner Schnauze.* Because this smart-aleck tone resembles New Yorkese, the novel is surprisingly undated.

The urban cynicism was contagious; the novel contains few positive figures, although to demand such models is a tribute to Mann's later, moralistic image. A modern reader may not regret the absence of heroes. While Thomas Mann was composing *Buddenbrooks,* a novel so steeped in tradition that it cannot imagine a world beyond itself, *Cockaigne* depicts a society where novelty reigns. Both Manns depend on the powerful description of gestures and objects to make rhetorical argument unnecessary. But the phenomena of *Buddenbrooks*—furniture, books, clothes, meals—come hallowed with associations, whereas in the "lazy man's heaven" of *haut* Berlin even the antique is newly minted. A society is inventing itself, cut loose from ethics and history. East German critics argue that Mann's is the first novel to fully depict capitalist

Germany; the Berlin novels of Theodor Fontane, his immediate predecessor, portray a much less materialistic society. In Cockaigne money is the universal lubricant. The speculator Türkheimer is compared to Roman generals and Renaissance princes, and while the allusion is sheer parody, his power over investors, employees, and the kaiser himself makes this crude trader Cockaigne's regent, a veritable pope of capitalism.

His minion, court jester, and rival is Andreas Zumsee. More than an alphabet separates the latter from his provincial roots: he even renames himself Zum See (it sounds more distinguished), although he already feels a racial superiority over the Jewish parvenus whose favor he seeks. The social ranks Mann celebrated in 1895 have fallen: in Cockaigne, one is a bum or a millionaire; the *Mittelstand* has disappeared. Capitalism subverts the institutions—family, culture, religion—that meant so much to the younger Heinrich. Thus when families draw together, it is only to plot sexual revenge (Mr. and Mrs. Türkheimer conspire to punish their former lovers by marrying them to each other, a ghastly fate in this novel) or social advancement (a workman pimps for his daughter). The spiritual exists in absurd reduction: at one point Andreas sees his bout with Türkheimer as the conflict between spirit and power; he also considers himself a proletarian avenging his class by sleeping with Mrs. Türkheimer. But either Mann lacks purchase on this dialectic, or Andreas is a poor exponent of spirit. He pretends to Catholic piety, but merely as a way of one-upping a Zionist rival while tantalizing his Jewish mistress. Religion becomes avant-garde, sexy: she loves him for devising so recherché an origin.

The stock market bankrupts investors, skyscrapers are built for obsolescence, furniture deconstructs, and the beer gives off a poisonous stench. Yet Mann's evocation of capitalist evils does not make this a radical novel. Communism is one more stale metaphor: in a nexus that links Türkheimer and his friends, it translates into a trickle-down economics for top people. The proletariat hastens to sell out its principles, not to mention its children. Even the cultural idols are shot down with wisecracks. A pretty parvenu contemplates statues of Heine, Nietzsche, Poe, Baudelaire, and Verlaine and says, "Don't let those guys spit in our soup."

Mann has fun with the Berlin Grub Street, the hacks and pedants who dismiss an aspiring artist like Andreas until he is taken up by society. Only the unsuccessful novelist Koph sees through their games: we know that he speaks the novel's truth because the ingenuous parvenu considers him an aristocrat. But Andreas must learn for himself the snares and delusions of a lazy man's heaven. We begin to think that a responsible press will expose the general corruption, but while nothing is sacred, very little is profane. The readers of Berlin tabloids appear shockproof. Andreas becomes a playwright, not through any pressing aesthetic urge but to enjoy the favor of the girls in the orchestra boxes. He considers art the product of a "neurasthenic" imagination; talent is simply what pays the bills.

In a heady mix of dramatic action, psychological revelation, and cultural commentary, Mann uses theatrical performances to convey his characters' inner natures. Residents of Cockaigne attend the theater much as an earlier bourgeoisie patronized Wagner's Bayreuth. A working-class play is put on—an obvious parody of Gerhard Hauptmann's *The Weavers* (1892). With a hilarious lack of comprehension, the bosses are spellbound by the workers' revolt. Some women become hysterical; others get voyeuristic thrills from seeing brawny workers assault the boss's wife. Only Andreas recognizes the massive hypocrisy. He proceeds to satirize his former editor, a man who supports radical theater in the literary supplement but changes his tune on the editorial page. But for whom does Andreas engage in such blunt criticism? His new mistress, Adelheid Türkheimer, is the boss's wife in the flesh. And poor Adelheid, ignoring

his cynicism and seeing only the talented mimicry, exclaims, "You can do anything."

An authentic Berlin tone arrives with the appearance of the workman Matzke and his scrawny, fractious daughter. Despite their dubious politics, their street slang comprises the novel's most revolutionary gesture. The girl becomes Türkheimer's mistress, acquiring a new name, Bienaimée, and a fancy house and wardrobe to go with it. Andreas finds himself increasingly drawn to her although she has neither the cultural veneer nor voluptuous profile he likes in women. (Adelheid is downright fat.) He isn't her ideal either. She has a dream prince; she saw him once on a box of soap powder. While this revelation allows Andreas cheap shots at her bad taste, it is also the novel's final proof of the commercialization of desire.

The novel's most spectacular scene is a masquerade ball held at Bienaimée's villa. Dressed in costume, the Berliners appear sillier than usual—one garbed as the Spirit of Song, another as German Culture—and also a bit crazed. By the night's end they sway like zombies: "The pale, perspiring faces . . . bore the mark of an ecstasy drowned in itself, possessed by its own idea." Matzke gets drunk and reverts to street talk, calling one grande dame "pancake face" and dismissing her sugar daddy as "moneybags." Somebody starts hurling the cutlery, and before long the leaders of society are tossing plates as if they were Frisbees. When they snap to they realize they have succumbed to "mania." The shock is something like that in Thomas Mann's *Mario und der Zauberer* (*Mario and the Magician*, 1930), when a roomful of citizens loses its collective will.

In a similarly prophetic scene the right-wing Zionist Liebling buys off Andreas and Matzke with Türkheimer's money. Andreas tries to make a Greek myth of their fall from grace. Liebling replies, "Why don't you talk German? We Germans understand nothing but German now and we're proud of it." Such xenophobia receives a far more chilling incarnation years later in *Der Untertan* (*Man of Straw,* 1918). But it does not matter that Mann cannot make more of what he has observed. It is sufficient that he has discovered a new literary subject in the mad comedy of capitalist Berlin. His novel has aged well, perhaps because so little has changed. Young writers still hustle; fame and fortune, theater and commerce, still cohabit in public spectacle. Like Andreas some poets still "walk with the king," but the highway remains booby-trapped.

Cockaigne was a critical success, not a popular one, although Thomas Mann took envious note of the publisher's "advertisements" (undoubtedly an unwitting reference to the baffling situation in which a writer attacks commerce while depending on its apparatus). Heinrich's next major effort involved a change of subject and era. *Die Göttinnen, oder die drei Romane der Herzogin von Assy* (The Goddesses, or Three Novels of the Duchess of Assy) appeared in 1903. It is a trilogy (*Diana, Minerva, Venus*) about an Italian noblewoman, Violante. In each novel she sups at the smorgasbord of modern culture, appearing first as a political activist, then as a patron of the arts, and finally as a full-time sybarite. But this female Quixote finds her windmills to be papier-mâché. In 1901 Mann wrote that he intended to portray "a whirl of paganism, modern swindle affairs, voluptuous artifices, classic mysteries, etc." The result was a peculiar mix of graphic scenes and prose poems evoking the conspicuously nonhuman charm of sun, wind, and sea.

These more mannered sections attracted aesthetes like Gottfried Benn and Rainer Maria Rilke. The latter wrote, "Who else has invented landscapes so splendidly in order to have them, quite simply, enter the bloodstream of an action?" The trilogy's problem is not simply that aestheticism clashes with melodramatic action. Mann's characters are meant to signify the exhaustion of tradition in a series of perverse swoons. (Nietzsche had socialized such longueurs in his *Genealogy of Morals* [1887], had made them exemplary if

unappealing.) Rather, the problem is that for an explorer of the heart, Violante is a cold fish. She traffics with political and religious zealots but has to hold her nose: they sweat too much. In turn they think she speaks "without feeling." She is notably hard to move. After her first sexual experience she wonders why "such an unimportant occurrence" should allow verbal or psychic intimacy. While this is an early literary instance of a woman's postcoital *tristesse,* it tends to belie her name.

Mann may have known her too well. His own narrative voice is often so cold and austere that it seems broadcast across a vast space, one no doubt populated at judicious intervals by classic sculpture. The Mann brothers were never known for their sociability. Both complained that people found them severe while confessing that intimacy did not come easily to them. (Thomas' wife Katia knew Heinrich for fifty years and took special care of him during his last years, but they never advanced from *Sie* to *Du* in their conversations.) Violante duplicates Heinrich's strenuous attempts at normal passion. Her soliloquy recalls the way he located himself between races and cultures: "Where is my family? To what country do I belong? To what people? . . . What do I represent? What community justifies me? Woe unto me if I weaken!"

The novel opens with an image of Violante appearing before a group of revolutionaries. She strips—only to reveal herself clothed: a highbrow tease. Nudity is reserved for heavily bosomed women, her stepmother and some artists' models: Mann's pleasure in their size is not winning, although the obsession does allow a grotesquely funny (and very German) description of a woman whose "flesh tended to glide in lumps" from section to section, cheeks to toes, "as if it would dissolve into jelly on the floor." This same unassured whimsy is found in descriptions of Violante's childhood. An old Voltairean counsels her never to believe more than half of what she hears. So "naturally she questioned facts; she believed only in dreams." She is anachronistically Debussyan (having been born in 1850), falling into reveries of a nude Daphnis while chatting with some friendly lizards. She feels herself the frail descendant of giants, the spawn of primeval monsters. If such emotions were ever felt, they surely would not prepare one for radical politics.

But in *Diana* they do. After a brief, unconsummated marriage to a wealthy relative, she has flings with a Slavic poet (so inauthentic that he fixates on her couch's ducal crown at the moment of orgasm), a Garibaldean agitator (too much her psychic twin—"we are both courageous visionaries"—to elicit her fancy), and a cynical journalist. Her political commitment dissolves when she realizes that the people do not want education, justice, and prosperity. Revolutionaries make themselves "obnoxious," interfering with the masses' natural conservatism. Anyway, she no longer sees them as animal half-gods, strutting heroically beside "heaps of garlic and olives and gigantic, round jars of clay." She comments, "On so much beauty I wanted to found a realm of liberty." These are not notes for anybody's revolution. Thomas Mann's Tonio Kröger lusting after his dim-witted beauties is a political firebrand beside the deluded Violante.

In the novel's most quoted passage a painter describes his art as Hysterical Renaissance:

"I have discovered a genre of my own. I call it secretly the Hysterical Renaissance! Modern paucities and perversions I dress up and put make-up on with such superior cleverness that they seem to share in the full humanity of the golden age. Their misery arouses no disgust but rather titillation. This is my art!"

Violante's erratic behavior makes her less a Renaissance woman than a hysteric. Even the book's poetry bespeaks neurasthenia.

Like his brother, Heinrich continued to turn out stories and novellas between his longer novels. For all the strengths of *Buddenbrooks,* some readers prefer Thomas Mann's early

tales clustering around *Tonio Kröger,* and similar cases have been made for his brother's shorter fictions. They too juxtapose cultural observations with a private melancholy. The narrator of "Drei Minuten Roman" (Three-Minute Novel, 1904) is a wealthy aesthete who moves to Paris. One night when a prostitute takes him home, a trick contraption sends him down a shaft, sans money and sans pleasure, but not before he overhears the woman and her pimp laughing at their mark. The sounds may emanate from a nightmare but they soothe him. From this point on he lives to realize perverse expectations. In Florence he attends a pantomime and falls for the Pierrot, a woman in disguise. He desires her so much that he becomes her beautician—a form of identification that may be unique with Heinrich Mann!—but as long as she is a star, she has no time for him. Eventually she becomes syphilitic, loses her job, becomes a streetwalker, and is finally reduced to boarding with him. As she sleeps, he gazes at her moribund form . . . and writes. (The parallels with Thomas Mann's *Death in Venice* [1913] are clear: the artist receives an almost sexual inspiration from a love object whom he cannot possess in the flesh, although he spiritually dominates his androgyne—she is a Pierrot; Tadziu is a nymph.) In the course of a few sentences the two volley insincere pledges of love. He realizes, "I had never loved her; I had only wished to love her," but he nevertheless considers the hour spent weeping over her corpse his life's great moment.

His next lover is a woman who desires only their mutual happiness. He finds her altruism stupid, and she quickly wearies of him. Precisely then he "compels" her to become his mistress. Although the story long predates Marcel Proust's great novel, it reaches a similar conclusion: Proust's Swann weds Odette after the fact, his love having long since died; similarly, it takes the death of love to make our hero experience desire. For him—as for Swann—union becomes "proof of . . . unbroken solitude." All this Mann conveys in four pages. The velocity of his prose reflects the mercurial nature of modern love.

Mann's best-known novella may be *Pippo Spano* (1905). A summary of its plot reads a bit like a shaggy dog story. Mario Malvoto, a self-conscious writer, meets an uninhibited girl, a "miracle" in Mann's rather sentimental phrase. Her passions rise as high as his rhetoric. But when the tabloid press exposes their affair, she decides they must commit suicide. He encourages her and even guides the knife as she stabs herself. But as she commands the poor schlemiel to join her, he pauses (one can't help remembering Jack Benny's response to the mugger's command, "Your money or your life": "I'm thinking! I'm thinking!"). She dies, cursing him as a murderer, while he insists that he is almost ready. But he is not; the "curtain" will not set on this "player."

Malvoto does not imitate his girlfriend's final operatic gesture because he believes that unless he remains alive as a witness, she will have died for nothing. As she summons him, he quips that a comedy does not end in suicide. Her eyes glaze; she proclaims, "I'm ready!"; she is gone. The unfortunate timing is so comic that it is hard to see Malvoto as villainous; he is too much the Mannian artist working out the permutations and combinations of his aesthetic solitude.

Years later Mann referred to *Pippo Spano* as one of his dress rehearsals for fascism, along with *Professor Unrat oder das Ende einer Tyrannen* (1905; translated variously as *Small-Town Tyrant* and *The Blue Angel* [in honor of its 1930 cinematic adaption]) and *Man of Straw*. Critics have noted the hero's identification of art and war, but a modern reader may as easily infer Mann's sense of art's amorality, a perception he shared with his brother. In Thomas' story "A Weary Hour" (1905) Schiller observes his sleeping bride and silently warns her that she can never wholly possess him; the artist must live for himself. In Heinrich's *Pippo Spano,* a similar situation prevails. Malvoto knows that he is an actor and an opportunist and that he will exploit Gemma's love

to his aesthetic advantage. He writes to her that he is a player, not a person, that he will be unfaithful to her with every woman he meets— at least in his heart—and worse, will betray her with a counterfeit Gemma of his own devising. He has "falsified" the characters she loves most in his books; she too will be changed utterly. What a pity, he thinks, rather proud of his concept. But he destroys the letter, his most egregious act, and she returns. Briefly her passion uplifts him. In a characteristic Heinrich Mann formulation, he finds himself "translated body and soul into the strength of a woman's being." This is Mannian empathy, just as Malvoto's self-criticism of artists—of their vindictiveness, their vanity, and their passion for fame—resembles his creator's strictures.

The novella "Die Branzilla" (1908) contains the story of an opera diva. The world revolves around her career; her binoculars focus exclusively on the stage. In the course of her life she murders a rival, turns away lovers, and, with an idiot-savant's concentration, masters her art. In comparison with Branzilla, Malvoto is an amateur. Age does not disturb her: "Who says that we are old! You, sure, you are old! . . . I am still Branzilla." Forty years later Mann was an exile living in Hollywood when Billy Wilder, another émigré, helped conceive *Sunset Boulevard* (1950). The film's heroine, Norma Desmond, is a latter-day Branzilla ("I *am* big; it's the pictures that got small"), another creature of brilliantly calculated effect. Mann's understanding of the performer's temperament jibes very well with Hollywood's.

His next novel, *Die Jagd nach Liebe* (The Hunt for Love, 1903), again depicts an actress, this one suggested by his sister Carla; it was written three years before her suicide. The roman à clef provoked a minor scandal in the family. Proper Thomas was particularly incensed, although he later employed vivid descriptions of Carla's last moments in his memoir and in *Doktor Faustus* (1947). Heinrich's novel is hardly remembered, but two years later he published his first masterpiece, *Professor Unrat, oder das Ende eines Tyrannen.*

Numerous accounts of the period from 1870 to 1914 have described the horrors of Prussian education: émigrés from Hitler often located the origins of Nazi tyranny in the German classrooms; the director Fritz Lang merely needed to summon up visions of his old professors to create a movie ogre; and Albert Einstein felt that his teachers had nearly ruined him—he fled them and Germany when he was sixteen. For both men the typical teacher was Mann's Professor Unrat.

His real name is Wolfgang Raat, which his pupils vulgarize into Unrath ("garbage"; the English translator calls him Mut to allow the wordplay on "mud"). The very language undermines this grammarian. He returns the insult by traducing the culture—his pedantic disassembling of Friedrich von Schiller makes the poet unreadable for future generations—and its values—he reduces politics and ethics to militarism and "old school" chauvinism. Concepts like "friendship" and "love" are only words to him. His archenemy is a student whose idols are Heinrich Heine and Émile Zola. They contend over a woman, but language is a big source of their conflict.

Raat is a monstrous victim. His tyrannical aspect is evident: we learn immediately that he is a "tyrant"—not, as Tonio Kröger is called, "an artist"—"with a bad conscience." But his isolation is so thorough, his pleasure so fleeting, that the reader is shocked into a kind of horrid sympathy. Many artists and intellectuals were unhappy in their childhood; without friends, taunted by their classmates, they considered their schooldays pure torture. But for this man the extremes of infantile panic are elaborated in adult life. With every corner he turns, he anticipates the awful syllables "Unrath." School is hell, and school is everywhere. When he looks down from the town prospect, he imagines fifty thousand students coming up with jokes at his expense. His paranoia is vast, a universe in itself, dizzy with contradictions. Like the Proustian hypochondriac who

gets upset when told she is sick and furious when told she is well, Raat despises those who mock him but truly hates those who do not. Lohmann, the young Heine disciple, becomes for him "the very worst of all" simply because he will not use the epithet that comprises Unrath's exclusive identity.

Tracking Lohmann and his friends to a cabaret, the Blue Angel, he meets their idol, Rosa Fröhlich. Not a very gifted singer, she is best known for her specialty number, "I'm Just an Innocent Girl." She appears to him in fragments; as the curtain rises, he perceives bare flesh but is not sure whether he sees neck, arms, or leg. Then he hears a voice that is all "personified shriek." The Homeric scholar receives his epiphany in a dive.

Rosa becomes the wrinkle in his pattern; her charm overwhelms his plans. However, she is not the naughty Lola who destroys Emil Jannings in the movie. This Rosa has a fast, sharp tongue—a mixture of *Berliner Schnauze* and show-business cheek—but she is not uncaring toward her "old fellow," the first adult to treat her with respect. In another prediction of *Sunset Boulevard,* he discovers the source of her allure: makeup. The pots, puffs, and paints make her a queen. With this perception he grows "disillusioned and initiated." Sounding more like Heinrich Mann than himself, he decides that artifice is wonderful—the most complex response Mann allows him—and becomes a makeup artist. Like the hero of "Drei Minuten Roman," he helps manufacture the object of his desire. Leaping from participles to cosmetics, Unrath has vaulted over the school walls.

As he begins to acquire friends among the workers who patronize the Blue Angel, he starts making political judgments. His schoolboy nemeses are placed on trial, accused of various corruptions, including dalliance with Rosa. He has his day in court, defending her honor, though his self-hatred leads him to suspect the worst: surely Rosa has preferred the young Lohmann. His attack on the unfairly privileged students leads to his dismissal, although a group of discontented citizens comes to regard him as their champion. (It is a sign of Mann's still tentative liberalism that his novel does not endorse any larger socialist perspective. Unrath's radicalism is reduced to sour grapes.)

Instead of revolution, he plots a tyranny. Like the hero of André Gide's *The Vatican Swindle* (1914), he announces that conventional morality is insufficient for the truly great. He is thrilled to realize that "his example could be dangerous to others." Garbage will pollute the community. Attended by his consort, the former teacher becomes a master of revels. He makes their home an after-hours gambling den where "ambiguous" pleasures seduce his former students. As Mann coalesces the novel's twin themes of cabaret and school, the salon becomes a giant dressing room where students playing hooky can spend the night.

The town is drowning in a whirlpool of orgies, and Unrath's enemies topple in succession, bankrupt or imprisoned. Yet Rosa is not content; she tries to love her old fellow, but learning Greek is easier. In one more scene anticipating Proust, Unrath spends a night waiting for his unfaithful wife, whom he has tricked into an assignation with yet another enemy. When he hears her footsteps, he hops into bed and fakes sleep. Manipulating appearances but terrified of consequences, this is the same masochist who used to turn corners half-hoping to hear his name. For a moment Mann dangles the prospect of redemption before him: he considers going straight, but he won't sacrifice his power, for "the tyrant had turned anarchist." Crime has rejuvenated him. No more a creature of pathos, he exults in his name: "Remember you're dealing with Old Garbage."

But it is too good or bad to last. Lohmann returns and figures out the "misanthrope": Unrath is a demagogue, the kind of man who leads a mob to burn down the palace, and the civilized aesthete is obliged to cleanse society of its garbage so that the palace can remain pristine. Rosa flirts with Lohmann. Unrath discovers them, goes mad, and tries to strangle her. Revealing his conventional streak, Lohmann calls for the police, and to his chagrin Rosa is arrested along with her man. A crowd gathers, suddenly restored to their senses. They merely stare at Rosa, who appears clinging to Unrath, filled with remorse. But they come alive with the appearance of Old Garbage. All his paranoid fears are realized: he can never escape his enemies; they will trail him forever. As the novel ends, a former student shouts the name, stripped of its cachet, a renewed obscenity.

If the novel is read as a political parable, this is a qualified happy ending, since the tyrant is toppled. But Lohmann's own plans— to rise above the fleshly "like Parsifal" and join the cavalry, a self-possessed Wagnerian warrior—make him seem equally awful. While Unrath is a sociopath, his sphere of influence is less the courthouse than the nightclub, and who wouldn't prefer the Blue Angel to a gymnasium? It may be a sign of Mann's unfinished ideas that he does not make the nightclub more an arena of emancipation, as he later does the opera house. One enjoys the austere Mann's engagement with the irrepressible Rosa, a far cry from his Italian noblewoman. He seems to see in her a cultural force so attractive that it may overwhelm high art. The apprehension that vernacular culture is the force to beat indicates that his *Weltschmerz* is in remission; Heinrich Mann was no longer writing for an audience of one.

Zwischen den Rassen (Between the Races, 1907) elaborates his earlier self-assessment. His mixed-breed persona in this work is a woman, Lola, a German-Brazilian like himself, and he bisects the male world by dividing her allegiances between Pardi, a hot-blooded, seductive Italian, and Acton, a clever but passive German. She marries Pardi, whose violent behavior obliges Acton to confront him in a duel. Once again the forces of reason are provoked to an unprecedented action. But the heroine's ambivalence reflects Mann's own lingering attraction to any form of passionate energy.

Acton distinguishes the Italian and German concepts of freedom. The German is a true conservative; his freedom is internal, contained within "four walls." Outside the Kaiser may reign; in his house the German enjoys an imperial power. But in Italy "the people . . . are rarely in their four walls. . . . They descend to the plazas, . . . and, like real young people who still live by reason and vision, know no difference between inner and outer experience." This casts a light on Mann himself, who at thirty-six was still a young man. It also anticipates recent attempts by writers like Hannah Arendt and Jürgen Habermas to posit a public space where people can enact their freedom. Today the four walls do not bar the public world so much as they embrace it in the form of media representations; the new imperial pastimes allow one to cultivate a private vision of public matters, compact as a disc, manipulable as a button. With that development in mind it is not surprising that when Mann puts public-spirited Italians out on the streets, he does so in the already old-fashioned form of an opera.

Die kleine Stadt (*The Little Town*, 1909) is his most technically complex novel. Polyrhythms and counterpoint prevail: Mann realizes a simultaneity unusual in literature, limited in cinema to crosscutting but uniquely possible on the stage. A large cast is trundled on and off, regrouping in all manner of formations. This is his most operatic work; the monologues resemble arias, expressing a heightened passion at the price of realism. The narrative concept is a grand one. A touring opera company arrives in a small Italian town; the company is a mélange of giddy chorines, romantic tenors, wizened managers, and cynical sopranos. In short order they provoke a minor civil war between the devotees of art and progress and the supporters of a reactionary priest. The troupe's sponsor is the town lawyer, a liberal committed to the service of "hu-

manity" and, like his creator, terrified of anarchy or class warfare. But his legalistic rhetoric verges on song. Mann adored Italian opera; he spent his last waking moments listening to recordings of Puccini. *The Little Town* may be read as a contra-Wagner novel, with the public-spirited melodies of Giuseppe Verdi complementing the text.

Once again this is a performers' world. Even the lawyer is dismissed by his enemies as being in cahoots with the actors, if not an actor himself. Nello, the lyric tenor, is an appealing figure. He delights in trilling his high D (the note with which Luciano Pavarotti made his fortune). He is not very bright or talented, simply a poor boy from Verona whose high notes provide a passport out of the ghetto. The novel includes three impassioned women, two of them in love with him. But he leaves the mezzo and coloratura to fight it out over him. Meanwhile, his lover is too "great" for him; she would sing out a real-life tragedy, but he is only "fit for stage blood." Alas, she gets him anyway in what resembles a Verdian *Todeslied*.

The novel's most interesting duet involves Don Tadeo, the village priest, and Flora Garlinda, the prima donna. Their conflict is not sexual. He pines for a soubrette while she flirts with the conductor. But as high priestess of art she becomes his Whore of Babylon. While her lover Dorlenghi yearns to compose for the masses, her attitude toward the public is ambivalent: she love-hates them because they are "wicked and dangerous." The conductor and the soprano divide between them Mann's lifelong confusion: he craves a public, and he distrusts them. This big woman finds her match in Tadeo: "He's a furious fanatic and stronger than you all." Their confrontation recalls Thomas Mann's closet drama, *Fiorenza* (1905), which includes a similar dialogue between a religious fanatic and a beautiful woman.

A more blatant literary parallel exists. After a fire occurs and Tadeo disappears, the local demagogue—a journalist—turns the town against the lawyer and singers. A vigilante mood takes over. But the priest returns and summons the faithful to church, where he preaches a sermon of such vehement self-hatred that women scream and roll in the aisles. Unwittingly Mann predicts the Pentecostal frenzies of the American South through a nineteenth-century Italian town. In his *mea culpa,* the priest admits that he has loved God in the spirit but not man in the flesh. He rips off his cassock and reveals—not a Scarlet Letter but similar evidence that he has been consumed by the flames: holes burnt in his cassock, for the union of art and society.

In this fictional manifesto there is little editorializing. An old writer observes that nothing really changes: "Again and again, humanity will have to overthrow its masters, and spirit be matched against might." But spirit has driven Tadeo crazy, and thus the novel subverts itself. Likewise, when the conductor declares, "You have no idea how good a man must be in order to create," he doubtless articulates Mann's credo. But Flora overhears and, a Wagner to his Puccini, mutters "Nothing great is kind." The novel concludes with a rapid sequence of virtuoso arias. The conductor pounds the piano like some delirious composer in a 1940's movie; Tadeo dedicates himself to humanity, having cut himself off from more modest and intimate satisfactions; and Nello and his lover lie dead while a senile old man bows to his invisible public.

Both Mann brothers have said that *The Little Town* is Heinrich's best work. It may be his most stylized, but a modern reader will more likely prefer *Der Untertan*—the translated title, *Man of Straw*, misses the subservience implicit in the German title. By the time of its composition Mann's liberalism had been announced in several essays, particularly *Geist und Tat,* his manifesto of 1910, and that same year's essay "Voltaire—Goethe," in which Mann castigates the German for his lack of humanity, his disregard for equality and freedom, these two rights being identified as coterminous. Mann appended a modern liberal's argument that inequality damaged

the oppressor as much as his victim. *Man of Straw* is a product of his prewar liberalism; it was composed between 1910 and 1914 although it wasn't published until 1918. By then, with all the prescience of hindsight, it seemed a prophetic book. The creator of Zumsee and Branzilla was reborn a Cassandra.

The first sentence introduces Diederich Hessling, "a dreamy, delicate child, terrified of everything." For a moment it seems that we are encountering another Hanno Buddenbrooks, a self-absorbed aesthete doomed in his cradle. But by the paragraph's end we discover instead a coquette and a sneak. Already, in adolescence, Diederich bullies the defenseless and cringes before authority. The Buddenbrooks clan was in decline; the Hesslings are parvenus, one generation away from the working class. Something of a German Snopes, Diederich dedicates himself to the destruction of his town's most distinguished family, the Bucks.

He develops into a figure alternately terrifying and hilarious. While growing up he is essentially an "as if" personality, acquiring his coloration from whatever figure dominates his milieu. He studies in Berlin, where he joins a dueling club, getting by on bravado, happiest when he can act the toady to an older brother. He acquires a mentor who sounds like the 1890's Heinrich Mann, preaching against "Jewish liberalism" and dismissing the Jews as social outsiders. His various needs for order and authority merge in a fanatical devotion to the emperor. When a band of unemployed workers petition Wilhelm for "Bread! Work!" the monarch is too preoccupied with his "personality and performance" to notice them. Politics is simply a theatrical routine, and Diederich is its most gullible fan. The first chapter ends as Diederich, rushing after the kaiser to apologize for the benighted masses, stumbles and plops in a puddle. The ruler takes him for a madman; then, recognizing a true subject, he bursts out laughing. But Diederich is impervious to insult; he lives to be patronized.

While in Berlin he has an affair with Agnes, a young woman who briefly arouses "the man he should have been." But she is a refugee from another Mann story. Her memories of a motherless youth—in which she feared that people would despise her until she realized that they wouldn't even pay attention—alarm him. He ridicules the art and literature she lives by: Schiller is romantic Quatsch, and no museum offers a lovelier prospect than the window of a delicatessen. Shades of *Pippo Spano,* she sends him a pathetic letter. But he responds without feeling; in an amusing if heartless dialogue he answers her written despair with a "there you go again."

He prefers the company of a man, Wolfgang Buck, the son of his town's first family. Old Buck, a veteran of the 1848 revolution, symbolizes the rapidly disappearing values of liberal humanism. His son is less idealistic, as evidenced by his striking remark that "the actor is the perfect modern type." Since their schooldays Diederich has despised Wolfgang's verbal prowess, but the two become buddies of a sort. Wolfgang finds him a fascinating case, and Diederich is awestruck by the other's fluency. His anti-Semitic nature is perversely aroused by this son of a Jewish actress.

He returns to his hometown and takes over the family business. Mann depicts a workplace pastoral ruined by Diederich's arrival. He weasels his way into public attention. First he dismisses a workman caught necking on the job; then, when the fellow is shot after cursing an officer, he exults in this demonstration of "imperial power." He provokes Lauer, Wolfgang's Jewish brother-in-law, to say that some German nobility have Jewish relatives, and he engineers Lauer's trial for public libel. Diederich quivers before each victory, astonished by his audacity. But when he testifies against Lauer, he assumes the fluency of a Buck. Wolfgang applauds his playing to the crowd, exclaiming, "A mad hit! A winner!" with a "hostile joy" that reveals his moral indolence.

He sums up his rival's nature: what makes Diederich "a new type is simply the gesture, the swaggering manner, the aggressive nature of an alleged personality, the craving for effect at any price." He refuses to see Diederich in terms of class or nationalism. The preferred metaphor is theatrical. In our post-economic era "public life becomes wretched mummery," and Lauer's "truth" becomes Hessling's "comedy." Diederich sits entranced by Buck's critique, having forgotten that he is the subject of it. But Diederich wins anyway, and Wolfgang rather enjoys his own defeat. Later he greets Diederich in all friendliness: "Admit it Hessling, nobody ever got your number like I did. In fact I was much more taken with your role than my own. Why, I've even imitated you in front of the mirror. The next step is clear. You will take over the town, and I must go on the stage." In such passages Mann makes moral conflict extremely dramatic.

True to form, Diederich is a domestic tyrant. Chaperoning his termagant siblings, he tells a prospective suitor, "Here is family bliss. Take a look!" He makes an equally absurd lover. No more Agneses: his new women are bawdy Valkyries. He marries Guste, a vulgar arriviste, and their lust becomes another source of political humor. On their wedding night Diederich interrupts his orgasm to salute the emperor, dedicating his pleasure to the monarch's glory. His wife giggles that he is no Lohengrin, a cute reference to Wagner, the only artist admissible in this patriot's pantheon. (Later she acquires a "revolutionary smile" and assumes the dominant role in their marriage.) They honeymoon in Rome, spending more time indoors than out. Coincidentally the emperor is also visiting Rome, and once again the two face each other under a benign sky. It is as close to mystical union as Diederich will get. He has often marveled at the affinity of their words and thoughts, but when he finally stands before his king, he has nothing to say.

Mann deepens his analysis by endowing Diederich with inchoate desires. No matter how he conspires against Old Buck, he is invariably moved by the patriarch's dignity. The hero of 1848 recognizes that Diederich is the wave of an awful future, but he is too humane, too simply paternal, to condemn any of his figurative offspring. Diederich thus comes to resemble characters imagined by Franz Kafka, Hermann Broch, and Robert Musil—men who seem to want nothing so badly as a wise father.

Man of Straw is obviously a major indictment of right-wing reaction. It contains prophetic passages: Diederich posits eugenic ("hygienic") solutions to racial conflicts; when he finally testifies against Old Buck, his innuendo is as slippery as that of Senator Joseph McCarthy accusing witnesses; his fatuous remark that the German spirit is fundamentally tragic looks forward to Thomas Mann's propaganda during World War I, while his tributes to family and church predict the Moral Majority, and his contention that young people are patriotic capitalists anticipates the Republican party line of 1984. Yet this is not a revolutionary novel; it lacks both party and program. The left is represented by Diederich's foreman, a master of realpolitik who prefers to form a block with the "patriots" rather than with the bleeding-heart liberals. Old Buck gives moving speeches addressed to "We the People," a classification that dissolves class divisions. Father and son deplore the infatuation with heroes; Wolfgang considers the emperor a second-rate performer. But they regard the power of genuinely great men as more beneficent than "social legislation." Sounding like the Violante of *Diana,* Old Buck laments that the Germans were not ready for 1848, since they were lacking in "political education." The Bucks are republican aristocrats; as so often in the work of both Mann brothers, democracy is decreed from on high.

In a spectacular finale Diederich convenes the town's citizens at the inauguration of a public building. During the ceremony he receives an imperial citation. But his glory is evanescent: a storm erupts, the crowd scrams, and he stumbles and winds up again with a soaked backside. He manages to hold fast to his decoration: even nature can't undermine the kaiser's power. To reassert his dignity he decides to visit the Bucks. Rained out or not, he will show those snobs that up against the power of "money" and "fists," their spirit hasn't a chance. The novel ends ambiguously. As Old Buck lies dying he hallucinates a "nation" worthy of a last outburst of "spiritual joy": one expects Beethoven on the soundtrack. But he catches a glimpse of Diederich, all puffed up "on general principles," and collapses from the shock. His inimitable self vanishes from his triumph, more clown than beast.

Man of Straw dramatizes what Hannah Arendt called "the banality of evil," a concept that irritated Americans but made perfect sense to other émigrés, most of whom had read Mann's novel. He expresses the right-wing mentality with a surprising empathy, as he breathes, nay hyperventilates, along with Diederich. The real ambivalence is saved for Wolfgang, and even as Buck asserts himself by quitting show business when police chiefs start applauding his routines, Mann reconsiders his role as an artist. Having imagined a professor become beautician and a lawyer turned actor, he now merges belletrist and propagandist. Unwittingly, he became the hero Wolfgang Buck refused to be.

When World War I began, few intellectuals were immune to the prevailing spirit of militarism and chauvinism. Among those who resisted, no German writer was more outspoken than Heinrich Mann. He paid a price: the serialization of *Man of Straw* was halted. Meanwhile his brother was turning out patriotic essays, hedged somewhat by ironic evasions but sufficiently rabid to grieve Heinrich. Thomas asserted the virtues of a German temperament—inbred, more musical than literary, anti-democratic, fundamentally tragic. Heinrich opted for another national identity, contending that after 1789 France was simply the homeland of those who preferred life to death.

In 1915 he published the essay "Zola," in which he decries a German form of intellectual treason. He begins by identifying political error with aesthetic immaturity: "A creator reaches manhood only relatively late in life—it is those who appear natural and worldly-wise in their early twenties who are destined soon to dry up." Heinrich saw himself retracing Zola's footsteps: both were aesthetes converted to radical politics; both were ostracized; and both would be vindicated by history, while their enemies would be revealed as hacks, "entertaining parasites."

A mortified Thomas picked up on the equation. Who else could Heinrich mean when he spoke of precocious talents? The use of the noun form "man" rankled further. Taking the essay personally, he proceeded to write the longest expression of sibling rivalry in literature. His *Reflections of an Unpolitical Man* (1918) was an apology for his pro-German positions—apology in both senses, perhaps, since toward its end he began to modify his attacks on democracy. The bulk of this huge work reiterates his earlier positions in a series of aesthetic and psychological variations: Germany is culture, tragic and profound; France is civilization, glib and shallow. He introduces the figure of Civilization's Literary Man, a chirping, chatty salesman for such inane concepts as "Humanity" and "Progress." This was a direct hit at the rather vague uplift of Heinrich's essay; it demoted the author from artist to journalist, poet to publicist. His literary past was held against him: the prophet of a "Hysterical Renaissance" was now an exponent of "Hysterical Democracy." Without naming Heinrich, Thomas employed fraternal imagery throughout the book. He also gave away family secrets by noting that this self-proclaimed altruist was actually a careerist more concerned with prose rhythms than with any platitudinous vision of peace.

In December 1917 Heinrich wrote to Thomas, "There is no I in my public remarks, and consequently no brother." His words had been aimed not at Thomas but at a legion. Despite their "intellectual hostility," he trusted that Thomas did not regard him as an enemy. The letter enraged Thomas. He replied that Heinrich was always trying to one-up him, always asserting his superior character without allowing him to "react with as much as a sentence." As for Heinrich's sentences, they reeked of "a truly French spitefulness": language and national identity had become the integers of fraternal conflict. Heinrich's attempts at the high road were dismissed as "moral smugness and self-righteousness." Rage made Thomas maudlin: you and your friends may call me a parasite, but I have a public and "I have helped them to live." Heinrich's reply offered an aphorism for Thomas' condition—and a simple formula for returning him to his senses: "Stop relating my life and action always to yourself." Having been bettered in an argument, you think I'm gloating in triumph, but a ruined continent and ten million dead are not my idea of debating points. As for the power of language, I don't know if any writer can help people live, but let's not use our words to help them die!

This feud estranged the Mann brothers for several years. It was a major loss for Heinrich, but there were professional compensations. Throughout the war he had solidified his reputation as a liberal intellectual. One of his plays, *Madame Legros* (1913), caused a sensation in Berlin during 1917. It depicts the efforts of a petit bourgeois housewife in pre-revolutionary France to proclaim the innocence of a falsely accused nobleman. The play reveals Mann's divided loyalties—his aristocrats are decorous and subtle, his masses anarchic brutes. A disaffiliated cavalier similar to Wolfgang Buck is the play's most sympathetic figure. Monsieur Legros is more conventional, and he—and Mann—find it perfectly natural that, having fulfilled her public function, his wife should return to domestic subjugation. Nevertheless the play was considered a major progressive statement. Another drama composed in wartime, *Die Unschuldige* (Not Guilty), reveals some more familiar Mann obsessions. Its heroine is accused of murdering her first husband. She marries her attorney and spends the play teasing him with hints of her guilt. Mann has it both ways: she is provocatively suspect but is in truth innocent, a smarter Emma Bovary with an unblemished record.

Heinrich had never sold well; Thomas was the family star. But in 1917, thanks to the promotion of his new publisher, Kurt Wolff, he emerged as a leading German author. A new edition of *Cockaigne* sold 60,000 copies, and *Man of Straw* astonished everyone by selling 150,000 copies. Ironically the war had bequeathed him a public. He also found himself engaged in practical politics. During the short-lived Munich revolution, he participated in a "Political Council of Intellectual Workers," although he distanced himself from the radicals and continued to distrust any appeals to class interests. After the Munich government fell he pledged his loyalty to the German republic. Like Old Buck genuflecting before "We the People," he envisioned a post-class society that had done away with socialists and bourgeoisie. He urged workers not to strike but to stand by their government, the best one imaginable under postwar circumstances. He continued to support it throughout the 1920's, aware of its dubious alternatives. Similarly, while he gradually overcame his initial revulsion toward Bolshevism (Lenin's "dictatorship of the proletariat" was a nightmare fulfilled), he believed that Communism was an Eastern phenomenon and would not work in Germany.

By the late 1930's he had transferred his absolute loyalty from the Weimar Republic to the Soviet Union. But that may simply have proved his need for order as well as his unfortunate penchant for always being a step behind politically: he was a liberal in radical Munich, a fellow traveler under Stalinism. However, during the 1920's he was simply the most famous German exponent of democratic values. He lectured widely and acquired an international reputation as Germany's most progressive mainstream intellectual. By then

the brothers had reconciled. Another latecomer, Thomas proved an equally ardent supporter of the Weimar government. He wrote rave reviews of Heinrich's novels and political essays for the foreign press.

But while a political sea change served to enrich Thomas's art—during the 1920's, he wrote *The Magic Mountain* (1924) and received the Nobel Prize for Literature (1929)—politics was a less happy influence on Heinrich's fiction. He made *Man of Straw* the first part of a trilogy, *Das Kaiserreich* (The Era of the Kaiser), which was supposed to examine all the classes. *Die Armen* (The Poor, 1917) revolves around Balrich, an employee of Diederich Hessling's. From an enraged activist he develops into a "son of the spirit" and winds up a lawyer, buying into the system to fight its exploiters. Even the novel's characters question his choice of vocation. Once again Mann draws his hero to the theater, but when Balrich attends a play he can make no sense of it, a lament on Mann's part that his new subject was not a likely reader of his fiction. In the third novel of the trilogy, *Der Kopf* (The Chief, 1925), the forces of authority are counterposed with two largely impotent intellectuals. Their peregrinations across the ideological landscape only confuse the reader; politics seems reduced to a metaphor for the peripatetic writer.

The novella *Kobes* (1925) is more intriguing. The title figure is a profiteer, a latter-day Türkheimer, and once again all Germany is at his feet—in 1923 Mann observed that "the wealthiest people" had conquered the country without a putsch. Kobes' only enemy is an employee of his Propaganda Department, Cabaret Division, who hopes to satirize the boss out of existence. It is typical that Mann conceives political dissent as a cabaret routine. (George Grosz contributed sketches to the book's first edition, indicating a congruent assessment of the Berlin robber barons.) But the efforts fail, the satire is misunderstood, and the intellectual commits suicide, a confirmation of the artist's impotence in the face of despotism.

Mann wrote tributes to youth and the working class, aware that for neither was he a convincing spokesman. His books stopped selling, and he wound up doing free-lance work, newspaper articles, radio lectures, even an appearance at a Berlin department store. His writings of the late 1920's support a bewildering range of positions, from the acutely critical to the amorphously spiritual. He complained that young people were "monarchorepublicans" who lived solely for pleasure. But then he attempted a series of entertainments, trying to compete with movies and potboilers, so desperate was he to recapture his public. His always brilliant literary essays began to discover the origins of modern politics: in an essay on Stendhal he discerned the "fascists of capitalism" flourishing before the French Revolution. This certainly sounds like dialectical materialism. Yet he so despised the uninflected materialism that had seduced his audience that he began to extol "spirit" no matter where he found it. The lifelong agnostic suddenly hailed the church as "the only form in which the West has seen the spirit triumphant over non-spiritual powers. . . . The church has become a power in itself." Later he said, "We must found our church," shortly before he placed his trust in Stalinism.

His brief homage to religion suffused his worst novel, *Mutter Marie* (Mother Mary, 1927), in which a reckless woman and her spoiled protégé are spiritually transformed, she, quite literally, when she regains her childhood faith in Jesus. Like Diederich Hessling she vanishes as the novel ends, but if he retires to his banal hell, the whore-saint has flown to heaven. *Eugénie, oder Die Bürgerzeit* (The Royal Woman, 1928) is his best novel of the 1920's. Its heroine, Gabrielle, is a Frenchwoman, married to a German, living in Mann's hometown, Lübeck. She is yet another Madame Bovary, bored by suburbia and lured to the city's fleshpots, where she is tempted by a crooked speculator. Her savior is not her husband but a platonic friend, Von Heines (likely a salute to the great German-Jewish poet Heinrich Heine). He writes a play and casts the speculator as Na-

poleon III and Gabrielle as his wife, Eugénie. Once again a drama provides both catalyst and catharsis. Never afterward did Mann imagine a writer exerting such control of events. The novel's subtitle, "A German Play" (about French characters, written in joint homage to Nietzsche and Flaubert), signifies the implausibility of his imaginative schemes. In art and politics alike he appeared increasingly eccentric.

Things looked up briefly. In 1929 a new edition of the racy *Cockaigne* sold one hundred thousand copies. In 1931 he married Nellie Kröger, a Berlin barmaid, his very own Rosa Fröhlich, although she later acted more like the movie's heartless Lola. His epithalamium was *Ein ernstes Leben* (The Hill of Lies, 1932), another entertainment, another flop. Yet at sixty he was perceived as an almost institutional figure. That same year he was elected president of the Prussian Academy of Arts, a largely ceremonial position. One American writer described him as a broad-shouldered, resolute presence; the critic Hermann J. Weigand saw him and his brother as the authors of Germany's political redemption.

Such optimism was short-lived. The Nazis became an active threat, and, together with the artist Käthe Kollwitz, Mann sought to unify socialists and Communists in opposition to Hitler. Although he had come to respect Communism, he "lived too far west" to share its values, and he considered the party's refusal to work with socialists a murderous error. As late as January 1933 he wrote *Das Bekenntnis zum Übernationalen* ("Supernational Manifesto") exposing the counterrevolutionary cliques that had wrecked the republic as early as 1919, making sarcastic fun of "the Fatherland," and imploring Germans to come to their senses. His toughest essay, it infuriated the Nazis, who had been publishing cartoons showing Heinrich's old head attached to Marlene Dietrich's legs. No doubt they would have done worse after they achieved power later that month. But on the advice of a French diplomat he fled the country in February. Weeks later his books went up in flames. The Diederichs had their revenge on the Bucks; as Mann wrote, they burned the books they could not write.

He moved to France, briefly boarding with the novelists Hermann Kesten (the gadfly of the literary emigration) and Joseph Roth (an astonishingly versatile novelist whose work manages to combine Trotskyism, Jewish folklore, neo-Catholicism, and loyalty to the Habsburgs, whom he depicts as the heroic obverse of *Man of Straw*'s Hohenzollerns). He was perhaps the first émigré to attack Fascism in print, using as a forum *Die Sammlung* (The Collection), a journal edited in Holland by his nephew Klaus Mann. While his only colleagues at this time were Marxists—Hitler's first victims—he continued to maintain his aristocratic principles as homage to tradition and as evidence that he stood above internecine (read "class") squabbles: "I am from an old family of the old Germany, and he who has tradition is guarded against false feelings. Tradition enables us to understand and makes us inclined toward skepticism and kindness. Only upstarts behave at times like barbarians." This benevolent tone was ill-conceived. The Nazis were much more than a disgruntled mob, and "skepticism and kindness" would not disarm them.

While in France Mann resided chiefly in Nice, although he became a citizen of Czechoslovakia in 1937. He wrote a series of dispatches for a provincial newspaper, the *Dépêche de Toulouse,* and published three collections of political essays, *Der Hass: Deutsche Zeitgeschichte* (Hatred: Essays in Modern German History, 1933), *Es kommt der Tag* (There Will Come a Day, 1936), and *Mut* (1939). During the period from 1933 to 1936 Thomas Mann kept a conspicuous silence, hoping thereby to retain his German readership. After his famous letter to the dean of Bonn University he was transformed into the most famous anti-Fascist intellectual, ultimately more unforgiving than Heinrich. But émigrés never forgot who had been the first

lonely voice. Heinrich became a hero of the Popular Front, establishing French and German exile branches of the movement. In addition to his work with the PEN Club, he addressed congresses of left-wing intellectuals. Some historians regard the Mann of the 1930's as the quintessential fellow traveler. Whatever the nature of his comrades in the war against Hitler, he had long outgrown the solitude of 1904 (although given the vagaries of politics it might have been better for his reputation had he maintained it).

He returned to fiction, and in one of the happiest ironies of emigration he recovered his talent in the process of losing his audience. Having been stirred by the first installments of his brother's mythic epic, *Joseph and His Brothers* (1933–1943), he devised his own, a massive two-volume novel about Henry of Navarre, *Die Jugend des Königs Henri Quatre* (*Young Henry of Navarre,* 1935) and *Die Vollendung des Königs Henri Quatre* (*Henry, King of France,* 1938). The gap between the brothers' heroes may be exemplary: Thomas's Joseph, the wily androgyne, the seductive courtier, is isolated and refined; Heinrich's Henry, the democratic monarch, the earthy sensualist, is incapable of introspection. Heinrich's Henry was his best-realized, most fully imagined hero, perhaps because resemblances between author and character were so tenuous. His story allowed bountiful room for sensuous descriptions and magisterial judgments. It was an astonishing instance of creative rebirth in old age.

His first sentence, "The boy was small, the mountains enormous," conveys the pathos of Henry's task, dwarfed as it were by time and space. It also announces a style in which every abstract issue is steeped in sensuous reality. Henry is a little model of polymorphous perversity: raised on garlic and roast pigeon, he is accustomed to the odor of sweat, smoke, and herbs and is content to bathe nude with peasant boys and girls. He lives among the people, happiest when speaking their language. Good French and the common cause become coter-

minous: he ultimately derives the same satisfactions from clear expression, physical work,
and lovemaking. From childhood he is the
most sexually liberated of Mann's heroes. He
bears traces of his master's obsessions—his
first wife happens to be the buxom "Fat Margot"—but in truth Henry loves women of all
sizes: he even flirts with a dwarf, and when the
agitated creature urinates in excitement, he
declares her aroma the court's sweetest perfume: "It was woman that bound him to his
people. In her he knew them; in her he made
them his"; Henry is the king who, by sleeping
with their daughters, makes love to the nation.
Much is made of his "blood"—a residue of
Mann's interest in the principles of heredity—
but Henry is compromised too often to attempt
an elitist posture. To the intellectual Mann
he offers the unprecedented example of someone totally in touch with his public. There
is a complete synchronization of sensibilities,
which is why Henry can identify for his subjects their political desires before they discover
them for themselves.

A man of action, he learns best from visceral experience. After his mother dies, he
finds out that she was still having affairs. His
grief is diminished, but years later, when he
finds himself lusty in middle age, he salutes
her precedent and apologizes for being such a
prude. Likewise it is only after the St. Barthol-
omew's Massacre that he realizes that his
naiveté combined with a childish bravado
have blinded him to the potential for violence
and that an unreflective sybarite makes a bad
king. In order to combine both tendencies, the
sensuous and the regal, he needs a theory, and
he derives an almost sensuous pleasure from
the intellectual guidance he receives from
Montaigne. The philosopher tantalizes him
with his formulation "How do I know?"—
particularly when he adds that even our bodies
escape our apprehension. (Like Thomas Mann
Heinrich enjoys contemplating his literary
mentors and underlining their common interests.) Montaigne's ethics refresh the shell-
shocked Henry. For a period the Latin apho-

rism *Nihil est tam populare quam bonitas*
(Nothing is as popular as goodness) is his
one consolation: a faith in the *vox populare*
(people's judgment) that his time, much less
Mann's, scarcely supports. Montaigne's skepticism is the mind-set that best fits Henry's
nature. Polymorphous perversity is reflected
in political pluralism.

After an intellectual development that is
measured in anecdotal episodes, Henry comes
to question dogma, to bypass doctrine, and, in
an ecumenical gesture, to merge Catholic fes-
tivity with Huguenot self-regard. The formal
product is the Edict of Nantes, the codified gift
of "freedom of conscience with all its consequences." In one of the novel's great sentences
Mann writes, "At last he knew himself strong
enough to say to them, 'You are free to believe
and to think.'" The novel's distinction is that it
makes a political position seem the dramatic
culmination of a lifetime of thought and action.

Mann's joy in his hero extends to Henry's
women, of whom Margot is the most provocative. A scholar-poet, she displays a greater
range of affect and idea than her husband.
When she discovers that her mother and
brother are plotting against Henry, her attempt
to extract some good out of a hopeless situation is depicted with great subtlety: Mann has
found a woman worthy of his excessive attentions. But she is also Henry's sensual twin, as
frank about desire, as quickly aroused. Her
potential for erotic violence is a sanitized
legacy of her mother, the murderous Catherine
de Medici. Mann's ultimate fat woman, her
cheeks spongy, her gait waddling, her mental
fleetness belying an obscene girth, Catherine
possesses a kind of aesthetic genius that stops
time: "For those whose life is action, all time is
the present; in it are absorbed both the future
and the past." She winds up commanding the
interest, if not the sympathy, of Henry, whose
mother she murdered; she is an irresistible
character. The other women range from the
fanatical Catholic Duchesse de Montpensier,
who plots Henry's murder, to the intellectual
Protestant Madame de Mornay, whose terrible

death instructs the fame-obsessed monarch (and perhaps his author) that "glory" comes only before the grave . . . "and after it—nothing."

There may be more smart women in this novel than in all of Thomas Mann's major works, not to mention those of Musil, Broch, Kafka, or—arguably—André Gide and Marcel Proust. But Henry and Mann reserve their most loving attentions for the comparatively simple Gabrielle d'Estrée, the mistress of Henry's middle years. As emotionally constricted as her unreflective king, she exhibits an atavistic, nearly animal loyalty that makes his devotion seem almost frivolous. Her death provides the novel's most rending pages, as gruesome as Echo's death in *Doktor Faustus*. (As Mann anticipates one novel, he echoes another. In shades of *The Magic Mountain* Henry studies a sketch of his wife's poisoned entrails much as Hans Castorp gazes at an X ray of Claudia Chauchat.)

The novel also depicts a homosexual subculture that flourished in "The New Court" of Margot's brother, Henry of Valois. In passages worthy of Proust, buccaneers and statesmen are shown salivating over pretty boys, fellows they would mistreat in other circumstances. But these common soldiers are transformed by "art," the makeup that beautifies Rosa Fröhlich. Sexual desire is inseparable from artificial display: the men get most aroused when they see the young soldiers performing in a *tableau vivant*. But the spectacle grows deathly when one of the king's favorites pretends to be poisoned by his rival. Fat Margot spies on the all-male gathering and concludes that these warriors in drag have gone from parody to murder. Caught in his act, the young poseur is beaten; rigid in his terror, he gives his best performance. Mann's Brechtian gloss is "Truth beats any impersonation." Yet Margot fully understands her brother's attraction to young men; her own is similarly debilitating. And Henry tells Valois that he regrets his inability to enjoy another form of love: "A certain side of human nature remains closed to me." Considering the potent homoerotic desires of Thomas Mann, this may be read as a tactful expression of fellow feeling between brothers.

Less obscure are the many allusions to Fascist politics. Several of Henry's Catholic enemies resemble Hitler and his henchmen. The most bloody excesses occur when the mob and the burghers join forces with "hot-headed youth," as they did in Nazi Germany when students burned Mann's books to the encouragement of the petit bourgeoisie. In a passage as prophetic as any in *Man of Straw*, Mann distills the banality of evil when a zealot kills a woman and then pauses to stroke her dog. As Mann notes, evil on this order is temporary: he will only kill today, but he will stroke a dog every day.

In such scenes Mann achieves a cinematic perspective with an intellectual resonance unique to literature. He tends to frame a sequence by reminding the reader of Henry's position in history, his previous representation in letters and portraits; coming after the most intimate close-ups these frames serve to distance us, yet paradoxically our identification with Henry is intensified. At its most vivid, his language conflates mimesis and analysis. For instance, Henry gallops over French soil, and the temporal-spatial movement duplicates a historical development, registered by the senses. Similarly, when the unhappy Valois finds himself dancing in the mirror, he cannot recognize the graceful creature, "innocent of memories," decapitated by the mirror frame. His innate morbidity overwhelms the physical image.

Mann utilizes all his verbal skills to stake his ultimate claims for language. In one scene he shows Henry surrounded by his followers. The king wonders, What if he could read the future in their faces? The book proceeds to do so. The game lies in the fact that Henry cannot; the wit lies in seeing that Mann—and literature—can. Turning reality on its head, Mann makes time language's vehicle. When Henry has his first affair with a peasant girl,

Fleurette, he calls her name as if recognizing that she is the first of thousands; and years later, when they meet again, he thinks like everyone else that she has died because the legend of first love requires it.

The monstrous Catherine de Medici lives so boldly in the novel that when she is finished off in a mere sentence—"she, in the meantime, did die"—the narrator questions her departure. The motive is so weak—she is blamed for a murder that for once she didn't commit and dies of exasperation—that language almost seeks to revive her. But she is gone, as will be Henry's great love, Gabrielle. He learns that she has died and mourns her while she is still struggling for life, sustained by the hope that he will soon join her. Coming after a medical catastrophe as horrible as any in literature, the disjunction between his past tense and her subjunctive breaks the heart.

Mann's most audacious verbal gesture is the composition of long passages in French. (He had sufficient practice composing items for the *Dépêche de Toulouse.*) At times he indulges in a donnish wit: one French passage describes Henry in Marxist categories as a man who will not act for thinking. When Henry dies, murdered by religious fanatics, his heart is carried through the land, and throngs of poor people regard the dismembered organ as a portable icon. Mann justifies their delusion by saying three times that Henry was the only king they ever loved. His final repetition is in French, the language of their covenant. In a coda Henry writes in French to his readers in 1936, consoling them with the message: "Vous me continuez. Gardez tout votre courage. . . . Il est toujours des oppreseurs du peuple. . . ." (I live on before you. Remain courageous. . . . The people always have oppressors. . . .) I had the French League; you have the Nazis. But like William Butler Yeats Henry affirms his identity with "mes amis" by simply recalling Gabrielle, "morte avant moi" (dead before me). As his people knew him, he lives and dies a lover.

The novel about Henry may constitute

Mann's masterpiece, the happiest of his works despite the circumstances of its composition. Yet even it did not make its author a literary celebrity among Anglo-American readers. The first volume had a modest American success; the second volume didn't sell. If Americans wanted to read a Mann, they bought Thomas.

A rare publication in English was the 1938 essay *The Living Thoughts of Nietzsche.* Writing out of an intimate involvement with his subject, an almost embarrassing identification with Nietzsche's loneliness, austerity, and cultural ambivalence, Mann tries to separate the propagandist who anticipates Fascism from the critic who provides a model of intellectual resistance. Admitting the impossibility of reading Nietzsche again with a young man's eyes, he satirizes the original audience of self-appointed supermen—youths like himself—each convinced that Nietzsche wrote expressly for him. The vision devolved into a performance; the "heroic" personality into a showman; the intellectual Valhalla into a Philistine Bayreuth. Mann turns the vexed friendship of Wagner and Nietzsche into a cautionary fable. More didactically he condemns the nineteenth century's unmediated faith in science, predicting the later attacks of the Frankfurt School.

He indicts Nietzsche for the thoughtlessness of his rhetoric, for dismissing as "nothing" the potential "sufferings of little people," a nothing consisting of ten or twenty million "butchered souls." Nietzsche called for eugenics; Mann says not to worry, the Nazis are getting there, but he trusts that a revived Nietzsche would vomit over the actions of his fabled "blond beasts." Discovering atypical solecisms in the normally lucid philosopher, Mann stresses that his language failed him when his thought went wrong. Yet Nietzsche was also a militant opponent of German nationalism, a non-socialist who heralded the working class's rise to power, an artist expressing his urge to create without regard to his own happiness, a man who valued politeness—in so many words, a forerunner of Mann himself. By making ethical questions interesting, he reclaimed moral dilemmas for serious literature, so today, when intellectuals are "violently irritated" by Nietzsche's students, they respond with a "good conscience" they inherit from him alone. Mann may write so well about Nietzsche because he felt himself equally trapped in the dilemma of fame, an "embalmed mask" totally subject to commerce and mass appeal yet necessary for influence and authority.

After a flight over the Pyrenees—the same mountains that drew young Henry—Mann arrived in Spain, accompanied by his nephew Golo Mann and the Franz Werfels. His sorrow upon leaving Europe was immense. Alma Mahler Werfel recalled that during their voyage to America Mann remained in his cabin, where he was found drawing sketches of bosomy women, the exile's fetish and nurture. After arriving in America, he traveled cross-country to Hollywood, where he celebrated his seventieth birthday at the celebrated Mabery Road salon of Salka Viertel. Before dinner his brother saluted him with a lengthy speech; when Thomas had finished, Heinrich rose with his own copious reply. The old-world formality signified Heinrich's distance from American life.

He joined several other émigré writers under contract to the Hollywood studios in a high-class form of welfare. But he received no assignments. He wrote an essay for Klaus Mann's magazine *Decision,* in which he discerned in Nazism a familiar German sabotage of French principles. He also echoed a concept beloved of French writers—that the well-lived life was like a novel. On his arrival in California he determined that the novel had reached its climax.

But ahead of him lay almost a decade of misery. His wife, Nellie, went mad. She would welcome guests in the nude, complaining about her silly old man. After being arrested for drunken driving, she committed suicide in 1944. Mann's only American publication was his 1933 call to reason, "The Supernational Manifesto," published in a volume edited by Klaus Mann and Hermann Kesten. Some royalties came in from the Soviet Union, but without his brother's assistance he would have been destitute. As it was he spent his time dodging creditors. (Thomas' enemies Brecht and Döblin spread a false rumor that he had abandoned Heinrich.)

Willfully isolated from his new countrymen, he remained obsessed with matters German. He became affiliated with the Committee for a Free Germany, a group based in Mexico, where most radical émigrés had been re-routed by the United States government. The group's position on German guilt was much less punishing than Thomas Mann's; members like Brecht considered him wickedly obtuse in his failure to see the vast pockets of German resistance, while Thomas considered them naively optimistic about the average German's culpability. After Auschwitz Thomas appeared the more realistic observer, and Heinrich marveled that he now was the more tolerant brother. With lower expectations of the German character he had less to forgive. But he refused to denounce Thomas, as his fellow Free Germans like Brecht desired. Nevertheless his affiliations came to the government's attention. The FBI kept a thirteen-year file on Mann: the Bureau intercepted his correspondence with his friends in Mexico and copied Nellie's police records. But the FBI investigators eventually concluded that he was too frail to pose a danger. The postwar attacks on Hollywood leftists frightened the old man, as he saw friends like Brecht and Hanns Eisler hounded out of the country. If he had known the identity of Whittaker Chambers, the Alger Hiss case would have provided one more astonishing coda to his life's novel, for Chambers had translated *Mother Mary,* his religious novel, and at this point, strengthened by his Catholic conversion, was tattling on Mann's comrades.

In 1949 he wrote a friend, "In fifty years, I have not been so completely disregarded as now." Although East German Communists were rereading *Man of Straw,* he did not want to survive as the author of a fictionalized editorial; the fame he sought would attend more to the range of his artistry than the correctness of his politics. He wrote a lengthy memoir, *Ein Zeitalter wird besichtigt* (An Age Is Surveyed, 1945). The survey was oddly dispirited; he admitted that Nellie's death had struck him to the heart. While all the world saw him as a Communist, the book's enthusiasms were ecumenical. His tributes to Stalin irritated the West, but the East was disturbed by his equally fervent homage to Churchill, de Gaulle, and Roosevelt. In private he told friends that society must be led by an intellectual vanguard, conspicuously not by the working class.

Still, East Germany needed a grand old man of letters, and he was invited to return. Funds were raised for the trip, but he died in March 1950, a month before his planned departure. In one of his final letters he reviewed a decade devoted to a ceaseless scrounging for funds: "If we had no need for dollars, we would laugh. At least let me smile."

His last novels, *Empfang bei der Welt* (Reception of the World, 1956) and *Der Atem* (The Breath, 1949), were never translated. Both are intensely private, filled with allusions to his earlier work, written as if without hope of their finding a sympathetic audience. In the ironically named *Empfang bei der Welt* an old man in an apocryphal California wills his spiritual legacy to his grandchildren, having concluded that his materialist offspring will squander it. In *Atem* a dying countess—based in part on Nellie—spends her last hours fleeing a fascistic banker. The novel takes place in Nice, and the German-born countess speaks more French than King Henry. A red duchess, a Violante converted to Communism, she is Mann's final theatrical figure; her epiphany occurs when she remembers a commedia del arte play in which despair was assuaged by kindness, and she dies at the moment her enemy is defeated, as melodramatic coin-cidence dissolves into a vision of simple *Menschenfreundlichkeit* (human friendship). Thomas Mann thought the novel exhibited an unprecedented "avant-gardism of old age." He felt Heinrich's late work conveyed a New World idiom: "It was so moving to see in his fiction and essays how a highly cultivated, austere and brilliant mind sought plainness, strove to reach social community and the common people, without the slightest surrendering of his aristocratic quality."

Thomas' summation evokes the great theme of Heinrich's career, the struggle of a mandarin intellectual to achieve a refined plainness. Heinrich thought that "simplicity" of genius only came after a lifetime of complications. But who would be left to recognize the mental turmoil behind the relaxed fluency of his prose? "In the eyes of the very next age," he wrote in 1938, "one is but a survivor, making demands from which posterity looks away and maintaining laws it misunderstands." In time Mann may find a new age more friendly to his work. Perhaps then, thanks to his preternatural sense of memory and desire, he will be reckoned a German Proust. After that, he will be honored for the attention he gave to political and social issues that few moderns have contemplated so long, with such variety, in so hard a life.

Selected Bibliography

EDITIONS

INDIVIDUAL WORKS

NOVELS AND NOVELLAS
In einer Familie. Munich, 1894.
Im Schlaraffenland: Ein Roman unter feinen Leuten. Munich, 1900.
Die Göttinnen, oder Die drei Romane der Herzogin von Assy (Diana, Minerva, Venus). Munich, 1903.
Die Jagd nach Liebe. Munich, 1903.
Flöten und Dolche. Munich, 1904. Includes "Drei Minuten Roman."
Pippo Spano. Munich, 1905.

Professor Unrat, oder Das Ende eines Tyrannen. Munich, 1905.

Zwischen den Rassen. Munich, 1907.

Die Bösen. Leipzig, 1908. Includes "Die Branzilla."

Die kleine Stadt. Leipzig, 1909.

Die Armen. Leipzig, 1917.

Der Untertan. Leipzig, 1918. Privately published in 1916.

Der Kopf. Berlin, 1925.

Kobes. Berlin, 1925.

Mutter Marie. Berlin, 1927.

Eugénie, oder Die Bürgerzeit. Berlin, 1928.

Ein ernstes Leben. Berlin, 1932.

Die Jugend des Königs Henri Quatre. Amsterdam, 1935.

Die Vollendung des Königs Henri Quatre. Amsterdam, 1938.

Der Atem. Amsterdam, 1949.

Empfang bei der Welt. Berlin, 1956.

DRAMA

Madame Legros. Leipzig, 1913.

Drei Akte: Der Tyrann, Die Unschuldige, Variété. Leipzig, 1917.

ESSAYS AND AUTOBIOGRAPHY

"Zola." First published in the journal *Die weissen Blätter: Eine Monatsschrift*, pp. 1312 ff. (November 1915).

Geist und Tat: Franzosen 1789–1930. Berlin, 1931.

Das Bekenntnis zum Übernationalen. Berlin, 1933.

Der Hass: Deutsche Zeitgeschichte. Amsterdam, 1933.

Es kommt der Tag. Zurich, 1936.

Mut. Paris, 1939.

Ein Zeitalter wird besichtigt. Stockholm, 1945.

CORRESPONDENCE

Briefe an Karl Lemke und Klaus Pinkus. Hamburg, 1965.

Letters of Thomas Mann, 1889–1955. Selected and translated by Richard and Clara Winston. New York, 1975.

Thomas Mann—Heinrich Mann, Briefwechsel. Berlin, 1965.

TRANSLATIONS

Berlin: The Land of Cockaigne. Translated by Axton D. B. Clark. London, 1929.

The Royal Woman. Translated by Arthur J. Ashron. New York, 1930.

The Hill of Lies. Translated by Edwin and Willa Muir. New York, 1935.

The Blue Angel. No translator cited. New York, 1979.

Henry, King of France. Translated by Eric Sutton. New York, 1985.

Letters of Thomas Mann, 1889–1955. Selected and translated by Richard and Clara Winston. New York, 1975.

The Little Town. Translated by Winifred Ray. London, 1930.

The Living Thoughts of Nietzsche. Translated by Barrows Mussey. New York, 1939.

Man of Straw. No translator cited. New York, 1984.

"Pippo Spano." Translated by Basil Creighton. In *Tellers of Tales*, edited by W. Somerset Maugham. New York, 1939.

"The Supernational Manifesto." In *The Best of Modern European Literature*, edited by Klaus Mann and Hermann Kesten. Philadelphia, 1945.

Young Henry of Navarre. Translated by Eric Sutton. New York, 1984.

BIOGRAPHICAL AND CRITICAL STUDIES

Gross, David. *The Writer and Society: Heinrich Mann and Literary Politics in Germany, 1890–1940.* Atlantic Highlands, N.J., 1980.

Hamilton, Nigel. *The Brothers Mann: The Lives of Heinrich and Thomas Mann.* New Haven, Conn., 1979.

Heilbut, Anthony. *Exiled in Paradise: German Refugee Artists and Intellectuals in America from the 1930s to the Present.* Boston, 1984.

Roberts, David. *Artistic Consciousness and Political Consciousness: The Novels of Heinrich Mann, 1900–1938.* Bern, 1971.

ANTHONY HEILBUT

MARCEL PROUST
(1871–1922)

LIFE

MARCEL PROUST, who counts as one of the two most influential novelists of the first half of this century (the other being James Joyce, whom Proust briefly met toward the end of his life), led a comfortable existence but one that was poisoned by poor health from childhood onward. He was born on 10 July 1871 in Auteuil, a pleasant suburb of Paris, at a time when the country was still reeling from the shock of defeat by the Germans in the Franco-Prussian War. His parents, very recently married, had remained in Paris throughout the two sieges of the city in 1870–1871—that of the German army and, after the armistice, that of the French government troops at Versailles fighting to put down the working-class Commune that had seized power inside Paris. Starvation rations and shortages of fuel during a bitterly cold winter, along with the shelling of the civilian population and the bloody and desperate street fighting of May 1871, constituted the worst possible conditions for a young woman carrying her first child, and it is perhaps not too fanciful to trace Proust's chronic ill health to the hardships his mother had to endure in the months before he came into the world.

Jeanne Weil was of Jewish birth, the daughter of a wealthy stockbroker; her husband, Dr. Adrien Proust, was a Catholic, the brilliant son of a family of small retail shopkeepers set-tled at Illiers, a little town not far from the cathedral city of Chartres in Île-de-France. In 1853 he came to Paris to study medicine and went on to achieve, in the course of a long life laden with honors, a reputation as one of the outstanding medical luminaries of his age. His specialty was public hygiene, and his greatest success lay in the field of sanitation; it was he who, after extensive travels, established the methods of control that made it possible to defend Europe from the periodic incursions of cholera from Asia. Thus Marcel Proust was born a member of the upper echelons of the professional middle classes, with plenty of money in the family. Like his contemporary André Gide but unlike nearly all the other great French writers who preceded him—Honoré de Balzac, Charles Baudelaire, Gustave Flaubert at the end of his life and Émile Zola at the beginning of his—Proust never had to cope with any serious financial problems and never needed to pursue a career other than that of letters.

His parents, it is true, did not at first view with equanimity his apparent determination to lead what must have seemed to them a life of culpable idleness, given up to frivolous society pursuits. Asthma, the illness that dogged him all his life, first appeared when he was nine, on a walk with his parents in the Bois de Boulogne; the attack was so violent that they thought they were going to lose him, but it proved a capricious complaint, causing only occasional absences from the school he attended. Nor did it prevent him, later on, from doing his military service as a volunteer cadet in 1889–1890; in fact, this year under the colors was perhaps the most carefree in his life. But then, on his release from the army, he was required by his family to prepare himself in all earnestness for one or another of the professions considered suitable for a young man in his station in society, and accordingly he enrolled as a student in the law faculty at the Sorbonne and also took courses in politics in case he might eventually want to enter the diplomatic service.

He does not seem to have taken either of these branches of study very seriously, being far more concerned at this period with his position in fashionable society, where his native charm, intelligence, and perfect manners made him a welcome guest at afternoon gatherings, dinner parties, and literary soirées. Although gratified to some extent by his social success, neither his father nor his mother was particularly pleased that he spent so much time in the drawing rooms of the celebrated hostesses of the period. They could not have foreseen that their son was unconsciously accumulating the material destined to serve him, long after they had both died, for the cycle of novels that has assured him a place in the first rank of creative writers of the twentieth century. There were constant rows at home about his extravagance, about the late hours he kept in disregard of his health, and about his failure to embark on a "proper" career. In this last respect, Marcel compared poorly with his younger brother, Robert, the only other child born to the Prousts, who was already starting to follow in his father's footsteps as a medical practitioner of distinction. It does not appear, however, that there was any overt sibling rivalry between the two boys. Robert, of a totally different disposition from Marcel, kept a discreet eye on his brother all his life and watched over him during his final illness. Having inherited, as next of kin, the mass of manuscript material discovered after his death in Marcel's study-bedroom, it was he who arranged for its eventual publication after World War II.

Eventually the Prousts resigned themselves to the idea that only the younger son would bring credit to the family name, while little more could be expected of the elder than that he should continue dining out at restaurants, where he became notorious for overtipping the waiters, and flirting in the salons of wealthy society ladies both in Paris and, during the summer season, at the Normandy resort of Cabourg. For an exhaustive list, replete with entertaining anecdotes, of the numerous friendships Proust formed with young men and women in the 1890's, it is necessary to consult George Painter's detailed biography. Here, we can note only that among the people he met at this time figured a few celebrities—although none exactly of the top rank—whose names have survived: the elderly novelist Anatole France, the musician Reynaldo Hahn, the poetess Anna de Noailles, and particularly the flamboyant and vainglorious writer Count Bertrand de Montesquiou, who was the principal model for Proust's unforgettable creation Baron de Charlus.

The period during which Proust was leading this outwardly dissipated but inwardly formative existence is usually known by the French as *la belle époque*—an expression best rendered in Robert Shattuck's phrase "the Banquet Years"—which can be considered to extend over the twenty or twenty-five years preceding the outbreak of World War I. It was an age marked by every kind of fruitful experimentation in the arts: in painting, by the emergence of the group known as the Fauves and the development of cubism; in music, by such figures as Claude Debussy (one of Proust's favorite composers), Maurice Ravel, and eventually Erik Satie; on the stage, by Alfred Jarry; and in poetry by Guillaume Apollinaire. But in addition it was a time of violent ideological upheaval in France, with the rise of the Socialist Party and, most notably and most dramatically, with the Dreyfus Affair, which split the country in 1897 and had long-term political and social repercussions thereafter, to which Proust makes constant allusions in his writings. From the start he and his brother were active in defense of the Jewish army captain who had been sentenced for high treason on trumped-up evidence; they were among those who busied themselves collecting signatures for the famous "manifesto of the intellectuals," a petition in favor of Dreyfus eventually signed by three thousand writers, artists, and university teachers. Finally, the period was also one in which, in France as elsewhere, scientific discoveries and technical innovations came thick and fast: telephones, bicycles, cameras, automobiles, and eventually airplanes, at first amazing novelties, became commonplace, and all of them find a place in Proust's great novel. As Charles Péguy wrote in 1913, "The world has changed less since Jesus Christ than it has in the last thirty years"—a statement that Proust, whose major work spans the whole period from the concluding years of the Second Empire to the first years of the postwar era, may be said to have endorsed at least by implication.

In 1895 he received his degree and a few months later started his dilatory career as an unpaid assistant librarian at the Bibliothèque Mazarine. The following year his first book, a collection of sketches and sentimental love stories, was published under the title *Les plaisirs et les jours (Pleasures and Days)*, by which Proust intended a facetious reference to Hesiod's *Work and Days*, a lengthy Greek poem urging the need for every man to work for his living. Proust's few readers were for the most part confirmed in their opinion that the young author was one who would always put pleasure before work. But in this they were mistaken, for over the next few years he was in fact busy with his first long novel, *Jean Santeuil*, which he finally abandoned as unsatisfactory. The manuscript, contained in a bundle of exercise books in Proust's handwriting, remained unknown to the wider public until in 1952 it was disinterred and published, arous-

ing considerable interest—less for its literary merit than for its evident status as an early version of his great novel, *A la recherche du temps perdu (Remembrance of Things Past, 1913–1927)*.

Proust, however, did not embark on this more mature work until some ten years later. In the interval his father, that indulgent but uncomprehending parent, died (1903), and two years afterward he lost his mother, with whom his ties had always been close. It is arguable that this double bereavement, once the shock was over, released some hidden spring in the writer's inmost self; it may be that at this time his life assumed in his mind its definitive shape. Realizing that it might not extend over many more years and sensing the hugeness of the task that lay before him, he came to see as in a vision the ultimate pattern of the work and the underlying ideas that inform it. He shut himself up in his apartment and in July 1909 began writing.

From then until his death thirteen years later, nearly all his time was devoted in one way or another to the gradual elaboration and creation of *Remembrance of Things Past*. The first part, *Du côté de chez Swann (Swann's Way)*, was published in 1913. It appears that Proust may originally have intended the entire work to consist of three parts: *Swann's Way*, to be followed by *Le côté de Guermantes (The Guermantes Way*, 1920) and then *Le temps retrouvé (Time Regained*, 1927). But with the outbreak of war, publication of the two sequels to *Swann's Way* had to be deferred until a more propitious moment, and in the meantime the work was expanded internally, ballooning under the pressure of Proust's endless creative inspiration, so that *A l'ombre des jeunes filles en fleurs* (translated as *Within a Budding Grove*, 1918) was written for interpolation before *The Guermantes Way*, and three other novels, *Sodome et Gomorrhe* (translated as *Cities of the Plain*, 1921–1922), *La prisonnière (The Captive*, 1923), and *La fugitive (The Fugitive*, 1925), were written as forerunners to *Time Regained*. Throughout the war years and

547

in the immediate postwar period, Proust remained for the most part immured in his town apartment, the walls of which he had workmen line with cork to provide him with the peace and quiet he needed. He had still not finished the work to his own satisfaction when he died, and the last volumes were published posthumously, in versions deciphered and assembled by the first editors as best they could from the untidy galley proofs and manuscript sheets the author had left. It was only much later, in 1954, that an authoritative edition prepared by two expert literary scholars was published in three compact volumes, each running to well over a thousand pages. This is the so-called Pléiade edition. (All page references in this essay refer to this edition.)

WORKS

In nineteenth-century Europe the novel came into its own, not just as entertaining reading matter but also because in France, Germany, and Russia this form attracted some of the most prominent writers of the age. Stendhal, Balzac, Flaubert, Zola, Theodor Fontane, Leo Tolstoy, and Feodor Dostoevsky—each in his distinctive way combined to endow the European novel with its own special characteristics. Proust, whose life span straddles the two centuries, emerged as a novelist in the early part of the twentieth century with a work that signaled a dramatic break with the tradition established by his forerunners. Among the many innovations Proust introduced, two are particularly noteworthy: the first has to do with narrative convention and the second with novelistic structure.

The great masters of the European novel in what can be called its classical period almost invariably used the narrative convention that presupposes an omniscient narrator. The author was never numbered among the dramatis personae; rather, he posed as a kind of chronicler, but one with special knowledge of the inmost thoughts and private motivations of the characters he chose to present. Hence he became omniscient, a sort of recording angel from whom nothing was hidden and thanks to whose revelations all mysteries were unraveled in due course.

Proust observed this convention in *Jean Santeuil,* in which—apart from a brief introductory section—the narrator plays no part; but he abandoned the technique almost completely in *Remembrance of Things Past,* where the only episode not told from the limited viewpoint of the narrator is that constituting the second part of *Swann's Way,* "Un amour de Swann" ("Swann in Love"). Except in this episode, the reader is always acutely conscious of the narrator as he unfolds the story, speculating on the other characters, drawing his own conclusions about them, meditating on this or that vast and intractable social, moral, or metaphysical problem. Yet there is no absolute equation between narrator and author. *Remembrance of Things Past* remains a fiction, not an autobiography, although its fabric is inevitably woven from bits of Proust's personal experience. For example, the presence in Proust's own childhood of a younger brother must have had a considerable effect on his development, giving scope to the protective side of his nature but also, through competition for his parents' affection, nurturing the rudimentary impulses of jealousy; but the Narrator in *Remembrance of Things Past* (whom hereafter, for the sake of clarity, we shall dignify with an initial capital) is presented as an only child. His father comes into the story as a kindly, conscientious parent, although far less close to the child than his mother; but he is no longer a famous physician—Proust has turned him into a senior civil servant, a permanent secretary at a ministry, possibly in order to free Proust to vent his sarcasm on the medical profession as a whole. Above all, although the novel includes a fascinating investigation of both male and female homosexuality, the Narrator examines the issue from the outside; his own tastes being strictly heterosexual; but we know that Proust always had homosexual tendencies, either combined with heterosexual urges or masked by them, and that he wrote with inside knowledge of the subject, although presenting it in his narrative on the whole unsympathetically, as being basically an unnatural vice.

Thus *Remembrance of Things Past* is far from being a strictly autobiographical novel, if indeed such a thing can ever be. Although we are always hearing his voice, the Narrator emerges as a curiously shadowy character. We know that he is not of robust health; we perceive that he drifts through life, apparently reluctant to take charge of his destiny; we deduce that he must have considerable social gifts, since he is much in demand in society, but we are rarely given any specimens of his conversation. He has no money problems, although apart from occasional references to legacies received, we are not told from what source he derives the income that permits him always to stay at the best hotels, give Albertine expensive presents, and afford chauffeur-driven cars to tour the countryside. He appears as the central character because his is the seeing eye; all the other major characters, each of them strongly individualized and quite unforgettable, are presented according to his judgment of them, but he himself is strangely insubstantial. Even when he is undergoing some violent emotion like love or jealousy, he is shown ultimately as merely obeying certain universal laws of human psychology, in the same way as Swann obeys them when he experiences much the same feelings for Odette as the Narrator comes to feel for Albertine.

The second distinction that can be drawn between Proust's novel and the nineteenth-century novel concerns its structure. Earlier novels have definite plots, sometimes simple, sometimes intricate and devious, that tend toward some dramatic climax, usually the death of the protagonist. *Remembrance of Things Past,* on the other hand, can almost be described as a novel without a plot. Certainly one event follows the next, but by a kind of natural drift along the sluggish current of lapsed time, with no startling shifts and few chance accidents or dramatic coincidences. We are never aware of the fashioning hand of a master storyteller, as we invariably are when reading a novel by, say, Thomas Hardy (whom Proust nevertheless seems to have held in considerable esteem).

It is possible to summarize the sequence of events in Proust's novel, despite its enormous length, in no more than a couple of paragraphs. The first part of *Remembrance of Things Past, Swann's Way,* covers his childhood in the Normandy village of Combray and his subsequent calf love for Gilberte Swann in Paris, with the already-mentioned episode "Swann in Love" intercalated. The second part, *Within a Budding Grove,* explains how the Narrator broke with Gilberte and then passes on to his first holiday at the seaside resort of Balbec with his grandmother. Here he becomes friendly with a group of young girls, among whom he singles out one in particular, Albertine, and falls in love with her but is ultimately repulsed. Also on this holiday, he meets Saint-Loup, a young aristocrat who becomes his close friend, Saint-Loup's uncle Charlus, and the talented painter Elstir. In *The Guermantes Way* we are back in Paris. The Narrator's family having moved into an apartment in the town mansion of the duke of Guermantes, he develops a romantic passion for the duchess, attracted as much by the glamour of her name as by her personal charms. A visit to the garrison town of Doncières, where Saint-Loup is stationed, cures him of this infatuation. On his return to Paris he is invited to various social functions by different members of the Guermantes family: first to an "at home" at the house of an aunt of the duchess, Mme de Villeparisis, whom he had met earlier in Balbec, then to a dinner party given by the duke and duchess, and finally to a reception held in the house and grounds of the prince and princess of Guermantes. The account of this last social gathering is reserved for the early part of the fourth book, *Cities of the Plain,* which begins with a kind of prologue in which Charlus' homosexuality is revealed to the Narrator. The scene then moves again from Paris to Balbec, where the Narrator spends more and more time in Albertine's company. He also makes the acquaintance of the Verdurins, a wealthy bourgeois couple whom the reader has already encountered in the episode "Swann in Love." The Verdurins invite him to the château they have rented in the neighborhood, and there he meets many of Swann's old friends about whom he has heard, and also Charlus with his most recent conquest, the young violinist Morel.

By the end of *Cities of the Plain,* the Narrator has decided he cannot be parted from Albertine, and in the sequel, *The Captive,* he has virtually imprisoned her in his parents' apartment in Paris, where they lead an unhappy life together, the Narrator consumed by a jealousy that Albertine can never allay. On the very last page or so he learns that she has left, and the opening part of *The Fugitive* describes his despair and his efforts to trace her, which continue for some weeks until a telegram arrives with the news of her death in a riding accident. It takes him a long time to recover from the shock and to learn how to do without her, but he is eventually reconciled to his loss. The last pages of *The Fugitive* deal with a trip to Venice with his mother and to his growing friendship with Gilberte, who is now the wife of Saint-Loup. In *Time Regained,* the final part of the work, there is mention of a long period during which the Narrator had withdrawn from society to be treated for his illness in a sanatorium. His life there is not related, one possible reason being that Proust, who insisted on staying in his Paris apartment in spite of his deteriorating health, could not have drawn on his own experience to write this part of the novel. But in 1916 the Narrator is discharged, and there follows a vivid account of Paris during wartime.

After a further spell in another sanatorium, the Narrator emerges sometime after the war to attend one final social function given by the princess of Guermantes. The long interval of time has been responsible for many changes: some of his friends have disappeared (Saint-Loup was killed in the war); others have aged to such a point that he can no longer recognize them, some, like his old friend the duchess, have suffered a decline in reputation; while others have come up in the world. His hostess, the lady who bears the title princess of Guermantes, is not the same person he knew under that name in former days; she has died, and the prince has now married Mme Verdurin, also widowed. The last person he is introduced to is a girl of sixteen, fresh and virginal; she is Mlle de Saint-Loup, the child of Gilberte and Robert de Saint-Loup, and the introduction is made by the princess, who in her earlier days as Mme Verdurin had introduced Swann to Odette, the girl's two maternal grandparents, and had favored their liaison, which led to the birth of her mother, Gilberte.

There is, then, no plot, as the word is usually understood, in *Remembrance of Things Past.* It is closer in this sense to Tolstoy's *War and Peace* (1862–1869) than to the same author's *Anna Karenina* (1873–1876). *War and Peace* similarly covers a long passage of years; the characters grow up, marry, have children; some of them die, some are killed in battle. *Anna Karenina,* on the other hand, is far more typical of the European novel in the nineteenth century as it was commonly structured: it is about the life of one woman who is tempted and succumbs; the book moves toward a single dramatic climax, ending with her tragic suicide. Essentially the same subject had been used by Flaubert a few years earlier in his *Madame Bovary* (1857). Death provides the characteristic ending of the nineteenth-century novel, especially as it developed in France: Ellénore's death in Benjamin Constant's *Adolphe* (1816), Julien Sorel's death on the scaffold in Stendhal's *Le rouge et le noir* (*Scarlet and Black,* 1831), Père Goriot's death from a broken heart in Blazac's novel of that name (1834), the terrible death from smallpox of the heroine of Zola's *Nana* (1880). But Proust's novel ends on a note of hope: in addition to the vision of Mlle de Saint-Loup as "still rich in hopes, full of laughter," the last twenty pages of the book also show the Narrator finally deciding, by virtue of a liberating discovery he has made that very day, to write his novel, which is, of course, none other than *Remembrance of Things Past.* Thus the novel's ending leads in, or back, to its beginning, and instead of the linear structure favored by earlier novelists, we realize that Proust has patterned his work in the form of a vast circle and that his whole novel cycle is best described by the cabalistic symbol for eternity, a serpent with its tail in its jaws.

Remembrance of Things Past can be considered plotless, however, only on a superficial plane. It lacks the proliferation of interlocking incidents, the play of dramatic irony, and the clash of wills that for the ordinary reader constitute the essential interest of fiction even to this day, but beneath its cyclical structure the novel has a deeper, less formal one that it owes to the persistent reappearance of a number of interlinked themes: love and jealousy, memory, time, the persistence and modification of the self, and the problem of death and of survival in a new form of being. These themes will be explored in the latter part of this essay, but it is first necessary to consider the social scene as Proust depicted it, for his novel embodies a multitude of characters, all strongly individualized; it covers a specific period in the history of France, a period now receding into the past; and it has a great deal to say about the evolution of that society and about the reasons why it evolved in the way it did.

Society

Proust deals with a fairly narrow social spectrum: he is concerned principally with the very rich—the old aristocratic families who had survived the French Revolution with their estates and revenues intact, together with those middle-class families who had, since the Revolution, amassed a sufficiently large fortune to enable them to enjoy the same standard of living. These people have their attendant phy-

sicians, they patronize certain writers, painters, and musicians, they pay well-known actresses to recite in their homes, and of course they occasionally converse with the largely anonymous flock of those who minister to them: waiters, chauffeurs, coachmen, lift attendants in hotels, and domestics of all kinds. Members of the industrial working class never figure in *Remembrance of Things Past,* nor do the peasant farmers who at the time still constituted the largest section of the French nation. Interestingly, the clergy, too, is virtually absent, its sole representative being the parish priest at Combray. While this old man no doubt celebrates mass, comforts the sick, and hears confession, we encounter him only when he is discoursing on the etymologies of local Normandy place-names, the study of which happens to be his hobby. Organized religion plays no part whatsoever in *Remembrance of Things Past,* and churches—the church at Combray and that at Saint-Jean-de-la-Haise that attracts Albertine as the subject for her watercolor painting—are discussed simply as relics of the past possessing certain aesthetic qualities. Compared with Balzac's vast panorama of types, ranging from gangsters to millionaires, and with the equally broad social sweep encompassed by his successors Zola and Guy de Maupassant, Proust's exploration of the contemporary social scene must appear distinctly limited. Yet it is not without its insights.

His assessment tends to be critical, whether he is dealing with the rich or with the large class of those whom they pay to look after them. The outstanding representative of the servant class is Françoise, the cook-housekeeper whom the Narrator knows as a child and who is still in his service at the end of *Time Regained.* His earliest memory is of tipping her on New Year's Day—the cash nexus that links master to servant having thus been impressed on him even at that tender age. She is then in the service of Aunt Léonie, a hypochondriac recluse in whose home at Combray the Narrator's family traditionally spends the summer months. As is natural, the little boy sees a great deal of her here and comes to distinguish between Françoise's good qualities—her loyalty and her excellence as a cook, which especially impresses him—and her bad ones—notably her strange hostility toward other women of her own class, over whom she is put in a position of authority. This trait comes to light when the family is surprised by the regular appearance of asparagus at every meal, until they discover the reason: Françoise has noticed that preparing asparagus gives her kitchen maid attacks of asthma.

There is a hard side to Françoise's nature, attributed by Proust to her peasant origins, that shows itself not just in her inexplicable aversions to certain people (at a later stage it will be to Albertine) but also in her callousness to the sufferings of even those to whom she is genuinely attached. She is, for instance, devoted to the Narrator's grandmother and in her final illness nurses the sick woman tirelessly night and day, but she has no scruples about abandoning her when an electrician turns up and Françoise feels that he must be entertained with polite conversation while he is doing his job. However much a part of the family Françoise feels herself, she judges them all quite distantly and sometimes quite unjustly, forming her opinions on the slightest word she overhears, on her employers' tones of voice or chance gestures, and expressing them so obliquely that they cannot reasonably take her to task. Proust compares her in this respect to writers living under a despotic political regime: "She managed to embody everything that she could not express directly in a sentence for which we could not find fault with her without accusing ourselves, indeed in less than a sentence, in a silence, in the way she placed an object in the room."

Impertinent servants of both sexes have figured for a long time in literature (although less often in novels than in stage comedy), and they are usually firmly put in their place by their masters, as happens, for instance, to Dorine in Molière's *Tartuffe* (1664). But Fran-

çoise's peasant cunning is such that no one could properly accuse her of rudeness; on one of the rare occasions when the Narrator tries to react, it is for her mispronunciation of words that he rebukes her sarcastically but, as he later admits, most unjustifiably, since Françoise's so-called mistakes in French are simply dialectic variants testifying to a more ancient form of the language than that which he uses. Given the style in which the wealthier classes lived in those days, servants were indispensable, but the relationship between them and their employers was clearly an uneasy one, apt to slide into impatience on the one side and suppressed resentment on the other.

Society in the narrower sense, fashionable society or "high society," occupies a great deal of the Narrator's life, as it is recounted in the books placed in the middle of the cycle, *The Guermantes Way* and *Cities of the Plain*. But his initial desire to enter it can be traced back to certain boyhood yearnings that have more poetry than snobbery in their composition. One of his playthings at Combray is a magic lantern representing Golo and Geneviève de Brabant. He learns that this legendary lady, whose story dates back to the time of the Merovingian dynasty, is supposed to have founded the Guermantes line. In the church at Combray there is a tapestry depicting the crowning of Esther: the queen's face is copied, so the story goes, from the features of a celebrated beauty who also belonged to the Guermantes family. The Guermantes Way is a walk in the direction of the Guermantes family seat that he and his parents sometimes take, although they never go as far as the château; but he daydreams that the duchess of Guermantes invites him to stay with her there, conducts him round her estate, and talks to him encouragingly about his literary projects. He can do no more than imagine what she looks like until one day she actually appears in church on the occasion of a wedding, and he sees in the Guermantes pew a blue-eyed woman with a florid complexion and a big hooked nose who cannot be anyone but Mme de Guermantes. The shock of disappointment caused by the discrepancy between her appearance as he had imagined it and the reality he now sees before him lasts only a moment. Then he reminds himself of her ancient lineage, of her proud position in modern society, and so succeeds in mentally reconstituting her prestige and even, when she absentmindedly beams on him in church, in falling a little in love with her.

Later, when he has grown up and his parents, as we have seen, move to an apartment in the Paris residence of the duke and duchess, the family has lost much of the romantic aura it used to possess, thanks to the deflationary revelations of the duchess's nephew, Robert de Saint-Loup. Nevertheless his boyhood passion for her revives, and he starts daydreaming again, imagining her ruined at the same time as he has grown immensely rich so that he can offer her his protection. His adoration of her, though mute, becomes obvious to Mme de Guermantes, and her annoyance shows in the frigid stares she gives him when he takes off his hat to her in the street. However, thanks to Saint-Loup, he is invited to an afternoon reception given by the duchess's aunt, Mme de Villeparisis, and this marks his first entry into the fashionable world.

Mme de Villeparisis' salon does not rate particularly highly in Paris society; the reason is that in her youth she had been keenly interested to know what the literary and artistic intelligentsia were thinking, and consequently she surrounded herself with cultivated commoners despite the offense this might give to her aristocratic friends. These friends gradually stopped coming, much to Mme de Villeparisis' distress in later years, when she finds that it is easier to lose one's friends than to win them back. The duchess of Guermantes, however, has not fallen into the same trap—as yet. As the old lady's niece she is bound to put in an appearance, but she barely consents to recognize any of her aunt's other visitors, and as soon as she sees Odette Swann entering the

room, she takes her leave. Although she has kept up with Swann, a friend of many years' standing, she flatly refused to meet his wife when he married and has maintained this embargo ever since—more, it appears, to punish him for getting married than because she has any particular aversion to Odette or to Gilberte, the child of the marraige.

She does, however, give the Narrator an invitation to dinner on this occasion, and thus he penetrates at last into the social holy of holies. The guests, he finds, include the princess of Parma, a member of a royal house related to all the reigning families of Europe but intellectually a totally insignificant person. The Narrator has never been to Parma, but the name suggests to him both the perfume distilled from Parma violets and Stendhal's novel *La chartreuse de Parme* (*The Charterhouse of Parma*, 1839). Confronted by this royal personage, the Narrator finds himself obliged to undertake the task of

> expelling . . . all the essential oil of violets and all the Stendhalian fragrance from the name of the princess and implanting there in their place the image of a little dark woman taken up with good works and so humbly amiable that one felt at once in how exalted a pride that amiability had its roots.
>
> (2:427)

The princess of Parma, like so many other aristocrats with high-sounding titles whom he meets at this dinner party and later at the reception given by the prince of Guermantes, is known by a name steeped in romance but is herself devoid of the slightest particle of interest, let alone glamour.

This is not the only sense in which this dinner party turns out to be a major source of disillusionment for the Narrator. The table talk consists mainly of petty scandalmongering, some of it rather vulgar. When they venture on the subject of literature, these elegant ladies and gentlemen of rank display an abysmal ignorance and a total lack of any standards of appreciation: one of the guests cannot remember Flaubert's name and the duke supposes Balzac to be the author of *The Mohicans of Paris,* one of Alexandre Dumas *père*'s less notable novels, while Mme d'Arpajon, an ex-mistress of the duke, expresses the opinion that Victor Hugo had a poor command of French. It is only when the duke begins talking genealogies that the Narrator listens with real interest; though far less knowledgeable about the subject than they, he is sensitive to the poetic resonance of the historic names they bandy about, and the discussion that ensues enthralls him, for the illustrious ancestors they refer to in passing confer on the Guermantes family tree a prestige of which they themselves are unaware, like "ploughmen or sailors speaking of the soil or the tides, realities too little detached from their own lives for them to be capable of enjoying the beauty which personally I undertook to extract from them." In the same way, at a later dinner party over which Mme Verdurin presides, he is fascinated by the endless erudite talk about the derivation of place-names that Brichot, a university professor, engages in. The others suppose the Narrator to be joking when he maintains how interesting he finds it all, and his hostess is even a little annoyed that he has been "taken in" by her pet pedant.

Mme Verdurin, although she poses in some respects as an unconventional woman, has in fact all the conventional social ambitions of her class. Her salon is the first we encounter, at the beginning of the episode "Swann in Love," the events of which take place before the Narrator's birth. She has established the salon not long since, but already the principles according to which her weekly dinner parties, always held on a Wednesday, are conducted have been tacitly laid down; they are still maintained a generation later. The company consists of a certain number of "the faithful," always the same, who first appear in "Swann in Love" and reappear in *Cities of the Plain* although of course by that time they are no longer in their first youth and have also, for the most part, won distinction in their various

professions; for Mme Verdurin has an uncanny knack for sensing which men are most likely to make their way in the world and for cultivating them but also bullying them, for she is a masterful woman, aptly nicknamed "la Patronne" (the Boss). Her guests are expected to keep every Wednesday free during the season; nothing must be allowed to interfere with the overriding duty of the faithful to attend her dinners. Desertion is unthinkable: Elstir, who had been a regular habitué but who later drifted away, is never forgiven by Mme Verdurin, who affects to admire only the works he painted in his earlier period, when he was still a member of the "little clan," and to decry the art of his maturity. Her rule is that no one of rank will ever be found under her roof; she could not endure them, referring to them indiscriminately as "bores" (in which of course she is not far wrong, as the Narrator discovers in due time). On the other hand she knows they have a certain magnetism, being all of them counts, marquises, or dukes, none of whom would dream of inviting her to their exclusive gatherings. So, by way of taking unnoticed revenge, she pretends to exclude them in her turn.

By the time we meet Mme Verdurin again, in *Cities of the Plain,* she is already beginning to compromise these principles. One of "the faithful" is a genuine princess—though a Russian, having no connections with the French nobility. She allows Charlus, a member of the Guermantes family, to join the circle, although only on the pretext that he is a friend of the young violinist she has recently "discovered," Morel. And the Narrator, who has heard (no doubt from Swann) that they do not dress for dinner, finds on his first visit that he is the only one not wearing evening dress. In *The Captive* we see the Verdurins still evolving toward their ultimate, secret goal, to be accepted by high society; they treat their unfashionable "old faithfuls" with growing contempt, and Mme Verdurin's salon is now definitely in the ascendant. Her great asset is, as it always has been, her flair for artistic novelties—the Russian ballet, Vinteuil's music—for she has a keen sense of what is likely to create a furor in the world of art. During the war she becomes one of the queens of Paris society and later still, her husband having died, she marries into the cream of the aristocracy, becoming princess of Guermantes.

When he meets her for the last time at the afternoon party she invites him to—the account of which occupies the final part of *Time Regained*—the Narrator is in a fair way to understanding that fashionable society, although self-satisfied, clinging to the past, and convinced of its own impermeability to change, nevertheless does evolve by an almost imperceptible process, so that at this reception he meets a number of people who formerly would never have been seen in an aristocratic drawing room but who are now clearly no longer regarded as outsiders. The fastidious exclusiveness of the Guermantes family has at last broken down and been swept away. Ancient historic names, the all-important passports to social acceptability, no longer retain their unique prestige; other names have become as prominent, and newcomers do not find it easy to distinguish old families from the newly rich. Thus society is seen not to be cast in a fixed mold of mutually exclusive circles where, as the wit J. C. Bossidy said of Boston at a Harvard dinner in 1910, "The Lowells talk to the Cabots, / And the Cabots talk only to God." If one lives in society long enough, the Narrator reflects, one realizes that the social universe is regulated by mysterious laws that cause certain stars, no matter how firmly fixed they appear to be in the heavens, to sink while others rise. People of a certain political affiliation or belonging to a certain race are, at one point in time, never to be seen in the very "best" society. Those who frequent this "best" society imagine that it will always be so and are astounded when one fine day they start meeting radicals or Jews in what they had thought of as the most exclusive of assemblies. The only social law that seems to have absolute validity is the law of perpetual change, the

law of the "social kaleidoscope," as Proust calls it in *Within a Budding Grove*. Nothing is fixed, and time will eventually efface all prejudices, though only to replace them with new ones.

Love

It is difficult to think of a single novel intended for adult reading that does not concern itself, to a greater or lesser extent, with the passion of love. *Remembrance of Things Past* is no exception to this general rule, but the analysis of love that Proust provides—copious, far-reaching, and wide-ranging—differs profoundly from any that previous authors had offered and constitutes one of the most controversial aspects of his work. It is presented through five major case studies, two involving the Narrator (his affairs with Gilberte and with Albertine) and the other three concerning, respectively, Swann and Odette, Saint-Loup and the actress Rachel, and Palamède de Charlus with his evil genius, Charlie Morel. All of these have their distinctive features but also a certain broad similarity, which may be due to unconscious imitation (there are occasions when the Narrator realizes that in his dealings with Albertine he is influenced by what he has heard of Swann's affair with Odette) but is much more likely to result from the operation of certain universal, unvarying laws that Proust shows to govern the behavior of each of these pairs of lovers. Proust's ideas about the origin, progress, and ebbing away of love are at complete variance with what most writers who have thought about the problem have assumed to be true. This is why his views, however persuasively presented, fail to win acceptance with the majority of readers while striking the minority, who privately espouse them and have never seen them so brilliantly argued and illustrated anywhere else, as totally convincing and irrefutable.

The first point to notice is that Proust is concerned with the psychology of love, not with love's physiological aspects, not with "having sex" as that expression is commonly understood today. A relationship between a man and a woman or between one man and another interests him only once it moves off the plane of purely physical desire. Love turns into a seething passion only when the cravings of the flesh lose importance and the demands of the intellect become correspondingly more imperious. This contrasts with the earlier view held by most novelists that lovers are consumed by passionate desire only so long as congress has not taken place; once the sexual appetite is sated, other considerations gain force. This, broadly speaking, is the scenario Constant postulates in tracing the affair between Adolphe and Ellénore, or Tolstoy in relating the tragic story of Anna Karenina. But it is quite otherwise in Proust. Swann remains almost indifferent to Odette until the night they first have sexual relations; but from that point on, his love for her becomes totally obsessive. Even more strikingly, at the end of *Within a Budding Grove,* Albertine, having invited the Narrator to her bedroom in the Grand Hôtel, is seized with sudden fright, refuses his ardent kiss, and pulls the bell rope to summon help; his passion for her is immediately abolished, put out as effectively as a bonfire by a cloudburst. According to popular conceptions of love, Albertine's behavior at this point might well have added fuel to the flames. But a few years later, back in Paris, she becomes his mistress willingly and unprotestingly, and his obsession with her grows steadily from that point on. On the other hand, his earlier passion for Gilberte Swann is violent and painful while it lasts, although the two hardly exchange a kiss. Thus, in Proust's view, love develops more or less independently of physical desire, which is certainly present but which constitutes a relatively minor element in the whole pattern.

What, in this case, causes a man to fall in love with a woman, sometimes a totally unsuitable one in the judgment of outsiders? On his first visit to Balbec, the Narrator, in poor health, is advised by his doctor to spend more time in the open air, and his grandmother accepts Mme de Villeparisis's offer to take them for drives in the countryside. In the meadows beside the road he glimpses the occasional cornflowers and also, walking, cycling along, or riding in a farm cart, some pretty girl,

> one of those creatures—flowers of the sunny day but differing from the flowers of the fields, for each of them secretes something that is not to be found in any other and that will prevent us from gratifying with any of her peers the desire she has aroused in us.
>
> (1:711)

These girls awake in him more than a longing of the senses; as he expresses it a little naively: "From the moment I realized that their cheeks could be kissed, I had become curious about their souls. And the whole world had seemed to me a more interesting place." What the Narrator has still to learn is that this curiosity about their souls can never be satisfied: partly because, being locked in his own subjectivity, he can never enter into another's and partly because this other always shrinks from the indiscreet probing of the interrogator lying beside her. A woman may take off her clothes for her lover, but it requires more love than she commonly feels to lay bare her soul.

As for what may follow this initial curiosity, that transmutation of the personality known as "falling in love," this is closely bound up, according to Proust, with jealousy; whenever the lover suspects that the girl who has attracted him has another life into which he cannot follow her, his earlier mild inclination turns into a frantic passion. There is a preliminary instance of this phenomenon in "Swann in Love." Swann has for some weeks been accustomed to meet Odette at the Verdurins' of an evening and occasionally visits her home in the afternoon to drink tea. He guesses that she is ready to put their relations on a more intimate footing but feels no particular urge to press his advantage until one evening when, delayed by the importunity of his current mistress, he arrives late at the Verdurins' and finds that Odette has already left. This disappointment provokes in Swann a violent reaction hardly proportionate to its cause. Oblivious of the fact that he will certainly see her the following day, he sets off in his carriage, stopping at every café where he has a chance of finding her; but the evening wears on into night and the search proves fruitless. Proust then comments:

> Of all the means by which love comes into being, of all the germs that spread that sacred infection, there are few more efficacious than the great wind of agitation that sweeps over us from time to time. For then the die is cast, the being in whose society we take pleasure at that moment is the one we are fated to love. It is not even necessary for that person to have attracted us hitherto more, or even as much as, some other. What was needed was that our longing for her should become exclusive. And that condition is fulfilled when—in this moment of deprivation—in place of the search for pleasure that we found in her company, suddenly we experience the anxious need for her very being, an absurd need which the laws of the universe prevent us ever from satisfying and from which we can wean ourselves only with difficulty—the irrational, agonizing need to possess her.
>
> (1:230–231)

Late that night Swann finally locates Odette and, primarily as an expression of his relief and gratitude, makes her his mistress, possessing her, it is true, but only in the physical sense. Thereafter he pays her regular evening visits, to the neglect of his social duties. He gets to know her, discovers her to be hard, mercenary, lacking in culture, taking pleasure in tasteless entertainments, having nothing in common with him, and appreciating him only because of his position in society. He suspects her of deceiving him with other men but can never be sure of anything, since she has an answer for everything or, in default, refuses to speak, pretending that his suspicions offend her. He realizes that most men find her desir-

able, and "the attraction that her person held for them had aroused in him a painful longing to master her completely in the smallest corners of her heart." But this, of course, he can never do, however carefully and lengthily he cross-examines her, for he has no means of checking the truth of what she says. His jealousy becomes all-devouring and with it his suffering, more particularly since the Verdurins give up inviting him to their dinner parties and to the excursions they make, while continuing to ask Odette along. When, as now seldom happens, he and she find themselves both at the same social gathering, and she permits him to take her home afterward, it crosses his mind that were he to marry her, such a return together in the same carriage would be normal, commanded in fact by social convention. But he soon dismisses this idea of normalizing the situation, reflecting that the tranquillity that marriage brings would deal his love a mortal blow; and he would rather go on suffering the deadly pangs of jealousy than be cured of love. (Swann does eventually marry Odette, but only in order to give his name to Gilberte.)

In due course the Narrator, too, experiences the same "irrational, agonizing need to possess" Albertine as Swann does with Odette; but in his case it affects him many months after the act of physical possession has taken place, whereas, as we have seen, Swann's "need" precedes his physical possession of Odette. The act of sexual union is no more than an incidental, almost irrelevant event in the whole process; and similarly it seems that physical fidelity is less important to the lover than his belief that he counts for everything in his partner's affections. It is the fear of loss that lies at the root of all jealousy. In the case of the Narrator, it was in earliest childhood that he first experienced the agony brought about by the suspicion that she whom he loved had other pleasures in her life that she preferred to him. The very first episode in *Swann's Way* encapsulates the story of how his mother omitted, one evening when she was entertaining company, to leave her dinner party and come upstairs to give him his usual good-night kiss. This caused the child acute agony; he felt that Swann, the principal guest, would have ridiculed him, for at that point the Narrator could not have known of Swann that

> a similar anguish had poisoned his life for many a year, and no one, perhaps, could have understood me as well as he; to him, the anguish that comes from knowing that the object of one's love is in some place of enjoyment from which one is banished and to which one cannot follow her—to him that anguish was revealed by love, love to which it is in a sense predestined.
>
> (1:30)

The dread of loss, of being deprived of the comfort and reassurance of a kiss of reconciliation, can perfectly well precede the awakening of sexual instinct.

Years later, living under the same roof as Albertine, he experiences a momentary reversion to that evening in Combray when his mother (with the best of intentions, it should be said) refused to come up to his bedroom, left unanswered the little note he had sent her begging her to do so, and so made it impossible for him to go to sleep. He and Albertine have had some lovers' tiff, and Albertine has left his room crossly to go to hers. The same anguish as of old grips him by the throat,

> as though all my feelings, in dread lest I should not be able to keep Albertine by my bedside, at once as a mistress, a sister, a daughter, and as a mother too, for whose regular good-night kiss I was beginning to feel once more the childish need, had begun to coalesce, to become unified in the premature evening of my life, a life that seemed destined to be as brief as a winter's day.
>
> (3:111–112)

Proust, it seems, had some notion of Freud's ideas concerning the significance of infantile experiences in affecting adult behavior, for this is not the only traumatic memory from earlier days that recurs later to affect the Nar-

rator's life. During his adolescence, exploring on his own the countryside surrounding Combray, he finds himself as twilight falls at a spot called Montjouvain, near the isolated house where Vinteuil, the composer who has recently died, used to live with his daughter. There, through the lighted window, he witnesses Mlle Vinteuil and her girlfriend making love in front of the photographic portrait of her father, who had been driven, so he has heard, into an early grave by knowledge of his daughter's lesbianism. Years later, the Narrator comes to suspect Albertine of having similar tendencies; but she conceals them so well that he has practically dismissed the idea from his mind when by sheer chance he mentions to her that he must remember, the next time he sees Mme Verdurin, to ask her for some information about the life of Vinteuil, in whose music he has become interested. Albertine replies that she can help him there, since she is in touch with Vinteuil's daughter's best friend and is to meet her shortly at Cherbourg, whence they plan to undertake a long journey to the Austro-Hungarian city of Trieste. Immediately the image of the scene at Montjouvain returns to him,

> in order to inaugurate for me a terrible new life and one richly deserved, in order, too, perhaps to make blindingly clear to me the dreadful consequences which wicked acts engender to the end of time, not only for those who have committed them but for those who have done no more, or thought they were doing no more, than to contemplate a curious and amusing spectacle.
>
> (2:1115)

This is the point at which the Narrator persuades Albertine, instead of going to Trieste, to return with him to Paris, where he can keep her continually under surveillance. And even when she escapes his vigilance, flees the house, and is shortly afterward killed, he, driven by a morbid curiosity, continues to pursue his patient, tireless, but unavailing investigations to try to determine whether Albertine was indeed a lesbian.

A curious aspect of Proust's treatment of homosexual love in *Remembrance of Things Past* is that much greater moral guilt appears to be attached to lesbianism than to male homosexuality; of the two cities of the plain, it is in Gomorrah, where the women dwell, rather than in Sodom that the fire from heaven falls. Male homosexuality sometimes gives rise to comic scenes, whereas lesbianism is always treated with the sort of horror that only the gravest of sins can provoke. The reason for this is partly, of course, that in any affair between two women where a man is in love with one of them, the rival he confronts is one whose attractions he can never hope to compete with; as the Narrator reflects, "this rival was not of the same kind as myself, had different weapons. I could not compete on the same terms, give Albertine the same pleasures, nor even form a clear idea what these pleasures might be exactly." But there is also, in the Narrator's case, the fact that the first lesbian scene he inadvertently witnessed at Montjouvain had been colored by a lurid hint of parricide; Vinteuil's death had been hastened by his grief at realizing that his daughter was not merely wanton but, as he would judge, perverted, and even after his death the girl set up the photograph of her father prominently in the room where she was entertaining her friend, and the Narrator heard this other woman propose that they should spit on the "monkey-face." Thus what was commonly viewed at the time Proust wrote as no more than an unnatural practice is overlaid in his novel by a sense of deep damnation, of filial ingratitude extending to the symbolic desecration of a father's grave.

Death and Love

Proust was not the first writer to consider love as a sickness that once contracted runs its feverish couse but from which one happily recovers in the end. Whatever suffering it causes, the disease is never mortal. As Rosalind remarks in Shakespeare's *As You Like It,* "Men have died from time to time, and worms have eaten them, but not for love." Love dies, but the lover survives.

For Proust the death of love is brought about in only one way: by the separation of the two lovers—the equivalent, to continue the metaphor, of starving a fever. In the case of Swann's great love, the cure starts when Odette is absent from Paris for a whole year, cruising in the Mediterranean on the Verdurins' yacht. At the end of this time Swann chances to run across one of the members of the party, who mentions that during the cruise Odette constantly talked about him in appreciative and affectionate terms. He listens gratefully but feels no resurgence of the old passion, for now "to the diminution of his love there corresponded a simultaneous diminution in his desire to remain in love. For a man cannot change, that is to say become another person, while continuing to obey the dictates of the self that he has ceased to be."

This comment provides the key to what can be called Proust's theory of the death of love, of how one gets over love and leaves behind all the painful jealousy and irritation it causes. It is not so much that love dies as that the part of one's self that had been in love perishes. If the lover has enough energy, willpower, and resilience, then he can stifle the love within him; but he does this only by killing the self that was in love. This is how the Narrator manages to end his first, foredoomed affair with Gilberte Swann. Everything seems to favor him at first. He meets her regularly in the Champs-Elysées and her parents, persuaded that he exerts a good influence on their daughter, encourage the relationship, inviting him to tea parties at their house, where he can meet her. The threat to his love seems to come from no external source but, paradoxically, from the very fact that he is completely happy. Happiness is an abnormal state in any love affair, according to Proust: "In reality there is in love a permanent torment, which joy can neutralize, make latent, defer, but which can at any moment become what it would have been long before if one had not obtained what one wanted, that is to say an atrocious suffering." However, the Narrator cannot fail to see that Gilberte herself resents his presence in the house, and so he finally decides to forgo the pleasure of seeing her there, imagining that she will miss him and start longing for him to return.

This tactical move has a long-term effect that he does not foresee: instead of stimulating Gilberte's love, it eventually destroys his. He continues to visit the Swanns' home but always at an hour when he can be sure Gilberte will be out, hoping that his absence will make her heart grow fonder. As he resolutely though regretfully declines all invitations from Mme Swann to come and take tea with her daughter, he suffers excruciating misery: "It was to a long and cruel suicide of the self which, within myself, was in love with Gilberte that I was perpetually having to steel myself." The only compensation, of which he himself is unaware at the time, is that in strangling his love he is in fact bringing to life a new self that is indifferent to Gilberte. It is a suicide since, according to Proust's way of thinking, we are composed not of one identical, unified, enduring self, but of a multiplicity of selves that flourish at different times in our lives and then wither away. One of them the Narrator has, by self-discipline and in the mistaken belief that he will bring Gilberte to look on him more kindly, caused to perish; but he has simply cleared a space, as it were, for a new self to germinate, spring up, and take the place of the one he has tugged up by the roots. And this new self, having no memory of the agonies he suffered when he was in love with Gilberte, will be ready to fall in love with Albertine or any of the other charming nymphs he later meets on the beach at Balbec.

Proust's meditations on the nature of the self lead to more than just this neat explanation of what happens when one "falls out of love." They introduce us to his profoundest speculations about the nature of memory and about the possibility of survival beyond the grave, for, as he observes in "Swann in Love," "it is a point of resemblance between love and death . . . that they cause us to probe more deeply, lest its reality elude us, into the mys-

tery of the human personality." The first death that deeply affects the Narrator is that of his grandmother, who had loved him with disinterested affection; and even then her passing does not move him so greatly at the time it occurs as it does a year later, when he pays a second visit to Balbec and is abruptly reminded of an incident, since forgotten, that occurred on his first arrival in what was then a strange and unfamiliar hotel room. He had been tired and depressed, and his grandmother had helped him off with his boots. Now, as he bends down to unlace them himself, he is reminded of this earlier occasion and bursts into tears. The paradox, on which he reflects fleetingly here, is that his grandmother's love must still be present and active since he can feel it so acutely; but she herself is no more. That night he dreams of her, or rather he dreams that his father is dissuading him from going to see her and is reluctant to give him her address, saying that she has grown very weak but is in good hands and adding that the woman in charge of her may refuse to let him see her.

However, the fact that the dead appear to us in dreams or in remembered incidents does not by any means prove that they are still living in another sphere of existence. The Narrator is led to reflect on this question again a little later, when he revisits Doncières and is curiously reluctant to comply with Saint-Loup's suggestion that he renew contact with the various army officers in this garrison town whose company, on his earlier stay, he had so much enjoyed. He realizes that he has outgrown them in the interval, has become detached from them, or, more properly perhaps, has become detached from and outgrown his earlier self.

We long passionately for there to be another life in which we should be no different from what we are in this one. But we do not consider that even in this life, before we enter on to the next, after an interval of a few years we are unfaithful to what we have been and to what we wished to remain for ever and a day. Even without the possibility that death might alter us more than the changes that occur in the course of our lives, if we were to meet in that other life the self we once were, we would turn aside from ourselves in the same way as we turn aside from people with whom we were once on friendly terms but have not seen for a long time.

(2:859)

For Proust the experience that comes nearest to that of death and resurrection is what happens when one resurfaces after a long night of dreamless sleep; this happens to the Narrator on his first visit to Doncières in consequence of the unusual physical exercise he has engaged in during the day. The French expression for a dreamless sleep is *un sommeil de plomb*, a leaden sleep; Proust finds the expression apt, since

> it seems we are ourselves, during the first moments after such a sleep ends, no more than a lead soldier. We are nobody in particular. How then, searching for one's thoughts, for one's personality as one searches for an object one has mislaid, does one end by lighting on one's own self rather than on some other? Why, when our mental processes start up again, do we not take up residence in some other personality than the previous one? It is hard to see what dictates the choice and why, among the millions of human beings we might be, it is precisely on the being we were the previous day that we invariably alight. What is it that guides us, when there has been a real interruption—whether it be that our sleep has been dreamless or that the dreams have been utterly alien to us? Death has really supervened, as when the heart ceases to beat and we are revived by artificial respiration. No doubt the room, even if seen only once before, awakens memories, to which other memories are attached; or else some lie dormant within us, and we now become conscious of them. The resurrection at our awakening—after that health-giving fit of mental alienation that sleep is—must be analogous after all to what happens when we recall a name, a line of poetry, a tune we had forgotten. And it may be that the resurrection of the soul after death is conceivable as a phenomenon of memory.

(2:88)

Memory

Christians, curiously materialistic in this respect, speak of the resurrection not of the soul but of the body, perhaps because each man's memory is thought of as located in his own body, in his brain, his muscles, his involuntary reflexes. But for Proust it seems that his memory might as well be thought of as situated in the things that habitually surround him, that— as the Narrator discovers on his first miserable evening at the Grand Hôtel in Balbec—it is not so much that we regretfully remember the old, familiar furniture of the room we are accustomed to as that it remembers us and mourns our absence, while in the new and unfamiliar environment, the furniture—the crossly ticking clock, the silently hostile curtains draped over windows looking onto strange streets—cannot remember us, and so regard us as intruders, until after a few days they become used to us and so cease to force themselves rudely on our attention. At this point in the narrative, halfway through *Within a Budding Grove*, the idea that inanimate objects retain memories could be dismissed as the sick fancy of a neurotic boy, were it not that the notion has already been presented to the reader, more convincingly no doubt, at the beginning of *Swann's Way*, in the celebrated episode of the madeleine and the lime tea.

The Narrator, now middle-aged, tired, and depressed, comes in one cold winter evening, and to cheer him up his mother sends for tea and for a particular variety of rich, scallop-shaped cake known as "little madeleines." Unthinkingly he breaks off a morsel of the cake, dips it into a spoonful of tea, tastes it, and is immediately suffused by an extraordinary pleasure apparently deriving from the mixture of the crumbs and the tea. Concentrating his attention, he realizes finally what the experience reminds him of: his aunt Léonie, on Sunday mornings at Combray, used to give him a piece of madeleine dipped in tea when he paid her a duty visit. Since those far-off days, he had seen madeleines frequently enough in pastry cooks' shops but had never eaten one nor known the mingling of their particular taste and smell with the taste and smell of the tea; the immediate result is to resurrect for him a host of magical memories of those tranquil childhood days in Combray. In his mind all the inhabitants of the little town come to life, the flowers that grew by the roadside and the water lilies on the surface of the river start blooming again, and the church and the little gray houses—things he had forgotten or rather let fall from his conscious memory—now rise to the surface, having been preserved intact by those tiny cake crumbs acting on the two humble senses of taste and smell, which Proust compares here to "spirits remembering, waiting, hoping, while all else lies in ruins, bearing indefatigably, on their all but impalpable droplet, the immense edifice of memory."

This strange experience and others like it seem to have haunted Proust all his life. His first published work, *Pleasures and Days,* contains a story, "A Girl's Confession," in which it is the scent of lilacs that evokes the past: when the central character smells their fragrance, she thinks, it is "within me, but at the same time far away and outside myself, that the soul that was mine at fourteen still awakens." There is also a long, semi-philosophical development of the question in *Jean Santeuil.* In *Swann's Way* the Narrator insists on a number of key characteristics of such an experience, in particular that the fragments of the past that are evoked in this way may have been devoid of charm at the time (the weekly visit to his old, invalid aunt was not something the small boy undertook with any great pleasure), but the experience of its resuscitation fills the man of forty or so with utter bliss, even before he realizes precisely what the memory is. Further, the joy he feels arises not from the mere repetition in the present of an insignificant experience from the past but from the essence that is common to them both, so that what one experiences is neither in the past nor in the present but is outside time altogether, perhaps in a universe where time has no meaning, a

paradise where everything is bathed in the radiance of eternity.

It was a phenomenon that others had noticed before Proust and that a few writers, chiefly poets like Baudelaire and Gérard de Nerval, had made use of in their works. But none studied it so closely as Proust, teasing out its significance and turning it into the lynchpin of his life's work. Critics commonly refer to it as "the involuntary memory" in contradistinction to the voluntary memory, the power of recall operated by the will, which we all possess and which serves, for instance, when we want to remember the date of a friend's birthday or the details of some notable incident in a vacation trip. One of the principal objections to the otherwise highly evocative title that Proust's great English translator, Scott Moncrieff, chose for the work is that it conveys almost the reverse impression from what Proust intended. The phrase "remembrance of things past" is taken from one of Shakespeare's sonnets, the opening lines of which run:

> When to the sessions of sweet silent thought
> I summon up remembrance of things past. . . .

Shakespeare refers here to the voluntary memory, which alone can summon up at will what has been pigeonholed in the conscious mind. Proust, however, whose title translated literally would be "In Search of Lost Time," was thinking of those dim, wispy, golden memories that cannot be summoned up, that hover at the back of the mind or flit around in the depths of the subconscious, to which some trivial sense impression seems obliquely to refer but which it requires determination, concentration, and the absence of all distractions to bring up to consciousness. The Narrator, when he tastes the madeleine mixed in the tea, has no idea at first why he should feel such elation; he drinks a second spoonful, then a third, but it is only by pondering long and deeply, by shutting off the sounds from the next room, that at last he can feel the involuntary memory as it lies quivering in the depths, striving to provide him with the visual scene that corresponds to the olfactory impression. It almost rises to the surface, then sinks again, and the Narrator is about to give up the task and turn his thoughts to mundane worries and preoccupations when at last, as if to reward him for his persistence, the memory stands shimmering before him in its pristine clarity.

This is only the first such instance mentioned in the book, but we are given to understand that it occurred late in the Narrator's life, no doubt sometime after most of the events narrated in the constituent volumes of *Remembrance of Things Past* have taken place. Other instances of involuntary memories are quoted in the early volumes. Thus in the first part of *Within a Budding Grove,* which deals with his meetings with Gilberte in the Champs-Elysées, he is called away from a game one morning by Françoise, who always goes with him on these outings and who wants to visit the public lavatory. As he waits for her at the entrance he notices the "cool, fusty smell" exuded by the damp walls of the little wooden pavilion. This fills him with a rapture different from the uncertain pleasure of playing with Gilberte— one that is "solid and consistent, on which I could lean for support, delicious, calm, richly endowed with a lasting, unexplained but incontrovertible truth." Unfortunately, the chatter of the lavatory attendant distracts him from the effort required to trace it to its source. The memory comes to him a little later, on his return home. The same musty smell had been that of his great-uncle Adolphe's room at Combray, but at this point he is too young and inexperienced to work out why one odor reminding him of another identical one should give him so much pleasure.

The same strange sensations assail him from time to time in his maturity but awaken no more than transitory curiosity. The first fire lit by Françoise after the end of summer fills him with joy, not because of the warmth but because of the scent of the twigs burning in the hearth, which strike him as being "like a fragment of the past, an invisible ice floe detached from some bygone winter advancing into my room"—although which particular winter he cannot say; this is possibly a composite memory of all the cosy occasions when he sat reading before a fire, oblivious to the rain and cold outside. Later still, an odor usually considered far from fragrant, the smell of gasoline, calls back to mind the memory of the car rides he had taken with Albertine the previous summer, and the odor "caused to blossom either side of me, for all that I was lying in my darkened bedroom, cornflowers, poppies, and red clover, intoxicating me like a country scent." But he merely notes the impression, being too lazy and too preoccupied with Albertine even to consider puzzling out why this involuntary memory should have so exhilarated him.

At this time of his life, when he is still absorbed in the social round, involuntary memories occur more rarely and are more fugitive in their effects, for they can never be dwelt upon. The presence of importunate friends and the sense of duty that obliges him to pay attention to them prevent him from doing more than merely registering these fleeting impressions. For example, on a foggy evening in Paris the street lamps gleaming in the murk transport him back in memory to an occasion in Combray when, returning at an unusually late hour, he saw the lights in the little town shining in just the same way. The connection between past and present, based on so apparently insignificant an analogy, fills him with "an enthusiasm which might have borne fruit if I had remained alone, and would thus have saved me the detour of many a useless year which I was still to traverse before the invisible vocation of which this book is the history could declare itself." For the Narrator has always felt that his vocation was to be a writer and has also had the vague premonition that the subject of his unwritten masterpiece was to be precisely the mystery hidden in the "enthusiasm" aroused by these strange impressions of the past recovered, of "time regained," which rise up before him unbidden, like reproachful spectres, at various moments in his life. On this occasion, alone in the stationary cab, he reflects for a few minutes on the problem posed by the involuntary memory and realizes that what separates the present impression from the past instant is not so much the gulf of years fixed between them as "the distance that there would be between two separate universes whose matter was not of the same substance." At this point in his meditations he is rejoined by Saint-Loup, with whom he is dining out at a fashionable restaurant and who had momentarily quitted him to give the cabdriver instructions. And the Narrator has to abandon his cogitations in order to devote himself once more to the trivial obligations of friendship.

Mission Accomplished

It is only after the Narrator has withdrawn completely from the world—his gradually deteriorating health making it imperative, as we have seen, for him to spend a long period of time in a nursing home—that the secret is at last revealed to him. After his discharge he receives an invitation to a party being given by the princess of Guermantes, and he decides to accept, since the name, even though now he knows it to grace only that energetic arriviste Mme Verdurin, still preserves for him some of the magic it possessed in the prewar world. Walking through the busy streets he finds himself reflecting resignedly on the collapse of his earlier literary ambitions and on how the "invisible vocation" never actually succeeded in declaring itself—thoughts that had filled him with melancholy on his train journey back to Paris. Then, abruptly, his doubts and discouragement vanish. A passing tram causes him to step back onto a loose paving stone on the sidewalk, and the same mysterious joy floods over him: he has a vivid impression of a deep blue vault, of dazzling light, and of coolness. It is, he realizes, the same kind of experience he had when tasting the madeleine; the

difficulty of discovering what lies behind it remains the same, but again he perseveres, rocking to and fro on his loose paving stone and disregarding the bystanders' stares until finally the connection is made. The memory evoked is that of Venice, where he had spent a vacation with his mother many years previously, and specifically of two uneven flagstones in the baptistery of the Cathedral of Saint Mark. He had barely noticed the odd sensation of imbalance at the time, but now, evoked afresh, it restores to him all the other pleasures of that trip to Venice, just as the little madeleine had recalled to him all the forgotten days in Combray. But the essential mystery remains: "Why had the images of Combray and of Venice, at those two different epochs, given me a joy that was like a mathematical certainty and which sufficed, without any further proof, to make death itself a matter of indifference to me?"

Almost immediately, a second and then a third involuntary memory appeal to his senses and challenge his intellect to discover the truth they conceal. He arrives at his destination and the butler shows him into the library, so as not to disturb the rest of the company, who are listening to a musical recital. In the silence of the empty room he hears the chink of a spoon against a saucer in the corridor outside and is inexplicably flooded by sensations of a warm day, a smell of smoke, and the greenery of woodland. He recognizes without much difficulty this insignificant memory of the day before, when a railwayman tapped the wheels of the train during an unscheduled stop in the depths of the forest. The majordomo, who has recognized him, then brings him a plate of petits fours, a glass of orangeade, and a napkin to wipe his mouth. As he does so, the Narrator has a vision of a bright day, the scent of seaweed in the air, and the sound of gulls crying far off,

for the napkin I had taken to wipe my mouth had exactly the same kind of starchy stiffness as the towel with which I had found it so awkward to dry myself, standing in front of the window on my first arrival at Balbec; and now, as I stood in front of the bookcase in the Guermantes mansion, this napkin shook out before me, as if it were distributed among its folds and flat surfaces, the plumage of an ocean green and blue like a peacock's tail. And it was not just those colors that delighted me, but a whole moment in my life which had raised them up and denoted perhaps some aspiration toward them which I was prevented from enjoying at Balbec through some feeling of tiredness or depression but which now, freed of all that is imperfect in external perception, pure and disembodied, made my heart swell with happiness.

(3:869)

The reason that these three recalls and all the similar ones described throughout the book give the Narrator so much joy is that each of them places him simultaneously in past and present time, to the extent that momentarily he has difficulty knowing whether he is living then or now. He has been transported for an instant into a universe existing outside time, where the clocks do not tick nor the pages of the calendar flick past. This explains why, tasting the madeleine, he is delivered from anxiety about death, since at that moment in time he is no longer subject to time and consequently is untroubled by any fear of what the future might bring; for in eternity there is neither past nor future.

Is there any way, he wonders, that he can conjure up at will such magic moments, compared to which the pleasures of love and friendship, intellectual conversation, and the pageant of social life are nothing? Return journeys, to Venice or Balbec, are clearly pointless, since places are never what one remembers them to have been. One's friends and the women one has loved change beyond recognition with the passage of time, as he discovers a little later, when he is admitted, the concert having finished, to the assembly rooms where so many of his past acquaintances have gathered. To try to recover the past by going back to it is fruitless, since the truly living reality lies

not outside but within each one of us. But by remembering everything that has happened, by suffusing it all in this radiant atmosphere of eternity of which the vision has been vouchsafed to him, he will be able to give not the historical record, as a memorialist might, but rather transfiguration of time past into a work of art.

Thus Proust (or the Narrator, for at this point in the discussion they are one and the same) arrives at a theory of literature that flatly contradicts that of the realist school of writers that preceded him. The work of transfiguration of which he speaks is a work of personal creation in the elaboration of which no one else can replace him. Many are challenged to undertake the task and many are the alibis by which they evade the challenge. Writers who claim they have a social mission to which they must devote their art are in fact merely inventing pretexts for shirking their real function, which is infinitely more important. The realists were right in supposing that art is based on the discovery of reality, but they were wrong in supposing that the real world is "out there." As the Narrator has now discovered, reality lies within us, and what the writer is required to do is to reveal what is real to him, not what he is tempted to think is real for everyone. It is not the appearance of external reality that has to be expressed but the interiorized reality that exists within each of us and is uniquely specific to every individual.

A constant tendency among writers is to look at any experience for that part of it that can be communicated to others and that therefore does not correspond to anything distinctive in the writer himself as an individual; objects are described so as to be recognizable to any reader. But objects are never just themselves; they are inseparable from our mood at the time we encounter them and from the associations they have for us and for no one else:

Since every impression is twofold, half sheathed in the object, half buried within us, and since this second half is the one that only we have knowledge of, we make haste to reject it—though it is the only one we should concentrate on—and fix our attention on the first half, which cannot be explored in depth because it is purely superficial. . . . To try and trace the little furrow left in us by the sight of a church or a flowering hawthorn is too troublesome a task.

(3:891)

For Proust, realist art can never be more than a record of what the eye sees and what the intellect grasps. True art seeks the living truth that lies within each of us but is hidden to most because they will not make the effort to discover it.

One may object that the writer, if he confines himself in this way within the bounds of his own subjectivity, will not be able to communicate properly with his readers. To this Proust replies that, on the contrary, the writer gives us a sense of the qualitative difference between reality as we apprehend it and reality as another mind perceives it, thus permitting us to gain insight into another's consciousness, which is the truest and perhaps the only valid form of communication. Furthermore, to create such a work of art is, he concludes, "the only way to rediscover lost time." The hours that he thought he had wasted listening to pointless gossip and that he therefore thought of as lost (the French phrase *temps perdu* can mean either "lost time" or "wasted time") stand revealed as having provided the raw materials of the work he will now be able to settle down and write:

> They had come to me in frivolous pursuits, in indolence, in tenderness, in unhappiness; I had stored them up without any more idea of their ultimate destination or even whether they would survive than a seed does when it stores within itself all the elements that will be needed for the nutrition of the plant. Like the seed, I might die once the plant had developed, and I realized that I had lived for the sake of the plant without ever understanding what I was doing, without seeing any contact between my life and the books I would like to have written and for which, when formerly I would sit down at my desk to begin

writing, I could never think of a subject. And thus my whole life down to the present day might and yet might not have been summed up under the heading, "A Vocation."

(3:899)

His is a hidden, unconscious vocation, since he had never suspected toward what sort of book he was slowly toiling; but a vocation nonetheless, since every experience had left some deposit that he would be able to use in his book.

This summary, necessarily truncated and simplified for the sake of clarity, of the long passage extending over some fifty pages toward the end of *Time Regained* constitutes at one and the same time Proust's justification for the nature of his work and the triumphant refutation of his critics' objections. It offers a theory of art that overthrows many of the preconceptions of the nineteenth century and points to many of the directions that art and literature have taken in the twentieth century. But now that we have allowed Proust his say, how convinced are we? And does all this make Proust any the more approachable? It is true that the enormous length of *Remembrance of Things Past* has deterred and will continue to deter many a reader who either "takes Proust as read" or contents himself with an isolated fragment, "Combray" or "Swann in Love." It is also true that the endlessly winding sentences, the paragraphs that stretch unbroken from page to page, the seemingly convoluted syntax with intercalated digressions, the similes piled one on top of the other do no more to commend Proust to impatient readers of today than they did to his bewildered contemporaries. But the style remains inseparable from the man, and the occasional attempts that have been made by would-be translators to simplify the writing by breaking up the sentences into manageable parts have come to nothing. To read Proust requires time and patience—time above all, but it will not be "time lost." One finds oneself, after a while, borne along by the majestic surge and undercurrents of the narrative, one's path lit up by the sheer brilliance of the style, one's imagination solici. d by the innumerable company of the characters, one's vision of mankind and womankind enriched by the extraordinary if controversial insights offered into the secret springs of human motivation, while some may even find greater consolation in Proust's meditations on good and evil, on life, death, and the afterlife, than they can derive from any moralist or religious teacher.

Selected Bibliography

EDITIONS

INDIVIDUAL WORKS
Les plaisirs et les jours. Paris, 1896.
Pastiches et mélanges. Paris, 1919.
Chroniques. Paris, 1927.
A la recherche du temps perdu. Published as 9 vols. Paris, 1913–1927. Contains Du côté de chez Swann (1913); A l'ombre des jeunes filles en fleurs (1918); Le côté de Guermantes, I (1920); Du côté de Guermantes, II (1921); Sodome et Gomorrhe, I (1921), Sodome et Gomorrhe, II (1922); La prisonnière (1923); Albertine disparue (1925); and Le temps retrouvé (1927).
Jean Santeuil. 3 vols. Paris, 1952.
Contre Sainte-Beuve. Paris, 1954.
Textes retrouvés. Edited by Philip Kolb and Larkin B. Price. Urbana, Ill., 1968.

COLLECTED WORKS
A la recherche du temps perdu. 3 vols. Edited by Pierre Clarac and André Ferré. Paris, 1954. Volume 1 contains Du côté de chez Swann and A l'ombre des jeunes filles en fleurs. Volume 2 contains Le côté de Guermantes and Sodom et Gomorrhe. Volume 3 contains La prisonnière, La fugitive, and Le temps retrouvé. This is the so-called Pléiade edition, to which two more volumes have been subsequently added: Jean Santeuil, précédé de Les plaisirs et les jours, and Contre Sainte-Beuve, précédé de Pastiches et mélanges et suivi de Essais et articles. Edited by Pierre Clarac and Yves Sandre. Paris, 1971.

TRANSLATIONS BY PROUST

Ruskin, John. La Bible d'Amiens. Paris, 1904.
————. Sesame et les lys. Paris, 1906.

CORRESPONDENCE

Correspondance. 12 vols. Edited by Philip Kolb. Paris, 1970– . In progress.
Correspondance générale. 6 vols. Edited by Robert Proust and Paul Brach. Paris, 1930–1936.

TRANSLATIONS

WORKS
By Way of Sainte-Beuve. Translated by Sylvia Townsend Warner. London, 1958.
Jean Santeuil. Translated by Gerard Hopkins. London, 1955; New York, 1956.
Pleasures and Regrets. Translated by Louise Varèse. London, 1950. Reissued as Pleasures and Days and Other Writings. Translated by Louise Varèse, Gerard Hopkins, and Barbara Dupee. New York, 1957.
Remembrance of Things Past. 7 vols. Translated by C. K. Scott Moncrieff and Stephen Hudson. London 1922–1931. Contains Swann's Way (1922); Within a Budding Grove (1924); The Guermantes Way (1925); Cities of the Plain (1927); The Captive (1929); The Sweet Cheat Gone (1930); and Time Regained (1931).
Remembrance of Things Past. 3 vols. Translated by Terence Kilmartin. London, 1981. Based on the 1954 Pléiade edition. The same titles as in the Moncrieff edition are used here, except that Albertine disparue, translated by Moncrieff as The Sweet Cheat Gone, appears here as The Fugitive.

CORRESPONDENCE
Letters of Marcel Proust. Selected and translated by Mina Curtiss. New York, 1949; London, 1950.
Marcel Proust: Letters to His Mother. Translated by George D. Painter. London, 1956; New York, 1957.
Selected Letters. Edited by Philip Kolb. Translated by Ralph Manheim. New York and London, 1983.

BIOGRAPHICAL AND CRITICAL STUDIES

Beckett, Samuel. Proust. London, 1931; New York, 1957.
Bell, Clive. Proust. London, 1928.
Bersani, Leo. Marcel Proust: The Fictions of Life and of Art. New York, 1965.
Blumenthal, Gerda R. Thresholds: A Study of Proust. Birmingham, Ala., 1984.
Brée, Germaine. Marcel Proust and Deliverance

from Time. Translated by C. J. Richards and A. D. Truitt. New Brunswick, N.J., 1955; London, 1956.

Cocking, J. M. *Proust: Collected Essays on the Writer and His Art.* Cambridge, England, 1982.

Deleuze, Gilles. *Proust and Signs.* Translated by Richard Howard. New York, 1973.

Fowlie, Wallace. *A Reading of Proust.* Garden City, N.Y., 1964.

Graham, Victor E. *The Imagery of Proust.* Oxford, 1966.

Hindus, Milton. *The Proustian Vision.* New York, 1954.

————. *A Reader's Guide to Marcel Proust.* London, 1962.

Houston, John P. *The Shape and Style of Proust's Novel.* Detroit, 1982.

Kilmartin, Terence. *A Guide to Proust.* London, 1983.

Mauriac, François. *Proust's Way.* Translated by Elsie Peel. New York, 1950.

Maurois, André. *The Quest for Proust.* Translated by Gerard Hopkins. London, 1950.

Mein, Margaret. *Proust's Challenge to Time.* Manchester, England, 1962.

Moss, Howard. *The Magic Lantern of Marcel Proust.* New York, 1962; London, 1963.

Painter, George. *Marcel Proust: A Biography.* 2 vols. London, 1959, 1965.

Rivers, J. E. *Proust and the Art of Love.* New York, 1980.

Rogers, B. G. *Proust's Narrative Techniques.* Geneva, 1965.

Shattuck, Roger. *Proust's Binoculars: A Study of Memory, Time, and Recognition in "A la recherche du temps perdu."* New York, 1963; London, 1964.

————. *Proust.* London, 1974.

F. W. J. HEMMINGS

PAUL VALÉRY
(1871–1945)

IN MARCH 1921 the French literary review *La connaissance* proclaimed Paul Valéry the greatest living poet. The assessment was based on a survey of poets and critics in which the forty-nine-year-old writer had polled over three thousand votes. Valéry reacted to the news by writing in his *Cahiers* (Notebooks, 1957–1961), "I am neither great nor a poet, nor they three thousand, but only four in some café or other." The comment reveals not only Valéry's dislike of literary politics but also a major paradox: that the acclaimed prince of poets did not even consider his work poetic, at least not in his contemporaries' meaning of the term. "My feeling was of not being similar to anyone," he wrote in a notebook jotting from 1928. "Of not being a poet, a writer, a philosopher, in the usual sense of these notions; but that if I had to be them, then [it would be by] being *against them.*" Valéry viewed the two collections of poetry and the "lyrical drama" *La jeune parque* (*The Young Fate,* 1917) that together had made him famous not so much as aesthetic milestones but as "exercises" for working out problems of language and prosody. By considering verse to be an application of certain deep-seated laws of thought, he sought to go beyond a literature whose aim was the transmission of mere beliefs or emotions. This calculated and formal approach to writing not only set him at odds with the increasingly fashionable surrealist movement but also distanced him from many of the earlier symbolists such as Paul Verlaine and Stéphane Mallarmé (to whom he is often compared). For while most of their work had been predicated on the gradual evocation of an emotion through a poem's metaphors, "the expression of feeling," according to Valéry, was "always false, *useless.*"

The paradox of Valéry's fame deepens when we consider that the poems on which his celebrity rests were almost all written within the space of five years, from 1917 to 1922. He had abandoned poetry in 1892, at the age of twenty-one, after publishing some early symbolist pieces, and although a few more poems appeared before 1917, he devoted the next twenty years to abstract reflections on mathematics, philosophy, and language. Some of these reflections found form in his essays "Introduction à la méthode de Léonard de Vinci" ("Introduction to the Method of Leonardo da Vinci," 1895) and "Une soirée avec Monsieur Teste" ("An Evening with Mr. Teste," 1896), while others left their trace in a series of notebooks that Valéry compiled from 1894 onwards. Rising at five o'clock each morning, he would work on his notebooks for the next three hours, so that "by eight I felt that I had already lived a whole day through my mind and that I had earned the right to be stupid up until nighttime." By the time of his death in 1945 he had filled 261 of these *Cahiers,* which were eventually published in twenty-nine facsimile volumes. After the appearance in 1922 of his second collection of poems, *Charmes,* Valéry put poetry aside once again and wrote no more verse of any importance. His influence on European intellectual life, however, had already made itself felt, and it grew in the remaining twenty years of his life through his frequent lecture tours outside France, his acquaintance with the leading scientists and mathematicians of the time, and his numerous essays on literature, painting, and dance.

As Valéry's ideas on various subjects came into general currency, the systematic nature of his thought gradually emerged, with the result that even his detractors could not ignore his arguments. One of these, the French poet Yves Bonnefoy, wrote in 1963 that in order to understand modern poetry today "we must forget Valéry"; history, however, has proved the contrary. The dominant literary review in France of the 1960's and 1970's, *Tel quel,* borrowed its title from a collection of Valéry's essays, and, ironically, Bonnefoy himself was elected in 1981 to the Collège de France's Chair of Comparative Studies of the Poetic Function, named in large part after the first Chair of Poetics, created especially for Valéry in 1937.

While posterity may have confirmed his sudden rise to celebrity in the 1920's, Valéry's paradoxical rejection of traditional poetic aims is only beginning to be understood. With the first thematically organized and indexed edition of his monumental *Cahiers* appearing in two dense volumes in 1973 and 1974, readers are finally able to retrace the complex crisscrossings of his thought and to form an accurate, detailed picture of this modern Renaissance man. Many of those who met him remarked that he seemed to have stepped straight out of the French Enlightenment—a view that amused Valéry since he did not consider himself to be of true French blood at all. He was born in the French Mediterranean port of Sète on 30 October 1871 to an Italian mother and a Corsican father who was employed as a customs officer. After beginning his education in a Dominican school that overlooked the calm Mediterranean and the

tightly huddled buildings of Sète, he moved inland with his parents at the age of thirteen to the provincial center, Montpellier. There he completed his secondary studies and enrolled as a law student at the university. He later admitted to having been "a rather poor student," gaining "the usual asinine diploma" along with "a disgust for prescribed things and a love for his own fantasy." Such fantasy had arisen from Valéry's early fascination with architectural balance and form—a subject to which he returned in his dialogue *Eupalinos, ou l'architecte* (*Eupalinos, or The Architect,* 1921) and his "melodrama" *Amphion* (1931)— but at the university his imagination took a literary turn in a series of poems published in minor reviews. The best-known of these is "Narcisse parle" ("Narcissus Speaks," 1891), in which the Greek mythological hero voices his last thoughts before suicide:

Adieu, reflet perdu sur l'onde calme et close,
Narcisse . . . ce nom même est un tendre parfum
Au coeur suave. Effeuille aux mânes du défunt
Sur ce vide tombeau la funérale rose.

Farewell, lost reflection on the sealed up waters,
Narcissus . . . this very name is a tender fragrance
To the gentle heart. For the shades of the departed
Sprinkle this empty grave with petals from the
*   funereal rose.*

(30–33)

While these lines illustrate many of symbolism's tenets (for instance, the fusing together of disparate elements—a "name," a "fragrance," a "heart"—into one symbolic evocation by which the name *becomes* the fragrance, which in turn exchanges its delicate [*suave*] nature for the "tender" one associated with the heart) and reiterate tragic aspects of the search for self that Mallarmé had explored in his poem "Hérodiade" (1887), they also pinpoint two issues that Valéry transformed into hallmarks of his own writing. The first is an exploration of the conjoined meaning and sound properties of certain words (a poem, for

Valéry, being but "a prolonged hesitation between sound and sense." In the quatrain above, the name "Narcisse" gives birth both phonetically and semantically to the symbolic equation already mentioned: phonetically, by the repetition of "n" (*nom*), "ar" (*parfum*), and "ss" (*suave*) in the words that immediately follow the name, and semantically by the development of the flower code ("fragrance," "petals," "rose"), which is both a metaphor for transient beauty and the context for the literal meaning of the term "narcissus." Consequently, the aural qualities of this particular word, in conjunction with its verbal associations, make it the "very name" for the sadness-in-perfection that the poem unfolds.

The other revealing trait of this early poem is the figure of Narcissus itself. Not only did this figure appear in four variations on the myth at different stages of Valéry's poetic career (an irregular sonnet written in 1890, a fragment of fifty-three lines published in 1891, the revised version given above and published in 1920, and then a longer poem, "Fragments du Narcisse" ["Fragments of Narcissus"], of 314 lines that appeared in 1926), but it also recurred throughout his prose writings. Seeing in Narcissus "the pure difference of selves"—that is, the ever-present distance between the observing self and the self observed—Valéry adopted the figure as an emblem for his investigation into the structures of the human mind. Rather than remain captivated by his own beauty, this modern Narcissus is more intent on apprehending the source *behind* both the observing and observed selves—the source, or "pure self" (*moi pur*), that makes both of these derivative selves possible and that grounds the structures they have in common. Such a "fleeing to the source" of the "fathomless Self" is especially evident in the final "Fragments of Narcissus," but it is also present in the earlier "Narcissus Speaks," where the natural spring in which the hero first glimpses his reflection becomes a metaphor for the original unity of which he dreams.

Around the time he was working on "Narcissus Speaks" Valéry was introduced to Mallarmé by their mutual friend Pierre Louÿs. Mallarmé's was the only poetry that Valéry held in great esteem, largely because Mallarmé had succeeded in detaching poetic language from its everyday descriptive function so that it could attain a self-sufficiency similar to that of a musical tune in which each note, rather than name a pre-existing meaning, creates a new meaning through its relation to all the other notes in the tune. (The analogy between poetry and music was a favorite symbolist notion.) The early Mallarmé had allied the self-sufficient nature of poetry to the Parnassian ideal of the beautiful (put forward notably in the poetry of Leconte de Lisle [1818–1894]), but his later work moved poetic language beyond the notion of "art for art's sake" and gave it an even loftier role as an instrument for humankind's spiritual fulfillment. The ideal "Book" of which Mallarmé dreamed but which he never completed (leaving behind only cryptic notes referring to "le Livre" and equations that were supposed to explain its function) was to be an ultimate, self-explanatory work that would resolve, like a modern-day version of the Bible, the metaphysical dilemmas of its audience. While Valéry was impressed by the internal coherence of Mallarmé's work and its fathoming of structures inherent in language (in which it opposed the romantic tendency to seek the value of poetry in factors outside the works themselves—in the poet's creative ecstasy or in the view of nature that a work expressed), he did not subscribe to Mallarmé's dream of an ideal literature. "I differ from many (and most especially from Mallarmé)," he wrote in his notebook, "on this point: that they ascribe an "absolute" value to Literature—that is to say, the value of an ultimate goal—while I give it only the value of developing possibilities of expression or of construction." He went on: "My goal is not a literary one. It is not so much to act upon others as upon myself—Self—insofar as this self can be seen as a work . . . of the mind. . . . My literary principle is anti-literary. . . . I enjoy writing only things that teach *me* something."

Literature, in other words, was but an *application* of certain patterns of thought; the patterns themselves and what they revealed about the thinking subject were what really interested Valéry. At the time of his acquaintance with Mallarmé, Valéry had also found much stimulation in the work of Edgar Allan Poe—both in Poe's constructivist principle of poetry put forward in his 1846 essay "The Philosophy of Composition" (where the American author described how his poem "The Raven" had "proceeded, step by step, to its completion with the precision and rigid consequence of a mathematical problem") and in the fame that Poe acquired in France through the translations of his work by Charles Baudelaire and Mallarmé. In particular, Baudelaire's characterization of Poe as "that marvellous mind forever wide-awake" struck Valéry as a rallying call to the task of perfecting his understanding of the mind. This task became especially urgent to him around 1892 as he suffered emotionally from an unsuccessful love affair. His notes from the period tell of the turmoil this event caused and of its climax in early October 1892, a key moment that later became known as "the night at Genoa." Awake the whole night in the midst of violent thunderclaps and lightning flashes, Valéry imagined the storm outside as a series of conflicts within his own mind. ("My whole destiny was being played out in my head," he later confided.) This experience led him to realize that his ideas, emotions, and fears all followed certain prescribed patterns and that by examining the patterns he not only freed himself from the hold of these powerful ideas and emotions (by reaching "a degree where consciousness no longer suffered from its opinions"), but also better understood their nature. "All these [i.e., all the inner changes he was undergoing] are mental phenomena," he concluded. Consequently, the most important enterprise ahead was no longer the writing of

poems but the systematic study of thought itself. Valéry emphasized this point in his terse remark "Others form books. I form my mind," which develops the comment made three hundred years earlier by Michel de Montaigne in speaking of his essays, "I have not so much made my book as my book has made me." Such a venture would ideally proceed by reconstructing and classifying the patterns and rules that thinking appeared to follow: "I am a transformation table—that wanted to reorganize itself."

This was Valéry's project for the next two decades. At the end of 1892 he moved to Paris and took up lodgings in a student hotel, where he remained for two years, engrossed in his reflections. Partly out of financial need he also accepted a commission to write an article on Leonardo da Vinci for *La nouvelle revue*, run by Juliette Adam, a French literary patron whose fame among symbolist writers increased with the publication of her memoirs, *Mes souvenirs*, in 1896. In 1894 he went to London and worked for a while in the press service of the Charter Company. He returned to Paris in the same year, then applied for a post as draftsman for the War Ministry in 1895, was accepted, but did not start work there until 1897. In 1900, the year of his marriage, he gave up civil service work and became private secretary to Édouard Lebey, director of the Havas news agency. This was just the sort of position Valéry had been seeking, since the financial security it gave him required only a few hours of work each day, leaving him ample time to pursue his own meditations. It was only in 1922, when his employer, Lebey, died, that Valéry gave up his secretarial position, but by then his fame as a writer was sufficient to allow him a livelihood from his pen.

Although it was a commissioned work, "The Introduction to the Method of Leonardo da Vinci" was an opportunity for Valéry to test many of his arguments on the nature of thought in general. (Indeed, Valéry's conception of "mental phenomena" was so wide-ranging that he had no trouble fitting the many commissions given him during his lifetime into the framework of his own research. "What is more stimulating for thinking than the unexpected?" he wrote in his notebook in 1935. "That's why I made myself accept those undreamed-of tasks, which I finished off by the hundreds.") Freely admitting the limitations to his own knowledge of Leonardo's life and works, Valéry set himself the more interesting goal of unearthing "the methodical unity" that lay behind the great Italian's dazzling creativity. A key to this unity lay in Leonardo's technique of viewing all phenomena with the eye of an engineer, so that the modern distinction between artistic and scientific thinking appeared irrelevant. As an example, Valéry mentions Leonardo's sketches of the water patterns around a swimmer, in which each pattern is molded to the intertwining movements of the man's muscles. While these swirling diagrams formed the basis of many cloud and water backgrounds in Leonardo's paintings, their joint aesthetic and scientific value lay not in their depiction of an empirical phenomenon (for such water currents are barely visible to the naked eye) but in their *formal reconstruction* of the effects produced by muscular forces. Leonardo's imagination had sketched out the causal chain underlying the water movements spotted by the eye, and his abstract reasoning had accurately hypothesized a play of forces that was not confirmed until three hundred years later with the advent of photography, as Valéry points out in a marginal note added to the 1930 edition of his essay. So, rather than the amazing observer we have come to know through legend, Leonardo was in fact a methodical reasoner whose genius we ought to compare not to the painter's roving eye but rather to the step-by-step constructions of an engineer-logician. In reconstructing his subjects, whether the Mona Lisa's smile or a bird's aerial mechanics, the Renaissance master not only explained their physical and aesthetic dimensions, he also gave us a glimpse of "the unknown logic," the hidden operations of universal thought, that ground all human achievement. He realized

that the strength of any construction, whether of "stones, colors, words, concepts, or people," lies not in its material enactment but in the play of forces exploited by the construction—forces he described as the "general conditions underlying [its] music-like form and in which [the particular materials used] play only the role of tones."

Valéry's constructivist version of Leonardo owes much to his reading of René Descartes, who was the first to argue for the primacy of logical relationships in scientific inquiry. Indeed, Valéry's awakening at Genoa to the fact that his thoughts formed a self-enclosed system, sustained not by their links to the external world but rather by their own internal logic, is curiously similar to the discovery made by Descartes during his legendary night of 10 November 1619 in a small town in Germany. It was then, as biographers of the French philosopher are fond to point out, that Descartes glimpsed the existence of universal mathematical laws that allowed the creations of human reason (for example, the laws of physics) to fit (and hence explain) the variety of phenomena in the material world. In Valéry's second published essay, "An Evening with Mr. Teste," these Cartesian undercurrents come to the surface. Indeed, through its portrayal of the fictional Monsieur Teste, the essay retraces the intellectual profile of the seventeenth-century thinker. To begin with, *teste* is the Old French word for "head," the cerebral connotations of which are prolonged by the name's proximity to the Latin word *testis* (witness). Teste is, in fact, the ultimate witness: he not only studies everyone else's behavior—while at the theater he completely ignores the action onstage in order to spend his time contemplating the audience—but he also looks at his own ideas from the standpoint of a detached observer. Such Cartesian impersonality also leads him to downplay the importance of feelings, which merely obscure the logical connections between thoughts. "Consider one's emotions as idiocies," he cautions, ". . . like seasickness or a fear of heights, which are humiliating." Everything about Teste, down to the plainness of his room with its bed and two armchairs, echoes the "indefinable simplicity" of his character as well as his ideal goal of becoming "the man of glass," or a person totally transparent to himself.

Valéry's original essay was later supplemented by three more chapters and a series of notes, all of which were published together in 1946 under the title *Monsieur Teste*. The second chapter is a letter written by Teste's wife to the narrator of the original essay, concerning her husband. No intimate details are revealed, however, because Teste (whose first name is not even mentioned in the letter) is the very antithesis of instinctive affection: love, he once remarked to his wife, is merely "the ability to be silly together." What we do learn is that Teste never reads anything (the letters he receives are read aloud by his wife) but instead spends his time wrapped up in reflection, occasionally punctuating his silence with comments that his wife does not even pretend to understand. She is not alone in her incomprehension, however, for at the end of Valéry's initial essay the narrator admits to being totally lost when Teste starts mumbling a string of numbers that seem to have some deep significance. And yet this curious habit, along with Teste's stubborn lack of interest in others' opinions and with the mental transparency to which he aspires, does begin to take on meaning when we view it through the Cartesian prism of "clear and distinct ideas." It is not merely by accident that Teste should be fascinated by numerical calculations since, as Descartes pointed out, it is precisely in such operations that consciousness attains ideal transparency. When I add 2 and 3 together, for example, my calculation contains no blind spots, for although habit might push me straightaway to the answer 5, I can always decompose the operation into a string of absolutely elemental (distinct) and self-evident (clear) ideas: $1+1+1+1+1 =$ ———. The rigor and certainty inherent in calculations of this kind

are what Teste and Valéry try to transpose to every area of human inquiry.

Nevertheless, Descartes' model soon breaks down, for while the rationalist philosopher was able to rebuild the edifice of human knowledge on a few self-evident ideas, Teste realizes that much of what we know can never be attached to firm foundations. "I distrust all words," writes one of Teste's friends, "since the slightest reflection makes one's faith in them absurd." The friend goes on to compare words to "slender planks spanning an abyss, and that withstand a quick crossing but no pauses." He continues, "A man moving quickly can use them and be off, but if he were to dwell even the shortest time on one point then this instant would break the planks and everything would disappear into the depths." The moral of the tale is that "he who hurries has *understood;* one must not put too much stress on words." In a few key paragraphs about language in the *Cahiers* Valéry develops this insight into the tenuous links between words and their meanings. Unlike Descartes, who had argued that the only way to purge thought of its uncertainty was to *reform language* by tying it to self-evident truths, Valéry argues that what needs reforming is our entire conception of the link between language and thought. As the plank-over-the-abyss analogy suggests, it is not words themselves that come up lacking but rather the *ideas* that we erroneously imagine to be underlying them. "Words do not cover up mysteries [that is, hidden realms of thought]," remarked Valéry. "Words cover up coincidences." He further observed that "there are neither concepts, nor categories, nor universals, nor anything of the sort. What we mistakenly name with such terms are *signs indicating certain transformations* whose mechanisms escape us."

Valéry elaborates on this novel theory of meaning in a set of notebook paragraphs composed under the heading "Gladiator." The "transformations" that he believed to underlie our words are not psychological in nature, but mathematical and linguistic. This becomes clear when we consider that a sentence is not the sum total of the meanings of its constituent signs but rather a complete unit in itself whose sense depends both on the interaction between the signs (*"There is no word in isolation"*) and on the specific aim of the sentence—for example, the statement "Please hand me the newspaper" functions properly when it triggers its intended reaction. By stressing that it is through their *use* that words acquire meaning and that language is a tool lending itself to *multiple* uses, Valéry shifts away from a mimetic conception in which words are pictures of thoughts, and instead shows the system of pragmatic calculations underlying both our speaking and our thinking. (We can judge the innovativeness of such ideas by considering that it was a quarter-century later that philosophers such as Ludwig Wittgenstein and J. L. Austin proposed their revolutionary notions of "language-games" and "performative utterances"—notions that bear more than a passing similarity to Valéry's.) The ability to speak is one that we all gradually learn to master by making the calculus-tool of words fit into our handling of certain tasks: "The child plays with his language as if he were playing with his limbs, and *speaks with himself*—there's the beginning of 'thought.'" Consequently, an understanding of how language works will come from an understanding of our ability to "play games" with words—childlike games at first (with purely playful goals), but then sophisticated, and sometimes deathly, ones: "Games . . . are the most generalized figure of [human] activity, from war up to arts, sciences, love, and business." And what lies at the core of these games is our skill in combining the elements (or words) that the rules of each activity offer: "[Games are] the model for the combining of chance with necessity . . . for calculating."

The notion of a "calculus" underlying language use is the key to Valéry's theory. For if one manages to grasp the general rules governing this calculus (i.e., the patterns common to all language combinations, from "Pass me the newspaper" up to the most sophisticated texts of literature or philosophy), then one will have grasped the extent of human potential, or what Valéry termed "action after calculation." This was Monsieur Teste's dream, and it is also the ideal summed up in the fictional "Gladiator" of the *Cahiers:* "'Gladiator' in brief would be the Code—the sacred book of *pure action*—of power in the realm of the possible—and that would (thanks to *the System* [of combinations that it revealed]) put thought, the mental, back in its proper place." Gladiator is not so much the name of a character as a figure for training and combat—for struggle with our own limited image of what we can do. By comparing the amazing feats of an athletic *body* to what could be achieved by mental training that focused on our virtually limitless ability to combine *words,* Valéry speculates on the vast potential that lies before him: "The horse could not conceive of jumping over barriers, and doesn't know that it can jump over them, until the moment when the spur, the voice, and other aids channel this brilliant system of muscles into doing what it has never done before." A later notebook entry adds: "All gymnastics moves toward the divine—or rather, toward a perfect point, probably so that it can go beyond this point. . . . Gladiator achieves *one* of the *man-works* that were already part of his potential."

For Valéry there were three activities that offered this ideal training for the mind: "writing verse, improving one's understanding of mathematics, drawing." "They are the three artificial things," he went on, "in which man can sense from afar, and yet precisely, his transformative machine." While he dabbled in the latter two, it was verse that Valéry used most frequently for sharpening his understanding of the calculus-system that is built into the heart of language (and that consequently comes to inhabit its users). Creating rhymed poetry, more than any other activity, draws out the formal patterning inherent in words (a patterning that has both phonetic and semantic dimensions, as we saw earlier in the extract from "Narcissus Speaks") and so gives us a glimpse of the formal system underlying such patterning: "Every poetic device rests on an enveloped mathematical fact." A poem's meaning, moreover, like that of any linguistic construct, depends on the calculated effect it produces in its readers. In this respect the mysterious power of poetic language, or what Valéry called a poem's *charme* (enchantment), resembles the pragmatic force of even commonplace utterances (such as "Please pass me the newspaper").

Given such far-reaching reflections on the nature of poetic language, from the late 1890's onwards, it is not surprising that Valéry returned to writing poems. The circumstances that determined the timing of his return, however, were largely accidental. In 1912, with the help of the publisher Gaston Gallimard, André Gide persuaded his friend to put together a volume of his early verse—a task that led to a major reworking of these pieces, culminating eight years later with their publication under the title *Album de vers anciens, 1890–1920* (*Album of Old Verses*, 1920). Along with the reworking there gradually appeared a new poem, begun in 1913, which was to be a companion piece to the earlier ones. But after almost five years of work (and eight hundred pages of notes), Valéry decided to publish the poem separately as *The Young Fate*. This long dramatic monologue of five hundred lines continues the questioning of self and of thought that had figured so prominently in the poet's notebook jottings over the previous two decades. Indeed, with the opening lines the goal of the inquiry is made clear:

Qui pleure là, sinon le vent simple, à cette heure
Seule, avec diamants extrêmes? . . . Mais qui
   pleure,
Si proche de moi-même au moment de pleurer?

Who is weeping there, if not the simple wind, at
   this hour
Alone, with far-off diamonds? . . . But who is
   weeping,
So close to myself at the moment of weeping?

The twice-repeated question "Who is weeping?" not only situates the poem's bare narrative (in which a young woman, the mythological Fate of the title, is awakened by her own crying one night beneath the "far-off diamonds" of the stars) but also underlines the main issue of the monologue: What is the voice of self-consciousness that the Fate feels "so close to myself [and yet distinct] at the moment of weeping"? This problem of self-identity reaches its climax when the Fate exclaims, "Mystérieuse MOI, pourtant, tu vis encore!" ("Mysterious SELF, and yet you are still alive!")

Although the remainder of the poem downplays the Fate's self-questioning by replacing her nocturnal speculations with the joy she feels for the sunrise and the new day that follows, the issue of how the thinking subject is to reconcile its own selfhood with an existence in the outside world remains at the forefront. Valéry's very choice of the Fate as protagonist points to the universal nature of the question, since her mythological role consists precisely of setting down the limits to human life. The Fate's gender is important too because it points to her metaphorical role as a model for the soul's dialogue with itself (*âme*, or soul, in French being a feminine noun). Such a dialogue was Valéry's ideal for poetry. "The most beautiful poetry," he remarked, "has the voice of an ideal woman, Miss Soul. For me the inner voice serves as a reference mark." Insofar as the Fate's inner voice is the subject of *The Young Fate*, such a voice also dissolves the apparent dualisms presented by the poem—thought versus language, or pure reason (the Fate's desire to grasp her own essence via her intellect) versus emotion (her awakening to sexuality). For what underlies both rational thoughts and the unexpected feelings of the body is an *inner voice* of consciousness. Consequently, after the Fate offers a preliminary reply to her questions "Who is weeping and why?" by postulating that a serpent's bite has wounded her or that a "secret sister" is pulling her away from a purely rational self-consciousness, both culprits turn out to be fictions of her thought. She is her own secret sister and her own serpent inasmuch as her consciousness is perpetually conscious of its own activity. Valéry highlighted the self-enclosed, serpentine structure of the poem when he remarked that it was "a fabric's weft that has neither a beginning nor an end, but knots," and that he wanted it to sound like a single phrase from the opening to the final line.

This last analogy brings out the important musical model on which the poem is based. Valéry admitted to being influenced by the vocal passages in Christoph Gluck and Richard Wagner, and what interested him especially in opera was the genre's special blending of dialogue and music, which resulted in the audience's being carried along by a combined verbal and musical melody. Rather than decipher the individual words sung by the opera's performers, we gradually become aware of a mood that the singing produces and that directs our attention to the pure form of the operatic voice. The musical effects produced by the carefully balanced structures of rhyme and rhythm in *The Young Fate* produce a similar effect by giving a harmonic unity to the Fate's inner voice, the poem's subject. Such "harmonic calculations" are not unique to this one text, however, since Valéry believed that in general "[a] poem has no sense without ITS voice."

The most famous illustration of Valéry's notion of the blending of thought into a pure, voiced, musical form is his poem *Le cimetière marin* (*The Graveyard by the Sea*), published three years after *The Young Fate*, in 1920. Claiming that *The Graveyard by the Sea* first came to him as "an empty rhythmical figure, or at least as one filled with useless syllables," Valéry considered the poem to be the ultimate proof that the inspiration lying behind his poetry was not "verbal" and did not "proceed according to words—but rather according to musical forms." The poem's formal structure is indeed striking since it uses the rare ten-

syllable line, grouped into six-line stanzas, to counteract the dominant French twelve-syllable alexandrine (which Valéry had used in *The Young Fate*) and thus to produce some startling harmonic effects. The opening stanza, for instance, modulates the steady movement of the tide (line 4) with the overall calmness of the land and seascape (line 6)—an effect achieved by alternating the 4+6-syllable line with its counterbalance, the 6+4-syllable line:

> Ce toit tranquille, où marchent des colombes,
> Entre les pins palpite, entre les tombes;
> Midi le juste y compose de feux
> La mer, la mer, toujours recommencée!
> O récompense après une pensée
> Qu'un long regard sur le calme des dieux!

> This peaceful roof where doves are walking
> Pulses between the tombs, between the pines;
> Noonday the just composes out of fires
> The sea, the sea, forever recommencing!
> After a thought, O then what recompense
> A long gaze at the gods' serenity!
>
> (Martin trans.)

In contrast to this perfect balancing of sound, the poem's closing stanza (with its staccato repetition of the 4+6 syllabic count) erupts with spontaneous energy, scattering the poem's previous verses (line 4) just as the breaking waves shatter the serenity of the shoreline (lines 5–6):

> Le vent se lève! . . . Il faut tenter de vivre!
> L'air immense ouvre et referme mon livre,
> La vague en poudre ose jaillir des rocs!
> Envolez-vous, pages tout éblouies!
> Rompez, vagues! Rompez d'eaux réjouies
> Ce toit tranquille où picoraient des focs!

> The wind rises! . . . Life calls to be attempted!
> The boundless air opens and shuts my book,
> Bravely the waves in powder from the rocks
> Burst! Take to your wings, dazzled pages!
> Break, waves! Break with delighted water
> This peaceful roof where sails were pecking!
>
> (Martin trans.)

Valéry was so wrapped up in the poem's musicality that it was only after the chance intervention of Jacques Rivière, editor of the literary journal *Nouvelle revue française*, that the poem acquired its definitive form. Visiting Valéry one day in April 1920, Rivière found the poet absorbed in his text and in a whole set of revisions and additions to its verse structure. Rivière read the manuscript and was immediately won over by it, insisting that it be published in his review—which it was, with some of its stanzas reordered. Twenty years later, Valéry admitted to being one of the few people enamored with the poem who could not recite it by heart, precisely because he viewed it not so much as poetic statement but as a "calculated" work in which the message was adapted to fit the poem's formal demands.

There is, however, a message in *The Graveyard by the Sea,* and a key to understanding it lies in its very proximity to the poem's vocal properties. The opening and closing stanzas quoted earlier not only present two contrasting poles (serenity/pure energy), but together they mark out a cyclical trail that the intermediate verses follow. Consequently, the final line—"[Break] this peaceful roof where sails were pecking!"—returns us to the poem's point of departure—"This peaceful roof where doves are walking"—and in so doing explains the initial metaphor of the poem: the doves walking on the roof are in fact sailboats bobbing on the sea. By calling for the breakup of this initial metaphor, however, the poem is not only bringing its own movement to a close. It is also undoing the dove metaphor in line 1 by questioning the analogy that the metaphor establishes between the peaceful seascape and "the gods' serenity" (line 6), an analogy implicitly contained in the spiritual associations of the word "dove" and also developed in stanzas 2 to 4. In other words, by the time we reach the end of the poem, we have been taken beyond the belief that happiness must be a state akin to the contemplation of sunlight dancing on a calm ocean—the seductive com-

parison with which the poem begins. The shift away from this identification between human fulfillment and divine contemplation is brought about precisely by the intrusion of the narrator and of his voice:

Beau ciel, vrai ciel, regarde-moi qui change!
Après tant d'orgueil, après tant d'étrange
Oisiveté, mais pleine de pouvoir,
Je m'abandonne à ce brillant espace,
. . . .
O pour moi seul, à moi seul, en moi-même,
Auprès d'un coeur, aux sources du poème,
Entre le vide et l'événement pur,
J'attends l'écho de ma grandeur interne.

Look at me, sky of truth and beauty, me
The changeable! For after all my pride,
My singular but potent idleness,
Now to this brilliant space I abdicate,
. . . .
For me alone, to me, within myself,
Close to the heart and at the poem's spring,
Between abeyance and the pure event,
I await the echo of my secret depths.
(31–36, 43–46)

Unlike the (seemingly) immutable sun at noontime, which looks down like a god on the splendors of the earth below, the figure of the poet speaking through his text is forever changing. Even in the "idleness" of his silent thoughts a "potent" force waits to spring forth in the form of the poem's words. When these words do appear, it is change, rather than immutable truths, that they bring to their creator and his readers.

Nevertheless, the mention of poetry also suggests that the message of a poem confers immortality on its creator—the sort of immortality-through-fame that writers have always dreamed of. The middle section of *The Graveyard by the Sea* develops this dream by linking it to the theme of death contained in the poem's title. "I breathe the elusive smoke I shall become [when I am dead]," remarks the narrator in line 28, and the peace that comes with death is strikingly underlined by an extended metaphor from stanzas 10 and 11:

Ce lieu me plaît, dominé de flambeaux,

. . . .

La mer fidèle y dort sur mes tombeaux!

Chienne splendide, écarte l'idolâtre!
Quand solitaire au sourire de pâtre,
Je pais longtemps, moutons mystérieux,
Le blanc troupeau de mes tranquilles tombes.

This place appeals, commanded by its torches,

. . . .

And sleeping on my tombs the faithful sea.

Resplendent watchdog, keep your guard against
The idolater! When I, a solitary,
A smiling shepherd, pasture long my sheep,
The white mysterious flock of peaceful tombs.

Just as the sea is compared to a sheepdog, guarding the graveyard on its shoreline, so the narrator becomes a shepherd looking after the sheeplike tombs in his care. This metaphorical tranquillity does not last, however, since the peaceful immobility of death (like that of the sun earlier in the poem) turns out to be an illusion. The bodies buried beneath the earth are not in fact frozen in a perpetual state of bliss, but instead are changing, decomposing, and giving *life* to the earth and the earthworm:

Le vrai rongeur, le ver irréfutable
N'est point pour vous qui dormez sous la table,
Il vit de vie, il ne me quitte pas!

The real, the irrefutable gnawing worm
Is not for you, asleep beneath the table,
He lives on life, he never gives me rest!
(112–115)

It is because of the omnipresence of life-through-movement that the poet must renounce his dreams of a "gaunt immortality" (line 103) through writing and embrace the potential that only *temporal* existence can offer us:

Non, non! . . . Debout! Dans l'ère successive!
Brisez, mon corps, cette forme pensive!
Buvez, mon sein, la naissance du vent!
Une fraîcheur, de la mer exhalée,

Me rend mon âme. . . . O puissance salée!
Courons à l'onde en rejaillir vivant!

No, no! . . . Stand up! Into succesive time!
Breathe, my lungs, the birth of the wind! Shatter,
My body, this reflective attitude!
A freshness, exhalation from the sea,
Restores to me my soul. . . . Salt potency!
Let's run to the waves and be flung back alive!
(127–132)

It is significant that what should be rejected here is a bookish form of contemplation ("Shatter . . . this reflective attitude!"), since it is precisely in contrast to the *dead* words inscribed in books that the final words of the poem burst forth: "The wind rises! . . . The boundless air opens *and shuts* my book" (lines 139–140, emphasis added). The "soul" that the sea restores to the poet in line 131 is the soul of a *speaking* (and singing) person whose "living words" are implied in the rich auditory effect of the poem. In this way, the obsessive rhythmical form that constituted *The Graveyard by the Sea* for Valéry also comes across as the underlying meaning of the poem for us, its readers. For the poem has gradually led us to identify this rhythm with the crashing sea (and the life it symbolizes) that echoes in the poem's final verses.

Consequently, the rallying call of the last stanza, "Il faut tenter de vivre!" ("We must try to live!"), is neither the sigh of a philosophical Valéry who has failed in his attempt to grasp his own essence intellectually, nor the spontaneous outburst of an emotional Valéry who repudiates reason in favor of sense-knowledge. Instead it is a rational solution to the dilemma of human existence, since neither the contemplative life (of a god) nor the instinctive life (of an animal) can yield human happiness. Only the peculiarly human blend of thought-about-action, and thought (or speech) *in* action, can produce such contentment. Human life (as well as thought) thrives on change and activity in the public world. As we saw earlier, it was toward this pragmatic conclusion that the *Cahiers* had been moving, and the Fate's final acceptance in *The Young Fate* of her own bodily existence (lines 333–334) reinforces the importance of the lesson even more: "Regarde: un bras très pur est vu, qui se dénude. / Je te revois, mon bras. . . . Tu portes l'aube. . . ." ("Look: an arm of great purity is seen, which is baring itself / I see you anew, my arm. . . . You are carrying the dawn. . . .")

To cap off the amazing success of *The Young Fate* and *The Graveyard by the Sea*, Valéry published one final volume of poems entitled *Charmes* in 1922. He remarked that the composition of the new collection, in contrast to the painstaking labor forced on him by the two earlier works, was like fencing with a foil after getting used to a bar of lead. Certainly the structure of the poems is much less ponderous, with sonnets and odes interspersed between longer pieces, and the whole collection has a dazzling variety of verse forms (ranging from classical alexandrines to lines of 8, 6, and even 5 syllables). The lightness of the subject matter, too, is often a surprise for readers acquainted with the earlier poems. In "Le Sylphe" ("The Sylph"), for instance, Valéry deliberately pokes fun at the highly abstract and involved commentaries that his poetry tended to evoke:

Ni vu ni connu
Je suis le parfum
Vivant et défunt
Dans le vent venu!

Ni vu ni connu,
Hasard ou génie?
A peine venu
La tâche est finie!

Ni lu ni compris?
Aux meilleurs esprits
Que d'erreurs promises!

Neither seen, nor known
I am the scent
Living and dying
In the passing wind

Neither seen, nor known
Mere chance or genius?

Hardly have I come
And the task is finished!

Neither read nor understood?
To the best minds
So many errors are predicted!

By conflating the mythological sylph (or wind spirit) and the voice of poetry itself, these lines question the aesthetic hold that poems exert over their readers. Where does the hold come from? It does not seem to be the mere arrangement of a poem's words but rather something "neither seen, nor known" that both gives the poem its spark of "genius" and eludes the rationalizations of even the "best [critical] minds."

Although lighthearted in tone, "The Sylph" touches upon the inquiry suggested by the title of the collection, *Charmes*—an inquiry into the "enchantments" that poetry produces in its reader. By reactivating the etymological root of this word, the Latin noun *carmen* ("a magical song"), Valéry establishes the key link between the delight produced by enchantment and the special powers of verse. In the 1942 edition of the volume he made the connection quite obvious by changing the title to *Charmes: C'est-à-dire Poèmes* (Charms: In Other Words Poems). The French word *charmes* extends the metaphorical links even further by associating such delight with female beauty and seduction (*les charmes d'une femme*). This comparison between woman and poetry is explored in more than a third of the book's twenty-two poems, finding its most provocative treatment in the long piece "La Pythie" ("The Pythia"). As Apollo's priestess at the oracle of Delphi, the Pythia was a Greek maiden who sat on a tripod over a crack in the sacred rock through which Apollo was believed to speak. When suppliants would come to consult the oracular rock the Pythia would fall into a divinely inspired ecstasy and utter incoherent words that would then be interpreted as the god's awaited answer. Valéry uses this ancient setting to propose his own theory of poetic inspiration and aesthetic power. When the Pythia cries out, for instance, in the third stanza,

—*Ah! maudite!* . . . *Quels maux je souffre!*
Toute ma nature est un gouffre!
Hélas! Entr'ouverte aux esprits,
J'ai perdu mon propre mystère! . . .
Une Intelligence adultère
Exerce un corps qu'elle a compris.

—Oh accursed woman! . . . What evils I endure!
My whole nature is an abyss!
Alas! Half open to the spirits,
I have lost hold of my own mystery! . . .
An adulterous Intelligence
Practices its power over a body it has understood,

we realize that she is a profoundly modern character. We are led not only to sympathize with her cruel fate but also to reflect on the criticism of divine (and poetic) ecstasy that these lines offer. The poem was written when the surrealists were affirming the need to let the unconscious dictate a poet's writing, but as we can see from the Pythia's following outburst, such an abdication of human control runs contrary to Valéry's principles:

Qu'ai-je donc fait qui me condamne
Pure, à ces rites odieux?
Une sombre carcasse d'âne
Eût bien servi de ruche aux dieux!

What then have I done that condemns me
Pure as I am, to these heinous rites?
The dark carcass of an ass
Would have served well for the gods' hive!
(121–124)

Poetry does not spring from a quasi-divine illumination, as the surrealists (and their romantic precursors) maintained:

Va, la lumière divine
N'est pas l'épouvantable éclair
Qui nous devance et nous devine
Comme un songe cruel et clair!
Il éclate! . . . *Il va nous instruire!* . . .

Non!
. . . .
N'allez donc, mains universelles,
Tirer de mon front orageux
Quelques suprêmes étincelles!
Les hasards font les mêmes jeux!

Away with you, divine light
Is not the terrifying spark
That precedes us and reads our fate
Like a cruel but limpid dream!
It bursts forth! . . . It will teach us! . . .
No!
. . . .
So, hands of all men, do not
Drag from my stormy forehead
Some supreme shafts of illumination!
Chance plays the same games!
(151–156, 161–164)

In the poem's final stanza Valéry offers an alternative model to the theory of divine furor that the Pythia has systematically repudiated. Not surprisingly, we find it is language itself (understood as a self-enclosed formal system) that gives poetry its magical power:

Honneur des Hommes, SAINT LANGAGE,
Discours prophétique et paré,
Belles chaînes en qui s'engage
Le dieu dans la chair égaré,
Illumination, largesse!
Voici parler une Sagesse
Et sonner cette auguste Voix
Qui se connaît quand elle sonne
N'être plus la voix de personne
Tant que des ondes et des bois!

Honor of Men, HOLY LANGUAGE,
Embellished discourse of prophecies,
Beautiful chains that trap
The god in distracted flesh,
Illumination, bounty!
Here speaks a Wisdom
And resonates that majestic Voice
That knows itself when it resounds
To be no more the voice of anyone
Than of the waves and the woods!

The voice of poetry is indeed "the voice of no one," since no person or god possesses it.

581

PAUL VALÉRY

Existing as a potential system outside its particular uses and users, such a voice is the authority of the formal patterning that language has imposed upon the world, or of the "beautiful chains" that give meaning both to ourselves and to "the waves and the woods."

The longest poem in *Charmes*, "Ebauche d'un serpent" ("Sketch of a Serpent"), was written at the same time as "The Pythia," but whereas the latter is an almost tragic treatment of a classical theme, the former is a playful re-creation of the earliest tragedy of all—Eve and the serpent. Through the serpent's narration we are told of how Adam's mate was fooled not by some formidable demon but by a mere voice:

> *Elle buvait mes petits mots*
> . . . .
> *Le plus rusé des animaux*
> *Qui te raille d'être si dure,*
> *O perfide et grosse de maux,*
> *N'est qu'une voix dans la verdure!*
> *—Mais sérieuse Eve l'était*
> *Qui sous la branche l'écoutait!*

> She drank in my little words
> . . . .
> The craftiest of animals
> Who is mocking your seriousness,
> O false-hearted woman, laden with evil,
> Is but a voice in the greenery!
> —But serious was Eve
> Who listened to him from beneath the branches!
> (211–220)

Parody here turns into self-parody, since the serpent not only chides Eve for her error but implicitly admits his own insubstantiality. Indeed the serpent's entire monologue is a glorification of the principle of nonexistence, or of what the poem's concluding line terms "l'étrange Toute-Puissance du Néant" (the strange Omnipotence of Nothingness). Even the serpent's seductive language is parodied in a series of exaggerated alliterations and assonances (lines 181–182) that mock the serious subject of his own pronouncements:

"Dore, langue! dore-lui les / Plus doux des dits que tu connaisses!" ("Cover them in gold! O language, for her cover in gold / The sweetest of all the sayings that you know!") Such virtuoso playing with the power of language is not only the basis of the poem's appeal (James Joyce considered "Sketch of a Serpent" to be Valéry's masterpiece), but also a key to the work's meaning. The "allusions, fables, subtleties [of meaning]" and the "thousand chiseled silences" of the serpent's speech (lines 183–184) are precisely the sort of rich poetic effects that always abounded in Valéry's own poetry. The original biblical allegory is therefore extended to become a satirical look at how all language (and especially figurative language) has duped a whole line of Eves (or innocent listeners and readers) throughout the centuries. The devil-as-serpent in Valéry's poem is, from the outset (lines 1–2), blended into the Tree of Knowledge with which he tempts the unsuspecting Eve: "Parmi l'arbre, la brise berce / La vipère que je vêtis" ("Amid the tree, the breeze cradles / The viper that I am cloaking"). The Tree, the serpent, and the seductive voice of (poetic) language are thus one, with the result that the true villain and true victims of the revised allegory are, respectively, language itself and us, its users, who believe that words bring knowledge:

> *Arbre, grand Arbre, Ombre des Cieux*
> *Irrésistible Arbre des arbres,*
> . . . .
> *O Chanteur, ô secret buveur*
> *Des plus profondes pierreries,*
> *Berceau du reptile rêveur*
> *Qui jeta Eve en rêveries*
> . . . .
> *Tu peux repousser l'infini*
> *Qui n'est fait que de ta croissance*
> *Et de la tombe jusqu'au nid*
> *Te sentir toute Connaissance!* . . .

> Tree, great Tree, Shade of the Heavens
> Irresistible Tree of trees,
> . . . .
> O Singer, O secret drinker

Of the deepest gems,
Cradle of the dreamy reptile
Who cast Eve into her dreams
. . . .
You can push back the infinite
That is made only out of your growth
And from the grave up to the nest
You can feel youself to be all Knowledge! . . .

(271–294)

The Tree of Knowledge that rocks the "dreamy" serpent is not a literal tree but the metaphorical language that "sings" to us in all trees—an "irresistible Tree of trees." This language can reach up to the stars (or imbibe their "deepest gems") and can even plunge into the "infinite" truths of the heavens. It can do all this, however, only because it has itself *created* such realms of truth ("You can push back the infinite / That is made only out of your [own] growth"). Consequently, Valéry's poem ends up parodying not only the serpent's claim to knowledge but also the claim to absolute understanding that is inherent in language itself (and that has been believed throughout the history of humankind). The parody is repeated in the poem's very emblem of a serpent biting its own tail, a favorite figure that Valéry sketched more than once in his *Cahiers.* In 1944 he wrote:

> The serpent bites its own tail. But it is only after a long period of mastication that he recognizes the serpent taste in what he is devouring. So the serpent stops. But after a certain while, finding nothing else to eat, he starts chewing again. Then he comes to the point of having his head in his mouth. That's what he calls "*a theory of knowledge.*"
>
> (*Cahiers,* 1.756–757)

In the next, and the penultimate, poem of *Charmes,* "Le Rameur" ("The Rower"), Valéry portrays himself as a rower engaged in a metaphorical journey upstream, against the flow of words and towards the source of language's authority. Just as the rower's boat cuts through the reflected water images, so its abstract counterpart (reversing the itinerary of Arthur Rimbaud's "Le bateau ivre" ["The Drunken Boat," 1871]) pierces beyond the familiar objects of the world in order to reach the source of their meaning:

Arbres sur qui je passe, ample et naïve moire,
. . . .
Déchire-les, ma barque, impose-leur un pli
Qui coure du grand calme abolir la mémoire
. . . .
Je remonte à la source où cesse même un nom.

Trees over which I pass, wide and watery
  simplicity,
. . . .
Tear them up, my boat, give them a wrinkle
That might run from this great calmness and
  abolish memory
. . . .
I am going back to the source where even names
  cease.

(9, 11–12, 16)

Not only does this backward journey upturn the dominant romantic symbol of a voyage (of poetic discovery) to the sea, but it also ends up repudiating in its final line the goal of Valéry's early mentor, Mallarmé. For by concluding "Je m'enfonce au mépris de tant d'azur oiseux" ("I plunge deeper to the contempt of so much azure idleness") the rower brings an end to an entire poetic tradition that had sought perfection in the azure sky of a transcendent poetic heaven.

The general acclaim that greeted the publication of *Charmes* seemed to confirm the volume's underlying argument that the value of poetry is to be found in the pleasurable effect its textual "machines" produce. It is doubtful, however, that many of the volume's early readers were alerted to the radical theory of linguistic creativity that the poems were illustrating. Admirers were more enthralled by the metrical and harmonic virtuosity of the verse, considering such qualities to vindicate classical French prosody against the iconoclastic dadaists and surrealists whose "automatic writing" dispensed with meter and rhyme. Indeed,

Valéry came to be a standard target of the surrealist's scorn for traditional literary values, a role that seemed only to be reinforced by his election to the conservative Académie Française in 1925, where he occupied the chair previously held by Anatole France. Among the duties he performed as an Academician were the delivery of a welcoming address to Marshal Pétain (who entered the Académie in 1931) and an obituary speech on the death of the philosopher Henri Bergson in 1941. Valéry received many other official posts and honors in the remaining twenty years of his life (for instance, the presidency of the Commission for Intellectual Cooperation at the League of Nations, and the chief administrator's position at the Centre Universitaire Méditerranéen in Nice, both in 1933), and with each new assignment his celebrity increased. Such public visibility was a startling reversal of the quiet and anonymous life of writing and reflection that he had lived until his mid-forties, and one senses in his last work, the unfinished play *Mon Faust* (*My Faust*, 1945), that public life did not give Valéry great pleasure. As the character Faust remarks in the second act, "It is embarrassing and tiresome to play the role of a great man: those who derive pleasure from it can only be pitied."

After 1922 Valéry published only prose works—essays, dialogues, aphorisms, but no novels (since the idea of anecdotal fiction was abhorrent to him). His thoughts on the European political and intellectual scene were printed in 1931 under the title *Regards sur le monde actuel* (*Reflections on the World Today*), while extracts from the *Cahiers* were developed and brought out in the volumes *Mauvaises pensées et autres* (*Bad Thoughts and Others*, 1942) and *Tel quel* (*Just as They Are*, 1941–1943). The latter work is a collection of ideas on such diverse subjects as philosophy, dreams, moral lessons, literature, and love. Some of the reflections follow a developed argument of a few paragraphs' length, but most appear as short aphorisms isolated between large empty spaces. The aphorism form was ideally suited to Valéry's self-critical thinking, in which the most obvious notions would be first questioned and then upturned, often giving rise to some startling new maxims for human conduct. Typical of this style are such comments as "What has been believed by everyone, always, and everywhere, has every chance of being wrong," "Men lean against their death like the conversationalist with his back against the fireplace," and "Each thought is an exception to the general rule of not thinking." Indeed, the title of the two volumes of reflections, *Tel quel*, reinforces their appearance as gems of wisdom that dart spontaneously, as it were, from their author's pen.

Valéry's most innovative writings in his last twenty years were a series of short works modeled on the Socratic dialogues of Plato: *Socrate et son médecin* (*Socrates and His Physician*, 1941), *L'Âme et la danse* (*Dance and the Soul*, 1921), and *Eupalinos, or The Architect*. The latter work is the longest, as well as the most famous, of the three, and the Austrian poet Rainer Maria Rilke considered the language of the text—whose translation into German was the last work he finished before his death—to be unrivaled in its balance and profundity. As in Valéry's earlier essay on Leonardo and his final work, *My Faust*, in which we find another thinker (Leonardo or Goethe) used as a cover for Valéry's own intellectual ends, these modern Socratic pieces owe only their form to Plato. The content of their argument is quite different from that of the classical texts, in which the wise Socrates gradually extracts from his interlocutors the many truths of metaphysics that only he had managed to glimpse. Indeed, in *Socrates and His Physician* Valéry offers us a remarkably troubled and anxious Socrates who pleads with his doctor, Eryximachus (a character borrowed from Plato's *Symposium*), not to leave him while he is in pain. This leads us to the main problem posed by the work, which is that Socrates' renowned self-knowledge appears curiously helpless when it comes to curing the ailments of his own body.

584

Only when Eryximachus assures the philosopher that the pain will soon subside is the latter's mind put at rest. Trying to extract a lesson from this change in his thoughts, Socrates remarks to Eryximachus, "It is strange that you should know a thousand times more than I do about myself and that I should be as it were transparent to the light of your knowledge, while I am for myself quite obscure and opaque." Then comes the disturbing paradox that gnaws at Socrates' authority:

> If you show me you know me better than I do myself, and can foresee even my next mood . . . must I not conclude that my whole effort is puerile, that my intimate tactics [for self-knowledge and self-control] vanish in the face of your entirely exterior art, which envelops my body and soul at once in a network of particular points of knowledge woven together, thereby capturing at single stroke the universe of my person?
>
> (*Collected Works*, 4:8)

The problem is not solved by the doctor's conciliatory remark that "if you know what I know, you could not know what you know" and it comes back to haunt Socrates' closing words in the dialogue: "My mind . . . repeats to itself as an oracle a strange and ambiguous saying: EVERYTHING RESTS ON ME—I HANG UPON A THREAD. . . ."

In *Eupalinos, or The Architect* Valéry returned to a meditation on the laws of construction revealed in architecture that he had started in his 1891 essay "Paradoxe sur l'architecte" ("Paradox on the Architect"). These laws were not merely rules of engineering but, as he made clear in his course on poetics at the Collège de France (beginning in 1937), were principles that underlie all constructions, from those of language (like a poem or a mathematical proof) to the three-dimensional edifices that we erect in the natural world. Valéry borrowed the etymological root of the term "poetry," namely the Greek verb *poiein* (to make or fabricate), in his special, generalized use of the word "poetics" for his famous course. We can see the outlines of Valéry's

ideal "poet-maker" in the fictitious architect Eupalinos, who is first introduced to us in the dialogue by Phaedrus. After spending the night meditating on the dimensions and form of a commissioned building, the next day Eupalinos would give the builders such expert plans that "his instructions and their acts [i.e., those of the builders] fitted together so happily that it seemed as though these men were nothing more nor less than his limbs." Remarking that such blending of calculation and execution "is the very way of God," Socrates goes on to use Eupalinos as the exemplary creator in every realm. Eupalinos scorns idle meditation that is not tied to active construction, remarking that he is "niggardly of musings, [and] conceive[s] as though [he] were executing." In this way his body plays an equal role in building to that of his mind, since his body limits the mind's imaginary creations to only those that can be achieved in the three-dimensional world. His greatness, then, comes from his perfecting the fusion of thought and bodily gesture in "their true relationship, their act"—an important point reinforced by Socrates' remark tht since he and Phaedrus are now disembodied souls, talking in the land of the dead, they can only bewail the loss of their own bodies "and consider that life which we have left with the same envious eye with which we formerly looked on the garden of happy shades [i.e., the afterworld]."

The artistic blending of thought in bodily activity is seen by Socrates to be at the basis of the power of music as well as that of architecture, and the remainder of the dialogue is an attempt to pinpoint exactly how these two arts achieve their divine blending. By pointing out that both disciplines "should . . . by means of numbers and relations of numbers engender in us not a fable, but that hidden power which makes all fables," Socrates leads Phaedrus to concede that the artistic value of music and architecture (and hence of the other arts) comes from their unveiling the all-pervasive powers of *language* that underlie what the mind can act out in harmony with the body.

"And so language is a constructor," admits Phaedrus—a radical Valéryan truth whose modernity Socrates hides by remarking that in Greek, "the very word that signifies language is also the name . . . for reason and calculation; a single word says these three things." Having progressed from a literal form of construction (namely, architecture) to the metaphorical activity of calculation-and-enactment through language, Valéry ends the dialogue with a mythical story of creation to illustrate his theory. As in Plato's *Republic,* where Socrates closes the discussion of the ideal state with a cosmic fairy tale (the myth of Er), apparently justifying the argument he has previously put forward, so Valéry's Socrates tells us of how he imagines the creation of the universe by God-the-constructor. Rather than impose his own order upon the original chaos, this divine poet instead extracts a hidden order from his materials by putting into opposition such elements as ice and fire and then by drawing out the consequences of such oppositions (hot and cold, night and day, and so on). Unlike Plato's philosophical treatise, however, where even myths appear true, *Eupalinos* ends with Socrates' lighthearted comment to Phaedrus that such a myth is indeed a fiction, spawned by "some rhetorician of the other world [i.e., Valéry] who has used us as puppets."

In the third dialogue, *Dance and the Soul,* we find Valéry's Socrates again wrapped up in a fictional account of artistic creativity. This time the blending of thought through language-in-action has dance as its illustration—a discipline to which Valéry returned in his 1936 book *Degas danse dessin (Degas, Dance, Drawing).* The equation between dancing and perfect artistry had already been drawn by Mallarmé in his theatrical reviews "Crayonné au théâtre" ("Theater Jottings," 1887) and even Valéry considered that his illustrious master "had exhausted the subject insofar as it belongs to literature." But in his own dialogue Valéry goes beyond Mallarmé's view of dance as "the theatrical form of poetry par excellence" by arguing, through the com-

ments of Socrates, that dance exemplifies not only an ideal form of art but also the goal to which all human life aspires. Two-thirds of the dialogue is a description of the graceful dance movements performed by Athikte in front of Socrates, Eryximachus, and Phaedrus. According to the latter, Athikte's dance is supremely Socratic in that, by showing the audience the artistic potential of their own walking steps, it teaches them, "in the manner of walking, to know [them]selves a little better." Socrates goes even further in his interpretation of Athikte's movements, concluding that in the complete merging of the dancer's body with the movements it performs there is a model for all human creativity. According to this model, action would completely dissolve the sterile opposition between pure thought and bodily existence (an opposition already attacked in *The Graveyard by the Sea*) by putting thought into action and thus perfecting both the mental and the physical. Athikte's dance reaches its climax in one final turn: "See. . . . She turns. . . . A body, by its simple force and its act, is powerful enough to alter the nature of things more profoundly than ever the mind in its speculations and dreams was able to do!" After this ultimate turn Athikte falls to the floor apparently dead, but in fact transported by her perfection, as we can judge from her exclamation, which closes the dialogue: "O Whirlwind! I was in thee, O movement—outside all things. . . ."

To expire in such a moment of triumph might very well have been Valéry's own wish. Certainly, the state funeral he received in July 1945 confirmed the glory that his thoughts and writings had brought him. But if we consider Valéry first and foremost as a great thinker, we have to bear in mind his own definition of the term:

Thinker! That ridiculous name—and yet one could find a man who would be neither a philosopher nor a poet, not definable by the object of his thought nor by his quest after some exterior goal, such as a book, a doctrine, a science, *the* truth . . . but who would be a *thinker* in the same way as one is a *dancer,* using his mind the way the dancer uses his muscles and nerves . . . an artist not so much of knowledge but of himself.

(*Cahiers,* 1.334)

Just as Valéry's ideal dancer redefined for him what dancing (and its counterpart, walking) was all about, so Valéry has shown us better what thinking and its pedestrian counterpart, speaking, really are.

Given the breadth of this achievement, it is not surprising that Valéry's influence has been felt more by philosophers and literary critics than by poets. It is true that his constructivist view of writing can be spotted behind some of the poetic innovations in France over the last thirty years (for instance, in the Oulipo group's formal derivation of poems via mathematical transformations). It is also true that Valéry's highly self-conscious, philosophical writing had an important influence on a certain intellectualist strain of poetry in the English-speaking world (notably on the work of T. S. Eliot and Wallace Stevens; the latter called *Eupalinos* "one of the most perceptive texts of modern times.") The far-reaching consequences of his ideas on literature and meaning have been drawn out not in poetry, however, but in recent literary criticism. By showing how meaning is created through a text's own internal relationships, as well as through its links to other texts (irrespective of the author's intentions or of the situations to which the specific work refers), structuralist critics of the 1960's and 1970's have confirmed many of Valéry's insights into the self-enclosed nature of literary language. Their resurrection of the Aristotelian term "poetics," designating the study of the general laws underlying all literary texts, also owes much to Valéry's earlier application of the term to general laws of symbolism underlying the production of any art work. In the neighboring realms of philosophy and linguistics Valéry's writings seem to have been similarly prophetic. His insistence on the common thread connecting a game's conventions to those of everyday speech, as well as his understanding of the overall pragmatic dimension of language, shows him to have been a precursor of the major thinkers in linguistic philosophy—the dominant philosophical movement since the 1950's. His investigations into mathematical symbolism, moreover, show that he was clearly aware of the connections between formal languages (such as algebra) and the so-called "natural" languages that we use in our daily lives (and that quickly lose their "naturalness" once we submit them to scrutiny). In short, the emblem in the *Cahiers* of a snake biting itself, or of language seeking to grasp its own nature (and hence understand everything else), may be not just the figure for the private obsessions of a symbolist poet, but rather a prefiguring of the main intellectual obsession of our times.

Selected Bibliography

EDITIONS

INDIVIDUAL WORKS

"Introduction à la méthode de Léonard de Vinci" (1895). In *Les divers essais sur Léonard de Vinci.* Paris, 1930.

"Une soirée avec Monsieur Teste" (1896). In *Monsieur Teste.* Paris, 1946.

La jeune parque. Paris, 1917.

Album de vers anciens, 1890–1900. Paris, 1920.

Eupalinos, ou l'architecte, précédé de L'Âme et la danse. Paris, 1921.

Charmes, ou Poèmes. Paris, 1922.

Amphion. Paris, 1931.

Regards sur le monde actuel. Paris, 1931.

Degas danse dessin. Paris, 1936.

Pièces sur l'art. Paris, 1936.

Socrate et son médecin. Paris, 1941.

Mauvaises pensées et autres. Paris, 1942.

Tel quel I et II. Paris, 1941–1943.

Mon faust. Paris, 1945.

COLLECTED WORKS

Oeuvres. Edited by Jean Hytier. 2 vols. Paris, 1975–1977.

PAUL VALÉRY

JOURNALS

Cahiers. Edited by Judith Robinson. 2 vols. Paris, 1973–1974.

CORRESPONDENCE

André Gide—Paul Valéry: Correspondance 1890–1942. Edited by R. Mallet. Paris, 1953.

TRANSLATIONS

The Collected Works of Paul Valéry. 15 vols. Edited by Jackson Mathews. Various translators. Princeton, N.J. 1956–1975.

Martin, Graham D. *Le cimetière marin. The Graveyard by the Sea.* Edinburgh, 1972. Bilingual edition.

BIOGRAPHICAL AND CRITICAL STUDIES

Crow, Christine. *Paul Valéry and the Poetry of Voice.* Cambridge, England, 1982.

Derrida, Jacques. "Qual quelle: Les sources de Valéry." In *Marges de la philosophie.* Paris, 1972.

Genette, Gérard. "La littérature comme telle." In *Figures I.* Paris, 1966.

Henry, Albert. *Langage et poésie chez Paul Valéry.* Paris, 1952.

Hytier, Jean. *La poétique de Valéry.* Paris, 1953.

Ince, W. N. *The Poetic Theory of Paul Valéry: Inspiration and Technique.* Leicester, 1961.

Kao, Shuhsi. *Lire Valéry.* Paris, 1985.

Lawler, James. *Lecture de Valéry: Une étude de "Charmes."* Paris, 1963.

————. *The Poet as Analyst: Essays on Paul Valéry.* Berkeley, Calif., 1974.

Nash, Suzanne. *Paul Valéry's "Album de vers anciens": A Past Transfigured.* Princeton, N.J., 1983.

Robinson, Judith. *L'Analyse de l'esprit dans les cahiers de Valéry.* Paris, 1963.

Todorov, Tzvetan. "La 'poétique' de Valéry." In *Cahiers Paul Valéry,* 1 (1975).

Whiting, Charles. *Valéry, jeune poète.* Paris, 1960.

STEVEN WINSPUR